W9-BLX-383

J D Strauss
LCC f LCS
1967

CHURCH AND STATE
IN THE
UNITED STATES

Historical Development and Contemporary Problems of Religious Freedom under the Constitution

Courtesy Charles Francis Adams and Frick Art Reference Library

THOMAS JEFFERSON, 1743-1826

A portrait by Mather Brown (1761-1831) painted in 1786. Jefferson shares with Madison the honor of being the most constructive American statesman in the field of Church-State separation and religious freedom. He was author of the Virginia Statute for Religious Freedom. See IV, 8, (10).

CHURCH AND STATE IN THE UNITED STATES

VOLUME II

A Historical Survey, Source Book, and Interpretation of Documents and Events Showing the Growth of Religious Freedom under the Friendly Constitutional Separation of Church and State, and the Resulting Influence of Religion in All Major Phases of National Development; also a Study of the Status of Churches including Synagogues and Other Religious Groups under Federal and State Constitutions, Statutes, and Judicial Decisions; Authoritative Opinions of Courts, Church Bodies, Statesmen, Religious Leaders, and Publicists on Matters at Issue; and a Discussion of Contemporary Problems of Adjustment

ANSON PHELPS STOKES, D.D., LL.D.
Former Secretary of Yale University
Former Canon of Washington Cathedral

Introduction by
RALPH HENRY GABRIEL, PH.D.
Sterling Professor of American History in Yale University

IN THREE VOLUMES
ILLUSTRATED

HARPER & BROTHERS
Publishers *New York*

CHURCH AND STATE IN THE UNITED STATES
Copyright, 1950, by Harper & Brothers. Printed in the United States of America. All rights in this book are reserved. It may not be used for dramatic, motion- or talking-picture purposes without written authorization from the holder of these rights. Nor may the book or part thereof be reproduced in any manner whatsoever without permission in writing except in the case of brief quotations which may be freely used in reviews, serious articles and books. For information address: Harper & Brothers, 49 East 33rd Street, New York 16, N. Y.

FIRST EDITION
D—Z

BOOK I

Foundations and Historic Adjustments Through the Civil War

(continued)

James Strauss

Gratis

9 August 84

6304

Part Four

CHURCH–STATE PROBLEMS PRECEDING, DURING, AND FOLLOWING THE CIVIL WAR

Chapter XIV

THE CONNECTION OF THE CHURCH WITH HISTORIC NATIONAL ISSUES BEGINNING SHORTLY BEFORE THE CIVIL WAR

There have been many national issues in which the Church, as such, has played an important part—sometimes trying to direct or stimulate, sometimes to restrain, the arm of government. At other times the line of cleavage has been horizontal rather than perpendicular—the struggle being between liberal groups, both within and without the Churches, supporting measures to advance the cause of political and civil freedom and justice, and conservative groups in opposition.

We have already considered the efforts of representative Christian statesmen individually[1] and collectively[2] to assure religious toleration by the State, and the relationship of the different religious bodies to national independence[3] and to the general subject of State control.[4] Now we are concerned with the major problems of national policy in which the Church has been interested in the course of the past century and a half.

The slavery question, involving the greatest moral issue of all, was the one in which the Church was the most concerned. It will be given a long chapter (XV). But it must be preceded by the present chapter on "The Connection of the Church with Historic National Issues Beginning Shortly Before the Civil War," and followed by another (XVI) dealing with "The Connection of the Church with Historic National Issues after Reconstruction."

In the present chapter we shall deal with:

1. The Antidueling Campaign
2. The Sunday Mail Controversy
3. The Antimasonic Campaign
4. The Antilottery Campaign
5. Religious Journalism
6. Temperance and Liquor Control
7. The Mormon Theocracy and Independence
8. Nonsectarian Public Education
9. The Annexation of Texas (1845)

10. The Mexican War (1846–48) and the Annexation of California (1848)
11. The Diplomatic Representation at the Vatican
12. The Communistic and Other New Religious Communities

The points of contact between Church and State in the broad field of social legislation are so varied, and are still so acute and complicated, that they will be dealt with in a separate later chapter (XX), even though the roots of many present-day problems will then have to be traced back to the period now under consideration. Similarly, "The Problems of Adjustment in Fields of Racial and Religious Restrictions" (XVII), "Education" (XVIII and XIX), and "Modern War and the Peace Movement" (XXI) will have separate chapters.

The "reform" tendency of American Protestantism is well known, and goes back mainly to the strong Puritan strain of New England and the inheritance of the middle-class ideals of English Methodism, which have had such a profound influence on this country. Most of the "anti" movements have had behind them Protestant groups led by their ministers.

This reforming tendency of the Protestant Churches—as far as directly influencing the policy of the State is concerned—had its effective origin in the first and second decades of the nineteenth century. Lyman Beecher (1775–1863) may be considered the outstanding leader in the movement. We find him preaching as early as 1803 a sermon published the following year with the title of *The Practicability of suppressing Vice, by means of Societies instituted for that purpose*. A decade later (1813) he published *A reformation of morals practicable and indispensable*. This sermon went through two editions and was "a forerunner of the temperance reformation."[5] It dealt with many of the moral problems of the time. Among other things he said:

> . . . Our institutions, civil and religious, have outlived that domestic discipline and official vigilance in magistrates which rendered obedience easy and habitual. The laws are now beginning to operate extensively upon necks unaccustomed to the yoke, and when they shall become irksome to the majority, their execution will become impracticable. To this situation we are already reduced in some districts of the land. Drunkards reel through the streets day after day, and year after year, with entire impunity. . . .[6]

Discussing events in the spring of 1813, he tells about "organizing a society for the promotion of reform." It was "a new thing in that day for the clergy and laymen to meet on the same level and cooperate," and he believes that it was the first meeting of the type that had ever been held in Connecticut. Those present included seven or eight of the leading lawyers of New Haven, President Dwight, and some of the representative Congregational clergy. This led to Beecher's sermon on the subsequent evening based on the text from Psalm CIII, "The fear of the Lord is the beginning of wisdom."

The list of section headings shows that many of the issues considered in this chapter were of an "anti" or reform character; others involved the attitude of the Church, or of large portions of it, toward events of national importance.

Section 1. THE ANTIDUELING CAMPAIGN

There had been sporadic opposition against dueling from the seventeenth century on, and some of the fathers of the republic—notably Washington, Franklin, and Jefferson—opposed the practice. But they accomplished relatively little. The duel continued a recognized method of settling disputes in certain parts of the American colonies, especially those where cavalier or other aristocratic European traditions were strong. We find here and there a clergyman supporting the custom. For instance, in February, 1778, the Reverend Wm. MacFee, preaching before the army at Valley Forge, defended it.[7]

Dueling had been connected with aristocratic groups on the one hand, which gave their names to the "South Carolina" and "New Orleans" codes,[8] and with frontier conditions on the other. It was strongly opposed by the organized Protestant forces of the country. Their position was largely responsible for the adoption in various states—especially after the killing of Alexander Hamilton by Aaron Burr in 1804—of constitutional provisions against dueling and statutes making it illegal. These generally made a person incapable of holding, or being elected to, any position under the state government, who challenged or accepted a challenge to fight a duel, and in other ways tried to discourage the custom.

In 1802 a Congressman from Virginia moved the House to appoint a committee to inquire into the expediency of a law to disqualify any person from holding an office under the government who should thereafter be concerned in a duel. The House however refused to carry out this proposal,[9] although four years later an act was passed forbidding dueling in the army.

By his oration before the New York State Society of the Cincinnati, July 31, 1804, commemorative of Hamilton, the Reverend John M. Mason (1770–1829), then one of the leading Protestant ministers of the country, gave nation-wide impetus to the effort to secure antidueling legislation. In the course of this address he said:

> Fathers, friends, countrymen! the grave of HAMILTON speaks. It charges me to remind you that he fell a victim not to disease or accident; not to the fortune of glorious warfare; but, how shall I utter it? to a custom which has no origin but superstition, no aliment but depravity, no reason but in madness. . . . The wise and good turn with

disgust from the man who lawlessly aims at his neighbor's life. Is it honorable to serve your country? That man cruelly injures her, who, from private pique, calls his fellow citizen into the dubious field. Is fidelity honorable? That man forswears his faith, who turns against the bowels of his countrymen, weapons put into his hand for their defence. Are generosity, humanity, sympathy, honorable? That man is superlatively base, who mingles the tears of the widow and orphan, with the blood of a husband and father. Do refinement, and courtesy, and benignity, entwine with the laurels of the brave? The blot is yet to be wiped from the soldier's name, that he cannot treat his brother with the decorum of a gentleman, unless the pistol or the dagger be every moment at his heart. Let the votaries of honor now look at their deeds. Let them compare their doctrine with this horrible comment. Ah! what avails it to a distracted nation that HAMILTON was murdered for a punctilio of honor? . . . My countrymen, the land is defiled with blood unrighteously shed. Its cry, disregarded on earth, has gone up to the throne of God; and this day does our punishment reveal our sin. It is time for us to awake. The voice of moral virtue, the voice of domestic alarm, the voice of the fatherless and widow, the voice of a nation's wrong, the voice of HAMILTON'S blood, the voice of impending judgment, calls for a remedy. At this hour, Heaven's high reproof is sounding from Maine to Georgia, and from the shores of the Atlantic to the banks of the Mississippi. If we refuse obedience, every drop of blood spilled in single combat, will lie at our door, and will be recompensed when our cup is full. We have then our choice, either to coerce iniquity, or prepare for desolation; and in the mean time to make our nation, though infant in years, yet mature in vice, the scorn and the abhorrence of civilized man?[10]

The same year (1804) the Reverend Timothy Dwight (1752–1817), the influential president of Yale College, preached a sermon in the college chapel on "The Folly, Guilt, and Mischief of Duelling." This was twice printed in 1805 and had a wide circulation. It was also preached in the old Presbyterian Church in New York City. It was occasioned by the Burr–Hamilton duel, and was significant both because of the preacher's important standing and because Aaron Burr was his first cousin. Dwight again discussed the problem before the students of Yale in 1814. He came to the conclusion that dueling is not justifiable, and quoted with some pride his belief that only five duels had ever taken place in New England, and that the participants in at least two of these were from outside the colony or state.[11] It is evident that the Puritan churches with their strong emphasis on "reform" had taken a stand against dueling, and one that was more justified than their opposition to all forms of the theater.[12]

The evening before his duel with Burr, Alexander Hamilton (1757–1804) wrote his will and enclosed with it a paper giving his opinion of dueling and his reluctance, for various reasons affecting the welfare of others, to face the combat. The first paragraph in this statement well sums up the attitude of thoughtful people then and today on the subject: "My religious and moral principles are strongly opposed to the practice of duelling, and it would ever give me pain to shed the blood of a fellow creature in a private combat, forbidden by the laws."[13]

The Reverend Eliphalet Nott (1773–1866), afterward president of Union College and one of the most representative ministers of religion in the United States, preached about the same time a sermon in the North Dutch Church, Albany, in which he referred to the same event.

I tremble [he said] to think that I am called to attack from this place a crime, the very idea of which almost freezes one with horror, a crime, too, which exists among the polite and polished orders of society, and which is accompanied with every aggravation, committed with cool deliberation, and openly in the face of day. . . . That barbarous custom which, like a resistless torrent, is undermining the foundations of civil government, breaking down the barriers of social happiness, and sweeping away virtue, talents and domestic felicity, in its desolating course. . . . Another and an illustrious character—a father, a general, a statesman, the very man who stood on an eminence and without a rival among the sages and heroes, the future hope of his country in danger,—this man, yielding to the influence of a custom which deserves our eternal reprobation, has been brought to an untimely end. . . . It [dueling] originated in a dark and barbarous age. The polished Greek knew nothing of it. The noble Roman was above it. Rome held in equal detestation the man who exposed his life unnecessarily, and him who refused to expose it when the public good required it. . . . But though Greece and Rome knew nothing of duelling, it exists among us—the most *rash,* the most *absurd,* and the most *guilty* practice, that ever disgraced a Christian nation.[14]

The general attitude of the Church toward dueling may be shown by recalling that on his deathbed Hamilton sent for Bishop Richard Channing Moore (1762–1841) and the Reverend Dr. John Mitchell Mason (1770–1829), expressing the desire to receive the communion, and stating that it had been his intention for some time to unite with the Church. The bishop explained his trying position under the circumstances, and then asked: "Should it please God to restore you to health, sir, will you never be again engaged in a similar transaction? And will you employ all your influence in society to a discontinuance of this barbarous custom?" His answer was: "That, sir, is my deliberate intention."[15]

Soon after Hamilton's death, General Charles Cotesworth Pinckney (1746–1825) of South Carolina, speaking as vice-president of the Society of the Cincinnati, of which Hamilton had been president, said:

Is there no way of abolishing, throughout the Union, this absurd and barbarous custom, to the observance of which he (Hamilton) fell a victim? Duelling is no criterion of bravery; for I have seen cowards fight duels, and I am convinced that real courage may often be better shown in the refusal than in the acceptance of a challenge.[16]

These opinions well expressed the enlightened opinion of representative public men early in the last century on the evils of the duel of honor, and they did much to create a general sentiment in opposition to its continuance. But it was a sermon[17] preached by Lyman Beecher (1775–1863) on New Year's Day, 1806, advocating that citizens refuse to vote for any duelist that did more than anything else to stir up the American people against dueling and to bring about legislation to prevent it.

In his *Autobiography* the following interview between Dr. Beecher and his daughter Catherine tells the essential features of the story:

About this time I wrote my sermon on Dueling, that had such a run.

C. "That was the first you ever published, was it not?"

It was the first that was much known. The first was a sermon on the History of East Hampton, preached on New Year's day, 1806.

C. "What led you to preach on dueling?"

Why, Aaron Burr fought a duel with Alexander Hamilton, and killed him. There never was such a sensation as that produced through the whole country.[18] When I read about it in the paper, a feeling of indignation was roused within me. I kept thinking and thinking, and my indignation did not go to sleep. It kept working and working, and finally I began to write. No human being knew what I was thinking and feeling, nor had any agency in setting me at work. It was the duel, and myself, and God, that produced that sermon.

I worked at it, off and on, for six months, and when it was done, without consultation or advice, I preached it to my own people, and in obscure villages on the north side of the island, to see how it would sound. Finally, I preached it before Presbytery at Aquebogue, April 16, 1806.

The brethren all stared that I should venture on such a subject in such a place, but they eulogized the discussion, and thought it should be printed. . . .

. . . So I had it printed. Still it seemed destined to speedy oblivion. Its circulation was at first local, on the mere extremity of Long Island. Besides, some of my people were Democrats, and feared it might injure their political idols; for these were the days when Democracy was swelling higher, and beating more and more fiercely on old Federalism and the standing order. And my publisher was a man of little capital. However, some copies strayed to New York.

Hooker, of New York, afterward of Goshen, Connecticut, got up an association against dueling, and called on Dr. Mason to get his name, and showed him this sermon. Immediately his great mind roused up and kindled.

"You are too feeble in your beginning," he said. "We have been too negligent on the subject. Stop a little, and I will write a review of that sermon."

So the doctor reviewed the sermon, and drew up a constitution, and publicly recommended the object.

Not long after, Synod met at Newark, New Jersey, and I brought up a resolution recommending the formation of societies against dueling. I anticipated no opposition. Every thing seemed going straight. But next morning a strong reaction was developed, led by Dr. ———. The fact was, a class of men in his parish, politically affiliated with men of dueling principles, went to him and said the thing must be stopped. He came into the house and made opposition, and thereupon others joined, and it suddenly raised such a storm as I never was in before nor since. The opposition came up like a squall, sudden and furious, and there I was, the thunder and lightning right in my face; but I did not back out. When my turn came, I rose and knocked away their arguments, and made them ludicrous. Never made an argument so short, strong, and pointed in my life. . . .

An impression was made that never ceased. It started a series of efforts that have affected the whole Northern mind, at least; and in Jackson's time the matter came up in Congress, and a law was passed disfranchising a duelist.

And that was not the last of it; for when Henry Clay was up for the presidency, the Democrats printed an edition of 40,000 of that sermon, and scattered them all over the North.[19]

The following are quotations from this sermon, which did so much to influence public opinion and legislation.

When we intrust life, and liberty, and property to the hands of men, we desire some pledge of their fidelity. But what pledge can the duelist give? His religious principle is nothing; his moral principle is nothing. His honor is our only security. But is this sufficient? Are the temptations of power so feeble, are the public and private interest so inseparable, are the opportunities for fraud so few, that, amid the projects of ambition, the cravings of avarice, and the conflicts of party, there is no need of conscience to guarantee the integrity of rulers? The law of honor, were its maxims obeyed perfectly, would afford no security. . . .

Duelling is a great national sin. With the exception of a small section of the Union, the whole land is defiled with blood. From the lakes of the North to the plains of Georgia is heard the voice of lamentation and woe—the cries of the widow and fatherless. This work of desolation is performed often by men in office, by the appointed guardians of life and liberty. On the floor of Congress challenges have been threatened, if not given, and thus powder and ball have been introduced as the auxiliaries of deliberation and argument. . . . Atheists may scoff; but there is a God—a God who governs the earth in righteousness—an avenger of crimes—the supporter and destroyer of nations; and as clay in the hand of the potter, so are the nations of the earth in the hand of God.

. . . Be not deceived. The greater our present mercies and seeming security, the greater is the guilt of our rebellion, and the more certain, swift, and awful will be our calamity. We are murderers, a nation of murderers, while we tolerate and reward the perpetrators of the crime. And shall I not visit for these things? saith the Lord. Shall not my soul be avenged on such a nation as this?[20]

Leonard Bacon (1802–81) paid his tribute to the influence of this discourse first preached in a small Long Island town:

That sermon has never ceased to be a power in the politics of this country. More than anything else, it made the name of brave old Andrew Jackson distasteful to the moral and religious feeling of the people. It hung like a millstone on the neck of Henry Clay.[21]

This last reference is to the duel fought in 1826 between Clay and John Randolph.

Leonard Bacon's son, in *The History of American Christianity,* discussing Beecher's sermon, brings out clearly the influence of the pulpit in this controversy:

Words such as these resounding from pulpit after pulpit, multiplied and disseminated by means of the press, acted on by representative bodies of churches, becoming embodied in antidueling societies, exorcised the foul spirit from the land.[22]

It was not unnatural, in view of the special influence of the Beecher family in Connecticut and their identification with the antidueling cause, that Connecticut should have been the first of the states to go on record against dueling. Its constitution of 1818 included conviction for dueling, along with bribery, forgery, and other offenses, as disqualifying a person from being an elector—that is, voter.[23]

Many of the states now passed laws against dueling. In the early part of the nineteenth century (1819) Virginia, a state in which dueling had been particularly prominent, passed a most stringent law with the following preamble:

Whereas experience has evinced that the existing remedy for the suppression of the barbarous custom of duelling is inadequate to the purpose; and the progress and consequences of the evil have become so destructive as to require an effort on the part of the Legislature to arrest a vice, the result of ignorance and barbarism, justified neither by the precepts of morality, nor by the dictates of reason; for remedy whereof, Be it enacted, . . .[24]

The mention of the inadequacy of the existing remedy had reference merely to the common law as it might then be applied. The 1819 act is an elaborate one, providing among other things that any person killing or mortally wounding an antagonist in a duel was guilty of murder and should suffer death by hanging.

Similarly in Alabama under the constitution of 1819 it was specified that

The general assembly shall have power to pass such penal laws to suppress the evil practice of duelling, extending to disqualification from office or the tenure thereof, as they may deem expedient.[25]

Tennessee, by its constitution of 1834, carried the proposal of Alabama into effect by adopting this constitutional provision:

Any person who shall, after the adoption of this constitution, fight a duel, or knowingly be the bearer of a challenge to fight a duel, or send or accept a challenge for that purpose, or be an aider or abettor in fighting a duel, shall be deprived of the right to hold any office of honor or profit in this State, and shall be punished otherwise in such manner as the legislature may prescribe.[26]

Such legal enactments have of course become dead letters, for dueling as a method of settling disputes has been practically nonexistent in the United States since the Civil War period in the South.

Many antidueling societies were established in the South in 1825–26. Bishop John England (1786–1842), the eminent Roman Catholic Bishop of Charleston, was one of the active sponsors of the South Carolina Anti-Duelling Association. In November, 1827, he delivered an address in the cathedral of Charleston before the members of the association *On The Origin and History of Duelling,* a work which had a broad influence.[27] But public opinion in that state, where the code of honor between gentlemen was strong, did not easily result in making dueling illegal. This was first effected by the Reconstruction constitution of 1868.[28] But the movement against dueling was growing in the South, its stronghold.

Henry Clay (1777–1852), who had himself been in a well-known duel only twelve years earlier, speaking in Congress in 1838 on a bill to prohibit dueling in the District of Columbia, said as the final word in the debate: "When public opinion is renovated and chastened by religion, reason and humanity, the practice of duelling will be at once discontinued."[29] As a result, the bill passed with only a single vote against it.

Again in 1852, when the question of a duel was being considered by two Southern Senators in Washington over a difference which had arisen between them, Senator Robert Barnwell Rhett (1800–76) of South Carolina said:

. . . For twenty years I have been a member of the Church of Christ. The Senator knows it—everybody knows it. I cannot and will not, dishonor my religious profession. If he, or anyone else, supposes that I am so much afraid of his insults, or the opinion which requires them to be redressed in the field, as to be driven by them to abandon the profession of twenty years, he is entirely mistaken. I frankly admit that I fear God, and that I fear Him more than man. . . . I trust I have the courage to support the right and defy the wrong, although backed by an overwhelming public opinion north and south.[30]

Several of the Southern state constitutions, such as those of North and South Carolina and Georgia, adopted at the close of the Civil War, had stringent clauses against the practice. For instance, Mississippi, in its Bill of Rights in 1868, stated:

No person's life shall be perilled by the practice of duelling, and any person who shall hereafter fight a duel, or assist in the same as second, or send, accept, or knowingly carry a challenge therefor, or go out of the State to fight a duel, shall be disqualified from holding any office under this constitution, and shall forever be disfranchised in this State.[31]

In the revision of 1890 this clause was still further strengthened so as to leave no loophole, implying that the custom had not yet entirely disappeared:

Human life shall not be imperiled by the practice of duelling; and any citizen of this State who shall hereafter fight a duel, or assist in the same as second, or send, accept, or knowingly carry a challenge therefor, whether such act be done in the State, or out of it, or who shall go out of the State to fight a duel, or to assist in the same as second, or to send, accept or carry a challenge, shall be disqualified from holding any office under this constitution and shall be disfranchised.[32]

Now a majority of the states, twenty-six out of forty-eight, have constitutional provisions against dueling. These are generally of one of three types: disqualifying duelists from officeholding and the franchise; making duels illegal; or specifically authorizing the legislature to pass appropriate legislation to prevent the practice.[33] Sometimes two or more of these provisions have been adopted. In other states there is no mention of dueling in the constitution, since the custom has entirely disappeared—an encouraging example of the effect of an awakened public opinion in which the Church played a large part.

Section 2. THE SUNDAY MAIL CONTROVERSY

The frictions between Church and State over the matter of Sunday observance will be dealt with in a later section,[34] where we shall see that the old idea of the strict keeping of Sunday was specially characteristic of the Puritans, but was generally followed even in Virginia and other states until after the Civil War period. Louisiana was perhaps the only state where Sunday observance was based more on continental traditions than on those of seventeenth-century England. The Puritan Sabbath gradually gave way with the growth of more liberal ideas. This change was due to many factors: the demands of workingmen as the modern industrial system with its grinding routine developed; urbanization; immigration from continental Europe and Ireland; foreign travel; growing humanitarianism and liberalism; improved means of transportation, especially the automobile; the rise of commercialized recreation and sport; and the loosening grip of theological dogmatism.

Here we are concerned with a single manifestation of this controversy, the question of the Sunday mails. This went back to the fact that all the American colonies had laws against Sunday travel—these being merely reflections of old English laws on the same subject—which were only gradually modified under the republic. For instance, as late as 1792 Massachusetts passed laws giving the authorities power to deter forcibly those traveling on Sunday. This created a good deal of trouble with the United States government because of the carrying of the mails. The Massachusetts Supreme Court, speaking through Chief Justice Theophilus Parsons (1797–1882), determined that the indictment against the driver of a mail coach could not be maintained. Not long after this, the question of the delivery of the mail on Sundays became a matter of Congressional discussion. By an act of April 30, 1810, "to regulate the post office establishment," it was required that post offices be open "every day on which a mail or bag, or other packet or parcel of letters shall arrive." Up to that time the practice had not been uniform; but in the larger towns it had become customary, since the early years of the century, to have the offices open through local arrangement for a small portion of Sunday. Congress soon after the passage of the new act began to receive strong remonstrances. The following year the Postmaster General reported that he had issued instructions to the effect that

> At post-offices where the mail arrives on Sunday, the office is to be kept open for the delivery of letters, etc., for one hour after the arrival and sorting of the mail; but in case that would interfere with the hours of public worship, then the office is to be kept open for one hour after the usual time of dissolving the meetings, for that purpose.[35]

The Seventh Day Baptists, who have always been opposed to Sunday legislation, quoted these instructions in a later petition to Congress on Sunday legislation for the District of Columbia.[36] They called attention to Postmaster General Granger's statement at the time that an officer had been prosecuted in Pennsylvania for refusing to deliver a letter on Sunday which had not been called for within the time prescribed, and added that he doubted whether mail could be legally refused to any citizen at any reasonable hour on any day of the week.

The Churches became deeply interested in the question. According to Lyman Beecher's *Autobiography,* their organized attempt to discontinue the delivery of mails on Sunday originated in action proposed by him at a meeting of Connecticut Congregational ministers in 1814. Discussing the matter of Sunday observance, he says:

We took hold of it in the meeting at Fairfield, June, 1814, and I brought in a report, which was adopted, recommending among other things a petition to Congress. That was the origin of the famous petitions against Sunday mails.[37]

For the next twenty years this question was frequently before Congress and fully discussed. In 1825, when the various acts regarding the post office were coordinated, Congress enacted a law to the effect

That every postmaster shall keep an office in which one or more persons shall attend on every day on which a mail shall arrive, by land or water, as well as on other days, at such hours as the Postmaster-General shall direct, for the purpose of performing the duties thereof; and it shall be the duty of the postmaster, at all reasonable hours, on every day of the week, to deliver, on demand, any letter, paper, or packet, to the person entitled to, or authorized to receive, the same.[38]

As a result of this action Congress was flooded with protests, petitions, and counter-petitions, showing that feeling on the subject ran high.

Jeremiah Evarts (1781–1831), the secretary of the American Board of Commissioners for Foreign Missions, whose long service as editor of *The Panoplist* had given him great influence with Christian public opinion, was one of the leaders of the movement. In 1828 a committee was organized in New York which petitioned for the closing of the post office on Sundays and the discontinuance of the Sunday mails. Some twenty-five thousand signatures were obtained to this and similar memorials—Boston, New York, Albany, and Charleston, South Carolina, being among the petition centers.[39] This petition campaign was significant, because, though it failed of its purpose, it laid the foundations for similar campaigns on the slavery issue which had important results.[40]

It may seem to the liberally minded public today that the petitioners were asking the government to turn the clock backward, but it must be remembered, as they pointed out, that at that time the post office in London was closed on Sundays, and post offices in English provincial towns were open for only a very short period. Furthermore, our country did not then have a large cosmopolitan urban population, accustomed to European continental conditions, and it was a day when old traditions were still strong. As late as 1892—as I remember because of my personal humiliation at the time—the greatly respected rector of St. Paul's School, Concord, New Hampshire, the Reverend Henry Coit (1830–95), asked the sixth formers in sacred studies to mention the "two bulwarks of human society." We all rightly named "marriage" as the first, but none of us thought of mentioning what the rector considered the second—"the observance of the Sabbath." Perhaps he was not as far wrong as we thought, if the word "observance" is interpreted broadly to emphasize re-creation and not merely recreation.

The committee of the Senate on the post office and post roads, to which the petitions for discontinuing the Sunday mails were referred, reported on January 19, 1829, adversely to the proposal, and requested that it be discharged from further consideration of the subject. The report, presented by Senator Richard M. Johnson (1781–1850) of Kentucky, is so able and so pertinent to our subject that we quote from it at considerable length:

That some respite is required from the ordinary vocations of life, is an established principle, sanctioned by the usages of all nations, whether Christian or pagan. One day in seven has also been determined upon as the proportion of time; and, in conformity with the wishes of the great majority of citizens of this country, the first day of the week, commonly called Sunday, has been set apart to that object. The principle has received the sanction of the National Legislature, so far as to admit a suspension of all public business on that day, except in cases of absolute necessity, or of great public utility. This principle the committee would not wish to disturb. If kept within its legitimate sphere of action, no injury can result from its observance. It should, however, be kept in mind that the proper object of government is to protect all persons in the enjoyment of their religious as well as civil rights, and not to determine for any whether they shall esteem one day above another, or esteem all days alike holy.

We are aware that a variety of sentiment exists among the good citizens of this nation on the subject of the Sabbath day; and our Government is designed for the protection of one, as much as for another. . . .

With these different religious views the committee are of opinion that Congress cannot interfere. It is not the legitimate province of the Legislature to determine what religion is true, or what is false. Our Government is a civil and not a religious institution. Our constitution recognizes in every person the right to choose his own religion, and to enjoy it freely, without molestation. Whatever may be the religious sentiments of citizens, and however variant, they are alike entitled to protection from the Government, so long as they do not invade the rights of others.

The transportation of the mail on the first day of the week, it is believed, does not interfere with the rights of conscience. The petitioners for its discontinuance appear to be actuated from a religious zeal, which may be commendable if confined to its proper sphere; but they assume a position better suited to an ecclesiastical than to a civil institution. They appear, in many instances, to lay it down as an axiom, that the practice is a violation of the law of God. Should Congress, in their legislative capacity, adopt the sentiment, it would establish the principle that the Legislature is a proper tribunal to determine what are the laws of God. It would involve a legislative decision in a religious controversy, and on a point in which good citizens may honestly differ in opinion, without disturbing the peace of society, or endangering its liberties. If this principle is once introduced, it will be impossible to define its bounds. Among all the religious persecutions with which almost every page of modern history is stained, no victim ever suffered but for the violation of what Government denominated the law of God. To prevent a similar train of evils in this country, the constitution has wisely withheld from our Government the power of defining the divine law. It is a right reserved to each citizen; and while he respects the equal rights of others, he cannot be held amenable to any human tribunal for his conclusions.

Extensive religious combinations to effect a political object are, in the opinion of the committee, always dangerous. This first effort of the kind calls for the establishment of a principle, which, in the opinion of the committee, would lay the foundation for dangerous innovations upon the spirit of the constitution, and upon the religious rights of the citizens. If admitted, it may be justly apprehended that the future measures of Government will be strongly marked, if not eventually controlled, by the same influence. All religious despotism commences by combination and influence; and when that influence begins to operate upon the political institutions of a country, the civil power soon bends under it; and the catastrophe of other nations furnishes an awful warning of the consequence. . . .

Senator Johnson's report then takes up other aspects of the problem. He states that it is the opinion of the committee "that the subject should be regarded simply as a question of expediency, irrespective of its religious bearing." It is not a matter for Congressional legislation. "It rests, as it ever has done, in the legal discretion of the Postmaster General, under the repeated refusals of Congress to discontinue the Sabbath mail. . . ."

Nor can the committee discover where the system could consistently end. If the observance of a holiday becomes incorporated in our institutions, shall we not forbid the movement of an army, prohibit an assault in time of war, and lay an injunction upon our naval officers to lie in the wind while upon the ocean, on that day? Consistency would seem to require it. Nor is it certain that we should stop here. If the principle is once established that religion, or religious observances, shall be interwoven with our legislative acts, we must pursue it to its ultimatum. We shall, if consistent, provide for the erection of edifices for the worship of the Creator, and for the support of Christian ministers, if we believe such measures will promote the interests of Christianity. It is the settled conviction of the committee that the only method avoiding these consequences, with their attendant train of evils, is to adhere strictly to the spirit of the constitution, which regards the General Government in no other light than that of a civil institution, wholly destitute of religious authority.

What other nations call religious toleration, we call religious rights. They are not exercised in virtue of governmental indulgence, but as rights, of which Government cannot deprive any portion of citizens, however small. Despotic power may invade those rights, but justice still confirms them. Let the National Legislature once perform an act which involves the decision of a religious controversy, and it will have passed its legitimate bounds. The precedent will then be established, and the foundation laid for that usurpation of the divine prerogative in this country, which has been the desolating scourge to the fairest portions of the old world. Our constitution recognises no other power than that of persuasion for enforcing religious observances. Let the professors of Christianity recommend their religion by deeds of benevolence; by Christian meekness; by lives of temperance and holiness. Let them combine their efforts to instruct the ignorant; to relieve the widow and the orphan; to promulgate to the world the gospel of their Savior, recommending its precepts by their habitual example: Government will find its legitimate object in protecting them. It cannot oppose them, and they will not need its aid. Their moral influence will then do infinitely more to advance the true interests of religion, than any measures which they may call on Congress to enact. . . .[41]

Mr. Johnson, who failed of re-election to the Senate, became a member of the House of Representatives in the 21st Congress. Here he presented another able statement on the same subject the following year. In it he said:

That the memorialists regard the first day of the week as a day set apart by the Creator for religious exercises, and consider the transportation of the mail and the opening of the post offices on that day the violation of a religious duty, and call for a suppression of the practice. Others, by counter-memorials, are known to entertain a different sentiment, believing that no one day of the week is holier than another. Others, holding the universality and immutability of the Jewish decalogue, believe in the sanctity of the seventh day of the week as a day of religious devotion, and, by their memorial now before the committee, they also request that it may be set apart for religious purposes. Each has hitherto been left to the exercise of his own opinion, and it has been regarded as the proper business of Government to protect all and determine for none. But the attempt is now made to bring about a greater uniformity, at least in practice; and, as argument has failed, the Government has been called upon to interpose its authority to settle the controversy.

Congress acts under a constitution of delegated and limited powers. The committee look in vain to that instrument for a delegation of power authorizing this body to inquire and determine what part of time, or whether any, has been set apart by the Almighty for religious exercises. On the contrary, among the few prohibitions which it contains, is one that prohibits a religious test, and another which declares that Congress shall pass no law respecting an establishing of religion, or prohibiting the free exercise thereof. The committee might here rest the argument, upon the ground that the question referred to them does not come within the cognizance of Congress; but the perseverance and zeal with which the memorialists pursue their object seems to require a further elucidation of the subject; and, as the opposers of Sunday mails disclaim all intention to unite church and state, the committee do not feel disposed to impugn their motives; and whatever may be advanced in opposition to the measure will arise from the fears entertained of its fatal tendency to the peace and happiness of the nation. The catastrophe of other nations furnished the framers of the constitution a beacon of awful warning, and they have evinced the greatest possible care in guarding against the same evil. . . .[42]

William McCreery (1786–1841) presented a minority report, March 5, 1830, of which the following paragraphs show the line of argument adopted:

All Christian nations acknowledge the first day of the week to be the Sabbath. Almost every State in this Union has, by positive legislation, not only recognized this day as sacred, but has forbidden its profanation under penalties imposed by law.

It was never considered by any of those States as an encroachment upon the rights of conscience, or as an improper interference with the opinions of the few, to guard the sacredness of that portion of time acknowledged to be holy by the many.

The petitioners ask not Congress to expound the moral law; they ask not Congress to meddle with theological controversies, much less to interfere with the rights of the Jew or the Sabbatarian, or to treat with the least disrespect the religious feelings of any portion of the inhabitants of the Union; they ask the introduction of no religious coercion into our civil institutions; no blending of religion and civil affairs; but they do ask that the agents of Government, employed in the Post Office Department, may be permitted to enjoy the same opportunities of attending to moral and religious instruction or intellectual improvement on that day which is enjoyed by the rest of their fellow-citizens. They approach the Government, not for personal emolument, but as patriots and Christians, to express their high sense of the moral energy and necessity of the Sabbath for the perpetuity of our republican institutions, and respectfully request that Congress will not, by legislative enactments, impair those energies.

Among the many reasons which might be advanced that it is both expedient and a duty to grant the prayer of the petitioners, the following only are submitted:

The petitioners ask the enactment of no law establishing the first day of the week as the Christian Sabbath; they only ask the extension and application to one Department of Government of a principle which is recognised, and has, since the foundation of our Government, been acknowledged in every other Department. The principle embraced in the petitions has been recognised by Congress, by adjourning over the first day of the week. At the first session of the first Congress a law was passed establishing judicial courts, and in that law Sunday is excepted from the days on which that court may commence its sessions. All the other Executive Departments of Government are closed on that day. Congress has never, by this, considered itself as expounding the moral law, or as introducing any religious coercion into our civil institutions, or making any innovations on the religious rights of the citizens, or settling by legislation any theological question that may exist between Jews, Sabbatarians, and other denominations. The good of society requires the strict observance of one day in seven. Paley, and other writers on moral philosophy, have shown that the resting of men every seventh day; their winding up their labors and concerns once in seven days; their abstraction from the affairs of the world, to improve their minds and converse with their Maker; their orderly attendance upon the ordinances of public worship and instruction have a direct and powerful tendency to improve the morals and temporal happiness of mankind. . . .[43]

The able reports of Senator Johnson, who was later Vice-President of the United States (1837–41), rendered national service. For instance, the General Assembly of Indiana, impressed by his views on religious liberty under the

Constitution, adopted and sent to Congress a memorial indorsing his Senate report. The memorial, dated February 15, 1830, reads as follows:

That we view all attempts to introduce sectarian influence into the councils of the nation as a violation of both the letter and the spirit of the Constitution of the United States and of this State, and at the same time dangerous to our civil and religious liberties.

That all legislative interference in matters of religion is contrary to the genius of Christianity; and that there are no doctrines or observances inculcated by the Christian religion which require the arm of civil power either to enforce or to sustain them.

That we consider every connection between church and state at all times dangerous to civil and religious liberty.[44]

The state of Illinois followed suit the next year when it adopted these resolutions:

Inasmuch as it is believed that such an innovation upon our republican institutions would establish a precedent of dangerous tendency to our privileges as freemen, by involving a legislative decision in a religious controversy on a point in which good citizens may honestly differ; and whereas, a free expression of sentiment by the present general assembly on the subject may tend, in a great degree, to avert so alarming an evil as a union of church and state; therefore,—

Resolved by the people of the State of Illinois, represented in the general assembly, That the able report made by Col. Richard M. Johnson, of Kentucky, in the Senate of the United States on the 19th January, 1829, . . . meets our decided approbation.[45]

Alabama, in spite of its being in what is now called the "Bible Belt," took similar action, resolving that the opinion expressed by the committee of Congress "is entitled to the highest consideration of the friends of the Constitution, and every lover of civil and political freedom."[46]

Apparently Senator Johnson's arguments had carried weight, and the attempt to prevent the "Sunday mail" failed. But, as we shall see later, a similar Congressional controversy arose half a century later in connection with the opening of the World's Fair in Chicago. This will be discussed when the modern development of Sunday legislation is considered.[47]

It is an interesting fact that though the Protestant clergy as a whole were active in trying to stop the transportation of the mails on Sunday, a Protestant minister, Reverend O. B. Brown, living in the District of Columbia, was largely responsible for the preparation of Senator Johnson's able opposition report, based largely on the noninterference by the Church in purely secular affairs and on the importance of maintaining religious freedom.[48] He was chief clerk of the Post Office Department and also an active Baptist preacher. It is not without significance that he and Amos Kendall, who revised the report, were both active members of the Baptist Church, a denomination with strong convictions on Church–State separation, though generally inclined to rigid Sabbatarian views.

The Senate report, based on the sound theory that our government is "a civil and not a religious institution," made Senator Johnson a national hero of the more liberal-minded and radical groups, to which he also appealed by his opposition to imprisonment for debt. Among his ardent supporters was the then notorious Frances Wright, who believed that he had struck a heavy blow at a union of Church and State, and asserted that the mail question "betrayed the whole soul of priestcraft. . . . A standard is reared under which all the party-coloured bands of orthodoxy may rally into one phalanx."[49] Many radical and workingmen's papers joined in her attack.

The Sunday mail controversy is not the only one in which the United States Post Office has borne the brunt of a battle between the Churches and the State. The successful antilottery campaign[50] was another. During the slavery debate the question of the delivery of abolition literature through Southern post offices became an acute national issue in which the Churches were indirectly involved through the antislavery societies. John C. Calhoun (1782–1850) tried to have enacted in 1836 a postal censorship bill which would have prevented the delivery in any state whose own laws forbade it of "any pamphlet, handbill, or other printed paper, or pictorial representation, touching the subject of slavery." Henry Clay (1777–1852) declared the proposal unconstitutional, and Daniel Webster (1782–1852) pointed out that "Congress may under this example be called upon to pass laws to suppress the circulation of political, religious, or other publications which produced excitement in the States."[51] The bill was defeated.

Section 3. THE ANTIMASONIC CAMPAIGN

In a previous section[52] attention has been given to Freemasonry as a factor in uniting the colonies and in laying the foundations of separation of Church and State. We have shown that it held an honorable position among the fathers of the nation and that Church and Masonic membership by the same person was not considered inconsistent by Protestants. In the early days of the republic, however, there are evidences of friction between Church and State on the matter. For example, as early as 1808 the New York Baptist Association considered this question from one of its member churches, "Is it proper or expedient to admit a Free Mason, tho apparently a believer, into a church?" The answer agreed upon was clear and specific. "No person continuing to associate with Free Masons ought to be considered a proper subject for Church Fellowship."[53] Similarly, in 1820, the Presbyterian Synod of Pittsburgh pronounced Masonry "unfit for professing Christians."[54]

But such an attitude was then uncommon. It was not until somewhat later that any real controversy arose between the Church on the one hand and secret societies, especially the Masonic order, on the other.

The organized Antimasonic movement, beginning with the Morgan trials in western New York in 1826, secured the active support of many religious bodies, and as the movement developed the first national third party it brought churches into a political controversy. Although the Roman Catholic Church had been long opposed to Freemasonry and its members subject to excommunication if they joined the society and Pope Clement XII had issued the first papal pronouncement against it in 1738,[55] the extreme Protestant opposition came much later. There had always been some suspicion of secret societies among Americans, as witness the furore at the close of the eighteenth century over the New England Illuminati[56] with which the Freemasons were believed involved. But the fact that George Washington and many of the founders of the nation were Masons led to their being generally accepted and honored, as we have seen in the discussion of the influence of Freemasonry on the ideals of the Republic.[57] It took the kidnapping and alleged slaying in 1826 of William Morgan (b. 1775), a bricklayer of Batavia, New York, because of the report that he was about to publish a revelation of Masonic secrets, to cause a vigorous campaign against the order. Because of its secrecy people came to believe that it was trying to control the State, and to do so in a way inimical to Christianity. And so Masonry got drawn into the Church–State issue.

In the trials which followed Morgan's disappearance in 1826 much was made of the alleged fact that the Masonic oath prevented a Mason from acting as a juror in cases where a Mason of like degree was a party and his opponent was not. Though American Masons were all necessarily theists, there was the possibility of the controversy developing into a serious issue. The forces of organized religion had for some time felt that the lodge was usurping in many cases the place of the Church, and "opposition to Masonry was taken up by the churches as a sort of religious crusade."[58]

The Morgan incident and the ensuing public discussion resulted in a serious decrease in Masonic membership. For instance, in New York many Masons renounced their vows, and the membership dwindled from about twenty thousand to about three thousand in the decade from 1826 to 1836. The churches became aroused; partly because it was felt that a secret society of this character was dangerous in a democracy, and partly because interest in Masonry was believed to detract attention from the Church and religion. The Presbyterian, Methodist, Baptist, and Congregational Churches in New England and New York, and also the Quakers, Moravians, and some other groups in Pennsylvania, were specially involved—congregations being frequently split over the issue.

Masons were in many cases excluded from admission to church membership and from participating in the communion, while pastors who were Masons were barred from some pulpits.

It was a time of much ferment in religious matters. Congress was being deluged with petitions against the Sunday mails, a Christian Constitution party was in process of formation (which some identified with the Antimasons), and liberals and conservatives were forming into hostile groups. In Massachusetts the orthodox were accused of trying to elect a legislature and to secure courts favorable to their view. Everywhere new religious movements were under way and religious passions aroused. Such was the psychology of the period when the national Antimasonic political convention of 1830 appointed a committee "to consider the nature, principles, and tendency of Freemasonry as regards its effect on the Christian religion."[59]

This brought the religious issue formally into the national political arena. Many Antimasonic party gatherings, especially in 1830 and 1831, took the ground that Masonry was antagonistic to Christianity and should be opposed. John Quincy Adams (1767–1848) says in his *Diary* that Antimasonry is "nothing more than orthodoxy in disguise."[60] He saw that it was attacking liberal groups such as Unitarians and Universalists as well as the Masons. The historian of the movement notes this same tendency. He says:

> The Antimasonic party, having so many of the prominent religious men of the country in its ranks and being at this time in a crusade in which "churches were distracted," naturally entered as another element in the religious distress of the period. In New England this was especially true as the party there was composed of the ultra religious country people already in opposition to the liberal spirit of the cities. It can be easily seen from these circumstances that the party soon received the stigma of the "Christian party in politics."
>
> Indeed if there was a religious party in existence it was the Antimasonic, for it wielded religion as one of the strongest weapons. Not only was every effort directed against Masonic preachers and laymen, but the churches in their councils condemned the order. . . .[61]

The press of the movement was almost always marked by a "religious" tone and was extensive. It was estimated in 1830 that there were about one thousand newspapers in the United States, and of these 124 were "founded exclusively upon the principle of opposition to free masonry or so conducted." Most of these —about three-quarters—were published in New York and Pennsylvania.[62] Perhaps the most influential was the *Albany Evening Journal,* founded in 1830, of which Thurlow Weed (1797–1882) was editor. The Antimasonic party, attracting many of the same social-economic groups that later supported prohibition, was strong enough in 1831 to nominate a national presidential candidate,

William Wirt (1772–1834) of Maryland, and in the election of 1832 to secure 2.65 per cent of the popular vote and seven electoral votes—all from Vermont.[63] It was also relatively strong in Pennsylvania, where it had the support of Thaddeus Stevens (1792–1868), and elected a governor, as it did in Vermont. This was the first "third party" with its own national ticket. Incidentally, its convention was the first to adopt a written platform.

The close connection between Antimasonry and some of the churches is shown by a study of the first "United States Anti-Masonic Convention," held in 1830, the one which nominated the political candidates just referred to. This appointed a committee to inquire into the effect of Freemasonry on the Christian religion. Its report to the convention, referring to Masonry, said:

> . . . It is not Christianity, or the handmaid of it, but an impious substitute for it. By estranging the mind from the doctrines of the gospels, it inevitably prepares its chambers for the lodgement of infidel principles. It harmonizes as well with the tenets of the Jew, the Pagan, and the Mahometan as with those of the humble followers of Christ. . . . It is a formidable objection to freemasonry, that it attempts a connexion with religion, and presents, in miniature, to the view of the American people, the abhorred union of church and state, revolting to the feelings of every freeman, and condemned by every principle of republicanism.[64]

The convention acknowledged that there were many ministers of religion in the order, but called upon them to leave it, stating that its secret oaths were not binding.

The new party drew support away from Clay and thus helped the victory of Andrew Jackson (1767–1845)—a high degree Mason; but its separate existence was short-lived, since by 1838 it had merged with the Whigs.[65] The slavery issue had become so acute that Masonry was politically almost forgotten.

Antimasonry seems to have had particularly strong support from the Presbyterians, Baptists, and Methodists. The Presbyterian synod in Pittsburgh in 1821 condemned Masonry as an institution "unfit for professing Christians," and Wirt writes that he had been told that the Presbyterians were coming to his aid in the presidential campaign; while a New England paper in 1830 said "that nearly every Anti-masonic press is under Presbyterian surveillance," a religious designation which at that time in New England would probably include Congregational. A Presbyterian pastor in New York published in 1833 a typical pamphlet[66] entitled, *Masonry proved to be a work of darkness repugnant to the Christian religion and inimical to the Republican government.*

The Methodist Church was also torn by the Antimasonic movement. As early as 1823 a Methodist conference in Pennsylvania had prohibited its ministers from becoming Masons, and in the excitement of the fall of 1829 a Lancaster paper asserted that "No religious sect throughout the United States has done more for the Antimasonic cause than the Methodists."[67]

Organizations of Baptists, Mennonites, Dunkards, Quakers, and Dutch Reformed joined in the attack. The action of the Dutch Reformed General Conference in 1831, when the political excitement over Masonry was at its height, was particularly significant, since it not only condemned the institution but also forbade its members to enter the order.[68]

The elements which made up the Nativist parties of the future were largely behind political Antimasonry. Extreme groups of Protestants saw similarities between the emphasis on ritual and secrecy (whether oath or confessional) of Masons and Roman Catholics. "Popery and Freemasonry" were denounced together; both were declared to have something of the Inquisition about them and to be dangerous to democratic institutions. The Antimasons were, in the opinion of many, determined to have the control of the State captured by Protestant Christian protagonists. They carried this religious emphasis in public life so far that they were frequently charged with trying to tie up politics with religion.

This point came out clearly in the Pennsylvania campaign of 1835 of the Reverend Henry Augustus Mühlenberg (1782–1854), who had served for a quarter of a century as pastor of the important Trinity Lutheran Church in Reading until he resigned because of ill health. Later, after serving in Congress, he became the Democratic candidate for governor. His opponents in the party who had supported the faction of the long-time governor and advocate of public schools, George Wolf (1777–1840), accused him, as many had accused other active Antimasons, of being an advocate of Church–State union. The Chester *Democrat* said:

> For upwards of eighteen years H. A. Mühlenberg professed to be a minister of the Message of Peace. . . . History portrays in glaring characters the danger of the unity of the civil with religious power. . . . Would every Pennsylvanian resist the encroachments of religious upon civil power, let him on this ground alone refuse to give his vote to Rev. Henry A. Mühlenberg.[69]

Governor Wolf was thereupon attacked by his political opponents for having appointed a man to office through the influence of a Roman Catholic priest. "We have read much about church and state in this contest," said a Pittsburgh paper, "and from whom has it come? none other than those who for the last six years have priest-ridden the Commonwealth." It was frequently declared in the campaign that "Catholicism, Masonry, and infidelity were combined to crush the liberty of the Republic." This, we are told, "was the beginning of the strong anti-Catholic feeling in Pennsylvania with which so many prominent

Antimasons, especially in the western part of the State, were later connected. . . ."[70]

Opposition to the Masons, due largely to their being a secret society, died down before the middle of the last century, but it has occasionally revived. For instance, in 1868 the National Christian Association was founded in Aurora, Illinois, with the special object of opposing secret societies or orders such as the Masons and the Jesuits, as well as Mormons, atheists, spiritualists, and advocates of free love. It published from 1867 to 1871 a weekly journal, *The Christian Cynosure*.

In these ways the active identification of large portions of the American Church with the Antimasonic cause resulted in organized religion becoming confused with politics in the public mind.

Section 4. THE ANTILOTTERY CAMPAIGN

Lotteries were accepted as a matter of course in colonial times, and many churches and educational institutions profited by them. Among the colleges were Harvard, Yale, and the College of New Jersey. Among the churches were several prominent Episcopal and Presbyterian churches in Pennsylvania;[71] though one much-advertised plan to construct pleasure grounds and public baths through funds secured in this way resulted in organized opposition from the clergy and others. As a result, a law was passed by the state legislature in 1761 declaring lotteries, whether public or private, to be public nuisances, and a heavy fine was decreed for opening any new one. But existing lotteries were allowed to continue,[72] especially those under state or municipal auspices; and half a century was to pass before the antilottery movement gained much headway. Even Faneuil Hall in Boston, "the cradle of American liberty," was rebuilt with the help of a public lottery in 1761 after the fire; and the Continental Congress in 1776 authorized a lottery for the benefit of soldiers in the field. The Church, which frequently profited by them, raised no effective voice of opposition, though as early as 1699 an assembly of Boston ministers attacked them as "cheats" and their promoters as "pillagers of the public."[73] As late as 1775, the handsome First Baptist Church of Providence, where Brown University holds its commencements, was built largely with the proceeds from a lottery.

Private philanthropy was seldom organized, and when public funds were not available for some important public purpose, such as a college or a library, it was generally considered proper to resort to a lottery, as long as it was duly authorized by the legislature and properly conducted. A striking case was that of a lottery in the interest of Dartmouth College in 1791. The drawing of tickets was held on the preacher's desk of the college chapel, "to the scandal of some worthy people."[74] Similarly, a little later (1803) a lottery was resorted to to build a Roman Catholic parochial school in Baltimore.[75] The development of the new capital city in Washington was aided by the same expedient. Legislatures also frequently granted permission for lotteries for educational purposes. For instance, Dr. Eliphalet Nott (1773–1866), president of Union College, secured permission from the New York legislature in 1805 for four lotteries of $20,000 each, and in 1814 a bill was adopted authorizing him to raise in this way $200,000 for Union; $40,000 for Hamilton College; $30,000 for the New York College of Physicians and Surgeons; and $4,000 for the Asbury African Church of New York.[76]

It was not until the nineteenth century was well under way that, as a result of the growing Christian conscience in matters social and the development of private philanthropy, the movement against this form of gambling received wide statutory recognition. Antilottery legislation was adopted by New York in 1821, and lotteries were suppressed both by New York and Massachusetts in 1833. Other states followed their example,[77] such as Connecticut in 1834 and Maryland shortly afterward, and Virginia in 1850.

Among the clergymen who took a lead in the early movement against public lotteries was the Reverend Dr. John M. Mason (1770–1829), professor in the Union Theological Seminary, New York, and later provost of Columbia College. He wrote a series of papers entitled "Considerations on Lots." The series begins with this statement:

> The frequency of public lotteries, the enormous system of private frauds which has grown out of them, the extensive ramifications of their *principle* through the community, and the facility with which many well disposed persons are seduced into the support of that principle, seem to require an investigation of the true nature and use of the *lot*. We shall accordingly devote some papers to that subject.
>
> A lot is an action, intended to decide a point without the aid of human skill or power. This definition includes every form of the lot, or every decision which in common language is said to be *left to chance*. Thus, whether the lot or the chance consist in drawing a ticket at random out of the lottery-wheel, after it has been turned round to prevent collusion, or in the position of a die which is thrown after rattling it in the box, or in the particular distribution of cards after a promiscuous shuffle, or in the tossing up of a piece of money, is a matter of no moment. The principle of the action is still the same; the decision to be effected is put avowedly out of the control of human skill and power.[78]

His major argument against lotteries—that since all things are determined by Divine Providence lots must be so determined—seems to the modern reader far-fetched and untenable; but his essay is valuable as evidence of the amount of gambling which then existed and of the growing public opinion against it.

New York state, where Dr. Mason lived, was a special offender. In 1830, the year when the state, stimulated by civic and religious efforts, put in its new constitution a provision that the legislature could never grant the right to conduct lotteries, $9,270,000 was expended on them.[79]

Pennsylvania seems to have had a specially difficult time in doing away with the lottery evil; Philadelphia was its principal center of activity in the United States.[80] In 1833–34 three events took place which had a wide influence. The passing by the legislature of strong antilottery legislation; the publication of a book entitled *A Brief Survey of the Great Extent and Evil Tendencies of the Lottery System of the United States* by Job Roberts Tyson (1803–58), a prominent Philadelphia lawyer who was active in public and philanthropic matters; and the founding of the Pennsylvania Society for the Suppression of Lotteries.

The essential parts of the legislative acts, which were given broad national publicity by Tyson's book and by the new antilottery society, deserve quotation.

An Act for the Entire Abolition of Lotteries

. . . Sect. 1. Be it enacted, by the Senate and House of Representatives of the Commonwealth of Pennsylvania, in General Assembly met, and it is hereby enacted by the authority of the same, That from and after the thirty first day of December, one thousand eight hundred and thirty three, all and every lottery and lotteries, and device and devices in the nature of lotteries, shall be utterly and entirely abolished, and are hereby declared to be thenceforth unauthorized and unlawful.

Sect. 2. And be it further enacted by the authority aforesaid, That from and after the day aforesaid, any person or persons who shall sell or expose to sale, or cause to be sold or exposed to sale, or shall keep on hand for the purpose of sale, or shall advertise or cause to be advertised for sale, or shall aid or assist, or be in any wise concerned in the sale, or exposure to sale, of any lottery ticket or tickets, or any share or part of any lottery ticket, in any lottery or device in the nature of a lottery within this commonwealth, or elsewhere, and any person or persons who shall advertise or cause to be advertised, the drawing of any scheme in any lottery, or be in any way concerned in the managing, conducting, carrying on, or drawing of any lottery or device in the nature of a lottery, and shall be convicted thereof in any court of competent jurisdiction, shall, for each and every such offence, forfeit and pay a sum not less than one hundred dollars, and not exceeding ten thousand dollars, or be sentenced to undergo an imprisonment not exceeding six months, at the discretion of the court.[81]

A month later the legislature adopted resolutions to provide for the wider distribution of the Act.

Whereas, lotteries are an acknowledged evil of great magnitude, vitally injurious to the morals and industry of any community: And whereas, the public and private injuries resulting from lotteries can only be remedied by their total abolition: And whereas, one state cannot effectually suppress the sale of lottery tickets, and the pursuit of this mode of gaming, without the co-operation of the other states of the Union: And whereas, the state of Pennsylvania has recently enacted that all lotteries shall be totally abolished in said state from and after the thirty-first day of December next, and has prohibited the sale of any ticket or tickets within the same, after said period. Therefore,

Resolved, by the Senate and House of Representatives of the Commonwealth of Pennsylvania, in General Assembly met, That the governor be requested to transmit a copy of the first and second sections of the act of Assembly, passed March 1st, 1833, entitled, "An act for the entire abolition of lotteries," together with a copy of these resolutions, to the governor of each state, with a request that he will, at the earliest period, lay the same before the legislature of his state, and request their co-operation in the effort of this commonwealth to effect the entire abolition of lotteries.

And be it further resolved by the authority aforesaid, That the governor be requested to transmit a copy of the said sections and of these resolutions to the president of the United States, with a request that he will at the earliest period lay the same before congress, and use such measures as may in his opinion be best calculated to effect the entire abolition of lotteries within the District of Columbia.[82]

Tyson's book, from which these quotations have been made, showed the bad moral and public effects of lotteries, especially in Pennsylvania, but also to some extent in the twenty other states where they existed legally. There were then more than two hundred offices for the sale of lottery tickets in Philadelphia alone, in spite of the act of the legislature designed to discontinue lotteries after the close of the previous year. The clergy and other thoughtful citizens were much aroused,[83] and the new society tried with much effect to show their extent, bad moral effect, and financial waste. The evil was so prevalent in most parts of the country that it has been estimated that 420 lotteries with $53,000,000 in prizes were functioning about 1830.[84]

An important step forward was taken in 1842, when the Federal government passed "An act to suppress the vending of lottery tickets in the District of Columbia." It is interesting, as showing the condition at the time, that this Act was obliged to provide for an exception in the case of then existing contracts regarding lottery tickets authorized by the common council of the city of Alexandria, at that time a part of the District of Columbia. The closing paragraph of the Act provided

That it shall not be lawful, under color of any contract made with the Common Council of the said city of Alexandria, as aforesaid, to vend or sell tickets, or parts of tickets, or shares, in any lottery or lotteries, authorized by the Legislature of any State or Territory within the United States, or any foreign Government.[85]

The part played by the Church in suppressing the Louisiana Lottery and various modern forms of commercialized gambling will be dealt with in a later section.[86]

Section 5. RELIGIOUS JOURNALISM

What is generally considered the first newspaper in what is now the United States was *Publick Occurrences.*[87] This appeared in a single issue only, in Boston, September 25, 1690. The editor announces his purposes, the first two of which bring out the double interest of our people in Church and State.

> *That which is herein proposed, is,* First, *That* Memorable Occurrents *of* Divine Providence *may not be neglected or forgotten, as they too often are.* Secondly, *That people everywhere may better understand the Circumstances of Publique Affairs, both abroad and at home; which may not direct their* Thoughts *at all times, but at some times also to assist their* Business *and* Negotiations.[88]

The issue opens with an account of a Thanksgiving Day, an event which for more than three centuries has represented a point of important contact between the religious interests of the Church and the public activities of the community.

> The Christianized *Indians* in some parts of *Plimouth,* have newly appointed a day of Thanksgiving to God for his mercy in supplying their extream and pinching Necessities under their late want of Corn, and for His giving them now a prospect of a very Comfortable Harvest. Their Example may be worth Mentioning.[89]

The regular American press began with the first issue of the *Boston News-Letter* on April 24, 1704. This had as its major feature extracts from London papers "concerning the present Danger of the Kingdom and of the Protestant Religion"—again linking Church and State with a speech of the Queen to Parliament on the subject. But this did not make the *News-Letter* a religious journal. Its second editor, however, taking over the paper in 1723, gave it what the author of *Journalism in the United States from 1690 to 1872* calls a "semi-religious character." In the publisher's advertisement he says:

> It being my Desire to make this as profitable and entertaining to the good people of this country as I can, I propose to give not only the most material articles of intelligence, both foreign and domestic, which concern the political state of the world; but also because this is a country, that has yet, through the mercy of God, many people in it, that have the State of religion in the world very much at heart, and would be glad, if they knew how to order their prayers and praises to the Great God thereupon, I shall endeavour, now and then, to insert an article upon the state of religion. I shall, therefore, from time to time, wait upon such as I may know to cultivate a correspondence with the most eminent persons in several nations, who may please to communicate to me, and thereby to the public, such things as all good men cannot but receive with satisfaction.[90]

Religious journalism in this country as distinct from secular also goes back to Boston, in the period of the Great Awakening[91] when *The Christian History* appeared for two years, 1743–45.

The first definitely denominational periodical was the *Arminian Magazine,* which appeared in 1789–90 under the editorship of two great Methodist leaders —Thomas Coke (1747–1814) and Francis Asbury (1745–1816). It was followed by similar periodicals published in behalf and often under the official auspices of the Baptist, Unitarian, Universalist, Episcopalian, Presbyterian, Congregational, and Roman Catholic Churches. These publications were for the most part interested not merely in religious faith and church work, but also to some extent in the issues of the day such as Deism, education, and slavery—the last-named splitting the periodicals of the North and South into two hostile camps. It is noticeable that in the middle of the century "religious fervor was giving way to reform,"[92] and this was reflected in the religious press.

Perhaps the most noteworthy of the early strictly religious periodicals was *The Churchman* of New York City. From 1804 until the present it has been an effective and on the whole representative organ of the liberal elements in the Protestant Episcopal Church, and it has appeared without interruption except during the War of 1812 and the Civil War. Recently it has become undenominational, though its editor continues to be an Episcopalian. It has fearlessly attacked public abuses and been a strong supporter of the separation of Church and State, but not always tolerant of the ecclesiastical views of others.

A period of larger usefulness for the denominational press opened after the War of 1812. It began in 1819 with *The Christian Watchman,* which in 1848 absorbed *The Christian Reflector,* and became the leading Baptist periodical, as *The Watchman and Reflector,* of Boston. During and after the Civil War *The Examiner* became even more influential.[93] It was followed by the *New York Observer,* a large, and long a favorite paper in Presbyterian homes, and by another influential Presbyterian paper, the *New York Evangelist;* the *Christian Register,* Unitarian; the *Christian Intelligencer,* Dutch Reformed; and still others—all by 1830.

The Methodists started all sorts of publications bearing the "Advocate" name, of which *The Christian Advocate,* founded in 1825 and published in New York, was the most influential. In its early days it was conservative, while its rivals, the *Northern Independent* and *Zion's Herald* of Boston, were earlier in taking a strong antislavery stand.

Nearly all these papers have been from their early days interested in reforms —antislavery, protemperance, favorable to Sunday legislation, and supporting the reading of the Bible in the public schools. *The Christian Advocate* is still a vigorous denominational organ of Methodism, in 1948 in its one hundred and thirteenth year. Although primarily interested in advancing the cause of religion through the Methodist Church, it has taken strong ground on many public questions, especially as a supporter of prohibition.

Let us turn now to a group of periodicals which developed into the strong modern undenominational Protestant religious press of which *The Christian Century* is the most conspicuous representative. In 1806 a somewhat broader type of religious journalism received an able recruit in the person of the Reverend John Mitchell Mason (1770–1829), a professor in the Union Theological Seminary. He projected the *Christian Magazine*. But even broader in its scope, and perhaps the most influential in its public policy, was the monthly *Panoplist* of Boston, edited from its foundation in 1805 to 1810 by the Reverend Jedidiah Morse (1761–1826), "Father of American Geography," and later (1822) author of the report to the secretary of war on Indian affairs. From 1810 to 1820 Jeremiah Evarts (1781–1831) was the editor. He was an active and respected layman who was secretary of the American Board of Commissioners for Foreign Missions, and editor of its *Missionary Herald,* with which the *Panoplist* was merged in 1821. He was deeply interested in having the Christian churches contribute to the amelioration of the nation's social and political ills. In some matters, such as protecting the rights of the Cherokee Indians,[94] the problems of temperance, and Sunday rest, he was the national spokesman of America's Christian conscience. As Evarts stated in 1817, "If the *Panoplist* has any merit it consists in the aid which our pages impart to the various plans of Christian benevolence now in operation."[95]

Another feature which gave it an enviable and all too rare position in the field of religious journalism of the last century was the note of Christian charity which generally marked its editorial policy in dealing with controversial Church issues. Although theologically conservative and opposed to Unitarianism, the editor proclaimed that "in controversies with the enemies of the truth, the law of love is never to be transgressed."[96] Would that this note had more generally marked our denominational periodicals!

Roman Catholic journalism in the United States really began with *The Shamrock, or Hibernian Chronicle,* published in New York from 1810 to 1817. Its purpose may be taken as characteristic of most of the nineteenth-century Catholic papers in the United States. Charles O'Conor (1804–84) speaks of his father, its editor, as having his pen "ever directed in vindicating the fame of Ireland, the honor of our United American States, or the truth and purity of his cherished mother the Apostolic Church."[97]

Bishop John England (1786–1842) of Charleston, South Carolina, followed in 1822 with *The United States Catholic Miscellany,* "the first continuing Catholic Newspaper in the United States."[98] Of this paper the bishop himself, writing in 1832, said that during upwards of ten years he and his associates have, at a very serious pecuniary loss, not to mention immense labour, published a weekly paper, "The United States Catholic Miscellany," in which the cause of Ireland at home and Irishmen abroad, and of the Catholic religion through the world, has been defended to the best of their ability. This paper is published every week on a large sheet of eight pages containing twenty four pages of letter press, in the city of Charleston.[99]

With the second quarter of the century and the large influx of Roman Catholic immigrants came a great development of the Catholic press. The *Truth Teller,* which appeared in New York in 1825, was perhaps the most prominent journal. It merged in 1855 with the *Irish American.* In 1830 came the "first strictly Catholic magazine," the *Metropolitan, or Catholic Monthly Magazine* of Baltimore. This was followed in 1839 by the *Catholic Register,* which soon combined with the well-known *Freeman's Journal,* established the same year. This paper was for several years under the control of Bishop John Hughes (1797–1864). It became particularly well known in the years from 1880 to 1888 when Maurice Francis Egan (1852–1924)—afterward professor in the Catholic University—was its editor.

A group of Roman Catholic papers arose in the middle of the nineteenth century which were largely ecclesiastical, political, and social in character. They battled against the attacks of the Know-Nothings and the Nativists, and supported the Irish and Catholic cause. Some of these still exist—*The Catholic Telegraph* of Cincinnati, founded in 1831; *The Boston Pilot,* 1837; *The Freeman's Journal,* already mentioned. Of these the *Pilot* was specially influential in the Civil War period as a strong supporter of the Union cause.[100]

The *Ave Maria* has had a large circulation in the West since 1865. There have also been any number of Catholic magazines from 1830 on, as well as Catholic quarterlies since the time when Orestes Brownson (1803–76), having been converted to the Church, transformed his old *Boston Quarterly Review* into *Brownson's Quarterly Review,* in 1844.[101]

Some 550 Roman Catholic periodicals were started in the United States in the period of about one hundred years from 1809 to 1911, but only five of those published during the first half of the nineteenth century survived until 1911. About two-thirds of the then existing periodicals were in the English language.[102] It was estimated that the total weekly circulation of Catholic periodicals in the United States about a decade ago was from seven to ten million copies.[103]

In general Roman Catholic religious journalism in this country has concerned itself mainly with advancing the interests of the Church and defending it against misunderstanding and abuse. This defense was particularly important in the middle of the last century when the Know-Nothings and the Nativists were so active. The two political and social matters which have most attracted its attention have been the cause of free Ireland, and the attempt to secure public financial support for parochial schools.[104] Other recent public interests[105] have been the warfare against Marxian Communism as developed by Soviet Russia; the demand that the United States government take heed of the plight of the Mexican Church, frequently under attack by the State; and that in the recent civil war in Spain (1936–39) and since, our government should recognize General Franco, a practicing Catholic believing in Catholicism as the State Church, but including among his followers many reactionaries who showed themselves glad to secure German Nazi and Italian Fascist help. The issue was complicated during the war because Franco's opponents, the Loyalists (Republicans), favored complete separation of Church and State but included some extreme leftists and Communists in their leadership. Outside of the issues named, and recently the question of birth control,[106] the American Catholic press has probably not given itself so much to public political issues as has the Protestant denominational press. The old charge, which has had some truth in a few municipalities, that the Catholic press was politically controlled can no longer be maintained as a general thesis. For historic reasons which identified the Church, and especially the dominant Irish element, with the Democratic party, the leading Roman Catholics of the United States have generally been and are today Democrats, but there are many notable exceptions. Furthermore, in World War II from 1939 on, in spite of the neutrality of Ireland, many Roman Catholic leaders and periodicals came out strongly on the side of England.

During the war the presidential campaign of 1940 took place, and the diverse attitudes of different Roman Catholic papers were notable. For example, many if not most diocesan papers held entirely aloof from the campaign. Of the journals of opinion two of the most influential, *America,* the Jesuit weekly, and *The Catholic World,* came out clearly against a third term for the Democratic candidate, Franklin D. Roosevelt, and the same was true of *Social Justice,* Father Coughlin's paper, which some Catholics however repudiate. On the other hand, the editors of *The Commonweal,* a highly respected magazine, announced that its editorial board was divided; a majority favored Mr. Roosevelt, while a minority favored Mr. Willkie or were "on the fence." Many Roman Catholic papers editorially urged independent voting, and took an impartial attitude. Noteworthy among these was *The Catholic Herald Citizen* of Milwaukee, which accepted and reprinted (October 5, 1940) the views of the Reverend Maurice Sheehy of the Catholic University.

The effort to coerce any Catholic group, as a Catholic group, to support a particular party or candidate, would in this country lead to disaster. I can foresee no greater tragedy for the Catholic Church in the United States than that which would be involved in alliance with a political party. Such an alliance might seem temporarily expedient, but in the long run it would mean persecution, intolerance, and a loss of that prestige which has been gained by remaining aloof from political campaigns. It reflects great credit upon our Catholic laity that it is horrified when a priest so forgets his spiritual office as to take sides publicly in a political campaign.[107]

One of the editors of *The Commonweal,* to whom we are indebted for many of the above facts, after making a broad study of "The Catholic Press and the Election," summed up his conclusions by saying: "In general, then, it might be said that the Catholic press as a whole has not expressed its preference in the current presidential election."[108] Such a statement from a responsible source would scarcely have been possible a generation earlier, when Irish freedom was a live American political issue.

The Occident, founded in 1843 and long edited by Isaac Leeser (1806–68), was the pioneer in Jewish periodical literature. It interested itself in public issues, and is credited with large influence in the ultimate victory which made Jews for the first time eligible for public office under the constitution of North Carolina (1868).[109]

We must now give some attention to religious journals of more than denominational significance and of broad public influence.

In the last half of the century *The Independent* came to the fore. The first issue appeared December 7, 1848. It had two major purposes: to advance Congregationalism through home missionary efforts, especially in the West, and to oppose slavery by supporting the "Free Soil" movement. It was a weekly religious newspaper under a series of able and influential editors—Leonard Bacon (1802–81), Joseph P. Thompson (1819–79), and Henry Ward Beecher (1813–87), all Congregational ministers. In 1856 it had a circulation of some twenty-five thousand. When Beecher, who for a score of years had been contributing editor, became the editor in 1861, it gave up its sectarian connection and became broadly representative of liberal Protestantism, largely increasing its number of subscribers and its influence, especially in the antislavery campaign. It engaged in a memorable tilt with its more conservative rival, the *Evangelist.* This incident is quoted in a standard history of the press in the United States as an illustration of the fact

that a portion of the religious press became somewhat vitiated in its contact with scheming politicians, and that the rough and dirty Pool of Politics was not the soft and sight-giving Pool of Siloam to the editors of these publications. One illustration we have given in the tilt between the *Independent* and *Evangelist.* . . .[110]

In 1870 Beecher was succeeded by a layman, Henry C. Bowen (1813–96), the son-in-law of Lewis Tappan (1788–1873), well-known abolitionist. Beecher then became editor of *The Christian Union,* whose circulation went up to over one hundred thousand. It went in for religious articles rather than for news, and was generally considered the best representative of the religious press of the time.[111] In 1875 Lyman Abbott (1835–1922) became its editor; later it became highly influential as *The Outlook*. This magazine was a factor of importance in broadening the social-welfare interests of the American Churches, and in adapting their theological views to square with the conclusions of modern scholarship and science. Theodore Roosevelt (1858–1919) after retiring from the presidency served for some time as contributing editor, and helped to make the periodical influential in supporting a broad international ("manifest destiny") policy as well as movements of liberal political and social reform. It was in some ways the predecessor of *The Christian Century.*

The first definitely religious newspaper, as distinct from a weekly or monthly journal, was *The Recorder,* established in Chillicothe, Ohio, in 1814, by a minister of the gospel. Similarly, the *Boston Recorder* was founded in 1816 by Nathaniel Willis (1780–1870), father of the poet, with Sidney Edwards Morse (1791–1874) as editor. It had some five hundred subscribers and continued until 1827, being more successful than most papers of this character. It later merged with *The Congregationalist.*

Other Christian daily papers followed at intervals. They were generally short-lived, like *The North American* of Philadelphia, 1839. Two papers with familiar titles were started in New York City in 1860 for definitely moral and religious purposes—*The New York Sun* and *The New York World;* but they continued this specific character for only about a year. *The Boston Daily News,* 1869, and *The New York Daily Witness,* 1871, followed. No such newspaper made itself a broad influence in the nation until *The Christian Science Monitor* was established by Mrs. Mary Baker Eddy (1821–1910), November 25, 1908. Under able editorship this has shown religious journalism at its best, but it dates from a much later period than the one we are now discussing.[112]

The Sunday newspaper has frequently been a matter at issue between the Churches on the one hand and the public and public authorities on the other. The first Sunday paper, *The Observer,* appeared in New York on February 17, 1809, published by William Elliot. It was suspended with the issue of August 6, 1809.[113] When another one was announced in the same city in 1832, the *New York Evening Post* said:

> . . . One of the evils of which the sober and religious part of the community of London have had much cause to complain—the violation of the Sabbath by the regular publication of newspapers on that day—has not hitherto been adopted in New York. Henceforward, however, we are to exhibit this as an additional feature of resemblance

to "the common sewer of Paris and Rome." An evening paper, we are sorry to perceive, announces an intention of issuing regularly hereafter, beginning on the 31st inst. a Sunday newspaper. . . . We should be well pleased if the experiment were to end in showing the persons who have undertaken the matter that there is too much moral sense in our community to allow of such a speculation proving profitable.[114]

Originally in this country the so-called Sunday papers were issued Saturday afternoon, but during the Civil War, when there was insistent demand for the latest news from the front, Sunday editions began to appear. Stimulated by the Churches, efforts were made to have the public authorities stop the hawking of these papers in the streets, as opposed to old laws still on the statute books. In New York and Philadelphia the papers continued the practice, their publishers being arrested from time to time, and paying the fines for their agents.

The public secular journals have recognized the importance of religion in many ways. The *New York Herald* was a pioneer in this field. It began in 1839 to publish full accounts of the annual meetings of the great religious societies. In 1844 it started the custom of publishing long extracts from the Sunday sermons of representative preachers—first on the Tuesdays following delivery, then on the Mondays—a custom which has become general throughout the country. "The religious page" is now an institution. Perhaps the most striking example of this development was the publication in the issues of the *Chicago Times* and the *Chicago Tribune* on Sunday, May 22, 1881, of the Revised New Testament, the *Times* receiving most of the text by telegraph from New York.[115] To be sure, these are examples of co-operation between the public press and religion, rather than between Church and State, but they are interesting as showing the interest in religion on the part of large masses of our citizens.

During the Civil War there were two notable clashes between religious periodicals and the public, represented in one case by the State, in the other by a mob. The *Freeman's Journal* (Catholic) was suppressed on August 24, 1861, by the Federal government for its extreme views. Originally it was a vigorous critic of the South, but later it became a critic of Republican conduct in the North and was offensive to the administration.[116] The ban against it was in force about eight months.

The other case is that of the Reverend Elijah Pomeroy Lovejoy (1802–37), Presbyterian clergyman and abolitionist, editor of *The Observer,* a St. Louis religious journal which attacked slavery without mercy. Three times his presses were destroyed. While defending the building in Alton, Illinois, to which place he had removed his fourth press for safety, he and one of his companions were killed November 7, 1837. He is widely recognized as a martyr to the cause of civil and religious liberty, and especially of the freedom of the press.

The religious press has played historically an important part in the determination of several national issues, such as:

(1) *The Nativistic Campaign* of the second third of the nineteenth century. As far as this was an effort to maintain American ideals of government and of separation of Church and State, it was in some ways praiseworthy, but when —as all too often—it was unfair to and abusive of Roman Catholics, it is to be severely censured. *The Protestant,* established in New York in 1830, followed by the *Downfall of Babylon,* the *American Protestant Vindicator,* and other "No Popery" organs, was characteristic of the reprehensible side of this movement. We have considered the influence of these papers on the policies of the State in a former section.[117]

(2) *The Antislavery Campaign.* Here almost the entire religious press of the nation began by opposing slavery as an unchristian institution. Then, as the abolitionists of the North and the proslavery advocates of the cotton states became more extreme, they divided, and the religious press of each section took a sectional view—the South basing its arguments largely on Old Testament precedent, the North on New Testament teaching and its implications. As we look back three-quarters of a century on the Northern religious press of this period, the weekly *Independent* of New York seems to have been the most influential.[118] It carried much weight in creating a strong Christian sentiment against slavery, and by giving the cue to many other influential papers. The author of a standard work on journalism in the United States calls special attention to the service thus rendered by religious journals to the antislavery cause. He says:

> What is called the religious press of the country, after it became an institution, and was confirmed as such by the people, entered the political arena, and aided the cause of the Republican Party and the abolition of slavery with all its gigantic moral power.[119]

(3) *The Temperance and Prohibition Campaign.* The campaign which resulted in the good and the ill of county and state prohibition over more than half of the area of the country, and finally in the Eighteenth Amendment, could not have succeeded without the influence of the denominational Protestant press and other religious publications which supported it almost unanimously,[120] and frequently with undue heat and animosity.

The tendency of our religious press has been twofold—to advance constructively the interests of religion in general and of some single denomination in particular, and to oppose some public tendency or political activity believed to be vicious. In this way the Protestant denominational press has taken up not only the great movements mentioned, but many others, such as Antimasonry,[121] as in *The Christian Cynosure* (1867–71); antiwar[122] (at least in times of peace), as eloquently represented by the ablest of present-day Protestant periodicals, *The Christian Century;* and the purification of the moving picture business,[123] as effectively advocated by many Roman Catholic magazines and *The Churchman* (then Episcopalian). These are merely a few examples taken almost at random.

A few of the religious weekly journals of today have considerable influence in the larger world of thought and action. This is specially true of *The Christian Century*—a religious periodical whose views on public questions are more quoted in the secular press than any others since the time—a quarter of a century earlier—when *The Outlook* was at its peak.

It is interesting to note that these two highly influential and progressive journals should have taken diametrically opposite points of view of America's duty to aid Great Britain with her military and naval forces in a contest with Germany's efforts to extend her territory by force. In World War I *The Outlook* was a vigorous supporter of American entry, while the strong tendency of *The Christian Century* in the early days of World War II was toward a relatively isolationist attitude, giving at least indirect support to pacifism. This led a group of eminent Christian scholars and divines, wishing to have America support Great Britain more adequately in protecting democracies and world peace, to found, in 1941, *Christianity and Crisis.* This is edited by one of the ablest of American thinkers, the Reverend Reinhold Niebuhr (1892–   ).

On the whole, the independent religious press has served an important public purpose not only for the cause of religion and for co-operation among the Churches, but also as a critic of government policies and as a supporter of movements for social reform. As to denominational papers, which have been much more numerous, they have with some notable exceptions inclined to be ecclesiastically narrow and politically conservative; but they have done much to advance the interests of their respective Churches in such important public causes as Negro education, the evangelizing of the West, and the needs of the immigrant.

The statistics of religious journalism in the United States are impressive. The Roman Catholics had in 1940 151 newspapers—including nine dailies—with a total circulation of about 3,000,000. Nine-tenths of these papers were weeklies. There were 208 Catholic magazines, reaching about 5,000,000 subscribers.[124] The Catholic Press Association gives as an approximate total for their press in 1946 about 12,700,000 copies—nearly one-fifth dailies and four-fifths magazines.

The influence of this group of publications on the public and private attitudes of citizens is enormous, and it is doubtless mostly good, though some of the eighty diocesan magazines are criticized in Protestant as well as some Catholic sources for narrowness and unfairness; a criticism that can be brought with equal force against some Protestant denominational journals. Among the important national Catholic journals today are *The Catholic World, The Commonweal,* a magazine of literary quality, and the Jesuit *America,* a scholarly journal discussing ecclesiastical and political problems. According to a survey of a decade ago, the largest circulation of any Catholic periodical was that of the *Denver Register,* which then had a chain of twenty-seven diocesan papers and a circulation of well over 2,000,000.[125]

The Roman Catholic diocesan weeklies have no counterpart in the Protestant world. They are newspapers serving their constituency in much the same way that small-town secular weeklies meet local needs. They give the news of the locality, the state, the nation, and the world, with emphasis on items of special interest to Catholics, and also contain much church and religious material. The special articles are provided for the most part by the National Catholic Welfare Conference with its "News Service" and *Catholic Action,* or one of their related organizations. Through these papers the Church has a large influence on public opinion.

As to comparative figures for the non-Catholic religious press, it is difficult to get anything authoritative. The Religious News Service reports that the approximate Protestant total for 1947 was 5,000,000. The largest circulation of any Protestant paper is probably that of *The Christian Advocate* (Methodist). The average circulation of national Protestant magazines was reported in 1941 as about 25,000, 70 per cent of the subscribers being laymen and only 30 per cent clergymen, though in the case of *The Christian Century* the percentages are almost exactly reversed.[126]

The Yiddish press has a total circulation of about 400,000, including dailies and other publications. Two Jewish weeklies in English, the *National Jewish Post* (Indianapolis) and the *Brooklyn Examiner,* have over 100,000 each; while the *National Jewish Monthly,* published by B'nai B'rith, has a circulation of 350,000. There are in all 166 Jewish publications, of which 117 are in English, 26 in Yiddish, 10 in Hebrew, or Hebrew and Yiddish, and the remainder scattering. The most influential Jewish daily is *The Daily Forward,* with a circulation of about 100,000.[127] The most broadly influential monthly is *The Commentary,* published under the auspices of the American Jewish Committee.

Ayer's *Directory of Newspapers and Periodicals* for 1947 lists 546 regular religious publications in the United States: 382 Protestant, 155 Roman Catholic, and 9 Jewish, or if those devoted to Zionism, Yiddish, and other Jewish interests are included the last number rises to 94 Jewish and the total to 631. These figures, which do not include parish or minor periodicals, probably give a good present-day picture of religious journalism.[128]

Section 6. *TEMPERANCE AND LIQUOR CONTROL*

The effective temperance movement in this country began with the publication by Dr. Benjamin Rush (1745–1813) in 1785 of his *Inquiry into the Effects of Ardent Spirits on the Human Body and Mind.*[129] This gave a good scientific basis for temperance instruction and, because of the author's standing as a patriot and a physician, it carried weight. He was not an advocate of prohibition by State action, but believed that the Churches should take the lead in promoting temperance. As he wrote to Jeremy Belknap:

> From the influence of the Quakers and Methodists in checking this evil, I am disposed to believe that the business must be effected finally by religion alone. Human reason has been employed in vain, . . . we have nothing to hope from the influence of *law* in making men wise and sober. Let these considerations lead us to address the heads of the governing bodies of all the Churches in America.[130]

In 1811 he presented a thousand copies of his *Inquiry* to the General Assembly of the Presbyterian Church, which the following year adopted a report placing the assembly behind the temperance movement. The Methodist General Conference and the Congregational Associations of Massachusetts and Connecticut followed suit, and in 1826 the American Society for the Promotion of Temperance was organized—Protestant ministers taking the lead in its advocacy, and providing seven of the sixteen members of its first board. In 1836 a more radical organization, known as the American Temperance Union, was formed by a merger of various societies. It adopted the principle of total abstinence. Stimulated by these groups the frontier churches did much to advance the temperance cause.

It is probable that the Reverend Lyman Beecher (1775–1863), the father of Henry Ward Beecher, who was greatly impressed by Dr. Rush's essay, did more to promote the temperance cause—which ultimately resulted in prohibition—than anyone else in the second quarter of the nineteenth century. His *Six Sermons on the Nature, Occasions, Signs, Evils and Remedy of Intemperance,* first preached in Litchfield, Connecticut, ran through many editions from 1827 on, and their teachings became part of the general ethical equipment of the Christian preachers and revivalists who spread through the growing Middle West at this time. His *Autobiography* is full of references to the subject, such as his lament over the "apparently universal" drinking when he became pastor in Litchfield;[131] his services as chairman of the committee appointed by the General Association of Connecticut in 1811, to deal with the problem;[132] his activity in forming voluntary associations "to aid the civil magistrates in the execution of the law";[133] and his many sermons on the subject, including one in 1825 in which he advocated prohibition.

"What, then, is this universal, natural, and national remedy for intemperance?" he asked. His answer was clear:

> IT IS THE BANISHMENT OF ARDENT SPIRITS FROM THE LIST OF LAWFUL ARTICLES OF COMMERCE BY A CORRECT AND EFFICIENT PUBLIC SENTIMENT, SUCH AS HAS TURNED SLAVERY OUT OF HALF OF OUR LAND, AND WILL YET EXPEL IT FROM THE WORLD. . . .
>
> . . . Like slavery, it [the traffic in ardent spirits] must be regarded as sinful, impolitic, and dishonorable. That no measures will avail short of rendering ardent spirits a contraband of trade is nearly self-evident.[134]

John B. Gough (1817–86) was the most effective of the temperance advocates; Father Theobald Mathew (1796–1856), an earnest Irish priest, was another great leader. After founding his Total Abstinence Society in Ireland in 1838, Mathew spent two years—1849–51—lecturing in this country, and had a profound influence; nearly 500,000 Catholic Americans are said to have taken the pledge during his visit.[135] Largely as a result of the movement which he started, the Catholic Total Abstinence Union was formed in 1872. This was followed two years later by the Women's Christian Temperance Union, which under the able leadership of Miss Emma Willard (1839–98) became a national force in uniting the women of most Protestant churches behind the total abstinence and prohibition movements. It was significant of the trend of the time that she declared herself "profoundly interested in politics as the mightiest force on earth except Christianity."[136]

In 1837 Neal Dow (1804–97), who had inherited from his Quaker upbringing a strong opposition to the liquor traffic, established, with the backing of leading Protestant ministers, the Maine State Temperance Society. Its purpose was to control the policy of the state legislature in matters dealing with the liquor evil. This society secured the first definite legal prohibition of intoxicating liquors in the United States, brought about by the Maine law of 1851 which prohibited their manufacture, sale, or keeping for sale. In the following four years twelve states in New England and in the North Central Division, and two Western states adopted similar laws. Many Protestant groups supported the legislation, but Roman Catholics, Episcopalians, Lutherans, and some others held aloof. They were for temperance but not for prohibition.

It is interesting to note that Abraham Lincoln (1809–65), who had become an advocate of total abstinence, drafted in 1855 a law prohibiting the liquor traffic in Illinois, which was passed by both houses of the legislature, but was finally rejected by the state on a referendum vote. After 1855 the situation began to return to a modified licensing system, giving up prohibition, so that twenty years later only three states, Maine, Vermont, and New Hampshire, retained their prohibitory legislation. This change in public sentiment was largely due to the increase of immigration from abroad, especially from Germany, and the growing industrialization of the country, which meant that the urban vote was increasing in its influence on state and national legislation. The European immigrants and city dwellers wanted their light wine and beer, especially the latter, and whiskey was all too popular, especially on the frontier.

The later history of the efforts of certain Protestant Churches to deal with the liquor evil through state and national prohibition will be dealt with in another chapter.[137]

Section 7. MORMON THEOCRACY AND INDEPENDENCE

The Mormons, or as they call themselves, "The Church of Jesus Christ of Latter Day Saints," represent in their peculiar way the nearest approach to a theocracy on a large scale which this country has known since early Puritan days. They are now a self-respecting and industrious group with over half a million members, recognizing fully the distinction between the functions of Church and State under our government; but in their earlier history there were many misunderstandings and conflicts. They were founded as an independent sect in 1830, in Fayette, New York, as a result of the alleged revelations to Joseph Smith (1805–44) contained in the *Book of Mormon,* of which, according to the first edition, he was "Author and Proprietor." The founder was an extraordinary person, combining religious enthusiasm, an eye for business, capacity for leadership, imagination, and some dramatic instincts. His followers, moving West, became a missionary body attracting large numbers of adherents in Ohio, Missouri, Illinois, and elsewhere, and suffering severe persecution, especially in the last two states. In Jackson County, Missouri, a mass meeting of several hundred citizens demanded that they move away, razed the printing shop of their newspaper, and tarred a Mormon bishop. The Mormons appealed to Governor Daniel Dunklin (1790–1844) for troops. They asserted that "no republican will suffer the liberty of the press and liberty of conscience to be silenced by a mob," and "that every officer, civil and military, with a very few exceptions, has pledged his life and honor to force us from the country, dead or alive."[138]

After a pitched battle and the calling out of the militia Smith decided to move with his people to Illinois. But before they left they suffered much more. The governor recognized their constitutional rights but did little to protect them. He wrote,

Your case is certainly a very emergent one. . . . For that which is the case of the

Mormons today, may be that of the Catholics tomorrow and after them any other sect that may become obnoxious to the majority of the people of any section of the state.

Later Governor Dunklin wrote these further words, for which he should be honored:

I am fully persuaded that the eccentricity of the religious opinions and practices of the Mormons is at the bottom of the outrages committed against them. . . . They have the right constitutionally guaranteed to them, and it is indefeasible, to believe and worship Jo Smith as a man, an angel, or even as the only true and living God, and call their habitation Zion, or the Holy Land, or even heaven itself. Indeed, there is nothing so absurd or ridiculous that they have not the right to adopt it as their religion, so that in its exercise they do not interfere with the rights of others.[139]

It must be remembered that at this time polygamy had not yet been officially advocated.

Failing to get satisfactory action protecting them and their rights from the governor, they addressed a petition, April 10, 1834, to President Jackson, saying that no sect had endured such persecution since the Declaration of Independence; that they were suffering unjustly, as the county court records carried no name of a Mormon in connection with any crime; and praying that they be restored to their lands in Jackson County and protected by armed force. Secretary of War Lewis Cass (1782–1866) replied that the laws of Missouri had been violated, not those of the United States, and that the latter could interfere only if the state applied for help on the ground that an insurrection existed. A petition to Congress was answered in the same way through the judiciary committee.[140] This was prior to the adoption of the Fourteenth Amendment.[141]

Being thwarted in their attempt to gain legal protection, they organized a militia of their own and became aggressive, incurring the armed opposition of the state. Governor Lillburn W. Boggs (1792–1860), commander-in-chief of the Missiouri militia, sent a dispatch on October 27, 1838, since known as the "Boggs Exterminating Order," in which he said:

Since the order of the morning to you, directing you to cause four hundred men to be raised within your division, I have received . . . information of the most appalling character which changes the whole face of things and places the Mormons in the attitude of open and avowed defiance of the laws, and of having made war upon the people of this state. . . . The Mormons must be treated as enemies and must be exterminated, or driven from the state if necessary, for the public good. Their outrages are beyond all human description.[142]

A few days later occurred the massacre of Haun's Mill, in which seventeen Mormons were killed or mortally wounded. The provocation was undoubtedly great, and yet the Haun's Mill incident is one of the most tragic that the historian of Church–State difficulties in this country must relate, and the governor's action, especially considering the wording of his order, was entirely out of keeping with the best American traditions.

In 1839, driven out from Missouri, where they had become a political factor, voting practically as a unit, the Mormons laid out and established an incorporated colony of many thousand people at Nauvoo (first called Commerce), Illinois, which was in effect an independent, self-governing theocracy under their "Prophet," who acted as head of the administrative, judicial, and military departments.[143] Here again they came into serious conflict with the neighboring communities.

The charter secured from the Illinois legislature, through Mormon influence with the Whig party, contained clauses assuring all religious sects freedom of speech and worship, but it was really contrived to deliver all control into the hands of Smith, and to create a situation which made it improbable that any non-Mormons would settle in the city. It said:

The city council shall have power and authority to make, ordain, establish, and execute all such ordinances *not repugnant to the Constitution of the United States or of this State* as they may deem necessary for the benefit, good order, regulation, convenience, and cleanliness of said city.

This, according to Mr. Beardsley, the biographer of Smith already quoted,

set up Nauvoo as a separate political entity, co-extensive with the State of Illinois, deriving its powers from the same constitution, but with authority to interpret that constitution as it might see fit, regardless of the laws of the State. The city of Nauvoo was superior to the statutes of Illinois, acknowledging only the sanctity of the constitution from which the statutes derived their authority.[144]

The charter established a municipal court with the mayor as chief justice and the four aldermen as associate justices. It was empowered to issue writs of habeas corpus, and to try the sufficiency of those issued by other courts, and even the original action in the case in which the writ was issued.

This extraordinary court was designed to protect Joe [Smith] and his followers from legal action on the part of Missouri and was so used throughout its existence. Nauvoo was also given power to deal in real and personal property for speculative purposes, a privilege granted no other city in the State.[145]

Some idea of Smith's conception of its political independence is shown by the fact that the Mormons petitioned Congress that it be made a separate territory![146]

Smith, as mayor, lieutenant general of the Nauvoo Legion, chief justice, etc., was virtually a dictator, though technically a legal one under his extraordinary charter. He was also head of the Mormon Church, prophet, president of Nauvoo University, a rich real estate speculator, political boss, husband of twenty-eight "celestial wives," and a candidate, in 1844, for the presidency of the United States on an extraordinary platform which he signed as "the friend of the people and of unadulterated freedom."[147] Of all these positions the one most ominous was his headship of the local militia, which at one time had several thousand members well armed by the state; its officers responsible not to higher officers of the state militia, but only to the governor.[148]

The dominating character of the general attitude of the founder of Mormonism may be derived from the contemporary account of the famous Methodist circuit rider, the Reverend Peter Cartwright (1785–1872). Referring to an argument with Smith, probably in January, 1843, Cartwright said:

My friend, Joe Smith, became very restive before I got through with my narrative; and when I closed, his wrath boiled over, and he cursed me in the name of his God, and said, "I will show you, sir, that I will raise up a government in these United States which will overturn the present government, and I will raise up a new religion that will overturn every other form of religion in this country!" . . .[149]

Some idea of his views on matters of public policy at this time may be derived from his speeches and sermons. For instance, speaking at a large town meeting at Nauvoo on June 30, 1843, Joseph Smith said:

It has been asserted by the great and wise men, lawyers, and others, that our municipal powers and legal tribunals are not to be sanctioned. . . . If there is not power in our charter and courts, then there is not power in the State of Illinois, nor in the Congress, nor the Constitution of the United States. For the United States gave unto Illinois her constitution or charter, and Illinois gave unto Nauvoo her charters, ceding unto us her vested rights which she has no right, or power, to take away from us. All the power there was in Illinois she gave to Nauvoo, and any man that says to the contrary, is a fool. . . .

I want you to hear and learn, O Israel, this day, what is for the happiness and peace of this city and people. If our enemies are determined to oppress us and deprive us of our constitutional rights and privileges, as they have done, and if the authorities that are on the earth will not sustain us in our right, nor give us that protection which the laws and Constitution of the United States and of this State guarantee unto us, then we will claim them from a higher power—from Heaven—yea, from God Almighty![150]

Things had come to a head that month in the struggle between the non-Mormon citizens of the county and some anti-Smith Mormons on the one hand, and the organized forces under Smith on the other. The local paper had criticized him severely; therefore, though Smith was insistent on the freedom of the Mormon-controlled town—then one of the largest in the Middle West—to do as it wished under his dictation, he showed in this order that he cared not at all for another freedom, that of the press:

Headquarters
Nauvoo Legion
June 10, 1844

To Jonathan Dunham,
Acting Major–General of the Nauvoo Legion:

You are hereby commanded to hold the Nauvoo Legion in readiness forthwith to execute the city ordinances and especially to remove the printing establishment of *The Nauvoo Expositor,* and this you are required to do at sight under the penalty of the laws; provided the Marshal shall require it and need your services.

Joseph Smith
Lieutenant–General, Nauvoo Legion[151]

The state militia had to be called out to secure the surrender of the Legion—a striking example of a Church–State conflict in a limited area but in an extreme form. Joseph Smith and his brother were arrested for treason and while awaiting trial were killed by a mob.

Even during his lifetime he attracted converts from afar. Over four thousand English followers sailed from England in the years from 1840 to 1846. Scandinavia was another large center of missionary activities. His representatives preached everywhere the doctrine of economic and religious salvation under their leader. Such was the career of an astounding man who was the founder of a new religio-economic sect numbering today some 1,500 churches and 700,000 people, most of them self-respecting, temperate, and law-abiding, and showing large capacity in various social and philanthropic fields. We have dealt only with a few incidents that brought him and his followers in the early days into contact with the State. It is not strange that one of his leading biographers, who went to Nauvoo to collect material for a book on ghost cities and then decided to write a novel based on the life work of Smith, finally decided that facts were stranger than fiction, and produced a biography of this extraordinary "prophet," who was forceful and full of imagination.

After Smith's death in 1844 and a brief interregnum, Brigham Young (1801–77), president of the council, succeeded him as president of the Church. He led his followers west to Salt Lake Valley in 1846–47 and established "the State of Deseret"—"land of the honey bee." He administered the government autocratically through his church position, and without any regular authorization. He appointed all civil and ecclesiastical officers. He later served, by appointment of the president of the United States, as first governor, from 1850 to 1854, of what was named officially the Territory of Utah. He also continued as president of the

Church. Under the Mormon system the Church is the only channel of divine revelation, so that when polygamy—"revealed" to Joseph Smith in 1843—was first advocated publicly in 1847, after his death, and first proclaimed by his successor, Brigham Young, in 1852, to be a doctrine of the Church, the government was unwilling to grant Utah's application for statehood. Here, it was thought, was the beginning of a dangerous *imperium in imperio,* rendered doubly dangerous by its extraordinary religious foundations.

The story of the Church–State battle over this question and of the closely related legal phase of the polygamy issue will be considered in a later section.[152]

Section 8. NONSECTARIAN PUBLIC EDUCATION

(1) THE BACKGROUND

A brief historical survey of the development of our schools in relation to government in this country is necessary for an understanding of most of the following sections, especially as the public school has become one of the main bulwarks of democracy. Public education of all of the people at public expense had scarcely been dreamed of in the Europe of three centuries ago. "When the period of settlement opened, the idea of free and compulsory education supported by public taxation for the children of all classes had nowhere occupied the thought of statesmen."[153] Such education as a matter of public right under direct State, rather than Church, auspices was not known until, as we shall see in the next section, it was tried in the Massachusetts of the seventeenth century. From the breakup of the Roman Empire until the seventeenth century the Church had been the dominant factor in all forms of institutional life, especially intellectual, moral, and social; hence it was natural that education had been considered primarily a function of the Church or of endowed institutions closely related to it and having a definitely religious character. A few exceptions, such as in some cities of Northern Italy at the time of the Renaissance, only prove the general rule. Furthermore, those who have studied most carefully American education, and who realize its secular but not antireligious character, recognize fully that it grew out of the ideals nurtured by the Reformation. It is "the child of American Protestantism,"[154] and was born in the Calvinistic tradition of Geneva.[155] The typical process of transformation from the church school of colonial Massachusetts to the public school of today will be studied to indicate the various steps taken. This will show that the Protestant Churches have at times yielded their control willingly, sometimes unwillingly, and, though differing on such matters as Bible reading in the schools,[156] have been agreed that although the spirit of the schools should remain Christian, and their general attitude one of profound respect for religion, they should provide no sectarian or dogmatic teaching.

Probably the fathers of the republic would be surprised if they should return today and find most schools entirely divorced from the Church, and religion as a regular curriculum subject of study practically excluded in the public schools of all states. They had been accustomed in the colonies to the teaching of religion in virtually all schools; and since education was not mentioned in the Federal Constitution, they doubtless expected the old colonial arrangements and the early State provisions which grew out of them to continue, being merely adjusted and expanded to meet new conditions. But it was generally realized that, except in parts of New England and in a few large towns, educational facilities for the masses were woefully inadequate.

The "academies," which were prominent both North and South, only partly met the need. They were generally privately endowed or controlled, as in the case of Franklin's Academy in Philadelphia chartered in 1753, or more generally founded and supported by some denomination, but their clientele seldom included the lower ranks of society. They formed chronologically and in general spirit a bridge between the earlier Latin grammar schools in the big towns and the present public high schools. The first school of this character was planned in Virginia in 1621, but the Great Massacre of the following year, and the failure of the Virginia Company, prevented its development. The earliest firmly established and most famous of the Latin schools was that in Boston, 1635. The Massachusetts law of 1647 requiring a grammar school in every town of a hundred families stimulated their growth, and by the middle of the eighteenth century every colony except Georgia had such schools.

The academies prospered greatly in the first half of the nineteenth century. There were about a thousand such incorporated institutions by 1830, and by 1850 they had increased several fold.[157] Although the most famous were in the North, such as those established by John Phillips (1719–95) in Andover, Massachusetts, 1778, and Exeter, New Hampshire, 1781, the South had an even larger number for its population. The Presbyterians and other denominations founded many of them. They did much for the education and culture of the upper and middle classes, and formed the foundation on which many colleges were built. They also provided for the education of women. But these institutions, many of which represented an important contribution of the Church to public education, were generally under self-perpetuating boards of trustees and were seldom aided by the State. They provided the conventional classical and religious education.

Only a few statesmen, like Thomas Jefferson (1743–1826), were educationally minded. Indeed, we are told that only five states seriously considered educational provisions in the constitutions of the Revolutionary period. Most of the leaders expected the old endowed schools and the churches to continue to provide all necessary education outside the home, and even where new schools were started or old academies given state aid it was generally assumed that religious instruction would be continued. For example, one of the most prominent and respected laymen in the country in the early years of the Republic was Dr. Benjamin Rush (1745–1813), the signer, and recognized leader of the medical profession. He spoke for most of the thoughtful citizens of his time in urging the study of the Bible in public schools. In *A Defense of the Use of the Bible as a School Book*, he took the ground that it provided the only adequate basis for a useful education. He stressed not only its moral and religious character but its possession of the very soul of democracy—equality of men, respect for just laws, and the essential virtues.[158]

The first attempts to remedy the unsatisfactory educational conditions were made not by the state or municipal governments but by philanthropic individuals and societies. Prominent among the new movements was the introduction of the plan of Sunday schools, first developed in England by Robert Raikes (1735–1811) in 1780. He employed women on Sundays to teach the elements of secular and religious subjects to the neglected children of the masses. The First Day or Sunday School Society in America was organized in Philadelphia in 1790 to carry out this plan. It was an encouraging sign of the new spirit of unity and tolerance in the country that Episcopalians, Quakers, Roman Catholics, and other groups united for this purpose. After the War of 1812 the movement spread, and by 1824 a national society—the American Sunday School Union—was founded. Little by little the English plan was departed from in that the teaching of reading and writing was given up, the schools becoming religious only, and no longer confined to the very poor, but, as was more appropriate in a democracy, open to all.[159] The general estimate of their significance in the 'twenties is shown by the fact that the legislature of Delaware in 1821 passed an act granting aid to Sunday schools from state funds—a move due, however, at least as much to their potentiality in reducing illiteracy as in encouraging religion.[160]

But the Sunday school, Latin grammar schools, and privately endowed academies were evidently entirely inadequate to meet the educational needs of the youth of the nation. It was necessary if our democracy was to succeed that public schools, publicly supported, and with curricula determined by public authorities, should be developed. Private and church schools and colleges need not be interfered with; they would always continue to meet a public need. But it was clear that the State itself would have to assume the responsibility for the direction and support of common schools for the education of the majority of its future citizens. No other agency had the resources for so vast an enterprise in a democracy, and no other agency could properly provide these and take into account the opinions of parents and religious organizations, the two groups heretofore most concerned with education. The State, it was believed, could best determine the elements of an educated citizenship, and see that they were realized through education.

(2) THE ACHIEVEMENT OF NEW ENGLAND UNDER MASSACHUSETTS LEADERSHIP (HORACE MANN)

The Massachusetts School Law of 1647 established "the first system of public education in the American colonies." Some towns had of their own initiative established schools, and a law had been adopted by the colony in 1642 calling for the instruction of children in reading; but this was the first general school law. It is specially interesting from the point of view of this study as showing clearly how public education in what is now the United States arose from the needs of "church and commonwealth," and had specially in mind the danger which would face a people who could not themselves read and study the Bible.

> It being one chiefe proiect of ye ould deluder, Satan, to keepe men from the knowledge of ye Scriptures, as in formr times by keeping y^{m} in an unknowne tongue, so in these lattr times by perswading from ye use of tongues, y^{t} so at least ye true sence & meaning of ye originall might be clouded by false glosses of saint seeming deceivers, y^{t} learning may not be buried in ye grave of o^{r} fathrs in ye church and commonwealth, the Lord assisting o^{r} endeavors,—
>
> It is therefore ordred, y^{t} evry towneship in this iurisdiction, aftr ye Lord hath increased ye number to 50 housholdrs, shall then forthwth appoint one wth in their towne to teach all such children as shall resort to him to write & reade, whose wages shall be paid eithr by ye parents or mastrs of such children, or by ye inhabitants in genrall, by way of supply, as ye maior part of those y^{t} ordr ye prudentials ye towne shall appoint; provided, those y^{t} send their children be not oppressed by paying much more y^{n} they can have y^{m} taught for in othr townes; & it is furthr ordered, y^{t} where any towne shall increase to ye number of 100 families or househouldrs, they shall set up a grammer schoole, ye m^{r} thereof being able to instruct youth so farr as they shall be fitted for ye university, provided, y^{t} if any towne neglect ye performance hereof above one yeare, y^{t} every such towne shall pay 5 pounds to ye next schoole till they shall performe this order.[161]

Such was the beginning of public education in North America under Massachusetts leadership. Since New England until very modern times continued to lead in the evolution of the American public school system, its experience in developing Church–State relations is particularly important. A standard history of education states that each little New England town was originally established as a religious republic, with the Church in complete control. The governing authorities for church and civil affairs were much the same. When acting as church officers they were known as Elders and Deacons; when acting as civil or town officers they were known as Selectmen. The State, as represented in the colony legislature or the town meeting, was clearly the servant of the Church, and existed in large part for religious ends. It was the State acting as the servant of the Church which enacted the laws of 1642 and 1647, requiring the towns to maintain schools for religious purposes. Now, so close was the connection between the religious town which controlled church affairs, and the civil town which looked after roads, fences, taxes, and defense—the constituency of both being one and the same, and the meetings of both being held at first in the Meeting-House—that when the schools were established the colony legislature placed them under the civil, as involving taxes and being a public service, rather than under the religious town. The interests of one were the interests of both, and, being the same in constituency and territorial boundaries, there seemed no occasion for friction or fear. From this religious beginning the civil school, and the civil school town and township, with all our elaborate school administrative machinery, were later evolved.

The erection of a town hall, separate from the meeting-house, was the first step in the process. School affairs were now discussed at the town hall, instead of in the church. Town taxes, instead of church taxes, were voted for buildings and maintenance. The minister continued to certificate the grammar-school master until the close of the colonial period, but the power to certificate the elementary school teachers passed to the town authorities early in the eighteenth century. By the close of this century all that the minister, as the surviving representative of church control, had left to him was the right to accompany the town authorities in the visitation of the schools. Thus gradually but certainly did the earlier religious school pass out from under the control of the Church and become a state school. When our national government and the different state governments were established, the States were ready to accept, in principle at least, the theory gradually worked out in New England that schools are state institutions and should be under the control of the State.[162]

The secularization of education, it is held, should

not be regarded either as a deliberate or a wanton violation of the rights of the Church, but rather as an unavoidable incident connected with the coming to self-consciousness and self-government of a great people.[163]

It became a necessity to secure the education of the great mass of our citizens under State auspices in such a way as would not create religious antagonisms and would insure the best interests of democracy. Beginning with New Hampshire in 1792 and Connecticut in 1818, it was specifically provided in state constitutions that public funds must be expended only on schools under public authority, and that no religious sect should have any share in such funds. Congregational ministers continued, however, in many cases to supervise town schools.

It is in Massachusetts that we can best study the slow growth of the movement which resulted in state systems of public schools, and in religious education being dropped out of the tax-supported schools of the United States. This is partly because this state has been until very recent days generally considered the center of educational movements in America, and partly because the development and decline of religious education under public auspices in its history have been made the subject of the most exhaustive and thorough study.[164]

The colonial background of Massachusetts has been of influence on the state in advancing the cause of religion. The General Court from its origin concerned itself with the spiritual welfare of the churches—originally all Congregational. In fact, "Religion and education were equally under the patronage of the State and all for the glory of God."[165] It was only with the rise of the Quakers, and later of the Baptists and Episcopalians, that there was any opposition to the State support of religion.[166]

> ... Throughout the colonial period there was never a time when Massachusetts did not apply the principle that it was a function of the state to promote religion and when the majority did not believe that taxation for religious purposes was justified. Whatever concessions were made were partly due to interference from England and partly to the importunity of those who held a different theory of church and state, or, in the case of the Episcopalians, who did not object to the theory, but did object to its application in favor of Dissenters and to their disadvantage.[167]

Furthermore, in all the schools, whether tax-supported or not, and in Harvard College, which received many grants from the state, the teaching of religious subjects and the training of a religious spirit were considered fundamentally important. During this period toleration had been established for all except Roman Catholics, though all taxpayers had to support the religious worship approved by the majority of each town, except that Episcopalians might have their tax transferred to their own minister, and Quakers and Baptists, if members of a regular church society, were exempted out of respect for their conscientious scruples.[168]

This attitude however was to be considerably modified as a result of the American Revolution, as may be seen from the constitution of the Commonwealth of Massachusetts adopted in 1780, which has the distinction of being the only constitution of one of the original states to have been adopted in the eighteenth century and to be still in existence with few modifications.[169] The portion regarding religion and education was largely the work of John Adams (1735–1826). The document has been reproduced at length in an earlier section, where the struggle for religious freedom in Massachusetts is discussed.[170] Here it is necessary to quote only the small portion necessary for the understanding of the constitutional situation in the field of education.

As the happiness of a people, and the good order and preservation of civil government, essentially depend on piety, religion and morality; and as these cannot be generally diffused through a community, but by the institution of the public worship of God, and of public instructors in piety, religion, and morality: Therefore, to promote their happiness, and to secure the good order and preservation of their government, the people of this commonwealth have a right to invest their legislature with power to authorize and require, and the legislature shall, from time to time, authorize and require, the several towns, parishes, precincts and other bodies politic, or religious societies, to make suitable provision, at their own expense, for the institution of the public worship of God, and for the support and maintenance of public protestant teachers of piety, religion and morality, in all cases where such provision shall not be made voluntarily.

And the people of this Commonwealth have also a right to, and do, invest their legislature with authority to enjoin upon all the subjects an attendance upon the instruction of the public teachers aforesaid, at stated times and seasons, if there be any upon whose instructions they can conscientiously and conveniently attend.[171]

The practice of catechizing in the schools and the religious character of many of the textbooks of this period indicate clearly the definitely religious quality of the instruction. Indeed, until the educational law of 1827, which gave school committees power over schoolbooks, and prohibited the introduction of books of a sectarian character, there had even been sectarian instruction in many schools. The wording of the new law is important:

Provided, also, that said committee shall never direct any school books to be purchased or used, in any of the schools under their superintendence, which are calculated to favour any particular religious sect or tenet.[172]

The Bible or the New Testament was still used as a reader in most schools, the nearest competitor being the *National Reader*. This laid emphasis on readings regarding "a sublime and catholic religion,"[173] though religion was taught incidentally rather than directly.

Several factors profoundly affected the interest in public education at this period. Such were the popular Democratic presidential administrations (1829–1837) of Andrew Jackson (1767–1845); the gradual freeing of the suffrage from property qualifications; the large immigration of European laborers ignorant of English and of our democratic traditions; the rapid growth of urban industrial centers; and the need of providing schools in the newly settled states of the Middle West. These and other factors attracted national attention to the problem of education in the second quarter of the nineteenth century. It was realized that the Churches and privately endowed or supported institutions were entirely inadequate for the task. Massachusetts took the lead in the resulting movement for greatly strengthening the public schools and for making attendance at some school obligatory for all children of certain ages.

The relation between the state of Massachusetts and public religious education under the state constitution up to the establishment of the Board of Education in 1837, is illuminating as showing conditions during the first half century of the republic in the state which was the most advanced educationally. Such education

> provided directly through churches supported by public taxation compulsory for all except Quakers unless voluntarily given, until 1833; and after that churches might levy tax on their own members. The teaching of piety was enjoined in the statutes and under this provision religious education continued in the public schools in a decreasing degree until the end of the period, through the catechism, the Bible as a reading book, daily Bible reading and prayer, the exhortations of ministers at the annual visitation, and the use of the prevalent textbooks and oral instruction. By 1827 sectarian doctrinal teaching had practically disappeared, and that situation was made legally requisite by excluding sectarian books from the schools and in the spirit of the law at least disapproving of oral sectarian instruction. During the remainder of the period the textbooks were free from such material, and there appears to have been only a negligible amount of it from the catechism or oral instruction. But Bible reading and visual and oral instruction in the general principles of Christianity accepted by the Protestant denominations in common was not illegal, but rather expected; the extent to which it was practised depended on the local community.[174]

The Board of Education—the first state Board of Education in the United States—elected as its secretary Horace Mann (1796–1859), a man of untiring energy, great ability, and boundless enthusiasm for public education. That the new movement was in no way hostile to the Churches, indeed that they were as a whole prepared to give it active support, is shown by the fact that in 1844 a majority of the board—five members out of eight—was made up of clergymen.[175]

Under the leadership of Mann, the greatest of American public school exponents, the state developed a compulsory education system of secular schools under state auspices, which became particularly effective after the legislature adopted in 1842 the principle of compulsory education. This system, as well as the increase in membership of the Roman Catholic Church and other non-Congregational churches, and the influence of Unitarian ideas, brought about by 1855 complete elimination from publicly supported schools of sectarian as distinct from religious instruction.[176] Mann wished however to maintain the fundamentally religious character of the schools while at the same time making them completely nonsectarian. He maintained that the education law of 1789, to the effect that all instructors of youth in the commonwealth should use their best endeavors "to impress on the minds of children and youth committed to their care and instruction the principles of piety and justice and a sacred regard for truth,"[177] required by the use of the word "piety"— still on the statute books— some form of instruction in the fundamental principles of the Christian religion based on the Bible.

In his *First Report* to the Massachusetts Board of Education, on January 1, 1838, Mann gave his fundamental views of the relation of public education to religion.

In regard to moral instruction, the condition of our public schools presents a singular, and, to some extent at least, an alarming phenomenon. To prevent the school from being converted into an engine of religious proselytism; to debar successive teachers in the same school, from successively inculcating hostile religious creeds, until the children in their simple-mindedness should be alienated, not only from creeds, but from religion itself; the statute of 1826 specially provided, that no school books should be used in any of the public schools "calculated to favor any particular religious sect or tenet." The language of the Revised Statutes is slightly altered, but the sense remains the same. Probably, no one would desire a repeal of this law, while the danger impends it was designed to repel. The consequence of the enactment, however, has been, that among the vast libraries of books, expository of the doctrines of revealed religion, none have been found free from that advocacy of particular "tenets" or "sects," which includes them within the scope of the legal prohibition; or, at least, no such books have been approved by the committees and introduced into the schools. Independently, therefore, of the immeasurable importance of moral teaching in itself considered, this entire exclusion of religious teaching, though justifiable under the circumstances, enhances and magnifies a thousand fold, the indispensableness of moral instruction and training. Entirely to discard the inculcation of the great doctrines of morality and of natural theology has a vehement tendency to drive mankind into opposite extremes; to make them devotees on one side, or profligates on the other; each about equally regardless of the true constituents of human welfare. Against a tendency to these fatal extremes, the beautiful and sublime truths of ethics and of natural religion have a poising power. Hence it will be learned with sorrow, that of the multiplicity of books used in our schools, only three have this object in view; and these three are used in only *six* of the two thousand nine hundred and eighteen schools, from which returns have been received.[178]

In this and some subsequent reports Mann had specially in mind the attempt of the American Sunday School Union to have its "select library," approved by the union at its annual meeting in 1837, accepted for use in the schools. Both he and the governor of Massachusetts declared this to be a sectarian proposal. The union's agent, Frederick A. Packard, pressed in particular the acceptance of Abbott's *Child at Home,* and there resulted the famous Packard-Mann correspondence, especially in the *Boston Recorder* in 1838. Packard contended that this book was Christian but not sectarian, while the secretary of the Board of Education showed that its doctrinal basis regarding the last judgment, sin, and other matters, represented orthodox doctrines not accepted by such religious groups as the Unitarians and Universalists. Mann felt that since the schools had children of all denominations in attendance they must, while supporting the fundamental religious and ethical truths of the Bible, decline to teach anything in the way of sectarian doctrines. He won, and it was an important victory.[179]

In a Fourth of July oration delivered in Boston in 1842, Mann remarked:

> I have said that schools should have been established for the education of the whole people. These schools have been of a more perfect character than any which have ever yet existed. In them the principles of morality should have been copiously intermingled with the principles of science. Cases of conscience should have alternated with lessons in the rudiments. The multiplication table should not have been more familiar nor more frequently applied, than the rule to do to others as we would that they should do unto us. The lives of great and good men should have been held up for admiration and example; and especially the life and character of Jesus Christ, as the sublimest pattern of benevolence, of purity, of self-sacrifice, ever exhibited to mortals. In every course of studies, all the practical and perceptive parts of the Gospel should have been sacredly included; and all dogmatical theology and sectarianism sacredly excluded. In no school should the Bible have been opened to reveal the sword of the polemic, but to unloose the dove of peace.[180]

In his eleventh annual report Mann stated further:

> The use of the Bible in schools is not expressly enjoined by the law, but both its letter and its spirit are in consonance with that use; and, as a matter of fact, I suppose there is not, at the present time, a single town in the Commonwealth in whose schools it is not read. Whoever, therefore, believes in the Sacred Scriptures, has his belief, in form and in spirit, in the schools; and his children read and hear *the words themselves* which contain it. The administration of this law is entrusted to the local authorities in the respective towns. By introducing the Bible, they introduce what all its believers hold to be the rule of faith and practice; and although, by excluding theological systems of human origin, they may exclude a peculiarity which one denomination believes to be true, they do but exclude what other denominations believe to be erroneous. Such is the present policy of our law for including what all Christians hold to be right, and for excluding what all, excepting some one party, hold to be wrong.[181]

In his final report, that for 1848, he took some forty-eight pages to discuss religious education of a nondenominational character, on which he laid great emphasis, while vigorously opposing all sectarian instruction in the public schools.

> I believed then (1837), as now, that sectarian books and sectarian instruction, if their encroachment were not resisted, would prove the overthrow of the schools.
>
> I believed then, as now, that religious instruction in our schools, to the extent which the Constitution and the laws of the State allowed and prescribed, was indispensable to their highest welfare, and essential to the vitality of moral education.
>
> I avail myself of this, the last opportunity which I may ever have, to say in regard to all affirmations or intimations that I have ever attempted to exclude religious instruction from the schools, or to exclude the Bible from the schools, or to impair the force of that volume, that they are now, and always have been, without substance or semblance of truth.
>
> Our system earnestly inculcates all Christian morals; it founds its morals on the basis of religion; it welcomes the religion of the Bible; and in receiving the Bible, it allows it to do what it is allowed to do in no other system, to speak for itself.

Dr. Mann went on to say that the religious education which a child receives at school

> is imparted for the purpose of enabling him to judge for himself, according to the dictates of his own reason and conscience, what his religious obligations are and whither they lead. But if a man is taxed to support a school, where religious doctrines are inculcated which he believes to be false, and which he believes that God condemns, then he is excluded from the school by divine law, at the same time that he is compelled to support it by human law. This is a double wrong.[182]

He supported his theory not only by arguing its positive value to the pupil, but by the process of elimination. There were, he thought, only four other possibilities, namely, purely secular schools; the teaching of a definite system of religion; local option, leaving it to the majority in a community to decide; or the leaving of all education to private agencies. Eliminating these, he decided that free schools for all with a basis of religious education which all parents could add to as they saw fit was the wisest plan.[183] His views prevailed. As a result, the Roman Catholics in Boston, as in New York and other places, developed parochial schools of their own, and in at least one place, Lowell,[184] secured public support for their schools intended for Irish immigrants. The town required that these schools should meet three tests:

> 1. That the instructors be examined as to their qualifications by the committee, and receive their appointments from them.
>
> 2. That the books, exercises, and studies should all be prescribed and regulated by the committee, and that no other should be taught or allowed.

3. That these schools should be placed, as respects the examination, inspection, and general supervision of the committee, on precisely the same footing with the other schools of the town.[185]

The Catholics supported their proposal on the ground that in New York, prior to the passage of the law of 1842 prohibiting public school money going to sectarian teaching, school funds had been divided among different religious denominations, such as the Dutch Reformed, Episcopalians, Baptists, and others. Public opinion was coming around definitely, however, to the position which has since been generally maintained in all American states, that public school money should not be applied to any sectarian institution. In 1853 with this object in mind the following amendment to the Massachusetts constitution was proposed:

All moneys raised by taxation in the towns and cities for the support of public schools, and all moneys which may be appropriated by the state for the support of common schools, shall be applied to, and expended in, no other schools than those which are conducted according to law, under the order and superintendence of the authorities of the town or city in which the money is to be expended; and such moneys shall never be appropriated to any religious sect for the maintenance, exclusively, of its own schools.[186]

This was ratified by the people two years later. But even this law was not quite stringent enough to meet American ideas. There was a lull in the controversy during the Civil War period, when the slavery question absorbed public attention, but at its close the discussion was renewed by many debates. The arguments pro and con may be profitably studied in a book published in Boston in 1876, in which Bishop Bernard McQuaid (1823–1909), one of the ablest and most effective of the advocates of parochial schools, presented his point of view, and Francis E. Abbot (1836–1903), editor of *The Index, A Boston Journal of Free Thought,* presented that of liberalism.[187] An interesting feature of Bishop McQuaid's presentation is that he did not emphasize state financial support of parochial schools, but rather the importance of Roman Catholics themselves providing such schools for their own youth at their own expense.

The 1853 law continued in force until 1917, when the following amendment —still the law of the State—was adopted by a vote of 206,329 to 130,357.

Section 1. No law shall be passed prohibiting the free exercise of religion.

Section 2. All moneys raised by taxation in the towns and cities for the support of public schools, and all moneys which may be appropriated by the commonwealth for the support of common schools shall be applied to, and expended in, no other schools than those which are conducted according to law, under the order and superintendence of the authorities of the town or city in which the money is expended; and no grant, appropriation or use of public money or property or loan of public credit shall be made or authorized by the commonwealth or any political division thereof for the purpose of founding, maintaining or aiding any school or institution of learning, whether under public control or otherwise, wherein any denominational doctrine is inculcated, or any other school, or any college, infirmary, hospital, institution, or educational, charitable or religious undertaking which is not publicly owned and under the exclusive control, order and superintendence of public officers or public agents authorized by the commonwealth or federal authority or both, except that appropriations may be made for the maintenance and support of the Soldiers' Home in Massachusetts and for free public libraries in any city or town, and to carry out legal obligations, if any, already entered into; and no such grant, appropriation or use of public money or property or loan of public credit shall be made or authorized for the purpose of founding, maintaining or aiding any church, religious denomination or society.

Section 3. Nothing herein contained shall be construed to prevent the commonwealth, or any political division thereof, from paying to privately controlled hospitals, infirmaries, or institutions for the deaf, dumb or blind not more than the ordinary and reasonable compensation for care or support actually rendered or furnished by such hospitals, infirmaries or institutions to such persons as may be in whole or in part unable to support or care for themselves.

Section 4. Nothing herein contained shall be construed to deprive any inmate of a publicly controlled reformatory, penal or charitable institution of the opportunity of religious exercises therein of his own faith; but no inmate of such institution shall be compelled to attend religious services or receive religious instruction against his will, or, if a minor, without the consent of his parent or guardian.[188]

This amendment made the prohibition of sectarian teaching statutory. It does not, however, prevent the teaching of the elements of Christianity as long as this teaching is not of a "denominational" character, hence Bible reading is still the rule. The amount of religion in the public schools, within the constitutional restrictions, is determined by local committees who have authority to approve parochial school attendance as a substitute for attendance at public schools.[189]

It should perhaps be added that during the period we have been mainly considering, from the start of the state Board of Education in 1837 on, state support was gradually withdrawn from sectarian higher institutions. Such institutions continue to be incorporated by the state, with the stipulation that there shall be no religious test for faculty or students in ordinary collegiate institutions.[190]

In 1839 Massachusetts opened at Lexington the first state normal school in the United States—an event of far-reaching importance. It had been prepared for by a Congregational minister, Samuel Read Hall (1795-1877), who conducted from 1823 to 1830 the first teacher-training institution in the country in a small town in Vermont, and published what is generally considered the first American textbook on the subject six years later in Boston. It was called *The Instructor's Manual, or Lectures on School-Keeping*. Its influence may be understood when it is recalled that in 1832 the New York state commissioner of education ordered ten thousand copies, and two years thereafter the state made its earliest provision for the professional training of teachers.[191]

We have considered at some length the history of the public school system of Massachusetts in relation to religious education because it is to a large extent typical of that of other sections of New England and of the early settled parts of the Middle West influenced by it, and because Massachusetts took the lead in most of the progressive steps.

In Connecticut the development was much like that in Massachusetts. Regular religious instruction was part of the accepted program of the colonial schools. It continued, only slightly modified so as to be on a simple nonsectarian basis, in the tax-supported schools of the early days after the establishment of the state; but it was not until after Church and State were separated by the constitution of 1818 that the movement for public schools entirely divorced from the local Congregational churches became strong. We have dealt in another place[192] with this struggle over the "standing order" in Connecticut. This involved indirectly the whole question of the control of public education, which had been gradually passing from the supervision of the local minister to that of the state, exercised mainly through locally elected school boards. Here we are concerned with the early efforts to secure efficiently directed nonsectarian public education. These go back to Henry Barnard (1811–1900), who as a member of the Connecticut legislature in 1838 secured the passing of an act to provide for the better supervision of the common schools. He became the secretary that year of the state Board of Education, and did for his state the same type of work that Horace Mann (1796–1859) was doing at the same time for Massachusetts. His work in Connecticut, and later in Rhode Island and Wisconsin, and as the first United States Commissioner of Education, and founder and editor of the *American Journal of Education* (1855–81), was of epoch-making importance in building up the nonsectarian public school system of the United States.

Little by little definite religious instruction was given up in the Connecticut schools, but as late as 1846 a great majority of them still reported the use of some part of the Bible as a reading book.[193] By about the middle of the century all formal religious instruction had been generally given up, and nothing was left except "formal Bible reading, hymns, and prayers, as opening and closing exercises."[194] This meant that religious training was mainly restricted to the home, the church, the parochial or private school, the Sunday school, and some endowed academies.

The Connecticut point of view was thus expressed by Horace Bushnell (1802–76) in 1840:

The great point with all Christians must be to secure the Bible its proper place. To this as a sacred duty all sectarian aims must be sacrificed. Nothing is more certain than that no such thing as a sectarian religion is to find a place in our schools. It must find a place for the Bible as a book of principles, as containing the true standards of character and the best motives and aids to virtue. If any Christian desires more he must teach it himself at home. To insist that the State shall teach the rival opinions of sects and risk the loss of all instruction for that, would be folly and wickedness together.[195]

In addition to its conservatism in the matter of retaining a basic religious note in the public schools, Connecticut deserves credit for its liberalism in being the first state definitely to restrict the use of the "school fund" to the public schools. The constitution of 1818 has this important provision:

SEC. 2. The fund called the SCHOOL FUND shall remain a perpetual fund, the interest of which shall be inviolably appropriated to the support and encouragement of the public or common schools throughout the State, and for the equal benefit of all the people thereof. The value and amount of said fund shall, as soon as practicable, be ascertained in such manner as the General Assembly may prescribe, published, and recorded in the Comptroller's office, and no law shall ever be made authorizing said fund to be diverted to any other use than the encouragement and support of public or common schools, among the several school societies, as justice and equity shall require.[196]

(3) THE STRUGGLE IN VIRGINIA

Although no states can compare with Massachusetts and Connecticut in their influence on the development of the public school system, which resulted in New England's giving the note in this field to the nation as a whole, it is necessary to tell briefly the struggle for public education in a few other states, beginning with Virginia. Here the situation was completely different from that in New England. Instead of the Congregational Church with its democratic traditions, the Anglican Church was dominant, and it had not up to the nineteenth century shown any deep interest in the general education of the rank and file of youth.

The detailed history of the relations of Church and State in the Old Dominion during this struggle for an educational system free from Church control may be found in a work entitled *The Church, the State, and Education in Virginia.* This shows that the basic principle of the colonization of Virginia was that it was an extension of the civil and religious government of England, and that consequently educational legislation was to be in harmony with that in the mother country. The first charter provided that the religion to be established was to be "according to the Rights and Doctrine of the Church of England."[197] This meant that prior to the Revolution, except during the brief Commonwealth era, there was little opportunity for an entirely independent educational policy.

Virginia, in fact, had an established Church. Indeed, even the Act of Toleration of 1689 was not recognized by its government until the last year of the century, and then inadequately.[198] Even this recognition was not due to the voluntary act of the government, but mainly to the earnest efforts of Francis Makemie (1658–1708), the founder of Presbyterianism in America. At about this time, in 1689, an important step was taken by drawing ecclesiastical affairs from the hands of the governor and placing them in the hands of the Church and the people. This laid the foundations for developing local interest in the Church and education[199] and gave the vestries large power.

The real history of education in Virginia goes back to the establishment of the College of William and Mary in 1693. It stood for the aristocratic ideals of the South, and although it had preparatory branches supplied by ministers and tutors, it was not deeply concerned with public education in the colony as a whole. Two other colleges established under Presbyterian auspices, namely, what is now Washington and Lee University, founded in 1749, and Hampden–Sidney College (1776), represented the only other important colonial efforts in Virginia to provide education aside from private means.

With the Revolution, and the Declaration of Rights adopted by the Virginia Assembly in 1776, a new day came. Dissenters were soon freed from taxation for the support of the established Church. The support of the clergy was left to voluntary contributions, the payment of their salaries by the legislature being given up. The adjustment to the new conditions was made with less difficulty than was anticipated.[200]

A historian of education in Virginia thus states the significance of the change:

> The suspension of salaries resulted in virtually breaking the union of church and state; not only in that the precedent once established, it was easy to renew the suspension annually until 1779, when all previous legislation for the support of the clergy was repealed,[201] but also, in that it gave those in favor of complete separation added encouragement in their battle to eliminate every trace of the previous establishment.[202]

The Episcopal churches were left only as much of their property as was used for definitely religious purposes, while in 1802 the assembly ordered their glebes sold, the proceeds to be appropriated to the poor or to such other nonreligious objects as the majority of the voters in the county should designate; the theory being that this property had really been public property and should revert to the public.[203]

The constitution of 1776 had nothing to say about education, and this was even true of the constitution of 1830. This shows how backward the state was in providing a system of public education, in spite of the farseeing efforts of Thomas Jefferson, who in 1779 introduced into the Virginia Assembly his "Bill for the more general diffusion of knowledge." Even though it did not pass, some of its sections are worth quoting. His idea was that young people

> endowed with genius and virtue, should be rendered by liberal education worthy to receive, and able to guard the sacred deposit of the rights and liberties of their fellow citizens, and that they should be called to that charge without regard to wealth, birth or other accidental condition or circumstance. . . .[204]

Under this plan every county was to be divided so that "all the children within each hundred may daily attend the school to be established therein."[205] These schools were to be erected by duly elected aldermen of the county. Section VI provided that

> At every of those schools shall be taught reading, writing, and common arithmetick, and the books which shall be used therein for instructing the children to read shall be such as will at the same time make them acquainted with Graecian, Roman, English, and American history. At these schools all the free children, male and female, resident within the respective hundred, shall be intitled to receive tuition gratis, for the term of three years, and as much longer, at their private expence, as their parents, guardians, or friends shall think proper.[206]

Overseers were to be appointed over these schools by the aldermen, and the general plan of instruction was to be developed by the visitors of William and Mary College. There were also to be a sufficient number of grammar schools with boarding facilities for each convenient group of hundreds. In these

> shall be taught the Latin and Greek languages, English Grammar, geography, and the higher part of numerical arithmetick, to wit, vulgar and decimal fractions, and the extrication of the square and cube roots.[207]

By a system of scholarships the best boys in the local schools were to be chosen to the grammar schools, and from the grammar schools the best scholars to William and Mary College, their expenses being met from the public funds. The plan was the most ambitious one for public education separated from the Church devised in the United States in the first half century after independence; but nothing came of it as far as Virginia was concerned.

In 1796 Virginia passed her first school law, entitled "An Act to Establish Public Schools," but it was optional and consequently ineffective. Instruction was to be free for three years, and thereafter tuition was to be paid.

In 1803 a charter was secured for an academy, given statutory existence in 1819 as the University of Virginia; an institution which, under Jefferson's leadership, stood for the separation of Church and State in public education.[208]

In 1815 the beginnings of a state board of education, termed a Board of Trustees of the Literary Fund, was established, and asked by the legislature to report

a system of education, including a university, to be called the University of Virginia, and such additional colleges, academies, and schools as should diffuse the benefits of education throughout the commonwealth.[209]

As a result, the legislature adopted in 1818 a plan of public education. This was however merely a charity school system by which the courts, counties, cities, and towns were to appoint school commissioners to arrange for the education of the poor, a fund of $45,000 annually being appropriated from the Literary Fund for this purpose.

In 1836 a law was enacted which provided for boards of school commissioners who were to establish schools in every district, to which all resident white children above the age of six were to be admitted free. The cost of maintaining these schools, above what was provided from the income from the Literary Fund, was to be met by a county school tax. But even this law was optional, since the counties could accept or reject its provisions; and again little was accomplished, only nine counties adopting the plan.

As late as 1843 the governor in his message to the legislature stated that as a result of nearly thirty years of effort to advance public education there was provision for only sixty days of schooling for about half the indigent white children of the state. There was not yet any state provision for Negro education.

The constitution of 1851 made the first constitutional mention of education by providing a capitation tax on white persons for the purposes of education in primary and free schools, a provision which was retained in the revision of 1864.

During all this period the various religious bodies, especially the Anglicans and Presbyterians, provided most of the worth-while education in the state through their academies, of which some 317 with 9,068 pupils were reported in 1850.[210] The Presbyterians seem to have first conceived popular education in a large way without reference to a strictly denominational emphasis. It was not until the law of 1870 that the basis of a really effective state school system, with a state superintendent and an ex officio state Board of Education, was established under the leadership of Dr. William H. Ruffner (1824–1908), a Presbyterian minister, who showed himself to be a man of uncommon good sense, energy, and vision.

(4) THE DEVELOPMENTS IN NEW YORK AND OTHER STATES

The state of New York passed in 1795 an act for the encouragement of schools. As a result, societies were organized to provide free schools, in many places where public education did not exist, or to promote the movement to have such schools started and supported by the state. In 1805 a permanent state school fund was created, and in 1812 a state system of schools was authorized under a superintendent of common schools. De Witt Clinton (1769–1828), governor of the state from 1817 to 1823 and from 1825 to 1828, was a strong advocate of public education at state expense, believing that a system of tax-supported schools was "the palladium of our freedom" and that it should care for the children of the state for ten years. "Upon education," he said, we must "rely for the purity, the preservation, and the perpetuation of republican government."[211]

The situation in the city of New York reflects this development. In 1801 the state legislature had passed an act to the effect that:

The mayor, aldermen, and commonalty of the City of New York shall pay to the vestry of the Episcopal Church, the vestry of Christ's Church, the trustees of the First Presbyterian Church, the minister, elder, and deacon of the Reformed Dutch Church, and trustees of the Methodist Episcopal Church, the Scotch Presbyterian Church, the African School, the United German Lutheran Church, the German Reformed Churches, the First Baptist Church, and the United Brethren or Moravian Church, each one-eleventh part of all money remaining in their hands from the Acts of 1795 and 1799. The income from the said apportionment to be used for the education of poor children.[212]

Similarly, by the act of 1813 the commissioners of the school fund were directed to distribute its income, plus an equal amount to be raised by tax on the city, to the trustees of various institutions named, "and of such incorporated religious societies, in said city as now support or hereafter shall establish charity schools," the distribution to be based on the number of children from four to fifteen years old taught free therein during the preceding year.[213] The New York Free School Society, organized in 1805, began two years later to receive grants from public funds, and in 1825 it became the sole recipient of public funds for education in the city—grants to church schools being discontinued. Up to this time such grants had persisted, though decreasing in number and amount.

It is well for us to remember such legislative acts as these in our early history, made in almost all cases at the request of Protestant churches, if we would understand the attitude of the Roman Catholic Church today in its attempts to secure public funds for parochial schools.

In 1825, when such grants were discontinued by the state, the New York Free School Society changed its name to the Public School Society of New York, and was permitted to levy a tax. It provided some "nonsectarian" religious instruction, but because this was based on the King James translation of the Bible it was unsatisfactory to Roman Catholics. This situation continued until 1842, when a city board of education was created, and the society handed over to it its buildings and property. In 1853 it disbanded.[214]

In 1840 Governor Seward recommended that "foreign children" should have schools with teachers of their own faith and language, which was interpreted as favoring public funds for parochial schools.[215] In the same year Bishop Hughes appealed in behalf of public aid for seven New York City parochial schools which were doing an important work among the Irish and other immigrant children. When his request was denied by the corporation of the city, he presented it to the legislature, where it passed the Assembly but was voted down by the Senate.[216]

In 1841 the state superintendent advocated in his annual report applying to the city of New York the principle of local control by which "each district suits itself, by having such religious instruction in its school as is congenial to the opinions of its inhabitants."[217] But the city decided that "Religious *instruction* is no part of the common school education."[218]

It was not until after the close of the Civil War that a comprehensive system of universal free education was established in the state.

Pennsylvania was only a few years behind New York, as in 1834 its legislature passed an act to establish a general system of education for public schools.[219] The Pennsylvania Society for the Promotion of Public Schools was very active.

In the South, North Carolina with its vigorous and democratic Scotch-Irish population took the lead in establishing democratic common schools, creating a permanent school fund in 1825, and passing a public school law in 1839. But state schools, as distinct from private and denominational ones, were not organized in anything like an effective system until the appointment in 1853 of a state superintendent of public schools.[220]

From 1844 on, all states amending their constitutions, and new states when admitted to the union (except West Virginia, which later corrected the omission), provided in their fundamental laws against any diversion of public funds to denominational purposes.[221] The state constitution framers were in the great majority of cases sympathetic with the cause of religion but anxious to keep the functions of Church and State distinct.

By 1860 all Northern states and several Southern states had laid the foundations of the American system of public schools free for pupils and free from denominational control. Some grants from public funds were still being made to church and private schools, mostly on the secondary level, but the movement for a completely public controlled public school system had become well established, with laws in most states permitting public taxation for such purposes. There had also been progress in the development of public high schools, normal schools, and state universities, as well as for responsible superintendents and boards of education. The framework of the American system had been laid in the East, Middle West, and upper South, and the superstructure was to be erected all over the country as soon as the Civil War and its immediate aftermath had passed.

(5) THE GROWTH OF NATIONAL INTEREST IN THE SEPARATION OF PUBLIC EDUCATION FROM CHURCH CONTROL

This brief survey of the development of public schools in the most representative states shows that the beginning of the movement for an adequate public school system goes back to the 'thirties and 'forties of the nineteenth century. Up to that time, though there were some public schools conducted by cities, counties, and townships, no general system of state schools supported by taxation had been developed. There were still many parochial schools conducted by Protestants or Catholics, a few schools conducted for private profit, and many schools of a high order conducted by charitable foundations. Some of this last group still continue, such as the Phillips Academies in Andover and Exeter, but most of them were absorbed by the public school system through the application of the cy-pres doctrine. Many of the schools founded and largely supported by churches were also taken over by public authority, being conducted until the middle of the century about as they had been in the past.

It was the enormous Irish immigration of the middle of the century, with the growing urbanization that accompanied it, that contributed more than any other new factor to the determination to develop a public school system which, while entirely undenominational, should conserve all that was considered best in the American educational tradition as developed mainly under New England leadership. It was essentially a democratic and constructive movement, for there were large elements in the population that showed a definite fear that the new immigrants, whose usefulness to the country was somewhat reluctantly granted, might, without a new emphasis on public education unconnected with any Church, introduce unwelcome changes in the American creed.[222] The extreme Know-Nothing party, which characteristically called itself the American party, was powerful in the 'fifties, carrying in 1855 a number of New England and border states, and might have won the national election in 1856, if it had not become hopelessly split over slavery. Its platform in that year contained this statement of policy:

> Resistance to the aggressive policy and corrupting tendencies of the Roman Catholic Church in our country by the advancement to all political stations—executive, legislative, judicial or diplomatic—of those only who do not hold civil allegiance, directly or indirectly, to any foreign power, whether civil or ecclesiastical, and who are Americans by birth, education and training, thus fulfilling the maxim "Americans only shall govern America."
>
> The education of the youth of our country in schools provided by the State, which

schools shall be common to all, without distinction of creed or party, and free from any influence or direction of a denominational or partisan character.

And, inasmuch as Christianity, by the Constitutions of nearly all the States; by the decisions of most eminent judicial authorities, and by the consent of the people of America, is considered an element of our political system, and the Holy Bible is at once the source of Christianity and the depository and fountain of all civil and religious freedom, we oppose every attempt to exclude it from the schools thus established in the States.[223]

Although Massachusetts and some other states, faced by the wave of European immigration, took the necessary steps a generation earlier, it was not until after absorption in the Civil War was a thing of the past and the Union had been restored, that the importance from a national standpoint of an adequate system of public schools under state auspices was fully realized. The most striking and effective presentation of this view, and of the danger of giving public moneys to parochial schools, was expressed by President Grant (1822–85) in his address September 29, 1875, to the Army of the Tennessee at Des Moines, Iowa:

The centennial year of our national existence, I believe, is a good time to begin the work of strengthening the foundations of the structure commenced by our patriotic forefathers one hundred years ago at Lexington. Let us all labor to add all needful guarantees for the security of free thought, free speech, a free press, pure morals, unfettered religious sentiments, and of equal rights and privileges to all men, irrespective of nationality, color or religion. Encourage free schools and resolve that not one dollar appropriated for their support shall be appropriated to the support of any sectarian schools. Resolve that neither the state nor the nation, nor both combined, shall support institutions of learning other than those sufficient to afford every child growing up in the land the opportunity of a good common school education, unmixed with sectarian, pagan or atheistical dogmas. Leave the matter of religion to the family altar, the church, and the private school, supported entirely by private contributions. Keep the church and state forever separate. With these safeguards, I believe the battles which created the Army of the Tennessee will not have been fought in vain.[224]

The following year, in the Hayes–Tilden presidential controversy, the matter came prominently to the fore when the Republican national platform called for an amendment to the Federal Constitution forbidding "the application of any public funds or property for the benefit of any school or institution under sectarian control."[225] When James G. Blaine (1830–93) submitted the proposed amendment in a strengthened form to Congress on August 14, 1875, it failed to receive the necessary two-thirds majority in a strictly party vote, the Republicans voting for it and the Democrats against it.[226] The exact wording of the proposed amendment was as follows:

No State shall make any law respecting an establishment of religion, or prohibiting the free exercise thereof; and no religious test shall ever be required as a qualification to any office or public trust under any State. No public property, and no public revenue of, nor any loan of credit by or under the authority of, the United States, or any State, Territory, District or municipal corporation, shall be appropriated to, or made or used for, the support of any school, educational or other institution, under the control of any religious or anti-religious sect, organization, or denomination, or wherein the particular creed or tenets shall be read or taught in any school or institution supported in whole or in part by such revenue or loan of credit; and no such appropriation or loan of credit shall be made to any religious or anti-religious sect, organization or denomination, or to promote its interests or tenets. This article shall not be construed to prohibit the reading of the Bible in any school or institution; and it shall not have the effect to impair rights of property already vested. Congress shall have power, by appropriate legislation, to provide for the prevention and punishment of violations of this article.[227]

The second sentence is all-important. One point raised may now be considered to have been settled, namely that there is only rarely an attempt to get public schools to provide denominational instruction as distinct from some voluntary released or dismissed time outside the school. As the Supreme Court of Iowa stated in a well-known case in 1918:

If there is any one thing which is well settled in the policies and purposes of the American people as a whole, it is the fixed and unalterable determination that there shall be an absolute and unequivocal separation of church and state, and that our public school system, supported by the taxation of the property of all alike—Catholic, Protestant, Jew, Gentile, believer and infidel—shall not be used directly or indirectly for religious instruction, and above all that it shall not be made an instrument of proselyting influence in favor of any religious organization, sect, creed or belief.[228]

Although the Blaine amendment was not passed by Congress, it was clear that the overwhelming majority of its members were in favor of a public school system divorced entirely from religious affiliations. Nine of the ten states admitted to the union since this time—Idaho being the only exception—have been required as a condition of admission to agree, by an ordinance irrevocable without the consent of the United States and of the people of the new state, that provision be made "for the establishment and maintenance of a system of public schools, which shall be open to all the children of the state and free from sectarian control";[229] and eight of these states have literally complied with this condition. Four of the other newer states of the West had also forbidden such control by their own action prior to this time, and two others, Wisconsin and Nevada, had forbidden sectarian instruction in the public schools. These latter restrictions have since been substantially copied by most of the states, especially in the Far West. The resulting constitutional provisions will be discussed in a later section.[230]

The development of the public school system with its tendency to secularize education has grown apace in the past half century, and especially since World War I.

It is part of a universal movement and has had many able advocates, of whom none has been more distinguished or influential than John Dewey (1859-). The movement to develop education for the great mass of our citizens under State auspices cannot and should not be stemmed, but there is nothing in American Constitutional law or national traditions to prevent the development for the pupils of these schools of voluntary religious courses, in which separate provision is made when called for by Protestants, Roman Catholics, and Jews, due attention being paid to the requirements of Church–State separation laid down by the Supreme Court in the recent Everson and McCollum cases.[231]

Much more serious is the matter of state financial aid to parochial schools. This was the major matter at issue in the proposed Blaine amendment. Zollmann gives a chronological list, dating from 1877 through 1913, showing that thirty-three states in this period forbade such expenditures by constitutional provisions.[232] As he[233] has generally been considered an authority in America on this matter in its legal and political aspects, and as his important work, *American Church Law,* is used even at the Catholic University of America, it is worth while to note his mature conclusion that the State should not contribute direct financial aid to denominational or parochial schools—a conclusion in which a considerable number of Catholic laymen unite, as may be shown by frequent letters on the subject in the daily press and even in such a Catholic publication as the *Commonweal.* He writes:

> There can be no question but that this solution is the only feasible one, no matter what hardships it involves for those who retain their parochial schools. Any arrangement by which parochial schools are allowed to participate in the public school funds cannot but result in political pressure. The first result is a close public control over the denominational schools. The next result is the entry of those schools into politics in order to shape this control to suit their own purposes. Where one denomination or a combination of them becomes strong enough, a shift of such control becomes inevitable. Instead of the public agencies regulating the parochial schools, the latter will control the public schools.[234]

Realizing fully, however, the evils of the present system, which result in most of the children having no religious instruction in the schools, he has become a strong supporter of a system of voluntary religious instruction on week days, which he believes that the courts will increasingly support; in other words, he favors a plan of religious day schools which will co-operate with the public schools rather than compete with them. This plan is discussed at length in another section.[235]

The Supreme Court of Illinois in a decision in 1917 puts the matter as follows:

> The constitution not only forbids the appropriation for any purpose or in any manner of the common school funds to sectarian or denominational institutions, but it contemplates that the separation between the common school and the sectarian or denominational school or institution shall be so open, notorious and complete that there can be no room for reasonable doubt that the common school is absolutely free from the influence, control or domination of the sectarian institution.[236]

This weighty opinion has recently been supported in substance by the United States Supreme Court.[237]

Much space has been given to the consideration of the history of state aid to sectarian schools, for it is not at all impossible that it may become an acute national problem. The Roman Catholic Church has always favored a liberal immigration law and has opposed birth control. In both cases this has been due in part to conscientious convictions based on religious and humanitarian grounds, and in part to a desire that the elements of the population it represents should increase in number so that in time they may be the dominant religious element in the American scene. As we have seen, there are already several states in the union in which there are more members of the Roman Catholic Church than of all Protestant communions combined,[238] though in no states does this proportion hold good of adherents as distinct from members. Consequently up to the present, in spite of strenuous efforts in Ohio, Massachusetts, and other places, Roman Catholics have not been able to secure an amendment to a state constitution that would permit grants from public funds to parochial schools. It is not at all impossible, however, that in the course of the next couple of decades the Church may be powerful enough to secure such an amendment in one or two states. If a state supreme court should—as is unlikely—declare it constitutional, the matter would then have to come before the Supreme Court of the United States to determine whether the plan is consistent with the guarantees of religious freedom in the Federal Constitution. There is very little chance that the Supreme Court would permit such a change in a state constitution to continue, for it seems reasonably clear that it is contrary to the fundamental guarantees of the Bill of Rights as interpreted by the Fourteenth Amendment.

The next step would then probably be an attempt to secure an amendment to the Federal Constitution which would legalize such grants from public funds to parochial schools. It is, of course, impossible to predict what will happen in the course of the centuries; but there is no reasonable likelihood that any such proposal would in the foreseeable future meet with the approval of the Congress of the United States and of the three-fourths majority of the states necessary for a Constitutional change. Consequently, though it is believed that the Roman Catholic hierarchy* will press these proposals at some future time, as they have a perfect right to do, and will receive the active support of a large majority of our Roman Catholic citizens, they are not likely to succeed, at least in the course of the next few generations. The problem is extremely complicated, because unquestionably the Church, through its parochial schools, does educational and moral work that is highly significant and influential.[239] Most thoughtful Protestants wish Catholics well in their present efforts to provide for large numbers of their own youth in urban centers a good education with a strong religious foundation; but direct financial aid from the State for denominational schools, whether Protestant, Roman Catholic, or Jewish, would in the long run seem distinctly disadvantageous in a democracy with our many racial and religious backgrounds, and with our traditions of separation between Church and State. Indeed, if put into force, such State aid might prove very dangerous to the cause of religious freedom, and react to the detriment of the Church which advocates it.

This whole question of maintaining the separation of Church and State in public education will recur frequently in these pages, especially when modern problems of adjustment in education between the State and the Churches are considered,[240] and when decisions in recent Supreme Court cases are discussed.[241]

Section 9. *THE ANNEXATION OF TEXAS (1845)*

With the early history of that part of New Spain that came to be called Texas we are not here concerned. Suffice it to remind the reader that in 1682 a Spanish settlement was made near El Paso, and that from about 1700 on Roman Catholic missionaries were active in the region, which was under Spanish and Catholic control. In 1821 Moses Austin of Connecticut, known as the "Father of Texas," secured from the Spanish governor a large grant of land for three hundred families. They were to be farmers and mechanics, Catholic in religion, and willing to take the oath of allegiance to the Spanish king. Concessions were made

* As this section is being read in proof Cardinal Spellman has issued his welcome statement regarding his recent controversy with Mrs. F. D. Roosevelt. In it he says that whereas the Church is seeking the extension of government auxiliary services to the pupils in its parochial schools, similar to those which are provided pupils in public schools and which have been declared Constitutional, it is not seeking direct government grants for the erection of parochial school buildings or their maintenance, or the support of teaching in them. It realizes, he says, that under existing Constitutional provisions and their interpretation by the Supreme Court such aid would be unconstitutional. This statement may prove of great significance in re-establishing more friendly Church-State relations. *N. Y. Times,* June 27, 1949, and August 6, 1949. See XIX, 10.

to others under similar circumstances, emphasis being placed on character and religious faith. Within a decade there were about twenty thousand settlers, more than had been brought in under three hundred years of Spanish rule.[242] In 1836 the territory, which had been for fifteen years under Mexico, won its independence under General Samuel Houston, and in 1845 it was annexed to the United States. The state, coming under American control without passing through the normal territorial status, or even the early American military rule in force in California, must be considered separately, since it involved new problems of Church–State adjustment. The constitution of the Republic of Mexico (United Mexican States, of which what is now Texas was then a part), adopted in 1824, stated that

The Religion of the Mexican Nation is, and will be perpetually, the Roman Catholic Apostolic. The Nation will protect it by wise and just laws, and prohibit the exercise of any other whatever.[243]

Similarly, the constitution, adopted in 1827, of the "Free State of Coahuila and Texas"—that is, the two northeastern provinces of Mexico—which were formed into a self-governing State, semi-independent of "the other adjoining States of the Mexican Federation," had this provision: "The Apostolic Catholic Religion is that of the State; this it protects by wise and just laws, and prohibits the exercise of any other."[244] Furthermore, the following section made the Church–State bond perfectly clear:

The State shall regulate and defray the expenses which may be necessary for the preservation of worship, in conformity with the regulation of the Concordato, which the Nation shall celebrate with the Holy See, and by the laws it shall dictate relative to the exercise of patronage in the whole Federation.[245]

It was also provided that "the catechism of the Christian religion" should be taught in all the common schools.[246]

These constitutional provisions are clear and specific, and in accordance with historic precedent in Catholic countries; but there were influential minority elements in the population, who either, as liberals, wished to see Church and State separated, or, as Protestants (a small group), wished to worship God according to the dictates of their own consciences. Consequently, when the delegates of the people of Texas, meeting March 2, 1836, unanimously declared for entire independence from Mexico, they included among their grievances against the Mexican government:

It denies us the right of worshipping the Almighty according to the dictates of our own conscience, by the support of a national religion calculated to promote the temporal interests of its human functionaries rather than the glory of the true and living God.[247]

The convention which drafted this declaration of independence also adopted a fortnight later, March 17, 1836, a constitution for the "Republic of Texas." This was based definitely on United States precedents, and marked an almost complete break with the old Catholic-Mexican tradition. It provided for the introduction by statute as early as practicable of the common law of England; the exclusion of priests and all other ministers of the Gospel from Congress and the presidency, as they are "by their profession, dedicated to God and the care of souls"—a phrase found in some of our early state constitutions;[248] and adopted a bill of rights including a guarantee of complete religious freedom:

No preference shall be given by law to any religious denomination or mode of worship over another, but every person shall be permitted to worship God according to the dictates of his own conscience.[249]

The story of the reasons which led the Republic of Texas to seek for admission into the United States need not be entered into here. Suffice it to say that in 1845 Congress consented to the formation of the state of Texas into a new state of the union on certain conditions, of which the most important was that the constitution, when duly drafted by representatives of the state, should be laid before Congress for its approval. Such a constitution was unanimously adopted at a convention held in the city of Austin, Texas, in 1845, and on submission to the people was ratified by an overwhelming vote. It contained in Article I the following clauses based on the experience of the American states:

Sec. 3. No religious test shall ever be required as a qualification to any office or public trust in this State.

Sec. 4. All men have a natural and indefeasible right to worship God according to the dictates of their own consciences; no man shall be compelled to attend, erect, or support any place of worship, or to maintain any ministry against his consent; no human authority ought, in any case whatever, to control or interfere with the rights of conscience, in matters of religion, and no preference shall ever be given by law to any religious societies or mode of worship; but it shall be the duty of the legislature to pass such laws as may be necessary to protect every religious denomination in the peaceable enjoyment of their own mode of public worship.[250]

The constitution took over from the old republican administration the provision disqualifying priests and other ministers of the Gospel from eligibility to the legislature. It was duly submitted to the Congress of the United States and approved, the state of Texas being "admitted into the Union on an equal footing with the original States in all respects whatever."[251]

This completes the outline of an interesting chapter in American Church-State relations, namely, the transformation of a portion of the Roman Catholic Mexican nation first into an independent republic, and then into a state which is part of the American union with complete religious freedom. It was with reference to this change that the Texas Supreme Court in 1848, in a well-known case, stated that by the constitution of 1845 the Roman Catholic religion was reduced "from the high privilege of being the only national church to a level and an equality with every other denomination."[252] As we have seen, however, the transformation was not quite as sudden as the court indicated, because the constitution of the republic, as adopted in 1836, nearly a decade before admission to statehood, had granted religious freedom.

Section 10. THE MEXICAN WAR (1846–48) AND THE ANNEXATION OF CALIFORNIA (1848)

The Mexican War from 1846 to 1848 provides an admirable opportunity of studying the relation of the Churches to the State in matters of governmental policy a century ago. Participation in the war on the part of the United States, following the annexation of Texas in 1845, has never since completely satisfied the ethical sense of the American people, and it did not at the time. "Manifest destiny," the great argument used for the war, does not commend itself as an adequate ground for the part played by this country. Its first recorded use was in the *Democratic Review* for July–August, 1845, where the editor spoke of "our manifest destiny to overspread the continent allotted by Providence for the free development of our yearly multiplying millions."[253] This was with specific reference to the annexation of Texas, but its use became general in the next few years, and the idea behind it was specially applicable to the Mexican War.

(1) THE ATTITUDE OF THE CHURCHES TOWARD THE WAR

It is particularly interesting to study the attitude of the Roman Catholic Church, for at the beginning of the war many Protestants predicted that its members in the United States would not take up arms against a Catholic country; but their fears proved ungrounded. The Church, in accordance with its historic tradition, took no part in bringing on the war, but when it was once decided upon by constituted authority its members on the whole supported it. The Sixth Provincial Council was in session in Baltimore when news of the war's outbreak arrived. It took no action regarding it, but in its *Pastoral Letter* the hierarchy stated to American Catholics that obedience to the pope was

> in no way inconsistent with your civil allegiance, your social duties as citizens, or your rights as men. . . . You can bear witness that we have always taught you to render to Caesar the things which are Caesar's, to God the things which are God's.[254]

Many of the leading Church papers, such as the *Freeman's Journal* and *Cath-*

olic Register of New York, agreed that as the war had been undertaken it should be brought to a successful conclusion. On the other hand, a small group of the Roman Catholic press maintained a position of editorial silence on the subject, but condemned the Churches which had seemed to favor the war as a means of carrying on Protestant proselytizing work in Mexico.

The Mexican War produced a highly important event in our Church-State relations: the use by the government of the United States of Roman Catholic priests, whose duties were partly spiritual and partly political or diplomatic, to commend the United States to their coreligionists in Mexico. Up to this time the relatively small number of Roman Catholic soldiers in the Army had been expected to attend such services as were conducted by Protestant chaplains. To this they naturally objected. President Polk (1795–1849) therefore seized the opportunity presented by the Mexican War, with its latent causes of Protestant-Catholic friction, to relieve the situation. Since his day, Roman Catholic chaplains have been regularly appointed, and their services have met with general approval. They are now fully as numerous in proportion to their Church membership as those of any other communion.

The following references in President Polk's *Diary* tell the story of their introduction. An entry under May 19, 1846, reads:

> Mr. Buchanan [then Secretary of State] called whilst some of the members of the Cabinet were still in my office and introduced Bishop Hughes of the Catholic church in New York. I requested Bishop Hughes [1797–1864] to call with Mr. Buchanan at 7 P. M. Bishop Hughes had come to Washington upon an invitation given by Mr. Buchanan upon consultation with me some days ago. Our object was to procure his aid in disabusing the minds of the Catholic Priests & people of Mexico in regard to what they most erroneously supposed to be the hostile designs of the Government and people of the U. S. upon the religion and church property of Mexico.
>
> Bishop Hughes called with Mr. Buchanan at 7 O'Clock. Mr. B. having already conversed with him on the subject, retired, and I held a conversation of an hour with him. I fully explained to him the object[ions] which we would probably have to encounter from the prejudices of the Catholic Priests in Mexico, and the false impressions they had of the hostile designs of this country on their religion. . . . Bishop Hughes fully agreed with me in the opinion I expressed that it was important to remove such impressions. I said to him that the great object of my desiring to have this interview with him, was to ask whether some of the Priests of the U. S. who spoke the Spanish language could be induced to accompany our army as chaplains and others to visit Mexico in advance of the army, for the purpose of giving assurance to the Catholic clergy in Mexico that under our constitution their religion and church property would be secure, and that so far from being violated, both would be protected by our army, and in this way avoid their active hostility in the pending war. Bishop Hughes at once said he thought such a visit to Mexico and having a few catholic priests with the

army would have a good effect, & expressed his entire willingness to cooperate with our Government in giving such aid as was in his power. He said he knew personally the Arch-bishop of Mexico, & expressed his willingness to visit Mexico himself if the Government desired it. I found Bishop Hughes a highly intelligent and agreeable man, and my interview with him was of the most satisfactory character. . . .[255]

On May 20, 1846:

Col. Benton called with the Catholic Bishop of Missouri. I had before held a conversation with Col. B. and he had concurred with me in the importance of having with our army in Mexico a few Catholic Priests, who would be able to allay the fears of the Mexican Catholics in regard to their religion and church property. I had a short interview with Col. B. and the Bishop. Col. B. said they had just seen the Secretary of War, and that a number of Priests would be designated by the Bishop to accompany the army. . . . The interview with Bishop Hughes on yesterday and this interview with the Bishop of Missouri to day was for the purpose of having their aid in conveying true information in relation to the free toleration of all sects of religion under our constitution to the Mexican Priesthood & people, & giving them assurance that our invasion of Mexico was not for the purpose of interfering in any way with their religion. . . .[256]

Secretary of War Marcy, under date of May 29, 1846, wrote to Major General Taylor giving the names of the Roman Catholic priests chosen and adding:

Although the President cannot appoint them as chaplains, yet it is his wish that they be received in that character by you and your officers, be respected as such and be treated with kindness and courtesy, that they should be permitted to have intercourse with the soldiers of the Catholic faith, to administer their religious instruction, to perform divine service for such as may wish to attend whenever it can be done without interfering with their military duties, and to have free access to the sick or wounded in hospitals or elsewhere. . . . As these gentlemen do not speak Spanish they have been desired by the President to associate with them another clergyman who both understands and speaks it; such person recommended by them you will receive on the same footing as themselves.[257]

The appointments caused something of a furore in some Protestant circles. In comparison today there are hundreds of Roman Catholic chaplains, and they have proved their patriotism and the value of their services.

President Polk now introduces us to a man of marked ability and zeal but known for his asperities as a controversialist, the Reverend William L. McCalla (1788–1859). He was an influential Presbyterian minister with "a rough tongue, which lent itself to telling epigram and kept its owner all his life in hot water."[258]

Polk writes on October 14, 1846:

After the Indians left I was occupied for more than an hour by the Rev'd Wm. L. McCalla of the Presbyterian church, & brother of the 2nd Auditor of the Treasury.

His ostensible object was to be appointed a chaplain in the army. I found him to be a fanatic, proscriptive in his religious opinions, and most unreasonable. . . . His petition was a violent & most intolerant attack on the Roman Catholics & a censure on the administration for employing, as it represented, two or three Roman Catholic Priests with the army in Mexico as chaplains. The prominent idea, aside from its abuse of Catholics & its fanaticism, was that unless I appointed the Rev'd Mr. McCalla a chaplain, the petitioners intended to go before the public & attack the administration upon religious grounds because of the employment of these Catholic Priests. I felt great contempt for Mr. McCalla and for his religion and gave him my mind freely. I told him that, thank God, under our constitution there was no connection between Church and State, and that in my action as President of the U. S. I recognized no distinction of creeds in my appointments to office. . . . I told him it was known that Mexico was a Catholic country, and that their Priests had great influence over that ignorant people, and that they would probably deceive them by representing that the U. S. was waging war against them to overturn their religion, and that if they succeeded in imposing such a falsehood as this upon the people of Mexico they would infuriate them and induce them to carry on a desperate and more sanguinary war against our army, and that to undeceive the Mexicans two or three Catholic Priests who spoke their language, it was thought, would be useful with the army. I told him that these were the reasons and these alone which induced their employment. I told him that Col. Benton and other members of Congress who were well acquainted with the Mexican people had advised their employment for these reasons. I told him that they were not chaplains, that there was no law authorizing the appointment of chaplains for the army, but that they were employees, such as armies often require, who had been sent out for the purposes stated. I told him further that in the Navy, where Chaplains were authorized by law, I had appointed several since I came into office, without regard to the sects of religion to which they belonged, and that I had appointed no Catholic Priests. He intimated that he wished to have an appointment of Chaplain in the Navy. . . . I could not resist the conclusion that one of two things was true; either that Mr. McCalla expected to alarm me into his appointment to avoid an attack before the public from him, or that he hoped to be refused so as to give him a pretext to make such attack. If either was true I had great contempt for him, and I gave him distinctly to understand that I would not appoint him. . . . To attempt to connect me with religious feuds between sects, either for the purpose of coercing me to give him an office or to give him a pretext to attack me upon affected or pretended religious grounds if I did not, proves him to be a man destitute of both religion and principle. . . . I have a great veneration and regard for Religion & sincere piety, but a hypocrite or a bigotted fanatic without reason I cannot bear. . . .[259]

Polk continued to discuss the same matter. On July 29, 1847, he wrote:

. . . The subject of a publication of a letter of the Rev. Wm. McCalla in the newspapers, relating to the employment of two Catholic Priests to attend the army, was one of conversation. The letter of Mr. McCalla contains a positive and absolute falsehood, to wit, that in conversation with him I had informed him that I had sent them to the army nominally as chaplains, but really as spies. It was stated that the letter was attracting much public attention, would likely produce some excitement, and the question was whether the falsehood should not be contradicted in the newspapers. Upon this point there was doubt. . . . I sent for the Secretary of State, who thought no notice should be taken of it, but if there was, it should be a very positive but short denial of his statement by the Editors of the *Union*. The matter was finally left open & undecided. The conduct of Mr. McCalla in this matter is of the basest character. He called on me some time ago and applied to me to appoint him a chaplain in the army. . . . He wished to know why I had appointed two Catholic clergymen to attend the army in the character of Chaplains. I told him that by law I had no power to appoint & commission chaplains, but that there were always many employes in an army, such as teamsters, labourers, bearers of despatches, couriers to bear & bring back information, &C. I informed him that early after the war with Mexico broke out, great efforts had been made to impress the mexicans with the belief that our object was to destroy their churches & make war upon their religion; that if this false impression should prevail generally among the mexicans, it would make the war one of ferocity & fanaticism. . . . His object is to produce a religious controversy in the country. He is a Whig & a religious fanatic, and from his publication it is clear to my mind that he is unprincipled.[260]

The Reverend Mr. McCalla's view of the Catholic "chaplains" supports other evidence of the bitter campaign carried on at this time by the Native American group. It is characteristic that his charges were given to the public by the publication of a letter which he wrote on the subject to a leading Native American of Philadelphia. Some Protestant organs of public opinion also severely criticized the appointment of this new group of chaplains by the president. The *New York Observer,* one of their most representative and influential papers, called it "a flagrant outrage upon the constitution," thus virtually implying that the American government was necessarily linked with the Protestant groups, many of which had urged the appointment of additional Protestant chaplains.[261]

President Polk also tried to make use of Bishop (later Archbishop) John Hughes (1797–1864) as an informal mediator in clearing up difficulties between Mexico and this country, but there was again so much opposition from Protestant sources that the bishop reluctantly refused to act.

As far as is known, only one Roman Catholic paper, that edited by the able but erratic recent convert, Orestes Brownson (1803–76), condemned the war, on the ground that it would bring the slavery conflict to a head, thereby injuring the South and destroying the Union.[262] In general it may be said that though the Roman Catholic Church in the United States took no official stand on the war, the rank and file of Catholics considered it their duty to respond when called on. The fact that they did themselves credit as patriotic citizens had a good effect in allaying at least for the time the tendency to regard Roman Catholics as "foreigners," not interested in American democracy.

The Episcopal Church attitude was similar.[263] The bishops' *Pastoral Letter* of 1847 regretted the war, but prayed that the Kingdom of God might be advanced by it. The diocesan conventions made little or no reference to it. Evidently they were noncommittal, questioning the justice of the war, but on the ground of patriotism supporting it when called upon, though without enthusiasm. Of the attitude of the Church Professor Ellsworth says:

> . . . The disestablishment of the Anglican Church during the Revolutionary period had forcefully shown the Episcopalians the wisdom of limiting the church's activity to the sphere of worship, some of the High Church clergy going so far as to refuse to vote. Throughout the fury of the slavery controversy, which, by the time of the Mexican War, had sundered two of the major churches, the Episcopal Church remained united by a policy of avoiding participation in any controversy outside the field of dogma. Within the field of dogma the church was preoccupied by the Tractarian storm raging on both sides of the Atlantic. That the Low Church Episcopalians, who were strongly anti-Catholic, did not defend the war indicates that then, as now, the Episcopal Church put less emphasis than many Protestant denominations on expansion through evangelization and conversion.[264]

The Lutheran Church took about the same position as the Episcopal Church. Very little attention was given to the war in the denominational press or in sermons. There was nowhere any enthusiasm for it. The various Reformed Churches were also noncommittal.

As to the other Protestant Churches, on the whole the groups that were the most favorable were the Southern Methodists and Baptists. A hundred ministers from the Baltimore Conference at the close of the annual meeting in 1847 called on President Polk to assure him that the Methodists were prepared to serve their country under all circumstances in peace or in war; though only a little later the New England Conference passed resolutions against the war, objecting to its cost in life and money, and to its irreligious tendencies, especially in the matter of Sabbath desecration.[265]

Most of the Methodist religious press was prowar after the conflict began. "My country, right or wrong," was at times their motto. The influential *Christian Advocate and Journal* of New York, an official organ of Northern Methodism, questioned the justness of the war, but believed that it was God's way of punishing Mexico for its sins, and that it would have the happy result of weakening the power of the Roman Catholic priesthood, for which it had no high regard. The only strong opposition among Methodist papers to the war was relatively mild and was confined to the North.

The Southern Baptists were definitely on the prowar side, and this largely because of Protestant evangelistic ideas, and opposition to "papal oppression." The Northern Baptists were much divided. An encouraging statement was that in the *New York Recorder,* which questioned the popular Protestant justification of the war:

> The plea that this war will be over-ruled for the advancement of Christianity with us has no force. We believe it will be, but this does not change the divine law against doing evil that good may come. We have yet to see that we are called upon to regenerate Mexico at the expense of our own degeneracy.[266]

To the Old School Presbyterians the war was a scourge of God, but it might be overruled for good by the opening of Mexico to the Gospel. The religious press of the denomination laid special emphasis on the debased character of popular religion in Mexico and the opportunity the war should give for Protestant evangelism. Very few antiwar sermons were preached in the pulpits of this denomination. They were less vocal than the Methodists and Baptists, taking a somewhat more spiritual attitude, such as calling for a day of prayer for forgiveness of individual and national sins, but nonetheless tending to support the war. The New School Presbyterians showed no uniform pattern, but were more often in opposition than support.

The most encouraging ethical attitude was that of the Quakers, Congregationalists, and Unitarians. The first named, that is the Society of Friends, were almost unanimous in opposing the war. They flooded Congress with petitions from their yearly meetings.[267] The Congregational press also opposed the war. A quotation from the *Boston Recorder* shows their opposition.

> While Humanity is outraged, our country disgraced, the Laws of Heaven suspended, and those of Hell put in force, by the conduct and continuance of the Mexican war, we shall not cease (to attempt at least) to rouse the public mind to a sense of the awful guilt brought upon this nation by what has been deservedly called "the most infamous war ever recorded upon the page of history."[268]

The state associations became increasingly sharp in their references to the dehumanizing aspects of the war—its probable result in extending slavery, and the unfortunate infectiousness of the war spirit. The North Conference of Churches of Worcester, Massachusetts, went so far as to "dissuade any persons from enlisting in this service."[269] The Reverend Horace Bushnell (1802–76) was a leading pulpit spokesman of the Congregational attitude, and his words carried great weight.

The Unitarians opposed the war and urged a peaceful solution. They were much criticized for their "flat-footed" opposition, and were accused of taking "a purely political attitude."[270]

The Ellsworth study of "The American Churches and the Mexican War," some of whose findings I have quoted, shows that the opposition was almost entirely from New England and Ohio, and that the support was strong in the southwest central region. It is interesting to note that of the whole population of New England only one in twenty-five hundred enlisted, while in Texas there was one in nineteen, and in Louisiana one in thirty-two!

The author quoted thus summarizes the motives that influenced the Churches in their attitude toward the war:

. . . On the question of the Mexican War in particular some factors were conducive to support: desire to regain public approval, evangelical emphasis, anti-Catholic feeling, tradition permitting "just" war, and substantial stakes in the territory adjoining Mexico. Other factors made for opposition: belief in the injustice or inexpediency of the present war, belief in the principle of absolute pacifism, concentration of the membership at a distance from the war. No church with its members concentrated in the Southwest or with a strong stake there opposed the war.[271]

The conscience of the North on the subject of the war is best expressed by the "Biglow Papers," a masterpiece of satire in Yankee dialect by James Russell Lowell (1819–1891). These appeared during the war years, 1846–48, and held up to scorn the advocates of slavery and of the imperialistic military venture in Mexico. As Lowell states in the introduction to the second series, he felt that the Mexican war was "a national crime committed in behoof of Slavery, our common sin," and he decided to show it up through the views of the Reverend Mr. Wilbur, "pastor of the first church in Jalaam" and his parishioner Hosea Biglow.[272] A few stanzas from "What Mr. Robinson thinks" tell the story:

Gineral C. he goes in fer the war;
He don't vally princerple more 'n an old cud;
Wut did God make us raytional creeturs fer,
But glory an' gunpowder, plunder an' blood?
So John P.
Robinson he
Sez he shall vote fer Gineral C.

We were gittin' on nicely up here to our village,
With good old idees o' wut's right an' wut aint,
We kind o' thought Christ went agin war an' pillage,
An' thet eppyletts worn't the best mark of a saint;
But John P.
Robinson he
Sez this kind o' thing's an exploded idee.

The side of our country must ollers be took,
An' Presidunt Polk, you know, *he* is our country.
An' the angel thet writes all our sins in a book
Puts the *debit* to him, an' to us the *per contry;*
An' John P.
Robinson he
Sez this is his view o' the thing to a T.

Parson Wilbur he calls all these argimunts lies;
Sez they're nothin' on airth but jest *fee, faw, fum;*
An' thet all this big talk of our destinies
Is half on it ign'ance, an' t'other half rum;
But John P.
Robinson he
Sez it aint no sech thing; an', of course, so must we.[273]

These and similar lines caused a smile throughout the country as the modern knight errant jousted with the foibles, sins, and hypocrisies of the time, but they served their purpose of making the war seem unnecessary and wrong, especially to the Congregationalists and Unitarians, who then provided New England with most of its independent thinking.

(2) THE SUBSEQUENT CHURCH–STATE PROBLEMS IN THE ANNEXATION OF CALIFORNIA

The conquest of California—long Catholic Mexican territory—by the United States took place in 1846–47. General John C. Frémont (1813–90), Commodores John Drake Sloat (1780–1867) and Robert Stockton (1795–1866), and General Kearny (1794–1848) were the officers mainly responsible. Kearny was appointed governor and held the office from March until June, 1847. In keeping with the American tradition and by instruction of the president, he declared that he would "respect and protect the religious institutions of California" and "take care that the religious rights of its inhabitants are secured in the most ample manner. . . ." These pronouncements and the subsequent steps to protect the Catholic missions are discussed in another section.[274]

By the original draft of Article IX of the subsequent Treaty of Guadalupe Hidalgo (1848) between the Mexican Republic and the United States, at the close of the Mexican War, it was provided that Mexicans who did not decide to retain the title and rights of Mexican citizens, pending their being admitted "to the enjoyment of all the rights of citizens of the United States according to the principles of the Constitution," should be "secured in the free exercise of their religion without restriction."[275] The government of the United States in ratifying the treaty made one or two changes, including the substitution of the third article of the 1803 treaty purchasing Louisiana for this Article IX. This was to the same effect, namely:

The inhabitants of the ceded territory shall be incorporated in the Union of the United States, and admitted as soon as possible, according to the principles of the Federal constitution, to the enjoyment of all the rights, advantages and immunities, of citizens of the United States; and, in the mean time, they shall be maintained and protected in the free enjoyment of their liberty, property, and the religion which they profess.[276]

This article was doubtless incorporated to satisfy the large Catholic population and to maintain the American tradition of religious freedom. In 1849, General Bennett Riley (1787–1853), the provisional governor, called a convention which drafted a constitution. After this had been ratified by a popular vote of over ten to one, it was presented to the United States government. It was accepted on the ground that it was "republican in its form of government"—this being in accordance with the provision of the American Constitution that "The United States shall guarantee to every State in this Union a Republican Form of Government." Whether a state constitution which provided for a State-Church would have met this test a century ago is open to some doubt, but in this case there was no difficulty, as the constitution submitted contained a declaration of rights that was explicit on the subject of religious freedom:

The free exercise and enjoyment of religious profession and worship, without discrimination or preference, shall forever be allowed in this State; and no person shall be rendered incompetent to be a witness on account of his opinions on matters of religious belief; but the liberty of conscience hereby secured shall not be so construed as to excuse acts of licentiousness, or justify practises inconsistent with the peace or safety of this State.[277]

This clause, similar to those adopted in some other states, such as South Carolina in 1790, formed the basis for the wording of religious freedom guarantees in the constitutions of several Western states. In most cases it was expanded by Congress in admitting these states to include further guarantees that civil and political rights would not be denied because of religion; that every citizen would be protected against the necessity of contributing to any ministry or place of worship; and that no preference would be given by law to any religious denomination. These provisions were also voluntarily incorporated in other state constitutions.

Section 11. *THE DIPLOMATIC REPRESENTATION AT THE VATICAN*

(1) THE FIRST EXPERIMENT, 1848–67

It should be remembered that the Papal States then included an extensive area in central Italy. For many centuries the states had an area of about sixteen thousand square miles and a population of over three million. Today the papal domain is restricted to 109 acres, and its normal population is a little over one thousand. Its present importance is entirely due to its being the residence of the pope and the center of the various activities of the Church of which he is head. It has no regular commercial or industrial activities, no port, and no natural resources.

The question of diplomatic representation at the Vatican represents one of the most interesting historical phases in American Church-State relations. In 1797, a native of Rome by the name of John B. Sartori was commissioned as the first consul to represent the United States in the papal dominions.[278] Though technically only a consular representative, he was, through the courtesy of the papal government, permitted to exercise the functions of a diplomatic official.[279] There were also consular representatives at one or two other places in the Papal States. The question of diplomatic representation had arisen as early as 1779. John Adams wrote the Continental Congress that he hoped it would "never send a minister to His Holiness," nor receive a Catholic nuncio to this country.[280] About seventy years were to pass before the consul was to be followed by the appointment of a duly commissioned American diplomatic agent. This was due to the enthusiasm created in 1846 by the election of Pius IX (1792–1878) to succeed Gregory XVI as pope. His election was very popular in this country, as it was believed at the time that he was a liberal who would work for greater freedom. He started his administration by various reforms of a most encouraging character. He released political prisoners, granted more freedom to the press, established a constitution, made many improvements in the field of public works, and even placed a box at the Vatican to receive complaints![281]

Lord Acton (1834–1902), a devout Catholic who was chosen Professor of Modern History in Cambridge University, has well expressed the rejoicing of liberally minded Roman Catholics and of all friends of freedom at the auspicious opening of the new pontiff's rule.

> . . . The reforms which followed soon made Pius the most popular of Italian princes, and all Catholics rejoiced that the reconciliation of the Papacy with modern freedom

was at length accomplished, and that the shadow which had fallen on the priesthood throughout the world was removed with the abuses in the Roman Government. . . .[282]

It was felt that the papacy was taking a liberal position that would mean much for Italy, and much for the Roman Catholic Church throughout the world. The legislature of New York praised the new pope's efforts to improve the condition of the people of Italy and to "bestow upon them the incalculable blessings of national independence and constitutional freedom."[283] Apparently the first definite proposal that formal diplomatic relations be established between the United States and the government of the Papal States was in a dispatch to the secretary of state June 1, 1847, when the American consul at Rome stated that high officials of the papal government and the pope himself had expressed to him the desire that such relations be formally inaugurated.[284]

The rejoicing over the new pope's election found expression in a demonstration held at the Broadway Tabernacle, a well-known Protestant center in New York, November 29, 1847, at which a sympathetic address presented by Horace Greeley (1811–72) was adopted and sent to Rome. Mr. Greeley was at that time editor of the *New York Tribune*. The *Tribune,* however, laid special emphasis on the fact that the mass meeting was not to be in any way denominational or ecclesiastical. It was "to express our sympathy as Americans and Republicans with the enlightened and generous efforts of Pope Pius IX," and the appeal was "to no sect, no party, no class, but to the generous and manly American heart. . . ."[285]

The *New York Herald* recommended diplomatic representation at the papal court as the fittest expression of American sympathy and admiration. In an article on November 23, 1847, after reviewing the situation in Italy and declaring that the influence of the liberal and tactful new pope had extended into Sardinia, Tuscany, and Naples, the *Herald* went on to say:

His Holiness is equal to the spirit of the age; He is coming back again to the first principles of Christianity—those principles which throbbed in union with the liberties of the people in opposition to old imperial Rome. He is combining the destiny of the Roman Church with the intelligent movement of the age.[286]

Then the editor asked,

Ought not the United States, the greatest of all free countries in Christendom at this day, open diplomatic relations and express its sympathy with the illustrious Pontiff?[287]

The *Herald* hoped that President Polk would act on this suggestion, and felt that in addition to other worthy reasons the Roman Catholic population of the United States, which was estimated then at nearly a million and a half, would specially appreciate this recognition.[288]

The mass meeting was apparently a great success. The *Tribune's* report filled five and a half columns, and included the address to the pope, the resolutions adopted, and extracts from the speeches delivered.[289]

A similar demonstration was held in Philadelphia. The legislature of New York followed, expressing admiration for the efforts of the new pope to ameliorate the condition of the Italian people. Somewhat similar resolutions of the legislature of Louisiana went further, stating that it would be a source of gratification should the United States government open diplomatic relations with the court of Rome.[290]

The message of President Polk (1795–1849) to Congress December 7, 1847, contained the following statement:

> The Secretary of State has submitted an estimate to defray the expense of opening diplomatic relations with the Papal States. The interesting political events now in progress in these States, as well as a just regard to our commercial interests have in my opinion rendered such a measure highly expedient.[291]

The proposal met with a warm debate in Congress. It was opposed on the ground that under our Constitution the government could have nothing to do with ecclesiastical matters; that there were no American commercial interests to protect in the Roman States; that the recognition would strengthen the hands of the Jesuits; and for other reasons. A Congressman from Pennsylvania who had been a leader of the American or Nativist party, said in his speech: "Pass your bill, and from that hour Native Americanism means only defense of Protestant rights and Protestant freedom against Papal tyranny and Jesuit aggression."[292]

On the other hand, a Congressman from Alabama on the Foreign Affairs Committee took the ground that the new pope was emphatically a reformer, and that though he himself was a strong Protestant he believed that "toleration is the wisest as well as the noblest policy."[293] After enumerating the reforms recently introduced by the pope, he said:

> Our true policy is to extend our peaceful relations with the world. We have nothing to fear from an intercourse of that kind with other powers. Truth is clad in more than triple steel; and I would bid her spread her standard in the very midst of the world, and take her station in front of the Vatican. By keeping the Papal See isolated, you strengthen it. Bring it upon the open field; do not shun it; bring it into open intercourse with a free Protestant nation, and civil and religious liberty will achieve new triumphs.[294]

There were, of course, accusations that the president was playing politics, trying to seek the Roman Catholic vote. His proposal before the House was finally passed 137 to 15 in favor of providing funds to send a chargé d'affaires to

Rome. This was the more remarkable as there were only two Roman Catholics in the House at the time, and one of them was opposed to opening the proposed mission.[295]

In the Senate similar arguments were used on both sides. There was some fear that Protestant Americans would look with disfavor upon the mission as conferring a favor upon the pope. John C. Calhoun (1782–1850) opposed the plan because the situation in Italy at the moment was so unsettled as to make it advisable to oppose the opening of diplomatic relations; but the mission was favored by others on various grounds, especially because the pope seemed in his liberal reforms "to borrow light from this country, and to diffuse it through the dominions in which he has a rule."[296] Senator Dix of New York favored the mission primarily from a commercial point of view, and he did not consider the question in any way a religious one. The American government had rights in China, Turkey, and Africa, where people denied the authority of the Christian faith, so he found it impossible to believe that Protestant feeling would be wounded by sending a diplomatic representative to the pope

> because he is also the head of a most respectable and important branch of the Christian Church. Sir, I cannot comprehend this feeling and I am, therefore, disposed to doubt its existence. At all events, I shall vote for the appropriation and trust to my Protestant friends for a just appreciation of my motives.[297]

After a long discussion the large vote in the Senate (36 to 7) favoring the proposal was highly significant. The first chargé was Jacob L. Martin (d. 1848), secretary of the legation in Paris. He was a former Protestant who had become a convert to Roman Catholicism. His instructions from the secretary of state, James Buchanan (1791–1868), under date of April 5, 1848, stated that

> Informal intimations had reached the Department from different quarters, that Pope Pius IX would be pleased to open diplomatic relations with this Government: and the President did not hesitate, upon my suggestion to recommend to Congress, in his annual message of December last, to provide for the outfit and salary of a Chargé d'Affaires to the Papal States. Hence the origin of your highly honorable and important mission.
>
> There is one consideration which you ought always to keep in view in your intercourse with the Papal authorities. Most, if not all the Governments which have Diplomatic Representatives at Rome are connected with the Pope as the head of the Catholic Church. In this respect the Government of the United States occupies an entirely different position. It possesses no power whatever over the question of religion. All denominations of Christians stand on the same footing in this country,—and every man enjoys the inestimable right of worshiping his God according to the dictates of his own conscience. Your efforts therefore, will be devoted exclusively to the cultivation of the most friendly civil relations with the Papal Government, and to the extension of the

commerce between the two countries. You will carefully avoid even the appearance of interfering in ecclesiastical questions, whether these relate to the United States or any other portion of the world. It might be proper, should you deem it advisable, to make these views known, on some suitable occasion, to the Papal Government; so that there may be no mistake or misunderstanding on this subject.

The President and people of the United States have observed, with great satisfaction, the wise and judicious measures of the Pope to reform ancient abuses in his Government, and promote the welfare of his people. Whilst our established policy renders it impossible that we should interfere with the forms of government or the domestic institutions of other independent States, the American people can never be indifferent to the cause of Constitutional freedom and liberal reform in any portion of the world.[298]

Similar instructions, based on an interesting historical summary, were given in 1862 by Secretary William H. Seward (1801–72) to Richard M. Blatchford (1798–1875), who was appointed minister resident of the United States to the Papal States:

This Government has not now, it seldom has had, any special transaction, either commercial or political, to engage the attention of a Minister at Rome. Indeed, till a very late period the United States were without any representation at that ancient and interesting capital. The first colonists in this country were chiefly Protestants, who not merely recognised no ecclesiastical authority of the Pope, but were very jealous lest he might exert some ecclesiastical influence here which would be followed by an assumption of political power unfavorable to freedom and self-government on this continent. It was not seen that the political power of the Catholic Church was a purely foreign affair, constituting an important part of the political system of the European continent. The opening of our country as an asylum to men of all religions, as well as of all races, and an extension of the trade of the Union, in a short time brought with them large masses of the faithful members of that Church, of various birth and derivation, and these masses are continually augmenting. Our country has not been slow to learn that while religion is with these masses, as it is with others, a matter of conscience, and while the spiritual authority of the head of their church is a cardinal article of their faith, which must be tolerated on the soundest principles of civil liberty, yet that this faith in no degree necessarily interferes with the equal rights of the citizens, or affects unfavorably his loyalty to the republic. It is believed that ever since the tide of emigration set in upon this continent the head of the Roman Church and States has freely recognized and favored the development of the principle of political freedom on the part of the Catholics in this country, while he has never lost an opportunity to express his satisfaction with the growth, prosperity and progress of the American people. It was under these circumstances that this Government, in 1848, wisely determined that while it maintained representatives in the capitals of every other civilized State, and even at the capitals of many semi-civilized States which reject the whole Christian religion, it was neither wise nor necessary to exclude Rome from the circle of our diplomatic intercourse. Thus far the new relation then established has proved pleasant and beneficial.

Just now Rome is the seat of profound ecclesiastical and political anxieties, which, more or less, affect all the nations of Europe. The Holy Father claims immunity for the temporal power he exercises as a right incident to an ecclesiastical authority which is generally respected by the European States.

On the other hand, some of those States, with large masses in other States, assert that this temporal power is without any religious sanction, is unnecessary and pernicious. I have stated the question merely for the purpose of enabling myself to give you the President's view of what will be your duty with regard to it. That duty is to forbear altogether from taking any part in the controversy. The reasons for this forbearance are three: First, that so far as spiritual or ecclesiastical matters enter into the question they are beyond your province, for you are a political representative only. Second, so far as it is a question affecting the Roman States it is a domestic one and we are a foreign nation. Third, so far as it is a political question merely, it is at the same time purely an European one, and you are an American Minister, bound to avoid all entangling connexion with the politics of that continent.

This line of conduct will nevertheless allow you to express, and you are therefore instructed to express to His Holiness the assurances of the best wishes of the Government and of the people of the United States for his health and happiness, and for the safety and prosperity and happiness of the Roman people. And you will farther assure him that the United States constantly preserve a lively remembrance of the many generous and liberal manifestations they have received of his goodwill and friendship, and that he may confidently rely upon them for the practice of all the duties which grow out of the relations of the two countries as independent members of the family of nations.[299]

During the twenty years of this diplomatic relationship matters moved on the whole quietly, without serious difficulties. There were important incidents, such as that in connection with the coming of Monsignor Cajetan Bedini (1806–64), the papal nuncio to the United States, and the question of his exact status as an apostolic delegate; the virtual recognition by the Papal States of the Southern Confederacy; the important part played by the American legation in protecting Vatican property at the time of Garibaldi's entrance into Rome; the saving by the American minister in 1849 of two thousand copies of a Protestant edition of the Bible published in Italian and ordered destroyed;[300] and the refusal by the Washington Monument Association in 1852 of a block of marble for the monument sent by the pope.[301] There was also at the time considerable discussion of the possible removal of the pope to the United States. This is referred to in these terms in a letter from the Honorable Rufus King (1814–76) to Secretary of State Seward, under date of November 20, 1866:

. . . The near approach of the period fixed for the departure of the French garrison lends new and daily increasing interest to this question. Indeed it is the one topic of conversation in all circles and opinions are greatly divided both as to the probability of the Pope's departure and the consequences likely to follow so decisive a step. Within the past few days the subject has been brought specially to my notice by intimations I have received from several officials of the Papal Government, that the presence of the American Ship of War at Civita Vecchia was highly desirable and that if the Pope felt compelled to abandon Rome *he might seek a refuge in the United States.* General Kansler, the Minister of War, and Monsignor Nardi, Domestic Chaplain to the Pope —both, it must be presumed, in his Holiness' confidence—each expressed very explicitly the opinion, that the only country in which the Pope could seek and find a suitable and secure Asylum was the great Republic of America. General Kansler added the expression of his earnest hope that the Pope would take this course and seemed anxious to know how I thought it would be received in the United States. I contented myself with replying, in general terms, that our country was the home of civil and religious liberty, as well as the refuge of all who fled from political, and other troubles in the old world; and that his Holiness, should he see fit to go to the United States, would no doubt meet with a kind welcome and be left to pursue, unquestioned and unmolested, his great work as Head of the Catholic Church. I cannot but think, from these and other similar indications, that this project of going to America is seriously entertained by a portion, at least, of the Pope's most trusted friends and counsellors and I know that his Holiness himself has spoken of it more than once and in terms that seemed to imply approval.[302]

The possibility of the pope's moving to America was discussed pro and con in the American press, but as far as known it was never seriously considered by our government. Developments made it unnecessary for him to remove the papal see even though he became a "prisoner" in the Vatican.

But the most difficult matter that arose in connection with American representation at Rome had to do with Protestant worship within the walls of the Holy City. Such worship outside an embassy chapel apparently seemed to the papacy inconsistent with the idea of Rome as the hallowed center of the one Universal Church—a jurisdiction which should according to this view be exclusively Catholic.[303]

Under date of March 9, 1850, the American minister, Mr. Lewis Cass, Jr. (*c.* 1810–78) wrote to Secretary Clayton:

I have the honor to inform you that religious worship, according to the forms of the Protestant Church, is now permitted, for the first time, by the Pontifical Government, to citizens of the United States, in the city of Rome. At the conclusion of the first service of this character, the Reverend Mr. Hastings, an ordained clergyman, from New York,[304] who officiated on that occasion, received a communication from the Police authorities, enjoining upon him a discontinuance of such exercises in future, upon penalty of expulsion from the Roman States. As soon as this circumstance came to my knowledge, I solicited an interview with the Cardinal Secretary of State, whom I apprised of this order. I informed him that the Constitution of the United States forbids the establishment of religion by law; but that it protects every person, who does not interrupt the peace of Society, in the exercise of his religion, of whatever denomination. I said, moreover, that in the absence of any convention or treaty, I did not feel authorised to demand, as a right, the same full and unrestricted liberty of worship for citizens of the United States, in Rome, as is guaranteed by our Constitution to subjects of the Pope, as well as to all other nations; but that as a concession, granted by the Head of the Catholic Church, such a privilege, I doubted not, would be highly gratifying to my Government, which had taken the initiative in the establishment of political relations between the two countries. In a spirit of religious freedom and liberality most commendable, the Cardinal Secretary of State, after a brief consultation with other members of the Government, acceded to my request; and it is with great pleasure that I announce to you, Sir, this honorable act of toleration on the part of the Papal authorities.

Of the right to which I am entitled, as Chargé d'Affaires, by the Laws of Nations, to private worship—and in which any citizens of the United States are allowed to participate—there has been no question whatever. This restriction, however, is attended with many inconveniences, and the desire of relieving our countrymen, of whom there is an unusually large number now in Rome, from all impediments to the enjoyment of public worship, together with other considerations, of a still higher character, induced me to prefer this request, which has been thus readily granted.

In the course of this interview, the Secretary of State alluded to the protection which it was in my power to afford to individuals and property, during the anarchy which prevailed at the close of the late siege; and I am charged by him to say to you, that it is the intention of the Pope, when he returns to Rome, to express to the President his sense of the services received from the Government of the United States, through my agency, at that period.[305]

Following this there were persistent rumors that these services under Protestant auspices were being discontinued. It is true that there were many protests in Rome against continuing them, but as long as they were held in the legation and it was not conducted as a Protestant missionary propaganda institution but merely for American Protestant worshipers, there was no serious trouble. But when property was taken outside the legation to accommodate the two or three hundred American visitors who frequently attended services, serious difficulties followed, especially as the English and Scotch had to go outside the walls of Rome to conduct their Protestant services other than those in the English legation chapel.[306]

It is not necessary to enter into all the details; but inasmuch as reports of the incident were the major cause for the discontinuance of the American legation at the Vatican, the following extracts from a letter to Secretary of State Seward from the Honorable Rufus King (1814–76), the United States minister, under date of February 18, 1867, are important:

In the brief despatch which I had the honor to address to the Secretary of State, under date of February 11th, referring to the action taken by the House of Representatives, on the rumored closing, or removal of "the Protestant Church, meeting at the American Embassy in Rome," I contented myself with a simple denial of the alleged fact; reserving for a future communication, a fuller history of the case. I now submit a detailed statement of the matter, for the information of the Department and of the public.

In Wheaton's *Elements of International Law,* Sixth Edition, page 304, the existing rule, as to freedom of religious worship, is thus laid down: "A minister resident in a foreign country is entitled to the privilege of religious worship in his own private chapel, according to the peculiar forms of his national faith, altho' it may not be generally tolerated by the laws of the State, where he resides." The laws of Rome do not tolerate any other form of public religious worship, than such as conforms to the teachings of the Roman Catholic Church; but the right of any foreign Minister at the Papal Court to hold religious services under his own roof and in accordance with the forms of his national, or individual faith, has never been questioned, or interfered with. Thus, the Russian, the Prussian, the American and other representatives of foreign powers in Rome, have always exercised and still enjoy, unmolested, the freedom of religious worship in the several chapels, connected with their respective legations. These chapels, of course, are open to all compatriots of the different ministers, desirous of joining in their religious services.

So long as the number of Americans visiting Rome was comparatively limited, it was not difficult for the Minister, in securing apartments for himself and family, to make suitable provision, as well for a Chapel. But of late years, with the very great increase of travel, this has been no easy matter. It has not unfrequently occurred that the congregation, worshipping under the Minister's roof, has reached the number of two hundred and fifty, or three hundred; and more than once has been much larger than could be accomodated in the apartments provided. These, of course, once set apart and suitably furnished for religious worship, could be used for no other purpose and hence it has followed that the largest and best rooms in the Minister's residence were practically inaccessible to him, except on Sundays and Holy Days.

In 1859, I think, while Mr. Stockton was Minister Resident here, Grace Church in Rome was regularly organized and placed under the jurisdiction of the Presiding Bishop of the American Episcopal Church. It is under the auspices of this organization that religious worship has since been conducted, in connection with the American Legation in Rome. In the Spring of 1865, the Revd. Dr. T. B. Lyman, formerly of Pittsburg, Penna., was regularly elected by the Wardens and Vestry of Grace Church, as their Rector. He accepted the charge; entered upon his trust, in the fall of the same year, and has since continued to discharge its duties to the general acceptation of all who united in the services.

During the winter of '65–'66, the residence of the American Minister was in the Salviati Palace and there the Congregation of Grace Church, as well as all American Protestants, desirous of uniting with them, met regularly for purposes of religious worship.[307] At times, the number attending was in excess of the accomodation provided, comparatively ample tho' it was, and attracted a good deal of attention. The holding of Protestant worship under Duke Salviati's roof and the crowd thereby gathered, were not agreeable to the proprietor and he declined to renew the lease of the Minister's Apartments for another year, except upon the express condition that there should be no chapel connected therewith. Repeated efforts to obtain other quarters, suitable for the Minister's residence and free from the restriction attached to the Salviati Palace, proved unavailing. It was under these circumstances that Dr. Lyman and the Vestry of Grace Church decided to hire an apartment, themselves, separate from the Legation, where they could hold religious services; confident in the belief that they would not be interfered with by the local authorities. Rooms were accordingly procured, fitted and furnished in the Vicolo D'Alibert, a central and convenient locality, and there since early in November, our American fellow-citizens have assembled for public worship, and still continue to assemble, without let, or hinderance [*sic*].

Having traced the history of the American Church up to 1866 the minister turns to compare the situation of the British and American congregations in 1867.

The English, who annually flock to Rome in large numbers, have been accustomed, these forty years past, to hold religious services, in accordance with the forms of their National Church, in a large building, just outside the Porta del Popolo. They have never been interfered-with by the authorities. During the last five, or six years, the Scotch Presbyterians, perhaps thirty, or forty in number, have met, for purposes of religious worship, in a private house within the walls of Rome. A few months since, a second Scotch Presbyterian congregation was formed; the line of separation between the two being the same that divides the Established, from the Free Kirk of Scotland. This division and the presence and participation of the Duke of Argyle, who chanced to be here, attracted the notice and led to the interference of the local authorities. It was intimated to the Ministers of the two Scotch Congregations, that their services were contrary to law and must be held outside the walls. They have transferred them accordingly to the building immediately opposite the one so long occupied by the English Protestants. There I presume, they will be allowed to meet and worship, unquestioned and unmolested.

It was supposed by many that the closing of the American Chapel, being apart from the residence of the Minister, would necessarily follow that of the Scotch places of worship. To prevent, if possible, a step which I knew would excite a great deal of feeling at home and subject our countrymen here to much annoyance and inconvenience; and, at the same time, to give ourselves at least the colour of right to assemble where we did for religious worship, I directed the Arms of the American Legation to be placed over the building in which the American chapel is located. This seems to have satisfied the requirements, or scruples of the authorities and thus far no one has interfered with us. Nor do I believe that we shall be disturbed during the present season.

Thus stands the case at present. But it is not so easy to see what future provision is to be made for the American church in Rome. The authorities may, possibly, hereafter insist upon the rule, that it shall be held under the Minister's roof. On the other hand, the Minister will always find increasing difficulty in securing apartments, that will accommodate his family and himself and, at the same time, include suitable provision for a Chapel. Very good rooms can be obtained in the same building, in which the English church is located, and I have the assurance of the Cardinal Secretary of State, himself, that no interference would be attempted with Americans choosing to assemble there for religious worship; even though separate and apart from the Legation. But the locality is objected to on the ground, that it is outside, tho' just outside the walls. One solution, indeed, of the difficulty has been suggested; but I am by no means sanguine that it will find favor in the eyes of Congress. This is, to purchase, or hire for a term of years, a building for Legation purposes; including ample accomodation for a Chapel. Under such an arrangement, there would be no further question as to the right of American Protestants to assemble for public worship within the walls of Rome; while an official residence might be provided, suitable to the position of the American Representative at the Papal Court and not unworthy the character, dignity and influence of the American Government and People.[808]*

As a result of this difficulty, which had been exaggerated in the public mind, growing sympathy with the aspirations of Italians for a united Italy, and other factors, Congress refused to appropriate any more money for a Roman mission, and, as there was no definite provision for it, it ceased to exist in 1867, without any specific action formally discontinuing it. Apparently both President Johnson and Secretary Seward favored this disposition of a difficult matter, and no formal message of explanation was sent to the supreme pontiff. The last dispatch of any importance on the subject shows that as long as the Protestant Church in Rome was conducted under the aegis of the American legation it was allowed to be continued. In an unofficial letter to Secretary Seward under date of May 7, 1867, after acknowledging the secretary's letter informing him that Congress had refused to appropriate more money for the Roman mission, Mr. King said:

Ever since I received (April 2nd) your despatch No: 55, apprising me that Congress had refused to appropriate any more money for the Roman Mission, I have been expecting instructions as to what course I was to take, in closing up the affairs of the Legation, paying my parting respects to the Pope, etc. etc. But, as yet, I am without a line and am really at a loss what to do. It is all the more awkward, since, if asked *why* the Legation is suppressed, I can only say, that Congress acted under the belief

* See Addenda.

that American Protestant worship had been excluded from Rome; the *truth* being, that it has *not* been interfered with, in *any* way; but on the contrary, we have been allowed, all the past season, to hold our services *apart* from the residence of the Minister and that for no other reason than that the Papal Court desired to show their good will towards the American Government and People. You will see, however, from my official despatch of this date, that if our Minister *is* withdrawn, American Protestants will be obliged to go *outside* the walls of Rome to exercise religious worship and that they will owe this exclusion, not to the Pope, but to the action of *their own Congress*.[309]

As we have seen, the only basis on which this Protestant service was permitted was that it was in what was considered "a Chapel connected with the U. S. Legation."[310]

Thus ended this interesting chapter in American Church–State relations. It should be noted that during the existence of the American ministry to the Vatican there was no reciprocal representation of the Papal States at Washington.

And yet at this time—that is prior to the fall of Rome in 1870 and its becoming the capital of Italy the following year—the pope continued to exercise temporal as well as spiritual authority in the Papal States, which since 1860 had been reduced to a very small area. The temporal power of course disappeared from 1870 until the Lateran Treaty and Concordat with Italy in 1929 recognized the political independence of Vatican City, a small territory of slightly over one hundred acres with a population of about one thousand people.

It was during this period—in 1873—that St. Paul's Episcopal Church, the first Protestant church inside the city of Rome, was erected and dedicated.

(2) THE IDEA REVIVED, 1939

Several recent steps have clearly indicated an effort to revive the formal representation at the Vatican and to make it reciprocal. These have included legislation by Congress in 1938 permitting the American consul in Rome to act as authenticating agent for documents of record in Vatican City "until the United States shall have a consular representative in the State of Vatican City . . . ;"[311] the special honors shown by the American government and its ambassador to Italy, to Cardinal Mundelein (1872–1939), in his visit to Rome; the building in 1938 of the impressive new building for the "Apostolic Delegation" of the papacy, opened in Washington on March 20, 1939; the marks of special respect shown by Congress in February, 1939, after the death of Pope Pius XI; the sending by President Franklin D. Roosevelt of the American ambassador to the Court of St. James, a Roman Catholic, to the coronation of his successor, Pius XII, as his personal representative;[312] and the naming in December, 1939, of a representative of the president for further co-operation between pope and president in European peace moves.

On the other hand, a spokesman for the Vatican was quoted from Vatican City in March, 1939, as making a statement discouraging the plan of regular diplomatic interchange. He said:

> The position of the Catholics in America is excellent. They are permitted free exercise of their religion, and enjoy the benefits of complete freedom of conscience.
>
> An exchange of diplomatic representation formalizing the relations between the Vatican and Washington would raise a multitude of difficult and embarrassing questions. The Holy See does not intend to take any step which might be construed, however erroneously, as an opening wedge for Catholic or church interference with American politics, foreign or domestic.[313]

American Catholics, a semiofficial source added, do not feel the need of a nunciature or papal embassy, since all business concerning Vatican-American relations is amply taken care of by the present apostolic delegate to Washington.

When the president sent his Christmas letter of greeting to the pope, Pius XII, in 1939, saying that he was planning to appoint a personal representative to the papacy, and accompanied it with a statement that he would remain for the duration of the war, so that "our parallel endeavors for peace and the alleviation of suffering may be assisted," the proposal was, on the whole, favorably received at first by the secular press of the country. This impression was due in part to the fact that the State Department let it be known that the president's choice for this mission—Mr. Myron C. Taylor (1874-), an Episcopalian personally acquainted with the pope, and a man of high reputation—would have merely the title of "Personal Representative of the President of the United States of America to His Holiness, Pope Pius XII" and that his appointment did "not constitute the inauguration of formal diplomatic relations with the Vatican," though it carried the rank of envoy extraordinary. Furthermore, it was announced that he would serve without personal compensation. As a matter of fact, the *Pontifical Directory* for 1940 lists his name at the foot of the list of thirty-eight accredited ambassadors and ministers, separated from the others by a dash, as "representative of his excellency, the President of the United States of America, with the rank of ambassador."[314] It will be noticed that Mr. Taylor was not considered by this country as a member of the regular diplomatic service of the government, nominated to and confirmed by the Senate. In keeping with this understanding he was not formally accredited by the State Department to the Vatican. He was thought of as the representative of our chief executive in a world crisis to the individual head of the Roman

Catholic Church—not as a full-fledged American ambassador to Vatican City.

The essential part of the president's letter to the pope, with whom he had enjoyed friendly associations when the latter visited America before his elevation to the Papal See, deserves quotation.

It is, therefore, my thought [he wrote] that though no given action or given time may now be prophesied, it is well that we encourage a closer association between those in every part of the world—those in religion and those in government—who have a common purpose.

I am, therefore, suggesting to Your Holiness that it would give me great satisfaction to send to you my personal representative in order that our parallel endeavors for peace and the alleviation of suffering may be assisted.

When the time shall come for the re-establishment of world peace on a surer foundation, it is of the utmost importance to humanity and to religion that common ideals shall have united expression. . . .

I trust, therefore, that all of the churches of the world which believe in a common God will throw the great weight of their influence into this great cause.[315]

An explanatory statement was given to the press by the White House at the same time. It began with this paragraph:

The President announced today that he had sent a Christmas letter to the Pope, as head of the Catholic Church, to Dr. George A. Buttrick, President of the Federal Council of the Churches of Christ in America, as a Protestant leader, and to Rabbi Cyrus Adler, President of the Jewish Theological Seminary of America, a leader of the Jewish Faith.[316]

The phraseology of this statement, and the reference in the president's letter to Dr. Buttrick that he had "sent a like greeting to the Pope as head of the Catholic Church," gave the public the definite impression that these two representatives of religion in America had also received a copy from the president of his letter to the pope, but this was not the case. The only concrete suggestion in the letters to the Protestant and Jewish representatives was made by changing the second paragraph quoted above in the letter to the Pope, to read:

I therefore suggest that it would give me great satisfaction if you would, from time to time, come to Washington to discuss the problems which all of us have on our minds, in order that our parallel endeavors for peace and the alleviation of suffering may be assisted.[317]

This suggestion of a conference was not sent to the pope or his American representatives.

The acknowledgment of Dr. Buttrick, sent as President of the Federal Council of Churches, before he had any knowledge of the President's specific proposal to the pope, was cordial.

This telegram gratefully acknowledges your Christmas message of hope and faith. We are glad that through your action we have this public opportunity to extend our cordial greetings to His Holiness the Pope and to Dr. Cyrus Adler and to all those whom they represent. We share your confidence that men and women in every land have a basic faith in God and therefore in human brotherhood, and that even in the present chaos and darkness they are preparing a better day.

We join you in the prayer that a lasting peace of justice and good will may soon bless mankind. Your invitation to a continued opportunity for conference is gratefully accepted. The Federal Council of the Churches of Christ in America pledges itself through you to the people of America and of every Church and land to seek under God a world order in which unmerited poverty and carking fear and the threat of war shall be banished.[318]

Dr. Cyrus Adler (1863–1940), to whom the president had also written because of his outstanding position among the leaders of Jewish thought, replied with equal cordiality, and the Rabbinical Assembly of America, representing three hundred rabbis, passed resolutions of appreciation and approval of the plan presented by the president to Dr. Adler.

The acknowledgment of the pope through the apostolic delegate to the Archbishop of New York regarding the selection of Myron C. Taylor read:

I am requested to express to the President His Holiness' profound gratitude for the choice of the Hon. Myron Taylor as the representative of the President of the United States of America, with the rank of Ambassador Extraordinary.[319]

The pope's personal reply came ten days later:

. . . We shall find a special satisfaction, as We have already informed Your Excellency, in receiving with all the honor due to his well-known qualifications and to the dignity of his important mission, the representative who is to be sent to Us as the faithful interpreter of your mind regarding the procuring of peace and the alleviation of sufferings consequent upon the war.[320]

The general position of Roman Catholics was that taken by the *Catholic News* of New York:

The Catholic Church and the United States are the two greatest influences for peace in the world today. Consequently they should co-operate to advance it.[321]

The Protestant press showed itself increasingly critical of the project as all the facts became known. It feared its ultimate implications. The objection was not to the president's appointee, who was recognized to be a man of character, ability, breadth, and experience, but to the naming of any representative with ambassadorial rank to the pope or the Vatican.

The Christian Century, the most representative journal of liberal Protestantism, immediately attacked the proposal as an entering wedge to the establishing of regular diplomatic relations between the Vatican and the American government, an action which, in the judgment of the editor, would be inconsistent with our inherited independence of Church and State. In his first editorial he said:

To strip away all camouflage, the President has, in reality, established diplomatic relations with the Vatican without legal authority. He has done so, we believe, not as a peace move but as a political move. Roman Catholics will be greatly pleased and can be counted on to remember it at the polls. Protestants and Jews are expected to be diverted by the sop in the invitations to Dr. Buttrick and Dr. Adler, and to forget it long before November. In that expectation we predict that the President will be disappointed. The American majority does not want to see relations established between this government and any religious body, and it will hold Mr. Roosevelt responsible for having tried to do this under the nearly sacrosanct cover of a campaign for peace.[322]

This was followed in the next issue with a long and carefully written editorial headed "An Un-American Appointment."

What Mr. Roosevelt intended to do by this action should be clear to anyone. He has deliberately undertaken to satisfy the insistent demands of the Catholic hierarchy for the establishment of political relations between the government of the United States and the government of the Roman Catholic Church, and to accomplish this without due process of public discussion or legislative action. This he could do in a devious and ambiguous manner by virtue of the fact that the Roman Catholic Church is a dual entity—it is both a church and a state. Mr. Roosevelt therefore adopted the ingenious device of appointing an ambassador who was accredited to neither church nor state and yet was accredited to both! By the use of subtle verbalisms, he left open a way of escape from criticism. When he is attacked for illegal action in recognizing the Vatican state, he can take refuge in the claim that he is recognizing only the Vatican church. And when this un-American innovation is attacked, he can take refuge in the claim that Mr. Taylor is only his *personal* representative!

Thus Mr. Roosevelt is able to perform an enormous service to the Roman Catholic Church, for which, no doubt, his intimate relations with representatives of the hierarchy have duly prepared him. His action is the next logical and appropriate step for him to take in his policy of establishing unique relations between the United States and the Holy See. His order to the American embassy in Rome to receive the late Cardinal Mundelein of Chicago with full diplomatic honors on the occasion of the latter's visit to Rome a year ago, was followed by the appointment of Ambassador Kennedy as special representative at the coronation of Pope Pius XII.

The appointment of Mr. Taylor as ambassador to the Vatican is a natural development of the special relations which Mr. Roosevelt is bent on establishing. The next step will be to make this ambassadorship permanent. It can be easily taken either by Mr. Roosevelt or by his successor.[323]

Somewhat removed from *The Christian Century* and the Federal Council in

69012

general outlook are the rank and file of Methodist and Baptist churches, especially those of the South, where suspicion of the political motives of the Roman Catholic Church continues strong. The Lutherans and Seventh Day Adventists also protested, and a restrained but nonetheless vigorous protest was sent by the Public Relations Committee representing the Northern, Southern, and National (Negro) Baptists. It said:

The Baptists of America find themselves heartily in accord with your efforts in the direction of peace. We feel that the detached and influential position of the nation, over which you preside as Chief Executive, gives promise of substantial results in any constructive program that may be inaugurated by you.

We are deeply concerned, however, lest your appointment of Hon. Myron C. Taylor, as your personal representative to the Vatican with the rank of Ambassador, may retard rather than promote such efforts. The distinctive theory, upon which this government has been founded, is the absolute separation of church and State, and any recognition, implied or otherwise, of the political status of any ecclesiastical organization constitutes, in our judgment, an assault upon this principle.[324]

The Baptist group arranged for an interview with the president to express their views. On leaving the White House on January 9, their spokesman, Dr. Rufus W. Weaver (1870–1947), a man respected far beyond his denomination, stated to the press that American Baptists were opposed to the establishment of diplomatic relations with any religious body. He added, however, that

Those who participated came away with the understanding that the appointment was a temporary expedient and grew out of the vast influence exerted by the Vatican over the large populations within the confines of those countries now engaged in war.[325]

It was quite clear that Protestant groups of many types who thoroughly favored informal conferences at the White House between representatives of different religious groups with the president on the peace problem, and who would have had little objection to the president's asking anyone whom he thought appropriate to confer on his personal behalf with the pope, objected when it was found that his representative was to receive the rank of ambassador. They feared it might lead to complications through the regular exchange of formal diplomatic relations between this country and the papacy.

Later, when reports were spread abroad that the interview had cleared up all difficulties, the Public Relations Committee of the three Baptist bodies issued a statement to the effect that

We appreciated fully what had been done and our fears lest a permanent ambassadorial relationship with the Vatican might be established were allayed only by the statement of the President that he had no such purpose in mind. All three groups (Baptist, Lutheran and Seventh Day Adventist) declared that the absolute separation of church and state was a principle which they were ready to defend to the utmost degree.[326]

The Executive Committee of the Federal Council took action on the matter on January 26. In view of the representative character of this agency for American Protestantism, and the fact that a month had elapsed since the announcement of the plan, thus giving adequate time for the weighing of public opinion and for careful consideration of the issues involved, its unanimous action at a largely attended and representative meeting is specially significant. It probably fairly represented the majority opinion of the country at the time, and was approved by Dr. Weaver, chairman of the Joint Committee on Public Relations of the Southern and Northern Baptist Conventions.

The Executive Committee of the Federal Council of the Churches of Christ in America, at its first meeting since President Roosevelt's announcement of the appointment to the Vatican of a personal envoy, "with the rank of ambassador," issued the following declaration of attitude and policy:

If the appointment should unfortunately prove a stepping-stone to a permanent diplomatic relationship, we should feel obliged in good conscience to oppose it, as a violation of the principle of separation of governmental function and religious function, which is a basic American policy and which both history and conscience approve, and as an ultimate injury to all faiths.

We assume, however, unless events disprove us, that the appointment is strictly temporary, unofficial, and centrally concerned with efforts for world peace. We can see ways in which it may help to bring peace and to avert wholesale bloodshed and a continuing disaster to civilization.

We pledge ourselves again to work with all faiths and with all men of good will for a just and enduring peace.[327]

The Christian Century was, however, far from satisfied. Here is its editorial reply:

We refuse to believe that these Baptist votes of approval really represented the Baptists of the United States, just as we refuse to believe that the Federal Council vote represented American Protestantism as a whole. As soon as the churches, the ministers, the members of congregations throughout the nation wake up to what has happened, its implications for Protestantism and for the democratic American doctrine of separation between church and state, we expect to see a rank-and-file uprising that will jar denominational and interdenominational headquarters, and register like an earthquake on the White House seismograph.[328]

The Federal Council now endeavored to have certain differences of interpretation which had arisen regarding the appointment cleared up by the president. In the issue of the *Federal Council Bulletin* for May, 1940, it published the correspondence, with the approval of the White House. In making it public, the Executive Committee on March 29 made the following comment:

We are gratified to receive the personal and official assurance of President Roosevelt that "this appointment does not constitute the inauguration of formal diplomatic relations with the Vatican."

This assurance, however, does not cover the entire ground of our apprehension. The unwarranted interpretation of the appointment to which Dr. Buttrick's letter called attention has not been explicitly denied.

We reiterate our declaration of January 26 and reaffirm our eagerness to join with men of all faiths in endeavors for world peace. We also declare again our unswerving adherence to the historic American principle of the separation of Church and State.

The exchange of correspondence between Dr. Buttrick, as President of the Federal Council of Churches, and President Roosevelt follows:

Dr. Buttrick's Letter

February 27, 1940.

The President of the United States,
The White House,
Washington, D.C.
My dear Mr. President:

A dispatch from Rome on February 13, 1940, reports that the Vatican, after a careful study of the status of Mr. Myron C. Taylor, has decided that he will be "just as much an ambassador to the Holy See as the representatives of other nations" and that he "could remain accredited to the Holy See even after Mr. Roosevelt ceased to be President."

This interpretation of your action plainly contradicts the interpretation which you have given and which was confirmed in the letter sent to me by the Assistant Secretary of State on January 23 in answer to my inquiry of January 16.

The misgivings among Protestants to which I then called your attention have not been allayed. They are deepening into grave apprehension. If you should care to see me personally, I could give many evidences of a growing disillusionment which augurs ill for inter-faith comity, for the success of Mr. Taylor's work for peace and for the health of our nation.

Therefore, because you have asked me to assist in "parallel efforts" for peace and in behalf of the Federal Council of the Churches of Christ in America, I do hereby respectfully request that you publicly state that the interpretation reported from the Vatican is contrary to your understanding of the appointment and is not accepted by you.

Faithfully yours,
GEORGE A. BUTTRICK, *President,*
Federal Council of the Churches of Christ in America.

President Roosevelt's Reply

THE WHITE HOUSE
WASHINGTON

March 14, 1940.

My dear Dr. Buttrick:

I have received your letter of February 27, 1940, concerning the status of Mr. Myron Taylor's mission to the Pope. I am sure that on further thought you will agree that no public statement is required, or indeed could be made, on the basis of a mere press report, which so far as I know has not emanated from a responsible source.

The status of Mr. Taylor's mission is exactly as Mr. Messersmith described it to you in his letter of January 25. Mr. Taylor is in Rome as my special representative. This appointment does not constitute the inauguration of formal diplomatic relations with the Vatican. The President may determine the rank for social purposes of any special representative he may send: in this case the rank corresponding to Ambassador was obviously appropriate. The reason for and circumstances surrounding his designation were made clear in my Christmas letter to the Pope; and in the letter which I gave to Mr. Taylor for presentation to the Pope, which conforms to the Christmas message.

Mr. Taylor was sent to Rome to assist parallel endeavors for peace and alleviation of suffering; and I am sure that all men of good-will must sympathize with this purpose.

There of course was not the slightest intention to raise any question relating to the union of the functions of church and state, and it is difficult for me to believe that anyone could take seriously a contrary view, or that the action taken could interrupt in any way the necessary and healthy growth of inter-faith comity.

Very sincerely yours,
(Signed) FRANKLIN D. ROOSEVELT.

The Reverend George A. Buttrick, D. D.,
President, Federal Council of the Churches of Christ in America,
297 Fourth Avenue, New York, N.Y.[329]

Now that the essential facts regarding the appointment of Mr. Myron Taylor in 1939 as special representative of President Roosevelt to Pope Pius XII, and the early reactions of the different Churches have been described, let us turn to later developments. In general it may be said that these showed no great variation from the early established patterns, except that the Protestant Churches became increasingly vocal against any permanent policy of diplomatic interchange between this government and the Holy See. To quote all official denominational actions and utterances would require a volume—such as will undoubtedly some day be published as a doctor's thesis—but we must quote a few representative ones and give some general conclusions, since the incident, and the reactions to it in this country, constitute an extremely interesting chapter in American Church-State relations.

In May, 1940, the annual Northern Baptist Convention was held in Atlantic

City. The Resolutions Committee considered among other matters "Threats to Spiritual Freedom." Three statements regarding the Taylor appointment were approved and adopted as recommended. They were:

(1) That we reaffirm our historic Baptist position regarding the separation of church and state. (2) That we restate our conviction that no privileges should be given to one religious body that are not accorded to all. (3) That we declare our irrevocable opposition to the establishment of diplomatic relations with any religious body whatsoever.[330]

The fourth proposal originally followed the *Christian Century* in demanding the "termination of the appointment at the earliest possible moment." This was modified so as to request the president to "reconsider the appointment." The resolutions met with the general approval of the two thousand and more delegates and were duly adopted.

The Methodists, Lutherans, and some other Protestant bodies took somewhat similar action; but the General Assembly of the Presbyterian Church in the United States (Southern) adopted resolutions to the effect that, owing to "the crisis in Europe," it was "not advisable or feasible" to discuss the Taylor appointment.[331] On the other hand, the General Assembly of the Presbyterian Church in the U.S.A. in 1940 passed a resolution requesting the president

to terminate at the earliest possible date the unconstitutional relations established between our government and the Vatican by the recent personal appointment of a representative with the rank of ambassador.[332]

It is difficult to ascertain the relative weight of public opinion in a controversial matter of this character, on which the public does not pass a direct vote, but from a consideration of the various polls made, the actions of different religious and civic groups, and editorial utterances, it seems to the writer that a majority of thoughtful citizens of the United States felt that, owing to the critical character of the European situation, the appointment of Mr. Taylor as the president's personal representative, with rank of ambassador, was justified at the time it was made. It is probably equally true that a majority of thoughtful non-Catholic citizens had at least serious doubts of the wisdom of following this appointment by establishing permanent diplomatic relations with the Vatican. Both points of view on this larger issue have been ably presented. Probably the ablest and fairest article presenting the reasons for direct and permanent diplomatic relations with the Vatican is the long letter to the *New York Times* by the Most Reverend James H. Ryan (1886–1947), Bishop of Omaha and former rector of the Catholic University. He took the ground that very definite advantages would accrue to the United States by the recognition of the Vatican as a State, and presented it as being "in all things independent and sovereign," receiving the ambassadors or ministers of thirty-six nations, among them England, France, Germany, Italy, the Argentine, Brazil, and Chile. He laid special emphasis on the Pan-American group, saying:

. . . The surest, safest and most realistic approach to understanding and cooperation between the Americas is along the road of morality and religion. In that large task the representatives of the Vatican in South America could play a really constructive role, were they instructed from Rome to cooperate fully with the forces advocating Pan-Americanism, the leadership in which has always been held by the United States.[333]

He further emphasized the fact that the formal recognition of the Papal State through diplomatic interchange would in no way commit the United States to the Catholic religious position.

. . . English or German recognition of the Pope as head of the Vatican state no more entails national acceptance of the Catholic religion than does recognition of the Shah of Iran involve acceptance of the religious claims of Mohammedanism.[334]

He felt that the United States could not play its part in the most intelligent and constructive way unless it had a regularly and permanently accredited representative who could avail himself, in the interest of this country, of the world-wide information obtained by the Vatican, the "Listening Post of Europe."

. . . The only sure way to obtain access to the Vatican is to be represented there, to have built up with the spokesmen of the Holy See a degree of confidence and intimacy which comes largely from personal contact, understanding and appreciation of each other's policies and motivations.

The Papacy is fundamentally a spiritual, not a political power. But so widespread and all-inclusive is the realm of the spirit, that it is difficult to segregate it from the political and to say that one thing is exclusively spiritual, the other exclusively political. . . .[335]

He added that such representation was particularly important today because of the claims of the totalitarian states to secure "complete domination of men's minds, wills and bodies."

The democratic regimes, on the other hand, respect the rights of the individual citizen, and in this action are backed up, philosophically and religiously, by the churches, both Protestant and Catholic, and particularly by the latter, whose basic creed is respect for the individual soul and its right.[336]

"The democracies and the Catholic Church are one in their opposition to totalitarian philosophies," he said, and they should co-operate, for

it would be, to put it mildly, fool-hardy for a democratic state, whose very existence is involved in the outcome of the struggle, to neglect to make friends with that religious power whose assistance is certain to be of such inestimable value.[337]

The moral leadership of the Papacy is not bound up with nationalistic policies or considerations. Essentially, it is supra-national. It therefore places the Pope in a position to regard the problems of peace and war, of national and individual welfare, divorced from the narrowness of nationalistic attitudes and ambitions. . . .

While emphasis is placed on the role of the Pope as an international teacher of morality—and in that function lies the real explanation of his world-wide influence—nevertheless, we cannot fail to mention, in any sound estimate of his position, that he is, at the same time, a temporal ruler—an independent sovereign with juridical powers as valid as those of the ruler of even the greatest empire. . . .

Should recognition be given to the Pope by the Government of the United States, the substantial benefits from the act would flow in the direction of this government, not in that of the Holy See. The Pope, and the church over which he rules, would gain prestige, but little else. The religious situation in this country is almost ideal, as far as freedom of action goes and respect for its ministers and teachings. The Pope could scarcely ask for more.

There can be little controversy over the fact that the United States Government stands to win much and lose nothing by recognition of the Vatican State. That is the reasoned judgment of almost every man connected with our diplomatic service, as it is of students of international affairs whose views stem from personal experience or the close study of political movements during the last century.[338]

Here we have the case in favor of diplomatic representation stated with authority and dignity.

On the other side, that of opposition to a permanent representative of the United States at the papacy, an excellent presentation is that given in an editorial in the *Federal Council Bulletin*. It is based on the fact that the council did not object to Mr. Taylor's appointment as a purely temporary one in the interest of peace and social welfare in a critical world situation, but that it had always said it would oppose it if it turned out to be a "stepping stone" to permanent relations.

What is the ground for such opposition? What real difference would it make if the American government should definitely decide to maintain an embassy at the Vatican?

It would make a tremendous difference,—and it is important that everyone should know why.

Although the particular phrase, "the separation of Church and State," may be vague and inadequate, what lies at the heart of the idea is of high moment. The fact that the Roman Catholic Archbishop of New York could recently refer to the separation of Church and State as a mere "shibboleth" indicates the necessity for our rethinking our heritage. If our fathers struggled and sacrificed for a shibboleth, it is time we knew it!

When our fathers embedded in the Constitution the principle that Congress should make no law "respecting an establishment of religion," it was no casual matter. They had abundant reason, both in European history and in their own experience in the New World, for appreciating the dangers of an official connection between Church and State. . . .

What our fathers thus established is one of the creative achievements of America. It has been the bulwark of religious liberty and has provided a setting in which every religious group has had full opportunity to develop its own inherent possibilities. Protestant, Catholic and Jew have all shared in this benefit. The whole movement of goodwill and friendly coöperation between Protestants, Catholics and Jews in America has developed within the atmosphere of the separation of Church and State, and the recognition of the legal equality of all religious bodies.

The "separation of Church and State," thus understood, is no "shibboleth"; it is one of the priceless treasures of American history, of as much importance today as it ever was.

If we would safeguard our heritage we must be vigilant against every encroachment upon it. That is the valid ground for concern over the possible establishing of diplomatic relations with the Vatican. Such an official connection would give one church a special status in relation to our government. It might thus prove to be the entering wedge for undermining a basic principle of American life.

Some of those who would see no objection to the diplomatic recognition of the Vatican argue that it is the Vatican State, not the Roman Catholic Church, with which relations are proposed. But in principle this involves a conception of the Church as a political entity, which is contrary to a recognition of the separation of Church and State. Moreover, in practice it is impossible to distinguish between the Catholic Church as a religious body and the Catholic Church as a political body. To have an ambassador at the Vatican State would be tantamount to placing the Roman Catholic Church in a special position with reference to our government.

The Roman Catholic pressure for the establishment of diplomatic relations with the Vatican therefore forces us to ask frankly whether the Catholic Church would like to change our historic American view as to the relation of Church and State. In general theory the Roman Catholic Church rejects that view, clinging to the idea of the union of the State with the Catholic Church. Pope Leo XIII in an encyclical of 1885 bluntly declared that "it is not lawful for the State to hold in equal favor different kinds of religions." Even so progressive and socially-minded an American Catholic as Msgr. John A. Ryan (in the book which he wrote jointly with Father Millar), after explaining that the Catholic theory does not have full application in a country like America, which provides in its Constitution for the separation of Church and State, adds that "constitutions can be changed and non-Catholic sects may decline to such a point that the political proscription of them may become feasible and expedient." It appears, then, that the Catholic Church accepts the American principle merely for temporary reasons of expediency because Catholics are now only a minority in America. Does the Catholic Church mean that if it should ever gain sufficient power it would be justified in discarding our cherished heritage? Do Catholics claim freedom and equality for themselves in America in the name of Protestant principles at the same time that they would (if they could) deny similar freedom and equality to Protestants and Jews in the name of Catholic principles?[339]

The secular position did not differ much from that of most of the Protestant press, though sometimes worded differently. In general it was effectively stated by the New York League for the Separation of Church and State. Its president was reported as criticizing the president's plan as "a breach, not only of the secular principle of our government, but a step with ominous implications." He remarked that Thomas Jefferson had said: "I consider the Government of the United States as interdicted by the Constitution from meddling with religious institutions."

Can it be [he said] that President Roosevelt is attempting to make political capital at the expense of the basic principles providing for the separation of church and state of these United States of America? Secularism, the separation of church and state, is the magic principle that has made this government the outstanding success among the nations of the world.[340]

Since these articles were written hundreds of resolutions, editorials, and other discussions for and against the Taylor appointment and its implications have been published without bringing out anything new of importance. When Mr. Taylor because of ill health returned from his mission, he continued his official position and his work *in absentia,* making occasional hurried visits to the Vatican, but a chargé d'affaires from the regular foreign service has generally acted as his deputy in Rome. The matter is likely to remain unchanged for some time, in view of its being full of "dynamite" from the point of view of American politics. When Mr. Taylor—who has served very acceptably, and is believed to have been able, through his Vatican position, to place important views and information at the disposal both of the president and the pope—retires, it is to be hoped that the question raised will be frankly that of regular diplomatic intercourse with the Vatican. It would be easier to debate that on its merits than the incomplete and partial arrangement of the recent appointment.

On this point, after four years' deliberation, the Federal Council of Churches at its biennial session in 1944 adopted a statement on the importance of retaining the separation of Church and State that deals specifically with the matter of regular diplomatic intercourse with the Vatican. It is believed from a study of newspaper comments on the Taylor incident and its aftermath that this represents the sober judgment of a majority of the citizens of the United States, both in its respect for the Roman Catholic Church as a Church, with its far-reaching religious and social work, and its belief that the Church as a political power should not, either for its own sake or for that of this country, be placed on a par with other political states in regular formal relations with the United States. As the question is sure to be raised frequently, the council's careful statement is here published in full:

For more than one hundred and fifty years our nation has cherished its heritage of the separation of Church and State. When this principle was first adopted and written into the Constitution of the United States it was an original experiment, without precedent in Europe. The formulation and the maintenance of this principle throughout our history has been one of the most important contributions of our country to political theory and practice.

The separation of Church and State has been our great bulwark of religious freedom in America. It has insured a policy of equal treatment of all religious bodies by the national government. It has afforded to every Church an equal opportunity to develop its inherent possibilities. It has thereby provided a spiritual climate favorable to good will and cooperation among Protestants, Roman Catholics and Jews.

All who treasure our historic achievement in religious liberty and a spirit of mutual respect and friendliness among the diverse religious groups must be zealous to maintain the principle of the separation of Church and State and to defend it against any measure that might prove to be an entering wedge for breaking it down.

It is for this reason that we are firmly opposed to the establishment of diplomatic relations between the United States and the Vatican. To establish diplomatic relations with the Vatican would confer upon one Church a special preferential status in relation to the American Government. Such an arrangement would be contrary to our American tradition.

A continuing official connection between our Government and the Vatican would also have the unfortunate effect of encouraging the un-American policy of a union of Church and State. The Roman Catholic Church has always advocated such a union; it regards itself, in fact, as both a Church and a State. Our nation, since the day of its birth, has rejected the union of Church and State. Other nations which do not share our traditions may feel that there are reasons of practical expediency for maintaining diplomatic relations with the Vatican. We do not regard such considerations as weighty enough to justify our country in compromising its historic position. A temporary contact for a clearly defined purpose of negotiation concerning a specific political or economic matter may be arranged if occasion arises, as for example, when William Howard Taft in 1902 dealt with the issue of the Friars' Lands in the Philippines. This, however, does not require the maintenance of regular diplomatic relations.

If it is argued that it is the Vatican as a State, not as a religious institution, with which diplomatic relations are established it must be pointed out that in practice it is impossible to separate the two. The Roman Catholic Church, according to its own conception, is a religious body and a political body at the same time. It has claimed temporal sovereignty even when it has had no territory over which to rule. Representation at the Vatican therefore involves a very different pattern of diplomatic relations from those which prevail among other states.

For the United States to have diplomatic relations with the Vatican would be to have diplomatic relations with the Roman Catholic Church. This procedure would set aside the American principle of according all religious bodies the same status in the eyes of our government. Such a departure from our historic past might even lead to an ultimate acquiescence in the doctrine enunciated by the encyclical of Pope Leo XIII on "The Christian Constitution of States," which bluntly declared that "It is not lawful for the State to hold in equal favor different kinds of religion." What this encyclical condemns is what the United States has practiced.

In taking this public stand we desire to make it clear that we are not speaking against Roman Catholicism as a form of Christian faith and worship. We recognize it as one of the great branches of historic Christianity. We earnestly seek every opportunity to cooperate with Roman Catholics, as Christian brethren, in common efforts for the welfare of mankind. But we find it necessary to make a sharp distinction between the Roman Catholic religion and the political power exercised by the Roman Catholic hierarchy for its own institutional ends.

We would also make it clear that we are not passing judgment upon the action of the President of the United States in sending a "personal representative" to the Vatican, provided this be now treated as a temporary measure of a wartime emergency character and not as a precedent for the future. We are appealing both to our Government and to public opinion for a faithful adherence to our American principle of the separation of Church and State. We are emphasizing the incompatibility of this principle with diplomatic representation at the Vatican. We are insisting that we should not now reverse an established policy of which the American people as a whole have been justly proud.[341]

The fear of the Protestant Churches that the continuance of the president's "personal representative" at the Vatican might be dangerous to the cause of Constitutional religious freedom in this country continued in the postwar years. The following action taken in June, 1946, is self-explanatory:

VOTED: That the Executive Committee of the Federal Council of the Churches of Christ in America has received with warm appreciation the report of the delegation, headed by Bishop Oxnam, which conferred with President Truman on June 5 and conveyed to him the united Protestant judgment that the present arrangement under which the President of the United States has a "personal representative to His Holiness the Pope, with the rank of ambassador," is contrary to the fundamental American principle of the separation of Church and State.

That the Executive Committee expresses great satisfaction in the report of the delegation that they were given assurance that the appointment of Mr. Taylor was a temporary expedient to give the President the fullest opportunity to make his contribution to the peace, that it might terminate at an early date but would certainly terminate with the signing of the peace treaties.[342]

Here the matter rests at the close of the period of World War II. The president's "representative" is still at the Vatican, but there can be no doubt that the

European situation is still an emergency one. The question involved will doubtless continue to be much discussed as an American Church-State problem which may create much honest difference of opinion and some bitterness. It appears at present, from a study of the religious and secular press, that outside the Roman Catholic group the majority opinion of thoughtful Americans is that some advantages of regular diplomatic relations with the Vatican in normal times would be more than balanced by possible disadvantages, especially when the safeguarding of our Constitutional religious freedom is borne in mind. The fact that the president in the summer of 1947 asked his representative, still Mr. Taylor, to make contact with the Archbishop of Canterbury and other religious leaders abroad may have some significance.

The two arguments most generally used for representation at the Vatican are that forty-one nations have official representatives there, and that the Vatican has nuncios or other official representatives at the capitals of these powers; and that the Vatican is the source of more information on internal conditions in other countries than any other agency. Both these statements can be accepted at their face value without influencing our decision as to whether in peacetime it is advantageous for the United States to have a regular representative at the headquarters of the Roman Catholic Church. The matter is further complicated by the fact that the Church is unquestionably both a religious and a political organization with a small Vatican State having its own courts, postal service, flag, currency, police force, etc. The pope, by official designation, is "Sovereign of Vatican City."

Section 12. THE COMMUNISTIC AND OTHER NEW RELIGIOUS COMMUNITIES*

Various self-governing communistic experiments were made in the thirteen colonies. The earliest was a Dutch Mennonite community on Delaware Bay in 1662, followed by the Labadist community of Protestant mystics in Maryland in 1680. These and others were not important, however, but in the eighteenth century came the Ephrata community, found in 1732, whose members should be specially remembered for their aid to the sick and wounded of Washington's army, in spite of their opposition to war; the Shaker communities, which began in 1786; the Harmony community of German Separatists in Pennsylvania, founded by George Rapp (1770–1847) in 1805 and continuing as a fairly

* The word "communistic" is used in this section in the old sense of "communalistic," implying common ownership of property and social equality, generally in a relatively small unit, without the rigid totalitarian and materialistic dogmas taught by Karl Marx (1818–1883).

successful agricultural and industrial experiment until the close of the century; the experiment of Robert Owen (1771–1858) and his son Robert Dale Owen (1801–77) at New Harmony, Indiana, in 1825, which differed from its predecessors in being nonreligious; the Hopedale community in Milford, Massachusetts, founded in 1842, along with the very different Brook Farm community of Transcendentalists founded the same year in the same state; and the Bishop Hill Colony in Illinois and the Oneida Society in New York in 1848.[343]

Of these, Brook Farm, or as it was legally known, "The Brook Farm Institute of Agriculture and Education," the center of Transcendentalism, was the best known and the most "high-brow" because of its identification with George Ripley (1802–80), the Unitarian minister who was its chief founder, Nathaniel Hawthorne (1804–64), Orestes Brownson (1803–76), Margaret Fuller (1810–50), Charles A. Dana (1819–97), and other eminent persons. It was short-lived —only five years—and conducted a successful and progressive boys' school. Its emphasis as a movement was much more literary and philosophical than economic and political, so, though it became a Fourierist "phalanx" in 1844, we must deal here with communities that come more directly within the scope of our theme. A full account of these, most of which represented a combination of pietism and socialism, may be found in the work of William Alfred Hines entitled *American Communities*. Here we merely call attention to the movement because of its interest from the point of view of Church–State relations; for most of these communities had a religious basis and were to a large extent self governing, conducting their own internal affairs in their own way with extremely little interest in the State or interference from it.

The longest lived and in many ways the most effective American communistic sect was the United Society of Believers in Christ's Second Appearing, commonly known as the Shakers. They were founded by Mother Ann Lee of Manchester, England, a woman of marked sincerity, piety, and ability, who came to this country in 1774. They had a Quaker background, but their tenets were those of a distinctive social religious group.

In 1787 the first organized Shaker Society was founded at what was then called Mount Lebanon, now New Lebanon, Columbia County, New York, just over the border from Berkshire County, Massachusetts. Between this date and 1794 eleven communities were established in New York and New England, and in the first quarter of the nineteenth century seven additional ones in Ohio, Kentucky, and Indiana. At the height of their prosperity, about the middle of the nineteenth century, they had eighteen communities with about six thousand members. In 1942 there were only four weak communities left with fewer than a hundred members. In 1949 they had virtually disappeared.

With the theological tenets of the Shakers we are not here concerned. Suffice it to say that they were a group of Christians who followed Christ but did not accept His full divinity. They believed that God had revealed Himself through the male principle in Christ and through the female principle in Mother Ann.

The Shakers became noted as farmers, mechanics, and artisans, and for their success in co-operative living and self-support. The latter was due to their remarkable skill in agriculture and various forms of home crafts. They lived pure lives, practicing celibacy, but admitting as junior members of their "families" young men and women who later became full members by mutual consent and by accepting the covenant. They preached and practiced twelve cardinal virtues: faith, hope, honesty, continence, innocence, simplicity, meekness, humility, prudence, patience, thankfulness, and charity—welcome ideals in the war-torn world of today!

Church–State relations were few. As a self-respecting and self-governing group they came into little touch with State authorities. During the American Revolution some of those who had settled at Watervliet, New York, were arrested because they were thought to be British spies, due mainly to the fact that Shakerism had been so recently imported from England. This experience and their Quaker background led during the War of 1812 to the development of their nonresistance attitude. Fines and abuse could not shake their determination not to serve in any army. During the war General William Henry Harrison granted their requests for military exemption and assigned many to hospital service. Later he presented to the Ohio legislature a petition for their relief from military duty, suggesting as a substitute three days' work on the highways, which the legislature granted.[344] Their pacifist attitude is shown and explained in a work published in Hartford in 1815 with this title: *A Declaration of the Society of People, commonly Called SHAKERS. Showing their Reasons for Refusing to Aid or Abet the Cause of War and Bloodshed by Bearing Arms, Paying Fines, Hiring Substitutes, or Rendering any Equivalent for MILITARY SERVICES.* They regarded the State as a more or less necessary evil, and neither voted nor were candidates for office. In spite of their inoffensive and religious ways of life these alleged unpatriotic attitudes led to their being much criticized.[345] In 1817 there was an attempt by the legislature of New York to pass an act which would have made the "Shaking Quakers" "civilly dead, their marriages dissolved, and all their children and property taken out of their hands." Jefferson's letter protesting against this proposal, which he thought would "carry us back to the times of the darkest bigotry and barbarism," is quoted in an earlier section.[346]

The Hopedale community had definitely Christian ideals and purposes. It was founded in 1842 in Milford, Massachusetts, by the Reverend Adin Ballou (1803–90), a Unitarian minister, its purpose being "an experiment in the science of a divine order of society, or an attempt to actualize in organic form the Kingdom of God on earth."[347] But this purpose did not prevent its being organized as a joint stock corporation. Two quotations from Mr. Ballou's prospectus of 1851 are pertinent. The religion of Christ was enjoined, but freedom in theological beliefs and social-welfare activities were emphasized.

> Each individual is left to judge for him or herself, with entire freedom, what abstract doctrines are taught, and also what external religious rights are enjoined in the religion of Christ. . . . In such matters all the members are free, with mutual love and toleration, to follow their own highest convictions of truth and religious duty. . . . But in practical Christianity this Church is precise and direct. There its essentials are specific. It insists on supreme love to God and man.[348]

The early members considered Hopedale "a miniature Christian Republic," in which the highest ideals of morality, religion, and social reform were emphasized, with due opposition to slavery, intemperance, and war. The prospectus states:

> Let each class of dissenting socialists stand aloof from our Republic and experiment to their heart's content on their own wiser systems. It is their right to do so uninjured, at their own cost. It is desirable that they should do so in order that it may be demonstrated as soon as possible which the true social system is. When the radically defective have failed there will be a harmonious concentration of all the true and good around the Practical Christianity Standard.[349]

The community existed for fourteen years.

The Amana Society, originally known as the Ebenezer Society, was established in 1843 when a group of German Pietists under the lead of Christian Metz (1794–1867), a man of religious consecration and business capacity, arrived in this country and purchased the Seneca Indian Reservation in western New York. Here they had a compact group of about eight hundred settlers living a common life. Their background was in the Society of True Inspiration, which dates from 1714, and represented a reaction against the arbitrariness and formalism of the State-Church. The society has until very recently been communistic, opposing oaths and participation in war, and managing its own extensive property—about twenty-six thousand acres—with relatively few external contacts either public or social. In 1854, partly because the suburbs of the city of Buffalo were encroaching on their desired isolation, and partly because they felt divinely guided to do so, they decided to move west, and the following year began to transfer to what they called the Amana villages in Iowa. Here they developed a successful experiment in co-operative agriculture, woolen goods manufacture, sawmills, dye works, etc.

The preamble to their constitution, adopted in 1859, shows their history and ideals.

> Whereas the Community of True Inspiration hath in the year 1843, and the following years emigrated from Germany into the United States of America, for the sake of enjoying the noble civil and religious liberty of this country, and hath settled at Eben–Ezer, in the County of Erie and State of New York, on the Buffalo Creek Indian Reservation, where they have existed, under the protection of God, in peace and prosperity; and whereas the said Community in the year 1854, according to the known will of God, resolved unanimously to sell the Eben–Ezer lands, and to undertake a new settlement in the western country, and hath consequently in the year 1855 and the years following, purchased a tract of land in the State of Iowa, and paid for the same out of the funds of the Community; and whereas since a beginning hath been made of this new settlement, with the purpose to continue and accomplish such resettlement by degrees, as the times and circumstances will permit.
>
> Now therefore, we the undersigned members of the Community of True Inspiration, feeling thankful for the grace and beneficence of God, to be privileged under the liberal laws of this state to an incorporation as a religious Society, do hereby associate ourselves anew under the corporate name of
>
> "The Amana Society,"
>
> in the town of Amana, and have adopted and do hereby adopt the following Constitution and By-Laws.[350]

In 1905 the society won in the courts a suit brought to effect its dissolution on the ground that, having been incorporated as a religious and benevolent society, it was illegally conducting a general business.

The society was reorganized in 1932 after nearly a century of considerable success as a communistic experiment. Now the religious and temporal affairs—their State and Church functions—were separated, being placed under two different boards. At the same time the organization adopted a profit-sharing rather than communistic basis.

The society is made up of respected and devoted "brothers all," with many distinctive characteristics and tenets. German remains the basis of instruction in the lower school grades. There are about fifteen hundred members.[351]

The Oneida Community was the most successful financially, and in some ways the most interesting, of the various communistic societies that developed in the United States in the second third of the nineteenth century. The society is especially interesting from our standpoint because it developed out of the religious experience and convictions of its founder, John Humphrey Noyes (1811–86).

Noyes was a graduate of Dartmouth College who studied theology at Andover and at Yale, and was licensed to preach by the New Haven Association

(Congregational). He soon developed doctrines that were either somewhat eccentric or radical for the time, such as that there was both a male and female principle in God, and that one could be saved from sin here and now. His conviction that it was possible for a person, through communion with God, to lead a perfect life, and to help in the establishment of the Kingdom of God in this world, led to his being called a "Perfectionist"; and the type of communistic society which he wished to organize resulted in the members of his group being frequently referred to as the "Bible Communists," a name taken from the title of a book published by Noyes in 1848.

In 1843 he entered into a "contract of Partnership" in Putney, Vermont, and founded the Putney Corporation or Association of Perfectionists. This association, much influenced by the teachings of the French socialist François Fourier (1772–1837), was practically communal. It embodied the founder's radical social and religious views, which led to much opposition in the Vermont village, especially because of his advocacy of "complex marriage." The opposition was so great that it seemed best to remove to Oneida, New York, with which the settlement is mainly identified, though it also had a branch in Wallingford, Connecticut.

At Oneida it had extraordinary success in the practice of community property ideas, through the manufacture of a steel trap for game and of steel chains for use with it. It also developed important agricultural canning industries and other activities. These were all well conducted and brought in a large income. The group had a high reputation in its neighborhood as being made up of industrious and responsible citizens. They were, however, a thorn in the flesh of the orthodox, partly because of their idea that "mine" and "thine," as contrary to the practice described in the early chapters of the Book of Acts, should not exist among Christians, and partly because of their rejection of monogamy, the practice of an elemental form of birth control, and the emphasis on eugenics. They were also opposed because of certain unorthodox religious views, such as their belief that Christ's second coming had actually taken place at the close of the Apostolic Age, and that consequently through vital communion with Him all selfishness could be done away with.

The opposition became so great, under the lead of a well-known Presbyterian divine, Professor John W. Mears (1825–81), that legislative action against the community was instigated. Finally in 1881 Mr. Noyes, the radical but idealistic founder of the community, advised it to "give up the practice of Complex Marriage, not as renouncing belief in the principles and prospective finality of that institution, but in adherence to public sentiment."[352] As a result, the community was transformed into a co-operative joint stock company. This has developed as an extremely successful organization, manufacturing game traps and other types of hardware, and various sewing and embroidery silks, as well as canning fruit, etc., in accordance with their historic tradition.

Aside from its Communism and its views on marriage, the most interesting feature of this community in its early days was its emphasis on mutual criticism, an idea which the founder derived from the missionary society known as "The Brethren," with which he had been identified at Andover.

As to the community life of the society, he said:

Our Communities are *families* as distinctly bounded and separated from promiscuous society as ordinary households. The tie that binds us together is as permanent and sacred, to say the least, as that of common marriage, for it is our religion. We receive no new members (except by deception and mistake) who do not give heart and hand to the family interest for life and for ever. Community of property extends just as far as freedom of love. Every man's care and every dollar of the common property are pledged for the maintenance and protection of the women and the education of the children of the Community.[353]

This society had no distinctive Church–State views, but it is interesting as an attempt to put Biblical ideas of property and community living into practice, to control offspring in the interest of eugenic principles, and to give women the same rights as men in the community organization. It felt that its treatment of all forms of labor as equally honorable was a contribution to social and industrial well-being and an effective substitute for the prevalent competitive economic system.

The so-called Bishop Hill Colony in Illinois was a religious communistic settlement which existed from 1848 to 1862. It was made up of a group of extreme Swedish Protestants known as Jansonists, and goes back to a devotional and evangelical reform of a pietistic nature in Sweden, beginning about 1825. It had some points akin to Methodism, but gradually added certain communistic features. The movement is connected particularly with one Eric Janson (1808–50), who interested people of Helsingland in 1842 in his views, and secured several thousand followers. Some of the group, persecuted by the Established Church of Sweden, came to America under their leader in 1846 with the purpose of establishing a colony that could practice religious freedom in their own way and without any interference by a State Church. When they reached America they arranged in 1846 for the purchase of land in Henry County, Illinois, as the center of their community. Other agents left in the homeland arranged for the migration of several thousand simple folk who wished to adopt the type of religious Communism which they thought the Bible taught. They erected log cabins and prepared dugouts; cleared the forest and began agriculture and the cultivating of flax; started simple manufacturing under very primitive conditions; established a gristmill; and erected a large frame church holding several thousand people. From our standpoint the interesting fact is that at the head of the community was one superior director, Eric Janson, who served both as temporal and spiritual ruler. He controlled everything and managed all the community's affairs. He was killed in 1850, and it is not necessary for us to follow further developments under his successors.[354] In 1855 the report of the trustees showed that the society owned 8,028 acres of land.

Another religious communistic society of significance, which had difficulties with the public and the State, is that of the so-called Hutterian Brethren, a body of Christians whose doctrines are in general accord with those of the Mennonites, but who differ from them in practicing strict communism based on religious principles. They originated in the sixteenth century in the Tyrol in the work of Jacob Hutter, an Anabaptist who was burned at the stake. Later, when they were driven out of Austria, they settled in Rumania and Russia, and then became prominent in Moravia.

In the early 1870's they turned to the United States, sending a petition to President Grant asking that they be exempted from jury duty and military service and given the right to administer their own schools in their own way. The president referred their petition to the Honorable Hamilton Fish, then secretary of state, with this notation:

> Of course no privileges can be afforded to foreign-born citizens not accorded to all other citizens. But it may be proper to state to these people that it is entirely improbable that they will be called upon to perform involuntary military service.[355]

When they received no encouragement from the State Department the Hutterites petitioned Congress for legislation authorizing the setting aside of tracts of government land upon which they might establish their colonies. This request also went unheeded; therefore some of the sect went to Manitoba, where they had been offered land on liberal terms.

In 1873 the Hutterite deputation purchased land in Dakota, that they might try out their communistic plan of social life and activity. In all perhaps a thousand immigrants joined the community. They prospered, and by 1918 there were some eighteen Hutterite colonies of from a hundred to a hundred and fifty members each. Each colony was governed by a body of elders, chief of whom was the pastor, who looked after the spiritual needs, and the *Wirt,* or manager, who was in charge of the colony's work. They lived a primitive life, with their own craftsmen making most of their garments from wool shorn from their own sheep, or from coarse cotton cloth bought wholesale. They engaged in agriculture, stock and poultry raising, and developed small flour mills and broom factories. For forty years they lived in peace with their neighbors and were happy among themselves; but during World War I they were accused of being pro-German and later of being Bolshevists. They were looked upon with increasing suspicion, especially as they refused to buy Liberty Bonds, to contribute to the Red Cross, or to heed the call to arms. As a result, some of these conscientious objectors were arrested and some imprisoned. The superpatriots of the neighborhood made it so difficult for those in the Janesville section that by 1925 only two of the seventeen Hutterite colonies still remained in South Dakota, the others having moved to Canada. But some of them returned in 1937, repurchased their old properties, and were received in a friendly way. A visitor who knows them well thus describes recent visits to the Janesville community:

> From my visit that day with the mild-mannered middle-aged pastor and from many subsequent visits with his intelligent, talkative brother and the members of his large family, I have learned much of the life and philosophy of the Hutterites. And I have come deeply to admire and respect them, equally because of their humble reverence for God, their fellow men and their government as for their unbending devotion to the principles they believe are right. We who would help to bring in the new world order of which humanity has dreamed so long can learn from the Hutterites to put first things first. The race still stumbles along, groping for a way. Only my friends the Hutterites seem certain of the road they must take. They are fully aware of the dangers that lie ahead, but for them there is no alternative.[356]

There are at present some eighteen hundred members of the sect, of which three colonies live in South Dakota, and two in Montana.

The Mormons were the largest and most important religious community in American history; but the Doweyites of Zion City have been the recently established group to receive most public attention. They are both dealt with at some length in other sections.[357]

Chapter XV

THE CHURCH AND SLAVERY

Section 1. THE COLONIAL BACKGROUND—THE EVIL RECOGNIZED

The first effective condemnations of conditions brought about by slavery in America were by ministers of the Gospel. The brave and vigorous protests of Bartolomé de Las Casas (1474–1566), a Roman Catholic secular priest who later joined the Dominican order, regarding the Indians in the mines of South America, are well known. He had been appointed "Protector of the Indians" by Cardinal Ximénez (1436–1517), and devoted his life to their service. His book entitled *Brevisima Relacion de la Destruycion de las Indias occidentales,* which appeared in 1552, created a profound impression. He did not in his early years oppose slavery or serfdom as such, but denounced their abuses, especially when applied to the American aborigines.

Similarly, in North America the first opponents of slavery were religious leaders and groups in Pennsylvania—Quakers, Mennonites, and Dunkers. No other group was as fearless and active in denouncing slavery as the Quakers. The first published protest against the institution in North America was by the monthly meeting of Friends in Germantown, Pennsylvania, in 1688. In 1693 the Philadelphia Yearly Meeting—the most influential of its kind in America—declared it should be the policy of Friends to buy no slaves "except to set free." They also agreed that they should aim to release their own slaves "after a reasonable time of service . . . and during the time they have them, to teach them to read, and give them a Christian Education."[1]

In 1743 one of the most beautiful and influential characters among the Quakers, John Woolman (1720–72), wrote his important tract *Considerations on Keeping Negroes Recommended to the Professors of Christianity of Every Denomination.* Another effective Quaker worker in the same cause was Anthony Benezet (1713–84), who came to Philadelphia from France in 1731, taught at the Friends' School, and founded and endowed a school for Negroes. His work, *Some Historical Account of Guinea,* published in 1772, had much influence on John Wesley and the Methodists. He was to a large extent responsible for the law passed in Pennsylvania in 1780 providing for the gradual emancipation of slaves.

In 1758 the Yearly Meeting, due largely to Woolman's influence, took action which, according to Whittier, made the meeting of that year "One of the most important religious convocations in the history of the Christian Church." Their statement reads:

After weighty consideration of the circumstances of Friends within the compass of this meeting, who have any negro or other slaves, the accounts and proposals now sent up from several quarters, and the rules of our discipline relative thereto; much time having been spent, and the sentiments of many Friends expressed, there appears an unanimous concern prevailing, to put a stop to the increase of the practice of importing, buying, selling, or keeping slaves for term of life; or purchasing them for such a number of years, as manifests that such purchasers, do only in terms, and not in fact, avoid the imputation of being keepers of slaves. This meeting very earnestly and affectionately intreats Friends, individually, to consider seriously the present circumstances of these and the adjacent provinces, which, by the permission of Divine Providence, have been visited with the desolating calamities of war and bloodshed, so that many of our fellow-subjects are now suffering in captivity; and fervently desires, that, excluding temporal considerations, or views of self-interest, we may manifest an humbling sense of these judgments, and in thankfulness for the peculiar favour extended and continued to our Friends and brethren in profession, none of whom have, as we have yet heard, been slain, nor carried into captivity, would steadily observe the injunction of our Lord and Master, "To do unto others, as we would they should do unto us," which it now appears to this meeting, would induce such Friends who have any slaves, to set them at Liberty,—making a Christian provision for them, according to their ages, &c. And in order that Friends may be generally excited to the practice of this advice, some Friends here now signified to the meeting, their being so fully devoted to endeavour to render it effectual, that they are willing to visit and treat with all such Friends who have any slaves: the meeting, therefore, approves of John Woolman, John Scarborough, John Sykes and Daniel Stanton undertaking that service; and desires some elders or other faithful Friends in each quarter, to accompany and assist them therein; and that they may proceed in the wisdom of Truth, and thereby be qualified to administer such advice as may be suitable to the circumstances of those they visit, and most effectual towards obtaining that purity, which it is evidently our duty to press after. And if after the sense and judgment of this meeting, now given against every branch of this practice, any professing with us should persist to vindicate it, and be concerned in importing, selling, or purchasing slaves, the respective Monthly Meetings to which they belong, should manifest their disunion with such persons, by refusing to permit them to sit in meetings for discipline, or to be employed in the affairs of Truth, or to receive from them any contribution towards the relief of the poor, or other services of the meeting. But if any cases of executors, guardians, trustees or any others should happen, which may subject any such Friends to the necessity of being concerned with such slaves, and they are nevertheless willing to proceed according to the advice of the Monthly Meetings they belong to; wherever such cases happen the Monthly Meetings are left to judge of the same in the wisdom of Truth, and, if necessary, to take the advice of the Quarterly Meeting therein.[2]

The influence of the Quakers on the antislavery cause was not confined to the North. They also stood by their colors in the South. They were particularly active in North Carolina and in Virginia. One of their petitions is worth quoting. In 1772 the Friends addressed the North Carolina Legislature:

Being fully convinced in our minds and judgments beyond a doubt or scruple, of the great evil and abomination of the importation of negroes from Africa: by which iniquitous practice great numbers of our fellow creatures with their posterity are doomed to perpetual and cruel bondage; without any regard being had to their having forfeited their natural right to liberty and freedom, by any act of their own or consent thereto otherwise than by mere force and cruelty, impresses our minds with such abhorance and detestation against such a practice, in a christian community; where experience fully makes it manifest that instead of their embracing true religion, piety, and virtue, in exchange for their natural liberty, that they are become nurseries to pride, and idleness, to our youth in such a manner that morality, and true piety, is much wounded where slavery abounds; to the great grief of true christian minds.

And therefore we cannot but invite our fellow subjects; and more especially the representatives in North Carolina (as much lies at their doors for the good of the people and prosperity of the province) to join heartily with their prudent brethren the burgesses of the colony of Virginia in presenting addresses to the throne of Great Britain in order to be as eyes to the blind, and mouths to the dumb; and whether it succeeds or not we shall have the secret satisfaction in our own minds of having used our best endeavor, to have so great a torrent of evil, effectually stopped, at the place where it unhappily had the permission to begin.[3]

In 1776 Pennsylvania Quakers went even further, and virtually decided to expel from membership those who did not emancipate their slaves. Other yearly meetings followed, and before the end of the century slaves of Quakers had practically all been set free.

New England's voice was also heard. Probably the earliest published attack on slavery in New England was that by Samuel Sewall (1652–1730). It was a tract written in 1700 for the Society for the Propagation of the Gospel in New England, and had the suggestive title of *The Selling of Joseph*. These quotations will show its character:

The numerousness of slaves at this day in the province, and the uneasiness of them under their slavery, hath put many upon thinking whether the foundation of it be firmly and well laid, so as to sustain the vast weight that is built upon it. It is most certain that all men, as they are the sons of Adam, are coheirs, and have equal right

unto liberty and all other outward comforts of life. GOD hath given the earth [with all its commodities] unto the sons of Adam (Ps. cxv. 16). . . .[4]
. . . Methinks, when we are bemoaning the barbarous usage of our friends and kinsfolk in Africa, it might not be unseasonable to inquire whether we are not culpable in forcing the Africans to become slaves amongst ourselves. And it may be a question whether all the benefit received by Negro slaves will balance the account of cash laid out upon them, and for the redemption of our own enslaved friends out of Africa, besides all the persons and estates that have perished there.[5]

It will be noticed that Sewall, who was trained for the Congregational ministry but later took up law, bases his argument against slavery largely on religion. He was a man of a great deal of independence. For instance, though a member of the court which took part in the decisions of the unfortunate witchcraft trial at Salem in 1692, he later confessed publicly that he had been mistaken. He stood up courageously in church while the minister read his confession of error and guilt, and thereafter kept annually a day of prayer and fasting for his offense.[6]

In 1710 the Reverend Cotton Mather (1663-1728), the leading Puritan minister in New England, published his *Essays to Do Good,* full of objection to slavery, and so clear-cut in denunciation of its injustice that the American Tract Society, reprinting it more than a century later, had to expurgate it to make it pass without undue criticism at a time when the slavery question was being debated.[7]

Such views appeared now and then among the eighteenth-century Congregational ministers and laymen of New England. They were based on Christian teaching, supplemented after the middle of the century by the natural rights theories of Locke and other European philosophers. The best example of this latter group I have noticed is the address by James Otis (1725-83) on *The Rights of the British Colonies Asserted and Proved,* delivered in 1764. In this he referred to the evils of slavery in no uncertain terms, but the incident has no direct bearing on our theme.

In Rhode Island and the neighboring colonies there had been in colonial days a good deal of domestic slavery, Negro servants being frequently found in the larger towns. The Puritans felt that they themselves were "God's elect," and it was not until the inherited Calvinism was modified in the course of the eighteenth century that any real sense of universal brotherhood was developed among them. Respectable church people in Rhode Island saw nothing inconsistent in sending ships to Africa with rum and having them come back laden with slaves. But it was in Newport, the leading New England center of the slave trade, that the Reverend Samuel Hopkins (1721-1803) fired the first effective gun in the antislavery campaign. He was the earliest of the New England ministers to preach in an outspoken way against slavery. He delivered a powerful sermon on the subject in 1770; and published in 1776, with a dedication to the Continental Congress, his *Dialogue concerning the Slavery of the Africans; showing it to be the duty and interest of the American States to emancipate all their African Slaves.* Here was a definite attempt by the Church to influence the State in the matter of slavery. Although he had been himself a slaveholder in his early days, and his Newport congregation contained many slaveholders and some slave traders, he succeeded in persuading his church to pass votes discouraging the holding of slaves by its members, and originated the Colonization Society idea by advocating sending back to Africa as missionaries two Negro members of his congregation. The words of the church resolutions are significant. They are

that the slave trade and slavery are a gross violation of the righteousness and benevolence which are so much inculcated in the gospel, and therefore we will not tolerate it in this church.[8]

In other words, in this Newport parish in the middle of the eighteenth century slavery is attacked as unchristian. The colored people of Newport were devoted to Dr. Hopkins, and many were found in his congregation.[9] It is encouraging to know that his views—based on a modification of Calvinism as influenced by Jonathan Edwards' ideas of "disinterested benevolence"—became dominant among New England Congregational ministers before the close of the Revolution. The ideas of "freedom" and "liberty" were in the air.

Another conspicuous Newport opponent of slavery was Ezra Stiles (1727–95), also a Congregational pastor and later president of Yale College. Hopkins and Stiles are known to have had a great influence on the humanitarian views of William Ellery Channing (1780–1842), founder of American Unitarianism.

Considering the influence of the Quakers and of these New England divines, we are reminded that as historians recognize that Christianity had a marked influence in ameliorating the condition of slaves under difficult circumstances in the Roman Empire, so its further influence under changed conditions was being increasingly shown in this country. The reader is referred to the statement from the *Encyclopedia Britannica* on this subject from which a long quotation is given in the notes;[10] to the account of the influence of the Christian religion and its various churches on American democracy;[11] and to the later developments in the relation of the Church to slavery outlined in this chapter.

The South was hampered in the early days by the fact that the Established Church could not break away easily from an old English law to the effect that a slave who had been baptized became free. There was consequently a good deal of opposition to baptism on the ground that it would encourage manumission.

But the Virginia Assembly in 1667 cleared up this matter by adopting resolutions to the effect that baptism did not alter the status of an individual as to his bondage or freedom, in the hope that this would encourage "the propagation of Christianity." Maryland in 1671 definitely approved slave baptism. Such actions tended to lay the foundations for the Christian teaching of the slaves, and indirectly for a more humane treatment of them. Little by little antislavery sentiment appeared in some quarters, until at the time of the Revolution, with ideas of human rights in the air, considerable opinion in favor of the ultimate freeing of slaves had developed.[12]

But the problem faced by the Southern planter was a difficult one. It is nowhere more frankly stated than by Patrick Henry (1736–99). Writing from his home in Henrico County, Virginia, January 18, 1773, to his friend Robert Pleasants (1722–1801), he said:

I take this Oppertunity to acknowledge ye receit of Anthony Benezets Book against the Slave Trade [*Some Historical Account of Guinea with an Inquiry into the Rise and Progress of the Slave–Trade,* 1772]. I thank you for it. It is not a little surprising that Christianity, whose chief excellence consists in softening the human Heart, in cherishing & improving its finer Feelings, should encourage a Practice so totally repugnant to the first Impressions of right & wrong: what adds to the wonder is, that this abominable Practice has been introduced in the most enlightened Ages. Times that seem to have pretentions to boast of high Improvements in the Arts, Sciences & refined Morality, have brought into general Use, & guarded by many Laws, a Species of Violence & Tyranny, which our more rude and barbarous, but more honest Ancestors detested; is it not amazing, that at a time when the rights of Humanity are defined & understood with precision in a Country above all others fond of Liberty: that in such an Age and such a Country, we find Men, professing a Religion the most humane, mild, meek, gentle & generous, adopting a Principle as repugnant to humanity, as it is inconsistant with the Bible & destructive to Liberty.—

Every thinking honest Man rejects it in Speculation, how few in Practice from consciencious Motives? The World in general has denied your People a share of its Honours, but the Wise will ascribe to you a just Tribute of Virtuous Praise, for the Practice of a train of Virtues among which your disagreement to Slavery will be principally ranked.

I cannot but wish well to a people, whose System imitates the Example of him whose Life was perfect.— And believe me I shall honour the Quakers for their noble Effort to abolish Slavery. It is equally calculated to promote moral & political Good.—

Would any one believe that I am Master of Slaves of my own purchase! I am drawn along by ye general Inconvenience of living without them; I will not, I cannot justify it. However culpable my Conduct, I will so far pay my devoir to Virtue, as to own the excellence & rectitude of her Precepts & to lament my want of conformity to them.—

I believe a time will come when an oppertunity will be offered to abolish this lamentable Evil.— Every thing we can do, is to improve it if it happens in our day, if not, let us transmit to our descendants together with our Slaves a pity for their unhappy Lot, and an abhorrence for Slavery.—

If we cannot reduce this wished for Reformation to practice, let us treat the unhappy Victims with lenity, it is the furthest advance we can make towards Justice. It is a debt we owe to the purity of our Religion to shew that it is at variance with that law which warrants Slavery. . . . I exhort you to persevere in so worthy a resolution; some of your People disagree or at least are lukewarm in the abolition of Slavery. Many treat the Resolution of your Meeting with ridicule: and among those who throw contempt on it are Clergymen, whose surest Guard against both Ridicule & Contempt is a certain Act of Assembly.

I know not when to stop. I would say many things on this Subject, a serious review of which gives a gloomy perspective to future times.[13]

This frank statement from an honest, high-minded Christian statesman, who was soon to be elected first governor of Virginia, shows both the pathos and the tragedy of slavery. It was easy to pass laws against the further importation of slaves, and for philanthropic individuals to arrange to enfranchise their own Negroes by will, but to do away with the institution was a different matter.

Henry and Pleasants—a Virginia Quaker who became president of an abolition society established in his state about 1790—had other correspondence on the same subject. Indeed Pleasants' letter to the governor under date of March 28, 1777, contains one of the clearest contemporary statements we have that slavery was inconsistent with the Declaration of Independence. He declared that "the representatives of the people have nobly declared *all men equally free*"; advocated manumission of slaves as "an acceptable offering to him who Rules in the Kingdom of men"; and urged that it was the duty of government "to establish a general, uniform and constant liberty, as well Civil as religious."[14] He showed his sincerity by freeing a large number of slaves the same year.

Section 2. THE REVOLUTIONARY AND EARLY FEDERAL PERIODS—A SOLUTION HOPEFULLY SOUGHT; ATTITUDES OF THE CHURCHES

During the Revolutionary period and in the early days of the republic much progress was made in almost all the states in ameliorating the lot of the slave; in freeing exceptional Negroes through manumission; and in developing a sentiment favorable to the gradual abolition of slavery. Thomas Jefferson was highly influential in advocating all these measures, and was representative of the best thought of the South in the matter. He included an antislavery plank in his suggestions to Virginia delegates to the Continental Congress. In his original draft of the Declaration slavery had been severely condemned as "cruel war against human nature itself, violating its most sacred rights of life and liberty."[15] This was unfortunately deleted in committee, but the well-known phrases on human equality and the inborn rights of life and liberty were retained,[16] and their implications gradually worked into the consciousness of the nation. He wrote much on the subject, but none of his statements is more impressive than the words incised on one of the four panels of the Jefferson Memorial at the nation's capital.

> GOD WHO GAVE US LIFE GAVE US LIBERTY. CAN THE LIBERTIES OF A NATION BE SECURE WHEN WE HAVE REMOVED A CONVICTION THAT THESE LIBERTIES ARE THE GIFT OF GOD? INDEED I TREMBLE FOR MY COUNTRY WHEN I REFLECT THAT GOD IS JUST. THAT HIS JUSTICE CANNOT SLEEP FOREVER. COMMERCE BETWEEN MASTER AND SLAVE IS DESPOTISM. NOTHING IS MORE CERTAINLY WRITTEN IN THE BOOK OF FATE THAN THAT THESE PEOPLE ARE TO BE FREE[17]

He was convinced that in the long run slavery was an uneconomic system and that its effect on master and slave alike was generally bad, but his main argument against it was based on his theory of the rights of man—the slave was a man created by God, and consequently he had the right of freedom.

Under Jefferson's leadership Virginia abolished the foreign slave trade in 1778, in keeping with the Continental Congress's nonimportation agreement, and she was soon followed by most other states, though the increase of slaves from the beginning of the eighteenth century to the Revolution—from about ten thousand to about two hundred thousand—represented a labor asset which it was hard for the South to dispense with on a large scale.

Jefferson was greatly disappointed when the ordinance which he drafted in 1785 for the government of the territories of the United States, providing for the exclusion of slaves after 1800, failed of passage by one vote.[18] This calamity was only partly met by the Ordinance of 1787 with its antislavery provisions, since the ordinance covered only the area north of the Ohio River.

Chancellor George Wythe (1726–1806) shared Jefferson's views, and during the ten important years, 1779–89, that he taught law at William and Mary, he was making some impression in favor of abolition; an influence which was sealed, as it was with other representative Southerners, especially in Virginia, by his giving his own slaves freedom and by trying to help them in the period of economic readjustment. It is probable that relatively few thoughtful persons in the new nation failed to recognize that slavery was inconsistent both with the ideals of the Declaration of Independence and of the New Testament.

As to the more drastic legal and constitutional methods to prevent the spread of slavery and gradually to eliminate it, there was consistent progress in the North, where, when the Revolution broke out, the total number of slaves was counted by the tens of thousands, rather than by the hundreds of thousands as in the South. This meant that there were then only a few more than fifty thousand (nearly half in New York) in a total slave population in the country of about half a million.

Rhode Island led the way by action taken on the very eve of the Revolution, and did so on fair and far-reaching grounds.

> Whereas, the inhabitants of America are generally engaged in the preservation of their own rights and liberties, among which that of personal freedom must be considered as the greatest, and as those who are desirous of enjoying all the advantages of liberty themselves should be willing to extend personal liberty to others. . . .[19]

Vermont was the first to act after the Declaration of Independence by placing in its constitution in 1777 a positive declaration against the legal holding of any man over twenty-one "to serve any person, as a servant, slave or apprentice," and the same for any female over eighteen. It based its action squarely on the natural-rights theory, which was stated as the conviction

> That all men are born equally free and independent, and have certain natural, inherent and unalienable rights, amongst which are the enjoying and defending life and liberty. . . .[20]

Pennsylvania, the Quaker stronghold, adopted measures for gradual abolition in 1780. More significant was the action of Massachusetts, where a Negro, Quork Walker, sued his master for freedom on the ground that the state constitution, following the wording of the Declaration of Independence, stated that "All men are born free and equal," and in 1781 won his suit, and slavery ended in that state.[21] The New Hampshire courts, interpreting a similar clause, freed the postnati. Connecticut and Rhode Island both took similar action before the adoption of the Federal Constitution, while New York and New Jersey did the same in 1784; other states followed. But most important of all, the Northwest Ordinance of 1787, as adopted by the Federal Congress at the suggestion of

Jefferson, excluded slavery forever.[22] This was highly significant, because Southerners legislating for territory outside the South favored the proposal—a condition far different from that which developed a half century later.

The year 1787 was for many reasons eventful in the slavery conflict. It saw the reinvigoration, under the presidency of Benjamin Franklin (who had long noticed the inconsistency between advocating liberty and permitting slavery),[23] of the Society for Promoting the Abolition of Slavery, established a decade earlier (1775), which was the prototype of many similar societies, North and South; a partial defeat for the opponents of slavery in the Constitutional Convention; a notable victory in Congress with the prohibition of slavery in the Northwest Ordinance; and in England four events that were to have a broad influence: the beginning of the effective public agitation against slavery by Thomas Clarkson, whose *Essay on the Slavery and Commerce of the Human Species* had appeared the previous year; the formation of the first society for the abolition of the slave trade, under the presidency of Granville Sharp, a leading Anglican layman who was a friend of the American colonies; the starting of a colony to be settled by emancipated slaves in Sierra Leone (chartered in 1791); and the assuming in the same year by William Wilberforce of the active parliamentary leadership of the cause of the abolition of slavery, which was crowned with success twenty years later (1807). Both in England and the United States the sentiment against slavery was growing fast.

Referring to the group behind this antislavery movement in England, the *Encyclopedia Britannica* says: "It is unquestionable that the principal motive power which originated and sustained their efforts was Christian principle and feeling."[24]

The Quakers took, as usual, an honorable lead in the matter. As early as March, 1790, they petitioned Congress against slavery, as did also the Pennsylvania Society for Promoting the Abolition of Slavery, which had been much influenced by the Quaker view that the traffic in slaves was unchristian. These were the earliest petitions to Congress on the matter.[25]

The Pennsylvania Society petition, which I have seldom seen quoted, is particularly significant because of its breadth of view, its recognition of the relation of Christianity and the Christian Church to the cause of abolition, and its being written by Benjamin Franklin. It is dated February 3, 1790, and starts with a statement about the history of the movement which includes these sentences:

> That from a regard for the happiness of mankind, an association was formed several years since in this State, by a number of her citizens, of various religious denominations, for promoting the abolition of slavery, and for the relief of those unlawfully held in bondage. A just and acute conception of the true principles of liberty, as it spread through the land, produced accessions to their numbers, many friends to their

cause, and a Legislative co-operation with their views, which, by the blessing of Divine Providence, have been successfully directed to the relieving from bondage a large number of their fellow-creatures of the African race. . . .[26]

Then comes this striking statement, which shows that Franklin and his associates believed that the Negroes should be granted the same rights as white men under the American system of government:

That mankind are all formed by the same Almighty Being, alike objects of his care, and equally designed for the enjoyment of happiness, the Christian religion teaches us to believe, and the political creed of Americans fully coincides with the position [my italics]. Your memorialists, particularly engaged in attending to the distresses arising from slavery, believe it their indispensable duty to present this subject to your notice. They have observed, with real satisfaction, that many important and salutary powers are vested in you for "promoting the welfare and securing the blessings of liberty to the people of the United States;" and as they conceive that these blessings ought rightfully to be administered, without distinction of color, to all descriptions of people, so they indulge themselves in the pleasing expectation, that nothing which can be done for the relief of the unhappy objects of their care will be either omitted or delayed.

From a persuasion that equal liberty was originally the portion, and is still the birth-right of all men; and influenced by the strong ties of humanity, and the principles of their institution, your memorialists conceive themselves bound to use all justifiable endeavors to loosen the bands of slavery, and promote a general enjoyment of the blessings of freedom. Under these impressions, they earnestly entreat your serious attention to the subject of slavery; that you will be pleased to countenance the restoration of liberty to those unhappy men, who alone, in this land of freedom are degraded into perpetual bondage, and who, amidst the general joy of surrounding freemen, are groaning in servile subjection, that you will devise means for removing this inconsistency from the character of the American people; that you will promote mercy and justice towards this distressed race, and that you will step to the very verge of the power vested in you for discouraging every species of traffic in the persons of our fellow-men.[27]

In 1791, Virginia, the most important Southern state, had an abolition society of some eighty members, mostly Quakers and Methodists, openly advocating the stopping of the African slave trade;[28] and by 1794 it was possible to hold "The American Convention for Promoting the Abolition of Slavery and Improving the Condition of the African Race," with half of its delegates from the Southern states. These were straws between independence and the close of the century showing the growing antislavery feeling.

It was also encouraging that Congress in 1808 exercised at the earliest date possible under the Federal Constitution the power given it to prevent the further legal importation of slaves into the United States. There was however considerable opposition to this measure both in New England and the South, although the Southern states had all individually forbidden the foreign importation of slaves prior to that time; indeed, nearly all of them had taken such action shortly before the adoption of the Constitution. This, it will be remembered, to meet the wishes of the Southern states, had provided that

> The Migration or Importation of such Persons as any of the States now existing shall think proper to admit shall not be prohibited by the Congress prior to the Year one thousand eight hundred and eight, but a Tax or duty may be imposed on such Importation, not exceeding ten dollars for each Person.[29]

Another weighty and slightly later contemporaneous evidence that thoughtful people in this country who lived at the time of the formation of our government considered slavery inconsistent with the Declaration of Independence is found in the early career of a later chief justice of the Supreme Court—Roger Brooke Taney (1777–1864), known for his unfortunate opinion in 1857 in the Dred Scott case. He upheld in 1818 before a Maryland court the right of a Methodist minister, one Jacob Gruber, to criticize slavery as a national "sin" and inconsistent with the Declaration. Taney spoke with horror of the slave trade, called slavery "a blot on our national character," and advocated gradual emancipation. He added:

> And until it shall be accomplished; until the time shall come when we can point without a blush to the language held in the Declaration of Independence, every friend of humanity will seek to lighten the galling chain of slavery, and better, to the utmost of his power, the wretched condition of the slave. Such was Mr. Gruber's object in that part of his sermon of which I am now speaking.[30]

This was different indeed from the chief justice's opinion forty years later!

This general attitude, which resulted in the freeing of slaves by Washington and many of his representative contemporaries, lasted for about a generation. We find it even after the War of 1812 and until the early 'thirties. Manumission of slaves based on a realization that slavery was inconsistent with the Declaration of Independence and the Christian Gospel was frequent. As late as 1831 we find a Virginian stating in his will his conviction

> that slavery in all its forms, is contrary to good policy, that it is inconsistent with republican principles; that it is a violation of our bill of rights which declares, that all men are by nature equally free; and that above all it is repugnant to the spirit of the gospel, which enjoins universal love and benevolence. . . .[31]

It would be hard to find a sounder statement of principles.

Examples of the relatively liberal attitude of representative Southerners of tidewater Virginia and South Carolina in the formative years of the nation on the subject of voluntary manumission of slaves and their ultimate freedom everywhere are not hard to find. Eaton in his chapter on "Aristocrats with Liberal Views" in his important work on *Freedom of Thought in the Old South* has brought together many such cases.[32] The Founding Fathers, irrespective of whether they favored early abolition of slavery, were almost a unit in believing it inconsistent with the rights of man and Christian teaching, and a temporary institution; and it must be remembered that a large majority of the white population of the South was never slaveholding. The question was not so much whether slavery should be discontinued as how and when the discontinuance could be most wisely brought about in the interest of black and white alike.

Three factors, separately discussed above,[33] greatly impressed the Churches during this early national period, and led to their taking an antislavery stand: the "Great Revival," which strengthened the religious note, and quickened the conscience of the evangelical groups in American Protestantism; the arguments in behalf of the liberation of the slaves as a Christian duty advocated by the Quakers, especially in Pennsylvania, by the Reverend Samuel Hopkins, the Reverend William Ellery Channing, and other Congregational and Unitarian ministers in New England, and by the new peace societies in various states; and the influence of the "rights of man" ideas which had been incorporated in the Declaration of Independence, the Federal Bill of Rights, and the state constitutions.

It is evident that in the early days of the republic, indeed for forty years after the establishment of the government, there was little fundamental difference of opinion in the Churches or between Church and State on the subject. All thoughtful groups, North and South, at least considered slavery inadvisable, and most believed that it should ultimately be done away with. There was difference of opinion as to the method, but as to the ultimate goal the Churches were virtually one and outspoken.

But this liberal attitude was to be drastically changed in a few decades, due to many factors, of which the most important were: the invention of the cotton gin (1793), which soon thereafter made cotton and its cultivation by slave labor financially highly profitable; the successful slave uprising in Santo Domingo under Toussaint L'Ouverture (1743–1803) in 1794, with the establishment soon thereafter of a Negro republic, with some lesser disturbances in the South giving rise to "the black terror"; and reaction against the extremes of the Northern abolitionists as symbolized by the publication of Garrison's *Liberator* in Boston in 1831.

Of the Churches, other than the Quakers, the Methodists were the earliest, after the separation from England, to take a definite antislavery attitude. This is not surprising in view of the fact that their ministers were very close to the masses of the people, and relatively little influenced by the aristocrats of the South who profited particularly by slavery—though even among them there were many who favored gradual emancipation. The earliest authoritative Methodist statement I have found was in 1780, when at their annual conference in Baltimore a "Yes" answer was given by the delegates to the following clear-cut question on the slavery issue:

Does this conference acknowledge that slavery is contrary to the laws of God, man and nature, and hurtful to society; contrary to the dictates of conscience and pure religion, and doing that which we would not that others should do to us and ours? Do we pass our disapprobation on all our friends who keep slaves, and advise their freedom?[34]

At the conference in 1784, also held in Baltimore, it was further decided that converts who had been previously warned and who buy and sell slaves were to be expelled if they bought them with no other design than to hold them as slaves. Local preachers who did not emancipate their slaves in states where the laws permitted it were to be borne with for another year in Virginia, but suspended in Maryland, Delaware, Pennsylvania, and New Jersey. In answer to the question, "What shall be done with our traveling preachers who now are, or hereafter shall be, possessed of slaves, and refuse to emancipate them where the law permits?" the answer agreed upon was "Employ them no more."[35]

This conference of 1784 was a particularly important one, because it adopted the first "Discipline" of the Methodist Episcopal Church. Question 42 had to do with an elaborate plan to "extirpate this abomination of slavery." It required each member within a year after notice given to him by the assistants, which notice they were required to give immediately, to execute legally and record an instrument

setting free every slave between the ages of forty and forty-five immediately, or at the furthest when they reach the age of forty-five; every slave between twenty-five and forty immediately, or at the furthest at the expiration of five years; and every one between the ages of twenty and twenty-five immediately, or at the furthest when they arrive at the age of thirty; and every slave under the age of twenty as soon as they arrive at the age of twenty-five.[36]

It also ordered that every infant born after the above-mentioned rules were complied with should be emancipated immediately. Those who did not comply within twelve months, nor withdraw, should be excluded, and no slaveholder should be admitted into the society or to the communion until he had complied with the rules. A remarkable postscript was, however, added as follows:

N.B. These rules are to affect the members of our Society no further than as they are consistent with the laws of the States in which they reside.

And, respecting our brethren in Virginia that are concerned, and after due consideration of their peculiar circumstances, we allow them two years from the notice given, to consider the expedience of compliance or non-compliance with these rules.[37]

Question 43, which follows, is also important:

What shall be done with those who buy or sell slaves, or give them away?

Ans. They are immediately to be expelled, unless they buy them on purpose to free them.[38]

In 1800 at the third regular general conference in Baltimore a committee was appointed to draft proper addresses to the state legislatures from year to year for the gradual abolition of slavery, and there are evidences that many such petitions were presented.

At the fourth general conference in 1804 an elaborate plan was adopted reaffirming the evil of slavery, instructing all concerned to be cautious in admitting persons to official stations when their attitude on slavery was in doubt, requiring security from slaveholders, and compelling traveling preachers who became the owners of slaves to forfeit their ministerial authority unless they executed legal emancipation agreements conformable to state laws. A Methodist preacher was required to speak fully and faithfully to slaveholders on the subject of slavery; and any member selling a slave, except at the slave's own request in cases of mercy and humanity duly approved by an investigating committee, was to be excluded. A member purchasing a slave should be excluded if he would not conform and execute a satisfactory legal document regarding emancipation, and further provide for the manumission of children. There was this clause at the close: "Nevertheless the membership of our societies in the States of North Carolina, South Carolina, and Georgia shall be exempted from the operation of the above rules."[39]

In 1808 the rule which prevented slaveholding among private members of the Church was dropped, leaving only the traffic in slaves as illegal.[40]

The general conference of 1816 adopted what was known as the "Compromise Law"—the law of the Church regarding slavery which remained in force for a score of years. It confirmed the recommendation of a committee which found

that in the South and West the civil authorities render emancipation impracticable, and they are constrained to admit that to bring about such a change in the civil code as would favor the cause of liberty is not in the power of the General Conference. They beg leave to submit the following resolution:

Resolved, That no slaveholder shall be eligible to any official station in our church where the laws of the State in which he lives will admit of emancipation, and permit the liberated slave to enjoy freedom.[41]

These quotations from the official records show clearly that the Methodists as a denomination in this country from the time of the Revolution to the 'twenties were clear in their opposition to slavery, and did what they felt feasible under the circumstances to encourage emancipation.

The Baptists have historically been deeply interested in civil and religious liberty, especially as affecting Church-State relations. They consequently were forced to face the slavery issue and to take a strong stand on it. In 1789 the general committee of the Church adopted the following resolution proposed by the antislavery leader, John Leland (1754-1841):[42]

Resolved, That slavery is a violent deprivation of the rights of nature, and inconsistent with a republican government, and therefore recommend it to our brethren, to make use of every legal measure to extirpate this horrid evil from the land; and pray Almighty God that our honorable legislature may have it in their power to proclaim the great Jubilee, consistent with the principles of good policy.[43]

This protest was not entirely effective, and we are told that the majority of Baptists soon reconciled themselves to slavery as an institution which "they were powerless to abolish, but which they would do everything in their power to mitigate by humane treatment and Christian instruction."[44] There continued, however, to be strong opposition to slavery on Christian grounds, especially in the North. For example, in 1808 the New York Baptist Association considered an inquiry from one of its constituent churches as to whether a person holding slaves could be a suitable person for church membership. The answer was, "The practice of slaveholding ought to be discountenanced as much as possible."[45] But it should be noticed that this wording did not prohibit slavery.

Since the Church was very strong in the Southern states an attempt was of course made to justify the institution on the basis of Old Testament teaching and on the lack of specific prohibition in the New Testament. The following sentence from a statement by the Reverend Richard Fuller (1804-76), more than once president of the Southern Baptist Convention, probably expressed the general sentiment of conscientious Southern Baptists of his time:

I am unwilling to appear in any controversy which can even by implication place me in a false and odious attitude, representing me as the eulogist and abettor of slavery, and not as simply the apologist of an institution transmitted to us by former generations—the existence of which I lament—for the commencement of which I am not at all responsible—for the extinction of which I am willing to make greater sacrifices than any abolitionist has made, or would make, if the cause of true humanity would thus be advanced.[46]

The official actions of the Presbyterian Church, both because of their completeness and the representative character of the Church, North and South, provide in many ways the best available index of the attitude at different times of the religious forces of the country toward slavery. Its earliest significant action on this subject was adopted by the Synod of New York and Philadelphia in 1787.

The Synod of New York and Philadelphia do highly approve of the general principles in favour of universal liberty, that prevail in America, and the interest which many of the states have taken in promoting the abolition of slavery; yet, inasmuch as men introduced from a servile state to a participation of all the privileges of civil society, without a proper education, and without previous habits of industry, may be, in many respects, dangerous to the community, therefore they earnestly recommend it to all the members belonging to their communion, to give those persons who are at present held in servitude, such good education as to prepare them for the better enjoyment of freedom; and they moreover recommend that masters, wherever they find servants disposed to make a just improvement of the privilege, would give them a *peculium,* or grant them sufficient time and sufficient means of procuring their own liberty at a moderate rate, that thereby they may be brought into society with those habits of industry that may render them useful citizens; and, finally, they recommend it to all their people to use the most prudent measures, consistent with the interest and the state of civil society, in the counties where they live, to procure eventually the final abolition of slavery in America.[47]

In 1801 the Reformed Presbytery, formed in 1774, representing a small group of conservative Presbyterians which had kept close to the Scottish Kirk, made the abandonment of slaveholding a prerequisite of church membership. Although most of its members were in Pennsylvania it had some in the South, and we are told that with one exception these complied with the new regulation.[48]

In 1811 the "Associate Synod"—that is, the short-lived group of Presbyterian churches in New Jersey and New York, which tried to avoid "the slackness of Congregationalism and the rigidity of Presbyterianism"—also took decisive action. Among the resolutions it adopted at this time these seem particularly significant:

That it is a moral evil to hold negroes or their children in perpetual slavery; or to claim the right of buying and selling, or bequeathing them as transferable property.

That in those States where the liberation of slaves is rendered impracticable by the existing laws, it is the duty of the holders of slaves to treat them with as much justice as if they were liberated; to give them suitable food and clothing; to have them taught to read, and instructed in the principles of religion; and when their services may justly deserve it, to give them additional compensation.

That those slave-holders who refuse to renounce the above claim and to treat their slaves in the manner now specified, are unworthy of being admitted into or retained in the fellowship of the Church of Christ. . . .[49]

With reference to the last clause it should be noted that slaveholders were not actually debarred from the communion until 1830.[50]

The 1818 utterance of the General Assembly of the Presbyterian Church in the U.S.A. was particularly important, because it showed the position of a representative and national cross-section of American Christianity toward the extension of slavery at a time when the conflict which resulted in the Missouri Compromise of 1820 was at its height.

We consider the voluntary enslaving of one part of the human race by another, as a gross violation of the most precious and sacred rights of human nature; as utterly inconsistent with the law of God, which requires us to love our neighbour as ourselves; and as totally irreconcilable with the spirit and principles of the Gospel of Christ, which enjoin that, "all things whatsoever ye would that men should do to you, do ye even so to them."

Slavery creates a paradox in the moral system—it exhibits rational, accountable, and immortal beings, in such circumstances as scarcely to leave them the power of moral action. It exhibits them as dependent on the will of others, whether they shall receive religious instruction; whether they shall know and worship the true God; whether they shall enjoy the ordinances of the Gospel; whether they shall perform the duties and cherish the endearments of husbands and wives, parents and children, neighbours and friends; whether they shall preserve their chastity and purity, or regard the dictates of justice and humanity. Such are some of the consequences of Slavery,—consequences not imaginary—but which connect themselves with its very existence. The evils to which the slave is *always* exposed, often take place in fact, and in their very worst degree and form; and where all of them do not take place, as we rejoice to say that in many instances, through the influence of the principles of humanity and religion on the minds of masters, they do not—still the slave is deprived of his natural right, degraded as a human being, and exposed to the danger of passing into the hands of a master who may inflict upon him all the hardships and injuries which inhumanity and avarice may suggest.

From this view of the consequences resulting from the practice into which christian people have most inconsistently fallen, of enslaving a portion of their *brethren* of mankind—for "God hath made of one blood all nations of men to dwell on the face of the earth"—it is manifestly the duty of all christians who enjoy the light of the present day, when the inconsistency of slavery, both with the dictates of humanity and religion, has been demonstrated, and is generally seen and acknowledged, to use their honest, earnest, and unwearied endeavors, to correct the errors of former times, and as speedily as possible to efface this blot on our holy religion, and to obtain the complete abolition of slavery throughout christendom, and if possible throughout the world. . . .[51]

1. We recommend to all our people to patronize and encourage the Society, lately formed, for colonizing in Africa, the land of their ancestors, the free people of colour in our country. We hope that much good may result from the plans and efforts of this Society. And while we exceedingly rejoice to have witnessed its origin and organization among the *holders of slaves,* as giving an unequivocal pledge of their desire to deliver themselves and their country from the calamity of slavery; we hope that those portions of the American Union, whose inhabitants are, by a gracious Providence, more favorably circumstanced, will cordially, and liberally, and earnestly co-operate with their brethren, in bringing about the great end contemplated.

2. We recommend to all the members of our religious denomination, not only to permit, but to facilitate and encourage the instruction of their slaves, in the principles and duties of the christian religion; by granting them liberty to attend on the preaching of the gospel, when they have the opportunity; by favouring the instruction of them in Sabbath Schools, wherever those Schools can be formed; and by giving them all other proper advantages for acquiring the knowledge of their duty both to God and man. We are perfectly satisfied, that as it is incumbent on all christians to communicate religious instruction to those who are under their authority, so that the doing of this in the case before us, so far from operating, as some have apprehended that it might, as an excitement to insubordination and insurrection, would, on the contrary, operate as the most powerful means for the prevention of those evils.

3. We enjoin it on all Church Sessions and Presbyteries, under the care of this Assembly, to discountenance, and, as far as possible, to prevent, all cruelty of whatever kind in the treatment of slaves; especially the cruelty of separating husband and wife, parents and children, and that which consists in selling slaves to those who will either themselves deprive these unhappy people of the blessings of the Gospel, or who will transport them to places where the Gospel is not proclaimed, or where it is forbidden to slaves to attend upon its institutions.—The manifest violation or disregard of the injunction here given, in its true spirit and intention, ought to be considered as just ground for the discipline and censures of the church.—And if it shall ever happen that a christian professor, in our communion, shall sell a slave who is also in communion and good standing with our church, contrary to his or her will, and inclination, it ought immediately to claim the particular attention of the proper church judicature; and unless there be such peculiar circumstances attending the case as can but seldom happen, it ought to be followed, without delay, by a suspension of the offender from all the privileges of the church, till he repent, and make all the reparation in his power, to the injured party.[52]

The minutes show that these resolutions "were unanimously adopted."[53] As there were apparently about one hundred commissioners present from different sections of the country at this Philadelphia meeting it was no merely sectional vote.

Probably no Church was more representative of the best public opinion both North and South than the Presbyterian; therefore this utterance to the effect that holders of slaves should show "their desire to deliver themselves and their country from the calamity of slavery" is impressive. Similar action was taken by the Associate Reform Synod a decade later, in 1830, and by the Synod of the Associate Church in 1831. Then came the great change of feeling due to reaction against the extremes of the abolition movement and other factors, as we shall see in the next section.

The resolutions quoted were, however, passed in the last moments of the Assembly and probably went further than the general opinion of the Presbyterian Church, which supported the Assembly in its recent expulsion by a large majority of a member for strong antislavery views. The resolutions, according to Professor Sweet, have been shown to be a "sop" to the antislavery group in the interest of unity.[53] But none the less they are of significance.

In 1788 the synod of the Dutch Reformed Church appointed a committee to translate and publish the doctrinal symbols of the Church and the articles of church government. It was found necessary to modify the articles in order to adapt them to American conditions. These were added to the eighty-four Articles of Dort in the form of "Explanatory Articles." No. LIX has this statement on Negro slaves:

> In the church there is no difference between bond and free, but all are one in Christ. Whenever, therefore, slaves or black people shall be baptized, or become members in full communion of the church, they shall be admitted to equal privileges with all other members of the same standing; and their infant children shall be entitled to baptism, and in every respect be treated with the same attention that the children of white or free parents are in the church. Any minister who, upon any pretense, shall refuse to admit slaves or their children to the privileges to which they are entitled, shall, upon complaint being exhibited and proved, be severely reprimanded by the Classis to which he belongs.[54]

The Congregational Church had inherited strong ideas of liberty, as we have seen above;[55] the Reverend Samuel Hopkins (1721–1803) and the Reverend Ezra Stiles (1727–95), afterward President of Yale College, were among the conspicuous leaders in the second half of the eighteenth century. In the nineteenth century they were succeeded by the Reverend Jonathan Edwards the Younger (1745–1801), the Reverend Lyman Beecher (1775–1863)—father of Henry Ward Beecher—and Jeremiah Evarts (1781–1831), a respected Christian lay leader, whose series of articles in the *Panoplist* of Boston in 1820 rallied the Church to new efforts against the extension of slavery. Samuel Hopkins's sermon in 1791 before the Connecticut Abolition Society, of which President Stiles was head, was specially influential. It was entitled *The Injustice and Impolicy of the Slave Trade and of the Slavery of the Africans.*

The Andover Theological Seminary became a center of the common antislavery effort. Its "Society of Inquiry" devoted itself largely to the question of uplifting the colored population of the country. It sent delegations to various parts of New England to speak in behalf of the cause. In 1823 this group published a report on "The Condition of the Black Population of the United States," of which the following is an extract:

> Excepting only the horrible system of the West India Islands, we have never heard of slavery in any country, ancient or modern, pagan, Mohammedan, or Christian, so terrible in its character, so pernicious in its tendency, so remediless in its anticipated results, as the slavery which exists in these United States. . . . When we use the strong language which we feel ourselves compelled to use in relation to this subject, we do not mean to speak of animal suffering, but of an immense moral and political evil. . . . In regard to its influence on the white population the most lamentable proof of its deteriorating effects may be found in the fact that, excepting the pious, whose hearts are governed by the Christian law of reciprocity between man and man, and the wise, whose minds have looked far into the relations and tendencies of things, none can be found to lift their voices against a system so utterly repugnant to the feelings of unsophisticated humanity—a system which permits all the atrocities of the domestic slave trade—which permits the father to sell his children as he would his cattle—a system which consigns one half of the community to hopeless and utter degradation, and which threatens in its final catastrophe to bring down the same ruin on the master and the slave.[56]

This report, which appeared originally in the *Christian Spectator,* was republished in pamphlet form and extensively circulated. It is interesting to note that there was even an edition published in Richmond, Virginia.

The Congregationalists at this time were so active that one of their leading historians, after giving the names of some of the antislavery preachers, closes by saying: "There was no adverse party."[57] This could have been said with a near approach to truth of several denominations as well as of public opinion in several states, North and South. Indeed, as late as 1831 a member denouncing slavery in the Virginia legislature as "the most pernicious of all the evils with which the body politic can be afflicted" is reported as saying, without being disputed, "By none is this position denied, if we except the erratic John Randolph."[58]

The attitude of the Unitarians was approximately that of the Congregationalists, of which they were an offshoot. Their most influential leader, William Ellery Channing (1780–1842), was an outstanding opponent of slavery.

The Roman Catholic Church, whose general attitude toward slavery will be discussed in a later section,[59] took no official action on the subject in this period. Indeed, one of its recent historians, referring to the vigorous denunciation of slavery by the Presbyterians in 1818 quoted above, says that "There is nothing in American Catholic history to parallel" it.[60] The same might be said of the

Episcopal Church, though it came out strongly for the Union cause in the war.[61]

In 1820 the Missouri Compromise, so earnestly advocated by Henry Clay (1777–1852), was adopted; Maine (which was sure to remain free) was admitted to statehood; Missouri was admitted as a slave state, and slavery was forbidden in all the remainder of the vast Louisiana Purchase north of 36° 30′ (that is, the parallel of the southern boundary of Missouri extended west). As a result, the slavery issue was relatively quiescent for a decade.

Matters remained in this situation until the 'thirties, when the slavery issue became again acute, and the division of most of the Churches between North and South occurred, as we shall see in a later section.

Section 3. THE EARLY 'THIRTIES—EFFECTIVE ANTISLAVERY SENTIMENT ORGANIZED

Various events in the 'thirties changed public opinion in the South. Among these were opposition to the fierceness of the attacks on slavery and slaveholders by the *Liberator*, founded by William Lloyd Garrison (1805–79) in 1831; the bloody insurrection of slaves that year in Southampton County, Virginia, which created terror throughout the South (Nat Turner's Rebellion); the great debate in the Virginia legislature in 1831–32; the resolutions of various Southern legislatures opposing antislavery views; the controversy over the status of slavery in the new Western states; and the abolition of slavery by the British in the neighboring West Indies (1833–38), which, though it stimulated the Northern abolitionists, created inevitable fears and reactions in the South; and perhaps most influential of all, the amazing, growing financial success of the "Cotton Kingdom," which felt itself dependent upon slave labor.

These events resounded through the South, and brought to an end in most of its sections all effective antislavery sentiment.

The old view of slavery as an unfortunate, unwise, and unchristian institution, which in some way and at some time must be superseded by a system of labor more in keeping with the humane conception of human dignity enshrined in the Declaration of Independence, was slowly yielding, especially in South Carolina and the deep South, to the view that it was an ideal system with divine sanction, and essential for the economic and political welfare of the South. This point of view reminds us of the defense of slavery by the Greek philosophers two thousand years earlier. John C. Calhoun (1782–1850) was among the ablest of its advocates, as he was also of the theory of state rights. In a speech delivered in 1838 he outlined this change in sentiment which had come over his section of the country.

Many in the South once believed that it [slavery] was a moral and political evil. That folly and delusion are gone. We see it now in its true light, and regard it as the most safe and stable basis for free institutions in the world. It is impossible with us that the conflict can take place between labor and capital, which makes it so difficult to establish and maintain free institutions in all wealthy and highly civilized nations where such institutions as ours do not exist. The Southern States are an aggregate, in fact, of communities, not of individuals. Every plantation is a little community, with the master as its head, who concentrates in himself the united interests of capital and labor, of which he is the common representative. These small communities aggregated make the State in all, whose action, labor, and capital is equally represented and perfectly harmonized. . . . Such are the institutions which these deluded madmen are stirring heaven and earth to destroy, and which we are called on to defend by the highest and most solemn obligations that can be imposed on us as men and patriots.[62]

This clearly shows the change that was beginning to appear among the political and economic leaders of the South. But the religious and humanitarian leaders there had not yet abandoned their desire to get rid of American chattel slavery if possible, and if not, to mitigate its ill effects; while in the North antislavery sentiment was growing steadily, especially in church circles, the while a strong effort was being made to prevent a split between the two sections of the country. Examples may be illuminating.

Two Presbyterian bodies adopted resolutions in the early 'thirties which were highly significant as showing public opinion at this time. The first is the action taken by the Associated Reformed Synod in 1830:

RESOLVED, 1. That the religion of Christ Jesus requires that involuntary slavery should be removed from the Church, as soon as an opportunity, in the providence of God, is offered to slave-owners for the liberation of their slaves.

2. That when there are no regulations of the State to prohibit it; when provision can be made for the support of the freedmen; when they can be placed in circumstances to support the rank, enjoy the rights and discharge the duties of freedmen, it shall be considered that such an opportunity is afforded in the providence of God.

3. That Synod will, as it hereby does, recommend it to all its members to aid in placing the slaves that are within the jurisdiction of this Synod in the possession of their rights as freedmen; and that it be recommended to them especially to take up annual collections, to aid the funds of the American society for colonizing the free people of color of the United States.

4. That the practice of buying or selling of slaves for gain, by any member of this Church, be disapproved, and that slave-owners under the jurisdiction of this Synod, be, as they hereby are, forbidden all aggravations of the evils of slavery, by violating the ties of nature, in the separation of husband and wife, parents and children, or by cruel or unkind treatment; and that they shall not only treat them well, but also

instruct them in useful knowledge and the principles of the Christian religion, and in all respects treat them as enjoined upon masters towards their servants by the apostles of our Lord Jesus Christ.[63]

The second Presbyterian action of importance in the development of antislavery sentiment in the Presbyterian churches in this period was taken in 1831 by the Synod of the Associate Church—long an opponent of slavery in the middle states.

RESOLVED, 1. That as slavery is clearly condemned by the law of God, and has been long since judicially declared to be a moral evil by this Church, no member thereof shall, from and after this date, be allowed to hold a human being in the character or condition of a slave.

2. That this Synod do hereby order all its subordinate judicatories to proceed forthwith to carry into execution the intention of the foregoing resolution, by requiring those church members under their immediate inspection, who may be *possessed of slaves,* to relinquish their unjust claims, and release those whom they may have heretofore considered as their property.

3. That if any member or members of this Church, in order to evade this act, shall sell any of their slaves, or make a transfer of them, so as to retain the proceeds of their services, or the price of their sale, or in any other way evade the provisions of this act, they shall be subject to the censures of the Church.

4. Further, that where an individual is found, who has spent so much of his or her strength in the service of another, as to be disqualified from providing for his or her own support, the master, in such a case, is to be held responsible for the comfortable maintenance of said servants.[64]

Some of the national Protestant Churches at this time were not prepared to go as far as these Presbyterian groups. They had all been equally opposed to slavery, and most of their members continued so, at least in theory, but in the interest of unity and harmony they tried to compromise in official statements of views so as to prevent secessions. For instance, the Methodists from 1831 to 1836 showed a real fear of the growing violence of the abolitionists and its possible results. During these years, we are told by a competent denominational authority, "bishops, conferences and ministers were studiously conservative."[65] But there were a few notable exceptions whose continued and growing conviction that slavery was unchristian would ultimately force a showdown and separation.

The fifteen years from 1830 on were years in which the Church in the North, speaking generally, identified itself more actively in the antislavery cause—giving it growing support, including that of the most prominent of its martyrs, the Reverend Elijah Lovejoy (1802–37). The extent of this activity has been brought out fully for the first time in a recent work published under the auspices of the American Historical Association.[66] This work lays emphasis on the fact that the religious revival begun under Charles G. Finney (1792–1875) in western New York in 1824–25 was largely responsible for the development. It broke away considerably from the old-time Calvinism, using the more liberal theology of Dr. Nathaniel W. Taylor (1786–1858) of Yale, which laid emphasis on the fact that salvation was the beginning of religious experience rather than its end, and that converts must begin a new life "in the interest of God's Kingdom. . . . They should set out with a determination to aim *at being useful in the highest degree possible.*"[67] This was significant, for it meant that the greatest revivalist of his time was encouraging men to do benevolent social work, not merely to try to increase their personal religious life. It meant placing the Churches behind practical Christian activity in a way that had not been known for generations. One of the ways in which the new movement was most felt was in the encouragement of the antislavery cause, which enlisted the support of some of Finney's leading converts, such as Theodore Dwight Weld (1803–95), to whom "salvation" instead of being an end was merely the beginning of a broad, benevolent activity. Finney had a powerful influence, and the great Christian awakening of 1830, with its definite interest in the improvement of human conditions, spread over the whole nation.

The "New York Philanthropists" were leaders in this group. Most of the important American philanthropic societies of the time, as we have indicated,[68] had their headquarters in New York, Philadelphia, and Boston, with Lewis Tappan and his brother as the most prominent members. These men were philanthropists not only in purpose but in life. They placed their means at the disposal of various movements in behalf of Christian education and social welfare, of which the abolition of slavery was perhaps the most important. Active benevolence had now become the vocation of one of the most representative groups in the metropolis.[69]

There were at this time two somewhat divergent movements in the interest of the Negro. Both were led by Christian laymen and ministers. Little by little the two groups separated into the more conservative "Colonizationists" and the more radical "Abolitionists." But in the early days some persons supported both. For instance, Lyman Beecher (1775–1863) said:

> I am not apprised of the ground of controversy between the Colonizationists and the Abolitionists. I am myself both, without perceiving in myself any inconsistency. Were it in my power to put an end to slavery immediately, I would do it; but it is not. I can only pursue the measures best calculated, in my judgment, to get the slaves out of bondage in the shortest time and best manner; and this, as I view the subject, is to make emancipation easy instead of difficult. . . .[70]

The American Colonization Society, founded in 1816, was interested in removing the American Negro, and more particularly the free Negro, to Africa. Its early advocates included many of the most representative and public-spirited men both North and South, with strong support in the border states. They believed that if they could develop a movement to have the free Negroes return to their "native home," a large migration might follow which would greatly reduce the seriousness of the slavery problem in this country. The Colonization Society's efforts accomplished some good, but they reached only a few thousand people, and could not, owing to the difficulties of transportation and other factors, be considered a major solution of the problem, so that after 1833 the main stress of American philanthropists was transferred to more radical measures. The Republic of Liberia, established in 1847, was, however, the result of this movement. It has had its ups and downs, but is significant today as a symbol of hope to many Africans rather than as an important contribution to the solution of the American Negro problem.

The other movement was interested in securing the complete abolition of slavery in the United States. This more radical group felt that the effort of the colonizers was merely a palliative and that it distracted attention from the major issue. Its members were greatly encouraged by the movement for the abolition of slavery in the British Empire. William Wilberforce (1759–1833), Thomas Clarkson (1760–1846), and their associates, who were mainly responsible for the efforts in England, succeeded in 1833 in having a law passed abolishing slavery in the West Indies. This was sufficiently near the United States to have a profound influence. As the *New York Evangelist* said, "Let us imitate our British brethren and open the flood gates of light on this dark subject."[71] Theodore Dwight Weld, a student for the ministry, to whom we have referred as one of Finney's disciples, was specially influenced by the British example, and made the American antislavery cause his own. With Lewis Tappan (1788–1873) and others the New York group proposed a plan for an American Anti-Slavery Society, but this did not assume definite form until the news arrived that the slaves in the West Indies were about to be emancipated. The New England Anti-Slavery Society had been formed two years before (1831); but the new organization was national in scope and was interested in having other sectional societies formed, from which they might have delegated representatives in the national organization. They launched the *Emancipator*, published antislavery pamphlets, and circularized the country with information about the British movement. They came out for "*immediate* emancipation," interpreting the words however rather broadly to gain support for any measure "if it be promptly commenced with the honest determination of urging it on to its completion. . . . In fine, it is *immediate* emancipation which is gradually accomplished."[72] Even more outspoken against the evils of slavery was Garrison's *Liberator*, conducted from 1831 until after the passing of the Thirteenth Amendment in 1866. As we shall see, it became more radical and more violent as the years passed.

From 1834 on, the situation even in the North became serious. In 1833 Lydia Maria Child (1802–80), later one of the most effective antislavery leaders, published her *Appeal in Favor of That Class of Americans Called African,* a veritable textbook of facts and arguments which was highly influential as the first extensive American book of its type. This and other works and activities of Mrs. Child gave rise to much discussion and added to the controversy. Especially in the large cities conflicts between slavery and antislavery groups were not uncommon. The congregation in the Chatham Street Chapel in New York, where the New York Anti-Slavery Society had recently been organized, was expelled. Other churches were attacked, and St. Philip's Episcopal Church (colored) was nearly torn down. Such events were especially prevalent in the summer of 1834, when the conditions in the city were so serious that all the local troops were under arms.[73] But rural regions were not free from trouble. Typical of extreme cases was that of a Methodist preacher in Northfield, New Hampshire, in 1835. While holding a meeting for the local antislavery society, he was dragged from his knees while at prayer, by virtue of a deputy sheriff's warrant accusing him of being "an idle and disorderly person . . . a common railer and brawler, going about . . . disturbing the common peace."[74] This time he was discharged, but a few months later, while addressing another meeting in a neighboring town, he was arrested in the pulpit and tried the same day. The sentence was three months' hard labor in the house of correction! These things happened not in the slaveholding South but in New England; as did also the arrest and imprisonment this same year of Prudence Crandall (1803–89) for conducting a school for colored children from different states in Canterbury, Connecticut, where the members of the school had been previously banned from public worship in the local Congregational church.

Many committees denounced abolitionists as much as they did slaveholders; and a group arose following in the footsteps of the Reverend Lyman Beecher (1775–1863), and founded in 1834 the American Union for the Relief and Improvement of the Colored Race. Its purpose was to avoid the extremes connected with Garrison and most of the abolitionists on the one hand, and on the other the tendency on the part of many Northerners to support the growing sentiment of the South in maintaining the status quo. This American Union advocated a "conciliating spirit, a Bible spirit," and expressed the belief that

> the hopes of the friends of the peaceful abolition of slavery in the United States depend upon securing the concurrence of slaveholders, procured by an appeal to their humane and Christian principles.[75]

Many clergymen were active in this movement.

William Lloyd Garrison[76] (1805–79), on the other hand, became increasingly radical. He started out by presenting the abolition cause from a Christian and Church standpoint, emphasizing that liberty is "a gift of God and nature." At an early period he said that

> Emancipation must be the work of Christianity and the Church. They must achieve the elevation of the blacks and place them on the equality of the Gospels.[77]

And again, he exclaimed:

> I call upon the spirits of the just made perfect in heaven, upon all who have experienced the love of God in their souls here below, upon the Christian converts in India and the isles of the sea, to sustain one in the assertion, that there is power enough in the religion of Jesus Christ to melt down the most stubborn prejudices, to overthrow the highest wall of partition, to break the strongest caste, to improve and elevate the most degraded and to equalize all its recipients.[78]

Dr. Charles Beecher (1815–1900), in the life of his father, Lyman Beecher, which appeared in 1863, says:

> The interval between this challenge [first number of the *Liberator,* January, 1831] and 1837, while gradually destroying Mr. Garrison's original sympathy with the theology of revivals and its kindred developments, added constantly to the intensity and power of his appeals. Yet the fact of this divergence of the Liberator from the theology of the Puritans does not nullify the fact that it was itself the child of that theology, albeit a wayward child. Its first numbers speak the dialect of Canaan—the dialect of faith, and prayer, and evangelical sympathy. "Take away the Bible," it exclaims (April 2, 1831), "and our warfare with oppression, and infidelity, and intemperance, and impurity, and crime is at an end; our weapons are wrested away, our foundation is removed; we have no authority to speak, and no courage to act."[79]

These quotations well express Garrison's point of view in his early years as an antislavery reformer. But later the leader of abolitionism became an opponent of the Church, and was opposed by it in turn because of his violence of utterance rather than because of his ultimate goal. His movement, which had become more and more extreme, became separated from the main stream of American Christianity. He called the Methodist Church a "cage of unclean birds and a synagogue of Satan"; ministers were "Dumb Dogs" (D.D.'s). Even the New England Congregationalists were "at the head of the most implacable foes of God and man"; while the Presbyterian Church was anathema.[80] Garrison's tirades against the Church were so bitter that at one time no church in Boston would open its doors for the annual meeting of his society.[81] But in spite of this change the Churches continued to advocate abolitionism as understood by the

New York philanthropists, even though many could not identify themselves with the extreme Boston leader. As the author of *The Antislavery Impulse* states:

> Garrison's terror of "the black-hearted clergy" was as much a delusion as was his certainty of his own primacy in the cause. From the beginning the movement had been inextricably bound up with the churches. The churches were its forums and the homes of its local organizations; from the churches it drew its justifying inspiration. It was an aspect of the churches, nonsectarian in organization but evangelical in character—a part of the benevolent empire. Everywhere in the organization clergymen were in control. Even in Garrison's own New England Anti-Slavery Society, clergymen composed nearly two thirds of the delegates in the typical session of 1835. In every aspect, the agitation was "a moral movement—a religious movement" drawing its life from the churches; and Garrison's "anti-clerical" obsession made him an enemy of the antislavery impulse itself.[82]

Garrison's sincerity of purpose and unselfishness have been increasingly recognized. He was the embodiment of devotion to a cause, even though his intense interest in it led him to many violent extremes of statement.[83] He placed abolition ahead of union, thus opposing Lincoln's views and policy. He was not, however, an advocate of force. Indeed, with the notable exception of John Brown's raid in 1859, the abolitionists—of whom many were Quakers—did not use force.[84]

The controversy over slavery may be seen in a striking way by what happened at Lane Theological Seminary in 1834. This institution had been started by the Reverend Lyman Beecher and some of his friends who were interestetd in training ministers to meet the religious and social needs of the West. It was in Cincinnati, Ohio, across the Ohio river from the border state of Kentucky. A leading spirit in the seminary was Theodore Weld (1803–95), whom we have already met as one of Finney's most ardent disciples. Beecher says of him:

> Weld was a genius. First-rate natural capacity, but uneducated. Would have made a first-rate man in the Church of God if his education had been thorough. In the estimation of the class, he was president. He took the lead of the whole institution. The young men had, many of them, been under his care, and they thought he was a god. We never quarreled, however.[85]

In February, 1834, the students decided to discuss the merits of abolitionism. They applied to Lyman Beecher, president of the institution, for permission. He at first consented. Later he advised the students to postpone the discussion, but the faculty did not support him in this, and the debate was held. It took the form of "a protracted meeting," lasting for some eighteen evenings. The debate began with a consideration of the question: "Ought the people of the slaveholding states to abolish slavery immediately?"[86] The debate was led by a Southerner who advocated abolition in the form of "gradual emancipation, immediately begun." On the ninth evening a vote was taken, and the entire body of theological students voted without dissent for immediate abolition. Weld wrote to Tappan: "The Lord has done great things for us here."[87] The second nine evenings were taken up with the question of whether the Colonization Society was entitled "to the patronage of the Christian community."[88] Almost unanimously at the close of the debate, the students, although knowing that their president, Dr. Beecher, believed in combining colonization and antislavery efforts, voted colonization down and organized an antislavery society.[89] The entire seminary, being converted to abolition, now devoted its efforts to elevating the free blacks of Cincinnati, equipping a library, a reading room, and a hall where evening classes, lectures, and Sunday schools were held. Outdoor relief and other forms of social welfare work were adopted.

The Lane debate reverberated throughout the nation. It was a striking evidence of the deep antislavery interest of the younger men in the Christian ministry. It was particularly significant as being held in Cincinnati, a city in the then West with a large Negro population. To be sure, the Lane trustees, being more conservative in their attitude, were opposed to what they thought to be the extreme views of the students. Indeed, they went so far as to vote to abolish the students' antislavery society and to expel Theodore Weld. The Executive Committee adopted a resolution August 20, 1834, declaring

> that rules ought to be adopted prohibiting any societies or associations in the seminary, any public meetings or discussions among the students, any public addresses by the students in the seminary or elsewhere, or appeals or communications to the students at their meals or when assembled on other ordinary occasions, without the approbation of the faculty.

The committee required that the Anti-Slavery Society and the Colonization Society of the seminary should be abolished, and that students not complying with these and other rules should be dismissed.[90] The authorities further took steps to terminate Weld's connection with the institution. The students arose almost to a man and left the seminary, and their action was supported by public opinion in the North. Beecher's conciliatory views had not prevailed, while the work of Finney and Weld, growing out of the "expanding benevolence" of the Great Revival which was deeply interested in improving human conditions, had triumphed. Beecher was equally interested in doing away with slavery, but he did not favor the methods of the abolitionists, even those of the New York philanthropists and the Lane Seminary students, who, though equally daring, were much more moderate in temper than Garrison and his Boston colleagues.

The important question was now what would happen to the fifty-three students who had taken the abolition stand at Lane Seminary. This is not the place to discuss the movement further than to say that most of them transferred to Oberlin College, which had just been established, especially as this college secured Finney as its first president and pledged itself to debar no student on account of color. It was Weld who persuaded Finney to accept, the vote in favor of admitting Negroes being passed by the trustees by the narrow margin of one vote. When the Lane rebels gathered for the spring term of 1835 at Oberlin, Finney praised their work for the free blacks of Cincinnati and justified the abolition creed which they had received from Weld, but warned them to avoid the censorious spirit which characterized the Boston group under Garrison. "A denunciatory spirit," he told them, "is unchristian, calculated to grieve the Spirit of God . . . and is injurious to the . . . slaves themselves."[91]

With this group of students as a nucleus, Weld, as agent of the American Anti-Slavery Society, drilled chosen students in the technique of proclaiming the abolition cause, until thirty of the fifty-four students who had signed the abolition statement were pioneering through the North for immediate action on the slavery question.[92] These young theological students and ministers trained at Lane and at Oberlin became evangelists of abolitionism, proclaiming the doctrine with great earnestness but in a more moderate and Christian spirit than characterized Garrison. They had learned their lesson from Finney and Weld. The work which Weld began in Ohio was followed in New York, Pennsylvania, and elsewhere, until he became the leader of what would be called today the antislavery lobby. His effort was directed primarily to converting to the cause individuals who would themselves become advocates.

A former Lane student selling Bibles and some other books in Tennessee in the summer of 1835 was arrested on the charge of being an abolition agent. The fact that he had some books against slavery for his own reading, and that some critical references to it were found in his journal, were thought incriminating by a committee of vigilance of sixty-two leading citizens, including seven Presbyterian elders. He was found guilty on three counts: that he was a member of an antislavery society in another state; that he had books of an antislavery tendency in his possession; and that he was *believed* to have circulated them! He was condemned to receive twenty lashes on his bare back in the public market place. He was forced to yield to this torture, being flogged with a cowhide, and having his books and papers taken from him and not returned. The only redeeming feature of the sad incident is that strangers cared for his wounds.[93]

The prevailing attitude of the Congregational churches in the Middle West on the slavery issue at this time may be seen by the action taken by the Congregational Association of Illinois in 1834:

I Resolved that this Association earnestly & solemnly renew their purpose by all proper means to effect the total overthrow of the system of Slavery as it prevails in the United States.
II That the existence of Slavery in the Church of Christ and its advocacy by Christians and especially by Ministers of the Gospel calls for deep humiliation and decided condemnation
Resolved 3rd, That we will endeavour to cherish feelings of kindness towards all who may be implicated in the sin of Slavery whether as Masters or Apologists
IV That we will bear our testimony against the sin of Slavery in public and private on all suitable occasions and lend our aid in the circulation of information through the medium of the press
V That we will ever maintain the right of free discussion and of petition and that we recommend to the community to withhold their support from all candidates for office who deny these rights
VI That we will remember the cause of the oppressed slave in our public prayers in the sanctuary and will not knowingly admit slaveholders into our pulpits
Voted to adopt the foregoing resolution as a whole. . . .[94]

This action represented a liberal rather than a radical attitude. Slavery is a sin and must be abolished, but the extreme denunciatory attitude of the abolitionists and their emphasis on immediacy are avoided. Here we have a typical and worthy expression of Church opinion from the section of the country best qualified to be impartial on the subject. The third section is prophetic of the attitude which was to mark Abraham Lincoln.

The American Anti-Slavery Society, established in 1833, and having as one of its major objects "to influence Congress" to abolish slavery in the District of Columbia,[95] was particularly influential at this time among the Presbyterians, Congregationalists, Methodists, and Baptists. We are told on good authority that more than two-thirds of all the abolitionists in New England were either Methodists or Baptists, these being groups very close to the needs of the common man.[96] Indeed, an analysis of the delegates to the New England Anti-Slavery Society meeting of 1835 shows that two-thirds of the delegates were ministers, and of these about two-thirds were Methodists.[97] But some of the most effective leaders were also found among Congregational and Unitarian ministers. A good example was the Reverend Samuel May (1797–1871), a Unitarian pastor with a long record of consistent opposition to slavery. As early as 1830 he was mobbed and burned in effigy in Syracuse, New York, for urging immediate emancipation—a prelude to six attacks upon him in New England for supporting Garrison's crusade.[98] He was active in the convention which formed the American Anti-Slavery Society, and in 1835 became the general agent of the Massachusetts Anti-Slavery Society. His career was typical of that of many New England ministers of the period who divided their time almost equally among public education, preaching, and reform.

In 1835 a Quaker meeting petitioned the United States Senate to abolish slavery and the domestic slave trade in the District of Columbia. This, according to Morison and Commager, really began the influence of abolition on national politics.[99] In the same year the antislavery offices in New York developed a nation-wide pamphlet campaign. These pamphlets went to representative citizens everywhere. Most of them, however, were mailed in large bundles to clergymen and postmasters accompanied by letters requesting them to distribute the pamphlets in their communities. The pamphleteers hoped to reach the conscience of the slaveholders. But when their campaign did not accomplish its purpose, they determined, as a result of the Ohio experience, to preach abolition as a great revival in religious benevolence, taking the ground that slavery was not only an evil but a sin. Weld's former band was increased to "The Seventy," the number being intentionally chosen from that of the early group of disciples referred to in the New Testament that was to convert the world to Christianity. All of them were clergymen or ministerial candidates, and it was due to these earnest Christian men that this new "revival" triumphed. As a result of this campaign hundreds of communities throughout the country developed strong antislavery convictions. The society therefore decided to devote its major attention to petitioning Congress for the abolition of slavery in the District of Columbia.

By 1835 the new petition campaign, started the previous year, was well under way, and by the beginning of 1836 it "headlined the news," and abolitionism was soon to enter vigorously the field of direct political action. John C. Calhoun (1782–1850), then in the United States Senate, was much aroused by it. The petitions

> do not come as heretofore [he said], singly and far apart, from the quiet routine of the Society of Friends or the obscure vanity of some philanthropic club, but they are sent to us in vast numbers from soured and agitated communities[100]

—words which might well have been repeated nearly a century later by those opposed to the campaigns for prohibition and other social movements. The part played by ministers in the petition campaign against the extension of slavery is clearly brought out by Dorchester. Two examples are worth recording. A mammoth memorial to Congress, two hundred feet long, bearing the names of 3,050 New England clergymen and beginning "In the name of Almighty God," was presented against the proposed extension of the domain of slavery. In a few months 125 separate remonstrances came from the ministers of these New England states.[101]

Calhoun charged that the petitions represented a Northern conspiracy against the "peculiar institutions" of the South, and he moved against their reception. His motion failed, but the discussion attracted much attention to the antislavery cause. In the House a similar motion was referred to a special committee, which recommended that

> all petitions relating . . . to the subject of slavery or the abolition of slavery, shall, without being either printed or referred, be laid upon the table, and . . . no further action whatever shall be had thereon.[102]

John Quincy Adams would not vote, but pronounced the measure a "direct violation of the Constitution of the United States, the rules of this House, and the rights of my constituents."[103]

This form of parliamentary obstruction, which certainly contradicted the provision in the Bill of Rights guaranteeing the right of petition, was known as the "Pinckney Gag," and it was repeated in various sessions until 1840, when it was made a standing rule of the House. The issue did much to unite the North in favor of abolitionism. Petitions which the Anti-Slavery Society with its clerical agents had done so much to encourage, were received and automatically laid on the table. The issue was fought in both houses of Congress. Its major result was to identify abolitionism with the Constitutional rights of citizens as laid down in the Bill of Rights.

The Honorable John Quincy Adams (1767–1848), former president of the United States and at the time a member of Congress, was the leader in presenting the petitions. He so much commanded the respect of all elements that he was extraordinarily effective as from week to week he presented appeals from all over the North on the slavery question. He accompanied them with comments designed to make the gag rule ridiculous. As the rules prevented his reading the petitions themselves, he gave the essential facts and was most resourceful. For instance, when a petition was presented from certain Lutheran ministers of New York praying that Congress would frame laws to carry out the principles of the Declaration of Independence in the District of Columbia, he declared that it did not come within the gag rule since it did not refer to slaves.[104]

Adams laid great emphasis on the Constitutional right of petition. He went so far as to present petitions that came to him praying for his own expulsion. He said that "The right of petition was co-extensive with the liberty of speech."[105] His whole purpose was to agitate the forbidden subject of slavery in every way that his ingenuity could devise. This became the passion of an old man of seventy who had rendered his country distinguished service. During the early years of this discussion he carefully avoided any official relation with the abolitionists, believing that he could accomplish more toward the overthrow of slavery by not being identified directly with a group that was believed to be extreme.

The agitation, which reached its height from 1837 to 1840, marked the change of the campaign from one of a mainly religious movement to political action. In 1833–34 there were about twenty thousand names on the petitions. In 1835–36, there were thirty-four thousand names, including a monster petition secured by Lane Theological Seminary students in Cincinnati; and so the numbers increased. Outside of the purely political field, it was the greatest piece of organized propaganda that had ever up to that time been attempted in the United States.[106] The campaign was mainly directed by three men: Henry B. Stanton (1805–87), who was to marry a few years later Elizabeth Cady (1815–1902), the woman suffrage leader; John Greenleaf Whittier (1807–92), the Quaker poet; and Theodore Weld (1803–95). The first and last had been connected with Lane Seminary. The other leaders of the American Anti-Slavery Society, namely, such men as Joshua Leavitt (1794–1873), James G. Birney (1792–1857), and Elizur Wright (1804–85), were occupied with other duties such as legislative conferences and editorial work. It is noticeable that most of these men were clergymen. They were in contact with over a thousand antislavery societies having a total membership of over one hundred thousand.[107] These societies were organized largely as a result of the work of "The Seventy," a group composed mainly of ministers, to which we have already referred.

The petitions were not always of the same type. Some were for abolition in the District of Columbia; some for the abolition of the interstate slave trade; others to forbid slavery in the territories. Signatures to these petitions were secured by agents, some paid, but mostly volunteers. Women such as Lydia Maria Child (1802–80), Susan B. Anthony (1820–1906), Angelina Grimké (1805–79) and her sister Sarah (1792–1873), and Elizabeth Cady Stanton (1815–1902), who gained great experience for their own emancipation in this effort to influence antislavery legislation, played a large part; more than half the signatures were those of women.[108] These women were recruited mainly from the Churches. It was felt that the talks that they had in securing petitions were of great value to the cause. The intellectual basis for their appeals was largely provided by Weld, whose *Power of Congress, Bible Against Slavery, Emancipation in the West Indies, Slavery As It Is,* and other books and pamphlets had an enormous circulation. The last named, which appeared in 1839, stirred special opposition in the South.

In 1839 the evangelical fervor in the petition campaign had died out, and a change had come over the Southern Church attitude, where an increasing group tried to present slavery as part of God's plan. The antislavery cause now moved its headquarters to Washington, in accordance with a plan made in 1837 by the American Anti-Slavery Society. This office was placed under Weld's direction. It is an interesting fact, however, that this lobby was established from within Congress rather than from outside. All the Congressmen involved were "professors of religion,"[109] and five were elders in the Presbyterian Church, several of them being Weld's own converts. They established what was known as "the Abolition House" directly in front of the capitol, and carried on a vigorous campaign. They kept in touch with leaders throughout the country, and especially with the antislavery movement in the West, which had a definitely religious character.

As we consider the first half of the 'thirties in retrospect, we see that the years were marked by two closely related movements. In the South we have noted a reaction on economic grounds toward the support of slavery, which it justified by moral considerations of its alleged usefulness to the blacks, who were considered incapable of effective work and development under other conditions; in the North the movement to prevent the extension of slavery and to bring about the freeing of the slaves was being effectively organized. In the South, church sentiment was swinging to the support of the status quo; in the North it was becoming increasingly outspoken in opposing slavery as incompatible with Christian teaching.

From about 1840 on, no member of any Southern college faculty could speak against the institution of slavery with impunity, and, its existence and justness having been "proved" from the Bible, abolitionism was not infrequently linked with atheism. The cleavage between the sections on this "peculiar institution" of the South had become marked and threatening. A tragic feature of the situation was that both sections were basing their moral arguments on incidents and "proof texts" from the same book, though the South appealed mainly to the letter of the Old Testament, the North to the spirit of the New.

Section 4. THE TWO DECADES BEFORE THE CIVIL WAR—NORTHERN AND SOUTHERN CHURCHES SEPARATE OVER SLAVERY

We come now to the most crucial period from the Church standpoint in the discussion over slavery; the decades that preceded the Civil War.

The "Civil War" is the term generally used in these volumes. The author is well aware that the "War between the States" is favored in the South; but neither this nor other substitutes seem entirely satisfactory. The fact is that the war was primarily a war between the Federal government and certain states which seceded and formed a separate government, so that the "War of the Secession" would have more justification than the "War between the States," since it was not, strictly speaking, a war between different states, but between the Union government, supported by most of the states, and certain other states. This has been recognized by some Southern historians. For example, the late Dr. Beverley Mumford, writing in *Virginia's Attitude toward Slavery and Secession,* refers to "the American Civil War, or to speak more accurately—the American War of Secession."[110] On the other hand, the old phrase common in the North during the war and immediately thereafter, the "War of the Rebellion," is naturally offensive to large groups of citizens and should not be used. "Civil War" seems therefore to be the term most generally accepted. "Confederate War," used at times in the South, is also unobjectionable.

Here we shall consider both the attitudes developed in leading denominations, North and South, which led to the crisis, and the incident of the Kansas Crusade, which reflected the growing determination of the Christian sentiment of the North to prevent the extension of slavery. It becomes increasingly necessary to show that in this period the Churches in the two main sections of the country were growing farther and farther apart on the slavery question. This was so marked that soon after the middle of the century the Mason and Dixon line represented almost a Chinese wall of intellectual separation, especially when the South, fearful of the effect of Northern abolition teaching, began to keep its students from attending Northern universities, and tried to introduce a blockade against books and periodicals dealing in any radical way with the slavery issue. Even the Churches had begun to separate into distinct organizations because of their radically different attitudes on this question.

(1) THE ATTITUDES OF THE DIFFERENT REPRESENTATIVE DENOMINATIONS

There were at the beginning of the second third of the nineteenth century four groups of churches which had the largest influence in the South: the Methodists, who were the first to separate (1844) over slavery; the Baptists, who separated in 1845; the Presbyterians, in 1858 and 1861; and the Episcopalians, whose Southern members carried on their work independently during the war years, but never completely broke their organic unity. The first three were the most numerous bodies; the Episcopal, though it had lost its pre-eminence after the Revolutionary period, continued highly influential among the planter aristocracy which held so much political prestige and power. The Roman Catholics, because division would have been inconsistent with the genius of their Church, did not divide. Outside of Louisiana and Maryland they were a very small group. A study of the slavery crisis as shown by the discussions and actions of these five bodies and of certain related groups is one of the most illuminating in the history of Church-State relations in the United States.

It will show a growing feeling among Southern members that slavery should not be abolished, though some of its evils should be removed by more Christian consideration on the part of slaveholders; and a growing feeling among Northern church members, first that slavery must not be allowed to spread, and later that it was intrinsically unchristian and must be abandoned or abolished. The part played by the Christian conscience in this latter movement has been clearly sensed by most recent historians. For example, the Beards state that

> Unquestionably, most of the men and women prominent in the anti-slavery agitation were deeply religious and made constant use of the teachings of Jesus in their appeals for support. . . .[111]

(a) *The Methodists.*—First, the Methodists, whose early record in this country in opposition to slavery has already been brought out.[112] There continued through the first third of the nineteenth century the conviction among members in all sections that slavery was an evil which should be removed. But about 1835 the changed situation—due largely to the fear engendered in the South by the extremes of Garrison and the Abolitionists (with a large A), and the growing conviction in the North that some method must be adopted to bring about the discontinuance of "the peculiar institution"—led to the matter becoming one of serious debate.

In 1833 the first Methodist abolition society was formed in New York. It was followed in 1835 by the establishment of similar societies by the New England and New Hampshire conferences. On the other hand, the Ohio Conference in 1835 declared against abolition. The line of cleavage between New England and most of the rest of the country was becoming clear, and it was inevitable that the matter would come before the next general conference. This was held in Cincinnati in 1836, and was forced to consider abolitionism, which was advocated in an uncompromising way by a New England delegate. After discussion, in which serious differences of opinion appeared, the following resolutions were voted by 120 to 14:

> *Resolved* by the delegates, That they disapprove in the most unqualified sense the conduct of the two members of the General Conference who are reported to have lectured in this city, Cincinnati, recently upon, and in favor of, modern abolitionism.
>
> Second, That they are decidedly opposed to modern abolitionism, and wholly disclaim any right, wish, or intention to interfere with the civil and political relation between master and slave as it exists in the slave-holding States of this Union.
>
> Third, That the foregoing preamble and resolutions be published in our periodicals.

This action showed that the current Southern attitude prevailed on the general subject of slavery, and the conference resolved that it is inexpedient to make any change in our book of Discipline respecting slavery, and that we deem it improper, therefore, to agitate the subject in the General Conference at present.[113]

The following year the Baltimore conference—significant as representing border-state opinion—declared itself convinced of the evil of slavery, but strongly opposed to the proceedings of the abolitionists.[114] On the other hand, the debates in the New England and New Hampshire conferences in 1837 showed that they were highly dissatisfied with this attitude—which was virtually that taken at Cincinnati—and believed that the Church must take a more vigorous stand against the evil of slavery. At the New England conference, in spite of the repeated efforts of the abolitionists, the presiding bishop, a Southerner by birth, refused even to present petitions which had to do with the question. He said:

Will you, brethren, hazard the unity of the Methodist Episcopal Church . . . by agitating those fearfully exciting topics, and that too in opposition to the solemn decision and deliberate conclusion of the General Conference? . . . Are you willing to contribute to the destruction of our beautiful and excellent form of civil and political government, after it has cost the labor, treasure and blood of our fathers to establish it? . . . I would that it [slavery] were obliterated from the earth; but in view of the terrible consequences that are likely to follow the agitation of those exciting topics, at the present I cannot consent to be participant in any sense or degree, in those measures which are advocated by modern abolitionists.[115]

The "irrepressible conflict" was now on in earnest within the Methodist Church, though the radicals were only a small minority. Young men who were abolitionists encountered opposition and even rejection when applying for admission to some conferences; others who would not take a definite antislavery stand, or who believed that slavery was the only possible condition in the interest both of American Negroes and of whites, were treated as though they were not Christians. Feeling ran high. Methodist antislavery conventions were held annually from 1837 on in the North, and the Southern Methodists were equally vocal in supporting their right to hold slaves if they wished to, and condemned Northern interference.

In such an atmosphere the 1840 General Conference of the Methodist Church was held. Just before it the various annual conferences in different sections of the country were asked to pass on a proposal from the New England Conference modifying the rule on slavery so that it should forbid "the buying or selling or holding men, women or children as slaves, except on purpose to free them."[116] But no conference outside of New England favored this specific proposal, and only four of the twenty-eight conferences asked for antislavery action.

Many features of the slavery problem came before the 1840 General Conference.

For our purpose one of the most illuminating was the case of a member of the Missouri conference, who had appealed from its decision that he was guilty of maladministration for admitting the testimony of a colored member against a white. The General Conference rejected a resolution confirming this decision, but the following day, by a vote of 74 to 46, passed a resolution proposed by a Georgia member to the effect

That it is inexpedient and unjustifiable for any preacher among us to permit colored persons to give testimony against white persons in any State where they are denied that privilege in trials of law.[117]

After various other resolutions had been proposed on the same subject, the following were adopted by a vote of 97 to 27:

1. *Resolved,* That in the decision of this conference, in the case of the appeal of the Rev. Silas Comfort, it is not intended to express or imply that the testimony of colored persons against white persons in church trials is either expedient or justifiable in any of the slave-holding States or Territories where the civil laws prohibit such testimony in trials at law.

2. *Resolved,* That it is not the intention of this conference, in the adoption of the resolution of the Rev. Ignatius A. Few, of Georgia, in regard to the admission of the testimony of colored persons, to prohibit such testimony in church trials in any of the States or Territories where it is the established usage of the church to admit it, and where, in the judgment of the constitutional judicatories of the church, such testimony may be admitted with safety to the peace of society and the best interests of all concerned.

3. *Resolved,* That it is not the intention of this conference, in either of the above cases or in any action had by this body, to express or imply any distrust or want of confidence in the Christian piety or integrity of the numerous body of colored members under our pastoral care, to whom we are bound by the bonds of the gospel of Christ, and for whose spiritual and eternal interests, together with all our fellow-men of every color and in every relation and condition in life, we will never cease to labor.[118]

Another matter of even greater historical significance this same year (1840) brought out clearly the Church–State difficulties of the slavery question. This was the "Answer of the General Conference" to a fraternal greeting from the British Wesleyan Conference in which, while it declined to advocate extreme measures, "opposition to slavery with earnest zeal and unflinching firmness" was urged from abroad upon all Methodist ministers.

The "Answer" is important.

Of these United States (to the government and laws of which, "according to the division of power made to them by the Constitution of the Union and the constitutions of the several States," we owe and delight to render a sincere and patriotic loyalty) there are several which do not allow of slavery. There are others in which it is allowed and there are slaves, but the tendency of the laws and the minds of the majority of the people are in favor of emancipation. But there are others in which slavery exists so universally, and is so closely interwoven with their civil institutions, that both do the laws disallow of emancipation, and the great body of the people (the source of laws with us) hold it to be treasonable to set forth anything by word or deed tending that way. Each one of all these States is independent of the rest and sovereign with respect to its internal government (as much so as if there existed no confederation among them for ends of common interest), and therefore it is impossible to frame a rule on slavery proper for our people in all the States alike. But our church is extended through all the States, and, as it would be wrong and unscriptural to enact a rule of discipline in opposition to the constitution and laws of the State on this subject, so also would it not be equitable or Scriptural to confound the positions of our ministers and people (so different as they are in different States) with respect to the moral question which slavery involves.

Under the administration of the venerable Dr. Coke this plain distinction was once overlooked, and it was attempted to urge emancipation in *all* the States; but the attempt proved almost ruinous and was soon abandoned by the doctor himself. While, therefore, the church has encouraged emancipation in those States where the laws permit it, and allowed the freedman to enjoy freedom, we have refrained, for conscience' sake, from all intermeddling with the subject in those other States where the laws make it criminal. And such a course we think agreeable to the Scriptures, and indicated by St. Paul's inspired instruction to servants in his First Epistle to the Corinthians vii. 20, 21. For if servants were not to care for their servitude when they *might not* be free, though if they might be free they should use it rather, so neither should masters be condemned for not setting them free when they *might not* do so, though *if* they *might* they should do so *rather*. The question of the evil of slavery, abstractly considered, you will readily perceive, brethren, is a very different matter from a principle or rule of church discipline to be executed contrary to and in defiance of the law of the land. Methodism has always been (except, perhaps, in the single instance above) eminently loyal and promotive of good order; and so we desire it may ever continue to be both in Europe and America. With this sentiment we conclude the subject, adding only the corroborating language of your noble Missionary Society, by the revered and lamented Watson, in their instructions to missionaries, published in the report of 1833, as follows:

"As in the colonies in which you are called to labor a great proportion of the inhabitants are in a state of slavery, the committee most strongly call to your remembrance what was so fully stated to you when you were accepted as a missionary to the West Indies: that your only business is to promote the moral and religious improvement of the slaves to whom you may have access, without in the least degree, in public or private, interfering with their civil condition."[119]

The majority report on slavery finally adopted by the General Conference was lamentably weak. It did little more than excuse inaction because of "the diversity of habits of thought, manners, customs, and domestic relations among the people of this vast republic," and "the diversity of the institutions of the sovereign States of the confederacy" (*i.e.*, Union)—note the capital "S" but the small "c."[120] The pastoral address adopted by the conference took the ground that in the interest of remaining "one and indissoluble they should leave the slavery controversy severely alone. In a word, the North, as represented by its antislavery leaders, lost, and the advocates of the Southern status quo were again triumphant.[121]

The results of this General Conference of 1840 were most unsatisfactory to antislavery men. Some formed small antislavery Methodist denominations, taking the Wesleyan name; others joined other denominations. The New England Methodists feared the effect of these withdrawals on the old denomination, with the result that abolitionist members held conferences to try to swing the Methodist Episcopal Church into line, even though this involved a break with their Southern annual conferences. They pointed out that within their Church there were about 200 travelling ministers holding 1,600 slaves, and 1,000 local preachers holding 10,000, in addition to about 25,000 slaveholding members. At a large convention of their adherents in Boston in 1843 a resolution was passed that

> slave-holding is sin; that every slave-holder is a sinner, and ought not to be admitted to the pulpit or the communion; that the Methodist Episcopal Church is responsible for slavery within its pale.[122]

It was now clear that a crisis within the denomination was inevitable, and this, with the resulting division of the major historic body of American Methodism, took place at the General Conference of 1844. The change which had come over the denomination in four years has been graphically described by the author of *Episcopal Methodism and Slavery.*

> In 1840, all factions believed that conservatism had won and that the unity of the Church had been preserved. In 1844, the Church was hopelessly divided. Garrison, Scott, Storrs and Sunderland, in the role of prophets of a new era of freedom, had changed the current of Methodist history. When the General Conference of 1844 convened at New York, two powerful groups—southern and anti-slavery—faced each other in a struggle which ended in Methodism's greatest catastrophe. Between these was the conservative faction which had formerly thrown its strength with the South. For more than a year, however, those who made up this fast vanishing minority had been rapidly assuming an attitude of antagonism to the South. A clash on the future policy of the Church was inevitable.[123]

The episcopal address tried to side-step the major issue; calling attention, with some justice, to a comparison between the fine Christian missionary work carried on by the denomination among the colored people of the South[124] and the condition in the North, where there were four annual conferences without a colored member, while in the remainder the membership was small. The conference, in spite of Southern opposition, voted the appointment of a committee on slavery with one member from each annual conference. It then considered the case of a member of the Baltimore conference, Francis A. Harding by name, who had been required by that conference to manumit certain slaves which came to him by marriage, as it held that it "cannot and will not tolerate slavery in any of its members."[125] The General Conference by a vote of 117 to 56 declined to reverse this decision—a striking victory for the antislavery side. Only two Southerners, and they not from the deep South, voted for reversal. Philadelphia and New Jersey divided, while the conference members from New York, New England, Maryland, and most of the North Central region were unanimous for confirming the Baltimore antislavery decision.

But this case was overshadowed in importance by that of Bishop James O. Andrew (1794–1871), who acknowledged that he had received by two bequests—one direct, the other indirect—two slaves, and that the previous year he had married a woman who had inherited slaves from her former husband. He added that it was obvious "that I have neither bought nor sold a slave; that in the only two instances in which I am legally a slave-holder emancipation is impracticable."[126] The bishop offered to resign when he found the strong sentiment in the North against his conduct, but the Southern delegates persuaded him not to.

Various resolutions were proposed and ably debated on both sides with much warmth. Moral, ecclesiastical, and Constitutional questions were thrashed out, as well as those of expediency.[127] Finally a vote was taken on the following resolution introduced by Ohio members:

> WHEREAS, The Discipline of our church forbids the doing anything calculated to destroy our itinerant general superintendency; and WHEREAS, Bishop Andrew has become connected with slavery by marriage and otherwise, and this act having drawn after it circumstances which, in the estimation of the General Conference, will greatly embarrass the exercise of his office as an itinerant general superintendent, if not in some places entirely prevent it; therefore,
>
> *Resolved,* That it is the sense of this General Conference that he desist from the exercise of this office so long as this impediment remains.[128]

The vote in favor was 111; against, 69. All Middle, Eastern, and Western votes were affirmative, except 17; all Southern votes negative, except 1.[129] This was followed by an unsuccessful attempt to have the resolution declared to be "advisory only, and not in the light of a judicial mandate."[130] After protests from the Southern delegates on the action of the conference regarding Bishop Andrew, and various attempts to bring about "an amicable adjustment of the difficulties now existing in the church on the subject of slavery,"[131] the conference adopted a plan of separation between the Northern and Southern churches which it took nearly a century to heal. This was drafted by the so-called Committee of Nine, and allowed ministers "to choose without blame the church to which they would adhere." The principal features of the plan for a "mutual and friendly division of the church" are given in these quotations from the resolutions adopted:

WHEREAS, A declaration has been presented to this General Conference, with the signatures of *fifty-one* delegates of the body, from thirteen Annual Conferences in the slave-holding States, representing that, for various reasons enumerated, the object and purposes of the Christian ministry and church organization cannot be successfully accomplished by them under the jurisdiction of this General Conference as now constituted; and,

WHEREAS, In the event of a separation, a contingency to which the declaration asks attention as not improbable, we esteem it the duty of this General Conference to meet the emergency with Christian kindness and the strictest equity; therefore,

Resolved, by the delegates of the several Annual Conferences in General Conference assembled,

1. That, should the delegates from the Conferences in the slave-holding States find it necessary to unite in a distinct ecclesiastical connection, the following rule shall be observed with regard to the northern boundary of such connection:—All the societies, stations, and Conferences adhering to the Church in the South, by a vote of the majority of the members of said societies, stations, and Conferences, shall remain under the unmolested pastoral care of the Southern Church; and the ministers of the Methodist Episcopal Church shall in no wise attempt to organize churches or societies within the limits of the Church South, nor shall they attempt to exercise any pastoral oversight therein; it being understood that the ministry of the South reciprocally observe the same rule in relations to stations, societies, and Conferences adhering, by vote of a majority, to the Methodist Episcopal Church; *Provided* also that this rule shall apply only to societies, stations, and Conferences bordering on the line of division, and not to interior charges, which shall in all cases be left to the care of that church within whose territory they are situated.

2. That ministers, local and traveling, of every grade and office in the Methodist Episcopal Church, may, as they prefer, remain in that church, or without blame attach themselves to the Church South. . . .[132]

9. That all the property of the Methodist Episcopal Church in meeting-houses, parsonages, colleges, schools, Conference funds, cemeteries, and of every kind within the limits of the Southern organization, shall be forever free from any claim set up on

the part of the Methodist Episcopal Church, so far as this resolution can be of force in the premises.[133]

The reference in the preamble is to a petition by the Southern delegates (and one from Illinois), expressing their conviction "that the continued agitation on the subject of slavery and abolition" in the Church and its General Conference, and "the extra judicial proceedings against Bishop Andrew" render "a continuance of the jurisdiction of the General Conference over these conferences inconsistent with the success of the ministry in the slave-holding States."[134]

A Methodist historian of the conflict over slavery thus summarizes the spirit and significance of this action which split the largest American Protestant denomination into two independent Churches.

Between the delegates of the two sections, goodwill and mutual forbearance seemed much in evidence. That they separated is not strange; that they did it peaceably seems incredible. True, the actual separation was contingent upon the necessity which southern conferences might find for such action, but no one in the General Conference of 1844 expected to see southerners sitting as delegates in the General Conference of 1848.[135]

At a convention in 1845 of the annual conferences of the Methodist Church in the South it was decided to organize a separate and distinct ecclesiastical connection. The following year the first General Conference of the Methodist Episcopal Church South was held with Bishop Andrew presiding, and the sectional break between Methodists over the slavery issue was complete.[136] Henry Clay (1777–1852) was among the statesmen who tried to prevent it, realizing fully its ominous significance. Writing on April 7, 1845, he said that he had

heard in the course of the past year of the danger of a division of the church in consequence of a difference of opinion existing on the delicate and unhappy subject of slavery. A division for such a cause would be an event greatly to be deplored, both on account of the church itself and its political tendency. Indeed, scarcely any public occurrence has happened for a long time that gave me so much real concern and pain as the menaced separation of the church by a line throwing all the free States on one side and all the slave States on the other.

I will not say that such a separation would necessarily produce a dissolution of the political union of these States; but the example would be fraught with imminent danger, and, in co-operation with other causes unfortunately existing, its tendency on the stability of the confederacy would be perilous and alarming.[137]

This letter from a public man of Clay's political acumen is evidence in support of the theory held by many that the break between North and South of the three largest Protestant bodies—combining as they did well over half of the white population in the South at the time—did much to bring on the Civil War and to bring to a head the political agitation over slavery.

At the next General Conference of the Methodist Episcopal Church (the parent body) in 1848, there was much ill feeling because of the alleged failure of the new Southern Church to live up to all the features of the plan of separation agreed to at the previous General Conference. As a result, a vote was passed to the effect that "this General Conference does not consider it proper at present to enter into fraternal relations with the Methodist Episcopal Church, South," and the plan of separation was virtually repudiated. It will surprise many to find the slavery issue the cause of such bitter sectional animosity in a great national Church in the 'forties. Incidentally, a point of special friction was the question of the Methodist Book Concern properties. The agreement regarding these involved long lawsuits. The Federal court in New York decided in favor of the South with reference to the New York branch of the Book Concern, while the Federal court in Ohio decided for the North with reference to the Western Book Concern of the Church. The South appealed the Cincinnati case to the Supreme Court of the United States. This gave a unanimous decision in 1854 in favor of the South.[138]

Of the future history of the Southern Methodists it is not necessary to speak here except to show their attitude toward slavery. This is clearly brought out by the action of their General Conference in 1858, when by a vote of 1,160 to 311 they voted to concur with the action of the Alabama Conference two years earlier urging the expunging from the General Rules of the Discipline of the historic statement forbidding "the buying and selling of men, women, and children with an intention to enslave them. . . ." But there was some question whether the vote gave the necessary three-fourths majority needed for a constitutional change, owing to the fact that some Western conferences had had no opportunity to vote on the resolutions. As a result, a committee was appointed, which adopted the following report by a vote of 141 to 7.

WHEREAS, The rule in the General Rules of the Methodist Episcopal Church, South, forbidding "the buying and selling of men, women, and children with an intention to enslave them" is ambiguous in its phraseology and liable to be construed as antagonistic to the institution of slavery, in regard to which the church has no right to meddle, except in enforcing the duties of masters and servants as set forth in the Holy Scriptures; and WHEREAS, A strong desire for the expunction of said rule has been expressed in nearly all parts of our ecclesiastical connection; therefore,

Resolved, 1. By the delegates of the Annual Conferences of the Methodist Episcopal Church, South, in General Conference assembled, that the rule forbidding "the buying and selling of men, women, and children with an intention to enslave them" be expunged from the General Rules of the Methodist Episcopal Church, South.

Resolved, 2. That, in adopting the foregoing resolution, this conference expresses no opinion in regard to the African slave-trade, to which the rule in question has been "understood" to refer.

Resolved, 3. That the bishops or others presiding in the Annual Conferences be, and are hereby, instructed to lay the foregoing resolutions before each of the Annual Conferences at their next ensuing sessions for their concurrent action. . . .

Resolved, 7. That the bishops are respectfully requested to set forth in the pastoral address the platform occupied by the Methodist Episcopal Church, South, on the relation of masters and servants, agreeably to the principle contained in the foregoing preamble and resolutions.[139]

At the General Conference of the Methodist Episcopal Church—that is, the original body—meeting in Buffalo in 1860, important action on the slavery question was taken after considering petitions signed by 45,857 individuals urging a change in the "Discipline" on the subject, as against petitions signed by fewer than a tenth of this number in opposition. The old section adopted in 1780 was then modified to forbid the holding of slaves. The revision involved this question and answer:

Question. What shall be done for the extirpation of the evil of slavery?

Answer. We declare that we are as much as ever convinced of the great evil of slavery. We believe that the buying, selling, or holding of human beings, to be used as chattels, is contrary to the laws of God and nature, inconsistent with the golden rule and with that rule in our Discipline which requires all who continue among us to "do no harm and to avoid evil of every kind." We, therefore, affectionately admonish all our preachers and people to keep themselves pure from this great evil, and to seek its extirpation by all lawful and Christian means.[140]

Thus the story of the separation of Methodism between North and South over slavery prior to the Civil War comes to a close as far as its main features are concerned. On the whole, it will be seen that the Methodists—except as the Southern members of the Church yielded to the pressure of what were believed to be the interests of their section in the two decades immediately preceding the war—were true to their antislavery principles. This was natural in view of their inherited interest in "the common man," their broad humanitarianism, and their closeness to the needs of the rural regions in which the overwhelming majority of slaves lived. Professor Alfred Whitehead (1861–), looking at history in its broad sweep from the vantage point of a detached philosopher, has this to say about the Methodists' contribution in the field under discussion:

They made the conception of the brotherhood of man and of the importance of men, a vivid reality. They had produced the final effective force which hereafter made slavery impossible among progressive races.

In the history of ideas the great danger is over-simplification. It is true that the Methodists produced the final wave of popular feeling which drove the anti-slavery movement to success. But the Methodist movement succeeded because it came at the right time.[141]

The United Brethren in Christ represent, as we have seen, an American evangelical denomination closely resembling the Methodists in doctrine and policy, and founded in this country in 1800. They are not to be confused with the *Unitas Fratrum* or Moravians, though resembling them in some particulars. Since their first general conference in 1815 the United Brethren in Christ had in their book of discipline strong condemnation of slavery, and from 1821 strong prohibitory legislation. They lived up to their convictions, which in the period under discussion did not permit ownership of slaves by members of the Church, under any circumstances whatever. As a result, outside of Maryland and Virginia, where the Church was fairly well established prior to the Civil War, it had little development in the South.[142]

(b) *The Baptists.*—At the Triennial Convention in 1841 in Baltimore, representing Baptists both North and South, it was decided, to prevent friction, not to discuss slavery. This was in keeping with the resolution of the Baptist Board of Missions passed in the winter of 1839–40, asserting the neutrality of the board on the slavery question. But it was clear that this situation could not last.

In the Triennial Convention of 1844 in Philadelphia, Richard Fuller (1804–76), a South Carolina clergyman of breadth and fine spirit, who had been educated at Harvard and left the Episcopal ministry to join the Baptists, introduced a resolution with the hope of preventing any allusion to slavery at the convention and making possible the continued co-operation of the North and South.

Whereas, Some misapprehension exists in certain parts of the country as to the design or character of this Convention, and it is most desirable that such misapprehension should be removed; therefore, Resolved, That this Convention is a corporation with limited powers, for a specific purpose defined in its constitution; and therefore, that its members are delegated to meet solely for the transaction of business prescribed by the said constitution; and that co-operation in this body does not involve nor imply any concert or sympathy as to any matters foreign from the object designated as aforesaid.[143]

Owing to opposition from the North the resolution was finally withdrawn and another substituted, which was unanimously adopted. This read:

Resolved, That in co-operating together as members of this Convention in the work of Foreign Missions, we disclaim all sanction, either express or implied, whether of slavery or of antislavery, but as individuals we are perfectly free both to express and promote our own views on these subjects in a Christian manner and spirit.[144]

In the course of the discussion on this resolution Dr. Fuller stated that he was not convinced that to hold slaves was a sin, but that he did regard slavery as a great evil, and though most of his brethren in the South did not, he hoped and prayed that the time would come when it would be done away with.[145]

Soon after this convention the Board of Foreign Missions took an increasingly active attitude against slaveholding missionaries, and it was generally understood in the South that slaveholders would be excluded from appointments as missionaries, agents, or officers of the board. There resulted some correspondence between Dr. Fuller and Francis Wayland (1796–1865), president of Brown University, who stood for all that was best among the Baptists of the North. They both based their arguments on ethical and scriptural grounds but came to different conclusions. Their letters, published in 1845—*Letters on Domestic Slavery*—are a valuable contribution to an understanding of the situation.

Late in 1844 the Alabama State Convention took the initiative in memorializing the Foreign Mission Board against its understood purpose to discriminate against slaveholders in the making of appointments. Some paragraphs from the resolution are worth quoting:

Whereas, The holding of property in African negro slaves has for some years excited discussion, as a question of morals, between different portions of the Baptist denomination united in benevolent enterprise; and by a large portion of our brethren is now imputed to the slave-holders in these Southern and Southwestern states, as a sin at once grievous, palpable, and disqualifying; 1. Resolved, . . . that when one party to a voluntary compact among Christian brethren is not willing to acknowledge the entire social equality with the other, as to all the privileges and benefits of the union, nor even to refrain from impeachment and annoyance, united efforts between such parties, even in the sacred cause of Christian benevolence, cease to be agreeable, useful, or proper. 2. Resolved, That our duty at this crisis requires us to demand from the proper authorities in all those bodies to whose funds we have contributed, or with whom we have in any way been connected, the distinct, explicit avowal that slave-holders are eligible, and entitled, equally with non-slave-holders, to all the privileges and immunities of their several unions; and especially to receive any agency, mission, or other appointment, which may run within the scope of their operations or duties.[146]

An officer of the board replied in a conciliatory way, refusing, however, the right of anyone, whether slaveholder or nonslaveholder, to appointment to positions at its disposal. The letter read in part:

In the thirty years in which the board has existed, no slave-holder, to our knowledge, has applied to be a missionary. And, as we send out no domestics or servants, such an event as a missionary taking slaves with him, were it morally right, could not, in accordance with all our past arrangements or present plans, possibly occur. If, however, any one should offer himself as a missionary, having slaves, and should insist on retaining them as his property, we could not appoint him. One thing is certain, we can never be a party to any arrangement which would imply approbation of slavery.[147]

This action, which was that of the executive, was virtually confirmed by the board itself, which adopted a report drafted by President Wayland, reading as follows:

1. The spirit of the constitution of the General Convention, as well as the history of its proceedings from the beginning, renders it apparent that all the members of the Baptist denomination in good standing, whether at the North or the South, are constitutionally eligible to all appointments emanating either from the Convention or the board. 2. While this is the case, it is possible that contingencies may arise in which the carrying out of this principle might create the necessity of making appointments by which the brethren at the North would either in fact or in the opinion of the Christian community become responsible for institutions which they could not, with a good conscience, sanction. 3. Were such a case to occur, we would not desire our brethren to violate their convictions of duty by making such appointments, but should consider it incumbent on them to refer the case to the Convention for its decision.[148]

This led to the formal withdrawal of the various Southern state conventions and auxiliary foreign mission societies from the national body; and at the suggestion of the Foreign Missionary Society of the Virginia Baptists the Southern Baptists met in May, 1845, to take independent action.

At about the same time there was difficulty in the Baptist Home Mission Society. This society had to consider the recommendation of the Georgia Baptist Convention, which wished a certain slaveholder as a missionary. Their representatives wrote:

We wish his appointment so much the more as it will stop the mouths of gainsayers. . . . There are good brethren among us, who notwithstanding the transactions of your society at Philadelphia, are hard to believe that you will appoint a slave-holder a missionary, even when the funds are supplied by those who wish his appointment.[149]

The board, however, decided at its meeting in October, 1844, that the proposal introduced the subject of slavery in direct contravention of the society's rules and that it was not at liberty to entertain the application. This decision added to the movement which was making inevitable the separation of Northern and Southern Baptists. This happened with relatively little bitterness, due to the high character of the leaders on both sides. The Southerners organized a Southern

Baptist Convention, May 8–11, 1845. They adopted an address to various groups, including "all candid men," in which they stated:

A painful division has taken place in the missionary operations of the American Baptists. We would explain the origin, the principles, and the objects of that division, or the peculiar circumstances in which the organization of the Southern Baptist Convention became necessary. Let not the extent of this disunion be exaggerated. At the present time it involves only the foreign and domestic missions of the denomination. Northern and Southern Baptists are still brethren. They differ in no article of the faith. They are guided by the same principles of gospel order. Fanatical attempts have indeed been made, in some quarters, to exclude us of the South from Christian fellowship. We do not retort these attempts, and believe their extent to be comparatively limited. Our Christian fellowship is not, as we feel, a matter to be obtruded upon any one. We abide by that of our God, his dear Son, and all his baptized followers. The few ultra-Northern brethren to whom we allude must take what course they please. *Their* conduct has not influenced us in this movement. We do not regard the rupture as extending to foundation principles, nor can we think that the great body of our Northern brethren will so regard it. . . .

We claim to have acted in the premises with liberality toward our Northern brethren. Thrust from the common platform of equal rights, between the Northern and Southern churches, we have but reconstructed that platform. . . . Have they thrust us off? We retain but one feeling in the case: *that we will not practically leave it on any account,* much less in obedience to such usurped authority, or in deference to such a manifest breach of trust as is here involved; a breach of covenant that looks various ways—heavenward and earthward. For we repeat, THEY WOULD FORBID US TO *speak unto* THE GENTILES. . . . "One thing is certain"—we must go everywhere preaching the word. "We can never be a party to any arrangement" for monopolizing the gospel; any arrangement which, like that of the Autocratical Interdict of the North, would first drive us from our beloved colored people, of whom they prove that they know nothing comparatively, and from the much-wronged aborigines of the country; and then cut us off from the whitening fields of the heathen harvest-labor, to which by cogent appeals and solemn prayers they have so often protested that, without us, they were inadequate. . . .[150]

Whatever the effects of separation may have been on the Christian Church as a whole, the intense loyalty of the South to its own institutions and the fact that conventions of the denomination were now held in that region, led there to the intensification of denominational loyalty.

The Southern Convention showed at its meeting in 1846 its desire to continue the work of evangelizing the Negro population.

Resolved, That in view of the present condition of the African race, and in view of the indications of Divine Providence toward that portion of the great family of fallen men, we feel that a solemn obligation rests not only upon the Convention, but upon all Christians, to furnish them with the gospel and a suitable Christian ministry.[151]

In spite of these resolutions the colored Baptists soon withdrew in most cases to state conventions of their own, and developed into a denominational force under the National Baptist Convention, U.S.A., Inc.

(c) *The Presbyterians.*—Let us turn now to the Presbyterians, who, it will be remembered, had twenty years before (1818) gone on record against slavery.[152]

As a result of the schism of 1837–38 the Old and New Schools were nearly equal in size, but the Old was stronger in property, while the New had been weakened by many of its member churches becoming Congregational. In the years immediately following the schism neither branch wished to take definite action on slavery. But the New School, though naturally more inclined to follow the declaration of 1818, was soon split over the issue, which was brought up vigorously by the New England group.

At the New School General Assembly in 1846 a declaration was adopted to the effect that slavery was wrong, and urging the Church to do away with the evil. This proposal had a large majority. In 1849 the General Assembly passed a resolution to the effect that "It is the duty of all Christians . . . as speedily as possible to efface this blot on our whole religion."[153]

The General Assembly (New School) in 1850 adopted the following:

We exceedingly deplore the working of the whole system of slavery as it exists in our country and is interwoven with the political institutions of the slave-holding States, as fraught with many and great evils to the civil, political, and moral interests of those regions where it exists.

The holding of our fellow-men in the condition of slavery, except in those cases where it is unavoidable, by the laws of the State, the obligations of guardianship, or the demands of humanity, is an offence in the proper import of that term, as used in the Book of Discipline, chap. i, sec. 3, and should be regarded and treated in the same manner as other offences.

The sessions and presbyteries are, by the Constitution of our church, the courts of primary jurisdiction for the trial of offences.

That, after this declaration of sentiment, the whole subject of slavery, as it exists in the church, be referred to the sessions and presbyteries, to take such action thereon as in their judgment the laws of Christianity require.[154]

The New Englanders had increasingly the support of Western groups, such as the synods of Utica, Genesee, and Western Reserve, in urging the General Assembly to make a clean break with slaveholders.[155]

The second paragraph quoted above was reaffirmed in 1853, when the Assembly proceeded to ask the Presbyterians in each of the slave states to provide full information regarding slaveholding by members. One of the presbyteries—that of Lexington, Kentucky—replied that its ministers and members were slaveholders both on principle and by choice. This attitude was severely condemned by the Assembly, and made the withdrawal of the Southern section of the New School almost inevitable.[156]

The Assembly in 1857, after long discussion, adopted resolutions condemning those who considered slavery "an ordinance of God," and in this country both "Scriptural and right."[157] The Southern churches, not in sympathy with these resolutions, had already decided to establish a Church in which the rights and wrongs of slavery would not be discussed. As a result, the United Synod of the Presbyterian Church was established. Later it merged with the Presbyterian Church in the Confederate States.

Among the Old School Presbyterians the matter came to a head in the Assembly in 1845. This declined to accept the demand of the antislavery delegates. By a vote of 168 to 13, though opposing any cruel treatment of slaves, it recognized no responsibility on the part of the Church to prevent these evils or to hasten emancipation.[158]

The church of Christ is a spiritual body, whose jurisdiction extends only to the religious faith, and moral conduct of her members. She cannot legislate where Christ has not legislated, nor make terms of membership which he has not made. The question, therefore, which this Assembly is called upon to decide, is this: Do the Scriptures teach that the holding of slaves, without regard to circumstances, is a sin, the renunciation of which should be made a condition of membership in the church of Christ.[159]

The Assembly found it impossible to answer this question in the affirmative without contradicting the teachings of the Bible. It consequently decided that it could not "denounce the holding of slaves as necessarily a heinous and scandalous sin."[160] It did not wish, however, to put itself on record as finding no evil in slavery.

In so saying, however, the Assembly are not to be understood as denying that there is evil connected with slavery. Much less do they approve those defective and oppressive laws by which, in some of the States, it is regulated. Nor would they by any means countenance the traffic in slaves for the sake of gain; the separation of husbands and wives, parents and children, for the sake of "filthy lucre" or for the convenience of the master; or cruel treatment of slaves in any respect. . . .

Nor is this Assembly to be understood as countenancing the idea that masters may regard their servants as *mere property,* and not as human beings, rational, accountable, immortal. The Scriptures prescribe not only the duties of servants, but of masters also, warning the latter to discharge those duties, "knowing that their Master is in heaven, neither is there respect of persons with him."

The Apostles of Christ sought to ameliorate the condition of slaves, not by denouncing and excommunicating their masters, but by teaching both masters and slaves the glorious doctrines of the gospel, and enjoining upon each the discharge of their relative duties. Thus only can the church of Christ, as such, now improve the condition of the slaves in our country.[161]

In view of the principles stated, the General Assembly took the ground "that the existence of domestic slavery, under the circumstances in which it is found in the southern portion of the country, is no bar to Christian communion," and thereupon declined "to make the holding of slaves in itself a matter of discipline," action which it believed would separate the Church, North and South.[162]

This action was reinforced in 1849, when the Assembly resolved

that in view of the civil and domestic nature of this institution, and the competency of our secular Legislatures alone to remove it . . . it is considered peculiarly improper and inexpedient for this General Assembly to attempt to propose measures in the work of emancipation.[163]

The leader in determining the Assembly's action in 1845 and 1849 was the Reverend Dr. Nathan L. Rice (1807–77), later moderator of the Church. He thus set forth his position:

The Presbyterian Church has stood at an equal remove from the extremes of Abolitionism and Pro-slaveryism. She has refused to pervert God's word to make it either denounce or sanction slavery. She has regarded it as a great evil, but as an evil inherited, an evil of long standing, and so interwoven with the very texture of society, that, like a chronic disease, it must require much time, and patience, and kind treatment, to eradicate it. She is fully persuaded, that for the evils under which mankind suffer, the Gospel is the great and only remedy. Refusing, therefore, to mingle in heterogeneous conventions, and to sanction their vague and unmeaning resolutions, she goes forward on her sublime mission, preaching the Gospel alike to master and slave, saying openly and boldly all the apostles said, and refusing to say a word more. And today she stands ready to compare notes, as to results, with her traducers.[164]

As a result, the Old School, which had tried to maintain a middle position, was apparently antiabolitionist, and a large group was getting ready to throw itself over onto the proslavery side. In 1861, when its Assembly met in Philadelphia with the border states fully represented, the Southerners, eight of whose states had already seceded, were generally in no humor to attend a convention in the North, and only sixteen attended. The Assembly by a vote of 156 to 66 adopted resolutions

in the spirit of Christian patriotism [to] acknowledge and declare our obligations to promote and perpetuate, so far as in us lies, the integrity of the United States, and to strengthen, uphold and encourage the Federal Government [defined by an explanatory clause as meaning merely "the central administration"] in the exercise of all its functions under our noble Constitution. . . .[165]

Even these mild resolutions in support of the Union were, however, too much for the South. Consequently, the Southern Old School constituency of the Presbyterian Church, being more interested in maintaining the institution of slavery than the Federal Union, broke away from their former Northern colleagues and formed later the same year (1861) the General Assembly of the Presbyterian Church in the Confederate States of America. Its remarkable address "To all the Churches of Jesus Christ throughout the Earth" is reproduced later when we discuss Church-State problems in the Confederacy.[166]

The Dutch Reformed Church, historically closely related to the Presbyterians, being almost entirely in the North, and supporting the Union side, was relatively little affected by the slavery controversy.

(d) *The Congregationalists and Other Closely Related Independent Churches.*—This was the period when the Congregationalists and Unitarians of New England were becoming very active in the antislavery cause. William Ellery Channing (1780–1842), Samuel Joseph May (1797–1871), Charles G. Finney (1792–1815), Horace Bushnell (1802–76), and Henry Ward Beecher (1813–87) were characteristic of the most influential antislavery preachers of this period. The work of these men is so well known as to require no extended statement here.[167] Less remembered today, but equally effective, was Theodore Parker (1810–60), a Unitarian minister who contributed powerfully to the antislavery cause. He was perhaps the most intellectual of the group, and, though he departed too far from orthodoxy to appeal to the masses in America of the mid-nineteenth century, his opposition to slavery came not only from his humanitarianism but from his deep religious sense. To him democracy was "the enactment of God's justice into human laws,"[168] and such laws could not tolerate slavery. He did much to awaken the conscience of the North, beginning with his sermon on the subject in 1841. He was not as extreme as Garrison and Wendell Phillips, but sympathized fundamentally with the abolitionists. He vigorously opposed the Fugitive Slave Law of 1850, took fugitive slaves into his own home, and attacked the institution of slavery from pulpit and lyceum throughout New England.

Another highly important Congregational influence at this time was the publication in 1851–52 by Harriet Beecher Stowe (1811–96) of *Uncle Tom's Cabin.* The book, descriptive of life under slavery, created such a furore both among advocates and opponents that it must be listed, with such national events as the Kansas-Nebraska bill two years later and the Dred Scott decision (1857), as among the events which hastened the Civil War. Mrs. Stowe was the product of the reform spirit as represented in Congregationalism; the daughter of a famous minister, the Reverend Lyman Beecher (1775–1863), the sister of a leading abolitionist, the Reverend Henry Ward Beecher, and the wife of a professor in a New England Congregational college (Bowdoin). Therefore the book—in spite of the fact that its author never allied herself with militant abolitionism—was always identified in the public mind with the typical religious attitude of New England toward slavery; an attitude hostile to the institution rather than to the slaveholder. Some three hundred thousand copies were sold in the first year, and more than a million by 1860. The book was translated into many languages, and dramatized, and secured the greatest audience of any novel up to its time.

When the Kansas–Nebraska bill, which threw overboard the Missouri Compromise and made possible and likely the extension of slavery in the Northwest, was under debate in Congress in 1854, the reaction of the New England clergy was "prompt, spontaneous, emphatic, and practically unanimous"[169] in protest, and they began active aid to the movement to settle Kansas with "Free-Soilers" —a movement to be discussed in a later section.[170]

It is particularly interesting to note the attitude of the German population. The Evangelical Association, which was strongest in Pennsylvania, is believed to have never wittingly had a slaveholder in its membership. In 1839 its General Conference took action declaring slavery and traffic in slaves a great evil, to be abhorred by every Christian, and strictly prohibiting any member from holding slaves or trafficking in them.[171]

(e) *The Quakers and Moravians.*—The Friends had always been interested in the cause of the Negro. Few of them held slaves, and many became active in the cause of emancipation, which they thought, in accordance with their general principles, should be brought about through moral suasion rather than through political action. They not only in general would not engage slave labor, but they refused to buy articles which had been grown or produced by it. They frequently bought freedom for slaves, especially in cases where they saw families being separated. They also frequently attended Negro gatherings so as to make them legal in states where such gatherings could not be held without the presence of white persons, and they taught many night schools for slaves. Aside from occasionally signing petitions they were not as a group identified with the political abolition cause. But they were very active, North and South, in anti-slavery societies. For example, by 1827 there were fifty such societies in North Carolina alone, with half as many in Tennessee, and these were mainly due to their activity.[172] As the Civil War approached they became less and less influential in the South, because most of those who had been active in the agitation against slavery had found conditions so unsympathetic that they had moved to Indiana and other places in the Middle West where their influence was to be effective in later years. They also were leaders in the Underground Railway and in the colonization societies.

The most prominent of the Quakers in the antislavery cause at the middle of the century was John Greenleaf Whittier (1807–92). His poems and articles did much to stimulate the movement, his *Songs for Freedom* being particularly effective. He appealed to the Christian conscience, and never advocated the use of force in the abolition of slavery.

Undoubtedly a large majority of the Friends, at least in the North and West, voted for Abraham Lincoln in 1860, believing him to be a representative of real freedom. There is an interesting correspondence between him and Eliza P. Gurney, who had made a visit to Lincoln on what she felt to be a divine mission regarding emancipation. That it was appreciated by the president is shown by the fact that it was found in his vest pocket after his death. In Lincoln's letter to her he showed his sympathetic understanding of the Quaker position.

> Your people, the Friends, have had and are having a very great trial. On principle and faith opposed to both war and oppression, they can only practically oppose oppression by war. In this hard dilemma some have chosen one horn and some the other. For those appealing to me on conscientious grounds I have done and shall do the best I could and can, in my own conscience, under my oath to the law.[173]

She replied by maintaining the position that wrong could not be set right by wrong,—that is, the use of force; but many nominal Quakers joined the Army. Relatively few of these, however, were actively identified with the Quaker faith, though it was a Hicksite Quaker who wrote the song "We are Coming, Father Abram." Many who enlisted were disowned by their yearly meetings; and in the South many Friends, in spite of much pressure and some persecution, refused to bear arms.[174] The Confederate government, realizing their predicament, created an exemption tax which many paid.

(f) *The Episcopalians.*—The Protestant Church which found itself in the most difficult position as the war approached was the Episcopal. It was one of the few Protestant Churches which had not taken, prior to the war, a position of direct opposition to Negro slavery. In many cases, such as those of the Methodists, Baptists, and Presbyterians, division between North and South on the slavery issue had had much to do with developing the sectional feeling that produced the war. The fact that the Episcopal Church had not divided on the subject had both disadvantages and advantages. It had the disadvantage of causing the Church to be regarded as having held aloof from a great national moral issue. But the Church had the advantage of retaining its unity, so that it did not share the difficulty of most other communions in bringing North and South together after the war. Its failure to take decisive action brought forth the rebuke of Bishop William Wilberforce (1759–1833), the great emancipator, who exclaimed with horror that

The Spirit of Missions, edited with the sanction of the Church, and with the eye of the Bishop of New York, proposes to endow a mission school in Louisiana with a plantation to be worked by slaves.[175]

The reasons why the Episcopal Church was not more clear-cut on the slavery issue are not hard to find. The Church was then absorbed in the split threatened between evangelical low churchmen and high churchmen influenced by the Tractarian movement. It had also not fully overcome the prejudices and disabilities inherited from the Revolution; and was deeply interested in strengthening its position in the East and South and carrying out missionary work in the West. Then too it had inherited, from its Church of England past, a feeling that Church and State held two very distinct spheres and that the Church should not get too much entangled in political questions. This idea was cultivated by the Southern members, who represented mostly the slaveholding planter class, and was strengthened by the fact that John Henry Hopkins (1792–1868), a pronounced high churchman, who became Bishop of Vermont in 1832, and presided, because of seniority, at the meetings of the bishops at the General Conventions in 1862 and 1865, was one of the relatively few prominent Northern clergymen who supported the slavery cause. This he did by several books, among which is *A Scriptural, Ecclesiastical, and Historical View of Slavery,* 1864. As a result of these and other factors the Episcopal Church, as such, seems to have taken no definite attitude on the slavery question in the years preceding the war, and when the war came on—as we shall see in the next section—though it came out strongly for preserving the Union, it did not deal with the slavery question nationally, in this respect being in the same position as the Roman Catholics. There was a strong minority group and there were individual leaders in the antislavery cause, but the Church as a whole was silent. The combination of Southern conservatives and Northern high churchmen prevented any constructive action against slavery.

The Church did not object when the Bishop of South Carolina denounced the "malignant philanthropy of abolition." It was at the time relatively stronger in the South than in the North, and in the South its membership was largely of the slaveholding group, while in the North it had only begun to regain the public standing it had lost because so many of its clergy were Tories in the Revolutionary War. So it felt that it was the part of wisdom not to identify itself too definitely with either side in a political issue. The leading Southern bishops opposed secession, but when it became a political fact they felt that it carried with it ecclesiastical separation. They retained the old idea that the national Church was made by a voluntary compact of autonomous state churches, and some of their leaders had even opposed the degree of unification of effort represented by the establishment of the General Missionary Society and the General

Theological Seminary.[176] These were to serve the needs of the whole Church, not merely of a diocese.

(g) *The Disciples of Christ.*—The Disciples of Christ were not active as a denomination in the slavery controversy. In the middle of the last century they were a relatively small denomination in the center of the nation, numbering only 40,000 in 1840, 118,000 in 1850, and 225,000 in 1860.[177] They were strong in Ohio, Kentucky, Indiana, Missouri, and the neighboring states, especially in the border states and counties; and consequently they took on the whole a moderate position. They were not well-to-do people and did not come from sections with many large plantations. They owned relatively few slaves, and since they found the master-slave relationship existing in New Testament times, they did not consider slavery morally wrong. They were inclined, however, to think it very inexpedient and a condition which the country should outgrow, but they had no patience with abolitionism. Probably the views of Alexander Campbell (1778–1866), their founder, and first president of their American Christian Missionary Society, may be taken as representative. In 1845 he wrote a series of articles on "Our Position to American Slavery." Some extracts will throw light on the denominational point of view:

> . . . Our position is not that of a politician, an economist, a mere moralist; but that of a Christian. Our premises are not the Declaration of American Independence, the bills of political rights or wrongs, natural religion, natural conscience, natural liberty; but the Christian Oracles. . . . I stand or fall by supernatural religion or revelation. . . .
>
> When I affirm that the New Testament recognizes *without censure* the *relation* of master and slave, I do not say that it sanctions the *legalized treatment* of either masters or slaves according to the American or any other code. I do not say that the New Testament authorizes a master to treat his servants as he treats his mules or his oxen; that if he feed, clothe, and house them well, find them abundance of wholesome food in health, medicine and medical attendance in sickness that then he has "rendered unto them that which is *just* and *equal*." They have souls as well as bodies; they have powers of reason; they have conscience, moral instincts, moral feelings, and are susceptible of spiritual enjoyments, of immortality, and eternal life. They have the rights of husbands and of wives—of parents and children; and any code that takes these away from them is not of God, but of men. Moral training, religious and moral instruction, they must have among their inalienable rights and privileges. These cannot be withholden by Christian masters without the forfeiture of Christian character and Christian privilege, no matter under what code of laws such injustice is perpetrated.
>
> When, then, I strongly affirm my long cherished and deeply impressed conviction that the New Testament sanctions the relation of master and slave, when such relation is providentially existing in any community, I do not maintain that it sanctions any

man in "man-stealing," in taking away the liberty of any man born free, or in withholding from those "born in his house or bought with his money" any of these specified rights, immunities, and privileges above enumerated. . . .[178]

In the following article he gives a carefully considered summary of his position:

To conclude, our views of American slavery and our position to it are summarily expressed in three propositions:—

1. That the relation of master and slave is not in itself sinful or immoral.

2. That, nevertheless, slavery as practised in any portion of the civilized world, is *inexpedient;* because not in harmony with the spirit of the age nor the moral advancement of society; because in itself, as fully demonstrated, not favorable to individual and national prosperity; and because it imposes on Christian masters and their families burdens and responsibilities not easily discharged in existing circumstances; and which, not discharged, prevent the refined and elevated personal and domestic happiness so desirable to any Christian household.

3. That no Christian community, governed by the Bible, Old Testament or New, can constitutionally and rightfully make the simple relation of master and slave a term of Christian fellowship or a subject of discipline, while in duty bound in this case, as in all others, to take cognizance of any neglect or violation of the relative duties obligatory on the parties. . . .[179]

Dr. Campbell declares that these expressions of his views—which he sums up by saying that he has always been "anti-slavery, but never an abolitionist"—have received the support "of all whose approbation and cooperation is desirable" and "from all parties."[180]

The Disciples do not seem, as an organization, to have taken any significant direct action on the question of slavery, but several related actions show their interest in improving the condition of the Negro. They acted in 1853 in favor of missionary work in Liberia; they suggested that a qualified Negro be freed and sent there as a missionary; they extended "the hand of Christian Love and Sympathy" to the Negro "Brother" chosen; they opposed secession; and when the war finally came on they not only started missionary work among the freedmen behind the lines in the border states, but the Board of Managers of the American Christian Missionary Society, meeting in Cincinnati in October, 1861, passed with only one dissenting voice this resolution:

Resolved, That we deeply sympathize with the loyal and patriotic in our country, in the present effort to sustain the Government of the United States. And we feel it our duty as Christians, to ask our brethren everywhere to do all in their power to sustain the proper and constitutional authorities of the Union.[181]

The Disciples of Christ were primarily interested in personal religion and evangelization, not in political and social reform. As a result, they were not active as a denomination in the slavery controversy, and they did not suffer any formal separation between North and South on the slavery issue or the resulting Civil War.[182]

(h) *The Lutherans.*—As the Lutheran Church had in 1840 twelve hundred congregations, one hundred thousand communicants and a constituency of nearly half a million,[183] its position on the slavery controversy was of some importance. The historic attitude of Lutheranism has been to make a fairly clear-cut distinction between the sacred and the secular, and consequently for the Church to take little part in public affairs.[184] Most of the synods and ministeriums, such as those of Missouri, New York, Ohio, and Pennsylvania, were extremely conservative in all matters. They tended to keep the Lutheran Church a thing apart both from other religious bodies and from all discussion of reform movements in the outside world. This attitude continued to be dominant during the period preceding the American Civil War, with only a few impressive departures from it. Even in the new West some synods took no action on slavery before secession, and, more important, the oldest Lutheran bodies in the country, the New York and Pennsylvania ministeriums, did not even officially consider the question during the whole period preceding the War.[185] But especially in Pennsylvania there were certain synods which remained outside of these groups.

It is an impressive evidence of the early aloofness of most Lutheran congregations from the political issue of slavery that the Church did not follow the usual Protestant pattern of dividing into Northern and Southern sections until the war was well advanced, 1863, when "The General Synod of the Evangelical Church in the Confederate States of America" was formed.[186] Georgia—where the Salzbergers, early opponents of slavery, had settled in 1734—North and South Carolina, and Virginia had a considerable Lutheran population.

The most striking exception to this general aloofness of the Lutheran Church on the issue of slavery, as distinct from that of union, was in northern New York. The Hartwick Synod, representing churches in Albany and to the west, had discussed the matter in 1836, and much difference of opinion appeared. Largely as a result of this a group of ministers who were opponents of slavery withdrew with their congregations in 1837, and formed the rival Franckean Synod. This was so radical on slavery and other moral reform subjects that it was denied admission to the relatively liberal General Synod until 1864.[187] The constitution of the new synod, unanimously adopted in May, 1837, by the representatives of twenty-one congregations and 1,650 communicants, provided that no minister could be a member who was a slaveholder, or who engaged in the slave traffic, or who advocated slavery; and no layman who was a slaveholder or in the liquor business.[188] The day after adopting the constitution certain advanced resolutions were passed under the heading of "American Slavery."

1. Resolved, That Slavery as it exists in the United States, . . . is a sin . . ., opposed to the spirit of the Gospel and a violation of the inalienable rights of man.

2. Resolved, That we do not deem it inexpedient for ecclesiastical bodies to interfere with the abolition of slavery; but that it is the duty of all such bodies of every evangelical denomination, to bear their decided testimony against the *Sin* of Slavery.

3. Resolved, That we have abundant cause for deep humiliation before God, that, as a denomination, we are so deeply involved in the *Sin of Slavery,* and that so many of our ministers practice the crime, and that so many others justify them in this iniquity.

4. Resolved, That we view the traffic in human beings as carried on in this country between the ministers of the Gospel and members of the churches, as revolting to humanity and as repugnant to the laws of Christ, as ever was the foreign slave trade.[189]

The Franckean Synod was so interested in the abolition of slavery that it adopted many other resolutions and reports on the subject from 1838 on, and published a journal, the *Lutheran Herald,* to advance its objectives. Its attitude was so advanced that it was condemned in 1839 by the General Synod.[190] But in spite of the rebuff it continued its agitation. In 1841 it went so far as to pass unanimously a resolution recommending to ministers and churches not to admit to their pulpits or to the Lord's Supper "any person who is a slaveholder or traffics in human beings . . . ,"[191] and, to promote its views, unanimously adopted a *Fraternal Appeal* on the subject of slavery to be sent to each evangelical Lutheran synod and to be published.[192] This had some influence. For example in 1844 the Allegheny Synod, probably due to proddings by the New York radicals, passed these resolutions:

Resolved, That the time has in our opinion arrived, when ecclesiastical associations are in duty bound to express their views on the system of American Slavery.

Therefore, Resolved, That we believe this system to be a moral, civil and religious evil, in conflict with the best interests of society, oppressive in its character and dishonorable to God and man.[193]

This was shortly followed by this support from the Ohio Synod:

In regard to a petition for an expression of sentiment on Slavery by the Synod, it was

Resolved, That this Synod regards slavery as an evil, which all Christians should deplore.[194]

The Synod of the West did not go as far, but its action shows the influence of the Franckean attitude:

Resolved, That we feel grateful to the Franckean Synod for their well meant attempt to enlighten us on the subject of American Slavery, and that our minds being always open to conviction on any subject, so soon as conviction has done its work, we will act; at the same time recommend to them the propriety of considering well the measures of abolitionists in the present day before they act.[195]

The leaven was working. The Pittsburgh Synod and the Synod of Wittenberg, Ohio, became specially active in opposing slavery.[196]

These favorable actions, as well as indifference in some places, and opposition to its views in most Lutheran synods, stirred the Franckean Synod to take more aggressive steps. In 1846 it condemned the Mexican War as carried on for the protection, perpetuation, and enlargement of American slavery;[197] in 1851 it strongly opposed the Fugitive Slave Law;[198] and in 1856 its "Report on Slavery" condemned the "Slave Power" in Texas, Kansas, Nebraska, Nicaragua, Cuba, and the Isthmus of Darien.[199] Evidently the leaders of this group had a deep and broad interest in the subject and were dead in earnest. We can, therefore, see that the Franckean Synod, which at about the peak of its influence in 1850 included only fifty churches and 3,213 communicants,[200] is a good example of how a small body with convictions and able leadership can wield a large influence in matters involving moral ideals.

Most of the Western synods took no action,[201] while the Southern Lutheran churches followed the pattern of their section and strongly opposed the Abolitionists, or in view of the Church's historical attitude of carrying the separation of Church and State to the point of expressing *no* views on public matters, remained silent. Typical synodical actions in the South follow:

The Synod of South Carolina, 1835:

1. Resolved, unanimously, that this Synod express their strongest disapprobation of the conduct of the Northern Abolitionists—that we look upon them as enemies of our beloved country; whose mistaken zeal is calculated to injure the cause of morals and religion.

2. Resolved, that we will hold no correspondence with the Northern Abolitionists, and that should they send to us any of their incendiary publications, we will immediately return them.

3. Resolved, that whilst we learn with heartfelt pleasure, that none of the ministers in our connexion in the United States, have adopted the sentiments of the Abolitionists; the members of this Synod pledge themselves, in behalf of their churches in connexion with them, that they will never countenance such doctrines.[202]

The same synod, 1836:

It having been stated, that some person or persons, in all probability of our own creed, living, perhaps, in the distant North, had made violent and unchristian attacks upon some of the clerical members of this Body by name, in some of the Northern prints, for holding property in the persons of Slaves, some expression of the opinion of this Body ensued, relative to the manner in which all attacks should be treated, and the impropriety and injustice of the interference or intermeddling of any religious or deliberative Body with the subject of *Slavery* and *Slave-holding, emancipation* or *abolitionism,* as agitated by the *affected patriots* and *self-interested,* and *more than rotten hearted benefactors* of this much commiserated race. As a full expression of the firm and unchanging determination of this Body, therefore:

XVI. Resolved, That this Synod will not at any time, enter into a discussion of Slavery, as agitated by the Abolitionists of the day, with such an entire absence of principle, and which has already produced such painful results in the deliberative councils and churches, in some branches of Christendom.[203]

The Synod of Virginia, 1835:

That this body view Abolitionism as a combination of ignorance, fanaticism, and dishonesty—alike opposed to our civil and religious institutions, and of a piece with all ultraism—folly.

Resolved, That we discountenance the circulation of all so-called religious papers, which are designed to support the cause of the abolitionists.[204]

The same Synod, 1839:

1. Resolved, That this body disclaims the ecclesiastical censorship of any particular Synod.

2. Resolved, That the pretensions of this description assumed by the Franckean Synod in regard to other ecclesiastical bodies, meet with our decided disapprobation, and that we totally discard any such arrogant assumption of synodical censorship.

3. Resolved, That we will not encourage the circulation of the "Lutheran Herald," published under the auspices of that body, among our members, and that we warmly recommend the "Lutheran Observer" to all who desire a religious paper. . . .[205]

It should be noted that these actions are in denunciation of abolitionism rather than defense of slavery. It should also be noted that some of the synods, such as that of North Carolina, gave attention at this time to the better care and religious instruction of slaves.[206]

In general then, with the notable exception of the Franckean Synod, the Lutheran Church, due to its historic position of serving the State almost entirely through its religious and moral efforts to transform individual lives, rather than to influence corporately its public policy, stood much more apart from the slavery issue than most Protestant bodies.[207] This is shown by the fact that a standard history of the Lutheran Church in this country makes practically no reference to the subject from the founding of our government to the beginning of the Civil War.[208] It was this same tradition of conscientiously abstaining from taking part in public issues even in a national moral crisis, that helped to account for the ineffective opposition of Lutheranism to Nazism in the early days of the Hitler regime, although later some Lutheran leaders took a heroic stand. But as we shall see, the Lutheran Church in this country is becoming definitely more "activist" as a denomination.[209]

(i) *The Roman Catholics.*—The attitude of the Roman Catholic Church in the period immediately preceding the Civil War differs from that of most other religious bodies, as it held practically aloof from the discussion of slavery then, and indeed throughout the war. Its attitude was due to historic and practical reasons. It found slavery in the world, and, although it worked steadily for the alleviation of the condition of slaves and most of its leaders did not favor slavery, the Church did not officially condemn the system.[210]

The Church in America was in a difficult position, for it had no evidence that the modern papacy had condemned slavery as such. The early Christian Church had done much for the slave. St. Paul's teaching was clear: "For by one Spirit we are all baptized into one body, whether we be Jews or Gentiles, whether we be bond or free. . . ." Slaves were admitted to the Church, and prior to the time of Gregory the Great (*c.* 540–604) even to offices in it; but the laws of the State regarding slavery were modified in the interest of humane treatment rather than by attempting to eliminate the institution. Manumission was encouraged but not demanded, and Augustine's predestinarian views, with their recognition of the natural inequalities of mankind, had large influence.[211] Therefore some slavery, including agricultural serfdom, continued on into the Middle Ages, but was gradually disappearing in Europe, due to economic and religious factors, until the discovery and colonization of America, with its demands for plantation labor, and the resulting African slave trade, caused its revival on a large scale both in the Catholic and Protestant territories of the New World. The Catholic Church made no effective protest; the lead in the abolition of African slavery was taken by the Protestant Christian humanitarians of England in the first third of the nineteenth century.

Only two or three of the popes had come out definitely against slavery; notably Pius II, who in 1462 called it "a great crime." Several forbade the enslavement of the Indians; but there was apparently no clear-cut condemnation of slavery, as distinct from the slave trade, in any of the Church councils or more important papal utterances.[212] In general the Church had compromised with it as a social evil which might be tolerated while at the same time the conditions of the slave were ameliorated.

Gregory XVI had issued on December 3, 1839, his apostolic letter[213] on slavery. This had been a strong condemnation of the *slave trade,* but it had nothing whatever to say against domestic slavery. An attempt was made by the secretary of state under President Van Buren, the Honorable John Forsyth (1780–1841), to influence the voters of Georgia against the candidacy of General Harrison for the presidency in 1840, by laying emphasis on what he believed to be the pope's condemnation of domestic slavery and consequent lining up with the abolitionists. As a result came the so-called "Letters of Forsyth,"[214] written by the leading Catholic prelate in the country at this time, Bishop John England (1786–1842) of South Carolina. In one of these letters Bishop England distinguished between the slave trade, as already prohibited by this country and by the European nations, and domestic slavery. He said: "The Pope neither mentions nor alludes to this latter in his Apostolic Letter, which is directed, as were those of his predecessors, solely and exclusively against the former."[215]

This point of view met with no protest from Bishop England's fellow prelates, and it is therefore clear evidence that they all understood the papal pronouncement and Catholic teaching in the same way. The apostolic letter had also been read at the recent council of Baltimore, and it has been authoritatively stated that

> If they had believed the letter contained a condemnation of domestic slavery they would have been obliged either to forward a protest to the Holy See or to take steps against the retention of slaves by the many Catholic slaveholders in their dioceses. We have no evidence that any one of the seven embraced either course.[216]

Furthermore, in a letter of October 7, 1840, Bishop England states that

> The existence of slavery is considered by our theologians to be as little incompatible with the natural law as is the existence of property. . . . Slavery, then, sir, is regarded by that Church of which the Pope is the presiding officer, not to be incompatible with the natural law.[217]

It may be said that in general the Roman Catholic Church had inherited the position that slavery under American conditions would be tolerated, but that every possible effort should be made to ameliorate the condition of slaves. It was not the "God-given institution" of some Southern advocates, nor did forced speedy abolition seem the wisest policy. Such was the general attitude of the Church as the war came on.

Bishop England's eighteen able letters defending the thesis that the Roman Catholic Church had never considered or taught domestic slavery to be immoral made many people think that he himself favored slavery, so under date of February 25, 1841, he wrote a letter to the editors of the *United States Catholic Miscellany*.

> I have been asked by many, a question which I may as well answer at once, viz: Whether I am friendly to the existence or continuation of slavery? I am not—but I

also see the impossibility of now abolishing it here. When it can and ought to be abolished, is a question for the legislature and not for me.[218]

The author of the monograph entitled *The Catholic Church in the United States During the Civil War Period (1852–1866),* the Reverend Robert Joseph Murphy, to whom I am indebted for most of the facts and quotations in this section, thus summarizes the situation brought out by the England correspondence:

This [letter of February 25, 1841] is the most positive statement we have from any Catholic authority. Together with the Letters of Forsyth it presents a crystallization of the three points in the Catholic attitude—slavery is not wrong; it is a system that must be done away with; the abolitionists are too immediate and radical in their demands—any action against it should be gradual, and should be accomplished only with the utmost respect for legal process.

It is safe to say that Bishop England's views can be taken as representing those of the majority of his fellow prelates. He was of the South and should for that reason have been even more favorable to slavery than most of the others who had Northern interests and sympathies. Dr. Hughes and Archbishop Kenrick were at one with him in their attitude toward abolition and emancipation, and nowhere do we find a Catholic bishop espousing this cause. It has been seen that Catholic distrust of abolition lasted through the Civil War.

One looks in vain through the records of the first seven Provincial Councils of Baltimore held at intervals from 1829 to 1849 for any mention of the slavery controversy or any allusion to the Catholic attitude. . . .[219]

The latest student of the subject after independent investigation reaches the same conclusion as to the attitude of the councils: "From none of these came any direct expression of opinion on the slavery question."[220]

When the First Plenary Council of the Roman Catholic Church in the United States was held in Baltimore in 1852 the slavery discussion was at its height, but "nowhere in Decrees, or in Pastoral Letter is there mention of slavery or abolition."[221] In other words, the hierarchy, following the historic tradition of the Church, refused to take sides in the issue of domestic slavery. Similarly, the Ninth Provincial Council of Baltimore in 1858 referred to domestic slavery only to dismiss it as a subject on which the Church would not take sides. A quotation from the pastoral letter issued by its bishops shows the point of view of the Church:

Our clergy have wisely abstained from all interference with the judgment of the faithful which should be free on all questions of polity and social order, within the limits of the doctrine and law of Christ.[222]

Although history plainly testifies that the Church has always befriended the poor and laboring classes, and effectually procured the mitigation of the evils attached to servitude, until through her mild influence it has passed away from the nations of Europe, yet she has never disturbed established order, or endangered the peace of society, by following theories of philanthropy.[223]

The peaceful and conservative character of our principles . . . has been tested and made manifest in the great political struggles that have agitated the country on the subject of domestic slavery.[224]

As a result of this factor, which was strengthened by opposition to the English, who had been active in abolishing slavery in their colonies, and the other considerations mentioned, most of the Church leaders either held aloof from the controversy, or, as in the case of such influential journals as the *Pilot* of Boston or the *Catholic Advocate* of Kentucky, condemned abolitionism as an unwise measure advocated only by extreme radicals with no regard for private "property," as inconsistent with Catholic ideals, and as representing an unworthy attempt by the Church to influence the political activities of the State.

In a word, the Church did not feel called upon to try to change the status quo. As the *United States Catholic Miscellany,* in October, 1856, stated:

Catholics as such are the only religious body exempt from fanaticism on the slavery question and bound by their creed to the support of the Constitution.

We have given the official attitude of the Church. It must not be thought, however, that all Roman Catholics were equally noncommittal. Many individuals, of whom Orestes A. Brownson (1803–76), editor of *Brownson's Review,* the somewhat erratic but able New England minister converted to Catholicism in 1842, though changing his position from time to time, was on the whole a strong opponent of domestic slavery. It must be remembered, however, that most Roman Catholics had affiliated themselves with the Democrats, who were then the slavery party.

It should be added that the Roman Catholic Church was theoretically inclined to accept in general state rights views; a tendency it has since shown in opposing Federal action on many matters of social legislation such as prohibition and child labor, believing it better that such matters should be left to State and Church decisions, and that the Constitutional powers of the Federal government should not be too broadly interpreted. Remembering the conflict of more than fifteen hundred years ago between "Caesar and Christ," it has not wished to see the central political power become too strong in internal matters. Of course there has been a strong group, of which the late Monsignor John A. Ryan (1869–1945) was a distinguished representative, which has taken a different view,[225] but this has been on the whole the tendency until very recent times; and it had striking exemplification in the slavery controversy.

An authority on Catholics and slavery thus sums up the evidence on the attitude of the Church and its major causes:

Community custom and thought, the conservative tradition of the Church, dislike of abolitionism, the affiliation of so many Catholics with the Democratic Party, the immigrant status of the church membership, each of these contributed in some measure to influence the tenor of Catholic opinion. Important also was the position of the hierarchy, most of whom agreed that slavery was a domestic problem, jurisdiction over which belonged to the states where the slave system was an established institution. Suspicion of centralized authority was in part responsible for this attitude. Stemming in all probability from European conflicts between Church and State, it has helped to give Catholic social thought in this country a pronounced state rights bias.[226]

The Church as a matter of fact denied that slavery per se was intrinsically wrong from a religious standpoint; it advocated the gradual eradication of evils which had developed in the administration of the system; it held that emancipation, which was ultimately desirable, could be brought about only gradually and with due recompense to slaveholders; it condemned the abolition movement of the time as extreme, but at the same time was opposed to the slave trade; and in general its attitude toward the existence of domestic slavery was so neutral that it was frequently believed to be proslavery. This belief, however, does not seem to have been justified, though general failure to condemn the institution authoritatively did not show much active opposition to it. The Church was praised by the South for restraint. Alexander Stephens (1812–83), long in Congress from Georgia and later vice president of the Confederacy, wrote of Roman Catholics:

They have never warred against us or our peculiar institutions. No man can say as much of New England Baptists, Presbyterians or Methodists; the long roll of abolition petitions, with which Congress has been so agitated for past years, come not from the Catholics; their pulpits at the North are not desecrated every Sabbath with anathemas against slavery. And of the three thousand New England clergymen who sent the anti-Nebraska memorial to the Senate, not one was a Catholic. . . .[227]

(j) *The Jews.*—The Jews, as we shall see in a later section,[228] played a considerable part in the Civil War, but in the agitation over slavery which preceded it they were not very active. In general they conformed in attitude to the pattern of their community. The leading Jewish student of the subject, after giving various isolated instances showing the point of view of individuals and groups, sums up his conclusions by saying that "As a body, however, the Jews in America took no action either *pro* or *con* on the slavery question."[229] They were naturally sympathetic with freedom, but the supporters of slavery, both Christian and Jewish, could turn to many Old Testament texts and incidents that seemed to give it as an institution sanction under some circumstances, though stressing the need of the humane treatment of slaves.

(2) THE EXTREME NORTHERN ATTITUDE—MILITANT ABOLITIONISM

We have shown how strong the sentiment of the Northern Churches was in favor of putting an end to slavery. They were opposed not only to its extension but to its continuing existence. And yet many of them found it impossible to go all the way with William Lloyd Garrison (1805–79). In the earlier stages of the controversy the religious forces of New England had largely supported him, as we have seen.[230] But as he became more extreme in demanding absolute and immediate emancipation irrespective of consequences, and became increasingly denunciatory of all slaveholders, of the Churches, and of the Constitution, which he declared to be "a covenant with death and an agreement with Hell," many former Church supporters broke with him entirely. They and their societies became in turn the target for his venomous attacks. The very thought of gradual emancipation, which many of the clergy favored, was anathema to him.

In the *Liberator* are certain resolutions proposed by Garrison, which were unanimously passed at the twenty-third anniversary of the American Abolition Society in 1856:

> *Resolved:* That (making all due allowance for exceptional cases) the American Church continues to be the bulwark of slavery, and therefore impure in heart, hypocritical in profession, dishonest in practice, brutal in spirit, merciless in purpose. . . .
>
> *Resolved:* That such a church is, in the graphic language of Scripture, "A cage of unclean birds" and the "Synagogue of Satan," and that such religious teachers are "Wolves in sheep's clothing," "Watchmen that are blind," "Shepherds that cannot understand," "That all look to their own way, every one to his gain from his quarter."[231]

Such language made most of the Churches, which were sympathetic with his ultimate goal of emancipation, unable to co-operate with him. An article in the *New York Observer,* May, 1855, shows the general attitude of the religious press at this time regarding the methods of the Garrison abolitionists:

> At a meeting of the American Antislavery Society held last week in this city, the following resolution was supported by Mr. Garrison from the Business Committee, and discussed, and, we presume, was unanimously adopted. If there is anything else in heaven or earth which these fanatics are disposed to denounce, it would be gratifying to know what and where it is:
>
> "*Resolved:* That the following religious organizations, viz., the American Board

of Commissioners for Foreign Missions, the American Home Missionary Society, the American Bible Society, the American Bible Union, the American Tract Society, the American Sunday School Union, the American and Foreign Christian Union, the American and Foreign Bible Society, the American Baptist Publication Society, the American Baptist Missionary Union, the American Baptist Home Mission Society, the Presbyterian Board of Foreign Missions, the Missionary Societies of the Protestant Methodists, Episcopal Methodists, Protestant Episcopal, and Moravian bodies, respectively, being in league and fellowship with the slave-holders of the South, utterly dumb in regard to the slave system, and inflexibly hostile to the antislavery movement, are not only wholly undeserving of any pecuniary aid or public countenance at the North, but cannot be supported without conniving at all the wrongs and outrages by which chattel slavery is characterized, and therefore ought to be instantly abandoned by every one claiming to be the friend of liberty and a disciple of Christ the Redeemer."

This resolution is submitted and supported by a man publishing a newspaper, in which he allows such blasphemy to be published from week to week as makes the blood run cold to read. In a recent number one of his correspondents says: "If God has the power to abolish slavery and does not, he is a very scoundrel." From this we infer readily that there is no God at all.

We suppose that among all the supporters of the resolution we have copied above there are very few who believe in the existence of the God of the Bible. The society which they represent is now the only American antislavery society having any vitality whatever. In thus planting itself in defiant opposition to the entire body of Christian philanthropists in the United States, and boldly proclaiming its hostility to the Church and to all the institutions of Christian benevolence, it discloses its true character and reveals the natural result of unregulated and unscriptural measures of reform. . . . Strike out of being the societies enumerated in the damnatory resolution given above, and what would be left in the matter of philanthropy and benevolence? Separate the clergy from the asylums and other charitable houses of relief for the poor and distressed, and how long would they be sustained? Infidelity makes a great outcry about its philanthropy, but religion does the work.[232]

That Garrison should support such a resolution shows the extreme to which he was willing to go to advance out-and-out abolitionism, and to try to discredit its opponents. It also explains why the leaders of the Northern Churches, though generally sympathizing with his ultimate objective, disapproved of the violent language and some of the methods he employed to accomplish his purpose.

(3) THE EXTREME SOUTHERN ATTITUDE—SLAVERY A DIVINE INSTITUTION

Slavery, according to the *Law of Negro Slavery in the United States,* the standard Southern work, published in 1858, and generally attributed to General Thomas R. Cobb (1823–62) of Georgia, in its more usual and limited signification, is applied to all involuntary servitude, which is not inflicted as a punishment for crime. . . . It has, at some time, been incorporated into the social system of every nation whose history has been deemed worthy of record. In the former condition the slave loses all personality: in the latter, while treated under the general class of things, he possesses various rights as a person, and is treated as such by the law.[233]

The author acknowledges that of the

right to private property the slave is entirely deprived. His person and his time being entirely the property of his master, whatever he may accumulate by his own labor, or is otherwise acquired by him, becomes immediately the property of his master.[234]

This ownership made all slaves vendable property, the child of slaves following the condition of its mother even when the father was a white man.[235]

This authoritative statement of the Southern point of view regarding slavery sounds worse than it often actually was in practice; but any institution which could be so defined was intolerable in the long view from a Christian standpoint, and inevitably carried with it in some instances gross abuses and extreme theories to rationalize and justify it. Indeed, most thoughtful Southerners recognized that the institution carried with it both dangers and evils which needed attention. Harriet Martineau, visiting America in 1855, recorded that in all her conversations with Southern planters she met only one who defended the system without reservation.[236] It must also be remembered that about three-quarters of the white population of the South did not belong to slaveholding families.[237]

In the South the Churches and the leaders of Christian thought, on the whole, in the two decades prior to the war, came increasingly to uphold slavery and did not wish to have it interfered with by the government. Many, especially in Virginia, had previously frankly recognized it as an evil and had advocated its gradual abolition, and almost all the more enlightened favored modifications in the laws which would legalize the instruction of slaves, the contraction of marriage, and the prevention of the forcible separation of husbands and wives, parents and children. But in the far South, and even in Virginia, as the Northern abolitionists became more extreme with the approach of the mid-century, the defense of slavery became more marked. Many Church leaders, though recognizing the evils involved, believed that it could be made "Christian," and pointed with pride to the good relations which existed with masters on the better type of plantations under responsible owners. They compared this to the "wage slavery" of the North, whose evils they painted in lurid colors.

But these leaders were increasingly being superseded in public influence by those who supported slavery as "a divine institution," and upheld it as a blessing both to the white men and to the Negroes of the South. We have seen how the Churches in the slave states—especially under the pressure of the economic threat to the section—broke away and started independent bodies supporting "the peculiar institution." Many of them were entirely sincere in their position; but they went to as great extremes as did the Northern abolitionists, and it is the testimony of impartial historians that they had far less justification. The theory that the Bible supports and inculcates slavery was advocated by a Presbyterian minister in Mississippi as early as 1833, but it did not become common doctrine until two decades later. *The Christian Doctrine of Slavery* was the title of a book published in 1857 by the Reverend George D. Armstrong, D.D. (1813–99), pastor of the Presbyterian Church in Norfolk, Virginia. He considered slavery "God's appointment" for certain people, and found it justified in the Bible in many ways, including apostolic example, precept, and injunction.[238] In such books isolated texts, especially from the early books of the Old Testament, were used at length, with little reference to Christ's fundamental teachings and their implication. The same view was also expressed in Congress. In 1858 a Southern member declared that slavery had the blessing of God, the Bible, the Constitution, and profane history![239] As we shall see when the Southern point of view in the Civil War period is discussed, extreme advocates of slavery not only considered it a divine blessing but believed that to expand its influence was to aid a great missionary agency.[240]

An article in the well-known New Orleans publication known as *De Bow's Review* for November, 1857, on "Southern Thought," took the ground that slavery has been proven necessary in all societies. Certain quotations from this article are worth quotation here:

> To protect the weak, we must first enslave them, and this slavery must be either political and legal, or social. . . . Slavery is necessary as an educational institution, and is worth ten times all the common schools of the North. Such common schools teach only uncommonly bad morals, and prepare their inmates to graduate in the penitentiary, as the statistics of crime at the North abundantly prove. . . . We, of the South, assume that man has all along instinctively understood and practised that social and political government best resulted to his nature, and that domestic slavery is, in the general, a natural and necessary part of that government, and that its absence is owing to a decaying diseased state of society, or to something exceptional in local circumstances, as in desert, or mountainous, or new countries, where competition is no evil, because capital has no mastery over labor.[241]

This is an extreme statement, but it shows the position of many of those in power in the South at the time—a position which the Churches of the section tried to modify in the interest of humanity, but not to overthrow. That the conviction reached was conscientiously held by tens of thousands of sincere people cannot be doubted, but it is nonetheless clear today that it was largely due to a rationalization based on what were believed to be the economic interests of the section, and to a failure to realize the potentiality of the Negro outside the slave status.

Slavery has been so associated in the view of a large portion of the reading public with the romantic life of the Old South that it is difficult for us to realize that its defense was primarily on economic and political grounds. Romanticism—derived in this country partly from the genial conditions of Southern cultural life and partly from the novels of Sir Walter Scott—stood for what were believed to be honor and chivalry, hospitality, support of the Church, pride of family and the defense of its women, *noblesse oblige,* valor, culture of the upper classes, an attractive plantation social life, or public service in the higher ranks—in a word the cavalier and aristocratic characteristics. They all had their significance, but they were too often cultivated at the expense of democratic ideals and with little regard for the welfare of the common man, especially when he was a poor white tenant or slave on a distant plantation—as distinct from house servants, and slaves about the resident planter's "big house," who were usually treated by master and mistress with the consideration that the slave status permitted. Those in the latter group were commonly given simple religious instruction and allowed to have their "sings," as well as being permitted to sit in the gallery of the white man's church, or in the larger communities to have simple chapels of their own.[242] But as the fear of slave insurrections increased, most Southern states passed laws restricting the religious freedom of the slaves. They were not legally permitted to have Negro ministers of their own or to worship without the presence of a white man—attempts to keep them from heeding the advice of such persons as the free Negro, David Walker. His widely disseminated *Walker's Appeal* (1829) instigated Negroes to insurrection,[243] and was so largely responsible for repressive measures in Southern legislatures in the 'thirties that by about 1835 the "black code" was practically complete. This was a unique phase in the suppression of religious freedom under the republic. It was due almost entirely to a fear of upheaval which might wreck the "peculiar institution" and have other ill effects on society—*salus populi, suprema lex.* Such laws were not often strictly enforced, but they were on the statute books as a deterrent, and went so far that, according to Eaton, Kentucky alone among Southern states in the period shortly before the Civil War, had no law prohibiting Negroes from learning to read or write.[244] In these matters the condition of the Negro slave had so far deteriorated in a generation that it would have shocked the great Virginia statesmen who played the leading part in establishing our form of Constitutional government, and in preparing the Declaration of Independence and the Bill of Rights.

For the development of the new and narrow Southern view of slavery no other personal influence was so great as that of John C. Calhoun (1782–1850), a man of high character and great ability, who felt that the best way to preserve the Union was to defend slavery as on the whole a righteous institution, and to suppress the Abolitionists, even if nullification of Federal laws was necessary to accomplish his purpose. His idea of democracy was that of Athens, where only a relatively small number were citizens and free, and where the slave's inferior status, without the ordinary civil rights, was definitely recognized. He consequently discarded all elements of Jeffersonian teaching inconsistent with his own political view, which was a combination of that of the Constitution, the Bible (especially the Old Testament), and Aristotle—all influenced, at least unconsciously, by what were believed to be the economic needs of "the Cotton Kingdom." As a result of Calhoun's influence and the other factors mentioned, the more moderate, less uncompromising views of his great political opponent, Henry Clay (1777–1852), were demolished, and the condemnation of slavery as an institution, so general among the thoughtful statesmen of the South in the early days of the republic, virtually ceased. Here and there some brave souls raised their voices in vain against the swelling tide: James G. Birney (1792–1857), of Kentucky, Presbyterian; Cassius M. Clay (1810–1903) of the same state; the Reverend John G. Fee (1816–1901), pastor of a Union Protestant Church and founder of Berea College, where in the early days whites and blacks were educated together; the Reverend Robert J. Breckinridge (1800–1871), Presbyterian, of Kentucky; Judge William Gaston (1778–1844), Roman Catholic, of North Carolina; Bishop William Meade (1789–1862), Episcopalian, of Virginia; Edward Coles (1786–1868), who went West to give his slaves freedom, and became governor of Illinois; the Reverend John Holt Rice (1777–1831), Presbyterian; Moncure Conway (1832–1907), Methodist, later Unitarian, of Virginia. The prominence of Kentucky and Virginia, of ministers of religion, and of Presbyterians in the list is noticeable. Yet the overwhelming majority of Southern pastors,[245] departing from the relatively liberal earlier tradition, had come to support slavery, and a large proportion of them—even among the frontier groups of Methodists, Baptists, and Presbyterians—held that it was sanctioned by the Bible. In spite of this, as the latest impartial study of the subject has pointed out, "from the southern ministry came a larger proportion of outspoken critics of slavery than from any other professional groups."[246] In other words—and this is important from the standpoint of the independence of Church and State—the ministry was more sensitive to the ills of the body politic than any other profession.

But free discussion of the tabooed subject virtually disappeared. "From 1835 to 1861 the South pursued a policy of silence in regard to the removal of slavery."[247] When it discussed the question in public at all it generally tried to defend the institution, or to revile the abolitionist leaders, many of whose utterances and methods were recognized by earnest friends of Negro emancipation in the North, including Abraham Lincoln, to be extreme and provocative. Even the Christian point of view, formerly so favorable to the gradual emancipation of the slave, had so changed that Bishop Leonidas Polk (1806–64), later famous as a general of the Confederacy, carried out in 1860 his plan for a University of the South at Sewanee, Tennessee, in which along with the Christian religion, and a curriculum emphasizing the classics and other cultural subjects, "sound" doctrines on slavery could be taught instead of having students "polluted" by attending Northern colleges.[248]

(4) THE KANSAS CRUSADE

Nothing better shows the desire of the Churches outside of the South to aid in preventing the extension of slavery than their part in the "Kansas Crusade." To understand this movement we must call to mind the intense feeling caused by the passage in 1854 of the Kansas–Nebraska Act, repealing the Missouri Compromise of 1820, and thereby permitting slavery north of the compromise dividing line of 36°30′ N. Lat., if desired by the people under the doctrine of popular sovereignty. The Northern churches believed with Lincoln that it was essential, if slavery were to be abolished, that the territory in which it was permitted should not be extended.

During the discussion in Congress over the Nebraska bill more than three thousand clergymen of New England under the lead of Lyman Beecher sent the following protest to Congress, dated Boston, March 1, 1854:

To the Honorable the Senate and House of Representatives in Congress assembled:

The undersigned, clergymen of different religious denominations in New England, hereby, in the name of Almighty God, and in his presence, do solemnly protest against the passage of what is known as the Nebraska Bill, or any repeal or modification of the existing legal prohibitions of slavery in that part of our national domain which it is proposed to organize into the Territories of Nebraska and Kansas. We protest against it as a great moral wrong, as a breach of faith, eminently unjust to the moral principles of the community, and subversive of all confidence in national engagements; as a measure full of danger to the peace and even the existence of our beloved Union, and exposing us to the righteous judgments of the Almighty; and your protestants, as in duty bound, will ever pray.[249]

Similar protests from ministers in other Northern states were also presented. For example, the clergy of New York, irrespective of denomination, and 151 strong, protested "in the name of religion and humanity"[250] against the guilt of slavery extension. A strong protest came even from the ministers in the northwestern states. Indeed, the Church was more active in this political issue than it had been in any other under the republic since the Sunday mail controversy.[251] The activity of the ministers of religion was both vigorously defended and vigorously opposed in Congress. A contemporary writer says that

This defiance of the clergy and then the "defense" of them . . . gave the long session of the 33d Congress for a time, the semblance of an ecclesiastical council more than that of a legislative assembly.[252]

Douglas bitterly condemned the ministers for "having prostituted the sacred desk to the miserable and corrupting influences of party politics," and asserted that they "ought to be rebuked and required to confine themselves to their vocation, instead of neglecting their holy religion."[253] This is a striking example of a situation which we have found repeated hundreds of times in this study when conservatives—especially among politicians and business men—strongly object to ministers of the gospel going outside the field of personal religion to advocate the application of what they believe to be Christian principles to social problems. The pros and cons of this general issue, frequently referred to as the "Church in politics," will be discussed in a later section.

The protests prepared the way for the Kansas Crusade. Let the leader of this movement, a New England educator, Eli Thayer (1819–99), who had become an ardent Free Soiler, tell his own story.

The influence of this action of the clergy and its rebuke by the Senate resulted in the creation of a mighty factor in aid of the Emigrant Aid Company, in securing freedom to Kansas, and in the destruction of slavery. In fact, the earliest reliance of our company was upon these clergymen and their churches. . . .[254]

Thayer's movement involved aiding the migration to "bleeding Kansas" of men and women capable of the highest type of citizenship who could build up a state that would not only exclude slavery but would be free from other evils. They must be of a heroic mold.

. . . The projected plan would call upon men to risk life and property in establishing freedom in Kansas. They would be called to pass over millions of acres of better land than any in the disputed Territory was supposed to be, land in communities where peace and plenty were assured, to meet the revolver and the bowie-knife defending slavery and assailing freedom. Could such men be found, they would certainly prove themselves to be the very highest types of Christian manhood, much above all other emigrants. *Could* such men be found?[255]

He counted heavily on the Church to advance his plan. The first person of any prominence to give him active support was the Reverend Edward Everett Hale (1822–1909), and his efforts with the clergy were most encouraging. Other Boston ministers threw open their homes or churches to the presentation of the cause. Then the campaign was carried into other parts of the state and neighboring states—Congregational ministers being specially active in the movement, both in arranging for meetings and in becoming members of the New England Emigrant Aid Company. This had been chartered by the Massachusetts legislature, as a result of Thayer's activities, in February, 1855, and took the place of the Massachusetts Emigrant Aid Company chartered the previous year "for the purpose of aiding emigrants to settle in the West."[256] The broader title of the reorganized society is suggestive—it was hoped to interest all of New England.

Here is a highly significant appeal to all the clergymen of this region. It will be noticed that it is signed by the Reverend Lyman Beecher (1775–1863) and the other ministers of Boston who had drafted the petition to Congress in 1854 against the passage of the Kansas-Nebraska bill, as well as by clergymen from neighboring towns and from Andover, Worcester, Hartford, and New Haven.

EDUCATION, TEMPERANCE, FREEDOM, RELIGION IN KANSAS

Dear Sir: We are engaged in an effort to have all the "clergymen of New England," made life members of the New England Emigrant Aid Company.

By insuring thus their cooperation in the direction of this Company, and by enlarging its funds at this period of its highest usefulness, we are satisfied that the Christians of New England will bring to bear a stronger influence in sustaining the principles of what was last year called the "Ministers' Memorial," than by any other means which Providence puts in their hands.

We ask such cooperation as you can give us; supposing that you may have been one of those 3,050 ministers, who in the Senate of the United States were pronounced to "know nothing of the facts, laws and votes involved in the Nebraska bill," and to have "no time to understand them." We are certain that you belong to that body of Northern ministers who have been prohibited from entering northwestern Missouri or Kansas, by those mobs of men who have attempted to take the law of that region into their own hands.

We beg your attention to the great work the New England Emigrant Aid Company has in hand. We ask your particular attention to the encouragement which divine Providence has given to its efforts. We beg you to observe all the facts in the case, before you give way to the false and discouraging impressions, assiduously circulated since the pretended election in Kansas, of March 30, which was the work, simply, of an invading army. You may rely on the following statements of the work of the Emigrant Aid Company, since it was established:

1. *For Freedom.*—It has assisted in establishing at commanding points the towns of Lawrence, Topeka, Osawatomie, Boston, Hampden, and Wabounse. In some of these

towns it has mills—in most of them some investment of value to the settlers. These towns are all peopled by "Free-State men," whose whole influence goes to make Kansas free. There are other towns already started of similar character. The only "Slave-State" town of commanding influence in Kansas is Leavenworth, on the Missouri frontier, separated from the other settled parts of the Territory by Indian reservations. We may say, therefore, that all the most important centers of influence have been established or assisted by the Emigrant Aid Company, and that their influence tells for the cause of Freedom. This Company has, in fact, directly transported between two and three thousand emigrants to Kansas. Not one man of them is known to have ever given a "Slave-State" vote. More than ten thousand, from free States of the Northwest, have been led there by its indirect influence here. To prevent the return of this tide, and to provide those who go with the assistance which capital only can provide, this Company wishes to supply saw-mills at important points, and other conveniences. For such purposes will it use any enlargement of its funds. The emigration is still very large; and wherever this Company can establish a saw-mill, with other conveniences, a "Free-State" town can be gathered. From the best sources of information, from the officers of the Company, and well-informed persons in Kansas and Missouri, we are convinced, as the result of what has been done, that the great proportion of settlers now in Kansas wish it to become a free State. At the election held on the 22d ult., to fill vacancies in the Legislature, nine "Free-State" members were chosen, and only three "Slave-State" members—the last in Leavenworth, which is separated by a ferry only from Missouri.

2. *For Religion.*—The officers of this Company have understood that, to make a free State, they needed, first of all, the Gospel. Every missionary sent there by different boards has received their active assistance. Divine service is regularly maintained in the towns where the company has influence, and, we believe, nowhere else. Every Sabbath school in the Territory has been formed with the assistance of the Company, or its officers. Every church organized has been organized with their cooperation.

3. *For Education.*—Schools will be in operation at Lawrence, at Topeka, at Osawatomie and Hampden before the end of July. These, which are the only schools in the Territory of which we have any account, are due to the exertions of the New England Emigrant Aid Company and its officers.

4. *For Temperance.*—The traffic in intoxicating liquors scarcely exists in any one of the towns founded with the Company's assistance, and any attempt to introduce it will be resisted by their citizens. This prohibition, intended in the first instance for the benefit of the towns, will approve itself to you as the only hope for the Indians still remaining in that Territory.

Such has been the work of this Company in one year. To carry further such operations in these towns, and to plant more towns at once in Kansas, so as to secure its future destiny before next January, the Company needs $150,000. We think it highly desirable that that sum shall be furnished by those who will continue to the Company the Christian direction which has always guided it. We address this statement of facts, therefore, to every clergyman in New England, asking for it their careful attention.

For each of those gentlemen we hope to obtain a single share in the stock of the Company, entitling him to vote at its annual meetings. He will thus be made a life member of the Company.

If it be in your power to obtain, at once, a subscription of twenty dollars, that sum will purchase a share for you, which will be at once taken in your name. For the shares not thus taken, we shall at once set on foot a subscription through New England, and take the shares in the name of the remaining clergymen. To this subscription we ask your assistance, if you and your friends are willing to subscribe less than twenty dollars, or more. It is desirable that this subscription be made at once, and we rely on some answer from you at your earliest convenience—if possible, before the 15th of July. A stamped envelope, already directed to one of our Secretaries, will be found within.

It is proper to state that the New England Emigrant Aid Company is incorporated by the Legislature of Massachusetts, and that no stockholder is liable, in any event, for anything beyond his first investment. Subscriptions of any amount will be at once acknowledged in the papers of Boston. This plan has been so favorably received before its general publication, that we believe the requisite number of shares will be readily subscribed for. The Essex South Conference of churches has provided, it is understood, for the shares of all its members. The Worcester Association has undertaken to make up the shares of all its members. From clergymen of all parts of New England we have assurances of sympathy and cooperation.

Yours, in Christian fellowship,

(Signed) LYMAN BEECHER,
BARON STOW, Rowe-st. Baptist Church,
CHARLES LOWELL, West Church, Boston,
S. STREETER, Pastor of First Universalist Church.
Committee on the Ministers' Memorial of 1854.

W. E. RICE, *Pastor of M. E. Church, Bromfield Street, Boston.*
JOHN H. TWOMBLY, *Pastor of M. E. Church, Hanover Street, Boston.*
EDWARD BEECHER, *Pastor of Salem-st. Church, Boston.*
T. STARR KING, *Pastor of Hollis-st. Church, Boston.*
JOHN S. STONE, *Brookline.*
HOSEA BALLOU, 2d, *President of Tufts College, Medford.*
CALVIN E. STOWE, *Andover.*
LEONARD BACON, *New Haven.*
JOEL HAWES, *First Church, Hartford.*
HORACE BUSHNELL, *North Church, Hartford.*

EDWARD E. HALE, Worcester,
H. LINCOLN WAYLAND, Worcester,
JOHN G. ADAMS, Worcester,
FRANKLIN RAND, Boston,
} *Secretaries.*

July 2, 1855.[257]

The four words at the top of the circular are not without special significance, for from that day three generations ago until today, "Education, Temperance,

Freedom, Religion" have been, along with agriculture, the dominant interests of the state of Kansas. This purpose to build up a free state which would be a real contribution to our American life is brought out in Thayer's statement, that he wished

> to go to the prairies of Kansas and show the superiority of free labor civilization; to go with all our free labor trophies: churches and schools, printing presses, steam engines and mills; and in a peaceful contest convince every poor man from the South of the superiority of free labor.[258]

With the circular and other activities of ministers in mind Thayer wrote:

> In this way many of the clergy became life-members of our company and were our stanch friends and supporters. In all my lecturing tours for uniting the people of the free States in the great work of securing freedom to Kansas, I found them invaluable aids. Their churches were everywhere open for my meetings, and almost without exception they reinforced my arguments with appropriate and effective appeals for patriotism and freedom.[259]

The efforts were not confined to New England. Writing after the movement was over and Kansas had become a free state, a Western correspondent who had been active in aiding Thayer, wrote to his society:

> The clergymen of the free States, with their congregations, were (as a rule), practically, Kansas Leagues, stimulating patriotic zeal, and constantly furnishing reliable reinforcements to the well-disciplined army of freemen who marched to the field of conflict under the guidance and protection of the Emigrant Aid companies. Let them be remembered with honor and gratitude.[260]

New York also became a center of activity; Thayer held meetings in many places, including the vestry of Plymouth Church, Brooklyn, the chapel of Columbia College, and the lecture room of the New York Tabernacle.

Sometimes small incidents do much to reflect public opinion; and three may be recalled here. When Douglas visited Chicago to speak in his own defense on the Kansas–Nebraska issue the church bells tolled for an hour! When Henry Ward Beecher was attending a meeting at which a deacon was raising money to supply weapons for a company to take part in the crusade, he declared that a Sharpe's rifle was a greater moral agency in this struggle than the Bible—an incident from which sprang the popular phrase "Beecher's Bibles."[261]

More significant is the eyewitness record of Leonard Woolsey Bacon (1830–1907), whose father was pastor of the First Church (Congregational) on the New Haven green at the time. He thus records from memory the stirring events of his early manhood:

> The appeal was to the same Christian sentiment which had just uttered its vain

protest, through the almost unanimous voice of the ministers of the gospel, against the opening of the Territories to the possibility of slavery. It was taken up in the solemn spirit of religious duty. None who were present are likely to forget the scene when the emigrants from New Haven assembled in the North Church to be sped on their way with prayer and benediction; how the vast multitude were thrilled by the noble eloquence of Beecher, and how money came out of pocket when it was proposed to equip the colonists with arms for self-defense against the ferocity of "border ruffians." There were scenes like this in many a church and country prayer-meeting, where Christian hearts did not forget to pray "for them in bonds, as bound with them." There took place such a religious emigration as America had not known since the days of the first colonists. They went forth singing the words of Whittier:

We cross the prairies as of old
  Our fathers crossed the sea,
To make the West, as they the East,
  The empire of the free.

Those were choice companies; it was said that in some of their settlements every third man was a college graduate. Thus it was that, not all at once, but after desperate tribulations, Kansas was saved for freedom. It was the turning-point in the "irrepressible conflict." The beam of the scales, which politicians had for forty years been trying to hold level, dipped in favor of liberty and justice, and it was hopeless thenceforth to restore the balance.[262]

The story of the Kansas Crusade and its results is part of American history. Thanks to Eli Thayer (1819–99); to such public-spirited businessmen as Amos Adams Lawrence (1814–86), the active treasurer of the Emigrant Aid Company, and others who subscribed to the undertaking from a combination—often criticized—of patriotic and investment motives; to the press, both religious and secular, of which the *Boston Daily Advertiser* took the lead; and to the Churches, about three thousand settlers went out from Boston in the crucial years. The members of the first party left July 17, 1854, and they were joined by nearly as many others on the way out.[263]

Several towns like Lawrence, Topeka, and Osawatomie were settled under the auspices of the New England Emigrant Aid Company, and their sturdy settlers had an important influence in the civil strife which resulted in making Kansas a free state. As Charles Robinson (1818–94), first governor under the free-state constitution and war governor, speaking at the quarter-centennial of Kansas, said:

Without these settlements Kansas would have been a slave state without a struggle, without the Aid society these towns would never have existed; and that society was born of the brain of Eli Thayer.[264]

He showed a very practical way in which the Churches and their members could influence public policy.

Section 5. THE WAR YEARS—THE ATTITUDES AND ACTIVITIES OF THE CHURCHES

Professor Sweet, in *The Story of Religion in America,* states that "there are good arguments to support the claim that the split in the churches was not only the first break between the sections, but the chief cause of the final break."[265] It is therefore a matter of importance to know the results in Church–State attitudes during the war among the adherents both of the North and of the South.

(1) IN THE UNION

We shall deal first with the attitude of the Protestant Churches during the war.

(a) *The Protestant Churches.*—The Northern Churches, almost without exception, came out definitely for the Union cause and against slavery during the period of the Civil War, while the Southern Churches with at least equal fervor and unanimity supported the cause of the Confederacy. The following typical actions taken by various Christian denominations during the first two years of the Civil War will show the contemporary attitude of the American Protestant bodies on slavery and related issues.

In March, 1861, the Methodist Episcopal New York Conference passed this resolution:

> *Resolved,* That we do here and now declare our earnest and entire sympathy with the cause of our country in this conflict, and our purpose to use all means legitimate to our calling to sustain the Government of the United States in defence and support of the Constitution and the nation's welfare.[266]

In June, 1861, the Hudson River Baptist Association of New York

> *Resolved,* That, in view of the death of our Lord and Saviour for men of every rank and class, of every nation, tribe, "kith or kin," we regard the brotherhood of man, the moral and spiritual equality of all the races of men, as an essential doctrine of the Christian religion; that it rests like a sure cornerstone upon the foundation that God hath laid in Zion; that whosoever falleth upon that stone shall be broken, but upon whomsoever it shall fall it will grind him to powder.[267]

In the same month the General Congregational Association of Illinois

> *Resolved,* 5. That, as the war is but the ripe and bitter fruit of slavery, we trust the American people will demand that it shall result in relieving our country entirely and

forever of that sin and curse, that the future of our nation may never again be darkened by a similar night of treason.[268]

In July, 1861, the Massachusetts Congregational Association

Resolved, That, believing the institution of Slavery to have been the fruitful source of the great trouble now upon us, we cannot but pray and hope that the present war may be overruled by Divine Providence for the ultimate removal of human bondage from our land.[269]

In the same month the General Congregational Association of Connecticut

Resolved, That it is the duty of all citizens, especially all ministers of the gospel and Christian people, to sustain at any and every sacrifice the Federal Government in suppressing this wicked rebellion; to repress, in the conduct of the war, all unhallowed passions and whatever is contrary to the will of God, and to exert all their influence against efforts, should any be made, to secure a peace by unreasonable concessions in the interest of slavery.

Resolved, That, regarding, as we do, the system of slavery in this country as mainly the cause of this treasonable war against the Federal Government, we wait reverently on the providence of God, in the earnest hope and prayer that he will so overrule this conflict and direct its issues that it may result sooner or later, and as soon as may be, in the peaceful and complete removal of this iniquitous and shameful system of oppression.[270]

In November, 1861, the Synod of New York and New Jersey (Old School Presbyterian)

Resolved, That, while we do not feel called upon to add any thing to the repeated testimonials of our Church on the subject of slavery, nor to offer any advice to the Government on the subject, still, fully believing that it lies at the foundation of all our present national troubles, we recommend to all our people to pray more earnestly than ever for its removal, and that the time may speedily come when God, by his providence, shall in his own good time and way bring it to an end, that nothing may be left of it but the painful record of its past existence.[271]

In 1861 also, the Miami Conference of the Christian denomination of Ohio

Resolved, That it is the duty of all loyal citizens, as Christian patriots, friends of human liberty, and brothers of the human family, to maintain and defend this Government, their institutions and liberties, by such means and measures as are necessary to disperse the traitors who threaten them.[272]

In the same year (1861) the members of the Ohio Baptist Convention avowed it to be their right and duty as Christian citizens to tender sympathy and support to those entrusted with the government, and they promised to uphold the armies "in their endeavors to crush the wicked rebellion" and to "offer up" their "prayers and supplications daily" in this behalf. They heartily approved the proclamation of the president declaring liberty to the slaves, and promised support in carrying out that proclamation "till our beloved country shall be purged of the accursed blot," which they declared to be "both the cause of the war and the chief means in our enemy's hands of carrying it on."[273]

A particularly interesting case is that of the Lutherans, a Church which generally considers it its duty to support the duly established government in any crisis. When the General Synod met in 1861, it sent a committee to President Lincoln communicating resolutions characterizing "the rebellion against the constitutional government of this land" as "most wicked in its inception, inhuman in its prosecution, oppressive in its aims, and destructive in its results to the highest interests of morality and religion."[274] It also practically read out of the Church the Southern synods which opposed the Federal government. But, unlike most religious bodies, it did not do this on the issue of slavery, but because of the "open sympathy and active co-operation they have given to the cause of treason and insurrection"[275]—things which always stirred the politically loyal Lutheran Church. The division was not fully healed until 1918.

In May, 1862, the Evangelical Lutheran Synod

Resolved, That it is the deliberate judgment of this Synod that the rebellion against the constitutional Government of this land is most wicked in its inception, unjustifiable in its cause, unnatural in its character, inhuman in its prosecution, oppressive in its aims, and destructive in its results to the highest interests of morality and religion.

Resolved, That in the suppression of this rebellion, and in the maintenance of the Constitution and the Union by the sword, we recognize an unavoidable necessity and a sacred duty which the Government owes to the nation and the world; and that, therefore, we call upon our people to lift up holy hands in prayer to the God of battles, without personal wrath against the evil-doers on the one hand, and without doubting the righteousness of our cause on the other, that he would give wisdom to the President and his counsellors, and success to the army and navy, that our beloved land may speedily be delivered from treason and anarchy.

Resolved, That, whilst we regard this unhappy war as a righteous judgment of God visited upon us because of the individual and national sins of which we have been guilty, we nevertheless regard this rebellion as more immediately the natural result of the continuance and spread of domestic slavery in our land, and therefore hail with unmingled joy the proposition of our Chief Magistrate, which has received the sanction of Congress, to extend aid from the General Government to any State in which slavery exists which shall deem fit to initiate a system of constitutional emancipation.[276]

In the same month, the Black River Methodist Conference, New York, resolved:

3. That we recognize slavery as the cause of the present rebellion and civil war, and are more than ever convinced that either slavery or the nation must perish; and therefore we hail with joy the recent emancipation of the slaves in the District of Columbia by Congress.

4. That we believe it to be the duty of all good men to sustain our national administration by prayer to God for its guidance and support, by their influence, and, if necessary, by their arms, recognizing, as we do, the very great responsibilities of our Chief Magistrate, and we confide in his integrity and his ability.[277]

In September, 1862, the United States Convention of Universalists

Resolved, That while in our judgment we must accept the existing strife as the natural and inevitable penalty of our national infidelity to our republican principles and of an attempt to reconcile freedom and slavery (which are essentially irreconcilable), we renewedly profess our faith in the justice of our cause and in the certainty of our final triumph, and renewedly tender to the President and his constitutional advisers the assurance of our sympathy amid the great responsibilities of their position, and of our hearty support in all proper and efficient efforts to suppress this atrocious rebellion.[278]

In October, 1862, the greatly respected American Board of Commissioners for Foreign Missions adopted a statement which included these words:

. . . And with our renewed prayer to the God to whose displeasure at the wickedness which fills the earth with sadness and oppression all history has testified, and who so often wrought deliverance for our fathers in their perils, we record our grateful confidence that the rebellion will be crushed, that slavery, its prime cause, will be removed, and that peace, prosperity, and righteousness will be permanently established in our land.[279]

In the same month the Philadelphia Baptist Association

Resolved, That, as Christian citizens of this republic, it is our bounden duty to renounce all sympathy with sin, to rebuke all complicity with evil, and cherish a simple, cheerful confidence in Him whose omnipotence flowed through a stripling's arm and sank into the forehead of the Philistine.

Resolved, That, in pursuance of this spirit, we hail with joy the recent proclamation of our Chief Magistrate, declaring freedom on the 1st day of January next to the slaves in all the then disloyal States, and say to him, as the people said to Ezra, "Arise, for the matter belongeth unto thee; we also will be with thee: be of good courage, and do it."

Resolved, That in the name of Liberty, which we love, in the name of Peace, which we would make enduring, in the name of Humanity and of Religion, whose kindred hopes are blended, we protest against any compromise with rebellion; and for the maintenance of the war on such a basis, whether for a longer or a shorter period, we pledge, in addition to our prayers our "lives, our fortunes, and our sacred honor."[280]

In May, 1863, the General Assembly of the Cumberland Presbyterian Church, which was strong in the border states, and consequently in a difficult position, adopted this compromise statement and resolution:

On the subject of American slavery, your committee submit that we should not view it as if it were about to be introduced, but as already in existence. We do not hesitate to declare that the introduction of slavery was an enormous crime, surpassed by few crimes that have disgraced the history of the world, and there are at present great evils connected with it, and that we believe will more or less be connected with it while it exists. As to the remedy for these, the greatest and best minds of our country and the world have greatly differed and been much perplexed: therefore we would recommend to those who in the providence of God have been placed in connection with this institution, to continue prayerfully to study the word of God, to determine their duty in regard to their slaves and slavery; and to those who are not thus situated, that they exercise forbearance towards their brethren who are connected with slavery,—as the agitation of this subject at the present time in that part of the Church where slavery does not exist cannot result in any good, either to the master or slave. Touching the subject of American slavery as set forth in the memorial before us, your committee are not prepared to make the simple holding of slaves a test of church-membership, as they understand the memorial before them to propose.

Resolved, That we disavow any connection with, or sympathy for, the extreme measures of ultra-abolitionists, whose efforts, as we believe, have been, and are now, aimed at the destruction of our civil Government in order to abolish slavery. The committee would say, in conclusion, that the report herein submitted is agreed upon as a compromise measure, to unite the whole energies of our beloved Church and harmonize all our interests in the future, and to bind the entire membership of our Church, if possible, in close bonds of Christianity and fellowship.[281]

In the same month the General Assembly of the Presbyterian Church, New School,

Resolved, That the system of human bondage, as existing in the slave-holding States, so palpably the root and cause of the whole insurrectionary movement, is not only a violation of the domestic rights of human nature, but essentially hostile to the letter and spirit of the Christian religion; that the evil character and demoralizing tendency of this system, so properly described, so justly condemned, by the General Assembly of our Church, especially, from 1818 to the present time, have been placed in the broad light of day by the history of the existing rebellion. That in the sacrifices and desolations, the cost of treasure and blood, ordained thereby, the Assembly recognize the chastening hand of God applied to the punishment of national sins, especially the sin of slavery; that in the proclamation of emancipation issued by the President as a war-measure, and submitted by him to the considerate judgment of mankind, the Assembly recognize with devout gratitude that wonder-working providence of God by which military necessities become the instruments of justice in breaking the yoke of oppression and causing the oppressed to go free; and, further, that the Assembly beseech Almighty God, in his own time, to remove the last vestige of slavery from the country, and give to the nation, preserved, disciplined, and purified, a peace that shall be based on the principles of eternal righteousness.[282]

In the same month also, the National Convention of the Young Men's Christian Association of the United States and the British Provinces, meeting in Chicago,

Resolved, That we are gratified at the steps already taken by the administration for the removal of the great sin of slavery,—"the sum of all villainies,"—and must express our candid conviction that the war will last so long as its cause morally exists, and that when we as a nation do *fully* right, God will not delay to give success to our arms.[283]

In June, 1863, the Conference of the Western Unitarian Association, meeting in Toledo, Ohio,

Resolved, That we give to the President of the United States, and to all who are charged with the guidance and defence of our nation in its present terrible struggle for the preservation of liberty, public order, and Christian civilization, against the powerful wickedness of treason and rebellion, the assurance of our cordial sympathy and steady support, and that we will cheerfully continue to share any and all needful burdens and sacrifices in the holy cause of our country.

Resolved, That we hail with gratitude and hope the rapidly growing conviction among the loyal masses of our countrymen that the existence of human slavery is inconsistent with the national safety and honor, as it is inconsistent with natural right and justice, and that we ask of the Government a thorough and vigorous enforcement of the policy of emancipation, as necessary alike to military success, to lasting peace, and to the just supremacy of the Constitution over all the land.[284]

The strengthening of the Methodist[285] position during war years is shown by the different statements issued in 1860 and 1864. In 1860 it is only the slave trade that is condemned; in 1864 it is slavery as such. In the former year, among the evils to be avoided by Methodists is "The buying and selling of men, women and children with an intention to enslave them." In 1864, the General Conference of the Methodist Episcopal Church adopted this statement, still published in the *Discipline:*

We declare that we are as much as ever convinced of the great evil of Slavery. We believe that the buying, selling, or holding of human beings as chattels is contrary to the laws of God and nature, and inconsistent with the Golden Rule, and with that Rule in our Discipline which requires all who desire to continue among us to "do no harm," and to "avoid evil of every kind." We therefore affectionately admonish all our Ministers and people to keep themselves pure from this great evil, and to seek its extirpation by all lawful and Christian means.[286]

This declaration was carried by a vote of 207 to 9. It may be considered as representative of the general Christian point of view in the North at all times since the founding of the government, and of the earlier Christian point of view of the South—that is, through the first third of the nineteenth century.

The conference which adopted it sent also a strong letter of loyal support to President Lincoln. We have his classic reply, preserved in the Library of Congress and reproduced in this volume.

Lincoln's tribute was deserved. He was doubtless somewhat "unorthodox" in some of his theological beliefs, but he is honored by men of all denominations for his profound faith in God, his religious nature, and his truly Christian spirit. He was a convinced believer in prayer, and valued the prayers that asked not so much for victory as for guidance. "In the present civil war," he said, "it is quite possible that God's purpose is something different from the purpose of either [contending] party."[288]

In the Episcopal Church the split between North and South was for certain reasons not as serious as in most other communions. For instance, the bishops of Virginia, Ohio, Tennessee, and Louisiana kept the promise, mutually given, that they would pray for each other by name every Sunday morning during the war,[289] and the General Convention, meeting in 1862 in New York City, called the roll of all the dioceses beginning with Alabama, just as though no war had separated them. This Triennial Convention was the only one in which the Southern states were not represented. It adopted strong resolutions in favor of supporting the Union without specifically discussing the slavery issue.

A special committee of nine, appointed on October 4, 1862, and consisting of the Reverend Drs. Mead of Connecticut, Higbee of New York, Wilson of Western New York, Totten of Iowa, Thrall of California, and Messrs. Winthrop of Massachusetts, Hunt of New York, Conyngham of Pennsylvania, and Goddard of Ohio, submitted the following report and resolutions on October 9:

The Special Committee of nine, to whom were referred the several propositions offered successively by Messrs. Brunot, Carpenter, Andrews, Hoffman and Warren, and by the Rev. Mr. Burgess and the Rev. Dr. Leeds,—all of them relating to the condition of our Church as affected by the condition of our country,—respectfully submit the following report:—

The Committee have been deeply impressed with the importance and with the difficulty of the duty assigned to them. They have examined with care all the various resolutions which have been referred to them, and have not lost sight of the subsequent suggestions, which have been made in debate, by members of the body from many parts of our country.

In framing the resolutions which they have at length, after much deliberation, agreed upon, they have had three leading objects in view. They have designed to leave no room for honest doubt, or even for invidious misconstruction, as to the hearty loyalty of this body to the government of the United States. They have desired to confirm and strengthen the unity of the Church, as represented in this Convention. And they have attempted so to refer to the course of our brethren who are not represented here, as to shut no door of reconciliation which is still open, and to afford the best hope that they may still be induced to reconsider and retrace their steps, and to renew their relations, in Christian love and loyalty, to a common Church and a common country.

The Committee have felt that it was not fit for this Convention to act or to speak as if they despaired, or in any degree doubted, of the ultimate restoration of the legitimate national authority over our whole land. They have felt, too, that the question before them was not so much as to what might be done, or what might be said, by this body, as a matter of stern justice, in vindication of the authority or the dignity of the Church; but as to what it was wise to do or say at this moment, consistently with our own convictions, and with a view to preserve, unbroken and undisturbed, every remaining link or tie of religious association and Christian sympathy, which might be of use hereafter in accomplishing the great end of restoring our National Union.

The Committee are unwilling to conclude their report without one other suggestion. While there could have been no hesitation, under any circumstances, in expressing, now and always, our earnest and abiding loyalty and devotion to our country, its constitution and its laws, and to all its duly constituted authorities, they have felt that there yet rested upon this Convention the most solemn obligation to abstain from entering upon any narrower questions, which peculiarly belong to the domain of secular politics. Our blessed Lord, in declaring that his kingdom is not of this world, and in directing us to render unto Caesar the things that are Caesar's, has clearly taught us, that, whether as Ministers or as Legislators and Councillors of his Church, we are to refrain from those matters which he has not committed to our care. There is, doubtless, a difficulty in the minds of many, in clearly discerning the precise boundary line between the subjects which come within our jurisdiction and the proper sphere of duty as Christian Ministers and Ecclesiastical Councillors, and such as belong exclusively to secular politics. But the Committee can hardly doubt the there will be a general concurrence in the opinion that, in this most critical period in the history of our Church and of our country, when words are things, and when rash utterances at one end of the Union may co-operate with rash acts at the other in extinguishing the best hopes which remain to us, it is wise for such a body as this to err on the safe side, if we must err at all; and to keep ourselves clearly within the limits which the Councils of our Church have hitherto so uniformly observed.

In accordance with these general views, the undersigned recommend the adoption of the following resolutions:—

Resolved, by the House of Clerical and Lay Deputies of this stated Triennial Convention, That, assembling, as we have been called to do, at a period of great national peril and deplorable civil convulsion, it is meet and proper that we should call to mind, distinctly and publicly, that the Protestant Episcopal Church in the United States hath ever held and taught in the language of one of its Articles of Religion, that "it is the duty of all men who are professors of the Gospel to pay respectful obedience to the civil authority, regularly and legitimately constituted;" and hath accordingly incorporated into its Liturgy "a prayer for the President of the United States and all in civil authority," and "a prayer for the Congress of the United States, to be used during their session;" and hath bound all orders of its ministry to the faithful and constant observance, in letter and in spirit, of these and all other parts of its prescribed ritual.

Resolved, That we cannot be wholly blind to the course which has been pursued, in their ecclesiastical as well as in their civil relations, since this Convention last met in perfect harmony and love, by great numbers of the ministers and members of this Church, within certain States of our Union which have arrayed themselves in open and armed resistance to the regularly constituted government of our country; and that while, in a spirit of Christian forbearance, we refrain from employing towards them any terms of condemnation or reproach, and would rather bow in humiliation before our common Father in Heaven for the sins which have brought his judgment on our land, we yet feel bound to declare our solemn sense of the deep and grievous wrong which they will have inflicted on the great Christian Communion which this convention represents, as well as on the country within which it has been so happily and harmoniously established, should they persevere in striving to rend asunder those civil and religious bonds which have so long held us together in peace, unity, and concord.

Resolved, That while, as individuals and as citizens, we acknowledge our whole duty in sustaining and defending our country in the great struggle in which it is engaged, we are only at liberty, as Deputies to this Council of a Church which hath ever renounced all political association and action, to pledge to the national government—as we now do—the earnest and devout prayers of us all, that its efforts may be so guided by wisdom and replenished with strength, that they may be crowned with speedy and complete success, to the glory of God and the restoration of our beloved Union.

Resolved, That if, in the judgment of the Bishops, any other forms of occasional prayer than those already set forth shall seem desirable and appropriate,—whether for our Convention, our Church, or our country, for our rulers or our defenders, or for the sick and wounded and dying of our army and navy and volunteers,—we shall gladly receive them and fervently use them.

Resolved, That a certified copy of the foregoing report and resolutions be transmitted to the House of Bishops, in evidence of the views and feelings of this body in reference to the afflicting condition of our Church and our Country.

Wm. Cooper Mead.
Ed. Y. Higbee.
W. D. Wilson.
Silas Totten.
S. C. Thrall.
Robt. C. Winthrop.
Washington Hunt.
John N. Conyngham.
Charles B. Goddard.

New York, October 9, 1862.[290]

On October 15, the resolutions were adopted by the following vote:

Dioceses as represented by the clergy vote: ayes, 13 (Delaware, Illinois, Iowa, Maine, Massachusetts, Michigan, Missouri, New Hampshire, New York, Ohio, Pennsylvania, Rhode Island, Western New York); nays, 6 (Kentucky, Maryland, Minnesota, New Jersey, Vermont, Wisconsin); divided, 3 (California, Connecticut, Indiana).

Dioceses as represented by the laity vote: ayes, 11 (Connecticut, Delaware, Maine, Massachusetts, Michigan, New Hampshire, New York, Ohio, Pennsylvania, Rhode Island, Western New York); nays, 5 (Illinois, Kentucky, Maryland, New Jersey, Vermont); divided, 1 (Minnesota).[291]

One lay deputy from Maryland opposed the action on the ground that a council of the Church should not concern itself in any way with political questions, and the presiding bishop, John Henry Hopkins (1792–1868) of Vermont, took a similar stand and refused to read the pastoral letter of the bishops. He stated that he thought that the introduction of politics into Church councils would be "high treason against God."[292] From the time of the adoption of the resolutions quoted, the whole weight of the Church influence was given to the Union side, a notable leader being Bishop Charles P. McIlvaine (1799–1873) of Ohio. He was one of the four ambassadors-at-large, informally appointed by President Lincoln, to help create a more favorable attitude toward the Union in England. He, along with the Reverend Henry Ward Beecher (1813–87), a Congregationalist, Archbishop John Hughes (1797–1864), a Roman Catholic, and Thurlow Weed (1797–1882) were very effective proponents of the Union cause.

In the meantime the Protestant Episcopal Church in the Confederate States of America had been organized in 1861, believing that it was "both necessary and expedient" that the dioceses of the Church in the seceded states should form an independent organization. All the states in the Confederacy except Texas were represented at the meeting when this action was taken, and all the bishops except Leonidas Polk (1806–64), a West Point graduate, who had entered the Confederate Army.[293] The diocesan system adjusted itself easily to the state rights theory.

When the General Convention met in Philadelphia in October, 1865, the roll of all the states was read as usual, the names having never been omitted. Two bishops from the South were present, and were treated with consideration upon signing the important declaration of conformity. There was difficulty when a thanksgiving service for "the restoration of peace and the reestablishment of the national government over the whole land" was proposed.[294] The Bishop of North Carolina said that he could not agree to the proposal in this form; Southern clergy would accommodate themselves to the result like all good citizens, but they could not be thankful for it. They were, however, willing to "return thanks for peace to the country, and unity to the Church," and a Northern bishop moved to substitute the Southerner's words. This proposal carried by a vote of 16 to 7.[295] In the House of Lay Delegates the vote on this substitute resolution was carried by a vote of 20 dioceses to 6, after vigorous discussion. "This action settled the question of reunion. The Southern Church met once more at Augusta, closed its affairs decently, and was no more."[296]

The attitude of the Moravians during the Civil War is clearly brought out by two resolutions adopted by synods held in Pennsylvania in 1861 and 1864. These show that whereas the Moravians in the North were loyal to the Union cause from the beginning, their interest in the slavery issue greatly developed in the course of the war. There had been previously no official objection to slavery, but the members of the Church were not large slaveholders. It will be noticed that the first resolutions do not refer to the irrepressible conflict, whereas the second resolutions come out strongly for the antislavery cause.

The first "Resolutions upon the State of the Country" were adopted at the Triennial Provincial Synod of the Northern District of the American Province of the Moravian Church of the United Brethren at their meeting from May 22 to June 2, 1861:

Whereas, the Provincial Synod of the Moravian church of the Northern District of the United States, now assembled at Lititz, Lancaster county, Pennsylvania, feels it to be just and proper, that, in common with our brethren of other religious denominations, we should express our deep interest in the present unhappy and gloomy condition of our once happy and prosperous country; inasmuch as it is a duty enjoined upon us by the Head of our church, in the commandment "to render to Caesar, the things that are Caesar's, and to God, the things that are God's;" therefore Resolved:

1. That, while, as citizens of the United States, and as members of the Moravian church, we deeply deplore the calamity of civil war in our land, we acknowledge the chastening hand of God, and humbly bow to the decrees of Him, who holds the destinies of nations in his hands.

3. [*sic*] That, while we acknowledge, and submit to *that Power,* we also acknowledge *"the powers that are ordained of God" over us,* and therefore declare our continued faithful, and unabated allegiance to the government and the constitution of the United States, and of the several States of which we are citizens.

3. That in acknowledging our constitutional government, and the liberty and blessings which we have been permitted to enjoy under it, we, as members of the Moravian church, deem it our duty to extend to it, our hearty support in its efforts and measures to uphold the constitution, to maintain the integrity of these United States, and to perpetuate to ourselves and to our children, the liberties and blessings of our republican institutions; so that we, as a church, "may continue to lead under them a quiet and peaceable life in all godliness and honesty."

4. That we will continue to unite in ardent prayer, that the Lord may grant unto the government of the United States, in these times of danger, His gracious counsel, and continue to be the gracious Protector of these United States, and of our national constitution; that He may defeat every evil design against us, and continue to show His tender mercies unto these United States as in days past; that He may in His tender mercy stop the effusion of human blood, and make discord and war to cease; and that to this end, He may put into the hearts of all citizens of these United States, thoughts of peace, that we may see it soon established, to the glory of his name.

5. That we will in our prayers, also remember those, who in obedience to the call of their country, have left their families and homes, and are gone forth to protect our insulted flag, and in support of our constitution and laws—that the Lord of Hosts may strengthen and uphold them, and in the hour of distress, especially when in the arms of death, prove to them their only trust and consolation; and that He may comfort and dry the tears of parents, of brothers, of sisters and of friends, and protect the widows and fatherless children of those who, under His Divine dispensation, sacrifice their lives in the cause of our beloved country.[297]

The second resolutions were adopted at a similar meeting of the synod, May 25 to June 4, 1864:

Resolved, 1. That, as the Provincial Synod of the Northern District of the Moravian Church in the United States, we are profoundly impressed with the peculiar character of the fearful and bloody war, now raging in, and desolating large portions of our beloved country, as an awful and deserved judgment of Almighty God upon this people.

2. That we regard it as clear and unquestionable, that African slavery, as it now exists in the Southern States, and was formerly connived at by the nation at large, is the primary cause of this war, not only in having generally led to it, but in being a great moral wrong, on account of which, in connection with other heinous sins, such as covetousness, pride, intemperance, profanity, Sabbath-breaking, and the cruel and heartless conduct of our people in their treatment of the aborigines of our land, largely prevalent in our country, God is visiting the nation with His judgment.

3. That this Synod recommend to our churches and people a humble confession and hearty repentance of these and all other sins of which we are guilty, that the judgment which has overtaken the nation may be speedily removed, and peace and prosperity restored to our beloved country.

4. That we most emphatically deprecate the interpretation of the Word of God, almost universal in the South, and still largely prevalent in the North, by which the Scriptures of Truth are sought to be perverted into an instrument of oppression, and the pure, sweet wine of the Gospel changed into gall and wormwood.

5. That we consider an earnest support of the Constitution and laws, which, in God's providence, have come down to us from our forefathers, and of our General and State Governments under them, a religious duty, and hereby express our willingness

to render the constituted authorities of our land all the aid in our power, to subdue unrighteous rebellion, and extend the rightful authority of the Government over every portion of our country.[298]

There was no formal break during the Civil War between Northern Moravians, centering in Bethlehem, Pennsylvania, and the Southern group, principally in and near Winston-Salem, North Carolina. Originally the members of the Church had been noncombatants, but during the war this attitude was abandoned, and there were many enlistments on both sides.[299]

During the Civil War there were several small denominations in the North that on the whole remained true to their nonresistance or pacifist principles. These included the Quakers and Mennonites—the two most numerous groups —and in addition the Dunkers (German Baptist Brethren), Shakers, Schwenkfelders, Christadelphians, Rogerenes, Amana Society (Community of True Inspiration), and certain Catholic orders, among which we note particularly the Benedictines.[300] But none of these groups was favorable to slavery, and all of them together represented only a very small percentage of the total population; hence it is safe to say that during the war, and especially after the issuing of the Emancipation Proclamation, the Northern Protestant Churches increasingly supported both the war and the antislavery emphasis.

Edward Wright, the author of *Conscientious Objectors in the Civil War,* tells us that figures are not available to show the total number of such objectors in the different denominations. He is however impressed by the preponderance of Mennonites, the largest and in some ways the most consistent of pacifist bodies; approached only by the Friends, who though less numerous had the most influential voice in behalf of their point of view.[301]

The attitude of the Quakers toward war service, war taxes, and fines, received much attention both within and without the denomination. Their position was difficult because they were and had always been outspoken opponents of slavery.[302] But they wished it abolished by peaceful means, and could not sanction a resort to force even to do away with such a recognized evil. Toward military service they maintained on the whole their historic position; few were actually in the armed forces. Similarly, they were nearly unanimous in opposing fines and bounty fees for nonresistants. For instance, in the records of the Baltimore Yearly Meeting we find this address to its members:

We are all united in the belief, that as we are opposed to war, in all its aspects and consequences, and cannot perform military services of any kind, we therefore cannot consistently or conscientiously, pay any *fines* imposed as a punishment "for non-performance of these services," or any thing connected therewith.[303]

In regard to the payment of taxes, much of which went for war purposes, there was less unanimity. The New England Yearly Meeting went so far as to recommend to its members to pay all taxes. It said:

The payment of taxes levied upon us, for the increase of public revenue has at this time claimed our consideration; and we would encourage Friends cheerfully to comply with the requisitions of our discipline, in regard to being punctual in the payment of every tribute which they can justly do, without attempting to make any impracticable distinctions respecting such taxes as may be imposed upon them for the support of our Government.[304]

This however takes a compromise position with which strict Quakers would scarcely agree.

The most interesting public document which the war provided indicating the Quaker attitude was the memorial which members of the society addressed under date of January 22, 1864, to the president, Senate, and House of Representatives, for exemption from military service. They outlined the basic position which they had held for over two hundred years, "that all wars and fighting were forbidden to them, as followers of Christ," calling attention to the fact that they came to America "for the free encouragement of civil and religious liberty." The petition is couched in language marked by a high moral tone and due consideration for the feelings of others. The last three paragraphs are worth quoting:

In thus defining our position, we enter not into judgment or condemnation of those who differ from us. We appreciate the difficulties that surround those upon whom rests the responsibility of guiding the nation through the awful perils of civil war.

We appeal to you under a sense of suffering—afflictions and mourning surround us, and sorrow hath filled our hearts.

Many of our young men, overcome by the spirit of war, have rushed into the conflict, where some of them have found an early death; some have purchased their release from the draft by the payment of money; others have remained steadfast to their faith in the hour of trial, thereby subjecting themselves to the penalty for desertion. Trusting in the mercy of our Heavenly Father, we desire that He may so touch your hearts and understandings with His wisdom, that you may grant our petition.[305]

Most Quakers gladly accepted some form of nonmilitary, humanitarian service, and were grateful to the government for making this possible. Here are the resolutions of one of the most influential Friends' groups in the country, that of the Meeting for Sufferings of the Philadelphia (Orthodox) Yearly Meeting (April 13, 1865):

The 17th Section of the "Mandatory enrolment Act" approved the 24th of 2nd month 1865 provides "that members of religious denominations, who shall by oath or affirmation declare that they are conscientiously opposed to the bearing of arms, and who are prohibited from doing so by the rules and articles of faith and practice of said religious denominations, shall when drafted into the military service, be considered noncombatants, and shall be assigned by the Secretary of War to duty in the hospitals, or to the care of freedmen, or shall pay the sum of three hundred dollars to such person as the Secretary of War shall designate to receive it, to be applied to the benefit of the sick and wounded soldiers: Provided no person shall be entitled to the provisions of this section unless his declaration of conscientious scruples against bearing arms shall be supported by satisfactory evidence that his deportment has been uniformly consistent with such declaration."

This, we believe, is the first recognition in the Statutes of the United States, of a religious scruple against war, and, coming in the midst of so mighty and desperate a struggle as that then pending, it may well be considered as a most important movement in favor of the Christian principle of "Peace on earth and good-will toward men."[306]

We may well bring to a close this summary of the attitude toward the war of the most representative group of American conscientious objectors by referring to an interview with the secretary of war, the Honorable Edwin M. Stanton (1814–69). The spokesman for a delegation of Friends who visited him on May 5, 1865, shortly after President Lincoln's assassination, said that

they felt unwilling to leave the city without calling to express their thankfulness to him for the uniform kindness and consideration with which he and his Department had treated Friends. . . . They were grateful not only for the relief afforded Friends, but especially for his and the Government's recognition of the rights of conscience, and the respect they had manifested for religious scruples. Several other members of the delegation expressed similar views.[307]

The substance of Stanton's reply has been preserved. He said

that he deeply appreciated the sentiments which had been expressed, and that in the administration of his department he had ever sought to respect the religious views of the Society of Friends and other religious bodies, and had been careful from the moment that he solemnly assumed the duties of his office, to endeavor to do no act which could, by displeasing the Almighty, bring his displeasure upon his country.[308]

In answering another representative delegation on June 1, 1865, Stanton, referring to President Lincoln, said that "He and myself felt that unless we recognized conscientious religious scruples, we could not expect the blessing of Heaven."[309]

That the Protestant Churches of the North were loyal, and that they felt a great moral issue to be at stake, in helping to preserve the union and to prevent the spread of slavery and thus provide for its ultimate abolition, is clearly shown by the president's utterances.[310] The lonely man in the White House seemed to rely increasingly on the moral support of the organized religious forces of the country. For instance, in May, 1862, he addressed a delegation of Evangelical Lutherans:

I welcome here the representatives of the Evangelical Lutherans of the United States. I accept with gratitude their assurances of the sympathy and support of that enlightened, influential, and loyal class of my fellow-citizens in an important crisis which involves, in my judgment, not only the civil and religious liberties of our own dear land, but in a large degree the civil and religious liberties of mankind in many countries and through many ages.[311]

In the same year the New School Presbyterian General Assembly sent him greetings:

Since the day of your inauguration, the thousands of our membership have followed you with unceasing prayer, besieging the throne of Heaven in your behalf. . . . When we look at the history of your Administration hitherto, and at the wonderful way in which this people have been led under your guidance, we glorify God in you.

Again in 1863 they presented loyal resolutions, with approval of Lincoln's antislavery policy. In replying, the president said that he had been happy "to receive testimonies of a similar nature from, I believe, all denominations of Christians." These gave him great satisfaction. He continued:

From the beginning I saw that the issues of our great struggle depended on the divine interposition and favor. . . . As a pilot I have used my best exertions to keep afloat our Ship of State, and shall be glad to resign my trust at the appointed time to another pilot more skilful and successful than I may prove. In every case and at all hazards the government must be perpetuated. Relying, as I do, upon the Almighty Power, and encouraged as I am by these resolutions which you have just read, with the support which I receive from Christian men, I shall not hesitate to use all the means at my control to secure the termination of this rebellion, and will hope for success.[312]

Lincoln's letter to the Quakers of Iowa is particularly significant.

It is most cheering and encouraging for me to know that in the efforts which I have made, and am making, for the restoration of a righteous peace to our country, I am upheld and sustained by the good wishes and prayers of God's people. No one is more deeply than myself aware that without his favor our highest wisdom is but as foolishness, and that our most strenuous efforts would avail nothing in the shadow of his displeasure. It seems to me that if there be one subject upon which all good men may unitedly agree, it is in imploring the gracious favor of the God of Nations upon the struggle our people are making for the preservation of their precious birthright of civil and religious liberty.[313]

These are but characteristic of the president's replies to delegations of Churches, Reformed, Presbyterian, Moravian, Methodist, Baptist, and others during the war. As the years advanced, and as the freeing of the slaves both for its own sake and as a means of preserving the Union became a definite objective, the Churches—especially those in New England and the Middle West—became even more outspoken in their support of the policy advocated by Lincoln at the Niagara Conference looking to the abandonment of slavery as the condition of permanent union and peace. In the autumn of 1864 the Congregationalists of New York, New Jersey, and Pennsylvania specifically adopted this policy through their General Association.[314]

Dr. Joseph P. Thompson (1819–79), who was pastor of the Broadway Tabernacle (Congregational) of New York during the war, and one of the most influential ministers in the United States during that period, has left us an account of a striking incident that shows the influence of the Church on public opinion and public events. It took place in 1863 when the president was hesitating whether to enforce the draft or to call for volunteers, and when there was much dissatisfaction in the North because their hopes for a speedy victory had not been realized, and when defeatism was strong. Dr. Thompson came into his pulpit at a Sunday service and made this plea:

> Of what avail are our churches if we shall no longer have a government or a country? Of what worth is our Christianity if it cannot preserve these? If the government cannot save the country, let the churches save both. Let this church call for volunteers; equip a regiment, and put it into the field, to show that *we* will never give it up.[315]

At the close of the service the congregation was asked to remain, and someone proposed a subscription for a church regiment. By evening upward of $30,000 had been collected and laid upon the altar. Two women in the congregation each sent $500, saying, "We cannot go: put men in our stead." The action of the parishioners made a remarkable impression on the country, bringing letters of thanks from senators, members of the cabinet, and generals of the Union Army. Dr. Thompson, who himself records the incident, closes his statement by saying: "It cheered the burdened heart of the President and gave new courage to the indomitable Minister of War."[316]

Among the most interesting Church–State issues during the war were several involving the attempt by Union officers to control in reconquered territory Southern Protestant churches and their services. A famous case of this sort arose in 1862 after the Episcopal Church in the Southern states in its revision of the *Prayer Book* had changed its prayers so as to make them for the Confederacy, instead of for the United States and its president. After this General Benjamin F. Butler (1818–93) issued an order to the effect that

The omission, in the service of the Protestant Episcopal Church in New Orleans, of the Prayers for the President of the United States, would be regarded as evidence of hostility to the Government of the United States.[317]

There was much discussion. This resulted in the forcible closing of some churches, the arrest of their rectors, and their being sent north as military prisoners; but on their arrival in New York they were at once set at liberty.[318]

In another case, in Mississippi, a young Union officer led an Episcopal clergyman to the door for omitting the usual prayer for the president. Then entering the pulpit, he read in the hearing of the Southern congregation the regular *Prayer Book* prayer "for the President of the United States, and all in Civil Authority!"[319]

In one state, Alabama, the bishop and the clergy were inhibited for their failure to observe the order. The churches were closed, and armed guards stationed at the doors. The bishop, however, wrote a letter to the president on the subject, which produced an immediate revocation of the obnoxious order.

Writing about conditions in Alabama just after the Civil War, the Right Reverend Richard H. Wilmer (1816–1900), the Episcopal bishop, referred to this incident:

Hearing that there were troubles brewing in Mobile,—I had refugeed in Greensborough,—I went there at once. I had been in the city but a few hours, when a servant came to my room, and told me than an officer had called to see me. Upon going to the parlor, a general of the Federal army introduced himself to me as an officer on the staff of the General commanding, and said that he had called by direction of said officer, to know when I meant to use the prayer for the President of the United States. I told him that that was a question the General had no right to ask, and that I answered no such questions if put in a tone of authority; that the Church had her sphere of action, and could not permit any intrusion. The officer was thrown aback, talked a good deal about the absoluteness of military power, and intimated, not obscurely, that I would have to succumb. I told him that he would see for himself the issue. After a considerable talk on his part,—I preserving entire silence,—he proposed that we should talk the matter over as "between man and man." I told him that I had no sentiment that was not open to the world, but none that could be extorted.

He then in a very familiar way put the question anew under the programme of, as "between man and man."—"When do you think you will use the prayer-book prayer for the President?"

I answered, "When you all get away from here." This particular prayer was for a government of the people's choice and affection,—the loyal prayer of the Church of England, rather servilely continued in our liturgy. "The fact is, sir, that the government, as it is over us now, and impersonated in the President, is a government for which I desire the least 'length of life' and 'least prosperity' that is consistent with the permissive will of God;" that we did ardently pray that he who held these reins of absolute power might have "grace" to execute judgment, and to maintain truth, etc., and hoped that our prayers would be answered. I then said to the officer, "Suppose our positions reversed; supposed we had conquered you, and, amid all your desolation and sadness and humiliation, commanded you to fall down upon your knees, and ask God to grant long life, health, and prosperity to our commanding officer,—would you do it?" I cannot quote his reply, for his excitement threw him off his balance; and he intimated in strong but profane terms, that he would be—something very dreadful—if he would. "Well," I said, "I am not disposed to use your phraseology; but, if I do that thing that you come to order me to do,—addressing the Almighty with my lips, when my heart is not in my prayer,—I run great danger of meeting the doom that you have hypothetically invoked upon your own head." He then left.

In the course of a few days, there came out "general orders," shutting up all our churches, and "suspending" me from all my functions. These orders were, on the part of the general commanding the military district, accompanied with a shower of bad language that could only fall with its foul savor on the head of him who gave vent to it.

Meanwhile, the churches were nearly all closed, and soldiers stationed at the doors to prevent entrance. Yet it is a great mercy that even military rule cannot entirely close our communications with Heaven. We worshipped in private houses; and I confirmed in churches which were not guarded by soldiers, issued Pastorals, etc., much to the indignation of the general who had suspended me from my functions.

After a while, the Council of the Church in the Confederate States held its regular triennial session at Augusta, Ga. There the whole question of "the prayer for those in authority" was settled by the adoption of the old form in the Prayer-Book. Coupled with this action, however, was a "resolution" that each bishop should exercise his own discretion as to the time for its introduction. Upon this modification, I had absolutely insisted.

By this action of the Council, it was competent for me at once to order the use of the prayer; but as the military intrusion still existed, I delayed the matter until the order should be withdrawn. It went hard with the General to do it; but he was compelled by a higher power, and poured out his wrath in language that could only defile the lips from which it issued.[320]

The general who suspended Bishop Wilmer from his functions was Gen. George H. Thomas (1816–70) of the Union Army. The president who went over the head of this officer and authorized the reinstatement of the bishop was President Johnson.[321] By this action he returned Church-State relations to their historic American position—that of separation—though it must be conceded that the bishop's form of statement was provocative.

Presbyterians in Missouri also had their troubles. A pastor in St. Louis, the Reverend Samuel B. McPheeters (1819–70), in the fall of 1862 refused to declare himself for the Union, and baptized a child with the name of a Confederate general. A provost marshal arrested him, taking control of the church. He protested to the attorney general. The matter was brought to the attention of President Lincoln, who wrote to General Curtis:

I tell you frankly I believe he does sympathize with the rebels, but the question remains whether such a man, of unquestioned good moral character . . . can, with safety to the government, be exiled upon the suspicion of his secret sympathies. . . . I must add that the United States Government must not . . . undertake to run the churches. When an individual in a church or out of it becomes dangerous to the public interest, he must be checked. . . . It will not do for the United States to appoint trustees, supervisors, or other agents for the Churches.[322]

But for some reason the pastor was not allowed to continue his ministrations, and Lincoln wrote that he had received a petition and letters from three dozen citizens relating to the case. "The petition prays, in the name of justice and mercy," said the president, "that I will restore Dr. McPheeters to all his ecclesiastical rights." Another correspondent inquired: "Is it not a strange illustration of the condition of things, that the question of who shall be allowed to preach in a church in St. Louis shall be decided by the President of the United States?" But Lincoln informed him of the contents of the letter he had written General Curtis nearly a year before. He added that no complaint had been received regarding the matter for nearly a year, and implied that Dr. McPheeters might perhaps be in trouble with his own congregation.

If, after all, what is now sought is to have me put Dr. McPheeters back over the heads of a majority of his own congregation, that, too, will be declined. I will not have control of any church on any side.[323]

Lincoln's general attitude in this case is shown in a letter he wrote to McPheeters early in 1863:

I have never interfered, nor thought of interfering as to who shall or who shall not preach in any Church, nor have I knowingly or believingly tolerated any one else to so interfere by my authority."[324]

A somewhat similar question arose in connection with Methodist churches in Southern communities occupied by Union troops. In 1862 the War Department issued an order signed by the secretary of war directing the commanding generals of the departments in the South to place at the disposal of certain bishops "all houses of worship belonging to the Methodist Episcopal Church, South, in which a loyal minister, who has not been appointed by a loyal Bishop of said church does not officiate." The order stated "that Christian ministers should by example and precept, support and foster the loyal sentiment of the people." The commanders were further instructed to supply the bishops named "with transportation and subsistence when it can be done without prejudice to the service" and to show them "courtesy, assistance and protection." Later additional Northern Methodist bishops were given jurisdiction over Methodist churches in other military departments of the South.

In 1864 orders similar in character were issued concerning the Southern Baptist churches. The military commanders were directed to turn over to the American Baptist Home Missionary Society those churches of the Baptist Church South "in which a loyal minister of said Church does not now officiate." The same procedure was followed with the United Presbyterian Church, both Old School and New School. "In every instance these orders were issued at the solicitation of some church official,"[325] and in some cases they required that churches should be opened to both white and colored people.

Memphis, Tennessee, was one of the places where this issue of what group should control a church was specially acute. Lincoln's orders were clear-cut. He wrote to the military commander:

> I am now told that . . . the military put one set of men out of and another set of men into the building. This, if true is most extraordinary. I say again, if there be no military need of the building leave it alone, neither putting one set in or out of it, except on finding some one preaching or practicing treason, in which case lay hands on him, just as if he were doing the same thing in any other building, or in the street or highway.[326]

Another related question which caused discussion and difficulty was that of granting passports or permits to Northern ministers to pass through the lines and occupy vacant pulpits in the South. Such permissions seemed necessary to the Union commanders in several cases where pulpits were vacant either because of their incumbents leaving voluntarily, or because they had been asked to leave for openly siding with the Southern cause. A typical order covering this point is that issued from the headquarters of Norfolk and Portsmouth February 11, 1864. It reads:

> General Orders, No. 3—All places of public worship in Norfolk and Portsmouth are hereby placed under the control of the Provost–Marshals of Norfolk and Portsmouth respectively, who shall see the pulpits properly filled by displacing, when necessary, the present incumbents, and substituting men of known loyalty and the same sectarian denomination, either military or civil, subject to the approval of the Commanding General. They shall see that the Churches are open freely to all officers and soldiers, white or colored, at the usual hour of worship, and at other times, if desired, and they shall see that no insult or indignity be offered to them, either by word, look, or gesture, on the part of the congregation. The necessary expenses will be levied, as far as possible, in accordance with the previous usages or regulations of each congregation respectively. No property shall be removed, either public or private, without permission from these headquarters. By command of
>
> E. A. Wild, Brig.–General.[327]

In a few cases officers of the Northern Army actually took over control of Southern churches. But President Lincoln protested against such action. He saw the serious Church–State issue involved, and wrote: "It will not do for the United States to appoint Trustees, Supervisors, or other agents for the Churches."[328] As in some other instances in our history where military officers have exceeded their authority, the president as commander-in-chief has overruled them in the interest of preserving Constitutional rights.

There was also much discussion over demanding an oath of allegiance to the government of the United States by ministers in Southern churches. The opposition was based on the ground that it was prescribing a religious test for the Church, but it was shown that this charge was not justified, inasmuch as the oath was merely an oath of loyalty to the Federal government.[329]

Before leaving this account of the Protestant Churches and the Union cause, we should at least notice the activity of religious groups and leaders in connection with the Underground Railroad. This loosely organized movement, in operation long before 1830, when it got its name, proved to be one of the most effective methods of freeing slaves in the Southern states by helping them to get to the North and to Canada. It aided about seventy-five thousand to escape North on various routes that became fairly well known, particularly in Ohio and Pennsylvania. The part played by the Protestant Churches in this movement has never been thoroughly investigated. We know, however, that members of these churches were its main workers. The Quakers were active in this project in North Carolina from early in the century; the members of the faculty of Oberlin College, a strong antislavery center, co-operated; the Wesleyan Methodists and Covenanters were active; Levi Coffin (1789–1877) became the so-called station master of the railroad in Cincinnati, an earnest Quaker who was generally considered the head of the movement; the Reverend Charles T. Torrey (1813–46), Yale graduate and prominent New England Congregational minister, gave up his church, and, after devoting his life to the freeing of nearly four hundred slaves in Maryland, died a martyr to the cause; the Reverend James M. McKim (1810–74), a Presbyterian minister, was recognized as one of the underground leaders. These examples will give an indication of what it is believed a thorough study of the part played by the churches in the underground railroad would probably bring out. The best known historian of the Negro in America states the case fairly when he says that the railroad was

> conducted by Quakers and militant abolitionists. This was not any well-known route controlled by a well-organized body. It was rather a number of Christian people scattered through the free States but united with their common purpose to promote the escape of slaves. . . .[330]

It should be added that many Negroes co-operated actively in the undertaking. Among these were William Still (1821–1902), a prominent Presbyterian layman who was the first historian of the movement, and Harriet Tubman (1821–1913), known as the "Moses" of her people, a remarkable woman who combined mysticism, force, and courage.

(b) *The Roman Catholic Church.*—The Roman Catholic Church during the war continued to refrain from taking sides as a Church on the slavery question. Thousands of its members served in both armies. Naturally, however, since the South had relatively few of the recent immigrants from Ireland, Germany, and the Latin countries of continental Europe, it was much stronger in the North. Consequently most of the hierarchy supported the Union side, which commended itself to the Catholic mind with its emphasis on the support of legitimate government and on Constitutional law. It was interested in removing the evils of slavery, but abolitionism, which seemed a radical and disruptive doctrine, made no appeal. The prevalent point of view of the Church was expressed in a letter written by Archbishop Hughes (1797–1864) to the secretary of war in October, 1861:

> The Catholics, so far as I know, whether of native or foreign birth, are willing to fight to the death for the support of the constitution, the Government, and the laws of the country. But if it should be understood that, with or without knowing it, they are to fight for the abolition of slavery then, indeed, they will turn away in disgust from the discharge of what would otherwise be a patriotic duty.[331]

The archbishop was not an advocate of slavery but an opponent of its forceful overthrow. In this position he had the support of the Church, as is shown by the statement in 1863 of Bishop Martin John Spalding (1810–72), who the following year was appointed Archbishop of Baltimore:

> In the very beginning of the war our Bishops in more than one provincial council publicly and officially declared in their pastorals that they had nothing, and the Catholic Church had nothing, to do with the causes which had induced the war, and that they would not on any account enter into the matter, except by daily prayers fervently recited before the holy altar for the public good, and for the return of peace and prosperity. This declaration on their part had a most happy effect on the public estimation, when all compared the difference between the true Catholic Church of all times and all nations and the local sects of yesterday, which furiously took one side or other in the midst of the tempest and fire and blood of war. Our holy Church thus truly showed itself the Church of God, who is not *Deus dissentionis sed pacis et caritatis.*[332]

Among the few prominent Roman Catholic dissenters on the slavery issue was the independent and somewhat erratic Orestes Brownson (1803–76), who advocated immediate emancipation.[333] Another Catholic editor who held decided views on the war issue was James Alphonsus McMaster (1820–86), who bought the *Freeman's Journal* from Bishop Hughes in 1848. He was a controversialist who quarrelled with the bishop on the Irish question, and with Orestes Brownson on his philosophy. He was an antiabolitionist and a strong state rights man. After the beginning of the Civil War his criticisms of President Lincoln and his administration resulted in his arrest (1861) and confinement for nearly a year in Fort Lafayette as a disloyal citizen. The *Freeman's Journal* was suppressed by the Federal government until April, 1862.

The attitude probably favored by most Northern Catholics was that of Archbishop Purcell (1800–83) of Cincinnati, a highly influential advocate of the Union cause. He showed his convictions by ordering the American flag to be flown from the spire of his cathedral in 1861. This action in a community where political feeling ran high, and the determined spirit behind it, were factors in helping to swing the Middle West into line to support Abraham Lincoln. It also incidentally provided an effective demonstration in combating Know-Nothingism.[334] It was of this incident that Rutherford B. Hayes (1822–93), later President of the United States, but at the time a prominent citizen of Cincinnati, said: "The spire was beautiful, but the Catholic prelate made it radiant with hope and joy for our country."[335]

(c) *The Jews.*—The Jews, being a minority group, have generally sympathized with other minority groups like the Negroes, because they were both seeking recognition and the removal of disqualifications imposed on them. This fact gave special zeal to the Northern Jews during the war—a zeal in opposition to the extension of slavery, and in behalf of Negro enfranchisement and progress. We have seen this tradition continued in our own day by several Jewish philanthropists, of whom the late Julius Rosenwald (1862–1932) is perhaps the most notable.

The Jews of the North made an excellent record during the war, as did also those of the South in their natural devotion to the Confederacy. There were about 6,000 Jewish soldiers in the Northern army alone, though the total Jewish population in the entire country was only about 150,000.[336] They were relatively most prominent at this time in cities like Savannah and New Orleans. New Orleans gave the Confederacy its secretary of state, the distinguished jurist Judah P. Benjamin (1811–84).

An unfortunate incident early in the war threatened the friendly feeling between this group and the State. It came soon after the Congressional authorization of Jewish chaplains in 1861.[337] On November 9, 1862, General Ulysses S. Grant (1822–85) issued instructions to General Hurlbut to refuse permits to pass south of Jackson, Tennessee. He added, "the Israelites especially should be kept out." He later issued orders to General Webster, referring to the Jews as "an intolerable nuisance." He also officially reported to Washington that "the Jews roam through the country contrary to the government regulations." Finally, on December 17, he issued a general order expelling all Jews "from his Department within 24 hours."[338] Probably the persons referred to were merely peddlers—who in that time and section were mainly Jews—but the form of the order discriminated against Jews as a group, a thing which of course could not be tolerated under our American system. It was clear to all thoughtful and unprejudiced people that in some way General Grant's orders, which were quite inconsistent with his later attitude of toleration, must be revoked.

The Jews of Paducah, Kentucky, a large town on the Mississippi, about fifty miles north of the Tennessee boundary, took the lead. They transmitted the following appeal to President Lincoln, the signers being all well-known merchants of the town.

Paducah, Ky., Dec. 29, 1862.

Hon. Abraham Lincoln, President of the United States.

General Order No. 11 issued by General Grant at Oxford, Miss., December the 17th, commands all post commanders to expel all Jews without distinction within twenty-four hours from his entire Department. The undersigned good and loyal citizens of the United States and residents of this town, for many years engaged in legitimate business as merchants, feel greatly insulted and outraged by this inhuman order; the carrying out of which would be the grossest violation of the Constitution and our rights as good citizens under it, and would place us, besides a large number of other Jewish families of this town, as outlaws before the world. We respectfully ask your immediate attention to this enormous outrage on all law and humanity and pray for your effectual and immediate interposition. We would especially refer to you the post commander and post adjutant as to our loyalty, and to all respectable citizens of this community as to our standing as citizens and merchants. We respectfully ask for immediate instructions to be sent to the Commander of this Post.

D. Wolff & Bros.
C. J. Kaskel.
J. W. Kaskel.[339]

This and other appeals had the necessary effect. The president notified General Halleck that the obnoxious order should be revoked, and he, in turn, notified General Grant. There was some delay in the transmission of the message, and the latter's revocation was not issued until January 7, 1863. A fortnight later, January 21, Halleck wrote to Grant:

It may be proper to give you some explanation of the revocation of your order expelling all Jews from your department. The President has no objection to your expelling traitors and Jew peddlers, which, I suppose, was the object of your order; but as it in terms proscribed an entire religious class, some of whom are fighting in our ranks, the President deemed it necessary to revoke it.[340]

This closed an incident to which General Grant made, as far as is known, no later reference. It is significant in Church–State relations in the United States as an isolated incident of its character, but one which fortunately ended in the only possible way consistent with our Federal Constitutional guarantees of religious freedom.

The correspondence has recently come to light between President Lincoln and the Jewish congregation Hope of Israel in Philadelphia. On April 23, 1862, the president of the congregation sent to the president of the United States a copy of a prayer written by its rabbi, Sabato Moaris, used in connection with the day set aside by the president "to humble ourselves" and to pray to God "whom we have forgotten" for forgiveness, as well as for "the restoration of unity and peace."[341]

Author of all good! We implore Thy Almighty protection on behalf of the American Republic of the North. Let Thine eyes, which never slumber, be open upon her, that she may not be erased from among the family of nations. Be with her in this struggle for life, that she may survive it, and wax greater and happier. Speak to the hearts of her disaffected children, and let them again throb with undying affection. Let both the weapon of aggression and that of defence be buried into the bottomless ocean, and cast Thou with it the spirit of acrimony that has sharpened its edge. Direct the hands into which the temporal welfare of this people is entrusted. Sustain them that their strength may never flag. Bless the President of the United States: Bless him for his sterling honesty, bless him for his firmness and moderation. Rekindle with joy his domestic hearth; pour on him the balm of divine consolation. Grant that the issues of his momentous obligations be a united and prosperous country. Grant that the end of his career be the maintenance of this Government, unimpaired and unsullied as bequeathed by our illustrious ancestors. So may it be, Amen.[342]

Lincoln wrote a letter under date of May 13, 1862, acknowledging the prayer "recently delivered at your Synagogue," and giving hearty thanks for the "expressions of kindness and confidence."

(d) *Co-operative Christian Enterprises.*—We come now to a group of movements which had their origin in the North and were specially effective in maintaining the morale of the troops.

The United States Sanitary Commission was the most important relief agency developed by the war. Founded in June, 1861, it did most of the work now carried on by the Red Cross—caring for the wounded and sick and their dependent families. It had as many as five hundred agents driving ambulances, conducting field hospitals and feeding stations, and engaged in other activities. Its leading founder was a respected Unitarian clergyman, the Reverend Henry

Whitney Bellows (1814–82). He was president of the commission during the war and administered it most effectively. Its funds were mostly raised by the churches, private contributions, and sanitary fairs.[343]

The American Bible Society, with headquarters in New York, also rendered conspicuous service to both Union and Confederate armies. The Board of Managers determined that either a Bible or a New Testament should be given every Northern and Southern soldier. An arrangement was effected with representatives of the government by which some 300,000 Bibles, Testaments, and Gospels, were allowed to pass through the military lines to Southern territory.[344]

The Centennial History of the American Bible Society tells the story in a graphic way.

> The decision of the Board was confirmed by a marvellous occurrence. When Bibles were sent South to nourish the souls of the men of the Confederate Army, the guards did not order a halt. Generals and their subordinates on both sides of the line let the Book travel under a sort of "Truce of God." Through this unparalleled respect for a holy enterprise, some three hundred thousand Bibles, Testaments and single Gospels during the war passed from New York, through the firing lines, to comfort the Southern soldiers. . . .
>
> Immediately after the first impulsive decision of the Board, in May, 1861, Secretary McNeill wrote to the Virginia Bible Society that the Southern Army would be supplied with Scriptures as well as the Northern. The first books sent in the West were held up as contraband of war. Early in 1862 Federal officers at Cairo, Illinois, stopped a parcel of New Testaments, as contraband, which was addressed to General (Bishop) Leonidas Polk's Army at Columbus, Kentucky. This may have been, however, because General Grant at that moment was beginning a movement in Kentucky which obliged General Polk to retire from Columbus, for later there was no further difficulty. Under the same system a goodly number of Testaments were sent directly to Richmond under flag of truce with the consent of the commanding officers of both armies. The Maryland Auxiliary reported in 1863 that it had sent to the South from the American Bible Society 86,424 volumes of Scripture during the year. Some five thousand of these volumes were sent, with the consent of the authorities, to prisoners of war in Richmond, all the difficulties which attended the plan to supply the South were removed, and by the middle of 1863 shipments of books in large quantities from New York were regularly forwarded under flag of truce by way of Fortress Monroe to their destination. The books mentioned above sent by the Maryland Bible Society were in fifty-seven cases, which were forwarded to Richmond by way of Fortress Monroe and City Point under permit from the Secretary of War; and the United States Government and the Norfolk Steamship Company paid all expenses of transport.[345]

Mr. Rhodes states that the Southern bishops and clergy appealed in 1862 to their brethren in the North for a few thousand *Prayer Books* and a quantity of church tracts. The United States government gave permission the following year for the passage through the lines of these publications.[346] It is believed that such Christian service under flag of truce as represented by these two incidents is perhaps unparalleled in modern history. In addition to providing Bibles or portions of the Bible to the troops in active service, about 35,000 volumes were given by the American Bible Society to Southern soldiers in Northern prison camps.

Another benevolent activity, and one even more directly related to the churches during the war, was that of the United States Christian Commission, which was organized in 1861 by a convention of the National Committee of the Y.M.C.A. An early official announcement of the Commission describes its objects:

> Their object is to promote the spiritual and temporal welfare of the brave men who are now in arms to put down a wicked rebellion. They propose to do this by aiding the chaplains and others in their work.
>
> 1. By furnishing to them religious tracts, periodicals, and books.
> 2. By aiding in the formation of religious associations in the several regiments.
> 3. By putting such associations in correspondence with the Christian public.
> 4. By cultivating, as far as possible, the religious sympathies and prayers of Christians in their behalf.
> 5. By obtaining and directing such gratuitous personal labor among the soldiers and sailors as may be practicable.
> 6. By improving such other opportunities and means as may, in the providence of God, be presented.
> 7. By furnishing, as far as possible, profitable reading other than religious, and, wherever there is a permanent military post, by establishing a general library of such works.
> 8. By establishing a medium of speedy and safe intercommunication between the men in the army and navy and their friends and families, by which small packages of clothing, books, and medicines, and mementoes of social affection, can be interchanged.
>
> We propose to encourage in them whatever is good and keep fresh in their remembrance the instructions of earlier years, and to develop, organize, and make effective the religious element in the army and navy. The field is open to us. We can have free access to their immortal souls; the chaplains desire and call for our aid; the Government wish it; and the men ask for and receive religious reading and teaching with an eagerness most touching. Thousands who at home never entered the house of God, and had none to care for their souls, now, in imminent peril, desire to know of Him who can give them the victory over death through our Lord Jesus Christ.[347]

During four years of service the commission distributed to the soldiers over four million books, Bibles, etc., and some three million dollars' worth of goods, and commanded the service as volunteers for six weeks or more each of nearly five thousand men. Lincoln said: "There is one association whose objects and motives I have never heard in any degree impugned or questioned; and that is the Christian Commission."[348]

The representatives in the field, who were everywhere cordially received, were known as "delegates." Each carried a "commission" addressed "To Officers of the Army and Navy of the United States, and others." This stated that

> His work will be that of distributing stores where needed, in hospitals and camps; circulating good reading matter among soldiers and sailors; visiting the sick and wounded, to instruct, comfort, and cheer them, and aid them in correspondence with their friends at home; aiding Surgeons on the battlefield and elsewhere, in the care and conveyance of the wounded to hospitals; helping Chaplains in their ministrations and influence for the good of the men under their care; and addressing soldiers and sailors, individually and collectively, in explanation of the work of the Commission and its delegates, and for their personal instruction and benefit, temporal and eternal.[349]

In other words, here was a voluntary organization backed by the Churches and devoted to improving morale among the soldiers at the front, and aiding the Army directly in ways open to an authorized and competent civilian.

The Christian Commission thus stated its spirit of co-operation with the military authorities and especially with the chaplains duly appointed by the government:

> . . . To meet the deficiency of chaplain service as far as possible by its delegate system, and to aid the tried and noble men who, through all perils, hindrances, and hardships, still remain to serve God and our country to the end of the war by supplying them with Scriptures, Hymns and Psalms, and the best issues of the religious press in every form, fresh, frequent, and copious as possible, is both wise, patriotic, and Christian.
>
> The idea, however, that this work of supplementing and supplying the chaplaincy, is or ought to be the main work of the Christian Commission, is extremely contracted, and would reduce the sphere of the Commission from that of a great national, religious, and relief agency between the people, the church, the home, the press, on the one hand, and the army and navy on the other, to that of little more than a mere receiving and distributing agency between publishing establishments and chaplains. With these facts in view, cooperation with chaplains has been a steadfast principle with the Commission from the first. Help has never been sought in vain within the boundaries of our objects and means by any chaplain; nor will it ever be.
>
> . . . In each military department, general hospital, permanent camp and separate post or station, the consent and counsel of those in command have been sought and obtained at the threshold.
>
> Delegates are strictly enjoined, in the prosecution of their religious duties, to offer every possible assistance to chaplains, but never to intrude uninvited upon their proper

domain. And in their work of ministering to the health and comfort of those under medical treatment and care, to do nothing without instructions from the surgeons in charge, and in all great emergencies on the battle-ground, or in the field hospital, or at points where the wounded are to be fed and cared for, during their removal from the front, always to report themselves to the medical director or surgeon in charge, and place themselves under his instructions for just that service which will most effectually aid him in the work of relieving and saving our wounded heroes. . .[350]

On the evening of February 22, 1863, the commission held a great public meeting in the hall of the House of Representatives in Washington, the presiding officer being the secretary of the treasury, the Honorable Salmon P. Chase (1808–73). At this meeting a letter was read from the president:

Executive Mansion, Washington, February 22, 1863.

Whatever shall be sincerely and in God's name devised for the good of the soldiers and seamen in their hard spheres of duty can scarcely fail to be blessed. And whatever shall tend to turn our thoughts from the unreasoning and uncharitable passions, prejudices, and jealousies incident to a great national trouble such as ours, and to fix them upon the vast and long-enduring consequences for weal or for woe which are to result from this struggle, and especially to strengthen our reliance on the Supreme Being for the final triumph of the right, cannot but be well for us all.

The birthday of Washington and the Christian Sabbath coinciding this year, and suggesting together the highest interests of this life and of that to come, is most propitious for the meeting proposed.

A. Lincoln[351]

This statement of the great war president may well be supplemented by the closing section of his second inaugural (1865), in which he gave classic expression to the nation's desire to have the will of God accomplished:

. . . Fondly do we hope—fervently do we pray—that this mighty scourge of war may speedily pass away. Yet, if God wills that it continue until all the wealth piled by the bondman's two hundred and fifty years of unrequited toil shall be sunk, and until every drop of blood drawn with the lash shall be paid by another drawn with the sword, as was said three thousand years ago, so still it must be said, "The judgments of the Lord are true, and righteous altogether."

With malice toward none; with charity for all; with firmness in the right, as God gives us to see the right, let us strive on to finish the work we are in; to bind up the nation's wounds; to care for him who shall have borne the battle, and for his widow, and his orphan—to do all which may achieve and cherish a just and lasting peace among ourselves, and with all nations.[352]

The subject of faith in God and the relation between religion and patriotism as represented in presidential Thanksgiving Day proclamations is treated in another section.[353] A similar section might well be written on the same subject as related to inaugural presidential addresses from the time of George Washington to that of Franklin Roosevelt. Here the inaugurals of Lincoln and Wilson would have a high place.

We may close this section by referring to a matter in which the Church was deeply interested—the observance, whenever possible, of Sunday worship in the Army. "General Orders No. 7" are famous.

Head-Quarters Army of the Potomac, Washington, Sept. 7 [1861].

The Major-General commanding desires and requests that in future there may be a more perfect respect for the Sabbath on the part of his command. We are fighting in a holy cause, and should endeavor to deserve the benign favor of the Creator. Unless in case of an attack by the enemy, or some other extreme military necessity, it is commended to commanding officers that all work shall be suspended on the Sabbath; that no unnecessary movements shall be made on that day; that the men, as far as possible, shall be permitted to rest from their labors; that they shall attend Divine service after the customary morning inspection, and that officers and men alike use their influence to insure the utmost decorum and quiet on that day. The general commanding regards this as no idle form. One day's rest is necessary for man and animals. More than this, the observance of the holy day of the God of mercy and battles is our sacred duty.

(Signed) Geo. B. McClellan.
Major-General Commanding.[354]

(c) *Lincoln and the Emancipation Proclamation.*—During the first year of the war some of the Church periodicals were very critical of the administration because of its failure to take immediate steps to free the slaves which fell into the hands of the Union forces.[355] The Northern Churches were therefore prepared to receive the news of emancipation most sympathetically.

The story of the Emancipation Proclamation is an extremely interesting one. By President Lincoln's own statement he reached alone his decision to issue it as "a covenant with God." It was natural, therefore, that in its closing sentence he invoked "the considerate judgment of mankind and the gracious favor of Almighty God." It has been said that this proclamation was "potentially more revolutionary in human relationships than any event in American history since 1776." It "lifted the Civil War to the dignity of a crusade. . . ."[356] It met with a response not only in New England and the West, but especially from the Protestant Churches; and it had a profound influence in England and France, as it became a rallying point for all liberals. This was specially true among evangelical and liberty-loving circles in England, which became highly influential in getting support for the Union cause.

Nicolay and Hay, who as Lincoln's secretaries were qualified to speak with authority, clearly realized both the interest of the Churches in the cause of emancipation and their approval of the president's action. They summarized the Church situation in the North by saying that "In all the Church conventions which met after the President's preliminary proclamation of the 22d of September, 1862, that act of liberation was greeted with the heartiest expression of approval and support."[357]

It is known that some of the Churches had for some time been urging on the president the emancipation of the slaves. For instance, the Central Ohio Conference of the Methodist Church in 1861 passed resolutions to the effect that the proclamation of universal freedom would be the only solution of the difficulties faced by the nation, and on September 22, 1862, it forwarded to the president this resolution:

> We believe the time is fully come when, from a material necessity for the safety of the country, such a proclamation should be made; and we earnestly beseech the President of the United States to proclaim the emancipation of all slaves held in the United States, paying loyal men a reasonable compensation for their slaves.[358]

Nine days before the issuing of the first emancipation proclamation, as we know from the *Diary* of Gideon Welles, then secretary of war, Lincoln received a delegation of a committee of clergymen from Chicago. The delegation was composed of the Reverend William Weston Patton (1821–1889), who served as chairman, and the Reverend John Dempster (1794–1863), president of the Garrett Biblical Institute. Patton was a distinguished Congregationalist, deeply interested in emancipation, and later chosen president of Howard University. Dempster was a Methodist. According to the unsympathetic *Chicago Times* for September 5, 1862, the delegates represented

> the religious community of Chicago who believe that the country is now suffering under Divine judgments for the sin of oppression, and who favor the adoption of a memorial to the President of the United States, urging him to issue a decree of emancipation, as a sign of national repentance as well as a military necessity.[359]

In his reply to the delegation Lincoln stated that he had been considering the matter for months. He had received opposite advice "from religious men who are equally certain that they represent the divine will." He knew that one side must be mistaken and thought it possible that on some points both were in error. He added:

> I hope it will not be irreverent for me to say that if it is probable that God would reveal his will to others on a point so connected with my duty, it would be supposed he would reveal it directly to me; for unless I am more deceived in myself than I often am, it is my earnest desire to know the will of Providence in this matter. And if I can learn what it is I will do it. These are not, however, the days of miracles, and I suppose it will be granted that I am not to expect a direct revelation. I must study the plain

physical facts of the case, ascertain what is possible, and learn what appears to be wise and right.[360]

Soon after this interview President Lincoln issued, on September 23, his preliminary proclamation freeing the slaves, to go into effect January 1, 1863. This was applauded by the Churches of the North, which believed, however, that the full enfranchisement of the Negro could come only when the forces of Christian education were adequately employed to support and implement the new policy of the State.

The final proclamation—still making emancipation a war measure applying directly only to persons held as slaves in those districts "wherein the people . . . are this day in rebellion"—invoked "the considerate judgment of mankind and the gracious favor of Almighty God."[361] This religious note was specially characteristic of Lincoln's feelings and of his public utterances during the war years, as his addresses and his Thanksgiving Day proclamations testify.[362]

(2) IN THE CONFEDERACY

No more illuminating statement of the Southern view of slavery that prevailed among those who supported secession can be found than the one made by Alexander H. Stephens (1812–83), the vice-president of the Confederacy, on March 21, 1861, shortly after his election to that office.

> The prevailing ideas entertained by . . . most of the leading statesmen at the time of the formation of the old Constitution were that the enslavement of the African was in violation of the laws of nature; that it was wrong in principle, socially, morally, and politically. It was an evil they knew not well how to deal with, but the general opinion of the men of that day was that, somehow or other in the order of Providence, the institution would be evanescent and pass away. . . . Those ideas, however, were fundamentally wrong. They rested upon the assumption of the equality of races. This was an error. Our new government is founded upon exactly the opposite idea; its foundations are laid, its corner-stone rests upon the great truth that the negro is not equal to the white man; that slavery—subordination to the superior race—is his natural and normal condition . . . in conformity with the ordinance of the Creator. . . . Our Confederacy is founded upon principles in strict conformity with these [Divine] laws. This stone which was rejected by the first builders "is become the chief of the corner"—the real "corner-stone" in our new edifice.[363]

This is important, as being the reasoned utterance of a man who was widely respected and a distinguished Constitutional lawyer. Though at times erratic and inconsistent, he was not a fire-eater or an extremist, but a high-minded, independent statesman with a broad knowledge of history. A believer in the Union, he had opposed secession in the Georgia convention of January, 1861, and only reluctantly followed his state in breaking away from the Washington government.

The close connection developed in the middle decades of the century between slavery and Protestant theological orthodoxy has been generally recognized. The defenders of slavery realized that though it was entirely inconsistent with the spirit and even the letter of Christ's teaching, there was a good deal in the Old Testament, when taken in a literal way, which could be used to defend it. Consequently the South, with its emphasis on verbal inspiration, laid the foundations of that extreme fundamentalism which was later to become characteristic of large areas of the section. The relative parts played by the need of developing a Biblical defense of slavery, the backward educational conditions of the rural South, and the aftermath of the Great Revival in bringing about this later movement of fundamentalism would make a fascinating study.

We come now to the attitude of the Southern Churches during the conflict. A representative of the extreme Southern point of view was the Reverend James H. Thornwell, D.D. (1812–62), a professor in the theological seminary of the Presbyterian Church at Columbia, South Carolina, and former president of the state college. In a sermon preached at the capital of the state a month before South Carolina withdrew from the Union, he urged the doctrine of secession on the ground of Constitutional right, with the alleged encroachments upon slavery as the main justifying cause. He frankly said that the Northern states "have been reluctant to open the Territories to the introduction of slaves, and have refused to restore fugitives to their masters,"[364] and he was indignant about it. Near the end of his discourse he went so far as to recognize that to protect the South and its institutions—slavery of course being mainly in mind—"our path to victory may be through a baptism of blood."[365] Immediately after the secession of the state he published an article in the *Southern Presbyterian Review* for January, 1861. In it he wrote that "Every slaveholding State has just ground for secession," and advocated open resistance on the ground that "The triumph of the principles which Mr. Lincoln is pledged to carry out is the death-knell of slavery."[366]

Similar sermons and addresses were delivered by equally representative men, such as the Reverend Benjamin M. Palmer, D.D. (1818–1902), of New Orleans, the Reverend Thomas Smyth, D.D. (1808–73), of Charleston, South Carolina, and many others. Smyth in an article in the *Review* for April, 1863, entitled "The War of the South Vindicated," stated:

> We have taken up arms for the defence of our civil and religious rights, and God, our country, and the world at large, call upon us to acquit ourselves like men, for our wives and our little ones, for our homes, our sanctuaries, and even our religion itself.

. . . The war now carried on by the North is a war against slavery, and is, therefore, treasonable rebellion against the Constitution of the United States, and against the word, providence, and government of God.[367]

. . . God is working out a problem in the physical, social, political, and world-wide beneficial character of slavery, as a great missionary agency, of unexampled prosperity and success, which He is now demonstrating to the family of nations. In this war the South, therefore, is on God's side. She has His word, and providence, and omnipotent government, with her. And if she is found faithful to Him, and to this institution, which He has put under her spiritual care, then the heavens and earth may pass away, but God will not fail to vindicate His eternal providence, and defend and deliver His people, who walk in His statutes and commandments blameless.[368]

The Right Reverend Leonidas Polk, D.D. (1806–64), Bishop of the Episcopal Church in Louisiana, and a distinguished major general in the Southern army, and several other representative Episcopal bishops took nearly the same position. They were supported by virtually every newspaper in the Southern states and by many in the border states.

A clear statement of this attitude is that given in the *Southern Presbyterian* of Columbia, South Carolina, in its issue for December 15, 1860:

We entreat our readers to let nothing mislead them on this point. The real contest now in hand between the North and South, is for the preservation or destruction of *slavery*. . . . We ask our correspondent, we ask all or any of the sober men of the North, if it is not the almost unanimous resolution of the Northern people to forbid The Extension of Slavery? We believe it is; and the Southern people, for a thousand reasons, must regard that as a wrong that cannot be submitted to.[369]

Some idea of the effect of the outbreak of war on the religious press of the South may be derived from the *Methodist,* a Northern publication of the time (1861). It says:

Religious journals were among the first to plunge madly into the current which was rapidly bearing the South on to anarchy, and they are now among the first to disappear.

Without commenting on the Southern Baptist publications of which seven have suspended, or those of Presbyterian and other denominations, which have suffered in a corresponding manner, let us note the condition of the Southern Methodist papers. [Eleven of them are then named.] Without a single exception these papers warmly espoused the rebel cause. The first three named [the *Southern Methodist Itinerant,* Parkersburg, Virginia; the *Intelligencer,* Holston, Tennessee; the *North Carolina Christian Advocate,* Greensboro] have ceased to exist—a sure and speedy retribution.[370]

This was of course written from the point of view of a Union sympathizer.

But we are interested here not so much in the utterances of individuals or of denominational journals, significant as they are, as in the official actions of the Southern Churches. We shall begin with the Presbyterians.

The General Assembly of the Presbyterian Church in the Confederate States was formed at a meeting of commissioners from all the Southern synods, in Augusta, Georgia, on December 4, 1861. It chose as moderator Dr. Benjamin M. Palmer (1818–82), an able and respected theologian and educator, whose fast-day sermon of 1860 had shown him to be a strong advocate of secession. A Confederate general said that "his services were worth more to the cause than a soldiery of ten thousand men."[371] The Assembly reaffirmed its devotion to Presbyterian doctrine; made only one change in the standards, namely, the substitution of the word "Confederate" for the word "United" wherever it appeared; and adopted the most important statement dating from this period attempting to justify the Southern position from the Christian standpoint. It was prepared by the Reverend James Henry Thornwell (1812–62), who had been president of South Carolina College.

Here are quotations from the address adopted "to all the Churches of Jesus Christ throughout the earth." After explaining that they had "renounced the jurisdiction" of the General Assembly of the Presbyterian Church in the United States of America, and "dissolved the ties which bound them ecclesiastically with their brethren of the North," they proceed:

> The Church, therefore, in these seceded States, presents now the spectacle of a separate, and independent, and complete organization, under the style and title of the Presbyterian Church in the Confederate States of America. . . .[372]
>
> . . . We have separated from our brethren of the North as Abraham separated from Lot—because we are persuaded that the interests of true religion will be more effectually subserved by two independent Churches, under the circumstances in which the two countries are placed, than by one united body.
>
> 1. In the first place, the course of the last Assembly, at Philadelphia, conclusively shows that if we should remain together, the political questions which divide us as citizens, will be obtruded on our Church Courts, and discussed by Christian Ministers and Elders with all the acrimony, bitterness, and rancor with which such questions are usually discussed by men of the world. Our Assembly would present a mournful spectacle of strife and debate. Commissioners from the Northern would meet with Commissioners from the Southern Confederacy, to wrangle over the questions which have split them into two confederacies, and involved them in furious and bloody war. They would denounce each other, on the one hand, as tyrants and oppressors, and on the other, as traitors and rebels. . . .[373]
>
> The only conceivable condition, therefore, upon which the Church of the North and the South could remain together as one body, with any prospect of success, is the rigorous exclusion of the questions and passions of the forum from its halls of debate. This is what always ought to be done. The provinces of Church and State are perfectly

distinct, and the one has no right to usurp the jurisdiction of the other. The State is a natural institute, founded in the constitution of man as moral and social, and designed to realize the idea of justice. It is the society of rights. The Church is a supernatural institute, founded in the facts of redemption, and is designed to realize the idea of grace. It is the society of the redeemed. The State aims at social order, the Church at spiritual holiness. The State looks to the visible and outward, the Church is concerned for the invisible and inward. . . .[374]

The Church has no right to construct or modify a government for the State, and the State has no right to frame a creed or polity for the Church. They are as planets moving in different orbits, and unless each is confined to its own tract, the consequences may be as disastrous in the moral world as the collision of different spheres in the world of matter. . . .[375]

The first thing which roused our Presbyteries to look the question of separation seriously in the face, was the course of the Assembly in venturing to determine, as a Court of Jesus Christ, which it did by necessary implication, the true interpretation of the Constitution of the United States as to the kind of government it intended to form. A political theory was, to all intents and purposes, propounded, which made secession a crime, the seceding States rebellious, and the citizens who obeyed them traitors. We say nothing here as to the righteousness or unrighteousness of these decrees. What we maintain is, that, whether right or wrong, the Church had no right to make them—she transcended her sphere, and usurped the duties of the State. . . .[376]

In addition to this, there is one difference which so radically and fundamentally distinguishes the North and the South, that it is becoming every day more and more apparent that the religious, as well as the secular, interests of both will be more effectually promoted by a complete and lasting separation. The antagonism of Northern and Southern sentiment on the subject of slavery lies at the root of all the difficulties which have resulted in the dismemberment of the Federal Union, and involved us in the horrors of an unnatural war. The Presbyterian Church in the United States has been enabled by Divine grace to pursue, for the most part, an eminently conservative, because a thoroughly Scriptural, policy in relation to this delicate question. It has planted itself upon the Word of God, and utterly refused to make slaveholding a sin, or non-slaveholding a term of communion. But though both sections are agreed as to this general principle, it is not to be disguised that the North exercises a deep and settled antipathy to slavery itself, while the South is equally zealous in its defence. Recent events can have no other effect than to confirm the antipathy on the one hand and strengthen the attachment on the other. The Northern section of the Church stands in the awkward predicament of maintaining, in one breath, that slavery is an evil which ought to be abolished, and of asserting in the next, that it is not a sin to be visited by exclusion from communion of the saints. The consequence is, that it plays partly into the hands of abolitionists and partly into the hands of slaveholders, and weakens its influence with both. It occupies the position of a prevaricating witness whom neither party will trust. . . .[377]

The address then goes on to vindicate the position of the Church in the slavery controversy and to give reasons for believing that it should keep hands off except for seeing that slaves were humanely treated.

And here we may venture to lay before the Christian world our views as a Church, upon the subject of slavery. We beg a candid hearing.

In the first place, we would have it distinctly understood that, in our ecclesiastical capacity, we are neither the friends nor the foes of slavery; that is to say, we have no commission either to propagate or abolish it. The policy of its existence or non-existence is a question which exclusively belongs to the State. We have no right, as a Church, to enjoin it as a duty, or to condemn it as a sin. Our business is with the duties which spring from the relation; the duties of the masters on the one hand, and of their slaves on the other. These duties we are to proclaim and enforce with spiritual sanctions. The social, civil, political problems connected with this great subject transcend our sphere, as God has not entrusted to his Church the organization of society, the construction of Government, nor the allotment of individuals to their various stations. The Church has as much right to preach to the monarchies of Europe, and the despotism of Asia, the doctrines of republican equality, as to preach to the Governments of the South the extirpation of slavery. This position is impregnable, unless it can be shown that slavery is a sin. Upon every other hypothesis, it is so clearly a question for the State, that the proposition would never for a moment have been doubted, had there not been a foregone conclusion in relation to its moral character. Is slavery, then, a sin?[378]

Now, we venture to assert that if men had drawn their conclusions upon this subject only from the Bible, it would no more have entered into any human head to denounce slavery as a sin, than to denounce monarchy, aristocracy, or poverty. . . .[379]

We cannot prosecute the argument in detail, but we have said enough, we think, to vindicate the position of the Southern Church. We have assumed no new attitude. We stand exactly where the Church of God has always stood—from Abraham to Moses, from Moses to Christ, from Christ to the Reformers, and from the Reformers to ourselves. We stand upon the foundation of the Prophets and Apostles, Jesus Christ himself being the Chief cornerstone. . . . And to this holy war it is the purpose of our Church to devote itself with redoubled energy. We feel that the souls of our slaves are a solemn trust, and we shall strive to present them faultless and complete before the presence of God.

Indeed, as we contemplate their condition in the Southern States, and contrast it with that of their fathers before them, and that of their brethren in the present day in their native land, we cannot but accept it as a gracious Providence that they have been brought in such numbers to our shores, and redeemed from the bondage of barbarism and sin. . . . We cannot forbear to say, however, that the general operation of the system is kindly and benevolent; it is a real and effective discipline, and without it we are profoundly persuaded that the African race in the midst of us can never be elevated in the scale of being. As long as that race, in its comparative degradation, co-exists, side by side, with the white, bondage is its normal condition.[380]

As to the endless declamation about human rights, we have only to say that human rights are not a fixed, but a fluctuating quantity. . . .[381]

Are we not right, in view of all the preceding considerations, in remitting the social, civil, and political problems connected with slavery to the State? Is it not a subject, save in the moral duties which spring from it, which lies beyond the province of the Church? . . .[382]

We have quoted at more than usual length from these resolutions because they represent the most consistent and carefully drafted statement of the point of view of Southern Christians. They are also of significance for their underlying view of Church-State relations, namely, that the Church should not interfere in matters that are political, even when such a great moral issue as slavery is at stake. Though the specific issue which they were prepared to meet is a thing of the past, these statements still have value as revealing a general view, still widely prevalent, of the attitude which their sponsors feel the Church should assume toward social problems generally dealt with by the State. The attitude—at least as applied to slavery—seems to us impossible, but it was that of many honest men a century ago.

To the next General Assembly (1862) the Committee on the State of Religion reported that Presbyterian congregations without exception in the Southern states evinced "the most cordial sympathy with the people of the Confederate States" to maintain their rights against the despotic power which was attempting to crush them. And they were convinced that "this struggle is not alone for civil rights, and property and home, but for religion, for the Church, for the gospel."[383]

The Southern Episcopalians also formed a separate Church, November 22, 1862, though fortunately the Protestant Episcopal Church in the United States continued to consider them members. As a result, there was no permanent schism. The words "Confederate States of America" were substituted for the old designation, but otherwise there were few changes. In the pastoral letter of the Southern bishops dated Augusta, November 22, 1862, after stating that they believed the providence of God had guided their footsteps and that secession was a civil necessity, they said:

It is likewise the duty of the Church to press upon the masters of the country their obligation, as Christian men, so to arrange this institution [slavery] as not to necessitate the violation of those sacred relations which God has created, and which man cannot, consistently with Christian duty, annul. The systems of labor which prevail in Europe, and which are, in many respects, more severe than ours, are so arranged as to prevent all necessity for the separation of parents and children, and of husbands and wives; and a very little care upon our part, would rid the system upon which we are about to plant our national life, of these unchristian features.[384]

The Southern Baptist Convention, representing more than 600,000 members, adopted resolutions in Savannah, Georgia, May 13, 1861, that included the following sentences:

Recognizing the necessity that the whole moral influence of the people, in whatever capacity or organization, should be enlisted in aid of the rulers, who, by their suffrages, have been called to defend the endangered interests of person and property, of honor and liberty, it is bound to utter its voice distinctly, decidedly, emphatically, &c. . . . Resolved, That we most cordially approve of the formation of the Government of the Confederate States of America, and admire and applaud the noble course of that Government up to the present time. . . . Every principle of religion, of patriotism, and of humanity, calls upon us to pledge our fortunes and lives in the good work.[385]

Finally, in April, 1863, the Methodists, Baptists, Episcopalians, Presbyterians, Lutherans, German Reformed, and other Churches in the South united in putting forth "An Address to Christians throughout the World," signed on behalf of these religious bodies by ninety-six ministers. They justified the position of the Confederate government, and said:

The recent Proclamation of the President of the United States, seeking the emancipation of the slaves of the South, is, in our judgment, a suitable occasion for solemn protest on the part of the people of God throughout the world.[386]

The part played by the Churches in defending the Southern cause has long been recognized, but a study of the facts also indicates that they had done much to bring on the conflict. An article in the *Southern Presbyterian* under date of April 20, 1861, entitled "The Church and the Confederate States of America," makes this remarkable statement:

This revolution has been accomplished mainly by the churches. I do not undervalue the name, and position, and ability of politicians; still I am sure that our success is chiefly attributable to the support which they derived from the co-operation of the moral sentiment of the country. Without that, embodying, as it obviously did, the will of God, the enterprise would have been a failure. As a mere fact, it is already historical, that the Christian community sustained it with remarkable unanimity. . . .[387]

On the other hand, it is equally clear that the influence of representative ministers in the border states did as much as—probably more than—any other cause to maintain their loyalty to the Union. The work of the Reverend Robert J. Breckinridge (1800–71) of Kentucky, of Bishop William Whittingham, D.D.

(1805–79) of the Episcopal Church in Maryland, and of the Reverend George Junkin, D.D. (1790–1868) in Virginia are examples of those who, while not able to save their states, took a strong position against secession. This had been the historic attitude of the Old Dominion, where the leading statesmen and churchmen had never fully given up the belief of Washington, Jefferson, and most of the other Founding Fathers of the republic that slavery was an evil which should be eliminated. This was in spite of the fact that slavery was in its least objectionable form in that state, which only reluctantly withdrew from the Union.

The difficult legal postwar questions of the ownership and control of property in the South which had previously belonged to national Church organizations but had been taken over by seceding religious groups will be discussed in a later section.[388]

An incident involving the Confederacy and the papacy is worth recording. In the course of the war Pope Pius IX made an appeal for its termination, addressing similar letters under date of October 18, 1862, to Archbishop Hughes in New York, representing the churches in the North, and Archbishop Odin of New Orleans, representing the churches in the Confederacy. These messages urged them to exhort the people and their rulers "that with conciliated minds they would embrace peace and love each other with uninterrupted charity."[389] The following year the pope received an envoy from Jefferson Davis bearing this letter expressing appreciation of Rome's attitude.

Richmond, September 23, 1863

VERY VENERABLE SOVEREIGN PONTIFF:

The letters which you have written to the clergy of New Orleans and New York have been communicated to me, and I have read with emotion the deep grief therein expressed for the ruin and devastation caused by the war which is now being waged by the United States against the States and people which have selected me as their President, and your orders to your clergy to exhort the people to peace and charity. I am deeply sensible of the Christian charity which has impelled you to this reiterated appeal to the clergy. It is for this reason that I feel it my duty to express personally, and in the name of the Confederate States, our gratitude for such sentiments of Christian good feeling and love, and to assure Your Holiness that the people, threatened even on their own hearths with the most cruel oppression and terrible carnage, is desirous now, as it has always been, to see the end of this impious war; that we have ever addressed prayers to Heaven for this issue which Your Holiness now desires; that we desire none of our enemy's possessions, but that we fight merely to resist the devastation of our country and the shedding of our best blood, and to force them to let us live in peace under the protection of our own institutions, and under our laws, which not only insure to every one the enjoyment of his temporal rights, but also the free exercise of his religion. I pray Your Holiness to accept, on the part of myself and the people of the Confederate States, our sincere thanks for your efforts in favor of peace. May the Lord preserve the days of Your Holiness, and keep you under His Divine protection.

(Signed) JEFFERSON DAVIS.[390]

The pope replied as follows:

ILLUSTRIOUS AND HONORABLE PRESIDENT,

Salutation:

We have just received with all suitable welcome the persons sent by you to place in our hands your letter, dated 23rd of September last. Not slight was the pleasure we experienced when we learned, from those persons and the letter, with what feelings of joy and gratitude you were animated, illustrious and honorable President, as soon as you were informed of our letters to our venerable brother John, Archbishop of New York, and John, Archbishop of New Orleans, dated the 18th of October of last year, and in which we have with all our strength excited and exhorted those venerable brothers that, in their episcopal piety and solicitude, they should endeavor, with the most ardent zeal, and in our name, to bring about the end of the fatal civil war which has broken out in those countries, in order that the American people may obtain peace and concord, and dwell charitably together. It is particularly agreeable to us to see that you, illustrious and honorable President, and your people, are animated with the same desires of peace and tranquility which we have in our letters inculcated upon our venerable brothers. May it please God at the same time to make the other peoples of America and their rulers, reflecting seriously how terrible is civil war, and what calamities it engenders, listen to the inspirations of a calmer spirit, and adopt resolutely the part of peace. As for us, we shall not cease to offer up the most fervent prayers to God Almighty, that He may pour out upon all the people of America the spirit of peace and charity, and that He will stop the great evils which afflict them. We, at the same time, beseech the God of pity to shed abroad upon you the light of His grace, and attach you to us by a perfect friendship.

Given at Rome, at St. Peter's, the 3d of December, 1863, of our Pontificate 18.

(Signed) PIUS IX[391]

This letter when made public in the North brought much criticism.

The papacy, and following it, the Roman Catholic Church as such, took no direct part in the political and military conflict over the continuance of domestic slavery in the United States. It devoted itself to its regular spiritual and humanitarian work. Its generally conservative attitude toward slavery has been discussed at some length in another section.[392]

Here and there, however, individual Catholics spoke out. We have referred to the outstanding Union and antislavery attitude of Archbishop Purcell of Cincinnati,[393] who was supported by his brother, the editor of the *Catholic Telegraph*. Another instance of Catholic independence and courage was that of Bishop Félix Dupanloup (1803–78), of Orléans in France, who in the midst of the Civil War issued a pastoral letter on April 6, 1862, condemning slavery and praying for the release of the unfortunate Negroes still held in bondage in the United States.[394]

Generally speaking, the Jews of the South naturally identified themselves with the point of view of their section and gave support to slavery. A striking exception was Rabbi David Einhorn (1809–79) of Baltimore, who wrote and preached courageously against it. There were also a few opponents of slavery even in the extreme South where the influence of Judah Touro (1775–1854), the respected philanthropist of New Orleans, and son of the well-known Newport rabbi, continued. He had emancipated his only slave and had aided others to obtain their freedom.[395]

Section 6. THE POSTWAR ACTIVITIES—SECURING EDUCATION AND CONSTITUTIONAL RIGHTS FOR FORMER SLAVES

The part played by the Church after emancipation in fitting the slave for his civil responsibilities was of national importance. Indeed, the education of the Southern Negro in its early stages after the war was due mainly to the missionary zeal of the Northern churches. This formed in many ways the most constructive work for the Negro during the decade of Reconstruction. It left its permanent impress for good on the South, not only through the institutions founded and the freedmen trained, but through stimulating public education by convincing the South that the former slave was capable of education and would profit by it. The Congregational Church, which stood behind the American Missionary Association, was a specially important factor in this movement. It had produced many antislavery leaders, and now did much of the educational work which in other countries would have been undertaken under similar circumstances by the State. It is necessary only to mention some of the institutions which it founded or fostered. Atlanta University, 1865; Fisk University, 1866; Talladega College, 1867; Hampton Institute, 1868, were characteristic of these. Howard University, chartered by Congress in 1867, should also be mentioned, for, though mainly supported by the government and undenominational, it grew out of a missionary meeting in the First Congregational Church in Washington in 1866; has had from the first a definitely Christian purpose; has generally had a minister of religion as its president; and has received much help from the American Missionary Association, especially for its School of Religion.[396]

The teachers in these institutions in the early decades were mostly New England men and women, and though they were sometimes open to criticism for not understanding Southern conditions and difficulties, and for overemphasizing a conventional academic education, their work was of inestimable importance. They trained the leaders of the Negro race, and were ever watchful to try to protect the freedmen's interests. All the other important religious bodies were also active in establishing and supporting schools and colleges for the Negroes. Characteristic of these were Penn School (1862), Quaker; Shaw University (1865), Baptist; Clark University, Atlanta (1870), Methodist Episcopal. Two institutions for Negroes were founded in the North just before the Civil War: Lincoln University (formerly Ashmun Institute) in Pennsylvania, by the Presbyterians in 1854; and Wilberforce, in Ohio, by the Methodists in 1856. The Quakers, though few in number, did much with their strong, century-old opposition to slavery, due largely to their great leader John Woolman (1720–72).[397]

Such institutions, established mainly by religious bodies, and supported by the contributions of church people, met the major educational needs for the training of Negro leadership in the years immediately after the war; and they still render vitally important service, though this may be relatively less conspicuous in a day of large support of public education.

It should also be remembered that a few Southern schools for Negroes, of which Tuskegee Institute is a conspicuous example, also arose in the Southern states though the action of their own citizens; and that the Reconstruction legislatures in which the colored people played such a large part did much, in spite of corruption and extravagance in other fields, to encourage Negro education. But in the earliest days of emancipation no factor was more helpful than that of the Negro schools founded by the Christian people of the North and supported by frequent visits of their officers to the Northern churches. This condition of large Northern Church support for Negro education continued through the nineteenth century, and is still important, though in this century the principal part in such education has been played increasingly by the public school systems of the South supported by Southern taxation.

In the period of Reconstruction the members of most Northern Churches—aside from the Roman Catholics, who continued to be wedded, at least locally, to the Democratic party—identified themselves with the Republicans, because they felt that only so could they safeguard the rights of the Negro, and the missionary work they had started in the South.

The Roman Catholic Church, which had had so little to say officially about the slaves and slavery during the days of national debate, now came out for extending to the freed Negroes "Christian education and moral restraint." The pastoral letter of the Plenary Council held in Baltimore in 1866, with both North and South represented, said:

We could have wished, that in accordance with the action of the Catholic Church in past ages, in regard to the serfs of Europe, a more gradual system of emancipation could have been adopted, so that they might have been in some measure prepared to make a better use of their freedom, than they are likely to do now. Still, the evils which must necessarily attend upon the sudden liberation of so large a multitude with their peculiar dispositions and habits, only make the appeal to our Christian charity and zeal, presented by their forlorn condition, the more forcible and imperative.[398]

In the South also the Churches began to interest themselves more actively in the cause of the freedmen.

The Alabama Baptist Convention in 1865 stated:

The condition of our colored population appeals strongly to the sympathy of every Christian heart and demands, at the hands of all who love the Saviour, renewed exertions for their moral and religious improvement.[399]

It recommended the establishment of Negro Sunday schools, and more adequate preaching of the gospel to the former slaves. The Protestant Episcopal Church took action the same year, the Bishop of North Carolina pointing out in his pastoral letter the ignorance and inexperience of the colored people. He warned his members of the danger of the Negro falling into mischievous hands, and urged the formation of Negro congregations in the towns and provision for the religious training of Negro children. Likewise the Methodist Episcopal Church, South, which had long before the Civil War interested itself in the moral and spiritual welfare of the slaves, renewed its activities in their behalf. By 1866 it had outlined a comprehensive plan for their development. They were to be formed into separate churches with their own quarterly conferences; colored persons were to be licensed to preach, and, where conditions justified, colored districts were to be organized, and later formed into annual conferences. When there came to be two or more annual conferences they were to be assisted in forming a separate Church. Thus in 1870 the Colored Methodist Episcopal Church was organized, consisting of the Negro members who had remained in the Methodist Episcopal Church, South.[400]

The part played by the Churches in abolishing slavery and educating the Negro has been much more adequately recognized in recent years. It has been referred to in another section.[401] Furthermore, the Church was probably the greatest single factor in the decade after the Civil War in educating the former slave for effective citizenship, and in advancing the good in Reconstruction, especially through developing a system of public education in the South, and checking the bad. It has given the colored man from that day until now many of his leading centers of training and inspiration. Today the liberal groups among the white Churches of the South, basing their claims on definitely religious grounds, are doing much to protect the Negro's rights and to advance interracial co-operation. The Negro Church has also been a factor of prime importance in the development of this highly significant minority group.[402]

In general it may be said that religion was the greatest inspiration of the Negro slave, as the "spirituals" so clearly show; that the religious motive was among the major underlying factors leading to the abolition of slavery, the education of the freedman, and the assuring to him of his Constitutional rights; and that the Negro Church, which the cleavages of the Civil War did so much to develop, has given the Negro his principal opportunity for self-expression and self-development. This is said with full recognition of the conservative character of most Churches and Church members, and of the fact that the Churches of the North, in spite of marked improvement since the beginning of World War II, have not fully kept up their generous attitude of two generations ago toward the Negro. But a relatively small and earnest group of thoroughly enfranchised Christian men and women, North and South, white and colored, has been mainly responsible for the progress made since emancipation, and is striving for the removal of those remaining barriers to the progress of Negro Americans that are inconsistent with the ideals of the Declaration of Independence and contrary to the letter and spirit of the Bill of Rights. They will get aid and support from the findings and recommendations of the President's Committee on Civil Rights, whose report was published in October, 1947.

As we survey the history of the long struggle to enfranchise the Negro slave both legally and spiritually, we are impressed by the contribution of the Christian Church. But in humility we remember that this enfranchisement has already taken nearly two thousand years, and is still far from complete: much remains to be done to overcome inherited prejudices and discriminations. It was the early Church, in the Roman world, which first among important organized groups recognized the slave as a human being and strove earnestly to ameliorate his condition; encouraging manumission but making no frontal attack on the institution of slavery. It was the medieval Church which improved his status through developing serfdom as part of the feudal system in place of chattel slavery. It was largely the spirit of the Founder of Christianity which little by little permeated the thought of Europe and led to the humanitarianism and democratic ideals of eighteenth century philosophers in England and France, even though many of them repudiated the Church—largely because its worldliness and ecclesiasticism had so nearly obliterated that breadth of human sympathy for the oppressed which Christ taught. It was the Church which directly inspired William Wilberforce (1759–1833), Thomas Clarkson (1760–1846), Zachary Macaulay (1768–1838), and their associates, who were mainly responsible in the early nineteenth century for the abolition of the African slave trade and for the final overthrow of slavery throughout the British Empire in 1833. It was the Church, through Quakers, Moravians, Methodists, Congregationalists, and others, which demanded in the early decades of the nineteenth century that slavery be discontinued in the United States. Speaking generally, it also was the Church—in spite of its defection in the South immediately preceding the Civil War, and in spite of its refusal to follow William Lloyd Garrison (1805–79) in his uncompromising attitude and violent language—which with effectiveness supported both Negro emancipation and Negro education.

An impartial British philosopher, Alfred Whitehead (1861–), now a professor at Harvard, gives us an interesting summary of the intellectual, social, and spiritual forces that led to the overthrow of slavery. He says:

> Thus in the evolution of the strands of thought which constituted the final stage in the destruction of the iniquitous slave-foundation of civilization, there is interwoven the insights and the heroisms of sceptical humanitarians, of Catholics, of Methodists, of Quakers. But the intellectual origin of the movement is to be traced back for more than two thousand years to the speculations of the philosophical Greeks upon functions of the human soul, and its status in the world of flux.[403]

Undoubtedly the origin of most intellectual and social ideas, as ideas, goes back to the philosophers of Greece, but it must be remembered that their civilization was largely based on the theory and fact of slavery, and that it was ultimately due mainly to the direct and indirect influence of Christianity that slavery was destroyed. Even when the organized Church seemed indifferent or slow to act, the spirit and letter of its Master's teachings, especially regarding brotherhood, and the record of the early Christian community, were always there on the written page of the New Testament to point the way to ultimate victory.

BOOK II

Modern and Contemporary Problems and Their Solution

Part Five

CHURCH-STATE PROBLEMS AFTER THE CIVIL WAR—POLITICAL AND SOCIAL ISSUES; EXPANSION; MINORITY RIGHTS; SCHOOLS

Chapter XVI

THE CONNECTION OF THE CHURCH WITH HISTORIC NATIONAL ISSUES AFTER RECONSTRUCTION

Introduction—The Rise of Social Christianity; Christian Socialism. The "social gospel" arose in America at the close of the Civil War, occasioned mainly by certain acute industrial problems which came to the fore in connection with immigration, urbanization, and the development of the industrial system. Its relationship and application to many problems and activities of the State and the community bring it conspicuously into our theme of Church and State in the United States. Its roots are clearly in the teachings of the Old Testament prophets, the pages of the Gospel, and the thought and activities of the Christian Church. The Church through most of its history has victories to its credit against social abuses, and in the Middle Ages through the guild system, the "truce of God," hostels, hospitals, and other activities, made Christianity the greatest power for unity and civilization in Europe. We have touched on these in dealing with the background of American democracy, religious freedom, etc.[1] Christianity was not satisfied merely with fitting the individual for eternal life; it was also concerned with the realization of the Kingdom of God on earth.[2] Such ideas were held and demonstrated in this country by the framers of the Puritan commonwealths, and later by groups as widely separated as the Roman Catholics and the Unitarians. The remarkably heroic work of the Catholics during the cholera epidemic of 1832, which received grateful acknowledgment from mayors of several of our larger cities,[3] and their care of the swarms of Irish immigrants, mostly arriving in great poverty, were two out of many examples of the public social services they early rendered in this country. But it was to Unitarianism, with its insistence on meeting the actual social needs of humanity, that we are perhaps most indebted for emphases in teaching which led to the effective beginnings of the movement that was to make the "social gospel" a national force. It was the principal "seedbed in which the ideological roots of social Christianity found themselves most at home,"[4] though the Quakers of Pennsylvania preceded it in some fields.

William Ellery Channing's (1780–1842) famous Baltimore sermon of 1819, with its emphasis on the dignity and divine possibilities of man, the immanence of God, and the importance of life in this world, is probably the best event to take as a starting point for the movement in the United States, though here and there other individual ministers had for a long time been proclaiming in one way or another a social as well as a personal message. Unitarianism's emphasis on the social side of Christianity is well expressed in Channing's essay *Honor Due to All Men* (1832):

> Among the many and inestimable blessings of Christianity, I regard as not the least the new sentiment with which it teaches man to look upon his fellow-beings; the new interest which it awakens in us towards everything human; the new importance which it gives to the soul; the new relation which it establishes between man and man. In this respect it began a mighty revolution, which has been silently spreading itself through society, and which, I believe, is not to stop until new ties shall have taken the place of those which have hitherto, in the main, connected the human race. Christianity has as yet but begun its work of reformation. Under its influences a new order of society is advancing, surely though slowly. . . .[5]

This may all seem commonplace to us, but a century ago it represented an important new emphasis.

It might also be mentioned, though Hopkins, the historian of American social Christianity, does not refer to it, that the basis of fellowship adopted by the Universalists in 1803 was definitely humanitarian in purpose. It refers to the nature of God as love; the restoration of "the whole family of mankind to holiness and happiness"; and the need "to be careful to maintain order and practice good works."[6]

These ideas were the inevitable reaction of American Protestantism stirred to activity by many crusades, from those early ones against slavery and intemperance to the later efforts after the Civil War to improve urban industrial conditions, conditions which were due largely to the influx into our eastern cities and industrial regions of "cheap" European labor.

Another influence came from abroad. It was the revived theory of progress (originally suggested by the Abbé de Saint-Pierre in 1737) associated with the name of a French Army officer who fought under Washington in the American Revolution—the Count de Saint-Simon. He was an erratic genius, sympathetic with the ideas of the new republic and with the theories of Condorcet. In 1815 he announced the coming perfection of the social order. He felt that the first step toward the goal of developing social happiness was the amelioration of the lot of the working classes, and this he believed to be the principal problem of government in reorganizing society. He thought that Socialism held the key.[7] His social philosophy, known as Saint Simonism, summed up in the manifesto of his followers issued in 1830, and based largely on his book *Système industriel, Nouveau Christianisme,* had considerable influence on advanced thinkers in this country.

The Unitarians started in Boston in 1826 "a ministry at large to the unchurched classes" which has been referred to as not only

> the first example of religious social service in America but also the first serious effort on the part of a religious body to cope with the social and religious problems of the submerged population of a sizable city.[8]

The fact is that a social conscience was coming into being, especially in and around Boston. Congregationalists were affected as well as Unitarians. The year after the Unitarian beginnings, Lyman Beecher (1775–1863) was active in forming in his church the "Hanover Association of Young Men." This was in January, 1827. Before the end of the year there were four other associations of the same kind in the city. They not only interested themselves in advancing the work of their church but also took up such matters as the violation of the Sabbath, the conditions of the colored population, work for the newly arrived Irish, the welfare of sailors, and so on.[9]

Ralph Waldo Emerson (1803–82), who began his career as a Unitarian minister, and the Transcendentalists also became factors in promoting social idealism,[10] believing as they did in the essential divinity of human nature. The Transcendentalist Club was founded in Boston in 1836, and their Brook Farm experiment started in 1842. Somewhat later the greatest leader of organized Unitarianism after Channing, the Reverend Theodore Parker (1810–60), who had been much influenced by the Transcendentalists, became a factor of importance in social reform movements. He gave up the pastorate of the First Parish Church (Unitarian) in West Roxbury in 1846, to become pastor of an independent group at the Melodeon in Boston. He used this, and later the Music Hall, as a center from which to stir the American conscience. His discourses before great congregations and his practical efforts in opposition to slavery and in behalf of temperance and prison reform were notable. His well-known motto, as he vigorously attacked abuses in the body social and politic, was "Religion rises every morning and works all day."

The evangelism of Charles G. Finney (1792–1875) in the 'thirties, and the publication by Horace Bushnell (1802–76) of his *Christian Nurture* in 1846, did much to break down the extreme individualism of the old Puritanism in the conservative Churches, and to turn men at least in the direction of a larger social emphasis.

About the middle of the century the writings of such English Christian Socialists as Frederick Denison Maurice (1805–72) and Charles Kingsley (1819–75) had a deep influence, especially in Episcopal Church circles.[11] These were supplemented by the appearance in 1866 of *Ecce Homo* by Sir John Robert Seeley (1834–95), a work which emphasized the significance of Jesus in terms of social life and the accomplishment of God's will on earth.

Certain other new factors of importance were influencing the United States from foreign countries. Among these were the European industrial revolutions in the late 'forties; the philosophic, social, and scientific thought that came from Germany (Kant and his successors), where Americans had begun to go for advanced studies; the theory of evolution, which in its accepted form dates back to Darwin's *Origin of Species* (1859); and Utilitarianism. This last, specially identified during the past hundred years with the name of John Stuart Mill (1806–73), a strong thinker outside of church circles, emphasizing "the greatest happiness of the greatest number," was not as powerful a force in America as in England, but it helped the movement for social reform through legislation, and especially for the alleviation of the working classes. Mill's opposition to slavery and his defense of liberty were also influential in this country.

But it was not until the slaves had been liberated by the Civil War that "the social impulse of Christianity" was set free to devote itself to the relief of the new industrial conditions which the war had helped to create. Up to that time public interests of the Church had been mainly absorbed in the question of slavery; now religion became "the most powerful drive behind the humanitarian movements of the age."[12] When Henry Ward Beecher (1813–87) wrote in his *Sermon on Christian Character,* published in 1869, that "All the details of human life" were to be influenced by Christianity, the social gospel was beginning to come into being. People began to think of the Kingdom of God as having to do with this world as well as the next. The first notable presentation of this view was made by President Samuel Harris (1814–99) of Bowdoin College, later Dwight Professor of Systematic Theology at Yale, who in 1870 gave a series of lectures to the students of Andover Theological Seminary entitled *The Kingdom of Christ on Earth*. He emphasized the fact that the Kingdom "proposed to realize on earth the universal reign of justice and love."[13] Similarly, in the years immediately following, Professor John Bascom (1827–1911) was teaching the students at Williams College that the Kingdom of God was a perfected society to be evolved here. Next came the efforts of a group of far-sighted men: Charles Loring Brace (1826–90), an earnest New York lay reformer; Washington Gladden (1836–1918), pastor after 1882 of the Congregational Church of Columbus, Ohio; Professor Richard T. Ely (1854–1943) of Johns Hopkins University; the Reverend Richard Heber Newton (1840–1914), Rector of All Souls Church (Episcopal) of New York City; and others. These men were deeply concerned with the application of Christianity to social and economic conditions. A striking example was an editorial by

Gladden, written while he was on the editorial staff of the *Independent* (1871–75). In reply to Boss Tweed's defiant "What are you going to do about it?" he wrote:

We are going to turn you and all your creatures out of your offices. . . .
We are going to get back as much as we can of the booty you have stolen.
. . . We are going to . . . send you to your own place, the penitentiary. . . .
We are going to make the city and the whole country too hot for you. . . .
God may have mercy on you; but as for us, we promise you that your ill-gotten booty shall be but a poor compensation for the inheritance of shame which shall be yours forever.[14]

Articles by Christian ministers began to appear in papers and magazines on prisons, boys' clubs, workingmen's clubs (of which perhaps the first was started at St. Mark's Church, Philadelphia, in 1870), co-operatives of the Rochdale type, child labor, the ethics of trade, and the reforming of factory conditions, such as the attempt by the Reverend Joseph Cook (1838–1901), Congregationalist, in Lynn, Massachusetts, beginning with 1871.

During this period when religious leaders were here and there trying to awaken the churches to a sense of Christian responsibility for the conditions of the poor, the unfortunate, and factory workers, there were some slight evidences that leaders of labor were also on their part invoking religious sanctions for their constructive efforts—at least we are fortunate that the labor movement in this country did not take on an antireligious slant. For example, Uriah S. Stephens (1821–82), the founder in 1869 of the first important American labor movement, the Knights of Labor, stated:

Creed, party, and nationality are but outward garments and present no obstacle to the hearts of the worshippers of God, the Universal Father, and the workers for man, the universal brotherhood. . . . The work to which this fraternity addresses itself is one of the greatest magnitude, that of knitting up into a compact and homogeneous amalgamation all the world's workers in one universal brotherhood, guided by the same rules, working by the same methods, practicing the same forms for accomplishing the same ends. Its work is the complete emancipation of wealth-producers from the thraldom and loss of wage slavery. The entire redemption of the world's toilers from the political tyranny of unjust laws, and the annihilation of the great anti-Christ of civilization manifest in the idolatry of wealth, and the consequent degradation and social ostracism of all else not possessing it, and its baneful effects upon heaven-ordained labor.[15]

The reform movements of the 'seventies were mostly sporadic, by individuals or small groups. The leading exceptions were the Episcopal Church Congress, the National Reform Association, and the Evangelical Alliance.

The constitution of the National Reform Association, organized in 1864 by representatives of eleven denominations meeting in Xenia, Ohio, contains the following statement, characteristic of the views of conservative religious leaders of the time:

Believing that Almighty God is the source of all power and authority in civil government, that the Lord Jesus Christ is the Ruler of all nations, and that the will of God is of supreme authority in civil affairs;

Remembering that this country was settled by Christian men, with Christian ends in view, and that they gave a distinctly Christian character to the institutions which they established;

Perceiving the subtle and persevering attempts which are made to prohibit the reading of the Bible in our Public Schools, to overthrow our Sabbath laws, to corrupt the Family, to abolish the Oath, Prayer in our National and State Legislatures, Days of Fasting and Thanksgiving, and other Christian features of our institutions, and so to divorce the American Government from all connection with the Christian religion;

Viewing with grave apprehension the corruption of our politics, the legal sanction of the Liquor Traffic, and the disregard of moral and religious Character in those who are exalted to high places in the nation;

Believing that a written Constitution ought to contain explicit evidence of the Christian character and purpose of the nation which frames it, and perceiving that the silence of the Constitution of the United States in this respect is used as an argument against all that is Christian in the usage and administration of our Government;

We, citizens of the United States, do associate ourselves under the following Articles, and pledge ourselves to God and to one another to labor, through wise and lawful means, for the ends herein set forth. . . .[16]

In 1867 this association, which drew large support from the Reformed Presbyterian Church, began the publication of *The Christian Statesman,* which still exists. The first issue stated its deep conviction that "National life must be pervaded with a religious spirit and purpose," and that "Governments are seats of power from which emanate some of the chief moral forces that act and re-act in human society." Consequently the "care and service of the State" is part of the Christian "patriot's duty to God." The journal interested itself in such matters as the Christian law of marriage, Sabbath observance, temperance, franchise limitations, the prevention of crime, the use of the Bible in the public schools, and "the frank and earnest discussion of political questions from the Christian point of view."[17] In a word, its purpose was to maintain what it understood to be the Christian ideal of the American republic.

The Episcopal Church Congress, established in 1874, discussed not only the Christian approach to the working classes, and the whole problem of the relation of capital and labor, but specifically the responsibility of Christian men in such matters as civil service reform, the tariff, charity organization, social service, and other contemporary problems. According to the historian of the *Rise of the Social Gospel in American Protestantism 1865–1915*, "Social issues first came to the semiofficial attention of a major American religious body in the early meetings" of this congress,[18] which brought together every year representative liberally minded clergymen and laymen.

The Christian Labor Union was another important movement. According to Hopkins it "set the first marker along the unpopular path of left-wing social Christian movements in the United States."[19] In Massachusetts it undertook to reform the relations between capital and labor, and maintained a precarious existence between 1872 and 1878. In 1874 it began publishing a magazine called *Equity: A Journal of Christian Labor Reform.* It took the ground that the attention of the Protestant Church

> has been so centered on the work in the heart of the individual, that the coordinate and equally essential work of reorganizing society has first been lost sight of and then denied. And so it has come about that our business system is pagan in origin, selfish in structure, and the deadly foe of Christianity; and yet Protestantism has no word against it. . . .[20]

This was followed in 1877 by a journal entitled *The Labor-Balance,* which was even more radical, coming out frankly for the socializing of land and the instrumentalities for the production of wealth, and having as its aim a "broad and generous objective Christian communism," to take the place of the Church's "narrow and selfish individualism."[21] Since this was the year of one of the most serious industrial strikes in American history, the paper had some significance.

Professor Arthur Schlesinger (1888–), writing of the *Rise of the American City* in the twenty-year period beginning with 1878, though implying that the organized Church was not yet very active in the cause of social amelioration, recognizes that "the humanitarian leaders of the day were deeply imbued with the Christian spirit and most of them were loyal Church members."[22] This suggests the case of Henry George (1839–97), whose early training in a deeply religious home left its marked impress upon him. He is principally remembered for his "single tax" views, but he also made a considerable contribution to social Christianity. He stated that "there is in true Christianity a power to regenerate the world,"[23] and that the social question is at bottom a religious question. His most important book, *Progress and Poverty* (1879), though primarily an economic textbook, showed a true concern for religion. He attacked religious institutions for their social failures, but felt that true religion, if applied to the problems of the time, would cure many of the world's ills. This was also the point of view of an influential book by Charles Loring Brace (1826–90), *Gesta Christi; or A History of Humane Progress under Christianity,* which appeared in 1882. Its author's conviction was that Christianity is "the *greatest* element in modern progress"; that Christ is "the central figure in the world's charity"; and that his teachings formed "a new moral force in the world's history."[24] *Socialism,* by Professor Roswald D. Hitchcock (1817–87), published in 1879, marked the beginning of a discussion that soon became one of the "focal points" of the social gospel.[25] But no other book in the fourth quarter of the nineteenth century did as much to get people interested in the application of religion to the problems of the nation as a work by the Reverend Josiah Strong (1847–1916), *Our Country: its possible future and its present crisis,* published in 1885. It reached a sale of over 500,000 copies. I can remember as a boy how it turned my attention to this field, which has ever since interested me greatly. It was followed by other books, including the *New Era* (1893), by the same author, who, as executive secretary of the Evangelical Alliance,[26] became a national power. He was convinced that a Christian America, building on its historic Protestant foundations, could become a great blessing to the world. He wrote from the side of the Church.

Strong was followed by a more incisive and scholarly, but not more influential, writer from the side of economic and political thought, namely, Professor Richard T. Ely (1854–1943) of Johns Hopkins University and later of the University of Wisconsin, whose essays on *The Social Aspects of Christianity* (1887) were the first important effort by a prominent American scholar to state "the social side of the Church's mission."[27] He was an active force in forming the American Economic Association, and it is significant that the third of its fundamental principles was to recognize "the Church, the State, and . . . Science" as the major factors in the solution of the vast social problems brought out by the conflict between labor and capital.[28]

The Christian note in Dr. Ely's early trail-blazing work in the interest of organized labor is important. Some of his writings on the labor movement in America first appeared in *The Christian Union* in 1884, and *The Congregationalist* printed his early studies of the co-operative movement. In a well-known statement to his working-class readers, he wrote:

> Christ and all Christly people are with you for the right. Never let go that confidence. This is a sure guarantee of the successful issue of every good cause, the righting of every wrong. Christ forever elevated labor and exalted the laborer. He worked himself and he sought his associates and the first members of his church among workingmen, rude and ignorant, and certainly no better than the workingmen of today. As Charles Kingsley has said, "The Bible is the rich man's warning, and the poor man's comfort."[29]

He added—this was two generations ago—that if we write down the names of the men outside the laboring class who are prominent for their advocacy of the cause of labor we shall find three-fourths of them clergymen. He quoted such men as Thomas Beecher, Washington Gladden, Heber Newton, Howard Crosby, and Newman Smyth.

The *Christian Union* under the editorship of the Reverend Lyman Abbott (1835–1922) gave the American Economic Association and all sound social experiments its hearty support; and efforts were made by Christian leaders to formulate a theology in which the social aspects would be given due attention. A brilliant early attempt of this type was by the Reverend Professor John H. W. Stuckenberg (1835–1903), an outstanding Lutheran liberal, whose sermons and lectures in Berlin, where he was pastor of the American Church in the early 'nineties, greatly impressed the author as a young student at the university. In his book, *Christian Sociology,* which appeared in 1880, he took the ground that all social problems should be solved from a Christian standpoint, and that the second commandment of Christ was as important as the first. It was his conviction that the teachings of Christ "are adaptable to all the needs of men."[30]

A notable interdenominational congress was held in Cincinnati in 1885, in which the Reverend Josiah Strong, Professor Richard T. Ely, the Reverend Washington Gladden—then becoming a great power in socializing the attitude of the Churches—and other leaders took part. But this may be considered as merely preparatory to the large conventions held under the auspices of the Evangelical Alliance in 1887, 1889, and 1893, and described in the next section.

Social Christianity was now being popularized. Nothing did more to accomplish this than the simple books of the Reverend Charles M. Sheldon (1857–1946), effective Congregational pastor of Topeka, Kansas, from 1889 on. The most significant of his books, *In His Steps: What Would Jesus Do?,* first published in 1896, had an amazing circulation and influence. It is believed that more copies of it were printed than of any other book written in this country. By 1925 it was estimated that over eight million copies had been printed in the United States. An equally large number were sold in England, and it was translated into twenty-one foreign languages, the total sales being estimated by its author in 1933 as 23,000,000 copies.[31] The author tried to answer the question: "What would Jesus do in solving the problems of present political, economic and social life?" It was preceded by a book by the well-known English journalist, William T. Stead (1849–1912), entitled *If Christ Came to Chicago* (1893). This book had a large influence on the reform of municipal conditions; more than 200,000 copies were sold. Its revelation of the crime and graft in which police and politicians were involved so aroused public opinion that the

Civic Federation of Chicago was formed. This did much to improve local conditions.[32]

Ray Stannard Baker (1870–1946) has given us the opinion of a competent witness of the conditions which Stead described:

> The difficulty was that the indictments made in Stead's book were generally true; and everybody knew they were true. The harlots were there, paying their wages of sin to corrupt policemen who passed on part of the loot to boodling aldermen and politicians; the gamblers were there, robbing Chicago of millions of dollars a year; the rich and greedy public-utility magnates were there, stealing franchises; the sleepy churches were there, unaroused to their duty. If Christ were to visit Chicago, Stead remarked that He would prefer to visit the City Hall, with all its wickedness, to remaining among the churches.[33]

This is a substantially true indictment of the attitude of the Churches toward the social ills of our great municipalities half a century ago. It took Stead, and Parkhurst, and Rauschenbusch, and many other reformers to awaken them from their lethargy.

The progress of all these and similar efforts to interest the Church in social reform may be studied with profit in the two editions of the *Encyclopedia of Social Reform* (1898, 1908), edited by the Reverend W. D. P. Bliss (1856–1926), who had organized in 1889 the first Christian Socialist party in the United States, and for four years thereafter served as rector of the Church of the Carpenter, which he organized in Boston. The new party declared that "The teachings of Jesus Christ lead directly to some specific form or forms of socialism."

In the last quarter of the nineteenth century leaders of the Churches were identifying themselves with almost all the social betterment movements of the time. They were interested in reforming the world. The essay of William Graham Sumner (1840–1910), *The Absurd Effort to make the World Over,* would not have seemed to them the voice of God. They did not think that "rugged individualism" was sufficient; they were more interested in the "social meliorism" of Lester Ward (1841–1913). They believed that man could to a large degree control for the better the destiny of his fellows. A case in point is provided by the charity organization societies. This movement, whose roots go back to the efforts of the Reverend Dr. Thomas Chalmers (1780–1847) in Edinburgh from 1819 to 1823, really started in substantially its present form in London in 1869. It was due mainly to a paper read the previous year by a Unitarian minister on "How to Deal with the Unemployed Poor of London," and to the earnest efforts of Edward Denison (1840–70), son of the Bishop of Salisbury. It was transported to this country in 1877, when an Episcopal clergyman, the Reverend S. H. Gurteen, organized the first American society in Buffalo.[36] Boston, New Haven, Philadelphia, Cincinnati, Brooklyn, and New York followed in that order in the five years following. Church leaders were prominent in almost all of these. In Cincinnati, as in Buffalo, a clergyman, the Reverend Charles W. Wendte (1844–1931), Unitarian, was the chief promoter.

There are now hundreds of such societies in American cities—frequently called Associated Charities or Family Service Associations. The important part played by the Church in their work is evidenced by the author's own experience as a resident of New Haven and Washington. In both places clergymen were the presidents during a large part of his years of residence, while in one an honored former minister was the executive secretary for some twenty years. These societies, as was frequently found with the organization of relief on a national scale during the depression of the 1930's, provide an important link between the Churches and the agents of the State. They serve alike members of all religious bodies, and generally have representatives of the three faiths on their boards of directors, but owing to the recognized efficiency of the Society of St. Vincent de Paul (Roman Catholic) and of various Jewish charities, their work in most cities, where Catholics and Jews are found in large numbers, tends to be mainly among Protestants and the unchurched.

The Church Association for the Advancement of the Interests of Labor (the C.A.I.L.) was formed at a meeting of Episcopal clergy in 1887, the plan of organization being proposed by the Reverend W. D. P. Bliss, whose social work we have already noted. It had a wide influence. Although its methods were conservative, its principles were for the time very liberal. They were as follows:

1. It is the essence of the teachings of Jesus Christ that God is the Father of all men and that all men are brothers.
2. God is the sole possessor of the Earth and its fulness; man is but the steward of God's bounties.
3. Labor being the exercise of body, mind and spirit in the broadening and elevating of human life, it is the duty of every man to labor diligently.
4. Labor, as thus defined, should be the standard of social worth.
5. When the divinely-intended opportunity to labor is given to all men, one great cause of the present widespread suffering and destitution will be removed.[37]

The fact that Bishop Frederic Dan Huntington (1819–1904) served as its president for seventeen years prior to his death, and was succeeded by Bishop Henry Codman Potter (1835–1908), indicates what substantial support it secured. It obtained from the Episcopal Diocese of New York a regulation that all printing should be given to firms paying standard wages; established an important Committee on Conciliation and Mediation; had an effective Sweatshop Committee that carried on aggressive work against this evil; and conducted a publication known as *Hammer and Pen,* advocating the cause of labor reform. It continued to exist until it had secured in 1926 the strengthening of the Department of Christian Social Service of the Episcopal Church, with a regular secretary for industrial relations.

The social settlement movement also owed much to the churches. Andover House, opened in Boston in 1892, the second settlement in this country; Kingsley House in Pittsburgh, 1893; the Chicago Commons, 1894; the Epworth League House in Boston, 1893, which developed the Good Will Industries; the Union Settlement Association in New York, 1895, are examples of the scores of settlements founded mainly under Church or religious auspices, and based largely on the model of Toynbee Hall in the East End of London (1885). These helped to relate sociologists and liberal religious leaders to the needs of the underprivileged urban population, and became centers where different American and foreign-born groups met and compared notes and where social-reform legislation was planned and stimulated.[38]

Jane Addams (1860–1935), founder of Hull House in Chicago (1889), the most influential of American settlements, well expressed the purpose which animated most of these new institutions. It was

> the impulse to share the lives of the poor, the desire to make social service, irrespective of propaganda, express the spirit of Christ—an impulse as old as Christianity itself.[39]

The Brotherhood of the Kingdom was established by the Reverend Walter Rauschenbusch (1861–1918) and some other Baptist friends in 1892. Among its aims were:

> Every member shall lay stress on the social aims of Christianity, and shall endeavor to make Christ's teaching concerning wealth operative in the church.
>
> On the other hand, each member shall take pains to keep in contact with the common people, and to infuse the religious spirit into the efforts for social amelioration.[40]

From this time on for many years Rauschenbusch was the leading exponent of the social gospel in the United States. He was most influential through his writings, and his fame will probably last longer than that of any of his contemporaries in the field of what became known as social Christianity and Christian socialism. His book of prayers, entitled *For God and the People—Prayers of the Social Awakening,* published in 1910, was highly significant. It includes prayers for various social groups and classes, such as "For Lawyers and Legislators," "For Judges," "For Public Officers," "For Immigrants"; also what he called "Prayers of Wrath" against war, alcoholism, the servants of mammon; and various prayers for the progress of humanity, including one for the "City and the Cooperative Commonwealth."

Moral and social reform now became one of the major activities of the Church. In the volume of the *History of American Life* dealing with this period (1898–1914) the author, speaking of reform measures in a chapter on "Religion and Reforms," says that "The hand of the church seemed everywhere."[41] Of course, this concern for public morality was not a new thing in American religion. The old election sermons in New England frequently took public morals as their theme, but it was then more an individual than a corporate matter. Now societies under Church auspices or founded by Christian leaders, for the prevention of crime, settlement houses, social-welfare conferences, movements of all kinds to eliminate the abuses connected with the saloon, gambling, immigration, Mormon polygamy, etc., became common.

It is impossible to name all the men and movements representing social Christianity in the United States during the first third of the twentieth century, but even the most casual summary would include some we have already mentioned in the earlier part of this survey, such as the Reverend Washington Gladden, a Congregationalist of Columbus, Ohio, whose books, such as *Applied Christianity* (1887) and *Social Salvation* (1901), were highly influential; the Reverend W. D. P. Bliss, founder of the Society of Christian Socialists (1889), publisher of *Dawn,* the first journal devoted to the cause of social Christianity in this country, and editor of the *Encyclopedia of Social Reform;* the Reverend Walter T. Sumner (1873–1935), Dean of the Episcopal Cathedral in Chicago, who presented the vice situation to the Federation of Churches and called upon the mayor to appoint a committee of citizens to investigate. This he did under the lead of Professor Graham Taylor (1851–1938) of the Divinity School of the University of Chicago. The resulting report, *The Social Evil in Chicago* (1911), was a document of importance.

The Reverend George Davis Herron (1862–1925), a Congregational minister, was another outstanding leader whose name must not be forgotten. His unfortunate marital affairs, which resulted in his being dropped from the ministry, and his virtual separation from historic Christianity at the close of his career, must not prevent our recognition of the contribution of his books to the understanding of the cause of "social redemption." It is worth noting that, like Gladden, Graham Taylor, and others, his work was done in the Middle West, especially from the E. D. Rand Chair of Applied Christianity at Grinnell College, Iowa, established for him in 1893. Among his books in the field of our studies are *The Christian State, a Political Vision of Christ* (1895) and *Between Caesar and Jesus* (1898).

The term "social gospel" first came into prominent use through the name of a magazine which appeared in 1898, *The Social Gospel, a magazine of obedience to the law of love.* It published reviews by the leading Christian reformers of the time.[42] It was the organ of the "Christian Commonwealth," an experiment in primitive Christian living undertaken in Georgia from 1896 to 1900. Shailer Mathews' (1863–1943) *The Social Teachings of Jesus* (1897) and *The Social Gospel* (1909), and Walter Rauschenbusch's *A Theology for the Social Gospel* (1917) gave the term a currency which is now well recognized. No book did more to promote the cause than the publication in 1900 of *Jesus Christ and the Social Question,* by the Reverend Francis Greenwood Peabody (1847–1936), founder of the Department of Social Ethics at Harvard University. This book gave a sound basis for the new emphasis in the teachings of Jesus himself. It was followed by many somewhat similar books, of which perhaps the most influential was that by Professor Jeremiah W. Jenks (1856–1929) of Cornell University, published by the National Y.M.C.A. in 1906, and entitled *The Political and Social Significance of the Life and Teachings of Jesus.*

Professor Rauschenbusch's *Christianity and the Social Crisis* appeared in 1907. Later he summed up the views of those who wished to reform "our semi-Christian social order," in a single sentence in his book entitled *Christianizing the Social Order,* which appeared in 1912. He said: "My sole desire has been to summon the Christian passion for justice and the Christian powers of love and mercy to do their share in redeeming our social order from its inherent wrongs."[43] Rauschenbusch's books were translated into French, Norwegian, Finnish, Swedish, Russian, Chinese, Japanese, and German. Dr. Hopkins says that his works "were undoubtedly the most significant religious publications in the United States if not in the English language in the first two decades of the new century."[44]

Rauschenbusch's presentation of facts and arguments made it impossible for the Church to keep out of the field of political and social reform. It is significant that his chair at the Rochester Theological Seminary originally included not only "New Testament Interpretation" but "Civil Government." His scholarship, clear literary style, vision, and religious fervor made a profound impression. He went beyond the ethics of mere personal Christian stewardship, and adopted the ideal of radical social change, believing that the then existing social system with its virtually uncontrolled capitalism must be substantially altered. He always, however, made a sharp distinction between socialism and Christian socialism, and emphasized in the latter a positive religious faith as opposed to a materialistic philosophy; stressing the value and social possibilities of the Church and religious regeneration as a factor in the salvation of society; asserting the reality and independent power of spiritual forces; and insisting on the sanctity of the family.[45]

Social Christianity has now become official with most representative Churches. The Evangelical Alliance,[46] its spiritual successor the Federal Council of Churches, and other religious groups, adopted social programs of broad significance. During the first decade or so of the twentieth century most of the larger religious bodies also appointed social-service agencies or commissions. A strong and aggressive minority, conscious of the social ills of the nation, and the responsibility of the Church to help relieve them, had forced the issue. The Presbyterians took the lead, with the work of the Reverend Charles Stelzle (1869–1941), who was called in 1903 to "a special mission to working men" by the Home Missions Board. He was to all intents and purposes the "Department of Church and Labor" of the Protestant Churches. He was himself a member of the International Association of Machinists, and had wide influence with labor organizations, using very effectively the approach of the noon shop meeting. He also in many cities secured the appointment of brotherhood delegates from local ministerial associations to the central city labor body; sponsored joint meetings of employers and employees; encouraged the development of Labor Sunday; gave out press releases for the unchurched working men of the United States; established the Labor Temple in New York; and provided a clearing house for information on all sorts of social problems and the relation to them of the Church.

The National Council of Congregational Churches, and the General Convention of the Protestant Episcopal Church, took official cognizance of the labor problem at their meetings in 1901. The latter appointed a standing committee on the relations of capital and labor, and in 1910 the General Convention reconstituted the committee into a Joint Commission on Social Service, which from 1913 on became a permanent body. It declared that

> The Church stands for the ideal of justice, and . . . demands the achievement of a social order in which the social cause of poverty and the gross human waste of the present order shall be eliminated; and in which every worker shall have just return for that which he produces, a free opportunity for self-development, and a fair share in all the gains of progress.[47]

The Methodist Church, North, organized the Methodist Federation for Social Service in 1907. Its purpose was

> To deepen within the Church the sense of social obligation and opportunity, to study social problems from the Christian point of view and to promote social service in the spirit of Jesus Christ.[48]

In 1908, at the Baltimore Conference, the Church adopted its highly influential

"Social Creed of Methodism,"[49] and provided for a program of social study and reform which has been a marked characteristic of its work ever since, and especially since 1912, when the Reverend Henry F. Ward (1873–), an outspoken liberal, and later Professor of Christian Ethics at the Union Theological Seminary, became its secretary.

The American Unitarian Society voted in 1908 to establish a Department of Social and Public Service. The National Baptist Convention in this same year, which was the year of its founding, took official cognizance of social problems, and three years later this influential Church provided for a Department of Social Service and Brotherhood. The Y.M.C.A. and the Y.W.C.A. and other Christian organizations added to the impetus of this movement, which by the time of the opening of World War I was markedly characteristic of American Protestantism. The Salvation Army also deserves mention. Founded in London in 1865 by William Booth (1829–1912), a Methodist minister, it gained little foothold in this country until 1889, and was not incorporated in New York until ten years later. In spite of its emotionalism and unconventional methods, its work among "down and outs," prisoners, drunkards, and the outcast gained for it much respect. Its lodging houses, soup kitchens, and workrooms became as characteristic as its gospel hymns, bands, and evangelical services. The Army and its offshoot (1896), the Volunteers of America, must be considered among the important Christian social-welfare agencies of our large towns and cities.

Another factor in the spread of social Christianity was the Chautauqua movement. Founded in 1874 as a summer assembly at Chautauqua Lake, New York, by Bishop John H. Vincent (1832–1920) of the Methodist Church and a layman, Lewis Miller (1829–99), its main original purpose was the better training of Protestant Sunday-school leaders. But the work was broadened in 1878 by the founding of the Chautauqua Literary and Scientific Circle, which under the leadership of such men as Professor William R. Harper (1856–1906) of Yale University and Professor George E. Vincent (1864–1941) of the University of Chicago, became a national factor for adult education not only through the main summer sessions at its home in New York but through smaller "Chautauquas" throughout the country, and through reading courses and study "outlines." All this made it, as President Theodore Roosevelt once said, "the most American thing in America." From our standpoint it is significant for bringing together on the same platform the leaders of various religious groups, and for emphasizing social reform and the part the Churches must play in educating and regenerating the nation. It formed a bridge between earlier camp meetings and modern university summer schools and extension courses. Religion, education, culture, and patriotism were combined in a way that met the needs of vast numbers of Americans.

It would be interesting to make a special study of the influence of Constitutional religious freedom on social reform in this country, but space forbids. It is clear, however, that its influence has been large. Freedom of religion and freedom of speech are closely connected, and as the State, within certain well-understood limits affecting its political security and moral integrity, does not interfere with the Churches. It has given them freedom to discuss controversial issues—slavery, polygamy, birth control, industrial relations, the status of woman, divorce, education, child labor, political corruption, liquor control, and so on. Only once, at least in time of peace, in the case of slavery, has government, and then a minority of state governments and not the Federal government, tried in any large way to interfere with this freedom; and this was one of the causes of the Civil War.[50]

The Churches as national organizations or other groups, or as local parishes, or through their individual members, have a right to air their grievances regarding the body politic or the body social, and to proclaim their panaceas, and the arm of the law will seldom try to interfere. This means that the cause of social reform is enormously stimulated, especially in a nation whose dominant religious note inherited so much from the Puritan reformers of Cromwell's day. This interest has more recently been stimulated from a very different source, the great papal encyclicals on social reform.

Section 1. *THE WORK AND INFLUENCE OF THE EVANGELICAL ALLIANCE*

With the early history of the Evangelical Alliance in the United States we are not specially concerned. It was a branch of the movement that started in England in 1846 for the purpose of bringing together Protestant Christians for closer fellowship and co-operation. The American Alliance was formed in 1867. It was not, however, until 1886, when the Reverend Josiah Strong (1847–1916) became its secretary, that the organization entered at all actively into the field of social Christianity and of Church–State relationships. He wrote books of large influence in the field of the relation of the Church to social problems, especially *Our Country* (1885), *The New Era* (1893), and *Religious Movements for Social Betterment* (1900). He was a vigorous and progressive leader of American Protestantism, deeply interested in making the influence of the Christian Church felt in solving the social problems facing the nation. As he stated in a letter to a friend:

> This movement sprang from a recognition of the perils which threaten our Christian and American civilization, and the great social problems which press for

solution. It is believed that the Gospel of Christ affords the only safeguard from these perils, and the only solution of these problems.[51]

In 1887 he persuaded the Alliance to issue a call, over the names of representative Christian lay leaders and some seventy of its most eminent ministers, to a conference at Washington. It began with these words:

Thoughtful men are convinced that the closing years of the nineteenth century constitute a momentous crisis in the history of the nation. There is a march of events which will not tarry. The necessity of planting Christian institutions in the formative West, and of strengthening them in older states, the duty of overtaking the rapid growth of our cities with adequate church provisions, the importance of closing the widening chasm between the church and the multitude, and of bringing the regenerative power of the gospel to bear upon every character and life, demand the instant attention of the Christian church and the full exercise of all its energies.[52]

President Cleveland (1837–1908), in greeting the Washington conference, said: "The purposes of this Alliance, as I understand them, are to apply the teachings of the Christian life to the problems and to the exigencies of our social and political life."[53] With the purpose thus expressed it seems that no thoughtful person could disagree.

This conference, attended by at least twelve hundred delegates, dealt with such subjects as capital, labor, immigration, misuse of wealth, and the temperance problem; but probably its major interest was trying to meet the problems that were developing in the Western states. Its printed report was entitled *National Perils and Opportunities.*

In 1889 the Alliance held another important meeting in which many problems touching on social Christianity and the responsibility of the Church to the nation were discussed. The proceedings were published as *National Needs and Remedies.*

The third of these conferences, in 1893, was held in connection with the World's Columbian Exposition in Chicago, and received national attention. The proceedings bore the title *Christianity Practically Applied.* During the week of its deliberations four general problems were discussed, namely, the religious condition of Christendom, Christian liberty, Christian union and co-operation, and the Church and social problems. The last received the major attention. Referring to this meeting, Dr. Strong wrote that its great object was

to point out the social mission of the church, and to present the practical methods of Christian work by which the church might accomplish her social mission, and thus meet the great perils and needs of the times.[54]

This conference heard from such representative men and women as the Reverend William S. Rainsford of St. George's Church, New York; Miss Jane Addams of Hull House, Chicago; Professor George D. Herron of Iowa College; the Reverend Charles H. Parkhurst, then in the midst of his fight against Tammany; Professor Graham Taylor of the Chicago Theological Seminary; and President E. Benjamin Andrews of Brown University. The opening address of President Andrews, on "A Plea for an Enlarged View of the Mission of the Church," set one of the keynotes of the convention, which was considered the climax of the influence of the Evangelical Alliance. Another highly influential paper was presented by Professor John R. Commons of Indiana University, on "The Churches and Social Reform."

The Alliance still exists, but since the formation of the Federal Council of Churches[55] in 1908 its activity in the field of social reform has been mainly taken over by the Council, which officially represents the co-operating Churches; whereas the Alliance is an association of individuals in many different countries primarily interested in the promotion of evangelical religion and religious toleration, and in co-operation among Protestants.

Section 2. THE WORK AND INFLUENCE OF THE INTERNATIONAL REFORM BUREAU

This organization, established in Washington in 1895, was due to the zeal of Dr. Wilbur Fisk Crafts (1850–1922),[56] an able and sincere Protestant minister of Methodist upbringing who incarnated much of the strength, and some of the limitations, of the group of reformers whom he represented. He resigned in 1893 from the editorship of the *Christian Statesman,* the official organ of the National Reform Association, to devote himself to more intensive efforts at the capital of the nation through what has been called "the first Christian Legislative Bureau in Washington." A circular issued by the International Reform Federation, successor of the Reform Bureau, in January, 1939, further describes its work.

> For nearly half a century it [has] stood on Capitol Hill as "The Watchdog of the Church at Washington," originating and supporting good legislation and exposing and opposing bad legislation in state and nation. Its campaigns have extended from coast to coast in opposition to crime, social impurity, gambling, salacious literature, objectionable motion pictures, Sabbath breaking, intoxicating liquor and the alliance of organized crime with politics.
>
> It was the first American Society to extend its work into foreign countries, combating alcohol in Europe and opium in Asia, to which it has sent its missionaries, and appropriated large sums of money, to be expended by accredited native agencies. It originated and secured the passage of eighteen laws in Congress, and obtained

treaties for the protection of native races against the ravages of drink and narcotics.

It has made investigations, gathered factual information, and hurled tons of printed ammunition against the citadels of perdition, fighting on a thousand fronts in local, state, national and international campaigns for social justice and civic righteousness in the name of Him, who was "manifested to destroy the works of the devil."

It has never compromised on a moral issue. Its home and foreign missionaries have been prophets for service and not servants for profit. Its publications have supplied the ammunition, and its platform and pulpit advocates the inspiration which has stimulated the reform forces of the nation in pulling down the strongholds of civic sin, and setting up a standard "to which the wise and prudent may repair."

The Bureau was intended to represent "the attitude of conservative evangelical Christians toward current social problems." Its founder called it the first "Christian lobby" established at our national capital to speak to government on behalf of all denominations, "as ancient prophets and apostles spoke to Kings of all righteousness, temperance and of judgment to come." The United States Senate published a volume entitled *Patriotic Studies,* containing extracts from Congressional documents tracing reform bills from 1888 to 1905, including a history and a description of the methods of the Bureau. Dr. Crafts was interested not only in securing legislation by Congress for the reform of intemperance, impurity, gambling, and "Sabbath breaking," but also in opposing the passage of legislation which might have a bad effect on the moral welfare of the country.[57]

The movement had particularly strong support from Methodists, Baptists, and certain groups of Presbyterians. Its tendency to be extreme in such matters as temperance legislation and Sabbath observance failed to gain for it the support of Episcopalians and certain other religious groups which felt that its propaganda, although sincere, was not always based on sound sociology and economics, and that it was inclined to be emotional.

The Bureau claimed at its twentieth anniversary in 1915 that it had to its credit "748 specific achievements."[58] It is still functioning energetically; its name has been changed to the International Reform Federation. Antiliquor, antigambling, Sunday observance laws, and law enforcement continue to be among the major interests of this militant organization. One of its officers once said to me in reply to a question as to the scope of its interests, it is "the whole gamut of reform," with prohibition in the forefront. In this last matter it has worked in close co-operation with the Anti-Saloon League and the Methodist Board of Temperance, Prohibition and Public Morals, and has adopted the same propaganda and political methods in trying to influence Congress and the electorate. Its officers and trustees are all outspoken Protestant leaders, mostly ministers, with the Methodist group prominent. They are men of character and zeal; but when they claim on their letterhead that "The Federation promotes those moral and social reforms on which the Churches generally agree" they make too sweeping a statement. For instance, the Roman Catholic, Congregational, Unitarian, and Episcopal Churches, and some groups of Presbyterians, would not wish to be included as supporting all their program, and even less the type of emotional and extreme statements which they make in their literature. Although these Churches are equally interested in the "social gospel," in the elimination of public evils, and in the Christianizing of the State, they see more clearly the danger of religious "pressure groups" in trying to control legislation. They frequently agree with the ultimate social ends sought, while disagreeing with the methods adopted to attain them.

Section 3. THE QUESTION OF POLYGAMY (THE MORMONS)

In a previous section[59] we have dealt with the origins and early struggles of the Mormons, taking up particularly the difficulties that arose because of their theocratic organization and their independent ways. In this section we deal exclusively with the question of polygamy, which became acute shortly after the middle of the nineteenth century.

This custom was euphemistically called "plural marriage." It was probably never indulged in by more than a small percentage of the Mormon population, but Brigham Young (1801–77) married in all twenty-seven women and left seventeen wives surviving. He was an amazingly effective organizer of a highly successful and thrifty co-operative community, which was virtually a theocracy under his control. The desert was made to "blossom as the rose," but his polygamous ideas and practices and his dictatorial methods resulted in much friction with the government—thus maintaining the reputation for conflict which his predecessor, Joseph Smith, Jr. (1805–44), had begun.

The government sent a military expedition to Utah in 1857–58 to bring the Mormons and their leader to terms, as they were believed to be interfering with the administration of the Federal court and were exercising power arbitrarily. In the background was the fact that their practice of polygamy was distasteful to most Americans, and that they were in frequent friction with non-Mormon Western pioneers and settlers. Of this the most important instance was the Mountain Meadows Massacre in September, 1857.

As early as 1862, the Federal government, stimulated by Christian public opinion, undertook to stamp out the polygamy evil, which was openly practiced, and was defended by Mormons on the ground of a divine revelation. In this year the first of several Federal laws forbidding it—the Morrill Act, "to punish and prevent the practice of polygamy in the Territories"—was adopted, and a vigorous effort was begun to have it enforced. The Mormon Church and its adherents fought this law in the courts, but the decision of the Supreme Court of the United States in 1878 (*Reynolds* v. *U.S.*) held that the practice of polygamy was unconstitutional.[60] The opinion took the ground, in harmony with Christian morality, that American law considers monogamous marriage as the basis of society, and looks upon polygamy as "an offense against society," and that therefore Congress was justified in passing laws to prohibit it. Such legislation is not contrary to the religious freedom guarantees of the Constitution, since, though laws "cannot interfere with mere religious belief and opinions, they may with practices."[61]

The court's opinion is too long to be quoted in full, but the historical introduction, the passages dealing with marriage, and the conclusion, are so important in defining the relations of Church and State that they are here given:

This is an indictment found in the District Court for the third judicial district of the Territory of Utah, charging George Reynolds with bigamy, in violation of sect. 5352 of the Revised Statutes, which, omitting its exceptions, is as follows:—

"Every person having a husband or wife living, who marries another, whether married or single, in a Territory, or other place over which the United States have exclusive jurisdiction, is guilty of bigamy, and shall be punished by a fine of not more than $500, and by imprisonment for a term of not more than five years."

. . . Congress cannot pass a law for the government of the Territories which shall prohibit the free exercise of religion. The first amendment to the Constitution expressly forbids such legislation. Religious freedom is guaranteed everywhere throughout the United States, so far as congressional interference is concerned. The question to be determined is, whether the law now under consideration comes within this prohibition.

The word "religion" is not defined in the Constitution. We must go elsewhere, therefore, to ascertain its meaning, and nowhere more appropriately, we think, than to the history of the times in the midst of which the provision was adopted. The precise point of the inquiry is, what is the religious freedom which has been guaranteed. . . . Amongst others, Mr. Madison prepared a "Memorial and Remonstrance," which was widely circulated and signed, and in which he demonstrated "that religion, or the duty we owe the Creator," was not within the cognizance of civil government. At the next session the proposed bill was not only defeated, but another, "for establishing religious freedom," drafted by Mr. Jefferson, was passed. In the preamble of this act religious freedom is defined; and after a recital "that to suffer the civil magistrate to intrude his powers into the field of opinion, and to restrain the profession or propagation of principles on supposition of their ill tendency, is a dangerous fallacy which at once destroys all religious liberty," it is declared "that it is time enough for the rightful purposes of civil government for its officers to interfere when principles break out into overt acts against peace and good order." In these two sentences is found the true distinction between what properly belongs to the church and what to the State.

In a little more than a year after the passage of this statute the convention met which prepared the Constitution of the United States. Of this convention Mr. Jefferson was not a member, he being then absent as minister to France. As soon as he saw the draft of the Constitution proposed for adoption, he, in a letter to a friend, expressed his disappointment at the absence of an expressed declaration insuring the freedom of religion, but was willing to accept it as it was, trusting that the good sense and honest intentions of the people would bring about the necessary alterations. Five of the States, while adopting the Constitution, proposed amendments. Three—New Hampshire, New York, and Virginia—included in one form or another a declaration of religious freedom in the changes they desired to have made, as did also North Carolina, where the convention at first declined to ratify the Constitution until the proposed amendments were acted upon. Accordingly, at the first session of the first Congress the amendment now under consideration was proposed with others by Mr. Madison. It met the views of the advocates of religious freedom, and was adopted. Mr. Jefferson afterwards, in reply to an address to him by a committee of the Danbury Baptist Association, took occasion to say: "Believing with you that religion is a matter which lies solely between man and his God; that he owes account to none other for his faith or his worship; that the legislative powers of the Government reach actions only, and not opinions,—I contemplate with sovereign reverence that act of the whole American people which declared that their Legislature should 'make no law respecting an establishment of religion or prohibiting the free exercise thereof,' thus building a wall of separation between church and State. Adhering to this expression of the supreme will of the nation in behalf of the rights of conscience, I shall see with sincere satisfaction, the progress of those sentiments which tend to restore man to all his natural rights, convinced he has no natural right in opposition to his social duties." Coming as this does from an acknowledged leader of the advocates of the measure, it may be accepted almost as an authoritative declaration of the scope and effect of the amendment thus secured. Congress was deprived of all legislative power over mere opinion, but was left free to reach actions which were in violation of social duties or subversive of good order. . . .

The opinion goes on to consider the bearing of English statutes on American Constitutional law, and to show that the latter must recognize such a primary sanction of morality as monogamy as an institution which the State has a right to protect.

By the statute of 1 James I. (c.11), the offence [bigamy], if committed in England or Wales, was made punishable in the civil courts, and the penalty was death. As this statute was limited in its operation to England and Wales, it was at a very early period re-enacted, generally with some modifications, in all the colonies. In connection with the case we are now considering, it is significant fact that on the 8th of December, 1788, after the passage of the act establishing religious freedom, and after the convention of Virginia had recommended as an amendment to the Constitution of the United States the declaration in a bill of rights that "all men have an equal, natural, and unalienable right to the free exercise of religion, according to the dictates of conscience," the legislature of that State substantially enacted the statute of James I., death penalty included, because, as recited in the preamble, "it hath been doubted whether bigamy or polygamy be punishable by the laws of this Commonwealth." From that day to this we think it may safely be said there never has been a time in any State of the Union when polygamy has not been an offence against society, cognizable by the civil courts and punishable with more or less severity. In the face of all this evidence, it is impossible to believe that the constitutional guaranty of religious freedom was intended to prohibit legislation in respect to this most important feature of social life. Marriage, while from its very nature a sacred obligation, is nevertheless, in most civilized nations, a civil contract, and usually regulated by law. Upon it society may be said to be built, and out of its fruits spring social relations and social obligations and duties, with which government is necessarily required to deal. In fact, according as monogamous or polygamous marriages are allowed, do we find the principles on which the government of the people, to a greater or less extent, rests. . . .

In our opinion, the statute immediately under consideration [against polygamy] is within the legislative power of Congress. It is constitutional and valid as prescribing a rule of action for all those residing in the Territories, and in places over which the United States have exclusive control. This being so, the only question which remains is, whether those who make polygamy a part of their religion are excepted from the operation of the statute. If they are, then those who do not make polygamy a part of their religious belief may be found guilty and punished, while those who do, must be acquitted and go free. This would be introducing a new element into criminal law. Laws are made for the government of actions, and while they cannot interfere with mere religious belief and opinions, they may with practices.

. . . Suppose one believed that human sacrifices were a necessary part of religious worship, would it be seriously contended that the civil government under which he lived could not interfere to prevent a sacrifice? Or, if a wife religiously believed it was her duty to burn herself upon the funeral pile of her dead husband, would it be beyond the power of the civil government to prevent her carrying her belief into practice?

So here, as a law of the organization of society under the exclusive dominion of the United States, it is provided that plural marriages shall not be allowed. Can a man excuse his practices to the contrary because of his religious belief? To permit this would be to make the professed doctrines of religious belief superior to the law of the land, and in effect to permit every citizen to become a law unto himself. Government could exist only in name under such circumstances.[62]

The same basic idea—that the act of polygamy is "in violation of social duties" and "subversive of good order," and that consequently it was Constitutional for Congress to ban it—is brought out in a subsequent decision of the Supreme Court regarding the disposition of the confiscated property of the Church of Jesus Christ of Latter Day Saints. Justice Joseph P. Bradley (1813–92), speaking for the Court, said:

The organization of a community for the spread and practice of polygamy is, in a measure, a return to barbarism. It is contrary to the spirit of Christianity and of the civilization which Christianity had produced in the Western world.[63]

It will be noticed that this decision goes even further than *Reynolds* v. *United States* in banning polygamy as a specifically unchristian form of conduct.

The contrast between the attitude of the courts toward the two forms of Mormon marriage, namely, marriages "for time" and marriages "for eternity" (sometimes called "celestial marriages"),[64] sheds a flood of light on the whole attitude of our government in matters of religious freedom. The actual *practice* by members of the Church of Latter Day Saints of their tenet of polygamy, representing marriages for this present world, was found unconstitutional by the United States Supreme Court. Such marriages were *acts* contrary to the best interests of society and of Christian civilization, and could not be tolerated. On the other hand, marriages for eternity, which were merely abstract, soul matches, as it were, which enabled certain Mormons to feel that they were ultimately to enjoy for all time the companionship of certain women of their choice, inasmuch as they did not result in actual polygamy, were not interfered with. They were purely matters of philosophical speculation and inward satisfaction. Zollmann sums up an interesting citation of cases by saying:

It follows that a believer in the Mormon religion, can, so far as the government is concerned, by "celestial" marriages or marriages "for eternity," create a harem for himself in the other world, provided he is able to avoid more than one terrestrial marriage at any one time."[65]

This distinction between definite concrete acts and mere thought or theory in matters of religious freedom is one that goes back in this country to Jefferson's Danbury address.[66] He held—and our courts have repeatedly upheld his opinion, which Chief Justice Waite quoted—that the government does not interfere with religious thought except where it eventuates in *acts* that are dangerous to the State or to society.

But the Federal government was becoming thoroughly aroused. In 1879 it even attempted to enlist the services of other countries in the crusade against polygamy. A circular letter was sent to the American ministers in Europe, asking them to call the attention of the governments to which they were accredited, to the American enactments against polygamy, and requesting that they prevent the preaching of Mormonism and the emigration of professed Mormons to the United States. This is, as far as I am aware, the only attempt of the American government to interfere with the religion of people in other countries, unless recently as to emperor worship in Japan. Lecky informs us that the governments of the countries where Mormon missionaries had been most successful replied that they could not undertake to inquire into the religious belief of emigrants.[67]

In 1882 Congress passed the Edmunds Act, which punished actual polygamy by disfranchisement, imprisonment, and other penalties. Five years later the corporation of the Church of Jesus Christ of Latter Day Saints was dissolved by the Federal government. Effective resistance was no longer possible. Hundreds of polygamists suffered fines and imprisonment, over one thousand were disfranchised, and much of the property of the Church was confiscated. In 1890 the head of the Church, President Wilford Woodruff (1807–98), issued a pronunciamento against polygamous marriages, stating that he would submit to the Federal law, and advising all Mormons "to refrain from contracting any marriage forbidden by the law of the land."[68] His action was promptly approved by a general conference of Mormon representatives, who accepted his "declaration concerning plural marriages as authoritative and binding."[69] The matter was not however conclusively settled until 1896, when the Territory of Utah was admitted as a state under a constitution whose third article, consistent with the Bill of Rights, reads:

> The following ordinance shall be irrevocable without the consent of the United States and the people of the state: Perfect tolerance of religious sentiment is guaranteed. No inhabitant of this state shall ever be molested in person or property on account of his or her mode of religious worship; but polygamous or plural marriages are for ever prohibited.[70]

Similar clauses guaranteeing religious freedom but making polygamy illegal were introduced in several other new Western States.

Thus came to an end a memorable controversy which had aroused the Christian people of the nation, who felt that polygamy was contrary to the Jewish-Christian moral code of the Bible, on which its ideals and law were largely based. They took the ground that the government could not tolerate any practice that was contrary to fundamental Christian ethics, and pointed to the many decisions of American courts taking this point of view.[71]

The Churches of the United States were not specially concerned about the theological views of Mormonism, or about its economic system. But they were disturbed by the attempts of a religious organization to control the policy of a state and to break down the law of Christian marriage. They maintained that a "Christian nation" had the right and duty to see to it that no flagrant disregard of this law was openly proclaimed or practiced by members of an organized and incorporated society which practically controlled a great territory seeking statehood. They pointed to the fact that the right of the State to use its police power had been explicitly stated or implied in the constitutions of all the States, and that it went back to early precedents, universally upheld by our courts.[72] For example, the New York constitution of 1777 provided that

The liberty of conscience hereby granted shall not be so construed as to excuse acts of licentiousness, or to justify practices inconsistent with the peace or safety of this State.[73]

An impression of the dangers of Mormonism from the point of view of some far-sighted leaders of the Christian Church in America a half century ago can be seen in *Our Country,* by Josiah Strong (1847–1916), published in 1885. It is interesting that its major emphasis was not on the evil of polygamy, serious as this was, but rather on that of a highly centralized and autocratic ecclesiastical power that was trying to dominate the state. Strong's attitude was that Mormonism was not merely a Church, but a State, "an *imperium in imperio* ruled by a man who is prophet, priest, king and pope, all in one."[74] He was the head of a population group of 138,000, of whom about one-fifth were said to be officials and missionaries in various capacities. As an evidence of the character and purpose of Mormonism at that time as a political force, Strong quotes an address shortly before (1881) by a Bishop Lunt of the Church of Latter Day Saints, who said:

. . . Our vote is solid, and will remain so. It will be thrown where the most good will be accomplished for the church. Then, in some great political crisis, the two present political parties will bid for our support. Utah will then be admitted as a polygamous state, and the other territories we have peacefully subjugated will be admitted also. We will then hold the balance of power, and will dictate to the country. In time, our principles, which are of sacred origin, will spread throughout the United States. We possess the ability to turn the political scale in any particular community we desire. Our people are obedient. When they are called by the church, they promptly obey.[75]

It was the feeling of the members of the Christian Churches that Mormonism was inimical to the United States both on moral and political grounds. To substantiate this position Dr. Strong refers to an address to the American public adopted by the pastors of churches and principals of schools in Salt Lake City. This said:

We recognize the fact that the so-called Mormon Church, in its exercise of political power, is antagonistical [*sic*] to American institutions, and that there is an irrepressible conflict between Utah Mormonism and American republicanism; so much so that they can never abide together in harmony. We also believe that the growth of this anti-republican power is such that, if not checked speedily, it will cause serious trouble in the near future. We fear that the nature and extent of this danger are not fully comprehended by the nation at large.[76]

An idea of the part played by the Churches in the antipolygamy campaign may be seen by looking over the records of the Forty-sixth, Forty-seventh, and Forty-eighth Congresses, especially for the period from December, 1880, through February, 1884. We find there memorials or petitions against polygamy from such representative religious groups as the General Association of Congregational Ministers of Michigan, the Methodist Episcopal Church Conference of Kansas, the General Council of the Reformed Episcopal Church, the Conference of the Church of Christ, the American Baptist Home Missionary Society, and the General Assembly of the Presbyterian Church of the United States.

The last two may be taken as characteristic of all. The Baptists petitioned Congress to take adequate measures to suppress the "pestilent system" of polygamy and its "attendant monstrosities."[77] The petition of the Presbyterians, adopted May 26, 1881, in Buffalo, New York, and presented to the House January 11, 1882, was particularly significant because it represented the view not merely of one state or locality, but of the delegates from all over the country of one of the most influential Protestant denominations in the nation. It reads as follows:

The standing committee on bills and overtures presented a report on overtures Nos. 8 and 9 from the presbyteries of Chicago and Logansport, praying the assembly to take further action on the subject of *polygamy*. Your committee would respectfully offer the following for adoption by the assembly:

Action condemnatory of polygamy has been taken at several recent meetings of the assembly. Yet, as the practice of this vice continues not only unsuppressed, but unabated, within the bounds of our national territory, and since a recent decision of the Supreme Court of the United States makes the attempt to strike it more difficult than before, the assembly feels that silence on the subject would now be inexcusable. This enormous wickedness has gradually grown through a period of years, organizing itself into a government for its own defense, under the eye of the national Government, until it has gained sufficient force to defy the legislative and executive power of the nation. It now stands more haughty and resolved than ever. Its efforts to strengthen itself by immigration of the weak and ignorant from Europe and by despotic suppression of liberty among its votaries and victims are systematically exerted. For its own fortification it is forcing its way from its original stronghold into adjacent territory, where, unobserved, it may take root and fasten on the land by finding quiet recognition in local laws.

Its spirit grows, with age, no less hostile to the law of Christianity, to the instincts of morality, to the essential principles of civilization, and to the existence of liberty for the people. It is condemned alike by the Church, by the State, by the family, and by the individual conscience. It is abhorred by God. It seems all the more detestable because it hides its crime for shelter under the garb of religion. It is growing, as slavery grew, from infancy to maturity of grasp upon the national life. The terrible conflict required for the extermination of the one should sound timely warning as to the latent perils of the other. The Territories in which polygamy yet exists are under the control of the President and of Congress, *i.e.,* of the national Government. The nation, as such, is therefore responsible for its continuance. The Christian citizens of the nation bear their share in this common responsibility.

Should these Territories become States, with polygamy maintained, the difficulty of reaching it would be vastly heightened. They are rapidly increasing in wealth and in population, and will soon be knocking for admission as States at the national door. Efficient action for its obliteration must then, if taken at all, begin without delay.

1. We, therefore, as an assembly, solemnly protest, before God and before men, against this heinous and abominable crime, as a foul blot on the face of our country, for the existence of which God will hold the nation to account, and for which He will surely call it into judgment, except the evil be speedily abated.

2. We rejoice in the determination of the President of the United States, as expressed in his inaugural address, to deal vigorously with this iniquity. And we assure him of our sympathy and support in all lawful and just efforts for its extinction, praying him not to withhold his hand.

3. We reiterate our hearty approval of the stand taken by Governor Murray, of Utah, and his counselors, and by the United States courts of the Territory, in hostility to polygamous marriages.

4. We respectfully memorialize the national Legislature to enact whatever laws may seem most wise and most efficient for the utter obliteration of this vice, whether as an organized system or as an individual practice.

5. And we urge our own members, without respect to party lines, zealously to exert their influence, in every lawful method, for the enactment of an amendment to the national Constitution that shall forever prohibit the existence of polygamy in the nation.

Your committee would also recommend that a copy of this action be officially laid before the President of the United States and the presiding officers of the two Houses of Congress, as conveying the unanimous sentiment of the ministry and membership of the Presbyterian Church in the United States.

The recommendations of the committee were adopted.[78]

The memorial of the Baptist Home Mission Society is also significant, for this Church was specially interested in helping to establish Christian conditions in the Western states, where polygamy threatened to be a serious evil. It was presented February 12, 1882, being entitled "A memorial to the President and to the Congress of the United States."

The American Baptist Home Mission Society, representing a church membership of about one million persons, and a constituency of five times that number of residents, chiefly of the Northern States, at its last annual meeting in May, 1881, authorized and instructed its executive board "to address a memorial to the President of the

United States, and through him to the National Congress, asking, in behalf of the great Baptist constituency in the land, that early measures be taken to remove and prohibit the practice of polygamy and its accompanying vices throughout all our borders."

In pursuance of these instructions, the executive board of this society, noting with profound satisfaction the popular feeling which has been aroused against this arrogant and blighting institution of Mormonism, hereby respectfully petition the Congress of the United States to take advantage of the present favorable state of public sentiment for the immediate passage of such acts as will effectually subdue this pestilent system, so far as it makes against good government and good morals.

As representatives of a society which seeks to extend the pure and loyal influences of the gospel of Christ over the very lands that are threatened by the presence of this evil, we have an especial interest in its due restraint; and we are authorized to pledge "the moral support of our society to the National Government in the exercise of its constitutional rights and legal obligations in taking early and vigorous measures to suppress and overthrow polygamy and its attendant monstrosities wherever they exist in our country."

As Baptists it is our pride to have been among the foremost champions of religious liberty. But the book from which we draw our inspiration and our warrant for maintaining the freedom of the human conscience, teaches us submission to righteous authority and the paramount blessedness of the marriage relation as established between one man and one woman; and it is our conviction that to admit the right of Mormonism to non-interference is to defend lust and treason behind the sacred ramparts of religious liberty.

Respectfully submitted.

By order and on behalf of the society:

H. L. MOREHOUSE,
Corresponding Secretary.

New York City, February 13, 1882.[79]

Such memorials as these coming from the Churches played an important part in abolishing polygamy. In these resolutions the threat of breaking down the Christian tradition of monogamy represented the major emphasis, but almost equally important in the mind of the country was the fact that Mormonism was developing a state within a state under a leader who had political ambitions for his Church as authoritarian and aggressive as those attributed by many Protestants of the time to the pope.

Although, as we have seen, the battles of public opinion and law against polygamy had been won before the nineteenth century came to a close, and Utah had been admitted as a state only on condition that polygamous or plural marriages were to be "forever" prohibited, the issue was not entirely dead. Such an entrenched practice necessarily dies hard, especially with a small group of

Mormon fundamentalists who do not believe that man-made law can take the place of what they consider divine revelation.

The Churches continued their watchful interest, owing to the continuing spread of Mormonism and their fear that polygamy might be revived. For example, as late as 1911 the General Assembly of the Presbyterian Church in the U.S.A., the parent body, "heartily approves the attempt to secure an amendment to our National Constitution prohibiting polygamy and polygamous living in the United States,"[80] and in 1918 it adopted these resolutions:

Resolved, 3. That we call upon the ministers of the Church and all who teach and exhort in the Church, that they aggressively attack the gigantic and growing evil of Mormonism, with its curse of polygamy and its pernicious and blasphemous teaching that the great Head of the Church, our blessed Lord and Saviour, Jesus Christ, was born in polygamy and was himself a polygamist by sanction and practice.

Resolved, 4. That in view of the grave possibilities of the situation, we refer the whole matter to the executive Commission for its earnest consideration and constant vigilance; and we pledge the support and resources of the Presbyterian Church of the U. S. A., in fighting polygamy to a complete finish.[81]

Section 4. THE ADMINISTRATION AND EDUCATION OF THE INDIANS

We have already dealt with early Indian problems in which Church and State came sometimes into friendly co-operation, at others into serious conflict, though generally pursuing their parallel courses with little direct contact.[82] Here we must confine ourselves to the problems which became acute after the Civil War, and especially to the Indian school question. As the Federal government has nothing to do with the actual conduct of the regular public schools in the different states, its policy regarding religious instruction and religious freedom on the Indian reservations subject to its jurisdiction is specially enlightening.

To understand the situation that arose we must remember that the Indians were theoretically considered from the beginning of the republic as "wards" of the nation, and that the government had encouraged missionary work among them. It had even, as we have seen, given this work financial aid, especially by the erection of school buildings on the reservations for the use of various missionary societies,[83] and also by the allotment of land for their mission stations and activities. In many cases the missions had originally occupied such lands without any regular title except the consent of the Indian tribes; but when the General Allotment Act was adopted the following clause confirming the validity of their land rights was incorporated by Congress:

And if any religious society or other organization is now occupying any of the public lands to which this act is applicable, for religious or educational work among the Indians, the Secretary of the Interior is hereby authorized to confirm such occupation to such society or organization, in quantity not exceeding one hundred and sixty acres in any one tract, so long as the same shall be so occupied, on such terms as he shall deem just; but nothing herein contained shall change or alter any claim of such society for religious or educational purpose heretofore granted by law.[84]

This action was particularly important, since the old conception of the Indian tribes as constituting independent "domestic nations," with treaty-making power and some other marks of sovereignty, had been given up by Congress in 1871, when the United States assumed responsibility for the administration of the Indians and their lands.

Now that the Negro had been enfranchised, as far as Federal Constitutional action made this possible, thoughtful citizens began to think increasingly of the welfare of the Indians, realizing that here was a large group of primitive people, many of them highly intelligent, who had not been fairly treated by the government. Politicians had played havoc with the Indian agencies, which, though some officials were honest and efficient, were marked by much lack of sympathy with their Indian wards and some corruption. In the winter of 1867–68 the Quakers, unselfishly interested in the Indians from early Pennsylvania days, took the matter up with the president, General Ulysses S. Grant (1822–85). He offered to make appointments of Indian agents from lists they submitted to him. They accepted the responsibility for some tribes, thus inaugurating the so-called "peace policy" of dealing with the Indians as "wards of the nation" and substituting education under religious auspices for military force.[85]

The policy with the Quakers seemed to be promising, though limited in scope, and it was expanded. A special case arose among the Chippewas. The government agent was placed by treaty under a board of three visitors chosen by the president "from such Christian denominations as he may designate."[86] The president chose three respected Church leaders—an Episcopal bishop, a Roman Catholic bishop, and a Congregational missionary. Similarly, the fund for the relief of the Sioux Indians was placed in charge of Bishop Henry B. Whipple (1822–1901) of the Episcopal Church, an honored name in the history of the Northwest, who accepted most reluctantly because of the financial responsibility involved.

The problem of the Indian was becoming more and more acute, owing to the settlement of the West and the building of transcontinental railroads. Consequently in 1869 Congress authorized the president to appoint a Board of Indian Commissioners "eminent for their intelligence and philanthropy, to serve without compensation." The appointments were made on nomination of the various religious boards, and a two-million-dollar fund was placed at their disposal, working in co-operation with the secretary of the interior, to whose jurisdiction Indian affairs had been transferred from the War Department when the new cabinet post was established in 1849. The board proved most sympathetic, and served as a useful intermediary between the government and the Indians.

In view of the success of the experiment with the Quakers and the religious leaders named, the president decided to take the nomination of Indian agents entirely away from the politicians, and from Army officers (whom Congress did not wish to have in civil offices), and asked the various missionary societies to nominate suitable men for these posts. In a letter sent by General Ely S. Parker (1828–95), Commissioner of Indian Affairs, to the Hicksite Friends, February 15, 1869, transmitting the president's request for a list of suitable persons for agents, they were informed

That any attempt which may or can be made by your society for the . . . education, and Christianization of the Indians under such agencies will receive from him, as President, all the encouragement and protection which the laws of the United States will warrant him in giving.[87]

The secretary of the Board of Indian Commissioners and the secretary of the interior thereupon allotted agencies to the various missionary groups, and a map was published showing the distribution. The list of allotments, as supplied by the Library of the Office of Indian Affairs, follows:[88]

LIST OF INDIAN AGENCIES ASSIGNED TO THE SEVERAL RELIGIOUS BODIES

Friends. The Northern Superintendency and the agencies therein, viz: Great Nemaha, Omaha, Winnebago, Pawnee, Otoe, and Santee, located within the State of Nebraska. B. Rush Roberts, Sandy Spring, Md.

Friends, (Orthodox).—The Central Superintendency and the agencies therein, viz: Pottawatomie and Kickapoo, in Kansas; Quapaw, Osage, Sac and Fox, Wichita, Kiowa and Comanche, and Cheyenne and Arapahoe, in the Indian Territory. Dr. Jas. E. Rhoades, Germantown, Philadelphia, Pa.

Methodist.—Hoopa Valley, Round Valley, and Tule River, in California; Yakima and Quinaielt, in Washington Territory; Alsea, Siletz, and Klamath, in Oregon; Blackfeet, Crow, and Fort Peck, in Montana; Fort Hall and Lemhi, in Idaho; and Michigan, in Michigan. Rev. Dr. J. M. Reid, secretary Missionary Society Methodist Episcopal Church, New York.

Catholic.—Tulalip and Colville, in Washington Territory; Grand Ronde and Umatilla, in Oregon; Flathead, in Montana; Grand River and Devil's Lake, in Dakota; Papago, in Arizona. Gen. Charles Ewing, Catholic commissioner Roman Catholic Church, Washington, D. C.

Baptist.—Union, (Cherokees, Creeks, Choctaws, Chickasaws, and Seminoles,) in the Indian Territory; and Pyramid Lake and Pi-Ute, in Nevada. Rev. Joseph F. Shoards, secretary American Baptist Home Missionary Society, New York.

Presbyterian.—Abiquiu, Navajo, Mescalero Apache, Southern Apache, Cimarron, and Pueblo, in New Mexico; Moquis Pueblo, in Arizona; Nez Perce, in Idaho; and Uintah Valley, in Utah. Rev. Dr. J. C. Lowrie, secretary Board of Commissioners for Foreign Missions of the Presbyterian Church, New York.

Congregational.—Green Bay and La Pointe, in Wisconsin; Red Lake, in Minnesota; Sisseton, and Fort Berthold, in Dakota; and S'Kokomish, in Washington Territory. Rev. Geo. Whipple, secretary American Missionary Association, New York.

Reformed.—Colorado River, Pima and Maricopa, and San Carlos, in Arizona. Rev. Dr. J. M. Ferris, secretary Board of Missions of Reformed Church, New York.

Protestant Episcopal.—White Earth, in Minnesota; Onca, Crow Creek, White River, Cheyenne River, Yankton, Spotted Tail, and Red Cloud, in Dakota; Shoshone, in Wyoming. Rev. Robert C. Rogers, secretary Indian Commission of the Protestant Episcopal Church, New York.

Unitarian.—Los Pinos and White River, in Colorado. Rev. Rush R. Shippen, secretary American Unitarian Association, Boston.

Free–Will Baptist.—Leech Lake, in Minnesota. Rev. A. H. Chase, secretary Free–Will Baptist Home Missionary Association, Hillsdale, Mich.

United Presbyterian.—Warm Springs, in Oregon.

There is no more striking evidence in American history of co-operation between Church and State than is indicated by this list, which shows the great religious bodies assuming important tasks as representatives of the government, and at its request. Some accepted their responsibilities reluctantly, owing to opposition in principle to all Church–State connections. It should be remembered, however, that the State reserved the right of confirming the nominees of the boards and the right to dismiss agents who were unsatisfactory. The Roman Catholic Church declined to co-operate in the plan, feeling that it had been assigned too few agencies, and as a result it established in 1874 in the District of Columbia its well-known Bureau of Catholic Indian Missions, which has continued to this time. It was largely through the activities of this agency that various advantages were secured by the Church. These included the right of Indian parents to choose the school to be attended by their children,[89] and grants for the benefit of Catholic "contract schools," payable from Indian tribal funds, an arrangement which received the Constitutional sanction of the Supreme Court in 1906.

Largely as a result of the bureau's efforts, seven schools supported by the government had been placed under Catholic missionaries and sisters by 1873. The peak in number of schools so conducted was reached in 1890, with forty-three boarding schools and seventeen day schools, and in the amount of compensation two years later, when the government expended $397,756 on such schools. During the period of the last quarter of the nineteenth century the Roman Catholics alone received $4,500,000 from the Federal government for the tuition and support of Indian children in mission schools.[90] Roman Catholics contributed largely to make these schools possible. One million and a half dollars was provided by the Drexel family of Philadelphia alone for their erection and equipment.

As a result of General Grant's new plan, Indian agents were appointed on the recommendation of the religious denominations during the decade of the 'seventies. Helen Hunt Jackson (1830–85), writing in 1881 in her influential book *A Century of Dishonor,* said that as a result of these new policies "More has been done to civilize the Indians than in any period of our history." The mission schools now flourished with government aid. From 1870 to 1897 (over a quarter of a century) government schools and Church schools, frequently aided by the government as we have shown in the case of Catholic schools, existed side by side—the mission boarding schools being an important feature from 1873 on. It is worth recording, however, that several of the Protestant Churches anticipated the government by deciding that it was better policy for them to discontinue receiving Federal aid. The Methodist General Conference took such action in May, 1892, and was followed by the Episcopalians in October of that year. This movement gained headway in the next few years. The American Protective Association,[92] a strong Protestant organization with an anti-Catholic bias, and active from 1891 on, played a large part in creating public opinion opposed to the continuance of the practice. It raised with some justice the Church–State issue, but at the very time it was doing so a well-known Methodist minister, the Reverend Daniel Dorchester (1827–1907), was serving as superintendent of Indian schools by appointment (1889–93) of President Harrison!

The question of continuing government grants to Indian mission schools was much discussed in Congress from 1894 on.[93] In the Appropriation Act of 1895 it was provided that such aid should be limited to the then existing contract schools, and should not exceed 80 per cent of what was then being applied. In the next Congress this was further reduced to 50 per cent, and a clause was added declaring it "to be the settled policy of the government to hereafter make no appropriation whatever for education in any sectarian school."[94] It was subject to these important provisos:

Provided, That the Secretary of the Interior may make contracts with contract schools apportioning as near as may be the amount so contracted for among schools of various denominations for the education of Indian pupils during the fiscal year eighteen hundred and ninety-eight, but shall only make such contracts at places where nonsectarian schools can not be provided for such Indian children and to an amount not exceeding forty per centum of the amount so used for the fiscal year eighteen hundred and ninety-five: *Provided further,* That the foregoing shall not apply to public schools of any State, Territory, county, or to schools herein or hereafter specifically provided for.[95]

As a result of this and subsequent actions, denominational schools as such ceased to receive Federal government grants, the appropriation bill of 1899 specifically declaring that it had now provided "the final appropriation for sectarian schools."[96] At this time, according to a government authority, there were in effect

a considerable number of so-called mission contracts paid from tribal funds: that is, money belonging to the tribes, as distinct from appropriations of public funds. It has been held (Quick Bear v. Leupp [210 U. S. 79]) that money belonging to individual Indians might be expended by the Government for the beneficiaries in schools of their choice, in which case the provisions of U. S. C. 278 do not apply. The majority of mission contracts paid from tribal funds are in effect with Catholic schools. There are, however, a few contracts with Protestant mission associations.

Tribal funds decreased in some cases to an extent which no longer warranted their use for payment of education of children in the mission schools. In some cases they have become entirely exhausted. Where no facilities are otherwise available for children requiring institutional aid there are in effect several contracts for care but not for education of children in mission schools. Education, though not covered by these contracts, is furnished by the mission from denominational funds, or gifts, at no expense to the Government or to the Indians.[97]

This letter was written in 1938.

The exception made in the case of Indian tribal funds—allowing them to be used for religious purposes—was based on the theory that denial of such use would, according to the Supreme Court, be an infringement of religious liberty, for it would have prohibited the "free exercise of religion."[98] Consequently, tribal funds are still being applied, at the wish of the tribes concerned, for education under both Roman Catholic and Protestant auspices. In 1933 about thirty-five denominational schools were thus drawing from tribal and treaty funds duly authorized amounts of from $223 to $32,500 each.[99]

The following provisions of recent laws show how mission schools receive *indirectly* this public assistance:

Rations to mission schools.—Mission schools on an Indian reservation may, under rules and regulations prescribed by the Commissioner of Indian Affairs, receive for such Indian children duly enrolled therein, the rations of food and clothing to which said children would be entitled under treaty stipulations if such children were living with their parents. (June 21, 1906, c. 3504, 34 Stat.)

Patents of lands to missionary boards or religious organizations.—The Secretary of the Interior is authorized and directed to issue a patent to the duly authorized missionary board, or other proper authority, of any religious organization engaged in mission or school work on any Indian reservation for such lands thereon as were prior to September 21, 1922, set apart to and were on that date being actually and beneficially used and occupied by such organization solely for mission or school purposes, the area so patented to not exceed one hundred and sixty acres to any one organization at any station: *Provided,* That such patent shall provide that when no longer used for mission or school purposes said lands shall revert to the Indian owners. (Sept. 21, 1922, c. 367, Par. 3, 42 Stat. 995.)[100]

There are still many mission schools in the reservations. The regulations regarding them are specific, and include certain important provisions:

The institution must agree to eliminate from its rolls as residents those children of Indian blood who live within a reasonable distance from any public or day school, except those children who are found to need special institutional care, and to limit its enrollment to such individual Indian children as are approved for enrollment by the agency superintendent or the superintendent of Indian education designated to approve enrollment or to handle payments under any contract entered into pursuant hereto. Indian children eliminated from Government boarding schools because of satisfactory home and school facilities nearby shall not be permitted to enroll in any school maintained by the institution or its responsible head, except at the personal expense of their parents or guardian, or at the expense of the institution.[101]

Such institution shall be subject to inspection at any time by the Commissioner of Indian Affairs or his duly authorized representative, and the institution shall agree in any contract entered into pursuant hereto that it will dismiss from its service any employee or employees who may be found by the Commissioner of Indian Affairs not to be qualified for the respective positions which they occupy in the institution.[102]

Closely related to this question of applying public funds to denominational schools was that of the wearing of a religious garb by their teachers. Both Protestant and Catholic schools taken over by the government retained for a time their religious character and influence, and in all government schools each denomination was allowed, under proper regulations, to use classrooms to teach its own doctrines. In this connection the Washington Secular League and some Protestant groups protested the use of the religious garb by Roman Catholic sisters, and in 1912 the Commissioner of Indian Affairs issued a circular ordering the laying aside of religious garb and the removal of denominational insignia from classrooms. The secretary of the interior, the Honorable Walter L. Fisher (1862–1935), revoked this order, and the revocation was later approved by President Taft. In explaining his ruling, the secretary, according to the summary by Gabel, a Catholic authority, declared that there was no statute against wearing the garb; that Indian regulations permitted the use of school buildings for religious services by any sect; that the Constitution did not forbid appropriation for religious purposes but the establishment of a State Church and union of Church and State; and that this prohibition was not violated by appropriations for religion since Congress supported chaplains in the Army and Navy, and appropriations for services rendered by persons wearing religious garb had been upheld by federal courts.[103]

By this ruling the government apparently put itself for the moment in disagreement with the opinion rendered by the New York Court of Appeals upholding a regulation of the state superintendent forbidding Catholic sisters employed as public school teachers from wearing any distinctive garb, on the ground that this would necessarily inspire respect, if not sympathy, for the religious denomination to which the teacher belongs.[104]

In August, 1912, however, Secretary Fisher stated that he

> had reached the conclusion that the matter of wearing garb was one of administrative policy and not of statutory or constitutional law; that the wearing of distinctive religious garb by teachers in Government Indian schools should not be permitted; that the extension of the practice should be definitely prohibited . . . ; that the mistake [of continuing to allow teachers to wear religious garb] should be corrected by ceasing to introduce into the service teachers of any sectarian religious schools; by filling all new positions and all vacancies in the teaching force from the eligible registers of the Civil Service; and by requiring all teachers . . . to refrain from all sectarian instruction or the use of their positions for sectarian ends.[105]

Gabel reports that in 1933 only five teachers wearing religious garb were left in government Indian schools, though the practice has increased in public schools—a 1947 study showed sixteen states where it was considered permissible.[106]

Some developments during the administration of President Franklin D. Roosevelt protecting religious freedom in the Indian reservations will be dealt with in a later section.[107]

Section 5. *THE EDUCATION OF THE WEST*[108]

In an earlier section[109] some account has been given of the part played by the Churches in developing public order and organizing education in the West through the first third of the nineteenth century. Here we are concerned with the later story; and as the Methodists, with their evangelistic note, played the most significant part in the earlier movement, so the Congregationalists and Presbyterians, with their emphasis on education, were perhaps the special heroes of the mid-century in the Middle West. But all the Churches, Protestant and Catholic, were active and helpful.

It was a period when the major part of the region—only recently opened up by settlers—was still under a territorial form of government. Conditions were in most places still somewhat crude, and there was a lack of responsible local government and of social stability and cohesion. This made the work of the Churches, especially in meeting under Christian influences the glaring gaps in educational facilities, of special importance.

The Illinois Band of seven students grew out of the essay on "The Call of the West" read by the Reverend Theoron Baldwin (1801–70) in 1828 before the Society of Inquiry at the Yale Divinity School. Baldwin and Julian M. Sturtevant (1805–88) were the leaders, and helped to found Illinois College, of which Edward Beecher (1803–95), a brother of Henry Ward Beecher, was the first president (1830). They and their associates, bearing commissions from the American Home Missionary Society, played a highly important part in the religious and educational work of the state, and in the struggle to keep it on the antislavery side. Baldwin became the secretary in 1843 of the "Society for the Promotion of Collegiate and Theological Education in the West"—popularly known as the "Western College Society"—which he helped to organize, and of which he was the driving force for twenty-seven years. By his work in this position, this modest Congregational minister earned the title of "the father of Western colleges," for no other organization was so effective in aiding the development of higher educational facilities in the West. Several of its colleges later developed into state universities.

A similar work was done by the Iowa Band—eleven strong. In 1843 they went out from the Andover Theological Seminary to assist Asa Turner (1799–1885) of the Illinois Band, who, after serving that state, struck out farther West to the territory of Iowa. Here they opened in 1848 Iowa College at Davenport, which later moved and became known as Grinnell College.

The Reverend Jason Lee (1803–45) was the pioneer missionary of the Methodists in the Northwest. He not only preached to the Indians and the white settlers, but took the lead in three times petitioning Congress for the organization of a territorial government. He also organized in 1838–39 a party of settlers who sailed from New York to Oregon with ministers, teachers, doctors, carpenters, farmers, and a blacksmith. The Federal government thought his expedition so important that it contributed $5,000 toward the total cost of about $40,000. The Methodist Missionary Society spent nearly $175,000 in ten years on its Oregon missions, of which Willamette University is one of the tangible and enduring outgrowths. But the most important result of Lee's labors was the success of his efforts to secure colonizers from the East, who, at a time of great rivalry between British interests, led by the Hudson Bay Company, and American interests, would create sentiment favorable to the permanent incorporation of Oregon as part of the United States. The fact that the meeting of settlers in 1843 voted for the establishment of a territorial government (by the small margin of 52 to 50), which meant that Oregon would become part of this country instead of Canada, was due in no small part to his efforts and those of other missionaries.[110]

Prominent among these were Father Pierre Jean De Smet (1801–73), a Jesuit founder of the Catholic Rocky Mountain Missions,[111] a zealous apostle of religion and education in the Northwest, and frequently a representative of the government in the 'fifties and 'sixties in difficult peace negotiations with the Indians, and Dr. Marcus Whitman (1802–47), a Congregationalist and a martyr, after whom Whitman College at Walla Walla was named. Whitman did not himself "save Oregon," as was once claimed, but he was largely responsible for directing the attention of the public to the Pacific Northwest and for attracting and aiding immigrants. He originally went out to make a missionary reconnaissance for the American Board of Commissioners for Foreign Missions, and it was for the purpose of persuading them not to discontinue certain phases of the work there that he made his famous ride East. On this he accomplished his purpose, and his interview with the secretary of war in Washington was doubtless mutually advantageous. In 1843 he personally guided some two hundred wagons with settlers to the Columbia Valley, and helped to prove that the route was feasible for the large immigration that followed.

Largely as a result of the influence of these American missionary groups and their colleagues, and of the settlers whom they influenced to go to the Northwest, Oregon was established as a territory in 1849. It was subdivided four years later by the establishment of the northern part as the Territory of Washington; and was admitted by Congress as a free state in 1859, with a constitution framed by its citizens two years before. The state had these ample constitutional guarantees of religious freedom and Church–State separation:

Sec. 2. [*Freedom of worship*] All men shall be secured in the natural right to worship Almighty God according to the dictates of their own consciences.

Sec. 3. [*Freedom of religious opinion*] No law shall in any case whatever control the free exercise and enjoyment of religious opinions, or interfere with the rights of conscience.

Sec. 4. [*Religious qualification for office*] No religious test shall be required as a qualification for any office of trust or profit.

Sec. 5. [*State aid to religion*] No money shall be drawn from the treasury for the benefit of any religious or theological institution, nor shall any money be appropriated for the payment of any religious services in either house of the Legislative Assembly.

Sec. 6. [*Religious tests of witnesses*] No person shall be rendered incompetent as a witness or juror in consequence of his opinions on matters of religion, nor be questioned in any court of justice touching his religious belief, to affect the weight of his testimony.

Sec. 7. [*Oaths of witnesses*] The mode of administering an oath or affirmation shall be such as may be most consistent with, and binding upon, the conscience of the person to whom such oath or affirmation may be administered.[112]

These provisions are important of themselves and because of their influence in other states of the Northwest.

Let us turn now to some of the successors of Lee, Whitman, and De Smet in laying the foundations of Christian civilization and good government in the Northwest.

The Reverend Samuel H. Willey (1821–1914) and the Reverend Sheldon Jackson (1834–1909) may be taken as characteristic of the Presbyterian missionaries to the West. Willey went to California in '49, and, with Padre Antonio Ramirez, served as chaplain of the constitutional convention in that year. In the same year he took the lead in the effort to found a college, which was chartered in 1855. As president of the board of trustees, he was a chief factor in developing the College of California, and later was one of the leaders in founding the state university. He organized, and during most of this period (1850–62) served as pastor of, the Howard Street Presbyterian Church in San Francisco.

The Reverend Sheldon Jackson was perhaps the most representative clerical figure in the Christianization of the Rocky Mountain region in the second half of the nineteenth century. After ten years of vigorous home missionary work in Wisconsin and Minnesota, he moved to Iowa, and with the completion of the Union Pacific Railroad in 1869 pushed on farther West. In thirty-three days that summer he organized eight churches in Wyoming, Montana, and Nebraska, travelling 2,300 miles by rail and 1,200 by stage coach.[113] Later he was also responsible for founding and fostering churches in Colorado, Utah, Arizona, and New Mexico, as well as continuing his earlier efforts in the other states mentioned, and even touching Nevada and Texas. But he is perhaps best remembered for his later pioneer missionary and educational work in Alaska. Here this man of God served also from 1885 on as the first "general agent" of education for Alaska, under the United States Bureau of Education. For twenty-three years he worked in this territory, building up an effective public school system, and aiding American citizens, Indians, and Eskimos in every way in his power; one of his great services being the introduction, in 1892, under government auspices, of herds of domesticated reindeer from Siberia. He was also a prominent factor in the organization of the territorial government. His combination of effective Church–State services is characteristic of many early Christian missionaries in the West.

This list might be almost indefinitely extended, but these examples should be sufficient to show the part played by the Church in aiding the State in opening up and educating the West. The missionary was to a large extent the pioneer who laid the civic and educational foundations on which the State built, as well as the person mainly responsible for providing moral and religious guidance for the settlers. Some appreciation of the significance of his work may be seen from the fact that the Baptist Home Missionary Society secured pledges from the Union and Central Pacific Railroads to deed to it land sufficient for a meetinghouse and parsonage in every city and town in the trans-Missouri regions. Sometimes it secured a whole block.[114]

We have dealt in a previous section[115] with the early development of American colleges and universities and the part played by the Church in the movement. Suffice it to add that Tewksbury has shown that of the 182 higher educational institutions founded in the United States prior to the Civil War 150 were established by the Protestant Churches. The Presbyterians were foremost in this movement, but Congregationalists, Methodists, Roman Catholics, and others played an extensive part.[116]

Fortunately the Church did not have to undertake the task of supplying most of the common school education, because when the trans-Mississippi region was settled the public school ideal was firmly implanted in the American system. It is worth remembering that John D. Pierce (1797–1882) of Michigan, who led the educational movement in the Middle West along the general lines laid down by Horace Mann (1796–1859) in Massachusetts and Henry Barnard (1811–1900) in Connecticut,[117] was a Congregational minister. He was mainly responsible for the Michigan free school law, served as superintendent of public education, published *The Journal of Education,* and gave expression to the democratic emphasis of a nation which had recently abolished the main remnant of the caste system in America—Negro slavery. He said:

> The common schools are truly republican. In the public schools all classes are blended together, the rich mingle with the poor, and both are educated in company. Let free schools be established and maintained in perpetuity, and there can be no such thing as a permanent aristocracy in our land: for the monopoly of wealth is powerless when mind is allowed freely to come in contact with mind.[118]

Any consideration of the public schools and the Christian forces in the education of the West must not overlook *McGuffey's Readers*. These were prepared by a Presbyterian minister, William Holmes McGuffey (1800–73), who spent most of his life teaching at various colleges in Ohio, but his last quarter century as Professor of Moral Philosophy and Political Economy at the University of Virginia. From the appearance of the *First Reader* at Cincinnati in 1836 until the end of the century some 120,000,000 copies were sold. No other book since the *New England Primer,* other than the Bible and *Webster's Spelling Book,* has had such an influence on youth in American schools. The *Reader* taught principles of morality, patriotism, proverbial wisdom, and religion. Defending himself against those who objected to his using so many selections of a religious character, McGuffey wrote, "In a Christian country the man is to be pitied who at this day can honestly object to imbuing the minds of youth with the language and the spirit of the word of God." He included in the *Third Reader* the Lord's Prayer, an evening prayer, and a hymn.

An interesting example of co-operation between Church and State in mid-century was the frequent use of courthouses and even Statehouses for purposes of worship. Dr. Robert Baird, a responsible observer whose book on *Religion in America* appeared in Glasgow in 1842, and in New York in 1856, referred to this.[120] He also refers to prototypes of union churches used both for religious purposes and for public education.

> In some places in the South-western States [he writes], the primitive and temporary churches built for all denominations, in the new villages or settlements, are called "republican churches;" that is, churches for the accommodation of the *public* rather than for any one sect. Large school-houses, also, erected for the double purpose of teaching and preaching, are called "republican meeting-houses."[121]

The use of public school buildings and even courthouses for various public purposes is still common, especially in rural districts, but the authorities seldom permit it for denominational religious services.

Section 6. *THE CAMPAIGN AGAINST THE LOUISIANA LOTTERY AND PUBLIC GAMBLING*

The most interesting and important event in the antilottery movement was that which resulted in the overthrow of the Louisiana lottery. This campaign, which had its effective beginning in 1890, when Congress authorized the postmaster general to prohibit the use of the mails for lottery purposes,[122] lasted until 1894, when the lottery was overthrown. The story illustrates in a striking way the force of public opinion expressed through the Churches and the public press in overcoming a dangerous socially entrenched activity.

The Louisiana lottery was developed in New Orleans soon after the Civil War, chartered by the legislature in 1868 for twenty-five years. It was given a reputable exterior by the association with it of men of known personal integrity and commanding position, including General Beauregard. It has been estimated that within twenty-five years about $300,000,000, drawn from the whole country, was "carried to, and disbursed from, or treasured in New Orleans."[123] The lottery had a state charter, which was about to expire when the movement in opposition to it became articulate in 1891. The "lottery crowd" was said to have offered a provisional gift of $1,250,000 a year for the Louisiana state schools if the lottery, which under its tax-exempt franchise brought the state regularly $40,000 a year, were continued for another twenty-five-year period.[124]

A professor of engineering at the Massachusetts Institute of Technology, Samuel Homer Woodbridge (1848–1926), who was visiting in New Orleans in the winter of 1890–91, was mainly responsible for organizing the movement which led to the overthrow of the lottery. He wrote a letter to the Reverend Lyman Abbott, then editor of the *Christian Union,* urging that the Christian forces of the country should do something to put an end to this moral menace. The letter was brought to the attention of General George Johnson, formerly of the Confederate Army, who had been sent North by the antilotteryites of New Orleans to seek moral and financial help. General Johnson went on to Boston to see Professor Woodbridge, and the two planned the campaign together. The letter to the *Christian Union,* according to its writer,

> recognized in the Church the earthly embodiment of moral and spiritual energy. It therefore urged that, on some fixed day preceding the then pending Louisiana election, from the pulpits of the whole land an appeal should be made to the Christian conscience and purse. It expressed the belief that the result for good in Louisiana of the knowledge that such a national move and effort was to be made would be overwhelming, both in its moral effect, and in the substantial monetary aid it would bring to those in sore need of such help.[125]

A circular was printed, signed by Bishop Phillips Brooks (1835–93), the Reverend Dr. Edward Everett Hale (1822–1909), and other leaders of Christian thought, and setting the second Sunday of March "as the day of the Church's advance on the foe."[126] But the circular, though printed, was not sent out, for knowledge of it reached New Orleans and gave the antilottery forces such strength that they secured a small majority of delegates to the Democratic state convention. According to the historian of the movement,

> It was then the nation's sympathy and help infused new vigor and strength into the anti-lottery ranks, and that the news came to Louisiana from Boston of a rising of the Church, that agent of the Almighty's strength in the pulling down of strongholds.[127]

It is not necessary to go into the details of the electoral and legislative struggle in Louisiana. Suffice it to say that Louisiana by a majority of 40,000 declined to renew the lottery franchise. This closed the Louisiana chapter of the story, as the state was now in the hands of responsible citizens determined that the lotttery should never again be allowed there. The lottery interests, finding laws and public opinion in all the states hostile, decided to open headquarters in Honduras, although, taking advantage of a Florida law, the actual publicity center was placed at Port Tampa. The new postal regulations, under the act of Congress of 1890, forbade the distribution of tickets and other lottery material through the mail, but they were transported by express all over the country and were advertised in theater programs, newspapers, almanacs, etc. The railroads and express companies had a financial stake and were profiting by the closing of the mails, and it became evident that nothing would stop the lottery evil except a stringent national law which would prohibit under severe penalty the sending by any means of lottery tickets, money, or material from one state to another, or from another country into our own. To secure such a law was now the purpose of the group with headquarters in Boston. Fortunately, the Interstate Commerce Act seemed to make such a law Constitutional.

Again Professor Woodbridge took the matter up with the Reverend Lyman Abbott, D.D. (1835–1922), then of the *Outlook*, and prevailed upon him to take the lead in the movement to secure the enactment of the necessary law by Congress. The national movement was started by an appeal to the country sent to about two hundred of its best known citizens by the leading clergymen of Boston and by some other representative leaders of public opinion. It resulted in a petition signed by thirty-eight bishops of the Episcopal Church, twenty-seven college and university presidents, Cardinal Gibbons and three archbishops, ten Methodist clergymen, the governors of eight states, and others. It is worth recording—as showing the lasting influence of such a document—that it was effectively quoted by the Massachusetts Civic League, Inc., in its successful efforts to arouse the Christian forces of the state in January, 1941, against five bills introduced into the Massachusetts state legislature to provide for a state lottery to increase state revenues. The advocates of this later move asserted that it would raise $25,000,000, which would take care of old-age assistance and eliminate some taxes. Cardinal O'Connell, Bishop William Lawrence, Rabbi Levi Olan, the Massachusetts Council of Churches, the Watch and Ward Society, and other religious leaders and religious and philanthropic organizations opposed it.[128]

The memorial favoring national legislation against the lottery evil, with accompanying bill, was presented to the Senate by Senator George F. Hoar (1826–1904) on February 15, 1894, and passed the Senate unanimously three months after its introduction, but was held up for some time in the House, as unanimous consent could not be secured for its consideration in spite of an overwhelming sentiment in its favor. There followed a national mail campaign which was extraordinary for its time. Religious newspaper subscription rolls, church registers, college catalogs, and other lists were secured, and about twenty thousand documents a week were sent out, all concentrated on securing favorable action in the House. The religious press of the country was particularly active; all religious papers with as many as 5,000 subscribers being sent documents wrapped and stamped, with the request that they be forwarded to the leading men and women on their lists.[129] Effort was particularly concentrated on the clergy of nine states whose Representatives in Congress were not favorable.[130] Finally the Lottery Act passed in 1895, after many trying and exciting incidents, and received the signature of President Cleveland. Its principal promoter says, with some justice, that

> The story of the Anti-lottery Crusade affords a unique illustration of the overwhelming power of moral energy when the social conscience is awakened and the social will is mobilized and directed against a recognized and menacing evil.[131]

There has been no event in our history where the influence of the Churches and their clergy has been more effectively secured in the interest of wise social legislation. The opening clause of this Act "For the suppression of lottery traffic through national and interstate commerce and the postal service subject to the jurisdiction and laws of the United States," reads as follows:

> Be it enacted by the Senate and House of Representatives of America in Congress assembled, That any person who shall cause to be brought within the United States from abroad, for the purpose of disposing of the same, (or deposited in or carried by the mails of the United States, or carried from one state to another in the United States) any paper, certificate, or instrument purporting to be or represent a ticket, chance, share, or interest in or dependent upon the event of a lottery, so-called gift concert, or similar enterprise offering prizes dependent upon lot, or chance, or shall cause any advertisement of such lottery, so-called gift concert, or similar enterprise, offering prizes dependent upon lot or chance, to be brought into the United States, or deposited in or carried by the mails of the United States, or transferred from one State to another in the same, shall be punishable in the first offense by imprisonment for not more than two years or by a fine of not more than $1,000.00, or both, and in the second and after offenses by such imprisonment only.[132]

The Act was finally upheld by the United States Supreme Court in 1903 as a valid exercise of power under the commerce clause of the Constitution. This decision is the basis on which later legislation excluding obscene literature, impure foods, etc., from interstate commerce has been adopted.[133]

The successful campaign against the Louisiana lottery has been recounted at some length as a striking example of the effect of an awakened sentiment working largely through the Churches against a public abuse. There have been many similar and successful state and local campaigns against other forms of gambling carried through under the leadership of the International Reform Federation, the Watch and Ward Society of New England, and similar organizations, whose main support has come from the Protestant Church group. A recent one was the defeat in Maryland, in 1938, of a proposed amendment to the Constitution which would have legalized lotteries. Public opinion credits the Council of Churches and Christian Education of Maryland with a large share of this success. But there is need of constant vigilance, as is shown by the fact that in recent years serious efforts have been made in Congress to provide in some Constitutional way for a national lottery as a means of increasing Federal revenues.[134]

The Federal Council, at its biennial session in 1940, adopted the following statement on the lottery danger, which is rapidly developing in some places considerable tension between State and Church:

> The Federal Council of the Churches of Christ in America has noted with increasing concern the rapid growth of the gambling evil among our people, as well as the high-powered propaganda which seeks to extend the vicious influence of this dangerous practice by establishing national and state lotteries and legalizing various forms of gambling and betting, on the alleged ground that great masses of our people are already indulging in these vices and millions of dollars which are now sent to other lands ought to be kept at home.
>
> It has also been charged in a recent survey that in many sections of our country a large percentage of raffles and games of chance are conducted under church auspices, and because of this complicity in evil the hands of many religious leaders are tied and the Church is robbed of much spiritual influence and power. In this, as in all other moral issues, judgment must begin at the House of God. History proves that all forms of gambling have a demoralizing influence upon character, and that in the end most of the losses are visited upon the poor. All our pastors and people should stand firmly against this evil, which has been gaining momentum by leaps and bounds, and it is the hope and prayer of the Federal Council of the Churches of Christ in America that no Christian congregation will foster, permit, or profit by any form of gambling under its auspices.[135]

This may be taken as characteristic of many national and local actions by Protestant groups.

The attitude of the Roman Catholic Church on the subect of raffles, lotteries, and various games of chance for church purposes is generally less condemnatory, though it differs greatly in different dioceses. The *Catholic Encyclopedia* thus states the position of the Church:

> Lottery. . . . Morally it is objectionable if carried to excess as it tends to develop the gambling spirit and distract people from earning a livelihood by honest work. How-

ever, if there is no fraud of any sort in the transaction, and if there is some sort of proportion between the price of a ticket and the value of a chance of gaining a prize, a lottery cannot be condemned as in itself immoral.[136]

The degree to which the Church permits bingo "at parish parties" may be seen in the full-page colored advertisement of accessories for use in the game in the *Official Catholic Directory* for 1948 (p. 18).

The influence of Protestant groups and of Cardinal O'Connell (1859–1944) was a decisive factor in preventing an attempt to legalize lotteries in Massachusetts in 1941. Such a proposal was defeated in the legislature—the House vote against it being 129 to 46, in spite of the fact that its proponents had cleverly tied up the plan with old-age pensions. The cardinal's objection was based on what seems to be incontrovertible moral ground, "the evils contingent to a public project based on the gambling instinct."[137] Other ecclesiastics, like the late Archbishop Curley,[138] have spoken out strongly against the gambling craze. Such dioceses as Buffalo, Pittsburgh, Albany, and Fall River have taken action against it, banning it from all church activities.

On the other hand, bingo is a form of gambling very common and popular in some Catholic dioceses, and justified by many ecclesiastics when played in the interest of Church purposes. Cleveland, Ohio, and Rochester, New York, are among the places where the Catholic churches have adopted this questionable method of raising money for religious objects.[139] Maryland and Connecticut have legalized it under certain conditions. In Wisconsin the game has been widely though not completely suppressed as a public nuisance. The Supreme Court of the state has declared it to be illegal even when played for philanthropic or religious purposes.

The bingo issue has been much to the fore recently in several communities, especially New York and Cincinnati. In New York the police commissioner issued a statement to the effect that bingo and similar games would be deemed unlawful except when conducted under the auspices of the Church. Mayor LaGuardia disagreed with this opinion, stating that

If a game is unlawful, the ultimate disposal of the funds, or the auspices under which the game is operated, or the place where the game is operated, does not make an unlawful game lawful. If bingo is unlawful in one place, it cannot be lawful in another.[140]

On the other hand, some Catholic priests felt that if the game were conducted for the benefit of the Church it would not be open to objection, though Archbishop Spellman stated that such gambling would be discontinued while the legal status of the matter was further probed before the courts. The mayor's action was promptly approved both by the Greater New York Federation of

Churches and by the Methodist Ministers Association. The Federation, through its general secretary, said that he thought bingo a reprehensible form of gambling, and expressed the hope that the mayor would proceed against "Protestant Churches or any other churches which resort to such a device to raise money." The Association, representing more than 700 churches, wrote through its president to the mayor:

> We heartily commend your action in barring bingo and similar games of chance from churches as well as places of entertainment. We pledge ourselves to aid you by the spoken word and also by our own churches.
>
> We believe bingo is bad morals, bad education and bad economics and as such should be condemned by an intelligent citizenry.[141]

In April, 1943, Governor Thomas E. Dewey of New York vetoed a bill which would have authorized local governing bodies, upon petition of 5 per cent of the local voters, to issue permits for the operation of bingo games by religious, social, fraternal, civic, and educational organizations. The governor based his disapproval of the bill on three main grounds. He felt that it was "clearly unconstitutional"; that it did not effectively bar professional promoters, who might take over an obscure fraternal organization and operate a central bingo game, transmitting the play to assembly halls throughout the state; and that the provision for voter petitions would annually stir up bitter political and moral issues in many localities.[142] The governor quoted an amendment to the state constitution adopted in 1939 which so clearly seems to bar bingo that the *New York Times* stated editorially that the only way to make this form of gambling legal in the state would be a further constitutional change. Other states have had similar proposals under consideration.

In Cincinnati the issue was particularly acute because the city fathers voted to permit the playing of bingo, though this was technically in violation of the state constitution and laws. The city manager disagreed with the other city authorities, and in the fall of 1942 ordered a police raid on a parochial school building where both slot machines and bingo were in use; thirty were destroyed. As a general result, a mandamus suit was brought by a woman active in the Kennedy Heights Presbyterian Church to compel the city authorities to do away with bingo, which had been the cause of large losses to many people in the city. The Council of Churches unanimously voiced its opposition to the game, and its support of those who were trying to ban it from the city.

These New York and Cincinnati cases may be considered typical of scores of local conflicts that have recently taken place and will continue to take place over this issue until Church, municipal, and state authorities, backed by public sentiment, unite in banning the game when used for public gambling.

Whether the underlying question of the legitimacy of public games of chance for money should generally be dealt with by law, when a strong majority support for the legislation is lacking, is open to debate; but it would seem unfortunate to have a distinction made between bingo in churches and elsewhere, or between the game when conducted for religious and philanthropic causes and for other purposes. Indeed, if public gambling, even for small stakes, is open to criticism, it would seem to be more open to criticism in churches than in other places, and at least as much open to criticism when practiced for religious as for other objects. It is doubtful whether a satisfactory argument can be made for church bingo on the ground that the end—the support of a church or of some worthy church enterprise—justifies the means.

There are two questions involved here in Church–State relations: the question of law observance, when laws against such forms of gambling exist; and the question of securing and enforcing more rigid laws. Speaking generally, Roman Catholic and Protestant ministers lay equal emphasis on law observance, but the latter—inheriting the Puritan tradition—are less tolerant of public gambling, and advocate much more rigid laws for its suppression, because they believe it to be demoralizing. They are well-nigh unanimous in feeling that the end does not justify the means when lotteries or bingo games are used for raising money for church purposes; whereas Roman Catholic priests are frankly divided on the subject, though generally opposed to bingo games if resorted to for other than church or charitable purposes.

Section 7. THE STRUGGLE OVER POLITICAL CORRUPTION AND GOOD GOVERNMENT

Although our great national religious bodies have deeply interested themselves in various social reforms and features of good government,[143] the fight against entrenched political corruption, as far as the Church is concerned, has been mainly by individual members, and by ministers and local ministerial groups in various municipalities. Probably the most impressive and illuminating case has been that of the Reverend Charles H. Parkhurst, D. D. (1845–1921), whose work was the main factor in the overthrow of the corrupt Tammany Hall administration in New York in November, 1894. Anyone interested in what an individual church led by a prophetic spirit can do in ridding a community of a government which is corrupt and a protector of crime should read Dr. Parkhurst's vigorous book entitled *Our Fight with Tammany*.[144] This tells the story of the Society for the Prevention of Crime and of the activities of Dr. Parkhurst, pastor of the Madison Square Presbyterian Church. The society, organized in 1878, had as its president a much respected Presbyterian minister, the Reverend Howard Crosby, D.D. (1826–91). On his death Dr. Parkhurst was elected president. Up to this time the society had tried to carry on its work in conjunction with the police, but the new president accepted the office on condition that henceforth it should deal with the police as its "arch-antagonist, making with it no alliance and giving it no quarter."[145]

What is generally considered the beginning of the campaign against Tammany Hall was the sermon preached in the Madison Square Church by Dr. Parkhurst February 14, 1892. It was on the text "Ye are the salt of the earth."[146] In it he said:

. . . In its municipal life our city is thoroughly rotten. Here is an immense city reaching out arms of evangelization to every quarter of the globe; and yet every step that we take looking to the moral betterment of this city has to be taken directly in the teeth of the damnable pack of administrative bloodhounds that are fattening themselves on the ethical flesh and blood of our citizenship.

We have a right to demand that the Mayor and those associated with him in administering the affairs of this municipality should not put obstructions in the path of our ameliorating endeavors; and they do. There is not a form under which the devil disguises himself that so perplexes us in our efforts, or so bewilders us in the devising of our schemes as the polluted harpies that, under the pretence of governing this city, are feeding day and night on its quivering vitals. They are a lying, perjured, rum-soaked, and libidinous lot.[147]

After stating that the only object of his appeal was

to sound a distinct note, and to quicken our Christian sense of the obligatory relation in which we stand toward the official and administrative criminality that is filthifying our entire municipal life, making New York a very hot-bed of knavery, debauchery, and bestiality, in the atmosphere of which, and at the corrosive touch of which, there is not a young man so noble, nor a young girl so pure, as not to be in a degree infected by the fetid contamination,[148]

he closed with these words:

. . . The good Lord take the fog out of our eyes, the paralysis out of our nerves, and the limp out of our muscles, and the meanness out of our praise, show to us our duty, and reveal to us our superb opportunity, making of every man and woman among us a prophet, instinct with a longing so intense that we shall not be afraid, loving righteousness with a loyalty so impassioned that we shall feel the might of it and trust it, and our lives become this day enlisted in the maintenance of the right, and thus show that Almighty God is mightier than all the ranks of Satan that challenge His claims and dispute His blessed progress.[149]

Many individuals and some organizations and publications supported Dr. Parkhurst, but he was generally reviled by men in office and by those in league with them. They took the ground that he should confine his activities to preaching the Gospel and keep out of politics. Tammany was furious, and the reforming pastor even received a presentment from the grand jury which declared that his charges, especially those against the district attorney in office, were unfounded and that their author had "no evidence upon which to base them, except alleged newspaper reports, which in the form published had no foundation."[150] The presentment added that his charges "can only serve to create a feeling of unwarranted distrust in the minds of the community with regard to the integrity of public officials, and tend only to hinder prompt administration of justice."[151] Thereupon Dr. Parkhurst decided to get evidence at first hand. With the aid of a detective and friends he secured in three weeks 284 affidavits, which he presented to the grand jury, stating that his sole object was "to secure in the general mind an indictment against the Police Department."[152]

He presented the evidence first in his pulpit on the morning of March 13, with the affidavits before him, taking as his text Psalms 12.8: "The wicked walk on every side, when the vilest men are exalted."[153] He said:

> I do not speak as a Republican or a Democrat, as a Protestant or a Catholic, as an advocate of prohibition, or as an advocate of license. I am moved, so help me Almighty God, by the respect which I have for the Ten Commandments, and by my anxiety as a preacher of Jesus Christ, to have the law of God regnant in individual and social life; so that I antagonize our existing municipal administration, because I believe, with all the individual exceptions frankly conceded four weeks ago, that administration to be essentially corrupt, interiorly rotten, and in all its combined tendency and effect to stand in diametric resistance to all that Christ and a loyally Christian pulpit represent in the world.[154]

Dr. Parkhurst's evidence of illegal open saloons, gambling places, houses of prostitution, "protection" by the police, etc., could not be refuted, and resulted in a sudden change in front and a presentment by the grand jury against the Police Department. This was the beginning of a movement which led to the overthrow of the corrupt Tammany administration. The next steps need not be recounted here. It should be enough to have shown how a great reform movement—without which the later honest and progressive administration of New York City by the late Mayor LaGuardia would have been most unlikely—began with the courageous attitude of a single minister of the Gospel. That his action was unconventional, that it was much more characteristic of an Old Testament prophet than of a modern Church clergyman, cannot be denied, but it was in the end extremely effective. It is hard to say to what extent the organized ministry of the churches co-operated, but what they said as individuals was unmistakable. Some, like Rabbi Henry Mendes and the Reverend Dr.

David J. Burrell, took an active part, and there is evidence that some of the most important religious groups strongly supported Dr. Parkhurst.

Among many other ministers of religion who have rendered vital service in advancing political causes where the ethical implications seemed uppermost, may be mentioned the Reverend John Witherspoon (1729–94), Presbyterian minister and president of Princeton, active in the Continental Congress and a signer of the Declaration of Independence; Henry Ward Beecher (1813–87), in his attacks on slavery and his defense of the Union cause in Great Britain; William G. Brownlow (1805–77)—"Parson Brownlow"—for many years an itinerant preacher of the Methodist Church, who, though not at the time opposed to slavery, became the leader of the Union antisecession cause in eastern Tennessee and later was elected Reconstruction governor and senator. He was editor of the last paper in the South before the war to continue to advocate remaining in the Union, one of his famous statements being that he would rather be imprisoned (as he was) than "recognize the hand of God in the work of breaking up the American government."

More recently we have had men like Dr. Graham Taylor (1851–1938), working through the Chicago Commons and in other ways to clean up one of the worst wards in Chicago;[156] and Norman Thomas (1884–), who before becoming the perennial national leader of the Socialist party was active as a minister of the Presbyterian Church in municipal reform in New York. Similarly, no men have done more in the United States to develop the social point of view in the Church[157] than Professor Walter Rauschenbusch (1861–1918), a Baptist minister of the Rochester Divinity School; Washington Gladden (1836–1918), pastor of the First Congregational Church in Columbus, Ohio; and Monsignor John Augustine Ryan (1869–1945), director of the Social Action Department of the National Catholic Welfare Council. No one else in this country has worked as effectively as Monsignor Ryan to secure the adoption by his Church of a wise, constructive, and progressive social-welfare program, based on sound economics.

An equally impressive case, and one perhaps more interesting for our purpose, is that of a Presbyterian minister, the Reverend Lester H. Clee (1888–) of Newark, who continued his pastoral duties while serving as speaker of the New Jersey Assembly (1935), member of the State Senate, Republican candidate for governor, and a vigorous and respected opponent of political corruption. The *New York Times* stated editorially:

> He has been faithful, zealous and constant in his religious functions, and he has felt that he owed a duty to his community and his State as well as to his congregation. He has been a good influence in the politics of New Jersey.[158]

Rabbi Louis Mann (1890–) of Chicago and Rabbi Stephen S. Wise (1874–1948) of New York may be taken as representative of the many Jewish rabbis, especially of Reform Judaism, who have identified their synagogues with liberal public causes in the interest of good government and social welfare.

Scores of such cases might be cited. But unless the moral issues involved are clear-cut, or the ministers act with great discretion, they inevitably create wide divergence of opinion between the supporters and opponents of the "Church in politics," as we shall see in a later section devoted to this issue.[159]

Section 8. THE PIOUS FUND CASES IN CALIFORNIA (1848–1902)

The so-called Pious Fund of the Californias, *Fondo Piadoso de las Californias,* was the first case decided by the Permanent Court of International Arbitration at The Hague. This was in October, 1902. The case goes back, however, for sixty years as a difficult matter of settlement, and its roots are in the close of the seventeenth century. In 1697 two Jesuits inaugurated the fund as the financial basis of their work in Lower California. It was for the purpose of converting the native Indians of Upper and Lower California to the Roman Catholic faith, and of maintaining the priesthood in these Spanish–Mexican territories. Here is a translation of the clause which caused so many difficulties:

> To have and to hold, to said missions founded, and which may hereafter be founded, in the Californias, as well as for the maintenance of their religious, and to provide for the ornament and decent support of divine worship, as also to aid the native converts . . . this fund shall be perpetually inalienable . . . so that even in case of all California being civilized and converted to our holy Catholic faith, the profits of said estates shall be applied to the necessities of said missions and their support.[160]

When Mexico became independent of Spain its government succeeded the Spanish crown in the trusteeship of this fund.

As is well known, the California missions had been very successful from the standpoint of law and order, and of agricultural and industrial development. They were also at least partly successful in the conversion of the Indians to the Christian faith and way of life. Some thirty thousand Indians came under their tutelage. But the old regulations contained a clause to the effect that after ten years in a mission it was expected that Indians should return to their pueblos and then be treated like other citizens—a provision which proved inadequate. The friars, under the leadership of the heroic Junípero Serra (1713–84), were the first agents of Western civilization in what is now California, and their work went on efficiently, according to their official records, from 1770 to 1831, when Governor Echeandia, the first governor under the Mexican flag, published his proclamation enforcing secularization.

During this time twenty-one missions had been developed, of which many are still objects of great religious and archaelogical interest. With Mexican independence of Spain, the plan for secularizing the missions, which had its origin in an unenforced decree of the Spanish Cortes in 1813, was carried out and the process was virtually completed by 1836; so that when the United States flag supplanted that of Mexico over the government house at the old capital of Monterey in 1846, the "carcass" of the missions "had been picked nearly to the bones."[161] The process had been hastened by the authorization of the sale or rental at public auction of the mission estates, so as to secure for the government money for the war against the United States.

At first it was understood that, in accordance with Spanish law, this would merely mean that the spiritual affairs of a mission—transformed into a pueblo —would be transferred from the order concerned to the bishop of the diocese, each mission being under secular parish priests, while the Indians retained control of the temporalities; but as practiced in California it virtually involved the turning over of mission property to political control. Indeed, a historian of secularization asserts that "in practice" the plan often resulted in the confiscation of the missionary property in lands by white settlers or government officials."[162] This whole procedure was opposed by the Franciscans, who felt that the land and all it produced, along with the livestock, buildings, etc., were really the property of the Indians to be held as a sacred trust for their benefit by the missions. There were no courts before which they could take their case, and as a result the mission property was little by little squandered, the missions neglected, and the missionary work greatly interfered with.

By a decree of the Mexican government, issued by President Santa Anna in 1842, the estates of the Pious Fund had been virtually confiscated and transferred to the public treasury. The government agreed, however, to pay interest at 6 per cent in perpetuity to carry out the original design of the donors, and the national revenue from tobacco was pledged for this purpose. But when Upper California became part of the United States by the Treaty of Guadalupe Hidalgo, which brought the war with Mexico to an end in 1848, the Mexican government refused to continue to pay the proportion of interest to which this section of the country was entitled. The matter had now become an international one. The Church appealed to the United States government for assistance, being encouraged to do so by its conviction of the justice of its case and by the wording of the proclamation which had been issued by Gen. Stephen Watts Kearny (1794–1848). This stated that

> He was instructed by the President of the United States to respect and protect the religious institutions of California, to take care that the religious rights of its inhabi-

tants are secured in the most ample manner, since the Constitution of the United States allows to every individual the privilege of worshipping his Creator in whatever manner his conscience may dictate.[163]

He also ordered that

the Missions and their property should remain under the charge of the Catholic priests until proper judicial tribunals should decide on the various claims to the Missions.[164]

On the whole, American occupation resulted in improved mission conditions, their control being returned to the diocesan authorities. Conditions seemed ripe to press the settlement of the Pious Fund case. The first Roman Catholic synod in California (1852) asserted the right of the Church to its share of the fund. The bishop brought the matter before the First Plenary Council at Baltimore, which advised his going in person to Mexico City to present his claims. This effort being unsuccessful, he appealed, on advice of counsel, to the secretary of state, Lewis Cass, but no action seemed possible until the establishment in 1868 of the Mixed Claims Commission. This was appointed to adjust claims between Mexico and the United States, with the understanding that if the commissioners appointed by the two States failed to agree, the matter was to be referred to an umpire. The archbishop and bishops of California presented their case to this commission, proposing that, as citizens of the United States, they were entitled

to demand from Mexico for the benefit of the Missions within their dioceses, a proper proportion of the sums which Mexico by the terms of the Santa Anna decree of October, 1842, had assumed to pay the Church in California.[165]

The United States duly entered their claim, but when no agreement could be reached the matter was submitted to the umpire, Sir Edward Thornton, then British minister in Washington.

In 1875 he found that there was due to the archbishop and bishops in Upper California, as administrators of the fund, an arrears of interest of $904,070.99, to be paid in Mexican gold. The main terms of this award were carried out by Mexico, the last installment being paid in 1890; but the payment of interest was withheld from October 24, 1868. The United States tried to collect the back interest without success, until in 1902 the Mexican and United States governments agreed to leave the matter to the Hague Court, which chose arbitrators and an umpire. The court in October, 1902, decided that the Thornton award must stand, and that the claim for interest was just, the only modification being that the interest due was to be paid in the then legal coin of Mexico, instead of in gold. But Mexico has not yet met this obligation.

The special interest of this case for our study is that it is one in which the government of the United States supported the claim of the Roman Catholic bishops in California for a settlement of debts, and carried the case successfully —as far as a decision was concerned—before an international tribunal.[166]

Section 9. THE SPANISH-AMERICAN WAR AND THE TREATY OF PARIS (1898)

The Spanish-American War was of very short duration—less than four months, from April 25, 1898, when war was declared, to August 12, when a protocol was signed by which Spain relinquished Cuba; but in spite of its brevity it had a profound influence on Church-State relations in and under the United States, and this for many reasons. The Protestant Churches were incensed at the sufferings of the people of Cuba, and believed that the Roman Catholic Church there was largely responsible because of its alleged shortcomings as a moral and spiritual force. They were convinced that Cuba offered a great opportunity for missionary work. The Churches themselves were active in various ways during the war, gaining an experience which was to prove invaluable in the World War of 1914–18. Furthermore, the Treaty of Peace—especially through the acquisition of the Philippine Islands—brought new and complicated problems, in view of the fact that the Philippines contained millions of devoted Roman Catholics with the Church legally established in the Islands, and that the Sulu Archipelago included a large Mohammedan population with certain practices inconsistent with those Christian standards which had become recognized as part of the American tradition. We shall deal with these and similar matters in the following pages.

The war is both far enough away and yet close enough to enable us to study objectively the attitude of the Churches toward it. The most important documentary material, especially the attitude of the Protestant and Catholic religious press, before, during, and after the war, has been well covered in a book recently published.[167] The attitude of the Churches was prepared for by the writings of Dr. Josiah Strong (1847–1916), a man of breadth, religious interest, and patriotism, whose works in the 'eighties and 'nineties of the last century did much to develop the idea of the part America should play in fulfilling Anglo-Saxon destiny as a civilizing and Christianizing power.[168] The same was also true of the missionary addresses of many men, and more especially of Dr. John R. Mott (1865–   ), whose *Strategic Points in the World's Conquest,* appearing in 1897, was broadly read and discussed. In general it may be said that, though a few independent groups, like the Friends and the Unitarians, opposed the entry of the United States into the war, most Protestant denominations either favored it or looked upon it as inevitable, especially after the report of Senator Redfield Proctor (1831–1908) showing the bad conditions in Cuba. The Roman Catholic attitude is of special interest, since Spain and Cuba were Catholic countries. The Catholic press urged that the matters at issue be arbitrated by the pope. Later, when this was shown to be impossible and war was declared, they were true to their major tradition, which is to support responsible government, especially when there seem to be—as in this case—moral issues involved. Some representative Catholic papers, however, expressed the hope that the occupation of the Philippine Islands would be temporary and that the Protestant missionary societies should not be allowed to try to proselytize in Catholic areas. In this connection it is interesting to note that under the leadership of Bishop Charles H. Brent (1862–1929) the Protestant Episcopal Church took somewhat the Catholic position, by deciding that the work of the Episcopal Church in the Philippines should be among the English-speaking population and among the non-Christian tribes, but not among Roman Catholics.

The restraint with which most of the religious press discussed the Cuban situation, and even the destruction of the battleship *Maine* in Havana harbor, changed to one of very strong criticism of Spain and of considerable sympathy for intervention after the speech of Senator Proctor in the Senate, March 17, 1898. He was a man whose character, record, and judgment carried weight with conservative Christian people, and his picture of the sufferings of the Cubans under Spanish rule created much sympathy.

It is interesting to note some comments[169] from denominational papers which are here arranged chronologically to bring out the development of opinion in this important Church–State situation.

In its issue of March 24, 1898, the influential Congregational *Advance,* which had denounced the sensationalism of the yellow press and had only a fortnight earlier declared that the conservative majority of the American people was opposed to intervention, accepted Senator Proctor's speech as confirming newspaper reports about conditions in Cuba, and came out strongly for Cuban independence.[170]

Similarly, on March 31, the *Evangelist* (Presbyterian) stated: "And if it be the will of Almighty God, that by war the last trace of this inhumanity of man to man shall be swept away from this Western hemisphere, let it come!"[171]

On April 13, when the issue of peace or war was still in the balance, the editor of the *Northern Christian Advocate* (Methodist) wrote: ". . . Should we now go to war, our cause will be just, and Methodism will be ready to do its full duty. Every Methodist preacher will be a recruiting officer."[172]

With the declaration on April 21 of the existence of a state of war the religious press became still more outspoken. Some journals of an extremely Protestant type began to indicate their belief that the war had significance from the point of view of Christian civilization.

On April 23, *The Standard,* although frankly recognizing the influence of the yellow press and other unworthy factors in bringing on the war, held that it was a "righteous war," which we had not entered for any selfish national purpose. Pratt summarizes this position as being that the United States "would go to Cuba with a loaf of bread at the end of its bayonet, with its warships laden with flour and shot. Its banners have been preceded by the Red Cross flag, and will be followed by school books and Bibles. . . . Christian citizens will uphold the president and stand by the flag."[173]

"Saving" Latin countries from the grip of the Roman Catholic Church was a favorite theme in the more extreme Protestant papers. For instance, in its issue of April 27, one journal connected with the Christian and Missionary Alliance took the ground that it was a war for humanity, and that it was God's instrument for striking a blow at that "system of iniquity, the papacy." The editor foresaw that not only Cuba and Porto Rico but the Philippines would be freed "from the intolerable yoke of Spanish oppression" and opened "to the Gospel of the Lord Jesus Christ. . . . God is beating down the long-closed doors." He scoffed at the idea that the Catholic powers of the Old World would prevent the United States from controlling the Philippines, saying: "God is stronger than either the Romish Church or the Catholic powers of Europe. We should pray not only that Cuba be free, but that these fair Eastern isles shall also become the scenes of Gospel triumphs and the salvation of countless souls."[174]

On May 21, the most influential of undenominational religious journals, the *Outlook,* the successor of Henry Ward Beecher's *Christian Union,* then edited by the Reverend Lyman Abbott (1835–1922), probably well expressed responsible Protestant Church opinion of the time when it said in an important editorial on "The Church in the War" that the Churches almost unanimously recognized that "the Nation had been moved to battle by the demand of awakened conscience answering to the call of outraged humanity."[175]

The Roman Catholic press was at first somewhat reserved, expressing frequently, and naturally, up to the day of final national decision (April 21, 1898), the hope that the matter might be referred to the arbitration of the pope. It criticized the proselytizing purpose which often appeared in the support of the war by Protestant religious journals. As late as May 7 the *Ave Maria* thus referred to the belligerency of many of the ministers of Protestantism: "The pulpits of the country resound with war-cries and calumnies against our foes. Many of the pious men who occupy them preferred war to peace, and war at any cost rather than peace as a result of the Holy Father's arbitration."[176] But in its issue of April 23 the *Catholic News* stated that the nation had entered the war purely from a sense of duty, and that "the spectacle we present today is a truly inspiring one." Somewhat later the American archbishops issued a circular to be read in all Catholic churches, directing priests to pray for an American victory, and declaring that whatever had been the opinions of individuals before the beginning of hostilities, there could "now be no two opinions as to the duty of every loyal American citizen," and that American Catholics were loyal to their country and obedient to the supreme authority of the Government.[177] The Church saw increasingly that it had both a great opportunity and a great responsibility to improve conditions in the former Spanish possessions by sending them American priests—a policy later carried out with notable results.

Almost the entire religious press agreed in the early fall of 1898 that whatever America's governmental relation to the Spanish islands might be after the war American Christians had a religious duty. A spiritual invasion must follow a military invasion. But how about the political invasion? As the war advanced, and victory seemed assured, the religious press gave more and more attention to the political responsibility of our government to the inhabitants of the Spanish islands.

As early as June 27 the *Religious Telescope,* a weekly of the United Brethren, thought that for the nation to decline to take the Philippines would be to refuse, for selfish reasons, "to assume the duty and the responsibility which a gracious Providence has thrust upon it." The editor felt that the same argument also applied to Cuba, Porto Rico, the Ladrone and Caroline Islands, and even to the Canaries![178]

The responsible *Methodist Review* of Nashville, in its July–August number, rejoiced that the war would "open up Cuba, Porto Rico, and the Philippines to the distribution and proclamation of the pure word of God," and teach America, along with Great Britain, its duties as a champion of the oppressed, defender of liberty, and protector of Christian preachers.[179]

The views of the representative Baptist *Watchman* are interesting. Its attitude in various editorials from August to December has been thus summarized:

> The *Watchman* suggested that the history of our dealing with the Indians cast grave doubt upon our fitness for bestowing benevolent government upon the Filipinos. If we were to govern alien races successfully, we must first clean up our government at home. It was, indeed, our responsibility to deliver the Filipinos from oppression and open their islands to civilization, but this could be accomplished through guarantees in the peace treaty; annexation was unnecessary. If we should nevertheless, assume the government of the Philippines, we must do so as trustees, not as exploiters. . . .[180]

Speaking generally, it may be said that after the signing of the armistice August 12 there was close to unanimity on the part of the religious press that the United States should hold the Philippines as a duty to its inhabitants, involving the provision of an honest and public-spirited government, and free scope for the ministrations of the Christian religion. Perhaps the most representative Church opinion at this time was that expressed by the *Independent* in its issues of October 6 and 20. It took the ground that we should be "possumists," not pessimists, "in the matter of the nation's ability to grapple with the problems of annexation." More specifically answering the charge of the *Springfield Republican* that the religious press had been seized by a "delirium of jingoism," its editors stated with conviction: "There is no delirium, no jingoism, in the acceptance by our religious people of the responsibilities put upon us by the war."[181]

But there was a small group of independent religious leaders who felt that there were grave dangers to our American democracy in adopting anything approaching an "imperial" policy. Bishop Henry Codman Potter (1835–1908) of New York was a representative of this group, but his colleague and friend, Bishop Arthur C. A. Hall (1847–1930) of Vermont, of English birth, thought otherwise, believing that the nation had been "used by Almighty God as an instrument for putting an end to a selfish system of misgovernment" and that it must face its responsibilities.[182]

Probably President McKinley's (1843–1901) experience and conclusions were in essence those of most American religious leaders. After nights of anxiety and prayer for guidance as to what course the nation should take regarding the Philippine Islands, he had become convinced that

> there was nothing left for us to do but to take them all, and to educate the Filipinos, and uplift and civilize and Christianize them, and by God's grace do the very best we could by them as our fellowmen for whom Christ also died.[183]

All that remained for the Churches to do was to organize their mission work, and this they did promptly, the Presbyterians taking the lead.

The activities of the Y.M.C.A. and of other Christian service agencies during the war[184] were on a relatively small scale compared with those in the World War fifteen years later, but the experience was valuable training for that later service. The general attitude of the Army and Navy was favorable to religious services, especially by ordained chaplains. The Army Regulations for 1895 and 1901—just before and just after the Spanish War—contain the following: "An orderly observance of the Sabbath by the officers and men in the military service is enjoined. Military duty and labor on Sunday will be reduced to the measure of strict necessity."[185]

Section 10. THE CHURCH AND STATE PROBLEMS IN THE PHILIPPINES

The acquisition by the United States of the Philippine Islands in 1899, as a result of the war with Spain, brought with it entirely new Church and State problems for the American government.[186] By the Treaty of Paris the Roman Catholic Church, as such, was recognized as a corporation. This fact differentiates the island possessions which came to the United States at the close of the war with Spain from all of our continental territory.[187] The new situation is brought out strikingly in an opinion of the United States Supreme Court in 1908, quoting words used by Governor William H. Taft (1857–1930) to Leo XIII in Rome in 1902.

> The transfer of sovereignty and all governmental property rights and interests from the Crown of Spain to the United States, in the Philippine Islands contained in the Treaty of Paris was a transfer from a government between which and the Church of Rome there had been in those islands the closest association in property, religion, and politics, to a government which by the law of its being is absolutely prevented from having such associations with any Church.[188]

In the Philippines there had been complete union between Church and State, and it had to be superseded under the American government by entire separation. As stated in the opinion of the Philippine Commission in dealing with the question of the control of the College of San José in the University of St. Thomas in Manila—a former Roman Catholic institution—the Treaty of Paris involved

> a transfer of sovereignty from a kingdom in which church and state were united, and one might say almost inextricably fused, to one in which church and state had to be kept entirely separate. . . .[189]

The letter given by President McKinley (1843–1901) for the guidance of the United States Philippine Commission contained the following instructions, which are important in our discussion.

> . . . That no law shall be made respecting an establishment of religion or prohibiting the free exercise thereof, and that the free exercise and enjoyment of religious profession and worship without discrimination or preference shall forever be allowed. . . .
>
> . . . That no form of religion and no minister of religion shall be forced upon any community or upon any citizen of the Islands; that, upon the other hand, no minister of religion shall be interfered with or molested in following his calling, and that the separation between state and church shall be real, entire, and absolute.[190]

It will be noticed that this takes as its basis the First Amendment to the Constitution of the United States, but as a result of American experience broadens it in two ways: by not restricting the guarantee of Federal Constitutional provisions for religious freedom to Federal cases, but extending it, as has recently been done by the Supreme Court's interpretations of the Fourteenth Amendment, to legislative acts of the Federal government's constituent parts in the United States—*i.e.,* the states; and by adding the last clause so as to prevent possible complications such as have arisen in some of our states.

The instructions also contained very specific principles to be borne in mind for the settlement of the difficult problems involved in the large land holdings of the friars:

> That the provision of the Treaty of Paris, pledging the United States to the protection of all rights of property in the islands, and as well the principle of our own Government, which prohibits the taking of private property without due process of law, shall not be violated; that the welfare of the people of the islands, which should be a paramount consideration, shall be attained consistently with this rule of property right; that if it becomes necessary for the public interest of the people of the island to dispose of claims to property, which the commission finds to be not lawfully acquired and held, disposition shall be made thereof by due legal procedure, in which there shall be full opportunity for fair and impartial hearing and judgment; that if the same public interests require the extinguishment of property rights lawfully acquired and held, due compensation shall be made out of the public treasury; . . .[191]

The provision for Church-State separation was confirmed in the fifth section of the Act of Congress of July 1, 1902. The most difficult question the commission had to settle was that of the ownership of the friars' lands, these being the lands held by Spanish monks of the Dominican, Franciscan, and Augustinian orders, and of the Recollects. These four orders owned more than four hundred thousand acres in the islands, mostly rich agricultural lands, and their income from them was estimated to approximate $450,000 Mexican, or $225,000 American gold.[192]

The friars had been mainly responsible for converting the inhabitants of the Philippine Islands to Christianity, but during the last nineteenth-century decades they had become unpopular among most groups in the Islands. This was due mainly to their political activities, their large ownership of land, and in some cases their demoralized lives. As pointed out by the friars themselves, their civil functions were large. The local friar-priest commonly served as president of various boards of health, charities, taxation, statistics, etc., and as inspector of primary schools, censor of municipal budgets, member of the board for partitioning crown lands, counselor for the municipal council, censor of plays, etc., etc.[193] Even the first governor general, the Honorable William H. Taft

(1857–1930), who respected the Christian Filipinos and was most anxious to protect their interests, was very critical of the friars. In a personal letter to a Roman Catholic friend in 1900, he wrote:

The truth is, that the friars ceased to be religious ministers altogether and became political bosses, losing sight of the beneficent purpose of their organizations. They unfrocked themselves in maintaining their political control of this beautiful country. Distance from Rome and freedom from supervision made them an independent quantity and enabled them to gratify their earthly desires for money and power and other things and they cut themselves off from any right to consideration by the church, by those who are in the church, or by those, who being out of it, respect it.[194]

The commission summed up the activities of the parish priest in the Philippines in the old days by saying that he

was not only the spiritual guide, but that he was in every sense the municipal ruler. . . . The truth is that the whole Government of Spain in these islands rested on the friars.[195]

They, of course, had "benefit of clergy," being entitled to hearings before an ecclesiastical court for all ordinary offenses. The Philippine Commission early realized the great importance of securing American Roman Catholic priests for the islands in addition to the better training of Filipinos for the priesthood, and also the necessity under the American system of government of having separation of Church and State in matters of education. It said in its first report:

. . . It would seem clear that any government organized under the sovereignty of the United States can not devote public money to the teaching of any particular religion. It has been suggested, however, that in any system of public education organized in these islands it would be proper to afford to every religious denomination the right to send religious instructors to the public schools to instruct the children of parents who desire it in religion several times a week, at times when such instruction shall not interfere with the regular curriculum.[196]

The commission in October, 1901, passed an act authorizing religious corporations of all denominations to hold land, and in April, 1906, the law of corporations (No. 1495) came into force. This authorized a bishop, chief priest, or presiding elder of any religious denomination to become "a corporation sole" for holding property in trust for the denomination, and also gave authority to any religious society or order, diocese, synod, or other organization to incorporate under specific conditions to administer its temporalities.[197]

Under existing laws

There shall be exempt from taxation burying grounds, churches and other adjacent parsonages or convents, and lands and buildings used exclusively for religious, charitable, scientific, or educational purposes and not for private profit.[198]

This does not, however, exempt glebe land used to procure revenue from being taxed. Bibles and hymnbooks are admitted free of duty, but all other objects used in the services of churches are dutiable unless purchased from or manufactured in the United States.

In general it will be seen that the regulations do not differ greatly from those in this country, except in one particular, namely, the provision for the teaching of religion in school buildings. The Educational Act (Act 74, sec. 16) provides:

> No teacher or other person shall teach or criticize the doctrines of any church, religious sect, or denomination, or shall attempt to influence pupils for or against any church or religious sect in any public school. If any teacher shall intentionally violate this section he or she shall, after due hearing, be dismissed from the public service; provided: however, that it shall be lawful for the priest or minister of any church established in the town wherein a public school is situated, either in person or by a designated teacher of religion, to teach for one-half hour three times a week, in the school building, to those public-school pupils whose parents or guardians desire it and express their desire therefor in writing filed with the principal teacher of the school, to be forwarded to the division superintendent, who shall fix the hours and rooms for such teaching. But no public-school teachers shall either conduct religious exercises, or teach religion, or act as a designated religious teacher in the school building under the foregoing authority, and no pupil shall be required by any public-school teacher to attend and receive the religious instruction herein permitted. Should the opportunity thus given to teach religion be used by the priest, minister, or religious teacher for the purpose of arousing disloyalty to the United States, or of discouraging the attendance of pupils at any such public school, or creating a disturbance of public order, or of interfering with the discipline of the school, the division superintendent, subject to the approval of the director of education, may, after due investigation and hearing, forbid such offending priest, minister, or religious teacher from entering the public-school building thereafter.[199]

An attempt in 1941 to modify this rule so as to make religious instruction by priests mandatory in the public schools, though embodied in a bill passed by the legislature, was vetoed by President Manuel Quezon (1878–1944), himself a Roman Catholic.

The adjustment of all these matters involved more intimate negotiations and dealings between the United States and the Vatican than had been customary heretofore. For instance, the apostolic delegate, namely, the archbishop of New Orleans, Most Reverend Placide Chapelle (1842–1905), appeared in Manila to represent the interests of the Church, while Judge William H. Taft (1857–1930), who had been the head of the Philippine Commission and first civil governor of the Islands, was appointed in 1902 chairman of a special mission to the Vatican to adjust various difficulties. His colleagues on the mission were Associate Justice James F. Smith (1859–1928), of the Supreme Court of the Philippines, the Right Reverend Thomas O'Gormon (1843–1921), Bishop of Sioux Falls, and a representative of the Judge Advocate's Department, U.S.A. In their instructions from the secretary of war, the Honorable Elihu Root (1845–1937), it was stated that the mission

will not be in any sense or degree diplomatic in its nature, but will be purely a business matter of negotiation by you as governor of the Philippines for the purchase of property from the owners thereof, and the settlement of land titles, in such a manner as to contribute to the best interests of the people of the islands.[200]

They frankly told the pope that the friars must leave, but that they wanted the Church to arrange in their place for suitable secular priests "whose presence would not be dangerous to public order,"[201] and assured the people that, though the United States was friendly to the Catholic Church, it treated all Churches and creeds alike.

The final agreement, reached the following year, provided for holding for Church uses of 10,000 acres of the 400,000 involved, and the payment therefor of $7,543,000, which was obtained by an insular bond issue raised under the authorization of Congress. The *New Catholic Dictionary* refers to this as "a handsome indemnity."[202] There can be little doubt that as a result, though the Roman Catholic Church lost in official power and in the varied types of its influence on the Catholic population, it nevertheless greatly strengthened the character of its representatives and their ministrations in the interest of religion and morality. At present there is little friction between Church and State, the bishops being Americans and Filipinos devoted to the interests of the people.

As the island of Porto Rico (or Puerto Rico) also came into the possession of the United States by the Treaty of Paris after the Spanish-American War, somewhat similar conditions had to be dealt with there as far as the Roman Catholic Church was concerned. The treaty protected the lawful owners "of property of all kinds of . . . ecclesiastic or civic bodies."[203] This meant that the Roman Catholic Church had to be duly recognized by our government as a corporation of which the pope is the head.

There have been many so-called "insular cases" before the Supreme Court of the United States which affect the liberties of the inhabitants of the Philippine Islands and of our other island possessions. The most important cases were decided between 1901 and 1922. In general, the court drew a distinction between outlying territories and possessions which were "incorporated" and those which were "unincorporated." The inhabitants of the former, considered to include Alaska and Hawaii, were assured all the rights of American citizens under the Constitution. Since the passing of the Jones Act (1917, amended 1927) Porto

Ricans have also been granted American citizenship. The Philippines, on the other hand, were considered "unincorporated" under these decisions, not having been taken in as organic parts of the United States, so that only the fundamental provisions of the Constitution would apply to them. These were specifically stated to include the guarantees against deprivation of life, liberty, and property without due process of law, and, consequently, religious freedom was legally assured in the Islands as long as they remained under the United States. In 1934 the independence of what was called the Commonwealth of the Philippines was guaranteed by the United States, to take effect in ten years—a period later extended because of the invasion of the Islands by Japan—and under the new constitution adopted by a constitutional convention, and approved by President Franklin D. Roosevelt in 1935, freedom of religion was specifically guaranteed. This is also true in the independent republic proclaimed in 1946.

The guarantees of religious freedom for the large Mohammedan population of the Sulu Archipelago are particularly significant. In the agreement entered into August 20, 1899, between General John C. Bates (1842–1919), representing the United States, and the Sultan of Sulu it is provided:

> ARTICLE III. The rights and dignities of His Highness the Sultan and his datos shall be fully respected; the Moros shall not be interfered with on account of their religion; all their religious customs shall be respected; and no one shall be prosecuted on account of his religion.[204]

Furthermore, in the later formal agreement (1904) between the governor general of the Philippine Islands and the Sultan, at the time of the latter's renunciation of sovereignty on March 22, 1915, following the abrogation by the president of the so-called Bates Treaty, it was provided that

> Whereas the Sultan of Sulu is the titular spiritual head of the Mohammedan Church in the Sulu Archipelago, with all the rights and privileges which under the Government of the United States of America may be exercised by such an ecclesiastical authority, and subject to the same limitations which apply to the supreme spiritual heads of all other religions existing in American territory, including the right to solicit and receive voluntary popular contributions for the support of the clergy, rites, and other necessary lawful expenses of an ecclesiastical character, . . .
>
> The Sultan of Sulu and his adherents and people of the Mohammedan faith shall have the same religious freedom had by the adherents of all other religious creeds, the practice of which is not in violation of the basic principles of the laws of the United States of America.[205]

These provisions have on the whole been carried out effectively in keeping with the American traditions of religious freedom for all religious groups, and are now well established. An impressive consequence of the friendly feeling developed was seen in World War II when many Moro leaders, trained largely at the school established for them by the late Bishop Charles H. Brent, showed their effective loyalty and co-operated with Christian groups in maintaining the independence of the Philippines from Japan.*

Section 11. *THE CONTEST OVER CHRISTIAN SCIENCE HEALING*

The general view of Christian Science on Church–State relations has been authoritatively stated by Judge Clifford P. Smith (1869–1945), the head of the Bureau of History and Records of the First Church of Christ, Scientist. He says:

> Christian Scientists are law abiding citizens, well disposed toward the legitimate functions of human government, and active in the promotion of social welfare. They have no wish to force any one to adopt their views. They respect the motives and attainments of the better class of physicians. They claim only the right to do Christian work and to be free from constraint in respect to their choice of religion and therapeutics.[206]

The Scientists feel that they have a right to have their sick treated in such ways as commend themselves to their judgment and conscience, and that any interference with this right is an interference with the Constitutional guarantees of religious freedom. As Governor Elbert Thomas (1883–   ) of Colorado, later an honored member of the United States Senate, stated in a veto message to a bill which had to do with the practice of medicine,

> The fundamental vice of the bill is that it denies absolutely to the individual the right to select his own physician. This is a right of conscience, and as sacred as that which enables the citizen to worship God as he may desire. It is indeed the same right manifesting itself in a parallel direction.
>
> It is a part of the law of this land, and no civil power is strong enough to deprive the citizen of its exercise. He may indeed select a healer of doubtful reputation or conceded incompetence, but that is his affair just as much as is his choice of a minister or attorney. His action may prove injurious, possibly fatal, to himself or to some members of his family. It is better so than to delegate to any tribunal the power to say "thou shalt not employ this man" or "thou shalt employ this one." That this bill produces such a result indirectly makes it the more objectionable. It is not the outspoken and aggressive assault upon individual liberty that men should fear, but the indirect or resultant blow that is masked and falls unexpectedly.[207]

The legislative debate over Christian Science began a few years after the publication, in 1875, by Mrs. Mary Baker Eddy (1821–1910) of her textbook *Science and Health with Key to the Scriptures*. It was most acute during the

* While this section has been passing through the printer's hands my attention has been called to a doctor's thesis at the University of Chicago, "Church and State in the Philippines," by D. D. Parker.

first two decades of this century, when, on the one hand, bills were introduced into practically all state and territorial legislatures to forbid the professional practice of the "healing" of disease without drugs, and on the other hand bills designed to recognize spiritual healing as a legitimate method of curing disease. Public opinion was specially inflamed in 1902, following the indictment in White Plains, New York, of three Christian Science practitioners after the death of a child under conditions which seemed to show neglect. As a result, Mrs. Eddy advised that "until public thought becomes better acquainted with Christian Science, the Christian Scientists shall decline to doctor infectious or contagious diseases."[208]

The opposition to Christian Science, as far as legislation was concerned, was mainly by medical practitioners. Usually the form of opposition chosen was the introduction of a bill to regulate the practice of medicine but containing a definition of medical practice so broad as to include Christian Science healing. The purpose was to eliminate Christian Science healers who could not meet the tests of the standard training required of medical practitioners, the point being that the practitioners of this new cult could not conscientiously attend the regular medical schools where most diseases were treated as due to physical causes.

Our interest in the controversy is due not to its theological implications, but to its bearings on Church-State relations. As we shall see, victories have in general resulted for freedom of conscience, religious freedom, where this does not involve the disregard of ordinary public sanitary precautions against contagious and infectious diseases. In this contest, though working primarily in the interest of their own Church, the Christian Scientists had the co-operation of many other groups, including those opposed to the old regular allopathic and homeopathic schools of thought, and the freedom they secured for themselves was often incorporated in statutes broad enough to include other "healing" sects.

The fundamental legislative acts affecting Christian Scientists are those which have to do with the practice of Christian Science as a healing profession. Occasionally the provisions are extended to exclude Christian Science practitioners from dentistry, midwifery, and nursing.

Here are some typical Federal, state, and territorial laws and regulations:

California—(Part of a law defining and regulating the practice of medicine.) "Nor shall this act be construed so as to discriminate against any particular school of medicine or surgery, or any other treatment, nor to regulate, prohibit or to apply to, any kind of treatment by prayer, nor to interfere in any way with the practice of religion."—*Deering's General Laws of California,* Act 4807, *sec.* 22.[209]

Canal Zone—(Part of an Executive Order by the President of the United States defining and regulating the practice of medicine.) "Provided, That nothing in this Order shall be construed to prohibit (a) the practice of the religious tenets of any church in the ministration of the sick or suffering by mental or spiritual means without the use of any drug or material remedy, whether gratuitously or for compensation, provided that such sanitary laws, orders, rules, and regulations as now are, or hereafter may be, in force in said Canal Zone are complied with."—*Executive Order No. 1448,* dated December 26, 1911.[210]

Hawaii—(Part of a law defining and regulating the practice of medicine.) "And further provided, that nothing herein contained shall apply to so-called Christian Scientists so long as they merely practice the religious tenets of their church without pretending a knowledge of medicine or surgery; provided, that the laws and regulations relating to contagious diseases are not violated."—*Laws of Hawaii* (1925), Act 26, sec. 1.[211]

Illinois—(Part of a law defining and regulating the practice of medicine.) "This Act shall not apply to . . . persons treating human ailments by prayer or spiritual means as an exercise of enjoyment of religious freedom."—*Cahill's Revised Statutes of Illinois,* chap. 91, sec. 29 (9).[212]

Kansas—(Part of a law defining and regulating the practice of medicine.) "But nothing in this Act shall be construed as interfering with any religious beliefs in the treatment of diseases: Provided, That quarantine regulations relating to contagious diseases are not infringed upon."—*Revised Statutes of Kansas,* sec. 1005.[213]

Louisiana—(Part of a law defining and regulating the practice of medicine.) "This law shall not . . . prohibit the practice of Christian Science or religious rules or ceremonies as a form of religious worship, devotion or healing; provided, That the person administering or making use of or assisting or prescribing such rely on faith and prayer alone, and do not prescribe or administer drugs or medicine, nor perform surgical or physical operations, nor assume the title of, or hold themselves out to be, physicians or surgeons."—*Acts of Louisiana* (1914), act 56, sec. 21, as amended and re-enacted (1918), act 54.[214]

District of Columbia—The situation in the District is regulated by an act of Congress regarding the practice of the healing art in the District adopted in 1928: "The provisions of this Act shall not be construed to apply . . . to persons treating human ailments by prayer or spiritual means, as an exercise of enjoyment of religious freedom: Provided, That the laws, rules, and regulations relating to communicable diseases and sanitary matters are not violated."[215]

This District of Columbia statute has special significance in view of the fact that the District is Federal territory and its laws are laws made by the United States Congress.

In studying the typical laws which we have outlined above we may well be impressed by the growth of the legal recognition of Christian Science beliefs in recent years. For instance, when Judge Smith published his book on the legal status of Christian Science in 1914 there were only twenty-six states or territories where the Christian Science practitioner was legally protected in his rights, whereas now there are only one or two states where the protection is not adequate. It must be remembered, however, that the Christian Scientists have secured their rights by strenuous efforts—by creating public opinion favorable to their cause; by submitting drafts of bills to the legislatures; and by taking cases to the courts. For our purpose in this study the important thing is that when the Christian Scientists have considered their religious freedom to be at stake, statutes and the courts in general have given them their desired relief as long as laws for the protection of public health, especially in the case of communicable diseases, are not infringed.

By action of the Ohio legislature in the summer of 1949 a statute was passed providing that

treatment of human ills through prayer alone by a practitioner of the Christian Science Church, in accordance with the tenets and creed of such church, shall not be regarded as the practice of medicine.

According to *Time* of July 18, which reported this action, this new law made Ohio the 48th state of the United States to legalize the public practice of Christian Science as a healing art.

Other legislation originating in difficulties between the Christian Science Church and the State which are not as yet fully settled have to do with such matters as vaccination, the physical examination and medical treatment of pupils in Church schools, the incorporation of churches, the exemption of Christian Scientists from school health instruction, and workmen's compensation benefits. A few typical state statutes on these matters are here given:

Vaccination:

(Part of a law authorizing physical examination of school children.) "No child shall be obliged to submit to physical examination or vaccination whose parents or guardians object thereto on the grounds of religious principles. Such objection shall be made in writing, shall be signed by the parents or guardians of such child and shall be delivered to the child's teacher or to the person who might order or conduct said examination in the absence of such objection; Provided, however, that exemption from physical examination and vaccination shall not be granted when in the judgment of the teacher, principal, superintendent, board of education or physician the child shows symptoms of physical defects or shows symptoms of or has been exposed to any contagious, infectious, obnoxious or communicable disease."—*Laws of Alaska* (1929), chap. 86, sec. 2.[216]

(Part of a public health law.) "No form of vaccination or inoculation shall hereafter be made a condition precedent, in this state, for the admission to any public or private school or college, of any person, or for the exercise of any right, the performance of any duty, or the enjoyment of any privilege, by any person."—*Compiled Laws of North Dakota, Political Code,* sec. 425a1.[217]

There have been one or two instances, however, where the courts have overruled the opposition of Christian Scientists to vaccination in schools, as in a Texas case where the ordinance was declared to demand merely a reasonable health regulation.[218]

Physical Examination and Medical Treatment of School Children:

(Part of a school law.) "Nothing in this Act shall be construed or operate so as to interfere in any way with the exercise of the child's or parent's religious belief, as to examination for or in the treatment of diseases; provided, that quarantine regulations relating to contagious or infectious diseases are not infringed upon."—*Revised Codes of Montana,* sec. 2510.[219]

Incorporation:

(Part of a law for incorporation of religious societies.) "It shall be lawful for any Church of Christ, Scientist, in this State, which is a branch of, and which is organized in accordance with the provisions of the Manual of The First Church of Christ, Scientist, in Boston, Massachusetts, hereinafter referred to as The Mother Church, to become incorporated under and by virtue of the provisions hereinafter stated."—*Cumulative Supplement to Compiled Statutes of New Jersey,* sec. 173–62s.[220]

Workmen's Compensation:

(Part of a Workmen's Compensation Act.) "Incidental compensation. TREATMENT. The employer shall supply such medical, surgical and hospital treatment, medicines, medical and surgical supplies, crutches, artificial members and appliances, or, at the option of the employee, if the employer has not filed notice as hereinafter provided, Christian Science treatment in lieu of medical treatment, medicines and medical supplies, as may be reasonably required for ninety days immediately following the injury, to cure and relieve from the effects of the injury and for such additional period of time as in the judgment of the commission will tend to lessen the period of time as the commission may deem advisable, not to exceed the period for which indemnity is payable, and in case of his neglect or refusal seasonably to do so, the employer shall be liable for the reasonable expense incurred by or on behalf of the employee in providing the same. . . ."—*Statutes of Wisconsin,* chap. 102.42 (1), (5), (7).[221]

Exemption from School Health Instruction:

(Part of a law relating to teaching physiology and hygiene in public schools.) "Physiology and hygiene, sanitation, the effects of stimulants and narcotics upon the human system, symptoms of disease and the proper care of the body, shall be taught daily for one-half of the school year in either the sixth, seventh or eighth grade, but no pupil shall be required to take such instruction if the parents shall file with the teacher a written objection thereto."—*Statutes of Wisconsin,* chap. 40.22 (2).[222]

NOTE ON THE COMMON COMMUNION CUP AND PUBLIC HEALTH

The only serious issues which have arisen in this country between Church and State on health matters have been with the Christian Scientists. This seems to be, therefore, the appropriate place to add a note on a latent issue involving the communion cup in which several denominations may become involved. Thus far it is largely a theoretical difficulty, but it is being used by the advocates of the individual communion cup to try to effect the "reform" they desire. In 1909 Kansas adopted regulations in the interest of public health against the use of the "common drinking cup" in public places. These applied at first only to railroads and educational institutions, but were later extended to hotels. Michigan and Mississippi followed the same year, and in 1910 Massachusetts enacted a law covering the matter. There was apparently no thought in this or later cases of having the laws apply to the communion cup, but their enactment had a broad influence in persuading many Protestant denominations to adopt the individual cup plan. By 1936 some sort of regulation regarding the common cup had been adopted in all but two states, and in eight—California, Colorado, Delaware, Maine, Maryland, Missouri, New Hampshire, and South Dakota—the law was made specifically applicable to churches; and this has also been done in some cities in other states.[223] In no case, however, is the communion cup mentioned. A typical law that includes churches is that of California:

> It shall be unlawful for any person, firm or corporation conducting, having charge of, or control of, any hotel, restaurant, saloon, soda fountain, store, theater, public hall, public or private school, church, hospital, wash-room, barber shop, railroad train, boat, or any other public place, building, room or conveyance, to provide or expose for common use, or permit to be so provided or exposed, or to allow to be used in common, any cup, glass, or other receptacle used for drinking purposes.[224]

The *Churchman* of New York, which has been actively interested in this matter for a decade, asserted editorially in two or three issues in 1943, when favoring "intinction" at the communion service, that the use of the common cup is illegal, but in this it was probably mistaken. As far as laws are now concerned, though in some cases churches and even Sunday schools have been specified, no attempt has been made to include the cup used at the Lord's Supper. There have been times of epidemic, such as that of influenza in 1918, when local health bodies have advised caution in the coming together of large numbers in public places, including churches, but no actual case is known of forbidding religious services. A leading authority on public health informs me that the Churches have generally been co-operative with health authorities.[225] Similarly, these authorities would be most unlikely to adopt any restrictions regarding the celebration of the holy communion or other Church rites except in cases of the gravest emergency.

Section 12. THE NATIONAL PROHIBITION EXPERIMENT

The beginnings and growth of the movements for temperance and liquor control in the United States have been dealt with in a previous section.[226] Here we are concerned with the development of prohibition after the Civil War.

Under the Internal Revenue Act of 1862, adopted under the pressure of need for money to carry on the war, Congress adopted the principle of licensing the liquor business, which thus received in a measure the sanction of the Federal government and was organized as an effective national industry. Similar taxes had been enforced during the Revolution and the War of 1812, but they had been removed soon after these wars were over. The new excise taxes now came to be considered as part of the regular revenue policy of the government. The open saloon increasingly prospered, especially in the large cities, where it became a center of political corruption and of moral degradation. The situation was serious, and as early as 1865 a convention was held that brought together various organizations in a new body, the National Temperance Society and Publication House. "Crusades" against saloons were organized, especially by women; and in 1869 the National Prohibition party was formed, committed to "the total prohibition of the manufacturing, importation and traffic of intoxicating beverages."[227] The Protestant Churches, led by the Methodists, were behind this and similar movements, of which the most effective at the time was the Women's Christian Temperance Union, established in 1874. In 1893 the Anti-Saloon League was organized in Oberlin, Ohio, one of the strongest Protestant religious centers of the Middle West. It soon described itself as "the church in action against the saloon."[228] Largely as a result of its efforts, a wave of prohibitory legislation began in 1907, so that by 1919 thirty-three states had by statute or constitutional provision prohibited the liquor traffic. The movement for a nationwide amendment was greatly stimulated by World War I, and the Eighteenth Amendment, proposed in 1917, was ratified by the necessary thirty-six states in 1919, and later by ten others.[229] The resulting Federal prohibition could not have been brought about had it not been for the larger Protestant Churches. The movement had the support of many other forces—educational, medical, industrial, social welfare, religious, and others, but undoubtedly the energy and political activity which carried the movement to success was supplied in a large measure by the Methodist Board of Temperance, Prohibition, and Public Morals.

This board, organized in 1916, organized and implemented inherited interest of Methodists in doing away with the evils of the liquor traffic. At the General Conference of 1883 drunkenness was declared to be an "immorality," and rules were adopted for proceeding against members drinking spirituous liquors.[230]

Three years later (1886) the General Conference decided to agitate actively the question of prohibition, and the Book of Discipline was amended to provide that anyone who engaged in the manufacture or sale of intoxicating liquor as a beverage should be dealt with as in cases of immorality.[231] In 1888 the permanent Committee on Temperance and Prohibition was established.

The Methodist board's effectiveness in this campaign was so marked that it seems well to quote the major clauses regarding its organization.

Board of Temperance, Prohibition, and Public Morals

Sec. 1. In order to make more effectual the efforts of the Methodist Episcopal Church in creating a Christian public sentiment, and in crystallizing opposition to all public violations of the moral law and to all attempts to undermine or destroy civil or religious liberties, the General Conference hereby approves the organization of a Board of Temperance, Prohibition, and Public Morals, of the Methodist Episcopal Church, with headquarters at the Methodist Building, Washington, D. C. The Board shall be incorporated under this title and work under the following Constitution: . . .

Sec. 3. Article II. The Management of this Corporation shall be vested in a Board of Managers consisting of two Bishops, one representative from each Episcopal Area in the United States, and ten members to be elected at large. The Board of Managers shall be nominated by the General Superintendents and elected by the General Conference. . . .

Sec. 5. Article IV. It shall be the duty of the Board of Managers to represent the Church officially in every wise movement for the promotion of voluntary personal total abstinence and the securing of prohibition of the liquor traffic by educational means; to promote public morals; to publish, approve, and distribute literature on the liquor traffic and the use of narcotics and manufactured articles containing a large percentage of alcoholic liquors; and to devise such plans and make such advices as shall enable the Church most successfully to accomplish the overthrow of the beverage liquor traffic; it shall also promote public policies which tend to the diminution of the use of narcotics; it shall actively oppose corrupting literature and degrading amusements; it shall work diligently for the suppression of lotteries and other forms of gambling, and in other ways it shall make use of the money that may be available for its purposes to the end that the moral interests of the nation may be promoted.[232]

The controversy over the proper attitude of the Church toward the Constitutional prohibition of the liquor traffic can be seen at its best in a study of the developments in the Methodist Episcopal Church, South, during the presidential campaign of 1928 and in the events which preceded and followed it. The study is particularly illuminating because the Church was definitely committed to the support of prohibition. The controversy was therefore entirely over the degree to which it should identify itself with a political party and with the adoption of political methods in securing the passage of the Prohibition Amendment.

The Methodist Episcopal Church, South, prior to the rise of the prohibition issue, had for the most part kept itself out of politics. For instance, the bishops of the Church in 1865, when the political situation due to the Civil War was very tense, issued an address in which they said:

> Know your high calling. Preach Christ and Him crucified. Do not preach politics. You have no commission to preach politics. The divinity of the Church is never more strikingly displayed than when it holds on its ever straightforward way in the midst of worldly commotions.[233]

Similarly in 1894 the Episcopal Address to the General Conference stated:

> It is not amiss to repeat what has often been declared—that our Church is strictly a religious and in no wise a political body. Our sole business is to preach and serve the kingdom of God. There are many questions—economical, social, and in part ethical—of burning interest in this day which our pulpit and Churches may be tempted to substitute for the simple gospel. . . . The more closely we keep ourselves to the one work of testifying to all men, the better shall we promote the highest good of our country and race. As a Church we are not related by affiliation or antagonism to any political party. As a citizen every man should carry his judgment and conscience into politics and all other spheres of life.[234]

But when the prohibition issue arose the Church became increasingly concerned. Resolution after resolution was adopted favoring national prohibition. For instance, the General Conference in 1910 adopted the following:

> Whereas, the Methodist Episcopal Church, South, has ever gone before the world as the unalterable foe of the liquor traffic, and is a prohibition church, which will never consider a compromise with this heinous sin; and whereas greater strides have been made in temperance in the home of Southern Methodism—in the South—than in any other part of our union in recent years, to the furtherance of which our Church has been one of the principal factors:
>
> Resolved, that we hereby appeal to the President and Congress of the United States to take immediate action and pass this bill (regulating interstate shipments of liquor) for the protection of the people from this great curse.[235]

In 1926 the episcopal address signed by all the bishops stated that "The

National Prohibition Law is the most remarkable social enactment by any great nation to promote the general welfare by the restriction of the activity of the individual."[236] This refers to the Eighteenth Amendment to the Federal Constitution, which became effective in 1920.

These quotations, which might be multiplied a score of times, show clearly that the Methodist Episcopal Church, South, was squarely committed to prohibition. The question at issue in 1928 that interests us is purely that of the Church as such getting into politics to advance the cause to which it was morally committed. On this question there was a definite cleavage. Four bishops, namely, Edwin D. Mouzon, John M. Moore, Horace M. DuBose, and James Cannon, Jr., believed that it was right for them to enter party politics to advance what they believed to be a great moral cause, and they acted accordingly. Two other bishops, Collins Denny and Warren A. Candler, strongly opposed this view. They were equally strong believers in prohibition, but they were opposed to the Church as a Church entering the political field to advance it by supporting the Republican party, and by denouncing the Democratic party which was opposed to prohibition and in favor of the repeal of the Constitutional amendment providing for it. The seven remaining bishops took no clear and definite stand at the time on the question.

Bishops Candler and Denny called attention to the spiritual nature of the Church, quoting from the Book of Ritual of the Church the following clause:

> The Church is of God, and will be preserved to the end of time, for the promotion of his worship, and the due administration of his word and ordinance—the maintenance of Christian fellowship and discipline—the edification of believers and the conversion of the world.[237]

It is not necessary to enter at length into the controversy; suffice it to say that Bishop Cannon (1864–1944) and a group of like-minded associates—mostly earnest and sincere, even though they seemed to many thoughtful people misguided—called a conference at Asheville, N. C., to organize the Anti-Smith Democrats. This group, with the support of many Southern papers and of most of the leading organs of the Methodist Episcopal Church, South, carried on a vigorous campaign both in opposition to Governor Smith and frequently against the Roman Catholic Church, of which he was a member. (The Smith campaign will be discussed later.[238]) A characteristic sample of the vituperative language used in the campaign appears in the resolutions unanimously adopted by the Methodist Preachers Meeting in Atlanta on July 24, 1928. Here occur such statements as the following:

> As patriots who hold principle above party we are undisturbed by the denunciation of party enthusiasts and partisan editors. Men of character and courage are only

amused at being dubbed "dry fanatics," "intolerant bigots," "prejudiced cranks," "party disruptionists" and other complimentary epithets inadmissible here. Oh, consistency! read us out of the party because we cannot conscientiously vote for your soaking wet Tammanyite, but go your limit to secure the Republican farmer-labor vote, the foreign-born, criminal wets of New York, Chicago, and similar hyphenated American cities and sections, and accept as the chairman of your campaign committee, one who confesses himself "an independent" and is even now a member of a Republican club.[239]

The controversy was bitter. There can be little doubt that most thoughtful people outside the Methodist Episcopal Church, South, believed that Bishop Cannon and his associates had gone too far, and that he would have done better to remember Francis Asbury's (1745–1816) farewell address to William McKendree, the first American-born Methodist bishop. In this Asbury wrote:

As to temporal power what have we to do with that in this country? We are not senators, congressmen, or chaplains; neither do we hold any civil office. We neither have nor wish to have anything to do with the Government of the states, nor, as I conceive, do the states fear us. Our kingdom is not of this world.[240]

The whole sordid story of the Cannon campaign may be read from the point of view of the anti-Cannon group in a competent book written by Dr. Rembert Gilman Smith entitled *Politics in a Protestant Church*. He had kept his head during the controversy, and in the North Georgia Conference of 1929 made an address which deserved the publication that was then denied by the conference. In it, among other things, he said:

When the church goes into personal and party politics, the prestige of her preachers will be sadly lowered, and this is no matter of theory. Preachers are accustomed to speak with dogmatism the truths of religion, and they should so speak, and when they make stump speeches, they use the same dogmatism, although they are then in the field where differences of convictions exist between equally good men.

There has never been in the United States a political battle in which there were not equally good men on opposite sides, but this fact, preachers turned politicians, are almost sure to forget. When the pulpit, or the press, or other agencies, of a church go into personal and party politics, there is real danger. . . .

The motive of church leaders in going into politics is frequently very high, and their courage is often very praiseworthy. They do this because of their strong love for some reform, but when they take it to one party there is very great hazard. No one party will stay in power all the time, and when that party which the church champions loses, prohibition is in a serious plight.[241]

The following year, 1930, he proposed to the conference a resolution which was not passed, but which is quoted here as a courageous statement of what

I believe to be the right attitude of the Church toward the extremes of political activity. To understand it we must remember that as a result of the 1928 presidential campaign, when Governor Alfred E. Smith, attacked as a "wet" and a Roman Catholic, was the Democratic candidate, the South associated prohibition, which it ardently favored, with the cause of Protestantism.

(1) That we reaffirm the historic doctrine of American Methodism that the Roman Catholic citizens of this nation have and should have equal political rights with other citizens.

(2) That we assure them of our abiding neighborly and brotherly love.

And whereas, we believe that this innovation, namely opposition to the political rights of Roman Catholic citizens by Methodist leaders, agencies and papers, is inconsistent with Methodist history, inimical to the internal peace of the nation, and perilous both to religion and to freedom.

I, the undersigned minister of this conference, after prayerful deliberation, do hereby record, with the brotherly permission of this body, my most earnest protest.

In the name of our forebears in church and state, whose memories we revere; in behalf of our children, whose burdens we would not increase; in anxiety for our children's children, whose dangers we would not enhance, we utter this word of warning, beseeching our fathers and brethren, who have initiated this innovation in our church, to retrace their steps.[242]

The liquor dealers of the country realized that the members of the various Methodist churches were their most effective opponents. In 1914 the secretary of the Liquor Dealers' Association said:

It is only necessary to read the list of those preachers who are active in the present propaganda for legislative prohibition to realize that it is the Methodist Church which is obsessed with the ambition to gain control of the government.[243]

The wording of this statement is extreme; but there can be no question that the Methodist Church, as the largest Protestant group in the country, and containing many able and sincere propagandists, did exert almost a controlling influence in favor of having the government—both Federal and state—ban intoxicating liquor for beverage use. From then until the final repeal of the Prohibition Amendment in 1933 the primary public interest of the Methodist and Baptist Churches was for the Eighteenth Amendment. This was particularly true in the South, where both were so powerful. Speaking of their influence and that of some other Protestant groups at this time in prohibition, and incidentally in the antievolution and various other restrictive legislation of a Puritanic type, a recent foreign publicist, who had been studying Southern conditions, said that "during the 1920's clergymen may almost be said to have dominated the South."[244]

We have devoted our major attention to the Methodist Church because it was clearly the most active in the prohibition movement. But the Baptist Church was a close second in its zeal for the cause, and its actions were very similar in scope and content. The Presbyterians were next, and since the denomination is of large national importance and generally somewhat conservative, its actions will appropriately serve to fill out the Protestant denominational picture. I quote from the resolutions passed by the Presbyterian Church in the United States of America in 1910, 1911, 1920, 1933, and 1938. These may be taken as typical of Protestant public opinion in this country at the dates indicated. It should be remembered that the Federal Prohibition Law (Volstead Act) was passed in 1919 and became void after the repeal of the Eighteenth Amendment in 1933.

1910

Resolved, That while rejoicing in the progress of Prohibition, and encouraging our people to assist in such campaigns, we nevertheless believe there is urgent need for the inculcation of total abstinence principles, for the dissemination of the latest results of scientific temperance, for the uncompromising proclamation of the sin of drunkenness, as essential to ground our people in true temperance and make permanent the progress of the Temperance Reform.

Resolved, That this Assembly authorize its Temperance Committee to memorialize Congress as follows:

(1) For the passing of the Gallinger–Bennet Bill, for the District of Columbia.

(2) For the passing of the Hamilton–Owen–McGuire Bill, establishing a prohibition zone of twenty-five miles around Indian reservations.

(3) In behalf of legislation creating a Commission of Inquiry to investigate and report upon every phase of the liquor traffic.

(4) In behalf of such legislation as will adequately protect prohibition territory against interstate shipments of liquors.

(5) Entering earnest protest against the National Government's sharing any complicity with the liquor traffic by the issuance of Federal tax receipts, and to enter protest against such rulings of the Treasury Department as tend to shield the violators of State or local liquor laws.

Resolved, That this Assembly reaffirms its solemn warning against the use of intoxicating beverages, and enjoins its members from engaging in the manufacture or sale of such liquors, or renting property for such purposes, or signing applications for saloon licenses or presenting the same in Courts, or endorsing bonds of saloon-keepers, or in any other way aiding or abetting this heinous evil.

Resolved, The Presbyterian Church must ever be the open, active, and persistent enemy of the liquor traffic in all its forms. We declare any form of license, under any name or guise, as . . . un-Christian.

We solemnly admonish our people to keep themselves socially, financially, and politically "separate and apart" from the liquor traffic, and to "touch not the unclean thing," to the end that this traffic may, by organic law, be expelled from our land, and our people be saved from its despoiling influence.[245]

1911

Resolved, That we endorse Senate Bill No. 1,523, known as the Curtis Bill, or some other measure which will adequately protect prohibition territory against interstate shipments of intoxicating liquors, and that we urge upon Congress the speedy passage of the same; and that the General Assembly communicate such action by telegram to the Judiciary Committee of the Senate and House of Representatives.

Whereas, We, as a nation, have abolished the use of intoxicating beverages from both Houses of Congress and our Army and Navy, and

Whereas, The example of this nation has a powerful influence over other nations, therefore, be it

Resolved, That this General Assembly hereby petitions the authorities of our Government to discontinue the use of intoxicating beverages at all diplomatic functions, both at home and abroad, and that a copy of this resolution be sent to the Secretary of State.[246]

1920

Resolved, That this Assembly composed of 900 ministers and elders, in equal numbers, authoritatively representing the Presbyterian Church in the U. S. A., with a membership and a constituency of millions of people solemnly protest against any modification of the Volstead enforcement code of the prohibition amendment to the Federal Constitution which would permit the manufacture or sale of wine and beer, or any other change capable of weakening the purpose or effectiveness of said amendment.[247]

1933

The Congress of the United States of America having submitted a resolution affording to the states an opportunity to vote upon the repeal of the Eighteenth Amendment this Assembly reaffirms its unaltered opposition to the repeal of the Amendment. We believe it has produced more beneficial results than any method of liquor control ever tried. No substitute, as yet suggested, gives promise of being equally beneficial and so-called state control promises only a return to the saloon with its intolerable evils. We believe that enforcement of the law, not repeal, is the solution.

In the crisis that immediately faces us we call upon the leadership of the Presbyterian Church and its constituency, to ally themselves with all organizations, the object of which is the retention of the Eighteenth Amendment.

We pledge our church to provide an intensive educational campaign that our youth may have adequate instruction within the church and to promote a campaign of secular education in the public schools to the end that all the youth of our land shall have adequate information as to the reasons for the prohibition of the traffic in this habit-forming narcotic.

We believe that the elimination of the liquor traffic is primarily a spiritual problem. The solution of this problem must find its dynamic in the Gospel. We, therefore, call upon all of our pastors to preach the Gospel with renewed faith and force and upon all of our people to seek a closer fellowship with God to the end that they may more effectively promote His Kingdom.[248]

1938

We note with alarm the continued increase in the consumption of alcoholic liquor in our country. We call upon our people to practice total abstinence as a mode of life for themselves and as an example to their children. We urge the continued stressing of scientific temperance instruction in our church schools and young people's societies, and call upon our pastors to inform and warn their people of the insidious propaganda being disseminated by those who for profit would extend and increase the consumption of such liquors. We urge our school authorities to provide more adequate scientific temperance instruction in the public schools.

We deem the present governmental policy of permitting the promotion of the sale and consumption of liquors by advertising of all kinds, by the employment of hostesses, and by other practices designed to lure trade as particularly vicious, inimical to temperance, and contrary to public welfare. We urge adequate state and Federal laws to prevent the advertising of liquor by the radio, newspapers, bill boards, or by any other means. We favor the enactment of laws requiring scientific test of drivers involved in automobile accidents who are suspected of being under the influence of alcohol.

We call attention to the growing crime rate, to the increasing number of motor fatalities and accidents incident to drinking, and to the greater number of first admissions for alcoholism to our state hospitals for the insane, and urge better enforcement of existing restrictions in liquor laws and the enactment of more stringent regulations and prohibitions. We pledge our best efforts to the authorities in the enforcement of the laws as they may at any time exist.

We commend the temperance activities of our Board of Christian Education, and also the work of the W.C.T.U. and the Anti-Saloon League, and pledge our cooperation in all practical plans for the promotion of temperance. Believing that our country took a long step backward in repealing the 18th Amendment, we pledge our great Church to unite with other Christian bodies in working and praying for a return of national prohibition.[249]

The Federal Council of Churches was heartily in favor of prohibition, but it never took such an extreme stand for it as did the Methodist and Baptist groups. It did not denounce those who conscientiously opposed prohibition, and throughout the discussion it laid special emphasis on the importance of removing abuses in administration, and continued to emphasize the vital importance of temperance and temperance education.

In September, 1925, it published its well-known Research Bulletin No. 5

strongly supporting prohibition but criticizing in some respects its administration, and discussing the matter with a good deal of objectivity. Sections of this report received much favorable comment from the opponents of prohibition and equally strong condemnation from its ardent supporters. As a result, the Federal Council was forced to reconsider the whole matter carefully, and at the meeting of its executive committee in December adopted a statement which represents so well the general attitude of the Protestant Churches at the time that it is here reproduced in full:

In view of the widespread interest attracted by the report of the Research Department of the Federal Council of the Churches of Christ in America on the prohibition situation, and of the serious misunderstandings which have arisen in connection with that report, the Administrative Committee of the Federal Council, composed of representatives of the church bodies which are members of the Council, has authorized the following statement of its conviction as to principle and policy.

First of all, the Committee would emphasize its unequivocal support of national prohibition, as expressed in many public utterances and reaffirmed by the quadrennial session of the whole Council in Atlanta last December. We declare our strong conviction that the policy of prohibition is the deliberately and permanently established policy of this nation, that this policy has not failed, but on the contrary has already yielded results which fully justify its adoption, that the liquor traffic and the saloon must not come back again, and that the Churches must set themselves with new purpose to see that prohibition is enforced by law and sustained by the national conscience.

The statement adopted by the Federal Council in December, 1924, as the authoritative expression of its attitude toward the prohibition amendment, declares that "the effect upon the physical, economic, social, and moral life of the nation of the extraordinary effort of society to protect itself from the liquor traffic has been so beneficial that it is now generally agreed that the law will stand, based as it is upon the unassailable purpose 'to promote the general welfare'." The present-day duty of the moral citizenship of the nation we believe to be:

"1. To magnify the value of the principle of total abstinence and the obligation upon the law-abiding citizens to practice the same;

"2. To make unmistakably clear to both the lawless sellers and the lawless buyers of intoxicants that the liquor traffic has been permanently outlawed in the United States as the enemy of society;

"3. To urge local, state and federal governments to cooperate with increased vigor against the present organized resistance to the prohibition law until as adequate an enforcement of that law has been secured as of any other social legislation."

The Administrative Committee of the Federal Council has seen nothing in the report of the Research Department to justify any modification whatever of the position thus taken by the Council on the prohibition issue. The policy of national prohibition, as the report shows, was adopted by the American people by the overwhelming votes of their elected legislative assemblies. This policy has been reaffirmed by increasing majorities wherever it has been challenged.

We would remind those otherwise good citizens, who by their personal example and public utterances are lending countenance to those who violate their country's laws, of the reasons which led to the adoption of the Eighteenth Amendment. It rests upon three fundamental considerations: first, the belief that in dealing with gigantic social evils like disease or crime individual liberty must be surrendered in the interest of effective social control; second, the belief that the liquor traffic is such an evil—a conviction which is gaining strength all over the world, and which has recently found official expression in the report of the special Commission on Drink of the Universal Christian Conference on Life and Work at Stockholm; third, the experience gained by a generation of experiment with substitutes, which has led the advocates of temperance to conclude that only drastic federal action could bring about the eradication of the evils they were fighting. Prohibition was not a policy adopted hastily or without due consideration, and it is not to be set aside merely because great difficulty or even temporary reverses are encountered in carrying it out.

The report makes clear the remarkable social gains which followed upon the adoption of prohibition: a lowering of the death rate from alcoholic disease, a remarkable lessening of dependency due to alcoholism, a great reduction in drunkenness, and other results of a socially desirable sort. It also calls attention to the part undoubtedly played by prohibition in improving business and economic conditions, and, above all, points out the indisputable advantage gained by the abolition of the saloon. At the same time, the report reminds us that national prohibition has not yet been given a fair opportunity to vindicate its full value to the physical, economic, social and moral life of the nation and calls attention to serious dangers to which it is at present exposed.

The Federal Council gratefully recognizes the splendid service which has been rendered by the agencies especially authorized by the Churches which for many decades have labored persistently and effectively to secure the adoption and the maintenance of prohibition. The Council pledges its active cooperation with all agencies which are ready to make a sustained and constructive effort to uphold the prohibition regime in order that there may be a conclusive demonstration of its merits as a national policy. It urges the friends of prohibition in other countries not to be deceived by the attempts which have been made by opponents of prohibition to interpret the report as a confession of failure, or even of discouragement on the part of the Federal Council or of its constituent church bodies.

The statement of the council closes by laying special emphasis on the importance of an effective public opinion and of education in carrying through such a great moral reform as the attempt to eliminate the liquor traffic.

The Federal Council calls upon the churches to undertake a renewed moral crusade to strengthen the hands of those who are responsible for prohibition enforcement, and in particular to give a greater measure of moral support to the newly reorganized activities of the Federal Government. It urges upon all citizens who believe in prohibition the necessity of supporting the law by an irresistible volume of public opinion. Of those who may be out of sympathy with prohibition as a social measure, or who question the wisdom of the particular method by which it was adopted, it asks voluntary compliance with the law in the interest of orderly government and in order that the policy it represents may be adequately tried. It appeals for a new measure of fair-mindedness and goodwill on the part of all in connection with this vitally important issue in order that the outcome of the great moral effort may be determined by reason rather than by prejudice and self-interest.

Especially does the Federal Council urge upon the churches the necessity for a more adequate program of education on the moral issues involved in the liquor traffic. We strongly emphasize the need for a far greater attention to this problem in the Church's program of religious education. In the last analysis, law depends for its support upon the public opinion which sustains it and the conscience of those who live under it.

There can be no greater mistake than to suppose that legislation can relieve us of the necessity of training our youth in habits of temperate living, self-control and the practice of Christian citizenship. To foster such habits and to cultivate such practice is the special and peculiar responsibility of the Church, to be ignored only at the peril of the nation.

It is our hope and confidence that the report of the Research Department on the prohibition situation, calling attention as it does to the real dangers with which we are confronted, will stir the churches to a renewed sense of their responsibility, not only for the enforcement of the prohibition law, but also for rallying the conscience of the nation to its support.[250]

It is clear that most of the Churches, except the Episcopalians and Roman Catholics, heartily favored the plan. The movement was undoubtedly actuated by high idealism, and was designed to deal with a great national evil, but the more thoughtful elements in the community—outside of the leaders of Methodism and some other denominations—increasingly believed that the specific plan adopted to bring about a temperate nation was not the wisest, and in 1933 the prohibition law was repealed. It is charged by the supporters of prohibition that repeal was effected by the Liberty League and other groups which carried on high-powered propaganda with the financial backing of a small group of very rich men.[251] That such a movement existed cannot be doubted, but it never would have succeeded had not the majority of thoughtful American citizens believed that, in spite of the serious evils of the liquor trade, the Eighteenth Amendment was not, in the existing state of public opinion, the wisest way to overcome them. Indeed, the high-pressure methods used to secure the adoption of Federal Constitutional prohibition did not give the nation great confidence in the plan of *direct action* by the Church in State matters.

That prohibition sentiment was not killed by repeal is shown by the action taken by the Methodist Episcopal Church at its General Conference in 1936:

The Methodist Episcopal Church does not retreat in this trying hour. It has accepted no discharge in the war for a saloonless nation free from the domination of legalized liquor. We do not blind ourselves to the trail of moral wreckage across the years of repeal. Increased crime, the open saloon under new dress and name, depressed morals, wrecked homes, debauched youth, mounting traffic tolls, broken pledges, and other glaring evils almost without number, shout the call for a reawakened conscience that will meet this crisis. We look to Almighty God for strength to meet this issue.

The function of the State is the protection of its citizens. It is intolerable that any government through participation in revenues should be a party to a business which thrives upon the physical, social, moral, and spiritual decay of its people. We demand that such participation cease. We declare for an intensified program of education and agitation for creation of a national conscience that will never countenance the iniquitous liquor traffic.

Total abstinence is the keystone of the Arch of Prohibition.[252]

. . . As a consistent first step in the Church's new advance against the liquor evil, we do now agree that: the future General Conferences of the Church shall be held only in cities that will provide adequate and appropriate accommodations in hotels and restaurants that will not sell or serve alcoholic beverages during the term of the Conference. In keeping with the General Rules of our Church, we challenge the people called Methodists to have no part in the infamous liquor traffic through any financial gains received therefrom. . . .[253]

Similarly, the bishops of the Methodist Church, South, and the United Presbyterian Church General Assembly, both meeting in May, 1938, adopted strong resolutions against the ill effects of repeal. They both supported a return to prohibition. Even more significant is the action of the biennial session of the Federal Council of Churches the following year, which, while not coming out in favor of re-enacting the Federal prohibition amendment, strongly opposed the commercial traffic in liquor for beverage purposes.

The Federal Council also places on record its opposition to the beverage liquor traffic as the enemy of the great aims of the Church of Jesus Christ. We especially urge adequate state and federal laws to prevent the advertising of liquor by the radio, newspapers and magazines, bill-boards, or by any other means. Many statements by constituent bodies of the Council concerning the liquor traffic indicate that they regard the liquor traffic as an enemy of the aims and purposes of the Christian Church.[254]

Two later actions of Protestant bodies that were supporters of the former national prohibition law will show how the wind is still blowing in substantial groups of the population, especially outside the large cities and in the middle sections of the country. The first is the action of the Disciples of Christ in 1941.

We renew our avowal of former years, of determined opposition to the liquor traffic. Alcohol is a character-destroying poison, a prolific cause of crime, the cause of untold poverty and suffering, and the cause of an increasing loss of life in automobile accidents. We believe, therefore, that those who do not protest against the legalizing of this traffic are betraying their social responsibility.

Therefore, we urge upon our churches and upon individual Christians (1) that they renew and intensify their efforts toward outlawing this traffic by proper legislation; (2) that they maintain a firm and uncompromising abstinence from the use of liquor, oppose its use by members of their families, and bring tactful protest against its use within their own social circles; and (3) that they endeavor to secure the fullest possible program of education in homes, Sunday schools, public schools, pulpits, and otherwise, to the end of educating our communities to the dangers of the use of alcohol.[255]

Along somewhat similar lines were the resolutions on prohibition passed by the Northern Baptist Convention in 1942. It met in Cleveland with 2,700 delegates, and after an address by the president of Colgate University, Dr. George Barton Cutten, it "overwhelmingly" endorsed a resolution against war liquor. This called attention to the fact that wartime sacrifices are expected of all and that "scientific and social research prove the detrimental effects of alcohol." It said that "the failure of our army and navy authorities to restrict the sale and use of alcoholic liquors has brought about a condition greatly deplored by our people." It pointed out that the manufacture and sale of liquor use manpower, sugar, rubber, and transport, "all of which are urgently needed in our war program." It "resolved that we call upon the President and Congress of the United States to declare a state of emergency and to forbid, or pass such legislation as would forbid, the manufacture and sale of all alcoholic liquors except for medicinal and scientific purposes for the duration of the war." It declared prohibition necessary "if our nation is to win the war."[256]

In connection with this action it should be remembered that the original national prohibition amendment grew out of laws passed during World War I.

On January 5, 1939, the late Senator Morris Sheppard (1875–1941), of Texas, a sincere and widely respected advocate of prohibition, reintroduced the Prohibition Amendment in the Senate, adding as a third clause, "The twenty-first amendment to the Constitution is hereby repealed."[257] Few of the more representative national Protestant, Roman Catholic, or Jewish groups endorsed this proposal, but it was ardently advocated anew by the influential reform organizations of the more militant Protestant groups whose work has already been described—the International Reform Federation[258] and the Methodist Board of Temperance, Prohibition and Public Morals.[259]

The liquor situation in the United States in 1941 was carefully studied and may be summed up as follows:

There were two out-and-out prohibition states—Kansas and Oklahoma. Kansas has since, however, voted for local option.

Mississippi had statutory prohibition except for beer and wine.

Alabama, Georgia, and North Carolina had a combination of prohibition and local dispensaries.

There were seventeen states where the traffic in liquor was a state monopoly. These states were mainly in the South and West, but they included also Maine, New Hampshire, Pennsylvania, Vermont, and West Virginia. Most of these states had some form of local option.

Twenty-six states and the District of Columbia had the licensing system, including such important states as New York and Minnesota.

Maryland had a combination of license and local dispensary laws.[260]

The national situation has not greatly changed since 1941.

The forms of local option still include county option, municipal option, township option, etc. The "drys," under the influence of the Methodists, Baptists, and other groups which forced through national prohibition legislation, have apparently won about 60 per cent of local option elections since repeal. They are pressing for further legislation. It is noticeable, however, that even Kansas and Oklahoma, the prohibition states, now define intoxicating liquors as being beverages containing more than 3.2 per cent of alcohol by weight, thus permitting the popular light beers. This arrangement, however, is not satisfactory to the out-and-out prohibition leaders.

Since prohibition days the Protestant Churches have all continued their interest in the cause of temperance, but they are not unanimous on the public or legislative side. The Baptists, Methodists, and some other large evangelical denominations, especially in the South and Middle West, continue to believe that the national prohibition of alcoholic beverages is the only adequate solution, and continue to work for it, but they have been unable to convince some of their colleagues in the Federal Council of Churches. In December, 1946, at the biennial meeting, the council considered and adopted a report on the "Alcohol Problem." The view that is most significant for our theme will be seen from these extracts on the social control of alcoholic beverages.

> We have affirmed our belief in a vigorous program of continuing education, based on science, illuminated and motivated by Christian ethics. But we affirm also that education and public action go hand in hand; that the second will work finally only as it is based on the first, and that attention must be given to the second if there is to be any chance of achieving the first.
>
> It seems apparent that any program attempting to eliminate the production and

use of alcoholic beverages by legislation on a national scale would be unsuccessful unless supported by an overwhelming majority of the people.

If there is real progress in the care and treatment of alcoholics, in research on alcohol problems, and in alcohol education, we believe that it will be increasingly possible for a better-informed and voluntarily convinced public to institute and support more effective and stringent control measures over the alcoholic beverage trade.

We believe there are certain measures which can be initiated now or in the near future which can reduce some of the evil effects of alcohol, and which can aid the public in understanding the nature of the alcohol problem. These are not final steps. But if they are not earnestly sought and achieved, there will be slight chance of securing better social control. The following are, for the present, our operating principles for social control:

1. Revision of the alcoholic beverage tax structure. This should be in the direction of encouraging the dilution of proof spirits and fortified wines, through a tax program providing adequate incentive to distributors for such reduction.
2. Enforcement of laws regarding issuance of liquor licenses and regulation of hours of sale. This should be in the direction of strictly regulating and decreasing the hours when alcoholic beverages may be sold by package and for consumption on the premises.
3. Prevention of sales to minors. This would be chiefly a matter of encouraging the enforcement of existing laws, by a type of personnel concerned with the total welfare of young people.
4. Social use of public revenue from the sale of alcohol. The taxing power of the government should be used to discourage the consumption of alcoholic beverages and toward decreasing their alcohol content. . . .
5. Regulation of advertising of alcoholic beverages. We deplore the effect which the advertising of alcoholic beverages is destined to have, especially upon the mind of youth, through its unwarranted and false claims, which go beyond public presentation of brand names, common to all advertising, and which aim to invest the use of alcohol with prestige and desirability. This calls for regulatory practices which, if not voluntarily put into effect by advertising agents, should be imposed by appropriate organs of government.
6. Local or state elimination of traffic in alcoholic beverages. This means what is commonly known as local option, eliminating the trade or traffic in neighborhoods, communities or states where at least a majority of the citizens agree that such action shall be taken.
7. Indirect control of alcohol consumption. There are two basic means of indirect social control over the consumption of alcohol, and both concern the churches. The first is based on the fact that alcohol as a social problem is related to other social problems. Where such social evils as poor housing, inadequate recreational facilities, and broken homes can be eliminated or alleviated, an indirect attack is also being made upon the evils of alcohol. The

second means of indirect social control lies in the transforming power of the Gospel itself. . .

We anticipate that, as such a program is carried out, other measures of social control consistent with those named above will become apparent. We shall explore the field to find such additional measures.

Conclusion—

Beverage alcohol is a serious social problem, and cannot be ignored. It is also a complex problem and cannot be solved at once. As Christians we intend to act, taking those specific steps which we believe will lead us most surely toward Christian goals in relation to alcoholic beverages.[261]

It will be noticed that these resolutions, which are earnest and constructive but represent a compromise between different religious groups, are far more moderate than those adopted immediately before and during the early days of prohibition. But the Federal Council never went so far even then as many of its constituent bodies.

The position of the Roman Catholic Church has not changed; it is in favor of temperance for all and of voluntary abstinence, but is opposed to prohibition.

Closely related to prohibition is the campaign carried on by certain Protestant religious groups against the teaching of evolution in schools. Probably a majority of the prohibitionists were also antievolutionists, and probably nine-tenths of the antievolutionists were prohibitionists. The two have close relations, though it must be recognized that prohibition appeals to a certain group of educated and public-spirited men who are too intelligent to oppose the doctrine of evolution. The Middle West and South were strongholds of both; so were the Methodist and Baptist churches. It seems best, however, to consider the teaching of evolution in another section.[262]

Another related movement was that connected with anticigarette legislation. In 1921 there were eight Central and Western states with anticigarette laws. Prohibition leaders, backed by certain Protestant denominations, among which the Methodists were prominent, were largely responsible for these laws. The movement has declined in force in recent years.

Section 13. THE INDUSTRIAL STRIKES—CAPITAL AND LABOR

It is not our purpose here to deal with the struggles between capital, or management, and labor as such. These should have no place in these volumes, which are concerned with social and State problems only as the Church and religion are related to them. The general attitude of the Church toward industrial problems is discussed elsewhere.[263] Here we are concerned with those particular conflicts that have arisen in recent times in which the Church has been involved.

In fact, there has been no important strike or trial of labor "agitators" in the past thirty years in which many ministers of religion and some churches have not become directly or indirectly involved. As a result, Church and State have frequently come into conflict. Speaking very generally, the pastors of conservative churches in large towns have, with a few notable exceptions, been inclined to side with capital and the "ruling classes" in local disputes, but independent pastors in industrial regions in increasing numbers, including many Roman Catholic priests, have been siding with labor—especially where the living conditions among workingmen have been on a deplorably low economic scale. Indeed, there is a growing tendency for the more liberal churches, especially through their national organizations, to support the labor unions in all reasonable demands as long as strikers observe the law. The Mooney-Billings case of 1916 in connection with the Preparedness Day parade bombings in San Francisco, the case of the Scottsboro Negro boys charged with rape in 1931, and the case of the Harlan, Kentucky, miners in the same year are examples.[264] The Sacco-Vanzetti murder case in Boston, in 1920, was so complicated that relatively few Church bodies took specific action on it.

Cases where individual clergymen took part in industrial conflicts—generally on the side of labor but opposing violence—became frequent toward the close of the nineteenth century. Roman Catholic priests were then often active in trying to protect the rights of miners and factory workers. Protestant ministers also played their part. The Reverend W. H. Cawardine, a Methodist pastor in Pullman, Illinois, was an early representative of this group. His flaying of the Pullman Corporation for the strike of 1894 received much attention.[265] My old friend the Reverend Alexander F. Irvine (1863–1940), a Congregationalist, was active in many industrial conflicts near the turn of the century.[266] These are merely instances taken at random. Roman Catholic priests, and even members of the hierarchy, have played a creditable part in helping to settle industrial disputes through membership on boards of mediation and arbitration. It may be sufficient to mention the names of Archbishop Ireland (1838–1918) for his part in helping to settle two railroad strikes in the Northwest in 1894, of Bishop John L. Spalding (1840–1916), who served in 1902 as a member of President Theodore Roosevelt's Anthracite Coal Commission which settled the serious coal strike of that year, and Monsignor Francis J. Haas (1889–), who was active in the years from 1935 on as a Federal labor conciliator. Similarly, the Reverend John P. Boland (1888–), pastor of a Roman Catholic church in Buffalo, has served for many years as chairman of the New York State Labor Relations Board. Several ministers of prominence, such as the Reverend Albert E. Day (1884–), of California, formerly vice-president of the Federal Council of Churches, and Bishop G. Bromley Oxnam (1891–), resident Methodist bishop of the New York area, have also served as referees in labor disputes by appointment of the National War Labor Board. These are typical of many others.

Probably no single industrial dispute in the history of the United States will show more clearly the attitude of Churches, both locally and nationally, than the steel strike of 1919. The history of this strike from the point of view of the Protestant religious forces of the country, as represented in the Inter-Church World Movement and the Federal Council of Churches, can be studied in two important volumes, the *Report on the Steel Strike of 1919* and *Public Opinion in the Steel Strike*. These were both published under the auspices of the Inter-Church World Movement. That this was a representative group is shown by the fact that the Honorable Robert Lansing (1864–1928), formerly secretary of state, was the chairman of the general committee, that Dr. John R. Mott (1865–) was chairman of the executive committee, and that the commission that made the investigation included such well-known Christian leaders as Bishop Francis J. McConnell (1871–) of the Methodist Church and the Reverend Dr. Daniel A. Poling (1884–) of the Reformed Church in America.

It will be remembered that the strike came by vote of the American Federation of Labor in June, 1918, as a culmination of the battle over the closed shop. The twenty-four international unions that claimed jurisdiction over the trades in the steel industry co-operated to organize the workers in that industry, and held mass meetings in Pennsylvania mill towns. The companies replied by discharging union members; and the United States Steel Corporation ignored the request of President Samuel Gompers (1850–1924) of the Federation of Labor for a conference.

The strike began September 22, 1919, and ended January 8, 1920. The long hours of labor, recognition of the union, and conditions of work were the major issues, though wages in certain grades in the industry were also unsatisfactory. Public opinion was particularly concerned about the twelve-hour day, which a report of a committee of the stockholders of the Steel Corporation had shown to be required of more than 50 per cent of the employees in rolling mills and furnaces. This committee recommended a reduction in hours, but the Finance Committee refused at the time to grant the request. The struggle became serious, with freedom of speech and assembly denied, and there was much bitterness. At McKeesport, Pennsylvania, alone, 3,000 men were sworn in as special police subject to instant call; and on the first day of the strike some 365,000 men stayed away from work.[267]

Reports show that there was the greatest difference of opinion about the strike among the clergy in the region affected. Some Protestant and Catholic ministers who had large numbers of the corporation's officers in their parishes opposed it in the early days. Others with large numbers of the workmen's families favored it. Probably the resolutions passed by the Pittsburgh Council of the Churches of Christ on November 28, 1919, fairly well expressed the majority opinion in the Protestant Churches. It was entitled "Appeal to Americans." The opening and closing paragraphs were:

We appeal to you in behalf of our neighbors of foreign birth.

They are among us in large numbers. Thoughtless and mistaken policies toward them at this time will bring grave consequences, both for them and for us. Unfortunately the evidence is unmistakable that some erroneous policies are being followed.

These people in the main are open-minded, honest, industrious, peace-loving. They are mostly from the peasantry of Europe, a stock possible of development into excellent citizenship. . . .

We recognize the presence of some aliens in our midst who have come wholly for selfish purposes and as enemies of our American institutions, and we would have no one misconstrue this statement in such a way as to soften our utter condemnation of their treasonable and insidious attacks upon that which we hold most dear.

Yet the church would be derelict and censurable if it were to remain silent at a time like this, making no protest against these errors so fraught with potencies of evil. We therefore appeal to our fellow Americans for a different course and for prompt and earnest efforts to correct the evil already done.

We appeal to civil officers to be exceedingly careful not to be unjust.

We appeal to employers to give to their employees time and encouragement for cultured life.

We appeal to the public to treat foreigners with the same courtesy shown to an American, and to be real neighbors to them, patiently helping them to learn our language and to arrive at all that is best in our American life.

We appeal to members of the American churches that they manifest a real Christian attitude toward these people, many of whom have revolted against churches which they considered tools of tyranny in other lands, and in so doing have swung far into hostility against religion itself. This state of mind cannot last. Let us, by act and word, so interpret to these people the mind of God that, when their fundamental religious nature shall again assert itself, we shall be in position to help them find Him and find peace and joy for their souls.[268]

The Inter-Church World Movement began its investigation three weeks after the opening of the strike, and transmitted its report to President Wilson on January 27 of the following year, after a careful investigation by experts on the field, and the taking of much testimony. The commission found the conditions—especially the twelve-hour day seven days a week—most serious, but believed that they were "remediable without the inauguration of anything even resembling social revolution."[269]

The report had an extraordinary effect on public opinion. Indeed, after the publishing of its preliminary results the Steel Corporation announced on March 7, 1920, that two of the evils, namely, the seven-day week and the so-called "long turn at the change of shifts," had been entirely eliminated, and that an announcement concerning the twelve-hour day could be expected "in thirty days or a little more." On April 18 the chairman of the Steel Corporation stated to the stockholders:

The officers of the Corporation, the presidents of subsidiary companies and a majority of others in positions of responsibility are in favor of abolishing the twelve-hour day, and for this reason and because of the public sentiment referred to, it is our endeavor and expectation to decrease the working hours—we hope in the comparatively near future. We have been disappointed by our inability heretofore to accomplish our purpose in this regard.[270]

It is most interesting to read the reports of public men and newspapers at the time showing the deep distress created by the facts brought out by the study. For instance, the Honorable William G. McAdoo (1863–1940), former secretary of the treasury, said in September, 1920, that

. . . the findings of such a Commission, as indicated by the recent illuminating report of the Interchurch World Movement, would inevitably have turned public sympathy in favor of the just demands of the men!

And let me say here, that the recent report of the Interchurch World Movement on the conditions in the steel industry must shock the conscience of America. The truly patriotic and Christian men, who interested themselves in this investigation and brought to light such convicting facts, deserve the praise and support of every good citizen. Men must not be permitted to work 12 hours per day and 7 days a week in this country. Such conditions will not be tolerated by an enlightened public opinion.[271]

Even so conservative a paper as the *New York Tribune* was then stated on July 20, 1920:

The report of the Interchurch Commission, composed of men whose good faith will not be questioned, concerning conditions in the steel trust industry, is such as to require the Steel Corporation either to refute the charges or to change its policies.[272]

This may be taken as characteristic of American public opinion. It may be supplemented by the views of an eminent professor at the Harvard Law School, Zechariah Chafee, Jr. (1885–), chairman of the Committee on Coal and Civil Liberties, who, reporting to the United States Coal Commission, wrote with appreciation of the report of the Inter-Church Commission. He said:

If the Interchurch reports lead to the abolition of espionage, shackled assemblage, illegal arrests, police clubbing, a partial press, an uninformed pulpit, no one will have sounder cause to rejoice than the supporters of our present industrial system.[273]

The stand in the controversy taken by the churches was well expressed by the spokesman of the Federal Council, Professor Edward T. Devine (1867–1948), early in 1920.

Whether the long day is desired by the employer, in the interests of profits; or by the worker, in the interest of wages; it is equally disastrous to the family life of the workers and equally disastrous to the American community conceived as made up of self-governing citizens. The churches are interested in the character of individuals, in the homes of the nation, and in the kind of neighborhoods or communities of which the nation is made up, and it is their testimony, gentlemen, that the twelve-hour day, which as your own committee pointed out, means an absence of at least thirteen hours from the family, deprives the children of the parental over-sight to which they are entitled; deprives the mothers of the full partnership to which they are entitled from their husbands; deprives the men of the chance to get acquainted with their children and the free time which their physical and social well-being demands. It is the view of the churches, expressed in many platforms and resolutions, that a twelve-hour day for industrial wage earners means overwork. We are quite aware that farmers and professional men often work longer, but the compensations are so obvious that it would be an insult to your intelligence to dwell upon them. The question which we raise and press with all the earnestness at our command is whether any corporation has the right for any considerable number of years, to decrease the efficiency and lessen the vigor and virility [the language is that of the Report of the Stockholders' Committee of the Steel Corporation, made in April, 1912] of their men; whether any employing corporation, even if, for the bribe of overtime pay, the workers themselves acquiesce, has a right to deprive American families of the presence of the head of the family for thirteen hours of the day; or the right to deprive the community of the vigor and virility of its citizens. There is a true Americanization program and many false Americanization schemes, but it is a part of any sound plan of Americanization that workers shall have free time for their families, or self-improvement for the discharge of their community obligations.[274]

The significance of this whole movement is that at the time of the strike, as shown by the engineers' report, about half of the 300,000 twelve-hour workers in the United States were in the steel industry; that their employers were the last large group to yield; and that they yielded largely as a result of the pressure brought to bear by the religious forces of America.

The Social Service Commission of the Federal Council of Churches of Christ co-operated closely with the Inter-Church World Movement in its survey, and later its Research Department published, in June, 1923, a pamphlet entitled *The Twelve-Hour Day in the Steel Industry*. This dealt with the social consequences of this system with its long hours seven days a week, and with the practicability of its abolition. A further evidence of co-operation with the Churches is shown by the fact that three of the leading groups, namely, the

Commission on the Church and Social Service of the Federal Council of Churches (Protestant), the Social Action Department of the National Catholic Welfare Conference (Roman Catholic), and the Social Justice Commission of the Central Conference of American Rabbis (Jewish), issued a joint statement on the situation on June 6, 1923. This was after the report of the special investigating committee of the American Iron and Steel Institute had declined to abolish the two-shift twelve-hours-a-day system—the action being mainly based on economic grounds. The joint statement from the representative religious forces of the country, referring to the conclusion of the report of the Institute, said that it

shatters the public confidence that was inspired by the creation of the Committee a year ago at the request of the President of the United States. It is a definite rejection of the proposal for the abolition of the long day. . . . The testimony of competent investigators, including eminent engineering societies, is ignored, and the conclusion is put forth without supporting data that the twelve-hour day "has not of itself been an injury to the employes, physically, mentally or morally." This statement is made in face of the fact that the committee of stockholders of the United States Steel Corporation, appointed in 1912 to investigate this matter, expressed the opinion "that a 12-hour day of labor, followed continuously by any group of men for any considerable number of years means a decreasing of the efficiency and lessening of the vigor and virility of such men." . . .

The Steel Institute's Committee . . . exalts a misconceived "law of supply and demand" to a position of equal authority with the law of justice. It excuses inhumanities in the name of economic necessity. Furthermore, it overlooks an important series of demonstrations within the steel industry and elsewhere, of the practicability and superior advantages of the three-shift system. These demonstrations confirm in practice what no honest man can question in principle—that bad morals can never be good economics. . . .

. . . The forces of organized religion in America are now warranted in declaring that this morally indefensible regime of the twelve-hour day must come to an end. A further report is due from the Iron and Steel Institute—a report of a very different tenor.[275]

Later this same year, responding to the force of public opinion, which the Churches had done much to develop, the twelve-hour shift was abolished in the steel industry.

Of the serious industrial strikes which have characterized the period between the two World Wars the most significant from the standpoint of Church relations after the steel strike was that in the cotton mills at Gastonia, North Carolina, in 1929. It was an example of the relatively recent intrusion of Communism as an important factor in industrial disputes. Formerly we had labor and management on the inside, and Church, State, and public opinion on the outside.

Now we frequently have as an organizing force in a labor dispute nonresident Communists who are equally opposed to Church and State, are antagonistic to all management, and little interested in labor except as it can be used to promote party ends. This cotton strike was one of the relatively few on a large scale in which the local churches, because of their extreme social conservatism, were not an important factor either in preventing the conditions that produced the strike, or in bringing about settlement.

This strike was significant because there were more looms and spindles within a radius of a hundred miles of the city of Gastonia than in or near any other Southern city. The area included a total of some 570 textile plants,[276] and the county manufactured most of the fine-combed cotton yarn produced in the United States. The situation was important also because Gastonia reflected mill conditions in many Southern cities, with most of the operators and mill hands Protestant Church members, the two groups attending, however, to a large extent, different churches. For these reasons we are giving it more attention than otherwise it might call for.

The story has been told with ample documentation and objectivity in a book entitled *Millhands and Preachers,* by Liston Pope, Ph.D., then assistant professor of social ethics in the Yale Divinity School. This book is important because it brings out, as its title indicates, the relations between the Churches and the industrial situation.

The millowners are shown to have been conservative, reputable citizens, taking a somewhat paternalistic attitude toward their employees, but with little interest in improving basic industrial relations. They paid low wages and saw no injustice in child labor. To be sure they paid for fairly extensive social-welfare services and community workers,[277] but many impartial observers believed that this was done more to keep the mill hands satisfied than to meet modern ideas of just industrial relations. There was a tradition of local ownership and community sponsorship of most of the mills; absentee owners from the North came into prominence only somewhat later.

The mill hands were not what is commonly called "poor whites," but were chiefly the descendants of small independent farmers in the area who had become impoverished and lost their land. They were considered "docile," and were not in the closing decades of the nineteenth century, when mills began to rise into prominence, much interested in anything beyond a reasonable wage, and were willing to work hard to secure it. They had little or no close contact with the employers and the "uptown people generally."

They had separate churches. Their religious views were fundamentalist and generally rather emotional. The Baptists predominated, with the Methodist Episcopal Church, South, second, and the Presbyterians third. From 1920 on, the small revivalist sects, such as the Church of God and the Pentecostal Holiness Church, came into a good deal of prominence. Sectarianism was strong. The mill churches were sometimes built by the gifts of the millowners, who frequently contributed toward their support and toward the salary of their ministers, thus giving them considerable indirect control over their policies.

Neither the uptown churches nor the mill churches took, on the whole, any large interest in the social and economic problems of the textile industry. Though the denominations they represented frequently had adopted forward-looking resolutions, these had little or no effect locally. There was a great deal of what is called social quiescence.

Even the "Appeal to Industrial Leaders of the South," issued in 1927 over the signature of three Episcopal bishops, five Methodist bishops, and prominent pastors of all denominations in the South, which called for "the improvement of certain social and economic conditions, especially in the textile industry," and mentioned the isolation of the mill population, long hours, low wages, child labor, and the "general absence of labor representation in our factories"—in a word, a broad social document—created practically no stir in Gastonia.[278] It was scarcely discussed either by the uptown churches or the mill churches, or by the owners. Indeed, the ministers were almost as much opposed to all forms of unionization as were the mill owners themselves. They felt that the duty of the Church was virtually confined to the "changing" of individuals, and were scarcely interested in any social problem except that of prohibition.

It was in this set of conditions that the Gastonia strike of 1929, led by outside Communists, arose. It was an attempt to overcome paternalistic capitalism and to substitute social control of the Communist type. The Communists took advantage of bad conditions in one or two of the mills; and especially of the rigid regulations introduced by the manager of the largest of the mills, the Loray, which the United Textile Workers of America believed to be the logical place for operations to start. A local union had been formed there in 1929, resulting in the first strike in Gaston County. The strikers' criticism then was not so much of the wage scale, or the hours, or even of the fifty-five-hours-a-week shift, but mainly against the mill superintendent and the company's refusal to recognize the union.[279]

The strike was not successful, but the seeds of unionism had been sown. Later the Loray mill was united with other mills which became bound up economically with various mills in Rhode Island. The number of employees increased to approximately thirty-five hundred. The management tried to keep them happy by means of welfare workers, a playground and nursery, a community house, a company doctor, a sick benefit association, a summer camp, a company store, and other features. But the mill was now controlled from the

North, and the welfare program became "increasingly an impersonal force for labor discipline" rather than a positive force for social organization.[280]

There was little enough sympathy between the management and the workers, when in 1927 the superintendent arbitrarily increased the labor loads so as to help the company economically and thereby made relations with the workers really acute. Indeed, we are told that the "impersonal and arbitrary methods of the superintendent appeared to have been the most significant factors underlying the strike."[281] As a general result, the old friendly relationships of a decade earlier had disappeared, and the Loray village by the beginning of 1929 was an industrial camp rather than a community.[282] In fact, the general demoralization had gone so far that even the membership, attendance, and influence of the churches had "declined tremendously." They had not been able to absorb the new elements in the community, due to the large turnover.[283]

The strike began on April 1, 1929. It was organized by an experienced strike leader from New Bedford, Massachusetts, Fred E. Beal, who formed a secret union. A public meeting attended by a thousand mill hands was held on March 30, and on April 1 practically the entire working force walked out. The strike was under the leadership of the National Textile Workers Union. It stood for elimination of all piecework, a minimum standard weekly wage of twenty dollars, the forty-hour week, abolition of the doubling up of work, decent sanitary and housing conditions, recognition of the union, and other matters deemed to be fundamental. It considered the methods of the old United Textile Workers as class collaboration with the millowners, while the new union was a militant, fighting one which stood for an indictment of the general economic system and took the ground that the Loray strike was the opening wedge in the South for the organization of all its textile workers. Some twenty-three outside representatives of Communist organizations took part, and the *Daily Worker* was widely distributed. The strike was consequently interpreted as a Communist struggle. It had no connection with the churches. At first it did not attack religion, but it became more and more radical as it moved from the economic into the political sphere. Soon there were clashes between the strikers and the police, and the National Guard was called out. Attempts were made to get its members to join the workers, but without success. Mass picketing was resorted to; but after a couple of weeks the strike seemed to have been defeated, and by May 1 the number of strikers had decreased from two thousand to two hundred.[284]

Circulars were distributed by the mill management, branding the strikers as un-American and atheistic. One of the circulars said:

Our Religion, Our Morals, Our Common Decency, Our Government, and the very Foundations of Modern Civilization, all that we are now and all that we plan for our children is in danger. Communism will destroy the efforts of Christians of 2,000 years. Do we want it? Will we have it? No!! It must Go from the Southland.[285]

An advertisement in the local paper on April 3 read:

Let every man and woman in Gaston County ask the question:
Am I willing to allow the mob to control Gaston County?
The mob whose leaders do not believe in God and who would destroy the Government?[286]

Church members among the more active strikers were probably only about 30 per cent, and few of these were active. It was generally thought that the strike would have been more successful had the Communist leadership been more sympathetic with religion.

The officials of the American Federation of Labor and of the United Textile Workers repudiated any connection with the strike, which they considered Communistic in character and purpose. But the strikers who remained became more aggressive, with a tent colony which became increasingly extreme in its views. On June 7, when rumors of a raid on the strike center were rife, there was a serious clash, which ended in one striker and four policemen, including the chief of police, being wounded; he died the following day. Thus ended the Communist challenge to Gastonia. The attitude of the strikers now became merely one of defense.

It is worth noting that none of the religious associations or organizations adopted any resolutions or engaged in any institutional action with regard to the strike.[287] They were quiescent. In spite of the actions of religious bodies outside, the local churches retained their old tradition of keeping "out of politics," but in general they were unsympathetic with the strike. Probably not over two or three ordained ministers showed any sympathy with it,[288] though one lay preacher joined the strikers, conducting special services for them. A representative of the Federal Council of Churches who attended a meeting of the Gastonia Ministers' Association on April 11, wrote:

The attitudes revealed were defensive, cold, unresponsive to a degree I have never met before in a group of ministers. Evidently they have not yet thought of any connection between the mind of Christ and low wages or night work for women or child labor. A number of mill village ministers were present. They especially felt called on to defend the system.[289]

It was clear that the ministers were of a markedly conservative type; and the sermon topics during the strike, as they appeared in the Gastonia *Gazette,* were almost all on theological or Biblical themes, with little or no reference to the local crisis. The chief approach by the ministers to the problem was to encourage evangelism. They are said to have opposed mob terrorism and police brutality against strikers less, if anything, than they opposed the Communists.

As a result of this disturbance Beal and fourteen other strike leaders were arrested and put in jail. Their trial attracted national attention. The judge had a reputation for fairness and impartiality, but the Communists used the trial as an opportunity for party propaganda. To secure a jury took nine days and the examination of 408 veniremen. They were examined as to their beliefs about trade unions, religion, the sanctity of private property, and other matters. The panel chosen consisted of seven workers, four tenant farmers, and one grocery clerk—all but two church members.[290]

During the trial there were many serious local disturbances, creating a reign of terror in the county. A speaking platform used by the Communists was destroyed by dynamite; and a prominent supporter of the strikers was murdered in the presence of at least fifty persons, yet no conviction of the murderer was ever secured. A newspaper man, writing of the long series of criminal actions and trials, said:

> In every case where strikers were put on trial strikers were convicted; in not one case where anti-unionists or officers were accused has there been a conviction.[291]

The second trial was for an alleged unlawful conspiracy among strikers which the state alleged had resulted in the murder of the chief of police; but as a matter of fact the issue of Communism was always in the foreground, especially the question of the admissibility of evidence as to Communist views on religion and other matters. The judge in the second trial admitted testimony on religious belief in determining the credibility of witnesses, the atheism of Communists being used against them. Religion also entered into the final summations by the attorneys for the prosecution and by the solicitor representing the state. Biblical references were almost as common as they were in the Scopes trial. The jury brought in on October 21 a verdict of guilty, with sentences varying from five to twenty years in different cases. The defendants forfeited the bail which had been posted for them, and fled to Russia; four are believed to be still there; one died. Beal, the leader, became disillusioned in Russia and returned to the United States, where he served a prison sentence in North Carolina until January, 1942, and was then paroled.

The rest of the story is that the trials resulted in the rout of the Communists; company unions were formed after the strike; and the mills enlisted in 1929 the services of the four Loray ministers to endorse applicants before they could be hired as mill hands. This plan, continued for a decade, in the opinion of the mill management worked well. Monthly conferences were held between the mill superintendent and the village pastors, and the mills did more than ever to help finance and support the churches. Efforts were also made, through trained workers, "to offset the incoming tides of materialism, unbelief, and anti-Americanism."[292] General conditions, however, remained much the same until improvements were brought about in mill conditions by the National Recovery Act of 1933.

Communists state in their literature that they count the ministers and churches as having been among their worst enemies in the Loray strike, because they largely supported the status quo.[293] This was not true, of course, of some of the state and national denominations which they represented, which work for a broader interest by the Churches in the whole industrial situation.

I have given the Gastonia story this considerable attention partly because it brings together many of the industrial factors in which the Church is concerned today, partly because of its bearing on the relation of the Church to public affairs, and partly because it has been the cause of extensive discussion.

Section 14. THE ROMAN CATHOLIC ADJUSTMENTS TO AMERICAN DEMOCRACY

(1) BACKGROUND

Although the Roman Catholic Church throughout the world is one in its creed and one in its loyalty to the pope in matters of faith and morals, there have been two somewhat divergent tendencies in its modern development, the one conservative, the other liberal. The conservative is pretty well summed up in the word "ultramontanism." The term came into use after the Vatican Council in the middle of the last century to indicate those who agreed with Rome without qualification in matters of doctrine, discipline, and policy, and were not willing to allow much scope for national differences or for any considerable measure of what has come to be called self-determination.

The liberal tendency on its theological side has been called modernism; on the social side, liberalism; and both these tendencies in this country have been summed up in European thought in the word "Americanism." In France—where the liberal movement went further than in this country—it had many of its historical roots in what was known as Gallicanism. This goes back to Marsilius of Padua and other Franciscans of the fourteenth century, who denied the divine origin and primacy of the papacy.[294] The theory that the councils were superior to the pope found special favor in France under the lead of the French scholar Jean Gerson (1363–1429). By the Pragmatic Sanction of Bourges (1438) an attempt was made to regulate the administration of the churches in

France independently. This general theory was endorsed by the Sorbonne in 1663. Gallicanism, which not only gave the State and the State Church certain powers generally claimed by the papacy, but provided for an appeal from the pope to a future council, became a recognized tendency, and perhaps, from the standpoint of Catholic ideas of Church discipline, a somewhat dangerous one. Its most extreme representatives in recent time have been the Old Catholics of Switzerland and Germany, but something of its spirit has continued active in France.

In the United States there has been a tendency toward a more liberal view from the earliest times of the republic; a tendency due partly to its being a new country, partly to its democracy, and partly to its Constitutional separation of Church and State. These factors all influenced the first bishop of the hierarchy in the United States and the first Archbishop of Baltimore, John Carroll (1735–1815), whose strong desire to adjust Roman Catholicism to the democratic traditions of America has been outlined at some length in a previous chapter.[295] He was not very popular with Rome, because of his desire that the Americans should nominate their own bishops, his friendly attitude toward Protestants, his deep interest in the cause of civil and religious liberty, and for other reasons. His generous open-minded attitude was continued by John England (1786–1842), first bishop of Charleston, whose standing as an American patriot may be seen in his being invited to address the United States Congress in 1826.[296]

These men and other broad-gauge men like them had constant difficulties with some members of the hierarchy who were more wedded to the past, and less broad-minded and tolerant. The outstanding leaders of the group that was fighting to maintain the Church in strict keeping with European Catholic practice were such men as Archbishop Hughes (1797–1864), an ecclesiastic of great force of character, who, failing to secure financial grants from the State for Catholic parochial schools, fought many features of the public school system, and encouraged tendencies whose result was to keep Roman Catholics as a group largely apart from their Protestant fellow citizens; and Bernard McQuaid (1823–1909), Bishop of Rochester, leader of the opposition to many of Cardinal Gibbons' more liberal views.

(2) FATHER HECKER AND ORESTES BROWNSON

The liberal-minded leaders following Archbishop Carroll and Bishop England were entirely loyal to the Church and its head, but believed that this loyalty was consistent with certain adaptations—which did not compromise fundamental matters of belief—to make the Church more effective and more influential in the American democracy of the nineteenth century. Its three main representatives after the middle of the century were different in type and background, but all were men who deserve respect.

The first was Isaac Thomas Hecker (1819–88). He came from a German Protestant background, and, though his father professed no religious faith, his mother became an ardent Methodist. He early formed a friendship with Orestes Brownson,[297] the well-known independent Catholic lay publicist and editor. The latter did much to interest him in social reform. Hecker joined the Brook Farm group of Transcendentalists, whose idealism appealed to him; but their vagueness of thought and lack of a consistent and logical philosophy left him dissatisfied, and in 1844 he joined the Roman Catholic Church. He entered the Redemptorist order, was ordained abroad in 1849, and came to America with four fellow Redemptorists in 1851 to work among immigrant Catholics in our large cities. He became well known for his lectures on Catholic truth, and was particularly effective in presenting the claims of the Church to non-Catholics.

Cardinal Newman wrote one of Father Hecker's associates after his death that "there was a sort of unity in our lives, that we had both begun a work of the same kind, he in America and I in England."[298] The unity came from their non-Roman Catholic bringing up, their intellectual capacity, their conversion, and their interest in commending the Church to groups inclined to think of it as a "foreign" institution whose views could not be reconciled with modern thought and with the ideals of an age when democracy was on the march.

Hecker and four of his associates—also Americans and Protestants by birth—had some difficulties with the rector major of the order in Rome, as they believed that the Church would be relatively ineffectual in the United States unless it adopted methods of work and appeal more suited to the country and the time. Acting as the agent of his associates, he went to Rome in the hope of getting permission to establish a Redemptorist novitiate in America, but instead he was expelled from membership, the stated cause being that he had made the journey to Rome to promote his views without sufficient authorization. The pope dispensed him and his companions from their vows and authorized them to form a new congregation devoted to missionary work in the United States. As a result, we have the highly influential preaching order of the Paulist Fathers—legally known as "The Missionary Society of St. Paul the Apostle in the State of New York"—founded in 1858, an order small in numbers but strong in intellectual and spiritual qualities.

Hecker, who edited the influential *Catholic World* from 1865 until his death, was an ardent American, deeply interested in democracy, and anxious to adjust the Church to American conditions. He was a believer in American political institutions. For instance, the *Catholic World,* in publishing under his editorship a summary of the Pastoral Letter of the Bishops in 1884, said:

The hierarchy of the Catholic Church in the United States share the conviction that American political institutions are in advance of those of Europe in helping a man to save his soul, and that they promise a victory for Catholicism more perfect than its victory in Medieval times.[299]

This statement and others like it, such as that by Hecker's friend and supporter Archbishop Ireland,

An honest ballot and social decorum will do more for God's glory and the salvation of souls than midnight flagellations or Compostellan pilgrimages,[300]

were sure to cause alarm in Rome. Theodore Maynard (1890–), in his stimulating *Story of American Catholicism,* says that Hecker was not trying to accommodate Catholic dogma to the temper of the American Protestant public, and summarizes his general view by saying that "so far as it is compatible with faith and piety" he was "for accepting the American civilization with its usages and customs," because "leaving aside other reasons, it is the only way by which Catholicism can become the religion of our people."[301] These and similar views became known to the world at large through their condemnation in an apostolic letter known as *Testem Benevolentiae* addressed to Cardinal Gibbons by Leo XIII, on January 22, 1899. This refers to the preface of the French translation (1897) of *The Life of Father Hecker,*[302] a book which, with its introduction by Archbishop Ireland, had great influence in France. Groups of liberal-minded French Catholics were disturbed by the fact that their clergy were hostile to the republic and sympathetic with the monarchists; that they kept aloof from modern methods and modern thought; and that they put too little emphasis on individual conviction and activity, and too much on the routine of religious observances. It was largely because Hecker's views fitted so well into their own and had become so influential abroad, that when his biography was translated into French it seemed important to the papacy to disavow its views, especially as Monsignor O'Connell had given them some support at the Catholic Congress in Freibourg in 1897.

The apostolic letter took the view that in keeping with the teachings of the Vatican Council the Church must constantly adhere to the same doctrine in the same sense and in the same way, though modifications in the rules of the Christian life might, in the judgment of the Church, be made from time to time. The idea that the individual could follow his own bent in keeping with modern ideas of civil liberty could not be allowed. The views which were condemned included the alleged insistence on interior initiative in the spiritual life as distinct from direction by the Church; the tendency to give too much heed to natural virtues in place of supernatural ones; the feeling that the vows of religious orders tended to interfere with true liberty; and the minimizing of certain features of Catholic doctrine. The letter concluded with an exhortation for unity within the Catholic Church and against any spirit which tended toward developing a national Church different from the Church elsewhere. Here are the important clauses in the condemnation of Americanism:

If by that name be designated the characteristic qualities which reflect honour on the people of America, just as other nations have what is special to them; or, if it implies the condition of your commonwealths, or the laws and customs prevailing in them, there is no reason why we should deem that it ought to be discarded. But if it is to be used not only to signify, but even to commend the above doctrines, there can be no doubt that our venerable brethren, the bishops of America, would be the first to repudiate and condemn it, as being especially unjust to them and to the entire nation as well. For it raises the suspicion that there are some among you who conceive and desire a Church in America different from that which is in the rest of the world.[303]

The hierarchy in the United States, referring to the brief, "all but unanimously gave spontaneous testimony that Father Hecker had never countenanced any deviation from, or minimizing of Catholic doctrines."[304] But he unquestionably did help to adjust the traditions and practices of his Church and its appeal to conditions in a republic with a Protestant background and majority. He was a good Catholic, but distinctly an "American Catholic."[305] The general effect of the encyclical was probably, from the standpoint of the Church, to act as a brake against some who might tend to go too far along the road of adjustment and compromise.[306]

(3) ARCHBISHOP IRELAND

John Ireland (1838–1918), Archbishop of St. Paul, was one of the most vigorous and admirable leaders produced by the Roman Catholic Church in this country. Strangely enough, no full-length life of the Archbishop has yet appeared, but the admirable sketch in the *Dictionary of American Biography*, supplemented by references to his writings, gives a clear picture of the man and his work.

Born in Ireland, he migrated to this country with his father, a carpenter, in 1849, during the potato famine exodus. After stopping at various places in the East they caught the Western fever and moved to Chicago, where John had some schooling. They then went by prairie schooner to Galena, Illinois, and then by river boat to St. Paul, which they reached in 1853. This was then merely a trading post.

All this experience with a family migrating to the West was to leave its marked impress on the young man. After attending the cathedral school in St. Paul he was sent by the bishop, who was impressed by the youth, to France, where he studied theology. He returned to America in the fall of 1861 with a Union passport. Being ordained in New York City, he became a chaplain in the Union Army, gained invaluable experience, and made for himself a notable reputation by his sincerity, earnestness, and tolerance.

When he left the Army because of being stricken with fever, he returned to St. Paul, but continued the tradition of his old connection through the Grand Army of the Republic, in which he was always prominent. As pastor of the Catholic cathedral in the leading city of the Northwest he waged a vigorous campaign against the liquor interests, and was instrumental in organizing total abstinence societies, though he never advocated prohibition. He was active in securing the adoption of a high license act by the state legislature. He also took the lead in many other public causes, especially as a vigorous opponent of political corruption, and as a staunch advocate of American principles.

He became bishop coadjutor of St. Paul in 1875, succeeding to the see in 1884. He then became president of the St. Paul Law and Order League. Public movements for decency and patriotism, whether the closing of a bad dance hall, or using his influence with the governor to prevent a specially objectionable prize fight, received his earnest support.

He was particularly identified with two movements. The first was the attempt—in contrast to Bishop Hughes' efforts[307]—to get Catholic immigrants to leave the congested cities of the East and move to the West. He organized the Catholic Colonization Bureau with this purpose. He procured from the railroads tracts of land which colonists could purchase at low prices, and held himself responsible for the payment of the installments.

The second movement had to do with the public schools, as we shall see in another chapter.[308] The gist of his plan was outlined in an address before the National Education Association in 1890. There he said: "I am a friend and advocate of the State school. In the circumstances of the present time I uphold the parish school."[309] He urged a compromise by which the state would pay for the secular instruction at parish schools, which should be inspected by the state and free, the teaching being conducted by the denomination concerned. This was the plan put into effect at Faribault (from which it got its name) and at Stillwater—parochial buildings being leased to the city, which paid their running expenses. The religious instruction and devotions both before and after the regular school hours were under local pastors. This was an honest attempt to solve the Church-State problem in the field of education.

He lectured on various occasions, especially on subjects dealing with the relations of the Catholic Church to the United States. He encouraged his clergy and his people to take an interest in civic life, and was recognized increasingly, along with Cardinal Gibbons, as one of the outstanding American leaders of the Church. It was consequently not surprising that Yale University at its bicentennial gave him the honorary degree of Doctor of Laws. I well remember his impressive appearance on this academic occasion. Few more striking personalities have ever crossed my path. Ireland's sermon at the Third Plenary Council of Baltimore in 1884 on "The Catholic Church and Civil Society" was one of his best known and most characteristic utterances.

He joined Bishop John J. Keane in consulting with the pope on the establishment in this country of a Catholic university on a national basis and under the American hierarchy. Their efforts were successful, and the archbishop supported Bishop Keane heartily as rector. He also took a prominent part in helping Cardinal Gibbons in the movement against Cahenslyism,[310] which was an effort to provide foreign rather than American priests for foreign congregations in America. This opposition was characteristic of his American point of view, as was his effective insistence that English should be the language of instruction in all Catholic parochial schools.

Ireland was also a strong supporter of organized labor. He discussed its problems with breadth and force, fearlessly taking sides when it seemed to him justified, as in his support of President Cleveland in the railroad strike in 1894. He also did much to advance education in the Northwest, and secured grants from the General Education Board and gifts from James J. Hill and others for his higher Catholic schools and colleges. These gained an excellent reputation.

His independence was shown in many ways, as when he condemned Tammany Hall; interested himself in the membership of the New York State Board of Regents; opposed Bryanism and the adoption of bimetallism; urged the replacement of Spanish priests by Americans in the Philippines; commended the Taft settlement regarding the friars' lands, etc. In fact, he was always in politics, but always with clean hands and a definitely high purpose, and never in a way that identified him with petty matters.

His point of view was never better expressed than when at the twenty-fifth anniversary of his friend Cardinal Gibbons' consecration in 1893, taking as his subject "The Church and the Age," he eulogized Leo XIII, Cardinal Gibbons, and others of the more far-sighted and generous-minded leaders of the Church, and reminded his hearers that "The watchwords of the age are reason, education, liberty and the amelioration of the masses."[311] It would be hard to make a more impressive or admirable statement. It should not be thought, however, that because Archbishop Ireland gave so much attention to public affairs and reform movements he neglected the routine work of his diocese and of the

Church at large; nothing could be further from the truth. By his amazing energy and ability he made the Roman Catholic Church a force in the Northwest. Perhaps one of his proudest moments was when in 1907 he was able, in laying the cornerstone of the St. Paul Cathedral, to read both a cable from Rome and a telegram from President Theodore Roosevelt.

Furthermore, he was entirely loyal to the pope and to the doctrines of the Church, always maintaining that there was no inconsistency between his beliefs as a Catholic, and his devotion as a citizen to the democratic ideals of the United States. Indeed, he admirably demonstrated in his own career how Church and State can co-operate under the American Constitution and at the same time retain their independence in keeping with its religious freedom guarantees.

(4) CARDINAL GIBBONS

The late Cardinal Gibbons (1834–1921) did perhaps more than any other person in the past hundred years to commend the Roman Catholic Church to the people of the United States, and to interpret its views and adjust its work so as to make them effective under the conditions of religious freedom in our American democracy.

The cardinal was born in Baltimore on July 23, 1834. His parents, however, returned to Ireland when he was three, and James Gibbons received his education in a private classical school there. When he was eighteen, after the death of his father, his mother returned to the United States and settled in New Orleans, where the future cardinal was a clerk in a grocery store. There he decided, when twenty years of age, to enter the priesthood. He studied at St. Charles College and at St. Mary's Seminary in Baltimore. He was ordained in 1861, and was given charge of a mission in Maryland near Fort McHenry, where he served as a chaplain, ministering to Federals and Confederates alike. His sympathies were with the Union cause, but he had a warm affection for the Southern people and took no part in the contest. In 1865 he became Archbishop Spalding's secretary, and by him was made assistant chancellor of the Second Plenary Council of Baltimore in 1868. Then, when only thirty-two, he became vicar apostolic of North Carolina, and in 1868 was consecrated a bishop, being the youngest of twelve hundred Catholic bishops. His stay in North Carolina had a vital effect upon his life, especially because it brought him into contact with so many people who were not accustomed to the Catholic tradition. He preached in Masonic lodge rooms and courthouses, and even in Protestant churches when no Catholic church was available.

This close contact with the people in a typically American state with a dominantly Protestant population gave him an understanding of American conditions and points of view that was to prove invaluable. He attended the Vatican

Council of 1870, and in keeping with most other American prelates he did not question the truth of papal infallibility, though he did doubt the wisdom of declaring it at that time. He, however, voted "placet."

His trip to Europe was specially important to him as showing the conflicts between Church and State under the monarchical system, and this increased his conviction that the American plan of Constitutional religious freedom was wiser. It received his earnest support throughout his life.

In 1872 he was made bishop of Richmond, and in 1875 he became archbishop coadjutor in Maryland, succeeding to the archiepiscopate later the same year. The year was also notable for the publication of his *The Faith of Our Fathers,* a book of which 2,000,000 copies were sold in his lifetime, and which did much, by its reasonable and tolerant attitude, to commend the Church to the people of the United States. At the age of forty-three he began his career in Baltimore, which was to make him for nearly half a century not only the leading Roman Catholic figure in the United States but one of its most respected citizens.

It is impossible here to give the details of his career, except for a few incidents which seem particularly appropriate in these volumes.

The proximity of Baltimore to Washington helped Gibbons to become the intimate friend of Presidents Cleveland, Theodore Roosevelt, and Taft; and he had friendly relations with all the other American presidents during his lifetime. He was not a partisan in national affairs, but took the deepest interest in helping to create wise public opinion on important issues. For instance, in 1881 he issued a circular letter to the clergy of the diocese expressing horror at Garfield's assassination. In the same year, when the observance of Thanksgiving Day was still far from general, he issued what is believed to have been the first direction by a Catholic prelate in the United States for the day's observance.

He organized the important Third Plenary Council of Baltimore in 1884 and presided over it, guiding the council into taking a strong stand in behalf of American civil institutions.[312] Later Gibbons took a leading part in the establishment of the Catholic University at Washington, which he served as head from its beginning until his death.

In 1887, after going abroad to receive the red biretta at the hands of his sympathetic friend Leo XIII, he preached a sermon in Rome in which he declared that the great progress of the Catholic Church in this country was in large part due to the liberty guaranteed by the American Constitution. He expressed his gratitude at being the citizen of a country "where the civil government holds over us the aegis of its protection, without interfering with us in the legitimate exercise of our sublime mission as ministers of the gospel of

Christ," and added: "Our country has liberty without license and authority without despotism."[313]

On this visit he devoted much attention to securing ecclesiastical support for the labor movement. He was able, as a result of his influence, to receive the assurance that the Knights of Labor would not be condemned in the United States, and secured the lifting of the ban against them in Canada. His plea, addressed to the prefect of the propaganda, was published and created a remarkable impression, as did his efforts to prevent condemnation by the Church of Henry George's *Progress and Poverty*.

In the last decade of the nineteenth century he identified himself actively with the experiments Archbishop Ireland was making for co-operation between the Church and the public school authorities. He even favored the reading of the Bible in the public schools if no other form of religious instruction could be provided.[314] At the same time he rendered perhaps his most significant public service by leading the opposition to the so-called Cahensly movement, which advocated the appointment of bishops in this country on the basis of the nationality of the groups they were to serve. In a famous sermon delivered in 1899, when conferring the pallium on Archbishop Katzer in Milwaukee, then one of the most German of American cities, he said:

> Woe to him, my brethren, who would destroy or impair the blessed harmony that reigns among us. Woe to him who would breed dissension among the leaders of Israel by introducing a spirit of nationalism into the camps of the Lord. Brothers we are, whatever may be our nationality, and brothers we shall remain; we will prove to our countrymen that the ties formed by grace and faith are stronger than flesh and blood. This is our watchword—Loyalty to God's Church and to our country—this is our religious and political creed and faith. . . .[315]

The Cahensly movement was named after Peter Paul Cahensly (1838–1923), a Prussian merchant, who was founder and secretary of the Archangel Raphael Society for the Protection of German Emigrants, and visited the United States in 1883 to advance its work. Originally this society seems to have had as its major purpose a real interest in the spiritual welfare of emigrants, so as to prevent their being lost to the influences of the Church, but later it became to some extent the tool of the rising pan-German influences which insisted on the preservation of the nationality and language of those Germans who left Europe for other countries and especially for the United States.[316] The movement was particularly strong in Missouri, with its large German population. Here several petitions were addressed by a German priest to the pope requesting that German Catholics be required to attend German-speaking congregations. It was this type of separatist movement that Cardinal Gibbons opposed with all the force at his command, yet it was clear that the German-Americans constituted a special problem. In 1850 they were only 20 per cent as numerous as the Irish, but forty years later they were 40 per cent.[317]

In 1890 the Cahenslyites held an international congress in Lucerne and addressed a memorial to the pope stating that the Church had sustained a loss of more than ten million communicants in the United States—a statement which Cardinal Gibbons and others rejected as a gross exaggeration. To prevent this situation the society proposed that parishes, congregations, or missions of emigrants should be separately formed according to nationality, and that these parishes should be entirely under priests of the same nationality.

In this wise [the memorial set forth] the sweetest and most cherished relations of the fatherland would be constantly brought to the emigrants, who would love the Church all the more for procuring for them these benefits.[318]

It was in opposition to this plan to make a permanent dividing line between most Americans and European-Americans, and especially to continue the connection of German-Americans with the Fatherland, that what came to be known as Americanism developed as a strong force actively identified with such men as Cardinal Gibbons and Archbishop Ireland.

A letter has been preserved, written by Cardinal Gibbons under date of July 12, 1891, which tells of President Harrison's strong appreciation of what the Cardinal had done in this matter.

Cape May, New Jersey, July 12, 1891.

Right Rev. dear Friend:

Yesterday, while taking a walk with Rev. Dr. Magnien, I accidentally met the President of the United States, who happened to be walking toward me going to his cottage.

He greeted me most cordially, and invited me to walk with him. We went together for some time chatting pleasantly, till we approached his cottage. When I was in the act of saying "Good-bye" to him and continuing my walk, he kindly asked me to accompany him to his cottage. I cheerfully complied, of course.

After discoursing for some time on various things, Mr. Harrison, without any suggestion on my part, introduced the subject of the Cahensly memorials, and the agitation which they were causing in the United States. He then remarked to me:

"I have followed the question with profound interest, and I regard it as a subject of deep importance to our country at large, one in which the American people are much concerned. I have also conversed on the subject with Mr. Tracy, a member of my cabinet. Foreign and unauthorized interference with American affairs cannot be viewed with indifference."

The President then continued:

"I was very much pleased with the opinion which you expressed publicly in the matter. I had thought several times of writing to you, and offering you my congratulations on the remarks that you made, but I refrained from doing so lest I should be interfering with church matters. But I am glad to have the opportunity of expressing my satisfaction at the words you have spoken and of opening my mind. This is no longer a missionary country like others which need missionaries from abroad. It has an authorized Hierarchy and well-established congregations. Of all men, the Bishops of the Church should be in full harmony with the political institutions and sentiments of the country."

The President concluded by saying that I had his authority to make any use I thought proper of his remarks.

I told the President I was happy to inform him that on this very day I had a letter from his Eminence, Cardinal Rampolla, written by direction of the Holy Father, in which the Cardinal informed me that the Pope had rejected the Cahensly petition regarding the appointment of foreign Bishops. The President seemed to be much pleased in receiving this information. . . .

Believe me,
Your faithful friend in Christ,
J. Card. Gibbons.[319]

The cardinal's biographer thus interprets the significance of his efforts to prevent the Roman Catholic Church in this country from losing the American note which had been given it by Bishops Carroll and England and becoming engrossed in European political efforts which, as we know, were later to find their climax in Nazism.

If the United States is a unit, unbroken by divergencies and jealousies of race and language, the country owes a debt to him [Cardinal Gibbons] more than to any other single force for arresting the progress of a propaganda perhaps more ominous to the future of the nation than was the anti-slavery agitation in its beginnings. . . .[320]

On the desirability of separation of Church and State in the United States, the cardinal's utterances are clear and most satisfactory from the standpoint of believers in the American creed. In 1909 he wrote an article on "The Church and the Republic."

American Catholics [he said] rejoice in our separation of Church and State, and I can conceive no combination of circumstances likely to arise which would make a union desirable to either Church or State. We know the blessings of our arrangement; it gives us liberty and binds together priests and people in a union better than Church and State. Other countries, other manners; we do not believe our system adapted to all conditions. We leave it to Church and State in other lands to solve their problems for their own best interests. For ourselves, we thank God that we live in America, "in this happy country of ours," to quote Mr. Roosevelt, where "religion and liberty are natural allies."[321]

In 1912 in a sermon in his cathedral on "Will the American Republic Endure?" he emphasized the same point in a different way.

It is true, indeed, that we have no official union of Church and State in this country. But we are not to infer from this fact that there is any antagonism between the civil and religious authorities, nor does it imply any indifference to religious principles. Far from it. Church and State move in parallel lines.[322]

Again in 1913, in a sermon on his favorite theme of "Civil and Religious Liberty," we find these words:

The Church has tried official union of Church and State and she has tried friendly independence. In adhering to the first system she has often been hampered and restrained in her Divine mission by the encroachment of despotic governments. As far as our own country is concerned, I prefer our American system, where there are friendly relations and mutual cooperation, where both move in parallel lines without clash or conflict, each helping the other in the mission it has from God. . . . I do not wish to see the day when the Church will invoke and receive Government aid to build our churches or subsidize our clergy. For then the civil rulers might dictate the doctrines we were to preach. May the happy condition now existing among us always continue. . . .[323]

American Catholics and all patriots may well be proud of the great cardinal. Some idea of Cardinal Gibbons' place in American life may be had from a study of the accounts of the celebration in Baltimore in 1911 of the jubilee of his cardinalate. At a public meeting in the largest hall of the city addresses praising his services both to his country and to the cause of religion were made by such representative Americans as President Taft, ex-President Roosevelt, Senator and former Secretary of State Elihu Root, and the British ambassador, the Honorable James Bryce. In his reply to the greetings of these distinguished men and of the highest officials of his state and city, he urged the preservation of the Federal Constitution and obedience to the public authorities in the lawful exercise of their important Constitutional duties.[324]

During the early part of the twentieth century he also rendered service of importance in helping to adjust the difficulties between the friars in the Philippines and the United States government. During World War I he was president of the National Catholic War Council, and though past eighty he gave his country active support. A noticeable fact throughout his life was his friendly relations with Protestant leaders and the great respect in which they held him though he was always entirely loyal to his own Church and its doctrines.

His official biographer well sums up his public services:

His position for a third of a century as a brilliant ecclesiastic, the ranking prelate of the Catholic Church in the United States, and as a citizen whose patriotism was undoubted, exhibiting judgment, breadth of view, and vision in his public utterances, was unique in the history of the country. His greatest influence was shown as a far-sighted leader and administrator and in promoting the spirit of religious toleration.

To the attainment of the latter object he devoted the full resources of his dauntless spirit and rare intellect. . .[325]

It is largely because of his contribution to religious toleration that Cardinal Gibbons seems so worthy of recognition in a study devoted to Church-State relations under the American Constitution. A characteristic story is told by a Catholic authority of a civic function in Baltimore when the cardinal and Bishop William Paret of the Episcopal Diocese of Maryland met. The question was raised by someone as to precedence. The difficulty was solved by the cardinal's saying, "My dear brother, we will walk together."[326] If that spirit were more common many church problems in the United States would disappear.

It is worth noting that of the seven American cardinals—McCloskey, Gibbons (who was the most outstanding), O'Connell, Dougherty, Mundelein, Farley, and Hayes—all except Cardinal Farley were born in the United States, and he had his collegiate education at St. John's College, now Fordham University. Cardinal Gibbons always considered it the greatest good fortune of his life that he had been born in America, though his family returned to Ireland, where he passed some of his early years.

The fact of the American birth of these princes of the Church is an impressive example of its adjustment to American conditions. It must be remembered, however, that the American representation in the College of Cardinals, which normally has a membership of seventy, is extremely small. It will undoubtedly increase with the years and result in the relatively more open-minded influence of the American Church abroad.

Section 15. THE ATTEMPT TO FOUND A MODERN THEOCRACY—ZION CITY

We come now to a very different type of relation between a religious organization and a conservatively organized community. In a previous section[327] we considered the most important approach to a theocracy known in our national history—the Mormons. There have been other attempts to set up independent theocracies in some "Zion" in the United States—one worth mentioning in modern times. This was the Christian Catholic Apostolic Church in Zion. It originated in 1899 when John Alexander Dowie (1847–1907), born in Scotland, formed the Zion Land and Investment Association. In 1901 some thousands of acres of land were secured in Illinois, and on March 31, 1902, Zion City was organized and incorporated under its laws.[328] A week later the so-called "Theocratic Party" was organized and municipal officers elected. This political creed of Zion was adopted:

The Citizens of the City of Zion, Lake County, State of Illinois, being assembled in their first convention, held in Zion City, on the night of Monday, April 7, 1902, for the purpose of nominating the first officers of their city, do so on a Theocratic Platform, and desire to set forth their position and their reasons for the formation of this new party in political affairs of the U. S. of America, in the manner following:

First. We declare our loyalty to the Constitution and laws of the U. S. of America.

Second. We affirm that both the Constitution and the Laws are capable of amendment and improvement in a Theocratic direction; and we simply propose to advocate the making of such alterations in the manner provided by the Laws of the United States.

Third. We declare the motto of our party to be the unalterable and unassailable truth that

WHERE GOD RULES MAN PROSPERS.

Fourth. Our object is therefore the establishment of the Rule of God in every department of government, by the free will of the people.

Fifth. We declare our conviction that the Holy Scriptures which contain the ten commandments, and the inspired Gospel of Jesus, the Christ the son of God, constitute the principles of all righteous government for the individual, for the nation, and for the whole world.[329]

In spite of the reference in this document to the "Theocratic Platform" and the "Theocratic direction," there is no statement in it of Dowie's full claims. He had already shown that he possessed a dangerous Messianic complex, believing that he was doing the work of the "messenger of the covenant" prophesied by Malachi. As early as the winter of 1899–1900 he said: "I have the right to stand here and say in Zion you have to do what I tell you! Oh! The whole church? Yes! the whole church—Presbyterian, Congregational, Baptist, Episcopal." A little more than a year later, preaching in his auditorium which held at least four thousand people, he added: "You have to do what I tell you, because what I tell you is in accordance with that word, and because I am the Messenger of the Covenant, Elijah the Restorer."[330]

In 1902, after adopting their political platform, the members of his association, the Zion Restoration Host, duly acknowledged his exalted claims. They vowed to recognize Dowie as "General Overseer of the C.C.C. in Zion, . . . in his three fold office, as the Messenger of the Covenant, the Prophet foretold by Moses, and Elijah the Restorer." Here is the form of pledge or vow:

I promise to the fullest extent of my powers, to obey all rightful orders issued by him directly or by his properly appointed officers, and to proceed to any part of the world, wherever he shall direct, as a member of Zion Restoration Host, and that all family ties and obligations, and all relations to all human governments shall be held subordinate to this vow, this declaration and this promise.

This I make in the presence of God and of the visible and invisible witnesses.[331]

It will be seen therefore that Dowie the founder was considered the head of everything in the community, both civil and religious. His idea of his civil powers is shown in an interview published in the official journal of the movement, *Leaves of Healing*.

The city is governed municipally according to the law of the State of Illinois, and of the United States of America. We bow to these as good citizens, and we have our charter from the state. Our mayor is elected by the people, and our aldermen and judge are elected, and all officers. But I may as well tell you the people would not vote a ticket if I did not approve it. There is one ticket and one vote. In voting for Roosevelt the other day, I took pains with my people and instructed them in the issues before the nation, and in the political condition of things from our point of view as Theocrats—believers in the Rule of God. . . . I said, "Why shouldn't we all vote for Roosevelt?" Our city is a very young city, and a great many of our people could not vote. . . . We have to live a certain time in a place to be able to vote; and so of the ten thousand people less than 1,300 men could vote. We polled if I remember correctly, about 1,260 votes and they were all for Roosevelt. Only 16 Democratic ballots were cast, and they came in from outside country districts, and did not belong to Zion. We were President Roosevelt's banner city.[332]

Everything in the community was placed under the absolute ownership and control of Mr. Dowie, including banks, brickyards, printing, the publishing house, and so on. Seldom have all powers in a community been more centered in one man. An exception was made of land, whose ownership was in God—only long-time leases being made.[333]

The purpose of the community was religious, but moral principle did not always characterize those who organized and conducted it. It had many financial difficulties, for instance, in connection with Dowie's attempt to convert New York City by a mass attack by hundreds of the faithful, which cost the organization more than $300,000. The result was of course a fiasco. Mr. Dowie intended it as a preliminary to an attack on London, where he planned to take ten thousand of his people!

Dowie was deposed in 1906, because his extravagance and unwise management ended in a receivership. After a brief interregnum he was succeeded by Wilbur Glenn Voliva (1870–1942), an efficient manager, who had been minister of a Christian Church in Ohio. He continued to enforce Dowie's puritanical moral and social ideas. In 1909 the name of the theocracy was changed from Zion City to Zion. Voliva greatly developed the industrial activities of the community under a corporation known as Zion Industries and Institutions, Inc. Some idea of his activities may be gleaned from a statement he made about 1930:

I have built a community of 6,400 souls, all members of the Christian Catholic

Apostolic Church in Zion. I have established twenty-six industries and institutions, in addition to schools, colleges, publishing houses and what not. I am the biggest manufacturer of fig bars in the world. Last year we shipped 26,000,000 of them with a profit of $100,000.

I have just sold ninety-one acres of land at $1,000 an acre. I have 1,800 more acres to sell, and when that is sold I still will have room for a population of 100,000. I have a $156,000 radio station. Zion's schools cost me $175,000 a year. Our tabernacle, which seats 5,000, cost me $457,000 last year.

It's all worth $7,500,000, and I would not take $10,000,000 for it. It is all one big, harmonious institution. My people are well paid, own their own homes and are happy, economically, socially and spiritually.[334]

In spite of these successes Voliva predicted the end of the world in 1923; then when this proved erroneous, in 1927, 1930, 1935, and 1943!

The movement has been mentioned as an example of a community where locally Church and State functions have been at times virtually concentrated in a single organization under an authoritarian leader, and where at all times the Church has dominated the community. Lately there have been some changes. Voliva continued until his death in 1942 as general overseer of the church and president of Zion Industries, but the town is conducted much like other municipalities, except that provisions in leases and city ordinances prohibit the sale of pork or swine products, tobacco, alcoholic liquor, drugs, and medicines, and forbid dancing, theatrical performances, and secret societies.[335]

Section 16. THE RUSSIAN ORTHODOX CHURCH IN AMERICA AND THE RUSSIAN REVOLUTION

The effect of the Russian revolution during the last quarter of a century on the Russian Orthodox Church in America has been a most complicated and interesting chapter in the history of Church–State relations in this country. It culminated in 1945 in the refusal of the American hierarchy of the Church to recognize any administrative control by the Moscow patriarchate after the patriarchate had been recognized by the U.S.S.R. The Americans were willing only to grant its spiritual headship but insisted on their autonomy, fearing that Soviet government policy might in some way compromise their independence. The matter is referred to here only because the controversy over the status of the Russian Church has been historically an important event in American Church–State relations, but it will be discussed at some length in a later section dealing with the attitude of the Eastern Orthodox Churches toward our government.[336]

Chapter XVII

THE PROBLEMS OF ADJUSTMENT IN THE FIELDS OF RACIAL AND RELIGIOUS RESTRICTIONS

Section 1. RACE RELATIONS—THE NEGRO

There have been many race problems in the United States. The most important in the order of their development have been the Indian problem;[1] the early immigration of large numbers of European, especially Irish, Roman Catholics;[2] the problems of Negro slavery,[3] the Jews,[4] Asiatics,[5] and the Mexicans in our Southwestern states.[6] None of these problems has been as difficult as that of the adjustment between the Negro and American civilization, partly because we are dealing with a race long in slavery in Africa and in parts of this country, and partly because very different racial types and backgrounds are involved. The question also affects a larger number than in any other minority racial group.

It is increasingly recognized that the presence among us of some 13,000,000 people inheriting African blood, and the need of integrating them more completely into American life, constitute our most serious racial problem. Unless and until it can be solved our government and our civilization will be open to serious criticism. It is a challenge facing the Churches, involving as it does directly the welfare of one-tenth of our population, and indirectly that of our entire body politic. It necessitates many difficult adjustments between the dominant white group and the Negro group, which is constantly surprising us by its capacity to overcome handicaps and to develop effective leadership.

One of the ways in which this leadership has shown itself has been in the development of the Negro Churches, which will be discussed at some length in a later section [XXIII, 4, (14)]. Here it is necessary merely to call attention to one or two fundamental considerations. There is no such organized body in America as the Negro Church. Most Negroes belong to Negro denominations, but hundreds of thousands of them continue as members of dominantly white denominations, either in separate church buildings or chapels, or worshiping without segregation in the old churches. Consequently their racial influence on the State and its problems is both direct and indirect; and lately the Negro Churches, formerly interested mainly in worship and evangelism, have become increasingly concerned with the fundamental problems of rights. They have one advantage over their white brethren in that they are free from the prejudices of an inherited European background. Consequently, for example, although the overwhelming majority of Negroes in this country are Protestant Christians (in 1946 the Commission for Catholic Missions among the Colored People and the Indians reported only 313,877 Catholic Negroes), they have almost no anti-Catholicism. The same is true of anti-Semitism. Indeed, there is a certain bond among Jews, Catholics, and Negroes due to the fact that they are all minority groups.

The great historic struggle in the United States over Negro slavery and Reconstruction, in which the Churches took a large part, has already been discussed.[7] Now we have to consider the more recent tensions between Church and State, and especially the efforts of the Church to advance what it believes to be the cause of Christian freedom in the extremely difficult and complicated field of Negro-white race relations. It must be remembered that it was the Churches of the North which through the American Missionary Association and other agencies took the lead in providing education for the emancipated Negroes in the South after the Civil War, and that it has been the religious forces of the nation, including those of the South, that have appealed to the authorities of the State to prevent lynching and all other injustices and flagrant discriminations against Negroes as such. The women of the Southern Methodist Church; the clergy of the Protestant Episcopal Church; the highly influential Commission on Interracial Co-operation, with headquarters in Atlanta, Georgia, and led by such outstanding Southern religious leaders as Dr. M. Ashby Jones (1868–1947), Baptist, Dr. Will W. Alexander (1864–), a minister of the Methodist Church, South, until 1917, when he withdrew to devote his time to interracial work, and Dr. Cary B. Wilmer (1859–), Episcopalian; the Y.M.C.A. with its widely disseminated study groups on race relations first effectively organized by Dr. Willis D. Weatherford (1876–) of Tennessee; and various boards organized or directed by the late Dr. James Hardy Dillard (1856–1940), an active Episcopal layman of Virginia, have been outstanding examples. These organizations and groups,[8] representing the best Southern blood and traditions, have had a powerful influence on public opinion. They have effectively demanded that the states should take a firmer and fairer attitude in protecting the rights and interests of their Negro population. As a result there was relatively as much progress in race relations in the South as in the North in the period between World Wars I and II.

The effective help of the churches and of individual ministers of religion in establishing and developing the vitally important work of the Commission on Interracial Co-operation will be shown at some length in another section devoted to agencies promoting the Constitutional rights of American minority groups.[9]

The Federal Council of the Churches of Christ in America, representing nearly all the more influential Protestant Churches, North and South, has also been active in presenting the cause of interracial justice before Congress. The lynching evil, which, contrary to general opinion, is not exclusively a Southern problem, is a case in point. The council's presentation of the demand for more effective Federal and state action to prevent lynching contains such a good summary of the position both of the council and of representative Churches that it is here quoted from at length. It was presented in 1934 by Dr. Samuel McCrea Cavert (1888–), its general secretary, at the Senate committee hearing on the Costigan–Wagner Bill for Federal legislation against lynching. It was in the form of an appeal for wise and effective action rather than an endorsement in detail of any specific proposal.

For many years the Federal Council of Churches has been carrying on an educational effort directed to bringing the influence of the churches to bear upon the eradication of the lynching evil. This educational effort has been under the direction of the Council's Department of Race Relations, but the Council as a whole has again and again given voice to its deep conviction that the prevalence of lynching in the United States is a black stain upon a civilization that is called Christian. At almost every quadrennial meeting of the Council, made up of about 400 delegated representatives of the constituent denominations, strong protest has been made against the continuance of the lynching evil and the churches have been urged both to educate their own members in respect for law and also to interest themselves in securing adequate legislation for the protection of all people from lynching mobs.

For the past eleven years the Federal Council of Churches has published an annual roll of honor of those states which during twelve months were free from the lynching evil. We have been appalled to discover, as a result of watching the record of the various states year by year, how widespread the evil is. So far as we can learn, there are only five states which have no lynching record. During the year 1933 the lynching evil spread to the territory of a larger number of states than in any of the eleven years since the honor roll was instituted.

Equally appalling is the fact that, in spite of the thousands of people who have participated in lynchings, the number of those who have been convicted for the crime is negligible. Although there have been 1,880 recorded lynchings between 1900 and 1930, there have been only 12 known cases in which convictions have been secured. It seems too self-evident to require argument that local and state authorities in all parts of the country have proven themselves ineffective in handling the lynching problem.

Such conditions as these have gradually come to be recognized by the thoughtful leadership of the churches and have led to outspoken statements by many different church bodies and in many parts of the country. A few of these, gathered from a far greater number that might be cited, are as follows:

The Board of Bishops of the Methodist Episcopal Church, South, as long ago as 1922 declared: "We especially urge that everything possible be done to prevent lynchings.... This crime of crimes, which is not only a complete subversion of law, but a stroke at the very life of law itself, has discredited our nation in the eyes of other civilized nations and brought undying obloquy upon many of the states of the Union."

The Washington Conference of the Methodist Episcopal Church declared: "As representatives of the Christian Church, which stands for law and order, we urge those who are intrusted with the administration of civil government to search for and bring to justice those persons who are responsible for this outrageous assault on society and good government."

The North Carolina Baptist Convention, 1930, pledged itself to "support vigorous measures to blot out forever the curse of lynching from our midst."

The General Convention of the Protestant Episcopal Church has declared that "mob violence in every form is wrong" and that "it is a clearly defined and imperative Christian duty to sustain the civil authorities in the righteous exercise of their powers in seeing that even-handed justice is unfailingly administered according to due and lawful processes."

The Northern Baptist Convention in 1922, after deploring the lawlessness of lynching and mob violence, declared that "legislation is needed to remedy these conditions."

The Southern Baptist Convention made the following official declaration: "... Never should we be content until every vestige of this barbarity (lynching) is eradicated and every individual, black and white alike, has secured to him the right of life, liberty and the pursuit of happiness, unless and until deprived of it by due process of law administered by public officers, backed by public sentiment and held responsible to public sentiment for the faithful discharge of their duty."

The general staff of the Board of Christian Education of the Methodist Episcopal Church, South, at a meeting in 1933, after noting the increasing number of lynchings, said: "We urge officials, both Federal, state and county, to use their utmost power to prevent lynchings throughout the nation, and to mete out prompt and adequate punishment to those who may be convicted of this crime."

The Commission on Missions of the General Council of Congregational–Christian Churches at a meeting within the past month adopted a resolution approving the Costigan–Wagner Anti–Lynching Bill.

One of the most recent and at the same time most significant statements from a ministerial group is that of the Ministerial Alliance of Nashville, Tenn., which on February 1, 1934, gave their endorsement to the Costigan–Wagner Bill. This action was taken at a meeting called for the specific purpose of considering the bill and after copies of the measure had been sent to every minister a week in advance.

Jewish as well as Christian groups have gone on record as convinced that further legal measures are necessary. The Central Conference of American Rabbis at three different meetings declared that "federal legislation against lynching is needed."[10]

In the light of such widespread evidence of the aroused sentiment of the churches against lynching, the Executive Committee of the Federal Council of Churches, made up of the representatives of twenty-five Protestant denominations, has again and again addressed messages to its constituency and made public statements concerning the necessity for a more vigorous and effective effort to prevent lynchings and to punish lynchers. . .[11]

Two months later, on April 2, 1934, the Executive Committee of the Federal Council took official action favoring national legislation on the subject:

The recurrence of the monstrous evil of lynching in different sections of our country is a continued national menace and disgrace. This horrible crime jeopardizes the very authority and majesty of the law, threatens the fundamental principle of the sacredness of personality set forth in the Gospel of Jesus Christ and outrages every vestige of human conscience.

During the past decade many instances have occurred when action of state and local authorities has either been ineffective or absent in the face of mobs about to lynch victims or in the prosecution of lynchers after the act.

Within the past twelve months the governor of a state condoned a double lynching and promised pardon to any participant who might be convicted; the effort of another governor to apprehend lynchers resulted in a community uprising; and the effort of a third governor and his staff failed to secure conviction of admitted participants in a lynching.

THEREFORE, BE IT RESOLVED That the Executive Committee of the Federal Council of Churches, realizing that lynching has become a national shame, believes that national legislation is a moral necessity to bring the Federal Government into prompt and effective cooperation with state and local authorities in the prevention of lynching and the prosecution of lynchers.[12]

In the years since these actions were taken they have been supplemented by scores of other actions by Church and other public bodies, and the situation has greatly improved. This improvement has been due to many factors, of which an aroused public opinion created by the Southern Churches, the Commission on Interracial Co-operation[13] in Atlanta, and other sympathetic agencies is the one mainly responsible. Statistics show a fairly steady decrease of lynchings in the past half century since the peak year of 1892 with 231. Thirty years later (1922) there were 57, and the annual average in recent years has been under five. Although in the first fifteen years when accurate statistics were kept (1882–1896) more than 40 per cent of the lynchings were of whites, not only in the South but also in the Southwest and West, most of the victims now are Negroes. It is believed that this blot on American civilization, in all its hideous forms, will soon be a thing of the past.[14]

Among other legislative matters affecting Negro rights or welfare on which the Federal Council either through its Executive Committee or its Department of Race Relations has recently taken action on behalf of the Protestant Churches, are the following:

The plight of the share-tenants and share-croppers of the South [both white and colored], whose "situation urgently calls for measures which will make it possible for farmer-tenants to have farm homes on land of their own," urged by the Executive Council, April 26, 1935.

The importance of providing in the bill now known as the Social Security Act "a clause or clauses to provide that there shall be no discrimination on account of race or color in the administration of the services and benefits to any person otherwise eligible," as urged before the Committee on Finance of the United States Senate in 1935 by the Executive Secretary of the Department of Race Relations.

The importance of insuring that Negroes in the nineteen States which provide separate schools for white and colored pupils should receive their share of any benefits of educational funds granted by the Federal Government to the States, as recommended by the Department of Race Relations in April, 1937.

It will be noticed that in these and similar matters the Federal Council generally devotes itself to supporting Constitutional proposals which it believes will make possible social legislation more acceptable to the Churches. It generally considers the drafting of proposed laws or the details of legislation as outside its province.

These actions of a decade ago have been followed in recent years by much more significant decisions. From the standpoint of Church leadership in progressive public policies, perhaps the most important of these was made in the year 1946, when various representative religious groups came out squarely against legal segregation by the State and against practical segregation in the Churches, as representing an unchristian ideal. These actions will be dealt with at the close of this section. Their general position, as in the actions already cited, was that religion teaches that God is the Father of all men; that all men are consequently brothers; and that the Church must help the State in our democracy to see and carry out its duty to eliminate all forms of racial discrimination in law and in public custom. The Kingdom of God on earth—the rule of peace, good will, and justice under Divine leadership—is one of the major goals of the Church, both Christian and Jewish.

So far in this section we have been mainly considering three organizations which have been of great service in calling attention to the needs of the Negro and especially in later years to his civil rights under the Constitution, namely, the Interracial Commission,* the Federal Council of Churches, and the Cath-

* This developed, in 1944, into the Southern Regional Council.

olic Social Welfare Council. We should now mention a few other ways in which the Churches in recent decades have directly or indirectly aided the Negro to obtain justice.

(1) The Churches have established most of the colleges and higher schools of education for Negroes in the South, from which a very large proportion of the wise and able leaders of Negro public opinion and advance in civic and civil status have been graduated. Atlanta University and Fisk University have been remarkable for their leadership in this respect. These Christian Negro colleges have been among the best investments ever made by the American Missionary Society and the other agencies and groups which founded them.

(2) The Negro Church has been, on the whole, the greatest social institution developed by Negroes. In many places it is the only center where they have an opportunity to meet and make plans for their own improvement. These churches have done much to give hope to the Negro and to develop his capacities for leadership. Lately they have also become interested not only in his education and social welfare, but in his civil rights. Ministers of the churches are the leaders of Negro public opinion in most places outside the large cities. Here too they are not without influence, but frequently journalists and other leaders have been even more influential. An example of a Negro church in a city which is a great factor in social welfare is the Abyssinian Baptist Church in New York. It has a broad welfare program, and is one of the largest churches of any denomination in America. Its pastor is a member of Congress. Furthermore, wherever local campaigns are conducted for one of the two great national service organizations for Negroes—The Association for the Advancement of Colored People, or The National Urban League—ministers play a large part in them. The Association, though generally considered the more radical of the two, has a church secretary who is a Negro minister.

(3) The Negro is generally tolerant of others' opinions. He is naturally conservative in religious matters, but he has never been a heresy hunter, and hence has contributed to the cause of religious freedom. Originally he had to look to his master for protection. Then in the early days after emancipation he became accustomed to looking both to the Church and to the State. For years the Church was his greatest ally. Now increasingly he is turning to the State, and especially the Federal government, for protection and help.

The European situation developed from World War II has greatly helped the Churches to bring home to the American public the need of speeding the process of securing full justice with first-class citizenship for the Negro and other social minorities. We cannot consistently condemn Nazi and Fascist imperialism and ideas of racial superiority while we continue the same types of evil in our own country. Similarly we cannot prevent the spread of Communism as long as we refuse to the members of some minority groups their full Constitutional rights. To put into practice Christian ideals of human brotherhood is our best defense against European ideologies of either the extreme right or left.

A few dates from the past generation will show some of the achievements of the Church in his behalf:

1913—Hampton Institute establishes a ministers' conference—the forerunner of many similar movements.

1917—The white women of a Southern Presbyterian church hold at Tuscaloosa, Alabama, the first large conference in the South with colored women present.

1922—The National Board of the Y.W.C.A. appoints an interracial committee to study the history of the Negro and his present-day problems—the beginning of a most fruitful activity; and announces that hereafter its national conventions will be held only where delegates can share all facilities alike.

1923—The Federal Council of Churches appoints a committee on the Church and Race Relations and establishes Race Relations Sunday.

1931—Southern Church women organize the Association of Southern Women for Preventing of Lynching.

1933—Benjamin Mays and J. W. Nicholson publish *The Negro's Church.*

1934—Joseph H. Oldham publishes *Christianity and the Race Problem.*

1934—The establishment of the Catholic Interracial Council in New York.

1937—The Oxford Conference on Church, Society, and State, the most representative ecumenical conference in centuries, attended by many Americans both white and colored, adopts significant resolutions against segregation—"there can be no place for barriers because of race or color, especially in the Church's own life and worship."

1939—The Inaugural Encyclical of Pope Pius XII refers particularly to the importance of a Christian attitude on race relations.

1945—The Roman Catholic Church inaugurates interracial justice week.

1945—The Reverend Howard Thurman, a Negro, and dean of the chapel at Howard University, becomes a regular preacher at Yale University, and the following year is invited to give the Ingersoll lecture on immortality at Harvard.

1946—The Federal Council of Churches adopts the recommendation of its Commission on the Church and Minority Groups, coming out in favor of an unsegregated church and against segregation as an unchristian ultimate solution of racial problems.

1947—The Archbishop of St. Louis opens Catholic parochial schools to Negro students.[15]

These are but a handful of typical dates that show the progress of Negro interests in Church matters.

During World War II, partly as a result of Supreme Court decisions protecting Negro rights and partly because of the labor shortage and the liberal attitude of President Franklin D. Roosevelt, the recognition of interracial justice made great progress. This stirred up reactionary forces in various parts of the country and there were unfortunate clashes in urban centers where the Negro population was disturbed and often indignant, especially because of discrimination in the armed forces and inadequate housing and recreation facilities at home. Much was said and said truly of the inconsistency between our condemnation of Nazi racialism and our all too frequent superior attitude toward blacks. In the new movement of protest led by the militant National Association for the Advancement of Colored People—the NAACP—which had secured nearly 500,000 paying members before the end of 1945, and in 1947 sought a million members, an important part was played by Negro urban churches and their ministers in securing support for the Association, and at the same time for the Urban League with its similar objectives—though mainly concerned with the Negro's rights in industry rather than in government—and with more conservative methods. Similarly in this period the Churches, led by the Federal Council of Churches and the National Catholic Welfare Council, and supported by such other agencies as the Y.W.C.A. and the Methodist women of the South, have become much more active in demanding the abolition of all discrimination against Negroes as Negroes. These efforts reached their climax in March, 1946. At a special meeting of the Federal Council held in Columbus, Ohio, March 5 to 7, a report on "The Church and Race," prepared by a special national commission which had long studied the subject, adopted after careful consideration and without dissenting vote a report which included the following statement under the subheading "The Church Must Choose":

> Either the Church will accept the pattern of segregation in race relations as necessary, if not desirable, and continue to work within this pattern for the amelioration of racial tensions or it will renounce the pattern of segregation as unnecessary and undesirable.
>
> The Federal Council of the Churches of Christ in America hereby renounces the pattern of segregation in race relations as unnecessary and undesirable and a violation of the Gospel of love and human brotherhood. Having taken this action, the Federal Council requests its constituent communions to do likewise. As proof of their sincerity

in this renunciation they will work for a non-segregated Church and a non-segregated society.

The Church when true to its higher destiny, has always understood that its gospel of good news has a two-fold function, namely:

To create new men with new motives.

To create a new society wherein such men will find a friendly environment within which to live their Christian convictions.

The churches of America, while earnestly striving to nurture and develop individuals of racial good-will, have at the same time neglected to deal adequately with the fundamental pattern of segregation in our society which thwarts efforts of men of good-will. This must be corrected. Churches should continue to emphasize the first function; however, they must launch a comprehensive program of action in fulfillment of the second function. This is imperative now.

In the same month resolutions looking toward the same goal were adopted by national conventions of the Y.M.C.A. and the Y.W.C.A.[16] It is significant that these groups were not sectional but represented the country as a whole.

It was characteristic of interest in the Negro on the part of many Churches today that the Congregational Christian Churches, along with the Protestant Council of New York, the Northern Baptist Convention, and other religious groups, joined the friends of the court in standing for "a non-segregated church in a non-segregated society," in the Supreme Court hearing on January 17, 1948. This was regarding restrictive covenants designed to prevent Negroes from living in certain residential areas.

Section 2. ASIATIC EXCLUSION LAWS

The Churches, believing profoundly in the brotherhood of man, have always opposed all extreme Asiastic exclusion laws. They were particularly active in opposition to the abrogation of the "gentleman's agreement" by which immigration was controlled. The following action of the Executive Committee of the Federal Council of Churches in 1925 will show in general the attitude of American religious groups—Protestant, Catholic, and Jewish—toward this problem:

The Asiastic Exclusion section of the Immigration Law of 1924 has created an International situation that causes us grave concern. The manner of its enactment, the abrupt abrogation of the Gentlemen's Agreement without the conference requested by Japan, the insistence on a discriminatory law which Asiatics resent as humiliating, unjust and unchristian, and the affront to Japan's prestige as one of the great and equal nations of the world, have combined to wound and grieve a friendly nation.

Many expressions of resentment and of disappointment in the idealism, brotherhood and good will of America have come from India and China as well as from Japan. While Asiatics know and say that nothing they can do can change the situation or the law, they repeatedly declare their trust in the sense of justice which many of them still believe inheres in the American people and their confidence that the American people will ultimately set this matter right.

The careful consideration of this important and far reaching problem leads us to make the following observations:

1. No Asiatic nation was or is asking for the privilege of Immigration.

2. It was, and still is possible to assure full protection from all dangers of Asiatic labor Immigration and at the same time to give Asiatics complete equality of race treatment.

3. A fundamental factor in the situation is the recent interpretation of our law of Naturalization whereby eligibility to citizenship has been limited to persons of the white race and to persons of African birth or descent. This law was enacted when these modern problems were not before the Nation. This law debars as unfit for citizenship on the basis of color alone persons of all other races whatever their individual character or qualifications.

4. The Immigration Law of 1924 provides that on July 1, 1927, a new quota principle for the regulation of Immigration shall come into force. If that quota principle were applied to Japanese, Chinese and East Indians, the number of Immigrants annually admissible from those countries to the United States would be 150, 100 and 100 respectively.

5. President Coolidge has declared in his last message to Congress that "We ought to have no prejudice against an alien because he is an alien"; that "the standard which we apply to our inhabitants is that of manhood"; and that "it is fundamental of our institutions that they seek to guarantee to all our inhabitants the right to live their own lives under the protection of public law," which means "the full right to liberty and equality before the law without distinction of race and creed."

In view of the foregoing facts and observations we are impelled to record our convictions.

1. That the dictates of humanity and the welfare of the world demand the recognition by all governments of the brotherhood of man and the inherent right of all nations and races to treatment free from humiliation.

2. That the United States cannot afford to over-ride the principle of essential human equality embedded in the Declaration of Independence.

3. That no nation can afford needlessly to flout and wound the feelings of other nations and peoples.

4. That the maintenance of justice, humanity, courtesy, and goodwill between the peoples of the Far West and the Far East is essential to the permanent peace of the Pacific and of the world.

5. That we recognize the need of restriction of immigration in order to conserve American standards of labor and living.

6. That Asiatics in the United States should be accorded their rights as human

beings and also their rights to which they are entitled by the letter and the spirit of the treaties under which they came to the United States.

7. That, in the words of former Ambassador Woods this action of Congress referred to above was an International catastrophe.

8. That we see at present no better solution of the problem than the application to Japan, China and India of the quota law as it comes into force in 1927 which would result in the annual admission of 350 immigrants from those three sections of the Orient.

We therefore recommend to all right-thinking and peace-loving citizens of the United States, the importance of giving these matters earnest study to the end that in due time appropriate steps may be taken to reestablish right relations between the United States and the peoples of the Orient.[17]

Similar action was taken by the council in 1928:

The Federal Council of the Churches of Christ in America, in Quadrennial Session assembled, reaffirms the action of the Executive Committee of 1925, urging the importance of so amending our immigration and naturalization laws that they may be applied without discrimination to nationals of all countries now resident in the United States or who may be admitted later.

The present discriminatory laws are resented by all intelligent Orientals as humiliating and unChristian. They constitute a serious barrier both to international goodwill and also to the progress of the Christian movement in those lands. The United States cannot afford to override the principle of essential human equality embedded in the Declaration of Independence and proclaimed to the world as fundamental in America's contribution to a new world order. No nation can afford to flout and wound the feelings of other nations and peoples.[18]

Such repeal was effected for the Chinese as a result of World War II when China was our ally, and when the Chinese government was under the leadership of the able Generalissimo Chiang Kai-shek, whose wife was educated in the United States and highly honored here. It is worth recording that they were both members of the Christian Church, as were many of their leading collaborators.

The attitude expressed by the Presbyterian Church in 1934 and again in 1936 may be taken as representative of Christian public opinion in the United States.

In order to promote more friendly relations between our own and far eastern nations, we advocate the repeal of the exclusion act of 1924, and the admission of orientals on the quota basis now in effect with respect to other nations. . .[19]

These actions, which might be multiplied, are evidences of the deep and increasing concern of the American Churches in the fair treatment of Asiatics by our government. The growth of American missionary activity in the Far

East, especially through Christian colleges in China fostered by our citizens; the development of the ecumenical movement among the Churches of East and West, more particularly since the great world conferences at Oxford and Edinburgh in 1937; and a deeper study of the fundamental implications of Christian theism and its resulting sense of Christian brotherhood—these all lead the churches through inescapable logic to oppose all exclusion laws which discriminate against immigrants merely on the basis of race.

The special difficulties which arose in World War II because of the presence of a large number of Japanese in the West, and the part played by the Churches in relieving the lot of those who were moved from their homes as a precautionary measure, will be considered in a later section.[20]

The presence of a considerable number of Chinese on the West Coast has brought about at least one religious freedom case that should be mentioned. The treaty with China in 1868 included a clause to the effect that

> Chinese subjects in the United States shall enjoy entire liberty of conscience, and shall be exempt from all disability or persecution on account of their religious faith or worship.[21]

But in 1873 a measure providing for the humiliating cutting of the queues of Chinese prisoners in the local jail in San Francisco was defeated only by the veto of the mayor, who called attention to the fact that the Civil Rights Act of 1870 was applicable to the Chinese as well, and quoted the treaty provision referred to above. In 1876, however, the following order was passed by the supervisors of the city:

> Each and every male prisoner incarcerated or imprisoned in the County Jail of this city and county under or pursuant to a judgment or conviction, had by any court having jurisdiction of criminal cases . . . shall immediately upon their arrival at said County Jail . . . have the hair of their head cut or clipped to a uniform length of one inch from the scalp thereof. It shall be, and is hereby made, the duty of the Sheriff to have enforced the provisions of this order.[22]

When the constitutionality of this order was under consideration in a suit before the United States Circuit Court for California, Justice Stephen Field (1816–1899), speaking for the court, declared the ordinance unconstitutional.

> . . . the Supervisors had no power or authority to prescribe what amounted to an additional penalty. . . . The ordinance being directed against Chinese only, imposing on them a degrading and cruel punishment is also subject to the further objection that it is hostile and discriminating legislation against a class, forbidden by the Fourteenth Amendment which declares that no State "shall deny to any person within its jurisdiction the equal protection of the laws." . . . The complainant avers that it is the custom of Chinamen to shave the hair from the front of the head and to wear the

remainder of it braided into a queue; that the deprivation of the queue is regarded by them as a mark of disgrace, and is attended, according to their religious faith, with misfortune and suffering after death . . . and that the plaintiff has suffered great mental anguish, been disgraced in the eyes of his friends and relatives, and ostracized from association with his countrymen. . . .

Probably the bastinado, or the knout, or the thumbscrew, or the rack would accomplish the same end; and no doubt the Chinaman would prefer either of these modes of torture to that which entails upon him disgrace among his countrymen and carries with it the constant dread of misfortune and suffering after death. It is not creditable to the humanity and civilization of our people, much less to their Christianity that an ordinance of this character is possible.[23]

This is typical of hundreds of cases where the higher courts of the land prevent injustice by insisting on the observance of those fundamental provisions of law which the thought and conscience of a nation founded by men with the Christian tradition and ideal have embodied in our national Constitution.

A similar issue has been raised by the marriage of Orientals with Americans of white stock, and especially white women. There are several Western states which specifically forbid such marriages, thus almost paralleling for East Indians, Mongolians, and, in recent years, Malays, the laws of the Southern states forbidding whites to marry Negroes. This matter became specially serious after 1933 when the Supreme Court of California in the Roldan case decided that a Filipino was not a Mongolian and that consequently he was not included under the civil law forbidding the issuing of a marriage license for a white person and a Mongolian. But the state legislature promptly got around this particular difficulty by adding Malays to the groups named in the law—a particularly embarrassing action in view of the political connection of the Philippine Islands with the United States. The Roman Catholic Church has been specially active in opposing this legislation, which has been copied in some other Western states, and a Catholic chaplain, the Reverend Eugene Noury, O. M. I., has been the leader of the movement to try to get it changed. He recently asked the governor of California: "Why is a law that is against the law of nature, against the law of God and contrary to the spirit of the Constitution" allowed to rule Pacific Coast Christians?[24] It is interesting to know that the canon law recognizes no interracial impediments to marriage.

Section 3. ANTI-SEMITISM

This term did not come into use until 1879. As good a definition of it as I have seen is that incorporated in a bill "To prohibit Anti-Semitism and to prevent the pollution of the channels of interstate commerce and communication" introduced into Congress by the responsible National Committee to Combat Anti-Semitism. Whether this particular proposal represents a wise method of attacking a growing menace is doubtful, but the definition may be taken as authoritative.

> Anti-Semitism is the practice of discrimination against persons of Jewish faith or ancestry in employment, whether public or private, or in business relations such as the rental or sale of housing facilities, or in the enjoyment of political or civil rights or the holding up of persons of Jewish faith or ancestry to ridicule, shame and obloquy or as unfit to hold public office or private employment, or that doctrine, principle, teaching or precept which teaches or declares that persons of the Jewish faith or ancestry are not or cannot be loyal citizens of the United States, or that persons of the Jewish faith or ancestry are, as such, members of or affiliated with an international organization or conspiracy directed at the seizure of power over the government of the United States or which advocates, proposes, urges or affirmatively suggests that persons of Jewish faith or ancestry be made the objects of discrimination in employment, whether public or private, or in the enjoyment of political privileges, or holds them up to ridicule, shame, obloquy or as unfit to hold public office or private employment.[25]

It is not necessary here to enter into the long story of anti-Semitism in Europe. Suffice it to say that though in the early Roman Empire, before the rise of the Christian Church to power, Jews were frequently discriminated against and persecuted because of their religion, which kept them as groups apart, yet after the destruction of the temple in A.D. 70 had resulted in their dispersion over the world, they began to enjoy virtually the rights of citizenship under the constitution of Caracalla in A.D. 212. But these rights they lost in the medieval world, partly because of the attitude of the Church, which was based in large measure on the connection of Jews with the crucifixion, and on their unwillingness to accept Christianity; and partly because the medieval conception of citizenship was based not so much on State allegiance as on membership in some largely self-governing corporation or guild, or privileged estate; partly because of their separateness and alleged peculiarities; partly because of the false accusations of "ritual murder," a charge also made by the Romans against the Christians in earlier days; and perhaps mainly because of economic factors. It was in the later Middle Ages, beginning with the period of the Crusades and the terrible slaughter of Jews on the way to Palestine, climaxed at the capture of Jerusalem in 1099, that the restrictions on the Jews and their persecution were at their worst, with the ghetto, yellow badge, economic restrictions, expulsions, and other indignities. Many of the extreme discriminations and cruelties were opposed by the Church, especially by some of the popes; but the record of "Christian" Europe was on the whole far from good, and all too often foul slanders and rumors were accepted by the multitude, the Jews being even thought to be in league with the devil. It was not, speaking generally, until the era introduced by the American and French Revolutions and the rise of the so-called secular State, that the Jews regained the right which they once held under the Roman Empire to be treated like others before the law.[26]

In a previous section[27] we have traced the gradual enfranchisement of the Jews in the various American states after the adoption of the Federal Constitution and Bill of Rights, and have shown some of the points of tension—none very serious—which have developed between the Jewish Church and the American State. Here we are concerned entirely with the recent growth of anti-Semitism; which is directly contrary to the letter and spirit of American institutions, and especially to the Bill of Rights and the Fourteenth Amendment as recently interpreted by the Supreme Court.[28]

Organized anti-Semitism, as it is known today, did not appear in the United States on any large scale until toward the close of the nineteenth century, and was due largely to the wave of Jewish immigration that set in at that time. Up to then it had been mainly a matter of social ostracism, and of criticism of certain personal traits and economic tendencies that were considered by some groups to characterize most Jews. The so-called "Protocols of the Elders of Zion," which are now known to be spurious and to have been devised in the interest of anti-Semitism, did not appear in this country until after the first decade of the twentieth century. The whole movement seems to have been associated with the wave of reaction which followed World War I.[29]

The publication in *The Dearborn Independent,* sponsored by Henry Ford (1863–1947), of the "Protocols" in 1920 gave them much publicity, and the prejudice and bitterness they stirred up were great. The antagonism of the *Independent* toward the Jew was fanned by the revived Ku Klux Klan. It was founded largely on the alleged plan for Jewish domination of the world incorporated in three documents—"The Protocol of the Elders of Zion," "The Protocol of the Meetings of the Zionish Men of Wisdom," and "The Protocol of the Wise Men of Zion." These—as *The Times* of London proved[30]—emanated from anti-Semitic sources in Russia and were secretly circulated during World War I, reappearing in several countries after its close. They formed the basis of the seven-year attack against the Jewish people in Ford's widely circulated paper and in many other publications. The American Committee on the Rights of Religious Minorities was alarmed at the resulting situation, and on December 24, 1920, this representative group of Protestant, Catholic, and Jewish patriots issued a manifesto, which was, according to Dr. Everett Ross Clinchy (1896–), "the first united expression of opposition to religious and racial prejudice in the history of this country." The concluding words of the protest are worth quoting:

In this time of world unrest, when the minds of men are still torn by the passion of war, when suspicion, jealousy and fear deeply permeate the public thought, and when special and solemn responsibility rests upon the American people to help heal the world's wounds, we appeal to all people of good-will to condemn every effort to arouse decisive passions against any of our fellow countrymen; to aid in eradicating racial prejudice and religious fanaticism; and to create a just and humane public sentiment that shall recognize the Fatherhood of God and the brotherhood of man, and shall demand that no men shall be denied the inalienable rights of freedom of conscience and worship because they belong to another race or profess a different faith.[31]

The anti-Semitic movement was somewhat interrupted by Henry Ford's belated but manly retraction. In 1927—seven years after his paper had first given wide publicity to the protocols—he wrote a letter to Louis Marshall (1856–1929), president of the American Jewish Committee, and active in trying to secure justice for Jews and other religious groups. Mr. Ford said:

I confess that I am deeply mortified that this journal which is intended to be constructive and not destructive has been made the medium for resurrecting exploded fictions, for giving currency to the so-called "Protocols of the Wise Men of Zion" which have been demonstrated, as I learn, to be gross forgeries, and for contending that the Jews have been engaged in a conspiracy to control the capital and the industries of the world, besides laying at their door many offenses against decency, public order and good morals. . . .

I frankly confess that I have been greatly shocked as a result of my study and examination of the files of the *Dearborn Independent* and of the pamphlets entitled *The International Jew*. I deem it to be my duty as an honorable man to make amends for the wrong done to the Jews as fellow-men and brothers, by asking their forgiveness for the harm that I have unintentionally committed, by retracting so far as lies within my power the offensive charges laid at their door by these publications, and giving them the unqualified assurance that henceforth they may look to me for friendship and good will.[32]

The anti-Jewish movement subsided for a few years, only to be reawakened, about 1929, as a result of the depression and Nazi anti-Semitism.[33] It is noticeable that such outbreaks accompany almost every depression, because when people are unemployed they try as a defense mechanism to make some group the scapegoat and to prevent members of that group from securing employment. In this case the Jews suffered, not the Catholics. After more than a decade of this agitation, stimulated in very conservative centers by the exaggerated impression of the part played by Jews in determining some of the radical or liberal policies of the New Deal under President Franklin D. Roosevelt, there was grave danger that Nazi racial tendencies might become a serious menace in this country, fanning the flames of anti-Semitism. Many otherwise patriotic Americans who believed in crushing Hitler and his imperialistic policies apparently did not realize that any form of anti-Semitism or of extreme racialism was playing into his hands. Even since the close of the war the effect of Nazi anti-Jewish propaganda has continued its baneful influence.

Many groups in their legitimate opposition to Marxian Communism have fallen into the grievous error of trying to show that this has an inevitable connection with Jewish thought, and consequently developed the dangerous movement working under the misleading name of "The Christian Front." Father Charles Coughlin (1891–) has been closely related to this group, and it was a source of some surprise that he was allowed by his Church to continue so long his agitation. It was considered Fascist in tendency, and was opposed by most of the clergy on the ground that it tended to create bigotry and race hatred. The delay in clamping down on the Detroit "radio priest" may have been due to respect for freedom of speech in America, or to fear lest opposition might make a martyr of him. It is worth recording that a group of Catholic clergy and laymen opposed to Father Coughlin formed a "Committee of Catholics for Human Rights" and published a monthly, *The Voice*. This opposed such "Front" organizations as the "Christian Mobilizers," the "Silver Shirts of America," and other semimilitary groups which sought to identify Communism and the Jews and to fight against both with the weapons of bigotry. There is a similar fearless publication, *Christian Social Action,* in Father Coughlin's own diocese.[34] If the "radio priest" had confined himself to proclaiming constructively *Social Justice* (the name of his organ) as based on Christianity, his large following would have had much justification, but his denunciatory attitude toward his opponents, and his anti-Semitism and Fascist tendencies made him seem to many an agent of racial prejudice and reaction.[35] He has his counterparts in Protestantism. Perhaps the most notorious are a Baptist minister, formerly closely allied with the political machine of the late Huey Long, and more recently identified with various other movements of a Fascist tendency, the Reverend Gerald L. K. Smith of Detroit; and a militant leader of Nativistic views, the Reverend Gerald B. Winrod. The latter was defeated in an important election in Kansas in 1938 with the active help of the Friends of Democracy, an organization led by a respected Unitarian minister, the Reverend Leon M. Birkhead.[36]

The Roman Catholic and Protestant Churches in this country, as shown by the official utterances of their responsible agencies and spokesmen, are entirely opposed to anti-Semitism, condemning it both on patriotic and Christian grounds. This would seem to be a logical and inevitable result of the teachings of Christ and the Church, and of the historic origin of Christianity within Judaism. Unfortunately, however, selfishness, prejudice, and an ignorance of history and of anthropology have often in Europe, and occasionally in America, resulted in anti-Semitism, but in this country it has never had the encouragement or support of any representative religious group.

The Catholic Church had some very serious lapses into anti-Semitism in the Middle Ages and at the time of the Inquisition, such as the action of the Fourth Lateran Council (1215) imposing the wearing of a distinctive badge by Jews and excluding them from public office, and the action of Pope Paul IV (1476–1559) constraining the Jews of Rome in various ways, including the requirement that they live in a ghetto; but these are exceptions, as the article in the *Jewish Encyclopedia* on "Popes" shows. From the time of Gregory the Great's letter in 598 against the persecution of the Jews, permitting them to observe their worship and festivals; through the issuing of the bull *Sicut Judaeis* by Calixtus II about 1120, extending to the Jews "the shield of our protection";[37] and to the various effective utterances on the subject by Pius XI (1857–1939), who in a talk to Belgian pilgrims in 1938 said "Anti-semitism is inadmissible. We are spiritually semites,"[38] the record of the Roman Catholic Church in the United States has been on the whole in advance of public opinion. No Church is doing more, through the preparation and distribution of literature and in other ways, to condemn anti-Semitism as dangerous to the State, inconsistent with the principles of our government, and utterly opposed to the teachings and spirit of Christianity.

The Protestant Churches, both as shown by the Federal Council and by the strong resolutions of individual denominations, are outspoken in their condemnation of anti-Semitism in every form. Furthermore, the National Conference of Jews and Christians, the Committee on Religious Life in the Nation's Capital, and other organizations which combine Protestants, Roman Catholics, and Jews, as well as the serious study of interracial problems at many universities and special institutes, are working effectively to combat the cruel wave of anti-Semitism stimulated in Germany under the Third Reich.

The Federal Council has recently issued a circular entitled *Anti-Semitism—unAmerican and unChristian,* which gives the action of the Executive Committee on September 19, 1941.

On the occasion of the 5702nd new year in the Jewish calendar, a year which opens as one of painful suffering for the Jewish people, the Executive Committee of the Federal Council of the Churches of Christ in America desires to make a public statement of its attitude toward anti-Semitism. On many previous occasions we have expressed our abhorrence of the religious and racial intolerance which afflicts our world today. We have especially emphasized our opposition to unjust and unchristian attacks upon the Jews. In so doing we have been wholeheartedly supported by similar utterances officially made by the highest governing bodies of the great denominations which cooperate in the Federal Council of Churches.

Recent evidences of anti-Jewish prejudice in our own country compel us to speak again a word of solemn warning to the nation. Divisiveness on religious or racial grounds is a portentous menace to American democracy. If one group be made the target of attack today, the same spirit of intolerance may be visited on another group tomorrow and the rights and liberties of every group thus be put in jeopardy.

We condemn anti-Semitism as unamerican. Our nation is a free fellowship of many racial and cultural stocks. It is our historic glory that they have been able to live together in mutual respect, each rejoicing in the rich contribution which the others have made to the common good. Anti-Semitism is an insidious evil which, if allowed to develop, would poison the springs of our national life.

Even more strongly we condemn anti-Semitism as unchristian. As Christians we gratefully acknowledge our ethical and spiritual indebtedness to the people of Israel. No true Christian can be anti-Semitic in thought, word or deed without being untrue to his own Christian inheritance.

In behalf of the Christian churches which comprise the Federal Council we voice our renewed determination to unite in combatting every tendency to anti-Semitism in our country. We recognize that a special responsibility rests upon us, who belong to the numerically strongest group, to be staunch advocates of the rights of minorities. We pledge our best efforts in their defense.[39]

This statement, which has its counterpart in scores of resolutions passed by different religious groups in this country, may be taken to represent the opinion of the American Churches. It is reflected in the observance by many Churches on May 2, 1943, of a Day of Compassion for the Suffering Jews of Europe, an action commended by proclamation by many state governors.[40]

The effect of extreme Zionist views held by some Americans on anti-Semitism in this country is considered below when we come to consider political Zionism as an American issue.[41]

Section 4. ANTI-ROMAN CATHOLICISM

During the Civil War period slavery was the supreme issue in the Protestant Churches, hence anti-Catholic agitation was in abeyance. In the years immediately after Appomattox, the nation, and especially the rural South—the section of the country which is the most militantly Protestant—was absorbed in the problem of reconstruction. The Ku Klux Klan, originally founded in 1866, was concerned primarily with assuring white supremacy in the South and in counteracting the effect of "carpetbag" governors from the North and their

Negro legislative assistants. It was not until the most violent years of political reconstruction after the war were over that the anti-Catholic movement, developed earlier by the "Nativist" agitation and "Know-Nothingism,"[42] again came to the front. The fears behind this recurring movement were just then given an objective basis in the minds of many people by two authoritative pronouncements of great importance—the *Syllabus of Errors* of Pope Pius IX in 1864, and the Vatican Decree of 1870. We can hardly appreciate the questioning attitude of some thoughtful non-Catholic Americans toward the compatibility of Roman Catholic theory and democracy without understanding these two landmarks in Church history.

(1) THE EFFECT OF EXTREME CHURCH STATEMENTS

(a) *The Syllabus of Errors.*—Pius IX was obliged during his papacy (1848–71) to meet the first onslaught of modern liberalism, and did so in a way which has been ever since embarrassing to many Christian supporters of democratic government, including some of the more liberal American Roman Catholics. His statement of his views of Church-State relations is given in the well-known *Syllabus* of 1864, officially called the "Syllabus of the principal errors of our time, which are censured in the consistorial Allocutions, Encyclicals and other Apostolical Letters of our Most Holy Lord, Pope Pius IX."

A major purpose of the *Syllabus* is one with which most thoughtful people would agree—to point out the dangers of growing secularism and of failure to emphasize the importance of the Church in matters spiritual. But its presentation, being mainly in a negative form emphasizing the dangers of certain errors, rather than the importance of certain truths, justifies some adverse criticism. This is especially true of those sections which dealt with democracy and liberalism.

Here are some of the more significant "errors," each followed by reference to the papal utterance in which it is considered in detail, and condemned:

15. Every man is free to embrace and profess that religion which, guided by the light of reason, he shall consider true.—Allocution *"Maxima quidem,"* June 9, 1862; *Damnatio "Multiplices inter,"* June 10, 1851.

24. The Church has not the power of using force, nor has she any temporal power, direct or indirect.—Apostolic Letter *"Ad Apostolicae,"* Aug. 22, 1851.

27. The sacred ministers of the Church and the Roman pontiff are to be absolutely excluded from every charge and dominion over temporal affairs.—Allocution *"Maxima quidem,"* June 9, 1862.

42. In the case of conflicting laws enacted by the two powers, the civil law prevails.—Apostolic Letter *"Ad Apostolicae,"* Aug. 22, 1851.

45. The entire government of public schools in which the youth of a Christian state

is educated, except (to a certain extent) in the case of episcopal seminaries, may and ought to appertain to the civil power, and belong to it so far that no other authority whatsoever shall be recognized as having any right to interfere in the discipline of the schools, the arrangement of the studies, the conferring of degrees, in the choice or approval of the teachers.—Allocutions *"Quibus luctuosissimis,"* Sept. 5, 1851, and *"In consistoriali,"* Nov. 1, 1850.

47. The best theory of civil society requires that popular schools open to children of every class of the people, and, generally, all public institutes intended for instruction in letters and philosophical sciences and for carrying on the education of youth, should be freed from all ecclesiastical authority, control and interference, and should be fully subjected to the civil and political power at the pleasure of the rulers, and according to the standard of the prevalent opinions of the age.—*Epistle to the Archbishop of Freiburg, "Cum non sine,"* July 14, 1864.

48. Catholics may approve of the system of educating youth, unconnected with Catholic faith and the power of the Church, and which regards the knowledge of merely natural things, and only, or at least primarily, the ends of earthly social life.—*Ibid.*

67. By the law of nature, the marriage tie is not indissoluble, and in many cases divorce properly so called may be decreed by the civil authority.—Apostolic Letter *"Ad Apostolicae"*; Allocution *"Acerbissimum,"* Sept. 27, 1852.

80. The Roman Pontiff can, and ought to, reconcile himself, and come to terms with progress, liberalism and modern civilization.—Allocution *"Iamdudum cernimus,"* March 18, 1861.[43]

Views which may sound to some equally reactionary, or at least ultraconservative, in the scientific, ecclesiastical, and social fields were held at the same time by some Protestant divines, and may be partly attributed to the *Zeitgeist* and the natural conservatism of the Churches, and as such they would call for no special comment. But here we are considering formal, official pronouncements of the head of a Church which claims authority in the field of morals and religion over all its members, including citizens of the United States. As such the *Syllabus* has significance which merely out of respect for the Church itself we cannot overlook.

The theory accepted by most Roman Catholic liberals to provide a way out of the difficulties created by the sweeping denunciations of the *Syllabus* is to make a clear distinction between a thesis and a hypothesis. This was advocated with special force shortly after the appearance of the *Syllabus,* by Bishop Félix Dupanloup (1802–78) of Orleans. He held that the condemned liberties as *theses,* that is, as principles of universal application to human nature and to the divine plan, are rightly condemned, but as *hypotheses,* that is, arrangements "suitable to special conditions in this or that nation," they may well be legitimate.[44] It has seemed to many that this explanation, which had large support in the hierarchy, disregards the usual understanding that particulars should be included in universals. At any rate, whatever may be the explanation, the *Syllabus,* as the *Catholic Encyclopedia* states, is "a decision given by the Pope speaking as universal teacher and judge to Catholics the world over. All Catholics, therefore, are bound to accept the Syllabus."[45] The result was that many Protestants in the United States became fearful lest the Church of Rome might become antagonistic to certain cherished American traditions and institutions having to do with such matters as religious freedom, public school education, separation of Church and State, provision for divorce (at least in extreme cases), democracy, etc.

(b) *The Vatican Decree.*—The latent anti-Roman Catholic feeling in the country was given additional stimulus by the Vatican Decree of Papal Infallibility of 1870. Many thoughtful people who had no sympathy with the Know-Nothing and Ku Klux groups were alarmed at the concentration in the hands of the pope of so much power over members of the Church the world over. They feared that his declared supremacy in his ex cathedra utterances in the fields of "morals" as well as religion might result in friction between the American democracy and the papacy. "The Roman Pontiff cannot err in defining matters of faith and morals" was the passage from the decree which caused so many misgivings in its possible application to pronouncements bearing on American social legislation. The view of the group opposing this statement is well represented by one of the most honored and distinguished of Roman Catholic publicists of the last century. Shortly before the adoption of the constitution *Pastor Aeternus,* and foreseeing the probable result, Lord Acton (1834–1902) wrote:

> It makes civil legislation on all points of contract, marriage, education, clerical immunities, mortmain, even on many questions of taxation and Common Law subject to the legislation of the Church, which would be simply the arbitrary will of the Pope.[46]

This was the attitude of many leading Roman Catholic divines at the time. Indeed, there is high Catholic authority for the statement that about one-fifth of the delegates to the Vatican Council were opposed to the definition. Though most of these doubtless believed the dogma to be true, they must have realized that its formal adoption would cause serious embarrassment. The original opponents included most of the German and Austro-Hungarian members, half of the Americans, and a third of the French.[47] Among the prominent original supporters of the proposed decree were Archbishop Martin Spalding (1810–72) of Baltimore, and Bishop (afterward Archbishop) John Joseph Williams (1822–1907) of Boston. Among the original opponents were Archbishops Peter Kenrick (1806–96) of St. Louis and John Purcell (1800–83) of Cincinnati.[48] But only two members of the council, Bishop Aloisio Riccio of Cajazzo, Italy, and Bishop Edward Fitzgerald (1833–1907) of Little Rock, Arkansas, actually voted non-placet, with 435 voting placet. Of the 601 bishops attending the Vatican Council, over one hundred and fifty absented themselves before the final vote—a clear evidence that there was no enthusiasm in certain sections of the Church for the adoption of the decree.[49] "But the infallible Church in an infallible Council had defined the infallibility of a visible head."[50] This was a doctrine which created genuine alarm, as it was feared by some that issues might arise under it creating serious difficulties between Church and State in the United States and elsewhere. It is well known that at the close of the Franco-German War the German Government made the new dogma the excuse for the *Kulturkampf,* but no serious issue involving the American State has arisen or is likely to arise under the decree, although it creates some problems, at least in the field of Constitutional theory. It is open to question whether, had the issue arisen during the more liberal papacy of Leo XIII (1810–1903), the decree would have been adopted at all, or in its present form.

Almost as significant from the standpoint of possible Church-State friction was the constitution adopted by the same council on the Church of Christ, or, as it is often called, on the Pope of Rome.

> When, therefore, anyone says that the Pope of Rome has only the office of supervision or of guidance, and not the complete and highest power of jurisdiction over the entire Church not merely in matters of faith and morals, but also in matters which concern the discipline and administration of the Church throughout the entire world, or that the pope has only the chief share, but not the entire fullness of this highest power, or that this his power is not actual and immediate either over all and individual Churches, or over all and individual clergy and faithful let him be anathema.[51]

As long as this constitution stands the Roman Catholic Church in the United States cannot be a strictly self-governing body. It must yield final authority to the pope. This fact is mentioned not as criticism, because it has advantages in the interest of a universal Church, but merely that we may have a realistic view of the situation as it may affect Church-State complications.

The Vatican Decree and other factors resulted in a growing anti-Catholic spirit during the 'seventies. One glimpse of an event in Congress in 1883 reveals a situation that was alarming as showing that Roman Catholics were still considered somewhat suspect and a group apart. It was in the testimony before a Senate committee on October 15, 1883, by Father William McDonald, long a respected priest at Manchester, New Hampshire. He said that though there were many skilled Catholics in the factories there, he had never known one to be appointed foreman. Senator Henry W. Blair (1834–1920) of New Hampshire, chairman of the committee, interposed remarks which throw much light upon conditions at the time:

I have taken some pains during this investigation [he said] to become acquainted with Catholic priests—something that I had not done before—and I think that priests are not, many of them, inclined to assert the political influence they once did. . . . I should be glad to see the time when Catholics will be considered in the same light as the rest of the population. I think the more people mingle together, the more they will think alike. I do not belong to any church or denomination, although my early affiliations were Congregational, and I attend the Methodist church now. My affiliations are principally Protestant, but it is not a bad thing to associate a little with people of all opinions. . . .[52]

Unfortunately there is still a good deal of social separation in many communities between Protestants and Catholics, due to fault on both sides. Protestants sometimes seem to think that they are the only real Americans; and in some communities Roman Catholics, with their many religious, philanthropic, and social organizations, tend to be a more or less separate group.

(2) THE CLEVELAND CAMPAIGN (1884)

Religion has directly and indirectly played a considerable part in American political campaigns. Anti-Catholic parties, stimulated by the Quebec Act,[53] showed their heads as early as 1776, and scarcely a decade since has been without them. The most prominent of these in the middle of the last century, which resulted in the "Nativistic" and "Know-Nothing" campaigns, have been dealt with in an earlier section.[54] Here we are to consider the first incident after the Civil War period where the religious issue was definitely and prominently raised in national politics, namely, the Cleveland-Blaine campaign for the presidency in 1884. (The Hoover-Smith campaign of 1928, which brought the same issue to the fore, will be considered later.[55])

Few histories deal frankly with the issue involving the churches and their standards developed toward the close of the campaign of 1884. In this campaign the Republicans had as their candidate the brilliant "plumed knight," James G. Blaine (1830–93) of Maine, whose standards as a member and speaker of the House of Representatives in matters of public ethics had been considered at least questionable. He was specially criticized for his connection with the *Crédit Mobilier* scandals and for undue political influence in connection with Western railroad financing.

The Democrats nominated Grover Cleveland (1837–1908), whose record for courage, integrity, and intelligence as mayor of Buffalo and governor of New York had been admirable. As governor he had often antagonized the politicians of Tammany Hall, and was consequently opposed by large groups of influential Irish Catholics. Cleveland's statement that "public office is a public trust," the fact that his political record squared with this utterance, and the mistakes of his opponents, won him one of the closest and most bitterly fought of American elections.

The infusion of the religious issue was due to a variety of causes connected with desperate attempts to win votes. An effort was made to draw away Irish Catholics from their traditional support of the Democratic party, on the ground that Cleveland, who was the son of a Presbyterian minister, was "a Presbyterian bigot," while Blaine's mother was a Roman Catholic. Even so influential a journal as the *Irish World* ardently supported the Republican ticket. A "whispering campaign" was resorted to on both sides, and little by little certain alleged facts became matters of public record. In particular a Baptist minister of Buffalo was responsible for a story published in the *Buffalo Evening Telegraph* that Cleveland was the father of a seven-year-old illegitimate child and that he had been guilty of the "grossest licentiousness." A group of fair-minded Republican fellow citizens investigated the facts, admitted the former liaison, but denied the alleged abduction and seduction, as well as the charges of drunkenness and libertinism. The Buffalo Association of Ministers divided on the question of whether the facts as proved unfitted him for the presidency. The statement of one respected Protestant minister of New York expressed what was perhaps the best public opinion of the time. Although regretting the unfortunate incident in his early career, he respected Cleveland for his fine public record, and "for showing no attempt to evade responsibility, and doing all he could to meet the duties involved, of which marriage was certainly not one."[56]

The *New York Tribune,* with its strong Republican tradition, naturally supported Blaine, and was confident that the voters were not "so degraded" as to "care nothing for home, nothing for the attractiveness of domestic life, nothing for the offenses which the religious press so strongly censures."[57]

So influential a Protestant journal as the *Independent,* which did not like Blaine's public record, referred to the "sickening disclosures," and withdrew its advocacy of Cleveland. The religious press in general condemned him, and the "moral issue" was carried into the pulpit. Some religious leaders of high repute, such as Felix Adler (1851–1933) and Washington Gladden (1836–1918), felt unable to vote for either candidate.

At the eleventh hour in the campaign, when it looked altogether probable that Blaine would carry the pivotal state of New York, the Reverend Samuel D. Burchard (1812–91), a Presbyterian minister who advocated his election at a great Blaine rally at the Fifth Avenue Hotel, New York, on October 29, referred to his opponents as the party of "rum, Romanism and rebellion!" This unfair summary, with just enough truth in it to make it sting, was naturally and rightly bitterly resented by the Democrats, especially as it was not disowned by Blaine. It proved a boomerang. Cleveland carried New York, but only by a plurality of 1,047 votes in a total of more than a million. Blaine himself felt that the Reverend Dr. Burchard's unfortunate remark lost him enough Roman Catholic votes to turn the scales against him. Thus the religious issue brought into the campaign brought failure, and the voters of the country, most of whom were members of Christian churches, showed that they considered that a long career of honorable, devoted, and effective public service outweighed an earlier lapse in private morality for which all possible amends had been made.

(3) THE AMERICAN PROTECTIVE ASSOCIATION AND RELATED MOVEMENTS (1887–1914)

This association, commonly known as the A.P.A., was founded in Iowa in 1887. Of its seven initiators one was a Methodist, one a Baptist, one a Presbyterian, one a Congregationalist, one a Lutheran, and two of no professed sect. Two were Republicans, two Democrats, one a Populist, and one a Prohibitionist. The central idea that brought them together was opposition to Catholicism, and among the association's definite aims were the curbing of immigration, and the preservation of the public schools from what was considered the Catholic purpose to thwart their activity.[58]

The association received a great stimulus as a result of the panic of 1893, when the scarcity of jobs brought about a campaign in favor of the native American, and in opposition to the immigrant, especially the Roman Catholic. As usual, the association flourished in the rural Protestant areas and was in part a movement antagonistic to the urban Roman Catholic population, which had been demanding a share in the public school funds. It had a strength of about a million votes, which went almost entirely to the Republican party because of fear of the church connections of the Democrats, who under Irish leadership had secured the almost solid Roman Catholic vote.

This movement, which has produced a considerable literature,[59] died down after the McKinley campaign of 1896, which split its forces, but there arose in the next decade another that was equally threatening. Indeed, the most violent wave of anti-Catholic feeling to spread over the United States after the Know-Nothingism of the middle of the last century began in 1908. In that year the centenary of the erection of the diocese of Baltimore into a metropolitan see was celebrated, and in the same year the first American Catholic missionary congress met in Chicago, the largest body of prelates, priests, and laymen ever brought together in the New World. This was followed by the appointment of two additional cardinals for America. These and other events caused alarm in some Protestant circles. Inflamed by *Tom Watson's Magazine* and other journals, and especially by a most unfair and bitter sheet, *The Menace,* various organizations were established to combat what was considered to be the danger to American institutions from a large group of people holding allegiance to the pope. It was launched, according to its own statement,

> in the belief that the Roman Catholic Political Machine, in its political intrigues and its interference with established American institutions, is the deadliest enemy to our civilization and liberties.[61]

It is said that by the close of 1914 the circulation of *The Menace* exceeded 1,400,000.[60] Efforts were made to have the publication denied the use of the mails. The postmaster general took the ground that he was not empowered to exclude publications of the *Menace* type and referred the matter to the Department of Justice for the prosecution of past offenders, under Section 211, Penal Code. This prohibits the circulation through the mail of obscene, filthy, or indecent publications. In 1915 four officers of the *Menace* company were indicted for depositing "obscene, lewd, lascivious, filthy and indecent matter in the mail." The trial before a Federal court resulted in acquittal for the staff.[62]

As a result of the agitation, the Knights of Columbus, in 1914, appointed a Commission on Religious Prejudices which did a dignified and important work. It showed that in this very year anti-Catholic legislation had been attempted in more than forty state legislatures. All this agitation led to the re-establishment, in 1915 near Atlanta, of the "invisible empire" of the Ku Klux Klan. Among its many activities intended to inflame the public against the Roman Catholic Church was the publication of an alleged Knights of Columbus oath pledging members to many extremes against the American government and Protestants so as to secure papal supremacy in this country. The fraudulence of the charge has been often exposed, but it seems best to publish here the real oath, so as to show how the Knights have endeavored to assure that their organization shall serve both Church and country. It reads:

> I swear to support the Constitution of the United States. I pledge myself, as a Catholic citizen and Knight of Columbus, to enlighten myself fully upon my duties as a citizen and to conscientiously perform such duties entirely in the interest of my country and regardless of personal consequences. I pledge myself to do all in my power to preserve the integrity and purity of the ballot, and to promote reverence and respect for law and order. I promise to practise my religion openly and consistently, but without ostentation, and to so conduct myself in public affairs, and in the exercise of public virtue as to reflect nothing but credit upon our Holy Church, to the end that she may flourish and our country prosper to the greater honor and glory of God.[63]

The pledge to support the Constitution is important from the standpoint of these volumes, because it helped to dispel some entirely unjustified rumors.

During World War I anti-Catholic feeling was in abeyance, but shortly after its close there was another bad flare-up which will be discussed in a later section.[64] The problem is still with us; but developments as these volumes are being prepared for the press seem to look toward an alleviation of the situation, at least in the matter of public support for parochial schools—recently the most insistent issue (XIX, especially 10).

(4) THE STORER INCIDENT (1906) AND OTHER EFFORTS TO SECURE AN AMERICAN CARDINAL

The Storer incident is particularly illuminating. Bellamy Storer (1847–1922) was in turn minister or ambassador of the United States to Belgium, Spain, and Austria-Hungary (1902–06)—all strongly Catholic countries. He and his wife were devout Catholics, who desired, among other things, to have the American government prevent the sending of Protestant missionaries to the Philippines, and more especially to secure the advancement of Archbishop Ireland (1838–1918)—a universally respected prelate[65]—to be a cardinal. Mr. Storer apparently misinterpreted the devotion of Governor Theodore Roosevelt to the archbishop, and his assurance that he would personally be pleased to see the latter given the cardinal's hat, as a formal authorization to the ambassador to request the appointment. This and other indiscretions of Mr. Storer and his wife in trying to advance the interests of the Church through political means led to his resignation from the diplomatic service at the request of the president.

The story goes back to the time when Theodore Roosevelt was governor of New York. In March, 1899, Mr. Storer had suggested that his friend, Archbishop Ireland, was a Catholic whose views were those of the Republican administration, and that if he could be made a cardinal it would have an excellent effect, especially in the Philippines, where the problem of the friars[66] was acute. He therefore suggested that the governor write to President McKinley (1843–1901) on the subject. "I wrote to the President," Roosevelt replied, ". . . I absolutely agree with you as to Archbishop Ireland."[67]

Later in the same month, replying to a request for information from Mrs. Storer, Roosevelt wrote:

> I have written to the President stating my belief that it would be a most fortunate thing for this country . . . if Archbishop Ireland could be made a Cardinal. . . . While I would not like to have this letter published, you are welcome to show it to anyone you see fit.[68]

He added, in writing to Mrs. Storer on April 27 of the same year, "I am only too delighted that my letter was of the slightest use."[69]

The president's secretary (the Honorable George B. Cortelyou, 1862–1940), recalling the incident, wrote,

> . . . I have repeatedly heard President McKinley state that in all such matters he could not divorce himself from his position as President, and that he would not under any circumstances interfere with or attempt to influence the action of any religious organization here or abroad looking to the preferment of any of its members.[70]

President McKinley realized full well that in his position any attempt to influence the Vatican in an American ecclesiastical appointment would be inconsistent with the separation of Church and State in the United States, and would be charged with political dynamite. Mr. Roosevelt was less discreet. There was also a difference between being governor, without any direct responsibility in foreign affairs, and being president.

But Mr. Roosevelt, constantly goaded on by his persistent, forceful, and indiscreet friend, Mrs. Storer, wrote again to President McKinley the same year in behalf of the archbishop; but the result was the same. "I guess your position is the correct one," Roosevelt admitted. He added, "I felt grave doubts about writing to you at all."[71] The following year, 1900, when again approached by his friend, Roosevelt said that there was nothing more that he could do. But this did not end the appeals. In November, he was obliged to write Mrs. Storer: "I am very, very fond of you, and that is the reason your letters put me in a quandary. You want me to do all kinds of things that I cannot possibly do."[72]

When he succeeded to the presidency after President McKinley's assassination, he became, according to his biographer, "apprehensive regarding letters he had exchanged with 'Dear Maria'." So he wrote to Storer, "Ask Maria if there is any letter of mine to her . . . in the hands of anyone else?" Rumors were current that Cardinal Rampolla at the Vatican had a copy.

> I care very little [the President wrote] as far as I am personally concerned, for what I write I stand by, but it is obviously not wise on general principles that any letter of mine should be in the hands of anyone to whom it was not addressed, at this time.[73]

This letter was dated January 16, 1902, when Mr. Storer was American Minister to Spain, a post which he was to leave later the same year for the more influential ambassadorship to Austria-Hungary. But the ambassador was still trying to accomplish his purpose and thought he had secured the president's blessing. In a pamphlet which Storer wrote a few years later is this striking statement:

> . . . The President said to me that if I went to Rome he would like to have me see the Pope and say to him in person that the Archbishop was his friend, and that he

would be pleased to hear that he had received the honor of promotion to the cardinalate.[74]

Therefore Storer called on the pope and delivered what he believed to be the president's suggestion. The fact of the interview reached the press, and Mr. Roosevelt wrote his ambassador to be more careful in the future. Two of the president's letters should be quoted. The first was dated May 18, 1902:

As you know, I always treat Catholic and Protestant exactly alike, as I do Jew and Gentile, as I do the man of native American, German, Irish or any other kind of parentage. Any discrimination for or against a man because of his creed or nativity strikes me as an infamy. . . .[75]

Later the president stated:

. . . While I am President and you are ambassador neither of us in his public relation(s) is to act as Catholic or Protestant, Jew or Gentile, and we have to be careful not merely to do what is right, but so to carry ourselves as to show that we are doing what is right. I shall ask you not to quote me to any person in any shape or way in connection with any affair of the Catholic Church and yourself not to take action of any kind which will give ground for the belief that you as an American ambassador are striving to interfere in the affairs of the Church.[76]

Nevertheless it is not altogether clear that President Roosevelt acted with suitable restraint in such a delicate matter. He is known to have been disappointed when the archbishop's name was not presented to the consistory December 5, 1905, and showed his feeling that Mrs. Storer's indiscreet actions were partly responsible. According to her statement, Mr. Roosevelt

told me to write him a letter denying that he had ever, personally or officially, asked any favour of the Vatican. He *ordered me* to return him every letter he had written on the subject, and he wound up by declaring that if I did not comply with his demands, he would recall my *husband!*

The president felt that his name had been improperly used in the case

In March, 1906, Mr. Storer was asked to resign his ambassadorship. Thus ended this highly entertaining and illuminating incident in American Church-State relations. It should serve as a lesson not only to future presidents and diplomats, but to all American public men—and women!

The Storer incident in connection with Archbishop Ireland revived interest in the earlier alleged pressure from America to secure the cardinalate for Archbishop Hughes (1797–1864). The facts are somewhat obscure, but it appears from well-informed Catholic sources that there is nothing on record to confirm the report that representatives of the United States government, either at home or abroad, acted indiscreetly by making efforts to have Hughes made a cardinal either in 1851 or 1862. It is hard to differentiate in this case between fact and rumor. The Seventh Council of Baltimore, held in 1849, recommended that three new American archbishoprics be established—in New Orleans, Cincinnati, and New York. In October, 1850, Bishop John Hughes (1797–1864) of New York duly received the papal brief announcing his advancement to be Archbishop of New York. He soon sailed for Europe to be invested with the pallium by the pope. His biographer thus refers to the movement—which had popular if not political support—to secure for him the cardinal's hat:

The archbishop had not been long in Rome before it was reported, on what seemed to be good authority, that he was about to be advanced to the rank of cardinal. The matter was certainly discussed unofficially among the dignitaries of the papal court. It originated, however, not at Rome, but at Washington. It had not escaped the notice of the American government that Pius IX was disposed to make the college of cardinals more catholic than it had lately been, and it was thought by some of the cabinet that certain personal and political interests might be subserved by having an American prelate presented for this dignity. The United States minister at Rome actively promoted the scheme, though perhaps not strictly in his official character. It was generally understood that if it should be carried into effect, Archbishop Hughes would be the nominee most acceptable to all parties. So certain seemed his appointment that the Leopoldine society of Vienna actually offered to present him with a suitable outfit. Another prelate, who was in Rome at this time, introduced the subject during an audience with the Holy Father.

"I will tell you," said the Pope, smiling, "what there is of that. It is true that your government did ask me for *a* cardinal—*non pas celui la, mais un cardinal*" (emphasizing the indefinite article); "and I told them, which was true, that there was no place of cardinal priest vacant."

In the meantime the archbishop of Baltimore had written to Rome to say that in his judgment it was inexpedient to create an American cardinal, and it is understood that other bishops of the United States, as well as the Pope himself, were of the same opinion.[78]

The second occasion when the archbishop's name was associated in the public mind with American political pressure to secure for him the cardinalate was in 1862. He went abroad late the previous year with Thurlow Weed (1797–1882) at the request of the American government, to counteract the effect of the Confederate commissioners Mason and Slidell, who had run the American blockade, and to attempt to create a friendly opinion toward the Union cause. Hughes had been a long-time friend of the American secretary of state, William H. Seward (1801–72), with whom he had come in close contact when the latter was governor of New York. Bishop Hughes went to Washington at the secretary's request on October 21, 1861, when the plan was outlined to him, and the result was his informal embassy with Mr. Weed and the Episcopal Bishop Charles Pettit McIlvaine (1799–1873) of Ohio.[79] The results of the visit were gratifying to the administration, but there is no documentary evidence to support the claim of the archbishop's biographer that

An official intimation was conveyed to the Holy See that the President, unable to offer Dr. Hughes a reward that he could accept, would feel particular gratification in any honors which the Pope might have it in his power to confer upon him. It would appear . . . that his Holiness did contemplate advancing him in dignity. Indeed, I believe that he was much nearer the cardinal's hat in 1862 than in 1851.[80]

It is believed that when the new and authoritative life of Archbishop Hughes by Monsignor Guilday is published, it will dispose once and for all of the report so widely circulated and believed that President Lincoln and his Secretary of State tried to interest the Vatican in making Hughes a cardinal.[81]

It is to be hoped that these experiences, and especially that of Ambassador Storer, with some encouragement from President Theodore Roosevelt, will show all future officers of our government the unwisdom of their using official position to try to influence the selection of high Church dignitaries.

(5) THE TAFT PRESIDENTIAL CAMPAIGN (1908)

A somewhat similar but less serious situation than that involving Ambassador Storer arose in the presidential campaign of 1908, when there was considerable opposition by certain Protestant groups to William Howard Taft (1857–1930) on the ground that he was a Unitarian; also, though to a less extent, because he was thought to have been over-friendly to the Roman Catholic Church in the Philippines, and in his negotiations at Rome with the Vatican. This matter is referred to in the Lodge–Roosevelt correspondence. For instance, on October 19, 1908, Senator Henry Cabot Lodge (1850–1924) wrote to President Roosevelt that it was reported that the Ohio situation "is quite dismal," especially because "The religious issue has been revived on Taft's Unitarianism." He added a comment which does him credit: "Good Heavens, are we to elect Presidents on a creed? The mere reviving of the issue is intolerable."[82]

Two days later President Roosevelt, referring to this letter, wrote further regarding the Ohio situation:

. . . The more narrow-minded evangelical Protestants, especially the country clergymen of the Methodist, Lutheran, Baptist, and even Presbyterian creeds are showing a tendency to bolt him; some on the ground that he has behaved too well to the Catholics, but most of them on the ground that he is a Unitarian. I have received hundreds of letters chiefly from clergymen protesting against him on this ground. . . .[83]

At about the same time President Roosevelt wrote to an inquirer:

I thank you for your letter of the 14th instant. If asked by Mr. Taft, I should most emphatically advise against his making any declaration as to his religious belief such as your friend suggests. If there is one thing for which we stand in this country, it is for complete religious freedom and for the right of every man to worship his Creator as his conscience dictates. It is an emphatic negation of this right to cross-examine a man on his religious views before being willing to support him for office. Is he a good man, and is he fit for the office? These are the only questions which there is a right to ask, and to both of these in Mr. Taft's case, the answer must be in the affirmative. In my own Cabinet there are at present Catholic, Protestant and Jew—the Protestants being of various denominations. I am incapable of discriminating between them, or of judging any one of them save as to the way in which he performs his public duty. The rule of conduct applicable to Catholic, Protestant and Jew as regards lesser offices is just as applicable as regards the Presidency.[84]

The attitude of the president on this matter appealed to most sensible people. Taft received 321 electoral votes to 162 for William Jennings Bryan. His biographer quotes Mr. Taft as writing to his brother in 1899: "I am a Unitarian. I believe in God. I do not believe in the Divinity of Christ, and there are many other of the postulates of the orthodox creed to which I cannot subscribe." Mr. Pringle believes that had his political opponents found this letter the phrase as to the divinity "would have been more than enough to send Bryan to the White House in 1908!"[85] Mr. Taft when a professor at Yale, after the close of his presidential term, regularly attended the Sunday services in the University Chapel, which has a Congregational background.

(6) THE REVIVED KU KLUX KLAN (1915); THE SMITH PRESIDENTIAL CAMPAIGN

The Ku Klux Klan started in 1866 with the idea of saving the white civilization of the South by overthrowing the "carpetbag" and Negro regime. Its nomenclature, white-hooded garb, night parades, and secret rites appealed to a large Protestant group of the South, especially in the rural regions. It was not originally anti-Catholic, and at least one prominent Hebrew, Judah P. Benjamin (1811–84), who had been a member of the cabinet of President Davis, supported it. It was always intensely Protestant, but it was not until its revival in 1921 in Atlanta, Georgia, that its Nordic racial propaganda included a strong anti-Jewish and anti-Catholic program. It owed its religious intolerance more to the American Protective Association than to Know-Nothingism.[86] The old Ku Klux name was revived in 1915, and the Klan began to become a national factor in 1920, when it engaged professional promoters. "Native, white, Protestant supremacy" became its watchword, the first and third of these descriptive terms applying primarily to opposition to Roman Catholics, and secondarily to

Jews. The Klan of the early 'twenties was "the first considerable, organized anti-Semitic agitation on the American soil."[87] The official questionnaire of the revived order showed the following questions asked of candidates:

> Were your parents born in the United States of America?
> Are you a Gentile or Jew?
> Do you believe in the principles of pure Americanism?
> Do you owe ANY KIND of allegiance to any foreign nation, government, institution, sect, people, ruler or person?[88]

We are here concerned primarily with its anti-Catholic activities. The fact that the pope was an Italian, and that some twenty thousand or more Roman Catholic priests in the United States owed spiritual allegiance to him, was made much of. When eighty-three thousand Klansmen and Klanswomen marched through the streets of Washington in 1925 every one of them was believed to be an American Protestant. The Klan propaganda laid great emphasis on the fact that the pope was a political autocrat and that the Roman Catholics were gaining in political power. The growth of the Knights of Columbus (founded in New Haven, Connecticut, in 1882) and of the Roman Catholic Church frightened them. They circularized a bogus oath attributed to the Knights; passed from mouth to mouth stories of rifles buried under Catholic churches and under halls of the Knights; and made tens of thousands of ignorant people believe that there was danger of the government being seized by the hierarchy. Even the Protestant Episcopal Cathedral on Mount St. Alban in Washington was commonly reputed in certain circles to be a disguised Roman Catholic institution from which the capital of the nation could be dominated by the military forces of the pope! Some of the Klan publications, such as *The Searchlight,* published outrageous slanders against Roman Catholics and the priesthood. On the whole, the officers of the Church responded with quiet dignity, but the movement laid the foundation for the bitter anti-Catholic feeling that developed in certain parts of the country.

The work of the Klan came to a head in the presidential campaign of 1928, but it was almost equally prominent in 1924 in opposing the candidacy of Governor Alfred E. Smith (1873–1944), a Roman Catholic, for the nomination at the Democratic convention in Madison Square Garden, New York. The Committee on Resolutions was almost evenly divided as to whether the Ku Klux Klan should be mentioned by name; the Ku Kluxers—supported by certain politicians in the interest of party harmony—finally secured its elimination. These groups supported William Gibbs McAdoo (1863–1941), who, though not a member of the Klan, had differed from his opponent, Governor Smith, in not wishing to have opposition to it referred to specifically, and so secured large Klan support. The division was so violent between the two groups that a compromise candidate, John W. Davis (1873–), was finally selected. In accepting the nomination he did not specifically name the Klan, but clearly referred to it in his statements denouncing intolerance, bigotry, and race prejudice; and on August 22 he said: "I am unalterably opposed to the evident purpose of the secret organization known as the Ku Klux Klan, as disclosed by its public acts."[89] Both Democrats and Republicans found it expedient that year to reaffirm the Constitutional guarantee of religious liberty, following the precedent of the Democratic platform of 1896.[90]

One of the worth-while features of an unfortunate contest was the exchange of letters in the *Atlantic Monthly,* in April and May, 1928, between Charles Clinton Marshall (1860–1938), a New York Episcopalian and lawyer of high standing, and Governor Alfred E. Smith (1873–1944), a respected Catholic. Mr. Marshall took the ground that there existed an irreconcilable opposition between the root principles of the Roman Catholic Church and the American democratic State. The *Atlantic* for May contained a reply entitled "Catholic and Patriot: Governor Smith Replies." In an introductory note the editor, Mr. Ellery Sedgwick (1872–), stated:

This is an historic incident, historic for the country and for the Church. Now for the first time in the republic's history, under a constitution which forever forbids religious tests as qualifications for office, a candidate for the Presidency has been subjected to public questioning as to how he can give undivided allegiance to his country when his church restricts the freedom of his choice; and the candidate has answered—answered not deviously and with indirection, but straightforwardly, bravely, with the clear ring of candor. . . .[91]

Mr. Marshall's view was afterward put in more definite form in a book entitled *The Roman Catholic Church in the Modern State,*[92] frequently quoted in later sections.

This exchange of letters and the literature it produced, especially Mr. Marshall's book and the replies of the Reverend Dr. John A. Ryan (1869–1945) and others, are important in the literature of American Church–State relations.

The great majority of editorials in the American press felt that Governor Smith had on the whole successfully replied to Mr. Marshall's challenge, and that there was no reason why a liberal-minded, conscientious, and public-spirited Roman Catholic layman like Governor Smith should not be a candidate for any office in the American government. Senator Joseph T. Robinson (1872–1937), the Democratic leader in the United States Senate, stated the matter well when he said in the Senate on January 18, 1928:

. . . I believe, Mr. President, that one who is a Catholic has just as much right to apply for the favor of his party associates as one who is a Methodist or a Baptist, and I believe that when you deny that right you deny a fundamental principle of this government.[93]

The issue of Roman Catholic eligibility for high office was brought again definitely to the front when in June, 1928, Governor Smith was chosen as the party's candidate for the presidency by the Democratic convention at Houston, Texas, by an overwhelming majority. The permanent chairman, Senator Robinson of Arkansas, in his speech before the convention, said:

Jefferson gloried in the Virginia statute of religious freedom. He rejoiced in the provision of the Constitution that declares no religious test shall ever be required as a qualification for any office of trust in the United States.[94]

This resulted in a demonstration in which delegates of forty-three states paraded around the convention hall cheering with enthusiasm. The five remaining states—all Southern and much under the influence of the Ku Klux Klan—declined to take part in the demonstration.[95] And so began the campaign, which as far as the prohibition issue was concerned, is dealt with elsewhere.[96]

The Southern Baptist Convention, representing nearly four million people, had by unanimous vote warned the Democratic party against Governor Smith on religious grounds.[97] On the other hand, the Unitarians, meeting shortly afterward, declared: "No candidate for public office within the gift of the American people should ever be regarded as disqualified for such by reason of his particular form of religious belief."[98]

No finer statement on this subject was perhaps ever made than that by the late Senator William E. Borah (1865–1940) in his speech before the Senate of the United States on Wednesday, April 24, 1929, in replying to a resolution of Sen. J. Thomas Heflin (1869–   ), well known at the time as a very vocal opponent of the Roman Catholic Church.[99] It is unfortunately too long for inclusion here. It was fair-minded, based on the Constitutional provision for religious freedom, and in every way patriotic; a good antidote for Heflin's repeated assertion that Smith's candidacy was "the crowning effort of the Roman Catholic hierarchy to gain control of the United States. . . ."[100]

And so the battle went on. Prohibition was the major issue for the Methodists and some other Protestant groups, but the alleged Roman Catholic "menace" was always in the background. The Anti-Saloon League was undoubtedly the dominant force against Smith, but it did not take up actively the religious issue. There were also other grounds of opposition to the former governor of New York based on his Tammany affiliations and other matters, but the religious issue played a considerable part, as can be clearly seen in the cartoons of the time, which have been brought together in a book already quoted—*The Shadow of the Pope*. On the whole, though Governor Smith, who was not elected, referred to the religious issue only two or three times in his campaign, the general effect on intelligent American voters was to impress them with the fact that the Roman Catholic Church as such was not being used as a national political weapon.

There have been instances where it has been so used in state and especially municipal elections, but Archbishop John T. McNicholas (1877–) of Cincinnati, referring to the presidential election in November, 1928, could state:

> I speak officially when I say that the Catholic Church in Cincinnati is interested in no political party nor in political candidates of any party. It experiences no disappointment because of the defeat of one party nor does it rejoice in the victory of the other. . . . As an American citizen I protest against the insinuation made that my Church because of a Catholic candidate or for any other reason whatever in any way attempted to control my political affiliations or to give me the slightest indication how I or any other Catholic citizen of this jurisdiction should vote.[101]

This straightforward utterance, coming from a responsible and respected source, confirmed the impression of thoughtful Americans that outside of a few communities the Catholic vote could not be "delivered."

Indeed, the evidence against what were then the two great divisions of the Methodist Church for political activity in the Smith campaign is probably stronger than that against the Roman Catholics. The *New York Times* stated editorially on November 3, 1928:

> . . . Catholics have exhibited such wonderful restraint under attacks upon their Church. They have kept silent even in the face of notorious misrepresentation and calumny. No priest or Catholic publication of any prominence has noticed the violent challenges of Senator Heflin, Bishop Cannon and others. Had the Catholic hierarchy in any way entered the lists against its political assailants, the country would have resounded with clamorous and bitter cries that would have sounded in all ears and filled thoughtful Americans with a sense of public disgrace. . . .[102]

In various surveys of the activities of the Klan from 1912 to 1928 the Protestant Churches whose ministers were most often found supporting the Klan or opposing the Roman Catholic Church were shown to be, in the order of their frequency, Methodist, Baptist, and Disciples. These represented about three-quarters of all Protestant ministers prominently identified with the movement. The next largest group was among Presbyterians in the South.[103]

The Klan undoubtedly enrolled among its more than four million members at its height in 1924–25 tens of thousands of well-intentioned Americans who thought that through this organization they could help protect America's civil institutions. They did not realize the grave danger of the intolerance they were encouraging. The Klan drew its appeal from inherited prejudices and hatreds,

Courtesy Georgetown University

1. ARCHBISHOP CARROLL, 1735-1815

Portrait by Gilbert Stuart of the most distinguished leader of the Roman Catholic Church in the new Republic. An ecclesiastic respected by Catholics and Protestants alike, and a powerful factor in laying firm foundations for his Church in this country. See IV, 8, (9); XII, 2.

Courtesy Kaufmann and Fabry, Chicago

2. THE WASHINGTON-MORRIS-SALOMON MONUMENT

Laredo Taft (1860-1936) designed this group presented by the Patriotic Foundation of Chicago, which raised the necessary $50,000 by popular subscription. It was unveiled December 15, 1941. It is important from the standpoint of this book as Haym Salomon (c. 1740-85) was not only the leading Jewish American of his time, but an earnest supporter of religious freedom. The quotation from Washington on the base is characteristic. See XIII, 3.

Courtesy New York Public Library

3. FEDERAL HALL, NEW YORK, 1789

A rare engraving by Amos Doolittle of "The Seat of Congress," printed in 1790, although depicted April 30, 1789, in connection with Washington's inauguration there. It is used as a frontispiece of Volume III of I. N. Phelps Stokes' *Iconography of Manhattan Island*. The building was built as a city hall from 1699 to 1704, but remodeled as Federal Hall by L'Enfant, 1788-89. Here the Bill of Rights was adopted. Washington is shown being inaugurated President. See VIII, 2, (1).

THE Committees of both Houses of Congress, appointed to take order for conducting the ceremonial of the formal reception, &c. of the President of the United States, on Thursday next, have agreed to the following order thereon, viz.

That General Webb, Colonel Smith, Lieutenant-Colonel Fish, Lieut. Col. Franks, Major L'Enfant, Major Bleecker, and Mr. John R. Livingston, be requested to serve as Assistants on the occasion.

That a chair be placed in the Senate-Chamber for the President of the United States. That a chair be placed in the Senate-Chamber for the Vice-President, to the right of the President's chair; and that the Senators take their seats on that side of the chamber on which the Vice-President's chair shall be placed. That a chair be placed in the Senate-Chamber for the Speaker of the House of Representatives, to the left of the President's chair—and that the Representatives take their seats on that side of the chamber on which the Speaker's chair shall be placed.

That seats be provided in the Senate-Chamber sufficient to accommodate the late President of Congress, the Governor of the Western territory, the five persons being the heads of the three great departments, the Minister Plenipotentiary of France, the Encargado de negocios of Spain, the Chaplains of Congress, the persons in the suite of the President; and also to accommodate the following Public Officers of the State, viz. The Governor, the Lieutenant-Governor, the Chancellor, the Chief Justice, and other Judges of the Supreme Court, and the Mayor of the city. That one of the Assistants wait on these gentlemen, and inform them that seats are provided for their accommodation, and also to signify to them that no precedence of seats is intended, and that no salutation is expected from them on their entrance into, or their departure from the Senate-Chamber.

That the members of both Houses assemble in their respective Chambers precisely at twelve o'clock, and that the Representatives preceded by the Speaker, and attended by their Clerk, and other Officers, proceed to the Senate-Chamber, there to be received by the Vice-President and Senators rising.

That the Committees attend the President from his residence to the Senate-Chamber, and that he be there received by the Vice-President, the Senators and Representatives rising, and be by the Vice-President conducted to his chair.

That after the President shall be seated in his Chair, and the Vice-President, Senators and Representatives shall be again seated, the Vice-President shall announce to the President, that the members of both Houses will attend him to be present at his taking the Oath of Office required by the Constitution. To the end that the Oath of Office may be administered to the President in the most public manner, and that the greatest number of the people of the United States, and without distinction, may be witnesses to the solemnity, that therefore the Oath be administered in the outer Gallery adjoining to the Senate Chamber.

That when the President shall proceed to the gallery to take the Oath, he be attended by the Vice-President, and be followed by the Chancellor of the State, and pass through the middle door, that the Senators pass through the door on the right, and the Representatives, preceded by the Speaker, pass through the door on the left, and such of the persons who shall have been admitted into the Senate-Chamber, and may be desirous to go into the gallery, are then also to pass through the door on the right. That when the President shall have taken the Oath, and returned into the Senate-Chamber, attended by the Vice-President, and shall be seated in his chair, that the Senators and the Representatives also return into the Senate-Chamber, and that the Vice-President and they resume their respective seats.

Both Houses having resolved to accompany the President after he shall have taken the Oath, to St. Paul's Chapel, to hear divine service, to be performed by the Chaplain of Congress, that the following order of procession be observed, viz. The door-keeper and messenger of the House of Representatives. The Clerk of the House. The Representatives. The Speaker. The President, with the Vice-President at his left hand. The Senators. The Secretary of the Senate. The door-keeper, and messenger of the Senate.

That a Pew be reserved for the President—Vice-President—Speaker of the House of Representatives, and the Committees; and that pews be also reserved sufficient for the reception of the Senators and Representatives.

That after divine service shall be performed, the President be received at the door of the Church, by the Committees, and by them attended in carriages to his residence

That it be intrusted to the Assistants to take proper precautions for keeping the avenues to the Hall open, and that for that purpose, they wait on his Excellency the Governor of this State, and in the name of the Committees request his aid, by an order or recommendation to the Civil Officers, or militia of the city, to attend and serve on the occasion, as he shall judge most proper.

April 29th, 1789.

Courtesy New York Public Library

4. DIVINE SERVICE AT WASHINGTON'S INAUGURATION

Official broadsheet, dated August 29, 1789, giving the arrangements made by the Committee of both Houses of Congress. Note particularly the ninth paragraph, beginning "Both Houses having resolved to accompany the President after he shall have taken the Oath, to St. Paul's Chapel [New York City], to hear divine service, to be performed by the Chaplain of Congress, . . ." See VI, 1.

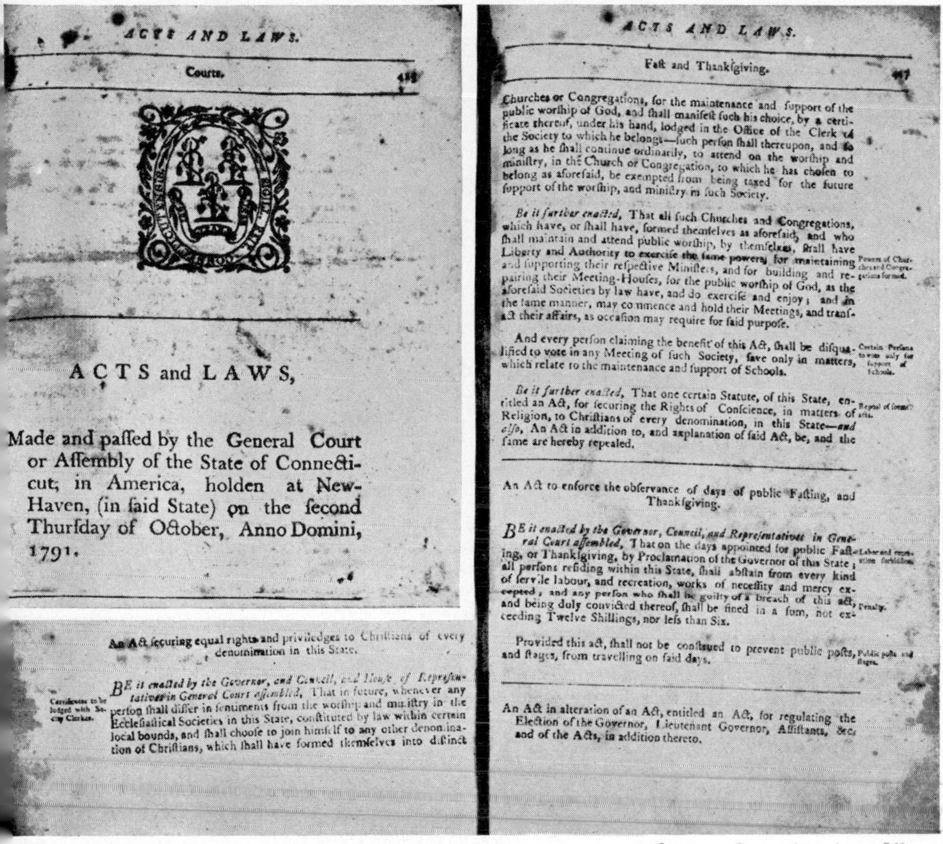

ACTS AND LAWS.

Courts. 418

ACTS and LAWS,

Made and paſſed by the General Court or Aſſembly of the State of Connecticut, in America, holden at New-Haven, (in ſaid State) on the ſecond Thurſday of October, Anno Domini, 1791.

An Act ſecuring equal rights and priviledges to Chriſtians of every denomination in this State.

BE it enacted by the Governor, and Council, and Houſe of Repreſentatives in General Court aſſembled, That in future, whenever any perſon ſhall differ in ſentiments from the worſhip and miniſtry in the Eccleſiaſtical Societies in this State, conſtituted by law within certain local bounds, and ſhall chooſe to join himſelf to any other denomination of Chriſtians, which ſhall have formed themſelves into diſtinct

Certificates to be lodged with Society Clerks.

ACTS AND LAWS.

Faſt and Thankſgiving. 417

Churches or Congregations, for the maintenance and ſupport of the public worſhip of God, and ſhall manifeſt ſuch his choice, by a certificate thereof, under his hand, lodged in the Office of the Clerk of the Society to which he belongs—ſuch perſon ſhall thereupon, and ſo long as he ſhall continue ordinarily, to attend on the worſhip and miniſtry, in the Church or Congregation, to which he has choſen to belong as aforeſaid, be exempted from being taxed for the future ſupport of the worſhip, and miniſtry in ſuch Society.

Be it further enacted, That all ſuch Churches and Congregations, which have, or ſhall have, formed themſelves as aforeſaid, and who ſhall maintain and attend public worſhip, by themſelves, ſhall have Liberty and Authority to exerciſe the ſame powers, for maintaining and ſupporting their reſpective Miniſters, and for building and repairing their Meeting-Houſes, for the public worſhip of God, as the aforeſaid Societies by law have, and do exerciſe and enjoy; and in the ſame manner, may commence and hold their Meetings, and tranſact their affairs, as occaſion may require for ſaid purpoſe. Powers of Churches and Congregations formed.

And every perſon claiming the benefit of this Act, ſhall be diſqualified to vote in any Meeting of ſuch Society, ſave only in matters, which relate to the maintenance and ſupport of Schools. Certain Perſons to vote only for ſupport of Schools.

Be it further enacted, That one certain Statute, of this State, entitled an Act, for ſecuring the Rights of Conſcience, in matters of Religion, to Chriſtians of every denomination, in this State—*and alſo,* An Act in addition to, and explanation of ſaid Act, be, and the ſame are hereby repealed. Repeal of former acts.

An Act to enforce the obſervance of days of public Faſting, and Thankſgiving.

BE it enacted by the Governor, Council, and Repreſentatives in General Court aſſembled, That on the days appointed for public Faſting, or Thankſgiving, by Proclamation of the Governor of this State; all perſons reſiding within this State, ſhall abſtain from every kind of ſervile labour, and recreation, works of neceſſity and mercy excepted; and any perſon who ſhall be guilty of a breach of this act, and being duly convicted thereof, ſhall be fined in a ſum, not exceeding Twelve Shillings, nor leſs than Six. Labour and recreation forbidden. Penalty.

Provided this act, ſhall not be conſtrued to prevent public poſts, and ſtages, from travelling on ſaid days. Public poſts and ſtages.

An Act in alteration of an Act, entitled an Act, for regulating the Election of the Governor, Lieutenant Governor, Aſſiſtants, &c. and of the Acts, in addition thereto.

Courtesy Connecticut State Library

5. CONNECTICUT ACT "SECURING EQUAL RIGHTS AND PRIVILEDGES TO CHRISTIANS . . ." 1791

From the *Acts and Laws* of the Connecticut Assembly, October 2, 1791, printed by Elisha Babcock. Although Congregational churches continued until 1818 to have certain privileges of a State Church, from now on no members of other Churches needed to contribute to the support of Congregationalism. To meet printer's needs, foot of title page is omitted. See III, 2, (1), (b); V, 6.

PROOFS

OF A

CONSPIRACY,

AGAINST CHRISTIANITY, AND THE GOVERNMENT OF THE UNITED STATES;

EXHIBITED

IN SEVERAL VIEWS OF THE UNION OF CHURCH AND STATE IN

NEW-ENGLAND.

By ABRAHAM BISHOP.

John Babcock, Printer, Hartford.

1802.

Courtesy Yale University Library

6. ABRAHAM BISHOP'S APPEAL FOR CHURCH-STATE SEPARATION, 1802

Connecticut's struggle for complete religious freedom was a long and bitter one. It did not result in Congregational disestablishment until 1818. Abraham Bishop was one of the most active of Jefferson's followers in the state, and this book was one of his effective attacks on the old standing order. See V, 6.

Courtesy Yale University Library

7. A WESTERN CAMP MEETING

The camp meeting was a great factor on the Western frontier, especially in the early decades of the nineteenth century. In spite of its emotional extremes it served the cause of democracy and religion, reaching every year tens of thousands of people. Methodists, Presbyterians, and Baptists were the leaders. The illustration entitled "Camp Meeting, Indiana, 1829" appeared in Mrs. Trollope's *Domestic Customs and Manners of the Americans,* 1832.

See X, 1.

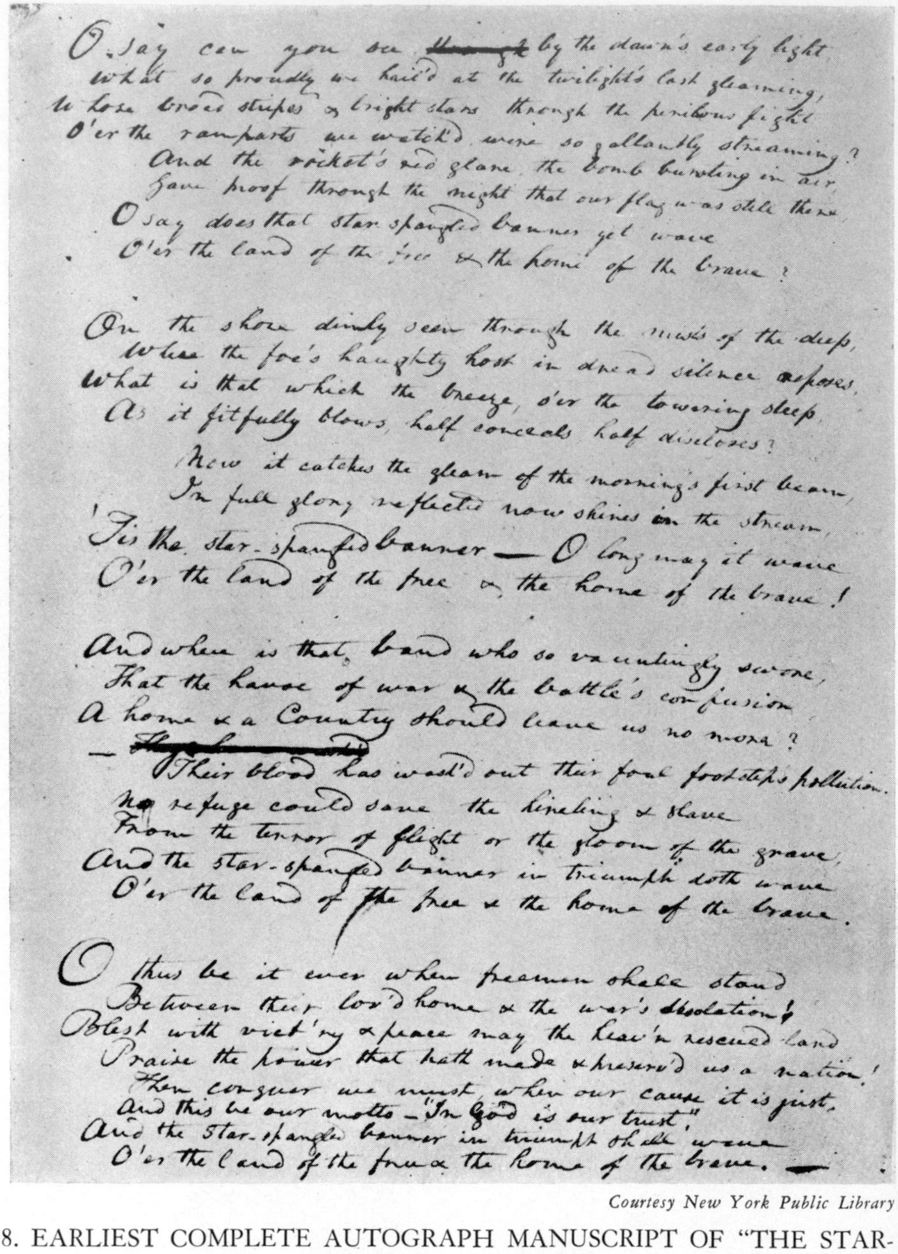

O say can you see by the dawn's early light
What so proudly we hail'd at the twilight's last gleaming,
Whose broad stripes & bright stars through the perilous fight
O'er the ramparts we watch'd, were so gallantly streaming?
And the rocket's red glare, the bomb bursting in air,
Gave proof through the night that our flag was still there,
O say does that star-spangled banner yet wave
O'er the land of the free & the home of the brave?

On the shore dimly seen through the mists of the deep,
Where the foe's haughty host in dread silence reposes,
What is that which the breeze, o'er the towering steep,
As it fitfully blows, half conceals, half discloses?
Now it catches the gleam of the morning's first beam,
In full glory reflected now shines in the stream,
'Tis the star-spangled banner — O long may it wave
O'er the land of the free & the home of the brave!

And where is that band who so vauntingly swore,
That the havoc of war & the battle's confusion
A home & a Country should leave us no more?
—
Their blood has wash'd out their foul footstep's pollution.
No refuge could save the hireling & slave
From the terror of flight or the gloom of the grave,
And the star-spangled banner in triumph doth wave
O'er the land of the free & the home of the brave.

O thus be it ever when freemen shall stand
Between their lov'd home & the war's desolation!
Blest with vict'ry & peace may the heav'n rescued land
Praise the power that hath made & preserv'd us a nation!
Then conquer we must, when our cause it is just,
And this be our motto — "In God is our trust,"
And the star-spangled banner in triumph shall wave
O'er the land of the free & the home of the brave.

Courtesy New York Public Library

8. EARLIEST COMPLETE AUTOGRAPH MANUSCRIPT OF "THE STAR-SPANGLED BANNER"

From the Henry Walters sale catalogue at the American Art Association, January 5, 1934. The manuscript was bought by Dr. Rosenbach, for $24,000, and promptly sold to the Walters Art Gallery, Baltimore. The song, written by Francis Scott Key in 1814, in the War of 1812, was adopted by Congress as the national anthem in 1931. The words "In God is our Trust" (cf. Psalm 31:1), are similar to the motto on American coins. See X, 6; XXIV, 5, (2).

Courtesy Essex Institute, Salem, Mass.

9. CHURCH AND STATE CARTOON, c. 1830

One of the early anti-Church cartoons in the United States. It was published in opposition to the attempt of the Churches to secure anti-Sunday mail legislation. It shows in a striking way the feeling of radicals at the time that the Church was trying to interfere with the distribution of the United States mail. The inscriptions, which may be read with a magnifying glass, are interesting, especially the one on the mail coach named Intelligence. Across the sides are the words, "What other Nations call religious privilege we call RELIGIOUS RIGHT." From the steeple of "The Church Visible" fulminations are being sent out against the religious liberty supporters. See XIV, 2.

Courtesy Corcoran Gallery of Art, Washington

10. SENATOR RICHARD M. JOHNSON, 1780-1850

Hero of Church-State separation in Congressional controversy over the Sunday mails. From the portrait by John Neagle. Johnson's reports were the ablest public utterances on the subject in this period in the United States. See Blakely, *American State Papers,* Fourth Edition, 1939, pp. 210-228. Senator Johnson was later vice president. See XIV, 2.

Courtesy St. Louis University, St. Louis

11. FATHER DE SMET, 1801-73, WESTERN PIONEER, MISSIONARY, SERVANT OF CHURCH AND STATE

Father Pierre-Jean De Smet (1801-73), Roman Catholic missionary to the Indians and the first western novitiate (1823), now St. Stanislaus Seminary, Florissant, Mo., which he established. The picture is taken from a circular of the Seminary issued in 1948, making an appeal for funds. See XVI, 4, 5.

Courtesy Yale University Library and Francis P. Harper, representing publishers of "Life, Letters and Travels of Father Pierre-Jean De Smet, S. J. 1801-1873"

12. FATHER DE SMET AS GOVERNMENT NEGOTIATOR WITH THE INDIANS

A sketch showing Father De Smet, unaccompanied, negotiating successfully for the United States Government in 1868 with Sitting Bull, Chief of the Sioux Indians, when they were threatening all white men. The services of this Roman Catholic missionary led General Grant to say, "He is worth a regiment of soldiers." See XVI, 4.

Courtesy New York Public Library and Senator Altgeld

13. THOMAS KENNEDY, 1776-1832—HERO OF JEWISH EMANCIPATION IN MARYLAND

Portrait of the Maryland Protestant legislator who devoted much of his life to securing full religious rights for the Jews of his state. Reproduced from frontispiece of *The Jews Struggle for Religious and Civil Liberty in Maryland* by E. Milton Altgeld. See XIII, 3.

Courtesy Ewing Galloway, N. Y.

14. JOSEPH SMITH, 1805-44, FOUNDER OF MORMONISM

This statue on the tabernacle grounds in Salt Lake City, commemorates particularly three events in Smith's life which his followers consider of prime importance: his vision of God, the revelation of the Book of Mormon, and the organization of the Church of Latter Day Saints. On the monument behind are medallions of the three alleged "witnesses" of the revelation of the Book of Mormon. See XIV, 7.

Courtesy New York Public Library

15. JOSEPH SMITH AS COMMANDER OF THE MORMON MILITIA

Contemporary picture of Joseph Smith as general in command of the Mormon militia—combining in his person both Church and State functions. Reproduced from T. B. Stenhouse, *The Rocky Mountain Saints*, 1873. See XIV, 7.

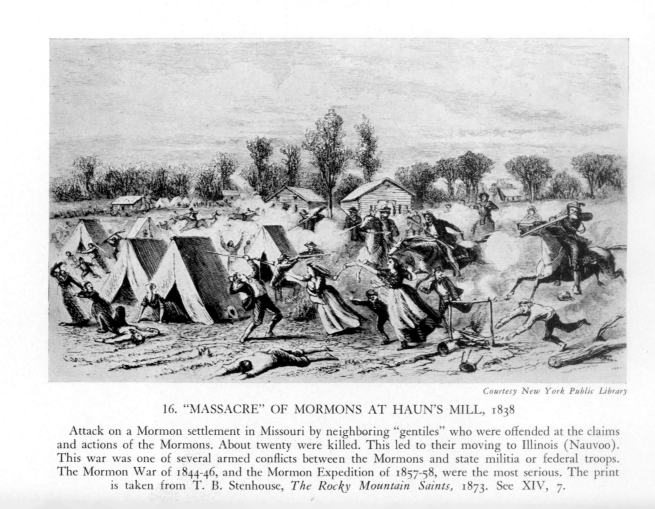

Courtesy New York Public Library

16. "MASSACRE" OF MORMONS AT HAUN'S MILL, 1838

Attack on a Mormon settlement in Missouri by neighboring "gentiles" who were offended at the claims and actions of the Mormons. About twenty were killed. This led to their moving to Illinois (Nauvoo). This war was one of several armed conflicts between the Mormons and state militia or federal troops. The Mormon War of 1844-46, and the Mormon Expedition of 1857-58, were the most serious. The print is taken from T. B. Stenhouse, *The Rocky Mountain Saints,* 1873. See XIV, 7.

Courtesy New York Public Library

17. NAUVOO (NAUVOE), CAPITAL OF THE MORMON THEOCRACY, 1839-46

Lithograph from the Phelps-Stokes collection drawn in 1846-47 by Henry Lewis and later published in his book *Das Illustrirte Mississippithal* (1857). The large temple just completed (May, 1856) may be seen on the crest of the hill. By 1845 Nauvoo had at least twelve thousand inhabitants, and was an *imperium in imperio*, which, with its Mormon militia, was in armed conflict with the militia of Illinois, until Smith's murder by a mob in 1844. See XIV, 7.

COMMISSION.

No. 4360

Office U. S. Christian Commission,

NO. 11 BANK STREET.

Philadelphia, 7th Feby 1865

To Officers of the Army and Navy of the United States, and others:

The **U. S. CHRISTIAN COMMISSION,** organized by a convention of the Young Men's Christian Associations of the loyal States, to promote the spiritual and temporal welfare and improvement of the men of the Army and Navy, acting under the approbation and commendation of the President, the Secretaries of the Army and the Navy, the Postmaster-General, the Surgeon-General, and of the Generals in command, have appointed

Frank H. Bradly Esqr of New Haven Conn.

A Delegate, to act in accordance with instructions furnished herewith, under direction of the proper officers, in furtherance of the objects of the Commission.

His services will be rendered in behalf of the Commission, without remuneration from or expense to the Government.

His work will be that of distributing stores where needed, in hospitals and camps; circulating good reading matter among soldiers and sailors; visiting the sick and wounded, to instruct, comfort, and cheer them, and aid them in correspondence with their friends at home; aiding Surgeons on the battle-field and elsewhere, in the care and conveyance of the wounded to hospitals; helping Chaplains in their ministrations and influence for the good of the men under their care; and addressing soldiers and sailors, individually and collectively, in explanation of the work of the Commission and its delegates, and for their personal instruction and benefit, temporal and eternal.

He is strictly enjoined, if with our forces when a battle is approaching, passing, or passed, to abstain from reporting any thing on the subject not authorized by the commanding officer, and in general strictly to observe all Army and Navy regulations, and abstain from casting reflections upon the authorities, military, medical and clerical.

All possible facilities, and all due courtesies are asked for him, in the proper pursuance of any or all of these duties.

Geo H Stuart

CHAIRMAN U. S. CHRISTIAN COMMISSION.

Courtesy Yale University Library

18. U. S. CHRISTIAN COMMISSION CERTIFICATE, UNION ARMY

A certificate of a delegate of the commission outlining his philanthropic duties and his work of "helping Chaplains in their ministrations." From an original in the Yale University Library. See XV, 5, (1), (d).

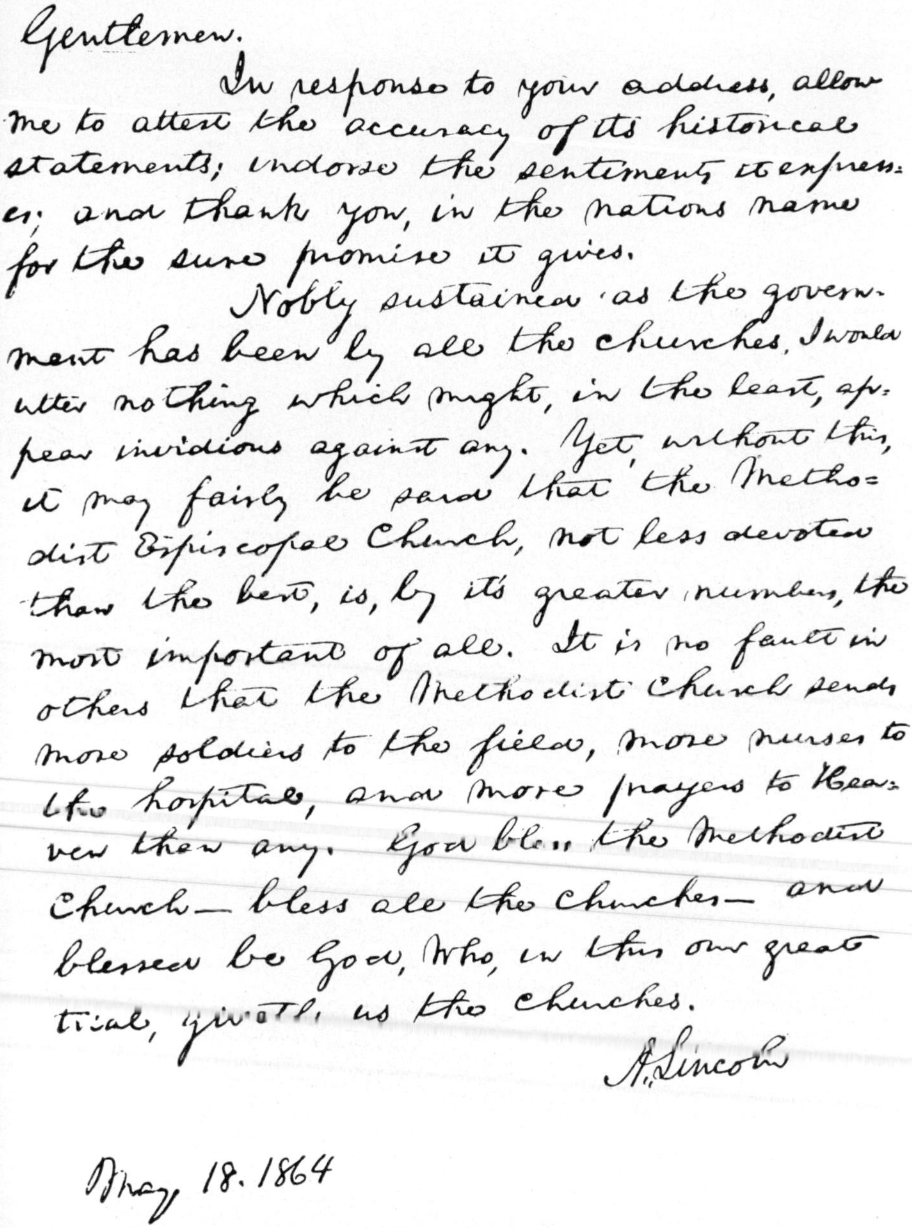

Gentlemen.
In response to your address, allow me to attest the accuracy of its historical statements; indorse the sentiments it expresses; and thank you, in the nations name for the sure promise it gives.
Nobly sustained as the government has been by all the churches, I would utter nothing which might, in the least, appear invidious against any. Yet, without this, it may fairly be said that the Methodist Episcopal Church, not less devoted than the best, is, by it's greater numbers, the most important of all. It is no fault in others that the Methodist Church sends more soldiers to the field, more nurses to the hospitals, and more prayers to Heaven than any. God bless the Methodist Church—bless all the churches—and blessed be God, Who, in this our great trial, giveth us the churches.

A. Lincoln

May 18. 1864

Courtesy Library of Congress

19. ABRAHAM LINCOLN'S TRIBUTE TO THE METHODISTS

The war president's letter to the Methodist Episcopal Church in 1864, in which he says, among other things: "Nobly sustained as the government has been by all the churches" yet it feels under special obligations to the Methodist Church "not less devoted than the best," for, because of its larger numbers, it sends "more soldiers to the field, more nurses to the hospitals, and more prayers to Heaven than any." A wonderful letter! See XV, 4, (1), (a).

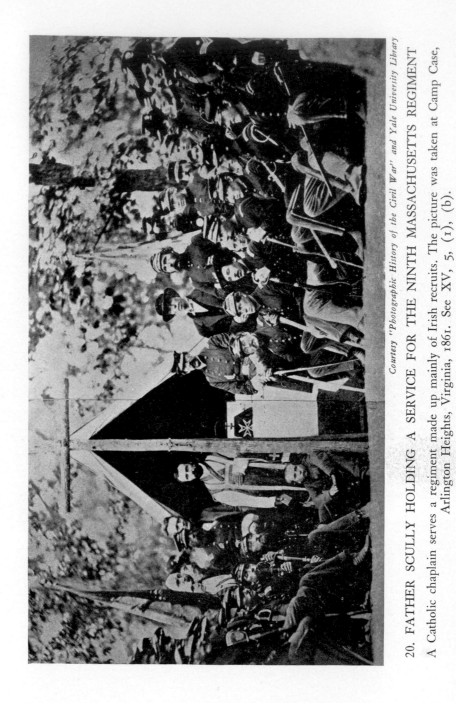

Courtesy "Photographic History of the Civil War" and Yale University Library

20. FATHER SCULLY HOLDING A SERVICE FOR THE NINTH MASSACHUSETTS REGIMENT

A Catholic chaplain serves a regiment made up mainly of Irish recruits. The picture was taken at Camp Case, Arlington Heights, Virginia, 1861. See XV, 5, (1), (b).

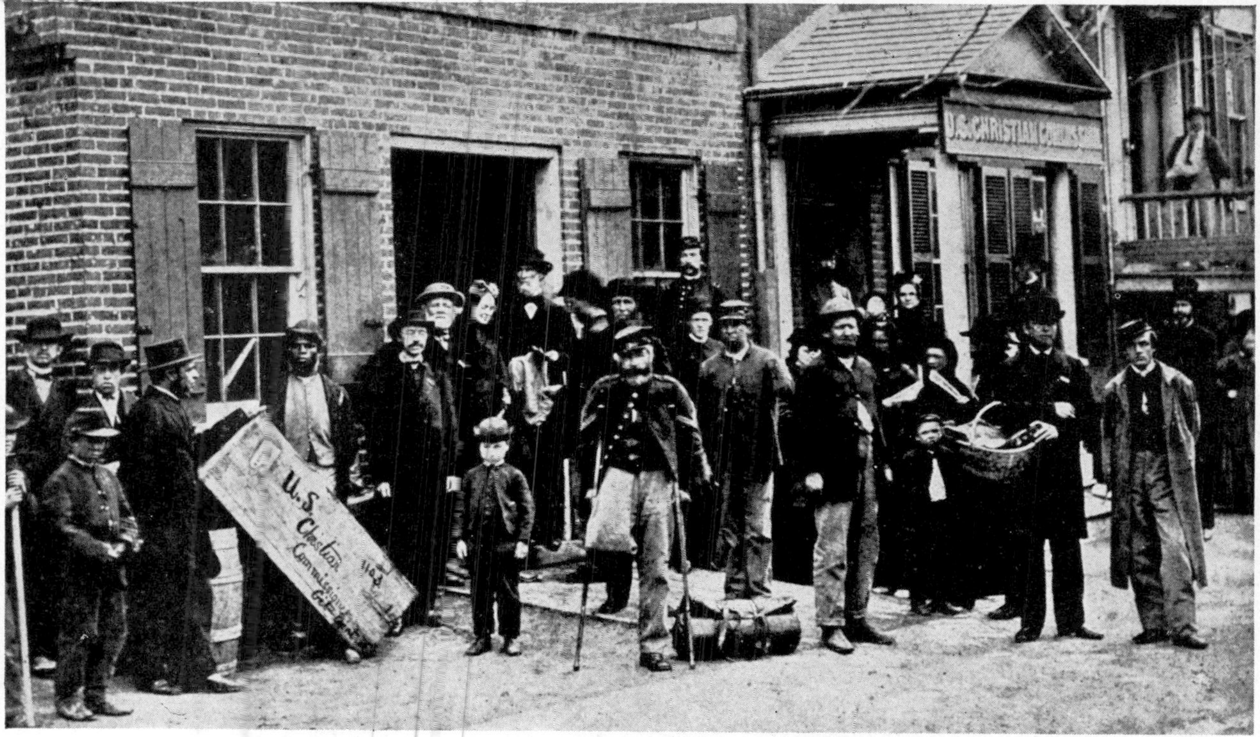

Courtesy "Photographic History of the Civil War" and Yale University Library

21. A FRONT HEADQUARTERS OF THE U. S. CHRISTIAN COMMISSION

The commission largely preceded the work of the Y.M.C.A. in World War I and the U.S.O. in World War II. It was established by the Y.M.C.A. October 28, 1861. Note in picture "U. S. Christian Commission" over door; ministers of religion and women aids in group; box with supplies addressed to City Point, Va., where the picture was evidently taken; a colporteur, etc. See XV, 5, (1), (d).

Courtesy Ewing Galloway, N. Y.

22. HENRY WARD BEECHER, 1813-87, PULPIT EXPONENT OF ANTISLAVERY CAUSE

A statue by Gutzon Borglum, erected on the property of Plymouth Church, Brooklyn, N. Y. showing Beecher appealing for the cause of the slave. One of the dramatic incidents of his ministry was the auction of a slave in Plymouth Church to cause resentment against this inhumane practice. See XV, 5, 1, (a).

Courtesy Yale University Library

23. THEODORE D. WELD, 1803-95—ANTISLAVERY LEADER IN THE CHURCHES

A daguerreotype taken from *William Lloyd Garrison, 1805-79.* Since the publication of Gilbert Barnes, *The Anti-Slavery Impulse, 1830-44*, it has been increasingly realized that Weld, a former student for the Congregational ministry, was one of the wisest and most effective of the antislavery agitators. He organized and instructed many bands of emancipation evangelists. See XV, 4.

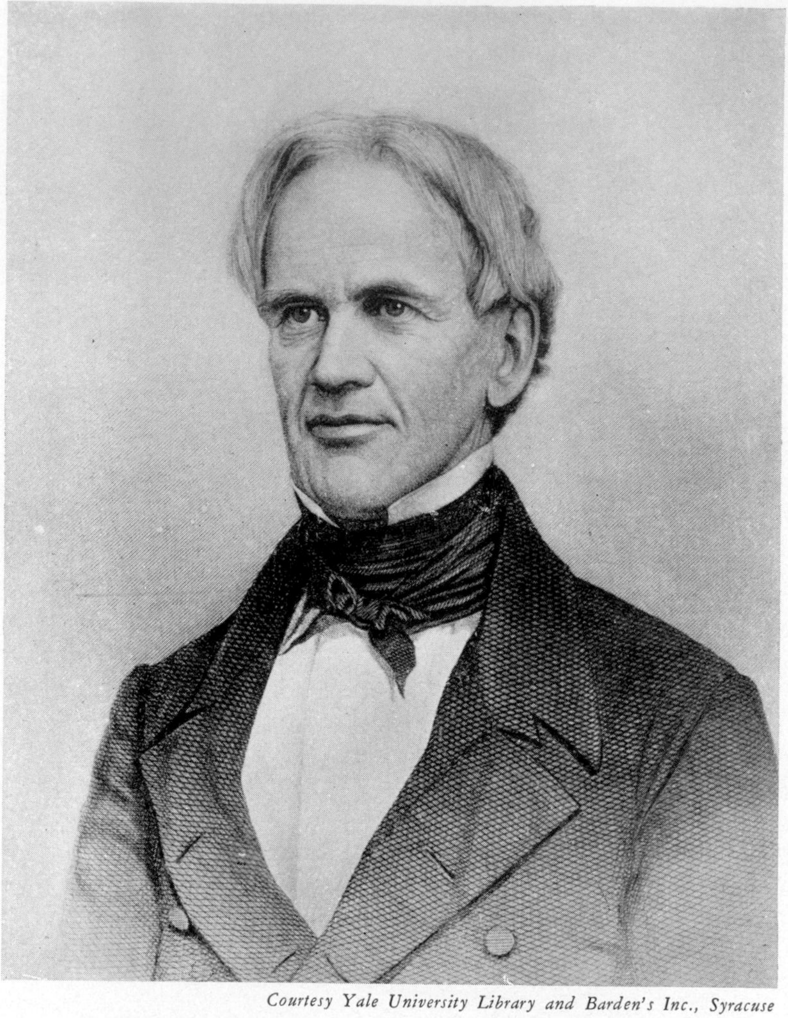

Courtesy Yale University Library and Barden's Inc., Syracuse

24. HORACE MANN, 1796-1859, EXPONENT OF PUBLIC SCHOOLS—CHRISTIAN IN ATTITUDE, BUT FREE FROM DENOMINATIONALISM

Horace Mann in Massachusetts and Henry Barnard (1811-1900) in Connecticut were the two greatest factors in the development of the American public school. Mann took the lead in freeing the schools from any Church connection but wished them to continue to have the Bible read without comment, and to permit the study of basic Christian teachings. From *American Educational Biography*. See XIV, 8, (2).

Sec. 13. And for extending the fundamental principles of civil and religious liberty, which form the basis whereon these republics, their laws and constitutions, are erected; to fix and establish those principles as the basis of all laws, constitutions, and governments, which forever hereafter shall be formed in the said territory; to provide, also, for the establishment of States, and permanent government therein, and for their admission to a share in the Federal councils on an equal footing with the original States, at as early periods as may be consistent with the general interest:

ARTICLE III

Religion, morality, and knowledge being necessary to good government and the happiness of mankind, schools and the means of education shall forever be encouraged. The utmost good faith shall always be observed towards the Indians; their lands and property shall never be taken from them without their consent; and in their property, rights, and liberty they never shall be invaded or disturbed unless in just and lawful wars authorized by Congress; but laws founded in justice and humanity shall, from time to time, be made, for preventing wrongs being done to them, and for preserving peace and friendship with them.

Courtesy Library of Congress

25. EXTRACTS FROM ORDINANCE OF 1787

The references in preamble to "the fundamental principles of civil and religious liberty" and in Article III to "Religion, morality and knowledge being necessary to good government and the happiness of mankind" were of enormous influence as the ordinance formed the foundation of all subsequent government in most of the West and Northwest. Taken from *Formation of the Union Documents.* See VI, 10.

Courtesy Oberlin Colleg

26. BEGINNINGS OF OBERLIN COLLEGE

In 1834 sixty-two people organized "The First Congregational Church of Christ in Oberlin." Rev. John J. Shipherd, principal founder of the college, was called as first minister. The church was built 1842-44, and is now the oldest building in Oberlin. When completed, it was considered the largest building west of the Allegheny Mountains. It was used for town hall and church and for college meetings. In 1908 and 1927 extensive repairs and alterations were made. As often in the West a church—generally Presbyterian, Congregational, Methodist, or Catholic—was the nucleus of a college. See XVI, 5.

Courtesy Oregon State Highway Commission, Salem

27. A WESTERN CIRCUIT RIDER

Equestrian bronze figure on East side of Oregon State Capitol, of the Reverend Robert Booth, by the sculptor, A. Phimister Proctor. It was dedicated April 19, 1924, to those "ministers of the Gospel, who as circuit riders became the friends, counselors and evangels to the pioneers on every American frontier." See X, 1; XVI, 5.

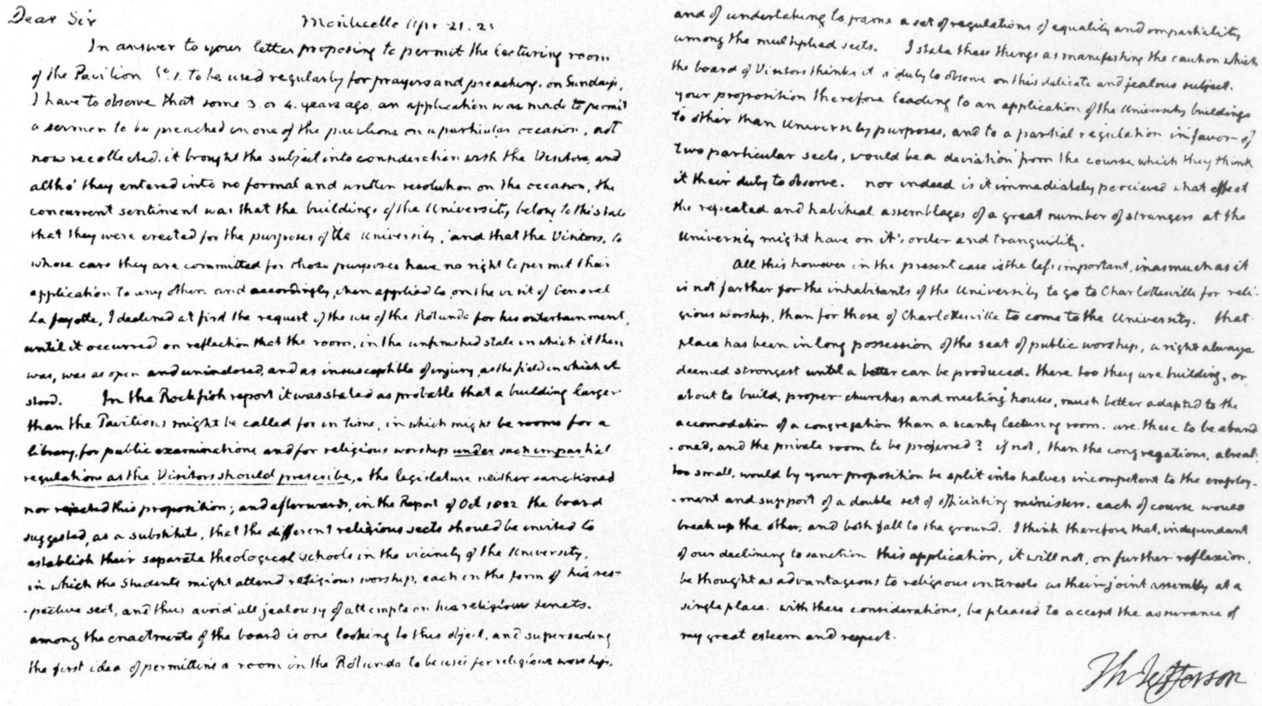

Dear Sir Monticello Apr. 21. 23

In answer to your letter proposing to permit the lecturing room of the Pavilion No. 1. to be used regularly for prayers and preaching on Sundays, I have to observe that some 3. or 4. years ago an application was made to permit a sermon to be preached in one of the pavilions on a particular occasion, not now recollected. it brought the subject into consideration with the Visitors, and altho' they entered into no formal and written resolution on the occasion, the concurrent sentiment was that the buildings of the University belong to this state, that they were erected for the purposes of the University, and that the Visitors, to whose care they are committed for those purposes have no right to permit their application to any other. and accordingly, when applied to on the visit of General La Fayette, I declined at first the request of the use of the Rotunda for his entertainment, until it occurred on reflection that the room, in the unfinished state in which it then was, was as open and unenclosed, and as insusceptible of injury, as the field in which it stood. In the Rockfish report it was stated as probable that a building larger than the Pavilions might be called for in time, in which might be rooms for a library, for public examinations and for religious worship under such impartial regulations as the Visitors should prescribe. the legislature neither sanctioned nor rejected this proposition; and afterwards, in the Report of Oct 1822. the board suggested, as a substitute, that the different religious sects should be invited to establish their separate theological schools in the vicinity of the University, in which the Students might attend religious worship, each in the form of his respective sect, and thus avoid all jealousy of attempts on his religious tenets. among the enactments of the board is one looking to this object, and superseding the first idea of permitting a room in the Rotunda to be used for religious worship, and of undertaking to frame a set of regulations of equality and impartiality among the multiplied sects. I state these things as manifesting the caution which the board of Visitors thinks it a duty to observe on this delicate and jealous subject. your proposition therefore leading to an application of the University buildings to other than University purposes, and to a partial regulation in favor of two particular sects, would be a deviation from the course which they think it their duty to observe. nor indeed is it immediately perceived what effect the repeated and habitual assemblages of a great number of strangers at the University might have on it's order and tranquility.

All this however in the present case is the less important, inasmuch as it is not farther for the inhabitants of the University to go to Charlottesville for religious worship, than for those of Charlottesville to come to the University. that place has been in long possession of the seat of public worship, a right always deemed strongest until a better can be produced. there too they are building, or about to build, proper churches and meeting houses, much better adapted to the accomodation of a congregation than a scanty lecturing room. are these to be abandoned, and the private room to be preferred? if not, then the congregations, already too small, would by your proposition be split into halves incompetent to the employment and support of a double set of officiating ministers. each of course would break up the other, and both fall to the ground. I think therefore that, independant of our declining to sanction this application, it will not, on further reflexion, be thought as advantageous to religious interests as their joint assembly at a single place. with these considerations, be pleased to accept the assurance of my great esteem and respect.

Th: Jefferson

Courtesy Lyman H. Butterfield, and University of Virginia Library

28. JEFFERSON'S VIEWS ON TEACHING RELIGION AT A STATE UNIVERSITY

Mr. Butterfield, assistant editor of "The Papers of Thomas Jefferson," states that he believes this letter has "never been published." It was in reply to a letter from Arthur Brockenbrough, bursar of the University of Virginia, as to whether a lecture room at the University might be used for Sunday religious services. Jefferson believes this inadvisable but is not opposed to denominational schools being separately established whose teaching and worship students could attend. See IV, 8, 10; XVIII, 9, 10.

Courtesy New York Public Library

29. " 'THE PROMISED LAND' AS SEEN FROM THE DOME OF SAINT PETER'S, ROME"

Thomas Nast shared the fears of many Americans after Garibaldi's capture of Rome in 1870, that the pope might transfer the papal see to the United States; this might solve a serious papal problem and aid the Church conquest of the United States, *Harper's Weekly*, October 1, 1870. See XXIII, 4, (1).

Courtesy New York Public Library

30. THE POPE ORDERS REMOVAL OF AMERICAN PROTESTANT WORSHIP FROM ROME

Nast's cartoons against the influence of the papacy in American affairs were often in bad taste but reflected much American opinion. From *Harper's Weekly,* February 9, 1867. This closing of the chapel was a cause of Congressional discontinuance of the Vatican mission. See XIV, 11, (1).

Courtesy American Library Service

31. A NIGHT RIDER OF THE KU KLUX KLAN

Frontispiece of Susan Lawrence Davis' *Authentic History, Ku Klux Klan 1865-1877*. The fiery cross and the hood covering the face are threatening what was to result from religious intolerance in rural regions, especially of the South with Negroes and Catholics as special targets for attack. See XVII, 1, 4, (6).

ROMISH POLITICS—ANY THING TO BEAT GRANT.

IRISH ROMAN CATHOLIC INVADER. "The Y. M. C. A. want the Bible in the public school, assuming that this is a Christian country. *We want the Priest, the Brother, and the Sister in our public schools, not assuming, but endeavoring to effect, that this is a Catholic country*."—*St. Louis Western Watchman*, July 13, 1872.

Courtesy Yale University Library

32. CARTOON ON THE BIBLE IN THE PUBLIC SCHOOL

A Nast cartoon from *Harper's Weekly*, August 17, 1872, showing the Protestant fear that Roman Catholic opposition to the reading of the Bible was a step in trying to make Catholic influence dominant. The Irishman debating with Horace Greeley, and the priest listening behind the doorway, will be noticed. The title "Romish Politics—Any thing to beat Grant" suggests Grant's declared opposition to government aid to parochial and other religious schools. See XVIII, 3.

Courtesy New York Public Library

33. "SECTARIAN BITTERNESS" OVER PUBLIC-SCHOOL FUND

Nast calls attention to dangers to public schools through "Political Influence" of the Roman Catholic Church. This blinds "Justice" so as to get funds away from the common schools, where "union is strength"—"free to all," "no sect," "no caste." From *Harper's Weekly*, February 26, 1870. See XIX, 2; 4, (3), etc.

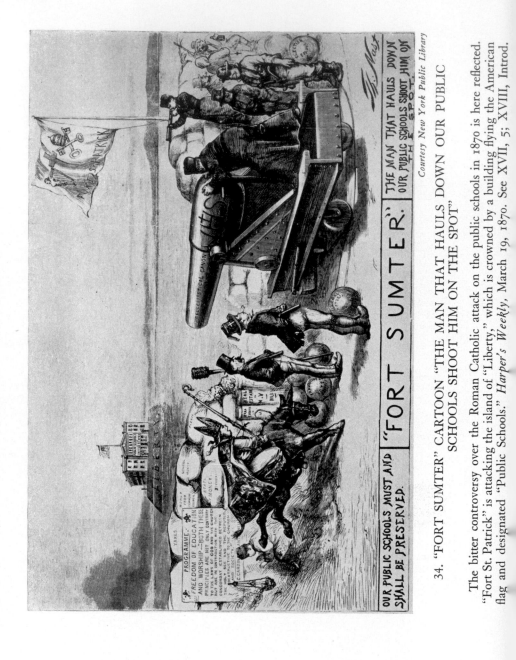

Courtesy New York Public Library

34. "FORT SUMTER" CARTOON "THE MAN THAT HAULS DOWN OUR PUBLIC SCHOOLS SHOOT HIM ON THE SPOT"

The bitter controversy over the Roman Catholic attack on the public schools in 1870 is here reflected. "Fort St. Patrick" is attacking the island of "Liberty," which is crowned by a building flying the American flag and designated "Public Schools." *Harper's Weekly,* March 19, 1870. See XVII, 5; XVIII, Introd.

FORESHADOWING OF COMING EVENTS IN OUR PUBLIC SCHOOLS.

"No, gentlemen, that will not do; and there is no help but in dividing the public schools, or in abandoning the system of public schools altogether."—*The Tablet*, Roman Catholic.

"It will be a glorious day for Catholics in this country when our school system will be shivered to pieces."—Cincinnati Roman *Catholic Telegraph.*

"Let the public school system go to where it came from—the devil."—Roman Catholic *Freeman's Journal.*

"We ask that the public schools be cleansed from this peace-destroying monstrosity—Bible reading."—Bishop Lynch, of New Orleans, Roman Catholic.

"We can not use the common schools, because they answer not our end nor satisfy our consciences."—Rev. Thomas Preston, Roman Catholic.

Courtesy New York Public Library

35. CARTOON AGAINST SUBSTITUTING CATHOLIC DEVOTIONS FOR HISTORY, THE BIBLE, AND SCIENCE IN PUBLIC SCHOOLS

Nast's drawings are sometimes too extreme to be reproduced here. This one, however, is valuable for its alleged quotations from Roman Catholic journals and priests as to the Church's intentions to divide the school fund or destroy the schools. See XIX, 4.

Courtesy New York Public Library

36. BRIGHAM YOUNG'S WIVES IN OLD MORMON TEMPLE

A public aspect of the polygamy problem from *Harper's Weekly*, September 26, 1874. This led to the most famous Church-State controversy before the Supreme Court in the nineteenth century. See XVI, 3.

Courtesy Union of American Hebrew Congregations

37. RABBI ISAAC MAYER WISE, 1819-1900

A Bohemian-born scholar who was a leader in Reform Judaism and did much to adjust traditional Jewry to American conditions. He was a true friend of Constitutional religious freedom. He was founder and president of the Hebrew Union College (1875) and of the Central Conference of American Rabbis (1889); also mainly responsible for the Union of American Hebrew Congregations. He combined religion with true patriotism. The photograph was taken in 1889 when Rabbi Wise was eighty years old. See XIII, 4; XXIII, 4, (4).

Courtesy National Park Service

38. STATUE OF LIBERTY ENLIGHTENING THE WORLD

Liberty holds in her right hand the torch of Freedom, under her left arm the Book of the Law—the Declaration of Independence. This is the cornerstone of American liberty, both civil and religious, for in direct antagonism to Marxian Communism, it refers to the rights of individual men, and bases the new movement for an independent government squarely on a religious foundation—that man is created by God—a truth Jefferson reiterates—and endowed by Him with "unalienable rights," of which Liberty is one. This heroic statue by Bartholdi was the gift of the French people to the people of the United States. See VI, 3.

"I AM NOW INFALLIBLE."

Courtesy New York Public Library

39. AMERICAN REACTION TO PAPAL INFALLIBILITY DECREE

This cartoon in *Harper's Weekly*, July 30, 1870, by Thomas Nast shows the dominant non-Catholic opinion in the United States that the new decree was splitting the world into two groups—one remaining connected with twentieth century liberalism; the other with ultramontane tendencies characteristic of the "Dark Ages." See XVII, 4, (1), (b).

Courtesy New York Public Library

40. "CHURCH & STATE"—THE CONTRAST BETWEEN EUROPE AND THE UNITED STATES, 1870

Nast in this cartoon depicts the theory of the Church State torn apart in Europe by the spirit of Liberty, while in the United States, where Liberty is enchained by the "fraudulent vote," the papacy is blessing the effort to unite Church and State across the country. *Harper's Weekly*, February 19, 1870. See XVII, 5; XIX, 10; XXIII, 4, (1).

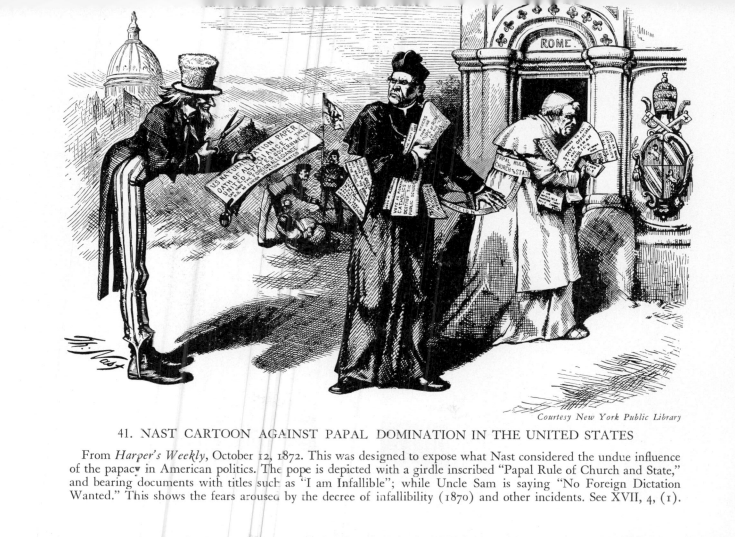

Courtesy New York Public Library

41. NAST CARTOON AGAINST PAPAL DOMINATION IN THE UNITED STATES

From *Harper's Weekly*, October 12, 1872. This was designed to expose what Nast considered the undue influence of the papacy in American politics. The pope is depicted with a girdle inscribed "Papal Rule of Church and State," and bearing documents with titles such as "I am Infallible"; while Uncle Sam is saying "No Foreign Dictation Wanted." This shows the fears aroused by the decree of infallibility (1870) and other incidents. See XVII, 4, (1).

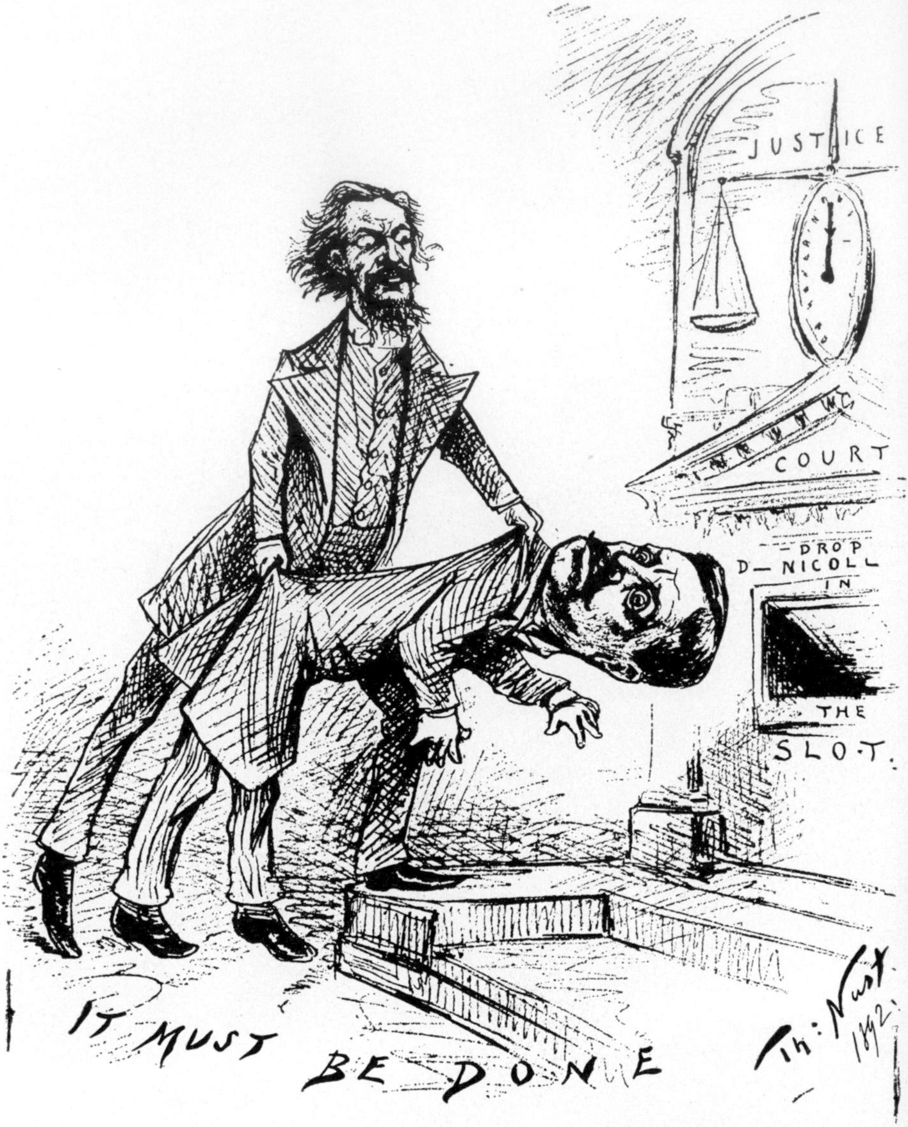
JUSTICE
COURT
DROP
D—NICOLL
IN
THE
SLOT.
IT MUST BE DONE
Th: Nast
1892

Courtesy New York Public Library

42. REV. CHARLES H. PARKHURST, 1842-1933, TRIES TO CLEAN UP NEW YORK POLITICS

A Presbyterian minister with a passion for public righteousness and justice reminiscent of the Old Testament prophets succeeded in the nineties in breaking much of the power of corrupt Tammany Hall. This Nast cartoon "It Must Be Done," from the *New York Gazette* of June 4, 1892, shows him getting rid of the Tammany District Attorney, DeLancey Nicoll—"Drop D—Nicoll in the Slot." See XVI, 7.

THE LESSON TAUGHT BY DR. PARKHURST, FOR THE PREVENTION OF CRIME.
OTHER CITIES DESIRING MUNICIPAL REFORM — TAKE NOTICE
FIRST — "RUN IN THE POLICE!"

Courtesy New York Public Library

43. REV. DR. PARKHURST AS "HERO OF THE PULPIT" HAS THE CORRUPT TAMMANY POLICE BY THE NECK

One of Thomas Nast's many cartoons showing a well-known Presbyterian minister as an effective New York City reformer. From *New York Gazette*, April 24, 1892. See XVI, 7. The Church, as represented by Dr. Parkhurst and a few other aroused clergymen and laymen, was largely responsible for bringing about the election of a reform mayor in 1894.

Andreas Steinhuber

Giralamo Maria Gotti

Jose Calasanz de Llevaneras Vives y Tuto

Serafino Vannutelli

Governor Taft

Mariano Rampolla del Pindaro

Governor Taft returning from the Vatican

Courtesy Yale University Library

44. JUDGE TAFT NEGOTIATES WITH VATICAN OVER PHILIPPINE FRIARS' LANDS

The Honorable William H. Taft, a Judge of the United States Circuit Court, and first Civil Governor of the Philippines by appointment July 4, 1901, was sent to Rome by President Theodore Roosevelt in 1902 to confer with the Vatican concerning purchase of the so-called Friars' Lands in the Philippine Islands. Cardinal Gibbons' good offices aided. The sum of $7,000,000 was paid by our Government for most of these lands. From *Harper's Weekly* of July 26, 1902. See XVI, 9, 10.

Courtesy Knights of Columbus Home, Baltimore

45. JAMES CARDINAL GIBBONS, 1834-1921

This was chosen by the Chancellor of the Baltimore archdiocese as the most suitable portrait of the cardinal for this book. It was painted in 1919 by Marie DeFord Keller. Gibbons was in the Catholic tradition of Carroll and England—a great churchman and a great American, and a firm believer in our Constitutional religious freedom. See XVI, 14, (4).

Courtesy Methodist Board of Temperance

46. THE CHURCH AND THE DRUNKARD—PROHIBITION

Cartoon by Somdal showing the Church trying to aid the alcoholic, victim of the corrupt "Liquor Traffic." See XVI, 12; XVII, 4, (6).

GILBERT O. NATIONS, Ph. D.
Editor

PRICE, 10 CENTS
$1.00 a Year

The Protestant

Ye shall know the truth, and the truth shall make you free.—John 8:32.

Vol. 8 **Washington, D. C., July, 1928** **No. 5**

Smith Must Be Annihilated

THE nation must choose between Herbert C. Hoover and Alfred E. Smith. Never before have we faced the issue now paramount. A typical wet Roman Catholic creature of Tammany Hall has been forced on a great party for the Presidency. He has been nominated but not elected. He has dealt with politicians and controlled newspapers. He must now meet forty millions of qualified voters.

In them the national sovereignty reposes. They are the court of last resort. The destiny of America and the world hangs on their decision. They will speak for our boys and girls, our homes, our schools and our churches. They have no sinister purpose. They are endowed with integrity that slush funds cannot corrupt. May the God of wisdom grant them discernment to pierce the glamour of deceptive propaganda, to see the candidates as they are, to take their true measure, to vote in the light of the whole truth.

No party fanaticism nor threadbare issues and traditions of the past should be permitted to complicate in the slightest degree the momentous duty confronting the voters. The vital issues that differentiated the Democratic and Republican parties in decades immediately after the Civil War no longer exist. There is nothing in the character or personality of the wet Tammany Governor of New York to endear him to southern compatriots of Robert E. Lee, Stonewall Jackson and Joseph Wheeler.

The time has come to save America, to fight a common enemy as Wheeler and a distinguished relative of Lee did in the Spanish-American War of thirty years ago. What incentive has Dixie to bare its breast for a candidate chosen from a great northern city notoriously corrupt and hostile to every principle cherished in the South? The pending election presents no party issue. It must turn on the choice between America and Rome, between decency and vice.

Though not the first choice of all good citizens, Mr. Hoover is personally a scholar and gentleman. He has no legal connection with papal Rome. He is not addicted to the excessive use of strong drink. He has no affiliation with the political underworld. He is a talented and successful business man. The men and forces responsible for his nomination are not entirely above reproach, but they are incomparably cleaner than those which triumphed at Houston.

He is believed to be favored by the great banking combinations, but not more so than others elected to the Presidency in recent years. He is certainly not more so than Governor Smith. The latter has been daily extolled and magnified in the Wall Street press more than a decade. He is obviously the beneficiary of many covert political deals between Tammany Hall and the reactionary combinations in the Republican party of New York.

Senator Curtis is a distinct asset of the Republican ticket. He is more agreeable to the western and southern farmers than Secretary Hoover or Governor Smith. Both Hoover and Curtis are men of culture. They have long moved in the highest moral and intellectual circles. They could meet the rulers and envoys of foreign powers with credit and decorum.

Regardless of personal preference concerning the men who sought the nomination at Kansas City, Hoover and Curtis are generally admitted to be a strong ticket. As against the ticket headed by the real and potential ruler of Tammany Hall, it should command the conscience and integrity of the nation. If all good citizens do their full duty in this grave national crisis, it will silence for all time to come the clamor for a Vatican subject in the White House. The wet papal following should be crushed beyond the possibility of resuscitation.

The forces and instrumentalities responsible for Smith have finished their service. He will no longer have a monopoly of the controlled press. It will continue friendly to him. Newspapers and periodicals notoriously vile may continue their partiality. But the better class of journals will not prefer him to Hoover.

It will now be possible to reach the public with a morsel of truth. For the first time in its history Tammany faces a real political fight to the finish beyond the borders of New York State. Campaign orators will dare unmask the tiger. The Smith ticket will have much to explain. It should be kept on the defensive.

The Tammany forces will have more difficulty in trading covertly with the up-state Republican machine in New York for the Presidency than for the Governorship. Above the Harlem the election this year will be reasonably clean. It is doubtful whether Smith can carry his own state. He can be defeated there if the

Courtesy New York Public Library

47. "SMITH MUST BE ANNIHILATED"

Typical of Protestant papers and newssheets opposing Alfred E. Smith for the presidency because he was alleged to be "a typical wet Roman Catholic creature of Tammany Hall . . ." while Mr. Hoover "has no legal connection with papal Rome." This number is specially directed to appeal to Southern voters. Its language is more temperate than that of the more extreme anti-Catholic journals. See XVII, 4, (6).

© Pillar of Fire, 1927. Al Smith and the Tammany Tiger will never reach the White House—See Editorial.

Courtesy New York Public Library

48. CARTOON ALLEGING ALLIANCE OF KU KLUX AND DRYS IN 1928 CAMPAIGN

Taken from a Protestant sheet published in rural New Jersey and devoted to "Educational, Political and Religious interests of the nation." It shows the Democratic donkey pulling an old wagon with an enormous crowned rum bottle. The driver is a Tammany tiger with "Al Smith" by his side. In the back is a priest depicted in a most uncomplimentary way. Ku Kluxers are preventing the group from reaching the White House. See XVII, 4, (6).

especially in the rural areas and small towns of certain sections in the South and Middle West where cultural standards were still relatively low. It capitalized the fear of alien influence. Its ritual, secrecy, and high-sounding titles all appealed to the ignorant and "frustrated" groups of the population. An insignificant clerk or farmer's hand felt when he donned imposing regalia that he was a person of some importance.

The most encouraging single thing about the controversy in 1928 was that it caused no recorded acts of physical violence or bloodshed.[104] This shows that the United States had learned one of the fundamental lessons of a democratic government. Another indirect good result was the organizing under the leadership of former Secretary of War Newton D. Baker (1871–1937) representing the Protestants, Professor Carlton Hayes (1882–), the Roman Catholics, and Roger Straus (1891–), the Jews, of the National Conference of Christians and Jews, which has ever since been a potent factor in preventing intolerance in this country.[105]

The Klan has become less aggressive in recent years, but some of its fellow-travellers among ministers of Protestant denominations have continued much of its spirit, especially such men as Gerald L. K. Smith and Gerald B. Winrod, editor of *The Defender Magazine,* both considered extreme Nativistic leaders. Smith has been a presidential candidate; and Winrod a candidate for the senatorship under Republican auspices in Kansas in 1938, but defeated largely by a campaign in behalf of tolerance by a group of Kansas ministers.

We have referred principally in this section to the Klan's opposition to Roman Catholics. Its opposition to Negroes, though equally open to criticism, does not come within our concern here, since it was not directly a Church–State issue. The anti-Jewish campaign it encouraged and directed was also serious, and has been discussed in another section.[106]

In general the Smith campaign helped to clear the air, and there followed a period of less acute anti-Catholicism. This was aided by the spread of education among all elements of the population; the experience of having hundreds of thousands of Roman Catholics in our public schools and state universities and in the Army and Navy; the recognized influence for good of Catholic parishes and Catholic welfare institutions, especially in the slums of our large cities; the sturdy insistence of the Roman Catholic Church that morality, public and private, is largely dependent on religion; the fine example set by Roman Catholics in regularity of church attendance and acceptance of religious duties; the leadership of the Church in standing for law and order and in combating the subversive tendencies of Marxian Communism; its constructive attitude in many social reforms, such as through the League of Decency in improving conditions in motion pictures; the fine record of Roman Catholics at home and abroad in both World Wars; the discontinuance of the agitation in behalf of Irish freedom by priests of Irish origin, owing to the virtual settlement of the most acute phases of the Irish question; the growth in culture and assimilation of American ideals by the second and third generation of Roman Catholic immigrants; the decline in immigration from Latin countries; the influence of American-trained bishops and priests; certain liberal Catholic journals, such as the *The Commonweal,* which are read by many thoughtful Protestants; the outstanding services to the nation of hundreds of devoted members of the Church in public life; and the influence of such organizations as the Conference of Christians and Jews, in dispelling prejudice.

As the years have passed, and as my own experience and studies have broadened, I have become increasingly convinced of the large actual services, religious, social, cultural, to the nation of the Church of Rome, the while I recognize that the reconciliation of ecclesiastical authoritarianism and political democracy still involves some serious difficulties. There are times, to be sure, as since the close of World War II, when complications on the home political front due to conditions here and abroad bring out latent ill feeling. This is kept alive by such Protestant prejudices as those shown in the Smith campaign, and too by some attitudes of the Roman Catholic Church on such matters as mixed marriages, birth control legislation, efforts to secure public financial aid for parochial schools, and the attitude of aloofness toward other religious bodies.[107] When all factors are taken into account it will be realized that the Roman Catholic Church has, on the whole and increasingly during the past century and a half, adjusted itself well to American life and institutions—better than many non-Catholics thought possible two or three generations ago because of its inherited totalitarian tradition. But this still occasionally causes difficulties when faced with modern American ideals of freedom and democracy. That these difficulties can be met is evidenced by the recent important announcement by Cardinal Spellman (August, 1949) that the Church will not seek government aid for the regular running expenses of its parochial schools (XIX, 10).

(7) THE EFFECT OF THE REVIVED PLAN FOR DIPLOMATIC REPRESENTATION AT THE VATICAN

Among the causes of the revived anti-Catholic sentiment in certain portions of the country and among certain groups has undoubtedly been the determination of the American hierarchy to secure full diplomatic representation from this country at the Vatican, with probably ultimately the same diplomatic interchange as exists with many other countries, including Great Britain. The matter was brought to a head in 1939 with the appointment of the Honorable

Myron Taylor, an Episcopalian, as the president's representative. Of his fitness for such a post and his useful service in it during the war and the period of postwar reconstruction there is little doubt among thoughtful people; but there has been grave concern among many non-Catholic groups of the danger, from the standpoint of Church-State separation, of continuing this policy permanently and making the president's representative a regular ambassador. This matter has been discussed when the plan was tried on a limited scale for two decades in the middle of the nineteenth century.[108]

(8) THE VARIOUS ANTI-CATHOLIC AND PRO-CATHOLIC FACTORS

In addition to the public anti-Roman Catholic developments outlined in this chapter there have been in recent years others discussed elsewhere in these volumes. The reader is referred especially to the following:

The problems related to public and parochial school education, and especially attempts by the Roman Catholic Church to secure financial aid for parochial schools from tax funds and to control public school education in certain matters.[109]

The question of birth control information legislation opposed by the Church.[110]

The questions related to marriage and divorce.[111]

The opposition of the hierarchy to Protestant missionary or educational work in countries historically closely related to the Roman Catholic Church, especially in Latin America.[112]

The dominance of Roman Catholic elements in certain prominent corrupt municipal administrations.[113]

The contrasting views of most Protestants and Catholics on Sunday observance,[114] certain forms of public gambling (especially raffles and "beano" in connection with Church charities),[115] and liquor control.[116]

The unwillingness of the Church to co-operate in many matters, such as union services and certain charities, with non-Catholic elements.[117]

The desire of the Church (in spite of its co-operative attitude in most international matters) to support Catholic regimes in other countries (such as Franco's in Spain and some regimes in Mexico), even when these are reactionary and totalitarian.[118]

The desire to prevent any criticism of the Church, even in past ages, in books used in public schools and generally available in public libraries.[119]

The question of permanent diplomatic representation at the Vatican.[120]

These developments and causes for anti-Catholic sentiment may be studied in the places indicated and by means of the index.

On the other hand, it must be remembered that there have been in recent years some important factors working effectively for the decline of anti-Catholic sentiment. Such factors have been:

The National Conference of Christians and Jews.[121]

The Boy Scout movement.[122]

The Catholic Social Welfare Conference, on the side of its social welfare pragram.[123]

The increased Americanization in the second and third generation of American Catholics.[124]

The removal of Ireland as a factor in American politics, and the increase of voting independence on the part of American Catholics.[125]

The constantly decreasing economic gap between the Roman Catholic population and most Protestants and others.[126]

The outstanding public services in peace and war of eminent Catholics.[127]

The patriotic attitude of the Church and its members in the late war.[128]

The more general recognition of the important spiritual, moral, and cultural contribution of the Roman Catholic Church to American life.[129]

The important service rendered by the Church in this country in combating anti-Semitism.[130]

The support by the Church of the United Nations.[131]

The development of an American-trained hierarchy and priesthood.[132]

The service of the Church in combating Communism.[133]

Section 5. THE IRISH QUESTION, THE CATHOLIC CHURCH, AND AMERICAN POLITICS

The Irish question has had many aspects. We are concerned here mainly with the political agitation for Irish freedom conducted by Irish-American Catholics, for this aspect of the question has had the most important reverberations in American Church-State relations. The matter bristles with difficulties that are in part due to the lack of distinction in early statistics between Protestant Scotch-Irish mainly from the north, and Catholic Irish mainly from the south, as well as to many emotional tensions, but the essential facts seem to be clear.

There was a serious and long-standing Irish problem in Ireland, and between Ireland and England, which we need not discuss in these pages further than to say that both sides must share the heavy responsibility for the bad conditions which resulted. But there was no serious Irish question in American politics until the nineteenth century had passed into its second quarter, when the enormous Irish-Catholic immigration began in earnest. This resulted in the development, as a protest and counterinfluence, of the latent Nativistic movement, whose unfortunate results we have elsewhere described.[134] The Irish were opposed for economic reasons, because they represented cheap competitive labor; for political reasons, because the old Federalist party saw that they became almost to a man Jeffersonian Democrats and had a flair for politics; for social reasons, because they congregated in the great cities, were accustomed to low living standards, and created serious housing and other social welfare problems; for emotional "patriotic" reasons, because they were "foreigners" inclined to stand together as a compact group; for educational reasons, because their percentage of illiteracy was high; and for religious reasons, because those coming over were dominantly Roman Catholic and inclined because of their historical antecedents to be strongly anti-Protestant—that is, opposed to what was then, even more than now, the prevailing American tradition. It is with the political and social conflict due to the last factor that we are mainly concerned here.

In 1790 less than 4 per cent of the Irish population of the United States was of Celtic-Irish stock, and this percentage included not more than 17,500 persons who could be classed as Irish Catholics.[135] In 1818 Bishop John Connolly (1750–1825), second bishop of New York, wrote in his notebook regarding conditions in the state:

> At present there are here about sixteen thousand Catholics—mostly Irish; at least 10,000 Irish Catholics had arrived in New York only within the last three years. They spread over all the large states of this country and make their religion known everywhere.[136]

This Irish Catholic element had begun to increase rapidly after the close of the War of 1812. Through the first quarter of the nineteenth century the Irish of Celtic stock in this country did not exceed the Scotch-Irish in number—the latter being especially the Protestant stock from which so many of the fathers of the country stemmed. In the decade beginning with 1820, 54,338 persons arrived from Ireland; in the next decade, 207,381; and in the decade closing with 1850, 780,719. The Irish-Catholic immigration was then on in full force, due especially to the potato famine in the late 'forties; religious, political, and economic discontent; and the large opportunities for the laboring man in the United States, whose freedom, in spite of some fears of Nativism, strongly attracted the Irish immigrant.

The Celtic element predominated in the Irish immigration from 1840 to 1870, being in some years as high as 80 per cent. This group came to America smarting under what it believed to be "oppression" in Ireland as a result of Protestant English rule, and it was not unnatural that it should agitate here for Irish freedom. As the Irish (we are not speaking here of the Protestant Scotch-Irish) were politically minded, socially cohesive, and ardent Roman Catholics, they congregated in New York and other great cities where they could have the ministrations and advice of their devoted priests—also mostly Irish—and could unite in politics and political agitation. They virtually all became Democrats, as was not unnatural in view of the political liberalism of the party; its successful overthrow in 1802 of the Federalist Alien Act of 1798, which required fourteen years instead of five for naturalization; its strength in industrial centers; and other factors. Indeed, as early as about the turn of the century a Federalist Senator reported that on a journey through Pennsylvania most of the Irishmen he had seen were "United Irishmen" and "the most God-provoking democrats this side of hell!"[137] It should also be added that most Irish-Americans also became ardent American patriots, and rendered notable service in the Civil War, which incidentally proved an important training ground for those who were later to advance the cause of Irish freedom. On the other hand, most of the Scotch-Irish, who desired Ireland to continue its union with England, were Republicans.

Irish Catholic political agitation showed itself in this country in several ways.

First and foremost, in aiding the cause of Irish freedom. This involved the Roman Catholic Church in the United States in our large cities for many years, as hundreds of priests and editors of Roman Catholic journals felt it their duty to advance this political objective.[138] This agitation by the Catholic press, and to some extent by the priesthood, lasted until Ireland (Eire) gained the legal recognition of her freedom by the Treaty of 1921 with Great Britain. Thereafter this and other questionable forms of political activity on the part of the Church—except as to the division of the school fund, birth control, and local issues in certain centers—became for the most part a thing of the past. Irish Catholics had many sympathizers among Protestant groups during these decades of struggle for at least a much larger measure of self-government in Ireland. Catholic Emancipation, the Fenians, the Irish land question, home rule, Sinn Fein—these terms, thanks to our Irish Catholic fellow citizens, became matters of intense discussion in American politics.

Second, in opposing England. Even Roman Catholic writers recognize this. For instance, Shane Leslie, referring to conditions in this country two generations ago, says that "the anti-British feeling was largely Catholic."[139] A striking example of this was the refusal of an Irish militia regiment in New York to parade in honor of the Prince of Wales when he visited this country in 1860.[140] Ireland never forgot that the United States had fought for and won her independence from Great Britain; this fact had an enormous influence on her hopes and plans. There is truth in the claim that Ireland has always believed that her freedom was due to her through American means.[141] A striking example of hostility of Irish-Americans to England was the defeat of the Anglo-American Treaty of Arbitration in 1897, due mainly to Irish influence in the United States Senate. But fortunately since the granting of freedom to the Catholic portion of Ireland after World War I this feeling largely disappeared, and in World War II we have seen many prelates of Irish descent supporting Great Britain.

Third, in promoting the interests of the Democratic party, which first interested itself in the Irish cause, thus tending to the unfortunate handing over of the Irish vote almost solidly, and until recent years often under ecclesiastical leadership, to a single party, just as unfortunately for decades the Negro vote went almost solidly to the Republicans.

In this whole matter it is necessary to remember that the Irish have been the dominant factor in the development of the Roman Catholic Church in the United States. The *Catholic Encyclopedia* (1913) puts the matter fairly when it says that

> they provided in turn the laity out of which new congregations were formed and the clergy which supplied to a large extent their spiritual needs. . . . There is hardly a diocese or archdiocese in continental United States but has been governed by prelates of Irish birth or descent.

It goes on to say that prior to about 1830 bishops of other nationalities, chiefly French, had the main share in governing the Church here, "but with the steady and large accessions of the Irish to the Catholic population, the latter acquired a predominance which has ever since been maintained."[142]

No Democrat who did not have Irish support could expect to be elected. Even Grover Cleveland's Irish blood through his mother, who was a Neal, helped him, especially as his Republican opponent in the campaign of 1884, James G. Blaine, could boast of an Irish grandfather. This was in the 'eighties when the Irish-American influence was so strong that it claimed forty-two Irishmen in the national House of Representatives.[143] It was in the Cleveland-Blaine campaign that the accusation that the Democratic party was the party of "rum, Romanism and rebellion" proved a boomerang that turned the scales in New York in favor of Cleveland and led to his election,[144] as described earlier in this chapter.

A few incidents from Catholic sources may show the extent to which Irish freedom became a political question among American Catholics, especially in the decades just prior to World War I. The incidents are taken from the book by Mr. De Valera's colleague and first appointed "Envoy of the Irish Republic to the United States," Mr. Patrick McCartan (1889–   ), *With De Valera in America,* and the *Catholic Encyclopedia,* both unimpeachable sources of information on the Roman Catholic point of view.

Mr. McCartan, soon after his arrival in America, in 1918, reported:

> Behind the activities of the Irish Progressive League stood the Carmelite Fathers. Their ramshackle Priory, at the Foot of East 29th Street, was a home for every Irish exile. Mellows and I, and later Boland and deValera, all shared the hospitality of these good Carmelites. Father Denis O'Connor, Father Slattery, Father O'Flanagan, and

Father O'Farrell were true representatives of the Church militant for the Faith and for the Irish Republic. But the virtual leader in New York during these stormy days was their Assistant-General, Father Peter E. Magennis.[145]

The first Catholic prelate publicly to espouse our cause was the Right Rev. Edward J. Hanna [1860–1944], Archbishop of San Francisco. On November 2nd, 1918, the following Washington dispatch appeared in the daily Press:—"Senator Phelan, of California, presented to President Wilson to-day a petition from the priests of the Roman Catholic archdiocese of San Francisco asking the President's support for Ireland's demand for Self-Determination. The signatures heading the list included those of the Right Rev. Edward J. Hanna, Archbishop of San Francisco; the Right Rev. Thomas Grace, Bishop of Sacramento; the Right Rev. John J. Cantwell, Bishop of Monterey and Los Angeles, and the Rev. A. J. McMahon, Provincial of the Dominican Order.[146]

Mr. McCartan further tells of the jubilation in American Irish Catholic circles when it was heard that on December 14, 1918, the Irish people voted to support the Irish Republic which had been proclaimed two years earlier. He says:

I was reading the latest edition of one of the evening papers when Maloney limped into the *Irish Press* Office, saying: "It is all over; we have won. In how many churches here can we have recited to-morrow prayers of thanksgiving for the peaceful establishment of the Republic of Ireland, in accordance with President Wilson's principle of the right of every people to live peaceably under the government of its own choice?"

I immediately telephoned Father T. J. Hurton and Joe McGarrity, and within half an hour the four of us were discussing Maloney's proposal with Monsignor Coughlan. Monsignor had been a Fenian in Ireland when a boy, and had remained true to the political tenets of his youth. He was esteemed in Philadelphia and had great influence with the priests of the diocese. We desired him to use that influence now for Ireland. After about five minutes he said: "I see. We regard it as a *fait accompli. Hibernia locuta est, causa finita est.* Excellent, get to the 'phone, Joe." Before he left that telephone thirty-four pastors had promised Monsignor Coughlan that they would, next morning, comply with his request.[147]

One more quotation from De Valera's representative is sufficient to show how definitely and wholeheartedly the hierarchy and priesthood of Irish extraction—and they were both in the majority—gave themselves to the cause of Irish freedom, in many cases speaking in its behalf and soliciting subscriptions even from the pulpit. As Mr. McCartan tells us,

. . . The action of Archbishop Hanna, the friendliness of Archbishop Dougherty, the interest of Cardinal Gibbons,[148] and the splendid speech of Cardinal O'Connell had shown that the American clergy were willing to lead their people to the support of Ireland in the United States.[149]

It is quite possible that Protestant ministers, if conditions in Ireland had been reversed, might have done the same thing. But that is not the point here. It is that the Roman Catholic Church was to a large extent "in politics" over the Irish issue in much the same way as the Methodist Church was "in politics" a few years later over prohibition. Each time the Church involved was criticized by its political opponents and each time its purely spiritual mission was somewhat diverted.

A great Irish race convention was held in Philadelphia on February 22 and 23, 1919, to support the recognition of the Irish Republic, whose independence had been proclaimed by the Dail on January 21. Arrangements were made for the universally respected Cardinal Gibbons to be present and present the resolutions. A leader in arranging for the meeting was Father Magennis, President of the Friends of Irish Freedom. As he was late in arriving, the Reverend Dr. Patrick Healy (1871–1937) of the Catholic University of America offered the following resolution, which was adopted by the convention, along with an amendment pledging the delegates to raise within six months the sum of one million dollars to advance the cause of Irish freedom:

We, therefore, in the name of many millions of American citizens of Irish birth and lineage who have contributed their full share to the winning of the war, and with the approval of the the overwhelming majority of the American people, now demand that President Wilson place before the Peace Conference and support with all his powerful influence Ireland's right of self-determination and secure for the elected delegates from her Constituent Assembly to the Peace Conference the same status and recognition which have been accorded to those of other small nations.[150]

Soon after this convention the envoy of the provisional government of Ireland in the United States tried to secure the support of the apostolic delegate in Washington to the cause of Irish freedom. In a letter to the delegate Mr. McCartan referred to the fact that "the Irish Race is the bulwark of the Church." He added:

. . . It was, however, felt that those in charge of the temporal affairs of the Church should be apprised of the fact that the Provisional Government of the existing Republic of Ireland, desirous of safeguarding the cordial relations which in the near future will doubtless link the Vatican and the Republic of Ireland, expected that there should be on the part of the Holy See at least benevolent neutrality towards the Republic of Ireland. I had the honour to communicate this expectation to Monsignor Cerretti during his recent visit to New York City; and he then gave me assurance that the Holy See had not issued, and—so far as he was aware—did not contemplate the giving of any instructions to the clergy in Ireland or elsewhere unfriendly to the existing Republic of Ireland. . . .[151]

Various resolutions favoring Irish independence, and later recognizing the Irish Republic, were introduced into Congress from time to time and received united Catholic and much Protestant support.[152] The acuteness of this issue in American politics drew toward an end on March 11, 1920, when the United States Senate ratified the Versailles Peace Treaty with the following reservation:

In consenting to the ratification of the treaty with Germany, the United States adheres to the principle of self-determination and the resolution of sympathy with the expectations of the Irish people for a government of their own choice adopted by the Senate, June 6th, 1919, and declares that when such government is attained by Ireland, a consummation it is hoped is at hand, it should promptly be admitted as a member of the League of Nations.[153]

Incidents might be repeated by the score. Some have been recorded not in any spirit of criticism but merely to establish the fact that the political question of Irish freedom was one which the hierarchy and priesthood of the Roman Catholic Church in the United States considered of vital importance and agitated almost unceasingly for years. As a result, the Church–State problem was considerably complicated, for most Protestants believed that Roman Catholics as such, in spite of many legitimate civil and social grievances, had already secured religious freedom in Ireland, and that the agitation had as a major ultimate purpose the setting up of an independent Roman Catholic State which would be unfriendly to England and Protestantism. However, the Irish Free State (Eire) when it came into existence, though recognizing the "special position of the Catholic Church as the guardian of the faith professed by the majority of the citizens," granted "freedom of conscience, and the free practice and profession of religion to all." Furthermore, all religions existing in the country at the time when the constitution went into force were recognized, and it was provided that no religion might be endowed by the State or subjected to disability of a discriminatory character[154]—relatively liberal provisions in view of the fact that about 93 per cent of the population of the new State were of the same religious body.

In all this agitation in the United States for the freedom of Ireland the Roman Catholic press took a leading and consistent part. As the names of so many representative Catholic newspapers and periodicals indicate, their major interest, next to the advancement of the Church in this country, was for years the Irish tradition and Irish independence. The *Shamrock, or Hibernian Chronicle, Irish American, American Celt, Catholic Advocate and Irishman's Journal, Erin, National Hibernian*—these were a few of the Catholic journals which showed in their titles the close bond between the Roman Catholic Church in this country and in Ireland. These and other Catholic papers in their day and generation vigorously and naturally supported the cause of a free Ireland. As De Valera's representative, speaking of the critical situation in 1918, stated:

> Through the championing of the Irish issue by the whole Catholic Press in America, the freedom of Ireland became a great question for the Bishops and clergy of the Church there. . . . Catholic and Irish were almost synonymous terms in the United States. And to the non-Catholic American it seemed only natural for the patriotic American Hierarchy to espouse the Irish cause.[155]

Section 6. THE CORELIGIONISTS IN OTHER COUNTRIES

The welfare of coreligionists in other countries is one which has created frequent contacts—some of friction but more of co-operation—between American Churches and the government. This has shown itself principally in two fields: the protection of American missionaries and their property and interests, especially in Asia; and the prevention of persecution in Europe. The cases of such friction go back more than half a century, but it seems best to consider the problem in this place because of specially important post-Versailles developments.

(1) FOREIGN MISSIONS AND MISSIONARIES

The first type of difficulty has occurred especially in places where there has been a lack of law and order, or where the government in control has been totalitarian, or unsympathetic to a given religious group, as with the Portuguese colonies in Africa and their Protestant missions, or certain Mohammedan countries and all Christian groups. The special difficulties of the Roman Catholics in Mexico in carrying out their regular religious and educational program, not being one of foreign missions, comes rather under our second head, the "Protection of Coreligionists in Other Countries."

In the early days of American Protestant missions it was assumed that the Churches could and should depend for the protection of property on the diplomatic support of the American government, and if necessary on the influence of the American Navy; but in the last twenty years a strong mission sentiment has grown up that the Church should not rely on armed protection from the American State. In 1928 the Foreign Missionary Conference of North America declared that

> . . . force for the protection of missionaries is in general a serious hindrance to missionary work and that the effort should be made to secure for those missionaries desiring it, the privilege of waiving their right to such protection.[156]

On the whole, American missionary societies have found the State Department most co-operative in protecting as far as possible the lives and property of American missionaries abroad. Many interesting situations have developed. This is especially true of China, partly because there are more American missionaries there than in any other country; partly because such a large proportion of the representative Chinese leaders of modern times have been educated in American mission colleges or at American universities; and partly because of a certain sympathetic understanding between Americans and Chinese—both with strong democratic traditions. In this connection it is worth noting that an ordained American medical missionairy, Dr. Peter Parker (1804–88), after many years of significant pioneer hospital service in Canton, resigned his position with the American Board and rendered important public service to China and the United States as a government official. After acting as secretary and interpreter of the American Embassy he served two years, from 1855 to 1857, as commissioner from this country. In this capacity he was given power to revise the treaty of 1844 between the United States and China, and was largely instrumental in securing the addition of the words "and temples of worship" in the clause permitting the leasing of ground in treaty ports and the erection of buildings for business and other specified purposes. These four words gave our missionaries a legal foothold in China.[157] Similarly, in the treaty "as to Commercial Relations," concluded by the United States with China in 1903 and ratified in 1904—a treaty which grew out of the Boxer Revolution—the following provision is made:

> The principles of the Christian religion, as professed by the Protestant and Roman Catholic Churches, are recognized as teaching men to do good and to do to others as they would have others do to them. Those who quietly profess and teach these doctrines shall not be harassed or persecuted on account of their faith. Any person, whether citizen of the United States or Chinese convert, who, according to these tenets, peaceably teaches and practices the principles of Christianity shall in no case be interfered with or molested therefor. No restrictions shall be placed on Chinese joining Christian churches.[158]

This provision in the treaty directly due to American missionary interests is one of the most clear-cut recognitions to be found in American official documents of the importance and value of the Christian religion.

The Boxer troubles involved the missions in other matters that are of interest from the standpoint of American Church–State relations. The revolution started as a protest by reactionary elements in China which had the sympathetic ear of the empress dowager, but not of the young emperor, against Western influences in general and Christian activity in particular. It began in 1899 and lasted until the fall of 1900, when the siege of Pekin was raised by an international military expedition that included American forces. The Boxers carried banners bearing the device "exterminate the foreigners and save the dynasty."[159] Two hundred and thirty-one foreigners were killed, including thirty-two American missionaries, and hundreds of their converts. Mission schools and churches and even entire Christian villages were destroyed. Later the United States, though declining to support extreme punitive measures, agreed to the terms of the indemnity. This included reparations for the cost of the military expedition to protect the legations and foreign nationals in Pekin, and suitable payments on behalf of the nations, societies, and individuals concerned, including the Chinese who had suffered, but not the Chinese Christians who had been martyrs because of their faith. Of the total indemnity, the United States received $25,000,000 gold. Largely as a result of the enlightened policy of Secretary of State John Hay (1838–1905), most of this indemnity, above the costs of the military and naval expeditions to relieve Pekin and the sums paid for losses in China, was returned to China. In this policy Hay was aided and abetted by American missionary effort, particularly that of Dr. Arthur H. Smith of the American Board, well known as the author of *Chinese Characteristics,* and of Miss Mary E. Woods of the Episcopal Board. The funds returned were to be used for educational purposes, especially for a new government institution, Ching-Hwa College in Pekin, and for scholarships to send Chinese students to America for college and university work.[160] Under the auspices of Ching-Hwa it has been customary to send from fifty to one hundred students a year during normal conditions. President Theodore Roosevelt definitely stated that the return of the money to China "was largely a result" of his conversation with Dr. Smith.[161]

This remission of the indemnity money created a most favorable impression in China. The Boxer incident also led not only to the full recognition of Christion missions and their converts referred to above, but to many reform measures.

The situation of American educational missions and missionaries in Japanese territory has at times been made extremely difficult because of the old governmental requirement that all students worship at Shinto shrines. As extraterritoriality had been abolished, Americans living in Japan or in other Japanese territory before the American occupation in 1945 were under Japanese law. They were therefore, if heads of schools, obliged to have their students conform to regulations inconsistent with their convictions, or to resign their posts. For example, in 1936 an American missionary, Dr. G. S. McCune of Heijo, Korea, was deprived of his position as president of two schools in the city because he refused to have the students of his school perform the required Shinto shrine rites in accordance with the orders of the Korean (Japanese) authorities. As a result of this incident he become *persona non grata* in Korea.[162]

This problem of Shinto has always been a difficult one for American missionaries in Japan. It has been complicated because there is a difference of opinion as to whether Shinto is to be considered merely a cult of patriotism or also a cult of religion. The evidence is somewhat conflicting, but increasingly in recent years the religious significance of the Shinto rites has been emphasized by Japanese philosophers, and consequently the issue of religious freedom has often arisen in the work of American missionaries. As far as the Roman Catholic Church is concerned, the matter was officially decided in 1936, when the Sacred Congregation of Propagation of the Faith in Rome (the Propaganda) issued instructions on the significance of State Shinto. These included this statement:

> The ordinaries of the territories of the Japanese empire shall instruct the faithful that, to the ceremonies which are held at the *Jinja* (national shrines) administered civilly by the government, there is attributed by the civil authorities (as is evident from the various declarations) and by the common estimation of cultured persons a mere signification of patriotism, namely, a meaning of filial reverence toward the Imperial Family and to the heroes of the country; therefore, since ceremonies of this kind are endowed with a purely civil value, it is lawful for Catholics to join them.[163]

As a result of this official utterance Roman Catholic propaganda in Japan immediately began to enjoy a State recognition and encouragement not known before. These were strengthened by the appointment of an apostolic delegate in Tokyo and the formal recognition by the papacy of Manchukuo—territory that had been seized and occupied by Japan.

The Protestant churches have not taken as definite action as did the Roman Catholic; but in 1930 fifty-five different Protestant organizations in Japan, including some missions then under foreign control, issued a statement to the effect that it was "unreasonable" for the government to treat the shrines of State Shinto as nonreligious. It requested the government to define the meaning of the word "reverence" when used in connection with shrine rites, and said that if these purely patriotic aspects were to be emphasized, intercessions, prayers, the conducting of funerals, and the making of offerings at Shinto altars and other religious functions, should be eliminated. On the other hand, the document stated, if shrine Shinto is to be considered within the field of religious activity its function should not be made compulsory. Here are some quotations:

> Recently the government in its efforts to foster national sentiment has promoted worship at the shrines of Shinto and even made it compulsory. This is clearly contrary

to the policy that Shrine Shinto is non-religious. Moreover, the question has often been raised whether at times it has not interfered with the freedom of religious belief granted by the constitution of the empire.

> In such movements as that for "the right direction of thought" and that for "the promotion of enlightenment," the consciences of individual subjects should be respected and regrettable issues like those created in the setting up of god-shelves and the compulsory worship at the shrines on the part of school children should be avoided [*i.e.,* by the authorities].[164]

In 1936 the National Christian Council went on record to the effect that "We accept the definition of the government that the Shinto shrine is non-religious."[165] But in 1940, under the pressure of war, a bulletin of the National Christian Council issued a statement from a study group which well represented the position at the time.

> The position of the Christian church of Japan on the shrine question is clear. The church of our country still possesses mission relationships, however, and foreign missionaries dwell among us. Especially in Korea, doubts on this issue have troubled missionaries for many years and even now they are not resolved. Because of this a large number of schools with mission connections have been closed. In this matter there are regrettable aspects in the attitudes assumed by missionaries, but at the same time we should remember that the issues concern things that are very difficult of comprehension on the part of foreigners and people of other lands who do not possess our traditional feelings, and that it is necessary that we make efforts to place ourselves in the position of mediators between the missionaries and the offices of the government concerned in order that they may arrive at a mutual understanding.[166]

So the matter stood until World War II, during which it became the more acute because of the wave of patriotic fervor which swept the country. The situation was the more serious for American missionary schools, and indeed for all Christians, in that the government had declared Shintoism to be "the perfect religion, the religion of religions."[167]

During the occupation General Douglas MacArthur abolished State support of Shinto, so that it now survives merely as a personal religion for its individual followers.

The whole question of shrine worship is related to Japanese mythology and history. The emperor was officially considered the descendant of Amaterasu Omikami. She is considered as the great Deity (*Kami*), and is specially worshiped at the shrine of Ise, though there are more than a hundred thousand other shrines throughout the country. The government, prior to the American occupation under General Douglas MacArthur (1880–) in the fall of 1945, claimed the emperor's divine descent from this goddess as the central dogma of the State, She is the Sun Goddess, and her activity was until recently believed by nearly all Japanese to give Japan a favored place over all other nations.[168]

Even so broad-minded a man as Prince Ito (1841–1909), who was largely responsible for the Constitution of the empire, wrote in his *Commentaries on the Constitution:*

> The Sacred Throne was established at the time when heaven and earth became separated. The Emperor is heaven-descended, divine, and sacred. He is pre-eminent above all his subjects. He must be reverenced and is inviolable. . . .[169]

The word *Kami* was in general use regarding the emperor, but its translation is difficult. Frequently it has been translated by such titles as "Manifest God" and "God Revealed as Man." Some interpret it in a less deistic way, but there seems to be a fairly general acceptance among objective students of Shintoism that the group acts of obeisance practiced throughout Japan in the direction of the imperial palace had the character of religious rites.

Even recently the problem of Shinto and shrine worship has again come forward. The United States Army Headquarters in Japan has found it necessary to publish a volume on *Religions in Japan,* including in its descriptions not only oriental cults but fourteen Christian denominations, and the various legislative acts, government regulations, and military directives under which religious activities are now directed.

In general our Protestant missionary societies, believing in the separation of the functions of Church and State, have not favored their missionaries assuming political posts, as distinct from service on various educational, relief, and other social-welfare commissions, without at least temporarily giving up their official connection with the home society. In the early days this policy was extended to disapproval of accepting financial grants for missionary educational work from foreign governments, especially when these were ruling native peoples. It was feared that missionaries might side with the government as opposed to the native population in whose interest they had gone to the foreign field. The records of the American Board of Commissioners for Foreign Missions are interesting in this connection. For example, in 1844 its Prudential Committee directed that letters be written to South Africa with a view to terminating the connection, "now existing to some extent, between the mission at Port Natal and the Colonial government."[170] Similarly, in 1850 the committee gave an opinion adverse to asking or receiving pecuniary aid from the British colonial government for support of missionary schools among the Zulus in South Africa.[171] Grants have, however, often been accepted for teachers' salaries, especially in British colonies.

American missionaries in China, Japan, Turkey, and other countries have often rendered conspicuous service to foreign governments, especially in their leadership of educational and humanitarian causes. An interesting example of such influence on public policy is found in the history of the Hawaiian Islands. Although the report that the missionaries definitely agitated for the annexation of the Islands to the United States is incorrect, since it was the sons of missionaries rather than missionaries themselves who were active, the Church has had a profound influence on Hawaiian history.

Seldom have American missionaries been of a higher type than those first sent to Hawaii in 1820 by the American Board (Congregational). From that date to the termination of the monarchy in 1893, that is, five years before annexation, though definitely "instructed by the Board not to get into politics, they necessarily exercised great influence in inculcating ideas of democracy and rights of person and property among chiefs and commoners alike."[172] This influence was seen when one of the early missionaries, in 1838, at the request of the Hawaiians, gave a course of lectures on the science of government. This was followed by a Declaration of Rights and an Edict of Tolerance (1839) and by the first constitution (1840). Other missionaries were detached for government service, some of them renouncing their allegiance to America and becoming subjects of the kingdom. In these positions, which they accepted at considerable sacrifice, they were of great service in the development of the whole fabric of government, and in laying the foundations of friendly race relations that still continue in the Islands. Prominent among these missionaries was Dr. Garritt Parmlee Judd (1803–73), who went to the Islands in 1828 as a physician of the American Board of Missions. In 1842 he severed his connection with the mission and became the royal government's recorder and interpreter. In 1843 he organized at the king's request the first Hawaiian cabinet, and later became minister of finance. Among his descendants have been a chief justice of the territory and other representative citizens.

Almost equally significant services to the Hawaiian State and its progress under the kingdom, republic, and territory, have been rendered by descendants of other missionary families—the Alexanders, Binghams, Castles, Cookes, Damons, Doles, Hartwells, Thurstons, and others. They have been constructive forces in the development of the Hawaiian Islands and in creating the remarkable spirit of good will among its heterogeneous racial groups.[173]

It is not true that the missionaries had anything to do with the deposition of Queen Liliuokalani (1838–1917). No member of the Committee of Safety of thirteen persons at that time was one of the regular missionaries, though several were missionary sons or grandsons. The criticism of missionary activity in Hawaii has been due mainly to misunderstandings, and to the fact that in the early days the foreign residents other than missionaries contained a large proportion of adventurers who "hung their conscience on the Horn" when they rounded the southern cape of South America.

The missionaries were particularly active in education under Christian auspices. General Samuel C. Armstrong (1839–93), the son of a missionary, carried their methods of industrial training to Hampton Institute, and from there they spread over the world.

The late Samuel Clemens (1835–1910)—Mark Twain—might not be expected to be enthusiastic about mission work, but after visiting the Islands and seeing the effect of the missions on the natives he said:

> The missionaries have clothed them, educated them, broken up tyrannous authority of their chiefs, given them freedom and the right to enjoy whatever their hands and brains produce, with equal laws for all, and punishment for all alike who transgress them. The contrast is so strong—the benefit conferred upon this people by the missionaries is so prominent, so palpable, and so unquestionable, that the frankest compliment I can pay them, and the best, is simply to point to the condition of the Sandwich Islanders of Captain Cook's time, and their condition today. Their work speaks for itself.[174]

The reader interested in this subject is referred to a paper by former Governor and Chief Justice Walter F. Frear (1863–1948), read before the Honolulu Social Science Committee in 1935, entitled "Anti-Missionary Criticism." He calls attention to the fact that the instructions for the missionaries, as officially defined in 1838, included the following:

> "Your views are not to be limited to a low narrow scale; but you are to open your hearts wide and set your mark high. You are to aim at nothing short of covering these islands with fruitful fields, and pleasant dwellings and schools and churches, and of raising up the whole people to an elevated state of Christian civilization. You are to obtain an adequate knowledge of the language of the people; to make them acquainted with letters; to give them the Bible with skill to read it; to turn them from their barbarous courses and habits; to introduce, and get into extended operation and influence among them, the arts and institutions and usages of civilized life and society"; and "you are to abstain from all interference with local and political interests of the people," and to "inculcate the duties of justice, moderation, forbearance, truth and universal kindness. Do all in your power to make men of every class good, wise and happy."[175]

The public services of American missionaries in various parts of the world would easily fill a book; and such an account would show many places where their contributions, direct and indirect, to the cause of good government and education have been comparable with those in Hawaii. Such a list, referring for the moment only to those no longer living, would begin with the services of Catholic and Protestant missionaries to the Indians.[176] It would include such names as these:

Samuel Wells Williams (1812–84), head of the American Board's Mission Press in Canton, later secretary and treasurer for the Peary mission which opened up Japan, who rendered long service to the United States government as secretary of legation both in Japan and China. He is best known for his standard work, *The Middle Kingdom*.

William A. P. Martin (1826–1916), missionary to China, active as interpreter to our legation, president and professor of International Law at Tung Wen College, Peking, for a quarter of a century, and frequently adviser to church officials; and first president of the Imperial University of China.

Guido Verbeck (1830–1898), whose name does not appear in most histories, but who is known to have been of great influence in persuading the Japanese government nearly three-quarters of a century ago to adopt many of the best features of Western civilization in education and other fields. One of his ablest coworkers was Daniel Crosby Greene (1844–1913), author of *The Christian Movement in Relation to the New Life in Japan*.

James L. Barton (1855–1936), missionary in Turkey, long the foreign secretary of the Amercan Board, and highly influential with the American government in all matters dealing with the Near East.

Arthur H. Smith (1845–1932), one of the most constructive of China's interpreters, and influential in determining America's policy toward China.

George Washburn (1833–1915), president of Roberts College near Constantinople, and a key man in the training of leaders for Turkey and the Balkans; his services have been specially recognized by Bulgaria.

Robert A. Hume (1857–1929), a missionary in India, to whom Queen Victoria gave the Kaiser-i-Hind Gold Medal for his public services.

Horace N. Allen (1853–1932), Presbyterian physician and the first Protestant missionary to Korea, who from 1884 to 1905 had a powerful influence on the political and social development of the Hermit Kingdom and on American-Korean relations. He was instrumental in establishing the Korean Legation in Washington, and at one time served as American minister-resident in Seoul. Some of his promotion plans and his relation to court intrigues were open to criticism, but his devotion to what he conceived to be the best interests of Korea was unquestioned.

In another section[177] we have noticed the earlier treaties in which religious freedom is guaranteed our nationals in other countries. The "Congo Basin" in Central Africa is an example of a large section of foreign territory where by international agreement not only our missionaries and missionary institutions are specifically protected but where we are given certain rights and responsibilities to protect the interests of the native population.

The Berlin Act of 1885, "adopted by the Conference of Berlin, relative to the development of trade and civilization in Africa, . . ." a conference in which the United States participated, contains in Article VI *Provisions relative to Protection of the Natives, of Missionaries and Travellers, as well as relative to Religious Liberty*. Among these provisions are the following:

Religious and other Institutions. Civilization of Natives

They [the Powers] shall, without distinction of creed or nation, protect and favour all religious, scientific, or charitable institutions, and undertakings created and organized for the above ends, or which aim at instructing the natives and bringing home to them the blessings of civilization.

Protection of Missionaries, Scientists, and Explorers

Christian missionaries, scientists, and explorers, with their followers, property, and collections, shall likewise be the objects of especial protection.

Religious Toleration

Freedom of conscience and religious toleration are expressly guaranteed to the natives, no less than to subjects and to foreigners.

Public Worship

The free and public exercise of all forms of Divine Worship, and the right to build edifices for religious purposes, and to organize religious missions belonging to all creeds, shall not be limited or fettered in any way whatsoever.

This Act was revised in 1919 at St. Germain-en-Laye by the United States, Belgium, the British Empire, France, Italy, Japan, and Portugal, and contains as Article 11 the following clauses:

The Signatory Powers exercising sovereign rights or authority in African territories will continue to watch over the preservation of the native populations and to supervise the improvement of the conditions of their moral and material well-being. They will, in particular, endeavor to secure the complete suppression of slavery in all its forms and of the slave trade by land and sea.

They will protect and favor, without distinction of nationality or of religion, the religious, scientific or charitable institutions and undertakings created and organized by the nationals of the other Signatory Powers and of States, Members of the League of Nations, which may adhere to the present Convention, which aim at leading the natives in the path of progress and civilization. Scientific missions, their property and their collections, shall likewise be the objects of special solicitude.

Freedom of conscience and the free exercise of all forms of religion are expressly guaranteed to all nationals of the Signatory Powers and to those under the jurisdiction of States, Members of the League of Nations, which may become parties to the present

Convention. Similarly, missionaries shall have the right to enter into, and to travel and reside in, African territory with a view to prosecuting their calling.

The application of the provisions of the two preceding paragraphs shall be subject only to such restrictions as may be necessary for the maintenance of public security and order, or as may result from the enforcement of the constitutional law of any of the Powers exercising authority in African territories.[178]

The issue of religious freedom as related to the American Protestant Churches working in Latin America has recently been raised in a serious way by the actions of the Catholic hierarchy. We have various treaties with these countries, generally treaties of amity or friendship, which give our citizens liberty of conscience and worship.[179] These countries also generally give us the protection of their laws providing for religious toleration, though perhaps half of them have some more or less close link with the Roman Catholic Church. Mexico, Brazil, Chile, Uruguay, and Cuba are among those in which the two powers have been separated. It is true that the overwhelming majority of the people throughout South and Central America are Catholic, and this situation requires that the Protestant missionary be unfailingly tactful and considerate of the inherited Catholic culture. But American Protestant missionaries have the same right as American Catholic priests to the sympathetic help of the American State Department in obtaining visas and in protecting their legal rights to carry on their work. Roman Catholics are in a minority of about one to five in this country, and Protestants are in a much smaller minority in Latin America, but in each case the majority should give, and in most cases does give, through the representatives of government, due regard to the rights of these minorities. In this connection it is important that many of the educational institutions supported by Protestants in Latin America have an overwhelming majority of Catholic students. Examples are the Colegio Ward in Buenos Aires, jointly administered by the Methodists and the Disciples of Christ, and the Colegio Internacional in Asunción, Paraguay.

The American hierarchy's protest against Protestant missionary work in Mexico and in Central and South America was made guardedly but clearly in the statement on "Victory and Peace" issued on November 14, 1942, by the members of the administrative board of the National Catholic Welfare Conference in the name of all archbishops and bishops of the United States. They said:

Citizens of these countries are bound to us by the closest bonds of religion. They are not merely our neighbors; they are our brothers professing the same faith. Every effort made to rob them of their Catholic religion or to ridicule it or to offer them a substitute for it is deeply resented by the peoples of these countries and by American Catholics. These efforts prove to be a disturbing factor in our international relations.[180]

This statement, since it obviously referred to the work of Methodist and other Protestant missionaries, proved offensive to American Protestant leaders.

The Federal Council of Churches issued a dignified reply in the form of a statement entitled "Our Heritage of Religious Freedom." This was duly approved by the Foreign Missions Conference of North America, and endorsed by many Protestant journals, such as *The Christian Century* and *Christianity and Crisis*. The council's statement deserves quotation:

It is with deep concern, therefore, that we have witnessed an effort now publicly endorsed in the United States by the archbishops and bishops of a sister Christian communion which constitutes a religious minority in this country, to set the relation of Protestant Christianity to Hispanic America in a perspective which does violence both to historical truth and to contemporary fact. We deplore the pretension of the Roman Catholic hierarchy to circumscribe the religious freedom of Protestant Christians in the proclamation of their faith, while by implication reserving for themselves the right to the universal proclamation of their own. We can imagine no policy more certain to project into the New World the baneful intolerance which is now producing such tragic consequences in the contemporary life of Spain. We accordingly feel it incumbent upon us to make the following simple and plain affirmations:

First: The Federal Council of the Churches of Christ in America stands, and will continue to stand, for the principle of religious liberty and for the rights of religious minorities in the United States and throughout the world.

Second: The churches represented in this council will continue to express solidarity with the national and autonomous Protestant churches in Hispanic America, whose numerous members are loyal and patriotic citizens of the countries where they dwell. They will also continue to avail themselves of the constitutional freedom which the republics of Hispanic America grant to the representatives of every faith. Their controlling aim in the discharge of their ministry will be, as it has always been, to have a part, however humble, in interpreting the significance of our Lord Jesus Christ for life and thought in those great and growing nations.

Third: We affirm, with full and first-hand knowledge of the facts, that, so far from Protestant institutions and the representatives of Protestant Christianity being a peril to good relations between the Americas, they are today, with some easily explained exceptions, and have been for decades, regarded with extreme favor by governments and peoples in the countries where they are located.

Fourth: While obliged by circumstances not of our seeking to make this statement in order to clarify the American Protestant position upon a crucial issue, it is nevertheless the judgment and desire of this council that Protestant and Roman Catholic Christians should combine their influence, in these days of supreme crisis, to work for religious freedom and the other freedoms both now and in the postwar world.[181]

The Roman Catholic press naturally supported the hierarchy and criticized the action of the Federal Council. One of the more restrained statements was an editorial in *America:*

In the United States we enjoy constitutional freedom of religion. Will that help us to enter upon the Latin-American field? Contrary to the later words of "Our Heritage," the Republics of Hispanic America do not grant constitutional freedom to the representatives of every faith, in the sense in which we in this country enjoy that liberty. Only Uruguay grants complete separation of Church and State, and something like equality to all religions.

Whether Protestant missions should be allowed to expand their work in Latin America today, is not a question for us in this country to answer. A reply to the petition must come from the people and Governments of Latin America. Nor would the American Catholic Bishops appear to be giving an answer to that request. Their statement assuredly went out as rather a plea that our Protestant missionaries do not attempt to embarrass the Latin Americans in their Catholic faith. And their observation that such attempts do factually disturb our international relations and directly make for disunity in the Western Hemisphere, conforms exactly with the testimony gathered from all sources of current information, diplomatic and scientific. It accords, likewise, with the recent pronouncement of prominent members of their own Protestant faith, such as John Erskine in *Liberty* for October 18, 1941 (cf. *America,* July 4, 1942); and John W. White in the Catholic *Digest* for December, 1942. "It is surprising," remarks Mr. White, in view of the anti-American feeling the Protestant missions have stirred up, "that protective measures were not taken throughout South America long ago."

There seems to be a tempest in a teapot. Men are so conscious of their own irks, so neglectful of another's situation. In most Latin-American countries, Protestant people receive very kind treatment. Undoubtedly they will continue to merit such treatment, and to receive it.[182]

This whole issue of religious freedom for American Protestant missionaries wishing to go to Latin America or engaged in work there has had many repercussions at home and abroad. Two quotations from Protestant and Catholic sources in Peru may be taken as typical.

In October, 1943, a group of Senators and Deputies presented to the Peruvian Congress petitions asking for "protection from the Catholic 'fight against Protestantism' which, it claimed, is being carried on despite constitutional guarantees of freedom of conscience. It was shown how the *Ley de Imprenta* has been used to justify the breaking up of Evangelist meetings by members of the Catholic 'Eucharistic Crusade.' . . .

"'We cannot believe,' the petitions say, 'that . . . when millions of men are sacrificing their lives on the battlefield in defense of Liberty and Democracy . . . it is a propitious hour in which openly to incite religious warfare . . . nor to expose ourselves to the severe and justified criticism which has appeared in some organs of the press of our sister countries.'

". . . The petition's specific requests were: (1) that the Minister of Interior and Police issue more energetic measures to prevent the subordinate authorities from 'continuing to commit abuses against the Evangelists'; (2) to provide all the necessary guarantees for the free exercise of their religion; (3) that the Minister of Foreign Relations and Religion give instructions that 'passports of persons desiring to come to Peru be visaed by the Consuls without taking into consideration the religious creed which they profess.' "

The Minister of Interior and Police informed the Senate that the Civil Guard and police have been ordered to give the protection requested in the petition.[183]

Here also are quotations from the pastoral letter issued by the Peruvian archbishops and bishops two months later. Referring to the above petitions "in favor of foreign sectarians," they say the incident "cannot fail to awaken our zeal and . . . alarm the national Catholic conscience."

We warn you therefore once more against the multitude of mercenary pastors who have invaded our native land. . . . You will understand ere this that we refer to Protestant propaganda.

Many years ago now Protestantism commenced to filter through into this nation. . . . The first groups, however, worked very much behind the scenes, since the Fourth Article of our Constitution declared the Apostolic Roman Catholic faith to be the state religion to the exclusion of all other forms of worship. The Protestant sects, however, in combination with anti-Catholic societies, refused to rest till they had succeeded by spacious pretexts in inducing our Legislative Chambers, first to mutilate and later repeal this Article, which constituted a sacred bulwark of our religious belief and a powerful restraint against sectarian audacity.

Scarcely was this protecting wall broken down and liberty of worship granted than the unrestrained violence of the sects overflowed in campaigns to propagate their doctrines; and, as though they now owned the country, they abused the hospitality so liberally extended to them and thought themselves quite within their rights in setting to work to demolish the secular edifice of our Catholicism by applying to it the incendiary torch of their heretical blasphemy.

In their eagerness to propagate their doctrine we behold them over-running towns, cities and country in the Coast, Sierra and Forest Region, armed with leaflets, tracts, periodicals and books, vehicles of their error and propagators of their virulence against the Catholic Church, all of which are distributed or sold profusely, the same as their Bibles, sometimes mutilated and always without the necessary ecclesiastical approval. With irritating cynicism we see them posing as teachers of religion, belching forth upon the ignorant populace from their soap-boxes in streets, plazas and parks, the whole content of their falsehood, pitifully disfiguring the very foundations of dogma and ethics, disguising the Word of God and deliberately falsifying historical truth. For the exercise of their religion and the greater success of their propaganda, they hold services in halls or rooms where their adepts and sympathizers gather and to which the curious and unwary are attracted.

. . . The Protestant invasion, beloved children, has demonstrated clearly that it is endangering our religious patrimony; therefore it is necessary that every son of the church and of our Catholic Nation prepare himself to defend it, putting the audacity of the invader within bounds and not wavering in a cowardly way or capitulating before dogmatic error. We would make ourselves accomplices and apostates by the very act of living together with its doctrines, attending its worship or agreeing to or supporting its campaign in this blessed land, where, since the majority are Catholics, the state is obliged by article 232 of the Constitution to defend their religion.

It is urgent, therefore, that we undermine and counteract the Protestant campaign, which is a Crusade of error and lies, opposing it with a sound and vigorous Crusade of Prayer and Apostleship. . . .[184]

The pastoral objects particularly because its signers believe the Protestants "deny the Sacrifice of the Mass," as well as the "prerogatives" of "the Immaculate Mother"; are hostile to the saints; fail to recognize "the divine Institution of the Catholic Church as the only true one founded by Jesus Christ; deny to its visible Head the powers that go with his high investiture, which were accredited by the Lord"; criticize unfairly the Catholic Church and its priesthood; and are guilty of many other errors and abuses, including the "hypocritical propaganda of defamation."

Fortunately in some other Latin American countries such as Chile, Mexico, and Colombia, the utterances of Roman Catholic authorities have been much more temperate.[185]

A reasonable position seems to be that as the message of the Roman Catholic Church has, along with some features that Protestants consider error, emphasized certain aspects of Christian faith and worship in this country which have enriched our American religious and cultural heritage, so it is felt that Protestant missionaries, especially those in the field of education, have greatly benefited Latin America. I remember fifteen or more years ago being in Santiago, Chile, after a eucharistic congress had been held there. A priest attacked the Methodist missionaries, but was answered by an archbishop who said that although he agreed that Catholicism had all the doctrinal truth, and Protestantism much error, there were certain highly important matters that we could learn from the attacked Methodists. He enumerated in particular three: their pastors were men of education; they lived clean lives; they were temperate. He added that these were all things that some Latin American priests needed, and that they should learn from the Methodist missionaries, rather than advocate their expulsion.

A joint committee on religious liberty was set up in 1942 by the Federal Council of Churches and the Foreign Missions Conference at the suggestion of the International Missionary Council. This council is aiding in the establishment of groups in various countries to promote religious liberty.

The council asked the Foreign Missions Conference of North America to be its representative in this matter in this country, and the conference invited the Federal Council to co-operate. The joint committee is taking up systematically the problems of religious liberty in other countries, especially as these affect the work of American missionaries.

The committee is one for study and recommendation, and is being aided by the permanent staffs both of the Federal Council and of the International Missionary Council.

Among the matters which have been discussed at the meetings of the Committee have been the possibility of drafting a charter of religious liberty—a brief statement of universal rights to be placed in the hands of statesmen; an analysis of the conception of religious liberty itself, with the differing attitudes toward it in different lands; the philosophic insistence on religious liberty as a fundamental human right; the distinction between toleration and liberty; the relation of religious liberty to the growth of culture; the best ways to advance religious liberty in other countries, whether by negotiations with governments, treaties, or patient working from within; the question of the inclusion of guarantees of religious liberty in peace treaties; and the consideration of some of the more difficult areas in which American missionaries meet, or wish to meet, the needs of those countries where Christian preaching and teaching, or at least Protestant preaching and teaching, are either forbidden or hampered. Such countries are the Moslem lands, certain Roman Catholic countries in Latin America, Spain, Portugal, and their colonies, and Russia, under the present constitution that forbids religious propaganda.[186]

Regions of special interest to the committee other than Latin America are the Belgian Congo and the Portuguese possessions in Africa, where the rights of Protestants under the Berlin Act of 1885 and the action taken at St. Germain-en-Laye in 1919 have not been fully observed.[187] In the Congo modifications in practices have been initiated by the government since World War II, which should go far toward removing the discrimination from which Protestant missionaries and especially Protestant schools have suffered in the past.

It is the committee's hope that its international efforts for religious freedom will gain support from the United Nations through its Commission on Human Rights. The committee published in 1945 a fair and well-documented book by M. Searle Bates, entitled *Religious Liberty: An Inquiry,* which deals with existing Church–State relations in all countries.

As a result of the joint committee's studies and consultations, especially in 1943, the text of a statement was decided upon and presented to the secretary of state by a delegation consisting of the secretary of the committee and officers of the Federal Council and the Foreign Missions Conference, both of whose executive bodies had duly approved it. The statement is so important as representing the most enlightened Protestant opinion in this country that it is here quoted in full.

We recognize the dignity of the human person as the image of God. We therefore urge that the civic rights which derive from that dignity be set forth in the agreements into which our country may enter looking toward the promotion of world order and be vindicated in treaty arrangements and in the functions and responsibilities assigned to international organizations. States should assure their citizens freedom from compulsion and discrimination in matters of religion. This and the other rights which inhere in man's dignity must be adequately guarded; for when they are impaired all liberty is jeopardized. More specifically, we urge that:

The right of individuals everywhere to religious liberty shall be recognized and, subject only to the maintenance of public order and security, shall be guaranteed against legal provisions and administrative acts which would impose political, economic or social disabilities on grounds of religion.

Religious liberty shall be interpreted to include freedom to worship according to conscience and to bring up children in the faith of their parents; freedom for the individual to change his religion; freedom to preach, educate, publish, and carry on missionary activities; and freedom to organize with others and to acquire and hold property for these purposes.

To safeguard public order and to promote the well-being of the community, both the State, in providing for religious liberty, and the people, in exercising the rights thus recognized, must fulfill reciprocal obligations: The State must guard all groups, both minority and majority, against legal disabilities on account of religious belief; the people must exercise their rights with a sense of responsibility and with charitable consideration for the rights of others.[188]

(2) PROTECTION OF CORELIGIONISTS IN OTHER COUNTRIES

Closely connected with the protection of missionaries in their lawful and helpful tasks is the welfare of Christians and Jews in other parts of the world where American churches believe they are being persecuted or oppressed, and therefore demand effective protests by our government. Notable among such oppressed groups in earlier years were the Armenians, in whose welfare American Protestants were especially interested; the Irish, about whom American Roman Catholics of Irish extraction were greatly concerned; and the Jews in Russia, Turkey, Rumania, Poland, and Nazi Germany, whose persecution outraged not only American Hebrews but all people of good will.

(a) *The Jews.*—The first modern instance of importance is probably that of the Jews in Turkey, after the persecution and massacres in Damascus in 1840. The American secretary of state addressed a dispatch on this subject on August 14, 1840, to John Gliddon, the United States consul at Alexandria, Egypt:

Washington, August 14, 1840.

Sir.—In common with all civilized nations, the people of the United States have learned with horror, the atrocious crimes imputed to the Jews of Damascus, and the cruelties of which they have been the victims. The President fully participates in the public feeling, and he cannot refrain from expressing equal surprise and pain, that in this advanced age, such unnatural practices should be ascribed to any portion of the religious world, and such barbarous measures be resorted to, in order to compel the confession of imputed guilt; the offenses with which these unfortunate people are charged, resemble too much those, in less enlightened times, which were made the pretexts of fanatical persecution or mercenary extortion, to permit a doubt that they are equally unfounded.

The President has witnessed with the most lively satisfaction, the effort of several of the Christian Governments of Europe, to suppress or mitigate these horrors, and he has learned with no common gratification, of their partial success. He is moreover anxious that the active sympathy and generous interposition of the Government of the United States should not be withheld from so benevolent an object, and he has accordingly directed me to instruct you to employ, should the occasion arise, all those good offices and efforts which are compatible with discretion and your official character, to the end that justice and humanity may be extended to these persecuted people, whose cry of distress has reached our shores. I am, sir,

Your obedient servant,
John Forsyth,
Secretary of State.[189]

Dr. Cyrus Adler (1863–1940) has called attention to the fact that this was the first instance of action taken by our government on behalf of Jews abroad; that there was no pretense that the persons referred to enjoyed American citizenship; and that only "the general right to intervene on behalf of justice and to alleviate human suffering was adduced by the President and the Secretary of State."[190] The latter also addressed a letter to the American minister in Turkey, instructing him to use his good offices with the sultan to prevent further trouble. In this letter occurs a statement which does credit both to President Van Buren (1782–1862) and Secretary Forsyth (1780–1841).

The President is of the opinion that from no one can such generous endeavours proceed with so much propriety and effect as from the representative of a friendly power, whose institutions, political and civil, place upon the same footing the worshippers of God of every faith and form, acknowledging no distinction between the Mohammedan, Jew and the Christian.[191]

But of even greater importance from an international standpoint was the protest of the State Department, at the instigation of American Jews, regarding religious freedom in Switzerland, a country now tolerant of all creeds. There was one particularly provocative instance where an American Jew resident in the country was asked to leave for apparently no reason other than his religious affiliation. Later, because of American protests, he was permitted to remain; not as a matter of right but merely as an act of grace. On February 13, 1851, President Fillmore transmitted to the United States Senate a treaty with the Swiss Confederation, negotiated by the American minister; but the president specifically stated that he objected to a clause which provided that Christians alone were entitled to its advantages. The secretary of state, Daniel Webster, and Henry Clay also protested against this clause. In the years 1852 and 1853 the matter received considerable publicity on the ground that the religious freedom of American citizens living abroad was involved. On April 19, 1854, Senator Lewis Cass (1782–1866) presented a petition, signed by a large number of American Jews, against the Swiss treaty. The treaty was thereupon slightly amended to make it less objectionable, but without meeting the fundamental issue in a satisfactory way. It was proclaimed on November 9, 1855. Since the Jews were still dissatisfied, the American minister in June, 1859, presented to the Federal Council of the Swiss Confederation, which left all questions of domicile to the cantons involved, the so-called "Israelitic Note." As a result, and because of the public opinion created, several cantons removed the restrictions against Jewish residents. This progress in toleration was due in large measure to the American protests. In 1874 the Jews were given legally all civil rights.[192] This was at the time of the adoption of the new constitution, when the federal power was increased. Full religious liberty was guaranteed, including freedom of worship not contrary to morals and the public peace, though the Jesuits and related religious orders were still excluded.[193] There continued to be trouble in some localities, but the Jews had gained their essential legal rights, and today they have more than twenty communities organized in full accord with the laws of the Confederation for associations.

Another typical case was the indignation of American Jews at the treatment of their coreligionists in Rumania. The Honorable William M. Evarts (1818–1901), secretary of state, wrote on November 28, 1879, to the American minister to Austria a letter in which the following paragraph occurs:

> As you are aware, this government has ever felt a deep interest in the welfare of the Hebrew race in foreign countries, and has viewed with abhorrence the wrongs to which they have at various periods been subjected by the followers of other creeds in the East. This Department is therefore disposed to give favorable consideration to the appeal made by the representatives of a prominent Hebrew organization in this country in behalf of their brethren in Roumania, and while I should not be warranted in making a compliance with their wishes a *sine qua non* in the establishment of official relations with that country, yet any terms favorable to the interest of this

much-injured people which you may be able to secure in the negotiations now pending with the Government of Roumania would be agreeable and gratifying to this Department.[194]

In pursuance of this same policy, and in the hope of satisfying the Jews of America, Secretary of State John Hay (1838–1905) issued on August 11, 1902, the well-known Rumanian Note which was sent to the representatives of the United States in France, Germany, Great Britain, Italy, Russia, and Turkey, the signatories to the Treaty of Berlin, which stipulated the equality of civil and religious rights in Rumania. The United States was not a party to this treaty, but our minister to Austria, the Honorable John A. Kasson (1822–1910), first suggested the inclusion of universal religious liberty clauses in the treaties to be negotiated at the Congress of Berlin in 1878.[195] The 1902 letter of Secretary Hay dealt particularly with the proposed naturalization treaty. It can be understood only as we realize the character of the laws adopted to oppress the Jews in Rumania. For instance, only a few months before it was sent a bill was passed designed to prevent Jews from earning a livelihood in many handicrafts and trades. The whole Hay document is significant. The following clauses are particularly suggestive, throwing light on the problem of immigration to the United States from Eastern Europe:

The United States welcomes now, as it has welcomed from the foundation of its Government, the voluntary immigration of all aliens coming hither under conditions fitting them to become merged in the body politic of this land. Our laws provide the means for them to become incorporated indistinguishably in the mass of citizens, and prescribe their absolute equality with the native born, guaranteeing to them equal civil rights at home and equal protection abroad. The conditions are few, looking to their coming as free agents, so circumstanced physically and morally as to supply the healthful and intelligent material for free citizenhood. The pauper, the criminal, the contagiously or incurably diseased are excluded from the benefit of immigration only when they are likely to become a source of danger or a burden upon the community. The voluntary character of their coming is essential; hence we shut out all immigration assisted or constrained by foreign agencies. The purpose of our generous treatment of the alien immigrant is to benefit us and him alike—not to afford to another state a field upon which to cast its own objectionable elements. The alien, coming hither voluntarily and prepared to take upon himself the preparatory and in due course the definite obligations of citizenship, retains hereafter, in domestic and international relations, the initial character of free agency, in the full enjoyment of which it is incumbent upon his adoptive State to protect him.

The foregoing considerations, whilst pertinent to the examination of the purpose and scope of a naturalization treaty, have a larger aim. It behooves the State to scrutinize most jealously the character of the immigration from a foreign land, and, if it be obnoxious to objection, to examine the causes which render it so. Should those causes originate in the act of another sovereign State, to the detriment of its neighbors, it is the prerogative of an injured State to point out the evil and to make remonstrance; for with nations, as with individuals, the social law holds good that the right of each is bounded by the right of the neighbor.

The condition of a large class of the inhabitants of Roumania has for many years been a source of grave concern to the United States. I refer to the Roumanian Jews, numbering some 400,000. Long ago, while the Danubian principalities labored under oppressive conditions which only war and a general action of the European powers sufficed to end, the persecution of the indigenous Jews under Turkish rule called forth in 1872 the strong remonstrance of the United States. The treaty of Berlin was hailed as a cure for the wrong, in view of the express provisions of its forty-fourth article, prescribing that in Roumania the difference of religious creed and confessions shall not be alleged against any person as a ground for exclusion or incapacity in matters relating to the enjoyment of civil and political rights, admission to public employments, functions, and honors, or the exercise of the various professions and industries in any locality whatsoever, and stipulating freedom in the exercise of all forms of worship to Roumanian dependents and foreigners alike, as well as guaranteeing that all foreigners in Roumania shall be treated without distinction of creed, on a footing of perfect equality.

With the lapse of time these just prescriptions have been rendered nugatory in great part, as regards the native Jews, by the legislation and municipal regulations of Roumania. Starting from the arbitrary and controvertible premises that the native Jews of Roumania domiciled there for centuries are "aliens not subject to foreign protection," the ability of the Jew to earn even the scanty means of existence that suffice for a frugal race has been constricted by degrees, until every opportunity to win a livelihood is denied; and until the helpless poverty of the Jew has constrained an exodus of such proportions as to cause general concern. . . .[196]

The Teachings of history and the experience of our own nation show that the Jews possess in a high degree the mental and moral qualifications of conscientious citizenhood. No class of immigrants is more welcome to our shore, when coming equipped in mind and body for entrance upon the struggle for bread, and inspired with the high purpose to give the best of service of heart and brain to the land they adopt of their own free will. But when they come as outcasts, made doubly paupers by physical and moral oppression in their native land, and thrown upon the long suffering generosity of a more favored community, their immigration lacks the essential conditions which make alien immigration either acceptable or beneficial. So well is this appreciated on the Continent that, even in the countries where anti-Semitism has no foothold, it is difficult for these fleeing Jews to obtain any lodgment. America is their only goal. . . .[197]

Whether consciously and of purpose or not, these helpless people, burdened and spurned by their native land, are forced by the sovereign power of Roumania upon the charity of the United States. This Government cannot be a tacit party to such an international wrong. It is constrained to protest against the treatment to which the Jews of Roumania are subjected, not alone because it has unimpeachable right to remonstrate against the resultant injury to itself, but in the name of humanity. The United States may not authoritatively appeal to the stipulations of the Treaty of Berlin, to which it was not and cannot become a signatory, but it does earnestly appeal to the principles consigned therein, because they are the principles of international law and eternal justice, advocating the broad toleration which that solemn compact enjoins and standing ready to lend its moral support to the fulfilment thereof by its co-signatories, for the act of Roumania itself has effectively joined the United States to them as an interested party in this regard. . . .[198]

Copies of the note were sent to the signatory powers of the treaty, the United States virtually serving notice on Rumania that by the obligations of international law, in which all civilized peoples are interested, and the rights of self-preservation, she had a right to protest. This note made a great impression on the world, but little was actually done to remove Jewish disabilities in Rumania until after World War I. The Treaty of Versailles had much to say about minority rights in Eastern Europe, in which American Jews were so deeply concerned, and, in spite of the continuance of some restrictions and the recurrence of occasional outbreaks, the Jews in Greater Rumania were at least nominally emancipated.[199]

This incident has been recorded at some length because it is illuminating as indicating how a religious body in the United States, supported by the public opinion of most Christian churches, may develop a state of tension with the government and ultimately prevail upon it to take strong diplomatic action.

Russia also created much difficulty in this period by her persecution of Jews, causing them to emigrate from the ghettos of eastern Europe in large numbers. As a result, the United States government published in 1892 the *Report of Commissioners of Immigration upon the Causes which incite Immigration to the United States.* This report, prepared for the House of Representatives, was a firsthand study of the nature and cause of persecution in various European countries, especially Russia, with its effect on emigration to this country. In this instance religious and racial persecution outside the United States constituted a serious American problem.

Another form of diplomatic difficulty for the United States, and one which created a *cause célèbre* lasting for a generation, was that of the rights of American Jews sojourning in Russia. This was closely related to the preceding issue. The pages of the *Congressional Record* and the files of the State Department are full of references to this controversy. Matters came to a head in 1902, when Judge Henry M. Goldfogle (1856–1929) of New York introduced the following resolution in the House of Representatives:

Resolved, By the House of Representatives of the United States, that the Secretary of State be, and he is hereby, respectfully requested to inform the House, if not incompatible with the public interest, whether American citizens of Jewish religious faith, holding passports issued by this Government, are barred or excluded from entering the territory of the Empire of Russia, and whether the Russian Government has made, or is making, any discrimination between citizens of the United States of different religious faiths or persuasions, visiting or attempting to visit Russia, provided with American passports; and whether the Russian Government has made regulations restricting or specially applying to American citizens, whether native or naturalized, of the Jewish religious denomination, holding United States passports, and if so, to report the facts in relation thereto, and what action concerning such exclusion, discrimination or restriction, if any, has been taken by any department of the Government of the United States.[200]

This resolution, duly passed by the House, received a reply from the secretary of state, the Honorable John Hay, before a somewhat similar resolution had been adopted by the Senate. Mr. Hay's reply was to the effect that American Jews were at no greater disadvantage in Russia than Jews of other countries; that the exclusion of naturalized citizens of Russian origin was due to a "conflict between national laws, each absolute within its domestic sphere and inoperative beyond it," and that such a conflict "is hardly to be averted"; that the effort to secure uniform treatment for American citizens in Russia had not been encouraging; and that the State Department was in the habit of sending all persons of Russian birth receiving passports an unofficial notice pointing out the provisions of Russian law liable to affect them, in order that they might not incur danger through ignorance.[201]

The history of further attempts to solve this problem is a long one. Many state legislatures urged the abrogation of the treaty with Russia unless an American passport were recognized as giving its possessor the right of domicile and travel in all parts of the Russian Empire. Congress followed with similar resolutions, and public opinion was so high that finally in December, 1911, President Taft instructed the American ambassador in St. Petersburg to serve formal notice on the Russian government that the Treaty of 1832 would be abrogated after the lapse of the required period of one year. Both Houses of Congress approved the President's act without a dissenting vote, "and the battle was won, as far as the American side of it was concerned."[202]

Up to World War II the principal trouble, as far as United States protests were concerned regarding the treatment of Jews, continued to be with the conditions in Eastern Europe. Since the Russian Revolution, though the United States has had many difficulties with Russia, these have not been on account of the treatment of Jews. Indeed, many think that the Soviet's greatest success has been in breaking down barriers of race under their flag.

The war completely changed the general situation. Nazi ideology and action in the matter of racialism in general and the Jews in particular shocked public opinion in this country. This was raised to fever heat at the close of hostilities when our officers abroad reported incontrovertible evidence that there had been a deliberate attempt on the part of the Nazi government to exterminate the great majority of Jews in Germany and conquered territories. Actually millions were put to death in concentration camps with specially built chambers for inflicting death by poisoning. No cruelty on a large scale so inhuman and revolting had been known in western Europe, and American Christians were as outspoken and unanimous as American Jews in demanding punishment, as an act of international justice, for those proved guilty by fair trial. This the Nuremberg trials of 1945–46 largely brought about.

Among the crimes in the indictment were those under count 4:

> Crimes against humanity, namely: murder, extermination, enslavement, deportation or other inhumane acts against any civilian population, before or during the war; or persecutions—political, racial or religious.[203]

This was specially directed against the Nazi attempt to exterminate the Jews, and American public opinion was largely responsible for it. The tragic story is so well known as a matter of recent world history that it need not be retold here, though the Jewish situation as related to Palestine, aggravated by war conditions in Europe, became such a controversial American political issue that it is described at some length elsewhere.[204]

The American Jews have been so active in trying to protect the rights of their coreligionists in other countries that they have developed a deep sympathy for the persecuted everywhere. An example of their breadth of sympathy was the action taken by the Central Conference of American Rabbis in 1936, when many of the clergy of the Roman Catholic Church were under serious persecution in Mexico.

> We Jews [said the resolutions adopted] as humanitarians and as religionists wish to voice our religious objections to the policy of any state which strikes at the very practice of religion. This stricture applies specifically to the treatment of the Catholics in our sister republic of Mexico.[205]

Many Protestant leaders took the same attitude.

(b) *The Catholics and Protestants.*—We turn now from Jewish to Christian coreligionists in other countries. There has been some friction between American Protestants and Catholics over Protestant missionaries in Latin

America. This has been due on the one hand to the position taken by the American hierarchy that their work is out of place in countries with Catholic traditions, and on the other to the hierarchy's alleged efforts to have our State Department seriously restrict the giving of passports to American Protestants wishing to take up such work.[206] This opposition is directed mainly against the Methodists, who are particularly offensive from the Roman Catholic standpoint because they have carried their educational and religious propaganda even to Rome itself.

An extreme case involving these ardent followers of the Wesleys and showing the difficulties involved in Catholic–Protestant relations in a foreign country is recorded in *Theodore Roosevelt and His Time.* The ex-president, who had always been most fair-minded in his attitude toward Roman Catholics, visited Rome on his return from Africa in 1910. He naturally wished to see the pope (Pius X) and was duly invited, the rector of the American Catholic College, Monsignor Thomas F. Kennedy (1858–1917), writing the American ambassador on March 23:

The Rector of the American Catholic College, Monsignor Kennedy, in reply to inquiry which I caused to be made, requests that the following communication be transmitted to you: "The Holy Father will be delighted to grant audience to Mr. Roosevelt on April 5, and hopes nothing will arise to prevent it, such as the much-regretted incident which made the reception of Mr. Fairbanks impossible."[207]

The reference to the former Vice-President Charles W. Fairbanks, a Methodist, is significant because the pope had refused to see him when he was in Rome shortly before, because of his visit to and interest in the Methodist headquarters in Rome.

The following self-explanatory correspondence ensued, and as a result the ex-president and the pope did not meet. Mr. Roosevelt wrote to the American ambassador:

Please present the following through Monsignor Kennedy:

It would be a real pleasure to me to be presented to the Holy Father, for whom I entertain a high respect both personally and as the head of a great Church. I fully recognize his entire right to receive or not to receive whomsoever he chooses for any reason that seems good to him, and if he does not receive me I shall not for a moment question the propriety of his action. On the other hand, I in my turn must decline to make any stipulations, or submit to any conditions which in any way limit my freedom of conduct. I trust on April 5 he will find it convenient to receive me.[208]

Ambassador Leishman thereupon, under date of March 28, transmitted the following message from Monsignor Kennedy:

His Holiness will be much pleased to grant an audience to Mr. Roosevelt, for whom he entertains great esteem, both personally and as President of the United States. His Holiness quite recognizes Mr. Roosevelt's entire right to freedom of conduct. On the other hand in view of the circumstances, for which neither His Holiness nor Mr. Roosevelt is responsible, an audience could not occur except on the understanding expressed in the former message.[209]

This closed an unfortunate incident which Mr. Roosevelt in a letter to the *Outlook* hoped would create no ill feeling, because of his high regard and friendship for Catholics and Protestants alike. It should be added in fairness to the pope that his action was probably dictated in part by offensive language regarding the papacy used by one of the Methodist officials in Rome. This was acknowledged and regretted by Mr. Roosevelt, who said that his colleagues were men of judgment who acted discreetly. As he had only just retired from the presidency, and was, according to his own statement, received everywhere, outside of Germany, as though he were still president, the incident was most regrettable and might have been serious had he not treated it so wisely and tactfully. It has its bearings on the Church–State issue involved in the diplomatic relations of the United States with the Vatican, a matter so complicated and so important that it has been dealt with at length elsewhere.[210]

The case of Spain has caused special difficulties. Here the Roman Catholic Church in this country was almost a unit in supporting General Franco in the recent Spanish War because he and his associates were "practising Catholics" and had the support of Rome. *The Commonweal* was virtually alone among leading organs of Catholic opinion in advocating caution when the Church clamored for the recognition of the Spanish dictator by the State Department, and for a break with the Republic under Señor Azana, which had support from Russia much as its opponents had the support of Fascist Italy and Nazi Germany. There was good and ill on both sides. The Loyalists included strong supporters of constitutional and administrative reform, popular rights, and religious liberty, but also, unfortunately, of antireligious Marxian Communism. Franco's supporters, on the other hand, were in general extremely conservative and "respectable" Spaniards, but they were out of sympathy with fundamental reforms and were definitely antidemocratic. Their victory in 1938 was in fact a victory for Hitler and Mussolini, and is increasingly recognized as having been unfortunate. The situation was complicated as far as American Church–State relations were concerned, because there was a definite attempt on the part of influential Catholic groups to get our country to support Franco; and on the part of liberal Protestants, who thought Nazi–Fascism an even graver world danger than liberalism tinged with Communism, to gain increased support for the liberal republican government in spite of some of its extreme tendencies. The identification of the Loyalists with "liberalism" tended to obscure the gravity of their cruel treatment of scores of Roman Catholic priests merely because these had often been connected with public reactionary activities; just as the identification of the Franco government with the Roman Catholic Church tended to obscure in the minds of American Catholics its intolerant totalitarianism. This included opposition to the Protestant churches in Spain in which some American denominations were deeply interested.

When such situations arise and protests are unavailing, boycotts by some religious group of imports from another country, or appeals for diplomatic recognition, or the breaking of diplomatic relations, or even, as in the case of Mexico, appeal by certain extreme groups for intervention, create at times tension between Church and State at home, as well as international friction.

One of the largest of the American churches, the Baptist, was greatly stirred in 1938 by attempts made in Rumania to discourage and virtually suppress the Rumanian Baptists with their 1,200 churches and 70,000 members. This was to be accomplished by enforcing a decree adopted July 18, 1938, which forbade all attempts by them at evangelization and made requirements so drastic that only about thirty of the churches could meet them. The matter received the careful attention of the State Department and of the American minister at Bucharest, who in a communication to the department explained the major difficulty. This was the fact that the Orthodox Church was the State Church, of which the prime minister was patriarch, and the minister of cults an archbishop. The Baptists and the Seventh Day Adventists were classed not as "recognized cults" but as "religious associations." These, according to the American minister, were "placed directly under the minister of cults and can only function with his special authorization which has been subject to frequent and sometimes disastrous change."[211]

Therefore, inasmuch as Rumania has been one of the leading centers of the missionary work of the large and influential Southern Baptist Church of the United States, and its members have established and supported a theological seminary and training school there, the issue was serious. Under the circumstances the Church asked and received moral support from the American State. As the Southern Baptist Committee concerned with the problem contained such representative public men as Senators George of Georgia and Bailey of North Carolina, the issue became a matter of Senate discussion in view of treaty understandings.

More recent evidence of deep Congressional interest in preventing persecution on religious grounds and the securing of religious freedom in all countries was the consideration in the spring of 1949 of a resolution favorably reported out by the Senate Committee on Foreign Relations. It protested against the recent trials of Protestant and Catholic clergymen in Hungary, Yugoslavia, and Bulgaria and their results as a violation of fundamental human freedoms guaranteed in treaties of peace and reaffirmed in the United Nations Charter. It asserted that these actions should be strongly protested in the United Nations or by other appropriate means.

The situation of American missionaries in Japan—already made difficult by the controversy over Shinto, previously discussed—became acute as a result of the Japanese government's decision, in the summer of 1940—the year before Pearl Harbor—to require all religions "to fit into the framework of Japan's new national structure." It formally recognized Christianity as one of the religions of the empire, but announced that no foreigner was to be allowed to hold an executive position in the Japanese Church and apparently no funds for missionary work were to be accepted from abroad.[212] One of the purposes was apparently to drive hundreds of missionaries out of the country, since the government realized that totalitarianism and Christianity were inconsistent, and that thousands of Japanese Christians were unsympathetic with Japan's war of aggression in China. Three American Episcopal bishops and an equal number of British bishops, all in the Japanese Anglican Church, were forced to give up their positions of leadership. The matter was one where the United States, wishing to protect the interests of American missionary organizations, was almost inevitably being forced by its treaty agreements into a Church–State controversy, when American entry into World War II intervened.

Section 7. THE MEXICANS IN THE SOUTHWEST—THE PENITENTES

The problem of our Mexican population, especially in the Southwest, that is, southern California, New Mexico, Arizona, and Texas, has become a somewhat difficult one, owing to the difference in traditions and customs from those of the dominant American population. After the Mexican War of 1845–47 there was considerable racial friction between Mexicans, who lived in the ceded regions, and the northern European-American stock. This friction increased in the last decade of the nineteenth century as the American settlers began to outnumber the natives, and again increased as there were evidences of further immigration from Mexico. It was due partly to cultural and partly to economic causes. The Mexicans generally have some Indian blood, and have a great devotion to the Roman Catholic faith, which in its practices and beliefs in some of the rural parts of this region has been somewhat affected by Indian customs. As a result, their adjustments to American political and social life have not been easy, though their religious freedom was early protected by treaty.[213] The problems that have arisen combine many of the difficulties experienced by immigrants from southern and eastern Europe in the eastern part of the United States, and those experienced by the Negro in the South. As the Mexicans—or Spanish-Americans, as they prefer to be called—have a lower living standard than that of the North Americans who settled in the Southwest, there have been many problems to face. Great progress has been made in recent years, but the fitting of people largely priest-ruled to the American democratic way of life is still far from solved, especially in remote regions; a complication due to the fact that the Mexicans are proud both of their Spanish and of their Indian blood. They also consider themselves superior to the small Negro population in the districts concerned.

The census of 1930 showed nearly a million and a half Mexican natives living in the United States, but the depression which followed reduced this number to approximately 1,200,000.[214] By 1940 it was further slightly reduced. Contrary to common opinion, these Mexicans do not live almost exclusively in the Southwest. They are also laborers in the Middle West and workers in industrial plants in Illinois and Michigan. Most Mexicans in this country, outside of the Southwest and a few places like New York City, are, however, seasonal laborers, especially on fruit farms and in the sugar beet industry. They accept small wages, and live generally in shacks or low-grade and unhygienic houses, apart from most Americans. Where they are numerous there is a tendency to segregate the school children.

There are in general three groups: the immigrants, who represent "cheap" labor; the educated political refugees from Mexico, who belong to the upper classes and live largely in southern California; and the large group of Mexicans who have dwelt in the Southwest since old Spanish times and are proud of their Spanish and Mexican ancestry.

The problems of education, housing, and recreation of these people are all serious, and cause great concern to many religious bodies. As the Mexican immigrants have their past religious life specially identified with some shrine, church, image, or patron saint, they feel uprooted when they come to this country. Many of them break with their old views of religious life.

Naturally, the Mexicans are almost all Roman Catholics, and the Catholic Church continues to care for them in this country. Some other religious bodies have however shown an interest in them. The Home Missions Council of the Presbyterian Church in the United States of America has published an interesting pamphlet entitled "The Northern Mexican," which shows that there is an interdenominational council dealing specially with Spanish-speaking people in this country. The list of its affiliated members includes the Northern Baptist Convention, the Southern Baptist Convention, Congregationalists,

Disciples of Christ, Friends, Methodists, Presbyterians (Southern), and United Brethren among the Churches other than the Roman Catholic which are interested. These all help the State by helping the Americanization process, but the major Church responsibility for them should continue to be Catholic.

An interesting Mexican group of Spanish descent which has caused occasional friction with the public and public authorities is that of the Penitent Brothers—*Los Hermanos Penitentes.* This is a secret religious organization or brotherhood existing among the Spanish population of rural New Mexico and contiguous regions at least since the seventeenth century, being probably an outgrowth of the Third Order of St. Francis. Their organization was found even earlier in Mexico, where it still exists in some rural regions, especially near the Rio Grande. The first public reference to it in modern times was in 1794 when Father José Bernal, a Franciscan, reported its existence to the civil authority.[215] It goes back to the *conquistadores* and through them to medieval Spain. Its avowed purpose is to dramatize the passion of Jesus Christ, thus emphasizing the expiation of sin through physical suffering. The secret character of the rites is of relatively recent origin, and is due to the notoriety and criticisms which arose as a result of the suffering inflicted and voluntarily assumed as a result of the flagellations, scourging, and other extreme practices connected with some of their Lenten ceremonies.[216] These have frequently resulted in excessive bleeding of the head (due to the crown of cactus thorns), hands, back, and feet, and to faintings, and even death.

The Church–State interest in this group of devotees is due mainly to two factors: the frequent incorporation of their local organizations as groups with legal protection, and the existence of cruelties which both Church and State hesitate to permit. There was so much public criticism two generations ago that in 1886 the Archbishop of Santa Fé ordered them to abolish flagellation and the carrying of heavy crosses. His orders to the elder brothers, the *hermanos majores,* were unheeded, as were the requests made of parish priests to induce the leaders to comply. The archbishop then (1889) ordered the societies to disband, but about the only effect was to make their rites more secret, and to abolish actual crucifixions with nails, which up to 1896 were annual on Good Friday in remote places both in New Mexico and Colorado, but which now do not go beyond the binding of the human *Christos* with ropes, and keeping him on the cross not more than about forty minutes.[217]

The *Catholic Encyclopedia* refers to the "barbarous customs" and "barbarous practices"[218] of the members of these secret societies, but some authors like Mary Austin call attention to their high ideal in seeking Christian perfection through suffering, the mutually helpful fellowship of the members, their desire to keep alive and potent the story of the Passion, and the fact that public pressure has mitigated their more extreme practices.[219] She believes that the days have passed when the *hermano major,* a secretly chosen life official of the brotherhood, was the arbiter in many local civil disputes, taking the place of the duly named government official, and that the order will no longer be used as an "instrument of political intrigue" by the native Spanish population of rural New Mexico against the *Americanos,* who are fast replacing their ideals and customs.[220] It is perhaps significant of this changing day that Miss Austin records witnessing the Penitentes' crucifixion scene near a New Mexico village during World War I, when the figure representing Caiaphas and Pontius Pilate combined had an American flag mounted on the tip of the high priest's hat!

The centers of these religious rites in many a remote village such as the author has visited between Santa Fé and Taos, with its *morada,* or council house, guarding the inevitable crosses and "chariot of death," used in processions, its *calvario* on a nearby hill, and the rare sixteenth-century ritual books, give the impression of a picturesque medieval survival with a deeply religious basis, but not fitted long to survive without further modifications in the interest of humane standards. It is probably a case, however, where public opinion in the Church and the local community should be relied upon, rather than the strong arm of the State, to do away with such abuses as still continue.

Section 8. THE INDIAN RELIGIOUS CUSTOMS

From the Civil War until World War I the major Indian problems in which the Churches were concerned had to do with education and with the administration of the reservations. These we have already discussed.[221]

In recent years, though these problems have not been completely solved, the question of native religions has come specially to the fore. For instance, a serious clash over a religious issue arose between the United States government and the Paiutes of Nevada in 1888. It had to do with a Messiah religion originated by a Paiute named Wovoka, known to the whites as Jack Wilson. This he evolved as a result of delirium during an illness. He preached that belief in his doctrine would bring about the restoration to the Indians of their hunting grounds, the return of their buffalo, and other blessings. The so-called ghost dances, in which the men wore ghost shirts and indulged in hypnotic utterances, were a feature of the excitement. The belief spread among the plains Indians and led to the Sioux outbreak of 1890–91. The Sioux in South Dakota became so affected that the Indian agent wired for troops, and many settlers left their homes, fearing a major Indian uprising. General Nelson A. Miles (1839–1925), commanding the troops, ordered the seizure of Chief Sitting Bull (1834?–1890); and he and six Indian police and eight of his followers were killed while resisting. This incident was followed by the unfortunate battle or massacre of Wounded Knee, in which two hundred or more Indians and twenty-nine whites were killed. The Sioux were compelled to surrender in January, 1891.

The incident is worth recording because it was a case where an extreme form of religious excitement threatened the public peace and had to be stopped, for, as has been pointed out several times in these volumes, though the Government guarantees religious freedom, this does not include freedom to disturb the public peace.[222]

It is sometimes difficult to make satisfactory adjustments between protecting the Indian's rights to his old religious customs and the work of Christian missions. In some places in the Southwest the Roman Catholic Church, in accordance with its traditions in parts of Latin America, has virtually accepted many of the old customs as being more or less harmless when diverted to higher purposes; but in other places, and especially among Protestant groups, difficulties have arisen from the desire of some missionaries to detach their adherents from such of their religious customs as seem inconsistent with Christianity. This brings up the question of religious freedom, and sometimes friction between Church and State.

This problem differs among different tribes. It came to a head during the administration of President Franklin D. Roosevelt when the commissioner of Indian affairs, John Collier (1884–   ), who was much interested in preserving many of the beautiful features of Indian art and religion, and who believed in religious freedom, felt that the missionary schools had become too dominant. In 1934 he issued an order that stated the policy of the Indian Office regarding religion. This order was published under the title "Indian Religious Freedom and Indian Culture." We quote the salient paragraphs:

> No interference with Indian religious life or ceremonial expression will hereafter be tolerated. . . . Violations of law or of the proprieties, if committed under the cloak of any religion, Indian or other, or any cultural tradition, Indian or other, are to be dealt with as such, but in no case shall punishment for statutory violations or for improprieties be so administered as to constitute an interference with, or to imply censorship over, the religious or cultural life, Indian or other.
>
> The fullest constitutional liberty, in all matters affecting religion, conscience and culture, is insisted on for all Indians.[223]

Commissioner Collier, after calling attention to the fact that this "injunction to the Indian Service" is in harmony with the provisions of the Federal Constitution, says:

Secretary Ickes and I felt compelled to issue the order from which the above sentence is quoted. We did so because we discovered that the Indian religions and the free choice of the Indians in religious matters were not given this Constitutional protection. We found, for example, that Indian children in the Government schools were subjected to compulsory denominational instruction, not through parental choice but by official coercion. School teachers were required to exact attendance and to maintain discipline at purely religious meetings. Physical persecution against the Indian religions has been indulged in from time to time, down to very recent years. Our present policy is to give to the Indians the same rights that other people in the country have, and have had, without question.

Regulations dealing with religious worship and instruction, approved January 15, 1934, applied this general policy to the religious training of Indian children in government schools. While we sternly insist that coercion shall be eliminated, we are going much further than previous administrations in cooperating with the denominations in placing the Christian invitation on a voluntary basis. The heart of these regulations is contained in the following paragraphs:

"Any denomination or missionary, including any representative of a native Indian religion, may be granted as a privilege the use of rooms or other conveniences in the buildings or premises of boarding schools, on condition that there are pupils who, by parental choice or by personal choice if the pupil is 18 years of age or over, request the services of such missionary or denomination."

"Any child at an Indian Service day school upon written request of his or her parents, knowingly and voluntarily given, shall be excused for religious instruction, including instruction in the native Indian religion, if any, for not more than one hour each week."

These regulations further direct employees "to cooperate with the missionaries by encouraging and facilitating attendance at the specified religious services," forbid compulsion upon the children, and proselytizing, and also direct that employees shall not be compelled to teach at Sunday School.

It is this Administration which introduced the general policy into Indian day schools of releasing children *during school hours* for religious instruction.[224]

It will be noticed that these regulations are entirely in keeping with the practice of most states of the United States, the only exception being that the Indian Office goes further than most of them in permitting the use of rooms in government boarding schools—which have been a feature of the reservations since 1873—for instruction by missionaries or, when specially requested, by the pupils or their parents. In this connection it is stated that

> Officials of boarding schools shall cooperate with the missionaries by encouraging and facilitating attendance at the specified religious services. Compulsion, however, shall not be used upon any child.[225]

Similarly, it is provided that Sunday school exercises may be conducted Sunday mornings "by the employees of the school, but compulsion shall not be used upon the employees to teach at Sunday-school or upon the children to attend it."[226]

There is no law preventing ministers of religion from teaching Indians in government schools. There are at present a few Protestant ministers, Roman Catholic priests, and nuns in charge of mission schools in which children are cared for by contract at government expense. Furthermore, according to Gabel, who made a special study of the subject, published in 1937,

> in government schools . . . pupils are expected to attend their respective churches, transportation is furnished at public cost if the church is at a distance, religious instruction is permitted to the various churches at specified hours, Bible reading and prayers are optional, an interdenominational service and Sunday school is conducted in some schools with chapel services on week days, and the opportunity is extended to the Y. M. C. A. and Y. W. C. A. to carry on "nondenominational" [Protestant] work among the pupils.[227]

This picture has been however slightly modified by regulations adopted after he made his inquiries.

Another interesting and difficult Church–State problem has recently arisen among the Indians of southern New Mexico. This concerns the powerful archbishop of Santa Fé; the Catholic parish in the pueblo of Santo Domingo; and the governor and council of the pueblo, duly elected by its citizens. There are some features about it that are obscure and complicated, but from the published statements of the parties to the controversy and talks with independent citizens of the neighborhood the essential facts seem to be these.

The pueblo is a large one, containing about a thousand Indians, most of whom are almost equally devoted to their ancient Indian religious customs and dances and to their local Roman Catholic parish, which, in accordance with the tradition of the old Spanish Southwest, has condoned many of these. The governor and council of the pueblo wished the Church to continue to baptize and marry their citizens and to say mass, but not to bury them or to hold required confessions, probably because some of their Indian burial customs were frowned upon by the Church, and the Indians did not wish to be forced to confess their part in them.

Matters came to a head in 1935 when the pueblo council—the local governing authority, with its governor and *principales*—was dominated by men devoted to retaining their Indian religious customs. It adopted measures to restrict such activities of the priests as were thought to interfere with these, though many of the Indians wished to continue all the practices of the Catholic faith, including confession and Catholic burial. The matter was complicated by the wish of the archbishop to secure land in the pueblo for a Catholic school and to send sisters to Santo Domingo to visit the sick and aid the priests in instruction. It was feared by the Indians that the influence of these representatives of the Church coming into the pueblo might result in further curtailing Indian religious customs, and might involve some of their important rights.

The archbishop held a seven-hour powwow with the civil authorities named, explaining to them that "the rights of liberty of conscience and practise of religion" under our laws were at stake, as these had been locally denied good Catholics by their action in attempting to curb some of the regular activities of the priests. As the governor and council were "stubborn" and declined to change their attitude, the archbishop declared an "interdict" against the entire pueblo. This meant in this case that, though not excommunicated, and remaining in communion with the Church, they were denied locally its rites and ministrations. The archbishop informed them in effect that they must accept all the Church's ministrations or none, and that because they wanted only certain rites and ceremonies to the exclusion of others he was forced to act in this way. The interdict lasted five years. The Church was left open, but the priests were not allowed to conduct any services. But in July, 1940, as a result of further long conferences with the pueblo governor and his officials, the ecclesiastical authorities announced that "everything was amicably settled. Full liberty to practise religion has been granted to the people. No one is to be coerced to attend any service, not even the Catholic." The archbishop himself said mass on Sunday, August 4—incidentally the date of the corn dance—but the Indians of the pueblo did not take part, and there were no mass baptisms or marriages. Most of the inhabitants were still defiant.[228] The interdict no longer holds. Although officially religious freedom won a temporary victory, as a matter of fact the battle continued for some time. The case is of interest in our study because it is a Church–State controversy whose solution has been attempted by conference between the parties concerned and not by recourse to the courts. But the last chapter in straightening out the difficulties has unfortunately not yet been written.

Section 9. THE MOVEMENT FOR PROTECTING THE RIGHTS OF MINORITIES AND FOR ENCOURAGING NATIONAL UNITY

During the past half century, and especially since the close of World War I, various national agencies have arisen devoted to the cause of removing friction and its causes due to religious and racial minorities in the United States. We are here not concerned with movements conducted by a minority, Roman Catholic, Jewish, Negro, or other, to protect its own interests, but rather with movements of a broader scope which make a large appeal to thoughtful citizens irrespective of their religion or race. We have in mind such national agencies as

(1) the Religious Liberty Association of America, 1888,
(2) the Commission on Interracial Co-operation, 1919, its Successor the Southern Regional Council, 1944, and related agencies,
(3) the American Civil Liberties Union, 1920,
(4) the National Conference of Christians and Jews, 1928,
(5) the Protestants and Other Americans United for Separation of Church and State, 1947,
(6) the Institute of Church and State, 1948.

All of these, except the Civil Liberties Union, which has also had many ministers connected with it, and the last named, have been to a large extent sponsored and supported by the Churches. Two special government agencies designed to accomplish similar purposes, namely the Civil Rights Section of the Department of Justice and the Committee on Fair Employment Practice (FEPC), were described when we considered the protection of the rights of citizens under the First and Fourteenth Amendments to the Constitution.[229]

These organizations do much to counteract the intolerance caused by such groups as the anti-Catholic Ku Klux Klan, the anti-Semitic National Union for Social Justice (Coughlinites), and various other organized movements that attempt to poison the minds of our citizens against minority groups, especially Roman Catholics, Jews, and Negroes. The same narrow spirit is also occasionally shown by opponents of Protestantism, but since this is the largest group it can generally defend itself even though hampered by its sectarian divisions.

We shall consider the voluntary movements in order.

(1) THE RELIGIOUS LIBERTY ASSOCIATION OF AMERICA

This came into existence in 1888 under the name of the National Religious Association. Its headquarters is Takoma Park, Washington, D.C., where it works in close co-operation with the Seventh Day Adventist movement. Indeed, it came into being in connection with a discussion in Congress providing for a Sunday rest law.

The association has taken a broad interest in the whole problem of religious liberty in this country, and publishes a quarterly "Magazine of Religious Freedom" entitled *Liberty*.[230] As it has nine affiliated regional associations and a representative in each state, it keeps in touch with all proposed legislation that seems to infringe on the basic religious-freedom guarantees of our government. It has been particularly active in opposing restrictive Sunday legislation, because the Seventh Day Adventists, for what they believe to be Biblical reasons, observe

Saturday instead of Sunday as the holy day. The association has recently adopted the following Declaration of Principles:

1. We believe in God, in the Bible, as the word of God, and in the separation of church and state as taught by Jesus Christ.

2. We believe that the ten commandments are the law of God, and that they comprehend man's whole duty to God and man.

3. We believe that the religion of Jesus Christ is founded in the law of love of God, and needs no human power to support or enforce it. Love cannot be forced.

4. We believe in civil government as divinely ordained to protect men in the enjoyment of their natural rights and to rule in civil things, and that in this realm it is entitled to the respectful obedience of all.

5. We believe it is the right and should be the privilege, of every individual to worship or not to worship, according to the dictates of his own conscience, provided that in the exercise of this right he respects the equal rights of others.

6. We believe that all religious legislation tends to unite church and state, is subversive of human rights, persecuting in character, and opposed to the best interests of both church and state.

7. We believe, therefore, that it is not within the province of civil government to legislate on religious questions.

8. We believe it to be our duty to use every lawful and honorable means to prevent religious legislation, and oppose all movements tending to unite church and state, that all may enjoy the inestimable blessings of civil and religious liberty.

9. We believe in the inalienable and constitutional right of free speech, free press, peaceable assembly, and petition.

10. We believe in the golden rule, which says, "Whatsoever ye would that men should do to you, do ye even so to them."[231]

The following clauses in a printed statement of 1936 of its aims and purposes are significant:

The Association has one object and one only, namely, the preservation to every man, regardless of his creed, of those inalienable rights which the founders of the Republic declared had been given by the Creator. No religious test is made a basis for associate membership in the Association. Citizens of every belief are equally welcome, provided only that they grant to others the privilege of choice which they seek for themselves.

The Association holds that the State may properly enact laws regulating the relationship of man to his fellow man, but that it has no right to pass measures which have to do with man's relationship to God or religion. The right to disbelieve may be as sacred as the right to believe. The right to dissent should be sacredly guarded.[232]

The association has distributed millions of copies of pamphlets under such titles as "The Church in Politics"; "Freedom—Civil and Religious"; "Your

Liberties Imperiled"; "The Fight for Freedom"; etc. It may be counted on to oppose any and all legislative measures that threaten to interfere with complete religious freedom for Jew, Protestant, and Catholic alike, though many in the last two groups may think it goes to an extreme in opposing certain forms of Sunday legislation designed to protect the day as a day of rest.

(2) THE COMMISSION ON INTERRACIAL CO-OPERATION AND RELATED AGENCIES

Because of the extraordinary influence of the Commission on Interracial Co-operation, it may be worth while to study the part played in its development and in the carrying out of its program by Christian leaders and Southern Churches.

The movement started early in 1919, when outstanding citizens of three of the strongest Southern denominations, Presbyterian, Methodist, and Baptist, met in Atlanta to make plans to improve the condition of Negroes in the South so as to prevent disillusionment on the part of Negro troops returning from Europe who had been fighting "to make the world safe for democracy." They felt that it was essential that the South should restudy the racial situation, and that it should adopt methods which would bring more consistent justice and a larger measure of opportunity to the colored people. The leaders in the movement were a Presbyterian businessman, John J. Eagan; a former Methodist minister, active in the Y.M.C.A. War Work Council, Dr. W. W. Alexander; and the pastor of one of the leading Baptist churches of the South, Dr. M. Ashby Jones.

From that day to this, ministers of the Churches and officers of the Christian Association have been active in promoting the work of the commission.* For instance, a study of the membership of the Interracial Commission, as it was composed in 1920, the year after its foundation, shows that of the fifty-four members, sixteen or 30 per cent were ministers of various Protestant religious bodies, and eight were Y.M.C.A. officers. This proportion of ministers has been to a large extent retained. The membership of the commission in 1941–42, excluding eight honorary members, was a hundred, of whom a quarter were ministers of the gospel.[233]

It is not merely in commission membership, but also in active support of the movement, that the Churches and their leaders have taken so prominent a part. The attitude of the Christian women of the South has been particularly significant. In 1920 a meeting of a hundred Southern women was called in Memphis, which issued a remarkable statement expressing

> a deep sense of responsibility to the womanhood and childhood of the Negro race and

* Since 1944 the Southern Regional Council.

a great desire for a Christian settlement of the problems that overshadow the homes of both races.[234]

A continuation committee of seven was created, representing the Methodist, Baptist, Presbyterian, Episcopal, and Disciples Churches, the Y.W.C.A., and the women's clubs. Such groups as these have rendered a service of great significance, especially in campaigns against lynching.

The same year (1920) there was held the Christian Leaders Conference on Interracial Co-operation. This brought together leaders in the Episcopal Church (including four bishops), the Methodist Episcopal Church, South, the Methodist Episcopal Church, the Southern Baptist Church, the Southern Presbyterian Church, the Presbyterian Church, U.S.A., the Disciples of Christ, the Congregational Churches, the Y.M.C.A., the Y.W.C.A., and certain educational agencies. This conference adopted "An Appeal to the Christian People of the South." It came out strongly against lynching, and in favor of legal justice for the Negro, as well as better traveling facilities, improved sanitation and housing, improved educational facilities, the support of the Interracial Commission, etc. Two paragraphs from the report are worth quoting:

> We urge the ministers of our churches to preach to and to teach their people on these vital inter-racial issues and to exhort them to an immediate and practical application of Christian principles in all of their relations with the colored race.
>
> . . . Reiterating our loyalty to the best traditions and convictions of the white people of the South and our unswerving and unalterable adherence to both the principle and the practice of race integrity, we call upon our fellow Christians of both races throughout the South to unite in a sincere and immediate effort to solve our interracial problems with the spirit of Christ, according to the principles of the Gospel and for the highest interest and benefit of all concerned.[235]

This conference and its manifesto made a marked impression. Following it, in the course of the years, most of the important Southern religious groups have come out strongly for improved race relations and justice for the Negro in the matter of his Constitutional rights. The following statements are characteristic:

The College of Bishops, Methodist Episcopal Church, South:

> We urge our people everywhere to do all they can for the uplifting of the Negroes into preparation for safe and helpful citizenship. This implies that they shall have complete justice where their lawful rights are concerned. We especially urge that everything possible be done to prevent lynchings, which are no less a disgrace to those who engage in them than they are an outrage upon the helpless victim.

The Southern Baptist Convention:

> In the broad matters of better education and more complete Christianization of the Negro, of better housing conditions, of better economic and industrial opportunity,

of a more evenhanded justice in the courts for the race, and of a better understanding between the two races and a more sympathetic attitude of each toward the other there is urgent need and an open door.

The Sewanee Provincial Synod of the Episcopal Church:

> It is of supreme importance for the peace and prosperity of our country that friendly relations between the white and Negro races should be maintained and that every agency which has in view the promotion of such friendly relations, and especially of securing justice and fair dealing to the weaker race, should be encouraged.[236]

The Association of Southern Women for the Prevention of Lynching has had a specially marked influence. It published in 1940 a list of the various organizations which were committed to a program of education to prevent this blot on American justice. This included the leading Christian forces of the South, as well as some women's clubs and other organizations. Furthermore, more than 41,000 white women of the South signed a statement not only repudiating lynching for any cause, but pledging themselves to an educational movement against lynching in their communities. They secured the active co-operation of more than 1,300 police officers, and are a vigilant and active force in the maintenance of law and order. Largely as a result of this and similar efforts in which the Church has been active, the number of lynchings has been greatly reduced.

An interesting development has been the conferences held from time to time between the leading white and colored Christian women in the South. The author was privileged to be at Tuskegee Institute a few years ago when such a meeting was being held, and was greatly impressed by the Christian spirit and ideals which dominated the gathering.

The National Association for the Advancement of Colored People, though not as close to the white Churches, which are sometimes inclined to think it too radical, has the support of nearly all progressive Negro religious leaders, and has done a highly important work in securing Constitutional rights for its minority group.

The Federal Council of Churches has also an active committee on race relations, and has recently appointed a commission on the Church and minority peoples, which has published an important report condemning segregation, especially in the Churches.

The Southern Regional Council, which succeeded the Commission on Interracial Co-operation in 1944, continues its work through the Churches, and publishes *The New South*. Its headquarters are in Atlanta.

These activities should give some idea of the part played by the Churches in the movement which has been steadily improving the status of the Negro in the South. More recently, as the problems of interracial adjustment have also become acute in certain Northern industrial centers, the National Urban

League has organized committees of white and Negro leaders who work together to improve local conditions.

(3) THE AMERICAN CIVIL LIBERTIES UNION

This organization was born out of the attacks made on civil liberties, especially freedom of speech, in the early days of World War I. The former American Union Against Militarism created a civil liberties bureau that soon became independent, and in 1920 expanded into the present American Civil Liberties Union. This has been an ably conducted organization dealing with all sorts of subjects involving civil liberties under the American Constitution—censorship of radio, press, moving pictures, and the stage; civil rights of employers, organized labor, and unorganized workers; defense of racial, religious, and radical minorities; freedom of speech on the platform, in schools and colleges; and the rights of conscientious objectors under conscription laws. The organization takes the ground that the law has a right to step in when overt acts dangerous to the State arise, but not merely when some individual or group has made a radical utterance. It states in its literature that its position on civil liberty is that of Thomas Jefferson, who said:

> It is time enough for the rightful purposes of civil government for its officers to interfere when principles break out into overt acts against peace and good order.[237]

The efforts of the union have been mainly before the courts, where its attorneys volunteer their services. Among the movements in which it has taken a special interest have been the attack on the political dictatorship of Mayor Hague in Jersey City and on the antievolution statutes in Tennessee and elsewhere; the support at all times of the Bill of Rights; the defense of certain labor unions; the insistence on the rights of Negroes in matters of the franchise; the necessity of maintaining Church-State separation, etc. The union follows measures proposed in Congress and in the various state legislatures, and when anything affecting civil liberties is proposed contrary to the Constitution it is heard from.

It is a corporation controlled by a national committee of sixty to seventy persons with a board of directors of half this number, and is supported by about five thousand contributors. The directors meet weekly in New York City. It functions mainly through committees on academic freedom, alien civil rights, education for civil liberties, and conscientious objectors, as well as through the National Council on Freedom from Censorship.[238]

The symbol of the "Goddess of Liberty Enlightening the World," and Patrick Henry's immortal utterance, "Eternal Vigilance is the Price of Liberty," are frequently found in its literature. This has lately included not only general references to religious liberty and a special study devoted to *The Persecution of Jehovah's Witnesses* (1941), but an admirable pamphlet printed in 1938 and reprinted in 1941, entitled *Religious Liberty in the United States Today*. This takes up such matters as the Constitutional guarantees of religious freedom, restraints on religious denominations, religion in public schools, oaths, freethinkers, atheists, compulsory military service (involving conscientious objectors), Sunday laws, and religious intolerance. The study of minority religious groups as varied as the Roman Catholics, Jews, Mormons, Jehovah's Witnesses, Christian Scientists, and Indians and their ancient religious tribal customs, all come in for discussion, while every attempt to introduce religion in the public schools is opposed.

Some liberally minded clergymen have been active in the union from its earliest days. Professor Harry F. Ward (1873-   ) of the Union Theological Seminary was long the national chairman, a position now held by the Reverend John Haynes Holmes (1879-   ); the late Monsignor John A. Ryan (1869–1945), Director of the Social Action Department of the National Catholic Welfare Conference, was for years a member of the national committee. This in a recent year included seven ministers of religion, among them a Methodist and an Episcopal bishop, while another Episcopal bishop, the Right Reverend Edward L. Parsons, was one of the three vice-chairmen.

These facts are mentioned merely to show that there is a considerable body of support among the clergy of the country to protect civil liberties in general through the American Civil Liberties Union, though this is frequently attacked by conservatives as a radical organization.

(4) THE NATIONAL CONFERENCE OF CHRISTIANS AND JEWS

The National Conference of Christians and Jews, originally called the National Conference of Jews, Protestants, and Catholics, was established in 1928 to provide an effective agency in which individuals from the three main religious groups in the country might work together on matters of common concern in their various communities. The late Dr. S. Parkes Cadman (1864–1936), long president of the Federal Council, the Honorable Newton D. Baker (1871–1937), formerly secretary of war, and Charles Evans Hughes (1862–1948), afterward chief justice of the Supreme Court, were among the leaders in the movement. The conference early took as one of its key sayings the words of Mr. Hughes that "When we lose the right to be different, we lose the right to be free." It has consequently upheld from the first the right of men to differ in their beliefs, but it has stood for something more than tolerance, namely, for a sympathetic understanding of religious views different from our own. As stated by the first Protestant cochairman of the conference, the Honorable Newton D. Baker,

The aim of the National Conference of Christians and Jews is to moderate—and finally to eliminate—a system of prejudices which disfigures and distorts our business, social, and political relations.[239]

With this in view the conference has authoritatively stated that it has three major objectives:

1. To analyze and allay prejudice arising among religious groups in the United States.
2. To establish a basis of cooperation for common ends while insuring the right of individuals and groups to differ.
3. To immunize the public mind and emotions against propagandas of misinformation and hatred by developing mutual understanding and appreciation—the only secure foundation for an abiding democracy.[240]

It is noticeable that the conference never tries to bring about any union or merger of religious bodies, nor does it undertake to represent religious denominations officially, nor to organize united religious services. It is an independent body made up of citizens who are sympathetic with it, and has had in recent years the financial support annually of something like twenty thousand people. It maintains a large staff of men and women, who conduct its educational work, education being the keynote of the conference program.

Among the features which have become well known are the "Trio Teams," made up of a priest, a minister, and a rabbi, or of laymen of the three faiths, which go from town to town presenting the point of view of their religious groups and meeting criticisms. The conference also sponsors National Brotherhood Week, held each year during the week of Washington's Birthday, as well as educational institutes such as those held at Williamstown, Massachusetts, and at Estes Park, Colorado. The conference has also issued useful books showing that the social programs of the three Churches have much in common. The method of round-table discussion has been largely used. The annual reports show the many efforts being made by this national organization to prevent intolerance and bring about national unity. Many of the pronouncements against anti-Semitism by Christian bodies have been due to the activities of this agency, which has been specially active in the field of religious news releases and radio. The weekly *Religious News Service,* sponsored by the conference, has arranged for broadcasting through scores of stations throughout the country.

In 1939 the executive committee requested the American Council on Education to undertake a national investigation of the question of religion in education. This investigation, whose report was published in 1947, should prove important in clarifying the issue of how objective knowledge of the great religions and of the facts of religious history could be made available to pupils in our public schools without interfering with our inherited tradition of Church–State separation and religious freedom. The report is opposed to the use of public schools for purposes of religious indoctrination.

It is an impressive fact that ministers of the different faiths have from the first taken a large part in conducting and supporting the movement. Its president, Dr. Everett Clinchy (1896–), is an ordained Protestant minister, and among its membership there are "thousands of clergymen including those of all three faiths."[241] The conference is the most representative of national bodies in its field. It has received gratifying support.

The National Conference of Christians and Jews is a group regarding which the bishops of the Roman Catholic Church have taken different views. Some permit its members as individuals to co-operate; some disapprove such action; others are neutral. *The American Ecclesiastical Review* of September, 1948, warned Catholics against the organization because it held meetings in which ministers, priests, and rabbis appeared together and spoke of the "common positive elements of all the faiths."[242] The Conference has been criticized by some Protestants for side-stepping public issues in which Catholics and non-Catholics disagree, but the criticism hardly seems legitimate as it is frankly an organization to emphasize points on which different religious groups are able to unite.

(5) THE PROTESTANTS AND OTHER AMERICANS UNITED FOR SEPARATION OF CHURCH AND STATE

This organization was formed in 1947 as a result of the fears of many Protestant leaders that the Roman Catholic Church was entering upon a campaign which if not checked might lead to the demand that parochial schools be supported by the State and that other infringements of Constitutional Church–State separation might take place. This agency, with headquarters in Washington, D.C., is dealt with in a later section [XIX, 5 (2)]. Its activities are limited exclusively to the Constitutional provisions involved, and to their observance by government.

(6) THE INSTITUTE OF CHURCH AND STATE

This organization was founded in New York City in the winter of 1947–48 by various liberals interested in Church–State separation and religious freedom. Its executive committee is composed largely of persons connected with Teachers College, Columbia University; New York University; and the New School of Social Research. Its chairman is Dr. John K. Norton of Teachers College; its secretary is an attorney, R. Lawrence Siegel. Its major purpose is to conduct research and disseminate information on the relation of Church and State.[243]

(7) THE OTHER AGENCIES

Among other agencies carrying on somewhat similar work in behalf of religious liberty, or Church–State separation, or both, are the following:

The American League for Religious Liberty, New York City.
The American League for Tolerance, New York City.
The American Society for Race Tolerance, New York City.
The American Tolerance Organization, Alameda, Cal.
The Committee on Religious Life in the Nation's Capital, Washington, D. C.
The Council Against Intolerance in America, New York City.
The Goodwill Commission of the State of New Jersey, Newark, N.J.
The Guardians of Religious Freedom, New York City.
The International Association for the Defense of Religious Liberty.
The Interfaith Movement, Inc., New York City.
The League for the Separation of Church and State, New York City.
The League Opposed to Sectarian Appropriations, Boston, Mass.
The Racial and Religious Tolerance Committee, South Bend, Ind.
Many national educational and philanthropic foundations and agencies.

The work of these organizations tends to aid the State by promoting tolerance and national unity, and is notable for the fact that most of their leaders have been active in the religious bodies of which they are members. There are also various national associations, among which the Boy Scouts are conspicuous, that foster the spirit of toleration and good will among various religious groups. Other organizations protect the reputation of religious groups. Among these is the Anti-Defamation League of B'nai B'rith.

It will be noticed that New York City is the center of most of the national movements against intolerance. It is probably true that no other American city has gone as far in integrating harmoniously Catholic, Jewish, and Protestant groups, including Negroes, into the political and public life of the community.

A movement in the interest of tolerance, but with a more definitely spiritual note, resulted in the Temples of Religion erected at the World's Fairs in New York and San Francisco in 1939 and 1940. The one in New York had impressively inscribed over the entrance the words "For All Who Worship God and Prize Religious Freedom." A characteristic feature was the presence during most of every day of some liberal-minded and spiritual minister of religion who was willing to talk over problems with consultants. Music was emphasized, but there were no specifically religious services or sermons.

To what extent the United Nations Commission on Human Rights will be able to aid the specific movement for religious liberty we cannot yet say, but its general influence on international difficulties due to different religious beliefs is sure to be salutary.

Section 10. *THE POLITICAL PARTY PLATFORMS ON RELIGION AND RELIGIOUS FREEDOM*

The first American political platform was adopted in a Congressional caucus in Philadelphia in 1800 by the new Democratic-Republican (Antifederalist) party. It contained this plank—the subject of these volumes: "Freedom of religion, and opposition to all maneuvers to bring about a legal ascendancy of one sect over another."[244]

Other party platform references to religion, religious freedom, and Church-State relations follow:

Liberty Platform of 1844:

1. *Resolved,* that human brotherhood is a cardinal doctrine of true Democracy, as well as of pure Christianity, which spurns all inconsistent limitations; and neither the political party which repudiates it, nor the political system which is not based upon it, nor controlled in its practical workings, by it, can be truly Democratic or permanent.[245]

9. *Resolved,* That the fundamental truths of the Declaration of Independence, that all men are endowed by their Creator with certain inalienable rights, among which are life, liberty, and the pursuit of happiness, was made the fundamental law of our National Government, by that amendment of the constitution which declares that no person shall be deprived of life, liberty or property, without due process of law.[246]

36. *Resolved,* that we cordially welcome our colored fellow citizens to fraternity with us in the *Liberty party,* in its great contest to secure the rights of mankind, and the religion of our common country.[247]

Other clauses in this document refer to the need for "our conformity to the LAWS OF GOD, and our respect for the RIGHTS OF MAN,"[248] and to the belief that "intelligence, religion, and morality" are "the indispensable supports of good government, . . ."[249]

The American (Know-Nothing) Platform of 1856:

X. Opposition to any union between Church and State; no interference with religious faith or worship, and no test oaths for office, except those indicated in the 5th section of this platform.[250]

The Democratic Platform of 1856:

Resolved, That the foundation of this union of States having been laid in, and its prosperity, expansion, and pre-eminent example in free government, built upon entire freedom in matters of religious concernment, and no respect of person in regard to rank or place of birth; no party can justly be deemed national, constitutional, or in accordance with American principles, which bases its exclusive organization upon religious opinions and accidental birth-place. And hence a political crusade in the nineteenth century, and in the United States of America, against Catholic and foreign-born is neither justified by the past history or the future prospects of the country, nor in unison with the spirit of toleration and enlarged freedom which peculiarly distinguishes the American system of popular government.[251]

The Republican Platform of 1856, at the time of the nomination of its first candidate for the presidency:

Resolved that we invite the affiliation and co-operation of the men of all parties, however differing from us in other respects, in support of the principles herein declared; and believing that the spirit of our institutions as well as the constitution of our country, guarantees liberty of conscience and equality of rights among citizens, we oppose all legislation impairing their security.[252]

The Liberal Republican Platform of 1872:

First: We recognize the equality of all men before the law, and hold that it is the duty of Government in its dealings with the people to mete out equal and exact justice to all of whatever nativity, race, color, or persuasion, religious or political.[253]

This plank influenced the Democrats, meeting two months later, to adopt substantially the same wording.[254]

The Prohibition Platform of 1872:

1. That while we acknowledge the pure patriotism and profound statesmanship of those patriots who laid the foundations of this Government, securing at once the rights of the States severally and their inseparable union by the Federal Constitution, we would not merely garnish the sepulchers of our republican fathers, but we do hereby renew our solemn pledges of fealty to the imperishable principles of civil and religious liberty embodied in the Declaration of American Independence and our Federal Constitution.

2. That the traffic in intoxicating beverages is a dishonor to Christian civilization, inimical to the best interests of society, a political wrong of unequalled enormity, subversive of the ordinary objects of government, not capable of being regulated or restrained by any system of license whatever, but imperatively demanding for its suppression effective legal Prohibition by both State and National legislation.

3. That while we recognize the good providence of Almighty God in supervising the interests of this nation from its establishment to the present time, having organized our party for the legal Prohibition of the liquor traffic, our reliance for success is upon the same omnipotent arm.[255]

The Democratic Platform of 1876:

Reform is necessary and can never be effected but by making it the controlling issue of the election and lifting it above the two issues with which the office-holding classes and the party in power seek to smother it:—

First—The false issue with which they would enkindle sectarian strife in respect to the public schools, of which the establishment and support belong exclusively to the several States, and which the Democratic party has cherished from their foundation, and is resolved to maintain without partiality or preference for any class, sect or creed, and without contributions from the treasury to any.[256]

The Prohibition Reform Platform of 1876:

8. The free use of the Bible, not as a ground of religious creeds, but as a text-book of purest morality, the best liberty and the noblest literature, in our public schools, that our children may grow up in its light and that its spirit and principles may pervade our nation.

9. The separation of the Government in all its departments and institutions, including the public schools and all funds for their maintenance, from the control of every religious sect or other association, and the protection alike of all sects by equal laws, with entire freedom of religious faith and worship.[257]

The Republican Platform of 1876:

7. The public school system of the several states is the bulwark of the true American republic; and, with a view to its security and permanence, we recommend an amendment to the constitution of the United States, forbidding the application of any public funds or property for the benefit of any school or institution under sectarian control.[258]

The National Liberal Party Platform of 1879:

Total separation of church and state, to be guaranteed by amendment of the national Constitution; including the equitable taxation of church property, secularization of the public schools, abrogation of Sabbatarian laws, abolition of chaplaincies, prohibition of public appropriations for religious purposes, and all measures necessary to the same general end.

National protection for national citizens in their equal civil, political, and religious rights, to be guaranteed by amendment of the United States Constitution and afforded through the United States Court.[259]

The Democratic Platform of 1880:

. . . No sumptuary laws; separation of Church and State, for the good of each; common schools fostered and protected.[260]

The Republican Platform of 1880:

The Constitution wisely forbids Congress to make any law respecting an establishment of religion; but it is idle to hope that the nation can be protected against the influences of sectarianism while each State is exposed to its domination. We, therefore, recommend that the Constitution be so amended as to lay the same prohibition upon the Legislature of each State, to forbid the appropriation of public funds to the support of sectarian schools.[261]

The Prohibition Reform Platform of 1880:

13. That we recognize the good province of Almighty God, who has preserved and prospered us as a nation, and, asking for his spirit to guide us to ultimate success, we will look for it relying upon his omnipotent arm.[262]

The American Prohibition National Platform of 1884:

We hold: 1. That ours is a Christian and not a heathen Nation, and that the God of the Christian Scriptures is the author of civil government.

2. That the Bible should be associated with books of science and literature in all our educational institutions.

3. That God requires and man needs a Sabbath.

4. That we demand the prohibition of the importation, manufacture, and sale of intoxicating drinks.[263]

The American Platform of 1888:

Resolved, That we reassert the American principles of absolute freedom of religious worship and belief, the permanent separation of Church and State; and we oppose the appropriation of public money or property to any church or institution administered by a church.

We maintain that all church property should be subject to taxation.[264]

The Republican Platform of 1888:

The political power of the Mormon Church in the Territories as exercised in the past is a menace to free institutions too dangerous to be longer suffered. Therefore we pledge the Republican party to appropriate legislation asserting the sovereignty of the Nation in all Territories where the same is questioned, and in furtherance of that end to place upon the statute books legislation stringent enough to divorce the political from the ecclesiastical power, and thus stamp out the attendant wickedness of polygamy.[265]

The Democratic Platform of 1892:

This country has always been the refuge of the oppressed from every land—exiles for conscience sake—and in the spirit of the founders of our Government we condemn the oppression practised by the Russian Government upon its Lutheran and Jewish subjects, and we call upon our National Government, in the interest of justice and humanity, by all just and proper means, to use its prompt and best efforts to bring about a cessation of these cruel persecutions in the dominions of the Czar and to secure to the oppressed equal rights.

We tender our profound and earnest sympathy to those lovers of freedom who are struggling for home rule and the great cause of local self-government in Ireland.[266]

The Prohibition Platform of 1900:

Sixth—One great religious body (the Baptist) having truly declared of the liquor traffic "that it has no defensible right to exist, that it can never be reformed, and that it stands condemned by its unrighteous fruits as a thing un-Christian, un-American, and perilous utterly to every interest in life"; another great religious body (the Methodist) having as truly asserted, and reiterated that "no political party has a right to expect, nor should receive, the votes of Christian men so long as it stands committed to the license system, or refuses to put itself on record in an attitude of open hostility to the saloon"; other great religious bodies having made similar deliverances, in language plain and unequivocal, as to the liquor traffic and the duty of Christian citizenship in opposition thereto; and the fact being plain and undeniable that the Democratic party stands for license, the saloon, and the canteen, while the Republican party, in policy and administration, stands for the canteen, the saloon and revenue therefrom, we declare ourselves justified in expecting that Christian voters everywhere shall cease their complicity with the liquor curse by refusing to uphold a liquor party, and shall unite themselves with the only party which upholds the prohibition policy, and which for nearly thirty years has been the faithful defender of the church, the State, the home, and the School, against the saloon, its expanders and perpetrators, their actual and persistent foes.

We insist that no differences of belief as to any other question or concern of government should stand in the way of such a union of moral and Christian citizenship as we hereby invite, for the speedy settlement of this paramount moral, industrial, financial and political issue, which our party presents; and we refrain from declaring ourselves upon all minor matters, as to which differences of opinion may exist, that hereby we may offer to the American people a platform so broad that all can stand upon it who desire to see sober citizenship actually sovereign over the allied hosts of evil, sin, and crime, in a government of the people, by the people, and for the people.

We declare that there are but two real parties to-day concerning the liquor traffic—Perpetuationists and Prohibitionists—and that patriotism, Christianity, and every interest of genuine republicanism and of pure democracy, besides the loyal demands of our common humanity, require the speedy union, in one solid phalanx at the ballot-box, of all who oppose the liquor traffic's perpetuation, and who covet endurance for this Republic.[267]

The Republican Platform of 1920:

The Republican party, assembled in representative national convention, reaffirms its unyielding devotion to the Constitution of the United States, and the guaranties of civil, political and religious liberty therein contained. It will resist all attempts to overthrow the foundations of the government or to weaken the force of its controlling principles and ideals, whether these attempts be made in the form of international policy or domestic agitation.[268]

The Democratic Platform of 1924:

PERSONAL FREEDOM

The democratic party reaffirms its adherence and devotion to those cardinal principles contained in the constitution and the precepts upon which our government is founded, that congress shall make no laws respecting the establishment of religion, or prohibiting the free exercise thereof, or abridging the freedom of speech or of the press or of the right of the people peaceably to assemble and to petition the government for a redress of grievances, that the church and the state shall be and remain separate, and that no religious test shall ever be required as a qualification to any office or public trust under the United States. These principles, we pledge ourselves ever to defend and maintain. We insist at all times upon obedience to the orderly processes of the law and deplore and condemn any effort to arouse religious or racial dissension.[269]

Such demands for religious freedom have continued to the present. For instance in 1944 the Republicans condemned appeals to racial and religious prejudices, and the Democrats stated, "We believe racial and religious minorities have the right to live, develop and vote equally with all citizens and share the rights that are guaranteed by our Constitution."[270]

These quotations indicate that there is a field here worth further investigation. Party platforms generally reflect the public opinion of large groups of American voters, and are consequently of value in determining American policy. They should be studied in relation to the various social and political movements of their time. It will be noticed that the major movements and the events which suggested them were the controversy over the Bible in the schools and over public grants to parochial schools, especially in the middle decades of the last century. The major parties have shown themselves, as far as the record goes, as favoring religious freedom and Church–State separation.

An evidence of the desire of the parties to be fair to the three principal religious groups in the country is the fact that increasingly in modern times their representatives have all been invited to make prayers at various sessions of the national political conventions.

Section 11. POLITICAL ZIONISM AS AN AMERICAN ISSUE

Zionism is to some extent part of the movement described above[271] when "Coreligionists in Other Countries" were under discussion. Because it has recently become important and has certain distinctive features of its own, it seems to deserve special treatment as a Church–State issue in recent American politics. In this respect the question of Palestine has assumed in the last two decades a controversial status in our political life in many ways similar to that of Ireland in the previous period. In both cases Washington has reverberated with the demands of Americans of a religious group regarding the government of a foreign country which they consider to be in one way or another their "homeland." In both cases the issue has dragged Great Britain into American politics.

The Zionist movement of recent years can be understood only as we realize certain facts in Jewish history. These explain the interaction between nationality and religion, nationalism and internationalism, traditionalism and "reform." They all go back to one fundamental question: are the Jews primarily a religious group, a national group, a cultural group, or a racial group? On the answer to this question depends the Jewish goal in the present and future; and it is this conflict in emphases, and especially the cleavage between religious and political ideals, that creates a Church–State problem for Judaism, and also for a country like the United States from which divergent Jewish aims are being aggressively pressed and financed.

There can be no question that when the Jews first appear prominently in history it is as a religious nation. It was their faith, centering in the worship of Jahveh (Jehovah), and their conviction that they were in a covenant relation with Him, that made them a "peculiar people." Abraham, and Moses with his inspired commandments, were Jahveh's servants in developing them into a nation out of related Semitic peoples. Nationality and religion were united in a theocracy, with a divine law and divine ceremonies. Every Hebrew was a member of a kingdom whose king in the Davidic line was none other than the vicegerent of Jehovah, originally conceived as a tribal God, who under the influence of Amos, Isaiah, and other prophets who flourished about 600 B.C. was to become a universal deity.

But the great events of 721 and 586 B.C. were to change this, for the Jews ceased to be a nation. In 721 B.C. the northern Kingdom of Israel was invaded by Sargon, King of Assyria, and most of its population was deported east to Mesopotamia and Media. In 586 B.C. the much smaller Kingdom of Judea, including Jerusalem, the religious and political capital of the old theocracy, was likewise invaded, this time by Nebuchadnezzar, King of Babylon, who destroyed the temple. The scattered Jewish people had to give up their nationality. They had neither land of their own, nor self-government, nor temple, nor capital. In this predicament two different proposals competed for acceptance.

The first was Zionist nationalism. The Jews must merely consider themselves in temporary exile, observing as far as possible their rites, ceremonies, and customs, and prepare for the time of restoration and of rebuilding the temple in Jerusalem. Ezra and Nehemiah were the great exponents of this view, which was aided by the action of the emperor Cyrus. When his Persians had defeated the Babylonians he gave the Jews, in 537 B.C., permission to return to Palestine and rebuild the temple. After the destruction of the second temple in A.D. 70

this view "became the standard ideology of orthodox Judaism and has remained so ever since."[272]

The alternative proposed during the exile, and revived after the destruction of the second temple, was that Judaism must be raised from a local and national religion to a universal one. Its adherents must be at home in every land. The destruction of national independence was even considered a spiritual blessing in disguise. The Jews in the various lands of "the dispersion" were to be "the light to the Gentiles." This was the view of the Second Isaiah, the spiritual author of chapters 40 to 66, and of several great exilic prophets. It was to become the accepted ideology of Reform Judaism. It was well expressed by the Pittsburgh conference of reform Rabbis in 1885:

We consider ourselves no longer a nation, but a religious community, and we therefore expect neither a return to Palestine nor a sacrificial worship under the sons of Aaron, nor a restoration of any of the laws concerning a Jewish state.[273]

Both groups believed in the coming of the Messiah, but the first interpreted the Messianic age largely in terms of the restoration of the old kingdom and the temple in Palestine. The ideal was that of Jewish nationalism.

But the second group saw the Jewish religion transformed and spiritualized, and irradiating the whole world. This was the ideal of Jewish universalism as a spiritual force, still advocated by Jews of the reform school. They recognize their people as a historic religious community but deny that they form a nation, and often have no special interest in re-establishing a Jewish state. They are rather concerned about Jewish religious, ethical, and cultural ideals which can be developed in the United States or any other country where they have freedom. Americans of this way of thought emphasize that the United States and not Palestine is now their homeland.

Sometimes both views have been combined by the same man, since the two emphases represent tendencies rather than sharply defined movements. At other times they have been combined with other factors; but they nonetheless represent the cleavage between Zionists and anti-Zionists, between traditional and Reform Judaism, which has lasted to our day.

These have been the two basic historic religious conceptions of Israel's mission, but a third was added in the nineteenth century. With the emancipation of the Jews as individuals in most countries of Western Europe, beginning with the action of the National Assembly of France in 1791, stimulated by constitutional discussions and actions in America, and with the rise and development of national ideologies,

Jewish nationalism became an instrument of secular politics. The establishment of a Jewish nationality came now to be regarded as on the one hand a method of affording protection to unemancipated or oppressed Jews [in Russia, Rumania, Poland, etc.], and on the other, as a means of focussing and crystallizing a group culture."[274]

Political Zionism, as we understand it—that is, the establishment of a Jewish State in Palestine—goes back for its actual modern beginnings to 1881, when Leon Pinsker, president of a Russian society known as the Lovers of Zion, sponsored agricultural settlements in the Holy Land. He wrote a book entitled *Auto-Emancipation*. This anticipated most of the views later outlined with clarity and force by Theodore Herzl (1860–1904), an Austrian, who in 1896 published *Der Judenstaat,* generally considered the foundation of modern Zionism; though his conception of a Jewish State was territorial rather than strictly political. Herzl had reluctantly come to the conclusion that given the prejudices against the Jews in continental Europe, as shown in a striking way by the Dreyfus trial, a strong Jewish community in Palestine was essential. Strangely enough, the movement had a prototype in the United States a half century earlier when Major Mordecai Noah (1785–1851) dedicated Ararat as "a city of refuge for the Jews" on Grand Island in the Niagara River, and invited his coreligionists from all over the world to come there. Indeed, he went so far as to say that

> The Jews never should and never will relinquish the just hope of regaining possession of their ancient heritage, and events in the neighborhood of Palestine indicate an extraordinary change of affairs.[275]

It is interesting that this seed-thought of a great world movement is found in New York state about a hundred years ago.

In the development of political Zionism we are not specially concerned here. It is merely appropriate that we should point out the Church–State connections of the movement in the United States, remembering that in its development it represents to a large extent the secularization of a religious ideal. It was in 1897 that the Federation of American Zionists was effected, immediately after the first International Zionist Congress, which met in Basle that year. It was not, however, until the Balfour Declaration of 1917 that the movement assumed definite political form and gained large support in this country. Mr. A. J. Balfour (1848–1930), then British secretary of state for foreign affairs, issued on November 2 from the foreign office a letter to Lord Rothschild conveying to him on behalf of his Government a declaration of sympathy with Jewish Zionist aspirations, approved by the cabinet, and suggesting that it be brought to the knowledge of the Zionist Federation. This read:

> His Majesty's Government view with favour the establishment in Palestine of a national home for the Jewish people, and will use their best endeavours to facilitate

the achievement of this object, it being clearly understood that nothing shall be done which may prejudice the civil and religious rights of existing non-Jewish communities in Palestine, or the rights and political status enjoyed by Jews in any other country.[276]

The Balfour Declaration was drafted in London, revised in New York and Washington, and issued with President Wilson's approval. It was made during War World I, and has since become the international foundation on which Zionist ambitions have been largely based. Two things should be noticed: The first is that it contains no specific statement that Palestine itself shall be constituted as a Jewish political state. The wording is clear, and to the effect that there should be "in" Palestine "a national home for the Jewish people." Furthermore, the second half of the declaration, which is generally not emphasized by extreme propagandists, definitely states that "nothing shall be done which will prejudice the civil and religious rights of existing non-Jewish communities in Palestine." This is particularly important, and undoubtedly had in mind primarily the Arabs, who at the time and until the events of 1948–49 formed a considerable majority of the population.

This declaration is embodied in the terms of the mandate to Great Britain for Palestine confirmed by the League of Nations on July 24, 1924, and carried into effect the following year. Article 6 provided that "The Administration of Palestine, while ensuring that the rights and position of other sections of the population are not prejudiced, shall facilitate Jewish immigration under suitable conditions."[277]

The Balfour Declaration was approved by the American Jewish Congress in December, 1918, in the name of the Jews of America, then over 3,000,000 in number. This congress also adopted a resolution urging Great Britain to assume the Palestine mandate, and appointed a delegation to represent American Jewry at the peace conference. The delegation presented to President Wilson a formal memorandum asking

that the Peace Conference recognize the aspirations and historic claims of the Jewish people in regard to Palestine; that such action be taken by the Conference as shall vest the sovereign possession of Palestine in such League of Nations as may be formed, and that the government thereof be entrusted to Great Britain as the mandatory or trustee of the League.[278]

Under the mandate commission regulations were made in 1927 for the organization of the Jewish population of Palestine as a religious community and its recognition as such by the government. It enjoyed autonomy for its internal affairs—religious, cultural, and communal—and had a restricted power to levy taxes. There were a chief rabbinate, local rabbinical officers, an elected assembly, and a general council, chosen by the assembly and representing the

Jewish community in its dealings with the government and with local committees. A good many Jews, however, opted themselves out of this community. Both the British government and the administration of Palestine recognized the Jewish agency, which included both Zionists and non-Zionists and was represented by a local executive in Palestine, as the agency of the Jewish people in all matters pertaining to the upbuilding of the Jewish national home.[279]

According to the official estimates made shortly before World War II, in 1938, there were about 1,400,000 people in Palestine, of whom nearly 900,000 were Moslems, 400,000 Jews, and over 100,000 Christians. The problems connected with their interrelations have been difficult, but are not considered insuperable, especially as most of the Arabs (Moslems) have been virtually obliged to leave the sections assigned the Jews in the partition. The Jews have developed more than two hundred agricultural settlements, more than half of them on land belonging to the Jewish National Fund established by the Zionist organization. There were prior to 1940 over 5,000 Jewish industrial establishments and artisans' workshops. Hebrew was one of the three official languages of the country, the others being English and Arabic. The Jews have provided almost all their own schools, having in addition a Hebrew university in Jerusalem, established in 1925, with distinguished scholars, and nearly 500,000 volumes in its library. There is also a large Hebrew technical institute.

It will be seen, therefore, that the interest in Palestine on the part of Jews throughout the world has been and is impressive. It has been very largely financed in the United States. By 1920 there were 171,000 American Jews contributing to the Zionist fund,[280] and they furnished a very considerable part of the hundreds of millions of dollars in contributions and investments which have made possible the large-scale immigration and colonization of the last quarter of a century.[281] This movement has received its support partly from the synagogue and partly from purely secular organizations.

All this as a voluntary interest on the part of American Jews in Palestine would not have special interest in a study of Church and State in the United States were it not that the American government and its leaders have from time to time interested themselves in Zionism, and that the program has political significance. All the presidents from Woodrow Wilson on have made frank and favorable statements on the general subject, though in almost every case following the Balfour Declaration in not committing our government definitely to the idea of Palestine (at least as a unit) as an autonomous Jewish State. The most important of these utterances are an early one of Woodrow Wilson and a later one by the late President Franklin D. Roosevelt. Mr. Wilson in August, 1918, stated:

I welcome an opportunity to express the satisfaction I have felt in the progress of the Zionist movement in the United States and in the Allied countries since the declaration by Mr. Balfour on behalf of the British Government, of Great Britain's approval of the establishment in Palestine of a national home for the Jewish people, and his promise that the British Government would use its best endeavors to facilitate the achievement of that object, with the understandings that nothing would be done to prejudice the civil and religious rights of non-Jewish people in Palestine or the rights and political status enjoyed by Jews in other countries.[282]

President Roosevelt's views are equally significant.

The interest which I have had and have frequently manifested in the rebuilding of the ancient Jewish homeland, is, I am persuaded, an interest which is shared by all who recognize that every people has the inalienable right to life, liberty and the pursuit of happiness. It is a source of renewed hope and courage, that by international accord and by the moral support of the peoples of the world, men and women of Jewish faith have a right to resettle the land where their faith was born and from which much of our modern civilization has emanated.[283]

The State Department has issued a pamphlet entitled *Mandate for Palestine* which contains all the documents exchanged between the United States and the League of Nations in drafting the mandate provisions. Among these papers is the letter that the secretary of state, Bainbridge Colby, wrote on November 20, 1920, to the British foreign secretary, Lord Curzon.

The United States [he said] is undoubtedly one of the powers directly interested in the terms of the mandates, and I therefore request that the draft mandate forms be communicated to this Government for its consideration before their submission to the Council of the League.[284]

More important is the joint resolution adopted by both Houses of Congress in 1922 and signed by President Harding on September 21 of that year. Its textual history is a matter of some importance. On March 30, 1922, Senator Henry Cabot Lodge (1850-1924) presented to the Senate resolutions adopted by the Commonwealth of Massachusetts the previous day, in which it was

Ordered, That the General Court of Massachusetts urges the Government of the United States of America formally to recognize the present status of the Jewish people in Palestine and thus to approve the fulfillment of its yearning desire for a national home in the land of its forefathers; and be it further

Ordered, That copies of this order be sent by the secretary of the Commonwealth to the President of the United States, to the presiding officers of both branches of Congress, to each of the Senators and Representatives in Congress from Massachusetts, and to the Zionist organization of America.[285]

On April 12, Senator Lodge introduced a resolution on the subject, which was referred to the Committee on Foreign Relations. Since it formed the basis of later national action in modified form it is here given.

Resolved, etc., That the United States of America favors the establishment in Palestine of the National Home for the Jewish People, in accordance with the provisions contained in the declaration of the British Government of November 2, 1917, known as the Balfour declaration, it being clearly understood that nothing shall be done which may prejudice the civil and religious rights of existing non-Jewish communities in Palestine, or the rights and political status enjoyed by Jews in any other country, and that the holy places and religious buildings and sites in Palestine shall be adequately protected.[286]

On June 30, the House, on motion of Representative Hamilton Fish (1888–) of New York, adopted the following:

Whereas the Jewish people have for many centuries believed in and yearned for the rebuilding of their ancient homeland; and

Whereas, owing to the outcome of the World War and their part therein, the Jewish people are to be enabled to re-create and reorganize a national home in the land of their fathers, which will give to the House of Israel its long-denied opportunity to re-establish a fruitful Jewish life and culture in the ancient Jewish land: Therefore be it

Resolved, etc., That the United States of America favors the establishment in Palestine of a national home for the Jewish people, it being clearly understood that nothing shall be done which may prejudice the civil and religious rights of Christian and all other non-Jewish communities in Palestine, and that the holy places and religious buildings and sites in Palestine shall be adequately protected.[287]

The form in which the joint resolution was finally adopted was based on that of the House. Here is its exact wording:

Favoring the establishment in Palestine of a national home for the Jewish people.

Resolved by the Senate and House of Representatives of the United States of America in Congress assembled, That the United States of America favors the establishment in Palestine of a national home for the Jewish people, it being clearly understood that nothing shall be done which may prejudice the civil and religious rights of Christian and all other non-Jewish communities in Palestine, and that the holy places and religious buildings and sites in Palestine shall be adequately protected.[288]

It is important that in discussing the highly controversial subject of political Zionism we should bear in mind both what was said and what was omitted in these resolutions.

The records of Congress show clearly the purpose of the action and the arguments that were used at the time, as well as the organized Jewish pressure that was exerted. Since, however, the resolutions favored merely "a national home for the Jewish people . . . in Palestine" and not the Jewish *state of* Palestine, and as the rights of all non-Jewish communities were fully protected, Christian public opinion also felt that the proposal was both fair and wise. There was little realization at the time that within a few years many extreme Zionists would read into these resolutions, and into the Balfour Declaration on which they were based, so much that was not originally contemplated.[289] This made it necessary in the winter of 1943–44 for high officers of the State and War Departments to urge the Foreign Affairs Committee of the Senate not to approve resolutions regarding Palestine urged by many political Zionists, on the ground that such resolutions would embarrass our government in carrying on the war in countries with a large Arab population.

The nearest approach I have found to any official American statement supporting the Zionists' full political position is that of President Wilson on March 3, 1919:

I am persuaded that the Allied Nations, with the fullest concurrence of our own government and people, are agreed that in Palestine shall be laid the foundations of a Jewish commonwealth.[290]

It will be noticed, however, that this is also very different from stating that Palestine itself was to be a Jewish State—the important "in" being still included.

It must be remembered that political Zionism—which is strongly opposed by the large Arab population of Palestine—does not appeal to all the leading Jews and Jewish organizations of the United States. Indeed, there is a sharp rift in sentiment with reference to it. It is chiefly a cleavage between those who think of Judaism primarily as a universal spiritual movement and consequently emphasize Judaism as a religion, and those who consider Judaism as representing mainly a racial group. These wish to have the Jewish people maintain to a large extent a separate national existence, with Palestine not merely as a homeland for hundreds of thousands of persecuted Jews from Europe and a center of cultural life, to which virtually all assent, but also as practically an autonomous Jewish State. Those who favor the latter were active in the movement to organize a Jewish Army in World War II—a movement opposed by the other group.

It should also be remembered that Zionism has been supported both by religious and secularist Jews. The late Louis D. Brandeis (1856–1941) of the United States Supreme Court, though not actively related to the synagogue, became an ardent Zionist. His views, as summed up in *The Jewish Problem—How to Solve It,* were thus stated:

My approach to Zionism was through Americanism, for it became clear to me that to become good Americans, we must become better Jews, and to be better Jews we must become Zionists.[291]

The Zionist movement is highly organized, constantly trying to exert pressure on the Federal administration and on public opinion in this country, and determined not only to complete the carrying out of the Balfour Declaration in favor of "the establishment in Palestine of a national home for the Jewish people," but to go further by interpreting this as involving an autonomous Jewish State covering most of Palestine. For example, the New Zionist Organization of America in 1943 promoted a large advertisement definitely referring to "Palestine—The Future Jewish State" and to the formation of "The Jewish Government in Palestine." Its appeal in large letters is thus summarized:

We appeal to all men of goodwill for active support of our following demands:

1) All Jews who can be saved from extermination should be immediately admitted to Palestine—the future Jewish State.
2) A Jewish Army to fight under a Jewish banner must be created.
3) The admission of the Jewish people to the councils of the United Nations as an equal partner in war and peace.[292]

In other words, many political Zionists in this country have been seeking, rightly or wrongly, to transform Palestine into a Jewish State with little regard for the wishes of the Arab and other "non-Jewish communities" referred to in the Balfour Declaration.[293] As to the Arabs, though some Zionist extremists still advocate their transference—voluntarily if possible—to lands further east, most supporters of the movement believe that these followers of Mohammed should be allowed to continue at least in the section of Palestine assigned them by the United Nations partition, observing their own religious, social, and communal life, while recognizing the authority of the new Jewish State within its own borders.

That the Zionist program in Palestine carried with it great extremes through the activities of various armed terrorist groups which tried to enforce it, has been acknowledged and deeply regretted by many Zionists in this country.

Reform Judaism, which emphasizes the adaptation of Jews to American conditions, and believes that the Jewish contribution to the life of today should be mainly on spiritual and cultural levels, has not generally supported political Zionism. The general view of this group regarding Palestine has been a moderate one. It has not favored a Jewish army and a totally separate Jewish State under Jewish control, or any movement which would bring Judaism into conflict with the Mohammedan world through the more or less forced emigration of the large Arab population of the Holy Land.

But there are many individuals of prominence in this liberal branch of

Judaism who have thrown themselves heartily into the Zionist cause. Among its rabbis the late Stephen S. Wise and among the laity Henry Morgenthau have been conspicuous exponents.

Here is a statement adopted by the American Jewish Committee in 1943, at the height of the controversy. It shows the deep interest of all Jews in Palestine, but gives no support to the extreme political Zionists.

To the extent that economic conditions in the war torn lands shall make emigration therefrom of their nationals necessary, we ask the implementation by those who shall frame the terms of peace of a program which shall under international supervision facilitate voluntary settlement elsewhere under the most favorable conditions.

We ask of the United Nations and those who shall frame the terms of peace, reaffirmation of the fundamental principle that Jewish citizens of every land, fulfilling their obligation of complete loyalty to their respective countries, shall be guaranteed the correlative right of complete equality. We applaud the recent statement of the Secretary of State, that we must have a world in which Jews like all others "are free to abide in peace and in honor."

Thus, while associating ourselves fully with all the purposes of human freedom and betterment proclaimed by the President of the United States, we have special concern with the two objectives, salvation of these suffering people and the preservation of the Jewish community as a spiritual force.

We recognize that there are now more than half a million Jews in Palestine who have built up a sound and flourishing economic life and a satisfying spiritual and cultural life, and who now constitute substantially one-third of the population, and that while this Palestinian immigration has been a blessed amelioration of the condition of this large number of Jews, and has helped to bring about a great development of the country itself, settlement in Palestine although an important factor cannot alone furnish and should not be expected to furnish the solution of the problem of postwar Jewish rehabilitation.

We affirm our deep sympathy with and our desire to cooperate with those Jews who wish to settle in Palestine.

With respect to the government of Palestine, we recognize wide divergence of opinion and that under existing conditions there should be no preconceived formula at this time as to the permanent political structure which shall obtain there. Since we hold that in the United States as in all other countries Jews, like all others of their citizens, are nationals of those nations and of no other, there can be no political identification of Jews outside of Palestine with whatever government may there be instituted.

We endorse the policy of friendship and cooperation between Jews and Arabs in Palestine and urge that every possible avenue be followed to establish good will and active collaboration between them.

We approve for Palestine an international trusteeship responsible to the United Nations for the following purposes:

(a) To safeguard the Jewish settlement in and Jewish immigration into Palestine and to guarantee adequate scope for future growth and development to the full extent of the economic absorptive capacity of the country.

(b) To safeguard and protect the fundamental rights of all inhabitants.

(c) To safeguard and protect the holy places of all faiths.

(d) To prepare the country to become, within a reasonable period of years, a self-governing Commonwealth under a Constitution and a bill of rights that will safeguard and protect these purposes and basic rights for all.[294]

The American Institute on Judaism and a Just and Enduring Peace, held under the auspices of the Commission on Justice and Peace of the Central Conference of American Rabbis, took very much the same moderate attitude regarding Palestine and Zionism as that just outlined. At its meeting in Cincinnati in December, 1942, it adopted this statement:

All Jews are bound by spiritual and historic ties to the Holy Land. Since the issuance of the Balfour Declaration, a tremendous impetus has been given to successful Jewish settlement in Palestine. Since the advent of the Nazi regime, there have been some years in which immigration increased to such a degree as to prove the extraordinary absorptive capacity of Palestine. After the war, conditions must be created to permit as large a Jewish immigration to Palestine as possible, in accordance with obligations assumed under the Balfour Declaration and the Palestine Mandate. Now more than ever the nations of the world must give fullest recognition to the right of Jews to a homeland in Palestine, and they must help facilitate in every way the work of rebuilding that land.[295]

This program, as distinct from that of the extreme Zionists, created no serious Church–State problem for the United States. It is not unlike that of the American Council for Judaism made up of Reform rabbis and prominent laymen. The Institute's pronouncement, published in the *New York Times*,[296] which has not been sympathetic with political Zionism, was roundly denounced by the Zionist leaders.

Perhaps the best statement of the more moderate group of Zionists was that adopted on September 26, 1943, by the representative American Jewish conference held in New York. It still interpreted the Balfour Declaration in favor of the establishment "in Palestine of a national home for the Jewish people" as intending "to constitute Palestine as the Jewish Commonwealth," but it says nothing of a Jewish army, or providing for transplanting the Arab population elsewhere, or carrying out some of the other views of extreme Zionists.

We call for the fulfillment of the Balfour Declaration and of the mandate for Palestine whose intent and underlying purpose, based on the "historical connection of the Jewish people with Palestine," was to constitute Palestine as the Jewish Commonwealth.

We demand the immediate withdrawal in its entirety of the Palestine White Paper of May, 1939, with its unwarranted restrictions on Jewish immigration and land settlement. . . .

The conference demands that the gates of Palestine be opened to Jewish immigration, and that the Jewish Agency, recognized under the mandate as the authorized representative of the Jewish people, be vested with authority to direct and regulate immigration into Palestine, to develop to the maximum the agricultural and industrial possibilities and the natural resources of the country, and to utilize its uncultivated and unoccupied lands for Jewish colonization and for the benefit of the country as a whole.

The measures here urged constitute the essential prerequisites for the attainment of a Jewish majority and for the re-creation of the Jewish Commonwealth.

In the pursuit of its objective of a Jewish Commonwealth, the Jewish people has steadfastly held before it the ideals which shall integrate Jewish Palestine within the new democratic world structure. The Jewish people pledge itself to scrupulous regard for and preservation of the religious, linguistic and cultural rights of the Arab population of Palestine, and to the civil and religious equality of all its inhabitants before the law. The inviolability of the holy places of the various religions shall be guaranteed. . . .[297]

These resolutions met with the approval of the overwhelming number of delegates, although opposed by a small group as involving political complications in wartime.[298]

Undoubtedly most American Jews in recent years have been Zionists favoring a Jewish State in Palestine. The percentage in the different groups is difficult to determine, but the Roper poll published on November 22, 1947, showed that 80.1 per cent of Jews queried were for a Jewish state, 10.5 per cent against it, and 9.4 per cent undecided.[299] Probably it is fair to say that at least 75 per cent of American Jews have favored political Zionism in some form.

The synagogue, or the temple, which has generally succeeded it in the nomenclature of Reform Judaism, is not only the place where the congregation worships, but also under Jewish law and tradition is a place of assembly and study. These two latter functions make it naturally a center where Zionism is discussed, generally sympathetically.

The intense distress of American Jews over the suffering of their fellow religionists in Europe is fully understood and shared by all thoughtful people in this country, as the cruelly violent anti-Semitism of Nazi Germany received universal condemnation, and even before the partition of 1948–49 there was agreement that further immigration into Palestine on a considerable scale was an important factor in the solution of this pressing problem. It was realized, however, that to disregard entirely the wishes and interests of the resident Arabs would not only be unjust but might well lead to a "holy war" involving large sections of the Middle East. On the other hand, if the demands of the extreme political Zionists could be waived, there appeared no reason why Palestine, which has made remarkable economic and social progress as a result of recent Jewish efforts and the British mandate, could not become prosperous and happy, either in a single state in which Jews and Arabs could each play a large part, dominating respective zones, but all united by a federal government, or by a joint commission under United Nations auspices; or in two separate states, one Jewish (Israel) and one Arab, with the United Nations controlling Jerusalem and perhaps certain ports of entry. The latter plan was in the spring of 1949 being worked out with probable success due largely to the tactful and persistent efforts of the United Nations mediator, the late Count Bernadotte of Sweden, and his American successor, Dr. Ralph Bunche. Several impartial international groups visited the Holy Land prior to the United Nations decision for partition, and no one of them favored the extreme Zionist demand for transforming all of Palestine into a Jewish political state. Similarly all favored increased Jewish immigration and spoke with appreciation of what the Jewish settlers and the British mandate had accomplished under very difficult circumstances, though generally feeling that the British made some serious mistakes of judgment, especially in the too drastic restriction of immigration.

Most important of these commissions are two in which the United States has been specially concerned; the Anglo-American Committee of Inquiry of 1946, and the United Nations Special Committee on Palestine of 1947. The first committee stated

> that Palestine is a Holy Land, sacred to Christian, to Jew, and to Moslem alike; and because it is a Holy Land Palestine is not, and can never become, a land which any race or religion can justly claim as its very own.[300]

This tried to do away with all extreme Jewish or Arab claims. The report did not favor either an Arab or a Jewish state, nor any sharp political partition, but the development of separate and mixed Jewish-Arab communities, with the country under United Nations trusteeship until it could stand alone. It emphasized the importance of doing away with restrictive land covenants of a racial character, and the need of economic and educational development which would bring the Arab population up to the living standard of the Jews.

The second report, that of the United Nations Committee, whose appointment was favored by the United States, also declined to accept either extreme Jewish or Arab claims, but the majority favored partition into Arab and Jewish states, with the administration of Jerusalem and its neighborhood under the United Nations, and an economic union between the states which would have large powers.[301]

The report of the United Nations Committee, somewhat modified, and with elaborate provisions to guarantee religious freedom, was accepted by the assembly on November 29, 1947, by a vote of 33 to 13, with ten nations abstaining, over a minority plan for a more unified federated State. This decision, which was far from accepting the extreme demands of American Zionists for a Jewish State embracing all Palestine, was nevertheless accepted as reasonably satisfactory by most Jews, including the Zionist element in this country. The group of citizens represented by the American Council on Judaism, which believes that the Jews' best future is in spiritual rather than political unity, and that their influence as a people should be through their integration into the life of the various nations of the world, regretted the decision. It was vigorously opposed by most Arab groups within and without Palestine. It is too early to predict results with certainty though prospects are encouraging. If, as seems likely, after certain territorial and other modifications are made under the auspices of the United Nations, it brings relative peace in Palestine and among American Jews, it will remove a bone of contention in the United States.

It is a fact of some significance that the resulting Zionist State, which claims to be in some respects the successor of ancient Israel, generally omits in its formal appeals and pronouncements any reference to God, belief in whose being and righteousness was the basic conviction of the old Jewish nation. The Israeli Declaration of Independence has, however, a final paragraph beginning with the words "with trust in the Rock of Israel we set our hands to this declaration. . . ." This phrase is said to have been the result of a bitter controversy between orthodox Jews who wanted mention of "God the Lord" and radical elements who voted for including no direct reference to the Deity. An English-born typist-translator, who believed that "Rock of Israel" would mean nothing to the English-speaking world, substituted the words "Almighty God," which, however, were omitted by the Tel Aviv censor and therefore were not included in the Associated Press dispatch which purported to publish the declaration in full on May 15, 1948.[302] In general the new state asserts its adherence to the cause of religious freedom, but seems to be somewhat "secular" in attitude, although regard is shown by many of its leaders for the Bible and the Sabbath, and a certain spiritual idealism of a historical, racial, and nationalist character marks the movement. The fact that outwardly at least the new state is being built mainly on racial and philanthropic lines rather than on religious ones is a reason why no Church–State issue has been raised in the discussions of diplomatic recognition of the government of modern Israel. But a recent visitor to Palestine calls attention in the *Jewish Spectator,* of June, 1949, to the fact that Israel has a Ministry of Religions; that the Cabinet has approved a budget equivalent to approximately two million dollars for the work of rabbis and other religious functionaries, of which one-third is to be appropriated by the national treasury and two-thirds by the fiscal agencies of the various cities; and that in Jerusalem and Tel Aviv synagogues are numerous and well attended.

It appears that two groups of ardent Jewish nationalists, devoted to the twofold cause of Jewish "restoration" of Zion and Jewish relief for the persecuted of Eastern Europe, have been mainly responsible for establishing Israel—the one made up of somewhat outspoken secularists, the other of extremely conservative religionists. Liberal Jews of the Reform school have played relatively little part in the political developments of Palestine except as outside supporters.

The draft of a constitution for Israel as prepared for the government has certain interesting Church–State provisions. The preamble states that the people of Israel resolve "to rebuild [their] commonwealth in accordance with the ideals of peace and righteousness of the People of Israel." A clause in the proposed constitution reads:

> . . . No discrimination of any kind shall be made by the State between the inhabitants of the State on the grounds of race, religion, language or sex. . . . This constitutional guarantee [freedom of speech] shall not extend to utterances or publications which are libelous, slanderous or obscene, or which are designed to stir up racial or religious hatred, or incite to violence or crime, or which advocate the suppression of human rights. . . .
>
> . . . The Sabbath and the Jewish Holy Days shall be days of rest and spiritual elevation and shall be recognized as such in the laws of the country. The Holy Days of other religious denominations shall equally be recognized as legal days of rest for the members of such denominations.[303]

The proposed constitution takes over from the provisions of the mandate the guarantees of the rights of the various religious bodies to their holy places and religious institutions.

Up to the present the adherents of Reform Judaism have not been able to secure recognition, and they have no temple in Israel. Only the orthodox are recognized in connection with Jewish marriage rites and certain other matters.

In the elections of 1944 and 1948 the Republican and Democratic national platforms vied with each other in trying to get the Jewish vote. Both came out in 1944 for unrestricted Jewish immigration into Palestine. The Republican platform also advocated that the country "may be constituted as a free and democratic commonwealth." The Democrats, meeting three weeks later, favored "such a policy as to result in the establishment there of a free and democratic *Jewish* [italics ours] commonwealth." This went further than customary, but it may be interpreted in the sense of President Wilson's nearest approach to a political Zionist statement that "*in* Palestine [italics ours] shall be laid the foundations of a Jewish commonwealth"—a plan advocated by many who believed that a section of Palestine might be so set apart, without in any way having the entire country created "a Jewish state." President Truman's later utterances show that he understands the difference. Such references to Palestine in party platforms and presidential utterances explain why this problem has had to be considered in a work on Church and State in the United States.[304]

In 1948 the platforms were similar, although taking into account the changed situation due to the partition of Palestine by acts of the United Nations in 1947 and 1948. The platforms of the major parties and of the Progressives are given in the *American Jewish Year Book 1948–1949,* which has an admirable chapter summarizing the situation at the time this work is being prepared for the printer.[305] The platforms show the desire of the people for recognition of the new State of Israel which has since taken place.

The Palestinian situation now is that active hostilities have been brought to a close, and the partition is generally recognized as an established fact. As announced by Secretary of State Acheson in his address at the opening of the United Nations General Assembly September 21, 1949, the most serious matter remaining is the determination of the status of Jerusalem. This is also the matter in which the Christian Churches are most concerned. Secretary Acheson's statement on this subject at the meeting referred to may be accepted as representing the fervent hopes and prayers of virtually all the American Churches.

> It is the hope of the peoples of all faiths that the General Assembly will be able to act successfully upon the report of the Palestine Conciliation Commission in respect to Jerusalem. In my government's view, it should adopt a practical plan for a permanent international regime in the Jerusalem area and for the protection of, and free access to, the holy places.[306]

Aside from the status of Jerusalem the question of the Arab refugees from the portion of Palestine now occupied by the Jewish State is the most serious problem. Another difficulty is the absorption of the unrestricted Jewish immigration, amounting in the autumn of 1949 to about 25,000 a month. The gates have been left wide open mainly because of an earnest desire to help the displaced Jews of Central Europe.

Chapter XVIII

THE PROBLEMS OF ADJUSTMENT IN THE PUBLIC EDUCATION FIELD

Adjustments in the relations between Church and State in the United States have proved difficult mainly in seven debated fields: Racial and Religious Restrictions; Public Education; Church Education; Social Legislation; War and the Peace Movement; Church Property; and Clergy Rights. The first-named has been already dealt with;[1] the others will be taken up in the chapters that follow.

INTRODUCTION—SEPARATION OF CHURCH AND STATE IN PUBLIC EDUCATION—THE MAJOR ISSUES INVOLVED

We shall consider here the Constitutional provisions for separation of Church and State in public education, and then the examples of co-operation and tension which have developed between them over educational matters.

It will be seen from the above analysis that many of the major issues in the United States between Church and State have been in the educational field. They have been due to the fact that the American public has shown an almost pathetic belief in the capacity of education—especially public education—to solve all the complicated problems facing democracy, with the resulting enormous development in public schools, of which a good example is the increase in high schools between 1880 and 1944 from 800 to 28,973.[2] Consequently, through Constitutional enactment, legislation, and court decisions the country has registered its determination to develop a system of public schools in harmony with American ideals, and with no loss of that religious freedom and the resulting Church independence which the founders of the Republic incorporated in the Bill of Rights.

At the outset it is essential to understand the Constitutional status of the public school as detached from every religious organization, and the Constitutional provision in many states prohibiting grants from public taxation to any form of parochial or denominational school. These specific provisions are found primarily in the state constitutions and bills of rights; inasmuch as general education is not a matter transferred by the states to the national government under the Federal Constitution, and is consequently reserved by the states, whose representatives in Congress have however authorized certain educational projects and financial appropriations in the interest of education by the United States. The principal exceptions are in such obvious cases as the education of Army, Navy, Marine, and Air officers,[3] and the education of the reservation Indians, who have been considered the special "wards of the nation."[4] The Federal government has also, and increasingly, aided other forms of public education through such agencies as the land-grant colleges and the National Youth Administration; but neither Congress nor the president nor any political party has ever adopted as a policy the transfer of major responsibility for the general conduct of public education from the community and the state to the nation as a whole. It must be constantly explained to visitors from abroad that American public schools are conducted *not* by Washington, but by thousands of towns and villages scattered through the country under general constitutional and statutory provisions of their respective states. These are and of course must continue to be consistent with the provisions regarding religious freedom in the Federal Constitution.[5]

Let us then turn to the fundamental provisions of representative states. We have chosen seven, the first two and last two alphabetically; Massachusetts, historically the most influential of all in the field of public education; and the two with largest population (New York and Pennsylvania). This means that we shall quote the determining constitutional provisions regarding public schools as they exist in the field outlined—generally in an article on "Education"—in states East and West, North and South, with varying religious and ethnic backgrounds. The years in which the constitutions were adopted also show a wide range.

ALABAMA (1901): Article XIV

Sec. 256. [Public school system] The Legislature shall establish, organize and maintain a liberal system of public schools throughout the State for the benefit of the children thereof between the ages of seven and twenty-one years. . . .

Sec. 262. [Superintendent of education] The supervision of the public schools shall be vested in a Superintendent of Education, whose powers, duties and compensation shall be fixed by law.

Sec. 263. [Aid to sectarian schools] No money raised for the support of the public schools, shall be appropriated to or used for the support of any sectarian or denominational school.[6]

ARIZONA (1912): Article XI

Sec. 1. [Public school system] The Legislature shall enact such laws as shall provide for the establishment and maintenance of a general and uniform public school system . . .

Sec. 2. [Supervision of school system] The general conduct and supervision of the public school system shall be vested in a State Board of Education, a State Superintendent of Public Instruction, county school superintendents, and such governing boards for the State institutions as may be provided by law.

Sec. 7. [Sectarian instruction] No sectarian instruction shall be imparted in any school or State educational institution that may be established under this Constitution, and no religious or political test or qualification shall ever be required as a condition of admission into any public educational institution of the State, as teacher, student, or pupil; but the liberty of conscience hereby secured shall not be so construed as to justify practices or conduct inconsistent with the good order, peace, morality, or safety of the State, or with the rights of others.[7]

Article IX, Sec. 10. [Aid to sectarian schools] No tax shall be laid or appropriation of public money made in aid of any church, or private or sectarian school, or any public service corporation.

MASSACHUSETTS (Amendment XLVI of 1917):

Sec. 1. No law shall be passed prohibiting the free exercise of religion.

Sec. 2. [Aid to sectarian schools] All moneys raised by taxation in the towns and cities for the support of public schools, and all moneys which may be appropriated by the Commonwealth for the support of common schools shall be applied to, and expended in, no other schools than those which are conducted according to law, under the order and superintendence of the authorities of the town or city in which the money is expended; and no grant, appropriation or use of public money or property or loan of public credit shall be made or authorized by the Commonwealth or any political division thereof for the purpose of founding, maintaining or aiding any school or institution of learning, whether under public control or otherwise, wherein any denominational doctrine is inculcated, or any other school, or any college, infirmary, hospital, institution, or educational, charitable or religious undertaking which is not publicly owned and under the exclusive control, order and superintendence of public officers or public agents authorized by the Commonwealth or Federal authority or both, except that appropriations may be made for the maintenance and support of the Soldiers' Home in Massachusetts and for free public libraries in any city or town, and to carry out legal obligations, if any, already entered into; and no such grant, appropriation or use of public money or property or loan of public credit shall be made or authorized for the purpose of founding, maintaining or aiding any church, religious denomination or society.[8]

The second part of this section takes the place of the words: "and such moneys shall never be appropriated to any religious sect for the maintenance, exclusively, of its own schools," the closing sentence of Article XVIII of the amendments to the constitution of 1780, as adopted in 1855.[9] It will be noticed that as a result of the experience of nearly a century and a half the Massachusetts constitutional convention adopted a much more rigid provision to prevent state aid to denominational schools.

NEW YORK (1938): Article XI
(The last two sections include amendments)

Section 1. [Common schools] The legislature shall provide for the maintenance and support of a system of free common schools, wherein all the children of this state may be educated. (Formerly Sec. 1 of Art. 9. Renumbered by Constitutional Convention of 1938 and approved by vote of the people November 8, 1938.)

Sec. 3. [Common school, literature and the United States deposit funds] The capital of the common school fund, the capital of the literature fund, and the capital of the United States deposit fund shall be respectively preserved inviolate and the revenue of the said funds shall be applied to the support of common schools and libraries. (Formerly Sec. 3 of Art. 9. Renumbered and amended by Constitutional Convention of 1938 and approved by vote of the people November 8, 1938.)

Sec. 4. [Use of public property or money in aid of denominational schools prohibited; transportation of children authorized] Neither the state nor any subdivision thereof shall use its property or credit or any public money, or authorize or permit either to be used, directly or indirectly, in aid or maintenance, other than for examination or inspection, of any school or institution of learning wholly or in part under the control or direction of any religious denomination, or in which any denominational tenet or doctrine is taught, but the legislature may provide for the transportation of children to and from any school or institution of learning.[10]

PENNSYLVANIA (1874): Article X

Sec. 1. [Public schools] The General Assembly shall provide for the maintenance and support of a thorough and efficient system of public schools, wherein all the children of this Commonwealth above the above of six years may be educated, and shall appropriate at least one million dollars each year for that purpose.

Sec. 2. [Aid to sectarian schools] No money raised for the support of the public schools of the Commonwealth shall be appropriated to or used for the support of any sectarian school.[11]

WISCONSIN (1848): Article X

Sec. 1. Superintendent of public instruction. The supervision of public instruction shall be vested in a State Superintendent and such other officers as the Legislature shall direct; and their qualifications, powers, duties and compensation shall be prescribed by law. . . .

Sec. 3. Free public schools. The Legislature shall provide by law for the establishment of district schools, which shall be as nearly uniform as practicable; and such schools shall be free and without charge for tuition to all children between the ages of four and twenty years; and no sectarian instruction shall be allowed therein.[12] [The same provision excluding sectarian instruction applies under Section 6 to the state university.]

WYOMING (1889): Article VII

Sec. 1. [Public schools] The Legislature shall provide for the establishment and maintenance of a complete and uniform system of public instruction. . . .

Sec. 12. [Sectarian instruction] No sectarian instruction, qualifications or tests shall be imparted, exacted, applied or in any manner tolerated in the schools of any grade or character controlled by the State, nor shall attendance be required at any religious service therein, nor shall any sectarian tenets or doctrines be taught or favored in any public school or institution that may be established under this Constitution.

Sec. 14. [Supervision of schools] The general supervision of the public schools shall be entrusted to the State superintendent of public instruction, whose powers and duties shall be prescribed by law.[13]

Article I, Sec. 19. [Sectarian aid] No money of the State shall ever be given or appropriated to any sectarian or religious society or institution.

Attention should be called to the fact that these constitutional provisions were all adopted prior to the recent Supreme Court decisions in the Everson and McCollum cases.

These provisions may be taken as typical. Zollmann shows that over thirty states, beginning with Massachusetts in 1855, within about sixty years adopted constitutional provisions forbidding the granting of public funds—in some cases with a few minor specified exceptions such as orphan asylums—to any denominational or sectarian institution.[14] The movement was greatly accelerated by the effort of President Grant in 1875 to secure a Federal Constitutional amendment on the subject.[15] This was generally thought unnecessary and undesirable, but the Federal government has shown repeatedly by its later actions its determination that none of its educational grants or appropriations should be made to denominational or sectarian institutions.[16] Furthermore, with the guarantees of the Federal Constitution, and with nearly 70 per cent of the states having special provisions against financial contributions from public funds to parochial or denominational schools, and the general provisions in the other states regarding public school education under public control, it is most unlikely that any law proposing to give direct financial aid to other than the regular public schools would pass the courts—both state and Federal.

From a study of the constitutions quoted and similar constitutional provisions in other states, five general conclusions emerge:

1. That though the Federal government, under the recent interpretations of the Fourteenth Amendment by the Supreme Court, protects religious freedom

in the states, all matters involving the administration and curricula of American public schools, except for a few groups like the Indians, are cared for by the states.[17]

2. That state constitutions lay great emphasis on public education under the control of duly elected or appointed state officials, but without any attempt to force pupils to attend public schools as distinct from private or parochial.[18]

3. That nearly 70 per cent of all states by constitution or statute have tried to prohibit any state funds reaching parochial or denominational schools, though they provide exemption of taxation for such schools,[19] and in some instances and under specified conditions permit free bus transportation, free textbooks, and even free lunches for their pupils.[20]

4. That sectarian or denominational teaching in public schools was specifically prohibited by most states even before considered unconstitutional by the Supreme Court in the McCollum case; that there is no specific prohibition of the teaching by public-school teachers of those common fundamentals of religion on which most citizens are agreed; and that there is much difference in state legal requirements on reading the Bible and repeating the Lord's Prayer at school exercises.[21]

5. That freedom of conscience in religious beliefs and worship is everywhere protected.[22]

It is clear that these provisions have come to be considered part of the American creed. They cannot be altered without state constitutional changes, and these in turn are subject to being ruled out if inconsistent with the guarantees of religious freedom in the Federal Constitution.

It is interesting to note that in the model state constitution prepared by the representative committee on state government of the National Municipal League, as issued in its third revision in 1933 after twelve years of study, among the twelve provisions of the proposed Bill of Rights are these two directly affecting the topic of our study:

Sec. 9. [Freedom of religion] The Legislature shall make no law respecting an establishment of religion, or prohibiting the free exercise thereof.

Sec. 10. [Aid to sectarian institutions] No public money or property shall ever be appropriated, applied, donated, or used directly or indirectly, for the use, benefit, or support of any sect, church, denomination, sectarian institution or association, or system of religion, or for charitable, industrial, educational, or benevolent purposes not under the control of the State.[23]

It is realized that the public school in a democracy is almost necessarily a secular institution, being intended for pupils of all religious groups. This however does not and should not imply that it is irreligious, and a people with our background should not permit it to become antireligious. Indeed, every such school should show its sympathy with a spiritual outlook that involves recognition of the existence of God as the Creator of the world and of man, and the Judaeo-Christian teaching of our duty to Him and to our neighbor. These are the foundations of our national creed based on the Declaration of Independence, the spirit of the Constitution, the Ordinance of 1787,[24] the decisions of our higher courts, and the papers of Washington, Jefferson, Lincoln, and our other great statesmen. What it all means is that the State, which is essentially a lay body, without trying to cover all education, and leaving certain vital tasks to Church and home, undertakes during a few hours each day to give mental and moral discipline, and instruction in certain secular subjects deemed essential for all future citizens[25]—the process being carried out in an atmosphere of social idealism.

In this connection it must be remembered that the religious training of youth, even more than their mental training, is not merely a matter of formal instruction. Religion may be aided by definite courses of study of the Bible and other books giving views of God, man, prayer, the future life, and human relations, but it cannot be advanced by instruction alone. It needs to be inculcated gradually over the years as a spirit permeating all activities. True religious spirit is awakened and cultivated by the example of parents and friends; by contact with spiritually minded people; by the observation of nature; by reading; by habits of prayer and worship; by the use of symbolism; by the customs of daily home life; by family tradition; and by other influences. In a word, we should bear in mind throughout this discussion that there are large areas which the day school must leave to the Church and the home. This means that even if all citizens were agreed on the advisability of religious instruction in public schools, such instruction might dispel much ignorance, but it would not alone solve the problem of the religious development of our future citizens. It is clear, however, that more effective instruction in the history and teachings of religion is needed for our youth. The only question is how best to bring it about.

The history of the inauguration and development of the public school system—which in the early days often involved a struggle with the Church—has already been treated.[26] Here we are concerned with problems that are still more or less acute, made so partly by the activity of various religious pressure groups, both Protestant and Roman Catholic, and less often Jewish; and partly by the determination of most thoughtful people in the United States to keep Church and State separate, and at the same time to see that our public schools co-operate in wise and legal ways with the moral forces represented by the Church (including the synagogue) and the home. It is generally conceded that neither the parochial school nor the Sunday school, nor both of these historic institutions together, important as they are, nor the modern vacation Bible schools, can completely solve the problem of aiding the Church and home in providing religious education for the young. The pupils of our public schools desiring religious instruction must consequently be reached by some specific and effective additional plan.

The two general plans which have received the most consideration will now be discussed, reminding the reader to consult recent court decisions [XVIII, 1, (3)].

1. Religious Education in the School Curriculum, generally as an Option
2. Religious Education by Churches for Pupils Desiring It, generally Outside Public School Buildings

The differentiation between the two groups varies, but generally the first is more official, more likely to be held in school buildings, and to have credit attached for successful examinations. These conditions, however, do not always prevail. Similarly in most cases the second, being provided by the Churches, involves "released" or "dismissed" time features. But there are many overlappings, border-line cases, and apparent inconsistencies, since this whole matter is one in which there is much experimentation in different states, and in different communities in the same state.

Section 1. RELIGIOUS EDUCATION IN THE SCHOOL CURRICULUM, GENERALLY AS AN OPTION

The question of adequate religious education in a democracy is both highly important and very complicated. The general absence of religion in the curriculum of our public schools, where most of our future citizens receive the major part of their education, means that large groups of youth not reached by the Churches have no regular religious or ethical instruction. The situation is more serious than most people realize. It is a result of our transfer from Church to State during the past century and a half of the major task of molding the minds and characters of our children, and of the belief of many that this transfer involves not only public neutrality in the whole field of religion, but also public indifference. We have seen a momentous change from religiously controlled to politically controlled teaching for the mass of youth. As Dr. Alexander Meiklejohn (1872–), though long a fighting liberal among American college presidents, has written,

> We have torn our teaching loose from its roots. We have broken its connection with the religious beliefs out of which it had grown. The typical Protestant has continued to accept the Bible as, in some sense, the guide of his own living but, in effect, he has wished to exclude the Bible from the teaching of his children. The teacher in

the modern school is commissioned to teach many things. But he is not commissioned —he is rather forbidden—to teach that "faith" upon which the community, for which he teaches, has built its own character and intelligence.[27]

The late President Nicholas Murray Butler (1862–1947) of Columbia University is among those who have realized the seriousness of the present situation because of the vital importance of religion in any complete education. In his report for 1934 he says:

The school child . . . is entitled to receive . . . that particular form of religious instruction and training which his parents and natural guardians hold dear. This cannot be done if the program of the tax-supported schools is arranged on the theory that religion is to be excluded from the educational process or treated merely incidentally as an element in home life.[28]

A more recent statement of his views, with interesting historical comments, is in his address at the rededication of Earl Hall, Columbia University, in 1940. He said in part:

. . . In this day and generation we are beginning to forget the place which religious instruction must occupy in education if that education is to be truly sound and liberal. We seem to forget that until some two hundred years ago religious instruction everywhere dominated education; religion guided education, shaped education and selected the material for education in every part of the world—in the Orient, in Europe and in the Americas. Then began, as a result of the rise of Protestantism and the spread of democracy, those sharp differences of religious opinion and of religious worship which unfortunately exhibited themselves in highly controversial form. One consequence was to lead men to turn aside from religious study and religious teaching in the attempt to avoid those unfortunate contentious differences which had become so common. Then, particularly in this democracy of ours, a curious tendency grew up to exclude religious teaching altogether from education on the ground that such teaching was in conflict with our fundamental doctrine as to the separation of Church and State. In other words, religious teaching was narrowed down to something which might be called denominationalism, and therefore because of differences of faith and practice it must be excluded from education. The result was to give paganism new importance and new influence. . . .

The Legislature of the State of New York has only just now passed a statute restoring the American system in the State of New York by providing that at a certain time each week all pupils in a public school shall be set free to receive such religious instruction as their parents may prefer from teachers of that form of religious faith which their parents choose. This statute realizes that the United States is not pagan but that it is a religious people and must have freedom of religious teaching and of religious faith. This particular system was first introduced in France when, after the political and social revolution which followed the war of 1870–71, the French Parliament in

1882 overturned the school system as then organized. In its new legislation it provided that the public school pupils should be set free on each Thursday and allowed to go to the church or religious institution or the teacher which their parents might select, for religious instruction. Of course, if their parents preferred paganism, that day would be for their children a holiday; otherwise, the children would receive religious instruction in the form which their parents desired.

It is just a little more than forty years ago that I presented my views on this subject before the Sunday School Commission of the Diocese of New York, my subject being "Religious Instruction and its Relation to Education." For the first time in years, I looked over that address to-day, it being printed in my volume, *The Meaning of Education.*[29] I do not find one single word in the argument which I then advanced that I would change to-day. Conditions as they then presented themselves have become even more serious, and the solution of the problem which I offered at that time is to me even more obvious to-day than it was then. . . .[30]

President Butler sees clearly that the fact that the scope of public school education has been so enormously broadened in recent decades makes the elimination of religion all the more serious, especially because of the psychological effect of this noticeable omission on students. Indeed, if the most influential American educational philosopher of today, John Dewey (1859–   ), is right in his emphasis on "the collective value of culture," and if, as all historians would agree, religion has played in the past an important part both in the formation of our culture and in its content, then it seems clear that no education can be complete which leaves it out of account. This does not mean that its tenets must be made a subject of regular instruction by the public school; this is impossible. But it does mean that pupils should at least know something of its origin, development, and character; otherwise much that they study in their history and literature classes will be without any deep meaning.

In general, Americans are almost equally concerned about two things: that sectarianism in every form shall be kept out of our public schools; and that the schools shall not be dominated by secularism or irreligion, which would be out of keeping with the best American tradition. "We must make our people realize that religious freedom is designed to protect, rather than to destroy, religious belief."[31]

The study of religious subjects in the public school curriculum has been thoroughly studied and the facts presented in a recent Columbia University publication.[32] From this and other reports we are able to cite some interesting recent experiments. These are worth study even though some late Supreme Court decisions make some of them no longer legally usable.

The Maine statute regarding normal schools is interesting as a rare survival: "Such schools, while teaching the fundamental truths of Christianity and the great principles of morality recognized by law shall be free from all denominational teachings. . . ."[33] Whether this provision—preserved in the revised statutes of 1916—is wise or not, it bespeaks the interest of the state in trying to insure that the teachers of youth shall be well grounded in those essential principles and ideals which are at the very foundations of our government.

In general the trend of legislative enactment is definitely against any required religious instruction as a regular part of the public school curriculum, though in the past few years there has been a growing tendency to provide for voluntary instruction of public school pupils in classes held outside the school building. The courts have decided that the legislature, subject to the Constitution, is the final authority concerning both curriculum and textbooks, unless this has been granted by statute to local school boards. Except for a few cases where high schools or the higher grades provide optional courses of Bible study for credit; some elementary schools, especially in the rural South, where Bible verses are learned by heart; and the state normal schools of Maine, there is relatively little that may properly be called the official study of religion *in* American public schools.

The states do not provide regular textbooks on religion, the nearest approach being the occasional printing at public cost of syllabi, which may be used as outlines for optional study, prepared by committees in which Jews, Catholics, and Protestants co-operate. In some places, as in Virginia, credit is given for the successful completion of such courses.

Special provisions are often made authorizing religious instruction for the inmates of state orphanages, industrial schools, reform schools, and penal institutions, but these always insure nondenominational education, or provide for visits from clergymen of different denominations when desired.[34]

(1) THE LEGAL STATUS OF RELIGIOUS AND MORAL INSTRUCTION IN PUBLIC SCHOOLS*

A study in 1922 of the attitude of the states toward religious instruction in public schools showed that twenty-eight states had laws prohibiting religious instruction; twenty-four states had laws forbidding the use of sectarian textbooks; forty-five states had constitutional provisions forbidding either sectarian religious instruction or religious texts in public schools; fifteen states had laws forbidding the exclusion of the Bible on the ground that it is a sectarian book, and prescribing the methods of its use; fourteen states set forth their educational aims without reference to religion; and five—all established more than a century ago—named it as an aim in education.[35] The matter is still further complicated by the fact that even in a given state there is often some diversity of practice due to the fact that local school boards, responding to local public

* See the McCollum decision of the Supreme Court, XVIII, 1, (3).

opinion, differ in interpreting and carrying out the requirements of state constitutions and statutes. A study twenty-five years later would probably show no marked statutory changes, though there undoubtedly has been a notable growth of voluntary courses in religious instruction available to public-school pupils.

Legal justification for including some fundamental religious instruction is perhaps implied in the constitutions of a few states, especially those which were originally part of the Northwest Territory.[36] For instance:

Michigan: "Religion, morality, and knowledge being necessary to good government and the happiness of mankind, schools and the means of education shall forever be encouraged."[37]

Mississippi: "Religion, morality, and knowledge being necessary to good government, the preservation of liberty, and the happiness of mankind, schools and the means of education shall forever be encouraged in this state."[38]

Ohio: ". . . But religion, morality, and knowledge being essentially necessary to the good government and the happiness of mankind, schools and the means of instruction shall forever be encouraged by legislative provision, not inconsistent with the rights of conscience."[39]

Such references to religion in state constitutions, however, are unusual.

The case of Ohio is particularly significant, for the association of religion with education is still found in Section 7 of Article 1 of the constitution, which makes it the duty of the assembly "to pass suitable laws to protect every religious denomination in the peaceable enjoyment of its own mode of public worship, and to encourage schools and the means of instruction." Although the Supreme Court of Ohio upheld in 1872 the Board of Education of Cincinnati in its regulation forbidding Bible reading and decided that this constitutional provision does not enjoin religious instruction in the schools, yet, as Gabel has pointed out, the people seem to have retained their belief in some form of religion in public education, for a large majority of the schools maintain Bible reading or devotional exercises.[40]

No better general statement has been made by public authority of the American attitude regarding the religious question in public education than was made in a decision some thirty years ago by the Supreme Court of Iowa. It reads:

If there is any one thing which is well settled in the policies and purposes of the American people as a whole, it is the fixed and unalterable determination that there shall be an absolute and unequivocal separation of church and state, and that our public school system, supported by the taxation of the property of all alike—Catholic, Protestant, Jew, Gentile, believer, and infidel—shall not be used directly or indirectly for religious instruction, and above all that it shall not be made an instrumentality of proselyting influence in favor of any religious organization, sect, creed, or belief.[41]

As far as religious instruction by the Churches in public school buildings on "released" time is concerned, the Constitutional questions involved have been settled, and settled adversely to the practice, in the Champaign, Illinois, case decided by the Supreme Court in 1948. This will be dealt with in a later section.[42]

Two other aspects of the subject have also received special treatment by the courts, namely, Bible reading and released time, and to these extensive sections will be devoted later.[43] We are concerned in this section primarily with the general legal problem of religion and religious education in public schools. It is difficult to deal with the problems in orderly sequence because the questions of Bible study, Bible reading, prayers, religious references in history courses, objective instruction in religion, released time, and so on, are often closely interrelated.

(2) THE VARIOUS PLANS ATTEMPTED AND PROPOSED

We have already discussed some of the efforts in the later decades of the nineteenth century to adjust the wishes of Roman Catholics regarding religious education to the historic American tradition in public education associated with great names such as that of Archbishop Ireland.[44] We shall discuss in the next section the many experiments made recently in excusing public-school pupils at certain times for religious instruction by the Churches. Here we are concerned with optional instruction on religion, especially in high schools, provided or authorized by the school authorities and generally involving scholastic credit. As the earlier proposals originated with liberal-minded Roman Catholics, so these about to be described are mostly of Protestant origin.

A survey made in preparation for the Oxford conference of 1937 showed that about a third of the religious leaders of America believed it possible to provide an elementary and general foundation for religious education in the schools by including in the curriculum such subjects as the history of religion and the ethical precepts of religion. About a quarter thought the best way to meet the problem was to have Church leaders teach voluntary courses in school hours, either inside or outside the school building, and a sixth were opposed to any regular plan of religious instruction to be carried on in co-operation with public school authorities.[45]

There have been five different types of proposals for making the fundamental data of religion known to public-school pupils in school which have seemed worthy of consideration as taking into account the sensibilities of all religious groups. Some of them have apparently been ruled out, at least for the present, by the recent decision of the United States Supreme Court in the Champaign, Illinois, released-time case,[46] but it nonetheless seems worth while to describe them, for they contain ideas which when modified to meet Supreme Court requirements may provide bases for Constitutional and otherwise sound educational projects.

The first might be called the "common denominator" or "three faiths" plan. Here the representatives of the Protestant, Roman Catholic, and Jewish churches agree on certain fundamental statements regarding the religious and moral teachings common to all three groups which will be taught as an optional course—any conscientious objectors being excused. This method at least shows that the importance of religion as a subject of study is recognized. Simple bibliographies refer pupils to books recommended for further study if desired.

This plan has been tried on a small scale in a few cases. It would probably pass the courts in most states, since the proposed instruction would be optional, and in no way sectarian. The major difficulty—not insuperable—is to get agreement on the part of all concerned as to the content of instruction. Some states with a large rural population have made successful attempts to issue such syllabi of Bible study, for which credit is given in optional high-school courses. For instance, the state board of education of Virginia issued in 1933 a series of courses in the Old Testament and in New Testament history and literature with the title *Official Syllabus of Bible Study for High School Pupils.* The commission included the state superintendent of education, a Protestant minister, a Roman Catholic priest, a Jewish layman, the president of a college, and two university professors. The courses proposed had the unanimous approval of this committee. The pamphlets contain carefully prepared "Directions for Securing High School Credit for Bible Study," given here in full. Special attention is called to the fact that references are provided from the King James, Douay, and Leeser (Jewish) versions. It is understood that the courses are entirely optional. Much emphasis is laid on memory passages.

I. To Religious Teachers, etc.

1. The Bible courses herein outlined are not intended to be made a *required* part of the public school courses, nor are public school funds to be used to provide this Bible teaching.
2. The responsibility for inducing pupils to elect Bible courses must rest solely upon their parents and religious advisers.
3. The teaching may be done in Sunday Schools, Sabbath Schools, Vacation Bible Schools, Y. M. or Y. W. C. A. classes or in private schools or classes. *Ninety recitation periods of at least forty-five minutes per period must be devoted to each course, and the class must be in charge of a teacher who will do and require faithful work.*

4. Teachers and superintendents or directors of religious instruction are earnestly cautioned not to certify the fitness of pupils to take the examinations until such pupils have been thoroughly prepared and tested, lest failure to pass may discourage them and others from further Bible study.
5. Religious bodies or individuals not caring to avail themselves of this provision for Bible credit for their children are in no way required to do so, as pupils who do not apply for such credit will take some one of the regular high school electives in lieu of it.
6. References are indicated for the three versions of the English Bible in common use among Protestants, Catholics, and Jews: The Authorized or King James, the Douay, and the Leeser. Where only one reference is indicated there is no difference in the three versions. Where there is a difference the Authorized version is in the text of the lessons; the Douay reference after it in parentheses; the Leeser version in a footnote. In Course II, Douay references are also in footnotes.
7. The spelling of many proper names differs radically in the three versions used, but it has been impractical to indicate the differences. The Authorized version has been followed. Teachers will have to aid pupils to find the equivalent name where other versions are used. With names, order of books, and the text of Biblical passages pupils must accurately follow whichever version they study.

II. To Pupils

1. High school pupils desiring credit for a course or courses in Bible study are permitted to substitute such courses for one of the regular electives.
2. They must take the course or courses under the instruction of a teacher, and preferably in an organized school of the religious body to which they or their parents belong.
3. In addition to regular attendance upon a class devoting ninety recitations of at least forty-five minutes' duration to each course, pupils must prepare their Bible lessons at home with the same thoroughness devoted to other studies.
4. Pupils intending to take an examination upon one of the Bible courses must notify the principal one month before the examination period.
5. For admission to the examination, pupils must present to the Principal a certificate, duly filled out and signed by the teacher with whom the pupil has studied Bible.
6. Pupils passing the examination on any of the three courses offered will be granted half a unit credit in Bible study. A maximum of one unit credit will be allowed upon the completion of two of the courses. Pupils may take examinations in all three courses, but only one unit of high school credit will be allowed in lieu of regular elective courses.

III. To Principals

1. Principals of high schools in which there are pupils preparing for Bible examinations should advise them as to what elective studies may best be omitted.

2. Principals should learn the number of pupils expecting to take Bible examinations, and which course, I, II, or III, they are taking, and promptly order the necessary number of uniform examination questions from the Superintendent of Public Instruction, Richmond.
3. Examination papers are to be given a numerical grade by the instructor of the class and then sent to the State Bible examiner for review of grades. The examiner will report back to the instructor so that uniform standards of grading may be maintained.
4. In case a pupil fails to make a passing grade of 75 he may be re-examined under the rules applying in the high school to re-examination in any other study.

Please follow these directions carefully to avoid needless trouble and delay. Copies of Syllabi and of examination questions for classes can be obtained only from the State Board of Education, Richmond, and directions as to where papers are to be sent will be found on the examination sheets. Correspondence concerning other details of the courses themselves may be addressed to Professor W. M. Forrest, State Bible Study Examiner, University, Virginia.[47]

This high school religious instruction under state auspices supplements the work of the Virginia Council of Religious Education, which in 1941, after eleven years of successful effort, had established centers in 235 local communities enrolling 28,217 pupils of grades one to seven of the common schools, where the work was conducted by thirty-six full-time and six part-time teachers, without expense to the state. The general subject was "Adventures in Christian Living," the studies being closely correlated with the latent religious resources in the school curriculum.[48]

West Virginia has a similar plan involving credit, with classes held sometimes in school buildings, sometimes outside.[49]

This plan is not necessarily inconsistent with the statement made negatively by Thomas Jefferson in connection with his advocacy of a public school system for his native state. He put his opposition to all denominational instruction in the schools in a way that might almost have suggested the idea from which the modern plan of the Virginia council has developed. After stating positively the proposed work of the schools, he added:

> But no religious reading, instruction or exercise, shall be prescribed or practiced, inconsistent with the tenets of any religious sect or denomination.[50]*

The state of Washington, through its legislature, preceded Virginia in a plan for the official recognition of religious instruction in the high school curriculum. It was however declared unconstitutional by the Supreme Court of the state in 1918. The court stated:

> The furnishing of an outline, setting an examination, reading the papers, and

* See Addenda.

determining the credit to be given for the study of historical, biographical, narrative, and literary features of the Bible, is "religious instruction," within the *Constitution,* Art. I, Sec. II. To give credit for the literary study of the Bible, pursued under sectarian agents is to give credit for sectarian teaching and influence contrary to the Constitution, Art. i, Sec. 4.[51]

Similarly, in 1930 the court denied a petition for a writ to include Bible reading in the public school curriculum.

It will be noticed that this plan requires the co-operation not only of Protestants and Catholics, as in England, but also, in many sections of the country, of Jews also. This is apt to be difficult where orthodox Jews as distinct from liberal are concerned. However, the National Education Association through its *Personal Growth Leaflets* has shown the possibility of providing at least a basis on which nearly all groups could agree. This consists of "selections for memorizing." Each begins with a Bible passage, and it is pointed out that if these are memorized throughout the usual twelve-year public school course the student will "become familiar with the basic material of the Bible."[52]

A modification of the plan outlined, which has much to commend it for older high-school students in some communities, would be to have each of the three faiths prepare a statement, entirely constructive in character, regarding its own history and tenets. If this were elected by all it would enable each group to learn the point of view of the other two groups. This would give a minimum of instruction on the basic facts of religion, to be supplemented outside the school by such classes as the different Churches might wish.

The plan of giving credit for some such courses as those outlined above was first tried out in 1912 in North Dakota and Colorado. In high schools, where the desire for credit is generally stronger than in the grade schools, there were in 1927 twelve states, all rural except Michigan, in which an authorized syllabus was commonly issued for Bible study. Montana and Michigan have used the same syllabus, over 150 pages in length, including such topics as Great Old Testament Characters, the Life of Christ, the First Century of the Christian Church, the Bible in the Making, the Bible as an Interpreter of the Interrelations of Social Institutions and a Guide to Right Living, and the Bible in Literature. There is also some memory work. Somewhat similar syllabi for Bible study have been issued by the Indiana state board of education (1926), the Dallas, Texas, board of education (1935), and some other official agencies. The classes are taught outside the schools.[53] In 1927 half of the states in the union—twenty-five out of forty-eight, and including New York and Illinois—permitted credit to high-school students who were reported by responsible groups to have completed satisfactory courses of Bible study.[54] The number has somewhat increased in recent years, until interfered with by the decision in the McCollum case.

The most notable movement in this direction was taken in Chicago in 1941, when the public-school authorities agreed to give high-school credits—a maximum of two out of the fifteen or sixteen required for graduation—for courses in religion that are offered as electives either on Saturdays or Sundays, or on released time on school days, in places and under instructors to be supplied by the Protestant, Roman Catholic, and Jewish groups. The school authorities reserved the right to pass on the competence of the teachers and the suitability of the syllabus of studies for credit. It was understood that the instruction could be definitely Protestant, or Catholic, or Jewish, and that in general it would be given in the buildings of churches or synagogues.[55]

As to the importance of a general knowledge of the Bible for the understanding of our literature, history, and ideals, the following recent statement by the Dean of St. Paul's in London, the Very Reverend Walter R. Matthews, D.D. (1881–), a liberal Anglican, at the Columbia University Convocation in the fall of 1938, is significant:

> . . . It is surely the duty of everyone who owes his own spiritual life to the Bible to do his utmost to insist that it shall take its proper place in the education of the people. I discern, I think, in England a new spirit in this respect. It is a remarkable achievement, I believe, that in every county in England there has been brought out an agreed syllabus of Bible teaching for all the schools in that area, a syllabus agreed upon by all the representatives of Christian churches in that area, so that there are now very few schools where the Bible is not regularly read and taught. . . . Your conditions, I know, in this country are quite different from ours, and it would be impertinent on my part to attempt to lay down lines of policy for you. I cannot help believing, however, that the principle is the same, that it is our duty constantly to urge that no education, from the most elementary to the most advanced, can be adequate which leaves students in ignorance of this fountainhead of all that is best in our common heritage.[56]

This English plan does not provide for participation of the synagogue in the preparation of syllabi, and therefore would not be possible here without modification; but its emphasis on matters of history and ethics rather than doctrine has made it broadly accepted.

That some degree of religious agreement among Protestants, Catholics, and Jews is possible is shown by the experiments outlined and by the "Declaration of Common Beliefs," issued in the winter of 1942 by a representative group of Protestant and Catholic clergymen and Jewish rabbis. This showed that they believed in one God "Creator and Sustainer of the Universe"; that man's mind reflects, even though imperfectly, God's mind; that they rejected all attempts "to explain man in merely material terms"; that God's will is the only ultimate sanction of human morality, and that man's freedom and happiness depend on his obedience to it; that recognition of man's dependence upon God "is essential to the progress of true civilization"; that God's Fatherly providence extends to every human being without recognition of the essential superiority of any one racial strain over another, and that consequently all men have "inalienable rights"; that the republican form of government is the most desirable "for our nation and for countries of similarly democratic traditions"; and that individual rights are an endowment from God.[57]

The second is the interdenominational Christian education plan. One of the cities which has gone furthest in providing voluntary religious courses of a definitely Christian character in public-school buildings is Elgin, Illinois. The plan was started in 1937, and the work has been carried on in the fourth and through the eighth grades, with a class for high school freshmen added in 1941. The courses have had an enrollment of some seventeen hundred boys and girls, or about 85 per cent of all the students in these grades.

A committee of the Elgin Council of Christian Education, after thorough discussion of the situation, came to the conclusion that the present "approach to the problem of living is hopelessly inadequate." It attributed "the breakdown of character and the failure to develop character" to the complexity of our present civilization; the breakdown of American homes; the growing materialistic attitude; and the cynical attitude toward morality. It was felt that the inadequacy of religious training provided by family and Sunday school was largely responsible for most of these conditions, and that something radical must be done about it. As a result, the Elgin Ministerial Association and the coordinating council appointed committees to investigate the feasibility of inaugurating a program of week-day religious training. The public-school principals endorsed the movement and favored the holding of the instruction in the public-school buildings. The following resolution was presented to the board of education:

> It is the opinion of the committee that religion supplies the motivating force and authority for all ethical action. In order that character may be based upon this necessary foundation the committee respectfully suggests that the public schools dismiss all children whose parents give consent for one hour per week, for the purpose of religious instruction in their respective churches to be taught by teachers who can meet public school requirements. In order that the children whose parents do not consent to their dismissal be not deprived of all character education it is suggested that the Board of Education provide opportunity for ethical instruction during the time the children are dismissed for religious instruction.[58]

The school board favored the resolution, and a committee was appointed to work with the committee of the ministers appointed to develop the plan. This joint committee made a thorough investigation of experiments in week-day religious education conducted in co-operation with the public schools, visiting such places as Gary, Indiana; Cincinnati and Dayton, Ohio; Oak Park and Batavia, Illinois; Madison, New Jersey; New York City; and Philadelphia. Its report showed the advantages and disadvantages of the different plans it found.

Among other findings of the committee was one to the effect that its members were "amazed at the interest and understanding with which the Roman Catholic Church has taken up and promoted this plan. We therefore anticipate no difficulty in securing the cooperation of the local Roman Churches." As a result of its study the committee presented to the Protestant ministers of Elgin various recommendations, including the following:

1. That we adopt Week Day Religious Education in Elgin.
2. That all classes be held in the public school buildings with the possible exception of churches with parochial schools.
3. That in view of the advice which your committee has gathered from all parts of the country we begin in public school grades 4, 5 and 6 in which enrollment is 1,250.
4. That we insist upon supervisors and teachers being required to have at least public school standard teachers certificates or the equivalent.
5. That our Council of Christian Education be re-organized to include the pastor of each church, a representative of religious education and a member of the official board, a member of the woman's organization and a member of the young peoples' group and one additional member at large for each 300 members of the church over and above the first 300 members. In addition there should be a representative from all affiliated organizations. Out of this group should be appointed a Council of Week Day Religious Education.
6. That this program be financed by a city-wide drive on the order of the Elgin Community Chest campaign and include the Budget of the Daily Vacation Bible School.[59]

This was a decade before the McCollum decision, which has ruled out as unconstitutional the holding of such classes in public-school buildings.

The council ratified the recommendations of its committee, and the plan was put into effect in 1938. The students were given the religious education work in the classroom, under trained teachers but on an interdenominational basis. The classes gave instruction in the fundamental teachings of the Bible, especially the outstanding characters of the New Testament, the later leaders of the Church, and the truths of Christianity. They took place one day a week, and were preceded by a devotional service led by one of the children, with the singing of hymns. The objective of the classes was "to release the dynamic of the

Christian religion" (that which has been revealed, not discovered) in the lives of the boys and girls, "in order that they may consciously experience and gladly share that 'abundant life' which is the portion of those who keep their values straight."[60] Its ultimate purpose was to provide through religion a basis for strong character. The budget, which amounted to nearly $10,000 a year, was raised by the seventeen Protestant churches represented in the Council of Christian Education. It was believed by those connected with the movement that it did much to encourage higher ideals and standards of conduct.[61]

Similar plans to that of Elgin have been tried in Vermont, some Southern states, and other parts of the country, especially in communities with a relatively homogeneous Protestant population. An example recently cited in the press is that of Somerville, Tennessee, a town of 1,300 people. Here in 1943 the Bible was placed in the regular curriculum as an elective, and was taken by all the 323 pupils in the grammar school and by many in the high school; regular credit was given in the latter.[62] In other places, such as Atlanta, Georgia, attempts to have the Bible taught regularly as an optional subject in the public schools have been opposed by the Baptists, on the basis of their historic opposition to any Church-State bonds, even though the proposal contained a provision that the churches would provide the salaries of teachers.[63]

If this plan—modified as to the place of instruction to meet Supreme Court requirements—is broadly adopted it would be necessary to provide officially for excusing those Roman Catholic, Jewish, agnostic, or other pupils whose parents might not find the proposed instruction acceptable, and who could be regularly cared for in some special ethical or historical course or in a study period.

This undenominational Christian education plan is sure to receive further attention in this country in the near future. It is the basis of the British government's plan first outlined in the White Paper on "Educational Reconstruction" issued in 1943. A few of its more important sections dealing with religion in public-controlled schools are reproduced in the notes for comparative purposes.[64]

The third might be called the "historical" method plan. It is to have an objective course in the history and teaching of religion given to all pupils in high schools. Its purpose is to recognize the important part played by religion in forming the ethics and culture of our day. There is no sectarian religious instruction, merely a frank recognition of the part which religion has played in the formation of our literature, history, government, art, moral standards, etc. This is done without offense in many high schools—indeed, to teach history leaving out religion entirely is quite impossible. Some advocate an extension of this plan. For instance, such a book as *The Bible of the World,* giving the sacred scriptures of all nations, with brief introductions, might be used as a textbook. It would not take the place of denominational instruction in Church Sunday school or at home, but would give students in simple form the story of the growth of religion from that of primitive people through polytheism to Christian theism. It would be an introduction to the more thorough courses in the history of religion and comparative religions as provided in colleges and universities.[65] It would also show that there is no necessary antithesis between religion and science. Many thoughtful people think that some such emphasis in instruction is important to prevent the growth of materialism and secularism.

An unofficial advocate of a slight modification of this plan, with special emphasis on highly trained professional teachers, is Dr. Charles Clayton Morrison (1874–), until his resignation in 1947, the able editor of *The Christian Century*. He believes that the state should employ teachers who would be expected to instruct pupils in the truths of religion historically and objectively. He thinks this entirely possible and necessary, because our Sunday schools, which now provide most of the routine religious instruction, are "merely a gesture towards education," and believes the state's active interest is needed because "We are not educating a citizenship spiritually minded enough to carry on democracy. . . ."[66]

Dr. Morrison outlined his views in two interesting addresses delivered before the Missouri State Teachers Association of Kansas City in May, 1941. He wishes to have some teachers' college inaugurate a course in the pedagogy of religion "designed to train teachers in the technique of presenting religious subject matter in public schools in a manner which should elicit the support of virtually the whole community."[67] This specialized training of teachers he considers a vital matter. He believes that there is "one commanding interest which the curriculum does not recognize. That interest is religion."[68] He adds: "An educational system which purports to reflect the major interests of its society and which excludes religion is falling short of its own theory and falling short at a most vital point."[69] He appeals for a public opinion in American communities which will be so stirred by the drift toward secularism in American culture, and by the fact that the task of fundamental religious instruction is too great for the Churches, that it will support the entering of the public school in this field of instruction at least on those elements of religion on which religious people agree. He concluded his second address with the statement:

. . . The churches which send their children to the public school have the right to ask that the school shall deliver to the community a body of youth furnished with a sufficient knowledge of religion to establish in their minds an understanding of its significance in the life of humanity and to afford the basis for an intelligent and reverent response to the spirit which the church embodies and the work it has been dedicated to do.[70]

The small but influential group holding these views is constantly calling attention to the fact that the boasted neutrality of the American public school in the matter of religion tends to be interpreted by many as an endorsement of antireligious secularism. The students become exposed to all the major social forces of the nation except religion, and consequently tend to think that the State does not consider this a matter of importance. This group believes that the home and the Church, especially those denominations that are not authoritarian in character, seem incapable of providing ample religious instruction—as distinct from facilities for worship, which most of its supporters think the school should not provide. They consequently believe that the only choices are (1) the development by Protestants, as well as Catholics, of parochial schools; or (2) the objective teaching by qualified teachers, using the historical method, of the basic facts of religion in the public-school curriculum. Recognizing the social values to democracy of the public school in which all groups meet, Dr. Morrison and those sharing his views dismiss the parochial school alternative as an undesirable general solution, while not denying the useful work of the Roman Catholic schools, and accept the plan of objective teaching by the historical method. They believe that religious subject matter, as distinct from religious devotion, should not be separated from other subjects of instruction, but should be a part of public education, omitting of course any attempt at denominational indoctrination—a matter which should be left entirely to the Church, the church schools, and the home. They also believe that though doctrinal teaching would be unconstitutional in public education there is nothing contrary to the Constitution in imparting the facts about the origin, history, and meaning of religion, treated historically, to Jew, Catholic, Protestant, and agnostic alike.[71]

The fourth is the method of incidental study of religion through the general liberal arts courses. This plan, related to the preceding, is advocated by those who do not believe that religion with a view to indoctrination can properly under our Constitution be specifically taught as a school course, but who think that it is unfair to religion and to society to have it entirely taboo in general schoolteaching. It advocates adequate objective references by teachers to religious subject matter in the study of such subjects as history, literature (including the Bible), social sciences, music, and art, and in community service. This is the general point of view of the distinguished Committee on Religion and Education appointed by the American Council on Education. This committee was named in 1944 to promote such studies and educational activities in the general area of religion and public education as might seem desirable; and the committee included such men of national standing as Professor Frederick E. Johnson, Rabbi Louis Finkelstein, President Frank P. Graham, and Father Frederick Hochwalt. The committee published in 1947 a significant study on the basic principles. *The Relation of Religion to Public Education—The Basic Principles.* The committee holds that the Judaeo-Christian tradition is an essential basis of our democracy, and that to disregard it in public education is "sheer madness," so that due regard should be paid the Bible, not in special Bible-study classes, but as part of the literature program. The point of view of those who advocate this solution is that such teaching would not be unconstitutional, even under recent Supreme Court decisions, if conducted by regular public-school teachers specially trained for the purpose. It would be merely the imparting of knowledge about religion to those wishing it, just as in a course in government the policies of Republicans, Democrats, Socialists, and Communists might all be presented without any attempt to convert a high-school student to any political party.

Various other ingenious modifications of this historical or cultural teaching of religion have been proposed. For example, at Hunter High School, New York—a tax-supported institution—a class in the "Problems of Democracy" has paid special attention to the historical place of the Church and its role in national life today. The course has included visits to a Jewish temple and to Catholic and Protestant churches, and at each of these a minister of the faith traced its history and basic beliefs. One of the results has been the discovery that the great religious bodies hold many truths in common.[T2] Similar plans have been tried in other high schools, and by some Protestant Churches.

In Indianapolis a plan was undertaken in 1940 which seems to have much promise, not necessarily as a substitute for other types of religious instruction but as an aid to them. The following explanatory letter was sent to principals and teachers of public schools.

Throughout the last year a committee of teachers and principals has been giving careful consideration to ways and means whereby our responsibilities to this phase of teaching can be met. The committee has unanimously agreed that there are certain elements of religious literature and music which should be known by all pupils in the schools; that we should make certain that every child *knows* certain passages of religious literature, a selected group of religious songs, and pictures which are accepted as a part of the cultural heritage of all educated people. Proceeding upon this thesis, the committee is recommending that as a beginning of such a program the list of materials mentioned herein be made *a matter of memorization by all pupils in the schools by the time they have completed the sixth grade.*

The committee recognizes that the rote memorization of these selections does not necessarily insure achievement in the direction of ethical character. The value of memorizing good poems and literary gems is so commonly recognized, however, that the committee has taken its cue from such procedures which are already generally accepted. For this reason it wishes to include in the memorization program materials which are taken from the Bible.[73]

Among the Biblical passages selected for memorizing are the Lord's Prayer, Psalms 1, 23, 100, and a number of the well-known excerpts from the Book of Proverbs. Among the hymns are "Come, Thou Almighty King," "O Worship the King," and the "Doxology" ("Old Hundredth"). A number of famous pictures are listed, including several Raphaels, Watts's "Sir Galahad," Hofmann's "Christ in the Temple," Leonardo da Vinci's "The Last Supper," and "Washington at Valley Forge."

The fifth is the ethical teaching plan. Many states realize that in the absence of religious instruction, standards of morals are apt to decline. Various attempts have therefore been made to provide instruction in moral conduct without any definite religious content. It is generally recognized that this is difficult if not impossible of accomplishment in any satisfactory way without postulating at least a theistic basis, and yet there is evidence that something can be accomplished. The U. S. Bureau of Education and the National Education Association have both interested themselves in the subject. At present California, Florida, Idaho, Indiana, Maryland, Massachusetts, Mississippi, Nebraska, Oregon, and South Carolina all have state laws requiring instruction in good behavior or morals and manners in the elementary schools. A provision of special interest is that of Florida, which requires the attempt "to inculcate, by precept and example, the principles of truth, honesty and patriotism and the practice of every Christian virtue."[74]

Most religious groups in this country are opposed to anything approaching regular religious instruction of a denominational character *in* the public schools, and believe the Supreme Court right in holding such instruction unconstitutional. As good a statement as I have seen on this subject is the petition to the Board of Education by the pastors of the Methodist Episcopal Church South in the District of Columbia a generation ago against the proposed introduction of religious education in the regular school curriculum. This petition stated:

We stand second to none in our loyalty to the Constitution and the established institutions of our country, chief among which is the American common school, established on non-sectarian principles by the separation of Church and State. We deny the principle that religious instruction, under any possible contingency, is a proper function of the American State, and brand all arguments and analogies drawn from the educational experience of European countries with a State Church as false and misleading for this country. We deny that the common school is responsible for the moral and religious crisis in the country, and protest against the proposed introduction of religious instruction into the public schools as reactionary, unAmerican, un-constitutional, illegal, subversive of civil and religious liberty, and, whether advocated wittingly or unwittingly of the vital principles involved, as inimical to the best interests of both Church and State, and tending to increase rather than cure the ills of society. Such reactionary school legislation, we believe, would justly expose our honorable Board of Education and the citizens of the District of Columbia to the ridicule and contempt of leading educators and all fair-minded, liberty loving American citizens the country over. . . .

The Constitution of the United States expressly forbids such sectarian teachings of religion and morals in the tax-supported school as is generally conceded to be necessary for complete moral character and American citizenship. The American common school was never designed to give complete preparation for American citizenship. No objection is made to the teaching of such a body of commonly accepted principles of morality as might be agreed upon. But we oppose thrusting upon the common school the extra burden of the home, the Sunday School, and the Church, in addition to its legitimate work as a branch of the State, as confusing and destructive to all. Such an educational policy would be suicidal.[75]

For the arguments in favor of teaching the foundations of religion in the public schools, not by denominational representatives, but by qualified public-school teachers, as far as this is permissible under Federal and state constitutions and laws, the reader is referred to a work embodying in book form many of the arguments used by Dr. Morrison in the articles quoted from above, *Church and State in Education,* by William Clayton Bower. This takes the ground that undenominational religious instruction of a scholarly character in the public schools is necessary if democracy is to survive. He holds that the schools are better fitted to provide satisfactory teaching on the subject than the home or the "denominational church."[76] For a recent presentation on the other hand of the need of a secular though spiritually sympathetic emphasis in public education, and the exclusion of religion from the curriculum, reference may be made to *School and Church: the American Way,* by Conrad Henry Moehlman.

The study of various communities where an attempt has been made to introduce courses bearing on religion in public schools makes clear that certain things should be borne in mind when and if such experiments are made in the future. These seem to be the basic requirements:

(1) That all plans for courses dealing with religious subjects should be strictly in keeping with the constitution and laws of the state and the nation and with our historic American separation of Church and State.

(2) That arrangements for such courses should be made after informal consultation with local Protestant, Catholic, and Jewish groups.

(3) That all courses should be of a scholarly character, and taught by well-trained teachers.

(4) That the point of view of teachers in all courses should be undenominational, and should show, when occasion arises, the common factors underlying theistic religion considered historically.

(5) That there should be no attempt to teach dogma, and no theological indoctrination, leaving these entirely to the Church, the religious school, and the home.

(6) That courses should show the contributions of religion to our modern civilization and culture.

(7) That the obligations of democracy to religion for its origin, growth, and present status in this country should be clearly brought out.

(8) That religious literature, especially that of the Bible, should be emphasized, each student being allowed to use the version favored by his religious group.

(9) That instruction should stress the importance of cultivating loyalty to one's own church (including the synagogue) and its institutions as a factor in local life.

(10) That the influence and responsibility of the Churches in meeting modern national and international problems should receive due attention.

(11) That religion should be broadly considered as fundamentally the worship of God and the service of one's fellow men as created in His image—truths taught in both Old and New Testament and in the fundamental American charters.

(12) That the needs of high-school students should be specially considered.

(13) That toleration and religious freedom should be emphasized.

(14) That the courses should be optional.

In the above statements it is understood that as a result of the decision of the Supreme Court in the recent Champaign, Illinois, case it will no longer be possible for the Churches to arrange for the teaching of religion in schooltime in public-school buildings, or for public-school authorities to use the "public-school machinery" for helping to carry out released-time programs in schooltime even outside school buildings.[77]

In this discussion we have been considering exclusively the debatable proposal that optional courses in religion, even though restricted to its literary significance and its historical contributions to thought, culture, and social welfare, should be provided by public-school authorities. We have therefore felt it necessary to restrict the plan suggested for discussion to a minimal basis which might receive general support in some communities, and would frankly offer little more than the historic framework for religious teaching in home, church, and religious school. It would not take the place of the latter, but would provide an introduction to an understanding of the meaning and significance of religion, and the part played by it in the modern world. When we come to discuss the development of religious courses by voluntary action on "dismissed" time and given outside school buildings, we shall be confronted by no such limitations of content and scope.

(3) THE SUPREME COURT DECISION IN THE CHAMPAIGN, ILLINOIS (MC COLLUM), CASE (1948)

This decision is of such importance for the future of religion in public education that it requires treatment at some length, especially since the Champaign method is used in Virginia and other states. It reverses the Illinois Supreme Court by clearly ruling out all instruction in religion by the Churches in public-school buildings, even though of an optional character. It probably also rules out some "released-time" programs conducted outside school buildings, though not necessarily interfering with such instruction on "dismissed time"—that is at the close of the school day. Whether it prevents the objective instruction of high-school pupils by qualified public-school teachers in the history, contents, and influence of religion is doubtful. This does not involve the "close co-operation" between Church and State in providing religious education as at Champaign, but it might be constitutionally objectionable on other grounds.

We must first give the background of this decision.

In 1945 a case was heard before the three judges of the Sixth Illinois Circuit Court on the legality of religious instruction in the Champaign public schools. It was brought by Mrs. Vashti McCollum, the wife of a University of Illinois professor, who as a "rationalist" objected to the religious instruction given to her ten-year-old son in a tax-supported school, on the grounds that the instruction was contrary to the First and Fourteenth Amendments of the Federal Constitution. The supporters pointed out that the thirty-minute classes once a week were voluntary, being available only when the parents consented, and were provided to children from the fourth to the ninth grades of the public schools by accredited teachers approved by the superintendent of schools. The case differed from many others in the country in that it involved instruction inside public-school buildings, and its defense was consequently more vulnerable than if given outside.[78] The courses, established in 1940, were provided gratuitously by the Champaign Council of Religious Education, and pupils could attend classes of their own faith under Protestant teachers, Catholic priests, or a Jewish rabbi; over fifty churches and synagogues were interested.

The suit was backed by the Chicago Civil Liberties Committee and by the organized opponents of instruction on "released time."

The decision of the circuit court in this case supported the Champaign school board as against Mrs. McCollum. After citing various U. S. Supreme Court rulings, the court stated:

> . . . So far as federal constitutional provisions are concerned, and conceding that they are binding upon the State of Illinois, and on the defendant school board, there is nothing in any expression of the Federal Supreme Court that remotely indicates there is any constitutional objection to the Champaign system of religious education.[79]

The court, in making this decision, fully agreed with Mrs. McCollum's counsel that the Fourteenth Amendment to the Federal Constitution extended the provisions of the First Amendment to the state of Illinois. It quoted various decisions favorable to its conclusion, and made the important comment that no case had been cited "where the purely voluntary participation in religious education classes, no part of the expense of which is borne by the tax payers, has been condemned."[80] It called attention to the fact that neither prayers nor hymn-singing were part of the classes; that sectarian differences were not taught or emphasized; that the courses had fostered tolerance rather than intolerance; that the Champaign Council of Religious Education which sponsored them was made up of representatives of Jewish, Roman Catholic, and Protestant faiths in the school district; and that the two last named conducted voluntary classes for their respective groups in public-school buildings on released time, that is during regular school hours, but that they were considered an "extra-curricular" activity, those not attending having their regular secular subjects supervised by the regular teachers during the instruction period.

When this important case came before the United States Supreme Court in the October term, 1947, the attorneys for Mrs. McCollum who had raised the original issue were supported by various Church and public service groups, and opposed by others.

The brief presented by the American Civil Liberties Union was specially significant, being signed by distinguished members of the bar from seven states. It took the ground that church, home, and the sectarian school were all proper places for religious education but not the tax-supported school. It called attention to the impossible Babel if denominational instruction in school hours in public-school buildings were permitted.

> They would be flooded with sectarian publications, crowded with religious teachers, many in clerical garb. Pupils would be classified and segregated according to their diverse beliefs or lack of belief. There would not be enough rooms to hold all the

classes. The public school system for all practical purposes would cease to exist and its ideal of secular education would be a mockery.

Answering the claim that the Champaign plan was justified as an act of "public welfare," the Civil Liberties Union lawyers said:

> . . . religion is not a civil function or a public matter. An education which includes religious teaching is a private matter and function. Practically every effort by the state and their agencies to break down the wall separating church from state is justified, at least in words, on the ground that it is in aid of the general public welfare or of some broad phase of the police power. History teaches that there have been few infringements of liberty that have not been justified in the name of righteousness and the public good. An approval of the Champaign plan would seriously interfere with the general welfare and tranquility of the whole country.

The brief concluded that the

> public ideal of secular education and the inspired concept of separation of Church from State should not be tarnished by compromise. They invade the religious rights of no one. They assure freedom for all.[81]

Other briefs opposing the constitutionality of the Champaign plan were presented by the General Conference of Seventh Day Adventists, the Joint Baptist Conference on Public Relations, the Synagogue Council of America, and other religious groups, while other organizations supported the released-time principle.

The court, after extensive deliberation, declared early in 1948, in an 8 to 1 decision, that the Champaign procedure was unconstitutional. It spoke through Justice Hugo Black (1886–), who held that the facts

> showed the use of tax-supported property for religious instruction and the close co-operation between the school authorities and the religious council in promoting religious education. The operation of the state's compulsory education system thus assists and is integrated with the program of religious instruction carried on by separate religious sects. Pupils compelled by law to go to school for secular education are released in part from their legal duty upon the condition that they attend the religious classes. This is beyond all question a utilization of the tax-established and tax-supported public school system to aid religious groups to spread their faith. And it falls squarely under the ban of the First Amendment (made applicable to the States by the Fourteenth) as we interpreted it in *Everson* v. *Board of Education,* 330 U. S. 1.[82]

The opinion goes on to repeat the *dicta* in the Everson case[83] and declines to change them, ending this brief but epoch-making opinion with these words:

> Recognizing that the Illinois program is barred by the First and Fourteenth Amend-

ments if we adhere to the views expressed both by the majority and the minority in the *Everson* case, counsel for the respondents challenge those views as dicta and urge that we reconsider and repudiate them. They argue that historically the First Amendment was intended to forbid only government preference of one religion over another, not an impartial governmental assistance of all religions. In addition they ask that we disinguish or overrule our holding in the *Everson* case that the Fourteenth Amendment made the "establishment of religion" clause of the First Amendment applicable as a prohibition against the States. After giving full consideration to the arguments presented we are unable to accept either of these contentions.

To hold that a state cannot consistently with the First and Fourteenth Amendments utilize its public school system to aid any or all religious faiths or sects in the dissemination of their doctrines and ideals does not, as counsel urge, manifest a governmental hostility to religion or religious teachings. A manifestation of such hostility would be at war with our national tradition as embodied in the First Amendment's guaranty of the free exercise of religion. For the First Amendment rests upon the premise that both religion and government can best work to achieve their lofty aims if each is left free from the other within its respective sphere. Or, as we said in the *Everson* case, the First Amendment has erected a wall between Church and State which must be kept high and impregnable.

Here not only are the state's tax-supported public school buildings used for the dissemination of religious doctrines. The State also affords sectarian groups an invaluable aid in that it helps to provide pupils for their religious classes through use of the state's compulsory public school machinery. This is not separation of Church and State.[84]

Of almost equal importance was the concurring opinion of Mr. Justice Frankfurter (1882–), joined by Justices Jackson, Rutledge, and Burton, the last two having also concurred in the court's opinion. These justices believed that the court was fundamentally correct in its decision, but wished to put on record certain facts and considerations to prevent the decision being taken as a precedent which would necessarily bar certain released-time programs of a somewhat different character from that in force in Champaign.

The first or historical portion of their opinion is important. Here are some quotations:

It is pertinent to remind that the establishment of this principle of separation in the field of education was not due to any decline in the religious beliefs of the people. Horace Mann was a devout Christian, and the deep religious feeling of James Madison is stamped upon the Remonstrance. The secular public school did not imply indifference to the basic role of religion in the life of the people, nor rejection of religious education as a means of fostering it. The claims of religion were not minimized by refusing to make the public schools agencies for their assertion. The non-sectarian or secular public school was the means of reconciling freedom in general with religious freedom. The sharp confinement of the public schools to secular education was a recognition of the need of a democratic society to educate its children, insofar as the State undertook to do so, in an atmosphere free from pressures in a realm in which pressures are most resisted and where conflicts are most easily and most bitterly engendered. Designed to serve as perhaps the most powerful agency for promoting cohesion among a heterogeneous democratic people, the public school must keep scrupulously free from entanglement in the strife of sects. The preservation of the community from divisive conflicts, or Government from irreconcilable pressures by religious groups, of religion from censorship and coercion however subtly exercised, requires strict confinement of the State to instruction other than religious, leaving to the individual's church and home, indoctrination in the faith of his choice.[85]

The Frankfurter opinion passes on from the well-documented historical phase of the subject to various dicta of significance for the future. Here are a few of them:

. . . The courses do not profess to give secular instruction in subjects concerning religion. Their candid purpose is sectarian teaching. While a child can go to any of the religious classes offered, a particular sect wishing a teacher for its devotees requires the permission of the school superintendent "who in turn will determine whether or not it is practical for said group to teach in said school system."[86]

. . . Separation is a requirement to abstain from fusing functions of Government and of religious sects, not merely to treat them all equally. . . . The public school system of Champaign actively furthers inculcation in the religious tenets of some faiths, and in the process sharpens the consciousness of religious differences at least among some of the children committed to its care. . . .[87]

If it were merely a question of enabling a child to obtain religious instruction with a receptive mind the thirty or forty-five minutes could readily be found on Saturday or Sunday. If that were all, Champaign might have drawn upon the French system, known in its American manifestation as "dismissed time," whereby one school day is shortened to allow all children to go where they please, leaving those who so desire to go to a religious school. . . .

We do not consider, as indeed we could not, school programs not before us which, though colloquially characterized as "released time," present situations differing in aspects that may well be constitutionally crucial. Different forms which "released time" has taken during more than thirty years of growth include programs which, like that before us, could not withstand the test of the Constitution; others may be found unexceptionable. We do not now attempt to weigh in the Constitutional scale every separate detail or various combination of factors which may establish a valid "released time" program. We find that the basic Constitutional principle of absolute separation was violated when the State of Illinois, speaking through its Supreme Court, sustained the school authorities of Champaign in sponsoring and effectively furthering religious beliefs by its educational arrangement.[88]

We renew our conviction that "we have staked the very existence of our country on the faith that complete separation between the state and religion is best for the state and best for religion." *Everson* v. *Board of Education,* 330 U.S. at 59. If nowhere else, in the relation between Church and State, "good fences make good neighbors."[89]

Justice Robert H. Jackson (1892–) filed a separate concurring opinion. He put on record certain reservations that may well be significant in future decisions:

I join the opinion of MR. JUSTICE FRANKFURTER, and concur in the result reached by the Court, but with these reservations: I think it is doubtful whether the facts of this case establish jurisdiction in this Court, but in any event that we should place some bounds on the demands for interference with local schools that we are empowered or willing to entertain. I make these reservations a matter of record in view of the number of litigations likely to be started as a result of this decision.

A Federal Court may interfere with local school authorities only when they invade either a personal liberty or a property right protected by the Federal Constitution. Ordinarily this will come about in either of two ways:

First. When a person is required to submit to some religious rite or instruction or is deprived or threatened with deprivation of his freedom for resisting such unconstitutional requirement. We may then set him free or enjoin his prosecution. . . .[90]

Second. Where a complainant is deprived of property by being taxed for unconstitutional purposes, such as directly or indirectly to support a religious establishment. We can protect a taxpayer against such a levy. . . .[91]

. . . While we may and should end such formal and explicit instruction as the Champaign plan and can at all times prohibit teaching of creed and catechism and ceremonial and can forbid forthright proselyting in the schools, I think it remains to be demonstrated whether it is possible, even if desirable, to comply with such demands as plaintiff's completely to isolate and cast out of secular education all that some people may reasonably regard as religious instruction. Perhaps subjects such as mathematics, physics or chemistry are, or can be, completely secularized. But it would not seem practical to teach either practice or appreciation of the arts if we are to forbid exposure of youth to any religious influences. Music without sacred music, architecture minus the cathedral, or painting without the scriptural themes would be eccentric and incomplete, even from a secular point of view. Yet the inspirational appeal of religion in these guises is often stronger than in forthright sermon. Even such a "science" as biology raises the issue between evolution and creation as an explanation of our presence on this planet. Certainly a course in English literature that omitted the Bible and other powerful uses of our mother tongue for religious ends would be pretty barren. And I should suppose it is a proper, if not an indispensable, part of preparation for a worldly life to know the roles that religion and religions have played in the tragic story of mankind. The fact is that, for good or for ill, nearly everything in our culture worth transmitting, everything which gives meaning to life, is saturated with religious influences, derived from paganism, Judaism, Christianity—both Catholic and Protestant—and other faiths accepted by a large part of the world's peoples. One can hardly respect a system of education that would leave the student wholly ignorant of the currents of religious thought that move the world society for a part in which he is being prepared.[92]

Justice Stanley Reed (1884-) filed a dissenting opinion in which he directed attention to the many instances of close association of Church and State in American society, such as the required attendance of cadets at West Point and Annapolis at the Academy Chapel or elsewhere. He felt that the decision went beyond the separation which Madison and Jefferson contemplated, and beyond the Constitutional prohibition of "an establishment of religion."

The phrase "an establishment of religion" may have been intended by Congress to be aimed only at a state church. When the First Amendment was pending in Congress in substantially its present form, "Mr. Madison said, he apprehended the meaning of the words to be, that Congress should not establish a religion, and enforce the legal observation of it by law, nor compel men to worship God in any manner contrary to their conscience."[93]

Mr. Justice Reed concluded with these passages asking for an open mind and due regard for American traditions in dealing with problems involved in the co-operation between public education and the religious forces of a community:

. . . The prohibition of enactments respecting the establishment of religion do not bar every friendly gesture between church and state. It is not an absolute prohibition against every conceivable situation where the two may work together any more than the other provisions of the First Amendment—free speech, free press—are absolutes. . . . This Court cannot be too cautious in upsetting practices embedded in our society by many years of experience. A state is entitled to have great leeway in its legislation when dealing with the important social problems of its population. A definite violation of legislative limits must be established. The Constitution should not be stretched to forbid national customs in the way courts act to reach arrangements to avoid federal taxation. Devotion to the great principle of religious liberty should not lead us into a rigid interpretation of the constitutional guarantee that conflicts with accepted habits of our people. This is an instance where, for me, the history of past practices is determinative of the meaning of a constitutional clause not a decorous introduction to the study of its text. The judgment should be affirmed.[94]

A careful study of all these opinions shows that though all members of the Court except Mr. Justice Reed clearly believed that the Champaign type of co-operation between the Churches and the schools in providing sectarian religious education in school buildings during regular school hours was unconstitutional, a majority indicated that it might have no objection to what is generally called "dismissed-time" instruction outside of such buildings, and held open many other possibilities of adjustment which would enable pupils in our public schools to learn the character, history, and influence of religion in Constitutional ways. In other words, the decision is clear on the major point at issue—it denies the right of the various Churches, with the co-operation of the public-school system, to enter public schools on school time to teach religion there. It does not, of itself, seem to prevent either the objective study of the history of religion in public schools under public-school teachers (which Dr. C. Morrison has so long advocated), or the dismissal of students to study religion in the churches or synagogues of their choice, such as is provided by the laws of New York and other states, and is advocated by many representative Protestant, Catholic, and Jewish groups.

The decision of the court was expected by many Constitutional lawyers. It disappointed most Roman Catholics[95] and Protestant Evangelicals but was praised by most Jewish agencies, by the *Christian Century,* Unitarians, and other liberal Christian groups, and even by many Baptists who saw its importance from the standpoint of Church–State separation. The author of these volumes anticipated it. He thought that as interpreted in the two concurring opinions, which took the ground that it did not necessarily affect other somewhat different released- and dismissed-time projects, it represented a step forward in supporting the Church–State separation and religious freedom clauses of the Constitution, though interpreting separation somewhat too rigorously.

The executive head of the International Council of Religious Education, which has done so much to advance the released-time principle in American education, expressed the views of many thoughtful religious leaders. He was naturally disappointed at the McCollum case decision, but stated that the Protestant Churches should do three things: seek clarification of the law; help week-day systems to conform to the law; and find other and more effective ways that are definitely Constitutional to combat increasing secularism.[96]

Unfortunately much of the discussion of the decision by the general public, and specially by those who opposed it, was based not on the Constitutional questions involved, but on the desirability of the religious time program from the standpoint of inculcating in public-school children some knowledge of religion. There was, however, a general recognition by responsible religious leaders that the form of religious instruction in public-school buildings by the Churches must be abandoned, and some "dismissed-time" or other Constitutional plan substituted as aids to home and Church in preventing the education of future citizens from being too dominantly secular.

In view of this decision various systems of released time are being tested for their constitutionality in the courts of many states. Among the early decisions the most important was in New York, where the New York Supreme Court held that the state law which permits public school students to be excused up to one hour a week for religious instruction *outside of school buildings and grounds,* and under the auspices of the Church of their choice, was not unconstitutional under the McCollum decision. In addition to the vital difference as to the place where the courses are held, the court pointed out other differences, such as that in New York no public funds are expended in connection with the classes and that the public school officials do not solicit or recruit pupils for religious instruction, or supervise or approve courses or teachers.[97]

A study published by the National Education Association in the early summer of 1949 entitled *The Status of Religious Education in the Public Schools* shows that the states are adjusting their programs of religious education to conform to the McCollum decision. For example, the Michigan State Board of Education has ordered all released-time classes stopped in that state. Oregon has required religious education classes to be moved away from public-school buildings. South Carolina—one of the most conservative of states—has announced that credit toward graduation will no longer be given for Bible study classes, and teachers will no longer be certified by the state for Bible teaching. Ohio has left the whole matter to local discretion after taking account of the McCollum decision. At least six states have announced that no changes are necessary, chiefly because their classes in religion are not held on school property. Undoubtedly many border-line cases will come before state courts, and some ultimately before the United States Supreme Court for review.*

Section 2. RELIGIOUS EDUCATION BY CHURCHES FOR PUPILS DESIRING IT, GENERALLY OUTSIDE SCHOOL BUILDINGS

In the previous section we have dealt with various plans attempted or suggested to offer voluntary religious instruction of an interdenominational character generally within public-school buildings and as a part of the school curriculum. Here we are concerned with attempts to meet the needs of the religious education of youth by the Churches, generally outside public-school buildings, but with the moral support of the school authorities, and on an entirely voluntary basis, under arrangements which do not infringe on the separation of Church and State.

This is a matter in which there is much current interest and a good deal of experimentation. Consequently, it is difficult to give any summary of the na-

* See Addenda.

tional situation which may not soon be outdated by court decisions and legislative action. But the background information here given, and the dated reports quoted, should give a clear idea of the origin, development, significance, extent, and current trends of the movement.

Assuming for the moment that some form of organized religious instruction for public school pupils is desired by a community, and that this can be constitutionally effected outside of school buildings and that the school authorities will give their moral support to such an interdenominational effort, various questions arise from the standpoint of the State, such as:

Should this instruction be on a "dismissed-time" or "released-time" basis? If the former, it means that pupils will be let out perhaps an hour earlier than usual on some one day of the week to attend such religious instruction as their parents may wish. If on the latter basis, it means that they will be similarly released at some time during regular school hours. Many persons prefer the former, as being in their judgment more in keeping with our national principle of Church-State separation.

Should bus service for voluntary religious courses outside public-school buildings be provided by the community?

Should the entire school be allowed to attend such classes at the same hour, or should the hours be "staggered"?

Should some fundamental syllabus be prepared acceptable to Protestant, Catholic, and Jewish groups which may form the basic outline of all instruction, to be added to by each group as it may desire?

Should public-school teachers be encouraged or permitted to conduct classes in voluntary weekday schools?

Should the school authorities be responsible for bringing these opportunities for religious study to the attention of the pupils, and should they keep a record of their attendance?

Should an hour of study or instruction in some such subject as ethics be required at the school for such students as do not wish to attend the religious education classes?

These questions will indicate the complexities of the problem, and the need of settling them wisely in the interest both of religious freedom and of giving moral support to all outside constructive efforts in behalf of high moral and spiritual standards.

The International Council of Religious Education, a responsible agency which has taken the lead in gaining a larger support for this program of the weekday Church school than for any other plan of bringing religious instruction to bear on public-school pupils, has summarized the conclusion of thirty years of experience. "A Ten Point Platform" to make these schools effective is proposed:

1. A year of planning before launching the program.
2. All religious groups working closely together.
3. Parents accepting their responsibility for the school and supporting it in every way.
4. Public school officials co-operating heartily without controlling.
5. A representative and reliable weekday church school board continuously on the job.
6. A course of education in religion as well planned and implemented to its purposes as the courses in the public schools are to theirs.
7. Teachers as well trained for teaching religion as the public school teachers are for their work.
8. A supervisor—trained, experienced, and religious—working with every school.
9. An expenditure per pupil (in proportion to the teaching time) equal to that for his public school education.
10. The spirit as well as the letter of the law preserved in all relationships.[98]

(1) THE HISTORY AND EXTENT OF THE MOVEMENT—"RELEASED" AND "DISMISSED" TIME

Co-operative weekday church schools, which according to President Butler had their origin in France after the overthrow of the old regime in 1882,[99] were first effectively organized in this country in Gary, Indiana, in 1914 by an able superintendent of schools, the late Dr. William A. Wirt (1874–1938).

Although the schools at Gary were on the so-called "released" time plan, that is, pupils were released from their regular school during school hours, there soon developed in other centers a significant variant of the plan known as "dismissed" time, which meant that students were generally let out or dismissed a half hour or an hour earlier one day in the week so that those who wished might attend religious courses, generally outside the school building. This has seemed to many less open to Constitutional and other objections. Sometimes the two systems were not clearly differentiated, as for instance in New York state, where the Education Law of 1940 merely stated that "Absence for religious observance shall be under rules that the Commissioner shall establish." This clearly permitted released time, but in adopting the regulation to control the procedure the state commissioner of education provided, on July 4, 1940, that "Such absence shall be for not more than one hour each week at the close of a session at a time to be fixed by the local school authorities." In other words, an experiment in religious education which permitted released time became practically a dismissed-time project. This fact was brought out clearly both by Mr. Justice Frankfurter in his concurring opinion and by Mr. Justice Reed in his dissenting opinion in *McCollum* v. *Board of Education* (1948).

Released time, as originally developed at Gary, did not involve some of the later dangers pointed out by the court in the McCollum case. Professor George A. Coe, formerly of Columbia University, one of the most active of the early leaders in this movement, in a letter to the author, on June 22, 1949, calls attention to the fact that Superintendent Wirt, the originator of the plan, insisted that the custody of a pupil was not to be shared between school and church either on school or church property or on the streets. He writes:

> . . . Ignoring this precaution, ecclesiastics began to exercise some of their functions upon school grounds; for example, making announcements and giving directions to children, in some instances assembling children of a given faith preparatory to guiding them in a body to the week-day church school. An equally real, though less obvious crossing of the line occurred when public-school teachers assisted in the promotion work of the churches in school hours and upon school grounds, and when records of attendance, work, and conduct at the week-day class in religion were submitted to and kept by the state school. The overlapping did not end even here, but these specimens are sufficient for present purposes. If the churches at Champaign and Urbana had heeded the judgment arrived at in the Religious Education Association so long ago, there never would have been a McCollum Case. . . .

Released-time classes were officially recognized in about three hundred towns during the twenty years following the Gary experiment. Groups of churches and ministerial associations secured the co-operation of boards of education and superintendents of schools in permitting classes in religious education during school hours. Classes were started as a result of the realization of educational leaders that it is difficult to provide adequate character education without some religious training, and surveys showed that not over 40 per cent of the population from five to seven years old in the United States was reached by Sunday schools. An important study, the "Inter Church World Survey," in 1920, showed only 63.3 per cent of the children in this country receiving systematic religious instruction.[100] The following statement, preceding a resolution of the Board of Education in Rochester, New York, in the same year, authorizing the starting of these schools, is significant:

> The importance of religious instruction, both to the individual and to the country, is generally recognized. By common consent, however, the free public-school system of this country cannot teach religion. The responsibility for such instruction must rest upon the home and the church, but the public school can and should cooperate to the limit of its power with the home and the church, to the end that the greatest possible number of our boys and girls may receive effective religious instruction.[101]

After this plan had been in force for some years a committee was appointed to survey the results and make recommendations. A summary of these follows:

Excuses to attend religious instruction should not be granted below the third grade; among the reasons mentioned for eliminating first- and second-grade pupils were the problem of control of traffic and the loss of school time in the case of many first-grade pupils who were attending half-day sessions.

All religious instruction classes are to be so organized that pupils from a single school grade shall be excused at the same time and avoid disturbing the same group more than once a week.

Assure careful checking of attendance at the religious instruction centers and place responsibility for absences after the pupil has left the public school upon the church school, which, in turn, will report to the parents.

Responsibility for the conduct of pupils either on the way to the classes or during the classes rests upon the religious instruction center. If a pupil's conduct is such as to reflect upon his school, permission to go should be canceled.

A uniform practice should be adopted as to the time allowed for religious instruction. Forty-five minutes is recommended, this to include the time necessary for preparation to leave the school. This involves the presence of "centers" which are near enough to require no more than 15 or 20 minutes of the pupil's time for transfer from the school. In the semidepartmental school the period would coincide with the regular class period.

It is considered unnecessary to have "consent" cards signed anew each year.

It is recommended that the board of education set a definite limit to the number of pupils to be placed in charge of one teacher; 100 or more is too large a number for adequate control and efficient instruction.

Pupils should not be taken from the schools until adequate control and instruction are provided for them in the religious classes.

The committee recommends that the religious instruction authorities be requested to make regular reports to the board of education.[102]

Somewhat similar recommendations were made by the Board of Education in Dayton, Ohio, in 1924:

1. That there should be a strong union of churches supporting the project and so organized that the superintendent of schools and board of education could deal with it rather than with individual churches.
2. That trained teachers must be engaged for the religious instruction classes, so that the quality of the instruction pupils received would be similar to that in the public schools.
3. A week-day report should be made to building principals of individual pupils' attendance and a schedule submitted to show the daily time and place of meeting of religious education classes, the teacher in charge, the grade taught. This ruling was to insure that pupils dismissed from school use the time as expected.
4. Classes organized must be graded.
5. Classes must be located in centers as near the schools as possible to assure a minimum amount of time for arriving from and going to the public schools.[103]

This general plan, of which there have been many variations,[104] has the advantage of being equally fair to all denominations, and, at least when the classes are held outside public-school buildings, does not run counter to the American tradition that public education should include no regular required religious instruction. An impressive 1939 case of its extension was in New York state, where the state on the advice of a commission headed by Owen D. Young (1874–) approved an experiment which is so important that it will be described in a separate section.[105] Such widely scattered states as Minnesota, Maine, Colorado, North Dakota, Virginia, Michigan, and Montana have more definite plans for optional Bible study for high-school students, generally with the understanding that they be held outside the public school.[106]

It is usually provided that such courses shall be given outside of regular school hours, or in the last school hour on "dismissed time," but there are hundreds of cases[107] where the educational authorities have permitted such attendance—within the regular school day, and sometimes in the school building. The movement grew rapidly prior to 1948. For example, in 1933 a comprehensive published survey showed only seven states whose laws specifically permitted the release of pupils in this way, sometimes only for confirmation classes, sometimes for more regular instruction. More commonly the law left the choice of the hours to the school authorities, merely permitting them to effect the necessary arrangements for such voluntary classes, generally but not always outside the public school buildings. In the following decade much progress was made. By 1941 the issue of legalizing the release of public-school children for religious instruction was an important one in such widely separated states as Massachusetts and California, both of which passed laws favoring the proposal, though in California the law was vetoed by the governor. The Massachusetts statute grants discretionary power to the local school committee, provided no public funds are used for the weekday religious program or for transportation incidental thereto, and provided the time is not more than one hour each week.[108]

Another typical recent case is that of Minnesota. Here the laws provide for such instruction when

> it is the wish of such parent, guardian, or other person having control of any child, that he attend for a period or periods not exceeding in the aggregate 3 hours in any week, a school for religious instruction, conducted and maintained by some church or association of churches, or any Sunday school association incorporated under the laws of this state, or any auxiliary thereof, such school to be conducted and maintained in a place other than a public-school building, and in no event, in whole or in part, at public expense. . . .[109]

In 1941 it was reported that approximately five hundred communities of all sizes in all parts of the country released children during school time for religious education.[110] This may be considered a fairly accurate statement for its date, in view of the reports received from the chief state school officers of forty-six states, the District of Columbia, Alaska, and some of our outlying possessions; but it must be remembered that it gave the situation as it was in 1940, and there was a large increase in the next decade. The statistics then showed that the school systems releasing pupils included only the elementary grades in 232 units, elementary and high-school grades in 130, and only high-school grades in 126, thus indicating a good deal of difference of opinion in experimentation. In Boston the eligible grades have been four to eight, and the assistant superintendent of schools, who supervises the program, reported in 1947 85 per cent of eligible students participating.[111]

The influential International Council of Religious Education reported in 1943 that the general plan of releasing children for weekday religious instruction which it endorses had been legalized in some way in forty-one states.[112]

In the early summer of 1949 the N. E. A. published *The Status of Religious Education in the Public Schools,* already quoted. This showed only four states —Maryland, Nevada, New Hampshire, and Wyoming—and the District of Columbia and Alaska reporting no religious education programs related to the public schools or their pupils. Of the 2,639 school systems reporting—urban, town, village, and county units—708 or 26.8 per cent showed that they were co-operating to some degree in or providing formal religious instruction; only 15.3 per cent had classes in public-school buildings during school hours. The largest group, 68.1 per cent, reported individual pupils released to attend classes away from the school—the public school keeping a record in about half the cases. About 14 per cent of all pupils covered by the survey were enrolled in some form of religious education class. Of the systems reporting, 510 or 11.8 per cent stated that for one or more reasons—in 52.3 per cent because of the United States Supreme Court decision in the McCollum case—they had given up their religious education program. These facts show the actual situation as it was early in 1949; the questionnaires for these studies had been sent out in December, 1948.

The amount of time given the optional courses provided by the Churches with more or less co-operation from the schools is generally about an hour a week. Those who do not belong to one of the three groups providing this instruction, or who do not wish to attend, generally remain in school for a substituted study hour. In addition to carrying out this general plan, other states by local custom permit pupils to absent themselves on holy days of their religion or for confirmation or similar special services. To religious classes outside the school building and outside school hours, school authorities are inclined to give every encouragement, even at times providing free bus transportation. Some such procedure will probably become more common in the future on the "dismissed-time" basis, but it is doubtful whether many states—in view of some of the dicta in the Champaign case decision—will permit such voluntary and private religious instruction to be credited as part of the regular public-school record.

It is hard to say how effective the weekday religious classes and schools have been,[113] but they have undoubtedly accomplished something in "dispelling spiritual illiteracy," and the movement they represent is likely to gain rather than lose headway after readjustments to conform to Constitutional requirements as laid down by the Supreme Court.[114] The schools are mainly in small cities and towns, though a few large cities, such as Chicago, Milwaukee, Kansas City, Rochester, Boston, New York City, St. Louis, and Pittsburgh, have adopted the plan. In St. Louis and Pittsburgh, and generally elsewhere, the parents of a high-school pupil decide which place of instruction their boy or girl shall attend. In Pittsburgh a credit system is included, based on a threefold attendance record—at church, Sunday school, and weekday religious school. The preamble to the St. Louis regulation of 1939 contains clauses which are particularly significant.

> Civil and moral delinquencies of both the juvenile and adult population have in large areas been found to be closely correlated with disadvantageous material and social environments. In both of these the schools can and should exercise constructive as well as ameliorative influences. Among these are pervasive civic and moral influences made effective by an enlightened socially pointed curriculum, the bases of which rest on spiritual and economic foundations, and the objective of which is found in culturally integrated individuals.
>
> In harmony with this view, the need for economic orientation has been increasingly emphasized in curriculum planning. On the other hand, attenuation of spiritual forces, particularly those inherent in religion, have, it is feared, weakened one of the bases of our educational structure and thus have hindered the attainment of our American educational goal.[115]

It must not be thought, however, that released time has been universally favored in American cities. The Baltimore Board of Superintendents, for example, in 1947, after considering a very thorough report on the subject opposed adopting the plan. Pertinent quotations from the school superintendents' action follow:

> Because of deep and continuous concern professionally and personally in the problem of character development among children and youth, we have given much con-

sideration to the various aspects of Character Education. We have examined and evaluated programs carried on in the past, both in Baltimore and elsewhere, programs now being conducted and plans which offer promise for further development in this very important phase of education. The members of this Board are unanimously of the opinion that every child, if his life is to be well based, must come under the effective influence of the church, the home, and the school. We do not believe, however, that it is either necessary or desirable that the child's contact with his church should occur during the time that he is required by law to spend in attendance at public school.

We are opposed to a program of Released Time Religious Education because such a program might have the effect of violating the principle of separation of church and state which is so fundamental a concept in American democracy. Moreover, we have found no indication either in the plans presented to us for the local program or in released time programs elsewhere which have been studied through observation and published reports that the purposes of education for character and citizenship would be furthered more effectively by work carried on outside of the schools than by the type of educational activity now being carried on in schools. . . .[116]

It should be emphasized that in Baltimore, as almost uniformly elsewhere, the importance of religious instruction was fully emphasized, but the responsibility for supplying it was placed squarely on the Church and the home.

Similarly in San Diego, California, the Board of Education after nearly a year's trial in ten schools, declined in 1947 to expand or continue the released-time program. Among the nine grounds stated were these:

5. Religious training is the special and particular sphere of the church. . . .

8. The year's trial of "Released time for religious education" has demonstrated that the program interferes with the progress of school work during the entire day, increases the work of principals and teachers, and results in certain confusion and loss of time to all children in the grade, both those who are released and those who remain. The evidence does not show growth of character or desirable behavior beyond that of the children who did not participate in the released time program. The results do not justify a continuation or extension of the plan.

9. The request for a continuation of the "Released time program" falls short of having the support of all the people or even of all the churches or church people.[117]

The Board of Education showed, however, its deep interest in the moral, religious, and spiritual problems involved. It adopted these resolutions:

RESOLVED that we urge the homes and the churches to continue and increase their efforts in spiritual and moral training in their respective spheres;

RESOLVED that we pledge the Board of Education and the schools to continue, in the future as in the past, to stress by every means at our disposal, the teaching of moral and spiritual principles, and character training; and

RESOLVED FURTHER, that we pledge earnest cooperation with all worthy plans for religious instruction outside of school time.[118]

The Dayton, Ohio, weekday schools of religion have developed an extensive literature that is largely used in religious schools where the Protestant ministers unite to give instruction in some building that is equally acceptable to students of the public schools. Among these books are *Building a Christian Character,* which develops the idea of God as a loving Father who desires the best possible of each of us. Another is *Building the Kingdom of God.* These books have even been used in the public schools in certain rural parts of Maryland and of other states that are predominantly Protestant. Similarly, the well-known "Christian Nurture Series" of books, originally prepared for use in Episcopal Sunday schools, has been adopted for general Protestant use in some of the schools in New York state; the experiment being first tried in Cortland, where successful weekday schools under the auspices of the Cortland Council of Churches have been in operation since 1925. The courses, which extend from the second through the sixth grades, take up in turn Trust in God, Obedience to God, God with Man, God's Great Family, and The Christian Seasons. These courses are not designed to take the place of denominational Sunday school instruction, but to give a common basis or supplement for it. The marks received by pupils are given for the benefit of parents on the regular school reports. About 90 per cent of the Protestant public-school children enroll. They are expected, in addition to their class studies, to learn hymns and to co-operate in certain forms of Christian service. The classes are opened and closed with prayer, and are on released time one day a week, at the close of the morning or afternoon sessions of the public schools. Teachers are chosen only from among college or normal school graduates who have had successful experience in religious education. A special feature is made of correlating the teaching with that of the public schools.[119] The founder of the Cortland experiment in 1942 conducted similar schools under the auspices of the Albany City Council of Religious Education.

The effort to co-ordinate voluntary religious instruction with the work of the public schools, of which we have given various examples, has been thus summarized by a special student of the subject.

The week-day church school

1. Is a church school, an essential part of the education program of the church and carried on under the direction of a local church or the churches of a community associated together in a council of religious education.

2. Is a distinct type of church school, to be differentiated from the vacation church school, the leadership training school, High School Bible-study-for-credit classes,

pastor's classes, boys' and girls' recreation clubs, societies, gymnasium classes, and other week-day classes in expansion of the Sunday session.

3. Is financed by the churches primarily, although the community is frequently called upon to share the cost.

4. Meets in church buildings wherever practicable, or in buildings that are rented or owned by the week-day church school board.

5. Is carried on by a specially appointed board or council (if cooperative) which is responsible for appointing and paying qualified teachers and supervisors, for setting up a program of courses and activities, and for providing the necessary place of meeting and equipment.

6. Has no organic relationship with the public school, but works in fullest cooperation with it. Its pupils of all grades are usually drawn from the public school by permission of the public school board.

7. Is conducted on "released time," or on "dismissed time," preferably, rather than on "free time," upon suitable arrangement with the public school officials.

8. Holds its sessions on the public school days of the week.

9. Receives children from the public school only on written request of parents.

10. Is not compulsory in the sense that public education is compulsory, but regular and prompt attendance is expected.[120]

The Federal government has shown its interest in weekday religious education by publishing through the United States Office of Education a special *Bulletin* on the subject.[121] This accepts as a satisfactory definition of the weekday church school one published in 1940 by the International Council of Religious Education in its pamphlet entitled *The Weekday Church School,* which describes it as

> a school of religious education, distinguished from all other weekday church groups by its close relationship with the public school, with which it cooperates, but with which it has no organic relationship. Weekday church school pupils meet in graded groups at regular intervals during the public school year to follow some organized course of religious education.
>
> The weekday church school is an essential part of the church's educational program, carried on under the direction of a local church or of several churches in a community associated in a Council of Religious Education, or Council of Churches and its Department of Religious Education.
>
> Its sessions are held in church buildings, or in buildings owned or rented by the weekday church school council or, where possible and advisable, in public school rooms. These sessions are held during regular public school hours, or during the last period of the day, or after school. (These arrangements are known as "released time," "dismissed time" and "free time," respectively.) In some cases, one period of 50 to 60 minutes is offered each class each week. In other instances, pupils meet two or three times a week. The weekday church school receives children on released time only upon

written request of parents. Attendance is elective as far as initial choice of parents is concerned, but it is usually compulsory for all children whose parents have signed request cards for dismissal from school for religious education.[122]

The *Bulletin* calls attention to the influence of the "White House Conference on Children in a Democracy" in 1940, which decried the inadequate meeting of the religious needs of many children and gave publicity to the estimate "that approximately one-half of the children and youth in the United States receive no religious instruction outside the home."[123] It is because of this fact that the released-time plan is being given serious consideration in so many states. When a proposal for authorizing it was before the Wisconsin legislature in the spring of 1947 it was stated by its advocates that the number of participating communities in this general plan had largely increased in four years. The proposal, supported by representatives of the Federation of Churches and the Roman Catholics, but opposed by Unitarian and Baptist ministers because of the Church–State issue, was defeated in committee.[124]

This Wisconsin story showed that there is no unanimity of opinion even among religious leaders as to the desirability of the plan. As a further example of this the experiment has recently been attacked in a book by Professor Conrad H. Moehlman, *The Church as Educator*. He opposes the plan for many reasons. He believes that it is unduly favorable to Roman Catholics, whose centralization and teaching system make them more effective in co-operating; that it destroys unity and democracy in the classroom, especially through magnifying differences between Protestants, Catholics, and Jews; that it encourages the breach between fundamentalists and liberals in religious education; that it creates conflict between Sunday school and weekday class standards; that it reaches only a small proportion of pupils, etc.

But it is fair to say that most intelligent observers are less critical, and believe that the plan, at least when used on the dismissed-time principle and outside public-school buildings, is promising. The courts are more likely to support the constitutionality of the method adopted if classes are held in the churches (and synagogues) or in places provided by them. This tends to minimize any Church–State complications, and is still the custom in about 60 per cent of the cases.

We have outlined the various suggestions made to meet the problem of providing adequate religious instruction for the public-school youth of this country, for we believe that it is highly important. Some more efficient method must be adopted by the Churches to reach the great majority of youth in the public schools. But this must be done in a way which does not entangle these schools in the question of denominational teaching, Catholic, Protestant, or Jewish, and which does not run counter to our ideals of religious freedom and of separation of Church and State.

Combining voluntary courses in religion with public education is successfully done in many state universities which have followed the so-called Toronto Plan of having colleges or hostels of residence established under the auspices of various religious groups, much as in Oxford—for instance, a Roman Catholic hostel, a Methodist hostel, or a Baptist hostel. In these members of a communion may live together under denominational auspices and receive such instruction as the Church concerned may desire, while at the same time they attend the regular courses in the degree-conferring university which is supported by the state and is entirely undenominational. In some cases, under the leadership of the Committee on Religion and Higher Education and other groups, it has been found possible, through the co-operation of university departments of philosophy and history, and of various religious forces in the community, to provide an integrated series of optional courses in religion, for which degree credit is given.[125] It is the theory of those who have developed this movement that religion is part of the cultural heritage of our race, and that no man can be considered truly educated who does not know something about the Jewish and Christian background that is mainly responsible for our spiritual and religious ideals.[126]

(2) THE LEGAL STATUS OF RELIGIOUS INSTRUCTION ON "RELEASED TIME"

The question of the legal status of released time is a difficult one to deal with satisfactorily because various phases of it are in process of consideration by the Supreme Court of the United States, and because related cases will come up later. The court has in the McCollum case regarding religious teaching by the churches in Champaign, Illinois,[127]* decided that the plan there used was unconstitutional. This involved primarily the holding of classes by churches during school hours in public-school buildings, and incidentally the use of public-school machinery for helping to secure students for these classes. Many other related questions are still unsettled, and there is nothing in this opinion that shows conclusively what the attitude will be toward them, and especially toward entirely voluntary released-time instruction outside school buildings that is not directly sponsored by the schools, and also toward that variant known as instruction on "dismissed" time where pupils are allowed once a week to go for religious teaching to the churches for thirty to sixty minutes before the normal close of the school day. In view of these uncertainties as to the Constitutional status of many such arrangements and as

* See Addenda.

to future laws, we come logically, after this introductory statement, to the developments in this field in recent decades. This is important in order that we may understand past, present, and future.

Granting that some provision for effective opportunity for religious education for public school children should be made by the religious forces of a community at their own initiative and expense, and with a friendly attitude on the part of the school authorities, it remains to decide whether this instruction can ever be allowed in regular school hours—that is, on "released time." This raises a difficult legal question, for several states permit it by statute, and at least thirty states[128] without any specific law on the subject have adopted this method of co-operating with Protestant, Roman Catholic, and Jewish groups in making religious instruction possible for those whose parents wish it.

The legal status of the plan at the close of 1947 just before the Supreme Court's decision in the McCollum or Champaign, Illinois, case may be studied in a pamphlet on *Legal Aspects of Release Time,* published by the National Catholic Welfare Conference. This gives the statutes authorizing the plan in typical states—California, Hawaii, Illinois, Indiana, Iowa, Kentucky, Maine, Massachusetts, Minnesota, New York, North Dakota, Oregon, Pennsylvania, South Dakota; also the provisions in some states, such as Michigan, for absence from regular school exercises for confirmation instruction. There is a historical introduction, and the more important court decisions are added.[129]

Some courts, like the Supreme Court of Washington, have declared it to be unconstitutional to give credit for released-time work.[130] On the other hand, the highly influential New York Court of Appeals, after contradictory opinions in lower courts, beginning in a well-known case before the Supreme Court in Westchester County,[131] decided in 1927 that a public school may release students in school hours for such instruction. This decision is of special interest because it was concurred in by Chief Justice Benjamin N. Cardozo (1870–1939), later a member of the Supreme Court of the United States, and recognized as one of the greatest of American jurists. The case had to do with an attempt to compel the commissioner of education of the state, Dr. Frank P. Graves (1869–), to order the school authorities of the city of White Plains to discontinue the regulation of the school under which, when requested by parents, pupils might be excused for a half-hour each week immediately before the close of the school session to receive religious instruction in church schools. It was a case where no public money was to be used to aid the church schools, although some slight use of the time of public-school teachers was required in registering pupils and checking excuses.

The court held that this practice was not a diversion of public funds sufficient to constitute a violation of the state constitution, which at the time prevented the use of public money "other than for examination or inspection, of any school or institution of learning wholly or in part under the control or direction of any religious denomination, or in which any denominational tenet or doctrine is taught," nor was it a violation of the law which requires that pupils "shall regularly attend upon instruction for the entire time during which the schools . . . are in session." In its decision the court stated that "It is impossible to say, as a matter of law, that the slightest infringement of constitutional right or of abuse of constitutory requirement has been shown in this case." It took the ground that to prevent pupils from being excused to attend religious instruction outside the public schools would be a discrimination against religion. It stated that as a child can be excused to take lessons in dancing or music, it should certainly be allowed to be similarly excused for instruction in religion—always understanding that this instruction is with the parents' consent and that no public funds are involved.[132]

The incident was brought to a close by the following statement of Commissioner Graves:

In my judgment this plan marks the limits to which public school officials should go in the matter of denominational religious education, and any extension may be regarded as an undue interference with the regular work of the schools. In fact, I believe it would be much better if pupils are to be excused at any time for religious instruction, to dismiss them half an hour earlier at the end of the week and permit them to go to their respective places for religious instruction, if they wish to go at all. No compulsion should be brought to bear by the school authorities to make them go. Of course the parents might do this, but the machinery of the school should not be used.[133]

Attorney General Paul Dever (1903–) of Massachusetts in 1941 gave a similar ruling. He informed the state commissioner of education that the state constitution did not bar the Boston School Committee from permitting pupils of the public schools to be released from school to attend voluntary religious instruction classes outside the school building. He said:

It is clear that no plan of weekday religious education would be constitutional which involved the teaching of religion by public school teachers, in public school buildings, through the employment of public school property or which in any other way required the expenditure of public funds.

Neither the 46th amendment nor any other article in the Constitution, however, discriminates against religion or religious instruction. The purpose is to separate the public school system from religious denominational instruction so that "denominational religion" . . . is put in its proper place outside public aid or support.

He then pointed out that the legislature in 1855 adopted a law requiring Bible reading, and that this had been qualified to exempt those who have conscientious scruples against this practice. He said that the New York Court of

Appeals permitted dismissal of school children to attend religious education classes, and "in my opinion the 46th Article of the Massachusetts Constitution" is to be construed in the same manner as the New York constitution. He then continued:

> I am therefore of the opinion that the Massachusetts Constitution does not prohibit the Boston School Committee from releasing pupils part time from school to receive religious education outside of public school buildings, at the request of their parents, provided the plan adopted involved no expenditure of public funds, the use of public property or loan of the public credit....
>
> In order to comply with the 11th article of amendment, guaranteeing equal protection to all religious sects and denominations, such plan must, of course, make similar provisions for pupils of all sects and denominations, not only of the Christian religion, but others as well. The Supreme Judicial Court has held that the guarantees of religious equality are not confined to adherents of the Christian faith and that it protects Jews as well as Christians.[134]

A few months after this opinion, voluntary religious education for public school pupils on released time was specifically legalized by the Massachusetts legislature.

In California in 1947 the State Supreme Court upheld as constitutional a law providing released-time religious instruction for public-school children. It affirmed the opinion of the District Court of Appeals which declared

> No one who keeps pace with the trends of modern society can deny that the instruction of youth in faith and morality is of the utmost necessity and importance....

The Court's opinion stressed that the framers of the California constitution were not opposed or hostile to religion as such.

> They proposed to insure separation of church and state, and to provide that the power and the authority of the state should never be devoted to the advancement of any particular sect or denomination.[135]

An interesting Constitutional question regarding released time has arisen in Porto Rico. In 1943 the commissioner of education, José M. Gallardo, realizing the poor moral conditions among the youth of the island, proposed to bring undenominational religious instruction into the public schools through the regular teaching staff. Finding that this would be unconstitutional under the American flag, he suggested a plan for released-time instruction. This was supported by the Roman Catholics, who are in the large majority, and opposed by the Lutherans, some Presbyterians, a few liberal Catholics, and the Masons. The opposition group maintained that the "Gallardo Plan" was inconsistent with the separation of Church and State.[136]

On the other side of the American world, in Hawaii, the problem has also come to the front. In 1947 the commissioner of public instruction limited the time to be given for religious instruction on dismissed time to the last hour of the school day instead of continuing the staggered plan. From Constitutional and school routine points of view the change was certainly called for, though objected to by the Churches because under the earlier plan they had been able to employ seven competent paid teachers who were able to go from class to class and from school to school, and thus reached in the final year of the plan 5,850 Protestants, about 5,000 Roman Catholics, and 1,200 Mormons. The commissioners made one concession—this was before the Champaign case was decided by the Supreme Court—that the dismissed-time plan could be carried on in school buildings instead of outside as before.[137]

As we read over the various court decisions and official rulings on the constitutionality of released-time instruction, and of its dismissed-time variant, it appears that the advocates of these plans would be on firmer Constitutional ground if they held their classes only outside of public-school buildings. This was the general purpose when such courses were started in various places a generation ago. Since the McCollum decision it is practically mandatory.

(3) A LEGISLATIVE ATTEMPT TO LEGALIZE "RELEASED TIME" WHICH FAILED—CALIFORNIA

One of the most significant battles over voluntary religious instruction for public-school children was waged before the California legislature in 1925. We quote at some length from the testimony because it brings out clearly the objections raised by some groups in many parts of the country to any formal recognition of religion by our public-school authorities. It all arose because a woman member of the assembly introduced the following bill (Miller Bill), which was referred to the Committee on Education:

An act to add a new section to an act entitled "An act to enforce the educational rights of children, and providing penalties for the violation of this act," approved March 24, 1903, as amended, to be numbered one a, providing for the excusing of children from school for religious instruction.

The people of the State of California do enact as follows:

SECTION 1. A new section is hereby added to an act entitled "An act to enforce the educational rights of children and providing penalties for the violation of this act," approved March 24, 1903, as amended, to be numbered one a, and to read as follows:

SECTION 1a. The board of education of any city, or city and county, or the board of trustees of any school district shall, upon the written request of parents or guardian, excuse his or her child for sixty to one hundred and eighty minutes in any week to permit such child to attend a week-day school giving instruction in religion. Said child may be excused at any hour of the day designated by the said school authorities, provided that such child so excused shall be held accountable for all work prescribed for his class in the public school.[138]

It will be noticed that this bill was considered vulnerable from the point of view of the historic American policy of separation of Church and State mainly because it permitted religious instruction *during* regular school hours. The ablest arguments against the proposal were those of Dr. Louis I. Newman (1893-), then Rabbi of Temple Emanu-El, San Francisco. He said:

We are opposed to the so-called Miller Bill (No. 128, Assembly, California State Legislature) for four main reasons. First, we oppose it in principle, as contrary to the spirit and teaching of our American system of public education and as opposed to the American belief in the complete separation of Church and State. Second, we affirm that, in practice, it will create chaos in the administration of our public schools; it will involve teachers, pupils and parents in situations embarrassing to their personal religious opinions. Third, we deem the Bill entirely unnecessary, inasmuch as those who desire religious instruction may secure it after school hours; the method suggested implies a wrong approach to the whole problem of religious education; the churches and synagogues ought to strengthen their own resources from within instead of appealing to the Legislature and other law-making bodies for assistance and pressure. Fourth, we believe that the sentiment of liberal religious leaders throughout the entire country will be found to be opposed to any intrusion into our public schools, and that the more we discuss plans such as the Miller Bill suggests, the more the opposition will crystallize, and in the end defeat any project to overthrow our established system of public secular and private religious instruction. Under these four main headings we may group the details of our objections to the Miller Bill.

Rabbi Newman then went on to develop each of these four arguments. Among his most telling points were these:

The policy of all those who prize American ideals of freedom of conscience and worship has been: hands off the public schools! For the public school is the great meeting-ground of the members of all races and faiths which constitute our Republic. In the public school, we are not Protestant, Catholic or Jew, but Americans all. We seek to teach in the classroom that knowledge which unites and does not divide us; we seek to find a common denominator of information whereby we may be comrades rather than adversaries. We have sought above all to keep religion and politics out of our public schools, our colleges and universities. In California we have developed the state university to its highest point largely through our unfailing insistence upon the doctrine that religion is a concern for the individual person and the individual family, and that secular knowledge—in the sphere of literature, art, science, linguistics, economics and allied subjects—is the concern of the school and college. We have kept sectarian religion from the schools because the value of this policy has been vindicated every time we have sought to depart from it. . . .

Under the seemingly harmless terms of the Miller Bill, there is the threat of compulsion leveled against both parent and child. The reason why its advocates will not listen to the proposal to shorten the number of teaching-hours for all pupils, to close the schools, dismiss all the children alike, and to leave the choice of spending the additional time for religious or other instruction to the individual family, is that thereby the entire essence and aim of the Miller Bill is destroyed. The plan aims to bring the pressure of the public school administration upon parent and child so that willy-nilly they must accept religious instruction. . . .[139]

We oppose the Miller Bill because we deem it completely unnecessary. The way to win our young people is not to make them feel that the public school and the state are in a conspiracy to drive them into the religious school and church, but to make our spiritual institutions so vital, so magnetic, so attractive in the richness of their resources, facilities and personalities, that our children and youngsters will voluntarily and delightedly choose affiliation with them. The task of the Church and the Synagogue is to strengthen their spiritual resources from within. To go to lawmaking bodies for assistance is a confession of weakness. The Jewish community has never asked for a single favor or privilege from the public school authorities on behalf of their children, although we believe we have been fairly successful in our religious education. *This has always been after school hours.* The *Hadorim* and *Talmud Torahs,* the Jewish Centers and Temple Houses which have grown up in every center of Jewish life in the United States perform their functions admirably by sheer force of their power to appeal to young people. . . .[140]

The Miller Bill was defeated after full hearings. The assembly vote was 41 to 33. Next to the Jews the Seventh Day Adventists were the strongest opponents of the measure. Some Unitarians and Roman Catholics joined them. As indicated above, it was the fact that the proposed instruction was to be provided in school time released for the purpose that caused the major antagonism. Had it not been for this one feature most of the arguments used by opponents would have carried little weight with the public, a large part of which is always interested in having adequate voluntary instruction in religion provided for public-school children after school hours.

(4) A SIGNIFICANT RECENT ATTEMPT—NEW YORK

The most important experiment in voluntary religious instruction for public-school students with state co-operation is that recently begun in the state of New York. The McLaughlin–Coudert Law, passed by the state legislature in its session of 1939–40 with the backing of many representative citizens and public organizations, provides that

Absence from required attendance shall be permitted only for causes allowed by the general rules and practices of the public schools. Absence for religious observance and education shall be permitted under rules that the commissioner shall establish.

Dr. Ernest E. Cole (1871–), the commissioner of education, announced the following rules:

1 Absence of a pupil from school during school hours for religious observance and education to be had outside the school building and grounds will be excused upon the request in writing signed by the parent or guardian of the pupil. 2 The courses in religious observance and education must be maintained and operated by or under the control of a duly constituted religious body or of duly constituted religious bodies. 3 Pupils must be registered for the courses and a copy of the registration filed with the local public school authorities. 4 Reports of attendance of pupils upon such courses shall be filed with the principal or teacher at the end of each week. 5 Such absence shall be for not more than one hour each week at the close of a session at a time to be fixed by the local school authorities. 6 In the event that more than one school for religious observance and education is maintained in any district, the hour for absence for each particular school in such district shall be the same for all such religious schools.[141]

The State Council of Churches, which supported the law and was pledged to aid in making it effective, was disappointed that this departmental ruling restricted the hours of instruction to the close of morning or afternoon sessions. It also felt that not permitting the religious instruction in school buildings might prevent the carrying out of the plan in some rural districts. Furthermore, since the wording of the law appeared to make the provision for religious education merely permissive, some boards of education did not seem disposed to put it into effect. In spite of these criticisms the New York experiment was on such a large scale as to attract national attention.

Encouraging beginnings were made in New York, Buffalo, and other cities. Roman Catholic, Protestant, and Jewish agencies co-operated, each group arranging for its own students. At first the proportion of students provided for at the experimental schools was relatively small, especially among the Protestants, where the problem in large cities of securing centers and competent teachers equally acceptable to all denominations was difficult. *The Commonweal* (Roman Catholic) summed up the situation after the first few months—pointing out at the same time how well prepared its communion was to provide effective instruction.

A method of procedure which takes prudent and forbearing and charitable account, not only of the child dismissed from school at a designated period to attend a religious class, but also of the child who is not dismissed, requires time to evolve. It will be evolved because in the circumstances it must be if the project is to endure. Meanwhile, some mistakes of zeal and judgment are inevitable. It was, for example, not very remarkable, if not very wise, that the children who left their schools for the initial religion classes should reappear wearing lapel buttons with question marks on them, designed to invite interrogation from the "left-behinds." This raised a mild furor about "proselytizing," which caused the buttons (properly) to disappear. Such small false starts are part of the trial-and-error whereby sound standards are worked out. It is notable that the press, aside from some die-hard opposition in correspondence columns, has given space and friendly comment to the classes, stressing, naturally enough as items of news, the differences that could be gleaned in the procedures of Catholic, Protestant and Jewish groups. It has begun well. May it grow and deepen into a fruitful tradition among us, symbolizing what of itself it cannot of course bring about: the revitalizing of religion in American life. Here Catholics have the special responsibility of exacter knowledge and completer faith. Happily they are well prepared to carry on their own training and give example, in a very concrete sense, to others. The Confraternity of Christian Doctrine has developed over a period of years an admirable curriculum for both vacation and year-round instruction of public-school children. Stress has been put largely on the grades, but the religious needs of high-school students have not been neglected. As an instance, the current *Journal of Religious Instruction* publishes an eye-opening account of the achievement in Brooklyn, where in 256 groups 38,855 high-school pupils are taught religion; in further conformity to the Confraternity design, a large number of the 991 teachers—670—are laymen and laywomen.[142]

In New York City, after the schools had been in regular operation under the new law for less than a year, the report of the Greater New York Interfaith Committee, based on official school statistics, showed that 101,633 pupils were enrolled.[143] At the beginning of the school year 1943–44 it was announced that nearly 150,000 were expected in New York and about 100,000 in Buffalo. This was considered encouraging. For the third year of the experiment the Public Education Association's report showed in New York City only 28 per cent of the children registered—the Protestants having 4 per cent, the Jews 1, and the Catholics 23.[144]

The general impression of those who are best informed is that the New York movement is a promising one worthy of further trial, but there continues considerable difference of opinion about it. An example of this was the discussion at the meeting of the New York Kindergarten 6-B Teachers Association in the spring of 1941, where able speakers denounced the law as inimical to Constitutional liberty, and others with equal vigor supported it. The released-time discussion was opened by Dr. Everett Ross Clinchy (1896–), president of the National Conference of Christians and Jews, who spoke in favor of the plan. He asserted that voluntary religious instruction on released time was not a threat to our Constitutional liberties, but that the existing lack of religious education among large elements of the population was a threat to them. He advocated co-operation in carrying out the plan, believing that it would benefit both the churches and the schools and would moderate tendencies to bigotry. The associate superintendent of schools of New York City argued that religious education must be an integral part of the total education of every child, and that released time might in spite of its difficulties be one of the ways of making this possible.

Dr. Clinchy was opposed by Dr. Kenneth Leslie, editor of *The Protestant Digest,* who said that it was an "administrative bridge" between the State and the Church, and would become "an effective weapon in the hands of clerical-fascism to develop a State-supported church school system and ultimately a church-controlled State."[145] He suggested that instead of continuing the plan then in use, a complete holiday be given on Wednesdays for children to go to religious classes if they or their parents so wished. Further opposition to the plan, on the ground that it was an opening wedge to public support of parochial schools and an interference with regular school work, was voiced by the principal of the Samuel J. Tilden High School. He felt that there was ample opportunity for religious schools on Saturday or Sunday, or after school hours. These were the major differences of opinion which arose regarding the plan.

(5) THE PROTESTANT, ROMAN CATHOLIC, AND JEWISH ATTITUDES

The Protestant, Jewish, and Roman Catholic attitudes toward religious education for public-school pupils differ somewhat on the subject of the released and dismissed-time projects.

Protestant Churches played the major part in developing the plan, and have given it official support through actions by many ministerial and church associations. They believe that with suitable regulations it constitutes an apparently Constitutional way of meeting, at least in part, the Roman Catholic charge that public education is godless, and that parochial schools provide the only substitute, in view of the fact that the American public will not permit religious indoctrination, by priests or other authorized teachers of any religious communion, in public schools. The determining part Protestantism has played in developing the plan has appeared in the previous sections.[146]

The Federal Council of Churches has not come out in favor of any specific form of religious instruction for public-school children. It is, however, deeply interested in working out some Constitutional plan by which religious illiteracy in so large a proportion of our youth may be combated. Its general attitude may be shown by the statement adopted in 1946 as part of its "Call to Evangelism." Under the heading of "Our Secular Society" occurs the following:

> We are grateful for the religious freedom we enjoy in our nation. However, we cannot be complacent in the face of a growing secularism, a gradual decline in moral

standards and a widespread indifference to organized religion. Millions are unreached by the teachings of Christianity. A prudential ethic is prevalent. Youth is adrift in a pagan and an abnormal world. Home life and childhood have suffered unspeakably during the war years.

It is most unfortunate that the children and youth of our nation receive no systematic religious instruction in our educational system because the American people have been led to believe that the separation of Church and State requires the exclusion of all religious subject matter from the school, whereas the legal and constitutional inhibitions actually concern sectarian indoctrination only.

We call upon the churches to fulfill their mission as the spiritual shepherds of our people; to expose our secularism, immorality and religious indifference to the claim and saving power of Christ; to reach the childhood and youth of this nation with the Gospel; and to co-operate with the public schools in providing religious instruction for our children of school age.[147]

The Roman Catholic Church has devoted its major attention in religious education to building up its parochial schools. It has generally felt that all supplementing of public-school education by special religious instruction outside of school hours was both inadequate and unsatisfactory. This view is well expressed by Father Richard Gabel, the historian and exponent of the movement to secure aid from public funds for church or parochial schools which are open to the public without charge. In 1937 he wrote:

> . . . Catholics desire all children in a Catholic school under Catholic teachers. Mere religious instruction does not suffice for it is necessary "also that every other subject taught, be permeated with Christian piety" and "that Religion may be in very truth the foundation and crown of the youth's entire training" in elementary, intermediate and higher institutions, as the Encyclical on *Christian Education of Youth* puts it.[148]

Recently, however, the Church has given evidence of interest not only in its own parochial schools, but in the religious training outside of school hours of all Roman Catholic pupils in public schools. The Confraternity of Christian Doctrine has this matter specially in charge. It has, according to its constitution, the following major objectives:

> a. Religious education of elementary-school children not attending Catholic schools, in vacation schools, instruction classes and correspondence courses.
>
> b. Religious instruction of Catholic youth of high-school age not attending Catholic schools, in suitable discussion clubs and by other successful methods.
>
> c. Religious discussion clubs for adult groups (including students attending secular colleges and universities, and out-of-school youth); inquiry classes for non-Catholics.
>
> d. Religious education of children by parents in the home.
>
> e. Participation as a society, and under the direction of the pastor, in sacred functions of public worship according to the norms of Canon 709:1. . . .[149]

The confraternity has recently estimated that there are 2,600,000 Catholic children not enrolled in parochial schools, and it is carrying on its work of reaching them with great vigor and intelligence and with strong support from the hierarchy and from Rome. It has sponsored the various national catechetical congresses, of which the first was held in Rochester, New York, in 1935.[150]

The confraternity is already caring for hundreds of thousands of Catholic public-school children—25,000 in Brooklyn alone; and at a recent session of the National Catechetical Congress Bishop Edwin V. O'Hara (1881–), chairman of the confraternity, announced its intention of aiming at religious instruction for all of their 1,750,000 high-school students. It is also emphasizing religious vacation schools for the 2,000,000 Roman Catholic students in public elementary schools. Here is a movement that is entirely Constitutional and patriotic, one for which American citizens generally should feel grateful. Bishop O'Hara has stated:

> The confraternity is a vigorous organization designed to put principles into practice. The world's denial of God for so long has resulted in the chaos we see abroad today.
>
> American democracy, too, is endangered and can readily fail unless God's supreme authority is recognized. That is why we insist on adequate religious instruction for all Catholics—to make them better Catholics and the finest type of citizens.[151]

A city where the Church has been specially active in this field of religious education for its public-school children is Pittsburgh. Here, under the inspiring leadership of a local priest, it began by securing rooms opposite public high schools and conducting classes two afternoons a week at the close of the regular school session. No charge is made for this instruction. This informal solution of the problem is being tried in many places both by Catholics and Protestants.

A statement of the Roman Catholic position with regard to encouraging voluntary religious instruction for public-school students may be quoted from a letter of the Most Reverend John T. McNicholas (1877–), Archbishop of Cincinnati, under date of June 30, 1936:

> While thanking God that our country is not opposed to religion, we must deplore the fact that it is indifferent to religion.... There is no thought that our government set up a State religion. We must thank God for the structure of our government which ensures freedom of religion. But we must go a step farther. We must have the encouragement of our government for the religious instruction of the youth of the land according to a plan which can and will satisfy all groups.[152]

A decade later, in 1947, in a letter to the National Education Association, he came out even more definitely in favor of the released-time project. This attitude seems to be growing, but it does not indicate any diminution of interest in the effort to provide effective parochial schools in all towns with a large Roman Catholic population.

The National Catholic Welfare Conference has not up to the present expressed itself officially on the released-time plan. The conference informed the author that "individual Bishops are meeting the situation as it arises in their own Dioceses."[153] But it has been co-operating with the Confraternity of Christian Doctrine in making a nation-wide study of the situation. It has sent out various news sheets which give a favorable Catholic reaction toward the essential features of the project. For instance, it has issued Monsignor Griffiths' statement criticizing some of the speakers at the meeting of the New York Kindergarten 6-B Association, already referred to. In this statement he declared:

> Any man or woman who would have the effrontery to state that such a law does not represent the will of the people must be ready to junk every pretense of democratic process. And what is more likely, such a man or woman is not merely opposed to education on released time but to all religious education and to religion itself.[154]

The conference has also issued a statement by the Reverend Cornelius B. Collins, LL.B., Director of the National Center Confraternity of Christian Doctrine, on "Religious Education of the Public School Child," in which the system is described. The writer states that

> Among the supports upon which the worker in the field of general religious education may lean, perhaps the most encouraging prop is the movement for the release of public school children for religious instruction in their own faith.[155]

It also quotes, with approval, the report of the "inter-faith" committee in New York to the effect that

> A pagan civilization cannot live. Morals, right living, character, depend finally on a religious foundation. Thus, a patriot wants religion included in education. Released time is one way of doing it.[156]

Father Collins adds that this is "a conclusion entirely in accord with the convictions of right-thinking Americans."[157] This opinion is being expressed by an increasingly large number of Roman Catholic leaders.

The Jewish attitude toward the released-time project has not yet become clearly articulate. It varies in different communities. We have already quoted the opposition of the Jews in California to the Miller Bill, which planned to provide religious education on released time.[158] That attitude received considerable support from Jewish sources. For instance, the leading reformed rabbis of the United States, constituting the Commission on Jewish Education, meeting in Cincinnati, Ohio, in March, 1925, discussed the issues. They sympathized in general with the view expressed by Rabbi Newman in opposing the Miller Bill, and unanimously passed a resolution to the effect that

> The Commission on Jewish Education endorses the efforts which are being made to procure more time for week-day religious instruction, and we recommend that for such purposes the public schools reduce their time schedule, schools be closed, and that the time thus put at the disposal of the children be used by the parents for their children as they desire.
>
> Furthermore, we are opposed to any form of religious instruction in the American public school system of education or in public buildings, or to any form of classification of children in the public school according to their religious affiliation.[159]

Since this commission was appointed by the Department of Synagogue and School Extension of the Union of American Hebrew Congregations and the Central Conference of American Rabbis, its action may be considered as representing the attitude of the leaders of liberal American Judaism at the time. Since then there seems to have been a swing in the opposite direction. For example the latest nation-wide test of public opinion was a referendum conducted by the National Council of Jewish Women of New York. As a result, the council took action in opposition to the released-time project.[160]

This was also true of the Central Conference of American Rabbis in 1947. It reaffirmed its opposition to "religious inroads in the public school system" including the released-time plan, and rededicated itself to "this struggle for the maintenance of the wall of separation between Church and State."[161] Similarly an officer of the Commission on Law and Social Action of the American Jewish Congress concludes a study of the subject by saying that the dangers and disadvantages outweigh "by far" the benefits. He lists four objections: it is a threat to the principle of Church–State separation; public school authorities often put pressure on children to attend the courses; Jewish children occasionally attend Christian classes regularly for fear of disclosing their religious differences; and the amount of religious instruction that can be given is negligible.[162]

Other Jewish opponents of the plan lay emphasis on the fact that children without available centers of study may be stigmatized; that going to different places of instruction may sharpen denominational differences; that social pressure may be placed on those who do not wish to conform; that the plan represents a dangerous intrusion in our pattern of Church–State separation; and that the amount of time available for religious instruction is inadequate.[163] There is some evidence, however, that liberal Judaism, impressed by the decline of religious faith and personal ethical standards in our larger communities, now includes those who advocate in principle the released-time project when the religious courses are held outside public school buildings.

Section 3. READING THE BIBLE AND RECITING THE LORD'S PRAYER IN PUBLIC SCHOOL EXERCISES

The laws of all the states forbid denominational instruction, though many of them permit, and some require, Bible reading without comment in the opening exercises. But this is opposed by some groups who fear that it may be an opening wedge for sectarian influence, and by others because of the difficulty in agreeing on an acceptable translation.

(1) THE HISTORY AND PRESENT PRACTICE

It may be interesting to call attention to the fact that Congress specially approved the publication of what is generally known as the Revolutionary Bible. This edition of the Authorized version was published by Robert Aitken in Philadelphia in 1782.[164] It was the first English Bible published on the American continent. Also in 1882 Congress authorized the repayment of duties paid on the 2,100 copies of the revision of the New Testament, undertaken under Protestant auspices, which had been sent to this country by the English revisers for the use and distribution of the American Revision Committee. It also authorized the same favor to be granted in the case of copies of the Old Testament when received.[165]

The Bible is not usually read at the opening exercises of Congress today, there being merely a prayer; but its reading by the public is frequently urged by government officials, as when President Wilson (1856–1924) made his public appeal for funds to give the Scriptures to all soldiers and sailors of the nation in World War I,[166] and when President Franklin D. Roosevelt (1882–1945) issued his message in behalf of Universal Bible Sunday, in which he said, "We know that the ancient truths of the Bible will prevail over all error because they constitute the teachings of God."[167]

Prior to the late 'thirties of the last century there was no serious objection by large groups to the then common practice of reading the King James version of the Bible at the opening exercises in public schools. There was only one state in the union during the first hundred years which made it obligatory by statute —Massachusetts, in 1826. Elsewhere it was merely continued from colonial tradition or agreed to by the local school authorities. The Massachusetts legislation was not followed by any American state until the twentieth century, when twelve states followed suit in the two decades following 1913.[168]

The first strong objection to the practice arose in certain Eastern cities which in the second quarter of the nineteenth century acquired through immigration a large Roman Catholic population. The controversy was particularly acute about the middle of the century, when the Roman Catholics were using the practice as an effective argument in favor of developing their own parochial schools. It had naturally been taken over from colonial times, when such reading was common and when capacity to read the Bible was required in some colonies by legislative enactment. As Professor Paul Monroe (1869–) has said, "Everywhere and at all times in the colonial period the religious element was prominent in the schools."[169] This meant that the Protestant point of view was emphasized. Under then prevailing conditions practically everywhere in the thirteen colonies, outside of parts of Maryland, no other attitude was possible. The Genevan version was the most used in Puritan New England and the King James version in the Anglican South; both were used in the middle colonies. But with the development of ideas of religious freedom under the republic, and with the growing power of the Roman Catholic Church and its sensitiveness on the subject of the King James version, whose use had become nearly universal among English-speaking Protestants, the practice of reading the Bible at the opening exercises of schools was given up in many places in the second third of the past century.[170]

The public issue of the question of Bible reading in the public schools was historically closely related to the development of the Roman Catholic parochial school movement. Opposition to the practice was considered only second in importance to the vital need of providing an education under Church auspices for the millions of immigrants arriving from Ireland, Germany, and other portions of Europe. The general subject, and particularly the latter phase of it, is discussed at length in an earlier section dealing with the cleavage between the developing of public and parochial schools, especially in Massachusetts.[171] Here belongs an incident from an Ohio experience of the same period—the 'thirties of the nineteenth century.

The Western Literary Institute and College of Professional Teachers (1829) had great influence in the Middle West. It favored from the beginning religious education in the public schools, with the Bible a reading book "from the infant school to the University." This represented the general Protestant position in Ohio. In 1837 Bishop John Baptist Purcell (1800–83), afterward archbishop of Cincinnati, pointed out the difficulty of making selections from the Bible for the common schools, and, though he preferred the whole Bible to selections, he urged that Protestant Bibles be not placed in the hands of Catholic youth; that teachers be forbidden to inject sectarian bias in their instruction; and that provision be made for children to be instructed by their own pastors once or twice a week.[172] An important debate ensued between the Reverend Alexander Campbell (1778–1866), a Baptist preacher, who was the real founder of the influential Church in the Middle West known as the

Disciples of Christ, and Bishop Purcell; this was in 1837. The Roman Catholic attitude, which Bishop Purcell had done so much to develop, was thus expressed in the pastoral letter of the Third Provincial Council of Cincinnati to the clergy and laity, 1861:

As this religious training is not possible in the Public Schools as at present organized and conducted, our children are necessarily excluded from them, as effectively as they would be by locks and bolts, . . . after paying our due proportion of common taxes for the support of Schools which are thus virtually closed against us, we feel constrained to erect others, at enormous expense for the Christian education of our own children. . . . In a country so divided in sentiment as ours is on the subject of Religion, the only system which would be fair and equitable to all, would be that which would make education like religion, and like all other important pursuits, *entirely free;* and if taxes are collected from all for its encouragement and support, to apportion the amount of these taxes fairly among the scholars taught certain branches up to a certain standard, no matter under what religious or other auspices. This system would elicit educational industry and talent, by stimulating competition; and we have not a doubt that it would lessen the cost of education, greatly extend its blessings, and render it both sounder and more widely diffused. It would satisfy all classes, and it would render the schools really *Public* and *Common* which they certainly are not at present except in name.[173]

A summary in 1934[174] showed that the practice of Bible reading in the public schools was specifically permitted by statute in seven states, and allowed by court or administrative decisions in a few others; considered optional in thirteen through the lack of any definite state law on the subject; prohibited in eleven—generally by interpretation by courts or educational authorities of state constitution guarantee of religious freedom, and/or the protection of public education from denominational instruction; and required in eleven and the District of Columbia. The required study clauses are mainly in Southern and Eastern states. In four cases the provision has been upheld in the state's highest court.[175] Although no comprehensive statistics are available, it is believed that a majority of public schools in the country still open their daily sessions with reading without comment from the Bible, and that a substantial minority open with a hymn and the Lord's Prayer. The latest careful survey I have seen (1946)—and this is not complete—showed that thirteen states including the District of Columbia required Bible reading in all public schools; twenty-five states permitted it; and in eight states no public schools read the Bible.[176]

It is noticeable that no state specifically prohibits public school Bible reading by statutory law,[177] though about three-fourths prohibit "sectarian" instruction or textbooks.[178] These two facts taken together clearly imply that lawmakers in general either do not consider Bible reading as practiced in the public schools to be instruction, or do not consider the Bible sectarian, or consider both of these arguments of opposers of the plan to be fallacious. From 1910 to 1930 eleven states enacted laws requiring Bible reading, and in one state, North Dakota, it is obligatory to have the ten commandments displayed on a placard in each schoolroom.[179] The decade from 1913 to 1923 was particularly productive of legislation requiring the reading of the Bible without comment in public-school exercises.[180] This "without comment" provision is generally included so as to prevent what is considered by most of the lawmakers as inspiring literature helpful to all, from being used for purposes of sectarian instruction.

The repeating of the Lord's Prayer at the opening exercises is very common, as is the making of a prayer by a Protestant or Catholic minister at graduation. The latter practice was even upheld as Constitutional in 1916 in Wisconsin, a state which, because of its large German population, has had the reputation of being somewhat secular in educational ideals.[181]

The Lord's Prayer custom has been occasionally criticized by Roman Catholics on the ground that the prayer as translated in the King James version is generally used rather than that of a recognized Catholic version, but the two are so similar as to make the objection of little more than academic significance today. Except for inconsequential differences in punctuation and capitalization, neither of which would be recognized in recitation, exactly the same form is being increasingly used both by Protestants and Catholics. For example, the commonly used wording of the prayer as given at the beginning of the holy communion service in the Episcopal *Book of Common Prayer* and in the authorized English translation of the Pater Noster in the *Ordinary of the Mass* is precisely the same, both being based on the accounts in Matthew 6 and Luke 11, as given in the King James version. Some Protestant groups going back to Wyclif's translation and that of the so-called Authorized or King James translation of Matthew 6:12, as well as the Douay version, use "debts" and "debtors" in place of "trespasses" and "those who trespass against us," and some add from St. Matthew's Gospel (6:13) the later ascription "For thine is the Kingdom," etc., at the end.[182] But these create no serious obstacles; and it is significant that at the great Congress of Religions at the World's Fair in Chicago, Christians, Jews, Mohammedans and other groups agreed to open their conferences with the Lord's Prayer.

Generally speaking there is in most states little legal or other objection, except on the part of a relatively few extremists, to the voluntary recital of the Lord's Prayer at opening exercises. The American Civil Liberties Union, however, in 1946 protested this practice in the New York public schools on the ground that it is contrary to the state constitution prohibition against using public funds to support schools in which "any denominational tenet or doctrine is taught."[183] But inquiries of the Board of Education of the city in December, 1947, merely elicited the reply from the superintendent of schools that the current by-laws of the Board of Education read as follows: "The regular assemblies of all schools shall be opened by reading to the pupils a portion of the Bible without comment."[184]

Courts in different parts of the country where the same issue has been raised differ on this matter, the major question generally being whether the use of the King James Bible version of the prayer is Constitutional on the ground of its not being denominational or sectarian. This question is closely related to that of reading the Bible in the schools.[185]

(2) THE LEGAL AND CONSTITUTIONAL ASPECTS

Most of the states now adopt one of two policies by acts of their legislatures, namely, either to forbid the use of any "sectarian" book or instruction, leaving it to the courts in any particular case to decide whether a book or instruction is sectarian; or to forbid the exclusion of the Bible on the ground that it is a sectarian book, and at the same time to prescribe the methods of its use.

Of the laws of the first character, which are by far the more general, the following may be named as typical:

Colorado: Among the powers of schools directors enumerated in the General Statutes of 1883 are: "To exclude from schools and school libraries all books, tracts, papers or catechisms of a sectarian character."[186]

Idaho: This State goes further by specifically forbidding in its constitution both sectarian teaching and any required attendance at religious worship:

"No religious test or qualification shall ever be required of any person as a condition of admission into any public, educational institution of the state, either as teacher or student; and no teacher or student of any such institution shall ever be required to attend or participate in any religious service whatever. No sectarian or religious tenets or doctrines shall ever be taught in the public schools, nor shall any distinction or classification of pupils be made on account of race or color. No books, papers, tracts, or documents of a political, sectarian, or denominational character shall be used or introduced in any schools established under the provisions of this article, nor shall any teacher in any district receive any of the public school moneys in which the schools have not been taught in accordance with this article."[187]

Kentucky: "No books or other publications of a sectarian, infidel, or immoral character shall be used or distributed in any common school," etc.[188]

Nevada: "No books, tracts or papers of a sectarian or denominational character shall be used or introduced in any school established under the provisions of this act; . . . nor shall any school whatever receive any of the public school funds which has not been taught in accordance with the provisions of this act."[189]

Washington: "Every board of directors unless otherwise especially provided by law, shall have power and it shall be their duty: . . . To exclude from schools and from school libraries, all books, papers, tracts or catechisms of an infidel, sectarian, or partisan character."[190]

This last clause should be interpreted in the light of the constitution of the state, which provides that

No public money or property shall be appropriated for or applied to any religious worship, exercise, or instruction, or the support of any religious establishment.

All schools supported wholly or in part by the public funds shall be forever free from sectarian control or influence.[191]

Of examples of the second policy, that is, one forbidding the exclusion of the Bible, or specifically authorizing its use, the following are characteristic:

Arkansas, by an initiative act as late as 1931 required the daily reading of the English Bible without comment in all the public schools of the state, including those of high-school grades.[192]

Iowa: "The Bible shall not be excluded from any school or institution in this state, nor shall any pupil be required to read it contrary to the wishes of his parent or guardian."[193]

Kansas: "No sectarian or religious doctrine shall be taught or inculcated in any of the public schools of the city; but nothing in this section shall be construed to prohibit the reading of the Holy Scriptures."[194]

Massachusetts: "A portion of the Bible shall be used daily in the public schools, without written note or oral comment; but a pupil whose parent or guardian informs the teacher in writing that he has conscientious scruples against it, shall not be required to read from any particular version, or to take any personal part in the reading. The school committee shall not purchase or use school books in the public schools calculated to favor the tenets of any particular religious sect."[195]

Mississippi: In only a single case, that of Mississippi, has a state constitution specifically allowed the use of the Bible in the public schools:

"No religious test as a qualification for office shall ever be required; and no preference shall be given by law to any religious sect, or mode of worship; but the free enjoyment of all religious sentiments and the different modes of worship shall be held sacred. The rights hereby secured shall not be construed to justify acts of licentiousness injurious to morals or dangerous to the peace and safety of the State, or to exclude the Holy Bible from use in any of the public schools of this state."[196]

North Dakota: "The Bible shall not be deemed a sectarian book. It shall not be excluded from any public school. It may at the option of the teacher be read in school without sectarian comment, not to exceed ten minutes daily. No pupil shall be required to read it nor be present in the schoolroom during the reading thereof contrary to the wishes of his parents or guardian or other person having him in charge."[197]

The practice in the District of Columbia, being Federal territory under the jurisdiction of the Congress of the United States, is specially important. It has no constitution, but its board of education has authority from Congress to draft rules for the public schools. The following is now in force:

Each teacher shall, as a part of the opening exercises, read, without note or comment, a portion of the Bible, repeat the Lord's Prayer, and conduct appropriate singing by the pupils.[198]

It is interesting to note that the Bible was also the standard reader and speller in the District of Columbia for a long time.[199]

It is clear that from the standpoint of state law the major question generally is whether Bible reading—that is, in the overwhelming majority of cases, the reading of the King James version—is "sectarian" instruction. Or to put it differently, is this translation of the Bible a sectarian book?

Many states have some related constitutional or legislative provisions which are involved. For instance, to quote merely a few typical cases, Wisconsin and Nevada have clauses in their constitutions against "sectarian" teaching in public institutions; Massachusetts and New Hampshire have laws against sectarian textbooks; Alabama and California have laws against sectarian instruction in state universities.[200]

There is also the question as to whether such reading is counter to the religious-freedom guarantees of the Federal Bill of Rights as interpreted by the Fourteenth Amendment.[201] Up to the present time in the cases brought before the Supreme Court it has assumed that under the Constitution this is a matter for each state to decide for itself.[202]

A few of the more important state court decisions on the Bible-reading question may now be quoted. As in the classifications already given, we are following an alphabetical arrangement of states as being on the whole the most convenient.

California:

An important case dealing with the Bible in general and its use in public-school libraries is dealt with later when some Church–State difficulties in the choice of books for public libraries are discussed.[203] Suffice it here to say that the court supported the Selma High School in purchasing copies of the King James Bible for the school library, and said that this decision would apply equally to the Douay version.

Illinois:

An important case dealing with the question of Bible reading in the public schools and the general question as to what constitutes religious or sectarian instruction is one decided by the Supreme Court of Illinois in 1910. Objection was raised by taxpayers of District Twenty-four, whose children attended the public schools, to the customary reading at the opening school exercises of portions of the King James version of the Bible and the reciting of the Lord's Prayer from the same version. The objectors were Roman Catholics who stated that as members of their Church, believing in its doctrines, faith, and forms of worship, they could not consent to having their children taught from a version of the Bible which they could not recognize and whose wording differed in important respects from the Douay version approved by their Church. They also took the ground that the laws of the state required children to attend school, and that as there was no private or parochial school in the county, they were compelled to attend what was virtually a place of worship against their consent and in violation of the Constitutional provisions regarding religious freedom. Majority and minority opinions were prepared. As they are among the more thoughtful which have been given by state courts on the subjects covered, the major portions are here reproduced:

The majority opinion in this case favored a secular ideal of public education, though fully recognizing the importance of religion:

> Our Constitution guarantees the free exercise and enjoyment of religious profession and worship without discrimination. The exercises mentioned in the petition constitute worship. They are the ordinary forms of worship usually practiced by Protestant Christian denominations. Their compulsory performance would be a violation of the constitutional guaranty of the free exercise and enjoyment of religious profession and worship. One does not enjoy the free exercise of religious worship who is compelled to join in any form of religious worship.
>
> The wrong arises, not out of the particular version of the Bible or form of prayer used—whether that found in the Douay or the King James' version—or the particular songs sung, but out of the compulsion to join in any form of worship. The free enjoyment of religious worship includes freedom not to worship.
>
> It is further contended that the reading of the Bible in the schools constitutes sectarian instruction, and that thereby the provision of the Constitution is also violated which prohibits the payment from any public fund of anything in aid of any sectarian purpose. The public schools are supported by taxation, and if sectarian instruction should be permitted in them, the money used in their support would be used in aid of a sectarian purpose. The prohibition of such use of public funds is therefore a prohibition of the giving of sectarian instruction in the public schools.
>
> Christianity is a religion. The Catholic church and the various Protestant churches are sects of that religion. These two versions of the Scriptures are the bases of the religion of the respective sects. Protestants will not accept the Douay Bible as representing the inspired word of God. As to them it is a sectarian book containing errors and matter which is not entitled to their respect as a part of the Scriptures. It is con-

sistent with the Catholic faith but not the Protestant. Conversely, Catholics will not accept King James' version, as to them it is a sectarian book inconsistent in many particulars with their faith, teaching what they do not believe. The differences may seem to many so slight as to be immaterial, yet Protestants are not found to be more willing to have the Douay Bible read as a regular exercise in the schools to which they are required to send their children, than are Catholics to have the King James' version read in schools which their children must attend.

The reading of the Bible in school is instruction. Religious instruction is the object of such reading, but whether it is so or not, religious instruction is accomplished by it. The Bible has its place in the school, if it is read there at all, as the living word of God, entitled to honor and reverence. Its words are entitled to be received as authoritative and final. The reading or hearing of such words cannot fail to impress deeply the pupils' minds. It is intended and ought to so impress them. They cannot hear the Scriptures read without being instructed as to the divinity of Jesus Christ, the Trinity, the resurrection, baptism, predestination, a future state of punishments and rewards, the authority of the priesthood, the obligation and effect of the sacraments, and many other doctrines about which the various sects do not agree. Granting that instruction on these subjects is desirable, yet the sects do not agree on what instruction shall be given. Any instruction on any one of the subjects is necessarily sectarian, because, while it may be consistent with the doctrines of one or many of the sects, it will be inconsistent with the doctrines of one or more of them. The petitioners are Catholics. They are compelled by law to contribute to the maintenance of this school, and are compelled to send their children to it, or, besides contributing to its maintenance, to pay the additional expense of sending their children to another school. What right have the teachers of the school to teach those children religious doctrine different from that which they are taught by their parents? Why should the state compel them to unlearn the Lord's Prayer as taught in their homes and by their Church and use the Lord's Prayer as taught by another sect? If Catholic children may be compelled to read the King James' version of the Bible in schools taught by Protestant teachers, the same law will authorize Catholic teachers to compel Protestant children to read the Catholic version. The same law which subjects Catholic children to Protestant influences will subject the children of Protestants to Catholic control where the Catholics predominate. In one part of the state the King James' version of the Bible may be read in the public schools, in another the Douay Bible, while in school districts where the sects are somewhat evenly divided, a religious contest may be expected at each election of a school director to determine which sect shall prevail in the school. Our Constitution has wisely provided against any such contest by excluding sectarian instruction altogether from the school.

We have been considering the case of the Protestant and the Catholic. Let us consider that of the Christian and the Jew. The Christian believes that Judaism was a temporary dispensation, and that Christ was the Messiah—the Savior of the world. The Jew denies that Christ was the Messiah and regards him as an impostor. Is it not the teaching of sectarian doctrine to his children to read to them daily from the

New Testament, every chapter of which holds up Christ crucified as the Savior of Men?

The only means of preventing sectarian instruction in the school is to exclude altogether religious instruction, by means of the reading of the Bible or otherwise. The Bible is not read in the public schools as mere literature or mere history. It cannot be separated from its character as an inspired book of religion. It is not adapted for use as a text book for the teaching alone of reading, of history, or of literature, without regard to its religious character. Such use would be inconsistent with its true character and the reverence in which the Scriptures are held and should be held. If any parts are to be selected for use as being free from sectarian differences of opinion, who will select them? Is it to be left to the teacher? The teacher may be religious or irreligious, Protestant, Catholic, or Jew. To leave the selection to the teacher, with no test whereby to determine the selection, is to allow any part selected to be read, and is substantially equivalent to permitting all to be read.

It is true that this is a Christian State. The great majority of its people adhere to the Christian religion. No doubt this is a Protestant state. The majority of its people adhere to one or another of the Protestant denominations. But the law knows no distinction between the Christian and the Pagan, the Protestant and the Catholic. All are citizens. Their civil rights are precisely equal. The law cannot see religious differences, because the Constitution has definitely and completely excluded religion from the law's contemplation in considering men's rights. There can be no distinction based on religion. The state is not, and under our Constitution cannot be, a teacher of religion. All sects, religious or even anti-religious, stand on an equal footing. They have the same rights of citizenship, without discrimination. The public school is supported by the taxes which each citizen, regardless of his religion or his lack of it, is compelled to pay. The school, like the government, is simply a civil institution. It is secular, and not religious, in its purposes. The truths of the Bible are the truths of religion which do not come within the province of the public schools. No one denies their importance. No one denies that they should be taught to the youth of the state. The Constitution and the law do not interfere with such teaching, but they do banish theological polemics from the schools and the school districts. This is done, not from any hostility to religion, but because it is no part of the duty of the state to teach religion—to take the money of all, and apply it to teaching the children of all the religion of a part only. Instruction in religion must be voluntary. . . .[204]

This opinion is in line with that of the Supreme Court of South Dakota, which declared that a school board violated the Constitutional guarantees of religious freedom in trying to compel Catholic children to listen to the reading of the "Protestant" Bible.[205]

The following are excerpts from the dissenting opinion of Justices Hand and Cartwright in the Illinois case:

The Bible is not mentioned in the Constitution, nor is there found therein any express inhibition against the giving of religious or moral instruction in the public schools, and while the Constitution is silent upon these subjects, it has been from the formation of our state government to the present time universally recognized by the people that there are certain fundamental principles of religion and morality which the safety of society requires should be imparted to the youth of the state, and that those principles may be properly taught in the public schools as a part of the secular knowledge which it is their province to instill into the youthful mind.

It has always been understood that those general provisions found in the several state Constitutions which usually appear in what are designated as a "bill of rights," and which provide that the enjoyment of the free exercise of religious profession and worship, without discrimination, shall be forever guaranteed to the people, and that they shall not be required to attend upon or support any ministry or place of worship against their consent, were primarily designed to prevent the establishment of a state religion or the compulsion of the citizen to support, by taxation or otherwise, an established ministry or places of established worship, it being the object of such constitutional provisions to work a complete divorcement of the state and the church, and to sever the relation between the state and church which had existed in the mother country prior to the Revolution and secure to the citizen freedom of conscience in the matter of religious belief and worship, and that the instruction which was to be imparted in the public schools did not fall within those provisions of the Constitution unless the instruction sought to be imparted degenerated into what may be properly designated as denominational or sectarian instruction, and falls within the inhibitions of those provisions of the Constitution which were enacted with a view to placing all religious denominations or religious sects upon an equality before the law. . . . We think it obvious, therefore, that all must agree that there can be no rational constitutional basis upon which this court can hold that the Bible can be excluded from the public schools of the state other than upon the ground that it is sectarian in character and falls within those inhibitions of the state Constitution which prohibit teaching in our public schools the beliefs and doctrines of the different denominations or sects into which the believers of the Bible have in the course of time divided.

None of the courts of last resort have held that the Bible, as an entirety, could be excluded from the public schools, upon constitutional grounds, as none of them have held that all parts of it were sectarian. . . .

We think it is apparent that it must be held, from a constitutional standpoint, that all parts of the Bible can be read in the public schools, or that it must be excluded as an entirety from the public schools. . . .

We do not think the Bible can be said to be a sectarian book or that its teachings are sectarian. Its plan of salvation is broad enough to include all the world, and the fact that those who believe in the Bible do not agree as to the interpretation of its teachings and have divided into sects, and are therefore sectarian in their beliefs, does not change the Bible or make it a sectarian book. To make the Bible sectarian it must be made to appear that it teaches the dogmas of some particular sect, and it is not sufficient, to show that it is sectarian, to establish that its teachings are so comprehensive that different phases of belief may be founded on argument based upon some of its parts which, when perhaps only imperfectly examined and partially understood, may seem to tend to support the doctrines of a particular sect and to overthrow the doctrines of some other sect.

We think the great weight of authority sustains the position that the Bible, or any version thereof, may be read in the public schools of this state, without comment, without violating those inhibitions of the Constitution which prohibit the giving of sectarian religious instruction in the public schools. . . .[206]

Kentucky:

The principal case in the state was tried before the Kentucky Supreme Court in 1910 after Thomas Hackett, a Roman Catholic public school patron, complained of the school exercises, which included singing of hymns, prayer, and the reading from the King James version of the Bible. Here are the main portions of the court's opinion.

There is perhaps no book that is so widely used and so highly respected as the Bible. No other that has been translated into as many tongues. No other that has had such marked influence upon the habits and life of the world. It is not the least of its marvelous attributes that it is so catholic that every seeming phase of belief finds comfort in its comprehensive precepts. Many translations of it, and of parts of it, have been made from time to time since two or three centuries before the beginning of the Christian era. And since the discovery of the art of printing and the manufacture of paper in the sixteenth century a great many editions of it have been printed.

The result has been that while many editions of the several translations have been made, those based upon the revision compiled under the reign of King James I, 1607–1611, and very generally used by Protestants, and the one compiled at Douay some time previous, and which was later adopted by the Roman Catholic Church, as the only authentic [English] version, are the most commonly used in this country.

That the Bible, or any particular edition, has been adopted by one or more denominations as authentic, or by them asserted to be inspired, cannot make it a sectarian book. The book itself, to be sectarian, must show that it teaches the peculiar dogmas of a sect as such, and not alone that it is so comprehensive as to include them by the partial interpretation of its adherents. It is not the authorship, nor mechanical composition of the book, nor the use of it, but its contents that give it its character. The history of a religion including its teachings and claim of authority, as, for example, the writings of Confucius or Mohammed, might be profitably studied. Why may not also the wisdom of Solomon and the life of Christ? If the same things were in any other book than the Bible, it would not be doubted that it was within the discretion of the school boards and teachers whether it was expedient to include them in the common school course of study without violating the impartiality of the law concerning religious beliefs.[207]

Michigan:

A characteristic decision was that of the Michigan Supreme Court, in 1898, in the case of *Pfeiffer* v. *Board of Education of Detroit,* to the effect that the use in the public schools for a quarter of an hour at the close of each day's session, of a supplemental textbook entitled "Readings from the Bible," emphasizing its moral precepts, when the teacher makes no comment and any pupil can be excused on application of parent or guardian, is not a violation of the state constitution.

The dissenting opinion took the ground that

> The elements of our population are so diverse, comprising as it does Protestants, Roman Catholics, Hebrews, atheists, orthodox Christians, heterodox Christians, and all shades of religious belief—that no system of religion can be taught which would not be objectionable to many of them. It is said that the school board has removed all objection to the religious exercises embraced in the stated reading of this religious book by excusing those children, whose parents may request it, from joining in it. If it is the duty of the schools under the ordinance of 1787 to teach religion, it is not easy to see how this duty can be abdicated: how some can be excused from it. Children should be taught to fear God and to love their fellow men. They should be made familiar with the truths of the Bible. They should be instructed to remember their Creator in the days of their youth, and to observe his commandments. But this is a branch of education which is not within the province of the State. It belongs to the parents, the home, the Sunday school, the mission, and the church.[208]

Nebraska:

In 1902 the state supreme court considered the case of *State* v. *School,* in which a teacher had received permission from her school board to have religious exercises during school hours. The court ruled that the particular exercises she conducted could not be allowed, because they constituted compulsory attendance at worship and sectarian instruction—both prohibited by the state constitution. It proceeded, however, to imply its belief that the mere reading of the Bible, as such, might be permitted by a school board. The following is an abstract of that part of the opinion referring to Bible reading.

> The Iliad may be read in the schools without inculcating a belief in the Olympic divinities, and the Koran may be read without teaching the Moslem faith. Why may not the Bible also be read without indoctrinating children in the creed or dogma of any sect? Its contents are largely historical and moral; its language is unequaled in purity and elegance; its style has never been surpassed. Among the classics of our literature it stands preeminent. The fact that the King James translation may be used to inculcate sectarian doctrines affords no presumption that it will be so used. The law does not forbid the use of the Bible in either version in the public schools; it is

not proscribed either by the constitution or the statutes, and the courts have no right to declare its use to be unlawful because it is possible or probable that those who are privileged to use it will misuse the privilege by attempting to propagate their own peculiar theological or ecclesiastical views or opinions.[209]

Ohio:

In 1872 the Supreme Court of Ohio handed down unanimously one of the most important decisions in the relations between Church and State in this country.[210] It upheld the refusal of the Board of Education to permit the reading of the Bible in the public schools of Cincinnati. It was interesting because it was prepared by men who believed that the spirit of Christianity was "the parent of good government, the sun which gives to government all its true light."[211] It also recognized the fact that in charitable, punitive, and disciplinary institutions the State may "take the place of the parent, and may well act the part of the parent or guardian in directing what religious instructions shall be given."[212] But this does not apply to public schools, whose children mostly live in their own homes. Here are two paragraphs from the decision:

To teach the doctrine of infidelity, and thereby teach that Christianity is false, is one thing; and to give no instruction on the subject is quite another thing. The only fair and impartial method, where serious objection is made, is to let each sect give its own instructions, elsewhere than in the state schools, where of necessity all are to meet.[213]

Legal Christianity is a solecism, a contradiction of terms. When Christianity asks the aid of government beyond mere impartial protection, it denies itself. Its laws are divine, and not human. Its essential interests lie beyond the reach and range of human governments. United with government, religion never rises above the merest superstition; united with religion, government never rises above the merest despotism; and all history shows us that the more widely and completely they are separated, the better it is for both.[214]

Pennsylvania:

Lincoln gives the following digest of a court decision in Pennsylvania on this matter in 1885:

The directors of the public school permitted the reading of the Protestant, or King James, version of the Bible in the school, and also the singing of Protestant hymns. The plaintiffs, Roman Catholics, protested against the King James version, insisting that the only correct version was that known as the Douay version. The reading of the Bible in the school was without note or comment, and was not intended for the purpose of imparting religious instruction. It appeared that a convenient room was set apart for the use of Roman Catholic children during the opening exercises, and that they were not compelled to attend such opening exercises where the Bible was read, and the hymns being sung.

One objection made by plaintiffs to the use of the Bible in the schools under defendants' control is that they use the Protestant, or King James version, which plaintiffs believe to be sectarian in character, and which has been so declared by the highest ecclesiastical court of the church to which the plaintiffs belong; and by the same tribunal has been declared an incorrect translation of the original writings through which the Deity has made himself known to men; also that the said Protestant Bible is incomplete, many portions of the true Bible having been omitted or excluded therefrom; and that the Douay version is the only correct one. The school directors maintained that the King James version was more nearly correct than the Douay version. The court said: "We have not been able to find authority or preference given by our law to any particular version of the Scriptures of truth, and must therefore conclude that all versions stand equal before the law. If the school directors have power to authorize the use of one version in the public schools, they had power to authorize the use of the other." The Bible is not sectarian in a legal sense.

The principle on which schools were established was not a regard for the children as individuals, but as a part of an organized community. The schools are a means adopted by the state to work out a higher civilization and freedom. They have not been founded for private benefit, but for the public weal. They are the outgrowth of state policy for the encouragement of virtue and the prevention of vice and immorality, and are based upon public conviction of what is necessary for public safety.

Education comprehends all that series of instruction and discipline which is intended to enlighten the understanding, correct the temper, and form manners and habits of youth, and fit them for usefulness in their future stations.

The morality which the state deems it important to cultivate must be the morality which is regarded necessary for the support of the laws and institutions of the state; this must be the morality on which they are based, and this is the morality of the Bible. It would seem to follow, therefore, that the source of that morality is not excluded, but that the Bible may be used for moral culture of the pupils in the public schools.[215]

Wisconsin:

The Supreme Court of Wisconsin in 1880 gave a unanimous decision to the effect that the reading of the Bible, even when unaccompanied by any comment, has a tendency to inculcate sectarian ideas, is sectarian instruction, constitutes an interference with the rights of conscience of pupils, and involves the appropriation of public money for the benefit of religious schools within the meaning and intention of the constitution and the statutes of Wisconsin.[216]

Here again, as in the Ohio case, the court strongly upheld the truths of the Bible, which it stated to be "priceless," but best given by the Church, Sunday and parochial schools, and parents. "Religion," said the opinion, "needs no support from the state. It is stronger and much purer without it." It added that the suit "brings before the courts a case of the plausible, insidious, and apparently innocent entrance of religion into our civil affairs. . . ."[217]

Gabel, in *Public Funds for Church and Private Schools,* Johnson, in *Church-State Relationships,* and Lischka, in *Private Schools,* all give summaries of the conflicting opinions in various states in recent years on this subject, and on the question as to whether use of the Bible is inconsistent with the Constitutional proscriptions against sectarian instruction. The summary prepared by Gabel in 1937 is as follows:

Such reading is not sectarian teaching, nor religious teaching (Illinois, 1910, minority; Kansas, 1910; S. Dakota, 1929, minority).

It does not violate religious liberty (Illinois; S. Dakota; Iowa, 1884); if pupil is excused or not required to attend (Kentucky, 1905).

Such reading is sectarian instruction (Illinois, majority; Wisconsin, 1890; Nebraska, 1902, majority); or aids sectarian purposes (Wisconsin).

It violates religious liberty (Nebraska, Illinois, and S. Dakota, majority; Minnesota, 1927, minority).

It is not religious worship (Illinois, 1880, and 1910, majority).

The Bible is a sectarian book (Illinois, 1910; Minnesota, 1927, minority).

The majority cannot determine its use (Michigan, 1898, minority).

The majority cannot compel the minority (Ohio, 1872; Michigan, 1898, minority).

The Bible inculcates religious doctrine (Illinois, majority).

Particular versions are sectarian (Illinois, majority; Nebraska, 1903; S. Dakota, 1929, majority; Georgia, 1922, minority).

Excusing pupils deprives them of equality and subjects them to stigma (Illinois, majority; Minnesota, minority); makes teaching sectarian (Michigan, 1898, minority); indicates version is sectarian (Louisiana, 1915); is cause of religious strife (Wisconsin, 1890).

Constitution forbids state to teach religion (Illinois, majority); does not compel religious instruction (Ohio, 1872).[218]

In Louisiana and Illinois the courts have decided that the reading of the New Testament violates the religious liberty of the Jews.[219]

These summaries, which still are substantially true to the facts, are significant, but they are open to possible misinterpretation unless studied in connection with the state constitutions and laws concerned and the legal cases specifically involved.

By way of final summary it may be said that most state supreme court decisions uphold the reading of the Bible as permitted in the absence of a statute to the contrary, and that most states, by legislative or board of education enactment, or by court decision, have permitted such reading at school exercises when this is desired by the local authority, and have taken the ground that the Bible is not a "sectarian" book.

Dr. Hamilton in his Columbia thesis on the subject of *The Courts and the Curriculum,* written in 1927, has made a careful study of these and other cases. From this he deduces the following four facts on which alone the courts seem to agree:

(1) That sectarian instruction in the public schools is prohibited, (2) that the public schools should not be subjected to sectarian influence, (3) that the public funds should not be appropriated or used in aid of sectarian purposes, (4) that no one should be compelled to attend or to support any worship against his will. However, when it comes to determining when the practices complained of constitute a violation of these propositions, there seems to be no general agreement.[220]

It is highly significant that the Supreme Court of the United States has consistently declined to take jurisdiction in the cases of state laws requiring Bible reading in the public schools because of the lack of a substantial Federal question involved. It is not impossible, however, now that the court has interpreted the Fourteenth Amendment as applicable to religious freedom cases under state laws, that the issue may come before the court. Up to the present the court has considered it a matter to be decided by each state without Federal interference.

A case of this kind was brought before the court as recently as 1931.[221] The state of Washington has an article in its constitution to the effect that "No public money or property shall be appropriated for or applied to any religious worship, exercises, or instruction, for the support of any religious establishment."[222] The Washington Supreme Court interpreted this provision as prohibiting the reading and teaching of the Bible in the public schools and in state educational institutions. The decision was appealed to the Supreme Court of the United States on the ground that it was contrary to the Declaration of Independence and a violation of the Federal Constitution, especially its preamble and the First and Fourteenth Amendments, and that it furthermore violated the enabling act admitting the state into the union, as well as the inherent rights of the petitioners. They contended that:

The several states and subdivisions thereof by appropriate legislation have the right to, and can require the reading or study of the Bible in the public and private schools, and they can likewise authorize religious instruction to the pupils so long as it is not restricted to any specific church, sect, or denomination; and such reading or study is not prohibited by the first amendment of the constitution, ratified finally in 1791, as it is only a restriction of the power of Congress and not of the several states, and only applies to "establishments" of religion as a specific church, sect or denomination. . . . The Bible and religious teaching thereunder is beneficial and uplifting to all and

> does not come within any of the teachings which the United States Supreme Court says the state can prohibit, therefore, the state cannot prohibit the reading and study of the Bible in either the public or private schools, and parents and pupils have the right to demand the reading and teaching of the Bible in the public and private schools of their communities.[223]

The Supreme Court of the United States declined to assume jurisdiction.

(3) THE POSITION OF CATHOLICS, JEWS, AND OTHER CONSCIENTIOUS OPPONENTS

In general the opposition to Bible reading in the schools comes from four very different groups: the Roman Catholics, the Jews, agnostics and atheists, and certain Protestants who believe that there are inherent dangers in such reading as inconsistent with Church and State separation in the United States.

As to the Roman Catholics, their objection is mainly on the ground that the King James version, which is generally used, is not the version approved by their Church. As is well known, they early adopted for use in this country the Douay (Rheims) version (1582–1609) as revised by Bishop Challoner in 1750. This, however, differs in only relatively slight particulars from that of the Authorized or King James version (1611). In 1941 the Confraternity of Christian Doctrine with the approval of the hierarchy published a new and admirable English translation of the Vulgate with critical notes and comments. A similar edition of the Old Testament has been issued since. These will doubtless succeed the Douay–Rheims–Challoner edition. May 18, 1941, was designated as Biblical Sunday by most American Roman Catholic bishops and archbishops, with the view of helping the movement "to place a revised New Testament in every Catholic home."[224] This is highly significant and encouraging. Roman Catholics assert that the King James version, having been made in England after the Reformation, inclines to a Protestant as distinct from a Catholic point of view, though freely granting that it has great literary beauty and significance and is deeply rooted in the literature of the language. The Roman Catholics frankly concede, however, that even if the Douay–Rheims or other version satisfactory to them were substituted for the King James version it would not result in their discontinuing their effort to build up a separate parochial school system. Indeed, the Douay version is permitted in some places without substantially altering the Church's position. The earliest reference I have noted of such use was in Connecticut in the 'fifties, when the matter of the version to be employed was left to the school committees.[225] Similarly, in the 'fifties the Douay version was specified for Catholic students in the public schools of Maryland.[226] In New York City, where Bible reading is still required, it has become common for teachers to use this version in schools with a predominantly Roman Catholic constituency, just as the Old

Testament alone is commonly used in the city public schools in Jewish districts. Even when the Douay Bible is used, the Roman Catholics generally are not satisfied, because they assert, with justice, that Bible reading alone, if considered from the standpoint of religious instruction, is entirely inadequate. Cardinal Gibbons, as we have already seen, was one of the few Catholic leaders who recognized that Bible reading in the public schools had definite advantages and should be supported when no other form of religious instruction could be provided. In a letter to the president of the Chicago Women's Educational Union, he wrote:

> The men and women of our day who are educated in our public schools will, I am sure, be much better themselves, and will also be able to transmit to their children an inheritance of truth, virtue and deep morality, if at school they are brought to a knowledge of Biblical facts and teachings. A judicious selection of Scripture readings; appropriate presentation of the various Scripture incidents, born of reflection on the passages read and scenes presented, cannot but contribute, in my opinion, to the better education of the children in our public schools, and thus exercise a healthy influence on society at large, since the principles of morality and religion will be silently instilled while instruction is imparted in branches of human knowledge.[227]

Most of the states which permit the reading of the Bible have either a constitutional provision or a statute to the effect that the Bible should be read "without written note or oral comment."[228] In this connection it should be borne in mind that the Roman Catholic Church has been cautious about commending the reading of the Bible by laymen, without authoritative notes giving the Catholic point of view, except when it can be interpreted by a priest or other authorized representative. But in spite of this opposition in principle, and often in action, to the reading of the Bible in the King James version, there are hundreds of thousands of Roman Catholic children in public schools where the Bible is so read without any active objection on the part of the local priests. Sometimes the version selected for the reading, or the reciting of the Lord's Prayer, depends on the teacher's choice.

The point of view of the Jews regarding Bible reading in public schools is based partly on their desire to maintain complete separation between Church and State, and partly on their fear that through the Bible Christological ideas which they cannot approve will be taught to their children. On the whole, they have been less active in their opposition to the reading of the King James version than the Roman Catholics; but their most representative and influential group, the Central Conference of American Rabbis, has adopted the report of its Committee on Church and State as contained in a pamphlet entitled *Why the Bible Should Not be Read in the Public Schools.* This was prepared in 1922, but its facts and conclusions still hold. Jewish opponents take the ground that their position is neither irreligious nor unpatriotic, but that it is in accord with the spirit of the Constitution, on the grounds stated by James Madison (1750/51–1836), that

> Religion is not in the purview of human government. Religion is essentially distinct from government, and exempt from its cognizance. A connection between them is injurious to both.[229]

They lay emphasis on the great difference between public and private schools, and declare that public schools "must be conducted in such a way that all those interested may have equal privileges, and receive exactly the same recognition."[230]

Though in general the Authorized Version is not unacceptable to Jews, they prefer that of Isaac Leeser (1806–68), a German-born American Hebraist, or that of the Jewish Publication Society, because they are translated from a Jewish point of view and are limited to the Old Testament. They fear that Bible reading may lead to the giving of sectarian views by teachers and to more definite religious instruction, calling attention to the fact that a Christian teacher would be likely to select passages giving specifically Christian truth, and that such reading "usually leads to the introduction of other religious exercises altogether sectarian in character."[231] They quote with approval the statement of President Grant:

> Leave the matter of religion to the family altar, the church and the private school supported by private contributions.[232]

They believe that the reading, being usually hurried and perfunctory, hurts rather than helps the cause of religious culture. They lay emphasis on the fact that if there is Bible reading it virtually amounts to a compulsory attendance at a religious service, which all would agree would be out of keeping with American traditions. For these and other reasons the Conference of Jewish Rabbis opposes the reading of the Bible in public school exercises. The pamphlet quoted contains in full the very able veto message of Governor Thomas E. Campbell (1878–1944) of Arizona, of a proposed law which would have permitted "reading the Bible, without comment, except to teach Historical or Literary facts. . . ."[233]

Jews and Catholics are not the only religious bodies that have protested against compulsory Bible reading. Occasionally Baptists and other Protestant groups have also done so. The most significant protest of this type was one recently issued by the Baptist General Association of Virginia. This association appointed the Honorable John Garland Pollard (1871–1937), who had retired from the governorship of the state in 1934, to draft their memorial, which was duly adopted and presented to the Virginia legislature. It is credited with having defeated proposed legislation which would have compelled teachers to read the Bible. The text of the document is worth reading in full. Among the points it takes up are these:

1. The Bible is distinctly a religious book, and when properly read is an act of worship which cannot rightfully be enforced by law. . . .

2. There are many versions of the Bible. One of these, commonly used by Protestants, is known as the King James Version; another used by Catholics, is known as the Douay Version, which contains entire books not appearing in the King James Version. . . .

3. The bill as proposed contains two provisions intended to protect the rights of conscience, but which disclose the inherent weakness of the whole proposition. It provides that at least five verses must be read without comment. It compels reading, but prohibits study. It also provides that pupils may be excused from the classroom during the reading of the Bible, upon written request of either parent. This provision is a recognition of the fact that any version of the Bible used will be looked upon by some as a sectarian book, and as a measure of justice to such, their children may withdraw from the classroom. . . .

4. The right to worship God according to the dictates of one's conscience is firmly established throughout America. But this is not all of religious liberty. It is broader. It means complete and absolute equality before the law of all religions. . . .

5. Some argue that the law should compel the reading of the Bible, not as a religious book, but simply as literature. But this is evidently not the viewpoint of the proponents of this bill, for, as if to minimize the wrong done sects who do not accept our Bible, they limit the reading to five verses, prohibit comment, and excuse pupils from attendance upon the reading. . . .

6. We wish it distinctly understood that we are in full accord with the proponents of the bill in their belief in the importance of training our children in the great religious truths taught in the Bible. Its importance cannot be overstated. The only difference between us is one of method, but that method involves a great underlying principle which is a part of our religious as well as our political faith. . . .

7. Baptists in this State would suffer no direct injury from the proposed law, for the Bible which would be read in the schools is the version which the Baptists use; but the Baptists of Virginia know historically what discrimination against their religion means. . . .

8. This matter seems trivial to some, who argue that the compelling of our teachers to read five verses of the Bible each day involves an infringement of their right so infinitesimally small that the law may well disregard it; but, to say the least, such a law would be a piece of petty pilfering of the rights of the minority sects, which would make us none the richer, but would brand us as offenders against the sacred rights of others, and render us easy marks for retaliation when circumstances are reversed.

The matter is in truth one of tremendous import, not perhaps in itself, but because it is a violation of principle; and one violation leads to another, until the principle itself is in danger. . . .

We therefore appeal to your honorable body to adhere to the doctrine, peculiarly bound up with the history of this commonwealth, which completely separates church and state, which refuses to exercise force in the realm of religion, and which places all religions on a plane of absolute equality before the law.[234]

The reasons stated in this protest seem valid as far as they go—namely, opposition to the required or "compulsory" reading of the Bible in the public schools. They are not, however, necessarily compelling if such reading is entirely voluntary, in the discretion of different communities, and if when such reading is done the rights of minority groups to absent themselves from such reading, or to read from some other Bible version or other inspirational work approved by their parents, are fully protected.

The memorial shows that Virginia Baptists still feel as they did a century and a half ago, that they must protest against any legislation which seems to them to endanger complete religious freedom.

In some places it has been found possible to have a representative committee of Protestant, Catholic, and Jewish citizens agree on certain passages of the Bible which are not of a Christological character, and without any translations objectionable to Roman Catholics, to be used in such cases. Such passages as some of the great Psalms and portions of Isaiah are used, along with the Beatitudes, the Summary of the Law, St. Paul's glorification of charity, and other quotations of a fundamentally ethical and theistic character. In Michigan the permissive use of such a book of selections, *Readings from the Bible,* has been declared constitutional by a state court.[236]

In this matter it should be remembered that where the reading of the Bible is permitted in schools it is with the understanding that there shall be no note or comment; and that the passages used are generally those to which Jews, Protestants, and Catholics would find no objection. Furthermore, in some cases where objection has been raised to Bible reading by Jewish or Catholic parents their children have been excused until the reading is over.[237]

The American Civil Liberties Union has been active in opposing Bible reading in public schools, on the ground that as long as it exists the clear separation between Church and State contemplated under our form of government is endangered. Probably most Protestants favor such reading without comment in communities where there is a strong public opinion favoring it, and oppose it otherwise. President Theodore Roosevelt took this position. In a letter to a New York legislator in 1915 he said:

I see you appeared against the bill making compulsory the reading of the Bible in the Public Schools. If I were in the Legislature or Governor, I should vote against or veto that bill, because I believe in absolutely non-sectarian public schools. It is not our business to have the Protestant Bible or the Catholic Vulgate or the Talmud read in those schools. There is no objection whatever, where the local sentiment favors it, for the teacher to read a few verses of the ethical or moral parts of the Bible, so long as this causes no offense to any one. But it is entirely wrong for the law to make this reading compulsory; and the Protestant fanatics who attempt to force this through are playing into the hands of the Catholic fanatics who want to break down the Public School system and introduce a system of sectarian schools. . . .[239]

The only large Protestant groups in which church opposition to Bible reading in public schools has been noted are the Universalists, the Unitarians, and occasionally the Lutherans and the Baptists, the latter being inclined to make a sharp separation between the sacred and the secular.[738] A possible plan for partly meeting the difficulty of religious education, and one which seems to the author worthy of consideration in some larger communities where there is great diversity of religious opinion, is what might be called the "Silent Bible-reading Plan." For instance, there might be a definite time, say fifteen minutes daily, at the beginning of school exercises, in which after the singing of "America," or some other appropriate national song, there should be a quiet time of Bible reading for all but the youngest groups. In this the Protestant could read from his copy of the King James version, the Roman Catholic from his copy of the Douay or Confraternity of Christian Doctrine version, and the Hebrew from his copy of the Leeser version. The Latin Vulgate might well be substituted by students in high schools qualified to read simple Latin. Should there be any students whose parents did not wish them to read the Bible at all in this hour, they might be allowed to read Emerson's *Essays* or some similar book of high ethical idealism not identified with any religious denomination. The plan would have the advantage of insuring the widespread reading of the Bible or other inspirational book and at the same time of preventing any criticism of partiality to any religious group. There would be no difficulty in arranging in each community for the authorized representatives of each of the three groups to prepare at the beginning of the year lists of passages to be read by those of his group. I have never happened to see the plan suggested but commend it for such consideration as it may deserve.[240] The same principle might well be applied to the Lord's Prayer. Indeed, I have known of cases in my own state, Massachusetts, where in the same school different versions of the Lord's Prayer are used, dependent upon the teacher.

A national movement has recently been under way to have copies of the ten commandments placed in public schools, on the theory that this is something on which Protestants, Catholics, and Jews could all agree. In at least one state, North Dakota, it is required that they be exhibited in every classroom; in another, Mississippi, a statute lays down the regulation that the "Mosaic Ten Commandments be included in a course on 'the principles of morality and good manners.'"[241] But this movement has run up against the problem of agreeing on the form of the commandments. This raises no serious difficulty between Protestants and Jews, but the Catholic version differs from the Protestant in combining the first and second commandments, as given in the King James edition, shortens the fourth, and divides the tenth into two so as to leave the number ten. The versions also differ somewhat in phraseology, such as the omission in the usual Roman Catholic catechism of the word "image" in the Protestant version of the second commandment and the substitution of "thing." These differences, though relatively minor, constitute real difficulties to be overcome. Recently, for instance, the board of education of Covington, Kentucky, declined to have plaques with the commandments put up in the schools. The whole question again shows how hard it is to come to an agreement on religious education under public auspices, especially where specific texts are involved.[242]

Somewhat related to the reading of the Bible in public schools is the idea of "Bible Week," which has been specifically commended by several governors. The most interesting and specific was the proclamation issued by Governor Leverett Saltonstall (1892–) of Massachusetts. He urged daily reading of the Bible by citizens "as a patriotic religious exercise." He stated that in the world crisis of the time "We need to be reminded not only that the deepest needs of our day remain spiritual, but also that the best things in American life are traceable to the Scriptures."[243]

Section 4. INCIDENTAL REFERENCES TO RELIGION IN TEXTBOOKS

It is recognized that no well-balanced cultural curriculum can possibly eliminate all references to religion. Religion has been so identified with the ideals and achievements of the human race that to leave it entirely out of historical or social studies is impossible. This fact creates some difficulty, for competent and conscientious teachers may occasionally and unwittingly color the presentation of important events in history, such as the Reformation, or the relations of Church and State in the Middle Ages, by their own religious convictions. American public high schools have nevertheless been increasingly successful in treating the fundamental facts of secular history that involve religious controversies or influences without bias or emotional appeal. This seems to be true of Protestant, Catholic, and Jewish teachers alike.

It is not possible here to give more than a few instances illustrating the difficulties that have arisen in our public schools because of references to religion or religious history. We must limit ourselves to a striking example from the early history of the schools in New York and then come to modern times with a few recent incidents.

The early incident goes back just over a hundred years to the time when Bishop John Hughes (1797–1864), who was appointed bishop coadjutor in 1838 and succeeded to the see in 1842, was carrying on his vigorous campaign to secure a share of the school fund for Catholic schools, and, when this proved impossible, to build up the separate parochial school system. It illustrates in an impressive way the experiences that have arisen time and again since then, but fortunately in decreasing number, because textbooks have been written with more care, scholarship, and breadth, and with few exceptions give today an objective view of those historical facts which most scholarly Protestants, Catholics, Jews, and even agnostics accept. The incident dates from a period when the public schools, as State-controlled institutions, were just coming into being, and when the Public School Society, a private organization, controlled their work.

At a general meeting of Roman Catholics held on September 21, 1840, in the schoolroom of St. James's Church, a petition to the Board of Aldermen was adopted, asking that a portion of the common school fund be allotted to the Catholic schools—eight schools were suggested—inasmuch as conscientious Catholics could not send their children to the schools of the Public School Society because, among other reasons, many of the books in use contained passages prejudicial to and critical of Catholics. On this point the petition stated:

> . . . Your petitioners have to state further, as grounds of their conscientious objections to those schools, that many of the selections in their elementary reading-lessons contain matter prejudicial to the Catholic name and character. The term "popery" is repeatedly found in them. This term is known and employed as one of insult and contempt toward the Catholic religion, and it passes into the minds of children with the feelings of which it is the outward expression. Both the historical and religious portions of the reading-lessons are selected from Protestant writers, whose prejudices against the Catholic religion render them unworthy of confidence in the mind of your petitioners, at least so far as their own children are concerned.
>
> The Public School Society have heretofore denied that their books contained any thing reasonably objectionable to Catholics. Proofs of the contrary could be multiplied, but it is unnecessary, as they have recently retracted their denial, and discovered, after fifteen years' enjoyment of their monopoly, that their books do contain objectionable passages. . . . With their intentions, your petitioners cannot enter into any question. Nevertheless, they submit to your honorable body that this Society is eminently incom-

petent for the superintendence of public education, if they could not see that the following passage was unfit for the public schools, and especially unfit to be placed in the hands of Catholic children.

They will quote the passage as one instance, taken from "Putnam's Sequel," p. 296.

Huss, John, a zealous reformer from popery, who lived in Bohemia toward the close of the fourteenth, and the beginning of the fifteenth centuries. He was bold and persevering; but at length, trusting to the *deceitful Catholics,* he was by them brought to trial, condemned as heretic, and burnt at the stake.

The Public School Society may be excused for not knowing the historical inaccuracies of this passage; but surely assistance of the Catholic clergy could not have been necessary to an understanding of the word "deceitful," as applied to all who profess the religion of your petitioners. . . .[244]

On October 19 both the Public School Society and the pastors of the Methodist Episcopal Church presented to the Aldermen remonstrances against the Catholic petition. The society had this to say of the books used in their schools:

The subject of objectionable matter in the books used in the public schools is so fully discussed in the papers now submitted to your honorable body, that little more would seem to be called for under this head. Finding their strenuous and long continued efforts to induce the Catholic clergy to unite in an expurgation of the books unavailing, the trustees commenced the work without them, and it is now nearly completed. If any thing remains to which the petitioners can take exception, no censure can by possibility attach to your remonstrants; and the trustees assert with confidence, that, if any has escaped them, there is now less matter objectionable to the Roman Catholics to be found in the books used in the public schools than in those of any other seminary of learning, either public or private, within this State.[245]

The Methodist remonstrance included the following:

The Roman Catholics complain that books have been introduced into the public schools which are injurious to them as a body. It is allowed, however, that the passages in these books to which such reference is made are chiefly, if not entirely, historical; and we put it to the candor of the Common Council to say, whether any history of Europe for the last ten centuries could be written which could either omit to mention the Roman Catholic Church, or mention it without recording historical facts unfavorable to that Church? We assert, that if all the historical facts in which the Church of Rome has taken a prominent part could be taken from writers of her own communion only, the incidents might be made more objectionable to the complainants than any book to which they now object. . . .

But this is not all. They have been most complaisantly offered the censorship of the books to be used in the public schools. The committee to whom has been confided the management of these schools in this city offered to allow the Roman Catholic bishop to expurgate from these books any thing offensive to him.

But the offer was not accepted;—perhaps for the same reason that he declined to decide on the admissibility of a book of extracts from the Bible, which had been sanctioned by certain bishops in Ireland. An appeal, it seems, had gone to the pope on the subject, and nothing could be said or done in the matter until His Holiness had decided. The Common Council of New York will therefore find that, when they shall have conceded to the Roman Catholics of this city the selection of books for the use of the public schools, that these books must undergo the censorship of a foreign potentate. We hope the time is far distant when the citizens of this country will allow any foreign power to dictate to them in matters relating to either general or municipal law.[246]

Ten days later the Aldermen held an open hearing on the subject of the petition and remonstrances. Bishop Hughes made a long address, in which he said:

... I defy you to find a reading-book in either public or private seminary, that in respect to Catholics is not full of ignorance. Not a book. For if it were clear of this, it would not be popular; and if they [the Public School Society] refer to this then, they refer to a standard which we repudiate. But it must be remembered those people can send their children to those schools or keep them at home. They are not TAXED for their support. But here we are. It is the public money which is here used to preserve the black blots which have been attempted to be fixed on the Catholic name. They say again (and it is an idea that will go exceedingly well with the public at large, for it will show how amiable and conciliating are these gentlemen)—that they have submitted the books to us as though we have nothing to do but to mark out a passage, and it will disappear. But are we to take the odium of erasing passages which they hold to be true? Have they the right to make such an offer? And if we spend the necessary time in reviewing the books to discover passages to be expurgated, have they given us a pledge that they will do it, or that they will not even then keep them in? ...

... They [the Methodists] assert that no history could be written which could either omit to mention the Roman Catholic Church, or mention it without recording historical facts unfavorable to the Catholic Church. If this be the case, I ask you whether, as citizens entitled to the rights of citizens, we are to be compelled to send our children to schools which *cannot* teach our children history without blackening us? . . . I contend that there are pages in Catholic history brighter than any in the history of Methodism; and that there are questions and passages enough for reading-lessons, without selecting such as will lead the mind of the Catholic child to be ashamed of his ancestors. . . .[247]

Theodore Sedgwick (1811–59), counsel to the Public School Society, replying to Bishop Hughes, said in part:

... As to the other branch of this double-headed objection, that the books used in the schools are hostile to Catholics, and promote the Protestant interest: if they are so, they ought to be expurgated; and if they cannot be satisfactorily expurgated, the books themselves ought to be abandoned, and their places supplied by others. The trustees have . . . expurgated whole passages of text from some books, and, in other instances, have pasted two leaves together, so as to annihilate completely the objectionable passages, until a new edition can be procured. This has been done, too, notwithstanding the refusal of the Catholic authorities to give the least aid; and surely it is not fair, when this has been done, to insist that these gentlemen were blamable for not discovering these passages sooner. I repeat, it is not common fairness.[248]

Hiram Ketchum of the Public School Society added certain discriminating remarks that have their lesson for us today, even though we recognize that the Roman Catholics had just cause for complaint. He said:

. . . It is affirmed that some of these books contain passages reflecting on Catholics. Now I submit to the candor of the gentleman, and of every one that hears me—because the books containing numerous extracts from numerous authors, collected together for the use of these schools, contain a few passages which I may conceive reflect on me, or on my religion, or on my politics; is that a good reason why I should have conscientious scruples and objections against the entire system? Let us see where it would lead. Here is the Catholic, in turning over perhaps a thousand pages, finds some fifty lines that reflect on his religion. I venture to say the Calvinists, on turning over those pages, would find something reflecting on them. I have not made the experiment, but I have no doubt that would be the result. Then comes the high churchman, and if he does not find something there bearing on his peculiarities, I am mistaken. Then there are the Methodists, and if they do not find something there bearing on what people call their fanaticism, it is extraordinary. Then there is the politician, and there may be something extracted from Jefferson used in these schools, and to this a certain class of politicians may say, I cannot have my children taught Jeffersonianism. Well, then, there is my particular, worthy friend, Daniel Webster, who may have contributed something to the pages of these books, and a Democrat, who takes up the books, may say, I cannot go Webster anyhow; I must have that expurgated. Now if all men must go on in this way, and conscientiously object to the system because in the reading-lessons they find some passages against their religious or political opinions, the whole of the books will be expunged. I do not mean to reflect on the conscientious scruples of any man, but I ask if we are not bound to take hold of this system in a fair and candid manner. We must have a public system; and it is impossible to have a public system to which some man may not have scruples and objections. . . .[249]

It was shown that some of the books to which objection was taken were not textbooks but merely books on the library shelves, and that even one of these to which objection was specially taken had been removed.[250]

The public hearing was continued on October 30, at which time representative pastors of Methodist, Dutch Reformed, and Presbyterian churches made addresses opposing the Roman Catholic petition. Bishop Hughes, replying, said in part:

. . . Why is the burning of Huss selected? why the burning of Cranmer? Why are our children taught, in the face of all sense and decency, that Martin Luther did more for learning than any other man "since the days of the apostles"? Why is "Phelim Maghee" represented as "sealing his soul with a wafer"—in contempt to the holiest mystery known to Catholics, the Sacred Eucharist? Why are intemperance and vice set forth as the necessary and natural effects of the Catholic religion? All this put in the hands of Catholic children by this Society, claiming to deserve the confidence of Catholic parents![251]

On December 19, the Public School Society made the following proposal:

In compliance with the request of the committee of the Board of Aldermen, the undersigned committee of the New York Public School Society submit the following propositions as a basis of a compromise with their Roman Catholic fellow-citizens on the subject of the public schools; which propositions they are willing to support before the trustees of the Society, and which they believe will be sanctioned by that board.

The Trustees of the New York Public School Society will remove from the class-books in the schools all matters which may be pointed out as offensive to their Roman Catholic fellow-citizens, should any thing objectionable yet remain in them.

They will also exclude from the school libraries (the use of which is *permitted* to the pupils, but not *required* of them) every work written with a view to prejudice the mind of the reader against the tenets or practices of the Roman Catholic Church, or the general tendency of which is to produce the same effect.

They will receive and examine any books which may be recommended for the use of the schools; and should such books be adapted to their system of instruction, and void of any matter offensive to other denominations, they shall be introduced so soon as opportunity may be afforded by a call for new books.

Any suggestions in reference to alterations in the plan of instruction or course of studies, which may be offered, shall receive prompt consideration; and, if not inconsistent with the general system of instruction now prevailing in the schools, nor with the conscientious rights of other denominations, they shall be adopted.

The building situated in Mulberry street, now occupied by Roman Catholic schools, shall, if required for the use of the Public School Society, be purchased or hired, on equitable terms, by the trustees, should such an arrangement be desired.

Every effort will be made by the Trustees of the Public School Society to prevent any occurrence in the schools which might be calculated to wound the feelings of Roman Catholic children, or to impair their confidence in, or diminish their respect for, the religion of their parents.

Anxious to keep open every avenue to such an arrangement as will lead to a general attendance of the Roman Catholic children at the public schools, and fully aware that some things may have escaped their observation which might be modified without violation of the conscientious rights of others, the undersigned wish it to be distinctly understood that, in offering the foregoing propositions as the basis of an arrangement, it is not intended to exclude other propositions which the Roman Catholics may make, provided they do not interfere with the principles by which the trustees feel themselves bound.[252]

This appears to have been a fair and conciliatory proposal.

On January 11, 1841, on the report of a committee which had considered all the evidence, and had also visited the public schools, the Board of Aldermen denied the petition of the Roman Catholics.[253]

To understand this decisive action we must refer to the work of a committee appointed by the society. Some of its recommendations and actions are not dated in the printed account of this incident, though all are from the school year 1840–41. The purpose of the committee was

to examine the books in use in the public schools, including those in the libraries, with a view to ascertain and report whether they contain any thing derogatory to the Roman Catholic Church or any of its religious tenets, with power to communicate with such persons of that Church as may be authorized to meet them in reference to such alterations.

This committee sent a set of the textbooks to Bishop Hughes at his request, inviting "a detailed specification of every passage by you deemed objectionable," but the bishop replied that he had no leisure time to devote to this object.[254]

The society's committee also wrote to the chairman of the Committee on Arts and Sciences and Schools of the Board of Aldermen to the effect

that it has ever been the intention of the trustees of the public schools to divest them, as far as practicable, of every thing of a sectarian character; and we are not aware that any of the books used in them have been deemed objectionable by any Church or society of religious purposes except the Roman Catholics.

It has been known and lamented for years that the clergy of this Church have discouraged the attendance of the children of its members at the public schools; and in 1834, a committee was appointed to wait on Bishop Dubois for the purpose of removing any reasonable objection he might have to the course of studies pursued and the books used in the public schools, and to assure him of the wish of the trustees to alter or discontinue the use of any book against which a reasonable objection may lay, and at the same time to invite the co-operation in the management of the public schools of any lay member of the Catholic Church who feels an interest in the literary and moral culture of youth. This committee made a full report, embracing all the points insisted on by the bishop as necessary to induce him to recommend the attendance of Catholic children at the public schools. Your committee will be furnished with a copy of this report, if desired; but it may be sufficient to remark, that, to comply with all his propositions, would have been to divest the schools of their neutral character, and make them such as would necessarily have excluded the children of Protestant parents. To this, of course, the trustees could not assent.

Desirous of doing all they could to induce the attendance of Catholic children, a teacher professing that faith was employed as principal of school No. 5, which is located near the cathedral in Mott street. This experiment did not, however, answer the expectations of the trustees. . . .[255]

The committee recommended various expurgations in textbooks including the following:

English Reader.—Page 51, strike out paragraph, "the Queen's bigoted zeal," &c., to "eternal welfare." Page 152, erase, "the most credulous monk in a Portuguese convent."

Sequel, Murray's.—The whole article, "Life of Luther." Pages 84 and 85, paste up "Execution of Cranmer." Page 279, erase, "and anon in penance, planning sins anew."

Putnam's Sequel.—Erase the article, "John Huss."

Maltebrun's Geography. . . . Page 140, erase five lines from the top, "and there is no doubt the lower classes of Ireland are so." Page 145, erase, "inflict the most horrible tortures." Page 148, erase, "Italy to be submitted to the Catholic bishop. . . ."

Hale's History of the United States.—Page 11, erase, "from the persecution of the Catholics," section 22.

Scripture Lessons.—Erase, in the title-page, the words, "without note or comment."[256]

Bourne sums up the subsequent actions in this statement:

The revision and expurgation of the books was continued under the direction of the board, and all the objectionable passages were either stamped with ink from a wooden block, or the leaves pasted together or removed, or a volume discontinued as a text-book or library-book. This course, however, on the part of the trustees, was not satisfactory, and did not in the least abate the demands of the applicants for a separate provision to be made for their schools from the schools' fund, and the controversy subsequently became more animated than ever before. The mutilated volumes were gradually worn out and rendered unfit for use, and were replaced by new books, which were permitted to go into the schools without change or expurgation, and the discussion in reference to the text-books subsided.[257]

And so this particular controversy came to an end. It has been recorded at some length because it illustrates an inherent difficulty in the matter of public-school teaching—that of being scrupulously fair to the facts of history without causing unnecessary offense to any religious group. It is clear that in this instance there were references in the textbooks of the time to which the Roman Catholics could legitimately take objection, and that the most serious were eliminated. It is also true that it would have been very difficult to have European history of the Reformation period, for example, taught in the schools objectively either by scholarly Catholic or Protestant teachers in a way to have entirely satisfied Bishop Hughes. Fortunately today, with the more tolerant attitude of both public school authorities and religious leaders, there is relatively little difficulty.

The impossibility of eliminating religious references in various humanistic studies may be further illustrated by two important official utterances in 1948. The first is by Mr. Justice Jackson in his concurring opinion in the McCollum case.

> . . . Perhaps subjects such as mathematics, physics or chemistry are, or can be, completely secularized. But it would not seem practical to teach either practice or appreciation of the arts if we are to forbid exposure of youth to any religious influences. Music without sacred music, architecture minus the cathedral, or painting without the scriptural themes would be eccentric and incomplete, even from a secular point of view. Yet the inspirational appeal of religion in these guises is often stronger than in forthright sermon. Even such a "science" as biology raises the issue between evolution and creation as an explanation of our presence on this planet. Certainly a course in English literature that omitted the Bible and other powerful uses of our mother tongue for religious ends would be pretty barren. And I should suppose it is a proper, if not an indispensable, part of preparation for a worldly life to know the roles that religion and religions have played in the tragic story of mankind. The fact is that, for good or for ill, nearly everything in our culture worth transmitting, everything which gives meaning to life, is saturated with religious influences, derived from paganism, Judaism, Christianity—both Catholic and Protestant—and other faiths accepted by a large part of the world's peoples. One can hardly respect a system of education that would leave the student wholly ignorant of the currents of religious thought that move the world society for a part in which he is being prepared.
>
> But how one can teach, with satisfaction or even with justice to all faiths, such subjects as the story of the Reformation, the Inquisition, or even the New England effort to found "a Church without a Bishop and a State without a King," is more than I know. . . .

It must be remembered that this was Mr. Justice Jackson's opinion even though he believed the released-time program for the teaching of religion by representatives of the Churches in public-school buildings in Champaign was unconstitutional. As such it carries the more weight.

The second statement is from the Illinois superintendent of education in an official bulletin, *Religious Education in Public Schools,* issued to implement the McCollum decision.

> The Bible as well as mythology can be called upon to provide a background for the study of English literature.

A course in history can include a study of the Crusades, the Reformation, and other examples in which religion has played a vital role in history.

Music is not banned because it happens to have been originally written for religious purposes. The High School Choral Group can still sing the Hallelujah Chorus.[258]

To show how religion is inseparably woven into a course of public-school study which is supposed to be entirely secular I have studied the curriculum in typical senior and junior high schools—those of the District of Columbia. This study, based on a pamphlet entitled *Course of Study in History, Geography, and the Other Social Studies,*[259] indicates that in the ninth grade in the courses on history, such matters are treated as the religions of early Greece and Rome, the birth of Christ and the importance of His teaching, the persecutions of the Christians, the recognition of Christianity by Constantine, the missionary work of the early Church, and the influence of Christianity on society. Under the subject "Mediaeval History," the significance of the coronation of Charlemagne, Mohammed and his religion, the power of the pope, excommunication, interdicts, and the punishment of heretics, are all discussed. Under the Reformation, Martin Luther, Calvin, Loyola, and the Jesuits are considered, as well as the rise of the English Church, the success of Protestant Holland in winning its freedom from Catholic Spain, the rise of the Puritans, and the Toleration Act.

Again, in the course on "Community Civics" in the ninth grade the Church is considered under three heads: development of religious beliefs; development of modern Churches; and work of the Churches for the community. Moral and spiritual ideals are discussed under the present-day problems of society.

In the tenth-grade study of "Modern European History" are included such matters as the outcome of the Protestant movement, the placing of the control of the Church in the hands of the State, and the significance of the Papal States.

Under "Economics" religion comes in, in the discussion of the aid of Church organizations to the poor and the prevention of crime through moral, religious, and vocational education.

A study of any good high-school course in literature would present almost equal difficulties for those who would eliminate all reference to religion. For instance, Milton's works, and Wordsworth's "Ode on Intimations of Immortality," and the writings of the Puritans, or Dante's poems, even in translation, cannot be separated from the discussion of at least their underlying religious ideas.

In New York City and other places where there is a large Jewish population there have been protests over the reading of Shakespeare's *Merchant of Venice* in the public schools on the ground that the character of Shylock gives the children an unfavorable and unfair impression of the Jews. In Buffalo it was banned from the regular curriculum in 1931 on the ground that it fostered intolerance. Similarly, in places where there is a large Roman Catholic population there have been difficulties, though less acute, over some passages in English literature that reflect on the Church of Rome in previous times. A public-school teacher of my acquaintance tells me that this has been particularly true of Chaucer's *Canterbury Tales,* in which, although there are some appreciative references to the priesthood, there are others that are critical. The same is true of certain passages in Milton's "Lycidas," which are taken as criticisms of the Church; but speaking generally, public-school teachers are trained to be fair and impartial and these matters cause relatively little difficulty.

A typical situation arose in the New York public schools in 1930. A well-known and much used textbook was then banned for a year because of criticisms based on the charge that it was socialistic, pro-Catholic, and anti-Protestant—charges that were unjustified as far as its general tenor was concerned. The book, *Modern History* (1923), was the work of two responsible historical scholars, both Catholics and professors at Columbia University, Carlton Hayes and Parker Moon. Matters came to a head when a little-known Episcopal clergyman who felt that the Church of England had not been fairly treated, especially in connection with the break with Rome in the sixteenth century, sent a letter of protest to the Board of Education, declaring that the book "deliberately defended Catholicism." Its chairman, a Roman Catholic, referred the letter to the superintendent of schools, a Presbyterian, who banned the book. In the meantime, the authors had, apparently independently, brought out a revised edition in which there were a few minor changes of phraseology, such as the use of Protestant "denominations" instead of "sects," the elimination of references to Henry VIII and Calvin as "Protestant Popes," and the tempering of criticisms of Luther. The book, which even in its original form had received the unanimous endorsement of the faculty of a representative Protestant divinity school (Berkeley), was now unobjectionable to the authorities, and was restored to the list of approved texts. The case has been mentioned to show how sensitive the public is to the maintenance of religious impartiality in public-school education.

Dickens' *Oliver Twist* is the latest important work of literature to be the subject of public-school controversy. This matter has been brought before the New York Board of Education.[260] The opposition is on the ground of the book's alleged anti-Semitism, as shown particularly in the character of the disreputable Jew, Fagin. There is some basis for this charge, but advocates of this classic maintain that it should be retained in public-school libraries because of its literary distinction, and its picture of English life in a previous age. They point out that if merely incidental criticisms of religious views or types, whether of Protestants, Catholics, or Jews, are considered sufficient ground for keeping a book out of a public-school library it might result in many exclusions, in the narrowing of the literary and historical "exposure" of youth, and in the development of an unfortunate censorship complex.

This summary will give a fairly good idea of the difficulties involved in selecting public-school textbooks and in teaching certain subjects in which the views and acts of the Church cannot be entirely disregarded. It is manifestly impossible to deal with the great problems of history and sociology, or to study the classics of literature, to say nothing of ethics and philosophy, without considering religion in general and Christianity in particular. As a result, there are from time to time complaints from Protestant, Jewish, and Catholic sources, as well as from the agnostic group, that the doctrines of some form of religion are being covertly introduced for propaganda purposes, though most such complaints are not justified. It is obviously impossible to understand the world in which we live unless something of the history of Christianity and its relations to society and the State are taken into account. The same is, of course, true of the teaching of the theory of evolution, a matter dealt with in a separate section.[261]

On the whole, there has been less trouble in connection with religious references in public-school textbooks than with social and economic references and attitudes. For example, there has been no such battle on this score as over the textbooks on American education, government, and civilization written by Professor Harold Rugg (1886–), which represent a liberal standpoint and are based on sound historical scholarship. Although millions of them have been used, they have been the subject of much criticism by conservative groups, including some organs of Church opinion, both because of their "modern" social and political philosophy, and their lack of emphasis on certain spiritual ideals.[262] Yet similarly serious issue has been taken with some references in public-school textbooks that are considered unfriendly to certain religious denominations. To meet this there has been during recent years a vigorous campaign by liberal-minded religious leaders and educators to remove all references to matters connected with religion or the Churches that are open to fair criticism. Under the direction of the National Conference of Christians and Jews this campaign to eliminate offensive passages in textbooks began at the Drew Theological Seminary, where studies were made of school material used in Protestant Church schools to discover passages which were conducive to prejudice and intolerance. Studies were made by the Synagogue Council of America, which has surveyed critically some five hundred volumes to discover antichristian bias. The Catholic Church, under the auspices of the Commission of American Citizenship, established by the Catholic University of America and other groups, has made similar studies, trying to eliminate prejudicial statements against Protestants and Jews in Catholic books. As Monsignor George Johnson, a leader in the movement, has stated:

There is no room in the Kingdom of Heaven for bigotry in any shape or form. The Catholic has an obligation to love and cherish all men, regardless of race or color or creed.[263]

As a result of these and similar efforts—which have had the support of the Federal Council of Churches, the International Council of Religious Education, the National Catholic Education Association, the American Jewish Committee, and other groups—it is the opinion of competent authorities that most intolerant or unfair statements have been removed from public-school textbooks, and that considerable progress has also been made in the matter of textbooks used in various Church and parochial schools.

Dr. Willard Johnson, assistant to the president of the National Conference of Christians and Jews, who was assigned to the textbook program, has pointed out that though there is still some anti-Negro bias in some textbooks, there are extremely few anti-Catholic or anti-Semitic references. He lays emphasis on work being done to prepare new textbooks and new methods of study which should result in bringing about a larger degree of intercultural education and sympathy. This whole movement is a good example of a constructive contribution by the Church to the State in preventing intolerance and creating a larger measure of national unity.[264]

This textbook matter as it has to do with references to religion is likely to come to the fore if, as seems likely, the plan for the necessary objective references to religion as a factor in cultural history in high schools becomes more articulate. Dr. Charles C. Morrison's proposals on this subject and those of the Committee on Religion and Education, appointed by the American Council on Education, are discussed at some length in an earlier section.[265]

Section 5. USE OF PUBLIC-SCHOOL BUILDINGS FOR RELIGIOUS PURPOSES

The question of the use of public-school buildings for religious meetings has often been a matter of controversy between Church and State authorities. The state regulations differ considerably. Some states specifically authorize such use under proper conditions, as for instance in Illinois, where school directors have the power

to have the control and supervision of all public school houses in their district, and to grant the temporary use of them, when not occupied by schools, for religious meetings and Sunday schools, for evening schools and literary societies, and for such other meetings as the directors may deem proper. . . .[266]

This law has been held to be Constitutional by the supreme court of the state in a case where a school board had granted the temporary use of the schoolhouse for religious meetings and Sunday schools at times which did not interfere with the regular work of the school. In some states, such as Arkansas, the doors are wide open to the discretion of the school board of the community for "any lawful meeting of its citizens." Similarly, in Massachusetts the school committee may allow individual and voluntary organizations to use school buildings in the interest of the community, adding that "the affiliation of any such association with a religious organization shall not disqualify such association from being allowed such a use for such a purpose."[267] In other states, such as Ohio, the use of school buildings may be determined by the vote of the people in a given district at their school meeting, or by the school authorities. In some sparsely settled rural districts where no churches are available such use is fairly common in many states. But, on the other hand, several states have decided that in the absence of express authority a school board may not permit the use of a school building for religious purposes.[268] Some states have gone even further and have adopted what was formerly known as the Connecticut rule, by which the courts decided that no schoolhouse might be used for religious meetings, Sunday schools, or other religious purposes even should the authorities of a community so desire.

A survey published in 1926 showed that even in those places where religious education was allowed on public-school time, only about one-sixth of reporting communities held these classes in public-school buildings.[269] The percentage has remained about the same. The N.E.A. report in 1949 shows about 15.3 per cent. The varying practices are partly a matter of law, partly of local tradition and public opinion. For instance, in some western states public-school buildings are almost never used for religious instruction, while in Vermont public-school buildings are frequently so used by voluntary religious groups organized by the Churches. In 1942 there were eighty-two communities in North Carolina which permitted the teaching of the Bible (without other textbooks), generally as a high-school elective for credit, and taught, as in Durham, by teachers with an A grade certificate, nominated by the council of churches and elected by the school board.[270] In New York state, I am informed on competent authority, 42 per cent of the experiments in weekday religious education on released time in 1941 were conducted *in* public schools;[271] but in 1943, Albany, through its board of education, declined the request of the local council of churches to set apart two rooms for this purpose.[272] These cases were of course prior to the United States Supreme Court decision in the Champaign, Illinois, case early in 1948.[273] On the other hand, the use of sectarian buildings for public-school purposes is usually considered legitimate in a temporary emergency.[274]

Generally most responsible groups see the danger of using public-school buildings for sectarian instruction of any kind, though advocates of the proposal are not lacking. For instance in the summer of 1938 the seven Roman Catholic dioceses of the state of New York called on the constitutional convention then in session to permit the teaching of religion in public schools "on consent of the parents."[275] An Iowa Supreme Court decision represents perhaps the general view outside of large urban centers.

> The use of a public school building for Sabbath schools, religious meetings . . . which, of necessity, must be occasional and temporary, is not so palpably a violation of the fundamental law as to justify the courts in interfering. Especially is this so where, as in the case at bar, abundant provision is made for securing any damages which the taxpayers may suffer by reason of the use of the house for the purposes named. With such precaution the amount of taxes any one would be compelled to pay by reason of such use would never amount to any appreciable sum. . . . Such occasional use does not convert the schoolhouse into a building of worship, within the meaning of the Constitution.[276]

It is not uncommon to have Christmas carols as well as simple Christmas plays and Christmas trees in public schools without giving offense; but occasionally there are protests when these are attempted in urban communities. For instance, Rabbi Israel, a much respected Jewish leader, appeared before the Baltimore School Board on January 1, 1930, to protest against Christmas exercises in a public school where a Roman Catholic priest officiated in his robes.[277]

An interesting and unusual experiment was made in the high schools of St. Paul and Minneapolis at the midwinter festival season in 1940 when Christmas Day and the Jewish Festival of Lights (Hanukkah) coincided. Christmas carols and Hanukkah hymns were sung by the students during the week preceding the holidays. Similarly, on the Jewish New Year in 1941 the "Shofar service" was sung before the entire student body at Hendrix College, Conway, Arkansas, though the enrollment of six hundred included only two Jews. Such evidences of sympathy and co-operation are generally encouraged by all but a small group.[278]

It is clear that public-school buildings, if used at all for religious purposes outside of school hours, must be made available on the same terms to all responsible groups in the community. Speaking generally, outside of rural areas where other suitable accommodations are not available, school buildings are so used only rarely. The most marked exception I have recently noticed is in New Haven, Connecticut, where, under the auspices of the Confraternity of Christian Doctrine, a series of ten conferences on Monday evenings was arranged in the winter of 1940 in the Hillhouse High School. They were all conducted by Roman Catholic priests, and included not only general themes, such as "Religion" and "The Christian Philosophy of Education," but more definitely denominational subjects, such as "The Holy Sacrifice of the Mass" and "The Catholic Readers Guide." The whole course constituted a school for thoughtful laymen in religion as believed in by Catholics. No admission fee was charged, but the confraternity paid the customary fee for the use of the hall. Each lecture was given twice an evening, followed by a discussion period. The course evidently met a public need, for it was attended by from fifteen hundred to over two thousand persons each of the early evenings. It was on the same lines as one conducted the previous year in Hartford, and was widely advertised, about twenty-five thousand leaflets being distributed.[279] The course itself seemed admirable and useful in purpose; but there is a serious doubt whether in principle a public-school building should be used, except in rare emergencies, for any purposes of religious education directly connected with one Church. In this New Haven case it should be remembered, however, that the meetings were of the nature of adult education rather than of regular instruction for public-school pupils, and that the Christian Scientists had been granted the use of the buildings for similar purposes, and the Jews for Zionist meetings.[280] The existing Connecticut law on the subject, enacted by the legislature in 1931, seemed to make the procedure legal.

I have discussed the matter with leading Protestant citizens of New Haven, some of whom feel that as long as similar privileges were accorded Protestants and Jews the experiment should be encouraged. Others think it a dangerous precedent from the point of view of Church–State separation. Among the latter group the *Christian Century* was quoted. It said editorially:

> . . . If this sounds like a Catholic effort to proselytize non-Catholics carried on in a public institution maintained at public expense, it is because that is exactly what it is. New Haven has numerous Catholic churches and well equipped parochial schools in which this effort to win Catholic converts might have been housed. The Protestant school of religious education, which meets in the same city, carries on its work in the Protestant churches. But the Catholics are using a public high school. Why? Perhaps New Haven's Catholic mayor, or its Catholic superintendent of schools, or the Catholic majority on its board of education know the answer. . . . At any rate, this New Haven incident should serve again to show why Protestants look with suspicion on the relation of Catholics to the non-sectarian public school system of America.[281]

This editorial called forth the following reply from a Methodist minister in New Haven:

Sir: In your editorial, "Sectarianism in a Public School," in the January 17 issue of The Christian Century, I fear your zeal to defend the non-sectarian public school system of America may lead to the charge of an anti-Catholic bias against The Christian Century. . . .

At least on one occasion I have with others applied for the use of the high school auditorium. That use has been granted, though I knew the city administration was not in sympathy with the ideas to be presented in the meeting. Because of a regard for our traditional American liberties of free speech and free assemblage, I believe our city fathers have pursued the wise course of granting to all responsible groups in the community who had the requisite rental the privilege of the public schools in the evening. To my knowledge, not only civic groups which are generally recognized as "respectable" have been allowed to use public property, but also socialist and communist meetings have been held in the school property. Now, at a time when wartime hysteria is forcing an abrogation of such rights in so many places, I must register my opposition to your editorial in seeing in this granting of permission to our Catholic brethren to the use of our schools an attempt to proselytize the non-Catholic community by quasi surreptitious and unethical means. If the policy which our board of education has adhered to in the past be continued, than any group, irrespective of political or religious belief, should have the same rights.

May I suggest that probably there is nothing more sinister in the fact that the Protestant school of religious education is meeting in a Protestant parish house than that its authorities saw no reason to pay our city treasury $27 a night which it did not have to.[282]

Some of the regulations of states on this matter of the use of public-school buildings for religious meetings may be of interest:

Illinois: The legislature of Illinois in 1872 enacted a law giving the directors of any school district power to grant the temporary use of school houses, when not occupied by schools, for religious meetings and Sunday schools, for evening schools and literary societies and for such other purposes as they should deem proper.[283]

Kansas: "The district board shall have the care and keeping of the school house and other property belonging to the district. They are hereby authorized to open the school house for the use of religious, political, literary, scientific, mechanical, or agricultural societies belonging to the district for the purpose of holding the public meetings of said societies."[284]

Ohio: "When in the judgment of any board of education it shall be for the advantage of the children residing in any school district to hold literary societies, school exhibitions, singing schools, religious exercises, select or normal schools, the board of education shall authorize the opening of such school houses for the purposes aforesaid."[285]

The reverse side of the shield in this matter is also interesting—namely, the question whether a public school may rent a church building for public-school purposes. There have been some interesting decisions which tend to show that under certain emergency conditions this is permissible. Here are the two most significant cases I have noted. The Illinois Court of Appeals decided that

Religious organizations are not under such legal bans that they may not deal at arm's length with the public in selling or leasing their property, when required for public use, in good faith.[286]

Similarly, the Iowa Supreme Court has ruled that such renting is permissible if made in good faith and not as a mere cover for an illegal fusion of a parochial with a public school.[287]

In a word, Church and State may co-operate in the use of buildings to meet emergency needs, but there must be a clear distinction between public and ecclesiastical functions, and no attempt by either party to confuse the distinction.

Section 6. GENERAL FREEDOM OF TEACHERS AND TEACHING; NUNS

The constitution of Arizona has a clause which defines clearly the general principle now accepted by the public-school systems of all the states in the employment of teachers. It is a rule to the effect that

No religious or political test or qualification shall ever be required as a condition of admission into any public educational institution of the state, as teacher, student, or pupil.[288]

Some states go even further, having adopted laws which prevent inquiry regarding a teacher's religious affiliations, the purpose being to prevent any discrimination. Similarly, one of the reasons given for opposition to the so-called "teachers' oaths" is that, though primarily designed to prevent the public schools having teachers with Communistic leanings, it is feared that they may become an opening wedge for other legislation interfering with the political and religious freedoms guaranteed under our Federal and state constitutions.

There is at times friction in certain communities where, in spite of the intended impartiality of the law, an active political group tries to secure a majority of Roman Catholic teachers or a Roman Catholic principal. This effort sometimes succeeds in the absence of a parochial school, as it has recently in some places in Rhode Island and Massachusetts. On the other hand there is occasional difficulty because of the opposition of some Protestants to Roman Catholic teachers. For instance, in communities where the Ku Klux Klan has been prominent and fundamentalism rampant, Roman Catholic teachers have at times been discriminated against. This was specially true in the mid-twenties of the century.[289] In this connection—though it should not be considered a discrimination but rather a reasonable attempt to prevent the identification of a public school with any one religious body—statutes have been adopted in several states to prohibit the wearing of a religious habit by teachers while engaged in the performance of their duties.

The first action of this type that I have noted was by the Pennsylvania legislature in 1895. The state supreme court has since declared this constitutional, on the ground that it is directed against acts and not against beliefs.[290] Similarly the New York Court of Appeals in 1906 upheld as reasonable a regulation of the state superintendent forbidding Catholic sisters from wearing a distinctive garb.[291] The question has never come before the Supreme Court of the United States.

In some states—now about fifteen—nuns wearing their religious garb are permitted as public-school teachers. Speaking generally, there is no more valid objection to an eligible nun being employed as a teacher than to a Protestant minister. They stand on the same footing from a public-school standpoint; but Protestant ministers engaged as teachers seldom wear a distinctive habit, and it is this which makes nuns in their regular garb open to comment and even criticism, because it is a constant reminder to the pupils of the Church connection of their teachers and is likely to cause misunderstanding. The practice has been specially prevalent in North Dakota, New Mexico, and Ohio. In North Dakota the issue came to a head in 1947, and the voters have since decided against the further employment of nuns while wearing their habit.[292] The New Mexico and Ohio cases are more serious. They are connected in some localities with the virtual taking over of certain public schools as parochial schools at the taxpayers' expense; they are described at length in a special section.[293]

These instances are typical of many others, though in all they represent only a small percentage of our public schools. The author knows, as a result of his own residence in New Haven, Connecticut, of two public schools there in dominantly Catholic neighborhoods where nuns wearing their garb have been regularly employed for years with the tacit consent of the school authorities. In one of these, the Hamilton Street school, the arrangement goes back more than half a century, and though an unfortunate precedent from the standpoint of Church–State separation it can claim some historical justification. The building was originally the home of a parochial school, but after the death of the priest in charge the local parish church in 1868 handed the building over to the city with the understanding, it is said, that the nuns were to be retained as teachers and paid by the city. A recent survey showed that 15 of a staff of 39, and the principal, were Sisters of Mercy.[294] The curriculum is that of the regular grade schools, and there is no formal religious instruction. Non-Catholic children so desiring may attend other public schools.

The issue of nuns wearing their garb while they are teaching in public schools was at one time an active issue in Federal government schools; the general matter is discussed where the Church and Indian schools are considered.[295]

Most Americans feel that it is undesirable and probably unconstitutional to have priests, ministers, rabbis, or nuns wearing a distinctive habit while they are regularly employed in the public schools, as tending to break down the Constitutional separation of Church and State. But it has been increasingly realized that the character, attitude, and example of lay teachers and their personal devotion to the Church of their choice represent indirect methods of commending religion in ways which are entirely proper and which laws cannot affect.

To insure entire impartiality in the selection of public-school teachers as far as religion is concerned, some states have adopted stringent legislation. For example, New York in 1932 enacted a law to the effect that

> No person, agency, bureau, corporation or association employed or maintained to obtain or aid in obtaining positions for teachers, principals, superintendents, . . . and no individual or individuals conducting or employed by or interested directly or indirectly in such an agency, bureau, corporation or association, and no board of education, trustee of a school district, superintendent, principal or teacher of a public school or other official, or employee of a board of education, shall directly or indirectly ask, indicate or transmit orally or in writing the religion or religious affiliation of any person seeking employment or official position in the public schools of the state of New York.[296]

This would seem to prohibit religious discrimination as far as legislation is concerned, but there is need of an alert and strong public opinion to make sure that it is observed. Fortunately most school boards are sympathetic and fair in this matter.

After World War I a wave of what was declared to be patriotic loyalty swept over the country. One of its manifestations in the late 1920's and the early 1930's was an attempt to prevent Communism in particular and radicalism in general from getting a foothold in the public schools. As a result some twenty-one states adopted what are called "teachers' oaths," in all cases demanding declarations of loyalty to the Constitution by teachers in the public schools. Twelve states imposed the same requirement on teachers in private schools. The laws involving these oaths have been effectively attacked not on the ground of their constitutionality but on the ground of their wisdom, especially as teachers alone of all public administrative servants of the state were at the time singled out for this particular requirement, though after World War II the Federal government imposed severe tests of loyalty also on officeholders and dismissed those believed to have Communistic affiliations.

The teachers' oaths were primarily intended to protect schools in urban centers from Communist teaching by demanding that teachers pledge themselves to support national and state constitutions and laws. In two states this ruling dates back to the years immediately after the Civil War, but in most cases it was established during the generations which followed. It has been opposed by many educational and religious bodies on the ground that it may serve as an entering wedge for regimentation of thought, and consequently for the weakening of academic and religious freedom. It is deemed specially unfortunate when applied to members of the faculties of a privately endowed university, as in Massachusetts,[297] or when worded, as in the "red rider" in an appropriation by Congress to the public schools of the District of Columbia a decade ago, so as to lead some superpatriots to try to prevent even classroom discussion of Communism. In Massachusetts two college professors who were Quakers were forced to resign for refusing, on conscientious grounds, to take the oath, while even at Harvard a considerable number of members of the faculty, both professors and instructors, took the oath only upon the urgent request of the university officers, accompanying their action by public statements opposing the implications of the oath. Their opposition was based sometimes on political grounds, sometimes on religious.

In some states officials have permitted an affirmation instead of an oath, and there have been cases where Quaker teachers who quietly declined to sign the oaths were not molested. The Protestant Churches have frequently been active in opposing such oaths, believing that they may ultimately be used to interfere with religious freedom. The Roman Catholics are so committed to a vigorous anticommunist campaign that they have taken little part in this opposition.

An oath of loyalty has long been required of applicants for passports, but this is of a general character, merely pledging support of the Constitution "against all enemies, domestic and foreign." The State Department has ruled in connection with passport oaths that they may be qualified to indicate that support of the Constitution by arms is not intended.[298]

Section 7. TEACHING OF EVOLUTION IN PUBLIC SCHOOLS—THE SCOPES TRIAL

The teaching of evolution in the public schools developed in the 1920's a controversy in which the Churches and the public were much concerned. It was not so much a struggle between Church and State as such, as a difference of opinion between certain reactionary groups in both Church and State on a matter in which religion was deeply involved.

The issue came to a head in 1925 in the so-called Scopes trial, at Dayton, Tennessee. The legislature that year passed an act thus specified in the State Code:

It shall be unlawful for any teacher in any of the universities, teachers' colleges, normal schools or other public schools of the state which are supported, in whole or in part, by the public school funds of the state, to teach any theory that denies the story of the divine creation of man as taught in the Bible, and to teach instead that man descended from a lower order of animals.

Any teacher violating the preceding section shall be guilty of a misdemeanor and fined not less than five hundred dollars for each offense.[299]

This legislation was mainly due to the fundamentalist and Ku Klux Klan activities prevalent in the central South at the time of its adoption. It must be remembered that fundamentalism as we understand it today has adopted as its major emphasis the verbal inspiration of the whole "infallible" Bible. It first began as an articulate public movement in 1910; the Ku Klux Klan was revived in 1915.

In 1922 fundamentalism became a national threat. It originally arose in the Baptist communion; but the Presbyterians were soon involved. In both cases the well-known New York preacher, Dr. Harry Emerson Fosdick (1878–   ), was one of the leading causes of contention, as a liberal Baptist who was serving as stated preacher in the First Presbyterian Church in New York. Perhaps no one was more responsible for the movement than Dr. Curtis Laws (1868–1946) of the *Watchman–Examiner,* who declared that 85 per cent of the members of his Church (Baptist) were fundamentalists, and that the movement which he was leading was "to do battle royal for the faith of our fathers."[300] It was he who coined the term "fundamentalist," in 1920, at a meeting of members of the Northern Baptist Convention at Des Moines, Iowa.[301] He outlined the five points of fundamentalism: the infallible Bible, the Virgin birth, the substitutionary atonement, the physical resurrection of Christ, and His second coming in the flesh. It is the first of these which concerns us mainly in this study, as it was the attempt to make the alleged teaching of the Bible on creation a requisite of public-school teaching, quite irrespective of the conclusions of modern science, that gave the antievolution campaign its motive and influence.

These views had gained such headway in conservative Protestant Churches by 1923 and had become such a threat against the teaching of evolution in public institutions, that a group of the leading scientists and religious leaders in the United States, including Professor Robert A. Millikan, physicist, and winner of the Nobel prize; Charles D. Wolcott, president of the American Association for the Advancement of Science; James R. Angell, psychologist, and president of Yale University; John C. Merriam, president of the Carnegie Institution; Bishop William W. Lawrence (Episcopalian) of Massachusetts; Bishop Francis J. McConnell of the Methodist Episcopal Church; Dr. William H. Welch, pathologist, and dean of American medicine; and others, issued the following statement:

> We, the undersigned, deeply regret that in recent controversies there has been a tendency to present science and religion as irreconcilable and antagonistic domains of thought, for, in fact, they meet distinct human needs, and in the rounding out of human life they supplement rather than displace or oppose each other.
>
> The purpose of science is to develop, without prejudice or preconception of any kind, a knowledge of the facts, the laws and the processes of nature. The even more important task of religion, on the other hand, is to develop the consciences, the ideals and the aspirations of mankind. Each of these two activities represents a deep and vital function of the soul of man, and both are necessary for the life, the progress and the happiness of the human race.
>
> It is a sublime conception of God which is furnished by science, and one wholly consonant with the highest ideals of religion, when it represents Him as revealing Himself through countless ages in the development of the earth as an abode for man and in the age-long inbreathing of life into its constituent matter, culminating in man with his spiritual nature and all his Godlike powers.[302]

But in spite of this and similar utterances from understanding friends of organized Christianity, the five-year period from 1920 on saw the movement gaining in strength. Even when evolution was not specifically mentioned, religious associations frequently passed resolutions which clearly had it in mind. For instance, the Ministers Association of Charlotte, North Carolina, in 1925 went on record as advocating that

> When the fact has been established that any president or teacher of our tax-supported schools is inculcating theories which tend to unsettle or destroy the faith of our boys and girls in the Old and New Testaments as the inspired Word of God, that such officer or teacher be promptly removed from his position.[303]

Some idea of the fundamentalist movement threat to religious liberty, especially through its advocacy of antievolution laws, may be gained from a statement of Dr. Albert Dieffenbach (1876–), editor of the *Christian Register,* which valiantly fought to stem the tide of intolerant obscurantism from 1922 on. In 1927 he wrote that his work as religious editor required his reading every week sixty representative American and English Church journals which speak with authority for their denominations, but not more than six of them ever mentioned liberty.[304] He gave his reason for thinking that in orthodox Protestant circles, especially the Baptist, Presbyterian, and Methodist Churches, the fundamentalists "have overwhelmed their liberty loving brethren." The evidence he produced to show that obscurantism was widespread is not always conclusive, especially regarding the Episcopalians, who, although they form what he calls a "creedal church," have allowed large freedom of interpretation of the creeds, and have seldom identified themselves with Biblical fundamentalism. Surely he is in error in stating that "liberty is dead" in these Churches.[305] It is clear, however, that true liberals have constituted a minority in them. The Roman Catholics, though insistent on theological dogma, took no part in the attempt to secure antievolution laws; nor did Episcopalians, Unitarians, Congregationalists, Lutherans, or Universalists. Dieffenbach felt, however, that "religious liberty is the greatest illusion extant in this country."[306] At the time of his writing seven states had adopted antievolution laws which, in his judgment, classified them as officially fundamentalist,[307] and in some fifteen others the issue was alive.[308] Fortunately there has been a great improvement in the general outlook since he wrote in 1927. For instance, it is believed that such an extreme utterance as that of Governor "Ma" Ferguson of Texas would scarcely be possible today. When the state Board of Education, at the time the excitement was at its height in the winter of 1925–26, ordered all passages on evolution deleted from the regular textbooks used by public-school teachers, the governor exclaimed, "I'm a Christian mother who believes Jesus Christ died to save humanity, and I'm not going to let that kind of rot get into Texas textbooks"![309] That is perhaps as extreme as any utterance of a person occupying an important public office produced by the unhappy evolution controversy, but the contemporary Scopes case was even more significant.

John Thomas Scopes (1901–) was a teacher in 1925 in the high school of Dayton, Tennessee, who could not support the antievolution doctrine recently adopted by the legislature. He used an authorized textbook in biology which stated that

> the earth was once a hot, molten mass, too hot for plant or animal life to exist upon it; the earth cooled, the sea formed, and a little germ of one cell organism was formed in the sea; this kept evolving till it got to be a pretty good sized animal, then came on to be a land animal, and it kept evolving and from this was man.[310]

Stimulated by friends, he taught these views as his own. As a result, he was arrested, and one of the most amusing, amazing, and pathetic trials in the history of American education took place. On one hand was William Jennings Bryan (1860–1925), sincere and earnest, but narrow-minded theologically, leading the forces of fundamentalism, antievolution, and reaction. On the other side were Clarence Darrow (1857–1938), a well-known agnostic, Arthur Garfield Hays (1881–), active in the American Civil Liberties Union, and others, protesting that the law was archaic and unconstitutional.

Bryan sought to prove that the Biblical account of creation in all its details was inspired by God. He claimed that the world was created in 4004 B.C., this being according to the chronology of Archbishop Ussher, who died in 1656. The idea that it was hundreds of millions of years old seemed to him preposterous in view of the statements in the Book of Genesis. He believed that Eve was actually and literally made out of Adam's rib. He took the ground that this was a fight between religion on the one hand and agnosticism or atheism on the other.

Darrow and his associates showed the inconsistencies in the Bible and the gaps between the Old Testament and modern science. They maintained that the law was unconstitutional on the ground that it fostered a specific type of religious instruction in the public schools, namely, that known as fundamentalism. They pointed out that the state constitution promised that "no preference shall ever be given by law to any religious establishment," and that "it shall be the duty of the general assembly in all future periods of this Government to cherish literature and science."[311] The defense also held that the statute was vague in that it did not state what Bible translation was to be adopted, nor what was meant by forbidding the "teaching" of evolution. Did it mean that it should not be taught as a fact, or that it should not be taught even by way of information as a theory? In general, the prosecution took the ground that since the public owned the school and paid the teacher, it had a right to determine what the teacher should teach, while the defense upheld the idea that, although the state could determine what subjects should be taught, it could not demand that they be taught falsely, and that evolution in a general sense was accepted by modern science. The following quotation from Mr. Darrow's argument is interesting, even though a later check showed that his references were not always accurate:

> Does this statute state what you shall teach and what you shall not? Not at all. Does it say that you cannot teach that the earth is round because Genesis says that it is flat? No. Does it say that you cannot teach that the earth is millions of ages old because the account in Genesis makes it less than six thousand years old? Oh, no. It does not state that. If it did you could understand it. It says you shan't teach any theory of the origin of man that is contrary to the Divine theory contained in the Bible.
>
> It makes the Bible the yardstick to measure every man's intelligence and to measure every man's learning. Are your mathematics good? Turn to Elijah i:2. Is your philosophy good? See II Samuel 3. Is your astronomy good? See Genesis, Chapter ii,

verse 7. Is your chemistry good? See Deuteronomy 6, or anything that tells about brimstone. Every bit of knowledge that the mind has must be submitted to a religious test.[312]

Mr. Darrow called the law "the most brazen and bold attempt to destroy liberty since the Middle Ages."[313]

A large amount of expert testimony on scientific and theological opinion was introduced by the defense, including that of eminent scientists who were also Christian believers. This was carried by the press all through the country and did much to inform the public on the meaning of evolution, but the judge ruled against it as inadmissible, as he did also a letter written a few years previously by President Wilson (1856–1924), in which he said that "like every other man of intelligence and education, I do believe in organic evolution."[314] But all this was lost on judge and jury. Judgment was rendered against the defendant without any facing of the broad issues involved.

Even though the leading counsel for the defense was an agnostic, which many thought unfortunate, there could be no question that on the fundamental issues at stake the defense was right in its contention that the law was an outrageous one and that Scopes should be set free. At the final session of the court he stood before the judge and said calmly:

Your Honor, I feel that I have been convicted for violation of an unjust statute. I will continue in the future, as I have in the past, to oppose this law in any way I can. Any other action would be in violation of my ideal of academic freedom.[315]

The argument on the appeal was heard in June, 1926, by the Supreme Court of Tennessee. Great emphasis was laid on the preference shown by the law for the fundamentalist Churches; on the fact that the law went beyond legislative power by a requirement of teachers to falsify the general conclusions of science; and on the indefiniteness of the law. This gave the court a way out without offending public sensibilities. Determined to prevent an appeal to the Supreme Court of the United States, the court decided that, though the law was not contrary to the Constitution, the conviction should be reversed on the ground that the fine had been improperly imposed by the judge.[316] It also directed the attorney general to nol-pros all proceedings in what it called a "bizarre" case, thus practically agreeing with a statement of the governor in his message on the law to the effect that it was a statute that would not be enforced. Although long on the statute books, it has become a dead letter, whereas the interest in the scientific theory of evolution has been greatly increased by the discussions that accompanied the trial of the case.

The chapter entitled "Freedom of Education" in Mr. Hays' book, which is devoted entirely to this case, in which he took so prominent a part, should be read for an amazing description of the religious atmosphere of Tennessee which was prevalent throughout the trial and which was mainly responsible for the antievolution law. He noted that the sessions of the court were opened with prayer by those who were definitely of the fundamentalist persuasion. This obvious attitude went so far that counsel for the defense stated that the prayers were "argumentative and helped to increase the atmosphere of hostility" to their client. But the court was "pleased to overrule the objection." Finally, however, on the receipt of a petition signed by Unitarians, Jews, and Congregationalists, the judge left the decision as to who should make prayers to the local "Pastors' Association," though counsel argued that this was a matter for judicial determination![317]

All things considered, there has probably never been another such extraordinary and pathetic exhibition of maladjustment in our Church–State relations as was brought to light in the Dayton trial. Little wonder that a distinguished American educator, Dr. Stephen P. Duggan, travelling immediately after it in Soviet Russia, when asking an officer of the government whether there was any such thing as freedom in Russia, was met by the retort, "How about Dayton, Tennessee?"

Two other Southern states of the "Bible belt" followed Tennessee in adopting antievolution legislation, Arkansas and Mississippi. The Mississippi statute is even more specific than that of Tennessee.

> It shall be unlawful for any teacher or other instructor in any university, college, normal, public school or other institution of the state which is supported in whole or in part from public funds derived by state or local taxation to teach that mankind ascended or descended from a lower order of animals and also it shall be unlawful for any teacher, textbook commission or other authority exercising the power to select textbooks for above mentioned educational institutions to adopt or use in any such institution a textbook that teaches the doctrine that mankind ascended or descended from the lower order of animals.[318]

Somewhat similar laws were introduced into the legislatures of other states, but nearly all failed of passage. About the same result, however, was accomplished in many places in the South and Southwest by local school board legislation.

After the effects of the Scopes trial had been digested, the movement by fundamentalists to secure laws to prohibit the teaching of evolution gradually waned. Its exponents were as vociferous as ever, but fewer thoughtful people were willing to encourage them. A typical extremist statement from the close of this period is that of the executive head of the World's Christian Fundamentals Association, the Reverend William B. Riley (1861–), a Baptist, author of *Daniel vs. Darwin* and a fighting champion of old-time doctrinal orthodoxy. Discussing evolution at the association meeting in 1927, he said:

> It is a religion or an irreligion. It is the religion of atheism. We are going to advise the passage of a uniform bill that will be based on the claim that State supported schools have no right to teach a philosophy that is unproven and is objectionable to a great majority of the patrons of these institutions. We plan to take three or four States a year and concentrate our forces there. Our program will be thorough, and will include New York, Pennsylvania, and other large States.[319]

The agitation was not confined to states south of the Mason and Dixon line, though there it found its most fertile soil. For instance, in Minnesota, at about the same time as the Tennessee action, an evolution law was proposed making it unlawful "to teach that mankind either descended or ascended from a lower order of animals" which specifically included in its scope all schools and colleges "supported in whole or in part by the public education funds of the state" as well as the University of Minnesota.[320]

Somewhat akin to the mentality and religious outlook of the opponents of the teaching of evolution in the public schools is the opposition to compulsory vaccination laws for school children. Such laws exist in several states to prevent the spread of smallpox. Occasionally parents refuse to have their children comply with the law, basing their opposition on medical or religious grounds. With the former we are not concerned here, but the latter brings up an interesting example of possible Church-State conflict. For example, in December, 1939, the Associated Press carried a despatch from Pittsburgh[321] that a family was moving from Pennsylvania to California to avoid compliance with the state vaccination law. The father of a public-school child stated that he had religious scruples against it. According to press reports, he had been arrested seven times because of his refusal to obey it. The child went to school, but the authorities refused to admit him because he had not been vaccinated and refused to be. It appeared that the boy's father was a fundamentalist, at least in believing the verbal inerrancy of the Bible. The vaccination law seemed to him to be contrary to the teaching of St. Paul: "Know ye not that ye are the temple of God, and that the Spirit of God dwelleth in you? If any man defile the temple of God, him shall God destroy; for the temple of God is holy, which temple ye are" (1 Corinthians 3.16, 17). In other words, some antivaccinationists base their opposition to the required inoculation of public-school pupils on the same ground as the antievolutionists we have been discussing—their interpretation of a Bible which they consider verbally inspired even in scientific matters.

Section 8. COMPULSORY SALUTE TO THE FLAG IN SCHOOLS

(1) JEHOVAH'S WITNESSES, FLAG SALUTE LAWS, AND THEIR VARIED EARLY INTERPRETATION

This simple mark of patriotism frequently creates tension between certain unconventional or extreme elements in the Church and the authorities of the State. The newspapers before World War II were full of reports of the children of Communists who were in difficulty with public school superintendents, and occasionally with the police, because they refused to salute the flag. This is also true of a group of followers of Pastor Charles T. Russell (1852–1916), founder of the International Bible Students Association and of the Watch Tower and Bible Society, Inc. (1884). It has been known since 1931 as Jehovah's Witnesses, a somewhat extreme Protestant group organized with Judge Joseph F. Rutherford (1869–1942) as president.[322] This group has no churches or regular religious services, but spreads its conception of the Christian gospel by tracts, public mass meetings, phonograph records, radio, and other forms of publicity. Its members generally use halls for meetings in substandard sections of a community.

Their propaganda usually takes the form of a house-to-house visitation. They carry a phonograph which reproduces some of the utterances of Father Russell or Judge Rutherford, and they sell the peculiar literature of their sect. The records and publications contain prophecies of the expected end of the world, together with exhortations to repentance and denunciations of most forms of organized religion, and more particularly of the Roman Catholic Church. The government of the United States, at least in peacetime, also comes in for its share of abuse. A literal view of Old Testament prophecies, which they apply to definite present and coming events in the ecclesiastical and political world, is their stock in trade. The fact that the founder of this movement, who died in 1916, predicted the end of the world as coming in 1914, and that later his followers chose 1918 for this event, and still later 1926, and so on, does not seem to weaken the faith of Russell's followers. The founder and his successor have been frequently before the courts. Father Russell was involved in selling alleged ancient Egyptian "miracle wheat," and in a long divorce suit brought by his wife, who made various serious charges against him. His successor, Rutherford, a Missouri lawyer and an effective speaker, who built up the organization, claiming more than 1,000 congregations and the sale of tens of million copies of his books, was sentenced in 1918 to serve twenty years for urging young men in army camps to resist military service. He was released after serving a few months in the Federal prison in Atlanta, and was later a frequent speaker over the radio, sometimes over international hookups. The extreme view of the group—which does not wish to be classed as a denomination—is thus officially stated in the *Year Book of Jehovah's Witnesses* for 1938:

Satan attempts to lull to complete silence everything that would expose him and his wicked operations. For that reason the religionists, Catholics, Protestants, Jews and others, all agree to say nothing that might provoke a controversy. They have induced the public press and the radio to refuse the publication of any truth concerning God's kingdom on the ground that it is controversial. They invoke every unrighteous rule against Jehovah's witnesses in their desperate attempt to keep the people in ignorance of everything pertaining to the kingdom of God, and this they do for the reason that they know the truth when told exposes the duplicity and crookedness of Satan and his religious agents.

Upon the false pretext of having peace those religionists insist that Jehovah's witnesses shall not be permitted to inform the people of God's kingdom, declaring that the Kingdom message is subversive and seditious; the very thing that religionists charged against Jesus when he was on the earth. The earthly ruling powers make laws which declare that the testimony given by Jehovah's witnesses concerning God and his kingdom is seditious and liable to cause a breach of the peace and therefore should be suppressed.[323]

This group has become principally known to the public for its refusal on conscientious grounds to salute the flag. It has been taught by its religious leaders that this act is un-Christian, as such a salute is believed to partake of idolatrous worship. Its other peculiarities which bring it into conflict with the State and the public are discussed elsewhere.[324]

In the cases which have come before the courts the ground for refusing to salute the flag has been in each case declared to be religious, because Jehovah's Witnesses—the only considerable group thus far directly involved—consider that the flag is a symbol "worshipped" by those who salute it, and that such worship should be rendered only to God. On the other hand, the salute seems to most legislators and school authorities to be a simple matter of elemental patriotism and school discipline; a view given in a recent district court decision in Massachusetts which sent two children of Jehovah's Witnesses to the State Training School as "habitual school offenders"![325]

In a pamphlet entitled *Reasons Why a True Follower of Jesus Christ Cannot Salute a Flag* the beliefs of Jehovah's Witnesses in this matter are set forth.

Each and every one of them has entered into an agreement or covenant with Jehovah God wherein they have consecrated themselves to do His will and to walk in the footsteps of Jesus.

The United States flag is the emblem of National sovereignty and authority. Men speak of it in highly laudatory terms, and the very attributes of Deity are ascribed to it. . . .

Children are taught to reverence it and to respect it and honor it. In teaching children to reverence, respect and honor the flag, a salute and pledge of allegiance is given as follows, to wit:

"I pledge allegiance to the flag of the United States of America and to the Republic for which it stands; one Nation, indivisible, with liberty and justice for all.

"The pledge is repeated facing the flag, with the right hand held over the heart. At the words 'to the flag', the right hand is extended, palm upward, toward the flag. This position is held until the last word is spoken." (Flag Code adopted by Flag Convention of June 14, 1923.)

Jehovah's Witnesses conscientiously object and refuse to salute the flag and pledge allegiance to it for the following reasons:

FIRST: TO SALUTE THE FLAG WOULD BE A VIOLATION OF DIVINE COMMANDMENT STATED IN EXODUS 20:3–5, TO WIT

"Thou shalt have no other Gods before me. Thou shalt not make unto thee any graven image or any likeness of anything that is in heaven above, or that is in the earth beneath, or that is in the water under the earth. Thou shalt not bow down thyself to them nor serve them. . . ."

The flag is the country's emblem. An emblem is an image or representation of something. The flag is the image or representation of the American nation.

The salute to the flag is the rendering of respect, reverence and devotion to the image of the United States government.

SECOND: THE SALUTE TO THE FLAG MEANS IN EFFECT THAT THE PERSON SALUTING THE FLAG ASCRIBES SALVATION TO IT, WHEREAS SALVATION IS OF JEHOVAH GOD. . . .

THIRD: FLAG SALUTING IS PART OF A CREED OF A SECT OF SO-CALLED PATRIOTS, TEACHING A RITUAL OF PATRIOTISM AND FROM SUCH ALL TRUE CHRISTIANS ARE COMMANDED TO TURN ASIDE. . . .[326]

Probably no other American religious organization since the early days of the Mormons has experienced as much persecution as have the Witnesses. It is true that they have brought this upon themselves quite largely by their methods of propaganda and by their attacks on various organizations, but the record of lawless attacks upon them is discreditable to the nation. The Department of Justice has on file some 335 instances of mob violence in forty-four states during 1940, involving 1,488 men, women, and children who were connected with this sect of zealots.[327] The intolerance against them has been mostly in small communities, where they are particularly active. Except on the single issue of the flag salute they are a law-abiding group. Their attitude toward the State is one of respectful obedience to all "righteous laws." They are opposed to military training but in general have observed the draft.

The peak of the violence was in May and June, 1940. The American Civil Liberties Union has published a pamphlet with a record of some of the most serious cases. These occurred in places as widely separated as Flagstaff, Arizona; Crocker, Missouri; Beaumont, Texas; Greenville, Illinois; and Kennebunk, Maine; although they are not as frequent in the East and extreme West as in other parts of the country.

In one or two cases the sheriffs refused protection. There were cases where women were beaten, where mobs yelled "Damn the law!" when members of the sect were arrested and put in prison without charges against them, where papers in small communities approved of violence, where large numbers of automobiles belonging to the Witnesses were wrecked, where halls in which meetings were held were attacked, and so on. It is to the credit of the American Civil Liberties Union, whose officers have apparently no sympathy with the purposes of the sect, that they should have defended its members on the ground of Constitutional religious freedom.

Largely as a result of its efforts, the solicitor general of the United States, the Honorable Francis Biddle (1886–), voiced a vigorous protest against lawlessness in a radio address on a national network in June, 1941. Among other things he said:

> A religious sect known as Jehovah's Witnesses have been repeatedly set upon and beaten. They had committed no crime; but the mob adjudged they had, and meted out mob punishment. The Attorney General has ordered an immediate investigation of these outrages.
>
> The people must be alert and watchful, and above all cool and sane. Since mob violence will make the government's task infinitely more difficult, it will not be tolerated. We shall not defeat the Nazi evil by emulating its methods.[328]

The legal issue of the flag salute has become acute in recent years in several places. The earliest state to adopt a law on the subject seems to have been Kansas in 1907. The second was Arizona in 1912. Representative Eastern states followed, such as New York in 1924 and Massachusetts in 1935, so that by 1939 there were seventeen[329] that had such legislation, and in others the same result was brought about by regulations of the school board. The present Massachusetts law, which has been much followed, is here quoted, with the new mandatory clauses added to the laws of 1911 and 1919 italicized:

> Par. 69. *United States Flags to be Furnished and Displayed; Penalties*—The school committee shall provide for each schoolhouse under its control, which is not otherwise supplied, flags of the United States of silk or bunting not less than two feet long, such flags or bunting to be manufactured in the United States, and suitable apparatus for their display as hereinafter provided. A flag shall be displayed, weather permitting, on

the school building or grounds on every school day and on every legal holiday or day proclaimed by the governor or the President of the United States for especial observance; provided, that on stormy school days, it shall be displayed inside the building. A flag shall be displayed in each assembly hall or other room in each such schoolhouse *where the opening exercises on each school day are held.*

Each teacher shall cause the pupils under his charge to salute the flag and recite in unison with him at said opening exercises at least once each week the "Pledge of Allegiance to the Flag." Failure for a period of five consecutive days by the principal or teacher in charge of a school equipped as aforesaid to display the flag as above required, or failure for a period of two consecutive weeks by a teacher to salute the flag and recite said pledge as aforesaid, or to cause the pupils under his charge to do so, shall be punished for every such period by a fine of not more than five dollars. Failure of the committee to equip a school as herein provided shall subject the members thereof to a like penalty. (1935, 258, appvd. May 13, 1935.)[330]

The New York law is less specific.

. . . It shall be the duty of the Commissioner of Education to prepare, for the use of the public schools of the state, a program providing for a salute to the flag, for instruction in its correct use and display and such other patriotic exercises as may be deemed by him to be expedient, under such regulations and instructions as may best meet the varied requirements of the different grades in such schools. . . .[331]

The Pennsylvania law merely permits local boards in their discretion to require teachers to take an oath of allegiance and pupils to salute the flag.

The American Civil Liberties Union, though probably none of its members belongs to the sect involved, has objected to the compulsory flag salute laws on four grounds:

a. These laws violate the common constitutional guarantees of religious freedom.
b. They violate the 14th amendment to the United States Constitution because they constitute a deprivation of liberty.
c. They may not be justified as an exercise of the police power of the state.
d. If applied to pupils and teachers in private schools, they violate the 14th amendment to the United States Constitution, because they deprive such schools of their property without due process.[332]

The statutes have been promoted by the same "patriotic" groups that have urged teachers' loyalty oaths.[333]

The matter has been before the courts in Massachusetts, California, New Jersey, Pennsylvania, New York, Georgia, and some other states, with conflicting results, prior to its judicial determination by the United States Supreme Court.

In Massachusetts the Supreme Court held in 1937 that the statute requiring the salute of the flag was constitutional; that it was within the competency of the legislature and did not exact anything either of pupil or teacher that was in opposition to religion. A similar result was reached in New Jersey in the same year by the Court of Errors and Appeals. The Massachusetts case was appealed to the United States Supreme Court, the American Bar Association's Committee on Civil Rights having filed with the court a brief *amicus curiae* urging that the court take jurisdiction, but to no avail.

The influential Court of Appeals of New York state took a conservative view of the flag salute statute, saying that "Our constitution requires that a religious belief, whatever it is, cannot interfere with the state's enactments for safety, preservation or welfare," a view from which Judge Irving Lehman (1876–1945) sharply dissented. He held that "the flag is dishonored by a salute by a child in reluctant and terrified obedience to a command of secular authority which clashes with the dictates of conscience."[334]

This latter view of the unconstitutionality of the required flag salute was also held by the Supreme Court of Georgia in 1938.

We need just glance at the current world scene to realize that the preservation of individual liberty is more important today than ever it was in the past.

The safety of our Nation largely depends upon the extent to which we foster in each individual citizen that sturdy independence of thought and action which is essential in a democracy.

Our country's safety surely does not depend upon the totalitarian idea of forcing all citizens into one common mold of thinking and acting or requiring them to render a lip service of loyalty in a manner which conflicts with their sincere religious convictions.

Such a doctrine seems to me utterly alien to the genius and spirit of our Nation and destructive of that personal liberty of which our flag itself is the symbol.

It follows that the regulation in question, however valid and reasonable it may be when applied to others, cannot constitutionally be applied to the plaintiffs as a condition of the right of Lillian and William to attend the public schools and of their father to have them to do so. . . .

Upon such a foundation of religious freedom our Commonwealth and Nation were built.[335]

The California Supreme Court took a similar attitude. It ordered the reinstatement of a child (a member of Jehovah's Witnesses) who had been suspended for her refusal to salute the flag.[336]

The year 1941 was marked by the frequent appearance of Jehovah's Witnesses before the courts. Here are a few examples of important decisions of the year.

The Supreme Court of New York in the May term, 1941, reversed the judgment of the Onondaga County Court, which declared a certain child, one Anson Reed, delinquent because of failure to pledge allegiance to the flag. The court ruled

> that this eight-year-old child's refusal to join with the other scholars in the salute to the American flag, as a part of the patriotic program prepared by the Commissioner of Education, [does] not, in our opinion, establish delinquency within the meaning of Sec. 486 of the Penal Code.[337]

Early in the summer the Supreme Court of Massachusetts, by a divided vote, reversed the lower court in the case of three children of Deerfield who had refused to salute the flag. They had been expelled from the public school and ordered committed to a reform school as "habitual school offenders."[338] In the opinion of the Massachusetts Supreme Court the flag salute law provided no penalty on the children for failure to salute the flag for conscientious reasons.

In a similar Jehovah's Witnesses case which came before the Honorable Arthur E. Moore, judge of the probate and juvenile courts of Oakland County, Michigan, about the same time, he outlined a plan that might perhaps be applicable elsewhere. He said:

> I am deeply desirous that these children banish any sense of conflict between religion and nation, but I am more concerned over millions of other children retaining their belief that there is no conflict.
>
> I understand that those who are "Jehovah Witnesses" refuse to salute the flag because of the old Testament teaching against "bowing down to any graven image." I also am informed that "Jehovah Witnesses" do profess allegiance to this Republic, our United States. If so, each of these children may harmonize his religious faith with his love of his country by merely omitting the words, "the flag," and pledging his allegiance to the United States.
>
> I therefore instruct each of you as children and you parents to cause these children to subscribe a pledge of allegiance to the United States reading as follows:
>
> "I pledge allegiance to the United States of America, . . . one nation indivisible, with liberty and justice for all."
>
> I believe the school board will accept this, for, after all, they are merely desirous of respectful and patriotic national attitudes, and to the enforcement of necessary discipline in the schools.
>
> I shall adjourn this hearing for one week to determine the results of my instructions.[339]

This is worth recording, especially as the children involved subscribed to the oath suggested, and there was apparently no further trouble with the school authorities.

(2) GOBITIS CASE AND THE SUPREME COURT; A SIGNIFICANT VICTORY FOR RELIGIOUS FREEDOM IN 1943

The most famous case involving a compulsory flag salute regulation was that of the Gobitis children. It is a case with a long court history, but it is so important that it needs to be told in some detail. It led, after various conflicting decisions, to what is believed to be final action by the Supreme Court of the United States. In June, 1943, the court handed down a six-to-three decision reversing itself and upholding the religious-freedom claims of Jehovah's Witnesses by declaring unconstitutional the forcing of the flag salute on children in public schools when it contravened conscientious scruples.

The court history of the case goes back to 1938, when a Federal judge in Pennsylvania ordered the reinstatement of certain pupils in a Minersville school, who had been expelled in 1935 because of their failure, on account of religious scruples as members of Jehovah's Witnesses, to comply with a school board regulation that made the salute to the flag compulsory. At the trial the former pupils (twelve and thirteen years of age), who were supported by their parents, stated that they had "dedicated" themselves to God and considered homage to the flag or other object contrary to this supreme allegiance. They were willing to "stand in respectful silence," but not to "bow down to a graven image." The judge, the Honorable Albert B. Maris (1893-), delivered an opinion in which he stated that he could personally see no "religious significance" in the salute to the flag, but that if the members of the family concerned conscientiously believed that it had such significance they were entitled to their belief under the Constitution. In giving his reasons for differing from the decisions of some courts in other states on the matter, he said:

> In so holding it appears to us that the courts overlooked the fundamental principle of religious liberty, namely, that no man, even though he be a school director or a judge, is empowered to censor another's religious convictions or set bounds to the areas of human conduct in which those convictions should be permitted to control his actions, unless compelled to do so by an overriding public necessity, which properly requires the exercise of the police powers.[340]

The case was carried to the Federal Circuit Court of Appeals, where a unanimous decision delivered by Judge William Clark (1891-) supported the district court. The court called attention to a statement by George Washington in 1789.

> I assure you very explicitly that, in my opinion, the conscientious scruples of all men should be treated with great delicacy and tenderness; and it is my wish and

desire that the laws may always be as extensively accommodated to them as a due regard to the protection and essential interests of the nation may justify and permit.

It added:

The school board of Minersville has failed to treat the conscientious scruples of all children with that "great delicacy and tenderness." We agree with the father of our country that they (the school board) should and we concur with the learned district court in saying that they must.[341]

This was the most important court decision given on this complicated and controversial issue prior to 1940. But we must now follow the case to the Supreme Court of the United States. Here, contrary to the expectation of many thoughtful people, the decisions of the district and circuit courts supporting the rights of the Gobitis children were at first overruled in an eight-to-one decision, Mr. Justice McReynolds concurring "in the result," but not necessarily in all of the reasoning. Justice Harlan Fiske Stone (1872–1946), later Chief Justice, in an able dissenting opinion which was later to influence the court to reverse itself, took the ground that the rights of religious freedom involved were so important that the lower courts should be upheld. It is thought by some that the serious international situation at the time, and the consequent need of supporting patriotism and law observance, as well as the extreme character of the Witnesses' views, interpretations, and actions, played some part in the majority opinion. It was criticized by many legal authorities, by some religious and secular journals, and by various agencies interested in upholding civil liberties, as running counter to the principle of religious freedom. For instance, the Jesuit weekly *America*—in spite of the Witnesses' attacks on the Roman Catholic Church—criticized the decision on the ground that it gave legislatures too unrestrained powers; while *The Christian Century* ended an editorial entitled "The Court Abdicates" with the words: "Courts that will not protect even Jehovah's Witnesses will not long protect anybody."[342]

The Supreme Court's opinion was written by Justice Felix Frankfurter (1882–), well known as a liberal. It is so important both in its *obiter dicta* and its conclusions that it and Mr. Justice Stone's historic dissent must be quoted at some length. The opinion of the court delivered by Mr. Justice Frankfurter held that:

A grave responsibility confronts this Court whenever in course of litigation it must reconcile the conflicting claims of liberty and authority. But when the liberty invoked is liberty of conscience, and the authority is authority to safeguard the nation's fellowship, judicial conscience is put to its severest test. Of such a nature is the present controversy.

Lillian Gobitis, aged twelve, and her brother William, aged ten, were expelled from the public schools of Minersville, Pennsylvania, for refusing to salute the national flag as part of a daily school exercise. The local Board of Education required both teachers and pupils to participate in this ceremony. The ceremony is a familiar one. The right hand is placed on the breast and the following pledge recited in unison: "I pledge allegiance to my flag, and to the Republic for which it stands; one nation indivisible, with liberty and justice for all." While the words are spoken, teachers and pupils extend their right hands in salute to the flag. The Gobitis family are affiliated with "Jehovah's Witnesses," for whom the Bible as the Word of God is the supreme authority. The children had been brought up conscientiously to believe that such a gesture of respect for the flag was forbidden by command of scripture.

The Gobitis children were of an age for which Pennsylvania makes school attendance compulsory. Thus they were denied a free education, and their parents had to put them into private schools. To be relieved of the financial burden thereby entailed, their father, on behalf of the children and in his own behalf, brought this suit. . . .

We must decide whether the requirement of participation in such a ceremony, exacted from a child who refuses upon sincere religious grounds, infringes without due process of law the liberty guaranteed by the Fourteenth Amendment.

Centuries of strife over the erection of particular dogmas as exclusive or all-comprehending faiths led to the inclusion of a guarantee for religious freedom in the Bill of Rights. The First Amendment, and the Fourteenth through its absorption of the First, sought to guard against repetition of those bitter religious struggles by prohibiting the establishment of a state religion and by securing to every sect the free exercise of its faith. So pervasive is the acceptance of this precious right that its scope is brought into question, as here, only when the conscience of individuals collides with the felt necessities of society.

Certainly the affirmative pursuit of one's convictions about the ultimate mystery of the universe and man's relation to it is placed beyond the reach of law. Government may not interfere with organized or individual expression of belief or disbelief. Propagation of belief—or even of disbelief in the supernatural—is protected, whether in church or chapel, mosque or synagogue, tabernacle or meeting-house. Likewise the Constitution assures generous immunity to the individual from imposition of penalties for offending, in the course of his own religious activities, the religious views of others, be they a minority or those who are dominant in government. *Cantwell* v. *Connecticut,* decided this Term, May 20, 1940.

But the manifold character of man's relations may bring his conception of religious duty into conflict with the secular interests of his fellow-men. When does the constitutional guarantee compel exemption from doing what society thinks necessary for the promotion of some great common end, or from a penalty for conduct which appears dangerous to the general good? To state the problem is to recall the truth that no single principle can answer all of life's complexities. The right to freedom of religious belief, however dissident and however obnoxious to the cherished beliefs of others—

even of a majority—is itself the denial of an absolute. But to affirm that the freedom to follow conscience has itself no limits in the life of a society would deny that very plurality of principles which, as a matter of history, underlies protection of religious toleration. Compare Mr. Justice Holmes in *Hudson Water Co.* v. *McCarter,* 209 U. S. 349, 355. Our present task then, as so often the case with courts, is to reconcile two rights in order to prevent either from destroying the other. But, because in safeguarding conscience we are dealing with interests so subtle and so dear, every possible leeway should be given to the claims of religious faith.

In the judicial enforcement of religious freedom we are concerned with a historic concept. See Mr. Justice Cardozo in *Hamilton* v. *Regents,* 293 U. S. at 265. The religious liberty which the Constitution protects has never excluded legislation of general scope not directed against doctrinal loyalties of particular sects. Judicial nullification of legislation cannot be justified by attributing to the framers of the Bill of Rights views for which there is no historic warrant. Conscientious scruples have not, in the course of the long struggle for religious toleration, relieved the individual from obedience to a general law not aimed at the promotion or restriction of religious beliefs.[343] The mere possession of religious convictions which contradict the relevant concerns of a political society does not relieve the citizen from the discharge of political responsibilities. . . . In all these cases the general laws in question, upheld in their application to those who refused obedience from religious conviction, were manifestations of specific powers of government deemed by the legislature essential to secure and maintain that orderly, tranquil, and free society without which religious toleration itself is unattainable. . . .

Situations like the present are phases of the profoundest problem confronting a democracy—the problem which Lincoln cast in memorable dilemma: "Must a government of necessity be too *strong* for the liberties of its people, or too weak to maintain its own existence?" . . .

The opinion goes on to consider how the demands of religious liberty and of the security of the State can best be reconciled.

The ultimate foundation of a free society is the binding tie of cohesive sentiment. Such a sentiment is fostered by all those agencies of the mind and spirit which may serve to gather up the traditions of a people, transmit them from generation to generation, and thereby create that continuity of a treasured common life which constitutes a civilization. "We live by symbols." The flag is the symbol of our national unity, transcending all internal differences, however large, within the framework of the Constitution. This Court has had occasion to say that ". . . the flag is the symbol of the Nation's power, the emblem of freedom in its truest, best sense . . . it signifies government resting on the consent of the governed; liberty regulated by law; the protection of the weak against the strong; security against the exercise of arbitrary power; and absolute safety for free institutions against foreign aggression. . . ."

The precise issue, then, for us to decide is whether the legislatures of the various states and the authorities in a thousand counties and school districts of this country are barred from determining the appropriateness of various means to evoke that unifying sentiment without which there can ultimately be no liberties, civil or religious. . . .

What the school authorities are really asserting is the right to awaken in the child's mind considerations as to the significance of the flag contrary to those implanted by the parent. In such an attempt the state is normally at a disadvantage in competing with the parents' authority, so long—and this is the vital aspect of religious toleration—as parents are unmolested in their right to counteract by their own persuasiveness the wisdom and rightness of those loyalties which the state's educational system is seeking to promote. . . .

But for us to insist that, though the ceremony may be required, exceptional immunity must be given to dissidents, is to maintain that there is no basis for a legislative judgment that such an exemption might introduce elements of difficulty into the school discipline, might cast doubts in the minds of the other children which would themselves weaken the effect of the exercise. . . .

That is to say, the process may be utilized so long as men's right to believe as they please, to win others to their way of belief, and their right to assemble in their chosen places of worship for the devotional ceremonies of their faith, are all fully respected. . . .[344]

The large majority of eight in favor of this view did not prevent the late Mr. Justice Stone from filing a vigorous dissenting opinion—one of the most influential in the modern history of the court.

I think the judgment below should be affirmed [he said, referring to the Gobitis children]. . . . They and their father are citizens and have not exhibited by any action or statement of opinion, any disloyalty to the Government of the United States. They are ready and willing to obey all its laws which do not conflict with what they sincerely believe to be the higher commandments of God. It is not doubted that these convictions are religious, that they are genuine, or that the refusal to yield to the compulsion of the law is in good faith and with all sincerity. . . .

The law which is thus sustained is unique in the history of Anglo-American legislation. It does more than suppress freedom of speech and more than prohibit the free exercise of religion, which concededly are forbidden by the First Amendment and are violations of the liberty guaranteed by the Fourteenth. For by this law the state seeks to coerce these children to express a sentiment which, as they interpret it, they do not entertain, and which violates their deepest religious convictions. It is not denied that such compulsion is a prohibited infringement of personal liberty, freedom of speech and religion, guaranteed by the Bill of Rights, except in so far as it may be justified and supported as a proper exercise of the state's power over public education. . . .

Government has a right to survive and powers conferred upon it are not necessarily set at naught by the express prohibitions of the Bill of Rights. . . . It may suppress religious practices dangerous to morals, and presumably those also which are inimical to public safety, health and good order. *Davis* v. *Beason,* 133 U. S. 333. But it is a long step, and one which I am unable to take, to the position that government may, as a supposed educational measure and as a means of disciplining the young, compel public affirmations which violate their religious conscience. . . .

So here, even if we believe that such compulsions will contribute to national unity, there are other ways to teach loyalty and patriotism which are the sources of national unity, than by compelling the pupil to affirm that which he does not believe and by commanding a form of affirmance which violates his religious convictions. . . .

The very essence of the liberty which they guarantee is the freedom of the individual from compulsion as to what he shall think and what he shall say, at least where the compulsion is to bear false witness to his religion. If these guaranties are to have any meaning they must, I think, be deemed to withhold from the state any authority to compel belief or the expression of it where that expression violates religious convictions, whatever may be the legislative view of the desirability of such compulsion. . . .

And while such expressions of loyalty, when voluntarily given, may promote national unity, it is quite another matter to say that their compulsory expression by children in violation of their own and their parents' religious convictions can be regarded as playing so important a part in our national unity as to leave school boards free to exact it despite the constitutional guarantee of freedom of religion. The very terms of the Bill of Rights preclude, it seems to me, any reconciliation of such compulsions with the constitutional guaranties by a legislative declaration that they are more important to the public welfare than the Bill of Rights. . . .

Here we have such a small minority entertaining in good faith a religious belief, which is such a departure from the usual course of human conduct, that most persons are disposed to regard it with little toleration or concern. In such circumstances careful scrutiny of legislative efforts to secure conformity of belief and opinion by a compulsory affirmation of the desired belief, is especially needful if civil rights are to receive any protection. Tested by this standard, I am not prepared to say that the right of this small and helpless minority, including children having a strong religious conviction, whether they understand its nature or not, to refrain from an expression obnoxious to their religion, is to be overborne by the interest of the state in maintaining discipline in the schools. . . .[345]

As a result of the decision of the court, later, as we shall see, to be overturned, the conscientious members of this extreme group were placed for the time being in a difficult position. In at least one place in New York state the Witnesses provided schools of their own, following the public school curriculum in all respects except for substituting the reading of the Bible for the flag salute. In another place, Pontiac, Michigan, a modified pledge of allegiance to the United States was adopted omitting the word "flag." The probate judge warned the parents that if they would not accept

the very gracious ruling of the school board and train the children better in Americanism, it will be the obligation of the court to take the children out of the homes long enough to give them environment and training to understand what Americanism is.[346]

The decision in the Gobitis case would have held for the flag salute in general had not a similar case come before the courts in 1942, which led the Supreme Court to reconsider the question. The West Virginia Board of Education adopted early in that year a regulation requiring all pupils in the public schools of the state to participate regularly in a salute to the flag, and stating that a refusal would be regarded as an act of insubordination and dealt with accordingly. The Board of Education acted under authority of the West Virginia Code of 1931 as amended by acts of the legislature in 1941, so it had strong state authority behind it.[347]

A suit attempting to enjoin the enforcing of the board's resolutions was brought before the United States District Court by three plaintiffs who were members of Jehovah's Witnesses and who had children of compulsory school age. They protested on the usual ground of their sect, that the act of participating in the flag-salute ceremony violates the Biblical commandment against bowing down to graven images. The district court found that the children had such religious scruples against the practice that they could not comply with the regulations. This meant that they would be expelled from the school and deprived of public school education, and that the parents would either have to pay to have their children educated in private schools or be subject to prosecution under the compulsory education law of the state for failure to send them to school. They declared that the regulation deprived them of the liberty guaranteed by the Fourteenth Amendment to the Constitution, which they assumed included the religious liberty guaranteed by the First Amendment. They also emphasized the fact that the regulation of the board had been superseded by a joint resolution of Congress adopted June 22, 1942, which, after describing the pledge of allegiance to the flag, provided that

> However, civilians will always show full respect to the flag when the pledge is given by merely standing at attention, men removing their headdress. Persons in uniform shall render the military salute.[348]

Under the lead of a judge of high standing and independence, the Honorable John Johnston Parker (1884–) of the United States Circuit Court of the Fourth Circuit, the court declined to follow the Gobitis decision, accepting in general the dissenting opinion of Mr. Justice Stone, who in the meantime had become Chief Justice of the United States.

With reference to Judge Parker's disregard of the Supreme Court's decision, Curtis in his stimulating book on the Supreme Court quotes with apparent approval the statement of Judge Learned Hand (1872–), one of America's leading jurists, that the measure of a lower court's duty "in the case of changes plainly foreshadowed" "is to divine, as best it can, what would be the event of an appeal in the case before it." He points out that that is what Judge Parker did.[349]

The American Bar Association's committee on the Bill of Rights interested itself actively in the case, which was appealed to the United States Supreme Court. The committee recognized that the Constitutional issues were the same as those in the Gobitis case. The major features of its argument were: The flag salute in its application to the plaintiffs and their children should be treated by this court as a religious ceremony; this impairment of religious liberty has no reasonable tendency to promote any public interest; the subsequent effect of the Gobitis case shows the soundness of the opinion of the present chief justice that the compulsory flag salute is unconstitutional as to these children.

The committee brought out that the legislation was of a sort entirely new to America in that it was "an attempt to *compel* a particular expression as distinguished from *restraints* on certain kinds of expression." It also stressed the fact that a careful examination of the best legal opinion after the Gobitis decision clearly supported the dissenting opinion of Mr. Justice Stone. A study of the twenty-two legal publications which had discussed the case showed that eighteen approved the dissenting opinion and only two agreed with the decision of the Supreme Court, the two others merely describing the case without taking sides. It also showed that state courts had tended to follow the reasoning of Mr. Justice Stone, and that in general the opinion had been considered a blow to religious liberty.

The decision of the Supreme Court in this new case came in June, 1943, when by a 6 to 3 vote it was decided that under the Bill of Rights public school children could not be compelled to salute the American flag if this ceremony conflicted with their religious beliefs. The change in the Supreme Court's attitude was the result of the addition to the court of two new members and the change in attitude of three of those who had taken part in the earlier majority opinion. The action of Messrs. Black, Douglas, and Murphy, in reversing an opinion they had only recently held, and doing so on an otherwise unrelated occasion, is believed to be without precedent in the history of the United States Supreme Court.[350] It is an important milestone in the history of religious liberty.

Statements from the majority opinion delivered by Justice Robert H. Jackson (1892–   ) are as follows:

We think the action of the local authorities in compelling the flag salute and pledge transcends constitutional limitations on their power and invades the sphere of intellect and spirit which it is the purpose of the First Amendment to our Constitution to reserve from all official control. . . .

To sustain the compulsory flag salute we are required to say that a Bill of Rights which guards the individual's right to speak his own mind left it open to public authorities to compel him to utter what is not in his mind. . . .

Justice Jackson also said that there was a doubt whether Abraham Lincoln "would have thought that the strength of government to maintain itself would be impressively vindicated by our conferring power on the State to expel a handful of children from school." Dwelling upon "the ultimate futility of such attempts he added:

To believe that patriotism will not flourish if patriotic ceremonies are voluntary and spontaneous instead of a compulsory routine is to make an unflattering estimate of the appeal of our institutions to free minds.

If there is any fixed star in our constitutional constellation, it is that no official, high or petty, can prescribe what shall be orthodox in politics, nationalism, religion, or other matters of opinion or force citizens to confess by word or act their faith therein.[351]

All the justices in their various opinions pro and con laid great emphasis on the importance of religious liberty, though the minority did not consider that religious liberty was enough affected in the case at issue to overrule the demands of national unity and patriotism.

No case in modern times involving religious freedom has been more discussed, or has brought out a more interesting literature. Those who wish to study the arguments underlying the latest, and what will probably prove to be the last, decision of the Supreme Court on this complicated issue, are referred to the earlier brief of the committee on the Bill of Rights of the American Bar Association on the *Constitutionality of the Compulsory Flag Salute,* originally submitted in the Gobitis case to the Supreme Court on April 25, 1940. Its convincing argument is summed up in this brief statement:

The committee believes that the compulsory flag salute regulation adopted by the petitioner Board of Education violates the constitutional prohibition against the deprivation of liberty without due process of law, because without sufficient justification it requires the suppression of a sincerely held religious scruple; and also because, apart from any religious aspect, it transcends the limits of governmental power in attempting to compel a particular form of expression without sufficient reason for such compulsion.[352]

Prior to the final decision the Department of Justice, through its Civil Rights Section, had sent to all United States attorneys a memorandum under date of July 18, 1942, which read in part as follows:

Attention is called to the Act of June 22, 1942, Public No. 623, 77th Congress, 2d

Session, by which Congress codified the rules and customs regarding the use of and respect due the flag of the United States. Section 7 of that Act recites the pledge of allegiance to the flag and describes the accompanying gesture of salute, but significantly notes that full respect for the flag may be shown by civilians when the pledge is given by merely standing at attention. Soldiers in uniform must give the military salute. The text of Section 7 is as follows:

"That the pledge of allegiance to the flag, 'I pledge allegiance to the flag of the United States of America and to the Republic for which it stands, one Nation indivisible, with liberty and justice for all,' be rendered by standing with the right hand over the heart; extending the right hand, palm upward, toward the flag at the words 'to the flag' and holding this position until the end, when the hand drops to the side. However, civilians will always show full respect to the flag when the pledge is given by merely standing at attention, men removing the headdress. Persons in uniform shall render the military salute."

The Department and the United States Attorneys have been repeatedly confronted with complaints from persons who have been mistreated or their children dismissed from schools and in some instances prosecuted for refusing to salute the flag because of religious scruples. It is felt that Section 7 of the above mentioned law lays down a Federal standard with regard to a matter which is primarily a concern of the national government and there is, therefore, a very real question whether any local regulation, ordinance, or statute prescribing a different measure of respect to the flag can be enforced.[353]

Jehovah's Witnesses have also been before the courts on other issues discussed at length elsewhere.[354] One of these cases, that of Newton Cantwell and his sons, arrested for breaking a Connecticut statute requiring previous permission from the secretary of the Public Welfare Council for certain specified activities, was of great importance. The unanimous opinion of the Supreme Court in deciding the case in their favor clearly held for the first time that the Fourteenth Amendment should be construed to guarantee in the states the religious freedom provided for under the Federal government by the Bill of Rights. It is quoted from at length where the Fourteenth Amendment is considered.[355]

Section 9. HIGHER EDUCATION

The tension between Church and State in the United States has been much less noticeable in the field of higher education than in that of the public schools, for obvious reasons, but especially because the number of students in all university and college groups is normally less than one-twentieth of those in the schools supported by taxation. Besides the total enrolled public-school population of 25,975,108 in 1938—a good year to consider since it just preceded abnormal war conditions—the number of university and college students (not including normal schools and teacher's colleges) was 1,205,256.[356]

By 1944, owing to war conditions, the number of public-school students decreased by more than two million, but of course many high-school boys were continuing some form of education in the armed forces.[357] By 1947 these army-trained men were flocking back into schools and colleges of all types, allowed under the G.I. Bill of Rights to attend Church schools and colleges as well as those under public auspices.[358] College attendance reached an all-time high, a fact which affected the Churches, since they conducted many of the higher educational institutions of the country. For instance, the *U.S. Department of Education Directory* for 1938 showed 692 out of a total of 1,686 institutions, or about 41 per cent, under Church control.[359] These last figures include both teacher-training institutions and junior colleges.

The Office of Education of the Federal Security Agency announced a total of 430,000 degrees conferred by state, private, and Church-controlled colleges and universities during the year ending June 30, 1949. Even masters' and doctors' degrees rose 20 per cent and 29 per cent respectively over the previous year, which had been the highest up to that time. The figures of the agency were based on statistics obtained from about one thousand out of twelve hundred institutions qualified to grant degrees.

The directory published by the United States Office of Education for 1947–48 listed 1,688 institutions of higher education, of which 782 were colleges and universities, and 427 junior colleges, with the others distributed among professional and other schools. The war has produced a very large increase in the number of state junior colleges and municipal colleges. These increases will probably mean a slight decrease in the relative percentage of Church institutions.

Most of the older colleges in America received royal charters under boards of trustees, which were to a large extent independent; and the colleges during most of the colonial period looked for their support mainly to tuition fees, private benefactions, and occasional lotteries. The colonies aided them from the public revenues, but, except to some extent in the earliest years at Harvard, they were not considered "State institutions." This development of great private, as distinct from State, institutions of higher learning continued to be the general tendency until, as a result of the establishment of the republic, the State felt a direct responsibility for directing and controlling the higher education of its future citizens.

Similarly the colonial colleges almost uniformly had clergymen as presidents, required chapel attendance and religious instruction, and from half to all their trustees were clergymen. For example, Harvard's first board, established in

1637 by an act of the General Court and later called the "Overseers," was made up of six magistrates and six clergymen,[360] and in the "theocracy" of Massachusetts Bay the two were closely related. The president, treasurer, and fellows or trustees named in the first charter, that of 1650 (which also continued the Board of Overseers), were given "perpetuall succession."[361] That is, they were self-perpetuating. There was no official representative of the colonial government on the trustee board known as the "President and Fellows," although such representatives were continued, along with the ministers of certain Congregational churches, on the Board of Overseers, whose consent was necessary in electing trustees.

Yale's trustees under the first charter, that of 1701, were to be "ministers of the gospel inhabiting within this Colony,"[362] and had power to elect their own successors. Furthermore, we have the famous statement about Harvard's founding in *New England's First Fruits* of 1643. It was "to advance learning and perpetuate it to Posterity; dreading to leave an illiterate Ministery to the Churches, when our present Ministers shall lie in the Dust."[363] Similarly Yale's earliest charter showed its founders actuated by "Regard to & Zeal for upholding & Propagating of the Christian Protestant Religion by a succession of Learned and Orthodox men. . . ."[364] Fortunately in neither case did they apparently have in mind what would today be called a divinity school, but rather a college of the arts and sciences wherein, as the Yale document states, "Youth may be instructed in the Arts and Sciences who through the blessing of Almighty God may be fitted for Publick employment both in Church & Civil State."[365]

What has been said of Harvard and Yale as essentially independent and self-governing cultural institutions of higher learning that emphasized giving men a broad training primarily as a basis for later theological study and secondarily for a public career, was also largely true of the other colleges established before the Revolution in New England, New York, and New Jersey—namely, Princeton, Brown, King's (Columbia), Queen's (Rutgers), and Dartmouth. It was also partly though less true of the other colonial colleges farther South—William and Mary, and the University of Pennsylvania. These two were less controlled by the clergy, and in early days were more directly interested in training men for practical and public life than their Northern sister institutions.

These general religious characteristics of most of the colonial colleges, and the close relation of the clergy to them, continued until the Revolution. Then the situation gradually changed.

The various influences on higher education of the establishment of an independent federal republic have been discussed in an earlier section.[366] Here we are concerned only with the later large development of public institutions under state control. Beginning with the charter of the University of Georgia in 1784 and that of the University of North Carolina in 1789, state universities began to be developed in the United States after the Revolution. Most of these early institutions differed relatively little from the older foundations in such matters as the teaching of Christian philosophy, the regular attendance of undergraduate students at Sunday worship, and the leadership of ministers of the gospel, or of men known to be sympathetic with historic Christianity as understood by most Protestants. The election of Thomas Cooper (1759–1839), a radical of the Tom Paine school, to the presidency of the University of South Carolina in 1821 created a sensation, and he was forced out of office after twelve years because of opposition, led by the clergy, to his liberal religious and political views.[367]

Of the new institutions, the University of Virginia, established by the Virginia legislature in 1819, soon became prominent for its departure from conservative tradition. The influence of Thomas Jefferson[368] on its ideas of freedom, on its system of democratic government, and on its curriculum, were all noticeable and were signs of a new day.

It may be sufficient here to give a single quotation from a letter he wrote to an English friend just as the university was being launched. It reflects a new spirit in American education.

> This institution will be based on the illimitable freedom of the human mind. For here we are not afraid to follow truth wherever it may lead, nor to tolerate any error so long as reason is left free to combat it.[369]

Of these state universities, the most representative in many ways was the University of Michigan, established in 1837. It was based on the conception that the university was the crowning feature of a system of public education, its Board of Regents being established as a constitutional part of the state government, and independent of legislative control. Under the long administration of President James Burrill Angell (1829–1916), from 1871 on, the university made history for higher education. It early adopted such far-sighted policies for a state institution as the abolition of compulsory daily and Sunday services, the broadening of the curriculum, and the development of professional schools of university grade.

Another state university which had large influence was the University of Wisconsin, established in 1849. This institution should be particularly remembered for its important stand in the matter of academic freedom. The Board of Regents published in 1894 the following statement which we now may accept as almost a commonplace, but which was then highly significant, especially considering that the university was a state institution, and that its distinguished

Professor of Economics, Dr. Richard T. Ely, was under vigorous attack for his liberal economic views.

As regents of a university supported by nearly two million of people who hold a vast diversity of views regarding the great questions which at present agitate the human mind, we could not for a moment think of recommending the dismissal or even the criticism of a teacher even if some of his opinions should, in some quarters, be regarded as visionary. Such a course would be equivalent to saying that no professor should teach anything which is not accepted by everybody as true. This would cut our curriculum down to very small proportions. We cannot for a moment believe that knowledge has reached its final goal, or that the present condition of society is perfect. We must therefore welcome from our teachers such discussions as shall suggest the means and prepare the way by which knowledge may be extended, present evils be removed and others prevented. . . . In all lines of academic investigation it is of the utmost importance that the investigator should be absolutely free to follow the indications of the truth wherever they may lead. Whatever may be the limitations which trammel inquiry elsewhere, we believe the great state University of Wisconsin should ever encourage that continual and fearless sifting and winnowing by which alone the truth can be found.[370]

This is not the place to take up the history of higher education in the United States. The point we wish to stress is that whereas prior to the formation of the American union universities were mostly endowed and privately supported institutions related to some religious denomination, there developed increasingly under the new government a system of state universities, so that today there is no state in the union without such a university or a state college that is developing into a university, at least in name. These institutions came into friendly competition, and sometimes into rivalry, with older private colleges, most of which had been developed under strong religious and denominational auspices. The religious forces of the country were at first inclined to strengthen their own institutions, and not to encourage the state universities, except for special lines of work such as agriculture, teacher training, applied science, and the professions; whereas the state was increasingly interested in its own publicly supported institutions and consequently tended to try to control directly or indirectly the private colleges. In this contest the Supreme Court's decision in the Dartmouth College case in 1819 was of great significance. The legislature of New Hampshire virtually tried to take over Dartmouth College and make it a state university; but the trustees held firmly to the independent rights granted them under their charter. Daniel Webster (1782–1852) argued the case for the college in the Supreme Court in one of the ablest speeches ever delivered in the United States. The decision, supporting the college, was of epoch-making importance. Chancellor James Kent (1763–1847) said of it:

The decision in that case did more than any other single act proceeding from the authority of the United States to throw an impregnable barrier around all rights and franchises derived from the grant of government; and to give solidity and inviolability to the literary, charitable, religious and commercial institutions of our country.[371]

This decision virtually stopped efforts by the State, as far as legislative control was concerned, to take over private educational institutions. But there have been various ways, such as the withholding of special grants, the limiting of tax exemptions of private foundations, and the granting of enormous sums to state institutions, which have been used to strengthen public higher education, as against the private higher education to which the older states of the East were accustomed. There is now, however, a general understanding that both groups of institutions are vitally important; the private institution is able to make experiments and uphold standards without political interference, and the state institutions are able to popularize education and to provide the natural capstone for the public education system.

There are still a few grants made annually by state legislatures to colleges under denominational control or influence. Maryland, Maine, Pennsylvania, and Vermont continue this practice in a few cases, for which Protestants are more responsible than Roman Catholics. In Massachusetts such grants were given to a few institutions as late as 1917, when they were discontinued by law.[372]

Although state universities must, under our separation of Church and State, be entirely detached from any religious body, there is nothing that prevents their offering elective courses in religion; and these are in fact rather frequent, especially courses in comparative religions and the history of religion. Indeed, in some cases there have been developed extensive groups of courses on religion included in the catalogue, and usually counting toward a degree. They are so important from the point of view of Church–State relations that they are dealt with separately in the next section.

The state universities differ considerably in what might be called their attitude toward religion. Some, like the University of Wisconsin, have maintained a very strict separation, and the religious forces have until recently had considerable difficulty in getting any strong foothold. As late as 1942 its Board of Regents even seriously discussed whether the University Press could properly publish a volume recommended by the Department of Philosophy on *The Religious Availability of Whitehead's God!*[373] The book was published as proposed. Other state universities in the South and in Iowa and Oregon have been sympathetic to religion.[374] I remember well the difference in atmosphere some twenty years ago between Wisconsin and Iowa; my address at the midweek convocation at Iowa was preceded on the printed program by the hymn "In the Cross of Christ I glory."[375]

Chapel services under university auspices are held at several state universities, especially in the South.[376] Their legality does not seem to have been questioned when they are on a purely voluntary basis. An interesting case came before the courts in Illinois in 1891 when it was decided that a rule of the university that required all students to attend chapel services, which consisted of reading from the New Testament, the repetition of the Lord's Prayer, the singing of a hymn, and so forth, was not prohibited by Constitutional provision (Art. 2, Sec. 3.), inasmuch as anyone might be excused who would sign a request to that effect.[377]

One Southern state university, Georgia, had a requirement as late as 1877 that "all officers elected or appointed for the university shall be of the Christian religion,"[378] and all presidents through the end of the nineteenth century were ministers. The University of South Carolina, whose revised statutes of 1873 provided that one of its departments should include "a school of mental and moral philosophy, sacred literature and evidences of Christianity,"[379] has a provision, adopted by act of the legislature in 1890, to the effect that the president shall not be an atheist or infidel.[380] I know of no similar provision elsewhere; though it is probably unnecessary, since it is doubtful whether any American university of standing would elect a president with such views, though there have been a few—very few—who could be classed as reverent agnostics. South Carolina still requires chapel attendance once a week for all freshmen and sophomores, and "about once a month the program is of a religious nature," though in general "chapel," in spite of its continuing the old name, is now scarcely to be considered a religious exercise.[381] Attendance at Sunday chapel exercises, which had hitherto been optional, was made compulsory a decade or more after the Civil War to meet the criticisms of the denominational institutions and "to show that the college was not an irreligious institution."[382] This plan was followed for more than ten years, but in 1894–95 there was substituted attendance at some church in the city (Columbia) for "All students, except those excused for special reasons by the President. . . ."[383]

A recent state university development that is interesting because it is at the University of Virginia, with its Jeffersonian tradition, and in a state dominantly Protestant, is the series of unofficial lectures arranged by members of the faculty every year since 1935. They are definitely Catholic in tendency, and are designed to give what President Hutchins of the University of Chicago has been advocating, an intellectual and spiritual unity in the various subjects of study. This series of lectures has really been based on the *Summa Theologica* of St. Thomas Aquinas. It was opened October 13, 1935, by a lecture by Dr. Stringfellow

Barr, an Episcopalian, later president of St. John's College, Annapolis, on "The Need for Dogma."

In the second year the lectures were on moral theology, natural theology, and dogmatic theology, and, as the prospectus states, the series was

based on the further premise, once more generally held, that theology is not a minute, isolated and remote subject-matter, but it is relevant to all the crises in the experience of human life.[384]

In 1938 lectures were divided into three sections—the "Theological Virtues"; the "Intellectual Virtues"; and the "Moral Virtues." This experiment in intellectual integration is not an official part of the university curriculum, but the lectures are held in university buildings with the collaboration of university professors. Furthermore each year Religious Emphasis Week is observed, with some college classes suspended so as not to interfere with a series of addresses on religious themes.

On the whole the presidents of state universities are sympathetic to the recognition of religion when it is broadly presented as an optional subject of study. This point of view has perhaps not been expressed better than by President Robert Gordon Sproul (1891–) of the University of California. In a recent book he has said:

For my part I believe that religion (not the sects) is basic to morals, central in our American culture, unique as a dynamic within the individual, able to save us from ourselves and lead us out into nobility. I believe that without religion we are forced to substitute weak conventions for permanent values and abiding standards; that, without religion, civilization with no adequate enforcement for the great strains that come upon it must yield . . . to disintegration and decay.

Believing these things, I believe also that the university which does not create in its sons and daughters a sensitiveness to the values of religion is likely to be a danger rather than a benefit to the state. Certainly it cannot serve its people as fully as it should unless it finds some way, as it has always done, to blend with knowledge and culture the rugged force of character and the spiritual power that give to these life and value. So only may knowledge become wisdom.[385]

This attitude has much support among undergraduates. For instance, *The Daily Iowan* of the state university of Iowa recently carried a remarkable editorial entitled "Take Us Back to Solid Ground," appealing for faculty help in re-establishing enduring spiritual foundations. The editorial said, among other things:

Religion is in medicine and commerce and physics too, and those of you who teach medicine and commerce and physics must teach religion too. . . . We want constant training in the constant things of life, the physical, mental, and spiritual things which have been the foundations of humanity since the civilizations of ancient China.[386]

Probably the greatest aid to religion, one which creates no difficulties in Church–State relations at state universities, is the personal influence through example and attitude of those members of the faculty with definitely spiritual ideals and convictions. The opportunities are great in almost all fields of teaching. They are frequently lived up to, especially by teachers of art, music, literature, philosophy, history, astronomy, geology—which seem to encourage the spirit of reverence for religion; less often by those in psychology, sociology, and the physical sciences. Here is a way in which, without any attempt at indoctrination, but by loyalty to a spiritual ideal, religious men can and do bear eloquent testimony to their convictions in ways that carry great weight with students.

There have been relatively few Church–State conflicts at state institutions that were due to the theological opinions of members of the faculty. Indeed, such cases have been much fewer than difficulties due to economic and political opinions. Most of those which have occurred have been in the South. An early one had to do with Jefferson's choice of the able and distinguished but radical and erratic Thomas Cooper (1759–1839) to be the first "Professor of Chemistry and Law"—an interesting combination—at the University of Virginia. In 1817 the Board of Visitors of the newly founded Central College extended an invitation to him, and in 1819, when the college had been transformed into the University of Virginia, the board duly appointed him to the chair of chemistry, mineralogy, natural philosophy, and law. This was done in spite of violent opposition on the part of some clergymen and laymen because of his alleged vagaries of conduct and his pronounced opposition to the Christian religion as interpreted by most of the churches. Even William H. Cabell (1772–1853) wrote to his brother Joseph, Jefferson's main supporter in the university project, that he feared

> Cooper's appointment will do the University infinite injury. His religious views are damnable, as exhibited in a book published by him shortly after the death of Priestley. You will have every religious man in Virginia against you.[387]

The influential *Evangelical Magazine* joined the opposition in a dignified but vigorous way. It stated that, as the university was now a state institution, and needed the support of the denominations, public opinion would object to the appointment of teachers of youth whose heresies, they thought, struck at the foundations of "social order, morals and religion."[388] It was in some ways a prototype of the furor raised 130 years later when the brilliant Bertrand Russell

(1872-) was called to a professorship in City College, New York, and there was effective opposition because of his unconventional views and attitudes on matrimony and other subjects.[389] In the earlier case the opposition was so acute that when Cooper offered his resignation a majority of the board was relieved and accepted it. In his last official communication to the university he said:

Whatever my religious creed may be, and perhaps I do not exactly know it myself, it is a pleasure to reflect that my conduct has not brought, and is not likely to bring, discredit on my friends.[390]

Later the same year (1819) Cooper was elected professor of chemistry in South Carolina College, and in 1821 became president by a vote of ten to nine, serving until 1833. He was frequently in hot water because of his deriding of the Christian Church, his attacks on theism, his critical attitude toward the Bible, and his advocacy of unpopular political views, all of which antagonized most thoughtful people in the state. Since he could not be removed except by action of the legislature, this body named a committee to examine him "and if they find that his continuance in office defeats the ends and aims of the institution that they be requested to remove him."[391] The trial took place in the hall of the House of Representatives before the trustees. He was acquitted by a divided vote, but the opposition continued so strong that he was prevailed upon to resign the presidency, but was allowed to continue to lecture on chemistry.

The same institution—now the University of South Carolina—dropped a professor of logic and philosophy in 1891 for his unorthodox views on the Trinity.[392] But such cases have been extremely rare in state institutions in recent decades. There has, however, been occasional discrimination on religious grounds both in faculty appointments and student admissions, especially at public and even more in private universities in urban centers with a large Jewish population, where a more or less informal quota system has been observed in law and medical schools. For example, during 1947 there was much discussion in New York state of racial and religious discrimination in the admission of students to some institutions of higher learning. This particularly affected Negroes and Jews. As a result the legislature passed the following year a law making it illegal for any college or university, except definitely religious or denominational institutions which wish to admit only those of their own faith, to refuse to accept a student because of color, race, creed, or national origin. New York is the first state to pass such a law, and it may have a broad influence.

Section 10. SCHOOLS OF RELIGION AT STATE UNIVERSITIES

One of the interesting educational developments in Church–State relations is the founding during the past twenty-five years of schools of religion or kindred organizations at several state universities. This movement has been closely related to the work of the Council of Religion in Higher Education.

The first proposal I have noticed for anything approaching a "Department of Religion" at a state university was the adoption by the state legislature of South Carolina in its session of 1864–65 of a statute, which was also repeated in the revised statutes of 1873 after the Civil War, to the effect that "A school of mental and moral philosophy, sacred literature, and evidences of Christianity" should be one of the departments of the university.[393] The university had long had a "Professor of Sacred Literature and Evidences of Christianity," but there is no evidence that the proposed "school" was ever developed.

The first effective step toward a real school of religion at a state university was taken fifty years later at the state university of Iowa, a university whose life has been influenced from its foundation by ideals inherited from the universities and colleges of New England, and which has always had on its faculty men deeply interested in religion. The plan was formulated in the years from 1921 to 1924 through the co-operation of members of the faculty, local pastors, the university secretary of the Council of the Church Boards of Education, the Y.M.C.A., and other groups. As a result, it was proposed to establish a school of religion whose governing board was to be "constituted in such a way as to secure the cooperative efforts of the religious bodies of the State and of the University in the support and control of the School."[394] The plan was approved by the president of the university and by the state board of education.

The organization was formed the following year at a meeting held in the senate chamber of the "old capitol," attended by representative Jews, Catholics, and Protestants. The group unanimously chose fifteen trustees, nine representing the churches and six the university at large. An executive committee representing the three groups, and including Monsignor W. P. Shannahan and Rabbi Eugene Mannheimer, was chosen. This committee secured a grant of $35,000 to test the experiment for three years and to incorporate the trustees.

A faculty was later selected, including a Jewish, a Catholic, and a Protestant professor, and an administrative director, Dr. M. Willard Lampe (1883–   ), who has been the major constructive force in the work of the school. The school, in addition to offering its regular courses, undertook to aid in the extra-curricular religious life of the campus, and through additional help from Mr.

Rockefeller a professor was added in 1930 with the primary purpose of developing the laboratory side of the enterprise.

Since 1933 the work of the school has been well integrated into the life of the university. It co-operated with the department of philosophy in providing a regular freshman course entitled "Religion and Ethics." The project was so wisely administered, in taking steps only when representatives of the three groups were unanimous about them, that it has had the hearty support of the university board and most of the members of the faculty.

These facts are taken from a bulletin of the university, published in 1936, entitled *The Story of An Idea.* I have seen no better statement anywhere of the responsibility of a state university in encouraging the forces of religion.

> The basic idea of our story is this: since religion is an essential part of all true education, there should be a way to teach it, not surreptitiously or indirectly, but unapologetically and comprehensively, *even* in an American state university. The significance of "even" lies in the fact that when people have started to play with this idea, they have commonly run into two blind alleys: first, the American tradition of the separation of Church and State with its corollary in the popular mind that public money must never be used for the support of religion under any guise; and second, the wild profusion of religious groups in this country which, like Joseph's gorgeous coat, adds color but not harmony to the scene and tends to frustrate every effort at concerted thinking or planning in this field.
>
> But in spite of these two blind alleys, the idea as stated persists, due chiefly to the pressure of two increasingly obvious facts: first, the fact that religion of some kind is always taught in a state university and that there is constant danger of its being taught in an unenlightened, unsympathetic and even disparaging way. Every teacher has some kind of a religion and he will not be able to fence it off from the minds of his students, even if he may earnestly desire to do so. It is foolish to think that a state university may teach everything but religion; it teaches religion willy-nilly. Second, it has become increasingly clear that there is no adequate substitute for religion formally integrated with university education. The only possible substitute is the organization of religion off, but near the campus. But religious education off the campus, no matter how fine the preaching, the teaching, or the pastoral and personal guidance may be, cannot be an educational or spiritual equivalent for religious education incorporated into the university itself and of the same quality as every other phase of the university's life.[395]

In the year 1938–39 there were more than four hundred students enrolled in credit courses, representing all three religious groups. The School of Religion has been regularly supported from state funds since 1937.[396]

In a recent article published in Spanish about the school by its administrative director, Dr. Lampe, a picture is given of the seven-man faculty including a

Roman Catholic priest, a Jewish rabbi, and a Protestant minister. It states that the school during its first twenty years has matriculated about a thousand students, or 15 per cent of those enrolled in the Faculty of Arts. It calls attention to the fact that the school—which grew out of the experience of Protestant, Jewish, and Catholic co-operation in World War I—is officially recognized by the university, which credits courses completed under its auspices toward the degrees of A.B., A.M., and Ph.D.[397] The late Dr. O. Delmer Foster, Secretary of the American Association of Religion, was instrumental in its formation and in securing the support of Archbishop Austin Dowling (1868–1930), then president of the National Catholic Council of Religion.

The school celebrated its twentieth anniversary on May 4 and 5, 1947. An interfaith vesper service featured Catholic, Protestant, and Jewish music. It has 1,798 students attending its courses given by professors of the three faiths. It offers one of the "core courses" which satisfy the B.A. degree requirements. The university provides classroom, office, and administration expenses, but the faculty salaries are paid from private subscriptions. The experiment has been highly successful.[398]

A second experiment of this kind was made at the University of Michigan. An inaugural meeting to create interest in the plan had been held in 1923. It was then stated that

> To meet the needs of students . . . they must be able to treat religion as one of the great provinces of human knowledge and interest; to study and make it their own in the same intelligent and effective way that they do history or economics or any other university subject. To meet this fundamental demand is the aim of the Michigan School of Religion which is to be established at Ann Arbor.[399]

The president of the state university, the late Dr. Marion Le Roy Burton (1874–1925), speaking at the meeting about religion as "a supremely necessary thing," said: "I submit to you that there must be some method by which this point of view can be incorporated in American education without doing violence to the principle of the separation of church and state."[400] The school was opened in 1925 as a result of the stimulus given by Professor Charles Foster Kent (1867–1925) of Yale University, the founder of the Council of Religion in Higher Education (1922), with the president and other officers of the university co-operating. It ran for four semesters with enrollments beginning at forty-five and going up to 193. Because of the lack of funds and the death of several of the leaders in the movement, the school was discontinued, and finally dissolved in 1937, its funds being used in later years for religious education. There has, however, been developed at the university a degree program in religion and ethics under the general leadership of Dr. Edward W. Blakeman, who was appointed by the president as adviser and counsellor in the field of religion. More than forty courses in several university departments were grouped to permit a student to take his A.B. (last two years), A.M., or Ph.D., in religion and ethics. This is not a special school or department, but merely a listing of courses. Though there are relatively few students, it is interesting to note that in this university, a leader among state universities, the courses have included such subjects as the history of religions; the history of Israel; the Gospels, the Acts of the Apostles, and the Pauline epistles in Greek; the Bible as literature; knowing the Bible; the philosophy of religion; the sociology of religion; and the history of religions (living faiths of the Near and Far East).

The university also supports a "Director for Religious Work" among students, who is a member of the university staff, and who is charged with the responsibility for developing an extracurricular program to help students gain a better understanding of religion. He works impartially with Jews, Catholics, Protestants, and students of Oriental faiths. Such an officer, sometimes called a "Counsellor in Religious Education," supported either by the university or by the churches, and with official or semiofficial status, is found at several American state universities.

The Hawaii School of Religion was made possible in 1930 by the co-operation of the various Protestant denominations and the Roman Catholic Church in the territory. It serves virtually as the Department of Religion at the university, offering courses in such subjects as problems in religious thought; Christian church history; comparative study of religions; and the teachings of Jesus. It is controlled, under its constitution, by a board of trustees of not fewer than thirteen members, of whom one represents the faculty of the university and is nominated by the university, nine representing the Protestant churches are appointed by the Collegiate Religious Education Commission, and three are appointed by the Roman Catholic Church. The Protestant teachers in the school are elected by the commission, the Catholic members are appointed by the bishop of the diocese, and the administrative officers are chosen by the board of trustees.[401]

President Donald Milton Erb (1900–) of the University of Oregon, discussing the establishment of a department of religion in the College of Social Science at the university, stated his belief that

it was educationally indefensible to have departments and courses devoted to a study of political, economic and social institutions generally, but a complete absence of any instruction in the field of religious institutions. In brief, the inclusion of religious instruction in our curriculum was judged to be proper under the character of the state and university, inasmuch as the right to give a well-rounded instructional program was unquestioned.[402]

The university has a department of religion supported by *state* funds.

Whenever courses on religion are proposed at state universities, land-grant colleges, or even municipal colleges like Hunter in New York City, it is encouraging to find that there are members of the faculty and local religious leaders qualified by scholarship, breadth of view, and religious conviction to provide satisfactory courses in many fields of Biblical theology, church history, the teachings of Christ, and related subjects.

A special problem appears in the state agricultural colleges for Negroes in the thirteen Southern states that give such helpful service in the rural regions. All of them conduct institutes for Negro ministers, 600 of whom attended in 1943. These institutes emphasize the social needs of suburban and country regions, and the ways in which the churches can co-operate. Students are also instructed in making church budgets and in conducting every-member canvasses to meet them, and are shown how contributions to the church can be made in kind or in labor. The courses are conducted by ministers, teachers, and farm agents. Each day's program begins with simple worship; in several states chaplains are provided to spend Sundays at the college and weekdays in extension work. The Home Missions Council (Protestant) co-operates with the colleges and various state departments in promoting this simple, effective form of nondenominational co-operation.[403]

A specially interesting type of organization to promote religion and social welfare at a state university is at the Southern Branch of the University of California in Los Angeles and at nearby Los Angeles City College. The so-called "University Religious Conference" is a corporation composed of what it considers the leading religious groups in the United States, namely, Baptist, Congregational, Disciples of Christ, Lutheran, Methodist, Presbyterian, Unitarian, Jewish, Church of Jesus Christ of Latter Day Saints (Mormons), Roman Catholic (archdiocese of Los Angeles), and Episcopal (diocese of Los Angeles and San Diego). Each of these bodies and the Y.M.C.A. are officially represented on the Board of Trustees, and the officers of the corporation rotate each year among four trustees representing officially the Roman Catholics, Episcopalians, Jews, and Protestant denominations. Various racial groups are also generally represented on the board. The conference carries on two types of activity—religious work, through the various agents supported by the denominations, and united community work. These denominations own in common property with a suitable building adjoining the campus of the university where each has its own offices, and they rent from the archdiocese a building for similar use at the college. They support a common budget, and engage in certain common enterprises for their mutual benefit and for community service. In the community program emphasis is placed on increasing understanding among Jewish, Protestant, and Catholic citizens of the area. This is accomplished through an extensive and well-organized program of addresses, round tables, and other activities, and through welfare work for children and youth.

The conference building was erected in 1932 without state help, by donations from denominations and private individuals. The only government assistance has been through the conference sponsorship of several National Youth Administration projects, with the project workers provided by the N.Y.A. office on the campus. It does not hold any formal religious services other than at Thanksgiving, and university vespers with a half hour of recorded music and reading every Sunday evening. It has no official university status, but enjoys the sympathetic support of the administration, faculty, and students. The university and the college do not permit organized denominational campus work, but at each there is a "Student Religious Board." The annual budget of $23,000 is about equally divided between campus religious work and community service.

Such are typical ways, outside the usual Y.M.C.A., Newman Clubs (Catholic), branches of the Menorah Society (Jewish), and similar student organizations, and student pastors supported by the leading religious groups, by which the cause of religion is advanced at state universities with the active co-operation and sometimes with the financial support of the university When the university is officially involved a special effort is made to have the work of high grade and equally acceptable to the three faiths. The various experiments recorded are evidence that it is practicable, without in any way infringing upon our Constitutional restrictions, to provide in state colleges and universities opportunities both for the study of religion in general and of Christianity in particular, and facilities for public worship. Of course these must all be on a voluntary basis.

A statement of the more liberal view at state universities on the part which religion may and should play in university life was made by a special committee of the alumni board of visitors of the University of California, appointed in 1947. The committee according to the *California Monthly,* April, 1949, came to these three conclusions:

1. The principle of the separation of the church and the state is sound.

2. That courses which deal with religion as a phenomenon in history and as an influence in human life deserve the same place in the curricula now accorded to art, music and literature.

3. The courses which indoctrinate or slant the teaching in a direction favorable or unfavorable to any religion or denomination have no place in educational curricula.

The committee further stated that the student body was in favor of expanding the study of religion on the campus, and it advocated the setting up of a department of world religion under able leadership, with a staff which, in addition to giving courses, might serve as counsellors in the "non-denominational areas of religion," thus supplementing the work of the denominational centers. The whole plan reminds one of that outlined by Thomas Jefferson in 1822 for the Universtiy of Virginia.

There are also many state institutions which have established chairs of religion financed by the state, exactly as though the chairs were in secular subjects. These include the state universities of Iowa, North Carolina, Oregon, and Florida, the Florida State College for Women, and Miami University.[404] The work at these and at many other institutions mentioned in this section has been largely aided by the National Council on Religion in Higher Education (1922), which during twenty-five years invested several hundred thousand dollars in fellowships for the training of college teachers of religious subjects. These have been mostly Protestant, but have included a few Catholic and Jewish students. Of these fellowship holders, according to a study in 1943, some 96 were in teaching and research; 28 in educational administration; 14 were ministers or rabbis; 24 were in social, religious, and educational agencies; and the others in miscellaneous professions and occupations. The original purpose of the council was to concentrate its attention primarily on state universities and colleges, helping them to organize schools or departments of religion; but it has increasingly stressed its fellowship program by which men and women of the highest character and broad view are trained for making a religious impress on the colleges and universities of this country.[405]

Dr. Richard H. Edwards (1877–), who has given most of his life to the leadership of religious forces at two state universities, Wisconsin and Cornell, has an excellent little pamphlet entitled *Three Basic Realizations about Religion at State Universities*. He gives the following as his main conclusions:

1. That the growth of persons including their religious growth is highly dependent upon voluntary group associations with more mature persons, and for religious growth to be vital in any state university community the religious groups within that community must be vital, that is, full of life.

2. That religious groups have it now laid upon them to minimize their differences, to magnify their common purposes, and to do their common job together without further quibbling.

3. That a state university community is to be recognized as one of the most significant of all settings for the lively operation of pure Christianity both in presentation and in life, because the Christian groups in such communities are in immediate juxtaposition to governmental agencies.

This section on ways in which religion can be wisely and constitutionally presented to state university students may well be brought to a close by reproducing a little-known—and apparently unpublished—letter from Thomas Jefferson written a century and a quarter ago. It is in reply to a request by certain representatives of Charlottesville churches—submitted by Mr. Brockenbrough, the university bursar—for permission to use the rotunda, the central University of Virginia building, for public religious services on Sundays. It shows both Jefferson's sympathy with providing opportunities for religious worship for students of the university and at the same time his belief that the buildings of the university should not be used for nonuniversity purposes, especially when the proposal seemed to favor "two particular sects."

To Arthur S. Brockenbrough

Dear Sir Monticello Apr. 21. 25.

In answer to your letter proposing to permit the lecture room of the Pavilion No. 1. to be used regularly for prayers and preaching on Sundays, I have to observe that some 3. or 4. years ago, an application was made to permit a sermon to be preached in one of the pavilions on a particular occasion, not now recollected. It brought the subject into consideration with the Visitors, and altho' they entered into no formal and written resolution on the occasion, the concurrent sentiment was that the buildings of the University belong to the state, that they were erected for the purposes of an University, and that the Visitors, to whose care they are committed for those purposes have no right to permit their application to any other. And accordingly, when applied to, on the visit of General Lafayette, I declined at first the request of the use of the Rotunda for his entertainment, until it occurred on reflection that the room, in the unfinished state in which it then was, was as open and uninclosed, and as insusceptible of injury, as the field in which it stood. In the Rockfish report it was stated as probable that a building larger than the Pavilions might be called for in time, in which might be rooms for a library, for public examinations, and for religious worship *under such impartial regulations as the Visitors should prescribe,* the legislature neither sanctioned nor rejected this proposition; and afterwards, in the Report of Oct. 1822. the board suggested, as a substitute, that the different religious sects should be invited to establish their separate theological schools in the vicinity of the University, in which the Students might attend religious worship, each in the form of his respective sect, and thus avoid all jealousy of attempts on his religious tenets. Among the enactments of the board is one looking to this object, and superseding the first idea of permitting a room in the Rotunda to be used for religious worship, and of undertaking to frame a set of regulations of equality and impartiality among the multiplied sects. I state these things as manifesting the caution which the board of Visitors thinks it a duty to observe on this delicate and jealous subject. Your proposition therefore leading to an application of the University buildings to other than University purposes, and to a partial regulation in favor of two particular sects, would be a deviation from the course which they think it their duty to observe. Nor indeed is it immediately percieved what effect the repeated and habitual assemblages of a great number of strangers at the University might have on it's order and tranquility.

All this however in the present case is the less important, inasmuch as it is not farther for the inhabitants of the University to go to Charlottesville for religious worship, than for those of Charlottesville to come to the University. That place has been in long possession of the seat of public worship, a right always deemed strongest until a better can be produced. There too they are building, or about to build proper churches and meeting houses, much better adapted to the accomodation of a congregation than a scanty lecturing room. Are these to be abandoned, and the private room to be preferred? If not, then the congregations, already too small, would by your proposition be split into halves incompetent to the employment and support of a double set of officiating ministers. Each of course would break up the other, and both fall to the ground. I think therefore that, independent of our declining to sanction this application, it will not, on further reflexion, be thought as advantageous to religious interests as their joint assembly at a single place. With these considerations, be pleased to accept the assurance of my great esteem and respect.

Th: Jefferson[406]

The attitude of Jefferson on this matter of religion at the University of Virginia has been further discussed in an earlier section [IV, 8, (10)].* Attention is here called specially to his statement on "Freedom of Religion at the University of Virginia," written in 1822, three years earlier than the above letter, and reproduced by O'Neill. It is interesting to note that in spite of Jefferson's attitude the University of Virginia now has on its faculty a "professor of religion," the incumbent for the past decade having been a member of the Church of the Disciples, a Church known for its broad and tolerant spirit.

Section 11. *PUBLIC AND PUBLIC-SCHOOL LIBRARIES*

Before considering Church-State problems that have arisen in connection with modern public libraries, we should perhaps notice the part which the Church played in earlier days in providing libraries in the colonies and the new republic. This part is apt to be overlooked at a time when public libraries are properly considered institutions to be supported mainly by state, county, and municipal funds. It is one of those cases, of which we have found so many in this study, where the Church has started a social-welfare or educational project and has carried it on in the days of small things, only to be superseded in ever-increasing measure by the State with its vastly larger resources.

A few "firsts" where the Church took a leading part are worth quoting.

1638—First library of a public character in the colonies started at Harvard College. This is always considered to be the beginning of the public-library movement in

* See Addenda.

America. Harvard at the time, as chartered by the colonial legislature, "the Great and General Court," was governed by a Board of Overseers made up half of magistrates and half of ministers, and its seals for the college corporation under the charter of 1650 contained the words *In Christi Gloriam,* and under the charter of 1692 *Christo et Ecclesiae.*[407]

1699—The Reverend Thomas Bray (1656–1730), appointed commissary for Maryland by the Bishop of London, begins his important work of providing parish libraries, which proved highly useful in their various communities. He established sixteen of these in Maryland soon after his arrival in 1700, and a few in other colonies, the total number being thirty-nine, some containing more than a thousand volumes, all brought over from England.[408] He proposed and started two influential societies, the Society for Promoting Christian Knowledge, and the Society for Propagating the Gospel in Foreign Parts. Few men in the early part of the eighteenth century did as much to encourage serious reading in America.[409]

1700—The first American library law adopted by the General Assembly of South Carolina. Its purpose is to provide for making a parochial library established by Bray a "provincial library."

1701—A group of ten Congregational ministers in Connecticut take steps to found Yale College. It is believed that their first formal act was meeting in Branford and presenting books for this purpose.

1703—The Reverend Thomas Prince, a Puritan divine of Boston, begins to collect New England manuscripts and documents, the first collection of such material to be brought together in this country. He presented it by will to the Old South Church. Such manuscripts and books as remain are now in the Boston Public Library.

1747—Abraham Redwood (1709–88), an active member of the Society of Friends, unites with others in establishing a society which collected books, and built in 1752 the Redwood Library, in Newport, R.I., the first public library building of its kind in the United States. It is still standing. He gave £500 for the purchase in London of standard works on literature, theology, history, and the sciences.

1763–69—The libraries of Columbia, Brown, Dartmouth, all started on the eve of the Revolution, are typical of those in colleges founded under religious auspices.

1790—Parochial libraries develop rapidly in New England about this time. They are mainly connected with the Congregational societies. President Stiles of Yale tells us in 1794 that lately "a spirit for parochial libraries spread itself in N. E." He adds that these libraries of from one hundred to three hundred volumes include such books as Rollin's *Ancient History,* Bruce's *Travels,* Robertson's *History of America* and *History of Charles V,* Guthrie's or Morse's *Geography,* etc., etc.[410] Writing two decades later, President Timothy Dwight, also of Yale, speaks in high terms of the broadening cultural interests of these "social libraries" both in the Congregational parishes and the towns.[411]

1793–1812—The colleges founded soon after the formation of the new government and mainly by representatives of the religious groups, such as Williams, Bowdoin,

Union, Middlebury, all lay stress on building up libraries. This is also true of the early colleges founded in the West, most of which are due to Church initiative.

1833—The first American free public library supported by public funds comes into being, in Peterborough, New Hampshire, as a result of the efforts of the Reverend Abiel Abbot.

These are just a few notes that indicate that the public in colonial times and in the early days of the republic was accustomed to look to the Church and to groups of philanthropically minded citizens rather than to the state for library facilities.

Of course during these years there were many other important movements leading to public libraries with which the Church had little or nothing to do, such as the starting of the Library Company of Philadelphia, a subscription or shareholding corporation established as a result of efforts by Benjamin Franklin, beginning as early as 1731; and the starting of the Library of Congress in 1800.

In 1838 New York state adopted a law providing for support by taxation for district school libraries; and in 1848 the Massachusetts legislature passed the first act enabling a municipality (Boston) to establish a tax-supported library, amending it three years later to permit any town in the state to do the same.

Thus the public-library movement grew, especially after the great benefactions of Andrew Carnegie (1835–1919); but its beginnings are found in the efforts of the Churches in colonial times and the early days of the republic, more particularly among the Congregationalists of New England and the Anglicans in Maryland, Virginia, and the Carolinas.

The right attitude toward possible conflicts between the Church and a library supported by public funds was defined by a well-known librarian in a paper read before the Library Department of the Religious Education Association in 1905. Dr. George F. Bowerman (1868–), director of the public library of the District of Columbia, speaking on "The Choice of Religious and Theological Books for Public Libraries," said:

> tho recognizing this almost universal religious need and aiming as fully as possible to aid in its satisfaction, the library can in no way be partisan. Since religion today is not a unit, but is manifested under various forms, the library cannot cooperate with the adherents of one form while discriminating against those of another.[412]

Dr. Bowerman goes on to show that in his judgment this policy should not result in excluding books of a scholarly character, and of literary quality, that are outspoken in trying to give the public what their authors believe to be the truth, or in playing up books of a controversial character. He cites several cases to illustrate his position. For instance, he refers to an incident in the Carnegie Library, Pittsburgh:

It is authoritatively reported that on the appearance of Edwin F. Dakin's *Mrs. Eddy; the Biography of a Virginal Mind* [1930], a committee from "the Christian Science church called at the Carnegie Library with a request that it be excluded from the collection." The director "decided that, while consenting to keep the book out of the *Monthly Notes* published by the library and off the shelves that are open to visitors, his duty to the people of Pittsburgh obliged him to carry it in his circulation department, and since that time it has been one of the most sought for of all present-day publications.[413]

The Committee on Publications of the Board of Directors of the First Church of Christ Scientist in Boston (the "Mother Church") was believed to be active in trying to suppress this volume, by working in co-operation with similar committees in the states, and advocating a boycott of bookstores which sold the volume.[414] Their efforts resulted in the book being removed from some public libraries and in others having it placed on the reserve shelves, where it was inaccessible to the general public. Such a book, critical in some ways of the founder of Christian Science and of its tenets, is considered by Christian Scientists to be obnoxious and to come under the provisions of their *Church Manual* to the effect that "A member of the Church shall not patronize a publishing house or bookstore that has for sale obnoxious books"[415]—a rule easily interpreted by loyal adherents of the Church to discourage their using public libraries where books severely critical of their movement may be found.[416] The publishers of the book, Charles Scribner's Sons, were faced with a serious effort to "smother" it as a result of pressure by Christian Scientists to have the book removed from sale by booksellers, and taken out of general circulation in public libraries. In this way the Scientists almost duplicated in intention, but not in success, the experience of twenty years earlier (1909), when Georgine Milmines' biography of Mrs. Eddy, which ran serially in *McClure's Magazine,* was so removed from general circulation as to be today a very rare volume. These efforts of course disregarded the spirit if not the letter of the First Amendment to the Constitution. Cases of friction between public libraries and Christian Scientists still occur occasionally, especially when the Scientists oppose the purchase and circulation of biographies of Mrs. Eddy which give an unfavorable impression of certain aspects of her career. Such incidents followed the publication of Lyman P. Powell's *Mary Baker Eddy* in 1930. Fundamentalists also caused some trouble a few years ago in protesting against scientific books which accepted the Darwinian theory.

Another example of the attempt of some Church interests to interfere with the freedom of a public library is taken from Dr. Bowerman's own experience as director of the public library in the nation's capital:

I have heard that in the case of some libraries attempts have been made by the Catholic interests to keep out books of scholarship at variance with the Catholic position, but I have never been able to verify them. . . . Once, a number of years ago, a Catholic University professor found on a display case a copy of Rénan's *Life of Jesus.* He brought it to my office with the remark that of course the library should have it but that he thought it ought not to be included among books especially recommended. To this I readily agreed. Note the mildness of the request and the reasonableness of the attitude.[417]

A somewhat similar situation is reported from the Rochester, New York, Public Library, where we are informed that the head of the Children's Department wrote to certain publishers, after the library had received a letter from the superintendent of schools in Rochester, objecting to one of the stories in Grimm's *Fairy Tales,* which was in their library collection:

We have been confronted by a problem in Rochester which may be of interest to you. The story of the Jew in the *Bramble-Bush,* which appears in many volumes of Grimm, has given offense to a number of Jews in our city. These objections have come from broad-minded people of culture and refinement who can see no reason why the particular rogue in the story should be a Jew, or why children of today should have a certain inherent racial prejudice which seems to be there fostered by the Fairy Tales which the Schools and Libraries provide for them. . . .

Although we have found no other libraries which have had difficulty with this particular story it has been decided that no more editions of Grimm which include it in this form may be purchased for the schools or in the public library. . . . My purpose in writing to you is to express the hope that at some future time you may see fit to replace the version you are now using of this particular story with some other equally funny but free from the barest possibility of keeping alive any one of our prejudices.

In reply the publishers thanked the writer for her letter and said that

We have examined the story in question and we see no reason for making the man a Jew. We agree with you that he might be an Italian, an Englishman, or a Frenchman. We have, therefore, deleted the word "Jew" as it appears in the story so that in future editions of the book there will be no race indication whatever. The copies of the book now in the trade are, of course, beyond our reach, but we shall have these changes made in all future copies.

Here was another example of the tactful handling of a difficult problem involving Church and State, although there is ground for difference of opinion as to the literary ethics involved in the change referred to.[418] In the regular public libraries in large cities—as distinct from school libraries—few such problems arise, since notable books of every point of view, religious, social, ethical, political, are available.

There is frequently correspondence in the religious papers covering this question, such as a letter in the *Christian Century*[419] from a correspondent in Bismarck, North Dakota, alleging that much more attention is given to displaying the Roman Catholic magazines than Protestant ones. Undoubtedly the opposite difficulty occasionally occurs where a narrow Protestant librarian is in charge. The matter was recently discussed in an article in *The New Republic,* and other cases have come to my attention, especially in Massachusetts.

In general, a wise librarian or library committee known to be objective in the purchase of books has no trouble, especially since it is the practice to have different groups in the community represented on the library board. Everything possible is therefore generally done to purchase important books representing the Protestant, Roman Catholic, and Jewish points of view, and to commemorate sympathetically by suitable exhibits important anniversaries observed by the different denominational groups. The Carnegie report on public libraries in the United States recognizes the fact that "in many library collections books that present the Protestant faith predominate to a degree that invalidates fair proportional balance";[420] a point of view that appears to be corroborated by a recent study of religious books published in *Booklist Books* of the American Library Association (1932–37) and in Wilson's *Standard Catalog for Public Libraries* (1934).[421] When such conditions are brought to the attention of librarians, with constructive recommendation of books of the necessary standard to meet objective tests, the defect is generally promptly remedied either by the purchase of books by the library or the acceptance of a gift of books by some church organization. The latter plan, in whose development the public library at Dubuque, Iowa, has taken a leading part, frequently involves the provision and maintenance of a "Catholic shelf." This is not thought by most librarians to compromise the independence of the library as a public institution, since the agreement provides that the librarian may reject any book thought unsuitable.[422]

A variation of this plan is a co-operative agreement between a public library and a denominational institution for the interchange of books desired by readers. Such an arrangement has been in successful operation in New York state between the White Plains Library and St. Joseph's Seminary (Roman Catholic) in Yonkers.[423]

The question of the version of Bibles to be provided by public libraries occasionally comes up for discussion. Naturally in most parts of the country where only one Bible is provided it is the King James version, because it is accepted by a majority of Americans, and because of its associations with English literature and with the history of this country. It seems reasonable, however, where there are numbers of Roman Catholics or Jews to provide versions satisfactory to them, such as for the Roman Catholics the Douay-Challoner version, or the admirable 1941 revision of the English Bible by a commission appointed by the American hierarchy, and for the Jews the Leeser version. This procedure usually avoids all difficulty. Indeed, all three versions should be available in all public libraries of any importance. It will surprise most people to know how slight are the differences among them.

There has been at least one important case before the courts of the question of the Bible in a library supported by public funds. It arose in connection with the Selma High School in California and was decided by the state supreme court in 1924. The issue arose because the local school board adopted a resolution authorizing the purchase of twelve copies of the King James version for the library of the school. Complainants, who apparently were Roman Catholic sympathizers, brought suit, believing that this action was contrary to the constitution and statutes of the state. The constitution states:

> . . . Nor shall any sectarian or denominational doctrine be taught, or instruction thereon permitted, directly or indirectly, in any of the common schools of the state (Article IX, Section 8).

A state statute published in the *Political Code* made it the duty of boards of education and school trustees

> . . . to exclude from school and school libraries all books, publications or papers of a sectarian, partisan, or denominational character (Section 1607, subdivision 3).

Furthermore, the same code provides that

> No publication of a sectarian, partisan, or denominational character may be used or distributed in any school, or be made a part of any school library; nor must any sectarian or denominational doctrine be taught therein.[424]

This is apparently the first time that the issue of sectarian influence was squarely raised before the highest court of a state in the matter of placing the Bible in a public school library. The court by unanimous decision, held (1) that the King James version of the Bible is not a sectarian book; (2) that neither the constitution nor the statutes would be violated by placing any version of the Bible in a public school library. One section from the opinion is worth quoting here:

> . . . Nor does the fact that the King James version is commonly used by Protestant churches and not by Catholics make its character sectarian. Its character is what it is, a widely accepted translation of the Bible. What we have said of the King James

translation is equally applicable to the Douai version. Both are scholarly translations of the Bible, and neither is a book "of a sectarian character" within the meaning of the statute relating to school libraries. Both are eligible to a place on the shelves of our public school libraries for reference purposes.[425]

Some school systems in California and elsewhere go further and permit, as in Santa Barbara, the Gideon Society, the Christian Commercial Travellers Society of America, which distributes copies of the Bible in hotels, hospitals, and other public institutions, to give Bibles to any public school pupil who may want them. The Bibles are given out under the supervision of the principals.

The most serious case that has recently arisen with reference to school library censorship is connected with the canceling by certain public-school boards in New York, New Jersey, and elsewhere of subscriptions to *The Nation,* because of a series of articles it has published by Paul Blanshard dealing in a critical way with the position taken by the Roman Catholic Church in regard to various matters such as birth control. It is a matter on which much is likely to be heard in the next few years. The New York state education commissioner has supported the school board in its view that it has the right and responsibility of deciding what publications may be included in school libraries.[426]

The American Library Association has seriously discussed ways of preventing religious censorship by groups in public-library boards. It has even considered publishing black lists of librarians yielding to undue pressure. At the annual meeting in 1948 the president of the Association warned his hearers that censorship was destroying intellectual freedom. He asked:

> Should a small religious minority be allowed to keep off the shelves of a library a biography of their founder that does not depict her as they feel she should be depicted? Should copies of *The Nation* ever be removed from library shelves? Should libraries in the South fail to have current books on the race problem or novels on the problem that may be offensive to perhaps even a majority of their constituents? Should witch hunts for subversive books persuade librarians not to stock a book because it is friendly to Russia or a communistic idea? The answer to all these questions is, of course, an emphatic no.[427]

Chapter XIX

THE PROBLEMS OF ADJUSTMENT IN THE CHURCH EDUCATION FIELD

We now turn logically from public, tax-supported, and controlled education to that offered by the Churches as a substitute.

Section 1. THE GENERAL POSITION OF THE STATE TOWARD PRIVATE AND PAROCHIAL SCHOOLS

It is necessary at the outset to have a clear conception of the difference between American public schools—known in England as "board schools"—and private schools. There are borderline cases, such as some early New England academies, a few normal schools, and some Negro colleges and schools originally private foundations which continue with some measure of private support and control, though taken over as public schools by the State or one of its subdivisions. But nonetheless there is in the overwhelming majority of cases a clear line of distinction between the two groups. The major differences are in control and support—that is whether these are public or private.

A Massachusetts court in 1866 defined the term "public" or "common" school as referring, under the legislation of the state, to schools

(1) "supported by general taxation,"
(2) "open to all free of expense,"
(3) "under the immediate control and superintendence of agents appointed by the voters of each town or city."[1]

The inference is that all schools that do not meet this threefold test are not public, and that consequently parochial and other private schools, even though they meet the second test, cannot be considered strictly public institutions, because they are not supported by taxation and are not under public control. This inference seems sound. But Father Gabel takes the position that

> it is neither tax support, nor gratuity of instruction, nor general admission to all pupils of a district or locality or state that differentiates the public from the private institution, but rather ownership, to which may be joined historical origin and control. Private schools are generally "public" in "use" and service.[2]

That parochial schools render a public service, and one for which the people of the United States should feel duly thankful, is freely granted, but this does not make them public institutions in the sense that they should be given public support from taxation. To admit Father Gabel's contention, which is, in general, that of the Roman Catholic Church, would be to overlook a fundamental thesis of democracy, namely, that the people through their own duly chosen agents alone have the right to determine the policy of publicly supported institutions or agencies, be they the Federal Army and Navy, or state forests, or local fire departments, or teachers' colleges, or elementary schools.

It is specially important to maintain this distinction in education, since the State has an inescapable responsibility for the education of youth; and though it does not and should not wish to invade the all-important functions of home and church and private school, it can generally spend tax money for education only through channels that it can control. Otherwise State funds will constitute a grab bag for all sorts of competing groups with different theories and ideals. These theories and ideals, if not inconsistent with the law and public policy, may well be allowed, and if they meet certain criteria encouraged, but the State should not foot the bill. In a word, the State accepts the theory that private schools may, and probably should, exist, but that it has a right to insist that they maintain certain standards and meet certain educational requirements which the State imposes.[3] Here we are concerned exclusively with Church schools carrying on general education. What the Churches do in the way of giving religious and ethical instruction in their regular Sunday or Sabbath Church schools is essentially their own affair as long as the laws of the State are observed in such matters as hygiene and conduct. And it is worth recording that, although in the churches and chapels of most religious bodies educational standards are inclined to be woefully inadequate, statistics for 1941–42 showed 209,963 such schools, with 22,495,047 pupils—a not unimportant group.[4]

Section 2. THE PAROCHIAL SCHOOLS AS SUBSTITUTES FOR PUBLIC SCHOOLS

The only serious problems in Church–State relations as far as Church schools are concerned is provided by the efficient parochial-school system of the Roman Catholic Church, whose purpose and development have already been discussed.[5] The question here is the demand of many of its advocates that it receive financial aid from the State, either directly by a share of the school fund, or indirectly through free bus transportation, free textbooks, or other services for its pupils. These desired forms of aid will be discussed from various points of view in a later section. They can be understood only as we remember that some Roman Catholics openly oppose the public schools on account of their allegedly "godless" character, and many conscientiously criticize them. An extreme example is the book by the Reverend Paul L. Blakely, S.J., *May An American Oppose the Public School?* with the imprimatur of Cardinal Hayes. He favors only schools in which textbooks, teachers, and curriculum are regulated by the Catholic Church, and quotes from the encyclical on education of Pope Pius XI (December 31, 1929) to support his views. The Lutherans, whose parochial school system stands second in importance, do not object to paying taxes for the public schools, and do not wish subsidies for their own schools. But as they give up their foreign language services the tendency is for their parochial schools to decrease in relative significance.[7]

Of other Church groups the Episcopalians and the Friends perhaps have relatively the largest number of denominational schools. The Friends schools are mainly confined to a few states; the Episcopalian, except for a few Negro schools in the South and Indian schools in the Northwest, are mainly private schools for persons who can afford to pay fairly large tuition fees. Outside of the Roman Catholic schools there is today no national system of parochial schools to cause any difficult adjustments in the relations of Church and State. The old system of what were virtually Congregational public schools in New England, and of an extensive Presbyterian parochial-school system, and of public support for various denominational schools in states like New York, has long ago been given up, leaving only a few isolated survivals.[8]

It is in some ways unfortunate that the Federal government has not published any adequate study of parochial schools—using this term to indicate schools conducted under the auspices of some denomination and available without charge, or at a nominal charge, to the members of a given denomination, and sometimes to others, and intended to take the place of the public grade schools. The Bureau of Education published in 1919 a report entitled *The Educational Work of the Church in 1916–1918,* but it is not complete, and in some cases, such as in that of the Lutherans, it is confusing in lumping together the real parochial schools with weekday religious schools—that is, schools giving merely religious instruction. Similarly, in the Federal government's *Biennial Survey of Education* for 1930–32, reports are given from 6,815 private elementary schools, the largest per cent being in the New England states, New York, Pennsylvania, the District of Columbia, and Delaware. In this particular study 96 per cent of the private-school pupils were in Roman Catholic schools, most of which provide virtually gratuitous teaching, while Protestant schools, outside of the Lutheran Church, were mainly pay schools and largely for special groups. The denominations reporting such schools were, in addition to the two groups already named, the Friends, Episcopal, Presbyterian, Methodist, Seventh Day

Adventist, Baptist, and Congregational. This study was far from complete, because many of the private and parochial schools (other than the well-organized parochial schools of the Roman Catholic Church) did not respond to the questionnaire; therefore it seems best not to publish its results in detail.[9] But from this and other studies by the leading religious bodies it appears that about 10 per cent of the children of school age in the United States are in private and parochial as distinct from public schools, and that of this 10 per cent about 90 per cent are in Roman Catholic parochial schools. The failure of the Congress to provide adequate financing for this decennial census of religious bodies, which was due in 1946, has resulted in inadequate official contemporary statistics on this subject. These may, however, be provided from organizational surveys. Recent statistics (1947) of religious or parochial elementary and high schools in the United States show the principal groups to be:

Roman Catholics	2,607,879	pupils	in	10,188	schools
Lutherans*	96,041	"	"	1,296	"
Seventh Day Adventists	35,219	"	"	970	"
Reformed Churches	21,175	"	"	120	"
Mennonites	2,106	"	"	35	"

* These are mainly in the Missouri and Wisconsin synods and the American Lutheran Church.

In each case the number of pupils and schools increased during the preceding decade.[10]

(1) THE ROMAN CATHOLIC SCHOOLS

The beginning of the parochial-school movement goes back to Philadelphia in 1782.[11] Indeed, Pennsylvania seems to have been the only American colony which would have permitted such schools.[12] The Penn tradition of liberalism, and the large immigration from the European continent, including a number of Roman Catholics whose needs had to be met, were responsible for its broader attitude. But the movement for parochial schools became at all general only as a result of the large immigration from Ireland and Catholic parts of Germany from 1820 to 1850.

(a) *The Decisions of Plenary Councils.*—The real development of parochial schools on a national scale goes back to the First Plenary Council of Baltimore, held in 1852, at the time when Catholic immigration was pouring into the country. This council adopted the following decree:

We exhort the bishops, and, in view of the very grave evils which usually result from the defective education of youth, we beseech them through the bowels of the mercy of God, to see that schools be established in connection with all the churches of their dioceses; and, if it be necessary and circumstances permit, to provide, from the revenues of the church to which the school is attached, for the support of competent teachers.[13]

During this period Bishop John Hughes (1797–1864), who was advanced to the archbishopric in 1850, was the most vigorous of Roman Catholic leaders. He bitterly attacked the public-school system. He tried hard, with the support of Governor William H. Seward (1801–72), an Episcopalian, to secure the support of Church schools by the New York legislature. He complained that if this were not done Catholics would be subject to "a second taxation, required not by the laws of the land, but the no less imperious demands of their conscience."[14] When his efforts to secure state support through political action failed he turned his forceful, fighting personality into the movement to build up the parochial-school system.

The Second Plenary Council, held just after the Civil War, was not able to do much more than restate the former decisions. It adopted, however, the following decree:

The best, nay the only remedy that remains, in order to meet these very grave evils and inconveniences, seems to lie in this, that in every diocese schools—each close to the church—should be erected, in which the Catholic youth may be instructed in letters and the noble arts as well as in religion and sound morals.

Following, therefore, in the footsteps of our predecessors, we urgently bid pastors of souls to devote their energy as far as they can to the erection of parochial schools, wherever this is possible. In these schools, carried on under the eyes of the pastors, the dangers which we have just said inhere in the public schools will be avoided; the pupils will be kept free from that indifferentism which is now so rampant; they will learn to walk in the Catholic way, and to bear the yoke of the Lord from their youth.[15]

Efforts were being made in various parts of the country by Roman Catholics to obtain stricter legislation regarding the attendance of their children at parochial schools, and in 1875 the Roman Congregation of the Propaganda, which had jurisdiction in American affairs, issued an "Instruction to the Bishops of the United States concerning the public schools." Since this had been approved and confirmed by the pope it is specially important. After calling attention to what it believed to be the dangers to faith and morals when Catholic children attended public schools as conducted, it included the following statements:

The Sacred Congregation is not unaware that circumstances may be sometimes such as to permit parents conscientiously to send their children to the public schools. Of course they cannot do so without having sufficient cause. Whether there be sufficient cause in any particular case is to be left to the conscience and judgment of the bishop. Generally speaking, such cause will exist where there is no Catholic school in the place, or the one that is there cannot be considered suitable to the condition and circumstances in life of the pupils. . . .

Parents who neglect to give this necessary Christian training and instruction to their children, or who permit them to go to schools in which the ruin of their souls is inevitable, or, finally, who send them to the public school without sufficient cause and without taking the necessary precautions to render the danger of perversion remote, and do so while there is a good and well-equipped Catholic school in the place, or the parents have the means to send them elsewhere to be educated,—that such parents, if obstinate, cannot be absolved, is evident from the moral teaching of the Church.[16]

This "Instruction" formed the basis of action for the Third Plenary Council of Baltimore in 1884, which was the most representative Roman Catholic assembly held in the United States up to that time, attended by eleven archbishops, sixty bishops, and the heads of many seminaries, religious orders, etc. About one-fourth of its decrees dealt with education in one field or another, one of its important acts being the establishment of the Catholic University at Washington.

To shut religion out of the school and to keep it for home and the church [said one decree] is, logically, to train up a generation that will consider religion good for home and the church, but not for the practical business of real life. But a more false and pernicious notion could not be imagined. . . .

Therefore we not only exhort Catholic parents with paternal love but we also command them with all the authority in our power, to procure for their beloved offspring, given to them by God, re-born in Christ in baptism, and destined for heaven, a truly Christian and Catholic education, and to defend and safeguard them from the dangers of an education merely secular during the entire period of childhood and youth; and therefore to send them to parochial schools or others truly Catholic, unless perchance the Ordinary, in a particular case, should judge that it might be permitted otherwise.[17]

The council recognized, however, that in some cases Catholic children would have to attend public schools. It therefore stated:

Since, therefore, for a sufficient cause, approved by the Ordinary, parents may wish to send their children to the public schools, providing the proximate dangers are removed by the necessary cautions, we strictly enjoin that no one, whether bishop or priest,—and this the Pope through the Sacred Congregation expressly forbids—should dare to repel such parents from the sacraments as unworthy, either by threat or act. And much more is this to be understood concerning the children themselves. Wherefore let pastors of souls, while they warn the faithful committed to them of the dangers of these schools, take great care lest, led by an immoderate zeal, they may violate, by word or deed, the most wise counsels and precepts of the Holy See.[18]

The council recognized that it had two objects before it: "To multiply our schools and to perfect them." To show the importance its members gave to the first of these they decreed that

I. Near each church, where it does not yet exist, a parochial school is to be erected within two years from the promulgation of this Council, and is to be maintained *in perpetuum,* unless the bishop, on account of grave difficulties, judge that a postponement be allowed.

II. A priest who, by his grave negligence, prevents the erection of a school within this time, or its maintenance, or who, after repeated admonitions of the bishop, does not attend to the matter, deserves removal from that church.

III. A mission or a parish which so neglects to assist a priest in erecting or maintaining a school, that by reason of this supine negligence the school is rendered impossible, should be reprehended by the bishop and, by the most efficacious and prudent means possible, induced to contribute the necessary support.

IV. All Catholic parents are bound to send their children to the parochial schools, unless either at home or in other Catholic schools they may sufficiently and evidently provide for the Christian education of their children, or unless it be lawful to send them to other schools on account of a sufficient cause, approved by the bishop, and with opportune cautions and remedies. As to what is a Catholic school, it is left to the judgment of the Ordinary to define.[19]

As to the second problem, that of perfecting existing schools, emphasis was laid on such matters as providing teaching of the principles of education to candidates for the priesthood, a closer personal relationship between the local pastor and the school, the conversion of the parish schools into free schools, the requirement of a teaching diploma, won by examination, for all teachers, the naming of school committees in each diocese for visiting schools, and the development of normal schools in certain communities.[20]

These decisions of the first three plenary councils between 1852 and 1884 laid the foundations for the remarkable development of Roman Catholic parochial schools which has since taken place. In general the position of the hierarchy has remained at least theoretically the same; Catholic parents are required to send their children to parochial schools when these are available, unless a dispensation is secured from the bishop. The press frequently contains admonitions to the faithful on the subject. For instance, the bishop of Mobile (Alabama) reissued in the fall of 1942 his annual warning that "the sacraments are to be denied to all parents not sending their children to the Catholic school." The *Catholic Week* reminded the faithful that "no priest of the diocese, be he pastor or curate, can grant this dispensation [of excuse]. It must come only from Bishop Toolen." But, said the *Week,* "if their [parents'] reasons are sufficiently weighty, he will grant the dispensation."[21]

Probably, however, there are many dioceses where these provisions are not strictly observed, and it is known that there are millions of Catholic children in the public schools. The greatest difficulty their parents have to overcome is the argument that the schools are "godless." Even a pope—Pius XII—in an encyclical letter on "True and False Prosperity," addressed to the American Church in 1939 in commemoration of the hierarchy in this country, referred to this matter with solicitation:

> And here we have a complaint to make, although in a most fatherly spirit, about many of the schools in your country. They despise or ignore Christ's Person, and are content to explain the whole of nature and of history without reference to religion, with science and reason for their guides.[22]

The general position of the Church is that parochial schools should receive financial support from government because they are public schools in that they serve the public interest by admitting students irrespective of their religion; that parochial schools by their educational work save the taxpayers much money contributed by the Church for their erection and support; that the sincere Roman Catholic is now in a position of having to pay what he considers "double taxation," when he does not use the public schools; that the First Amendment to the Constitution does not prevent financial aid to religious bodies so long as this is given impartially; that in adopting it Congress had in mind mainly to prevent the establishment of a single Church for the Federal union; that the phrase "separation of Church and State" does not exist in the Constitution or any of its amendments; that the support of religious schools by government, frequent in colonial days and in the early days of the republic, does not and should not involve government control.[23]

(b) *The Attempted Adjustments with Public Education.*—Of the various attempts at compromise between the supporters of parochial and public school education, that sponsored by Archbishop Ireland in Minnesota is the most significant. It is necessary, however, to know about the earlier Lowell and Poughkeepsie experiments in order to understand the more important Faribault plan.

The *Lowell plan*—in force from 1835 to 1852 in this Massachusetts mill town with its large foreign-born population. Here the Roman Catholic parochial schools were supported by public funds, as they had been on a small scale in New York City before 1824. The request of the Reverend Father Conelly for aid from the town for two parochial schools resulted in an agreement, by which the town required

> 1. That the instructors must be examined as to their qualifications by the committee [of the public school board], and receive their appointments from them.

2. That the books, exercises and studies should all be prescribed and regulated by the committee, and that no other whatever should be taught or allowed.
3. That these schools should be placed, as respects the examination, inspection, and general supervision of the committee, on precisely the same footing with the other schools of the town.[24]

The plan seemed to give a good deal of satisfaction locally, but many educators thought it "dangerous" in its unusual tying up of Church and State. At any rate, the wave of Know-Nothingism which swept over the state in the middle of the century doomed it to discontinuance.

The *Poughkeepsie plan* was intended to meet the legal objections to the Lowell plan. The arrangement, which had the formal sanction of the local school board, was in force for a quarter of a century—1873–99. Under this plan, which was copied in several other New York cities, the school board paid a nominal rent for the two local parochial-school buildings, the Roman Catholic nuns continuing as teachers paid from public funds. The common regulations for public schools were continued. The plan worked fairly well, and was discontinued only when the state superintendent of public instruction intervened on the ground of its unconstitutionality—a position supported by the supreme court of the state in a similar case involving a school in Lima a few years later.[25]

Somewhat similar schools were carried on before the Civil War in at least ten states.[26] According to Gabel, they are still in operation in some places,[27] but there must be very few of them, since the plan is definitely contrary to prevalent American public opinion, which has repeatedly shown its opposition to such a formal compact between Church and State, whether Protestants, Roman Catholics, or Mormons are concerned.

The *Faribault plan* is the most important compromise thus far attempted between the American public school and the Roman Catholic Church. It is identified with the name of Archbishop John Ireland (1838–1918), who did so much to bring greater harmony between Catholic tradition and American ideals in the Northwest.[28] He accepted the traditional Catholic doctrine that the education of the child belongs primarily to the parent and the Church, but frankly conceded to the State as an agent the right and duty of imparting instruction as well as the power of compulsory education.

Pointing out that the exclusion of religion from the school-room must lead to religious indifference as a creed in maturer years, and arguing that the interests of the Republic, no less than the preservation of Christianity, necessitated a return to the ideals of religious instruction that obtained in the earlier period of our national existence, he proposed as a solution of the problem the adoption of the denominational system of England and Prussia, or, in lieu of this, the compromise arrangement at Poughkeepsie.[29]

As a result, in 1891 the Catholic schools at Faribault and Stillwater, Minnesota, were practically placed under the control of the public-school boards during the regular school hours, and the members of the religious societies who were engaged as teachers were listed on the payroll as public-school teachers. It was a gentleman's agreement between the pastors and the school boards—a tacit understanding without written agreement. Cardinal James Gibbons (1834–1921) thus described the plan, which was developed with the hearty support of Archbishop Ireland:

> The schools are leased to the State authorities for one year, the contract being renewable at the pleasure of the two parties. The same teachers (Religious of St. Dominic) are retained. After hearing mass in the parish church, the children are marched to school. At 3:30 P.M., at the close of the school hours, the pupils are instructed in their catechism for an hour, and then dismissed. No text-books to which the Archbishop objects are retained. Instead of receiving a precarious and small compensation from the parents, the teachers now receive a salary of $50 a month each from the school authorities. The teachers as well as the pupils are subject to an examination by the school board, and this arrangement has benefitted both teachers and pupils. The schools are now more numerously attended than before.[30]

The Reverend Thomas Bouquillon, D.D. (1840–1902), professor of moral theology at the Catholic University, published in 1891 his much-discussed pamphlet entitled "Education: To Whom Does It Belong?" His theory was that "education belongs to men taken individually and collectively in legitimate association, to the family, to the state, to the Church, to all four together, and not to any one of these four factors separately," and that "education is one of those mixed matters in which many powers concur, and which is to be regulated amicably by the parties interested."[31] Dr. Bouquillon carried out his thesis with relentless logic. He said:

> If the state may coerce parents who neglect the education of their children, so also may it determine a minimum of instruction and make it obligatory. Who admits the former must admit the latter. The consequence seems to us logically necessary, and we are surprised that all do not see it. Consider, when are parents called negligent? Evidently, when they do not give their children a minimum of education. If then you grant the state power over cases of neglect, you at once give it power to define what is the minimum of education, and to exact that minimum by way of prevention and of general precept.[32]
>
> . . . If the state may exact on the part of teachers evidences of capability, on the part of the children a minimum of instruction, if it may punish negligent parents, it follows that it may also prescribe the teaching of this or that branch, the knowledge of which, considering the circumstances, is deemed necessary to the majority of the citizens. No more difficulty in the one case than in the other. Moreover, it is not

needed that we should remark that the state has over all schools the authority of inspection as to hygiene and public morality.[33]

During 1892 the so-called Catholic or Bouquillon controversy was at its height, as the religious press of the day clearly shows. Dr. Bouquillon's views even played an important part in some judicial decisions, as, for instance, in the test case of *The State of Ohio* v. *Rev. Patrick C. K. Francis Quigley, D.D.*, before the state supreme court. In this a Catholic school under the compulsory education law of the state was obliged to furnish the names, ages, and residences of its school children to the public board of education.

Although the Faribault plan was considered by most of its defenders as merely a tentative arrangement, it probably would have worked out fairly well as a practical local experiment had it not been brought into the controversy over Dr. Bouquillon's article. The Congregation of the Propaganda on April 21, 1892, made this decision:

The Decrees of the Baltimore Councils in respect to parochial schools remaining in full force, the agreement entered into by Archbishop Ireland relative to the schools of Faribault and Stillwater, in view of all the circumstances, may be tolerated.[34]

This is known as the *Tolerare Potest* decree, but the proposal was too much of a compromise to be satisfactory either to the State or the Church. In the fall of 1892 Cardinal Francesco Satolli (1839–1910), who was appointed the following year as the first apostolic delegate to the United States, came to represent the Holy See at the Columbian Exposition. He gave much attention to the school question, and was specially commanded by the pope to speak on the subject of Catholic education. He made the following statements as to the Church's attitude:

The Catholic church in general, and especially the Holy See, far from condemning or treating with indifference the public schools, desires rather that, by the joint action of civil and ecclesiastical authorities, there should be public schools in every State, according as the circumstances of the people require, for the cultivation of the useful arts and natural sciences; but the Catholic Church shrinks from those features of public schools which are opposed to the truth of Christianity and to morality; and since, in the interest of society itself, these objectionable features are removable, therefore, not only the bishops, but the citizens at large should labor to remove them, in virtue of their own right and in the cause of morality.[35]

Wherefore, if it be clear that in a given locality, owing to the wiser dispositions of public authorities, or the watchful prudence of school board, teachers and parents, the above named dangers to faith and morals disappear, then it is lawful for Catholic parents to send their children to these schools, to acquire the elements of letters and arts, provided the parents themselves do not neglect their most serious duty, and the pastors of souls put forth every effort, to instruct the children and train them in all that pertains to Catholic worship and life.[36]

. . . It is left to the judgment and the wisdom of the Ordinaries to decide whether, in a certain part of their respective dioceses, a parochial school can be built and kept up in a fitting condition, not inferior to the public schools, taking into consideration the temporal condition of the parents, while graver needs for procuring their spiritual welfare and the decent support of the Church are pressing.[37]

The proposal of Archbishop Satolli, who had become the apostolic delegate to the United States, did not settle the matter. In fact, a settlement was not reached until 1893, when the pope himself in a letter to Cardinal Gibbons said:

In order that, in a matter of so grave importance, there may remain no further room for doubt or for dissension of opinions, as we have already declared in our letter of the 23d of May of last year to our venerable brethren, the Archbishop and the Bishops of the Province of New York, so we again, as far as need be, declare that the decrees which the Baltimore Councils, agreeably to the directions of the Holy See, have enacted concerning parochial schools, and whatever else has been prescribed by the Roman Pontiffs, whether directly or through the Sacred Congregations, concerning the same matter, are to be steadfastly observed.[38]

There are still scattered here and there, especially in states of the Middle West, a few high schools conducted on some compromise plan—that is, public schools where, owing to the dominant Roman Catholic population of the neighborhood, there is a tacit understanding that only Roman Catholic teachers will be employed. Gabel lists Iowa, Illinois, Vermont, North Dakota, Kansas, Kentucky, Minnesota, Michigan, and Ohio as having such schools in 1937. Such informal agreements have, of course, no standing in law, and are open to the same objection that would be raised in a dominantly Protestant community if Roman Catholic teachers, as such, were virtually excluded. In the past decade some of the states named, Michigan for example, have made progress in eliminating this practice. In others, such as New Mexico, as we shall see later,[39] some parochial schools have been taken over with their teachers into the public school system.

This section should not close without record of the fact that many Roman Catholics have defended the public schools and urged their support by their fellow Catholics. There have also been a few who have gone further and advocated the support of public as against parochial schools. Most prominent among these was Father Edward McGlynn (1837–99), who was deposed for his liberalism on various subjects but afterward restored to good standing without recantation. On February 24, 1889, he stated:

If I could reach the mind and the heart of the whole of the American people, I would say: Cherish your public schools; listen not to their enemies, no matter whence they come. Make them as complete and perfect as you can. Show no favor to any rival system. If you will not exercise the right to forbid rival systems altogether, at least do not be guilty of the incredible folly of nursing and fostering, and actually, by appropriations and tax exemptions, encouraging rival systems. The rival systems, as a rule, are promoted by those, who, educated in foreign lands, are but half republican or but half democratic. Never be guilty of the folly of dividing your school fund among the various churches and sects. You, in such a case, would be guilty of destroying one of the greatest and most potent instruments for building up and maintaining one great, free, common nationality.[40]

But this point of view is not the orthodox one in the Church. The generally held Roman Catholic position in the matter of education in public and parochial schools has been well summarized by the late Monsignor John A. Ryan (1869–1945):

. . . As a matter of fact, the State maintains a system of schools which is not completely satisfactory to Catholics, inasmuch as no place is given to morality and religion. Since the Church realizes that the teaching of religion and instruction in the secular branches cannot rightfully or successfully be separated one from the other, she is compelled to maintain her own system of schools for general education as well as for religious instruction.[41]

(c) *The Status, Scope, and Justification Today.*—The education in the parochial schools follows in general the curriculum in the public schools, the main differences being that about 15 per cent of the time is given to religious instruction, and that the Catholic point of view is brought out in the treatment of historical and other subjects, just as the Protestant point of view might be emphasized in a Protestant school. Catholics point with pride to the fact that the overwhelming majority of those who later enter the priesthood have been trained in the parochial schools.

During the last two-thirds of the nineteenth century the weight of the hierarchy was placed behind the parochial-school movement and in favor of securing from the State financial aid for these schools as substitutes for the public schools for Catholic children wherever possible. But two tendencies of a somewhat different character received, as we have seen, support from responsible Catholic sources: some form of compromise with the public schools, in which several experiments were made; and the Bouquillon agitation regarding the right and duty of the State, and not merely of the Church, to provide public education for its children.

An impression of the scope of the educational work carried on in the United

States by the Roman Catholic Church under the general direction of its more than 150 bishops may be gained by a study of the general summary printed in *The Catholic Directory* for 1948 given later in this section. The most important facts for our purposes are that there were 2,198,212 pupils in elementary parochial schools and 320,929 in Catholic public high schools—the latter figure being lower than normal as a result of the War. It should be remembered that the largest relative percentage of Roman Catholic pupils—about 80 per cent of the total—attend the elementary parish schools, and that the relative number attending their own institutions decreases as the grade increases. For instance, a survey made for the Department of Education of the National Catholic Welfare Conference for the scholastic year 1923–24 showed 37,931 Roman Catholics in non-Catholic colleges and universities, that is, about 52 per cent of all the Catholics then in college.[42] This large number is particularly significant when it is realized that under the existing canon law a Roman Catholic student is not expected to attend a non-Catholic institution except with the specific approval of his bishop, who has the authority "to decide under what circumstances and with what safeguards to prevent loss of faith" Catholic children and youth may go to other schools.[43]

It is generally estimated that the number of Roman Catholic pupils in the regular parochial schools is about matched by the number in public tax-supported schools. Statistics show that the number of children in elementary parochial schools has remained about the same during the past two decades.

The entire control of the parochial school system is, of course, clerical, with sisters of scores of different orders playing the largest part in the teaching, and with priests, mostly Jesuits, in charge of most of the Catholic colleges and other institutions of learning. Eighty thousand teaching nuns comprise more than 90 per cent of the teaching force in the American Catholic elementary schools.[44] They do their work with great devotion. A few have received higher training at universities.

There are no exact statistics as to tuition fees, but the National Catholic Welfare Conference reports that their parochial schools, which constitute about 90 per cent of their elementary schools, are mainly supported, as their name implies, by their respective parishes. In some cases tuition is free, but normally a tuition fee of one dollar or one dollar and a half a month is charged. Textbooks are not generally supplied free,[45] except when so provided in some states by legislative act.[46]

The following statistics regarding the Roman Catholic Church in the United States were taken from the 1948 edition of *The Official Catholic Directory*. They will give some idea of the extent of the activities of the Church and the effectiveness of its organization. The major headings have been added by the author. Not all groups of statistics have been included, but only those of most significance from the Church–State standpoint.

Hierarchy and Clergy: Cardinals, 4; archbishops, 21; bishops, 153; abbots, 32; priests, 41,747; brothers, 7,335; sisters, 141,083.
Dioceses and Parishes: Archdioceses, 23; dioceses, 101; parishes, 14,905.
Educational Institutions: Colleges and universities, 221, with 220,226 students: diocesan and parochial high schools, 1,637, with 320,927 students; private high schools, 795, with 185,470 students; elementary parochial schools, 7,724, with 2,198,212 students; private elementary schools, 524, with 76,628 students; public-school pupils attending special religious instruction classes, 1,078,436; total youth under Catholic instruction, 4,138,695; full-time teachers, 101,944—of whom 6,779 are priests; 3,445 brothers; 372 scholastics; 79,952 sisters; 11,396 lay teachers; seminarians, 23,701.
Church Membership and Vital Statistics: Baptisms (in 1947), 1,022,508; converts, 115,214; marriages, 394,593; deaths, 262,991; Catholic population, 26,075,697 of total of 134,336,026.[47]

No statistics of mixed marriages or annulments are given in the "General Summary" from which these figures are taken. The diocesan summaries give marriages, e.g., Mobile, Catholic, 388; mixed, 676; New York, Catholic, 12,006; mixed, 3,213; Toledo, Catholic, 3,130; mixed, 1,046; Trenton, Catholic, 3,373; mixed, 1,016; Washington (D.C.), Catholic, 1,547; mixed, 1,709.

Monsignor Fulton Sheen (1895–), than whom no American Roman Catholic religious thinker and publicist reaches a broader public, in 1938 summarized the extent and significance of the parochial school system in the United States.

> Catholics are taking religion so seriously in reference to our country that, rather than see God perish out of our national life, we conduct 7,950 elementary schools and 2,175 public [high] schools, employing 58,000 and 15,000 teachers respectively. These two schools represent an investment of $750,000,000 for elementary schools, and $575,000,000 for high schools. To keep the system going we spend $58,000,000 a year on elementary schools and $10,000,000 a year on high schools and, figuring on the basis of public school costs, we save the taxpayers of the country $139,600,000 a year. Every cent of this money comes out of the pockets of Catholics, and why? Because we believe that the 2,177,000 children in elementary schools and 285,000 in high schools have a right to know the truth which makes them free. In other words, we take very seriously the Declaration of Independence which derives the rights of man from God.[48]

As to the Catholic argument for public support for parochial schools, I have not seen this better stated than by the Most Reverend Karl J. Alter (1885–),

Bishop of Toledo, Ohio. Writing in February, 1935, on "Does State Aid to Education Mean Union of Church and State?" he expressed the general Roman Catholic point of view. He said in part:

> . . . To support the Church is one thing, but to support the school is something quite different. Furthermore, we have not even asked full support of our educational establishments.
>
> We provide the buildings without cost to the State and also full equipment. We neither ask nor would we in any circumstances accept public money for the teaching of religion. We wish to maintain absolutely our independence of any State funds in this respect. We merely ask that the State help us to teach the secular branches which the State compels all children to study in order to prepare adequately for the duties of citizenship.
>
> In simple truth, to deny to our Catholic people any share in the new program of education support by state and not local taxes is to contradict the fundamental principles of justice in our distinctively American traditions. Even a minority has its rights to just treatment in any well organized civil society. This is particularly the boast of a democracy. But where are the rights of a minority safeguarded under this inequitable system of education which now obtains?[49]
>
> The real question at issue is not that of union of Church and State but the question of equality of treatment before the law of Christian conscience. We are fighting for the rights of Christian education as against the monopoly which a secular minded state has heretofore imposed upon all its citizens. We should reasonably expect to have the loyal support not only of our Catholic fellow citizens but of all friends of religion of any and every denomination, for their rights are equally involved with our own.[50]

But in spite of this authoritative statement there are devout Roman Catholics who question the wisdom of trying to duplicate the public schools outside the larger towns, and many more who believe that parochial schools should continue to be supported entirely by the Churches without attempts to secure financial grants from the public treasury. Such an article as that which appeared in the *Atlantic Monthly* in 1928 by an anonymous Roman Catholic priest is significant. He went so far as to say, "When the American bishops cease their school building crusade and begin the work of developing Christian character, there will be hope for the church in America."[51]

Even more significant is the statement made to me recently by a devoted Roman Catholic who has been mayor of an important American city. He said that he thought it would be wiser, and more in keeping with American traditions, for his Church to give up the attempt to secure public funds for their work, and that he had expressed his views on this subject frankly to members of the hierarchy. One of the best known and most respected priests in this country has also expressed the same conviction in a somewhat different way by saying that, although it be just and equitable for the State to contribute directly to the support of parochial schools, it would be neither civic nor expedient for the Church to urge or to accept such support.

There can be no doubt, I think, that representative Roman Catholics are in increasing numbers coming to realize that it is the part of wisdom to discontinue the agitation for direct aid from public taxation for parochial schools, and to be content, as far as tax help is concerned, with the less vulnerable proposals for indirect aid through certain services, such as free bus transportation and free textbooks (when these are the same as those in use in the public schools). These "liberals" take the ground that their parochial schools might properly, as a matter of equity, have some of the tax money paid by them go to their own schools, which they support independently at large expense, but that it is not advisable to press the issue. They realize that the American tradition of the last hundred years and American public opinion are against the contention of their Church in this matter, and that self-support gives their parochial schools an independence they could not long maintain if they were subsidized by the State. This view will receive strong support by the encouraging outcome of the controversy between Cardinal Spellman and Mrs. Roosevelt in the summer of 1949 (XIX, 10).

There was a time when the Church felt that it alone had the right to teach or supervise the teaching of youth, but that time has nearly passed away with the rise of democracy and the recognized right and duty of the people to fit citizens either directly or through schools approved by them for their duties as defenders of the State. This is why supporters of religious freedom properly lay so much emphasis on the free public-school system and on keeping it independent of control, direct or indirect, by any religious body. These schools are the very bulwarks of democracy; and though the Churches are right in urging that in some entirely Constitutional ways their pupils be exposed to the historical teachings of religion, they cannot be party to any officially approved indoctrination courses. Our citizens live too close to Quebec on the north and Mexico on the south to wish to see in this country either the dividing of the public-school funds, or the attempt by the Roman Catholic Church or any other Church to control education for its own ends. It would be disastrous to American freedom, democracy, and culture. Therefore the American public school must be protected and improved, and while no obstacles should be put in the way of parochial or other denominational schools for those who wish them—whether these be Roman Catholic, Lutheran, Episcopal, Jewish, or other—they must stand on their own merits without any direct government financial aid.

Here are the pros and cons of parochial schools when supported entirely by those that use them or who are specially interested in them, and when observing all state requirements.

Reasons Given for Parochial Schools

They represent the conscientious wishes of a large and important element of the population to advance at much personal sacrifice the cause of religion and education in ways they think best.

They are Constitutional, and the attempt by legislation to interfere with them by requiring practically all youth to attend public schools has been declared by the Supreme Court unconstitutional in the Oregon case.

They save taxpayers large amounts of money that would otherwise have to be expended in supplying extra accommodation in public schools.

They encourage discipline, moral standards, and especially the religious faith of those patronizing them.

Their standards, though differing widely, average about the same as those of the public schools, and the states can, if they will, make and enforce requirements as to teacher standards, health conditions, inclusion of courses in American history and government, etc.

Their teachers on the whole are men and women of character, unselfishness, and devotion who make a life work of their profession—in this latter respect having an advantage over most public-school teachers.

They form a natural early training ground for the priesthood and other religious professions.

They provide a social outlet for the work and interests of the normal parish and a bond among its members.

They have provided a useful transition factor between European and American life, and have helped to keep this country in touch with the main cultural tradition of western Europe.

Reasons Given against Parochial Schools

They separate a large segment of the population from a great American "educational melting pot" in which they could both give and get much of value, and they consequently encourage a cult of "separateness" that is unfortunate. They weaken the public schools by drawing away the educational interests of many citizens from the public schools.

They employ mainly as teachers nuns living in Roman Catholic convents and detached from the main stream of American life, who are trained to look unsympathetically at the Protestant religious viewpoint of most Americans.

They are constantly endeavoring to get financial help from public taxation, a plan which most Americans, following the Supreme Court, believe to be unconstitutional and fraught with grave dangers to our inherited freedoms.

Their teachers are not encouraged by training either to independent thinking or democratic action, being taught that they must teach and do what the Church demands. Their high character is therefore to be balanced against a tendency to narrowness and subserviency.

Their teaching, though loyal to the republic, is consequently apt to be so dominated by theological and ecclesiastical authoritarianism as not to fit pupils adequately to discuss impartially and independently in the classroom the great social and political problems which face the country.

They devote so much time to matters theological, ecclesiastical, and religious, and to old-time disciplinary subjects, as to leave too little time for the modern studies; or to put it another way, they tend to emphasize the European background rather than conditions of present-day America.

They or their superiors object so much to state inspection and standardization that such state laws as exist on this subject are likely to go by default.

They tend to present American history inaccurately. For example, a study of nine high-school texts prepared by Roman Catholic authors for use in their parochial schools showed an overemphasis on Roman Catholic contributions and the minimizing or overlooking of non-Catholic contributions. The net result is a warped understanding of the history of the nation, which reacts unfavorably on Catholic attitudes toward non-Catholics. In one of the texts examined at least a third of the book was devoted to Roman Catholic matters, while no other religious body was mentioned in the section on our national period, though the Church here at the time was relatively small and uninfluential.[52] Probably the regular public-school textbooks occasionally err on the other side, but they are almost never guilty of the systematic minimizing of Roman Catholic influence.

The reasons given above are based on the assumption that parochial schools are not receiving tax aid. If and when such aid is considered these arguments should be taken into account, and furthermore the point made by Mr. Justice Jackson in the New Jersey School Bus case [XIX, 5, (2)] that a Roman Catholic parochial school is not just another school, but is an integral part of the Roman Catholic Church, and therefore any use of public funds for parochial schools would seem to be violation of the principle of the separation of Church and State, as this has been understood in the United States.

I believe that any direct contributions to parochial or other denominational schools by the Federal government, the state, the county, or other local unit is in this country both unconstitutional and unwise, in view of the American tradition and Constitutional provisions. Only one suggested plan seems even remotely possible where a community thinks a taxpayer deserves "relief" from double financial support of a duly incorporated nonpublic school actually attended by one or more of his children and the public-school system. The suggestion is that whereas all citizens, irrespective of religion, must contribute their share of taxes for public schools as vitally important community projects, the parent who thinks he deserves relief might after paying these taxes apply for a small percentage rebate; provided, of course, that the state legislature had passed a law authorizing such procedure, and that the local community specially wished it applied within its limits. This plan however should not be applicable in any case where a parochial or other private school receives any direct public aid, as distinct from free bus transportation or other services to pupils. The proposal is not advocated by the author, but is mentioned as less open to criticism than some plans. Yet it would involve Constitutional and other difficulties.

After surveying the parochial schools in the United States the author is of the opinion that non-Catholic citizens would best give up any attempt to discourage them, and recognize their legitimacy and value in spite of some disadvantages. Non-Catholics should, however, continue their opposition to parochial or other denominational schools receiving any grants of public funds, except as aid may be given to pupils through certain widely recognized auxiliary services, and should insist that parochial schools and all other nonpublic schools should have regular state inspection and should conform to certain legal standards.

In view of the fact that the great majority of public-school teachers are sympathetic with the Christian faith and live lives of Christian unselfishness, and that probably a majority of them are church members, Roman Catholics should give up the attack on public schools as "godless." They should rather devote themselves even more earnestly, in co-operation with citizens of other faiths, to filling in Constitutional ways the large gap caused by the necessary lack of definite religious instruction in the regular public school curriculum.

A word should perhaps be added regarding two educational institutions of national significance to Roman Catholics, the American College in Rome and the Catholic University of America.

The American College in Rome was erected by Pius IX on August 18, 1858, and was made a pontifical institute in 1884. It was under the patronage of the Prefect of the Propaganda, though administered by the American hierarchy, and had as students only Americans recommended by their diocesan bishops.[53] The administration of this college in Europe under the aegis of the Vatican has up to the present created no serious complications with the United States. It is quite as reasonable for American Catholics to go to Rome to study theology at any institution that they may wish, as for Episcopalians to go to Oxford, or Presbyterians to Edinburgh; though, to be sure, the Roman Catholics in Rome are in an institution that is related both to a foreign religious power and to a foreign State.

The case of the Catholic University of America, an institution which has obtained broad recognition and respect, is more questionable from an American standpoint, because its rector is appointed by the pope,* customarily from among three names transmitted by the trustees, and the university is subject to the Sacred Congregation of Seminaries and Universities at Rome.

(d) *The Modern Attempts to Absorb the Parochial Schools into the Public School System.*—In earlier sections we have dealt with attempted adjustments more than half a century ago between the Roman Catholic Church and public education, and later with other and broader attempts to accomplish similar ends made by Archbishop Ireland.[54]

Here we are concerned with the fact that efforts have lately been made in several states not merely to secure, directly or indirectly, a controlling Roman Catholic influence in public schools, but to make arrangements by which a parochial school with its Catholic faculties, religious teachings, and traditions continuing, were taken into the public school system. Two cases of this kind, in Ohio and New Mexico, have recently been brought to public attention, and these may be considered typical of a small group of widely scattered cases in these states, as well as in Michigan, North Dakota, and elsewhere, where either parochial schools have been absorbed in the public-school system, or nuns wearing the garb of their order have been employed in considerable numbers, a practice legally permissible in about one-third of our states.

It will be worth while to consider the first case in some detail,[55] because it is recent and because it shows our Church–State problem in so striking a form that in 1947 the National Education Association called it "probably the most serious school situation now current in the nation." A similar plan to incorporate a parochial school into a public school system was also tried in Missouri, but in 1941 the supreme court of the state stopped it as unconstitutional.

The Ohio situation began to be acute in 1940 when St. Mary Margaret Parochial School in North College Hill, a small suburb of Cincinnati, with its teaching staff of eight nuns, was incorporated into the local public educational system by a board of education in which the Catholics had secured a majority of one. This resulted in leasing the school for $3,500 a year, paid to the archbishop, an amount ultimately increased to $6,000, although the school continued to be

* In 1948 the Vatican announced the establishment of a Washington archbishopric, with the incumbent ex officio rector of the university.

operated on the old parochial lines but with its name changed to the Grace Avenue School. The result was a community split and much ill feeling.

Owing to local indignation at the arrangement, so inconsistent with American public-school traditions and with the Constitutional separation of Church and State, the Catholic candidates were defeated in the election of 1942 and the new board of education terminated the arrangement. For the next four years the parochial school, though receiving no public funds, continued in existence, supported as it had been originally by the Roman Catholics.

The extent to which the Roman Catholic Church went to no avail to retain its new privileges is shown by the letter sent under date of October 30, 1941, by the Rector of St. Mary Margaret Parish, addressed to his parishioners, naming the five candidates for whom he asked them to vote. The closing paragraph is important as showing that a leading objective of the Catholic group—the Citizens School League—was to transfer the support of the parochial school from the parish to public tax funds.

> .If we do not elect the above five candidates we will lose the money paid by the Board of Education to the Sisters as salary; we will lose what can be made on the $3,500.00 as rental for the school; we will lose the $500 paid to the parish by the Sisters as rental for the cottages in which they live; we will lose the privilege of free text books; (formerly you paid four times more than you pay now for work books plus 25¢ for religion course). THE PUPILS OF OUR SCHOOL HAVE LOST NONE OF THE BENEFITS THEY ENJOYED IN THE PREVIOUS YEARS BUT HAVE BEEN GIVEN ADDITIONAL ONES. Children now pay 5 cents to see movies given at the school, whereas they used to pay 10 cents—a saving of 50%. To prevent all these heavy losses, please vote for the above candidates.[50]

In 1945, however, a normal slight non-Catholic majority in the school district of about 7,500 people relaxed its vigilance and lost, the main issue being the incorporation of the school. A strong point was made by the Citizens School League of the fact that under Ohio law a subvention from the state is made according to the number of pupils attending a public school, and that this subvention would be increased by the addition of the parochial school pupils.

Increased tension resulted when it appeared that not only was the parochial-school building to be rented again for public-school purposes, at an increased rental, the church retaining the basement for its own uses, but that an attempt was being made to place it, and to some extent all the other schools in the school district, under Roman Catholic domination. It was this more than the parochial-school incident that stirred up the community. The crisis came over the appointment of new teachers, whose nomination under Ohio law was vested in the superintendent. As he declined to be interfered with in this matter, or to turn over his teacher correspondence file to the board, he was charged with insubordination, and at its meeting in February, 1947, the board voted not to renew his appointment when it expired in July. When this decision was known some 700 students of the schools went on strike; and the situation seemed so serious that the National Education Association investigated, and severely criticized the school board and upheld the exceptionally able superintendent, Dr. William A. Cook (1881–), former professor of education at the University of Cincinnati. The Ohio Education Association blacklisted the school as "an unprofessional place" for teachers to work.

The N.E.A. made an eight-point indictment, including the board's "unwarranted action" in refusing to employ Dr. Cook, its ignoring the protest "of the great majority" of students and teachers, and its conducting "the affairs of the board in such a way that large sections of the community have been divided on religious grounds." As to the continuing character of the school as of the Roman Catholic parochial type, the report stated:

> This school enrolled only Catholic pupils and was taught largely by Catholic Sisters, wearing the garb of their religious order. It was conducted as a sectarian school, but paid for out of public funds. Sectarian religious instruction was given each day as a regular part of the school program. The symbolic decorations of the building were of a sectarian nature. The Sisters were paid from public funds under contract with the local board of education.[57]

The school board met April 15 in a public session, with about a thousand persons reported as attending in the large school gymnasium. The School Improvement Association, which supported the non-Catholic minority, and other citizens offered petitions for the reinstatement of the much respected principal, but the petitions were not considered. This created indignation, which grew still hotter when letters were received from twenty-nine of the thirty-three regular teachers in the schools resigning in protest. In the discussion that followed a fracas broke out that resulted in the arrest of several persons in the protesting minority. The whole situation was so serious that it threatened to spread its ill feeling over a wide area. This tension was reflected in the action of various non-Catholic organizations in the Cincinnati area. For example, the Council of Churches of Greater Cincinnati on April 28, at a meeting largely attended by ministers and laymen, commended the action of certain taxpayers who had brought suit in the Common Pleas Court to recover the money which they felt had been illegally paid from public funds for the rental of the parochial school. Furthermore, it authorized its headquarters committee to oppose the use of public funds "for the establishment and maintenance of sectarian religious schools or the teaching of sectarian religious belief or practice in public schools"; and issued a public statement which said among other things:

The principle of the separation of church and state was established on the basis that any state support, however slight, for any church or religious establishment would lead first to bitter wrangling between the adherents of different religions for tax favors and ultimately to that worst of all tyrannies, religious persecution. As President Madison pointed out in his famous "Memorial Against Religious Assessments," the first step towards church support, direct or indirect, from tax funds is the first step towards a return of the Spanish Inquisition. Recent disorders in North College Hill prove the soundness of the prophecy of bitter feelings when tax support for any church becomes a public issue. We dare not wait to see whether the rest of Madison's prophecy is sound. . . . The principle of separation of church and state is not a worn out slogan to be evaded by legal fiction. It is the keynote of our religious freedom. As such, it is worth protecting. For that reason, we shall support wholeheartedly the move to stop tax support for any church school, in North College Hill or any other place.[58]

Local Lutheran, Methodist, and Presbyterian churches also took similar action. The Presbyterians, through the General Council of the Cincinnati Presbytery, included this statement:

The Roman Catholic clerical program to invade the public school programs in North College Hill must be understood as a local spearhead of a nationwide movement to gain control of and to rule for their own advantage the free public schools of America.[59]

The statement further called attention, per contra, to the clause in the first constitution of the Presbyterian Church in this country adopted by the General Assembly in 1788:

The Presbyterian Church . . . do not wish to see any religious constitution aided by the civil power, further than may be necessary for protection and security, and at the same time be equal and common to all others.

It referred to the efforts of the Roman Catholic Church to gain control of public-school policies in many large cities, like Boston, Buffalo, Cleveland, Chicago, and St. Louis, with resulting deterioration of school conditions as shown by impartial reports. The statement acknowledged that an Ohio law permitted a board of education to lease or rent property where school buildings are inadequate and to hire any qualified teacher. The General Council of the Presbytery called attention, however, to the fact that many Roman Catholics in North College Hill were entirely out of sympathy with the attempt to use this provision for the purpose of allowing their Church to gain control of public schools. It added:

In North College Hill there are teachers who are faithful Roman Catholics in religion who nevertheless support Dr. Cook and oppose the clerical policy because they believe in democracy and in public schools free from sectarian control.[60]

The presbytery called for the defense of our public schools, and opposition to all "clericalism," as distinct from the Catholic faith.

The next important move came on June 17, when, yielding to public opinion at a large mass meeting, the Roman Catholic majority of three board members resigned. The Protestant minority, in the interest of a constructive solution, did the same, thus throwing the administration of the schools into the hands of Probate Judge Chase M. Davies of Cincinnati. After a public hearing, convinced that it was the only just and wise solution, he offered the superintendency again to Dr. Cook for a three-year term and the latter accepted it.

This was followed on November 2 by the election in a vote of about 2,400 to 1,600, of two Protestant members of the school board for the vacancies then to be filled. This was interesting for two reasons: it brought nearly all the voters to the polls, and it showed that though the town was fairly evenly divided between the two major religious groups, a large number of Catholics, believing that the former Catholic members had been wrong in trying to conduct the schools in a way inconsistent with our Constitutional Church–State separation, voted for the Protestant candidates.[61]

Thus the situation was restored to a Constitutional basis in keeping with the American tradition. Judge Davies appointed a new board of education of five members, of whom four were Protestants and one a much respected Catholic who had shown himself a moderate in school matters, who later resigned for reasons not connected with the school situation. At the November elections the members chosen were all Protestants, and for the first time in years a Protestant mayor and city council were chosen.

The incidents described above took place in a small community in the Middle West, but the reverberation was nationwide, since it was felt to be a test case of great significance; especially as Archbishop John T. McNicholas (1877–   ), of Cincinnati, was a national figure in Catholic education, being chairman of the department of education of the National Catholic Welfare Conference. The North College Hill case was undoubtedly influential in the decision of the group that founded "Protestants and Others for Separation of Church and State."[62]

Furthermore, the subject was a major matter of discussion at many educational gatherings; for example, at the eighty-fifth conference of the National Education Association in Cincinnati in the second week of July, 1947. Of special significance was the letter sent by Archbishop McNicholas to be read at each mass in each church in the archdiocese on Sunday, July 6, published in part in the papers the previous evening and in full in the *Catholic Telegraph Register* that Sunday. Besides a strong defense of the released-time program the

section shall be immediately discharged, his certificate to teach school revoked, and be forever barred from receiving any school moneys and employment in the public schools in the state. Provided, that this section shall not be construed to interfere with the use of school buildings for other purposes authorized by the county board after school hours.[65]

In 1947 the legislature declined to permit religious instruction in public schools by religious groups.

The dominant factor in the schools was the local priest, Father Ruppis, supported by Father Bradley, head of the parochial schools of the diocese. There were thirty-six pupils in the school. The standards were certainly not as high as in most parochial schools, though in this case the only public school provided and supported by the community and without its vote was virtually a parochial school.

Matters came to a crisis when, after the people of Dixon had raised $13,000 to build a new grade school where the first five grades could be taught by lay teachers, the county board sent word the day before the school was to open that in this new school a nun would be principal and several sisters teachers. The people protested to the county board of education, which referred them to the state board, which referred them back to the county board. The matter, however, reached the ears of the archbishop of Santa Fé, who wrote the following letter to all who were then teaching school within his archdiocese:

Venerable Religious: In view of the present agitation against Sisters in the public schools and to avert grave future difficulties that could prove disastrous to the continuation of Sisters in the public schools in the state of New Mexico, I request that no religious instruction be given in public-school buildings by the teachers on school days. . . .[66]

This letter is interesting when it is remembered that at the time it was written in 1947 there were 128 Catholic nuns teaching in the public schools. Somewhat similar conditions existed in other towns in New Mexico, such as in Costilla, where the town priest taught in the public high school and the diplomas were given out by the archbishop, the graduation exercises being held in the Roman Catholic church. In connection with this New Mexico situation it should be remembered that the state law said that

no appropriation shall be made for charitable, educational or other benevolent purposes to any person, corporation, association, institution or community not under the absolute control of the state.[67]

The *Christian Century* correspondent who studied the situation stated that more than $50,000 a year has been paid the Church for the educational services of the nuns in Dixon, and that in the state as a whole the annual payments out of school funds aggregated $375,657.60, to 136 nuns, brothers, and priests on the public payroll of the state.[68] The legality of these payments, tested in the Santa Fé district court, came to a decision in October, 1948. The judge declared that he would sign injunctional orders prohibiting 143 nuns and lay brothers from teaching in the public schools of the state, requiring the removal of sixteen public schools held in Roman Catholic buildings, and prohibiting, among other practices, both the teaching of sectarian doctrines in public schools and the payment of public tax funds to teachers in parochial schools.[69]

Further and corroborative information was given in a leaflet issued by the local free school committee in the summer of 1947. Here are two paragraphs:

> Six years ago the Catholic Church assumed control of the public schools in Dixon without the people's consent. Pupils and equipment were moved into Catholic Church property. The school then became known as the St. Joseph public school, but in the diocesan records it is listed as a parochial school. Our school buildings were either sold or abandoned. An expensive WPA-built structure with over $2,000 worth of oak flooring stands today without roofing, its doors are ripped off, windows broken out, the fine hardwood floors buckling from moisture—the result of neglect and vandalism.
>
> Dissatisfaction developed, due to the poor quality of instruction and the religious teachings daily forced on all children during school hours by garbed nuns. They are protected as teachers by the tenure law, if it is legal to hire them at all, which we question, so that after three consecutive years in a school system, it is almost impossible to replace them or remove them. Their salaries paid by state funds go out of the state as tax-exempt money to their mother organization. In our county alone this amounts to approximately $65,000; in the state to over one-fourth of a million dollars a year.[70]

Later, thanks to the initial efforts of this committee and to the later activities of the new national organization known as Protestants and Other Americans United for Separation of Church and State, there was considerable easing of the situation, including the decision by the state school board, formally approved by the diocesan authorities, that only laymen be employed in the new Dixon grade school, that no religious instruction be given during school hours, and that buses would arrive and leave the school on regular schedule.[71] Much more needs to be done, but the progress made in 1947 is an encouraging example of what can be accomplished by an awakened public opinion to protect our American Constitutional Church–State separation. New Mexico, owing to its large Catholic population and early historic association with the Roman Catholic Church, also has some Catholic philanthropic institutions closely related to the state.[72]

The Christian Century of October 12, 1949, states that the Protestant plaintiffs in this New Mexico case have filed an appeal, since a careful study of Judge Hensley's decision convinced the Free Schools Committee that its triumph had been moral rather than legal. According to their complaint ten parochial schools in the state have begun operations this fall in buildings formerly used for public schools, and nuns—though not those specifically excluded—are still teaching in public schools.

There is, however, some evidence that the tables may be turned, at least in part, from criticism of the Catholics to criticism of the Protestants, because suit was also filed in the summer of 1949 in the New Mexico District Court to restrain four teachers from using the public school at Lindrith to spread Protestant sectarian teaching. Those who brought the suit charged that Baptist and Presbyterian publications were used as textbooks in the school.

(2) THE LUTHERAN SCHOOLS

Among the Protestant Churches the one that has most nearly approximated the Roman Catholic parochial-school system is the Lutheran Church. Indeed, it may be considered as in many ways the effective founder of the modern parochial-school system of general education under religious auspices, having adopted it before the Council of Trent. The Catholic Church had developed the external schools conducted by monasteries, episcopal and cathedral schools, guild schools, city schools, and many other useful types of education, but it was the early Lutherans, confronted by their special problems in northern Europe, who most clearly emphasized the parish unit as the basis for humanistic education in addition to religious training. Therefore since Luther's time the parochial school has been a characteristic Lutheran institution.

When the Germans began to settle in the American colonies in considerable numbers during the eighteenth century they always emphasized the schooling of their children. All the German sects, which were particularly strong in Pennsylvania, had their parochial schools, that is, schools including the ordinary branches of education in addition to religion. The ministers were frequently the schoolmasters. Some of the Lutheran leaders, of whom Dr. Henry Melchior Mühlenberg (1711–87) was a conspicuous example, had been students of August Hermann Francke (1663–1727) at the University of Halle and were committed to his church school ideas. By 1750 all the congregations in Pennsylvania but one reported flourishing schools. These developed to such an extent that when the Pennsylvania Assembly in 1796 took steps to introduce free schools the Ministerium of Pennsylvania addressed a petition to it on the subject, fearing that the plan might injure their educational system. By 1820 there were 206 of these parochial schools and eighty-four congregations.[73]

Throughout the first half of the nineteenth century these parochial Lutheran schools were flourishing in the Ministerium of Pennsylvania and that of New York; but the absence of a seminary for the training of teachers, the growth of free public schools, and the gradual substitution of English for German as a language taught in the home, resulted in the decline of the system in the East. The same plan, however, was taken up very actively by the Evangelical Lutheran Synod of Missouri, Ohio, and Other States, established by the Lutherans of Saxon origin who sailed from Bremen in the late fall of 1838. When they reached St. Louis, which was to be their headquarters, a regular parochial school was opened in the basement of the Episcopal Church, now known as Christ Church Cathedral, in which the Lutherans worshipped for a time until the erection of their first church in 1842. These Saxon Lutherans were not the only active Lutherans in the Middle West, since the Pennsylvania Synod in 1838 sent a pastor into Ohio and Indiana. The new synod was formed in 1847; and among its purposes, according to Article III of its constitution, was "The training of teachers. . . . The publication of school books. . . . The furtherance of Christian parochial schools."[74] The first president of the synod, Dr. Carl F. W. Walther (1811–87), stated that "Next to the public ministry the chief means of preserving and spreading our Church is the solicitous promotion of our parochial School system."[75] By 1857 there were 114 schools with 5,561 students. In 1937 this synod had 1,354 parochial schools with 75,726 students and 2,299 teachers, of whom well over a thousand were engaged exclusively in teaching.[76]

Among the achievements of this "Missouri Synod" was the establishment in 1864 of Addison Lutheran Teachers Seminary at Addison, Illinois, in 1912 relocated at River Forest, Illinois, and called Concordia Teachers College. The parochial schools of this synod have been most effective; costing now nearly $3,000,000 a year, or about one-fourth of the total amount raised for home expenses. Most Lutherans belonging to the synod have been students in these schools.

There are certain clearly marked characteristics of the Lutheran school system, such as:

The predominance of men teachers over women. In this the Lutheran system, following the German tradition, is differentiated from the public school system of this country and from the Roman Catholic parochial schools. In 1937 in the Missouri Synod there were 1,307 installed men teachers in contrast to only 347 women.

The long service of regularly installed men teachers. For instance, statistics for 1937 in the Missouri Synod show their average service to be thirty-five years, while that of public-school teachers was only about one-fifth as long.[77]

The great emphasis on thorough Lutheran religious instruction, although otherwise reproducing the main features of the public school curriculum.

The regular instruction in German or one of the Scandinavian or other European languages with which the Church group is connected. This emphasis is declining.

The concentration of responsibility for the parochial school on the parish itself, which elects a committee, of which the pastor is generally chairman, to look after the school.

The thorough preparation of teachers at Lutheran colleges or teachers' seminaries.

The continued success of the Lutheran school movement in the North Central states, and at the same time its decline in the Eastern states, where English has become the dominant language of the home.

The frequent opposition to compromising their denominational convictions by uniting to support weekday schools under united Protestant auspices for the purpose of teaching "a general religion" after regular school hours.[78]

The providing of instruction at low cost, or free, at the expense of the congregation.[79]

The enthusiasm and loyal support of members of the churches, who normally send their children to their schools.

The dependence entirely on self-support and the unwillingness of the Church to ask for any support from public funds. In this respect there is a striking difference between the supporters of the Roman Catholic and the Lutheran schools.

The following action taken by the Missouri Synod in 1890 is suggestive in this connection:

. . . And we most cordially approve of combating with legitimate means such laws as have to the detriment and damage of our parochial schools been enacted in the States of Wisconsin and Illinois during the past year, while on the other hand we, for the same reason, condemn all demands upon the public funds for the erection or maintenance of parochial schools.[80]

That this general position continues to be held is shown by the action of the Albany (N.Y.) District Evangelical Conference in 1938, when the constitutional amendment permitting the legislature to provide free bus transportation for private and parochial school pupils was under consideration. It stated:

The position of all American, as well as Christian, citizens of whatever church body, should be clear and decisive. Parochial or religious schools are private schools, and should ask nothing of public treasuries. It may seem insignificant to divert small sums of public money for denominational or sectarian purposes, but experience has shown that beginnings must be resisted. Once the principle of demanding the clear-cut separation of church and state is surrendered the complete usurpation of public money for religious purposes will be inevitable.[81]

The character and purpose of the Lutheran schools are thus described in one of the standard pedagogical treatises of the denomination:

An Evangelical Lutheran congregational school is formed by the voluntary agreement and resolution of a Lutheran parish, or local church organization, to gather its children of a prescribed age in a place, properly fitted for the purpose, to the end of having them thoroughly instructed, within certain prescribed hours, by a common teacher, chiefly and primarily in the wholesome doctrine of God's Word according to the Lutheran Confessions, and to advance them in true godliness; next, to give them instruction and training, as far as practicable, in such knowledge and accomplishments as are necessary for all men in their civil status.[82]

The Lutheran schools have won their freedom. Their most serious crisis was when the so-called Bennett Law was adopted by the Wisconsin legislature in 1889. This law, which controlled the general school system of the state, and was designed to make all private schools conform to the public-school pattern or to put them out of existence, provided that

No school shall be regarded as a school under this act, unless there shall be taught therein as part of the elementary education of children, reading, writing, Arithmetic, and United States History in the English language.[83]

The Lutherans, who at the time had 380 parochial schools with about 20,000 pupils in Wisconsin, joined the Roman Catholics in protesting vigorously against the law on the ground that it interfered with their religious freedom. In the election of 1892 the party that had passed the law was overwhelmingly defeated, and the law was repealed, a compulsory attendance law being then adopted. This did not interfere with the instruction in the private schools.[84]

It is significant that the statistics of Lutheran parochial schools are included among their parochial statistics, for it is normal for a Lutheran parish of one of the conservative groups to have its parochial school. (By parochial schools we mean schools that are substitutes for the public schools, and not merely Sunday schools or other weekday religious schools.) In the *Lutheran World Almanac* statistics include, under what are called "Congregational Schools," three groups: Sunday schools, parochial schools, and other weekday schools. Colleges and academies are listed independently, not being parochial in character. We are here concerned only with schools of the second group, which look after the full education of children and youth, since they alone have direct bearing on the problem of Church and State.

According to the National Lutheran Council the total number of their parochial schools in 1948 was 1,439. The schools are mainly in the West and are related to conservative congregations, such as those of the "Evangelical Lutheran Synod of Missouri, Ohio, and Other States." This powerful organization, generally known as the Missouri Synod, had 1,204 of these. Though its headquarters are in St. Louis and its principal strength is in the Middle West, it had congregations affiliated with it in districts as widely scattered as the Eastern states and California.[85] It is a very well-organized and effective body, with a strongly conservative background. In 1937 the Church reported that parochial and other schools, other than Sunday schools, had 234,425 students and 8,043 teachers.

The statistics as given include all the branches of the Lutheran Church. Some of them are identified with such special national groups as Danish, Lutheran, Finnish, Slovak, etc., but the dominant note of distinctive Lutheran educational policy in this country has been given by the Missouri synod with its strong German background.

These figures should be supplemented by the fact that the baptized enrollment of the Lutheran churches in the United States when given out in 1937 was 4,533,002.[86]

The figures for 1947 for the two groups in the National Lutheran Council conducting a system of parochial schools show:

The American Lutheran Church, with about 600,000 baptized members, 42 schools, 97 teachers, 3,038 pupils.

The United Lutheran Church in America, with about 1,750,000 members, 3 schools, 9 teachers, 150 pupils.

The Missouri Synod (Evangelical Lutheran Synod of Missouri, Ohio and Other States) with about 1,420,000 members, 1,090 schools, 2,614 teachers, and 82,029 pupils.

In the other Lutheran groups, except for those coming from Northern Europe, parochial schools are scattering.[87]

These figures are illuminating as showing that Lutheran parochial schools continue to play an important part in the churches of the conservative Lutheran Missouri Synod in the Middle West and Northwest, but that in the more liberal churches affiliated with the National Lutheran Council, embracing nearly half the total number of baptized members, the part played by the parochial school is relatively small.

(3) THE PRESBYTERIAN SCHOOLS

It may surprise many readers of these volumes to know that the Presbyterian Church (Old School) made experiments in the middle of the last century with a nation-wide system of parochial schools. At one time it looked as though it might carry out such a plan for its own people on almost as extensive a scale, proportionately, as the Roman Catholic Church has done.

The movement lasted a quarter of a century, beginning about 1845 and ending in 1870. It was due in large measure to the same factors that had produced the Roman Catholic parochial schools, namely, dissatisfaction with the secularization of American public education, and desire to have a thoroughly Christian training in conformity with the tenets of the Church and under the auspices of the Church.

The spirit animating the movement may be seen in the resolutions passed by the Synod of New Jersey in 1845. It feared that the

> race of irreligious and infidel youth, such as may be expected to issue from public schools, deteriorating more and more, with revolving years, will not be fit to sustain our free institutions. In such hands they will first be thrown by anarchy into wild confusion; and then engulfed in one or more military despotisms. . . . Let all the churches of every denomination, in our country, engage in this great enterprise . . . and then citizens . . . may seek an alternative in the law. They may, with a fair prospect of success, apply for a Rule of the State, that every taxpayer, that every man, when he pays his tax for education, may signify to what denomination of Christians it shall be applied. . . . If any should decline exercising their privilege, their money would be entirely at the disposal of the State.[88]

The Presbyterians had been accustomed in Scotland and in Holland to Church-controlled schools, hence it was natural for them to try the plan in the United States.

The General Assembly in 1844 appointed a committee "to consider the expediency of establishing Presbyterian parochial schools" with instructions to report to the next meeting.[89] The report was adopted in 1846 and referred to the Board of Education of the Church. The general plan was still further worked out in a report presented to the General Assembly in 1847, which stated that a parochial plan should in general embrace the following particulars:

> 1. A school under the care of the Session of the Church; 2. Designed for children, say from five to ten or twelve years of age; 3. In which the usual branches of sound elementary education are taught; 4. *With the addition of daily religious instruction from the Bible;* 5. *Under the superintendence of a Christian teacher.*[90]

This assembly went on record to the effect that "Immediate and strenuous exertion should be made, as far as practicable, by every congregation to establish within its bounds one or more primary schools."[91] In the course of the debate on this subject so representative a man as the Reverend Charles Hodge (1797–1878) of the Princeton Theological Seminary stated his belief that parochial schools should receive State support from State funds.[92]

As a result of these efforts, some 264 parochial schools were established under church auspices in twenty-nine states.[93] The largest number were in Pennsylvania, New Jersey, New York, and Indiana. The schools declined for various reasons. Those enumerated by the historian of the movement are: Objection by ministers to the task of teaching; the emphasis deflected from elementary education; lack of interest and effort; lack of financial support; the maturing

American policy for controlling education; the failure of the "Bible in the Schools" controversy to turn the tide; the death of the real leader of the movement, Cortlandt Van Rensselaer, in 1860; and the effects of the Civil War.[94]

It is interesting to note that there were some cases of practical co-operation between Church and State, with the parochial school constituting in effect a unit in the public school system.[95] Furthermore, there were a few places where State aid was secured in small amounts, although the predominance of opinion in the Church was against the effort to secure funds from public sources, the ministers believing that if the Church were not satisfied with the public schools and wished to provide schools of its own it should meet the cost.[96]

(4) THE OTHER PROTESTANT PAROCHIAL SCHOOLS

When we consider Protestant parochial schools we should remember that in colonial times most schools in this country were conducted by some religious denomination, or were academies or other private foundations under self-perpetuating or appointed trustees whose educational objectives were largely religious. Indeed, there is some justification for the assertion that the Connecticut common schools were "Congregational parochial schools"[97] during most of this period. The same might be said of Massachusetts.

The work of the Lutheran parochial schools, discussed earlier in this chapter, has been and is so important that the early schools of the Reformed Church have been somewhat overlooked. These were mostly in New York, New Jersey, and Pennsylvania, where a majority of their churches had Church schools. For instance, in Pennsylvania during the eighteenth century, of 188 Reformed churches, 124 had Church schools.[98] The movement was growing through the century, so that some twenty new schools were opened in its last five years. In a few cases the Lutheran and Reformed Churches in the same community united their educational forces, and after the Revolution there was a tendency in some communities to develop "neighborhood" or "pay schools" in which all the different religious elements came together, but the separate Lutheran and Reformed schools continued in large numbers. The Reformed Church parochial schools were generally discontinued about 1880 with the gradual Americanization of the younger generation. There are probably today not more than a dozen schools where the parochial system still prevails, these being mainly in the Northwest.

In 1934 the Reformed Church in the United States and the Evangelical Synod of North America were united in what is now called the Evangelical and Reformed Church. Here too the parochial schools, which were so common in the early days of immigration from northern and central Europe, have gradually disappeared. The Board of Christian Education of the Church is, however, extremely active in trying to see that all its young people receive adequate religious instruction.[99] A recent pamphlet of the board, after referring to the schools of earlier days, says:

> These parochial schools have since given way to the public schools, but the Church has not surrendered to the State its responsibility for the religious education of its boys and girls and men and women.[100]

They have 550,000 pupils enrolled in Sunday schools.

The Episcopal Church has a large number of important private preparatory schools, but these are mostly institutions for those who can afford the type of education which the English "public schools" provide, in keeping with the Arnold of Rugby tradition. The Church also conducts under the American Church Institute a small group of representative schools for Negroes in the South, but it has nothing at all approximating the extensive Catholic or Lutheran school systems. An effort was made in 1938 to start one in connection with St. John's Church, Bridgeport, Connecticut. It was announced that tuition fees would vary from $100 to $150, according to the grade. The purpose was to provide a public-school education plus emphasis on "the fundamental ethics of Christian living." It seems hardly likely, however, that the Episcopal Church or any other Church not now in the field will try to duplicate on a large scale the public-school system.

This seems the best place to mention the peculiar situation which has arisen in Pennsylvania because of the refusal of a small ultraconservative German Baptist Mennonite sect, the Amish, popularly known for their banning of all buttons on their clothing and their peculiar bowl-shaped haircuts, to allow their children to attend a modern consolidated public school. Their opposition to the erection of this school, which they unsuccessfully contested in the courts, and to the closing of their local one-room schools near Lancaster, Pennsylvania, which they practically controlled, was intense. As a result, they attempted in 1938 to have the legislature authorize a separate school district for their use, where they could have a type of education conformable to their wishes. But the acts proposing to authorize this procedure failed of passage.[101]

These simple people have now purchased one or two of their old discarded schoolhouses, and, having engaged teachers, have a type of school to their liking.[102] In other words, the Amish people have in this case virtually adopted the parochial-school principle.

Sir Michael Sadler of Oxford, one of the most authoritative modern educational authorities, has taken strong ground in favor of permitting the free development of parochial and private schools. In his lectures delivered at Teachers College, Columbia University, in 1930, entitled *The Outlook in Secondary Education,* he stated that

Sooner or later in all countries, governments will have to find a synthesis which will give a place in the national system both to Catholic and to secular schools, and to that great variety of types of schools which lie between those sharp extremes.[103]

This is a statement with which I might agree if "national system" does not mean that all these different groups of nonpublic schools are to be government-controlled and -supported.

(5) THE JEWISH SCHOOLS

The Jews in the United States have been highly appreciative of the opportunities of the American public school system, and the overwhelming majority of Jews have availed themselves of its privileges. They have, however, supplemented this secular education by various forms of Jewish education, some of which go much further than most Protestant groups have gone in providing for adequate background religious instruction. This movement goes back to the early synagogue schools, and to the general Jewish Sunday school, not affiliated with any synagogue, as first established in Philadelphia in 1838; but it has been particularly strong since 1910, when the Bureau of Jewish Education was established in New York. This was the first time that an American Jewish community recognized its responsibilities to provide adequate educational facilities in keeping with Jewish history for its boys and girls. More than twenty-five other Jewish communities have since followed the New York lead by establishing a competent central community agency devoted to Jewish education.[104]

This agency was conceived on a broad plan to advance the religious education of Jewish youth. It had not much sympathy with the one-day-a-week Sunday-school idea, which it thought inadequate, or with the ordinary parochial school that included both secular and religious subjects, which it felt removed the Jewish youth too much from the rank and file of other Americans. It favored a communal school, not affiliated with any one congregation, to provide instruction in Hebrew, the Bible, and Jewish history. The idea was to build largely on the basis of the so-called Talmud Torahs—weekday schools unaffiliated with any specific congregations. There has also been some development of Jewish academies or parochial schools known as *yeshivoth,* the number of which in the period from 1917 to 1939 in New York City increased from five to fifteen with a total of 3,700 pupils. To what extent these schools, which combine, as do the Roman Catholic parochial schools, secular and religious knowledge, will develop is uncertain. But most people do not think that they represent the major tendency of American Judaism.

An effort is being made by the Bureau of Jewish Education in each large community to have all the Jewish schools, whether reform, orthodox, conservative, Yiddishist, parochial, weekday or Sunday, communal or congregational, related in some way to the bureau. This seems to favor the three-day-a-week school of one and one-half to two hours per session, thus providing about five hours a week for transmitting the essentials of Jewish history and Jewish religion. They laid great emphasis on a sufficient knowledge of Hebrew to understand and appreciate the Hebrew Bible and prayer book. It will be noticed that, though the type of religious education favored by the Bureau of Jewish Education provides time for much more thorough religious instruction than do ordinary classes on so-called released time, it does not necessarily interfere with the latter, where conditions do not permit the three-day-a-week school to be established.

In 1936 a thoughtful survey appeared entitled "Twenty-five Years of Jewish Education in the United States." Accepting such education as essentially a process in social adjustment and cultural self-preservation, it claimed about a quarter of the 800,000 Jewish children of school age in schools of their religion. Of these about 100,000 were in 1935 in officially recognized weekday schools (the Talmud Torahs); 3,000 in all-day parochial schools (Jeshibahs); 75,000 in Sunday schools; and the remainder in privately conducted weekday schools. For our purposes the Jeshibah is the most interesting type, since it tries to take the place of the public school with its general education, but religious instruction takes up most of the morning. Some of these schools carry their pupils through the equivalent of high-school grades. Nearly three-fourths of the cost of the instruction is met by tuition fees or membership dues.[105]

Section 3. THE EXEMPTION OF CHURCH–SCHOOL PROPERTY FROM TAXATION

The greatest single help given by the State to the Church in this country, other than sympathetic protection, is exemption from taxation. Such exemption, applied to the schools of all religious denominations alike, stands on an entirely different and far sounder basis than attempts often made by the Roman Catholic Church to secure direct financial help from public funds for their parochial schools.

But since the question of Church-school tax exemption is only part of the larger problem of the exemption of all property used for religious purposes, it will not be discussed at length until we come to the section in which we consider the whole problem of adjustments with the State in matters of Church property.[106] Here suffice it to say that church schools profit to the extent of more than $100,000,000 a year through tax exemptions, but it is generally believed that the State is saved a larger amount both by not having to provide education at its expense for more than 2,500,000[107] students in private and parochial schools, and by avoiding the necessity of caring for a larger number of later delinquents, as a result of the moral and religious instruction these schools give. The financial saving from the latter cannot be determined; that for the former may be roughly estimated by taking the United States Office of Education statistics for 1940, which show that even after the economies due to the depression we were paying more than $2,300,000,000 for more than 25,000,000 pupils enrolled in our public schools, an average of over $90 each.[108]

Section 4. THE DIRECT STATE FINANCIAL AID TO PRIVATE AND PAROCHIAL SCHOOLS

(1) THE GENERAL BACKGROUND OF THE DEBATE

Closely related to exemption from taxation, but much more controversial, is the question of direct State aid to Church schools.

We have discussed the struggle in the first half century of the republic to develop an adequate system of tax-supported schools free from all denominational ties or instruction,[109] and the factors which led to the development of parochial schools.[110] These were mainly the desire to give the children of Roman Catholics, especially the large number of Irish who arrived in the second quarter of the nineteenth century, the thorough training in religious faith and practice impossible in the public schools, and the objection to the reading of the King James version of the Bible at the beginning of school exercises.[111]

There has been and still is considerable opposition by Roman Catholics in the United States to being called upon to support two systems of education—the public schools maintained by the State, and the parochial schools maintained by the parish or other Church unit. Their feeling, which has been strongly expressed in the past and still has many ardent advocates, is that since their schools, to which they contribute generously, are open to public inspection and provide instruction free or practically so, they should be exempt from paying taxes to support the so-called "public" or "free common schools," or else receive State grants in aid of their parochial schools. They take the position that, whereas the modern public-school system of the United States, which derived much of its inspiration from Prussia, though fairly well adapted if adequately supplemented by Church or home to train citizens as such, is prevented by its secularity from meeting the higher spiritual needs of youth. Indeed, to the Catholic the civil government cannot truly educate youth in the full and deeper meaning of the term, because all such education will be inadequate except when it is under the direction and control of the Church or of those committed to the viewpoint of the Church.

There have been three groups in the Roman Catholic Church with reference to aid from tax funds for parochial schools. The first and largest group, represented in general by the hierarchy and priesthood, and most of the laity, believes that such grants are legitimate and strongly favors them; the second, represented by a small group of liberals, recognizes that such grants are probably unconstitutional federally under recent opinions of the Supreme Court, and that they are definitely unconstitutional under the constitutions or statutes of most of the states; the third group, also a small but thoughtful one, holds a somewhat intermediate position, believing that such grants are legitimate and that there are some precedents in American history for them, but that it is unwise to press the issue at this time because of the strong public opinion among nonCatholic citizens against financial grants from tax funds to any schools conducted by religious bodies.

On the other hand, the general feeling of non-Catholics is that the State should tax all its citizens for the support of public education, and that if any Church wishes to provide additional schools of its own it is entitled to do so but entirely at its own expense. This is a costly matter when large numbers in many centers are involved. Indeed, the Roman Catholics, in spite of their devotion to their Church, probably would not be able to meet the expense were it not that they can make use of a celibate clergy of various orders, lay and clerical, and of many nuns who are increasingly receiving special training for such work.

The question of financial aid to parochial schools has created much friction in some parts of the country, especially in large urban centers where Roman Catholics have a well-developed parochial-school system and consequently do not wish to be heavily taxed for public schools; and among Protestants in some places where there has been Roman Catholic opposition to the development at the expense of taxpayers of adequate public-school facilities. The Roman Catholic Church feels that the exclusion of religion from the public schools supported by taxation is so serious a matter that where parochial schools are provided it puts pressure upon its members to attend them.

It must be remembered that the omission of religious instruction from the public-school curriculum was not due originally to any opposition to religion, but merely to the desire on the part of the public to keep all sectarian teaching out of tax-supported schools. Non-Catholic citizens are practically united in their conviction that in order to maintain the entire separation of Church and State there should be no direct grants from public taxation in favor of those groups, mainly Roman Catholic and Lutheran, wishing parochial schools of their own. And as a matter of fact, the only case I have noticed in the past hundred years where an American state, as distinct from a few localities, has officially acted otherwise than in accordance with this basic conviction was in California, where in 1851, a year after joining the union, a school tax was levied from which parochial schools profited in the same way as public schools. But the law was repealed in 1855. There have been and still are a few isolated cases where for special reasons a parochial school receives some public aid, or where a public school has been virtually handed over to the Church to provide agreed-upon educational facilities; but these have generally been in disregard of the letter and spirit of the law, rather than because of specific legal provision.

(2) THE GROWTH OF OPPOSITION TO STATE AID TO DENOMINATIONAL SCHOOLS

The attempt to prevent state appropriations to denominational schools goes back to James Madison in his fight against the Assessment Bill in Virginia, and his *Remonstrance* [IV, 8(11); V, 3(5)]. This had its repercussions in other states, and doubtless had some influence on the broad wording of what is now the first clause of the Bill of Rights. Connecticut seems to have been the first state to put into a constitution a specific provision against grants to denominational schools. The constitution of 1818 included this important statement, which was repeated in letter or spirit in the constitutional or statutory requirements of nearly all the states:

> . . . no law shall ever be made authorizing such [school] funds to be devoted to any other use than the encouragement and support of public or common schools among the several school societies, as justice and equity shall require.

Father Parsons, who quotes this statement, says that he believes "this is the first time that the term 'public school' is used to denominate a school not under church auspices."[112]

The most notable issue that arose in the matter of State aid to parochial schools in the first half century of the republic was that in New York in the

1840's, when, under the leadership of Archbishop Hughes,[113] the Roman Catholic Church tried to secure the legalization of the appropriation of public money for sectarian schools. The matter went so far that a Roman Catholic ticket was placed in the field in the state elections. The controversy was settled by an act of the New York state legislature, April 11, 1842, which provides that

> No school shall be entitled to, or receive, any portion of the school moneys, in which the religious doctrines or tenets of any particular Christian or other religious sect shall be taught, inculcated, or practiced, or in which any book or books containing compositions favorable or prejudicial to the particular doctrines or tenets of any sect shall be used.[114]

The movement that led to constitutional action by the states to prevent the grant of public money to sectarian institutions reached a head in the decades immediately following 1850. Up to that time in many of the older states of the East it had been the custom to give grants, considerable in their total amount, to Protestant and Roman Catholic institutions, where for special historical or local reasons it seemed proper. Even New York state gave largely, especially to orphanages and reformatory institutions,[115] and in 1853 Episcopalians, Methodists, Baptists, and Roman Catholics all applied for appropriations from the school fund of the state. As late as 1894 a bill was introduced into the state legislature by the Honorable Michael C. Murphy which proposed that

> The schools established and maintained by the New York Catholic Protectory shall participate in the distribution of common school funds, in the same manner and degree as the common schools of the City and County of New York.[116]

But such proposals were doomed to failure; for all over the country the movement against sectarian appropriations from public funds, which got well under way about a third of a century earlier, was taking form in constitutional provisions designed to maintain the separation of Church and State contemplated by the Bills of Rights. For instance, Kansas in 1858, in revising its "Lecompton Constitution" of the previous year, added a provision to the effect that "No religious sect or sects shall ever have any right to, or control of, any part of the school funds of this State."[117] This early provision against sectarian appropriations, extended in 1859 to include university funds, is interesting because Kansas was in the throes of being admitted to statehood, a process not legally completed until 1861.

Louisiana in 1864 provided in its new constitution that "No appropriation shall be made by the legislature for the support of any private school or institution of learning whatever. . . ."[118]

Similarly, Illinois in 1870, when revising its constitution of 1848, made for the first time adequate legislative provision for public education. This revision ushered in the most active period of state enactments against appropriations from public funds to Church schools. Some twelve[119] states took action on this matter within a short time. For example, Article VIII of the new Illinois constitution was devoted to it. This contains the following provision against public financial aid to any sectarian institution:

> Neither the General Assembly, nor any county, city, town, township, school district, or other public corporation, shall ever make any appropriation, or pay from any pubic fund whatever, anything in aid of any church or sectarian purpose, or to help support or sustain any school, academy, seminary, college, university or other literary or scientific institution, controlled by any church or sectarian denomination whatever; nor shall any grant or donation of land, money or other personal property, ever be made by the state, or any such public corporation, to any church or for any sectarian purpose.[120]

The state supreme court, interpreting this article in 1888, went so far as to decline to authorize a payment to certain Roman Catholic institutions caring for 200 dependent girls, pending the completion of a state school for this purpose.

Such constitutional provisions and judicial interpretations are frequently found in the last quarter of the nineteenth century. Honorable Elihu Root, later secretary of state, and one of the most eminent of American lawyers, stated in 1894 in proposing the specific prohibition by the state of New York against the use of public funds for sectarian education,

> It is not a question of religion, or of creed, or of party; it is a question of declaring and maintaining the great American principle of eternal separation between Church and State.

This was effectively quoted by Mr. Justice Frankfurter in his concurring opinion in the Supreme Court case of *McCollum* v. *Board of Education* in 1948.[121]

The New York constitution of this period may be taken as representing the general attitude of American states:

> Neither the State nor any subdivision thereof, shall use its property or credit or any public money, or authorize or permit either to be used, directly or indirectly, in aid or maintenance, other than for examination or inspection, of any school or institution of learning wholly or in part under the control or direction of any religious denomination, or in which any denominational tenet or doctrine is taught.[122]

The revised constitution of 1938 permitting free bus transportation for children "to or from any school or institution of learning," not being a grant to schools, as such, but entirely to their pupils, has not been considered by the courts to contravene this provision.[123]

Pennsylvania in its new constitution of 1873, supplanting that of 1838, included the provision that "No money raised for the support of the public schools of the Commonwealth shall be appropriated to or used for the support of any sectarian school."[124]

New Hampshire also in its constitution as revised in 1877 inserted after the old provision for the public support of education the clause, *"Provided, nevertheless,* that no money raised by taxation shall ever be granted or applied for the use of the schools or institutions of any religious sect or denomination."[125]

And so the movement to prevent State aid to parochial and other denominational schools continued vigorously through the 'seventies and 'eighties. By the close of the century few states continued to give any direct aid to private or denominational schools. The principal exceptions were some old foundations of the academy type, which are today virtually undenominational. Grants to such schools in Maine in 1931 amounted to $105,000.[126] The movement was stimulated by the discussions in Congress of President Grant's proposal in 1875 for an amendment to the Federal Constitution which would forbid such aid.[127] The Evangelical Alliance[128] was specially active in this movement. It issued an appeal to the American people, December 22, 1888, in which it said:

> It is hardly necessary to repeat the declaration so often made by this Alliance and recently announced at the National Christian Conference at Washington, that while it must resist as American citizens and Christians all attacks upon our public schools or any of our institutions by a foreign power that has no sympathy with our advance as a Republic, we have no feeling but that of kindly regard for the American Roman Catholics who as American citizens, in good faith renounce all allegiance to a foreign potentate; who regard our common schools as essential to the common welfare, and especially to that of their own children; and some of whom have set the noblest example to the American people in their determined resistance to ecclesiastical encroachments upon religious freedom.[129]

Since then there has been increasing appreciation by the Roman Catholic Church of the value of democracy; and it is not true today that the Church as represented in the papacy has "no sympathy with our advance as a Republic." We have in general, and in spite of some reactionary sentiment, gone back to the earlier tradition identified with the honored name of Archbishop Carroll[130] in the formative days of the nation, which was temporarily weakened during the stress and strain of the second and third quarters of the last century because of the large new immigrant Roman Catholic population from Europe.

Most Protestants feel strongly on the subject today, but they would word their protest somewhat differently from that of the Evangelical Alliance. They would recognize the important contribution to education and citizenship made by the Roman Catholic parochial schools. But they do insist that, in accordance with the principle of Church and State separation carried out fully by the Lutherans and other smaller Protestant groups maintaining parochial schools at their own expense, no Church group should either ask or be granted public funds. It is believed that any other policy is sure in the end to compromise the independence of the Churches, including the Roman Catholic Church. This was the attitude of President Theodore Roosevelt (1858–1919) when in the New York legislature from 1882 to 1884 he opposed consistently all such appropriations to definitely Catholic or Protestant institutions on the ground that they were unconstitutional, and that religion and politics ought to be kept apart.[131] This has been the point of view, indeed the conviction, of the great majority of American statesmen.

A fair and temperate statement of the Protestant position was made by the Reverend David H. Greer (1844–1919), Episcopalian, later bishop of New York, in addressing the Alliance the year after it issued its appeal.

> . . . My point just now is this: that the public schools of this country being the creations of the state, which is itself secular, must be of a secular character, and that this secular character must not be tampered with or encroached upon by any religious body, Catholic or Protestant, on any ground or pretext whatsoever. They are for all creeds and for no creed, for Catholic, Protestant and Agnostic. They are for all nationalities, native-born and foreign, for the Irish, German, and Italian, as well as for the American child, and this impartial, secular and comprehensive character of the public schools is the only one which can be in this country consistently and safely maintained. . . .[132]
>
> As Christian people we believe that the social life of the country must be quickened and sanctified by the power of the Christian religion; that the children of the country must receive a Christian nurture; that the people of the country must be established in Christian character, and that the spirit of Christian righteousness must permeate all our affairs: and yet to do this great and needed work, the state, in this country, will not and cannot give us any assistance. . . .[133]
>
> Such then is the relation of the Christian church to civil society and political life in America,—something like the relation which existed between the Christian church and civil society in apostolic times, and never before since apostolic times, I think, did the evangelization of human society depend so entirely upon the unaided efforts of the Christian church as it does in this country to-day. . . .[134]
>
> Here the Christian faith must commend itself to the people as it did in apostolic days, by what it can show itself to be worth, and by the fruits which it can bring forth, and by nothing else. . . .[135]

The Federal Council of Churches has been slow in formulating a definite policy on state aid to schools, public and private, which would take into account recent Supreme Court decisions. But on September 20, 1949, its executive committee issued a clear statement favoring the reservation of public money for strictly public schools as far as general support is concerned. After approving Federal aid to public schools to secure "a national minimum of educational opportunity for all the children in all the public schools of all the states," the statement continues:

We believe that the sound and practicable way out of the legislative stalemate would be to treat aid to schools and the supplying of welfare services to children as separate projects. Each should be decided on its own merits. In accordance with previous statements of the council, we urge that prompt provision be made for federal aid for the maintenance of public schools, with assurance that in its administration there be no discrimination on account of race. We further urge that, as a separate matter unconnected with grants for schools, open-minded consideration be given by Congress to the need of all children of school age for certain welfare services. We believe that if federal aid is made available for such services, they should be administered or supervised by a public agency. By thus drawing a clear distinction between aid to schools and welfare services to children, we believe that necessary assistance can be given to education without making it the object of sectarian controversy or compromising the principle of separation of church and state, for which the council has always stood.

This would exclude parochial schools from direct financial aid from government, but would permit the matter of auxiliary aid to parochial school children to be debated and decided on its merits.

The fact that over the border in Canada separate schools for Roman Catholics and for Protestants and Jews are provided from public funds in most of the provinces has kept the issue much to the fore in certain Northern states with a large urban Roman Catholic population and with forceful bishops supporting the plan. One typical example may be quoted. The question was a political issue in 1933–34 in Ohio, where some Roman Catholic bishops went so far as to advise opposition to legislative candidates who did not favor state aid to parochial schools. After prolonged debate the legislature declined by a small margin, in spite of strong pressure, to "divide the fund" by granting public aid to parochial schools.[136] It was stated that the parochial schools of the state had been educating about 179,000 pupils and saving the taxpayers annually the equivalent of $15,000,000.

The Catholic argument was substantially this: no claim was made for any public school money, whether taken from the school fund or raised by taxation, or for money paid by any Lutheran or Methodist or infidel, or for any state aid in the teaching of religion, but simply for a small portion, not the whole amount, of public money paid by Catholics for the secular education imparted in parochial schools. Catholics paid one sixth of the taxes but as they were educating 16 per cent of the children of the state at an expense of over $17,000,000, besides paying regular taxes for public schools, they were already sustaining a double burden.[137]

Gabel further quotes with approval the view of those Roman Catholics who feel that by the compulsory education law the State virtually penalizes some of its citizens for maintaining their obligation of conscience. It is claimed that this is the equivalent for Catholics of paying a fine for not sending their children to the public schools.[138] Stress was laid on the emergency due to the depression, and that consequently it was necessary to continue all free tuition schools,[139] including of course all parochial schools.[140]*

(3) THE PRESENT STATUS OF THE MOVEMENT TO SECURE STATE AID FOR PAROCHIAL SCHOOLS

Fortunately the campaign for government aid for parochial schools is now generally conducted in an open way; there is no attempt to hide its purpose. Father Gabel's book *Public Funds for Church and Private Schools,* to which we are greatly indebted, is a frank statement of the facts that show the desire of the Roman Catholic Church for State financial aid. In recent years such proposals have encountered increased public opposition, and there are signs that the objections to them are realized by some leading ecclesiastics and parochial school leaders,[141] at least from the standpoint of the interest of the Church in the face of present public opinion. Furthermore, the improved financial status of the Irish majority group makes the problem of self-support somewhat less onerous, though this advantage is matched by rising costs.

An official utterance on the subject was made by the National Catholic Welfare Conference on November 8, 1940.

> The department of superintendents of the National Catholic Educational Association, at its annual meeting at the Catholic University of America here, today recommended that the Catholic school authorities "continue their efforts to secure for Catholic school pupils a just share of the funds which are annually expended by the federal government and the individual states and subdivisions thereof for the support of education in the United States."[142]

It is noticeable that this does not specifically refer to direct aid to parochial schools. The resolution was probably worded in this way to prevent controversy within and without the Church. But there is no denial by the Roman Catholic Church that public funds are occasionally sought, and applied to parochial schools, for such procedure has been in its judgment Constitutional and proper. For example the Jesuit weekly, *America,* recently stated that "public funds are

* See Addenda.

actually being allocated, in no less than 350 instances, to American parochial schools today."[143] But that was in 1947, before the McCollum decision and the interchange of letters between Cardinal Spellman and Mrs. Roosevelt (XIX, 10).

The problem from the standpoint of the Roman Catholic Church has two aspects—Federal and state.

From 1945 on the hierarchy increasingly attempted to get direct aid from increased Federal appropriations for general school purposes, taking the ground that parochial schools meeting the state tests of educational fitness should not be excluded. Some of the bills proposed here carried a proviso, however, that such aid is only possible where states specifically permit it; others like that introduced by Senator Aiken in the 79th Congress contained devices for direct payment to private and parochial schools which, if enacted, would have made it possible to by-pass state laws on this subject. These attempts, vigorously opposed by the National Education Association, although having solid Roman Catholic support and much other support in urban constituencies with many Roman Catholics, are likely, in view of the dicta of the Supreme Court in the Everson and the McCollum cases, to be thrown out by the courts, if adopted. This is true of the provision of direct aid but would probably not apply to indirect aid in the way of school buses, nonreligious textbooks used also by the public schools of a state, and health services.

From the standpoint of state aid the problem is even more complicated, as a large majority of states forbid state aid to denominational or parochial schools either by constitutional provision or statute, and public opinion is very much awake on this subject.

In cases where the question of direct state financial aid to parochial schools has come before the courts the decisions have been almost uniformly against the constitutionality of such proposals. An important recent decision of this character was that of the Supreme Court of Missouri in the May term, 1941. It had to do with a school in the town of Meta in that state established and well conducted as a parochial school under the direction of the parish priests, the teachers being members of the Sisters of the Most Precious Blood. The school adjoined the parish church and included a chapel. It was taken a few years previously into the state public-school system and supported by public funds, the only important change in its conduct being that the textbooks and course of study prescribed by the state superintendent were adopted.

It was continued as the St. Cecilia School, the three schoolrooms being rented from the parish priest by the school board. Sisters of the same religious order were engaged and paid by the board and constituted the teaching staff. There was no serious difficulty until 1913. Then a controversy arose, mostly among Catholics, as to the administration of the school, which continued to be conducted to all intents and purposes as a Catholic parochial school, the pupils going to the Catholic church for mass and being given religious instruction based on the catechism and an approved Catholic version of the Bible. In addition, on one or two days of the week the parish priest was accustomed to give religious instruction, and on Friday afternoons the pupils were regularly marched to the church for confession. As accessories to the religious instruction the schoolroom had pictures and symbols of the Roman Catholic faith, with holy-water fonts at the doors. The children were practically all Catholics, although occasionally one or two Protestants were enrolled.

The school board maintained a school for the second grade in the same town, attended entirely by Protestant children. The plaintiffs contended that the members of the school board, who were the defendants, were maintaining a parochial school at public expense contrary to the Constitution. They asked that the board be enjoined from using public funds in support of a parochial school, in employing as teachers persons garbed in the habiliments of a religious order, etc.

The school board issued a general denial. The chancellor of the state investigated, enjoined the use of religious textbooks and accessories, but did not prohibit the teaching of sectarian religion except by the parish priest within the school building. He did not enjoin the maintenance of a sectarian school by public officials at public expense. The plaintiffs then appealed this decision and received a unanimous verdict in their favor from the court. The opinion breathed a fine spirit of toleration, and of appreciation of the services of the parochial school system and of the Catholic Church generally, but it decided that

> the inclusion of the St. Cecilia School in the public-school system and its maintenance as a part of an adjunct to the parish church in its religious teaching and where children of every faith may be compelled to attend and have attended, constitutes a denial of our guaranty of religious freedom. . . .[144]

The opinion also took the ground that the virtual segregation of Catholic from non-Catholic children and their mandatory attendance at one or the other of the two grade schools according to their religion "constitutes a denial of complete religious freedom." The opinion quoted the clear statements in the constitution of the state against the aid from public funds of "any church, sect or denomination of religion, or in aid of any priest, preacher, minister or teacher thereof, as such," as well as another article which provided that

> Neither the General Assembly nor any corporation, shall ever make an appropriation or pay from any public fund whatever, anything in aid of any religious creed, church or sectarian purpose, or to help to support or sustain any private or public school, acad-

emy, seminary, college, university or other institution of learning controlled by any religious creed, church or sectarian denomination whatever; nor shall any grant or donation of personal property or real estate ever be made by the State, county, city, town or other municipal corporation, for any religious creed, church or sectarian purpose whatever.[145]

After full and generous recognition of the need of more religious instruction, the opinion continued:

Nevertheless, the question confronting us is one only of law; of upholding our Constitution as it is written which, as lawyers and judges, we have dedicated our professional life to do. The constitutional policy of our States has decreed the absolute separation of church and state, not only in governmental matters, but in educational ones as well. Public money, coming from taxpayers of every denomination, may not be used for the help of any religious sect in education, or otherwise. . . .[146]

In the opinion of the court: "The members of the school board have unintentionally but unquestionably violated our constitutional provisions in the respects noted."[147] As a result, the case was remanded to the chancellor with directions to give the plaintiffs relief in accordance with the views expressed in this opinion, which was written by the Honorable James Marsh Douglas (1896–).[148]

Exceptions to the ruling against the appropriation of state funds for private and sectarian schools have been made for special reasons by Pennsylvania and Maryland for some universities and colleges in their states. Maine has also given funds from the public treasury to certain old-established and partly endowed schools of the academy type, including some of a somewhat sectarian character.[149]

There are also decisions in one or two states which have permitted sectarian and private schools connected with orphan asylums to receive state aid,[150] and though the Congress of the United States declared in 1897 that it was "the settled policy of the government to hereafter make no appropriation whatever for education in any sectarian school,"[151] it has continued to draw on the income of certain "treaty" and "trust" funds held for the Indians for sectarian school purposes. The Supreme Court decided that this was not unconstitutional, since these are "the only moneys that the Indians can lay claim to as a matter of right; the only sums on which they are entitled to rely as theirs for education."[152] This has disposed of a very controversial matter.[153] The question of Federal aid to Church schools is discussed in a later section.[154]

A very interesting case where state aid was actually granted occurred in Vincennes, Indiana, from 1933 to 1937. The school board of the city paid during this period the operating expenses, including salaries of the teaching nuns, of three former parochial schools. The alleged cause of this unusual action was the fact that the Church authorities stated that they would be obliged to close the schools unless they could be supported by public money. *The Christian Century* in reporting the case says that there is "no convincing evidence that the whole affair was not conducted in good faith on both sides." The matter came before the supreme court of the state on a taxpayers' suit, their charge being that the closing of the parochial schools was not necessary but was merely for the purpose of transferring the support of the schools from the Church to the public. The court in 1940 confirmed the verdict of a lower court, whose effect was to sustain the legality of the action of the school board on the ground that public schools were actually conducted in the former buildings of parochial schools to meet an emergency. It is understood that the schools have now been returned to their original status. *The Christian Century* thus sums up the conditions which existed while the arrangement was in force:

Basic facts upon which the parties to the suit seem to have been in agreement are these: religious instruction was not given during school hours but was given before or after; the nuns, who continued to occupy their positions, were properly certificated as teachers; Catholic pictures and other symbols remained on the walls of the schoolrooms; and Catholic children from all parts of the city attended these schools.[155]

Later and on larger scale, notably in Ohio and New Mexico, there have been important instances where parochial schools with their regular teachers have been absorbed and financed from the public treasury,[156] cases clearly at variance with the dicta in important recent Supreme Court decisions.[157]

This brief review shows clearly that except for Roman Catholics the overwhelming, well-nigh unanimous, opinion of Americans as reflected in constitutions and statutes is opposed to any direct financial aid to denominational or parochial schools other than the usual exemption from taxation. It is believed that any other policy is fraught with grave danger to the principle of separation of Church and State, and the resulting religious freedom, which it seems important for a democracy like ours to maintain. There is general appreciation of what Roman Catholics are doing for religion and morality through their parochial schools, and a recognition of the disadvantages of a curriculum without religious instruction; but it is believed that in the long run the latter difficulty may be largely avoided by some plan that gives constructively objective historical data about the major world religions, supplemented by voluntary and inspirational instruction outside the school.[158] At any rate, the experience of some European States has shown the danger of State grants to denominational schools, and with our American background such grants would be sure to result in friction and bitterness, from which the Roman Catholic Church would itself be the loser. A recent expression of this conviction is given in the following temperate statement by the Federal Council of Churches:

We note with grave misgiving the attempts which are being made in various quarters to secure subsidies from public funds for the support of parochial and private schools. We register the strong conviction that such proposals are contrary to the cherished American principle of the separation of Church and State.[159]

Furthermore, Protestants agree in denying the assertion so often made by Roman Catholics that the alternative facing the country is secularism and some form of government aid to parochial schools, or some form of Church recognition in the public schools. As long as the spirit of the public schools is sympathetic to the importance of religion, as is generally the case, much may be accomplished to meet the undoubted religious needs of pupils by some Constitutional form of released-time or dismissed-time instruction outside of public-school buildings and by much greater emphasis on the major responsibility of Churches and homes in this matter of religious training and education. Fortunately, though our schools sometimes show indifference to religion, they almost never show antagonism. There is nothing approaching the Russian situation here.

Since the late Professor Carl Zollmann probably gave more attention to the legal aspects of Church–State relations than any other American scholar of his time, and since he was so fairminded that although a Protestant his book, *American Church Law* (1933), has an introduction by the dean of the Catholic University of America School of Law, his conviction of the need of maintaining entire fiscal separation between public and parochial schools is worthy of serious attention. He says:

This solution is the only feasible one, no matter what hardships it involves for those who retain their parochial schools. Any arrangement by which parochial schools are allowed to participate in the public school funds results in political pressure. The first result is a close public control over the denominational schools. The next result is the entry of those schools into politics in order to shape this control to suit their own purposes. Where one denomination or a combination of them becomes strong enough, a shift of such control becomes inevitable. Instead of the public agencies regulating the parochial schools, the latter will control the public schools. . . .[160]

It remains to sum up the present status of the question of State aid to parochial and similar schools conducted by religious or other private groups.

Nearly a third of the states have explicit provisions in their constitutions which forbid the appropriation of public money by the state or its subdivisions to institutions that are not under the absolute control of the State.[161] The group includes such states as California, Massachusetts, Pennsylvania, and Virginia. The Colorado constitution contains the following statements, which are similar to those of several other Western states:

No appropriation shall be made for charitable, industrial, educational, or benevolent purposes to any person, corporation, or community not under the absolute control of the state, nor to any denominational or sectarian institution or association. (Art. v, sec. 34.)

Neither the general assembly, nor any county, city, town, township, school-district, or other public corporation—shall ever make any appropriation, or pay from any public funds or moneys whatever, anything in aid of any church or sectarian society, or for any sectarian purpose, or to help support or sustain any school, academy, seminary, college, university, or other literary or scientific institution controlled by any church or sectarian denomination whatsoever; nor shall any grant or donation of land, money, or other personal property ever be made by the State, or any such public corporation to any church or for any sectarian purpose. (Art. ix, sec. 7.)[162]

Furthermore, almost all states which have no constitutional provisions on the subject accomplish the same purpose through legislative enactments and court decisions. A few, such as Virginia and West Virginia, have laws prohibiting any denomination from receiving special privileges or preference, and one, Utah, forbids in terms a "union of church and state." This, however, is implied in the various state bills of rights and in the whole history of their judicial interpretation since the Supreme Court included religious freedom in the states among the protections of the Fourteenth Amendment.[163]

Gabel sums up his thorough study of the matter of State aid to Church schools, written in 1937, in the following statement:

1) Thirty States with enactments against the appropriation of public money to denominational or sectarian institutions or to schools under sectarian control.
2) Nine States providing against appropriations to schools not under absolute control of the State (not including Massachusetts and North Dakota).
3) Six States with provisions against drawing on the treasury for the benefit of any religious sect, society, or theological institution.
4) Eight States with provisions against appropriations for any sectarian purpose, viz., California, Colorado, Idaho, Illinois, Mississippi, Missouri, Montana, Nevada.
5) Four States with provisions against the *control* of school funds by any religious sect (Ohio, Kansas, South Carolina, and Mississippi).
6) Two States forbidding the acceptance of any gift or grant for sectarian purposes (Nebraska and South Dakota).[164]

The situation has changed little since this authoritative survey was made more than a decade ago. There has, however, been on the one hand a definite increase of Roman Catholic pressure for direct State financial aid, and on the other more determination on the part of non-Catholic groups that such aid should not be granted to denominational or parochial schools as being both unconstitutional and unwise.

Section 5. THE INDIRECT STATE AID TO PRIVATE AND PAROCHIAL SCHOOLS

(1) FREE BUS TRANSPORTATION

The nearest approach to a compromise on State aid to parochial schools is the provision by direct legislative action or court decision that in ten or more states authorizes free transportation, under certain conditions, for parochial school students. For example, a 1936 Massachusetts law permits cities and towns to assign public funds to meet the cost of transporting pupils to private (including parochial) schools. Some Protestants think they see a danger in the law—an entering wedge for breaking down the traditional American separation between Church and State—and are seeking its repeal.[165] New York and New Jersey, as we shall see later in this section, have recently taken action similar to that of Massachusetts, and both are states with a large and politically powerful Roman Catholic population. Illinois, Kansas, Michigan, and Oregon are among those which have made the practice legal, and the movement is spreading.[166] In Louisiana free transportation was early authorized to nonpublic schools approved by the state board of education, and in Indiana and some other states when a child lives on a public school bus route.[167] The Roman Catholic voters of Maryland have been pressing for free bus transportation for parochial schools in counties where they have a large population, and this favor has been granted increasingly in later years.

Texas has an interesting reflection of this situation. In 1925 the state legislature passed a law providing half fare for students between the ages of twelve and seventeen "who are in actual attendance at some academic school of a grade not higher than that of the public high schools, and who are actually studying academic courses." In 1931 the law was extended to children attending school who were under twelve. This reduced fare transportation affects "all persons or corporations owning or operating street railways or motor busses in or upon the public streets of any city of not less than 12,000 inhabitants."[168] The plan was adopted mainly to help the parochial schools of the Roman Catholic Church, which in Texas are the only schools that profit to any large extent by the legislation. Similarly, in the District of Columbia and in many cities reduced fares are offered all school children on bus and trolley lines. In several states wherein such specific law exists the attorney general has interpreted existing public school free transportation laws so as to include parochial school pupils.

A recent case where the matter of free transportation of Catholic school children was the issue came up in New York state. The so-called Catholic bus bill, which was a prominent issue in the 1936 campaign for the governorship because originally vetoed by Governor Lehman, was declared unconstitutional by the court of appeals in the spring of 1938 by a divided vote of four to three. The bill required boards of education to provide transportation for students in parochial schools whenever similar transportation was provided for public-school students.

The majority opinion found that the statute

> in so far as it authorizes transportation for pupils to and from any school or institution of learning wholly or in part under the control or direction of any religious denomination or in which any denominational tenet or doctrine is taught, is repugnant to our fundamental law, unconstitutional and void.

The dissenting opinion was to the effect that the law did not give aid to the school but to its pupils, and hence the Constitutional provision was held not to apply.

The following quotation from the prevailing opinion may be accepted as authoritative. It seems to the impartial layman to be a fair one in view of the then existing (though since altered) fundamental law of the state of New York. It says that:

> . . . Since our organization as a State we have clearly and unequivocally indicated that there must be a complete severance between denominational or sectarian schools on the one hand and public common schools on the other.
>
> The argument is advanced that furnishing transportation to the pupils of private or parochial schools is not in aid or support of the schools, but rather in aid of their pupils.
>
> This argument not only ignores the spirit, purpose and intent of the constitutional provisions, but as well their exact wording. The wording of the mandate is broad. Aid or support to the school "directly or indirectly" is proscribed. The two words must have been used with some definite intent and purpose; otherwise, why were they used at all?
>
> Aid furnished "directly" would be that furnished in a direct line. Aid furnished "indirectly" clearly embraces any contribution, to whomsoever made, circuitously, collaterally, disguised or otherwise not in a straight, open and avowed aid of the school, that may be of benefit to the institution or promotional of its interests and purposes. How could then people have expressed in the fundamental law their purpose in more apt, simple and all-embracing language?
>
> Free transportation of pupils induces attendance at schools. The purpose of the transportation is none other than to promote the interests of the private school or religious or sectarian institution that controls and directs it.

Judge Harlan W. Rippey (1874–) explained that without pupils there could be no schools and asserted "it is illogical" to say that furnishing of transportation was not an aid to the institution while the employment of teachers, accommodations and other facilities were such an aid. He added:

If the cardinal rule that written constitutions are to receive uniform and unvarying interpretation and practical construction is to be followed, in view of interpretation in analogous cases it is idle to assert that the furnishing of transportation to the private or parochial school out of public money is not in aid or support of the school.

The minority opinion took the ground that the statute is

. . . not designed to maintain the institutions themselves, that the object of the 1936 legislation was apparently to insure the attendance of the children at their respective schools for the requisite period of instruction and, perhaps, to safeguard the health of the children.

The law says to the children and parents: having chosen a proper school, you must attend regularly. The school district has been given the power to add to that; where necessary, we shall assist them in getting there.

The statute in question does not have the effect of giving public money, property or credit in aid or maintenance of religious schools. The aid is given to the pupils who are legally attending such schools, to assist them to spend the required time in attendance upon instruction.[169]

A specific proposal to permit the legislature to provide for free transportation for children to private schools was approved by the New York constitutional convention of 1938 by a large majority (134 to 9), and was further approved when the various amendments adopted were presented to the voters for ratification. The existing law is now as follows, the last permissive clause having been added to the old regulation which was not otherwise changed:

Neither the state nor any subdivision thereof shall use its property or credit or any public money, or authorize or permit either to be used, directly or indirectly, in aid or maintenance, other than for examination or inspection, of any school or institution of learning wholly or in part under the control or direction of any religious denomination, or in which any denominational tenet or doctrine is taught, but the legislature may provide for the transportation of children to and from any school or institution of learning.[170]

It will be noticed that this action is permissive, not mandatory; but in May, 1939, Governor Herbert H. Lehman (1878–) signed a bill permitting city boards of education to provide free bus transportation for children in public, private, and parochial schools.[171]

The amendment, changing a long-established law, and one for "health and welfare service for all children," were fought by many agencies on the ground that they might prove an entering wedge for an attempt by Roman Catholics to secure direct financial aid for parochial schools. The New York League for the Separation of Church and State was formed in November, 1938, to organize opposition to these two amendments, and has since continued to combat other attempted "encroachments" of the Church on the State. The league carries on its letterhead a picture of President Grant and a quotation from his well-known speech before the Army of the Tennessee, beginning, "Resolved, that not one dollar of public money shall be appropriated to the support of any sectarian school. Keep the Church and the State forever separate." The card sent to voters read:

DO YOU KNOW:
THAT THE PROPOSED NEW STATE CONSTITUTION THREATENS OUR TIME HONORED PRINCIPLES OF RELIGIOUS LIBERTY?

Included among the 50,000 words of the nine proposed amendments of the Constitution are dangerous and vicious proposals which would destroy the basic American principle of the separation of Church and State.... Our Public Schools are open and free to all.... Private and sectarian schools must support themselves.... Supporting parochial schools means supporting a particular religious denomination, because these schools exist primarily for inculcating a particular religious creed.... To support these schools means a connection of Church and State which the founders of this Republic warned us against as a menace to our liberties.

Vote NO on Amendment 1	This proposition contains in it a provision which will permit free bus service for Catholic parochial schools. The Court of Appeals in a recent decision declared such an act passed by the Legislature to be "repugnant to our fundamental law." This crafty endeavor to circumvent the ruling of the highest Court in New York should be sternly rebuked by the people of this State.
Vote NO on Amendment 8	Do not be misled by the deceptive wording used on the voting machine for this amendment. Our present Welfare Laws amply provide for the care of the needy. Under the guise of "Social Welfare" are incorporated far-reaching provisions for the aid of denominational schools which are equally as destructive of the principle of the separation of Church and State as are the proposals of Amendment No. 1.

Unless these amendments are defeated on November 8th by the people of this State, they will prove an entering wedge for an eventual subsidy by the State of Catholic parochial schools, and place upon us the tax burden of additional millions of dollars to support religious opinions, doctrines and dogmas in which we do not believe. This will mean the beginning of the end of our historic American principle of the separation of Church and State.

VOTE AN EMPHATIC "NO" on AMENDMENTS #1 and #8!

The supreme court of Oklahoma in December, 1941, took the ground that under the state constitution public funds could not be used for the transportation of children to parochial schools. It consequently voided the law passed two years previously by the legislature, which was similar to that in some other states in that it provided

That whenever any school board shall, pursuant to this section or to any law of the State of Oklahoma, provide for transportation for pupils attending public schools, all children attending any private or parochial school under the compulsory school attendance laws of this State shall, where said private or parochial school is along or near the route designated by said board, be entitled equally to the same rights, benefits, and privileges as to transportation that are so provided for by such district school board.

This seemed to the court inconsistent with a provision of the Oklahoma constitution:

No public money or property shall ever be appropriated, applied, donated, or used, directly or indirectly, for the use, benefit, or support of any sect, church, denomination, or system of religion, or for the use, benefit, or support of any priest, preacher, minister, or other religious teacher or dignitary, or sectarian institution as such.

The gist of the opinion is in these words:

If the cost of the school bus and the maintenance and operation thereof was not in aid of the public schools, then expenditures therefor out of the school funds would be unauthorized and illegal. . . .[172]

The appropriation and directed use of public funds in transportation of public-school children is openly in direct aid to public schools "as such." When such aid is purported to be extended to a sectarian school, there is, in our judgment, a clear violation of the above-quoted provisions of our constitution. . . .

The brief for plaintiff in error emphasizes the wholesomeness of the rule and policy of separation of the church and the state, and the necessity for the churches to continue to be free of any state control, leaving the churches and all their institutions to function and operate under church control exclusively. We agree. In that connection we must not overlook the fact that if the legislature may directly or indirectly aid or support sectarian or denominational schools with public funds, then it would be a short step forward at another session to increase such aid, and only another short step to some regulation and at least partial control of such schools by successive legislative enactment. From partial control to an effort at complete control might well be the expected development. The first step in any such direction should be promptly halted, and is effectively halted, and is permanently barred by our constitution.[173]

Kentucky has been faced by the same problem. Its court of appeals in 1942 declared the 1940 act of the state assembly providing for a similar plan unconstitutional under the constitution and statutes of the state. The leading journal of public opinion in the region, the *Louisville Courier-Journal,* declared the decision "a sorry victory for constitutionalism," and censured those "persons who permitted their abstract respect for the suitable separation of church and state to obscure their sense of proportion."[174]

This same question was vigorously discussed in the New Jersey legislature in 1941. A petition was signed by 489,000 people asking for the passage of a bill to give free bus transportation to pupils in nonprofit private schools on the ground of the safety and welfare of the pupils. Emphasis was placed by proponents of the plan on the fact that ten states had already provided such legislation. Opponents stressed the dangerous precedent in leading to the breakdown of America's cherished Church–State separation.[175] The status and extent of the movement on the eve of the Supreme Court decision in the New Jersey case may be seen in a pamphlet published in 1946 by the National Catholic Welfare Conference entitled *School Bus Transportation Laws in the United States.*

A bill was passed by the legislature which was finally declared Constitutional by the Supreme Court of the United States. The opinion of the court and the dissenting opinions are so important not only for the specific issue but for their bearing on the whole question of Church–State separation and religious freedom that they are discussed in a separate section which follows.

The case of Wisconsin should also be considered before we take up the Supreme Court decision on the constitutionality of this free bus transportation matter. In November, 1946, the proposal to amend the state constitution to permit the use of public funds to provide "transportation of children to and from any parochial or private school or institution of learning" was defeated by a vote of 530,000 to 463,000 after a vigorous educational campaign on both sides. *The Christian Century* thought the result specially significant because out of a population of 3,000,000 there were about 750,000 Roman Catholics, 650,000 Lutherans, and 350,000 non-Lutheran Protestants. The Catholic group, led by the Knights of Columbus and other laymen and actively supported by the clergy through press and pulpit, took the ground that it was unjust to its pupils not to allow them to ride to their schools in buses provided in part by their parents' taxes. The Protestant group, through the state council of churches and various ministerial associations, emphasized religious liberty and Church–State separation. The Protestants asserted that if this proposed amendment referring to the aiding of pupils were adopted it would be followed in a few years, as in Maryland, with a law providing for a separate transportation system to be provided the Roman Catholic Church for its own schools—a provision which it is believed the higher Federal courts would not accept. It is a striking fact that in Wisconsin the Lutherans, in spite of their numerous parochial schools, opposed the amendment.[176]

(2) THE UNITED STATES SUPREME COURT AND THE EVERSON CASE

The so-called New Jersey bus law, as passed by the legislature in 1941, reads:

> Whenever in any district there are children living remote from any schoolhouse, the board of education of the district may make rules and contracts for the transportation of such children to and from school, including the transportation of such children to and from school other than a public school, except such school as is operated for profit in whole or in part.
>
> When any school district provides any transportation for public school children to and from school, transportation from any point in such established school route to any other point in such established school route shall be supplied to school children residing in such school district in going to and from school other than a public school, except such school as is operated for profit in whole or in part.[177]

The constitutionality of the law was contested before the New Jersey supreme court by a taxpayer, one Arch R. Everson, who challenged the right of the board of education of the township of Ewing to reimburse certain parents of parochial school students. He contended that the statute, and the resolution of the board passed pursuant to it, violated both the state and Federal constitutions. The resolution had authorized the transportation of Ewing pupils "to the Trenton and Pennington High Schools and Catholic Schools by way of public carrier as in recent years."[178]

The state supreme court held that the legislature was without power to authorize such payment under the state constitution. The New Jersey Court of Errors and Appeals reversed this decision, holding that the legislative action was not in conflict with the state and Federal constitutions. Both decisions, as so often happens in cases involving the relation of religion and education, were by divided courts.[179]

The United States Supreme Court supported in a 5 to 4 decision (February 10, 1947) the judgment of the Court of Appeals. The case attracted wide attention and resulted in able majority and minority opinions, which, though containing some inaccuracies and extreme deductions, are full both of pertinent historical facts dealing with the religious freedom guarantee of the First Amendment, and of reasoning valuable to the student of American religious liberty and Church–State separation. In addition to the arguments of contestants, briefs in support of the constitutionality of the New Jersey law were presented by the states of Illinois, Indiana, Louisiana, Massachusetts, Michigan, and New

York, which have similar laws. No state without such a law filed an opposing brief, although Justice Rutledge calls attention to the fact that at least seven states have held invalid acts of the character of the New Jersey statute—Delaware, Kentucky, Oklahoma, New York (prior to the new constitution of 1938, which specifically permits the same type of free bus transportation), South Dakota, Washington, and Wisconsin.[180]

It is important to remember that though the statute in question does not refer specifically to Roman Catholic schools, and presumably includes in its scope all denominational and private schools not conducted for private profit, the specific case tried involved only certain parochial schools under the supervision of a Catholic priest and with regular Catholic religious instruction. The opinion of the court, written by Justice Hugo Black (1886–), stated:

> The only contention here is that the State statute and the resolution, insofar as they authorized reimbursement to parents of children attending parochial schools, violate the Federal Constitution in these two respects, which to some extent, overlap. *First.* They authorize the State to take by taxation the private property of some and bestow it upon others, to be used for their own private purposes. This, it is alleged, violates the due process clause of the Fourteenth Amendment. *Second.* The statute and the resolution forced inhabitants to pay taxes to help support and maintain schools which are dedicated to, and which regularly teach, the Catholic Faith. This is alleged to be a use of State power to support church schools contrary to the prohibition of the First Amendment which the Fourteenth Amendment made applicable to the states.[181]

As to the first objection, the court held that the New Jersey legislature was of the opinion that "a public purpose" would be served by the proposed aid of all school children in schools not conducted for private gain, and asserted,

> . . . The fact that a state law, passed to satisfy a public need, coincides with the personal desires of the individuals most directly affected is certainly an inadequate reason for us to say that a legislature has erroneously appraised the public need.[182]
> . . . Insofar as the second phase of the due process argument may differ from the first, it is by suggesting that taxation for transportation of children to church schools constitutes support of a religion by the State. But if the law is invalid for this reason, it is because it violates the First Amendment's prohibition against the establishment of religion by law. This is the exact question raised by appellant's second contention, to consideration of which we now turn.[183]

Taking up the second objection to the constitutionality of the statute, the court said:

> *Second.* The New Jersey statute is challenged as a "law respecting the establishment of religion." The First Amendment, as made applicable to the states by the Fourteenth, *Murdock* v. *Pennsylvania,* 319 U. S. 105, commands that a state "shall make no law respecting an establishment of religion, or prohibiting the free exercise thereof. . . ."[184]

The court held through historical references that the purpose of the First Amendment to the Constitution was to prevent the compelling of people "to support and attend government favored churches."[185] Taxes imposed to pay ministers' salaries, and to build and maintain churches, was what aroused the indignation of the people of Virginia, as crystallized in the Parson's Case of 1763,[186] and resulting in the Virginia bill for religious freedom.

This Court has previously recognized that the provisions of the First Amendment, in the drafting and adoption of which Madison and Jefferson played such leading roles, had the same objective and were intended to provide the same protection against governmental intrusion on religious liberty as the Virginia statute.[187]

Then followed these statements, among the most important ever drafted by the Supreme Court in its efforts to define and protect religious liberty:

The "establishment of religion" clause of the First Amendment means at least this: Neither a state nor the Federal Government can set up a church. Neither can pass laws which aid one religion, aid all religions, or prefer one religion over another. Neither can force nor influence a person to go to or to remain away from church against his will or force him to profess a belief or disbelief in any religion. No person can be punished for entertaining or professing religious beliefs or disbeliefs, for church attendance or non-attendance. No tax in any amount, large or small, can be levied to support any religious activities or institutions, whatever they may be called, or whatever form they may adopt to teach or practice religion. Neither a state nor the Federal Government can, openly or secretly, participate in the affairs of any religious organizations or groups and *vice versa*. In the words of Jefferson, the clause against establishment of religion by law was intended to erect "a wall of separation between Church and State."

We must consider the New Jersey statute in accordance with the foregoing limitations imposed by the First Amendment. But we must not strike that State statute down if it is within the State's constitutional power even though it approaches the verge of that power. See *Interstate Ry.* v. *Massachusetts,* Holmes, J., *supra* at 85, 88. New Jersey cannot consistently with the "establishment of religion clause" of the First Amendment contribute tax-raised funds to the support of an institution which teaches the tenets and faith of any church. On the other hand, other language of the amendment commands that New Jersey cannot hamper its citizens in the free exercise of their own religion. Consequently, it cannot exclude individual Catholics, Lutherans, Mohammedans, Baptists, Jews, Methodists, Non-believers, Presbyterians, or the members of any other faith, because of their faith, or lack of it, from receiving the benefits of public welfare legislation. . . .

Measured by these standards, we cannot say that the First Amendment prohibits New Jersey from spending tax-raised funds to pay the bus fares of parochial school pupils as a part of a general program under which it pays the fares of pupils attending public and other schools. . . . That Amendment requires the state to be a neutral in its relations with groups of religious believers and non-believers; it does not require the state to be their adversary. State power is no more to be used so as to handicap religions than it is to favor them.

... It appears that these parochial schools meet New Jersey's requirements. The State contributes no money to the schools. It does not support them. Its legislation, as applied, does no more than provide a general program to help parents get their children, regardless of their religion, safely and expeditiously to and from accredited schools.

The First Amendment has erected a wall between church and state. That wall must be kept high and impregnable. We could not approve the slightest breach. New Jersey has not breached it here.[188]

Hence the court, though emphasizing the supreme importance of maintaining the "wall between church and state," and recognizing that the state in passing this legislation "approaches the verge" of its constitutional power, held that it did not exceed it.

A phrase in this majority opinion that seems seriously questionable is the one that rules out laws to "aid all religions."* This principle logically carried out would mean the abandonment of such established provisions as exemption of taxation for Churches, Army and Navy chaplaincies, Thanksgiving Day proclamations, etc. Professor Edward S. Corwin, the Constitutional authority of Princeton University, in an article written after the above implications were noted, took the same position on the paragraph in the opinion on the establishment of religion, namely, that "historical data support its last clause, but rule out its middle one." There is nothing unconstitutional about a law merely because it aids all religions, if this is done impartially without "preference to any religion, or any denomination.[189] As the three words referred to appeared only in dicta and are inconsistent with the American tradition, it seems likely that they may be omitted in future statements by the court defining the scope of the First Amendment. Such omission would seem desirable.

Chief Justice Fuller, speaking for the Supreme Court in a case involving Indian mission schools, stated what has heretofore been the established and well-recognized American position. This was that

the government can never act in a sectarian capacity, either in the use of its own funds or in that of the funds of others, in respect of which it is a trustee; because the government is necessarily undenominational. . . .[190]

This is far different from asserting (fortunately only in *dicta,* however), that the government cannot impartially "aid all religions."

The dissenting opinions in the Everson case were also highly important, and show both the complicated issues involved and the deep public interest in the problems of religious freedom and of Church-State relations in education.

* See Addenda.

Justice Robert H. Jackson (1892–) in his dissent, in which Mr. Justice Frankfurter concurred, felt that "undertones" of the court's opinion advocating "complete and uncompromising separation of Church and State were utterly discordant with its conclusion yielding support to their commingling in educational matters."[191] He reduced the question to a single simple one: "Is it constitutional to tax this complainant to pay the cost of carrying pupils to Church schools of one specified denomination?"[192] His answer was a very definite "no." He did not accept the theory of any vital difference, from a Constitutional standpoint, between giving financial aid to a parochial school and aiding pupils to be transported to such a school along with public-school students. He quoted from canons 1372 to 1374 and canon 1381 of the Roman Catholic Church to show the definitely religious character of these schools and their supreme importance from the standpoint of the Church; compared them with the essentially "secular" education of the public schools; and held that this should prevent the State from aiding them. He added:

> Our public school, if not a product of Protestantism, at least is more consistent with it than with the Catholic culture and scheme of values. . . .
>
> Catholic education is the rock on which the whole structure rests, and to render tax aid to its Church school is indistinguishable to me from rendering the same aid to the Church itself.[193]
>
> . . . But we cannot have it both ways. Religious teaching cannot be a private affair when the state seeks to impose regulations which infringe on it indirectly, and a public affair when it comes to taxing citizens of one faith to aid another, or those of no faith to aid all. If these principles seem harsh in prohibiting aid to Catholic education, it must not be forgotten that it is the same Constitution that alone assures Catholics the right to maintain these schools at all when predominant local sentiment would forbid them. . . .[194]

Mr. Justice Jackson closed his dissent by stating that the majority opinion is "unconsciously turning the clock's hand a backward turn."[195]

One feels that his argument in behalf of Church–State separation was unanswerable, but that much can be said on both sides as to the applicability of the Constitution to this particular law designed to enable school districts at their discretion to help children in nonprivate as well as public schools. It is auxiliary aid through pupils much like G.I. scholarships, which are available at public and private institutions alike, rather than direct aid to schools. Unquestionably, however, most of those who have discussed the decision in the law reviews have upheld the minority rather than the majority of the court.

The dissenting opinion written by Justice Wiley Rutledge (1894–1949) and concurred in by Justices Frankfurter, Jackson, and Burton should be read by every student of Constitutional religious freedom and Church–State separation. It refused to draw a distinction, from the standpoint of Constitutional interpretation, between aiding a religious school directly and aiding such a school indirectly by helping pupils to attend one. In this respect the opinion seemed to run contrary to that in the Louisiana textbook case,[196] in which, however, aid was permitted only in supplying under certain conditions free textbooks in secular subjects to students in parochial schools.

Mr. Justice Rutledge's dissent was the most detailed statement of the Constitutional grounds for a clear-cut, absolute, rigid separation of Church and State yet made by a justice of the Supreme Court. Some of his views and historical deductions in the *dicta* seemed, however, to go too far in its interpretation of the First Amendment, and if applied in other cases, might result in excluding church tax exemption, military chaplaincies, and other long-established forms of impartial co-operation between the government and religious bodies.

Mr. Justice Rutledge emphasized Madison's "Remonstrance" against taxation in Virginia for the support of the Christian religion, especially his claim that "there is not a shadow of right in the general government to intermeddle with religion." He felt that Madison's writings in behalf of religious freedom in Virginia should be considered "warp and woof" of our Constitutional tradition, and gave an illuminating commentary on its meaning.

This dissenting opinion also emphasized the danger of any financial appropriation, no matter how small, going directly or indirectly to the encouragement of religious institutions. As to the relation of this principle to the present case, it stated:

... Here parents pay money to send their children to parochial schools and funds raised by taxation are used to reimburse them. This not only helps the children to get to school and the parents to send them. It aids them in a substantial way to get the very thing which they are sent to the particular school to secure, namely, religious training and teaching.

Believers of all faiths, and others who do not express their feeling toward ultimate issues of existence in any creedal form, pay the New Jersey tax. When the money so raised is used to pay for transportation to religious schools, the Catholic taxpayer to the extent of his proportionate share pays for the transportation of Lutheran, Jewish and otherwise religiously affiliated children to receive their non-Catholic religious instruction. Their parents likewise pay proportionately for the transportation of Catholic children to receive Catholic instruction. Each thus contributes to "the propagation of opinions which he disbelieves" in so far as their religions differ, as do others who accept no creed without regard to those differences. . . .

New Jersey's action therefore exactly fits the type of exaction and the kind of evil at which Madison and Jefferson struck. Under the test they framed it cannot be said that the cost of transportation is no part of the cost of education or of the religious instruction given. That it is a substantial and a necessary element is shown most plainly by the continuing and increasing demand for the state to assume it. . . .[197]

The public function argument, by casting the issue in terms of promoting the general cause of education and the welfare of the individual, ignores the religious factor and its essential connection with the transportation, thereby leaving out the only vital element in the case. So of course do the "public welfare" and "social legislation" ideas, for they come to the same thing.[198]

It is not because religious teaching does not promote the public or the individual's welfare, but because neither is furthered when the state promotes religious education, that the Constitution forbids it to do so. . .[199]

The great condition of religious liberty is that it be maintained free from sustenance, as also from other interferences, by the state. For when it comes to rest upon that secular foundation it vanishes with the resting. . . .[200]

We have staked the very existence of our country on the faith that complete separation between the State and religion is best for the State and best for religion. . .[201]

To a layman like the author reading these majority and minority opinions objectively, both seem conclusive as to the importance of maintaining the separation of Church and State as far as public grants to denominational educational institutions are concerned. The question directly at issue was whether the type of indirect aid contemplated by the New Jersey law in providing transportation on public school routes to children attending Roman Catholic schools is contrary to the Constitution as it stands. On this point it is clear that competent Constitutional authorities differ. If a majority of our citizens think such aid constitutes a dangerous opening wedge which might ultimately break down our important inherited tradition of separation, and if the basic judgment is not later reversed—a reversal which seems possible in view of recent experience with Jehovah's Witnesses and other cases—then a Constitutional amendment, somewhat similar to that recently introduced by Congressman Bryson, but simplified, may be considered advisable. But this matter of indirect aid through pupils is both less clear and much less serious than direct financial aid from tax funds to parochial and other denominational schools.[202]

The Supreme Court's decision in the New Jersey bus case created extraordinary interest and important reactions. A few examples may be cited. The *New York Times* the following day (February 11, 1947) published a two-column dispatch beginning on the front page with large headlines. Two days later Arthur Krock's column on the editorial page of the same paper was devoted entirely to it, pointing out particularly the danger that the decision, unless reversed in a subsequent case, might be a first step toward attempts to secure "more extensive support of religious education by New Jersey."

The Roman Catholic press hailed the decision as an important victory for the rights of Catholic taxpayers, and for the cause of religious education, although *America,* the Jesuit journal (March 5, 1949) showed that the Rutledge dissent was supported by the great majority of law reviews.

The Protestant press, led by the *Christian Century,* the *Churchman,* the *Methodist Southern Christian Advocate,* and various Baptist publications, was uniformly severely critical or much alarmed, but sometimes evidently forgot that the Supreme Court's function is to interpret the Constitution as it stands, rather than to state what it believes to be best for the country; and also failed to realize that from the standpoint of Constitutional law the case was extremely complicated, as many divided court decisions on the issue in different states indicate.

Religious Liberty, "A Magazine of Religious Freedom" published for more than half a century under the auspices of an association representing the Seventh Day Adventists, devoted a large portion of one issue—that for the third quarter of 1947—to a strong editorial of its own on the subject and to editorial references from the secular press. From this compilation typical extracts may be quoted:

Chicago Daily Tribune, February 13, 1947.

As we said recently, in connection with the controversy over religious instruction in the schools of Champaign, Ill., the teaching of religion should be encouraged in every way so long as it is carried out by the citizen himself in his home or thru his church.

Evening Star, Washington (D.C.), February 14.

. . . As Justice Jackson ruefully remarked, it is an issue that can stir up the very sort of "bitter religious controversy" which our forefathers sought to end through separating church from state. And the unfortunate fact is that the decision opens the way for other claims against the State, not only in New Jersey but elsewhere, that inevitably will lead to further legal disputes, ill-feeling between religious groups and further action by the Supreme Court.

PM, New York, February 20.

There is no more essential doctrine in the American tradition than the separation of church and state. We have always recognized that this has a double meaning: the state must leave the churches free, but the churches must also be kept away from meddling with the state, and especially from using state funds. That doctrine has now been broken, under sufferance from a bare majority of the highest court . . .

At once the deepest and most brilliant treatment of the whole issue is in Justice Rutledge's long 35-page dissenting opinion. In the decade since Justice Brandeis' resignation from the Court I do not recall an opinion which more satisfyingly combined historical thoroughness, legal acumen and logic, and moral passion. "This is not," writes Justice Rutledge, "just a little case over bus fares." I agree. I think it is a case which—if its direction is followed any further in later cases—will embroil the nation in deadly religious controversies. . . . Religious controversies are fatal to democracy. The only way to avoid them is to stick to the rigid separation of church and state, and especially of church schools and state funds.

This alone can assure our country of religious liberty. For there is a double price, as Justice Rutledge points out, that we must pay for religious liberty. One is the immense effort to keep the state from interfering in the way a man worships his God. The other is the equally immense effort to keep the churches from using state strength to propagate one particular version of religious truth. Let us never forget that in order to assure religious freedom in the first sense, you must assure it in the second also. That the road away from one also leads away from the other has been amply shown not only by the religious despotisms in the Europe of Jefferson's day, but also by the even more terrible despotisms in Europe today.

Montgomery Advertiser, Alabama, February 13.

The *Advertiser* sees in this decision a grievous and incredible error. We do not desire to see public money going into Catholic, Baptist, Methodist, or any other variety of non-public schools.

Toledo Blade, February 17.

Though last week's decision is applicable to only one church and draws the line at which a church can receive support from the state, it lets down a historic barrier. From now on, all churches, creeds, and sects can scramble for public funds and set up schools to justify them. In which case, the American public school system could be sadly disrupted. And the consequences to American democracy might be disastrous.

Christian Science Monitor, February 12.

Separation of church and State is a bulwark of religious liberty. To remove a stone from that bulwark is to weaken the fortress of religious liberty. In our opinion the Supreme Court, by its decision permitting the use of public funds to pay for the transportation of pupils to sectarian schools, has torn down a whole section of that bulwark.

To these we may add a sentence from an editorial in the *Washington Post* of February 13 which has been widely reproduced:

. . . The fundamental error lies in the Court's assumption that the intrinsic merit of a private activity, such as financing transportation to church schools, may transform it into a public welfare function.

It held that "the Court appears to have struck a blow at religious freedom as well as the separation of church and state," in spite of its strong statement in support of both of these principles.

Various Baptist and other religious groups interested in Church–State separation soon got into action. The Seventh Day Adventists, a denomination which operates more than 900 day schools, mostly of an elementary grade, adopted, through the executive committee of its general conference, resolutions that show their consistent opposition to free transportation at public expense for children attending their schools.

WHEREAS, The question of transporting parochial school pupils free of charge on public busses is being widely discussed in view of the five-to-four decision of the United States Supreme Court, on February 10, 1947, in the New Jersey school bus case, *Everson vs. the Board of Education of the Township of Ewing, et al.*, . . .

Resolved, That we reaffirm our belief that for pupils to ride free of charge to and from Seventh-day Adventist schools in public busses is in principle contrary to the historic position of the Seventh-day Adventist Church, that church and state be kept separate, as indicated by our Lord when He said, "Render therefore unto Caesar the things which are Caesar's; and unto God the things that are God's" (Matt. 22:21); and further

We recommend, That because of the principles concerned Seventh-day Adventists do not use busses which are operated at public expense, for the free transportation of their children to and from our church schools."[203]

The bishops of the Methodist Church, meeting in Riverside, California, passed strong resolutions on religious freedom in general, and on the Supreme Court decision in particular. Extracts from their statement follow:

A simple rule might guide all of us as we face the issue of religious liberty, and that is to do unto others as we would be done by.

The recent decision of the Supreme Court, affirming the constitutionality of state legislation providing public funds for the transportation of children to parochial schools is, in our judgment, a departure from the American principles of the separation of church and state and carries with it a serious threat to our public educational system which is a bulwark of democracy.

We rejoice in the liberty this nation grants churches to maintain schools if they so desire, but we hold that the support from public funds of sectarian education is fraught with danger and must be resisted and ended. We shall resist all attempts of the Roman Catholic hierarchy to secure public support for such schools and other religious enterprises on the ground of the separation of the church and state because we believe that such action will create reaction here, as it has elsewhere, which may limit religious freedom. . . .

Are our Roman Catholic brothers, with whom we desire the friendliest of relations and for whom we demand the same religious liberties we insist upon for ourselves, to push their demands so far that we must in self-defense take steps that will protect our liberties and those of our children?[204]

The Presbyterian Church, U.S.A., at its general assembly meeting in the early summer of 1947, condemned "the continuing attempt of parochial school authorities of whatever denomination or faith, to obtain and use public tax funds for private education."[205]

The Baptist point of view is indicated by the statement issued February 11, immediately after the decision by the Baptist Joint Conference Committee on Public Relations, representing the three major Baptist conventions in the country. It reads:

We feel that the majority opinion must be acknowledged as turning back the hands of the clock as far as religious liberty and the separation of church and state are concerned in these United States.

We deplore this opinion and are convinced that it will divide the people of the nation at a time when unity is greatly needed. In view of the religious heritage of America, which Associate Justice Black so eloquently reviewed, the decision is all the more to be deplored.

As Baptists of the United States we are resolved that the struggle for religious liberty, in terms of the separation of church and state, must be continued. Having lost a battle, we have not lost the war.

We feel that the decision will, in many ways, help to clarify the whole church-state issue if reviewed in the light of the constitution and our religious heritage. This will be particularly true when similar bills are brought before the Supreme Court.

We have the conviction that the cause of religious freedom is an invincible one, and we stand unalterably opposed to the use of public funds for the support of private and church schools now, and at any time in the future.[206]

Most other Protestant Church resolutions were of a similar character.

The Supreme Court decision also had its effect on legislatures and courts. For example:

Maryland. The state approved a law extending free bus transportation to parochial school pupils in a county not covered by such legislation.

Pennsylvania. A Roman Catholic citizen of Kennett Square near Philadelphia, one Paul Connell, stimulated by the Everson decision, demanded that the joint board of school directors of the Kennett school board be required under the state school code to give his daughter free bus transportation to a parochial school. The board decided that using public funds for that purpose would be contrary to the state constitution provision that "no money raised for the support of the public schools shall be used for the support of any sectarian school." The supreme court of Pennsylvania upheld the board and a lower court. Mr. Connell brought the case before the United States Supreme Court, but later asked that it be dismissed.[207]

Iowa. The supreme court of the state decided unanimously that public-school buses might not be used to carry private or parochial school pupils. The court stated that this was a state case in which no Federal Constitutional question was involved. The court declared:

We hold public schools have no authority to transport other than public school children and that one doing otherwise has no right to reimbursement from the state school bus aid fund.[208]

Washington. Similar action to that in Iowa was taken by the superior court of Waatcom County. The case is interesting because it involved not a Roman Catholic but a member of the Christian Reformed Church.[209]

Wisconsin. While this all-important New Jersey bus case was being argued by the courts, and being given great publicity in the press, this Western state took action. In November, 1946, a proposal to amend the Wisconsin state constitution to permit the use of public funds to provide "transportation of children to and from any parochial or private school or institution of learning" was defeated by a popular vote by about a seven to six ratio. The contest was described earlier in this section. It was interesting that the Lutherans, in spite of their numerous parochial schools, opposed the amendment.[210] This action is again referred to here because though it was taken a few months before the final decision of the Everson case it was influenced by the New Jersey legislation, as well as by the arguments before various courts on its constitutionality and public discussion of its wisdom.

In some ways the most significant result of the Supreme Court decision in the New Jersey bus case was the forming of a new national organization in behalf of Church–State separation. The decision had climaxed and given support to what was thought by leaders of the new movement to be evidences of a growing determination of the Roman Catholic Church to secure certain types of support from government, which a strict construction of the Constitution evidently did not warrant. The new movement, according to press dispatches, started at a small meeting of interested persons—all Protestant leaders—May 15, 1947.[211] A second and larger conference, with sixty present and presided over by Bishop G. Bromley Oxnam (1891–   ) of the Methodist Church, was held in Calvary Baptist Church, Washington, on October 13. A strong committee on plans and policies with Dr. Charles Clayton Morrison (1874–   ), editor-emeritus of the *Christian Century,* as chairman, and a committee on legal approaches with a Washington attorney, E. Hilton Jackson (1869–   ) at its head, were announced. Dr. Joseph M. Dawson (1879–   ), executive secretary of the Baptist Joint Conference on Public Relations, acted as secretary. The choice of a name for the organization, tentatively called "The National Council of Citizens on Church and State," and of a chairman were postponed; but the conference unanimously adopted a resolution calling upon

all Americans who profess allegiance to Protestantism, Judaism or any other religious faith, and those who though professing no church allegiance believe in the American form of government, to join in demanding that legislatures and executives and courts shall defend the Constitution against all efforts to subvert it.[212]

The committee was formally organized under the name of "Protestants and Other Americans for the Separation of Church and State" at a meeting in Washington on January 11, 1948, and elected Dr. Edwin McNeill Poteat (1892–), president of Colgate-Rochester Divinity School, as president. It adopted a long manifesto outlining what the signers believed to be breaches by the Roman Catholic Church in the wall of Church–State separation, such as the New Jersey bus law; the president's continuance of his personal representative at the Vatican; attempts to secure public funds for parochial schools. It called upon all citizens interested to unite to protect the Constitutional guarantees which the committee believed were designed to prevent such actions.

The manifesto was published in full in the *New York Times* of January 12, 1948. The following program of immediate objectives was announced:

1. To enlighten and mobilize public opinion in support of religious liberty as this monumental principle of democracy has been embodied and implemented in the Constitution by the separation of church and state.

2. To resist every attempt by law or the administration of law further to widen the breach in the wall of separation of church and state.

3. To demand the immediate discontinuance of the ambassadorship to the Papal head of the Roman Catholic Church.

4. To work for the repeal of any law now on the statute books of any state which sanctions the granting of aid to church schools from the public school treasury.

5. To invoke the aid of the courts in maintaining the integrity of the constitution with respect to the separation of church and state, wherever and in whatever form the issue arises, and, specifically, to strive by appropriate constitutional means to secure a reconsideration of the two decisions of the Supreme Court upholding the use of tax funds (a) for providing the pupils of parochial schools with free text books, and (b) for the transportation of pupils to parochial schools.

6. To call out and unite all patriotic citizens in a concerted effort to prevent the passage of any law by Congress which allots to church schools any portion of a Federal appropriation for education, or which explicitly or implicitly permits the states to make such allotment of Federal funds. This purpose in no wise prejudices pro or con the propriety of a Federal grant in aid of public education.

7. To give all possible aid to the citizens of any community or state who are seeking to protect their public schools from sectarian domination, or resisting any other assault upon the principle of separation of church and state.

8. In seeking these objectives we are determined to pursue a course that cannot be justly characterized as anti-Catholic, or as motivated by anti-Catholic animus. As Protestants, we can be called anti-Catholic only in the sense in which every Roman Catholic is anti-Protestant. Profound differences separate us in the area of religious faith, but these differences have no relevancy in the pursuit of our objectives as clearly defined in this manifesto. The issue of separation of church and state has arisen in the political area and we propose to meet it there.[213]

Official and unofficial Roman Catholic replies appeared promptly. That of the Knights of Columbus was in the papers of January 13, and that of the highly important and authoritative National Catholic Welfare Conference on January 26, through the chairman of its administrative board, Most Reverend John T. McNicholas (1877–), Archbishop of Cincinnati. Extracts from the conference statement follow:

It is a departure from our custom to answer accusations made against us. It is distasteful for us to do so now.

We speak out, lest false statements of the manifesto be taken as true by some of our well-meaning fellow citizens who have not access to reliable sources of information on the issues raised. We are confident that the framers and signers of this manifesto do not speak for the great body of Protestants, nor for informed Jews and God-fearing Americans having no religious affiliation.

We deny absolutely and without any qualification that the Catholic bishops of the United States are seeking a union of church and state by any endeavors either proximate or remote.

If tomorrow Catholics constitute a majority in our country, they would not seek a union of church and state. They would then as now, uphold the Constitution and all its amendments, recognizing the moral obligation imposed on all Catholics to observe and to defend the Constitution and its amendments.

. . . The signers of the manifesto assume that their attempt to have the Supreme Court reverse its decision is a patriotic virtue, but that it is criminal for others to seek an interpretation of an amendment to the Constitution.

The manifesto also stigmatizes as unwarranted pressure the action of the Catholic hierarchy in presenting its views on proposed Federal legislation. At the same time the signers of the manifesto propose to do that very thing, by influencing legislatures, the judiciary and executives.

Despite the dogmatic assertions of the signers of the manifesto, there is no authoritative interpretation of the First Amendment, declaring unconstitutional Federal aid for children attending other than tax-supported schools. Our history shows many precedents of government aid to private schools.

The parents of America have basic and imprescriptible rights regarding the education of their children, which are guaranteed by the unanimous decision of our Supreme Court. That decision gives us the charter for the American system of education and guarantees its freedom. It rules out a monopoly of education for the public-school system of America. Parents—Jewish, Protestant, Catholic, as well as those who are creedless—should know their rights and insist that they be respected.

The First Amendment is being distorted today, especially by those who advocate secularism in education and in every department of our government.[214]

Much space has been given to this New Jersey decision and its immediate results, partly because it settled at least temporarily a highly controversial issue in Church–State relations, and perhaps even more for the significance of the vigorous insistence of all nine justices on the importance of maintaining the Constitutional separation of Church and State. The differences were not on this basic matter, for majority and minority opinions went out of the way in emphasizing, as we have shown, the need of maintaining what they believed to be Jefferson's and Madison's ideals in this respect. Indeed, it would be difficult to find a more inclusive statement of the vital significance of the Constitutional provisions in this matter than that quoted above from the majority opinion which permitted the New Jersey law to stand. The difference between the two groups was rather in their application of the idea of Church–State separation to this particular case. Here three factors seem to have played the most important part with the majority: first, that in their opinion the Constitution is not specific in clearly forbidding such indirect aid to parochial schools as that contemplated by the legislation; second, that the aid given was to pupils in the parochial schools, not to the schools themselves—a distinction which Chief Justice Hughes had emphasized in the Louisiana textbook case;[215] and third, that a state should be given much freedom in deciding what the "public welfare" demands in borderline Constitutional cases.

Supporters of religious freedom are divided as to the best future course. Some believe in pressing the issue further before the courts; others, recognizing that it was a borderline case, believe in accepting the court's decision, at least for the present, and devoting their attention to the more serious Church–State issues. Logic probably favors the former position; expediency, the latter.

(3) FREE TEXTBOOKS, LUNCHES, SCHOLARSHIPS, ETC.

In several states, such as Louisiana, New Mexico, and Indiana, free textbooks and free medical service have been provided for pupils in parochial schools, and the same privilege has recently been sought by bills presented in Ohio and several states west of the Mississippi. In Texas the issue has been raised frequently in recent years. In 1935 an amendment to the state constitution which would have permitted free textbooks to parochial school pupils passed the legislature but was subsequently voted down by public referendum. The proposed amendment failed again in 1941. But in this latter year Oregon passed a law providing free textbooks to pupils in private and parochial elementary schools,[216] and many other states are sure to follow.

In the well-known Louisiana textbook case, *Cochran* v. *Louisiana State Board of Education,* the United States Supreme Court, speaking through Chief Justice Charles Evans Hughes (1862–1948), upheld the constitutionality of such a law, declaring that it does not violate the Fourteenth Amendment, since the books are given to the children and not to the schools, and since they are the same as those used in the public schools.[217] This decision may well prove of epochal importance. It was rendered April 28, 1930. The essential clauses follow:

One may scan the acts in vain to ascertain where any money is appropriated for the purchase of the school books for the use of any church, private, sectarian or even public school. The appropriations were made for the specific purpose of purchasing school books for the use of the school children of the State, free of cost to them. It was for their benefit and the resulting benefit to the State that the appropriations were made.

True, these children attend some school, public or private, the latter, sectarian or nonsectarian, and that the books are to be furnished them for their use, free of cost, whichever they attend. The schools, however, are not the beneficiaries of these appropriations. They obtain nothing from them, nor are they relieved of a single obligation because of them. The school children and the State alone are the beneficiaries. . . .

What the statutes contemplate is that the same books that are furnished children attending public schools shall be furnished children attending private schools. This is the only practical way of interpreting and executing the statutes, and this is what the State Board of Education is doing. Among these books, naturally, none is to be expected adapted to religious instruction.[218]

The influence of this decision has been largely responsible for action in other states.

In 1941 the Mississippi supreme court decided that students in parochial and private schools are entitled to receive textbooks without charge under a free-textbook act voted the previous year. The majority opinion took the ground that a refusal to permit children in parochial or private schools the benefits of the provisions would constitute a denial of equal privileges on "sectarian grounds." Justice W. D. Anderson dissented, holding that such distribution of books was a "step toward breaking down the separation of the church and state."[219]

Another form of aid to religious bodies permissible under the laws of some states is payment for the care of needy children in denominational institutions, especially orphans in communities where there is no public orphan asylum. Such a provision was added by New York state to its constitution in 1938. This provides that

Payments by counties, cities or towns to charitable, eleemosynary, correctional and reformatory institutions and agencies, wholly or partly under private control, for care, support and maintenance, may be authorized, but shall not be required by the legislature.

No such aid however is possible for any child or other person

who is not received and retained therein pursuant to rules established by the state board of social welfare or other state department having the power of inspection thereof.[220]

Similarly, many students were supported in private and denominational institutions under the "student aid" and "work project" provisions of the National Youth Administration established within the Works Progress Administration in 1935. These young men and women were in high schools, colleges, and universities.

The Federal Food Distribution Administration also announced in 1943 that under a Congressional appropriation for school-lunch programs in the interest of national health, private and parochial schools and child-welfare institutions, if nonprofit organizations, could apply for the same aid as public schools—namely reimbursement per pupil up to nine cents a meal.[221]

This whole question was brought very much to the front in public discussion by the publication of the report of President F. D. Roosevelt's Advisory Committee on Education (1937–38). This committee, though opposed to the Roman Catholic demand to "share" the public school fund by having parochial schools supported from public taxation, advocated the use of Federal funds to provide under certain circumstances reading material, textbooks, transportation, and scholarships for students in parochial and other nonpublic schools.

Many of the services of public schools should be available to children regardless of whether they are enrolled in public schools for instruction. It is therefore recommended that such portions of the general aid as may be allocated in the joint plans to the purchase of reading materials, transportation, and scholarships, be made available so far as Federal legislation is concerned, for the benefit of pupils both in public and nonpublic schools. The Committee also recommends that local public schools receiving Federal aid be authorized to make local health and welfare services available to pupils in nonpublic schools. The conditions under which health and welfare services and aid for reading materials, transportation and scholarships may be made available for pupils in privately controlled schools should be determined by the States or by the local school jurisdictions receiving the grants if the States so determine.[222]

Attempts to put this proposal into effect by Federal legislation have been made in Congress but have failed.[223]

The American Association of School Administrators and other representative groups of educational leaders have by large majorities gone on record as opposing this type of Federal aid, fearing that it may prove an opening wedge for mixing politics and religion. Their view is expressed in the speech made at a recent meeting by a well-known educational leader, Professor George D. Strayer (1876–), of Teachers College, Columbia University. He urged:

Let's not have any church—Catholic, Protestant or Jewish—using public money to make propaganda for any policy or belief peculiar to itself. Let all these churches stand on their own feet. Let them not use the arm of government through controlled education to enforce their religious and political philosophies. History shows the tragedy of church-State-controlled education. Let's not have it repeated in America.

We have maintained the separation of church and State in our country. This principle is violated by the President's advisory committee in its recommendation that public funds be given to church schools. Some headway in vitiating our constitutional principle has already been made through laws in two States, which provide for expenditure for public funds for books for children attending church schools in Louisiana; for the transportation of children to church schools in public school buses in New York.

Let us have public schools in which all of the children of all the people, without regard to the religious affiliation of their parents, may work together. Let us hope that nothing in the practice of these schools shall set one group against another, or distinguish among those who are receiving that tuition which will prepare them for citizenship in our common country.[224]

It is interesting that conservative and liberal educators, though divided on many matters of policy, generally agree—their Roman Catholic colleagues being almost alone in dissent—that any direct financial aid from government funds to parochial and other denominational schools would be both unwise and unconstitutional. They are divided as to whether such restricted indirect use of public funds for nonpublic school purposes as those mentioned above, by aiding pupils rather than schools, constitutes a precedent of doubtful wisdom. At one meeting at the conference referred to, attended by about 800 persons, a resolution condemning a proposal for public financial aid to pupils in parochial schools as "a clear violation of the principle of separation of Church and State, therefore vicious and un-American," was adopted with only nine dissenting votes. Experience shows that this attitude is not dictated by hostility to parochial schools as such, but merely to their being supported by public funds or given aid from them—except, of course, in the form of tax exemption. This meeting would probably have voted by a large majority to favor the continuance of Roman Catholic or other parochial schools that conformed with state educational requirements if these continued to be supported by their own denominational constituency, without calling on the state for any direct financial aid.

Several bills have been proposed during recent years in various states to provide public funds or other assistance to private and sectarian schools. Representative cases are the following reported in a single year (1937):

California: (1) Whenever a district provides transportation (or payment to parents in lieu thereof) for public school pupils it shall also provide same for non-public school pupils. (2) State shall supply textbooks and district shall supply supplementary books free to pupils in private schools, as supplied to pupils in public elementary and secondary schools.[225]

Connecticut: (1) Upon a majority vote of any town or city board of education the sum of $2.25 may be donated for each registered child in private or parochial schools. Money to be used for books and supplies. To be paid by city treasurer from state funds received by him. (2) Treasurer of town in which is located a private school enrolling more than twenty-five children who are included in the enumeration shall pay to school that proportionate share which was derived from enumeration of children in said private school.[226]

Ohio: (1) Three and a half million dollars appropriated to pay parents (or guardians) with children in nonpublic schools: 10c per day of elementary school attendance; 15c per day of secondary school attendance. Not to exceed 180 days. (2) To provide free textbooks for *all pupils* in elementary, junior and senior high schools. (3) To provide free transportation for pupils of private and parochial schools when provided for public school pupils.[227]

Such proposals have increased in number during the past decade.

These examples will show the activity of the Roman Catholic Church in pressing for State aid for parochial schools or their pupils, thus hoping to relieve the heavy financial burden of maintaining unaided an efficient separate school system.

The extent to which the states co-operate with the Churches in giving support to the cause of religion for public school students, and aid for parochial schools, in addition to the usual exemption from taxation, may be thus summarized as of 1946:

In 18 states and one territory parochial school students were transported at public expense.

In 6 states the courts had declared the practice unconstitutional.

In 2 states the courts had upheld the practice.

In 5 states free textbooks (when they were the same as those used in the public schools) were furnished parochial school students.

In 35 states laws permitted the excusing of pupils to attend weekday religious classes under Church (or synagogue) auspices.

In 10 states voluntary religious instruction by Church teachers inside school buildings was specifically permitted.

In 13 states Bible reading at opening exercises was specifically required.

In 24 states such reading was permitted.

In 34 states laws permitted the use of public-school buildings for religious purposes after school hours.

In 16 states laws permitted the employment as public-school teachers of persons wearing a religious garb.

In 22 states such practice was not permitted under the laws.[228]

Only the first four items refer to the specific subject under discussion in this section, but the remainder are added to give the full picture. Free lunches for children in public and parochial schools were established in 1946.*

It remains to mention briefly a form of indirect Federal financial aid to denominational as well as to public institutions that in 1947 was in full operation with general public approval—an approval which would be doubtful if the funds were provided directly to institutions rather than to individual available students. We refer to the provision for permitting veterans of World War II to receive financial aid from the government. This makes no distinction between public, private, and sectarian institutions. By the Servicemen's Readjustment Act of 1944, popularly called the G.I. Bill of Rights, every veteran who has fulfilled the minimum period of service required for eligibility is entitled to at least one year's study at any approved school or training institution of his choice in any subject for which he is fitted. The government meets tuition and other fees, cost of books, supplies, equipment, and other necessary expenses not to exceed a maximum of $500 per school year, as well as providing a subsistence allowance during the period of from $65.00 to $90.00 a month, conditional on dependents. From our Church–State standpoint it is important to notice two things: that the grants, as in most cases of free lunches and bus transportation for school children, are made to the individual, not to the institution; and that students are not penalized if they wish to attend denominational schools or colleges. The Veterans Administration, which has charge of this and other services for ex-servicemen, announced in November, 1946, that 1,953,053 had already availed themselves of these educational privileges.[229] The government has also been helping theological students, along with other students, under the G.I. Bill and Vocational Rehabilitation Act because of services in the last war.[230] On the whole these arrangements seem justified in view of existing needs and Constitutional interpretations. But they must not be extended too far. Justice Cardozo called attention many years ago in *The Nature of the Judicial Process* to the fact that whenever a new principle is introduced into the statutes it tends to expand to the full limits of its inherent logic. This tendency should be borne in mind in connection with the further extension of borderline cases.

* See Addenda.

Section 6. THE QUESTION OF FEDERAL AID TO SECTARIAN INSTITUTIONS

In the early days of the republic it was assumed[231] that education, except for that at West Point and Annapolis, was exclusively a state matter; but after the Civil War, when the problem of educating the former slaves and the large number of immigrants from Europe arose, the United States Commissionership of Education was established (1867). There was then some discussion of the possibility of Federal aid to schools in general, and to the denominational and parochial schools that were struggling courageously to meet the major educational tasks facing the nation.

The earliest cases of such aid were on a small scale and were to Indian schools. The first considerable appropriation I have found recorded was through the Freedmen's Bureau. According to the best estimates available it gave nearly $250,000[232] between 1866 and 1870 to the American Missionary Association (Congregational) for buildings in the important Negro schools it was then founding in those parts of the South that were open to its activities.

(1) GRANT–BLAINE PROPOSALS

The first clear-cut declaration of the Federal government against the propriety of giving financial aid to sectarian institutions was made in 1875. President Ulysses S. Grant (1822–85), addressing the Army of the Tennessee, said:

> . . . Now, the centennial year of our national existence, I believe, is a good time to begin the work of strengthening the foundations of the structure commenced by our patriotic forefathers one hundred years ago at Lexington. Let us all labor to add all needful guarantees for the security of free thought, free speech, a free press, pure morals, unfettered religious sentiments, and of equal rights and privileges to all men, irrespective of nationality, color or religion. Encourage free schools, and resolve that not one dollar appropriated for their support shall be appropriated to the support of any sectarian schools. Resolve that neither the State nor nation, nor both combined, shall support institutions of learning other than those sufficient to afford every child growing up in the land the opportunity of a good common-school education, unmixed with sectarian, pagan, or atheistical dogmas. Leave the matter of religion to the family, altar, the church, and the private school supported entirely by private contributions. Keep the church and state forever separate. With these safeguards, I believe the battles which created the Army of the Tennessee will not have been fought in vain.[233]

It is interesting to note that the editor of the *Catholic World* which reported this interpreted the address as supporting the Roman Catholic opposition to the alleged Protestant sectarianism of the time in the public schools. He wrote:

. . . We agree with the President: 1st. No "sectarianism" in our common schools; and, therefore, not one dollar to our present system of schools, because they are sectarian. 2nd. "Not one dollar" to "Pagan" schools, in which God is ignored. 3rd. "Not one dollar" to "atheistical" schools, in which God is denied in the name of "science falsely so-called."[234]

Surely an impartial study will show that this was not the purpose of the address.

In his message to Congress later in the year (December 8, 1875) the president reverted to the same subject, which became a matter of large public interest. The resulting debate in Congress reflects the views of the time on this Church–State issue.

The journal of the House of Representatives for December 14, 1875, contains the resolution introduced by James G. Blaine (1830–93) of Maine, later speaker of the House, to carry the plan of the president into effect. It is based almost exactly on an amendment proposed in his message.

Resolved by the Senate and House of Representatives, That the following be proposed to the several States of the Union as an amendment to the Constitution:

Article XVI

No State shall make any law respecting an establishment of religion or prohibiting the free exercise thereof; and no money raised by taxation in any State for the support of public schools, or derived from any public fund therefor, nor any public lands devoted thereto, shall ever be under the control of any religious sect, nor shall any money so raised or lands so devoted be divided between religious sects or denominations.[235]

This resolution was referred to the Judiciary Committee.

On August 4, 1876, by a vote of 180 for, 7 against, and 98 not voting, the resolution was passed by the House with only slight verbal changes.[236]

When the resolution was read in the Senate on August 7, 1876, Senator Frederick Theodore Frelinghuysen (1817–85), a Republican of New Jersey, declared:

. . . The amendment only applies to a school fund and prohibits its being appropriated to schools under denominational control. There is not a word in the amendment that prohibits public money from being appropriated to theological seminaries, to reformatories, to monasteries, to nunneries, to houses of the Good Shepherd, and many kindred purposes. We know that in one State within a decade $1,200,000 was voted to Protestant institutions for which the Catholics of the country were taxed, and we know that in the same period several millions of dollars were voted to Catholic institutions for which Protestants were taxed.

Besides, sir, even in reference to schools this amendment only prohibits appropriating the school fund to denominational schools. It does not by any means forbid appropriations from the Treasury generally even to denominational schools.

He therefore proposed the following substitute:

Section 1. No State shall make any law respecting the establishment of religion or prohibiting the free exercise thereof; and no public property and no money raised by taxation in any State, Territory, or District, or derived from public lands, or other public source, shall be appropriated to any school, educational, or other institution that is under the control of any religious sect or denomination; and no such appropriation shall be made to any religious sect or denomination or to promote its interests; nor shall any public money, land, or property be divided between religious sects or denominations.

Sec. 2. The Congress shall have power to enforce by appropriate legislation the provisions of this article.[237]

Senator Aaron A. Sargent (1827–87) of California proposed still another substitute:

Section 1. There shall be maintained in each State and Territory a system of free common schools; but neither the United States nor any State, or Territory, county, or municipal corporation shall aid in the support of any school wherein the peculiar tenets of any religious denomination shall be taught.

Sec. 2. The Congress shall have power to enforce by appropriate legislation the provisions of this article.[238]

Senator Isaac P. Christiancy (1812–90) of Michigan offered the following:

No State shall make any law respecting the establishment of religion or prohibiting the free exercise thereof, nor shall Congress nor any State raise by taxation, donate, or appropriate any money or property for the support of any church or religious society, nor for the support or in aid of any theological school or seminary, or of any school or seminary teaching the peculiar religious doctrines, or subject in any respect to the control or direction of any church, religious society, sect, or denomination. And no special or denominational system of religion or religious belief shall in any State or Territory or in the District of Columbia constitute any part of the course of study or instruction in any school or institution of learning supported wholly or in part by taxation or by the donation of any money or property by any State or by the United States.[239]

The original resolution and all the substitutes were referred to the Committee on the Judiciary.

On August 11, 1876, the committee reported an amendment to strike out all after the enacting clause of the joint resolution and in lieu thereof to insert the following:

That the following article be proposed to the Legislatures of the several States as an amendment to the Constitution of the United States, which when ratified by three-fourths of the said Legislatures, shall be valid as a part of the said Constitution, namely:

Article XVI.

No State shall make any law respecting an establishment of religion, or prohibiting the free exercise thereof; and no religious test shall ever be required as a qualification to any office or public trust under any State. No public property and no public revenue of, nor any loan of credit by or under the authority of, the United States, or any State, Territory, District, or municipal corporation, shall be appropriated to or made or used for the support of any school, educational or other institution under the control of any religious or anti-religious sect, organization, or denomination, or wherein the particular creed or tenets of any religious or anti-religious sect, organization, or denomination shall be taught. And no such particular creed or tenets shall be read or taught in any school or institution supported in whole or in part by such revenue or loan of credit; and no such appropriation or loan of credit shall be made to any religious or anti-religious sect, organization, or denomination, or to promote its interests or tenets. This article shall not be construed to prohibit the reading of the Bible in any school or institution; and it shall not have the effect to impair rights of property already vested.

Sec. 2. Congress shall have power, by appropriate legislation, to provide for the prevention and punishment of violations of this article.[240]

In opposing this substitute and speaking in favor of the resolution as passed by the House, Senator Theodore Fitz Randolph (1816–83) of New Jersey said:

There is a general belief that good government requires by some sufficient means religious as well as secular education. Protestants and leading American Catholics agree in this.

Infidels and some other sects deny the necessity. The present issue as to where secular education ends and religious teaching begins is mainly between Protestants and Catholics. Agreeing in the main proposition, they are at irreconcilable difference as to the means. Most Protestants urge taxation for the support of public schools, in which they would have limited religious instruction. Catholics would have no general taxation for the purpose; or if any be had, then an equitable distribution of the moneys raised. The Catholic preference is for an education dependent upon the will of the parent, or the zeal of rival religious organizations. They contend that in the advanced position of the cause of education in the United States the widespread knowledge of the premium which society gives to intelligence will ever insure fair education to the masses. Protestants assert that history does not sustain this view.

Many even claim that the security of the state hinges upon the education of its people; that ignorance is the instrument of despotism, as intelligence is its foe. Thus it is argued the free state can only maintain its integrity through the education of its citizens. If this be strictly true then education must be *compulsory*. Then if you may compel my child to learn the lessons the state deems best, and those lessons be what a majority of the state, through temporary rulers, agree upon, what becomes of the priceless guarantee of liberty of conscience? . . .

I have indicated what seems to me to be, if persisted in, the ultimate of any system that antagonizes large bodies of citizens, attracting to them through sympathy—that oppression, real or fancied, ever begets—a large and constantly increasing number of non-religious citizens. As a Protestant, believing in the beneficence and desiring the advancement by fair means of my own religious doctrines, I protest against a public policy that brings so little of gain to me, and that promises so much to my differing fellow-citizens. . . .

Is it not wiser and safer that we who would place public education upon an enduring basis should so decide as to leave political affairs as the business alone of the state and religious teachings the duty of parents and of denominations and sects?. . . [241]

However, the Judiciary Committee's amendment to the House resolution was passed by a vote of 27 to 15.[242]

When the resolution as amended by the Senate came up for final vote on August 14, Senator Francis Kernan (1816–92) of New York said that he approved the first sentence but considered it unnecessary. The remainder of the amendment, however, he strongly opposed, saying in part:

. . . I cannot quite conceive what state of things there is to be in an orphan asylum, a hospital, or a reformatory. These charitable institutions will be founded and they will be managed by zealous hands and active feet belonging to one or the other of Christian denominations. They have their faith, and so believing they do not want to protrude their views upon others, but they gather up their own pauper children, their own pauper sick, their own pauper aged in these institutions. Yet you say the State shall not encourage them in their need by aiding from the treasury according to the will of the people of the State, because they teach that creed that makes them these ministering angels and zealous workers.

No city can aid the institution, no county can do it, no State can do it. While they can give to any other enterprise they shall not help with the public funds these zealous people who give their labors and their lives to this work. All Christian denominations have these zealous men and women, and by this amendment you say neither State nor city shall aid them. . . .[243]

Speaking in favor of the amendment, Senator Oliver P. Morton (1823–77) of Indiana said:

. . . It is in my opinion an essential principle of American liberty and one upon which the perpetuity of our Government depends that we shall have perfect freedom of religious worship, that there shall be no established church, no religion established by law that is taught by law, and that so far from the States being left free to establish a church if they see proper, or to establish denominational schools at public expense, I believe that the safety of this nation in the far future depends upon their being deprived of any such power. I believe that the example of one State establishing a religion, or doing what amounts to the same thing in principle, establishing denominational schools to be supported at public expense, endangers the perpetuity of the nation. The support of a school by public taxation is the same thing in principle as an established church.

. . . If any one believes that a particular church ought to be established by law or that children ought to be educated in peculiar doctrines at public expense, then he ought to oppose this amendment. But if he thinks that such education should be at private expense and that that given by the public should be general in its character, if he believes that no church should be established, why oppose this amendment? It is no more for Protestants than it is for Catholics. It is no more against Catholics than it is against Protestants; it puts all on the same level precisely, takes from one church precisely what it takes from the other. It is not a measure of favoritism. Let my friend bear it in mind that this is offered in a country where to-day the majority in every State are Protestants. It is offered in what may be called a Protestant country. But I trust that men of all parties, of all religions, and of every kind of education recognize the importance of maintaining this as a free country in which there shall be no established religion, and religion shall not be taught by law at public expense.[244]

The final vote by the Senate on the joint resolution was 28 for, 16 against, and 27 absent or not voting. Since there was not a two-thirds majority in favor, the proposed amendment could not be submitted to the states.[245]

Several factors conspired to bring about this result. Among these were a feeling that existing Constitutional guarantees were adequate; that the matter, as far as not already covered, would best be left to the states; that it was unwise to raise a nation-wide religious issue, especially so soon after the divisions of the Civil War; and strong Roman Catholic opposition. Inasmuch as similar proposals have since been occasionally made and are sure to be repeated, it has seemed well to record the history of the proposed amendment in some detail.

During the year of the early debates on the proposed Constitutional amendment to prevent public moneys from being used for denominational purposes, and otherwise to attempt further to protect religious freedom, both the Democratic and Republican parties were holding their conventions. Their planks on the subject of Federal financial aid to institutions under sectarian control have already been quoted.[246]

These Federal and party actions, whether wise or unwise in the exact forms taken, are evidence of the strong public opinion in this country two generations ago in favor of maintaining the separation of Church and State in all matters of education.[247]

Eleven Congressional attempts were made from 1870 (by Congressman Burdette of Missouri) through 1888, to secure an amendment to the Constitution which would specifically forbid government financial aid to parochial and denominational schools, and sometimes to set up other more rigid barriers between Church and State. Of these all except three were proposed between 1875 and 1878. The Blaine proposal just discussed was the only one that passed even one house of Congress with the necessary two-thirds vote required for submission to the states for ratification.[248] Congressman Bryson of North Carolina in 1948 proposed an amendment of this sort.

(2) RESTRICTIONS IN CONGRESSIONAL ENABLING ACTS FOR NEW STATES

Another and more successful attempt over a period of years to prevent Federal funds going to parochial or other denominational schools has been made in connection with the "enabling acts" authorizing the admission of the newer states of the West into the union. The earlier states, as we have seen,[249] were admitted under the general guarantees of the Federal Constitution, but these were not considered sufficiently specific, in spite of guarantees of religious freedom in state constitutions, to cover the issue later raised in several states as to the constitutionality of attempts made to secure public funds for parochial schools. Consequently Congress decided in the last quarter of the last century to go further.

Five Northwestern states admitted in 1889—Montana, the Dakotas, Wyoming, and Washington—were required to adopt ordinances guaranteeing that public schools would be established "free from sectarian control." The same wording was later used in connection with the admission of several other Western states, generally in the form of a compact. The purpose of Congress to prevent the use of public funds for sectarian purposes was made doubly clear by restricting the use of the township sections set apart for education not merely to "schools," as provided for in Ohio and some other states of the West early admitted to the union, but to "common" or "public schools," and in the latest cases, Arizona and New Mexico (1912), to "free public non-sectarian public schools."[250] It would be impossible for Congress to make its wishes and conditions more explicit.

(3) FEDERAL GRANTS TO SECTARIAN EDUCATION, AND RECENT ATTEMPTS TO PREVENT THEM

An impressive evidence of the will of Congress in this matter is contained in the District of Columbia Appropriation Act for 1897. The paragraph follows:

> And it is hereby declared to be the policy of the Government of the United States to make no appropriation of money or property for the purpose of founding, maintaining, or aiding by payment for services, expenses, or otherwise, any church or religious denomination, or any institution or society which is under sectarian or ecclesiastical control; and it is hereby enacted that, from and after the thirtieth day of June, eighteen hundred and ninety-seven, no money appropriated for charitable purposes in the

District of Columbia, shall be paid to any church or religious denomination, or to any institution or society which is under sectarian or ecclesiastical control.[251]

This provision was carried in identical language, except for the change of dates, in the appropriation for the succeeding year,[252] and these precedents have in general been since followed. A curious point about this paragraph is that it includes in one sentence a general provision of law with a clause limiting it to the District of Columbia. The fact that the District is, like all territories, directly under the control of Congress does not fully explain this anomaly.

A similar purpose was evidently in mind when the United States Office of Education, providing for part-time jobs for students under the Federal Emergency Relief Administration Act of 1934, stated that "no work of a non-public or sectarian nature should be included."[253]

Attempts have been made increasingly in recent years to include parochial schools in Federal grants for public education, but up to 1949 they have proved unsuccessful. Such proposals generally die in committee, or if they pass one House of Congress they are likely to be killed in the other. Furthermore, in view of the Supreme Court *dicta* in the Everson and McCollum cases it is probable that laws permitting such grants if passed would be declared unconstitutional. Among proposals of this character recently before Congress were one by Senator Robert A. Taft of Ohio and later by Senator Elbert D. Thomas of Utah, which would make grants applicable however only when the state concerned permitted them by law and when it was ready to duplicate the Federal grant; and another by Congressman Richard J. Welch of California which specifically mentions not only public schools but elementary and secondary parochial schools.[255] American public opinion, except for that of the Roman Catholic Church and of men in public life from centers with a large Catholic population, is generally opposed to all such grants as unconstitutional. But the question continues a live one, although rendered less serious by Cardinal Spellman's recent assurance (August, 1949) to Mrs. Franklin D. Roosevelt (XIX, 10).

The attitude of Congress toward aid to parochial schools prior to this was reflected in votes taken in May, 1949. The Senate by a vote of 58 to 15 approved an education bill (S. 246) which authorized vast sums to equalize educational facilities in the various states, and which included the parochial schools in the plan when public grants to them are permitted by state laws and when the state legislatures so decide. The whole matter was complicated by the fact that representative Roman Catholics and Catholic organizations had taken the ground that parochial schools are virtually public schools because they are open free or on small charges to all, and that consequently they could not favor any Federal aid to education that did not include such schools. It has been estimated that under existing state laws the amount of the grants to parochial schools under this bill would be over seven million dollars. This is of course in addition to what pupils of such schools get under existing grants for auxiliary services, which are to be supplemented under the National School Health Services Act of 1949. The Senate action on the education bill permitting grants to the states for parochial schools came after the defeat by a vote of 71 to 3 an amendment by Senator Donnell of Missouri which sought to exclude all aid under the bill to private and parochial schools.

It should be remembered that the Senate acted after the Supreme Court in its *dicta* in both the Everson and McCollum cases had clearly excluded all financial aid to such schools from public funds—an opinion shared by eight of the nine justices in the McCollum decision. If therefore this new bill becomes law it is likely to be voided by the court as unconstitutional.[255]

The Jesuit magazine *America* seemed to approve of the opposition to Federal aid for public schools unless Catholic schools also received help, but *Commonweal* has taken the ground that to do this "merely because parochial schools are not to receive the same degree of help, is evidence of a discouraging short-sightedness."[256]

The general policy of the Federal government is neither to make nor permit grants from public funds for any denominational religious purpose. Exceptions to this rule are trifling. Federal courts have permitted a few old Spanish, Mexican, and Russian grants of property for church purposes to stand; such as the grant by Russia of property for a Lutheran Church in Sitka, Alaska,[257] and a few grants by the Federal government to hospitals and other philanthropic institutions which render a public service to all, irrespective of creed. But these are merely exceptions which prove the rule.

The question of public aid to a legally secular philanthropic institution conducted by a religious body came before the supreme court of the District of Columbia in the case of *Bradfield* v. *Roberts*. It involved a Congressional grant to Providence Hospital in the District, an institution incorporated by an Act of Congress in 1864. Congress authorized the commissioners of the District to spend in their discretion $30,000 for the erection of two "isolating [*sic*] buildings" on the grounds of this and another private hospital. An injunction was sought by certain persons to prevent the carrying out of this grant, mainly on the ground that Providence Hospital was not strictly a public institution but virtually a Roman Catholic hospital. The supreme court of the District granted the injunction, which was overruled by the court of appeals, and the United States Supreme Court unanimously affirmed this latter judgment. The decision is important as indicating that the Supreme Court believes that the State is not prevented from aiding a philanthropic institution, which is entirely secular as far as its legal incorporation is concerned, even though it is actually under the auspices of a religious organization, if it is equally open to all citizens and not conducted in a sectarian spirit. It would be a mistake, however, to read too much into the court's opinion, which is mainly based on the fact that the hospital is actually doing exactly the work for which it was incorporated.

In the course of the opinion delivered for the court by Justice Rufus Wheeler Peckham (1838–1909) it was stated:

The act shows that the individuals named therein and their successors in office were incorporated under the name of "The Directors of Providence Hospital," with power to receive, hold and convey personal and real property, as provided in its first section. By the second section the corporation was granted "full power and all the rights of opening and keeping a hospital in the city of Washington for the care of such sick and invalid persons as may place themselves under the treatment and care of the said corporation." The third section gave it full power to make such by-laws, rules and regulations that might be necessary for the general accomplishment of the objects of the hospital, not inconsistent with the laws in force in the District of Columbia. Nothing is said about religion or about the religious faith of the incorporators of this institution in the act of incorporation. It is simply the ordinary case of the incorporation of a hospital for the purposes for which such an institution is generally conducted. It is claimed that the allegation in the complainant's bill, that the said "Providence Hospital is a private eleemosynary corporation, and that to the best of complainant's knowledge and belief it is composed of members of a monastic order or sisterhood of the Roman Catholic Church, and is conducted under the auspices of said church; that the title to its property is vested in the Sisters of Charity of Emmitsburg, Maryland," renders the agreement void for the reason therein stated, which is that Congress has no power to make "a law respecting a religious establishment," a phrase which is not synonymous with that used in the Constitution which prohibits the passage of a law "respecting an establishment of religion."

If we were to assume, for the purpose of this question only, that under this appropriation an agreement with a religious corporation of the tenor of this agreement would be invalid, as resulting indirectly in the passage of an act respecting an establishment of religion, we are unable to see that the complainant in his bill shows that the corporation is of the kind described, but on the contrary he has clearly shown that it is not.

The above-mentioned allegations in the complainant's bill do not change the legal character of the corporation or render it on that account a religious or sectarian body. Assuming that the hospital is a private eleemosynary corporation, the fact that its members, according to the belief of the complainant, are members of a monastic order or sisterhood of the Roman Catholic Church, and the further fact that the hospital is conducted under the auspices of said church, are wholly immaterial, as is also the allegation regarding the title to its property. The statute provides as to its property and makes no provision for its being held by any other than itself. The facts above stated do not in the least change the legal character of the hospital, or make a religious corporation out of a purely secular one as constituted by the law of its being. Whether the individuals who compose the corporation under its charter happen to be all Roman Catholics, or all Methodists, or Presbyterians, or Unitarians, or members of any other religious organization, or of no organization at all, is of not the slightest consequence with reference to the law of its incorporation, nor can the individual beliefs upon religious matters of the various incorporators be inquired into. Nor is it material that the hospital may be conducted under the auspices of the Roman Catholic Church. To be conducted under the auspices is to be conducted under the influence or patronage of that church. The meaning of the allegation is that the church exercises great and perhaps controlling influence over the management of the hospital. It must, however, be managed pursuant to the law of its being. That the influence of any particular church may be powerful over the members of a non-sectarian and secular corporation, incorporated for a certain defined purpose and with clearly stated powers, is surely not sufficient to convert such a corporation into a religious or sectarian body. That fact does not alter the legal character of the corporation, which is incorporated under an act of Congress, and its powers, duties and character are to be solely measured by the charter under which it alone has any legal existence. There is no allegation that its hospital work is confined to members of that church or that in its management the hospital has been conducted so as to violate its charter in the smallest degree. It is simply the case of a secular corporation being managed by people who hold to the doctrines of the Roman Catholic Church, but who nevertheless are managing the corporation according to the law under which it exists. . . .[258]

The opinion of the court was rendered in 1899. Whether the case would be similarly decided today may be open to question.

This decision is important in protecting the rights of a private institution under its act of incorporation. It is even more important for our present purpose because of its underlying assumption that if the institution could be proved to be a sectarian one in the ordinary understanding of the word it could not receive public funds. It is believed that the Federal government would hesitate to incorporate today a distinctly sectarian institution or give it any financial aid; but a few broadly conceived self-supporting educational institutions in the District of Columbia, whose privileges are not restricted to any one religious group, have been given their charter by Congress in the absence of any other legislative body which might have jurisdiction.[259]

It is not improbable, in view of the state of public opinion today, that Congress will propose to the states a Constitutional amendment that will specifically forbid both Federal and state direct financial grants to all parochial and denominational institutions. Such action need not of course go so far as to upset existing plans to help individual students in these institutions in such matters as free bus transportation and free textbooks or to aid former soldiers and certain other groups with free scholarships in any institution of good standing whether public, denominational, parochial, or private. Such an amendment has been proposed by Congressman Joseph R. Bryson, and is given in full in a later section where "The Changes Needed to Secure Complete Religious Freedom" are discussed.[260] It follows, in general, the provisions of various bills proposed in the Grant administration and outlined earlier in this section. A similar purpose, to exclude direct financial aid from the Federal government for the support of any but strictly public schools, is behind the Barden bill, proposed in 1949 by Congressman Graham A. Barden of North Carolina and given in full in a later section (XIX, 10), where the recent controversy between Cardinal Spellman and Mrs. Franklin Delano Roosevelt is discussed. Its supporters, following recent Supreme Court decisions, merely take the ground that government financial aid for the support of religious schools of any denomination is unconstitutional. The parochial schools have been almost entirely supported in the past by Roman Catholics without public aid. If this continues to be the policy and the few cases of state aid are eliminated, there will be more general appreciation by non-Catholics of the contributions which the Catholics are making to general education.

Section 7. THE INSPECTION AND STANDARDIZATION OF PRIVATE AND PAROCHIAL SCHOOLS

It is believed that the question of denominational schools has been wisely and finally settled by granting all groups freedom of educational action as long as they observe all Constitutional and legal requirements. The states however hold in reserve, even when it is not expressly stated in constitution or statutes, the right to maintain the educational courses and standards they consider necessary. Whether this involves the right of inspection of classroom instruction has been much debated. An attempt to have this provided for by law in Massachusetts in 1888 failed.[261] The somewhat similar Bennett law framed by the Wisconsin legislature in 1889 did not go as far. In New York the Board of Regents has long exerted a "limited supervision" over parochial and other private schools, and some other states have followed the same practice.[262] The Ohio compulsory education law, sustained by the supreme court of the state in 1892, required a Catholic school principal to furnish to the public educational authorities the names, ages, and residences of his students.[263]

In a Nebraska case, in which the United States Supreme Court declared a certain law passed by the Nebraska legislature in 1919 unconstitutional, it pointed out that a state may determine the curricula of its own schools, and may reasonably regulate all schools to the extent of supervising, inspecting, and examining them, including their teachers and pupils, and may require certain studies essential to good citizenship.[264] On the other hand, the right of parents, based on the old common law, to have their children taught at home or in some private or denominational school of their choice is duly protected, provided that the school chosen meets the lawful requirements of state statutes. Similarly the Supreme Court in deciding the Oregon school case in 1924 clearly implied the right of a state to inspect its private and parochial schools. It said:

> No question is raised concerning the power of the State reasonably to regulate all schools, to inspect, supervise and examine them, their teachers and pupils; to require that all children of proper age attend some school, that teachers shall be of good moral character and patriotic disposition, that certain studies plainly essential to good citizenship must be taught, and that nothing be taught which is manifestly inimical to the public welfare.[265]

The supreme court of Georgia has even allowed to pass as not infringing the Constitution a statute adopted by the state in 1916 providing among other things for the inspection of convents.[266] Here is the law:

> 59–401. Appointment of committee to visit and inspect certain institutions.—The grand juries in the respective counties shall at each regular term of the courts in their respective counties, appoint a committee of not less than five members from the grand jury, whose duty it shall be, as soon as practicable after they are named on said committee, to visit, inspect, and carefully inquire into every orphanage, sanitarium, sanatorium, hospital, asylum, House of the Good Shepherd, convent, monastery, house of correction, reformatory, penitentiary, school and college, for the purpose of ascertaining what persons are confined within said institutions and by what authority such persons are held within the same.[267]

This act is known as the Veasey bill or the Veasey inspection law. It will be noticed that it applies equally to all such institutions, irrespective of denomination, and that it does not specifically include any reference to their work and discipline. But inspectors carrying out their assigned tasks as agents of the state might well make mental notes of any abuses or defects found. A similar law was passed in Alabama in 1919.

The exact degree to which the state may supervise public schools has never been authoritatively stated. In the well-known Hawaiian foreign language case the Supreme Court of the United States ruled out certain legislative action as unconstitutional because it involved "affirmative direction concerning the intimate and essential details of such schools."[268]

One of the most informing cases indicating the measure of supervision which a state may employ was decided a few years ago by the supreme court of New

Hampshire.[269] This decision upheld the right of the state to regulate and superintend the education of children to the extent at least of requiring that they be trained in good morals and good citizenship. In this decision the court said:

> The power "reasonably to regulate," to require attendance, good character of teachers, studies to be taught and those to be prohibited, all look to laying down rules for future conduct. As the statute does not exceed the exercise of these powers, it is held to be constitutional.
>
> In the adjustment of the parent's right to choose the manner of his children's education, and the impinging right of the state to insist that certain education be furnished and supervised, the rule of reasonable conduct upon the part of each towards the other is to be applied. The state must bear the burden of reasonable supervision, and the parent must offer educational facilities which do not require unreasonable supervision. If the parent undertakes to make use of units of education so small, or facilities of such doubtful quality, that supervision thereof would impose an unreasonable burden upon the state, he offends against the reasonable provisions for schools which can be supervised without unreasonable expense. The state may require not only that educational facilities be supplied but also that they be so supplied that the facts in relation thereto can be ascertained, and proper direction thereof maintained, without unreasonable cost to the state. Anything less than this would take from the state all efficient authority to regulate the education of the prospective voting population.[270]

This seems consistent with the decisions in the two great Federal cases of *Meyer* v. *Nebraska* and *Pierce* v. *Society of the Holy Names of Jesus and Mary*—the "Oregon case," decided in 1923 and 1924 respectively.[271]

Although the Roman Catholic Church has resisted attempts at official inspection of its schools when they thought such inspection was actuated by unworthy and inquisitional motives, any citizen may visit the schools, and it is well known that their curricula, except for the addition of religious subjects, follows closely those in the public schools, and that patriotism is inculcated. In theory the Church supports the right of the State to see that the education in parochial schools is conducted in such a way as to be "in the name of the good of the general public." This is the authoritative view of a professor of the history of philosophy in the Catholic University of America. In discussing the principles of Catholic education, he says:

> In all schools, whether established by the Church or the State, or even by a group of families (so long as there are pupils received from different families) the State has the right to see that the laws of public health, public order, and public morality are observed, and if any school doctrines were taught subversive of public peace or otherwise opposed to the interests of the general public, the State would have the right to intervene "in the name of the good of the general public."[272]

In general, the State accepts the theory that private schools may exist, but that it has a right to inspect them and see that they maintain certain standards and ideals which legislatures believe to be essential. Such right is clearly specified in some state constitutions and is generally implied in all. For instance, the constitution of New York has long permitted the use of public money for the

> examination or inspection, of any school or institution of learning wholly or in part under the control or direction of any religious denomination, or in which any denominational tenet or doctrine is taught,[273]

and specifically states that this is the only lawful use of public moneys for such institutions, except as free bus transportation was legalized after the constitutional convention of 1938.

A recent study of the supervision of sectarian schools (i.e., parochial and other denominational) by public-school authorities was published by the National Educational Association in 1946. With five states not heard from, the results are given from the remaining forty-three states, the territories of Alaska and Hawaii, and the District of Columbia. There is generally the requirement for all privately conducted schools that English be the medium of instruction. Similarly, three-fourths of the states provide by law that education in parochial schools shall be equivalent to that in public schools. The following are the more important results of the study showing the states in which private and sectarian schools are inspected in the matters mentioned: Term equivalent to public schools, 20; certification of teachers, 15; registration with state department, 14; state-approved course of study, 19; U.S. Constitution, American history, civics, etc., in curriculum, 21; physiology and hygiene included, 19; effects of hygiene and narcotics taught, 18; standards for facilities and equipment, 15; attendance records filed, 27. Seven other states require inspection in most of these matters when formal state approval is sought.[274]

Educational policy is clearly within the police power of the state, and consequently the state has the right to outline those educational requirements that it believes necessary for the public welfare and to see that they are observed. This is emphasized, along with the right of inspection of denominational schools, in the government regulations for Indian schools adopted in 1937; but, as the Supreme Court stated in the Oregon case referred to above,

> The fundamental theory of liberty upon which all governments in this Union repose excludes any general power of the state to standardize its children by forcing them to accept instruction from public teachers only. The child is not the mere creature of the state; those who nurture him and direct his destiny have the right, coupled with the high duty, to recognize and prepare him for additional obligations.[275]

There are various ways in which the state sees to it that instruction in private schools is of acceptable character. It is everywhere conceded that such schools must abstain from any and all practices deemed inconsistent with the peace, good order, and safety of the state.[276] It is also recognized that the state may require certain subjects in the curriculum, such as a knowledge of hygiene, of the English language, and of American history and government. The state may also control the length of the school course and a reasonable regularity of attendance on the part of pupils, the qualifications for teachers' certificates, as in Alabama, South Dakota, Michigan, and Nebraska.[277] It also has in a few states the specific right of supervision, and the specific right of inspection in at least one-third of the states. Inspection is likely to increase. It is of course not to be carried out in any inquisitorial way, as in the unfortunate attempts to inspect convents in Massachusetts shortly before 1850.[278]

Section 8. THE RIGHTS OF PRIVATE AND PAROCHIAL SCHOOLS

There have been several cases in which the question of freedom in education, especially the right of parents to select their own schools, have been before the higher courts in the United States. Most of these have been brought up for decision as to their constitutionality by religious groups to protect themselves against laws in Western states which, in the interest of "Americanism," have tried to interfere in one way or another with Church schools, even going so far as to try to require public school attendance. Strangely enough, this movement in America came to a head before the recent development of the totalitarian state in Europe. It has been led by vigorous and conscientious but sometimes extreme Protestants, who have feared that the parochial schools of the Roman Catholic Church might prove inimical to democracy by educating a group apart, with supreme allegiance to Rome. The matter has been much to the fore in certain states with a predominantly agrarian population. The courts have generally decided, as stated by the Supreme Court of Ohio as early as 1877, that it is not the "public policy of the state that the children of the state shall not receive any education in any other schools than in one of the public schools established by itself."[279] This would seem a reasonable position, but, to prevent advocates of a superpatriotic type from making it illegal for parents to educate their children in parochial or private schools, one state, Kentucky, in 1891 adopted an addition to its Bill of Rights reading: "Nor shall any man be compelled to send his child to any school to which he may be conscientiously opposed."[280] The fact that the United States Supreme Court decisions about to be quoted make such a clause unnecessary in no way detracts from its historic significance. The following year (1892) the voters of Wisconsin repealed the Bennett law of 1889, to which the Lutherans and Roman Catholics had strenuously objected because it required the elementary education of children to be in the English language.[281]

There have been two specially important cases before the Supreme Court of the United States on this issue of freedom in education. The first was *Meyer v. Nebraska* in 1923.[282] The court, by a seven to two decision—the dissenters being two members seldom found on the same side in a divided court, Justices Holmes and Sutherland—decided that a parent had the right to educate his child in a parochial school. In this case there was under judicial consideration an act of the legislature of Nebraska in 1919 entitled "An act relating to the teaching of foreign languages in the state of Nebraska," the most important sections of which were these:

Section 1. No person, individually or as a teacher, shall, in any private, denominational, parochial or public school, teach any subject to any person in any language other than the English language.

Sec. 2. Languages, other than the English language, may be taught as languages only after a pupil shall have attained and successfully passed the eighth grade as evidenced by a certificate of graduation issued by the county superintendent of the county in which the child resides.[283]

The Nebraska Supreme Court had decided that a teacher in a school maintained by the Zion Evangelical Lutheran Congregation, one Robert T. Meyer, had unlawfully taught the subject of reading in the German language from a collection of Bible stories, to a child of ten who had not passed the eighth grade. The decision was reversed by the United States Supreme Court. The principle involved affected far more Roman Catholic than Protestant schools, as at bottom the whole question of the legality of parochial as distinct from public schools was involved. The case was decided on the ground that the Fourteenth Amendment, which forbids any state to deprive any person "of life, liberty, or property without due process of law," denotes among other things the right of the individual "to worship God according to the dictates of his own conscience."[284]

The questions of the court and the answers of counsel, the late Arthur Francis Mullen (1873–1938), a Roman Catholic, of Omaha, Nebraska, are significant. Justice James C. McReynolds (1862–1941), who wrote the opinion, was the questioner.

Q. I just want to see what you claim. What about the power of the State to require the children to attend the public schools?

A. That is what I will come to in a moment.

Q. You will admit that, will you not?

A. I do not admit that.

Q. You do not admit that?

A. I do not admit that. I deny that a State can, by a majority of the legislature, require me to send my child to the public schools. I submit this, however: I agree with the proposition that under the police power, the State has authority to regulate private schools. I distinguish between the right to abolish an institution and to regulate it.

After more questioning, in which Chief Justice Taft joined, Mullen proceeded.

It is now seriously argued that a legislative majority can, by its mere fiat, take my children and require me to send them to a public school, and have the course of study absolutely controlled by the State. I deny that any such power exists in a constitutional government.

That question is at the very base of this case. It is a blow at education; it is striking down the principle that a parent has control over the education of his child. I deny the power of a legislative majority to take the child from its parent.

These important questions have been discussed here very quickly. The right of a man to communicate with his family, and the right of a man to give religious instruction to his children; the right to be free in his home; the right to maintain private educational institutions, and in these matters to be let alone—surely these are "privileges and immunities" protected by the Constitution of the United States. And these rights should not be fixed or limited by narrow and devitalized definitions of constitutional liberty.[285]

This view won the support of Mr. Justice McReynolds and of a majority of his colleagues. These are the most important paragraphs in his highly important and influential opinion as adopted by the court:

While this court has not attempted to define with exactness the liberty thus guaranteed, the term has received much consideration and some of the included things have been definitely stated. Without doubt, it denotes not merely freedom from bodily restraint but also the right of the individual to contract, to engage in any of the common occupations of life, to acquire useful knowledge, to marry, establish a home and bring up children, to worship God according to the dictates of his own conscience, and generally to enjoy those privileges long recognized at common law as essential to the orderly pursuit of happiness by free men.[286]

The established doctrine is that this liberty may not be interfered with, under the guise of protecting the public interest, by legislative action which is arbitrary or without reasonable relation to some purpose within the competency of the state to effect. Determination by the Legislature of what constitutes proper exercise of police power is not final or conclusive but is subject to supervision by the courts.[287]

. . . Plaintiff in error taught this language in school as part of his occupation. His right thus to teach and the right of parents to engage him so to instruct their children, we think, are within the liberty of the amendment.[288]

. . . That the state may do much, go very far, indeed, in order to improve the quality of its citizens, physically, mentally and morally, is clear; but the individual has certain fundamental rights which must be respected. . . .[289]

The power of the state to compel attendance at some school and to make reasonable regulations for all schools, including a requirement that they shall give instructions in English, is not questioned. . . .[290]

The Oregon case,[291] unanimously decided in 1925 favoring the constitutionality of attendance by children at parochial and private as distinct from public schools, is the other United States Supreme Court decision of special importance in this field. It was based on the precedent of *Meyer* v. *Nebraska,* which we have just considered. The essential facts were these. By a popular referendum vote of about 115,000 to 103,000 the state of Oregon adopted a law requiring parents and guardians to send all children between the ages of eight and sixteen except those in a few categories "to a public school," failure to comply being punishable as a misdemeanor. The constitutionality of the law was contested in the United States Supreme Court by the Society of the Sisters of the Holy Names of Jesus and Mary, conducting orphanages, parochial schools, and junior colleges, and by the Hill Military Academy, a private school. A unanimous decision was rendered in 1925 invalidating the compulsory education act[292] as interfering with religious freedom. The court took the position that the carrying out of its provisions would practically force the closing of most private schools in the state, and supported the lower court in holding that the act was contrary to the provisions of the Fourteenth Amendment. It declared that

the right to conduct schools was property, and that parents or guardians, as a part of their liberty, might direct the education of their children by selecting reputable teachers and places. . . . Appellees asked protection against arbitrary, unreasonable, and unlawful interference with their patrons, and the consequent dissolution of their business and property. Their interest is clear and immediate. . . .[293]

The most important quotation from the Supreme Court opinion, written by the late Justice James C. McReynolds (1862–1946), follows:

Under the doctrine of *Meyer* vs. *Nebraska* 262 U.S. 390 . . . we think it entirely plain that the Act of 1922 unreasonably interferes with the liberty of parents and guardians to direct the upbringing and education of children under their control. As often heretofore pointed out, rights guaranteed by the Constitution may not be abridged by legislation which has no reasonable relation to some purpose within the competency of the state. The fundamental theory of liberty upon which all governments in this Union repose excludes any general power of the state to standardize its children by forcing them to accept instruction from public teachers only. The child is not the mere creature of the state; those who nurture him and direct his destiny have the right, coupled with the high duty, to recognize and prepare him for additional obligations.[294]

This has generally been considered one of the wisest and most important decisions of the Supreme Court in voiding a state law as unconstitutional. It is specially significant as being decided on its Constitutional merits when this country was at peace, and before Nazi totalitarianism made its threat against the United States. The court specifically stated that no question was raised as to the right of the State to require certain things of schools and make due inspection of them. In fact its comments on these matters are so important that they are treated at length elsewhere.[295]

Section 9. THE FOREIGN-LANGUAGE SCHOOLS WITH RELIGIOUS ASSOCIATIONS

The question of foreign-language schools in the United States and its territories and insular possessions has been a matter on which appeals are frequently made to the courts. These cases interest us in this study because Church schools have been very largely involved, such as schools conducted by German or Scandinavian Lutherans, or by Japanese Buddhists. In general the courts have taken the ground that the State may not interfere unduly in the education of children, and that if parents wish schools other than the public schools, even when such schools are conducted in a foreign language, the parents have the right to carry out their wishes provided certain essential requirements are met. The state merely retains such rights of oversight and regulation as may be necessary to prevent abuses and to insure good citizenship.

Such cases were particularly common during and immediately after World War I, when several states passed statutes forbidding the use of German, or of foreign languages in general, as a means of instruction to pupils under a certain grade. State courts in Ohio, Nebraska, and Iowa upheld such statutes, but on appeal to the United States Supreme Court they were decided to be unconstitutional. It was held that the right of parents to engage a teacher to instruct their children in German, for instance, is within the liberty of the Fourteenth Amendment, and that the statutes in question interfered with the parental prerogative and exceeded the limitations on the power of the state.[296]

In *Meyer* v. *Nebraska* (1923)[297] the question of religious liberty was indirectly involved. The pastor of the congregation in charge of the school concerned testified that his "ultimate and only object" for wishing German instruction was

> . . . for instance, so that the children can take part in the devotional exercises of the parents at home, attend public worship with the parents and worship with them—for that reason we wanted to have children learn so much German that they could worship with their parents.

The decision of the court on this point in the Oregon case was also particularly important.[298]

For our purposes the most interesting case involving foreign languages was that decided by the United States Supreme Court in April, 1927, with reference to an act to supervise and regulate foreign language schools in Hawaii, especially those that are often spoken of as "Buddhist schools." The act had been declared unconstitutional by the Ninth Appellate United States Court, and its decision was affirmed by the Supreme Court.

The case is known as *Farrington* v. *Tokushige,* Farrington being the governor of Hawaii, whose territorial legislature had passed an "Act relating to foreign language schools and the teachers thereof."[299] This Act, and the subsequent regulations of the territorial Department of Public Instruction to carry it out, were considered to infringe the rights of the owners of Japanese schools and of the parents whose children attended them. These schools had had their beginning three decades earlier in 1896. It was shown that there were 163 foreign-language schools in the territory. Of these 147 were Japanese schools, owned, maintained, and conducted, without help from public funds, by about 5,000 persons, and with an enrollment of about 20,000 pupils—"practically all" children who attended some public or recognized private school and who enrolled in the foreign-language school for supplementary instruction outside of regular school hours.

According to the court

> It is the declared object of the Act to fully and effectively regulate the conducting of foreign language schools and the teaching of foreign languages, in order that the Americanism of the pupils may be promoted, and the department is directed to carry out the provisions of the Act in accordance with its spirit and purpose.[300]

Although it was not brought out at the trial, we are told by the President's Advisory Committee on Education, quoting a survey under the direction of the United States commissioner of education, that "These schools were usually conducted on Church property by Church leaders."[301]

It is this that gives the case special significance in this study, for the right of religious and language groups to give an education supplementing that in the public schools without undue interference by the state was really at issue. The subjects covered by the curriculum of these schools were mainly the Japanese language, composition, reading, penmanship, history, geography, moral teaching, and the customs and traditions of the parents.[302] It was this last group of studies that was specially criticized by those who felt that the parents concerned could not be relied on to inculcate American ideals in their children.

The court, after outlining the main features of the Hawaiian legislation, gave the following opinion:

> The foregoing statement is enough to show that the school Act and the measures adopted thereunder go far beyond mere regulation of privately-supported schools where children obtain instruction deemed valuable by their parents and which is not obviously in conflict with any public interest. They give affirmative direction concerning the intimate and essential details of such schools, intrust their control to public officers, and deny both owners and patrons reasonable choice and discretion in respect of teachers, curriculum and text-books. Enforcement of the Act probably would destroy most, if not all, of them; and, certainly, it would deprive parents of fair opportunity to procure for their children instruction which they think important and we cannot say is harmful. The Japanese parent has the right to direct the education of his own child without unreasonable restrictions; the Constitution protects him as well as those who speak another tongue. . . .
>
> The general doctrine touching rights guaranteed by the Fourteenth Amendment to owners, parents and children in respect of attendance upon schools has been announced in recent opinions. *Meyer* v. *Nebraska,* 262 U. S. 390; *Bartels* v. *Iowa, id.* 404; *Pierce* v. *Society of Sisters,* 268 U. S. 510. While that amendment declares that no State shall "deprive any person of life, liberty or property without due process of law," the inhibition of the Fifth Amendment "no person shall . . . be deprived of life, liberty, or property without due process of law"—applies to the federal government and agencies set up by Congress for the government of the Territory. Those fundamental rights of the individual which the cited cases declared were protected by the Fourteenth Amendment from infringement by the States, are guaranteed by the Fifth Amendment against action by the Territorial Legislature or officers.[303]

As a result of this decision the territorial legislature abolished in 1927 the position of supervisor of foreign-language schools, and appropriated a sum of nearly $20,000 for the reimbursement of fees that had been paid in connection with non-litigating schools. The incident was thus closed. Since the schools decreased in number, had fewer teachers who had not mastered English, and were not apparently trying to take the place of the regular public or private schools, the agitation of two decades ago slowly disappeared. The process was aided by the fine record of Hawaiian Japanese-American troops in World War II. It is worth recording, however, that the joint committee on Hawaii, reporting to the Congress in 1938, stated that though there was no evidence of anti-Americanism in the existing plan

> it does offer a source of criticism, and undoubtedly the American people would be better satisfied if there was more supervision of these schools. If this cannot be done legally it would seem that the schools themselves should voluntarily submit to the supervision of the Department of Public Instruction of the Territory of Hawaii.[304]

But something was accomplished to which no thoughtful person can object. Under new laws these schools, like other private schools of all kinds, were placed nominally "under the supervision of the Territorial Department." They were required to "regularly report to the Department on numbers, nationality, etc., of teachers and pupils."[305] The requiring of such information and the right of general supervision involved are very different things from the detailed regulation of curriculum, textbooks, teachers, etc., contemplated in the Act that was declared unconstitutional.

California had a somewhat similar experience. In 1921 it adopted a law based on the territorial law for Hawaii, though not so extreme, to control the foreign-language schools. This remained in effect for six years, when, on the advice of the attorney general of the state, the state department of education ceased all activity in connection with these schools, due to the decision rendered by the United States Supreme Court in the Hawaiian case above referred to. The California law was intended to make sure that Americanism was advanced in these schools, and that the instruction was "approved" by the state board of education. Prior to the Japanese deportations from the West coast in World War II, such schools were sometimes under control of the Buddhist churches, sometimes of the Japanese community. They received no public aid and apparently gave only supplementary education,[306] hence it was believed that their constitutionality could not be questioned.

Section 10. *CONTROVERSY BETWEEN CARDINAL SPELLMAN AND MRS. ROOSEVELT*

While this volume has been in the hands of the printer, in the summer of 1949, a dramatic incident has occurred in the field of American Church-State relations that will have a broad and possibly permanent influence. The incident was the controversy between His Eminence Cardinal Francis Joseph Spellman (1887–) and Mrs. Franklin D. Roosevelt (1884–) regarding public aid to parochial schools. It has ended in an encouraging way which may prove historically important by removing a major cause of friction between the Roman Catholic Church and most of the non-Catholic citizens of this country. To understand the incident it seems necessary to give brief attention to eight matters:

(1) The historical background of the parochial school situation.

(2) The Barden Bill for direct Federal aid to public schools.

(3) Mrs. Roosevelt's defense of Church-State separation as applicable to the question of tax aid to parochial schools.

(4) Cardinal Spellman's attack on Mrs. Roosevelt for her attitude.

(5) The public reaction.
(6) Mrs. Roosevelt's reply to Cardinal Spellman.
(7) The cardinal's statement of his modified position.
(8) Mrs. Roosevelt's sympathetic comments.

(1) THE HISTORICAL BACKGROUND OF THE PAROCHIAL SCHOOL SITUATION

We have dealt at length in these volumes with the history of parochial schools in this country to show that their origin as an important factor in national life was due to the large immigration from Ireland and continental Europe in the second third of the last century.[307] The present chapter has dealt with the development of the parochial school system until today, when it is prominent in every state in the Union. The Roman Catholic position, in general, as taken by the Church in its Plenary Councils,[308] has been that where parochial schools are available Catholic children must be sent to them unless they receive from the diocesan authority special permission to go elsewhere; and since these schools have become increasingly expensive to maintain, there has been a definite movement on the part of the Church to secure Federal and state aid. This situation has been particularly acute lately not only because of mounting costs but because the new opportunities for women, such as those in nursing, social service, and business, have made it more difficult to secure an adequate supply of candidates for the various sisterhoods on which the Church depends so largely for the practically gratuitous teaching in its parochial schools.

The Church has also felt that as in Canada and in many European countries grants are made by the government to parochial schools, so they should be made in this country; otherwise their patrons are required to pay what they call "double taxation." Unfortunately for the Catholic position, the constitution or statutes of practically every American state prohibit grants from tax money to schools conducted by any religious body. This is one of the reasons that the effort has been made to secure direct financial aid from the *Federal* government, but here the Church faces a difficulty; for in the recent opinions in the Everson and McCollum cases[309] the Supreme Court has stated definitely that direct financial aid to schools under religious auspices is unconstitutional.

(2) THE BARDEN BILL

The Barden bill, though not specifically mentioned by Mrs. Roosevelt, was clearly the spark which caused the controversy between her and the cardinal. This bill, introduced by Congressman Graham A. Barden (1896–   ) of North Carolina on May 11, 1949, was to "provide for Federal financial assistance to the states in bearing certain costs of public elementary and secondary education." The use of the word "public" here should be noted, for though parochial schools are not excluded by name it is clear that they would be excluded under the provisions of this bill, which propose payment of $300,000,000 through the states "to assist them in making current expenditures for public elementary and secondary schools." An elaborate formula is provided to determine the amount of appropriations to the states, and also to the territories. The bill further provides that amounts paid under this bill "shall be expended only for current expenditures for public elementary and secondary schools within such State," and it adds definitely that in case any taxpayer feels that the provisions limiting this help to public schools is being violated or about to be violated, he may make application to the proper United States court for an order "enjoining such acts or practices, or for an order enforcing compliance with the first sentence of this section." Furthermore, where the facts warrant, an injunction or restraining order may be issued.

The "Definitions" accompanying the act specifically state under Section 7 (2):

> The term "current expenditures" does not include expenditures for transportation or for interest, debt service, or capital outlay, and does not include expenditures for health services for the prevention, diagnosis, or treatment of physical or mental defects or conditions.

They further state:

> The term "public elementary and secondary schools" means tax-supported grade schools, and high schools which are under public supervision and control.[310]

It is important to notice—especially since this matter has been often misstated in the press—that this bill has nothing to do with the transportation of school children or other auxiliary services. It does not apply to such services given to individual children, which have been held Constitutional by the Supreme Court (in a 5 to 4 decision in the Everson case), but to direct grants to the schools for their current expenses.

The Barden bill has been generally but not universally supported by non-Catholics, but opposed by Roman Catholics because it does not provide for direct aid to parochial schools where the states concerned so wish. In this respect it differs from the other educational aid bills before Congress which permit each state to decide such questions for itself.

Cardinal Spellman was among the members of the hierarchy who had long favored direct Federal aid to parochial schools.

(3) MRS. ROOSEVELT'S DEFENSE OF CHURCH–STATE SEPARATION

Mrs. Roosevelt's "My Day" column in the *World Telegram* on June 23 brought up issues which resulted in one of the most significant Church–State controversies of recent years. It was a very moderate article which did not refer specifically to the Barden bill, though this was clearly in her mind. It was followed by two other articles in the "My Day" column, which the cardinal also evidently had in mind. These appeared on July 8 and July 15. The first and most important of the "columns" is given in full below, with quotations from the others.

From the article of June 23:

The controversy brought about by the request made by Francis Cardinal Spellman that Catholic schools should share in federal aid funds forces upon the citizens of the country the kind of decision that is going to be very difficult to make.

Those of us who believe in the right of any human being to belong to whatever church he sees fit, and to worship God in his own way, cannot be accused of prejudice when we do not want to see public education connected with religious control of the schools, which are paid for by taxpayers' money.

If we desire our children to go to schools of any particular kind, be it because we think they should have religious instruction or for any other reason, we are entirely free to set up those schools and to pay for them. Thus, our children would receive the kind of education we feel would best fit them for life.

Many years ago it was decided that the public schools of our country should be entirely separated from any kind of denominational control, and these are the only schools that are free, tax-supported schools. The greatest number of our children attend these schools.

It is quite possible that private schools, whether they are denominational schools—Catholic, Episcopalian, Presbyterian, Methodist, or whatever—or whether they are purely academic, may make a great contribution to the public school systems, both on the lower levels and on the higher levels.

They will be somewhat freer to develop new methods and to try experiments, and they will serve as yardsticks in the competitive area of creating better methods of imparting knowledge.

This, however, is the very reason why they should not receive Federal funds; in fact, no tax funds of any kind.

The separation of church and state is extremely important to any of us who hold to the original traditions of our nation. To change these traditions by changing our traditional attitude toward public education would be harmful, I think, to our whole attitude of tolerance in the religious area.

If we look at situations which have arisen in the past in Europe and other world areas, I think we will see the reasons why it is wise to hold to our early traditions.[311]

From the article of July 8:

. . . I would like to make it clear once and for all that I believe in the right of any human being to worship God according to his conviction, and I would not want to see this right taken away from anyone. . . .

One of my correspondents asks me if I do not realize that government tax money is already being used by many young, returned veterans for education in Roman

Catholic schools and colleges and why should I object to that? The answer is that I do not have the slightest objection to that—the taxpayers' money in this instance is given to the boy or girl because of service during the war. . . .

In fact, I think there should be a great effort made to stress that education is not purely for material purposes, but is directed toward moral and spiritual aims and that religion plays a distinct part in achieving these ends.

But no school, private or public, can give any child a complete religious education. That must be done in the home, through the family and in the church. These, in co-operation with the schools, are the forces that must give our children the education that we want them to have.

But if we want our children in school to receive some particular sectarian church education, then we should pay for that education and it should not in any way lessen our interest and support of the public schools, which are attended by the vast majority of the children of our country and can be attended by all of our children if they so desire.

I do not want the public school system to be dominated by the Federal Government. That is why Federal aid should set only certain standards and not demand to control the schools of any state. But neither do I want church groups controlling the schools of our country. They must remain free.

From the article of July 15:

I am still getting letters from a few people who seem to think that in opposing aid from the taxpayers' money to any but public schools, I must have a particular bias against the Catholic Church. This must be because their parochial schools are more numerous than the schools of any other denomination.

I hate to continue an argument that many people think is based on prejudice, but something was written in a letter to me that seems worth mentioning.

A gentleman writes that the Barden bill was a discriminatory bill against the Negroes in the South. I have not read the bill carefully, and I have been rather careful not to say if I am for or against any particular bill or bills.

. . . This is no real reason why every school should not teach every child that one of the important aspects of our life is its spiritual side. It might be possible to devise a prayer that all the denominations could say and it certainly ought to be possible to read certain verses from the Bible every day.

It probably would do children no harm to learn to know some of the writings of other great religious leaders who have led other great religious movements.[312]

It will be noticed that there is only one reference in these three letters to the Barden bill, and that a general one, but that Mrs. Roosevelt came out clearly in support of the Constitutional separation of Church and State by opposing grants directly from public funds to parochial or other religious schools. In other words, she tacitly approved the principle of the Barden bill, which, without making any provision for *auxiliary services* to children in schools, whether public or parochial, confines direct Federal aid to public schools. Mrs. Roosevelt showed that she was not opposed in principle to auxiliary services in parochial schools, by her specific approval of aid under the G.I. "bill of rights" to ex-service men attending institutions of their own choice including "Roman Catholic schools and colleges." It will also be noted that Mrs. Roosevelt made no personal "attack" on Cardinal Spellman, and indulged in no "anti-Catholic" campaign. Her only reference to him was entirely courteous.

(4) CARDINAL SPELLMAN'S ATTACK ON MRS. ROOSEVELT

The following quotations give the introductory and final paragraphs and the more important intermediate statements in the cardinal's letter of July 21:

Dear Mrs. Roosevelt:

When, on June 23d in your column MY DAY, you aligned yourself with the author and other proponents of the Barden Bill and condemned me for defending Catholic children against those who would deny them their constitutional rights of equality with other American children, you could have acted only from misinformation, ignorance or prejudice, not from knowledge and understanding!

It is apparent that you did not take the time to read my address delivered at Fordham University; and, in your column of July 15th, you admitted that you did not even carefully read and acquaint yourself with the facts of the Barden Bill—the now famous, infamous bill that would unjustly discriminate against minority groups of America's children. . . .

I had intended ignoring your personal attack, but, as the days passed and in two subsequent columns you continued your anti-Catholic campaign, I became convinced that it was in the interest of all Americans and the cause of justice itself that your misstatements should be challenged in every quarter of our country where they have already spun and spread their web of prejudice. . . .

American freedom not only permits but encourages differences of opinion and I do not question your right to differ with me. But why I wonder do you repeatedly plead causes that are anti-Catholic? . . .

Now my case is closed. This letter will be released to the public tomorrow after it has been delivered to you by special delivery today. And even though you may again use your columns to attack me and again accuse me of starting a controversy, I shall not again publicly acknowledge you.

For, whatever you may say in the future, your record of anti-Catholicism stands for all to see—a record which you yourself wrote on the pages of history which cannot be recalled—documents of discrimination unworthy of an American mother!

Sincerely yours,

FRANCIS CARDINAL SPELLMAN,

Archbishop of New York.[313]

Mrs. Eleanor Roosevelt,

Hyde Park, N. Y.

It will be noticed that the cardinal did not specifically take issue with Mrs. Roosevelt's contention that tax funds should not be given to the direct support of parochial schools, but referred primarily to the importance of giving children in parochial schools the same benefits as those in public schools from public grants for auxiliary services such as free bus transportation, nonreligious textbooks, and health aid. Such services for schoolchildren—public, parochial, or private—had not been opposed by Mrs. Roosevelt in any of her three letters. Furthermore, the antagonistic tone of the cardinal's letter, with its lack of his usual courtesy, evidenced strong feeling on his part. To understand this we must remember that there had been several matters over the years in Mrs. Roosevelt's comments on public events which had irritated the hierarchy. This went back to her unsympathetic attitude toward the recognition of Franco in Spain, and to the fact that in early years when this country had Russia as a war ally, and later when it was co-operating with Russia in establishing the United Nations, she did not condemn Russian conditions as unequivocally as the Church thought called for.

(5) THE PUBLIC REACTION

No religious issue in recent years has brought a more immediate reaction. An interesting and valuable book could be written on the comments of press and public. This would show a well-nigh universal expression of regret at the tone of Cardinal Spellman's letter criticizing Mrs. Roosevelt, and assertion of her freedom from "bigotry" and fine record for religious toleration. As to the Barden bill and Federal aid to pupils in parochial schools through auxiliary services,[314] there was difference of opinion. There were some extreme statements on both sides, such as those of a Catholic ecclesiastic in Washington supporting the cardinal and condemning Mrs. Roosevelt, and that of a well-known Methodist bishop condemning the cardinal and his Church for their alleged attempt to control public policy in the interest of Roman Catholicism. But most statements were more moderate.

The non-Catholic press in general supported the view that public aid for the regular support of education should go only to public, not private or religious, schools, in accordance with the opinion of the Supreme Court in its interpretation of Federal Constitutional provisions, and with the constitutions or statutes of almost all states. On the matter of auxiliary aid, the cleavage in opinion was not strictly on religious lines. It reflected the 5 to 4 decision of the court in the New Jersey (Everson) case[315] permitting free bus transportation of parochial schoolchildren under certain conditions. Undoubtedly the comment which received widest attention and approval was that of ex-

Governor Herbert H. Lehman (1878–), who, the day after the cardinal's first statement, issued this comment:

I am deeply shocked at the attack of Cardinal Spellman on Mrs. Roosevelt. I strongly believe, as I have always believed, that in our American democracy every responsible citizen is entitled to express his or her views on public issues without being subjected to the accusation of being against any religion or any race.

The issue is not whether one agrees or disagrees with Mrs. Roosevelt on this or any other public question. The issue is whether Americans are entitled freely to express their views on public questions without being vilified or accused of religious bias.

Mrs. Roosevelt has been a public figure for twenty-five years. Her every act has been a matter of record. In that splendid record I do not know of a single act or word that would in the slightest degree indicate bias or prejudice against any religion or any race.

Her whole life has been dedicated to a constant fight for tolerance and brotherhood of men as children of one God.

She will, I am confident, retain the trust and the affection of all peoples irrespective of creed or race.[316]

The *New York Times* perhaps expressed the most general view of thoughtful people when it said editorially two days later:

IT IS THE CHILD THAT MATTERS

The unhappy controversy which has arisen over Mrs. Roosevelt's comments on the Federal Educational Finance bill and Cardinal Spellman's reply to those comments should not be allowed to obscure the important issue at stake. This is to what extent the Government may aid children attending sectarian schools without impairing the mandate of the First Amendment that "Congress shall make no law respecting an establishment of religion." The Supreme Court has been explicit on this point. Of particular pertinence is the New Jersey school bus case (Everson vs. Board of Education), on which a 5-to-4 decision was handed down on Feb. 10, 1947.

The whole Court would doubtless have concurred in the majority verdict that "No tax in any amount, large or small, can be levied to support any religious activities or institutions, whatever they may be called, or whatever form they may adopt to teach or practice religion." But the majority held that New Jersey did not breach the First Amendment when it provided "a general program to help parents get their children, regardless of their religion, safely and expeditiously to and from accredited schools"—among which sectarian schools meeting "the secular educational requirements" were included.

In these rulings we find a clear distinction. Local and state governments may in fact subsidize private schools by exempting them from taxation, but they cannot legally pay their teachers or maintain their buildings. A law appropriating federal funds to be used for the general purposes of private schools would not, on the record, be sustained by the Supreme Court. On the other hand, a law allowing such funds to be used for the direct benefit of school children's health or safety, no matter what kind of school each attends, seems both reasonable and proper. We are glad to note the favorable action taken yesterday by a House subcommittee on a measure already passed by the Senate specifically providing for health aid for all school children. We believe this is a sound principle and that the $35,000,000 provided in the bill might well be considerably increased.

Thus we arrive at what seems to us a sound conclusion. The Government cannot subsidize religious education as such. It cannot do so constitutionally and it cannot do so without danger both to itself as the representative of all the people and to the churches as free and voluntary organizations. The emphasis should be, as we are sure Cardinal Spellman would agree, on the child, not on the school. It is the child we must care for, protect and cherish. It is the child who must be treated everywhere on a fair and equal basis with all other children.

So far as the immediate controversy is concerned, we believe that Cardinal Spellman will come to realize that Mrs. Roosevelt cannot be justly charged with prejudice or bigotry. As she said in her syndicated column yesterday, she was "shocked" by what she "considered bigotry against the Roman Catholic Church" when she campaigned for the late Governor Smith and does not "wish to encourage anything of that kind." We do not believe she ever discriminated against Catholic soldiers, or those of any other faith, when she went the rounds of the war hospitals, or that she would be less compassionate toward a needy or hungry Catholic child than she is toward other children.[317]

Mrs. Roosevelt acted with so much restraint, fairness, and ability in this discussion that it gained her commendation from press and public,* even from those conservative groups which had been bitter against her because of her identification with President Franklin D. Roosevelt and the New Deal.

(6) MRS. ROOSEVELT'S REPLY TO CARDINAL SPELLMAN

Mrs. Roosevelt's letter was dated Hyde Park, N. Y., July 23, 1949. The most important paragraphs in it were as follows:

Your Eminence:

Your letter of July 21st surprised me considerably.

I have never advocated the Barden Bill nor any other specific bill on education now before the Congress. I believe, however, in Federal aid to education....

As we have developed in this country we have done more and more for our public schools. They are open to all children and it has been decided that there should be no particular religious beliefs taught in them.

I believe that there should be freedom for every child to be educated in his own religion. In public schools it should be taught that the spiritual side of life is most important. I would be happy if some agreement could be reached on passages from the

* See Addenda.

Bible and some prayer that could be used. The real religious teaching of any child must be done by his own church and in his own home.

It is fallacious, I think, to say that because children going to public schools are granted free text books in some states, free transportation, or free school lunches, that these same things must be given to children going to private schools.

Different states, of course, have done different things as they came under majority pressure from citizens who had certain desires, but basically by and large, throughout the country, I think there is still a feeling that the public school is the school which is open to all children, and which is supported by all the people of the country and that anything that is done for the public schools should be done for them alone.

I would feel that certain medical care should be available to all children, but that is a different thing and should be treated differently. If we set up free medical care for all children, then it should not be tied in with any school. . . .

You state: "And the Supreme Court of the United States has declared that health and transportation services and the distribution of non-religious textbooks to pupils attending parochial schools do not violate our Constitution." None of us will presume to decide questions which will come up before the Supreme Court of the United States, but all of us must think seriously about anything which is done, not only in relation to the specific thing, but in relation to what may follow after it and what we think will be good for the country.

Anyone who knows history, particularly the history of Europe, will, I think, recognize that the domination of education or of government by any one particular religious faith is never a happy arrangement for the people.

Spiritual leadership should remain spiritual leadership and the temporal power should not become too important in any church.

I have no bias against the Roman Catholic Church and I have supported Governor Smith as Governor and worked for him as a candidate for the office of President of the United States. I have supported for public office many other Roman Catholic candidates.

You speak of the Mindzenty case. I spoke out very clearly against any unfair type of trial and anything anywhere in any country which might seem like attack on an individual because of his religious beliefs. I cannot, however, say that in European countries the control by the Roman Catholic Church of great areas of land has always led to happiness for the people of those countries. . . .

I can assure you that I have no prejudice. I understand the beliefs of the Roman Catholic Church very well. I happen to be a Protestant and I prefer my own church, but that does not make me feel that anyone has any less right to believe as his own convictions guide him.

I have no intention of attacking you personally, nor of attacking the Roman Catholic Church, but I shall, of course, continue to stand for the things in our Government which I think are right. They may lead me to be in opposition to you and to other groups within our country, but I shall always act, as far as I am able, from real conviction and from honest belief.

If you carefully studied my record, I think you would not find it one of anti-Catholic or anti-any-religious group.

I assure you that I have no sense of being "an unworthy American mother." The final judgment, my dear Cardinal Spellman, of the worthiness of all human beings is in the hands of God.

With deepest respect, I am

Very sincerely yours,

ELEANOR ROOSEVELT.

(Mrs. Franklin D. Roosevelt.)[318]

It will be noticed that in this letter Mrs. Roosevelt stands out very definitely for the separation of Church and State. She shows no antagonism whatever to parochial schools, but in the matter of auxiliary financial aid to their pupils she leaves several points open.

(7) THE CARDINAL'S STATEMENT OF HIS MODIFIED POSITION

The country was much stirred and relieved when the papers of August 6, 1949, published a statement by Cardinal Spellman written in a different temper from that of his letter attacking Mrs. Roosevelt, and showing a constructive and Constitutional attitude toward the problems involved. The essential features of this statement follow:

It is important that everyone should understand clearly what we are asking for under constitutional law, and, for what we are not asking. We are not asking for general public support of religious schools. In the State of New York, as in practically every other state, the State constitution prohibits the use of public funds for the support of sectarian schools. The Supreme Court of the United States has interpreted the Federal Constitution in the same sense.

Under the Constitution we do not ask nor can we expect public funds to pay for the construction or repair of parochial school buildings or for the support of teachers, or for other maintenance costs.

There are, however, other incidental expenses involved in education, expenses for such purposes as the transportation of children to and from school, the purchase of non-religious textbooks, and the provision of health aids. These are called "auxiliary services." The Federal-aid controversy revolves around these incidental benefits to schoolchildren, and around them alone.

Our New York State Constitution expressly allows the use of public funds for the transportation of children to any school, public or parochial. Fourteen other states follow the same non-discriminatory practice. Moreover, in some states public funds are used to provide non-religious textbooks for the children in all schools, public and parochial. In all states many communities supply public health services to pupils in all schools. The Supreme Court of the United States has upheld these practices as constitutional.

What precisely are we asking for? We believe in Federal aid for needy states and needy children. We further believe that Congress should guarantee, as it did in the School Lunch Act, that all children of whatever race, creed or color no matter what schools they attend, will share alike in the "auxiliary services" for which these Federal funds are spent in the states.

We do not think it should be left to each state to decide for itself whether or not to distribute Federal funds in a discriminatory way. And above all, we ask that Congress guarantee the use of Federal funds for health and transportation services to the 2,800,000 of America's children attending parochial schools if they guarantee Federal funds for health and transportation services to other American children attending public schools.

We are asking Congress to do no more than to continue, in its first general aid-to-education measure, the non-discriminatory policy it has followed in the School Lunch Act and other Federal laws dealing with schools and school children. We do not want Congress, for the first time, to adopt a discriminatory policy in the field of education. . . .[319]

Some idea of the significance of the new attitude of the Church as stated by Cardinal Spellman may be gained if we remember that several Federal aid bills for educational purposes have been held up in Congress largely because there was no provision for parochial schools sharing directly in the appropriations for current expenses.

Cardinal Spellman's statement was of epoch-making importance as far as Church–State relations in the United States are concerned. It was the first time that the hierarchy, represented by one of its most prominent members, a cardinal of the Church of Rome, recognized publicly that direct aid for the support of parochial schools was, under existing constitutions, laws, and Supreme Court decisions, unconstitutional. Up to this time the Church had through many actions and through statements in authoritative utterances, and in books with the imprimatur of competent Church authority, stated frankly its conviction that parochial schools, being practically free schools, should share with public schools in the distribution of Federal funds for direct aid to education.

In the second place, the cardinal's statement, disowning any desire to secure tax money for the regular expenses of parochial schools, laid his entire stress on the importance of students in parochial schools receiving the benefit of auxiliary educational services such as bus transportation, which the Supreme Court by majority vote in the Everson case had declared to be Constitutional. In this connection it must be again pointed out that the Barden bill, which created the whole controversy, makes no provision of auxiliary services either to public, parochial, or private schools. It distinctly states that such aid is not in the purview of the bill.

The enunciation of these principles by Cardinal Spellman has enormously cleared the situation, for whereas any attempt to secure direct Federal aid for parochial schools would have created much bitterness, the matter of auxiliary aid was one which could be fairly debated. Such aid, under certain circumstances, had been considered Constitutional in the opinions in both the Everson and McCollum cases, though the majority recognized that it was a borderline issue, and though a strong minority of the court dissented from the majority opinion.

As the issue has now been concentrated by the cardinal's second statement on the question of certain auxiliary services, it may be well to quote the court's statements on this matter in the Everson case, which will be fully discussed later.[320]

The majority opinion held that free bus transportation for parochial school students, as provided for in the New Jersey statute, was not unconstitutional. It said, among other things:

> We must consider the New Jersey statute in accordance with the foregoing limitations imposed by the First Amendment. But we must not strike that State statute down if it is within the State's constitutional power even though it approaches the verge of that power. . . . While we do not mean to intimate that a state could not provide transportation only to children attending public schools, we must be careful, in protecting the citizens of New Jersey against state-established churches, to be sure that we do not inadvertently prohibit New Jersey from extending its general State law benefits to all its citizens without regard to their religious belief. . . .
>
> It appears that these parochial schools meet New Jersey's requirements. The State contributes no money to the schools. It does not support them. Its legislation, as applied, does no more than provide a general program to help parents get their children, regardless of their religion, safely and expeditiously to and from accredited schools.[321]

On the other hand, the four dissenting justices who opposed free bus transportation on Constitutional grounds also expressed their fear that it might be an entering wedge to unconstitutional demands for direct aid to parochial schools. They said:

> Transportation of pupils to their schools, public and private, is as essential to education as are text-books, lunches, athletic equipment, writing and other materials. If the New Jersey statute at issue, reimbursing citizens for transportation of pupils to Catholic schools and public schools, is upheld as a service to the "public welfare," then the states can appropriate fully to support all private religious schools. Thus the majority ruling establishes exactly what the First Amendment to the Constitution disestablished in erecting, as Jefferson said, "a wall of separation between church and state."[322]

(8) MRS. ROOSEVELT'S SYMPATHETIC COMMENTS

At the same time that Cardinal Spellman gave out his statement modifying his views on Federal aid to parochial schools he released a comment by Mrs. Roosevelt in which she called the cardinal's second statement both "clarifying and fair."

His Eminence, Cardinal Spellman, called me Thursday evening, August Fourth. He asked me to go over a statement which he would like to release. I have read it and think it a clarifying and fair statement.

Paragraph Number Two of His Eminence's statement emphasizes the point which to many citizens of the United States, is very important, namely, that no Federal Funds appropriated for public schools by the Congress shall be used except as provided in the Constitution.

That means that funds appropriated for school buildings, the maintenance of school buildings, the equalization of school terms throughout the country and the improvement in teachers' salaries, which would tend to equalize educational opportunities for all children, in all parts of our country and would obliterate any discrimination in public schools, can only be available to public schools.

The Cardinal's statement makes the point that the Supreme Court has declared it constitutional for States to use State or Federal funds for "auxiliary services." There has been a feeling among many citizens that the use of Federal funds for "auxiliary services" might lead to a change in the interpretation of the Constitution. The Cardinal's statement is clear on this Constitutional point.

I again wish to reiterate that I have no anti-Roman Catholic bias. I am firm in my belief that there shall be no pressure brought to bear by any Church against the proper operations of the government and that there shall be recognition of the fact that all citizens may express their views freely on questions of public interest.[323]

The statements of the cardinal and Mrs. Roosevelt were later brought to the attention of the Vatican by some newspaper reporters in Rome. The pope was loath to make any comment, but finally was willing to be quoted as saying that the exchange of correspondence had resulted in resolving the situation. This should mean that in the near future, at least, we are to understand: (1) that the Church will make no attempt to secure direct government aid for the running expenses of parochial schools; and (2) that it will continue a determined effort to see that such matters as free bus transportation, free textbooks on nonreligious subjects, and health services for pupils in parochial schools, are treated exactly the same in the matter of appropriations as for pupils in the public schools. The distinction between direct aid to schools and indirect aid through meeting certain needs of pupils, as in the case of the G.I.

bill, goes back to the unanimous decision of the Supreme Court in the free textbook case in Louisiana where this distinction was made, and a law making the free distribution of public school textbooks to parochial school pupils was declared Constitutional.[324]

In Mrs. Roosevelt's "My Day" column of August 22, 1949, there were further references to the matter of auxiliary services. Of these the most important were the following:

> When it comes to the auxiliary services, it seems to me that if we want the health services to amount to anything, they should be taken out of the actual school jurisdiction and put under the hospitals or public health services of the area. . . .
>
> Transportation I think a good argument can be made for where any free schools are concerned, whether they are public or private. Books I am doubtful about for so far these are all services which have come up for consideration in different states and it seems to me important now to consider only the need for federal aid to do a primary job—a job that will benefit every child in public schools throughout our country and in doing so the nation will be benefitted in the long run.[325]

The following day, August 23, Mrs. Roosevelt's column contained a reference to the fact that Cardinal Spellman had called to see her on his way to dedicate a chapel in Peekskill: "We had a pleasant chat and I hope that the country proved as much of a tonic to his spirit as it always is to my own."[326]

This brought to a close a most interesting and illuminating public discussion, the general results of which should prove of benefit to the country, even though many non-Catholics may differ on the question of auxiliary aids, and many Catholics may regret that the cardinal yielded on the matter of direct aid to parochial schools.

NOTES

Chapter XIV

1. III, 3; IV, 8.
2. V; VIII, 1, 2; etc.
3. IV, 6; XI.
4. V; XXIII, 4.
5. Dexter, F. B., *Yale Biographies and Annals,* V, 252, 253.
6. *Autobiography of Lyman Beecher,* I, 261, 262.
7. See abstract of sermon in Morris, B. F., *op. cit.,* pp. 376, 377.
8. See Sabine, Lorenzo, *Notes on Duels and Duelling; The Code of Honor.*
9. Patterson, A. W., *The Code Duello,* p. 73.
10. Mason, Ebenezer, *Complete Works of John M. Mason, D.D.,* IV, 520–522.
11. *President Dwight's Decisions of Questions . . .*, p. 310.
12. XX, 10, (3).
13. Millingen, John G., *History of Duelling,* I, 380.
14. Patterson, A. W., *op. cit.,* p. 72. The title of the sermon was *A Discourse . . . occasioned by the ever to be lamented Death of General Alexander Hamilton. . . .*
15. *Ibid.,* p. 20.
16. *Ibid.,* p. 73.
17. Beecher, *Autobiography,* etc., I, 155.
18. "The duel was forced upon Hamilton, who made repeated efforts for a friendly settlement. It is said that he fell mortally wounded on the very spot where, two years previously, his eldest son, twenty years old, had been shot in a political duel. Hildreth states that 'when the correspondence which preceded the duel came to be published, the outburst of public indignation against Burr was tremendous. He was charged with having practiced pistol-shooting for three months before the challenge; with having gone to the field clothed in silk as a partial sort of armor; and with having, while Hamilton lay on the bed of death, mirthfully apologized to his intimates for not having shot him through the heart.'" Note in *ibid.,* I, 150.
19. *Ibid.,* I, 150–154.
20. *Ibid.,* I, 155, 156.
21. Bacon, *op. cit.,* p. 264, footnote.
22. *Ibid.,* p. 264.
23. Thorpe, *op. cit.,* I, 544.
24. Patterson, *op. cit.,* p. 75, quoting the Revised Code of 1819, p. 583.
25. Thorpe, *op. cit.,* I, 109, quoting Art. VI, sec. 3.
26. *Ibid.,* VI, 3437, quoting Art. IX, sec. 3.
27. *Works of John England* (Messmer ed.), VII, 425–429.
28. Thorpe, *op. cit.,* VI, 3284.
29. Brace, C. L., *op. cit.,* p. 397.
30. Patterson, *op. cit.,* p. 71.
31. Thorpe, *op. cit.,* IV, 2071, sec. 27.
32. *Ibid.,* IV, p. 2092, sec. 19.
33. *Cf. Constitutions of the States and the United States* (1938), index, p. 1765, under "Duelling."
34. XX, 8.
35. Snow, Charles M., *Religious Liberty in America,* p. 404; *cf.* documents in *American State Papers,* XV, 45.
36. XX, 8, (1).
37. Beecher, *op. cit.,* I, 268, 269.
38. Snow, *op. cit.,* p. 405. Action taken Mar. 3, 1825.
39. Tracy, E. C., *Memoir of the Life of Jeremiah Evarts,* p. 320, note.
40. XV, 4.
41. *American State Papers,* VII, 211–212.
42. *Ibid.,* VII, 229. The date was Mar. 4, 1830.
43. *Ibid.,* VII, 231.

44. Snow, *op. cit.*, pp. 252, 253.
45. *Ibid.*, p. 253. The date was Jan. 21, 1831.
46. *Ibid.*, p. 254.
47. XX, 8, (1).
48. Schlesinger, *op. cit.*, p. 139, note 18.
49. *Free Enquirer*, Oct. 31, 1829; quoted by Schlesinger, *op. cit.*, p. 138.
50. XVI, 4.
51. Gales, *Register of Debates*, XII, part 2, p. 1675, quoted by Whipple, *op. cit.*, p. 111.
52. III, 4, (6).
53. *New York Baptist Association, held in the City of New York: Minutes*, 1808. Ref. from Argosy Book Stores (N.Y.), Catalogue No. 805.
54. Tyler, A. F., *op. cit.*, p. 356.
55. Guilday, *op. cit.*, p. 781.
56. IV, 3.
57. III, 4, (6).
58. *Cf.* art. "Anti-Masonic Party," *Enc. Brit.*, II, 127.
59. McCarthy, Charles, "The Antimasonic Party: A Study of Political Antimasonry in the United States, 1827–1840," in Amer. Hist. Assn. *Annual Report* (1902), I, 540.
60. *Diary of John Quincy Adams*, IX, 11.
61. McCarthy, Charles, *op. cit.*, pp. 540, 541.
62. *The Proceedings of the United States Anti-Masonic Convention*, Sept. 11, 1830, p. 41.
63. Morison and Commager, *op. cit.*, p. 926.
64. *Proceedings*, *op. cit.*, p. 81.
65. See art. "Anti-Masonic Movements," *D.A.H.*, I, 82; Weed, Thurlow, *Autobiography*, I, *passim*.
66. This was by Lebbeus Armstrong; see McCarthy, *op. cit.*, p. 542.
67. *Lancaster Antimasonic Herald*, Oct. 9, 1829, quoted by *ibid.*, p. 543.
68. *Pennsylvania Telegraph*, Sept. 21, 1831, quoted by *ibid.*, p. 543.
69. *Pennsylvania Reporter*, Sept. 25, 1835, quoted by *ibid.*, p. 469.
70. *Ibid.*, p. 470, which quotes the sources for this judgment.
71. Spofford, A. R., "Lotteries in American History," Amer. Hist. Assn. *Annual Report* (1892), pp. 175, 176.
72. *Ibid.*, p. 176.
73. Art. "Lotteries," Johnson, *Universal Cyclopedia*, V, 362.
74. Weigle, *op. cit.*, p. 308.
75. Guilday, *op. cit.*, p. 793.
76. Gabel, *op. cit.*, p. 206.
77. See Spofford, *op. cit.*, espec. pp. 181–188.
78. Mason, Ebenezer, *op. cit.*, I, 503, 504.
79. Tyson, Job Roberts, *Brief Survey of the Great Extent and Evil Tendencies of the Lottery System as existing in the U. S.* (Phila., 1833), p. 75, etc.
80. Art. "Lotteries," *D.A.H.*, III, 303.
81. Tyson, *op. cit.*, pp. 99–100. The Act quoted was passed Mar. 1, 1833. The resolutions were adopted Apr. 3, 1833.
82. *Ibid.*, pp. 100–101.
83. Spofford, *op. cit.*, p. 177.
84. *D.A.H.*, III, 303.
85. *U. S. Statutes at Large*, V, 578–579.
86. XVI, 6.
87. Stokes, I. N. Phelps, *Iconography of Manhattan Island*, IV, 964, mentions a still earlier paper, *The Present State of New England Affairs*, published in the autumn of 1689. A copy is in the American Antiquarian Society.
88. Hudson, Frederic, *Journalism in the United States from 1690 to 1872*, pp. 44–45.
89. *Ibid.*, p. 45.
90. *Ibid.*, p. 64.
91. III, 4, (5).
92. Art. "Religious Periodicals," *D.A.H.*, IV, 445.
93. *Cf.* Newman, A. H., *A History of the Baptists of the United States*, pp. 423, 424.
94. X, 10.
95. Tracy, E. C., *op. cit.*, p. 64.
96. *Ibid.*, p. 72.
97. Article "Periodical Literature," *Cath. Enc.*, XI, 692.
98. *Commonweal*, Feb. 7, 1941.
99. *Cath. Enc.*, XI, 692. For Bishop England, see VII, 7.
100. *Cf.* Mott, Frank Luther, *History of American Magazines*, II, 76.

101. For Brownson, see XII, 6.
102. *Cath. Enc.*, XI, 692.
103. Ahern, F. J., in an address on "The Catholic Church and American Culture," at tercentenary of the Harvard Divinity School, *Catholic Mind*, XXXIV, No. 17 (Sept. 8, 1936), 357, 358. *Cf.* "The Catholic Press and the Election," *Commonweal*, Nov. 1, 1940.
104. XIX, 4.
105. XVII, 6, (2).
106. XX, 3, (4).
107. *Commonweal*, Nov. 1, 1940.
108. *Ibid.*
109. V, 4.
110. Hudson, *op. cit.*, p. 304.
111. For these facts, see Mott, *op. cit.*, 3 vols. to 1865.
112. See Lee, James Melvin, *History of American Journalism*.
113. Stokes, I. N. Phelps, *op. cit.* V, 1501, citing art. by Clarence S. Brigham in Amer. Antiquarian Soc. *Proceedings* (1917), p. 472.
114. *Ibid.*, V, 1710, quoting *New York Evening Post*, Mar. 29, 1832.
115. Weigle, *op. cit.*, p. 222.
116. Baumgartner, Apollinaris W., *Catholic Journalism—A Study of its Development in the United States* (New York, 1931).
117. XII, 4, (4).
118. XV, 3, 4, 5.
119. Hudson, *op. cit.*, p. 304.
120. XIV, 6; XVI, 12.
121. XIV, 3.
122. XXI, espec. 3, 4.
123. XX, 10.
124. *Commonweal*, February 7, 1941.
125. Ahern, *op. cit.*, 358.
126. *Cf.* "A Study of the Religious Press," *Information Service*, May 23, 1942.
127. Letter from Religious News Service, N. Y. City, Nov. 25, 1947.
128. Quoted by Ward, Harry F., "Organized Religion in the United States," p. 122.
129. Weigle, *op. cit.*, p. 175.
130. Quoted from Tyler, A. F., *op. cit.*, p. 319.
131. Beecher, Lyman, *Autobiography*, I, 245.
132. *Ibid.*, I, 248, 253 (footnote).
133. *Ibid.*, I, 248.
134. *Ibid.*, II, 35–37.
135. See editorial in *America*, July 30, 1938; *cf.* art. "Temperance Movement," *D.A.H.*
136. Weigle, *op. cit.*, p. 209.
137. XVI, 12.
138. Whipple, *op. cit.*, p. 68.
139. Quoted by *ibid.*, pp. 69, 70.
140. *Ibid.*, p. 70.
141. VIII, 5.
142. Smith, Joseph Fielding, *Essentials in Church History*, p. 231, quoted by Beardsley, Harry M., *Joseph Smith and his Mormon Empire*, p. 176.
143. Bates, Ernest Sutherland, *American Faith*, p. 352.
144. Beardsley, *op. cit.*, pp. 208, 209.
145. *Ibid.*, p. 209.
146. Tyler, A. F., *op. cit.*, pp. 104, 105.
147. *Ibid.*
148. pp. 212, 213.
149. Beardsley, *op. cit.*, Strickland, W. P., ed., *Autobiography of Peter Cartwright, The Backwoods Preacher*, p. 345, quoted by *ibid.*
150. Beardsley, *op. cit.*, pp. 278, 279.
151. *Ibid.*, p. 344.
152. XVI, 3. Prof. W. W. Sweet has called my attention to a recent Ph.D. typed thesis at the Univ. of Chicago by Dr. Jensen on "Church and State in Mormonism."
153. Beard, Charles A. and Mary R., *Rise of American Civilization*, I, 166.
154. Moehlman, *School and Church*, p. 1.
155. III, 1, (9).
156. XVIII, 3.
157. Art. "Academies," *D.A.H.*, I.
158. Moehlman, *op. cit.*, p. 65.
159. Weigle, *op. cit.*, p. 272.
160. Gabel, *op. cit.*, p. 287.
161. Commager, *op. cit.*, I, 29.
162. Cubberley, E. P., *Public Education in the United States*, pp. 44, 45.
163. Ibid., p. 173.
164. Smith, Sherman M., *The Relation of the State to Religious Education in Massachusetts, passim.*
165. *Ibid.*, p. 18.
166. *Ibid.*, p. 22.

167. *Ibid.*, p. 24.
168. *Ibid.*, p. 68.
169. *Ibid.*, p. 70.
170. V, 7.
171. Smith, S. M., *op. cit.*, pp. 71–72, note 15.
172. Smith, S. M., *op. cit.*, p. 95.
173. *Ibid.*, p. 104.
174. *Ibid.*, p. 109.
175. Culver, R. B., *Horace Mann and Religion in the Massachusetts Public Schools*, p. 184.
176. Smith, S. M., *op. cit.*, p. 142.
177. *Ibid.*, p. 81.
178. *Ibid.*, pp. 61, 62.
179. Moehlman, *School and Church*, pp. 92, 93.
180. Culver, *op. cit.*, p. 170.
181. Smith, *op. cit.*, p. 175.
182. Mann, Horace, *Annual Report* (1845–48), IV, 308 ff. (Boston, 1891), quoted by Confrey, Burton, *Secularism in American Education, Its History*, p. 134, footnote 46.
183. Smith, S. M., *op. cit.*, p. 179; *cf.* testimony of Hon. Edward Twistleton, English visitor in 1851, *ibid.*, p. 181.
184. See Walsh, L. S., *The Early Irish Catholic Schools of Lowell, Mass.* (1901).
185. Smith, S. M., *op. cit.*, p. 193.
186. *Ibid.*, p. 206.
187. The book is *The Public School Question as Understood by a Catholic American Citizen, and by a Liberal American Citizen.*
188. Smith, S. M., *op. cit.*, pp. 294, 295.
189. *Ibid.*, p. 296.
190. *Ibid.*, p. 251.
191. Tyler, A. F., *op. cit.*, pp. 237–238.
192. V, 6.
193. Stewart, George, Jr., *A History of Religious Education in Connecticut*, p. 278.
194. *Ibid.*, p. 282.
195. *Ibid.*, p. 277.
196. Art. 8, sec. 2, quoted from Thorpe, *op. cit.*, I, 545.
197. Bell, Sadie, *The Church, the State, and Education in Virginia*, p. 37.
198. *Ibid.*, p. 59.
199. *Ibid.*, p. 77.
200. *Cf.* V, 3, (5); XI, 18.
201. Hening, *Statutes at Large* (Va.), X, III, 197.
202. Bell, S., *op. cit.*, p. 91.
203. V, 3, (5).
204. Wuntch, *op. cit.*, p. 77.
205. *Ibid.*, p. 78.
206. *Ibid.*
207. *Ibid.*, p. 80.
208. IX, 4.
209. Art. "Virginia," V, Monroe, *Cyclopaedia of Education*, 729.
210. *Ibid.*
211. Weigle, *op. cit.*, p. 276.
212. Confrey, *op. cit.*, p. 92.
213. *Ibid.*, p. 92, quoting act of Mar. 12, 1813.
214. Weigle, *op. cit.*, p. 273.
215. Gabel, *op. cit.*, p. 357, quoting Bourne, O. W., *History of the Public School Society of the State of New York.*
216. Sweet, *Story of Religion*, etc., pp. 393, 394.
217. Gabel, *op. cit.*, p. 357.
218. *Ibid.*, p. 359, note 16.
219. Weigle, *op. cit.*, p. 277.
220. *Ibid.*, p. 285.
221. Cubberley, *op. cit.*, gives table of dates on p. 100.
222. XII, 4, (4), (5).
223. Mode, Peter G., *op. cit.*, p. 468.
224. Hecker, *Catholics and Education*, p. 180; and *Religious Education* (1926), p. 82.
225. *Ibid.*
226. For an account of the debate, see *Congressional Record*, IV, Part 1, p. 5595.
227. *Ibid.*, IV, Part 1, p. 5580, quoted by *Religious Education* (1926), p. 83; for further reference to this and similar proposals, see XIX, 4, 5, 6.
228. *Knowlton* v. *Baumhover* (1918), 182 Iowa 691, 166 N.W. 202, 5 L.R.A. 841, 843, quoted by *Religious Education* (1926), p. 84.
229. *Ibid.*, p. 83; *cf.* Zollmann, *op. cit.*, p. 77 and note 31.
230. XVIII, introd.
231. XVIII, 2.
232. See lists in *Religious Education* (1926), pp. 84, 85, and Zollmann, *op. cit.*, pp. 78–80.

233. See references in preface and bibliography.
234. *Knowlton* v. *Baumhover* (1918), 182 Iowa 691, 166 N.W. 202, 5 L.R.A. 841, quoted by *Religious Education* (1926), pp. 85, 86.
235. XVIII, 2.
236. See *Cook County* v. *Industrial School for Girls* (1888), 125 Ill. 540, 563; 18 N.E. 183, 1 L.R.A. 437. See 1917 *Williams* v. *Stanton School District, S.W.* 1058, quoted by *Religious Education* (1926), p. 86.
237. XXIX, table of dates, 1947.
238. II, 1.
239. XIX, 2.
240. XVIII and XIX, espec. XIX, 4, 5, 6.
241. XVIII, 1, (3); XIX, 5, (7).
242. Beard, Charles A. and Mary R., *The Rise of American Civilization*, I, 587.
243. Thorpe, *op. cit.*, VI, 3476.
244. *Ibid.*, VI, 3495.
245. *Ibid.*, VI, 3496.
246. *Ibid.*, VI, 3519.
247. *Ibid.*, VI, 3529.
248. *Ibid.*, VI, 3536. For reference to a previous declaration of citizens demanding religious freedom, see *Niles Register*, Sept. 11, 1819, cited by *Pageant of America*, II, 235.
249. Thorpe, *op. cit.*, VI, 3542.
250. *Ibid.*, VI, 3547, 3548.
251. *Ibid.*, VI, 3569.
252. *Blair* v. *Odin*, 3 Tex. 288, 300, quoted by Zollmann, *op. cit.*, p. 16.
253. Art. "Manifest Destiny," *D.A.H.*, III, 332.
254. Ellsworth, C. S., "The American Churches and the Mexican War," *Amer. Hist. Rev.*, Jan., 1940, p. 302.
255. *The Diary of James K. Polk during his Presidency, 1845 to 1849*, I, 408–410 (printed in Chicago Hist. Soc. *Collections*, VI, 408–410).
256. *Ibid.*, I, 411.
257. *American Army Chaplaincy . . . , op. cit.*, pp. 22, 23.
258. Thompson, R. E., *History of the Presbyterian Churches in the United States*, p. 127.
259. Polk's *Diary, op. cit.*, II, 187–191 (Chicago Hist. Soc. *Collections*, VII).
260. *Ibid.*, III, 103–105 (Chicago Hist. Soc. *Collections*, VIII).
261. *Cf.* Billington, *op. cit.*, p. 239.
262. Ellsworth, *op. cit.*, *American Historical Review*, Jan., 1940, p. 303.
263. Manross, William Wilson, *A History of the American Episcopal Church*, pp. 218, 266, 289.
264. Ellsworth, *op. cit.*, *American Historical Review*, Jan., 1940, p. 324.
265. *Ibid.*, p. 304.
266. *New York Recorder*, Jan. 27, 1847, quoted by *ibid.*, p. 312.
267. Ellsworth, *op. cit.*, p. 317; *cf. Friends' Review*, I, 281, 343.
268. *Boston Recorder*, Jan. 21, Aug. 12, 1847, quoted by Ellsworth, *op. cit.*, p. 315.
269. Ellsworth, *op. cit.*, p. 314.
270. *Ibid.*, p. 315.
271. *Ibid.*, p. 326.
272. *The Poetical Works of James Russell Lowell* (Riverside Press ed., 1848), II, 155.
273. *Ibid.*, pp. 66, 67.
274. XVI, 8.
275. Thorpe, *op. cit.*, I, 381.
276. *Ibid.*, I, 389; III, 1360.
277. *Ibid.*, I, 391.
278. There was at least one colonial case where the authorities of what was to become U. S. territory came into official contact with the Papal States. In the *Historical Records and Studies* published by the U. S. Catholic Historical Society, Vol. II, p. 381, is an interesting article entitled "The Papal Flag in New York Harbor, 1757–8." This has to do with the coming of a Roman ship to New York and certain difficulties that were experienced.
279. Feiertag, Sister Loretta Clare, *American Public Opinion on the Diplomatic Relations between the United States and the Papal States (1847–1867)*, p. 6.
280. Stock, Leo Francis, *United States Ministers to the Papal States*, p. xxiii.
281. *Ibid.*, p. xxii.
282. Acton, John E. E., *The History of Freedom and other Essays*, p. 363.
283. Billington, *op. cit.*, p. 268.
284. Stock, L. F., *op. cit.*, p. xxii.

285. Feiertag, *op. cit.*, p. 9.
286. *Ibid.*, p. 6.
287. *Ibid.*, p. 6.
288. *Ibid.*, p. 7.
289. *N. Y. Daily Tribune*, Nov. 30, 1847.
290. Feiertag, *op. cit.*, p. 12; for the pope's reply, see *N. Y. Herald*, Dec. 26, 1847.
291. Feiertag, *op. cit.*, p. 15.
292. *Ibid.*, p. 17.
293. *Ibid.*
294. *Ibid.*, pp. 17, 18.
295. *Ibid.*, p. 20.
296. *Ibid.*, p. 22.
297. *Ibid.*, p. 25.
298. Stock, L. F., *op. cit.*, pp. 2, 3.
299. *Ibid.*, pp. 258–260.
300. Feiertag, *op. cit.*, p. 64.
301. *Ibid.*, pp. 78, 79, note 30. For the saving of the Propaganda College, see art. "Cullen, Paul," *Cath. Enc.*, IV, 565.
302. Stock, L. F., *op. cit.*, 394.
303. For a discussion of the historical incidents involved, see "A Diplomatic Incident," *Atlantic Monthly*, Oct., 1929.
304. Marraro, Howard R., *American Opinion on the Unification of Italy*, p. 95, quoting *N. Y. Herald*, says that Mr. Hastings, chaplain to the legation, was from Boston.
305. Stock, L. F., *op. cit.*, pp. 64, 65.
306. See Feiertag, *op. cit.*, p. 65, note 65; Stock, *op. cit.*, p. 84.
307. "To the horror of his very Catholic landlady, who, when the General changed his residence, had the room thoroughly cleaned and fumigated." Cesare, Raffaele de, *Last Days of Papal Rome*, p. 111.
308. Stock, L. F., *op. cit.*, pp. 414–416.
309. *Ibid.*, pp. 427, 428.
310. Letter from Mr. King to Secretary Seward, May 7, 1887, quoted by *ibid.*, p. 430.
311. Associated Press dispatch from Washington, in *N. Y. Times*, July 17, 1938.
312. A typical example of Protestant opposition to these actions is that of the Southern Baptists, who, at their annual convention in May, 1939, in Oklahoma City, adopted resolutions severely criticizing the sending of the Ambassador to Great Britain, Joseph P. Kennedy (1888–), a Roman Catholic, to Rome for the coronation of Pius XII, and the adoption by Congress of a message of sympathy on the death of his predecessor (*Newsweek*, June 5, 1939). These actions were in form based on the alleged danger to the American doctrine of separation of Church and State.
313. Cable of International News Service from Vatican City, in *Washington Post*, March 6, 1939.
314. Quoted by *Christian Century*, Jan. 31, 1940.
315. *N. Y. Times*, Dec. 24, 1939.
316. White House "Release," Dec. 23, 1939, p. 1.
317. *Ibid.*, p. 4.
318. *Federal Council Bulletin*, Jan., 1940, p. 9.
319. White House "Release," Dec. 26, 1939, p. 1.
320. *Ibid.*, Jan. 19, 1940, p. 2.
321. Quoted by *Christian Century*, January 24, 1940.
322. *Ibid.*, Jan. 3, 1940.
323. *Ibid.*, Jan. 10, 1940.
324. *N. Y. Times*, Jan. 5, 1940.
325. *Berkshire Eagle*, Jan. 22, 1940.
326. *Christian Century*, Jan. 31, 1940.
327. *Federal Council Bulletin*, Feb., 1940.
328. *Christian Century*, Feb. 14, 1940.
329. *Federal Council Bulletin*, May, 1940.
330. *Christian Century*, June 5, 1940.
331. *Ibid.*
332. *Deliverances of the General Assembly*, etc., *op. cit.*, p. 28.
333. *N. Y. Times*, May 12, 1940.
334. *Ibid.*
335. *Ibid.*
336. *Ibid.*
337. *Ibid.*
338. *Ibid.*
339. *Federal Council Bulletin*, May, 1940, p. 4.
340. *N. Y. Times*, Dec. 28, 1939.
341. *Federal Council Bulletin*, Jan., 1945.
342. *Federal Council . . . , Biennial Report*, 1946, p. 211.

343. See art. "Communities," *D.A.H.*
344. Wright, Edward N., *Conscientious Objectors in the Civil War,* p. 26.
345. The above facts are from art. "Shakers," in *D.A.H.,* by Andrews, Edward D., and conversations with its author.
346. IV, 8, (10).
347. Art. "Hopedale Community," *D.A.H.*
348. Tyler, *op. cit.,* p. 169.
349. *Ibid.*
350. Perkins, William R., and Wick, B. L., *History of the Amana Society, or Community of True Inspiration,* pp. 82–83, Appendix A, quoted from Wright, E. N., *op. cit.,* p. 28.
351. See espec. the writings of Bertha M. H. Shambaugh.
352. Art. "Oneida Community," *Enc. Brit.,* XX, 106.
353. *Ibid.,* XX, 107.
354. For facts, see Mikkelsen, Michael A., "The Bishop Hill Colony: A Religious Communistic Settlement in Henry County, Illinois," *Johns Hopkins University Studies in Historical and Political Science,* Vol. X (*Church and State*), pp. 1–80.
355. Goodhope, Nanna, "Must the Hutterites Flee Again?" in *Christian Century,* Nov. 13, 1940.
356. *Ibid.*
357. XIV, 7; XVI, 14.

NOTES

Chapter XV

1. Weigle, *op. cit.,* p. 162. For details, see Barnes, G. H., *The Antislavery Impulse.*
2. Mode, Peter G., *op. cit.,* pp. 555, 556; quoting *A Brief Statement of the Rise and Progress of the Testimony of the Religious Society of Friends against Slavery and the Slave Trade.* Reprint, *The Friend,* Vol. XVI, No. 51.
3. Weeks, Stephen B., *Southern Quakers and Slavery,* pp., 206–208.
4. Sewall, Samuel, *The Selling of Joseph,* quoted from Smith, Bernard, ed., *op. cit.,* pp. 15, 16.
5. *Ibid.,* p. 17.
6. III, 2, (4).
7. Bacon, *op. cit.,* p. 153.
8. *Persecution and Liberty* (Burr memorial vol.), chap. on "Agitation against the Slave Trade in Rhode Island," p. 475.
9. *Cf.* Walker, Williston, *Ten New England Leaders,* chap. on "Samuel Hopkins," espec. pp. 349–351.
10. To understand the antislavery movement it is necessary to go back to the teachings of Christ regarding man's nature and destiny and to the work of the early Church. "The rise of Christianity in the Roman world," says the *Encyclopedia Britannica,* XXV, 220, "still further improved the condition of the slave. The sentiments it created were not only favourable to the humane treatment of the class in the present, but were the germs out of which its entire liberation was destined, at a later period, in part to arise. It is sometimes objected that the Christian church did not denounce slavery as a social crime and insist on its abolition. . . . But the institution itself could not be at once seriously disturbed. The results must have been disastrous, most of all to the slave population itself. Before that end could be accomplished, an essentially new social situation must come into existence. But in the meantime much might be done towards further mitigating the evils of slavery, especially by impressing on master and slave their relative

duties and controlling their behaviour towards one another by the exercise of an independent moral authority. . . . The church also encouraged the emancipation of individual slaves and the redemption of captives. And its influence is to be seen in the legislation of the Christian emperors, which softened some of the harshest features that still marked the institution. But a stronger influence of Christianity appears in Theodosius, and this influence is at the highest in the legislation of Justinian. Its systematic effort is, in his own words, pro libertate, quam et fovere et tueri Romanis legibus et praecipue nostro numini peculiare est. . . . A new process of manumission was now established, to be performed in the churches through the intervention of the ministers of religion; and it was provided that clerics could at any time by mere expression of will liberate their slaves. Slaves who were admitted to holy orders, or who entered a monastery, became freemen, under certain restrictions framed to prevent fraud or injustice. . . ."

11. III, 1, (4), (6), (8) ff.
12. Rice, Madeline Hooke, *American Catholic Opinion in the Slavery Controversy,* pp. 25, 26.
13. Morgan, George, *Patrick Henry* (1929), pp. 246–248.
14. Henry, William Wirt, *Patrick Henry —Life, Correspondence and Speeches,* III, 49–51.
15. Art. "Abolition Movement," *D.A.H.; cf.* Thomas Jefferson *On Slavery.*
16. X, 1.
17. Early phrases are from Jefferson, *Notes on Virginia,* Query XVIII; last two phrases from his letter to Washington Jan. 4, 1786, in Randolph, T. J. ed., *Memoir, Correspondence and Miscellanies from the Papers of Thomas Jefferson* (1829), I, 394.
18. Tyler, A. F., *op. cit.,* p. 466.
19. Morison and Commager, *op. cit.,* p. 126.
20. Thorpe, *op. cit.,* VI, 3739, 3740.
21. Morison and Commager, *op. cit.,* p. 126.
22. VI, 10.
23. *Cf.* his letter to Benezet, Aug. 22, 1772.
24. Art. "Slavery," *Enc. Brit., XXV,* p. 223.
25. Whipple, *op. cit.,* p. 114.
26. Gales & Seaton, *Annals of Congress,* I, 1239.
27. *Ibid.,* p. 1240.
28. Weeks, *op. cit.,* p. 213.
29. Constitution, Art. I, Sect. 9.
30. Eaton, Clement, *Freedom of Thought in the Old South,* pp. 132–133, with references.
31. *Ibid.,* p. 18.
32. *Ibid., op. cit.,* pp. 18–19, citing Catterell, H. T., *Judicial Cases Concerning American Slavery and the Negro,* I, 317.
33. X, 1, XVI, 1, etc.
34. Buckley, J. M., *History of the Methodists in the United States,* p. 185.
35. *Ibid.,* p. 197.
36. *Ibid.,* p. 244.
37. *Ibid.,* p. 245.
38. *Ibid.,* p. 245.
39. *Ibid.,* p. 303.
40. *Ibid.,* p. 385.
41. Alexander, Gross, *History of the Methodist Church, South,* p. 8.
42. III; IV, 8, (13).
43. Newman, A. H., *History of the Baptist Churches in the United States,* p. 305.
44. *Ibid.*
45. *New York Bapt. Assoc'n. . . ., Minutes,* 1808, quoted from Argosy Book Stores *Catalogue* No. 805, Item 121 (1944).
46. Newman, *op. cit.,* p. 306.
47. Thompson, R. E., *History of the Presbyterian Churches in the United States* (Amer. Church Hist. Ser., Vol. VI), appendix, pp. 362, 363.
48. *Ibid.,* p. 363; *cf.* pp. 47, 75.
49. *Ibid.,* p. 363.
50. *Ibid.,* p. 91.
51. *Ibid.,* pp. 364, 365.
52. *Ibid.,* pp. 366, 367, 368; *cf.* "Extracts from the Minutes of the General Assembly of the Presbyterian Church in the United States of America, dated

A. D. 1818," pp. 28–30, in letter from acting stated clerk, Sept. 7, 1943.
53. Letter from Dr. W. W. Sweet, June 10, 1949.
54. Corwin, E. T., *History of the Reformed Church, Dutch* (Amer. Church History Ser., Vol. VIII, p. 179.
55. XI, 8.
56. Bacon, L. W., *op. cit.*, p. 272, quoting *Christian Spectator* (1823), pp. 493, 494, 341.
57. *Ibid.*, p. 273.
58. *Ibid.*, p. 274, quoting Wilson, *The Slave Power*, I, chap. xiv.
59. XV, 4, (1).
60. Murphy, Robert Joseph, "The Catholic Church in the United States During the Civil War Period (1852–1866)," Amer. Cath. Hist. Soc. *Records*, XXXIX, 273.
61. XV, 4, (1), and 5, (1) (a).
62. Calhoun, John C., "Remarks on the States Rights Resolutions in Regard to Abolition, January 12, 1838," *Works*, III, 180, quoted by Parrington, *op. cit.*, II, 80, 81.
63. Thompson, R. E., *op. cit.*, pp. 368, 369.
64. *Ibid.*, p. 369.
65. *Cf.* Swaney, Charles Baumer, *Episcopal Methodism and Slavery* (1926), p. 51.
66. Barnes, Gilbert Hobbs, *The Antislavery Impulse, 1830–1844* (New York, 1933).
67. *Ibid.*, p. 11.
68. X, 5.
69. *Cf.* Barnes, *op. cit.*, p. 21.
70. Beecher, *Autobiography*, II, 323.
71. Barnes, *op. cit.*, p. 33.
72. *Ibid.*, quoting *Zion's Herald*, VI, 21.
73. See Bowen, C. W., *Arthur and Lewis Tappan*, p. 10, quoted by Whipple, *op. cit.*, pp. 96, 97.
74. *Ibid.*, p. 100.
75. Barnes, *op. cit.*, p. 61.
76. Cf. XV, 4, (2).
77. Johnson, Oliver, *William Lloyd Garrison and his Times*, p. 68, quoted by Brace, C. L., *op. cit.*, p. 382.
78. Johnson, O., *op. cit.*, p. 106, quoted by *ibid.*
79. Beecher, *Autobiography*, II, 425, 426.
80. Barnes, *op. cit.*, p. 93.
81. *Ibid.*, p. 97.
82. *Ibid.*, p. 98.
83. For Garrison's later career and opposition to the Churches, see XV, 4, (2).
84. *Cf.* Whipple, *op. cit.*, p. 84.
85. *Autobiography*, II, 321.
86. Barnes, *op. cit.*, p. 66.
87. *Ibid.*, p. 67.
88. *Ibid.*
89. *Ibid.*, p. 68.
90. Beecher, *Autobiography*, II, 327.
91. Barnes, *op. cit.*, p. 77.
92. *Ibid.*
93. *Liberator*, V, 156, quoted by Whipple, *op. cit.*, pp. 87, 88. The student's name was Amos Dresser.
94. Sweet, W. W., *The Congregationalists, Religion on the American Frontier*, III, 201.
95. Barnes, *op. cit.*, p. 103.
96. *Ibid.*, p. 91.
97. *Ibid.*, p. 242.
98. Beard, Charles A. and Mary R., *op. cit.*, I, 708.
99. Morison and Commager, *op. cit.*, p. 408.
100. *Ibid.*, p. 110.
101. Dorchester, *op. cit.*, p. 472. See also Davis, Rev. Emerson, *The Half Century* (Boston, 1851).
102. Barnes, *op. cit.*, p. 110.
103. *Ibid.*
104. *Ibid.*, p. 123.
105. *Ibid.*, p. 124.
106. *Cf. ibid.*, p. 133.
107. *Ibid.*, p. 134.
108. *Ibid.*, p. 143.
109. *Ibid.*, p. 182.
110. Munford, Beverley, *op. cit.* (1909), p. vii.
111. Beard, Charles A. and Mary R., *op. cit.*, I, 699.
112. XV, 2.
113. Buckley, J. M., *op. cit.*, pp. 378, 379.
114. *Ibid.*, p. 386.
115. Sweet, W. W., *The Story of Religion in America*, p. 434; *cf.* Buckley, *op. cit.*, p. 387.
116. *Ibid.*, p. 394.
117. *Ibid.* The member was Silas Comfort.

This resolution was rescinded in 1844 (*ibid.*, p. 448).
118. *Ibid.*, pp. 395, 396.
119. "Journal of the General Conference," 1840, pp. 155, 156, quoted by *ibid.*, pp. 396–398.
120. *Ibid.*, p. 402.
121. Swaney, Charles B., *op. cit.*, pp. 99, 100.
122. Buckley, *op. cit.*, p. 406.
123. Swaney, *op. cit.*, p. 117.
124. Colored members in the South were then estimated to number 125,000; white members, 350,000.
125. Buckley, *op. cit.*, p. 410.
126. *Ibid.*, p. 413.
127. For debate, see *ibid.*, pp. 412–441.
128. *Ibid.*, p. 420.
129. *Ibid.*, p. 441.
130. *Ibid.*, p. 442.
131. *Ibid.*, p. 444.
132. *Ibid.*, pp. 693, 694.
133. *Ibid.*, p. 696.
134. *Ibid.*, p. 444.
135. Swaney, *op. cit.*, p. 139.
136. Buckley, *op. cit.*, pp. 460, 461.
137. *Ibid.*, p. 475.
138. Sweet, *op. cit.*, pp. 439, 440.
139. Buckley, *op. cit.*, pp. 625, 626.
140. *Ibid.*, p. 501. In 1864 this was further slightly modified so that the reference was made to forbidding "slave-holding, buying or selling slaves"—the "slave" question being then uppermost (*ibid.*, p. 511).
141. Whitehead, Alfred North, *Adventures of Ideas*, p. 28.
142. Berger, D., *History of the Church of the United Brethren in Christ* (Amer. Church Hist. Ser., XII), p. 368.
143. Newman, Albert Henry, *A History of the Baptists of the United States* (Amer. Church Hist. Ser., II), p. 444.
144. *Ibid.*, pp. 444, 445.
145. *Ibid.*, p. 445.
146. *Ibid.*, pp. 446, 447.
147. *Ibid.*, p. 447.
148. *Ibid.*, p. 448.
149. Sweet, *op. cit.*, pp. 430, 431.
150. Newman, A. H., *op. cit.*, pp. 451, 452.
151. *Ibid.*, p. 454.
152. XV, 2.
153. Sweet, *op. cit.*, p. 440.
154. Thompson, R. E., *op. cit.*, pp. 372, 373.
155. *Cf.* Beecher, *Autobiography*, II, 427.
156. Thompson, R. E., *op. cit.*, p. 135.
157. Sweet, *op. cit.*, p. 441.
158. Thompson, R. E., *op. cit.*, p. 136.
159. *Ibid.*, Appendix, pp. 369, 370.
160. *Ibid.*, p. 370.
161. *Ibid.*, pp. 370, 371.
162. *Ibid.*, p. 372.
163. Sweet, *op. cit.*, p. 442.
164. *Ibid.*, p. 443.
165. Thompson, R. E., *op. cit.*, p. 153.
166. XV, 5, (2).
167. See XV, 3; XV, 4, (2), (4).
168. Parrington, *op. cit.*, II, 420, quoting Parker, Theodore, *Additional Speeches*, I, 327.
169. Bacon, *op. cit.*, p. 284.
170. XV, 4, (2).
171. Spreng, Samuel P., *Hist. of the Evangelical Association*, p. 425.
172. Eaton, Clement, *op. cit.*, p. 237.
173. Thomas, Allen C., and Richard H., *History of the Society of Friends in America* (Amer. Church Hist. Ser., Vol. XII), p. 286.
174. *Ibid.*, p. 287.
175. McConnell, S. D., *History of the American Episcopal Church*, pp. 362, 363.
176. McConnell, S. D., *op. cit.*, p. 366.
177. *Year Book of Disciples of Christ* (1907), p. 500.
178. *Millennial Harbinger*, 3d ser., Vol. 2, No. V, May, 1845, pp. 236–240.
179. *Ibid.*, No. VI, June, 1845, p. 263.
180. *Ibid.*, No. VIII, Aug., 1845, p. 358. I owe these quotations to the Director of the Library of the United Christian Missionary Society (Disciples of Christ) in a letter dated Dec. 28, 1943.
181. *American Christian Missionary Society, Report of the Thirteenth Anniversary Meeting . . . , Oct. 22, 23, 24, 1861* (Cincinnati, 1861), p. 20.
182. Letter of Dec. 28, 1943, from the Director of the Library of the United Christian Missionary Society.
183. Fortenbaugh, Robert, "American Lutheran Synods and Slavery 1830–

1860," *The Journal of Religion,* XIII, 1, (Jan., 1933), p. 72.
184. XXIII, 4, (5); XI, 12.
185. Fortenbaugh, *op. cit.*, p. 74.
186. XV, 5, (1).
187. Fortenbaugh, *op. cit.*, p. 75.
188. *Ibid.*, p. 76.
189. *Ibid.*, p. 77.
190. *Ibid.*, p. 78.
191. *Ibid.*, p. 81.
192. *Ibid.*
193. *Ibid.*, pp. 81, 82.
194. *Ibid.*, p. 82.
195. *Ibid.*, p. 83.
196. *Ibid.*, pp. 85–87.
197. *Ibid.*, p. 84.
198. *Ibid.*, p. 86.
199. *Ibid.*, p. 91.
200. *Ibid.*, p. 86.
201. *Ibid.*, pp. 87–88.
202. *Ibid.*, p. 79.
203. *Ibid.*, pp. 79, 80.
204. *Ibid.*, p. 80.
205. *Ibid.*
206. *Ibid.*
207. Students wishing further information on the part played by the Lutheran Church in the controversy over slavery and in the Civil War are referred to Heathcote, C. W., *The Lutheran Church and the Civil War* (New York, 1919).
208. Jacobs, Henry E., *A History of the Evangelical Lutheran Church in the United States of America* (New York, 1897).
209. XIII, 4, (5).
210. *Cf.* Murphy, R. J., *op. cit.*, pp. 272, 273.
211. *Cf.* remarks of Troeltsch, *op. cit.*, I, 133.
212. See art. "Slavery," *Cath. Enc.*, XIV, 39.
213. For English trans. of the brief, see Messmer, Sebastian, ed., *Works of the Right Rev. John England,* V, 110–112.
214. *Ibid.*, V, pp. 183–311. The full title is *Letters to the Honorable John Forsyth on the Subject of Domestic Slavery,* originally published in *United States Catholic Miscellany* (1840–41).
215. Quoted by Murphy, R. J., *op. cit.*, p. 281.
216. *Ibid.*
217. *Ibid.*
218. *Ibid.*, p. 282.
219. *Ibid.*, pp. 282, 283.
220. Rice, Madeleine Hooke, *American Catholic Opinion on the Slavery Controversy* (1944), p. 63.
221. Murphy, R. J., *op. cit.*, p. 293.
222. *Ibid.*, pp. 275, 276.
223. *Ibid.*, p. 278, quoting *Pastoral Letter,* Ninth Provincial Council of Baltimore, 1858.
224. *Ibid.*, p. 296.
225. XX, 1, (2).
226. Rice, *op. cit.*, p. 155.
227. *Ibid.*, p. 157.
228. XV, 5, (1), (c).
229. Kohler, Max J., "The Jews and the American Antislavery Movement," Amer. Jewish Hist. *Publications,* V, 143 (1897).
230. XV, 3.
231. Thayer, Eli, *History of The Kansas Crusade,* p. 217.
232. *Ibid.*, pp. 128–129.
233. *Law of Negro Slavery,* quoted by Stanton, R. L., *The Church and the Rebellion,* p. 477.
234. *Ibid.*, pp. 477, 478.
235. *Ibid.*, p. 479.
236. Beard, *op. cit.*, I, 705.
237. Phillips, U. B., *Life and Labor in the Old South,* p. 40.
238. Weigle, *op. cit.*, p. 166.
239. Beard, *op. cit.*, I, 705.
240. XV, 5, (2).
241. Stanton, *op. cit.*, p. 103.
242. XI, 16.
243. Eaton, *op. cit.*, pp. 121–125.
244. *Ibid.*, p. 129.
245. *Cf.* Birney, James G., *American Churches, the Bulwark of American Slavery,* (1840).
246. Eaton, *op. cit.*, p. 271.
247. *Ibid.*, p. 174.
248. *Ibid.*, p. 214, citing Polk, W. M., *Leonidas Polk,* I, 209–212.
249. Thayer, *op. cit.*, p. 123.
250. Bacon, *op. cit.*, p. 284.
251. XIV, 2.
252. Johnson, Lorenzo D., *op. cit.*
253. Swaney, *op. cit.*, p. 272, quoting *Zion's*

Herald and *Wesleyan Journal,* April 12, 1854.

254. Thayer, *op. cit.,* p. 124.
255. *Ibid.,* p. 24.
256. *Ibid.,* p. 27.
257. *Ibid.,* pp. 130–133.
258. *Ibid.,* p. 31.
259. *Ibid.,* p. 125.
260. *Ibid.,* p. 136.
261. Nevins and Commager, *The Story of a Free People,* pp. 223, 225.
262. Bacon, *op. cit.,* pp. 341, 342.
263. Thayer, *op. cit.,* p. 57.
264. Art. "Eli Thayer," *Appleton's Cyclop.,* VI, 72.
265. Sweet, W. W., *The Story of Religion in America,* p. 449.
266. Morris, B. F., *op. cit.,* p. 683.
267. *Ibid.,* p. 687.
268. *Ibid.,* p. 692.
269. *Ibid.,* p. 691.
270. *Ibid.,* pp. 697–698.
271. *Ibid.,* p. 698.
272. *Ibid.,* p. 704.
273. Sweet, *op. cit.,* p. 451.
274. Jacobs, H. E., *A History of the Evangelical Lutheran Church in the United States,* p. 452.
275. *Ibid.*
276. Morris, *op. cit.,* p. 707.
277. *Ibid.,* p. 710.
278. *Ibid.,* p. 727.
279. *Ibid.,* p. 730.
280. *Ibid.,* pp. 743–744.
281. *Ibid., op. cit.,* p. 765.
282. *Ibid.,* p. 770.
283. *Ibid.,* p. 776.
284. *Ibid.,* p. 755.
285. For additional facts, see Swaney, C. B., *Episcopal Methodism and Slavery* (1920).
286. *Doctrines and Discipline of the Methodist Episcopal Church* (1936), p. 76; letter from the Librarian of the Methodist Historical Society of the City of New York, May 13, 1940; and Dorchester, *op. cit.* (rev. ed.), p. 465.
287. From original in Library of Congress.
288. *Complete Works of Abraham Lincoln* (Nicolay and Hay ed.), VIII, 52.
289. Johns, John, *Life of Bishop Meade,* p. 237, quoted by McConnell, S. D., *op. cit.,* p. 364.
290. *Journal of the Proceedings of The Bishops, Clergy, and Laity of the Protestant Episcopal Church in the United States of America, Assembled in a General Convention . . . in the year of Our Lord 1862,* pp. 51–53.
291. *Ibid.,* pp. 92–94.
292. *The Life of the Late Right Reverend John Henry Hopkins, First Bishop of Vermont, and Seventh Presiding Bishop,* by One of his Sons, p. 325.
293. McConnell, S. D., *op. cit.,* pp. 370, 371.
294. *Ibid.,* p. 377.
295. *Ibid.,* pp. 377, 378.
296. *Ibid.,* p. 379.
297. *Journal of the Triennial Provincial Synod of the Northern District of the American Province of the Moravian Church of the United Brethren, Convened at Lititz, Lancaster Co., Pa., from May 22d to June 2d, 1861,* pp. 55, 56.
298. *Ibid.,* p. 77.
299. Letter from Archives Committee, Southern Province, Moravian Church in America, Dec. 3, 1943.
300. Wright, E. N., *Conscientious Objectors in the Civil War,* p. 6.
301. *Cf. ibid.,* p. 223.
302. XV, 1.
303. Minutes of the Meeting for Sufferings of Baltimore (Hicksite) Yearly Meeting, p. 84, and *The Friend,* XXXVI, no. 2, p. 13, quoted from Wright, E. N., *op. cit.,* pp. 48–49.
304. Minutes of the Meeting for Sufferings of New England Yearly Meeting, 8 mo. 20, 1862, p. 274, cited from Wright, *op. cit.,* p. 48.
305. Mode, Peter G., *op. cit.,* p. 618, quoting McPherson, *The Political History of the United States during the Great Rebellion,* Appendix, pp. 503–504. This appendix on "The Church and the Rebellion" is valuable.
306. Wright, *op. cit.,* pp. 216–217.
307. *Friends' Review,* XVIII, no. 39, p. 617, cited from Wright, *op. cit.,* p. 128.
308. *Ibid.,* cited from Wright, *op. cit.,* pp. 128, 129.

309. Minutes of Philadelphia (Hicksite) Yearly Meeting, 1866, pp. 12–14, quoted from Wright, *op. cit.*, p. 129.
310. *Cf.* XV, 5, (1), (e).
311. Sandburg, Carl, *Abraham Lincoln: The War Years,* III, 370.
312. *Ibid.*, III, 376.
313. *Ibid.*, III, 377.
314. *Ibid.*, III, 376.
315. Thompson, Joseph P., *Church and State in the United States,* p. 123.
316. *Ibid.* The use of the term "Minister" was doubtless due to the fact that Dr. Thompson makes this statement in a book that was specially prepared for German readers.
317. McConnell, S. D., *op. cit.*, p. 372.
318. *Ibid.*
319. Sandburg, *op. cit.*, II, 157.
320. Wilmer, Richard H., *The Recent Past from a Southern Standpoint,* pp. 143–146.
321. Art. "Robert H. Wilmer," *Appletons' Cyclop. of Amer. Biog.*, VI, 543.
322. Sandburg, *op. cit.*, II, 156.
323. *Ibid.*, II, 410.
324. Sweet, *op. cit.*, p. 463.
325. *Ibid.*, pp. 460, 461.
326. *Ibid.*, p. 465. This was in May, 1864.
327. Stanton, *op. cit.*, p. 239.
328. Gabel, *op. cit.*, p. 508, n. 69.
329. Stanton, *op. cit.*, p. 270.
330. Woodson, Carter G., *The Negro in Our History* (5th ed.), p. 264.
331. Hassard, J. R. G., *Life of the Most Rev. John Hughes,* p. 437, quoted by Murphy, R. J., *op. cit.*, p. 279.
332. Quoted by Shea, J. G., *op. cit.*, IV, 385.
333. See *Brownson's Review,* October, 1861.
334. Art. "Purcell," *Cath. Enc.*, XII, 571.
335. Leslie, Shane, *The Irish Issue in its American Aspect,* p. 11.
336. Facts from the pamphlet *The Jew as Patriot and Soldier,* published by Christian Friends of Palestine, Washington, D.C., 1939; *cf.* also Wolf, Simon, *The American Jew as Patriot, Soldier and Citizen* (1895), p. 424.
337. XX, 6, (1).
338. Markens, Isaac, *Abraham Lincoln and the Jews,* p. 10.
339. *Ibid.*, p. 11.
340. Lincoln, Abraham, *Complete Works,* (Nicolay and Hay ed.), II, 304.
341. See XX, 9, (2).
342. I owe this material to the courtesy of Rabbi Moshe Davis of the Jewish Theological Seminary of America. The letter was discovered by him in the archives of Dropsie College in Philadelphia. Reproduced in *Congressional Record,* Feb. 29, 1944.
343. See Stillé, C. J., *History of the United States Sanitary Commission.*
344. *Bible Society Record,* LXXXVI, No. 1, (January, 1941), p. 3.
345. Dwight, Henry Otis, *The Centennial History of the American Bible Society,* pp. 262–263.
346. Rhodes, James Ford, *History of the United States,* V, 467.
347. Morris, B. F., *op. cit.*, pp. 780–781.
348. Weigle, *op. cit.*, p. 188.
349. *Ibid.*, quoting from a commission in the Yale Library.
350. Mode, *op. cit.*, pp. 620, 621, quoting *Second Annual Report (1863) United States Christian Commission,* pp. 15–21.
351. Morris, B. F., *op. cit.*, pp. 783–784.
352. *American Orations . . . ,* edited by Alexander Johnston, III, 247, 248.
353. XX, 9, (2), (a).
354. Morris, B. F., *op. cit.*, pp. 789–790.
355. Sweet, *op. cit.*, p. 451.
356. Morison and Commager, *The Growth of the American Republic,* p. 568.
357. *Complete Works of Abraham Lincoln* (Nicolay and Hay ed.), VI, 315.
358. Buckley, J. M., *op. cit.*, p. 509.
359. Welles, Gideon, *Diary,* I, 130, quoted by Swaney, *op. cit.*, p. 328.
360. *Complete Works of Abraham Lincoln* (Nicolay and Hay ed.), II, 234–236, quoted by Swaney, *op. cit.*, p. 329.
361. Original copy in author's possession of the Proclamation sent to the states.
362. XX, 9, (2).
363. Pendleton, *Alexander H. Stephens,* pp. 251–254, quoted by Parrington, *op. cit.*, II, 91.
364. Stanton, *op. cit.*, p. 157.

365. *Ibid.*
366. *Ibid.*, p. 160.
367. *Ibid.*, p. 171.
368. *Ibid.*, p. 172.
369. *Ibid.*, p. 186.
370. Mott, Frank Luther, *A History of American Magazines*, II, 61, citing the *Methodist,* as quoted in the *Friends' Review*, XIV, 727 (July 20, 1861).
371. Thompson, R. E., *op. cit.*, p. 156.
372. *Ibid.*, pp. 388, 389.
373. *Ibid.*, p. 390.
374. *Ibid.*, pp. 391, 392.
375. *Ibid.*, p. 392.
376. *Ibid.*, pp. 393, 394.
377. *Ibid.*, pp. 396, 397.
378. *Ibid.*, p. 398.
379. *Ibid.*, p. 399.
380. *Ibid.*, pp. 401, 402, 403.
381. *Ibid.*, p. 403.
382. *Ibid.*, p. 405.
383. Sweet, *op. cit.*, p. 453.
384. Stanton, *op. cit.*, p. 181.
385. *Ibid.*, pp. 182, 183.
386. *Ibid.*, p. 183.
387. *Ibid.*, p. 197.
388. XXII, 2, (1).
389. Mode, *op. cit.*, p. 470.
390. *Jefferson Davis, Ex-President of the Confederate States of America*, II, 445–446.
391. *Ibid.*, II, 446–448. A slightly different translation is given in Mode, *op. cit.*, pp. 470, 471.
392. XV, 4, (1), (i).
393. XV, 5, (1), (b).
394. *Records of the American Catholic Historical Society*, XXV, 18–29, cited from Rice, *op. cit.*, p. 108.
395. *Cf.* Kohler, M. J., "The Jews and the American Antislavery Movement," Amer. Jewish Hist. Soc. *Publications*, V, 137–155; IX, 45–56.
396. For the governmental status of Howard, *cf.* XXII, 3, (4).
397. XI, 9; XV, 1.
398. Rice, *op. cit.*, p. 153.
399. Sweet, *op. cit.*, p. 472.
400. *Ibid.*, pp. 472, 473.
401. XV, 4.
402. XI, 16.
403. Whitehead, *op. cit.*, p. 29.

NOTES

Chapter XVI

1. III, 1, espec. (4) and (6).
2. *Cf.* remarks of Troeltsch, Ernst, *The Social Teaching of the Christian Churches*, II, 727.
3. Guilday, Peter, *Life and Times of John England*, II, 223–227.
4. Hopkins, Charles Howard, *The Rise of the Social Gospel in American Protestantism 1865–1915*. I am greatly indebted to this book. It is cited hereafter as Hopkins, C. H., *op. cit.* (book), while the Ph.D. manuscript thesis on which it is based, and which is on file in the Yale Library, is cited as Hopkins, C. H., *op. cit.* (MS.). The original title of the thesis was *The Rise of Social Christianity in American Protestantism 1865–1915*. This frequently gives more extended quotations from resolutions, etc., than the published book.
5. Channing, William Ellery, *Honor Due to All Men,* quoted from Smith, Bernard, ed., *The Democratic Spirit*, pp. 239, 240.
6. Eddy, Richard, *History of Universalism,* p. 431.
7. Beard, Charles A. and Mary R., *op. cit.*, I, 731, 732.
8. Hopkins, C. H., *op. cit.* (book), p. 4.
9. *Autobiography, Correspondence, etc., of Lyman Beecher, D.D.*, II, 146.
10. X, 11.
11. For these and other facts in this sum-

mary, see Hopkins, C. H., *op. cit.* (book), introd.
12. Gabriel, Ralph H., *The Course of American Democratic Thought,* p. 161.
13. Hopkins, C. H., *op. cit.* (book), p. 21.
14. Gladden, Washington, *Recollections,* p. 206.
15. *Churchman,* Jan. 1, 1943.
16. Hopkins, C. H., *op. cit.* (MS.). I have given the longer quotation from the original Ph.D. manuscript, I, 125, 126, quoting the Association's *Annual Report for 1904.*
17. *Ibid.,* I, 106–109; *cf.* Hopkins, C. H., *op. cit.* (book), p. 17.
18. *Ibid.,* p. 38.
19. *Ibid.,* p. 42.
20. Hopkins, C. H., *op. cit.* (MS.), I, 115; *cf.* Hopkins, C. H., *op. cit.* (book), p. 44.
21. *Ibid.,* p. 46.
22. Schlesinger, Arthur, *Rise of the American City,* p. 349.
23. George, Henry, *Works,* III, 96.
24. Hopkins, C. H., *op. cit.* (book), p. 64.
25. *Ibid.,* p. 67.
26. See XVI, 1.
27. Hopkins, C. H., *op. cit.* (book), p. 106.
28. Hopkins, C. H., *op. cit.* (MS.), I, 312; *cf.* Hopkins, C. H., *op. cit.* (book), p. 116.
29. *Churchman,* Jan. 1, 1943.
30. Hopkins, C. H., *op. cit.* (book), p. 112.
31. *Ibid.,* p. 143.
32. See Asbury, Herbert, *Gem of the Prairie: An Informal History of the Chicago Underworld* (1940).
33. Baker, Ray Stannard, *American Chronicle* (1945), p. 31.
34. Beard, Charles A. and Mary R., *op. cit.,* II, 421.
35. This suggestive critical essay, which showed little sympathy with the "democratic" movements of the time, especially as applied to industry, appeared first in the *Forum,* March, 1894. It was reprinted (1940) in *Sumner Today.*
36. Watson, Frank D., *The Charity Organization Movement in the United States,* p. 53.
37. Hopkins, C. H., *op. cit.* (MS.), I, 448, 449; *cf.* Hopkins, C. H., *op. cit.* (book), p. 151.
38. Beard, Charles A. and Mary R., *op. cit.,* II, 422.
39. *Ibid.,* II, 421.
40. Hopkins, C. H., *op. cit.* (MS.), I, 490; *cf.* Hopkins, C. H., *op. cit.* (book), p. 132.
41. Faulkner, H. U., *The Quest for Social Justice,* 1898–1914 (*History of American Life,* Vol. XI), p. 205.
42. Hopkins, C. H., *op. cit.* (book), p. 196; *cf.* Hopkins, C. H., *op. cit.* (MS.), II, 753.
43. *Ibid.,* II, 800, quoting *Christianizing the Social Order,* p. x; *cf.* Hopkins, C. H., *op. cit.* (book), p. 219.
44. *Ibid.,* p. 216.
45. *Ibid.,* chap. XIII, "Walter Rauschenbusch Formulates the Social Gospel"; *cf.* Hopkins, C. H., *op. cit.* (MS.), II, 832.
46. XVI, 1.
47. Hopkins, C. H., *op. cit.* (book), p. 286.
48. *Ibid.,* p. 289.
49. XX, 4, (2).
50. Weigle, *op. cit.,* p. 201.
51. Sanford, Elias B., *Origin and History of the Federal Council of the Churches of Christ in America* (Hartford, 1916), p. 92, quoted by Hopkins, C. H., *op. cit.* (MS.), I, 336.
52. *Ibid.,* I, 336, 337.
53. *National Perils and Opportunities* (Evangelical Alliance, Washington, 1887), p. 342.
54. Hopkins, C. H., *op. cit.* (MS.), I, 342.
55. XX, 1, (1).
56. For Dr. Crafts' career and influence, see Hopkins, C. H., *op. cit.* (MS.), chap. XV, "Locking Horns with the Devil."
57. *Cf.* Hopkins, C. H., *op. cit.* (MS.), II, 581.
58. *Ibid.,* II, 584; *cf.* circular issued by the Bureau (Federation), January, 1939.
59. XIV, 7.
60. For a good historical summary, see art. "Mormons," *Enc. Brit.* (11th ed.).

61. *U. S. Reports,* XCVIII, 166.
62. *Ibid.,* XCVIII, 146–167, *passim.* (The references to Jefferson's *Works,* etc., given in the opinion, have been omitted.)
63. *Mormon Church* v. *U. S.,* U. S. Supreme Court, Oct. Term, 1889, p. 28.
64. For "Celestial Marriages," see Brand and Ingram, *op. cit.,* p. 165.
65. Zollmann, Carl, *American Church Law,* p. 42.
66. IV, 8, (10).
67. Lecky, William Edward, *Democracy and Liberty,* I, 548.
68. Weigle, Luther A., *American Idealism,* p. 246.
69. *Enc. Brit.,* XVIII, 846.
70. *Ibid.,* XVIII, 846, 847.
71. XXIV, 2.
72. See references in Zollmann, *op. cit.,* p. 41.
73. Quoted by Whipple, Leon, *Our Ancient Liberties,* p. 73.
74. Strong, Josiah, *Our Country,* p. 63. This address by Bishop Lunt is also quoted at some length by Dorchester, Daniel, *Christianity in the United States,* p. 648.
75. Strong, *op. cit.,* p. 63.
76. *Ibid.,* pp. 65, 66.
77. *Congressional Record,* Feb. 18, 1882, p. 1259, quoted by Myers, *op. cit.,* p. 215.
78. *Ibid.,* XIII, pt. 1, 367 (47th Cong., 1st sess.).
79. *Ibid.,* XIII, pt. 2, 1259 (47th Cong., 1st sess.).
80. *Deliverances of the General Assembly of the Presbyterian Church in the U.S.A.,* p. 51.
81. *Ibid.,* p. 52.
82. X, 9, 10.
83. X, 9.
84. *Indian Missions of the United States* (Dept. of the Interior, Office of Indian Affairs, Bull. No. 8, 1928), p. 4, citing 24 Stat. L., 390.
85. Rushmore, Elsie M., *The Indian Policy during Grant's Administration.*
86. Edwards, Martha L., "A Problem of Church and State in the 1870's," *Miss. Valley Hist. Rev.,* XI, 45 (June, 1924).
87. Gabel, Richard J., *Public Funds for Church and Private Schools,* p. 521.
88. From *Annual Report of the Commissioners of Indian Affairs,* 1875.
89. Art. "Indian Missions," *New Cath. Dict.* (1929), p. 477.
90. Art. "Indian Missions," *Cath. Enc.,* VII, 746.
91. Jackson, H. H., *A Century of Dishonor,* p. viii.
92. XVII, 4, (3).
93. For beginnings, see X, 9.
94. This important action was taken June 7, 1897, but some denominational appropriations are still made.
95. *U. S. Statutes at Large,* XXX, 79 (55th Cong., 1897–99).
96. Gabel, *op. cit.,* p. 529.
97. Letter from Office of Indian Affairs, Oct. 24, 1938.
98. *Quick Bear* v. *Leupp* (1908), 210 U. S. 50.
99. Gabel, *op. cit.,* p. 530.
100. Title 25, U. S. C., 279–280.
101. Circular issued by the Office of Indian Affairs July 14, 1937, entitled *Regulations Governing the Care of Indian Children in Mission and Other Contract Schools,* sec. No. 9.
102. *Ibid.,* sec. No. 14.
103. Quoted by Gabel, *op. cit.,* pp. 530–532.
104. Zollmann, *op. cit.,* p. 99; *cf.* also action of N. Y. legislature there quoted. For general question of nuns as public school teachers see XVIII, 6.
105. Letter from Office of Indian Affairs, November 16, 1938, quoting the substance of Secretary Fisher's letter of Aug. 24, 1912.
106. Art. "Religion and the Public Schools," *Churchman,* Aug., 1947. North Dakota's successful campaign early in 1948 to make illegal the wearing of a religious garb by public school teachers will probably be followed in other states. See XVIII, 6.
107. XVII, 8.
108. For the facts in this section I am indebted largely to Weigle, *op. cit.,* Thwing, Charles F., *History of Higher Education in the United States,* and Appleton, *op. cit.*

109. X, 1.
110. Facts from Weigle, *op. cit.*, p. 248.
111. X, 9.
112. *Constitutions of the States and United States*, 1938, p. 1298, Art. I, Secs. 2–7.
113. Weigle, *op. cit.*, p. 254.
114. Sweet, William W., *The Story of Religion in America*, p. 483.
115. IX, 4, and X, 1.
116. See Tewksbury, Donald G., *The Founding of American Colleges and Universities . . .* (New York, 1932), *passim*, and espec. pp. 84–87.
117. XIV, 8, (2).
118. Morison, Samuel E., and Commager, Henry S., *The Growth of the American Republic*, pp. 764, 765.
119. Art. "McGuffey's Readers," *D.A.H.*
120. Baird, Robert, *Religion in America*, p. 269, footnote.
121. *Ibid.*, p. 273, footnote.
122. Art. "Lotteries," *Enc. Soc. Sci.*, IX, 615.
123. Woodbridge, Samuel Homer, *The Overthrow of the Louisiana Lottery* (1921), p. 8.
124. *Ibid.*, p. 9; *Enc. Soc. Sci.*, IX, 615; and art. "Louisiana Lottery," *D.A.H.*, III, 307.
125. Woodbridge, *op. cit.*, p. 13.
126. *Ibid.*, p. 15.
127. *Ibid.*
128. A.P. dispatch, *Berkshire Eagle*, Feb. 13, 1941.
129. Woodbridge, *op. cit.*, p. 30.
130. *Ibid.*, p. 32.
131. *Ibid.*, p. 41.
132. *Ibid.*, supplement, pp. 1, 2.
133. Art. "Lottery Case"—*Champion* v. *Ames*, *D.A.H.*, III, 304.
134. *Christian Century*, May 11, 1942; *Federal Council Bulletin*, Nov., 1942, Jan., 1943.
135. *Ibid.*, Jan., 1939.
136. Art. "Lottery," *Cath. Enc.*, IX, 366.
137. *Progress*, May, 1941, p. 12.
138. By an order effective Jan. 28, 1939.
139. *Progress*, Apr. and May, 1941.
140. *Christian Century*, Dec. 16, 1942.
141. *N. Y. Times*, Dec. 3, 1942.
142. *Ibid.*, Apr. 17, 1943.
143. XIV, introduction.
144. Parkhurst, Rev. Charles H., *Our Fight with Tammany* (New York, 1895).
145. *Ibid.*, p. 5.
146. Matt. 5.13.
147. Parkhurst, *op. cit.*, p. 10.
148. *Ibid.*, pp. 23, 24.
149. *Ibid.*, pp. 24, 25.
150. *Ibid.*, pp. 41, 42.
151. *Ibid.*, p. 42.
152. *Ibid.*, p. 51.
153. *Ibid.*, p. 59.
154. *Ibid.*, pp. 60, 61.
155. Art. "Brownlow," *D.A.B.*, III, 177.
156. See his autobiography, *Pioneering in Social Frontiers.*
157. XVI, introd.
158. *N. Y. Times*, Nov. 30, 1941.
159. *Cf.* XXVI, 5.
160. *U. S. House Documents*, No. 4442 (Pious Fund), 284, quoted by Geary, Rev. Gerald J., "Transfer of Ecclesiastical Jurisdiction in California (1840–1853)," in U. S. Cath. Hist. Soc. *Historical Records and Studies*, XXII, 122.
161. Hunt, R. D., and Sánchez, Nellie, *A Short History of California*, p. 260. See various indexed references to "secularization."
162. Geary, G., *The Secularization of the California Missions 1810–1846*, pp. 11, 16.
163. Geary, *op. cit.;* U. S. Cath. Hist. Soc. *Historical Records and Studies*, XXII, 140.
164. *Ibid.*, XXII, 141.
165. *Ibid.*, XXII, 164.
166. Facts on which this statement is based are mainly taken from the work by Geary quoted above, and from the arts. in the *Cath. Enc.* on "California" (III, 182), and in the *Enc. Brit.* on "Arbitration, International" (II, 328).
167. Pratt, Julius W., *Expansionists of 1898* (Baltimore, 1936). The book deals with the war and the annexation of Hawaii and the Spanish islands.
168. XVI, introd. and I.
169. I am indebted to Pratt, *op. cit.*, for this group of comments from the religious press.
170. *Ibid.*, p. 284.

171. *Ibid.*, p. 285.
172. *Ibid.*, p. 283.
173. *Ibid.*, pp. 286, 287.
174. *Ibid.*, p. 289.
175. *Ibid.*, p. 286.
176. *Ibid.*, p. 282.
177. *Ibid.*, p. 288.
178. *Ibid.*, pp. 290, 291.
179. *Ibid.*, p. 295.
180. *Ibid.*, p. 292.
181. *Ibid.*, p. 302.
182. *Ibid.*, pp. 306, 307.
183. Olcott, C. S., *The Life of William McKinley*, II, 109–111, quoted by *ibid.*, p. 316.
184. See XXI, 1.
185. Art. 202. Letter from Office of Chief of Chaplains, Jan. 17, 1941.
186. In Texas, Roman Catholicism was originally an established religion under the Republic, but by the Constitution of 1845 it was—to quote a court decision—reduced "from the high privilege of being the only national church, to a level and an equality with every other denomination."—*Blair* v. *Odin* (1848), 3 Tex. 288, 300, quoted by Zollmann, *op. cit.*, p. 16. This is the only case of a State Church existing within the past century in what is now the continental United States.
187. Zollmann, *op. cit.*, p. 111.
188. See *City of Ponce* v. *Roman Catholic Apostolic Church in Porto Rico*, 210 U.S. 296.
189. *Lands Held for Ecclesiastical or Religious Uses in the Philippine Islands*, etc. (Doc. No. 190, 56th Cong., 2d sess., 1901), p. 43.
190. Forbes, W. Cameron, *The Philippine Islands*, II, 443, 444.
191. *Ibid.*, p. 27. The letter was dated Apr. 7, 1900.
192. *Reports of the Taft Philippine Commission* (Doc. No. 112, 56th Cong., 2d sess., 1901), pp. 27, 28.
193. *Ibid.*, pp. 25, 26.
194. Pringle, Henry F., *The Life and Times of William Howard Taft*, I, 223, quoting letter from Governor Taft to Mrs. Bellamy Storer, Dec. 4, 1900.
195. *Reports of the Taft Philippine Commission*, *op. cit.*, p. 26.
196. *Ibid.*, p. 33.
197. Art. "Philippine Islands," *Cath. Enc.*, XII, 16.
198. *Ibid.*, XII, 17.
199. *Ibid.*
200. Pringle, *op. cit.*, I, 226.
201. *Ibid.*, I, 229.
202. Art. "Philippine Islands," *New Cath. Dictionary* (1929).
203. Zollmann, *op. cit.*, p. 111, with discussion.
204. Forbes, *op. cit.*, II, 470.
205. *Ibid.*, II, 473.
206. Smith, Judge Clifford P., *Christian Science: Its Legal Status. A Defense of Human Rights*, p. 12.
207. *Ibid.*, p. 62.
208. Faulkner, H. U., *The Quest for Social Justice, 1898–1914* (*History of American Life*, Vol. XI), p. 167.
209. *Table of Statutory Provisions Favorable to Christian Science or to Freedom Concerning Health* (published by The Christian Science Publishing Society), p. 5.
210. *Ibid.*, p. 9.
211. *Ibid.*, pp. 11, 12.
212. *Ibid.*, p. 12.
213. *Ibid.*, p. 16.
214. *Ibid.*, p. 17.
215. *Ibid.*, p. 10.
216. *Ibid.*, p. 3.
217. *Ibid.*, p. 33.
218. Case of *New Braunfels* v. *Waldschmidt* (1918), quoted by Confrey, Burton, *Secularism in American Education*, pp. 113, 114.
219. *Table of Statutory Provisions*, *op. cit.*, p. 25. Similar provisions of law are found in several other states.
220. *Ibid.*, p. 29.
221. *Ibid.*, p. 49. Similar provisions of law are found in several other states.
222. *Ibid.*, p. 50.
223. Fromson, David, comp., *Regulatory Measures Concerning the Prohibition of the Common Drinking Cup* (New York, 1936), *passim*.
224. *Ibid.*, p. 13.

225. Letter from Prof. C. E. A. Winslow of Yale, Jan. 17, 1944.
226. XIV, 6.
227. Weigle, *op. cit.*, p. 208.
228. *Ibid.*, p. 210.
229. For a good summary, see art. "Prohibition," *Enc. Soc. Sci.*, XII.
230. Buckley, J. M., *History of the Methodists in the United States*, p. 640.
231. *Ibid.*, p. 641.
232. *Doctrines and Discipline of the Methodist Episcopal Church* (1936), pp. 469, 470.
233. Smith, R. G., *Politics in a Protestant Church*, p. 11.
234. *Ibid.*, pp. 41, 15.
235. *Ibid.*, p. 19.
236. *Ibid.*, p. 21.
237. *Ibid.*, p. vi.
238. XVII, 4, (6).
239. Smith, R. G., *op. cit.*, p. 105.
240. *Ibid.*, p. 129.
241. *Ibid.*, p. 165.
242. *Ibid.*, pp. 165, 166.
243. Quoted by Faulkner, *op. cit.*, p. 224.
244. Myrdal, Gunnar, *An American Dilemma* (1944), I, 458.
245. *Deliverances of the General Assembly of the Presbyterian Church in U.S.A.* (*1910–40*), pp. 52, 53.
246. *Ibid.*, p. 53.
247. *Ibid.*, p. 59.
248. *Ibid.*, p. 62.
249. *Ibid.*, p. 65.
250. Federal Council of the Churches of Christ in America, *Annual Report* (1925), pp. 180–183.
251. See Dobyns, Fletcher, *The Amazing Story of Repeal* (1940).
252. *Doctrines and Discipline of the Methodist Episcopal Church* (1936), p. 664.
253. *Ibid.*
254. *Federal Council Bulletin*, Jan., 1939.
255. *Schedules of Resolutions and Reports . . International Convention of Disciples of Christ, Wed., May 7, 1941* (mimeographed).
256. *Christian Century*, June 10, 1942.
257. *Progress*, Jan., 1939, p. 4.
258. XVI, 2.
259. See earlier in this section.
260. *Information Service*, Oct. 18, 1941 (XX, no. 33, p. 1).
261. *Federal Council . . . , Biennial Report* (1946), pp. 279, 280.
262. XVIII, 7.
263. XX, 4, (2).
264. These may be studied from the liberal standpoint of the outspoken advocates of freedom in Arthur Garfield Hays, *Trial by Prejudice* (1933). See also sec. on "Justice," XX, 5.
265. *Cf.* Schlesinger, *op. cit.*, p. 324.
266. See his *A Fighting Parson* (1928).
267. See art. "Strikes and Lock-Outs," *Enc. Brit.* (12th ed.), XXIII, 596.
268. McConnell, Francis J., *Opinion in the Steel Strike*, pp. 144, 145, 146.
269. *Ibid.*, p. vi.
270. *Ibid.*
271. *Ibid.*, p. 308.
272. *Ibid.*, p. 311.
273. Chafee, Zechariah, Jr., *The Inquiring Mind*, p. 171; *cf.* p. 163.
274. *The Twelve-Hour Day in the Steel Industry* (issued by the Research Department, Federal Council of the Churches of Christ in America), appendix, pp. 5, 6.
275. *Ibid.*, pp. 76–78.
276. Pope, Liston, *Millhands and Preachers*, p. viii.
277. *Ibid.*, p. 188, note 2.
278. *Ibid.*, p. 189.
279. *Ibid.*, p. 223.
280. *Ibid.*, p. 227.
281. *Ibid.*, p. 231.
282. *Ibid.*, p. 233.
283. *Ibid.*, p. 236.
284. *Ibid.*, p. 249.
285. *Ibid.*, p. 253.
286. *Ibid.*, p. 254.
287. *Ibid.*, p. 274.
288. *Ibid.*, p. 277.
289. Myers, James, MS., "Field Notes on Textile Strikes in the South," quoted by *ibid.*, p. 279.
290. Pope, Liston, *op. cit.*, p. 290.
291. Jones, Weimar, "Southern Labor and the Law," *The Nation*, CXXXI, 16 (July 2, 1930), quoted by *ibid.*, p. 295.

292. Pope, Liston, *op. cit.*, p. 327.
293. *Ibid.*, pp. 328, 329.
294. See III, 1, (6).
295. IV, 8, (9).
296. VII, 7.
297. XII, 6.
298. Art. "Hecker," *Cath. Enc.*, VII, 187.
299. Maynard, Theodore, *The Story of American Catholicism*, p. 512.
300. *Ibid.*, p. 514.
301. *Ibid.*, p. 515.
302. By Father Walter Elliott.
303. Art. "Testem Benevolentiae," *Cath. Enc.*, XIV, 538.
304. Art. "Hecker," *ibid.*, VII, 187.
305. *Cf.* Maynard, *op. cit.*, p. 517.
306. *Ibid.*, p. 519.
307. *Cf.* XII, 4, (4).
308. XIX, 2, (1), (b).
309. Art. "John Ireland," *D.A.H.*, IX, 495.
310. XVI, 14, (4).
311. Art. "John Ireland," *D.A.B.*, IX, 496.
312. XII, 3.
313. Art. "Gibbons, James," *D.A.B.*, VII, 240; *cf.* Will, A. S., *Life of Cardinal Gibbons* (1922), I, 498.
314. See XVIII, 3, (1).
315. Quoted from *Commonweal*, Aug. 23, 1940.
316. Will, *op. cit.*, I, 498; *cf.* art. "Emigrant Aid Society," *Cath. Enc.*, V, 403.
317. McSorley, *op. cit.*, p. 876.
318. Will, *op. cit.*, I, 501, citing *Collections in the Life and Times of Cardinal Gibbons*, III, pt. 3, pp. 7–9.
319. Will, *op. cit.*, I, 524–525.
320. *Ibid.*, I, 540.
321. *Ibid.*, I, 314.
322. *Ibid.*, I, 315.
323. *Ibid.*, I, 318.
324. Art. "Gibbons, James," *D.A.B.*, VII, 241.
325. *Ibid.*, VII, 242.
326. Maynard, Theodore, *The Story of American Catholicism*, 1941, p. 551.
327. XIV, 7.
328. Harlan, Rolvix, *John Alexander Dowie and the Christian Catholic Apostolic Church in Zion*, (Evansville, Wisconsin, 1906), p. 6.
329. *Ibid.*, pp. 6, 7.
330. *Ibid.*, p. 38.
331. *Ibid.*, p. 5.
332. *Ibid.*, p. 8, quoting *Leaves of Healing*, XVI, no. 20, p. 643.
333. Art. "Zion," *D.A.H.*
334. *N. Y. Times* obituary, Oct. 13, 1942.
335. Art. "Zion," *D.A.H.*
336. XXIII, 4, (11).

NOTES

Chapter XVII

1. X, 9, XVII, 8.
2. XII, 4, (4).
3. XV.
4. XIII; XVII, 3.
5. XVII, 2.
6. XVII, 7.
7. XV.
8. XVII, 9, (2).
9. *Ibid.*
10. Among the many Church organizations that have taken action against lynching similar to the extracts given above: the Woman's American Baptist Mission Society passed a resolution endorsing the Costigan-Wagner Bill. The Women's Missionary Society, M.E. Church, South, has pledged itself to do all in its power to prevent lynching. The Southern Church Leaders Conference, the Southern Methodist Episcopal Church's Commission on Cooperation with the Colored Methodist Church, the Diocese of Georgia, Protestant Episcopal Church, and the Church Women's Committee of the Federal Council's Department of Race

Relations, are among the other agencies that have condemned lynching and called for prevention of the evil and punishment of lynchers. The latest representative Church action taken on this matter was that of the Presbyterians in 1938: "We urge adoption of Federal legislation that will end the unspeakable evil of lynching in the United States. Eight persons were lynched in America in 1937. Fifty-five other attempts were made, but failed. Not one person was indicted for these crimes. Where the States have failed to guarantee a fair trial to persons accused of crime, the Federal Government is obligated to act on behalf of the most elemental of human rights." —Quotation from report of 150th General Assembly of the Presbyterian Church in the U. S. A., *N. Y. Times,* June 1, 1938.

11. Federal Council release to the press, Feb. 21, 1934.
12. *Ibid.,* Apr. 3, 1934.
13. XVII, 9.
14. *World Almanac* (1943), p. 662, Lynchings in the U. S. since 1900; and *ibid.* (1940), p. 309.
15. See Stokes, Anson Phelps, *Progress in Negro Status and Race Relations, 1911–1946;* and "American Race Relations in War Time," *Journal of Negro Education,* Vol. XIV, No. 4, Fall, 1945.
16. Mimeographed "Official Statement" on "The Church and Race" issued by the Federal Council in Mar., 1946.
17. Federal Council of the Churches of Christ in America, *Annual Report* (1925), pp. 188–190.
18. *The Churches and the World Covenant of Peace. A Declaration of Policy by the Quadrennial Meeting of the Federal Council of the Churches of Christ in America* (Dec., 1928), p. 10.
19. *Declarations of the Presbyterian Church in the U.S.A. . . . ,* p. 42.
20. XXI, 4, (4).
21. Whipple, *op. cit.,* p. 201.
22. *Ibid.,* pp. 201, 202. See *How the United States Treaty with China is Observed in California,* by Friends of International Right and Justice, for a complete account.
23. *Ho Ah Kow* v. *Matthew Nunan,* 5 Sawyer Reports 662, quoted by Whipple, *op. cit.,* p. 202.
24. "You Can't Marry a Filipino," *Commonweal,* Mar. 16, 1945.
25. Mimeographed copy supplied in 1943 by National Committee to Combat Anti-Semitism. The six words in brackets have been reconstructed, since the original cannot be traced.
26. Mahler, Raphael, *Jewish Emancipation,* pp. 5, 6.
27. XIII.
28. VIII, 5, (3).
29. *Cf.* Clinchy, Everett R., *All in the Name of God,* p. 118.
30. See the pamphlet published by *The Times* of London and reproduced by the *N. Y. Times, The Truth about the Protocols; cf.* Myers, *op. cit.,* p. 354.
31. Clinchy, *op. cit.,* p. 120.
32. Williams, Michael, *The Shadow of the Pope,* p. 130.
33. For facts and interpretation, see Strong, Donald S., *Organized Anti-Semitism in America* (Washington, 1941).
34. See art. "Catholicism and Father Coughlin," *Christian Century,* Jan. 24, 1940.
35. This matter is further discussed, XVII, 5.
36. Carlson, John Roy, *Under Cover* (New York, 1943), chap. X, "Poison in the Pulpit."
37. Art. "Toleration," *Cath. Enc.,* XIV, 762.
38. Sturzo, Luigi, *Church and State,* p. 528.
39. *Anti-Semitism,* pamphlet referred to in the text.
40. XX, 9, (2).
41. XVII, 11.
42. XII, 4, (5).
43. Quotations from the Syllabus of Errors, of Pope Pius IX, reprinted from *Dogmatic Canons and Decrees,* pp. 187–209.
44. Quotation from the *Civiltà Cattolica*

by Corrigan, Raymond, *The Church and the Nineteenth Century,* p. 298.

45. Art. "Syllabus," *Cath. Enc.*, XIV, 368, 369.
46. Marshall, Charles C., *The Roman Catholic Church in the Modern State,* p. 67.
47. Konrad, Rev. J. M. Kirch, S. J., in article "Vatican Council," *Cath. Enc.*, XV, 305.
48. *Ibid.*
49. *Ibid.*, XV, 307.
50. Corrigan, *op. cit.*, p. 200.
51. *Cath. Enc.*, XV, 309.
52. *Report on Relations Between Capital and Labor,* U. S. Senate Committee on Education, III, 215, 668, quoted by Myers, *op. cit.*, pp. 221–222.
53. IV, 2.
54. XII, 4, (5).
55. XVII, 4, (6).
56. Quoted by Schlesinger, Arthur M., *The Rise of the City 1878–1898,* p. 399. This is Volume X in the series known as "A History of American Life," to which I am indebted for most of the facts and quotations regarding the 1884 campaign.
57. Schlesinger, *op. cit.*, p. 399.
58. Myers, *op. cit.*, p. 219.
59. See Desmond, Humphrey J., *The Know Nothing Party* (1904); Gladden, Washington, "Anti-Catholic Crusade," *Century,* XLVII (1893–94), 789.
60. Williams, *op. cit.*, p. 117.
61. Myers, *op. cit.*, p. 267.
62. *Ibid.*
63. *Ibid.*, p. 300.
64. XVII, 4, (6).
65. XVI, 14, (3).
66. XVI, 10.
67. Storer, M. L., *Theodore Roosevelt, the Child,* p. 31, cited from Pringle, Henry F., *Theodore Roosevelt,* p. 456.
68. Pringle, *op. cit.*, p. 456.
69. *Ibid.*
70. *Works of Theodore Roosevelt* (Executive ed.), V, 888.
71. Pringle, *op. cit.*, p. 456.
72. *Ibid.*, quoting *Presidential Addresses,* V, 882–883.
73. Pringle, *op. cit.*, p. 455.
74. *Ibid.*, p. 456. This and some of the other letters quoted were published in the *N. Y. Herald,* Dec. 9, 1906.
75. *Works, op. cit.*, V, 884.
76. *Ibid.*, V, 891.
77. *In Memoriam Bellamy Storer,* p. 113, quoted from Maynard, *op. cit.*, p. 614, note; *cf.* Pringle, Henry F., *Life and Times of William Howard Taft,* II, 224.
78. Hassard, John R. G., *Life of The Most Reverend John Hughes, D.D., First Archbishop of New York, with Extracts from his Private Correspondence,* pp. 337–338, 340.
79. *Ibid.*, pp. 448, 449.
80. *Ibid.*, pp. 485–486.
81. Letter from Dr. Leo Stock of the Carnegie Institution of Washington, Jan. 14, 1941.
82. *Selections from the Correspondence of Theodore Roosevelt and Henry Cabot Lodge, 1884–1918,* II, 321.
83. *Ibid.*, II, 322.
84. *Ibid.*, II, 324, 325.
85. Pringle, Henry F., *The Life and Times of William Howard Taft,* I, 45.
86. For the rise of Nativism, see XII, 4, (5); and for the A.P.A., XVII, 4, (3).
87. Clinchy, *op. cit.*, p. 101.
88. *Ibid.*
89. Williams, *op. cit.*, p. 168.
90. Whipple, *op. cit.*, pp. 270, 351.
91. Williams, *op. cit.*, p. 170.
92. New and enlarged edition (New York, 1931).
93. Williams, *op. cit.*, p. 181.
94. *Ibid.*, p. 187.
95. *Ibid.*
96. XVI, 12.
97. Williams, *op. cit.*, p. 195.
98. *Ibid.*, p. 196.
99. *Cong. Rec.*, LXXI, pt. 1, pp. 448–449.
100. Myers, *op. cit.*, p. 311.
101. *The Catholic News,* November 24, 1928, quoted by Matheny, E. Stacy, *American Devotion,* pp. 254, 255.
102. Williams, *op. cit.*, p. 285.
103. For details of denominational Klan affiliations, see *ibid.*, pp. 317–319.
104. *Ibid.*, pp. viii, 297.

105. XVII, 9.
106. XVII, 3.
107. For this whole question as related to parochial schools, see XIX.
108. XIV, 11, (2).
109. XVIII, 1, (3); XVIII, 2, (5); XIX, 2, 4, 5, 6, 10.
110. XX, 3, (4).
111. XX, 3, (1), (2), (3).
112. XVII, 6, (2).
113. XVI, 7.
114. XX, 8.
115. XVI, 7.
116. XVI, 12.
117. XXI, 4, (3), (b) and (c).
118. XVII, 6, (2) (b); and XXI, 2.
119. XVIII, 4 and 11.
120. XIV, 11.
121. XVII, 9, (4).
122. XVII, 9, (7).
123. XX, 1, (2).
124. XVI, 14.
125. XVII, 5; XXIII, 4, (1).
126. XX, 4, (2); XXIII, 4, (1).
127. XVI, 14.
128. XXI, 4.
129. XXIII, 4, (1).
130. XVII, 3.
131. XXI, 4, (6).
132. XXIII, 4, (1).
133. XXI, 4, (7).
134. XII, 4, (5).
135. Art. "Irish Immigration," *D.A.H.*, III, 154.
136. Art. "The Irish," *Cath. Enc.*, VIII, 135.
137. Quoted by Morison and Commager, *op. cit.*, p. 260.
138. For the active part played by the Catholic press in promoting the cause of free Ireland, see XIV, 5.
139. Leslie, Shane, *The Irish Issue in its American Aspects* (New York, 1917).
140. Bagenal, Philip H., *The American Irish and their Influence on Irish Politics* (London, 1882), p. 144.
141. Leslie, *op. cit.*, pp. 4, 5.
142. Art. "The Irish," *Cath. Enc.*, VIII, 144, 145.
143. Leslie, *op. cit.*, p. 12.
144. XVII, 4, (2).
145. McCartan, Patrick, *With De Valera in America*, p. 40.
146. *Ibid.*, p. 56.
147. *Ibid.*, pp. 63–64.
148. This was at the Irish Freedom meeting in Madison Square Garden, New York, Dec. 18, 1918. *Ibid.*, p. 59.
149. *Ibid.*, p. 79.
150. *Ibid.*, pp. 84–85.
151. *Ibid.*, p. 104.
152. See the hearings before Foreign Affairs Committee of House, Dec. 13 and 14, 1919, on the Gallagher resolutions.
153. McCartan, *op. cit.*, p. 167.
154. *Statesman's Year Book* (1939), p. 463; based on constitution of 1936.
155. McCartan, *op. cit.*, p. 54.
156. *Annual Report of the Foreign Missions Conference of North America* (1928), p. 14.
157. Stokes, Anson Phelps, *Memorials of Eminent Yale Men*, I, 94.
158. 1 Malloy, 268, quoted by Zollmann, *op. cit.*, p. 13.
159. Art. "China," *Enc. Brit.*, VI, 204.
160. Letter from Professor Kenneth Latourette, November 30, 1944.
161. Malone, C. B., "Past and Future Uses of Boxer Indemnity Funds," *The China Mission Year Book* (1924), *passim.*
162. Letter from Rev. D. C. Holtom, an authority on Shinto, Apr. 2, 1942.
163. Holtom, D. C., "What Have Japan's Christians Surrendered?" *Christian Century*, Jan. 28, 1942.
164. *Ibid.*
165. *Ibid.*
166. *Ibid.*
167. *Christianity and Crisis*, June, 1942.
168. Holtom, D. C., "The Worship of the Sun Goddess," *Christian Century*, Feb. 4, 1942.
169. Holtom, D. C., "The Sacred Emperor," *ibid.*, Feb. 11, 1942.
170. MS. minutes of Prudential Committee, A.B.C.F.M., VI, 365.
171. MS. records of Prudential Committee for July 16, 1850, VIII, 169.
172. Letter from former Chief Justice Frear under date of January 17, 1939.
173. For a fair summary of missionary influence in Hawaii by a well-informed

scientific writer see Porteus, Stanley D., *Calabashes and Kings,* Chap. IV, "Myths and Missionaries."
174. Frear, Walter F., *Anti-Missionary Criticism With Reference to Hawaii,* p. 21.
175. *Ibid.,* p. 11.
176. X, 10; XVI, 4.
177. VI, 8.
178. Buell, Raymond Leslie, *The Native Problem in Africa,* II, appendix.
179. Zollmann, *op. cit.,* pp. 14, 15.
180. *Catholic Mind,* Jan., 1943, p. 6.
181. *Christian Century,* Dec. 23, 1942.
182. *America,* Dec. 26, 1942.
183. *Information Service,* Apr. 4, 1944, quoting *Inter-American,* N. Y., Jan., 1944.
184. *Ibid.*
185. *Cf.* art. by Dr. Guy Inman, *Churchman,* Nov. 15, 1943, and Howard, George P., *Religious Liberty in Latin America* (1944).
186. Mimeographed minutes of Joint Committee, Jan. 26, 1943.
187. Circular letter from Dr. Emory Ross, May 5, 1944. See also art. by Professor Ernest Hocking in *International Review of Missions,* Oct., 1931.
188. *N. Y. Times,* Apr. 25, 1944; *cf. Federal Council Bulletin,* Apr., 1944.
189. Adler, Cyrus, "Jews in the Diplomatic Correspondence of the United States," *Publications* of the Amer. Jewish Hist. Soc., No. 15, pp. 4–5.
190. *Ibid.,* p. 5.
191. Quoted from Matheny, *op. cit.,* p. 125.
192. *Jewish Enc.,* XII, pp. 356, 357.
193. Art. "Switzerland," *Enc. Brit.,* XXVI, 244.
194. Wiernik, P., *History of the Jews in America,* p. 346.
195. Kohler, Max J., "The Fathers of the Republic and Constitutional Establishment of Religious Liberty," Luzzatti, Luigi, *God in Freedom,* p. 702.
196. Wiernik, *op. cit.,* pp. 347, 348, 349.
197. *Ibid.,* p. 350.
198. *Ibid.,* pp. 350, 351.
199. *Cf. ibid.,* p. 352.
200. *Ibid.,* p. 316.
201. *Ibid.,* pp. 316, 317.
202. *Ibid.,* p. 318.
203. *World Almanac,* 1947, p. 903.
204. XVII, 11.
205. Landis, Benson Y., *Religion and the Good Society,* p. 56.
206. XVII, 6, (1).
207. Bishop, Joseph Bucklin, *Theodore Roosevelt and His Time,* II, 196.
208. *Ibid.,* p. 197.
209. *Ibid.*
210. XIV, 11.
211. Weaver, Rufus W., *The Roumanian Crisis,* p. 17.
212. *Christian Century,* Sept. 4, 1940.
213. V, 9, (3).
214. Schrieke, B., *Alien Americans,* p. 46.
215. Austin, Mary, "The Trail of the Blood," *Century Magazine,* May, 1924, espec. p. 36.
216. Art. "Penitent Brothers," *D.A.H.,* IV, 242.
217. Art. "Penitentes," *Cath. Enc.,* XI, 636; *Century, op. cit.,* art. cited, p. 41.
218. *Cath. Enc., loc. cit.*
219. *Century,* art. cited, *passim.*
220. *Ibid.,* p. 44.
221. X, 9.
222. See art. "Ghost Dance," "Messiah War," and "Wounded Knee, Battle of," *D.A.H.;* also Mooney, James, *The Ghost-Dance Religion and the Sioux Outbreak of 1890.*
223. Circular No. 2970, Office of Indian Affairs.
224. Letter of Commissioner Collier, Feb. 19, 1936.
225. Order of Commissioner Collier, Jan. 15, 1934.
226. *Ibid.*
227. Gabel, *op. cit.,* pp. 530–532.
228. See arts. in *The Santa Fé New Mexican,* July 21, Aug. 3 and 5, 1940.
229. See VIII, 6, 7.
230. See bibliography, under *Liberty.*
231. *Liberty,* XXXVI (1941), No. 3.
232. *Aims and Purposes of the Religious Liberty Association of America,* issued by the Religious Liberty Association [1936].
233. Facts in a letter from R. B. Eleazer, educational director of the Commission on Interracial Co-operation, Oct.

10, 1941, and from a list printed in 1920, *An Appeal to the Christian People of the South*. The work of the commission was largely taken over in 1944 by the Southern Regional Council.
234. Eleazer, Robert B., *Southern Women and the South's Race Problem*, p. 2.
235. *An Appeal to the Christian People of the South* (1920), pp. 8, 9.
236. *Southern Opinion and Race Relations*, published by Commission on Interracial Co-operation, Inc. (1938).
237. *The American Civil Liberties Union* (pamphlet).
238. *Ibid.*, p. 6.
239. *What is The National Conference?* (pamphlet), p. 1.
240. *Ibid.*
241. Letter from Robert A. Ashworth, of the national staff, Oct. 3, 1941.
242. Blanshard, *op. cit.*, p. 300; *cf.* statement of some bishops in *Commonweal*, July 14, 1944.
243. *The Churchman*, May 1, 1948, and letter from the secretary, Mr. R. Lawrence Siegel.
244. Blakely, William A., *American State Papers bearing on Sunday Legislation* (rev. and enlarged ed., 1911), p. 166.
245. Porter, Kirk H., comp., *National Party Platforms* (N. Y., 1924), p. 7.
246. *Ibid.*, p. 8.
247. *Ibid.*, p. 13.
248. *Ibid.*, p. 14.
249. *Ibid.*, p. 11.
250. *Ibid.*, p. 39.
251. *Ibid.*, p. 43.
252. *Ibid.*, p. 50.
253. *Ibid.*, p. 77.
254. *Ibid.*, p. 71; *cf.* Blakely, *op. cit.*, p. 170.
255. Porter, Kirk H., comp., *op. cit.*, p. 79.
256. *Ibid.*, p. 89.
257. *Ibid.*, p. 93.
258. *Ibid.*, p. 96.
259. Blakely, *op. cit.*, p. 170.
260. Porter, *op. cit.*, p. 99.
261. Blakely, *op. cit.*, p. 170.
262. Porter, *op. cit.*, p. 108.
263. *Ibid.*, p. 113.
264. *Ibid.*, pp. 139–140.
265. *Ibid.*, pp. 149–150.
266. *Ibid.*, p. 163.
267. *Ibid.*, pp. 227–228.
268. *Ibid.*, p. 447.
269. *Ibid.*, pp. 490–491.
270. *Liberty*, Fourth Quarter (1948).
271. XVII, 6.
272. "Jewish Nationalism: Preface and Prospect," *Contemporary Jewish Record*, June, 1942, a scholarly anonymous article to which I am largely indebted for the historical background of this summary.
273. *Ibid.*, p. 258.
274. *Ibid.*, p. 252.
275. Quoted by Janowsky, Oscar I., *The American Jew*, p. 232, from Isaac Goldberg's *Major Noah*, pp. 140, 194. See also XIII, 4.
276. From a facsimile reproduction provided by the Zionist Archives and Library, New York.
277. *Contemporary Jewish Record*, June, 1942, p. 315.
278. From material provided by Zionist Archives and Library, New York.
279. Art. "Palestine," *Statesman's Year Book* (1939), p. 195.
280. Janowsky, *op. cit.*, p. 243.
281. *Ibid.*, p. 244.
282. Letters provided by the Zionist Archives and Library, New York.
283. *Ibid.* In the 1944 campaign, both President Roosevelt and his political opponent, Governor Dewey, made statements in favor of a Jewish "commonwealth."
284. *Ibid.*
285. *Cong. Rec.* LXII (1922), pt. 5, p. 4758.
286. *Ibid.*, p. 5376.
287. *Ibid.*, pt. 10, pp. 9799, 9800.
288. Public Resolution No. 73, 67th Cong., from copy provided by the Zionist Archives and Library.
289. *Cf. Cong. Rec.*, LXII (1922), pt. 6, p. 5760; also *ibid.*, pt. 10, p. 9799 ff.
290. Letters, etc., *op. cit.* See note 282.
291. Janowsky, *op. cit.*, p. 240.
292. *N. Y. Times*, Feb. 23, 1943.
293. For further discussion, see XXI, 4, (5), "The Church and Postwar Reconstruction."
294. Adopted Jan. 31, 1943; quotation from *Information Service*, Mar. 13, 1943.

295. *A Statement from the American Institute on Judaism and A Just and Enduring Peace,* Dec. 1942, p. 15.
296. *N. Y. Times,* Aug. 31 and Sept. 1, 1943.
297. *Christian Century,* Sept. 2, 1943.
298. *Ibid.,* Feb. 14, 1948.
299. The pro and con Zionist literature within Judaism is enormous. For good statements of the former emphasis the reader is referred to *The Jewish Frontier;* for the latter, to the *Contemporary Jewish Record.*
300. Anglo-U. S. Committee Report, *N. Y. Times,* May 1, 1946.
301. United Nations Special Committee on Palestine Report, *N. Y. Times,* Sept. 1, 1947.
302. For facts and explanation see *Christian Century,* July 14 and Sept. 8, 1948.
303. *Churchman,* May 1, 1949.
304. *Cf.* platforms in *World Almanac,* 1945, pp. 718, 720; *cf.* "The Sorry Story of Palestine," *Christian Century,* Nov. 28, 1945.
305. *American Jewish Year Book 1948–1949,* "Palestine in the United Nations and the United States," pp. 336–267.
306. *N. Y. Times,* Sept. 22, 1949.

NOTES

Chapter XVIII

1. XVII, 1.
2. *World Almanac,* 1949, p. 374, and Monroe, *Cyclopedia of Education,* "High Schools."
3. XIX, 4, (2).
4. XVI, 4.
5. VIII, 1, 2, 5.
6. *Constitutions of the States and the United States* (Albany, 1938), p. 48.
7. *Ibid.,* p. 84.
8. *Ibid.,* pp. 790, 791.
9. Thorpe, *op. cit.,* III, 1918; Zollmann, *op. cit.,* p. 78.
10. *The Constitution of the State of New York, as Revised, with Amendments . . . , 1938* (Albany, N. Y., 1944), pp. 216, 217.
11. *Constitutions of the States and the United States,* p. 1345.
12. *Ibid.,* p. 1700.
13. *Ibid.,* pp. 1724, 5, 6.
14. Zollmann, *op. cit.,* pp. 78, 79.
15. XIX, 6, (1).
16. XIX, 6, (2), (3).
17. VIII, 5, (2), (3); IX, 4 (beginning); XIV, 8.
18. XIV, 8; XIX, 8.
19. XIX, 3, 8; XXII, 4.
20. XIX, 5.
21. XVIII, 3.
22. V, 1 to 9; appendix, 4.
23. *Constitutions, op. cit.,* p. 1816.
24. VI, VII, VIII.
25. *Cf.* some comments by Lecky, *Democracy and Liberty,* (rev. ed. 1899), II, 61.
26. XIV, 8.
27. Meiklejohn, William, *Education between Two Worlds* (1942), pp. 4 *ff.*
28. *Report of President of Columbia University* (1934), pp. 21–22.
29. Butler, Nicholas Murray, *The Meaning of Education* (rev. ed., 1915), pp. 179–200.
30. Art. "The Place of Religion in American Education," *Modern Churchman,* June, 1941, pp. 116–118.
31. *Religious Education,* 1926, p. 94.
32. Hamilton, Otto T., *The Courts and the Curriculum* (1927).
33. *Rev. Stat.* (1916), Title II, chap. 16, sec. 140, quoted by Confrey, *op. cit.,* p. 73.
34. *Cf.* Brown, S. W., *The Secularization of American Education,* chap. II, pp. 26–32.

35. See summary in *Why the Bible Should not Be Read in the Public Schools,* p. 12, based on study by Brown, S. W., *op. cit.*
36. See the Ordinance for the Government of the Northwest Territory, VI, 10.
37. *Constitution* (1909), art. XI, sec. 1, quoted by Brown, S. W., *op. cit.,* p. 98.
38. *Constitution* (1817), art. VI, sec. 16, and *Constitution* (1832), art. VII, sec. 14, quoted by *ibid.,* p. 99.
39. *Constitution* (1802), art. VII, sec. 3, quoted by *ibid.,* p. 99.
40. Gabel, *op. cit.,* p. 662.
41. *Knowlton* v. *Baumhover* (1918), 182 Iowa, 691, 166 N.W. 202, 206, 5 A.L.R. 841, 843, quoted by Zollmann, *op. cit.,* p. 78.
42. XVIII, 1, (3).
43. XVIII, 2 (2), and 3 (2).
44. XVI, 14.
45. *The Issues at Oxford. A Report* (1937), p. 6.
46. XVIII, 1, (3).
47. See "Directions for Securing High School Credit for Bible Study," issued by the state.
48. *Federal Council Bulletin,* Oct., 1941. See also McCasland, *The Bible in our American Life* (1942). The author is professor of religion in the University of Virginia.
49. Johnson, Alvin W., *Legal Status of Church-State Relationship in the United States,* p. 140.
50. Moehlman, *Church and School,* p. 84, citing Honeywell, R. F., *Educational Work of Jefferson,* 24, 232.
51. Confrey, *op. cit.,* p. 118, quoting *State ex rel. Dearle* v. *Frazier* (1918), 102 Wash. 369, 173 Pac. 35, L.R.A. 1918F, 1056.
52. *Information Service,* May 27, 1944.
53. Johnson, A. W., *op. cit.,* pp. 143, 145.
54. Davis, M. D., *Week-Day Religious Education* (1933), p. 22; but *cf.* Gove, F. S., *Religious Education on Public School Time,* p. 101.
55. *Christian Century,* Mar. 19, 1941.
56. *Columbia University Quarterly,* Dec., 1938, quoted by *Information Service,* Jan. 7, 1939.
57. *Federal Council Bulletin,* Mar., 1942.
58. From *Report of Committee on Week Day Religious Education* (n. d.), transmitted by the Reverend C. W. Brown, its chairman, p. 1.
59. *Ibid.,* pp. 4, 5.
60. Article "Modern School adding Religion to Three R's," *Forth,* Sept. 1941.
61. Correspondence with the Reverend Crawford W. Brown, of Elgin, Oct. 16, 1941.
62. *Bible Society Record,* Jan., 1944.
63. *Christian Century,* Aug. 18, 1943.
64. 36. There has been a very general wish, not confined to representatives of the churches, that religious education should be given a more defined place in the life and work of the schools, springing from the desire to revive the spiritual and personal values in our society and in our national tradition. The church, the family, the local community and the teacher—all have their part to play in imparting religious instruction to the young.

37. In order to emphasize the importance of the subject provision will be made for the school day in all primary and secondary schools to begin with a corporate act of worship, except where this is impracticable owing to the nature of the school premises, and for religious instruction to be given. At present this is the practice in the great majority of schools and this practice will receive statutory sanction and be universal.

38. This does not, of course, mean that all children will be required to participate in the corporate act of worship or in religious instruction. In this respect the old established rights of conscience will remain inviolate and it will be open to the parent to withdraw his child from all or any form of religious worship or instruction.

39. In county [provided] schools the religious instruction will, subject to a strictly limited exception to which reference is made at the end of this paragraph, be in accordance with an agreed syllabus, examples of which are

already in use in many areas. Provision will be made for such a syllabus to be drafted by those who can speak for the Church of England, the Free Churches, the teachers and the Authority. . . . — *Information Service,* Oct. 16, 1943, quoting White Paper on "Educational Reconstruction." The plan has met with large support outside of Roman Catholic circles.

65. For an interesting presentation of this plan, see "The Teaching of Religion," *School and Society,* June 29, 1940.
66. *Christian Century,* Nov. 12, 1941.
67. *Ibid.,* May 14, 1941, p. 654.
68. *Ibid.,* May 7, 1941, p. 619.
69. *Ibid.*
70. *Ibid.*
71. *Ibid.,* May 14, 1941, p. 654; e.g., See Morrison, Charles Clayton, "Protestantism and the Public School," *The Christian Century,* Apr. 17, 1946.
72. *Information Service,* Nov. 15, 1941.
73. *Ibid.*
74. *Florida School Law,* 1936, sec. 669.
75. *Why the Bible Should Not be Read in the Public Schools,* pp. 21, 22.
76. Pub. by Univ. of Chicago Press, 1944.
77. XVIII, 1, (3).
78. *N. Y. Times,* Sept. 16, 1945, and *Christian Century,* Sept. 28, 1945.
79. *Churchman,* Feb. 15, 1946.
80. Quotation from *Information Service,* Feb. 9, 1946.
81. *Churchman,* Jan. 1, 1948.
82. *McCollum* v. *Board of Education* (1948), 333 U. S. 203.
83. XIX, 5, (2).
84. *McCollum,* etc., *op. cit.,* pp. 7, 8.
85. *Ibid.* (Mr. Justice Frankfurter's dissenting opinion), p. 5.
86. *Ibid.,* p. 15.
87. *Ibid.,* p. 16.
88. *Ibid.,* pp. 19, 20.
89. *Ibid.,* p. 20.
90. *Ibid.* (Mr. Justice Jackson's dissenting opinion), p. 1.
91. *Ibid.,* p. 2.
92. *Ibid.,* pp. 4, 5.
93. *Ibid.,* (Mr. Justice Reed's dissenting opinion), p. 7; quoting 1 *Annals of Congress,* 730.
94. *Ibid.,* pp. 18, 19.
95. For the R.C. position see "The Supreme Court on Separation of Church and State," *Commonweal,* Feb. 18, 1949, and O'Neill, *Religion and Education Under the Constitution.*
96. *Christian Century,* Mar. 17, 1948; for school actions in representative communities, see *Churchman,* July 1, 1948.
97. *Amer. Bar Association Journal,* Jan., 1949.
98. *Information Service,* May 29, 1943.
99. Butler, N. M., *Liberty, Equality, Fraternity,* pp. 145, 147.
100. Gove, F. S., *op. cit.,* p. 4.
101. Davis, M. D., *op. cit.,* p. 13.
102. *Ibid.,* p. 14.
103. *Ibid.,* p. 12.
104. See Keesecker, W. W., *Laws Relating to Releasing of Pupils from Public Schools for Religious Instruction* (1933); Davis, M. D., *op. cit.*
105. XVIII, 2, (4).
106. Johnson, Alvin W., *op. cit.,* pp. 141, 143.
107. See statistics in Gove, *op. cit.,* p. 24.
108. *Federal Council Bulletin,* Oct., 1941.
109. Davis, M. D., *op. cit.,* p. 4, quoting *Laws of Minnesota Relating to the Public School System,* p. 83, sec. 319.
110. *Weekday Classes in Religious Education,* No. 3 (1941), p. v.
111. *Christian Century,* Dec. 24, 1947.
112. *Ibid.,* Mar. 10, 1943.
113. For a favorable view see reports of International Council of Religious Education; for unfavorable, Moehlman.
114. XVIII, 1, (3).
115. *Information Service,* XIX, no. 43 (Dec. 28, 1940).
116. *Liberty,* Third Quarter, 1947.
117. *Ibid.,* Fourth Quarter, 1947.
118. *Ibid.*
119. For this and additional information, see Cutton, George L., *The Cortland (N.Y.) Plan,* Morehouse Publishing Co., Milwaukee, Wis. [n.d., 1928?]; for the similar Virginia experiment, see XVIII, 1, (2).
120. Davis, M. D., *op. cit.,* pp. 2, 3, quoting Settle, M. D., "Week-day Church Schools from Coast to Coast," *Inter-*

national Journal of Religious Education, July, 1929.
121. *Weekday Classes . . . , op. cit.*
122. *Ibid.*, pp. 2, 3.
123. *Ibid.*, p. 1.
124. *Christian Century*, Apr. 30, 1947.
125. XVIII, 10.
126. *Cf.* Butler, Nicholas Murray, *The Meaning of Education*, Lecture I.
127. Previous section, XVIII, 1, (3).
128. *Religious Liberty in the U. S. Today* (1939), p. 27.
129. Prepared by Vincent C. Allred of the Legal Department.
130. *State ex rel. Dearle* v. *Frazier* (1918).
131. *Stein* v. *Brown* (1925).
132. *People ex rel. Lewis* v. *Graves* (1927), 245 N.Y. 195, 156 N.E. 663, affirming 219 App. Div. 233, 219 N.Y.S. 189, as summarized by Zollmann, *op. cit.*, p. 83; Johnson, A. W., *op. cit.*, pp. 131, 133, 134.
133. Quoted by *ibid.*, p. 134, and Zollmann, *op. cit.*, p. 83.
134. *Berkshire Eagle*, Jan. 10, 1941.
135. *Churchman*, June 1, 1947.
136. For an interesting account, see art. "Religion in Puerto Rican Politics," *Christian Century*, Oct. 11, 1944.
137. *Christian Century*, Aug. 27, 1947.
138. Newman, Louis I., *The Sectarian Invasion of Our Public Schools* (1925), p. 1—Assembly Bill No. 128.
139. *Ibid.*, pp. 5, 6.
140. *Ibid.*, p. 9.
141. Circular issued by State Education Department, Aug., 1940, entitled *Absence for Religious Observance and Education.*
142. *Commonweal*, Feb. 21, 1941.
143. *N. Y. Sun*, Jan. 16, 1942.
144. Moehlman, *School and Church*, p. 132.
145. *N. Y. Times*, May 19, 1941.
146. XVIII, 2, (1), (3), (4).
147. *Federal Council . . . Biennial Report* (1946), pp. 137, 138.
148. Gabel, *op. cit.*, p. 737.
149. Ahern, Rev. Michael, S. J., *Catholic Religious Education* [reprinted from *Education*, Jan., 1939].
150. *Ibid.*
151. *N. Y. Times*, Nov. 5, 1939.
152. Quoted by Matheny, *op. cit.*, p. 261.
153. See letter from the Department of Education of the National Catholic Welfare Conference, Nov. 26, 1941.
154. *N.C.W.C. News Service*, May 26, 1941.
155. *Ibid.*, School Supplement No. 6, Aug. 11, 1941.
156. *Ibid.*
157. *Ibid.*
158. XVIII, 2, (3). For a good bibliography on "The Jewish Attitude toward Religion and Public Education" covering the period from 1934 to 1941, consult the one published by the American Association for Jewish Education.
159. Newman, L. I., *op. cit.*, pp. 15, 16, quoting *Jewish Daily Bulletin*, Mar. 15, 1925.
160. *The Witness*, Aug. 20, 1942.
161. *Churchman*, Aug., 1947.
162. Pfeffer, Leo, *Religion and the Public Schools, Churchman*, Jan. 15, 1948.
163. *Contemporary Jewish Record*, Apr., 1942, p. 158.
164. VI, 6.
165. *Papers of the American Historical Society* (1888), II, 508, 509.
166. XXI, 1.
167. *Christian Century*, Dec. 18, 1940.
168. Johnson, Alvin W., *op. cit.*, p. 26.
169. Art. "Colonial Period," etc., Monroe, *Cyclop. of Education*, II, 119.
170. It has been pointed out that, though the opposition of the Roman Catholic Church was the major factor in eliminating the reading of the Bible from public schools in many states, the controversy among different Protestant groups regarding the content of religious instruction was almost equally responsible for the secularization of public schools. Dean Weigle cites as an example the strife between Trinitarians and Unitarians in Massachusetts. *Cf. Religious Education* (1926), p. 91.
171. XIV, 8, (2).
172. Gabel, *op. cit.*, p. 439, n. 12.
173. *Ibid.*, p. 442.
174. This is a summary of the data given by Johnson, A. W., *op. cit.*, pp. 26, 27.
175. *Ibid.*, p. 39.

176. *The State and Sectarian Education, N.E.A. Research Bulletin,* Oct., 1946, p. 36.
177. Gabel, *op. cit.,* p. 553.
178. *Ibid.,* p. 549.
179. *Ibid.,* p. 552.
180. Beale, Howard K., *Are American Teachers Free?* p. 211.
181. Zollmann, *op. cit.,* p. 33.
182. *Cf. The Book of Common Prayer,* New York [Certified, 1944, as conforming to Standard Book of 1928], p. 67; *cf.* p. 82; and *The Catholic Missal,* New York [with imprimatur of Patrick Cardinal Hayes, Archbishop of New York, 1934], p. 641.
183. *The Churchman,* Dec. 15, 1946; and letter from Civil Liberties Union.
184. Letter dated Dec. 8, 1947.
185. XVIII, 3.
186. Brown, S. W., *op. cit.,* p. 71.
187. Idaho State Constitution (1899), art. IX, sec. 6, quoted by Monroe, *Cyclop. of Education,* I, 374.
188. *Statutes* (1903), ch. 113, sec. 4368, act July 6, 1893, quoted by Brown, S. W., *op. cit.,* p. 72.
189. *General Statutes* (1885), sec. 1338. This provision is repeated in the Compiled Laws of 1900, sec. 1323, quoted by Brown, S. W., *op. cit.,* p. 73.
190. Act of Nov. 28, 1883, title IV, ch. 38, quoted by *ibid.,* p. 75.
191. Art. 7, sec. 11, art. 9, sec. 4, quoted by Johnson, A. W., *op. cit.,* p. 33.
192. *A Review of Educational Legislation of 1931 and 1932* ("Biennial Survey of Education").
193. *Statutes,* sec. 1764, quoted by Hamilton, O. T., *op. cit.,* p. 80.
194. *General Statutes* (1905), sec. 6816, quoted by Brown, S. W., *op. cit.,* p. 77.
195. *Revised Laws* (1901), pt. I, title I, ch. 42, sec. 19, quoted by *ibid.,* p. 78.
196. Thorpe, Francis N., *Federal and State Constitutions,* IV, 2092, constitution of 1890.
197. *Political Code* (1899), sec. 754, Laws of 1890, ch. 62, sec. 134, quoted by Brown, S. W., *op. cit.,* p. 80.
198. Letter from the superintendent of schools, Oct. 1, 1937.
199. See reports of the commissioner of education (1894–95), II, 1673–1698, and (1895–96), I, 331–336, quoted from Gabel, *op. cit.,* p. 179.
200. These facts from *ibid.,* p. 309.
201. See discussion, VIII, 5.
202. See summary at close of this section.
203. XVIII, 11.
204. *Northeastern Reporter* (St. Paul, Minn.), XCII, no. 5. (Aug. 2, 1910), pp. 251–266, quoted by Brown, S.W., *op. cit.,* pp. 135–139. Case is *The People* v. *Board of Education,* 245 Ill., 334.
205. *State ex rel. Finger* v. *Weedman et al.*
206. *People ex rel Ring* v. *Board of Education* (1910), 245 Ill. 334, 92 N.E. 251; quoted by Brown, S. W., *op. cit.,* pp. 121–123.
207. *Hackett* v. *Brooksville* (1905), 120 Ky. 608, 87 S.W. 792, quoted by Lincoln, Charles Z., *The Civil Law and the Church,* pp. 41, 42.
208. Art. "Bible in the Schools," Monroe, *op. cit.,* I, 375.
209. *State ex rel. Freeman* v. *Scheve* (1902), 65 Neb. 853, 91 N.W. 846 from the digest of the opinion in Lincoln, *op. cit.,* pp. 45, 46. *Cf.* Hamilton, O. T., *op. cit.,* pp. 26, 71, etc.
210. *Board of Education of Cincinnati* v. *Minor* (1872), 23 Ohio St. 211.
211. Zollmann, *op. cit.,* p. 26.
212. *Ibid.,* p. 46.
213. *Ibid.,* p. 95.
214. Johnson, A. W., *op. cit.,* p. 22.
215. *Hart* v. *School Directors of Sharpsville* (1885), 2 Lanc. Law Rev. (Pa.) 346, from the digest of the opinion in *ibid.,* pp. 43, 44; *cf.* Zollmann, *op. cit.,* p. 94, note 52.
216. Summary quoted from Johnson, A. W., *op. cit.,* p. 82, from *State ex rel. Weiss* v. *District Board* (1890), Wis. 177, 44 N.W. 967.
217. *Ibid.,* p. 83.
218. Gabel, *op. cit.,* pp. 716, 717.
219. *Ibid.,* p. 718.
220. Hamilton, O. T., *op. cit.,* pp. 154, 155.
221. *Clithero, George I., et al.,* v. *N. D. Showalter, as State Superintendent et al.; cf. State ex rel. Dearle* v. *Frazier* (1918), 102 Wash. 369.

222. Johnson, A. W., *op. cit.*, p. 35.
223. *Ibid.*
224. *Information Service,* October 4, 1941.
225. See Stewart, George A., *Religious Education in Connecticut*, p. 292.
226. Gabel, *op. cit.*, p. 390.
227. Will, A. S., *op. cit.*, I, 478.
228. Hamilton, O. T., *op. cit.*, p. 89.
229. *Why the Bible Should Not be Read in the Public Schools*, p. 3.
230. *Ibid.*, p. 4.
231. *Ibid.*, p. 6.
232. *Ibid.*, p. 7.
233. *Ibid.*, p. 15.
234. *Liberty,* Third Quarter, 1942, pp. 18–22. *Cf.* views of Professor Moehlman in his *School and Church,* chap. VIII, "Can the Bible Return to the Classroom?" His answer is "no."
235. See V, 3, (2).
236. Johnson, A. W., *op. cit.,* p. 60.
237. See references in Zollmann, *op. cit.*, pp. 94, 95, n. 53.
238. For further discussion, see Johnson, A. W., *op. cit.*, espec. pp. 77, 98; Hamilton, O. T., *op. cit.*, chap. V; and Brown, S. W., *op. cit., passim.*
239. Bishop, Joseph Bucklin, *Theodore Roosevelt and His Time,* I, 21.
240. This suggestion was written before the issuing of President F. D. Roosevelt's Thanksgiving Day proclamation in 1944. In this he proposed a somewhat similar idea: "To the end that we may bear more earnest witness to our gratitude to Almighty God, I suggest a nation-wide reading of the Holy Scriptures during the period from Thanksgiving Day to Christmas. Let every man of every creed go to his own version of the Scriptures for a renewed and strengthening contact with those eternal truths and majestic principles which have inspired such measure of true greatness as this nation has achieved." *N. Y. Times,* Nov. 4, 1944.
241. Johnson, A. W., *op. cit.*, pp. 26, 27.
242. See discussion in *Liberty,* Third Quarter, 1942.
243. *Christian Century,* Dec. 23, 1942.
244. Bourne, William O., *History of The Public School Society of the City of New York* (1873), pp. 192–193.
245. *Ibid.*, p. 198.
246. *Ibid.*, pp. 200–201.
247. *Ibid.*, pp. 208, 212.
248. *Ibid.*, pp. 237–238.
249. *Ibid.*, pp. 245–246.
250. *Ibid.*, pp. 251–252.
251. *Ibid.*, pp. 300–301.
252. *Ibid.*, pp. 321–322.
253. *Ibid.*, p. 323.
253. *Ibid.*, p. 325.
254. *Ibid.*, pp. 344–345.
255. *Ibid.*, pp. 345–347.
256. *Ibid.*, pp. 326–327.
257. *Ibid.*, pp. 348–349.
258. Quoted by O'Neill, J. M., *op. cit.*, p. 231.
259. This is published by the Washington Public Schools as School Document No. 1, 1936, rev. Apr., 1938. Mr. George J. Jones, head of the department of social studies, has kindly checked off the more important sections for me.
260. *N. Y. Times,* Apr. 4, 1949. For analysis of this general subject, see Beale, *op. cit.*, pp. 306–307.
261. XVIII, 7.
262. See "The Textbook War," *Information Service,* XX, no. 20 (May 17, 1941), and *Commonweal,* Oct. 31, 1941.
263. Art. "Ten Year Drive Cuts Bias in Textbooks," *N. Y. Times,* Feb. 14, 1943.
264. *Ibid.*
265. XVIII, 1, (2).
266. *Revised Statutes of the State of Illinois* (1931), chap. 122, sec. 123, quoted by Johnson, A. W., *op. cit.*, p. 157.
267. For the above and similar laws and regulations see Taylor, E. T., *Principles and Policies Governing the Use of Public School Property in the Several States,* a dissertation at Columbia University (1947).
268. *Ibid.*, p. 159.
269. Gove, *op. cit.*, p. 104; *cf. The Status of Religious Education in the Public Schools* (1949).
270. *Christian Century,* Jan. 6, 1943.

271. Statement of director of Albany Council of Religious Education, October 8, 1941.
272. *Christian Century,* Jan. 30, 1943.
273. XVIII, 1, (3).
274. Johnson, A. W., *op. cit.,* p. 160.
275. *N. Y. Times,* June 24, 1938.
276. *Davis* v. *Boget* (1878), 50 Iowa, 11, 15, 16. See notes, 31 L. R. A. (N.S.) 593, 5 A. L. R. 866; quoted by Zollmann, *op. cit.,* p. 97.
277. Hartogensis, B. H., "Denial of Equal Rights," etc., *Yale Law Journal,* XXXIX (1930), p. 663, n. 18, *Cf.* protest of Jewish rabbi, *N. Y. Sun,* Dec. 6, 1944; also XX, 9, (1).
278. *Christian Century,* February 19, 1941.
279. Information from New Haven superintendent of schools, Feb. 6, 1940.
280. *Ibid.,* Feb. 14, 1940.
281. *Christian Century,* Jan. 17, 1940.
282. *Ibid.,* Jan. 31, 1940.
283. Brown, S. W., *op. cit.,* p. 52.
284. General Statutes (1901), sec. 6194, quoted by *ibid.,* p. 53.
285. *Bates Annotated Statutes* (1906), Title III, ch. 8, sec. 3987, quoted by *ibid.,* p. 54.
286. Zollmann, *op. cit.,* p. 97.
287. *Ibid.,* pp. 97, 98.
288. Johnson, A. W., *op. cit.,* p. 166.
289. *Cf.* Beale, *op. cit.,* p. 220 ff.
290. Zollmann, *op. cit.,* p. 99, with references.
291. XVI, 4.
292. *Christian Century,* July 28, Aug. 4, 1948.
At the preliminary election on June 29, 1948, North Dakota voters decided 93,469 to 83,038 to make it illegal for Roman Catholic nuns and others wearing a distinctively religious dress to teach in the public schools. This action does not interfere with the same persons teaching if they do not wear a distinctive religious garb. The rival groups in the state organized under a "Committee for Separation of Church and State," which favored the proposed new law, and the "Committee for Defense of Civil Rights," which opposed it. The movement was brought to a head by the publication of the fact that the records of the state superintendent of public instruction for May, 1947, revealed that there were 74 nuns and eight priests teaching in twenty schools and receiving $71,475 of public school tax money in salaries. The bishops of the Church in North Dakota immediately announced that they would comply with the law.
293. XIX, 2, (1), (d).
294. *Christian Century,* Feb. 25, 1948.
295. XVI, 4.
296. Beale, *op. cit.,* p. 516, citing N. Y. Session Laws (1932), p. 617.
297. *Teachers Oaths,* bulletin of N.E.A., Oct., 1936.
298. For this and some of the other facts above recorded, see *Religious Liberty in the United States Today* (1939), pp. 30, 31.
299. Tennessee *Code* (1932), sec. 2344, 2345.
300. Dieffenbach, Albert C., *Religious Liberty,* p. 63.
301. *Ibid.,* p. 78.
302. *N. Y. Times,* May 27, 1923, quoted by Weigle, *op. cit.,* p. 229.
303. Beale, *op. cit.,* p. 220.
304. Dieffenbach, *op. cit.,* p. 11.
305. *Ibid.,* p. 36.
306. *Ibid.,* p. 39.
307. *Ibid.,* p. 40.
308. *Ibid.,* p. 144.
309. Beale, *op. cit.,* p. 311.
310. *American Year Book* (1925), p. 87. For another account of this incident, see Allen, Leslie H., *Bryan and Darrow at Dayton.*
311. Hays, Arthur G., *Let Freedom Ring,* p. 38.
312. *Ibid.,* p. 45.
313. Weigle, *op. cit.,* p. 229.
314. Hays, A. G., *op. cit.,* p. 63.
315. *Ibid.,* p. 78.
316. *Scopes* v. *State* 154, Tenn. 105.
317. Hays, A. G., *op. cit.,* p. 47.
318. Mississippi—*Code Ann.* (Hemingway, 1927), sec. 9493.
319. Dieffenbach, *op. cit.,* pp. 182, 183.
320. Lee, G. T., *Church and State. Can we*

Save the Country by Legislation? (Minneapolis [1927]).
321. *N. Y. Sun,* Dec. 14, 1939.
322. The movement functions through three nonprofit organizations: The Watch Tower Bible and Tract Society of Pennsylvania; the Peoples Pulpit Association of New York; and the International Bible Students Association of London, England. For interesting account of Jehovah's Witnesses, see *Boston Evening Transcript,* Aug. 10, 1940. See XXIII, 4, (15).
323. Quoted from *Religious Liberty in the U. S. Today* (1939), published by American Civil Liberties Union, p. 19.
324. XX, 10, (2) (a); XXIII, 4, (15).
325. *The Bill of Rights—150 Years After* (the report for 1938–39 of the American Civil Liberties Union), pp. 12, 46.
326. Fennell, William G., *Compulsory Flag Salute in Schools,* pp. 8, 9.
327. *The Persecution of Jehovah's Witnesses* (published by the American Civil Liberties Union, January, 1941), p. 3.
328. *Ibid.,* p. 22.
329. *Religious Liberty in the United States Today* (1939), p. 21.
330. *Annotated Laws, Mass.,* chap. 71, sec. 69, 1935, quoted in Fennell, *op. cit.,* p. 4.
331. Par. 712.
332. Fennell, *op. cit.,* pp. 10, 11.
333. See XVIII, 6.
334. *The Bill of Rights—150 Years After,* p. 46.
335. Quoted from *Philadelphia Evening Bulletin,* June 18, 1938.
336. Most of these cases, with references, described in Fennell, *op. cit.,* p. 2.
337. *Liberty,* First Quarter, 1942, p. 20.
338. *Christian Century,* August 20, 1941.
339. *Liberty,* Third Quarter, 1941, p. 20.
340. *N. Y. Times,* Nov. 11, 1939, quoting this previous decision.
341. *Ibid.*
342. *Christian Century,* July 3, 1940.
343. The court here gives in a footnote many authorities, espec. quotations from Jefferson, Madison, and Roger Williams.
344. *Supreme Court of the United States,* No. 690, October Term, 1939. Decided June 3, 1940.
345. *Ibid.*
346. *Christian Century,* Nov. 20, 1940.
347. *Brief of the Committee on the Bill of Rights, of the American Bar Association . . . ,* filed [before the Supreme Court] Mar. 8, 1943.
348. 56 Stat. 380; 36 U.S.C.A., 1942 Cum. Supp. Sec. 172.
349. Curtis, Charles P., Jr., *Lions under the Throne, A Study of the Supreme Court of the United States* (Boston, 1947), quoting 47 F. Supp. at 253.
350. See Heller, Francis H., "A Turning Point for Religious Liberty," *Virginia Law Review,* XXIX (1943), 440.
351. *N. Y. Times,* June 15, 1943.
352. *Supplement to the Bill of Rights Review,* Vol. I, No. 1, "Constitutionality of the Compulsory Flag Salute" [1939], pp. 2, 3.
353. Memorandum submitted by Wendell Berge, Assistant Attorney General, July 18, 1943.
354. See XX, 10, (2), (a); XXIII, 4, (15).
355. VIII, 5.
356. *World Almanac,* (1943), pp. 558, 572, quoting U. S. Office of Education.
357. *Ibid.* (1948), p. 357.
358. XXI, 4, (3), (a); and (5).
359. *U. S. Dept. of Education Directory* (1938), part III, p. 6.
360. Morison, Samuel E., *The Founding of Harvard College,* pp. 193, 194.
361. *Ibid., Harvard in the Seventeenth Century,* I, 6.
362. Dexter, Franklin B., *Sketch of the History of Yale University,* p. 10.
363. Quoted from Morison, *The Founding . . . , op. cit.,* p. 247.
364. Quoted from Dexter, F. B., *op. cit.,* p. 9.
365. *Ibid.,* p. 9.
366. IX, 4.
367. *Ibid.*
368. IV, 8, (10).
369. *Writings of Thomas Jefferson* (Monticello ed.), XV, 303.
370. Quoted by Weigle, *op. cit.,* p. 327.
371. Quoted by *ibid.,* p. 315.

372. Gabel, *op. cit.*, p. 285.
375. *Christian Century*, Feb. 18, 1942.
374. See Searles, Herbert Leon, *The Study of Religion in State Universities* (Iowa City, 1927).
375. This state university has a fine cultural tradition.
376. It will be interesting to note whether the designation of Rutgers University (originally under the Dutch Reformed Church, but later undenominational), which took effect in 1945, will result in any changes in the required chapel provisions. None is contemplated.
377. Confrey, *op. cit.*, p. 64.
378. Georgia *Code* (1861), sec. 1127, quoted by Brown, S. W., *op. cit.*, 40, 41; *cf.* letter from director of public relations of university, Jan. 27, 1940.
379. Brown, S. W., *op. cit.*, p. 25.
380. Green, Edwin L., *History of the University of South Carolina* (1916), p. 235.
381. Letter from director of public relations, Feb. 8, 1940.
382. Green, E. L., *op. cit.*, p. 234.
383. *Ibid.*
384. *Commonweal,* June 24, 1938, p. 34.
385. Sproul, Robert Gordon, "The Practical Aspects of Spiritual Training," in *The Obligation of the Universities to the Social Order* (New York, New York University Press, 1933), pp. 382–83.
386. Shedd, Clarence Prouty, "Religion in State Universities," *Journal of Higher Education,* XII, No. 8, Nov., 1941, p. 410.
387. Bruce, Philip Alexander, *History of the University of Virginia 1819–1919,* I, 204, note.
388. *Ibid.*
389. See XVIII, 6.
390. Bruce, P. A., *op. cit.*, I, 205.
391. Green, E. L., *op. cit.*, p. 41.
392. *Cf.* Simkins, F. B., *The Tillman Movement in South Carolina,* pp. 142–144.
393. *Session Laws* (1864–65), p. 313, no. 4748, and *Rev. Stat.* (1873), chap. 42, sec. 13, par. 5, quoted by Confrey, *op. cit.*, p. 109.
394. Lampe, M. Willard, *The Story of an Idea,* p. 9.
395. *Ibid.*, p. 7.
396. Letter from Dr. Lampe, Sept. 11, 1939.
397. Lampe, M. Willard, *La Vitalidad De Una Idea,* University of Iowa [n.d., about 1945].
398. *Christian Century,* June 4, 1947.
399. *Michigan School of Religion, Ann Arbor, Inaugural Meeting, Detroit, Friday, January 26, 1923,* p. 2.
400. *Ibid.*, p. 9.
401. *The Hawaii School of Religion Affiliated with the University of Hawaii* [1946]; and copy of constitution.
402. Shedd, Clarence Prouty, "Religion in State Universities," *The Journal of Higher Education,* XII, No. 8, Nov., 1941, p. 412.
403. Art. "Negro Pastors go to Rural Colleges," *Christian Century,* Jan. 5, 1944.
404. *Ibid.*, p. 415.
405. From circular of National Council on Religion in Higher Education, 1943.
406. The original of this letter is at the University of Virginia. It has been called to my attention by Dr. L. H. Butterfield, assistant editor of "The Papers of Thomas Jefferson." He says, "Jefferson's reply has (I believe) never been published." The reference number is 47770.
407. Morison, *The Founding of Harvard College,* pp. 194, 330.
408. Tiffany, Charles C., *A History of the Protestant Episcopal Church in the U.S.A.* (1895), p. 67.
409. For a good summary of the history of libraries in this country, see art. "Liraries" in *D.A.H.*, and Chap. XXIV, "Libraries," in Dexter, Edwin Grant, *A History of Education in the United States,* 1911.
410. *The Literary Diary of Ezra Stiles,* III, 528.
411. Dwight, Timothy, *Travels in New England and New York* (1823), IV, 298.
412. Bowerman, George F., *Censorship and the Public Library, with Other Papers,* p. 97.
413. *Carnegie Magazine,* Nov., 1929, p. 181, quoted by *ibid.*, p. 28.

414. Haight, Anne L., *Banned Books*, p. 74.
415. *Church Manual of The First Church of Christ Scientist, in Boston, Mass.* (1906), art. XXIX, sec. 9.
416. See art. in *Nation*, CXXX, 147–149 (Feb. 12, 1930); *cf.* similar arts. in *New Republic*, 1929 and 1930.
417. "Censorship and the Library," Bowerman, *op. cit.*, p. 29.
418. Yust, William F., "Censorship—A Library Problem," *Library Journal*, LVII (1932), 178–179.
419. Issue of Dec. 14, 1938.
420. Haines, Helen E., *Living With Books* (1937).
421. *Catholic Library World*, Oct., 1938, pp. 35, 36.
422. *Ibid.*, p. 36.
423. Letter from the seminary, Jan. 17, 1940.
424. Quoted by Hamilton, O. T., *op. cit.*, p. 74.
425. *Ibid.*, p. 75.
426. For a summary of this question see *Information Service*, Nov. 27, 1948, and *N. Y. Times*, May 28, 1949. See under Blanshard, Paul, in bibliography.
427. Blanshard, P., *op. cit.*, p. 194, quoting *N. Y. Times*, June 15, 1948.

NOTES

Chapter XIX

1. This definition and similar definitions are discussed in White, E. S., *Distinction Between Private and Public Schools as Shown by Court Cases*, unpublished Master's dissertation, University of Pittsburgh, 1931, referred to by Gabel, *op. cit.*, p. 1.
2. *Ibid.*, pp. 3, 4.
3. XIX, 8, where the Oregon school law case is discussed.
4. *Information Service*, Nov. 18, 1944.
5. XII, 4, (3).
6. XIX, 4.
7. XIX, 2, (2).
8. XIX, 2, (3), (4).
9. "Statistics of Private Elementary Schools for the Year 1930–331," *Biennial Survey of Education in the United States: 1930–1932*, p. 4.
10. *Information Service*, March 26, 1949.
11. For beginnings in the U. S., see XII, 4, (3).
12. McSorley, Joseph, *Outline History of the Church*, pp. 725–727.
13. *Decreta Conc. Prov. et Plen. Balt., 1829–1852* n. 13, p. 47, quoted by Burns, J. A., *Growth and Development of the Catholic School System in the United States*, p. 184.
14. Quoted in *American Historical Review*, Jan., 1931, p. 270.
15. *Decreta*, 430, 431, quoted by Burns, *op. cit.*, p. 188.
16. *Ibid.*, pp. 190, 191.
17. *Decreta*, p. 196, quoted by *ibid.*, pp. 192, 193.
18. *Decreta*, n. 199, quoted by *ibid.*, p. 195.
19. *Ibid.*
20. *Ibid.*, p. 196.
21. *Christian Century*, Oct. 21, 1942.
22. Rankin, Charles, *The Pope Speaks*, p. 254.
23. For an authoritative contemporary statement of this general position, see Wilfrid Parsons, S.J., *The First Freedom, Considerations on Church and State in the United States* (New York, 1948). For *pros* and *cons*, see XIX, 2, (1), (c).
24. Gabel, *op. cit.*, p. 322.
25. Art. "Schools in the United States," *Cath. Enc.*, XIII, 583.
26. Gabel, *op. cit.*, p. 305.
27. *Ibid.*, p. 493.
28. For further information regarding

somewhat similar plans in Hartford, Connecticut, and Poughkeepsie, New York, see Burns, *op. cit.*, pp. 253–258.
29. *Annual Report of the N.E.A.* (1890), p. 185, quoted by *ibid.*, p. 260.
30. *Civiltá Cattolica* (1892), I, 756, quoted by *ibid.*, p. 261.
31. Bouquillon, Thomas, in *Rejoinder*, p. 1, quoted by *ibid.*, p. 232.
32. Bouquillon, *op. cit.*, p. 26, quoted by *ibid.*, p. 236.
33. Bouquillon, *op. cit.*, pp. 27, 28, quoted by *ibid.*, p. 237.
34. *Ibid.* (Burns), p. 263.
35. *Ibid.*, p. 243.
36. *Ibid.*, pp. 243, 244.
37. Prop. IX, quoted by *ibid.*, p. 245.
38. *Ibid.*, p. 247.
39. XIX, 2, (1), (d).
40. Moehlman, *School and Church*, p. 78.
41. Ryan, Rt. Rev. John A., *The Citizen*, etc., *op. cit.*, p. 12.
42. *Religious Education* (1926), p. 399.
43. *Ibid.*
44. Blanshard, Paul, *op. cit.*, p. 67.
45. Letter from Information Section, N.C.W.C., Oct. 20, 1938. The literature regarding Catholic parochial schools is large. Among important books which may be consulted for additional facts are: Cronin, James T., and Donohue, Francis J., *Catholic Public Schools in the United States* (New York, 1937); Allen, William C., "The Application of the Doctrine of the Separation of Church and State in Education," unpublished Master's dissertation, Univ. of S. C., 1931 (not consulted); McLaughlin, Sister Raymond, O.S.B., Ph.D., *A History of State Legislation Concerning Private and Elementary Schools 1870–1945* (1946).
46. XIX, 3.
47. Figures from *The Official Catholic Directory* (1948), chart at close of Part II, after p. 1360.
48. Sheen, Fulton J., *Liberty, Equality and Fraternity* (New York, 1938), pp. 133–134.
49. *Catholic Educational Review*, Feb., 1935, p. 69.
50. *Ibid.*, p. 70.
51. Quoted by *Christian Century*, June 3, 1940, p. 734.
52. Letter from Prof. W. W. Sweet, May 23, 1949, and his arts. in the *Christian Advocate* on "American History in Roman Catholic Parochial Schools," June 22–29, 1922.
53. *Pontificia Americana* (Vol. XV of Catholic Univ. of America "Studies in American Church History," Washington, 1923), pp. 389 ff.
54. XIX, 2, (1), (6); XVI, 14, (3).
55. This sketch is based largely on two mimeographed "Reports" on the North College Hill situation dated June 27, 1947, and July 14, 1947, published by the Council of Churches of Greater Cincinnati, together with other material cited.
56. Copy of letter from Rev. Bernard J. Wellman.
57. Fey, Harold E., "The Stand for Free Schools!" *Christian Century*, July 2, 1947.
58. *Ibid.*
59. Fey, Harold E., "Preview of a Divided America," *Christian Century*, May 28, 1947, an article based on careful study on the spot, to which I am greatly indebted.
60. *The Facts and Implications of the School Trouble in North College Hill, Ohio*, issued by the General Council of the Presbytery of Cincinnati, Ohio . . . [1947].
61. *Christian Century*, editorial, Nov. 19, 1947.
62. XVII, 9, (5).
63. *Op. cit.*, "Report on the North College Hill School Situation," July 14, 1947.
64. *N. Y. Times*, July 11, 1947; special dispatch from Dr. Benjamin Fine.
65. *Christian Century*, June 23, 1948.
66. Art. "When Rome Takes Over," by Frank S. Mead, *Churchman*, Feb. 1, 1948. (Originally in *Christian Herald*.)
67. *Ibid.*
68. *Christian Century*, Jan. 14, 1948, and Mar. 10, 1948.
69. *Ibid.*, *Mar.* 23, 1949; *cf. ibid.*, July 6, 1949.

70. *Ibid.*, June 23, 1948.
71. *Ibid.*
72. XX, 6, (6).
73. Art. "Lutheran Church and Education in the United States," Monroe, *Cyclop. of Education,* IV, 96.
74. [Stellhorn, A. C.,] *A Century of Lutheran Schools in America,* p. 11.
75. *Ibid.*
76. *Ibid.*, p. 12.
77. *Ibid.*, p. 16.
78. See resolutions of the Missouri Synod in 1920, in Merkens, Albert G., *The Policies of the Evangelical Lutheran Synod of Missouri, Ohio, and Other States with Regard to Elementary Education by Means of Christian Day-Schools,* p. 15.
79. The following is an authoritative statement of the policy of the Missouri Synod in this matter of parochial school charges:

"As a rule, the congregational schools are maintained by voluntary contributions on the part of the members. However, the means of maintaining them used to be, and in some instances still are, secured by tuition, payable monthly in advance. About twenty-five per cent. of the schools in the Synod charge tuition. The tuition-fees, usually very low, having hardly ever sufficed to defray the expenses of the school, and the deficit is made up by members of the congregation through voluntary contributions. The Synod discourages the charging of tuition-fees and encourages its members, whether they have children or not, to support the school as a missionary enterprise." From *ibid.*, p. 5, quoting *Statistical Year-book of the Missouri Synod for 1932,* p. 163, and *Proceedings of the Thirtieth Convention* (1917), p. 50.

80. See resolutions of the Missouri Synod in 1920, in Merkens, *op. cit.*, p. 43.
81. *Churchman* (New York), Nov. 1, 1938.
82. Lindemann, J. C. W., *Amerikanisch-Lutherische Schulpraxis* (St. Louis, Mo., 1879), p. 7, quoted by Merkens, *op. cit.*, p. 3.
83. See, for full information, Vilas, W. F., *The Bennett Law in Wisconsin.*
84. *Ibid.*
85. Detailed information about 992 of the 1,378 parochial schools then connected with the synod may be found in the *Statistical Year Book of the Evangelical Lutheran Synod of Missouri, Ohio and Other States for the year 1936,* pp. 182–185.
86. See statistics in *Lutheran World Almanac* corrected in letter from the National Lutheran Council, Nov. 2, 1949.
87. Letters from secretary, United Lutheran Church in America, July, 1948.
88. Moehlman, *School and Church,* p. 67.
89. Sherrill, Lewis Joseph, *Presbyterian Parochial Schools 1846–1870,* p. 20.
90. *Ibid.*, p. 25.
91. *Ibid.*, p. 27.
92. *Ibid.*, p. 36.
93. See list, *ibid.*, pp. 73–82.
94. *Ibid.*, pp. 56–64.
95. See instances, *ibid.*, p. 99.
96. *Ibid.*, p. 101.
97. Gabel, *op. cit.*, p. 28.
98. Livingood, Frederick George, *Eighteenth Century Reformed Church Schools,* p. 199.
99. Information from letter from the Board of Christian Education of the Evangelical and Reformed Church, Jan. 25, 1939.
100. *Christian Education and a New Church,* p. 2.
101. See Acts Numbers 24 and 52 of the extraordinary session of the legislature for 1938, and letters dated Dec. 2, 1938, from the Legislative Reference Bureau, Harrisburg, and Jan. 13, from the State Department of Public Instruction.
102. *N. Y. Times,* Nov. 29, 1938.
103. Gabel, *op. cit.*, p. 769.
104. Greenberg, Simon, "Trends in Jewish Education," *Contemporary Jewish Record,* Apr., 1942, pp. 162 ff.
105. Chipkin, Israel S., "Twenty-five Years

of Jewish Education in the United States," *Amer. Jewish Year Book 5697*, XXXVIII (1936), *passim*, espec. p. 37.
106. XXII, 4.
107. 2,638,776 in 1935–36, according to the U. S. Office of Education in Washington. The number given in the *Official Catholic Directory* for 1942 as enrolled in Catholic schools is slightly smaller.
108. The exact figures, as quoted in the *World Almanac* (1943), p. 572, for 1940, the last year for which published figures were available, were 25,433,542 enrolled pupils, and $2,344,048,927 total expenditures.
109. XIV, 8.
110. XII, 4, (3).
111. See XII, 4, (4).
112. Parsons, Wilfrid, S.J., *op. cit.*, p. 60.
113. XII, 4, (3); XIX, 2, (1), (a).
114. Quoted from an account of "Denominational Schools" published in 1877 when the memory of this controversy was still fresh. See Kiddle and Schem, *Cyclop. of Education*, p. 218; *cf.* also XII, 4, (3), (4).
115. For some striking facts, see Dorchester, Daniel, *Christianity in the United States* (rev. ed.), espec. pp. 591, 592.
116. *Ibid.*, p. 603.
117. Thorpe, *op. cit.*, II, 1232, quoting art. VII, sec. 5.
118. *Ibid.*, III, 1446, quoting title XI, art. 146.
119. Gabel, *op. cit.*, p. 549.
120. Lischka, C. N., *Private Schools and State Laws* (1926). This and similar provisions found on pp. 188–194; *cf.* Thorpe, *op. cit.*, II, 1035.
121. Root, Elihu, *Addresses on Government and Citizenship*, pp. 137, 140.
122. Art. IX, sec. 4, in *Constitution of the States and the U. S.* (1938), III, 1130.
123. *World Almanac* (1939), giving abstract of "official summary" of convention, p. 142; and XIX, 5.
124. Art. X, sec. 1, in Thorpe, *op. cit.*, VII, 3142.
125. Art. 82, in *Constitution of the State of New Hampshire* (published by the Department of State, Concord, N. H. [1935]), p. 40.
126. *State Aid to Private and Parochial Schools*, p. 30.
127. XIX, 6, (1).
128. XVI, 1.
129. *National Needs and Remedies* (Evangelical Alliance, Boston, 1889), p. xiv.
130. IV, 8, (9).
131. Bishop, Joseph Bucklin, *Theodore Roosevelt and His Time*, I, 21.
132. *National Needs*, etc., pp. 200, 201.
133. *Ibid.*, p. 202.
134. *Ibid.*, p. 204.
135. *Ibid.*
136. See *School and Society*, Mar. 3, 1934. *Cf.* Master's thesis by Tollinger at Ohio State University in 1934 on "The Legal Status of State Aid for Private and Parochial Schools in Ohio"; also Beale, *op. cit.*
137. Gabel, *op. cit.*, p. 667.
138. *Cf.* "Tentative Statement of Catholic Position" (MS.), quoted by *ibid.*, pp. 668, 669.
139. *Ibid.*, p. 670.
140. For an able presentation of the Roman Catholic position, see "Does State Aid to Education Mean Union of Church and State?" *Catholic Educational Review*, Feb., 1935.
141. *Cf.* attitude of superintendent of schools for St. Paul archdiocese, *Christian Century*, June 4, 1947 and Cardinal Spellman's recent reply to Mrs. Roosevelt, XIX, 10.
142. *Christian Century*, Nov. 20, 1940.
143. *America*, July 29, 1947.
144. *Liberty*, First Quarter, 1942, p. 25; *cf.* *Christian Century*, Aug. 20, 1941.
145. Art. XI, sec. 11, quoted by *Liberty*, First Quarter, 1942, p. 26, footnote.
146. *Ibid.*, p. 26.
147. *Ibid.*, p. 27.
148. *Ibid.*
149. N.E.A. *Bulletin*, Mar., 1937, on *State Aid to Private and Sectarian Schools.*
150. Johnson, A. W., *op. cit.*, p. 155.
151. *Ibid.*, p. 199.
152. *Ibid.*, p. 203.
153. For a history of the "compromise plan" by which the state virtually takes over certain parochial schools, see XIX, 2, (1).

154. XIX, 6.
155. *Christian Century,* July 24, 1940.
156. XIX, 2, (1), (d).
157. XVIII, 1, (3), and XIX, 5, (2).
158. XVIII, 1, 2.
159. *Federal Council Bulletin,* Jan., 1939.
160. Zollmann, *op. cit.,* p. 80.
161. Gabel, *op. cit.* (13 in 1937), p. 541.
162. *Ibid.,* p. 543.
163. *Cf.* Zollmann, *op. cit.,* pp. 18, 19; and XVIII, 5.
164. Gabel, *op. cit.,* p. 548.
165. Van Dusen, Henry, ed., *Church and State in the Modern World,* p. 169.
166. *Information Service,* XIX, no. 43 (Dec. 28, 1940).
167. For these and other facts, see N.E.A., mimeographed bulletin (March, 1937), entitled *State Aid to Private and Sectarian Schools,* pp. 29–31; also *Newsweek,* June 5, 1939.
168. Art. 827 of the Penal Code of Texas.
169. *N.Y. Times,* May 25, 1938.
170. *Board of Elections in the City of New York,* being proposed amendments as submitted to the consideration of the voters Oct. 10, 1938, art. XI.
171. *Newsweek,* June 5, 1939.
172. *Liberty,* Second Quarter, 1942, p. 26.
173. *Ibid.,* p. 27.
174. *Christian Century,* Jan. 13, 1943.
175. *Churchman,* June 1, 1941.
176. *Christian Century,* Nov. 20, 1946, and editorial Oct. 30, 1946.
177. *New Jersey Laws,* 1941, c. 191, p. 581; *N J Rev. Stat.,* 18: 14–8, cited by 330 U. S. 1, note 1.
178. 330 U. S. 1. *Everson* v. *Board of Education* (Rutledge dissenting opinion), p. 33, note 59.
179. *Ibid.,* p. 26, note 47.
180. *Ibid.,* pp. 26, 27, notes 47, 49.
181. *Ibid.* (Black opinion), p. 3.
182. *Ibid.,* p. 4.
183. *Ibid.,* p. 5.
184. *Ibid.,* p. 6.
185. *Ibid.,* p. 6.
186. *Ibid.,* p. 9 (*cf.* V, 3).
187. *Ibid.,* p. 11.
188. *Ibid.,* pp. 13–16.
189. Corwin, *op. cit.,* "The Supreme Court as National School Board," *Thought* (Fordham University, Dec., 1948).
190. *Quick Bear* v. *Leupp,* 210, U. S. 50, p. 81. I am indebted for this reference to O'Neill, *op. cit.,* p. 131.
191. 330 U. S. 1, *op. cit.* (Jackson dissenting opinion), p. 1.
192. *Ibid.,* p. 4.
193. *Ibid.,* p. 6.
194. *Ibid.,* p. 9.
195. *Ibid.,* p. 10.
196. *Cochran* v. *Louisiana State Board of Education,* 281 U. S. 370, *infra* in this section.
197. 330 U. S. 1 (Rutledge dissenting opinion), pp. 17, 18.
198. *Ibid.,* p. 22.
199. *Ibid.,* p. 24.
200. *Ibid.,* p. 25.
201. *Ibid.,* p. 30.
202. H. J. Res. 187 (1947); *cf.,* XXVI, 6; also *cf.* model state constitution, VIII, 2, (1), close.
203. *Liberty,* Fourth Quarter, 1947.
204. *Churchman,* May 15, 1947.
205. *Op. cit.,* June 15, 1947.
206. *Op. cit.,* Mar. 1, 1947.
207. *Liberty,* Third Quarter, 1947, and Associated Press dispatch from Washington, Aug. 29, 1947; *Liberty,* Third Quarter, 1948.
208. *Churchman,* Nov. 1, 1947.
209. *Christian Century,* Oct. 29, 1947.
210. *Ibid.,* Nov. 20, 1946.
211. *The Churchman,* June 15, 1947.
212. *Christian Century,* Nov. 5, 1947.
213. *N. Y. Times,* Jan. 12, 1948.
214. *N. Y. Herald-Tribune,* Jan. 26, 1948.
215. XIX, 5, (3).
216. *Christian Century,* Apr. 16, 1941.
217. Johnson, A. W., *op. cit.,* p. 194.
218. 281 U. S. 370; quoted from Moehlman, Conrad H., *The American Constitutions and Religion,* p. 140.
219. *Christian Century,* Mar. 19, 1941.
220. Art. VIII, sec. 1.
221. *N. Y. Times,* Sept. 7, 1943.
222. *Report of the President's Advisory Committee on Education* (1938), p. 54.
223. See H.R. 3517 and 10340.
224. *N. Y. Times,* Feb. 28, 1938.

225. *State Aid to Private and Sectarian Schools,* p. 32.
226. *Ibid.*
227. *Ibid.,* p. 35.
228. Federal Council . . . *Federal Aid to Sectarian Education* (1947), pp. 11–13; based mainly on the N.E.A. Bulletin (1946), *The State and Sectarian Education.*
229. *World Almanac,* 1947, p. 808.
230. See XXIV, 5, (5).
231. VIII, 1.
232. Gabel, *op. cit.,* p. 520, n. 26.
233. *Catholic World,* XXII (Jan., 1876), pp. 434, 435.
234. Letter from education editor, *America,* Aug. 18, 1947.
235. *Cong. Rec.,* 44th Cong., 1st sess., IV, 205.
236. *Ibid.,* IV, 5189–91.
237. *Ibid.,* IV, 5245.
238. *Ibid.*
239. *Ibid.,* IV, 5246.
240. *Ibid.,* IV, 5453.
241. *Ibid.,* IV, 5455.
242. *Ibid.,* IV, 5456.
243. *Ibid.,* IV, 5583.
244. *Ibid.,* IV, 5585.
245. *Ibid.,* IV, 5595.
246. XVII, 10.
247. For other references to the subject in party platforms, see *ibid.*
248. For study of these amendments see Ames, Herman V., *Proposed Amendments to the Constitution of the United States, 1789–1889;* and O'Neill, *op. cit.,* pp. 122–125.
249. IX, 2.
250. I owe the facts in this paragraph to Gabel, *op. cit.,* pp. 524–526.
251. 29 Stat. 393, 411.
252. 29 Stat. 665, 683.
253. Gabel, *op. cit.,* p. 535, gives the references.
254. *Cf. Christian Century,* Jan. 29, 1947.
255. *Ibid.,* May 18, 1949. *Cf.* XVIII, 1, (3), and XIX, 5, (2).
256. *Liberty,* First Quarter, 1948.
257. See reference in Zollmann, *op. cit.,* p. 500.
258. *U. S. Reports,* CLXXV, 296–299.
259. See XXII, 3, (4).
260. XXVI, 6.
261. Burns, J. A., *op. cit.,* p. 278.
262. *Ibid.,* p. 219.
263. This case is fully discussed in *Compulsory Education. The State of Ohio vs. The Rev. Patrick Quigley, D.D.*
264. Johnson, A. W., *op. cit.,* p. 176; *cf.* XIX, 8, *Meyer* v. *Nebraska.*
265. *Pierce* v. *Society of Sisters,* etc., 268 U. S. 510. *Cf.* XIX, 8.
266. *Cf.* Gabel, *op. cit.,* p. 485. The case is that of *Sister Felicitas* v. *Hartridge,* 148 Ga. 832.
267. *Code of Georgia of 1933,* p. 1589; *cf. Acts* (1916), p. 126; (1918), p. 166.
268. *Farrington* v. *Tokushige,* 273 U. S. 284; *cf.* XIX, 8.
269. *State* v. *Hoyt* (1929), 84 N.H. 38.
270. *Ibid.,* quoted by Johnson, A. W., *op. cit.,* pp. 190, 191.
271. See next section, 8.
272. Turner, Rev. Dr. William, "Schools," *Cath. Enc.,* XIII, 558.
273. *Constitutions of the States and U. S.,* p. 1130, quoting art. IX, sec. 4.
274. *The State and Sectarian Education,* N.E.A. Research Bulletin, Feb., 1946, quoting *Revised Statutes of Nebraska,* 1943, vol. 4, chap. 79, sec. 1913, and General Laws of R. I. of 1938, Title 21, chap. 181, sec. 8. See espec. p. 47.
275. *Pierce* v. *Society of the Holy Names of Jesus and Mary* (1924), 268 U. S. 510, 45 S. Ct. 571, 69 L. Ed. 1070, 39 A. L. R. 468.
276. Zollmann, *op. cit.,* p. 101.
277. See Gabel, *op. cit.,* pp. 754, 755, for these and related facts.
278. XII, 4, (2).
279. *Gilmour* v. *Pelton.* References in Zollmann, *op. cit.,* p. 92.
280. The story of the part played by one far-sighted citizen, Edward John McDermott (1852–1926), in securing this amendment is told in *America,* July 30, 1938.
281. XIX, 2, (2).
282. 262 U. S. 390.
283. 262 U. S. 397.
284. Zollmann, *op. cit.,* p. 11.

285. Quoted from *America,* July 30, 1938.
286. 262 U. S. 399.
287. 262 U. S. 400.
288. *Ibid.*
289. 262 U. S. 401.
290. 262 U. S. 402; Justices Holmes and Sutherland united in a mildly worded dissenting opinion.
291. 268 U. S. 510; case of *Pierce* v. *Society of the Holy Names of Jesus and Mary;* 39 A.L.R.
292. The Act revising Sec. 5259, Oregon Laws, is found in 39 A.L.R., pp. 473, 474.
293. *Ibid.*, p. 476.
294. *Ibid.*, pp. 475, 476.
295. *Ibid.*, pp. 475, 476; XIX, 7.
296. *Meyer* v. *Nebraska,* 1923, in 262 U. S. 390–402, summarized by Zollmann, *op. cit.,* p. 92. See previous section, XIX, 8.
297. *Ibid.*
298. See previous section, XIX, 8.
299. Act 171, amending Act 30 of the Session Laws of 1920.
300. *U. S. Reports,* Supreme Court, October Term, 1926, CCLXXIII, 293.
301. Blauch, L. E., and Reid, C. F., *Public Education in the Territories and Outlying Possessions* (1939), p. 80.
302. *Ibid.*
303. *U. S. Reports,* Supreme Court, October Term, 1926, CCLXXIII, 298, 299.
304. *Statehood for Hawaii,* 75th Cong., 3d sess., Sen. Doc. no. 151.
305. See *Revised Laws,* 1935, sec. 732, 3. Information from letter of former Chief Justice Frear, Jan. 11, 1939. For additional information see Gulick, Sidney L., *Mixing the Races in Hawaii* (1937), pp. 176–180.
306. From letter from the deputy superintendent of public instruction, Dec. 27, 1939.
307. XXI, 4, (3).
308. XIX, 2, (1), (a).
309. XVIII, 1, (3) and XIX, 5, (2).
310. H. R. 4643, 81st Congress, 1st session.
311. *N. Y. Times,* July 23, 1949.
312. *Ibid.*, quoting *The World Telegram* of the days mentioned.
313. *N. Y. Times,* July 23, 1949.
314. XIX, 5.
315. XIX, 5, (2).
316. *N. Y. Times,* July 24, 1949.
317. *Ibid.*, July 26, 1949.
318. *Ibid.*, July 28, 1949.
319. *Ibid.*, Aug. 6, 1949.
320. XIX, 5, (2).
321. 330 U. S. 1.
322. *Ibid.*
323. *N. Y. Times,* Aug. 6, 1949.
324. XIX, 5, (3).
325. Release from Mrs. Roosevelt to United Feature Syndicate, Aug. 22, 1949.
326. *Ibid.*, Aug. 23, 1949.

261.7
St8
v.2
6304
3 4711 00228 1964